怪物讲师教学团队的 7,000 "单词"+"语法"

怪物讲师教学团队 ◆ 著

北京理工大学出版社
BEIJING INSTITUTE OF TECHNOLOGY PRESS

使用说明 User's Guide

我想买个新包。
囫 An apple a day keeps the doctor away. 一天一苹果，医生远离我。

0002 **able** ['eɪbl] a 能够的，会的
Jack hasn't been able to revise the article yet.
杰克至今没能修改文章。
同 capable 能干的　反 unable 不能的　短 be able to... 能做……

冠词 a 用在以辅音开头的单词前面；以元音开头的单词前面用 an。

语法重点
hasn't 是 has not 的简写，因为要表达"到目前为止还没有修改文章"，所以用现在完成时。

0003 **about** [ə'baʊt] prep 关于，在……的附近　ad 在四周
I know nothing about him.
我对他一无所知。
同 concerning 关于　短 be about to... 即将要
句 I know nothing about... 我对……一无所知

语法重点
nothing 的反义词是 everything。"对……了如指掌"可表达为 know everything about sth.。

1 | 单词 + 语法记忆法

"怪物讲师教学团队"独创的"单词 + 语法"学习法，左栏单词、右栏语法重点。一次学习，事半功倍！

符号图示说明
- n 名词　　pron 代词
- v 动词　　art 冠词
- a 形容词　同 同义词
- ad 副词　　反 反义词
- prep 介词　短 短语
- conj 连词　句 句型
- aux 助动词　重 使用重点

2 | 依程度分级，循序渐进学习

本书共分成6个Level，单词、例句、各种补充的难易度皆依Level代表的能力程度来量身打造。只要用心读完全书，英语成绩便能迅速提高，考到满级分更不是梦想！

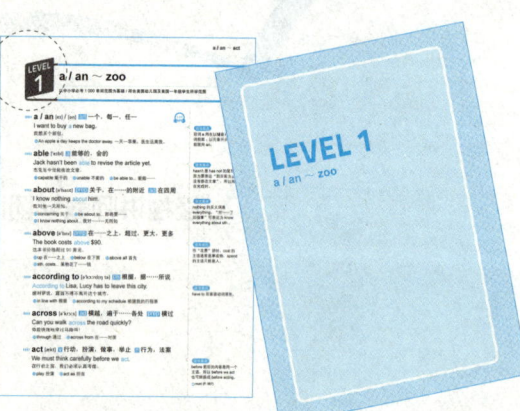

3 | 补充多元学习元素，培养延伸活用的能力

单词皆标示音标、词性、中文词义，并视考试重要性补充同义词、反义词、短语、句型、使用重点、语法等，延伸式的学习能帮助读者记忆，不仅节省额外背诵的时间，更能培养活用的能力。

0004 **above** [ə'bʌv] prep 在……之上，超过，更大，更多
The book costs above $90.
这本书价格超过 90 美元。
同 up 在……之上　反 below 在下面　短 above all 首先
句 sth. costs... 某物花了……钱

User's Guide

4 | 用Review自我检测，用Preview掌握重点

每个Level的最前面都设计预习与复习的内容，既可以检测之前的学习成果，也可以事先掌握学习重点。

Preview
语法重点预习，在开始之前先预习会让印象更深刻！

1 单词的词性分为：名词（noun，书中用 n 表示）、动词（verb，书中用 v 表示）、形容词（adjective，书中用 a 表示）、副词（adverb，书中用 ad 表示）、介词（preposition，书中用 prep 表示）、连词（conjunction，书中用 conj 表示）。
2 名词基本上可以分成可数名词、不可数名词。可数名词的复数形式，视名词的词尾或音节不同而在词尾加 s、es 或 ies；也有单复数同形及不规则变化的情况。
3 第一人称（I）的 be 动词使用 am，第二人称（you）和第三人称复数的 be 动词使用 are，第三人称单数（he、she、it）的 be 动词使用 is。
4 动词的变化：
 • 和第一人称、第二人称、第三人称复数搭配时，使用动词的原形。
 • 和第三人称单数搭配时，动词后面需加 s 或是 es（视动词的词尾或音节而定）。
 • 表示现在进行时时，动词后面需加 ing（视动词的词尾或音节不同而有不同的变化规则）。

5 | 像Ctrl + F般的"前寻、后找"

学英语最怕背了又忘、忘了又背。为了避免发生这样的情况，本书规划前寻后找的功能，让你随时能搜寻到想找的单词或是语法重点。（⊙ 表示之前学过的内容；➡ 表示之后要学到的内容）

...ts take is an absolute doddle.
...容易了
...cess of 在……的过程中
...，包括 n 盖子
...t for me every night.
...ver up 掩盖，盖住
...奶牛
...cows there are on the farm?
...牛仔，牧童
...the cowboy.

语法重点
"选课"是 take the course，"退课"是 drop the course.
⊙ adult (P. 004)

语法重点
例句叙述的是每天都要做的事情，所以用一般现在时。

➡ fascinate (P. 567)

6 | 7 000单词发音MP3完整收录

只会在纸上认出单词是不够的，现在英语听力越来越受重视，许多学校也将英语听力成绩纳入考试。本书由专业外籍老师录制MP3，让你随时随地都能听单词、背单词。

0001 **a / an** [eɪ] / [ən] art 一个，每一，任一
I want to buy a new bag.
我想买个新包。
谚 An apple a day keeps the doctor away. 一天一苹果，医生远离我。

★ 本书附赠音频为MP3格式 ★

目录 Contents

LEVEL 1 a / an ~ zoo 001

LEVEL 2 ability ~ zebra 119

LEVEL 3 aboard ~ zone 249

LEVEL 4 abandon ~ youthful 387

LEVEL 5 abide ~ zoom 519

LEVEL 6 abbreviate ~ zeal 663

LEVEL 1
a / an ~ zoo

LEVEL 1

a / an ~ zoo

Preview test

先来测验看看，Level 1 的单词，你会多少个？

1 garden　　▶ _____　　5 supper　　　▶ _____
2 least　　　▶ _____　　6 bottom　　　▶ _____
3 wash　　　▶ _____　　7 vegetable　▶ _____
4 practice　▶ _____　　8 knee　　　　▶ _____

Preview

语法重点预习，在开始之前先预习会让印象更深刻！

1 单词的词性分为：名词（noun，书中用 n 表示）、动词（verb，书中用 v 表示）、形容词（adjective，书中用 a 表示）、副词（adverb，书中用 ad 表示）、介词（preposition，书中用 prep 表示）、连词（conjunction，书中用 conj 表示）。

2 名词基本上可以分成可数名词、不可数名词。可数名词的复数形式，视名词的词尾或音节不同而在词尾加 s 或 es 或 ies；也有单复数同形及不规则变化的情况。

3 第一人称（I）的 be 动词使用 am，第二人称（you）和第三人称复数的 be 动词使用 are，第三人称单数（he、she、it）的 be 动词使用 is。

4 动词的变化：
  • 和第一人称、第二人称、第三人称复数搭配时，使用动词的原形。
  • 和第三人称单数搭配时，动词后面需加 s 或是 es（视动词的词尾或音节而定）。
  • 表示现在进行时时，动词后面需加 ing（视动词的词尾或音节不同而有不同的变化规则）。
  • 表示过去时或过去完成时时，动词后面需加 ed（视动词的词尾或音节不同而有不同的变化规则）。
  • 除了规则变化之外，还有其他不规则的动词变化，需额外记忆。

5 时态可分过去时、现在时、将来时。
  • 过去时：描述过去的事情、动作、状态……。
  • 现在时：表示客观事实、一般性的动作、经常发生的事情、习惯……。
  • 将来时：表示在将来的某个时间会发生的动作或情况。

6 表达"从过去的某一时间一直持续到现在的动作或状态"时要用现在完成时。
  表达"过去已经完成的事情"时要用过去完成时。

7 形容词的比较级、最高级变化：
  • 比较级：单音节单词于词尾加 er，双音节和多音节单词于形容词前加 more。
  • 最高级：单音节单词于词尾加 est，双音节和多音节单词于形容词前加 most。
  • 还有其他不规则的变化，需额外记忆。

正确答案　1 名词／花园　2 形容词／最少的　3 动词／洗涤　4 动词；名词／练习
　　　　　5 名词／晚餐　6 名词／底部　7 名词／蔬菜　8 名词／膝盖

LEVEL 1 a / an ～ zoo

以中小学必考 1 000 单词范围为基础 / 符合美国幼儿园及美国一年级学生所学范围

0001 a / an [eɪ] / [ən] `art` 一个，每一，任一
I want to buy a new bag.
我想买个新包。
● An apple a day keeps the doctor away. 一天一苹果，医生远离我。

> 语法重点
> 冠词 a 用在以辅音开头的单词前面；以元音开头的单词前面用 an。

0002 able [ˈeɪbl] `a` 能够的，会的
Jack hasn't been able to revise the article yet.
杰克至今没能修改文章。
● capable 能干的 ● unable 不能的 ● be able to... 能做……

> 语法重点
> hasn't 是 has not 的简写，因为要表达"到目前为止还没有修改文章"，所以用现在完成时。

0003 about [əˈbaʊt] `prep` 关于，在……的附近 `ad` 在四周
I know nothing about him.
我对他一无所知。
● concerning 关于 ● be about to... 即将要……
● I know nothing about... 我对……一无所知

> 语法重点
> nothing 的反义词是 everything。"对……了如指掌"可表达为 know everything about sth.。

0004 above [əˈbʌv] `prep` 在……之上，超过，更大，更多
The book costs above $90.
这本书价格超过 90 美元。
● up 在……之上 ● below 在下面 ● above all 首先
● sth. costs... 某物花了……钱

> 语法重点
> 作"花费"讲时，cost 的主语通常是事或物，spend 的主语只能是人。

0005 according to [əˈkɔːrdɪŋ tə] `ph` 根据，据……所说
According to Lisa, Lucy has to leave this city.
据利萨说，露西不得不离开这个城市。
● in line with 根据 ● according to my schedule 根据我的行程表

> 语法重点
> have to 后面接动词原形。

0006 across [əˈkrɔːs] `ad` 横越，遍于……各处 `prep` 横过
Can you walk across the road quickly?
你能快速地穿过马路吗？
● through 通过 ● across from 在……对面

0007 act [ækt] `v` 行动，扮演，做事，举止 `n` 行为，法案
We must think carefully before we act.
在行动之前，我们必须认真考虑。
● play 扮演 ● act as 担当

> 语法重点
> before 前后的内容是同一个主语，所以 before we act 也可转换成 before acting。
> ⊃ must (P. 067)

0008 action [ˈækʃn] n 行动，行为，措施
You should put your ideas into action.
你应该把想法变成行动。
≈ behavior 行为　● take action 采取行动，提起诉讼

> **语法重点**
> should 后面接动词时，用动词原形。

0009 actor / actress [ˈæktə] / [ˈæktrəs] n 男演员 / 女演员
She dreamed of being an actress.
她梦想成为一名演员。

> **语法重点**
> actor 通常指男演员，actress 通常指女演员。在不强调演员性别时，也可以用 actor 来泛指演员。

0010 add [æd] v 增加，补充
She was reluctant to add my name to the list.
她不愿意在名单上加上我的名字。
≈ increase 增加　↔ subtract 减少　● add up 合计
● sb. be reluctant to do... 某人不愿意做……

0011 address [ˈædres] n 地址 v 称呼，向……致辞
My friend is going to address the meeting tomorrow.
我朋友明天将在会议上致辞。
≈ greet 致敬　● address book 通信录　● be going to do... 将要做……

> **语法重点**
> address 作动词时是及物动词，所以后面直接放宾语 the meeting。

0012 adult [ˈædʌlt] n 成人 a 成年的，成熟的
Her behavior looks like very adult.
她的行为看起来很成熟。
≈ mature 成熟的　↔ childish 幼稚的　● adult education 成人教育

0013 afraid [əˈfreɪd] a 害怕的，担心的
I'm afraid that I can't lend money to you.
我恐怕不能借钱给你。
≈ scared 害怕的　≈ bold 大胆的　● I'm afraid (that) I can't... 恐怕我不能……

> **语法重点**
> lend money to sb. 是"借钱给某人"。"向某人借钱"可表达为 borrow money from sb.。
> ⊃ money (P.064)

0014 after [ˈæftə(r)] prep 在……之后，在后面
He planned to do housework after school.
放学后他打算做家务。
≈ behind 在后面　↔ before 在之前　● go after 追求

0015 afternoon [ˌæftəˈnuːn] n 下午，午后
Shall we go to swim this afternoon?
我们今天下午去游泳怎么样？

⊃ swim (P. 100)

0016 again [əˈgen] ad 再次，又
I need to wash the plate again.
我需要再洗一次这个盘子。
≈ repeatedly 重复地，再三地　≈ again and again 再三地

> **语法重点**
> again 与动词连用可用 repeat doing sth. 来代替。例句中 wash the plate again 可替换成 repeat washing the plate。

action ~ airport

0017 against [ə'genst] **prep** 反对，违反
There is no good for us to go against his decision.
反对他的决定对我们没好处。
- versus 对抗　- for 为了　- go against 违反，反对

0018 age [eɪdʒ] **n** 年龄，时代
It has been ages since we danced together.
我们好久没在一起跳舞了。
- era 时代　- of age 成年　- It's ages since... 好久没……

> 语法重点
> It has been ages since... 句型中，since 后面的句子要用一般过去时。

0019 ago [ə'goʊ] **ad** 以前，之前
Two years ago, we had finished the task.
两年前，我们就已经完成了这项任务。
- previously 以前　- hence 今后　- long ago 很久以前

> 语法重点
> 表达"过去已经完成的事情"时要用过去完成时。
> ⇒ finish (P. 039)

0020 agree(ment) [ə'griː] / [ə'griːmənt] **v** / **n** 同意，赞成
My father will not agree on my opinion.
我的父亲将不会同意我的观点。
- consent 同意　- object 反对　- agree with... 和……意见一致

0021 ahead [ə'hed] **ad** 在前方，向前
We should make contact with him ahead of time.
我们应该提前和他联系。
- forward 向前　- backward 落后　- go ahead 前进，进行

> 语法重点
> ahead 不能单独使用，一般位于动词的后面或介词的前面，和动词或介词连用。

0022 air [er] **n** 空气，空中
There is a scent in the air.
空气中有一种香味。
- atmosphere 大气，空气　- air ticket 机票

> 语法重点
> air 是不可数名词，不能用具体的数词修饰，但可以用定冠词 the 修饰。

0023 airmail ['ermeɪl] **n** 航空邮件，航空邮政
I would like to send a letter by airmail.
我想寄封航空邮件。
- airpost 航空邮件　- I would like to do... 我想做……

> 语法重点
> by airmail 中间不加任何冠词。

0024 airplane / plane ['erpleɪn] / [pleɪn] **n** 飞机 **v** 乘飞机
He did not leave the airport until the airplane took off.
直到飞机起飞，他才离开机场。
- aeroplane 飞机　- on a plane 在飞机上

> 语法重点
> 主句与从句的时态要一致。
> ⇒ leave (P. 057)

0025 airport ['erpɔːrt] **n** 机场，航空港
Tomorrow I will pick Lily up at the airport.
明天我将去机场接莉莉。
- international airport 国际机场
- I will pick sb. up at someplace 我将去某地接某人

> 语法重点
> 一般将来时表示在将来的某个时间会发生的动作或情况。

005

0026 all [ɔːl] a 所有的，全部的 n 所有一切
All of us hang on her sleeve.
我们都很依赖她。
同 entire 全部的　近 several 几个的　反 in all 总共，共计
派 hang on sb.'s sleeve 是固定搭配，sleeve 要用单数。

0027 allow [əˈlaʊ] v 允许，同意
We are not allowed to sneak about there.
我们不能在那里偷偷摸摸地行动。
同 let 允许，让　反 disallow 不允许　派 allow for 考虑到

➡ about (P.003)

0028 almost [ˈɔːlməʊst] ad 几乎，差不多
I almost never play football.
我几乎从没踢过足球。
同 nearly 差不多，几乎

语法重点
play 后面加某种球类运动名词可表达"打……球，踢……球"的意思。

0029 alone [əˈləʊn] a 单独的，独自的
We can't leave him alone in the kindergarten.
我们不能把他独自留在幼儿园。
同 isolated 孤立的，单独的　派 all alone 独立地，独自地

语法重点
alone 既可作形容词又可作副词，lonely 只可作形容词。
➡ kindergarten (P.182)

0030 along [əˈlɒŋ] prep 沿着，顺着
She saw me running along the road yesterday.
她昨天看到我沿着马路跑。
同 down 沿着　派 along the road 沿路

0031 already [ɔːlˈredi] ad 已经，早已
We have already lived here for two years.
我们已经在这里住两年了。
派 already over 已经结束　派 we have already done... 我们已经做……

语法重点
现在完成时可以表示一直持续到现在的动作或状态，"已经在这里住两年了"是从过去的某一时间到目前一直住在这里，所以用现在完成时。

0032 also [ˈɔːlsəʊ] ad 也，同样地
They also should pay attention to the air pollution.
他们也应该关注空气污染。
同 too 也　近 as also 同样，照样

语法重点
should 是情态动词，它没有人称和数的变化，通常后接动词原形。

0033 always [ˈɔːlweɪz] ad 总是，始终
I always try to help other people.
我总是尽力帮助别人。

语法重点
try to do... 表示试图去做某事，还没做；try doing... 表示试着做某事，已经在进行中了。

0034 am [əm] v （用于第一人称单数）是，在
I must admit that I am a lazy man.
我不得不承认我是个懒惰的人。

语法重点
be 在一般现在时有三种形式：第一人称单数用 am，第三人称单数及单数主语用 is，第二人称及复数主语用 are。

0035 **among** [ə'mʌŋ] `prep` 在……中，……之一
She is the only girl among us.
她是我们当中唯一的女孩。
● among 指在三者或是三者以上的人或事物之间。

0036 **and** [ənd] `conj` 和，以及
My brother and my friend are both reading a book now.
我的哥哥和我的朋友现在都在看书。
● and so on 等等，诸如此类

语法重点
and 连接两个或两个以上的人或物，表示同类或是并列关系。

0037 **anger** ['æŋɡər] `n` 生气，愤怒
Her anger is out of control.
她无法控制自己的愤怒。
● fury 暴怒　● sb. be out of control 某人失去控制

↪ control (P. 144)

0038 **angry** ['æŋɡri] `a` 生气的，愤怒的
She was very angry because I did not wait for her.
她很生气，因为我没等她。
● be angry over 因……生气，对……生气（= be angry at）。

0039 **animal** ['ænɪml] `n` 动物，牲畜
Animals can be divided into many species.
动物可被分为很多种。
● wild animal 野生动物，野兽　● be divided into... 被分为……
● species 是生物学方面的"物种，种类"，type 是物品的"类型，品种，样式"的意思，kind 是东西的"种类"。

↪ divide (P. 154)

0040 **another** [ə'nʌðər] `a` 另一个的，再一个的
Let's find another seat.
我们再找个座位吧。

语法重点
another 泛指三个或三个以上的人或物中不确定的另一个，the other 指已知的两个人或物中的另一个。

0041 **answer** ['ænsər] `v` / `n` 回答，回复
It is easy for me to answer the question.
我可以轻易地回答这个问题。
● reply 回答　● ask 提问　● answer back 应答，回复

0042 **ant** [ænt] `n` 蚂蚁
I'm afraid of ants.
我害怕蚂蚁。
● have ants in one's pants 因焦急、气愤等而坐立不安
● be afraid of sth. 是"害怕某物"，be afraid of doing sth. 是"害怕做某事"。

0043 **any** ['eni] `a` 任何的，任一的，一些
Any one of us is a good dancer.
我们之中的任何一个人舞都跳得很好。
● whatever 不管什么样的，任何的　● any time 任何时候，随时

语法重点
"当中的任何一个人"表示的是单数，所以 be 动词用 is。

007

0044 **anything** [ˈenɪθɪŋ] **pron** 任何事
I can do anything for you if you like.
如果你愿意，我可以为你做任何事。

> **语法重点**
> can 是情态动词，在表达"能，可以"的意思时，后面接动词原形。

0045 **ape** [ep] **n** 猿猴，模仿者
They say humans evolved from apes.
据说，人类是由猿猴演变而来的。

> **语法重点**
> evolve from... 表达"由……演变而来"的意思。"发展成为什么，演化成什么"可用 evolve into 表达。
> ⊃ evolve (P. 717)

0046 **appear** [əˈpɪr] **v** 出现，显露，看起来像
I hope he can appear on time tomorrow.
我希望他明天能准时出现。
🔵 emerge 浮现，显露   🔴 disappear 消失   🟢 appear to be 好像是
📘 I hope... 我希望……（后面接 that 从句）

0047 **apple** [ˈæpl] **n** 苹果
There is an apple on his table.
在他的桌上有一个苹果。
📘 apple 是以元音开头的单词，所以前面用冠词 an。

0048 **April** [ˈeɪprəl] **n** 四月
In April, I will return to my native town.
在四月份，我将回故乡。
📘 Apr. 四月   📘 April Fool's Day 愚人节

> **语法重点**
> will 是情态动词，用于一般将来时，后接动词原形。
> ⊃ native (P. 328)

0049 **are** [ər] **v** 是，在
We are looking forward to buying a new car.
我们期待买一辆新车。
📘 we look forward to doing... 我们期待做……

> **语法重点**
> look forward to 中的 to 是介词，所以后面接动词的 ing 形式。

0050 **area** [ˈeriə] **n** 区域，面积，地区，范围
It has a population of one million in this area.
这个地区有 100 万人口。
🔵 district 地区   🟢 rural area 农村地区

> ⊃ population (p.206)

0051 **arm(1)** [ɑːrm] **n** 手臂，武器，装备
His arm is longer than mine.
他的手臂比我的长。
🔵 weapon 武器   🟢 at arm's length 保持距离

> **语法重点**
> 形容词比较级 + than + 比较成分，可表达两者之间的比较。

0052 **arm(2)** [ɑːrm] **v** 武装，装备
It is necessary to arm the security guard with the advanced weapons.
用先进的武器武装保安人员是十分必要的。
🔵 equip 武装   🔴 disarm 解除武装   🟢 be armed to the teeth 全副武装

> **语法重点**
> arms 也可作名词，表达"武器"的意思，但它主要指"炸弹和枪支之类"；而 weapon 指"枪、刀、导弹等能造成人身伤害的东西"。

0053 army ['ɑrmi] **n** 军队，陆军
Without the army, people will have no sense of security.
没有军队，人民会没有安全感。

0054 around [ə'raʊnd] **prep** 在……四周，围绕，大约
My grandmother always says the moon revolves around the earth.
我奶奶总是说月球围绕地球运转。
- round 大约
- turn around 转身

> **语法重点**
> 表示客观事实或普遍真理用一般现在时。月球围绕地球运转是一种客观事实，所以句子用一般现在时。
> ⇨ revolve (P. 625)

0055 art [ɑːrt] **n** 艺术，美术，人文学科
My sister is good at art.
我妹妹擅长艺术。
- work of art 艺术品
- be good at... 在……方面擅长

> **语法重点**
> "表示主语的性格、能力、状态等"可用一般现在时表达。

0056 as [əz] **conj** 和……一样，像，当……时
As expected, she came here on time.
不出所料，她准时来到了这里。
- since 因为
- thus 所以
- as soon as 一……就
- as expected 与后面的句子要用逗号隔开。

> ⇨ expect (P. 162)

0057 ask [æsk] **v** 问，请求，邀请
I will ask Jim to clean the room.
我将要求吉姆打扫房间。
- ask the way 问路
- ask sb. ... to do sth. 要求某人做某事

0058 at [ət] **prep** 在……，以
Just at that moment, the boy burst into tears.
就在那时，这个男孩突然哭了起来。

> **语法重点**
> just at that moment 一般要与过去时连用。

0059 August [ɔː'gʌst] **n** 八月
Last August, I moved to this city from New York.
去年八月，我从纽约搬到了这个城市。
- I move to A from B 我从 B 搬到 A

> **语法重点**
> last 后面接上表示星期、月份等时间的名词，表示过去的某个时间。

0060 aunt [ænt] **n** 姑姑，阿姨，伯母，婶婶，舅母
I have to take care of my aunt tomorrow.
我明天得照顾阿姨。
- auntie 姑母，伯母，婶婶，舅母，阿姨
- uncle 姑父，伯父，叔叔，舅父，姨父

0061 autumn ['ɔːtəm] **n** 秋天，秋季
Autumn is my favorite season.
秋天是我最喜爱的季节。
- fall 秋季

> **语法重点**
> favorite 本身就表达"最喜爱的"，所以它没有比较级和最高级形式。

0062 away [ə'weɪ] **a** **ad** 离开，远离，在远处
I live twenty miles away from the company.
我住在离公司二十英里①远的地方。
同 near 靠近　　away from home 不在家，离家出走

> **语法重点**
> mile 是可数名词，所以表达"20 英里"时用复数形式。

0063 baby ['beɪbɪ] **n** 婴儿，宝宝
She just gave birth to a baby.
她刚生完小孩。
同 babe 婴儿　　baby sitter 保姆，临时照看孩子的人

> **语法重点**
> give birth to 除有"生孩子"的意思，还有"产生，造成"的意思。

0064 back [bæk] **n** 背部 **ad** 向后，后退地
Please remember to give back the book to me.
请记得把书还给我。
同 rear 向后　　反 fore 在前面　　give back 归还

> **语法重点**
> remember to do sth. 表达"记得去做某事，但还没做"。remember doing sth. 表达"记得已经做过的事"。

0065 bad [bæd] **a** 坏的，不好的，差的
I am bad at singing songs.
我不擅长唱歌。
I am bad at... 我在……方面不擅长

0066 bag [bæɡ] **n** 袋子，包
What has he got in the green bag?
他那个绿色的袋子里装的是什么？
同 sack 袋　　plastic bag 塑胶袋

0067 ball [bɔːl] **n** 球
She threw away that ball.
她把那个球扔了。
ball games 球类运动　　sb. throws away... 某人把……扔掉，丢弃

> **语法重点**
> this 和 that 都是指示代词，this 指近处的"这，这个"，that 指远处的"那，那个"。

0068 balloon [bə'luːn] **n** 气球 **v** 膨胀
I have a colorful balloon.
我有一个彩色气球。
反 shrink 收缩　　hot-air balloon 热气球

> **语法重点**
> have 和 own 都可表达"有"的意思，但 have 的含义较广，可以指"物质的或非物质的东西"，而 own 则更强调"个人的、私人的拥有"，通常指"拥有某物"。
> colorful (P. 142)

0069 banana [bə'nænə] **n** 香蕉，（美俚）喜剧演员
Eating bananas is good for the eyes.
吃香蕉对眼睛有好处。
doing sth. is good for... 做某事对……有好处

0070 band [bænd] **n** 乐团，带子
The band is very popular with people.
这个乐队很受人们的欢迎。
sb. / sth. is popular with... 某人 / 某物受……欢迎

> **语法重点**
> person 通常是指单个人，复数形式是 persons；people 则是泛指不确定数量的人们，不带任何色彩，其单复数形式一样。

①1 英里=1 609.344 米。

away ~ basketball

0071 bank(1) [bæŋk] **n** 银行，岸，堤
My mother withdrew some money from the bank.
我妈妈从银行取了一些钱。
- shore 海岸   - in the bank 在银行

> **语法重点**
> "把钱存到银行"可表达为 deposit money in the bank。

0072 bank(2) [bæŋk] **v** 堆积，开户
I usually bank at ICBC.
我经常在工商银行存钱。
- pile 堆积   - bank at 把钱存入银行，开立账户

> **语法重点**
> usually 通常用在一般现在时中，表达一般性的、经常性的动作。

0073 bar [bɑːr] **n** 棒子，酒吧，栅栏 **v** 禁止
I have never been to a bar.
我从来没去过酒吧。

0074 barber ['bɑːrbər] **n** 理发师 **v** 为……理发
The barber is very kind to the customers.
这个理发师对客人很和善。
- shaver 理发师   - at the barber's 在理发店

> ↪ kind (P. 054)

0075 base [beɪs] **n** 基础，底部 **v** 以……为基础
Most of the poor people are based at the house.
大部分穷人都被安置在这个房子里。
- bottom 底部，下端   - top 顶部   - production base 生产基地

> **语法重点**
> base 指有形的基础，侧重于指构成或支撑某一具体物体的基础，而 basis 指无形的基础，主要用作抽象或引申意义。

0076 baseball ['beɪsbɔːl] **n** 棒球，棒球运动
As is well known, she likes the baseball champion.
众所周知，她喜欢那个棒球冠军。
- baseball cap 棒球帽   - as is well known, ... 众所周知，……

> **语法重点**
> champion 是指赢得某项比赛的人，而 championship 是"冠军称号，锦标赛"的意思。
>
> ↪ champion (P. 270)

0077 basic ['beɪsɪk] **a** 基础的，基本的
Citizens enjoy basic human rights.
公民享有基本的人身权利。

0078 basket ['bæskɪt] **n** 篮子，筐
Please give me the basket.
请把这个篮子给我。
- bamboo basket 竹篮，竹篓   - Please give sb. sth. 请把某物给某人

> **语法重点**
> give 和 pass 都有"给"的意思，give 是指两者之间的"给予"，pass 是"传递"的意思。

0079 basketball ['bæskɪtbɔːl] **n** 篮球，篮球运动
I would rather play basketball than stay at home.
我宁愿打篮球而不愿待在家里。
- I would rather do... than do... 我宁愿做……而不愿做……

> **语法重点**
> 美式英语多用 stay home，描述的是一种状态，英式英语多用 stay at home，描述的是个人意愿。从语法上分析，stay home 的 home 是副词，stay at home 的 home 是名词。

0080 **bat**(1) [bæt] n 蝙蝠，球拍
People rarely see bats.
人们很少见到蝙蝠。
- blind as a bat 近乎全盲的，视力很差的
- rarely 是 rare 的副词形式，rare 表达"稀有的，罕见的"的意思。

0081 **bat**(2) [bæt] v 击球，(俚)反复推敲，眨眼睛
I hurt my legs while batting.
我击球时伤了腿。

0082 **bath** [bæθ] n 浴缸，沐浴，洗澡
I want to have a shower instead of a bath.
我不想泡澡，想要淋浴。
- I want to do A instead of B 我想做 A 而不做 B
- shower 指的是"淋浴"，bath 一般指在浴盆里"泡澡"。

> 语法重点
> hurt 指对身体或心灵造成的伤害，表示有强烈的疼痛感；wound 一般指外伤，尤其指在战争中、打斗中受伤，出现明显的伤口；injure 指在平时或事故中受伤。
> ⇨ hurt (P. 051)

0083 **bathe** [beɪð] v 沐浴，洗澡，弄湿
Do you like bathing in the river?
你喜欢在河里洗澡吗？

0084 **bathroom** ['bæθruːm] n 浴室，盥洗室，洗手间
Could you tell me where the bathroom is?
你能告诉我洗手间在哪里吗？
- washroom 盥洗室，洗手间
- go to the bathroom 上厕所

> 语法重点
> 当表达"想要、欲做某事"时用 like to do sth.；当表达喜欢做某事，而且以前就喜欢，还可能持续，用 like doing sth.。

0085 **be** [bi] v 是，在
If he doesn't want to join us, then so be it.
如果他不愿意加入我们，那就随他便吧。
- let it be 随它去
- if..., then so be it. 如果……，那就随……的便吧。

0086 **beach** [biːtʃ] n 海滩，湖滩，河滩
Mr. Brown is walking on the beach.
布朗先生正在海滩上散步。
- foreshore 海边，海滩
- on the beach 上岸，在海滩上

0087 **bear**(1) [ber] n 熊，粗鲁的人
She thinks that bears look very ugly.
她认为熊看起来很丑。
- gentleman 绅士
- polar bear 北极熊

> 语法重点
> look 后接形容词，表达看起来什么样的状态；look like 后接名词，表达看起来像什么东西。

0088 **bear**(2) [ber] v 容忍，负担，生育
I can't bear him any longer.
我再也无法容忍他了。
- endure 忍耐，忍受
- bear up 坚持下去，振作起来

> 语法重点
> bear 和 stand 常用于否定句，bear 强调忍受者对痛苦、忧虑以及责任的承受力，stand 强调不屈不挠或经受得起。

0089 **beat** [biːt] v 打，敲，打败
The rain is beating against the window, and I am sitting beside it.
雨敲打着窗户，我坐在窗户边。
≈ defeat 打败　≠ lose 失败　● heart beat 心跳

⇒ against (P. 005)

0090 **beautiful** ['bjuːtɪfl] a 美丽的，漂亮的
Lucy is the most beautiful girl I have ever seen.
露西是我见过最漂亮的女孩。
≈ pretty 漂亮的　≠ ugly 丑陋的　● so beautiful 如此美丽，如此漂亮

0091 **beauty** ['bjuːti] n 美人，美，美丽
A lot of people praise highly natural beauty.
很多人推崇自然美。
※ a lot of 还可替换成 many。

⇒ praise (P. 207)

0092 **because** [bɪ'kɔːz] conj 因为，由于
I went to sleep because it was too late to do anything.
我去睡觉了，因为太晚了什么也做不了。
※ "去睡觉" 还可表达为 go to bed。

0093 **become** [bɪ'kʌm] v 成为，变成
As he thought, James becomes a successful man.
正如他所想，詹姆斯成了一名成功的人士。
● get 变　● become one 成为一体，结合

⇒ successful (P. 230)

0094 **bed** [bed] n 床，河床
Do you want to have a rest in bed?
你想在床上休息一会儿吗？
● go to bed 上床睡觉　● Do you want to do...? 你想做……？

0095 **bee** [biː] n 蜜蜂，忙碌的人
I have found that my mother is as busy as a bee every day.
我发现母亲每天忙得像蜜蜂似的。
● honeybee 蜜蜂　● sloven 懒散的人　● queen bee 蜂王，社交界女王

语法重点
不定冠词用于表示泛指，可表示一类人或事物中的一个，句中的 a bee 泛指蜜蜂中的一个。

0096 **before** [bɪ'fɔːr] prep 在……以前，在……前面
I haven't listened to the song before.
我从来没听过这首歌。
※ song 是一首首的歌曲，music 则是音乐的总称。

0097 **begin** [bɪ'gɪn] v 开始，着手
When did you begin to learn Russian?
你什么时候开始学俄语的？
● start 开始　≠ end 结束　● to begin with 首先，第一

语法重点
begin to do 表示一件事情的开端，持续与否不确定；begin doing 强调持续性。

0098 **behind** [bɪ'haɪnd] prep 在……背后，在后面
There is a tree behind my house.
我家的后面有一棵树。
同 after 在……之后　　before 在……之前　　drop behind 落后

语法重点
house 主要指房屋，里面可以没什么东西；home 强调家，包括房子、家具和人等，有一种主观感情在里面。

0099 **believe** [bɪ'liːv] v 相信，认为
I don't believe she is our teacher's daughter.
我不相信她是我们老师的女儿。
同 think 认为　　反 doubt 怀疑

⇒ daughter (P. 028)

0100 **bell** [bel] n 铃，门铃
Can you hear the bell is ringing?
你能听到门铃在响吗？
同 buzzer 门铃　　alarm bell 警钟，警铃

语法重点
说话时铃声正在持续地响，所以用现在进行时。

0101 **belong** [bɪ'lɔːŋ] v 属于，附属
Does the book belong to him?
这本书是属于他的吗？
同 attach 附属　　belong to 属于

语法重点
belong 是不及物动词，后面不能直接接宾语，所以要与 to 连用。

0102 **below** [bɪ'loʊ] prep 在……之下，以下
The temperature is below 20 degrees now.
现在温度在二十度以下。

语法重点
below 指处于比某物低的位置，不一定在某物的正下方；under 指处于某物的正下方。

0103 **beside** [bɪ'saɪd] prep 在……旁边，在……附近
Do you like to sit beside me?
你喜欢坐在我旁边吗？
同 near 靠近　　beside oneself 极度兴奋，为某事而忘形

语法重点
near 指空间、时间上的距离，形容的距离一般比 beside 形容的远，beside 多指空间上的距离。

0104 **best** [best] a 最好的，最佳的
Who is your best friend?
谁是你最好的朋友？
反 worst 最坏的　　make the best of 充分利用

语法重点
best 是 good 的最高级形式。

0105 **better** ['betər] a 更好的，较好的
You'd better tell him the truth.
你最好告诉他实话。
反 worse 较坏的　　for the better 好转，向好的方向发展

0106 **between** [bɪ'twiːn] prep 在……之间　ad 在中间
You have to choose one between the two colors.
你必须在这两种颜色中挑选一种。
同 intermediately 在中间　　between... and 在……之间

语法重点
have to 表示客观的"必须"；must 强调说话者主观上的看法，是主观上的必要。

behind ~ blood

0107 bicycle / bike [ˈbaɪsɪkl] / [baɪk] **n** 脚踏车，自行车
The bicycle is a little cheaper than that one.
这辆脚踏车比那辆便宜一点儿。
≈ bike 脚踏车 ≈ racing bicycle 赛车

> 语法重点
> 比较级前可用 a little 或 much 修饰。

0108 big [bɪg] **a** 大的，巨大的，大型的
Which is the biggest room?
哪个是最大的房间？
≈ large 大的 ≠ small 小的 ≈ talk big 说大话，吹牛

> ↪ room (P. 083)

0109 bird [bɜːrd] **n** 鸟，禽
The bird flew from the south.
这只鸟从南方飞来。
≈ birdie 小鸟 ※ "北方"是 the north。

0110 birth [bɜːrθ] **n** 出生，出身
Although she was of rich birth, she led a simple life.
尽管出身富贵，她却过着简朴的生活。
≈ origin 出身 ≠ death 死亡 ≈ give birth to 生孩子

> 语法重点
> although 引导的从句不能和 but / however 连用，但可以和 yet / still 连用。

0111 bit [bɪt] **n** 小块，一点点，小片
I want to get rid of bad habits bit by bit.
我要一点儿一点儿地改掉坏习惯。
≈ little 一点 ≠ mass 众多 ≈ every bit 完全，从头到尾

> 语法重点
> "一点儿一点儿地"还可用 little by little 表达。
> ↪ habit (P. 173)

0112 bite [baɪt] **v** 咬，叮，刺
That dog often bites people.
那只狗经常咬人。
≈ pierce 刺 ≈ bite at 咬

0113 black [blæk] **a** 黑的，黑暗的
The black cat ran away from my home.
那只黑猫从我家逃跑了。
≈ black and white 白纸黑字，单色，黑白片

> 语法重点
> 例句中特指的是那只黑猫，而不是其他的猫，所以前面加定冠词 the。

0114 block [blɑːk] **n** 街区 **v** 堵塞，拦阻
Lily's home is nearby; it is only three blocks away.
莉莉的家就在附近，距此只有三条街。
≈ clog 阻塞 ≈ block up 阻碍，垫高，停用，阻塞

> 语法重点
> nearby 和 near 都可做形容词，但 nearby 指空间上的接近，near 指空间、时间和年龄上的接近。
> ↪ nearby (P. 194)

0115 blood [blʌd] **n** 血，血液，血统
I am going to faint at the sight of blood.
我一看到血就要晕过去。
≈ parentage 血统 ≈ blood pressure 血压

0116 blow [bloʊ] v 吹响 n 击，打击

I really enjoy the feeling of the wind blowing my hair.
我很享受风吹着头发的感觉。
🔄 strike 打击　　🔄 blow out 吹熄，爆裂

➔ enjoy (P. 160)

0117 blue [bluː] a 蓝色的 n 蓝色

The blue skirt is different from the red one.
这件蓝色的裙子和那件红色的不同。
🔄 out of the blue 突然地，意外地　　🔄 be different from... 和……不同

语法重点
one 可用来指代前文提到的同类但不是同一个的可数名词，所以句中后面的 skirt 用 one 代替。

0118 boat [boʊt] n 小船，艇

Who told you there is a boat here?
谁告诉你这里有一只船？
🔄 ship 船　　🔄 Who told you...? 谁告诉你……？

语法重点
boat 指的是小船；ship 指大一点儿的船，能装货物的船。

0119 body [ˈbɑːdi] n 身体，主体

Smoking is harmful to your body.
吸烟对你的身体有害。
🔄 whole body 全身　　🔄 be harmful to... 对……有害

语法重点
smoking 是个动名词，动名词作主语时，动词为单数，所以 be 动词用 is。

0120 bone [boʊn] n 骨头，骨骼

These two dogs are fighting for a bone.
这两只狗正为一根骨头打架。
🔄 skeleton 骨骼　　🔄 flesh 肉　　🔄 bone fracture 骨折

语法重点
fight 是不及物动词，后面不能直接接宾语 a bone，所以句中和 for 连用。

➔ fight (P. 038)

0121 book(1) [bʊk] n 书，书籍

Can I borrow your book?
我能借你的书吗？
🔄 literature 文献，著作　　🔄 second-hand book 二手书

0122 book(2) [bʊk] v 预订，预约

When do you want to book the ticket?
你想什么时候订票？
🔄 reserve 预订　　🔄 book in 预订

语法重点
ticket 是各种票的总称，可表达门票、车票等。

0123 born [bɔːrn] a 出生的，天生的

He was born with a speech talent.
他生来就有演讲天赋。
🔄 born and bred 土生土长的　　🔄 be born with... 生来就具有……

语法重点
ability 强调一种做事的能力；talent 强调的是一种天赋，一种与生俱来的能力。

0124 both [boʊθ] pron 双方的 a 两个的

Both of you must go to the dinner party.
你们两个都必须参加晚宴。
🔄 two 两个的　　🔄 neither 两者都不　　🔄 both the two 两者都

blow ～ bridge

0125 bottom [ˈbɑːtəm] **n** 底部，根基
We should stick to our own bottom line.
我们应该坚守自己的底线。
- fundus 基底 - peak 顶点 - at the bottom of 底部，基层

> **语法重点**
> stick 可作及物动词和不及物动词，作"坚持"讲时只能是不及物动词。
> ⇒ stick (P. 228)

0126 bowl [boʊl] **n** 碗，钵，碗状物
I'd like a bowl of porridge.
我要一碗粥。
- over the bowl 在酒宴上，一边喝酒，一边谈话

0127 box [bɑːks] **n** 盒子，箱，包
I sent a box of oranges to her.
我给她寄了一箱橙子。
- case 箱 - I send sth. to sb. 我寄某物给某人

0128 boy [bɔɪ] **n** 男孩，少年，儿子
The boy is cleverer than his elder brother.
这个男孩比他哥哥聪明。
- girl 女孩 - as happy as a sand boy 高兴极了

> **语法重点**
> cleverer 是 clever 的比较级，clever 的最高级是 cleverest。

0129 brave [breɪv] **a** 勇敢的，无畏的
If you were a brave man, you would be fearless in your daily life.
如果你是个勇敢的人，日常生活中你将无所畏惧。
- bold 勇敢的 - timid 胆小的

> **语法重点**
> if 既可表条件又可表假设，在该句中 if 表假设，所以从句用虚拟语气。

0130 bread [bred] **n** 面包，食物，生计
I almost eat bread every morning.
我几乎每天早上都吃面包。

> **语法重点**
> every morning 和 every day 用法一样，前面都不加 on 或 in 之类的介词。

0131 break [breɪk] **v** 损坏，破坏
The window glass was broken by the boy.
窗户玻璃被那个男孩打破了。
- destroy 破坏 - break through 突围，取得突破性成就

> **语法重点**
> the window glass 是句中的主语，句子是被动语态，所以用 break 的过去分词。

0132 breakfast [ˈbrekfəst] **n** 早餐
I don't understand why you don't have breakfast.
我不明白你为什么不吃早餐。
- supper 晚餐 - have breakfast 吃早餐

> **语法重点**
> have 加三餐的名词可表达"吃早、午、晚餐"，例如 have lunch 吃午餐。

0133 bridge [brɪdʒ] **n** 桥，桥梁，桥牌
There is not much clearance for us to pass under the small bridge.
这座小桥下没有能让我们通过的空隙。

> **语法重点**
> bridge 是可数名词，句中 bridge 前面加冠词 the，指"这座桥"。

0134 bright [braɪt] a 光亮的，聪明的
We all believe that Tom will have a bright future.
我们都认为汤姆会有一个光明的未来。
　bright and early 大清早　　sb. has a bright future 某人前途光明

> **语法重点**
> future 既可作名词，又可作形容词，句中 future 是名词。
> believe (P. 014)

0135 bring [brɪŋ] v 携带，引出
Can you bring me something to eat?
你能给我带些吃的东西吗？
　cause 引起　　take 带走　　bring home 清楚说明，带回家

> **语法重点**
> 句中 to eat 是动词不定式，表目的。

0136 brother [ˈbrʌðər] n 兄弟，同胞
My brother is a good boy.
我的弟弟是个好男孩。
　compatriot 同胞　　sister 姐妹　　blood brother 亲兄弟

0137 brown [braʊn] a 褐色的 n 棕色
I want to see the brown sweater.
我想看那件棕色的毛衣。
　do up brown 做得彻底，干得漂亮

> **语法重点**
> the 后面接表颜色的形容词 + 某种衣服可表达"特定的某种颜色的衣服"。

0138 bug [bʌg] n 虫，窃听器
Aren't you afraid of bugs?
你不害怕臭虫吗？

> **语法重点**
> 句子的肯定回答是 Yes, I am（不，我害怕），否定回答是 No, I am not（是的，我不害怕）。

0139 build [bɪld] v 建造，创立
They decide to build a new school.
他们决定建一所新学校。
　create 创立　　demolish 毁坏　　build up 逐步建立，增进，增强

> **语法重点**
> build 的过去式和过去分词都是 built。

0140 building [ˈbɪldɪŋ] n 建筑物，大楼
The man who is in front of the building comes of a good stock.
大楼前面的那个人出身世家。

> front (P. 042)

0141 bus [bʌs] n 公交车
Do you like to take a bus or be on foot?
你喜欢乘公交车还是步行？
　autobus 公交车，巴士　　bus stop 公交车站

> **语法重点**
> "乘公交车"还可表达为 by bus。

0142 busy [ˈbɪzi] a 忙碌的，繁忙的
She is busy cooking supper.
她正忙着做晚餐。
　engaged 忙碌的　　free 空闲的　　busy season 旺季

> supper (P. 100)

0143 **but** [bət] **conj** 但是，可是，却

I'm sorry, but I can't help you.
对不起，我不能帮你。
- however 可是
- but good 非常地，完全地，彻底地

语法重点
I'm sorry, but 后面常接 can't，表达委婉的拒绝。

0144 **butter** ['bʌtər] **n** 奶油，黄油

You should blend the butter and sugar together.
你应该把奶油和糖混合在一起。
- cream 奶油
- peanut butter 花生酱

语法重点
blend 指将一种东西一点点儿地溶于另一种中，其中各成分不再单独存在，而此混合物却具有各成分的性质。

0145 **butterfly** ['bʌtərflaɪ] **n** 蝴蝶，蝶，轻浮之人

Can you tell the difference between a butterfly and a moth?
你能说出蝴蝶和蛾的区别吗？
- butterfly stroke 蝶式

↻ difference (P. 153)

0146 **buy** [baɪ] **v** 买，购买

My friend bought a hairpin for me.
我朋友给我买了一个发夹。
- purchase 购买
- sell 卖，出售
- buy favor with flattery 以谄媚得宠

语法重点
buy 接双宾语，通常指人的间接宾语在前，指物的直接宾语在后。如果直接宾语位于间接宾语之前，那么其后须用介词 for 引出间接宾语。

0147 **by** [baɪ] **prep** 经由

I was tripped by a stone.
我被一块石头绊倒了。
- via 经由
- by and by 不久以后

0148 **cage** [keɪdʒ] **n** 笼子，鸟笼，囚笼

The bird was confined in the cage.
这只鸟被关在笼子中。
- coop 笼
- bird cage 鸟笼

↻ confine (P. 413)

0149 **cake** [keɪk] **n** 蛋糕

This cake tastes good.
这块蛋糕尝起来不错。
- a piece of cake 一块蛋糕，轻松的事
- sth. tastes good 某物尝起来不错

语法重点
taste 作感官动词，通常后接形容词，表"尝起来"。

0150 **call** [kɔːl] **v** 呼叫，叫喊，召集

People always call her Snow White for some reason.
出于某种原因，人们总是叫她白雪公主。
- do sth. for some reason 出于某种原因做……

语法重点
call 表达"把……叫作"的意思时是及物动词，后面直接接宾语。

0151 **camel** ['kæml] **n** 骆驼，浮船箱

We should let the camels drink some water.
我们应该让骆驼喝点儿水。
- oont 骆驼
- swallow a camel 默认难以置信的事

语法重点
some 可以修饰不可数名词，表示"一些"。

0152 camera ['kæmərə] n 照相机，摄影机
My camera was imported from Germany.
我的相机是从德国进口的。
● video camera 摄影机　● sth. be imported from... 某物从……进口的

语法重点
主语是无生命的物品 camera，所以用被动语态。

0153 camp [kæmp] n 营地，兵营
Now, many parents would like to attend the summer camp with their children.
现在，很多家长愿意和他们的孩子一起参加夏令营。
● in the same camp 在一个阵营里，志同道合

语法重点
attend 作"参加，出席"讲时是及物动词，所以后面直接放宾语。

0154 can(1) [kæn] v 能够，会，可能
Can you do me a favor?
你能帮我一个忙吗？
● cannot 不能，无法　● can be 可能，可以是

↪ favor (P. 163)

0155 can(2) [kæn] n 罐头，罐
On my way home, I bought a can of beer.
在回家的路上，我买了一罐啤酒。
● tin 罐　● "一瓶啤酒"是 a bottle of beer.

0156 candy / sweet ['kændi] / [swi:t] n 糖果 a 甜的
The little girl threw the candy to me.
那个小女孩把糖果扔给了我。

语法重点
描述发生在过去的事情时用过去时，throw 的过去式是不规则变化，变 o 为 e。

0157 cap [kæp] n 帽子，便帽
Who is the man in the duckbill cap?
戴鸭舌帽的那个男人是谁？
● hat 帽子　● go cap in hand 毕恭毕敬，卑躬屈膝

语法重点
cap 指无檐、无边的帽子，或是棒球帽、鸭舌帽等仅在前方有帽檐的帽子，而 hat 多指有帽檐的帽子。

0158 car [kɑr] n 汽车，轿车
The structure of my car is very simple.
我的汽车结构很简单。
● automobile 汽车　● car industry 汽车工业

语法重点
在介词 of 后面加名词也是所有格的形式，此形式多用于表示无生命的东西的名词的所有格。

↪ structure (P. 367)

0159 card [kɑrd] n 卡片，名片
I intend to send my father a handmade card on Father's Day.
我打算在父亲节送给父亲一张我亲手做的卡片。
● name card 名片　● I intend to do... 我打算做……

0160 care [ker] n 照顾，关心
We should take good care of ourselves when we leave our parents.
离开父母时，我们要照顾好自己。
● concern 关心　● disregard 漠视　● with care 小心地

语法重点
care 是名词，所以可用形容词 good 修饰。

0161 careful ['kerfl] a 小心的，仔细的

You must be careful when you open the bottle.
你打开这个瓶子时，一定要小心。
- cautious 小心的 - careless 粗心的

语法重点
be careful 后面经常和 in、with、of 连用，表达"小心……"的意思。

0162 carry ['kæri] v 提，搬，携带，运载

The weather forecast says it will rain today, so don't forget to carry your umbrella.
天气预报说今天有雨，因此你不要忘了带伞。

语法重点
天气预报说的都是将来的天气情况，所以要用将来时。

0163 case(1) [keɪs] n 事件，情况，病例，箱子

In most cases, the parents love their children with all their heart.
在大部分情况下，父母都是全心全意地爱他们的孩子。
- in case (of) 假使，以防 - with all one's heart 表示"全心全意地"意思。

0164 case(2) [keɪs] v 包围，把……装入

Next, we need to case the computer into the box.
接下来，我们要把电脑装到箱子里。
- surround 包围 - case the joint（行窃前）仔细勘察

语法重点
case 作动词时是及物动词，所以后面直接接宾语。

0165 cat [kæt] n 猫，猫科动物

Leopards and cats look alike.
豹和猫长得很像。
- puss 猫咪 - (as) sick as a cat 病得厉害、严重

语法重点
leopards 和 cats 用名词复数表示泛指，泛指豹和猫这两种动物。

0166 catch [kætʃ] v 捕捉，捉住，赶上，领会

Upon seeing me, she excitedly caught my arm.
一见到我，她就激动地抓住我的胳膊。
- seize 抓住 - loose 释放 - catch up with 赶上

0167 cause [kɔːz] n 原因，理由，事业 v 引起

What is the cause of the fire?
引起这起火灾的原因是什么？
- cause of death 死因

语法重点
cause 表示造成某一事实或现象的直接原因和起因，reason 是说明一种看法或行动的理由。

0168 cent [sent] n 一分硬币

Can you guess how many cents there are in my hand?
你能猜出我手里有多少一分的硬币吗？
- penny 分 - red cent 一便士，一分钱

语法重点
cent 是可数名词，问多少时用 how many。

0169 center ['sentər] n 中心，中枢 v 集中

The pillar is the center of my house.
这根柱子是我的房子的中心。
- centre 中心 - shopping center 购物中心

语法重点
center 多指物体的正中心，middle 则指中间或中部，它表示的位置不如 center 精确。

0170 certain ['sɜːrtn] a 确实的，肯定的，某些
It is certain that he likes high-tech products.
可以肯定的是，他喜欢高科技产品。
　sure 确定的　　uncertain 不确定的　　for certain 肯定地，确切地

> 语法重点
> high-tech 是 high technology 的缩写。

0171 chair [tʃer] n 椅子，主席
Did you see my chair?
你看到我的椅子了吗？
　bench 长凳　　put in the chair 选举……为主席、会长

> 语法重点
> 句子说的是发生在过去的事情，所以用过去时。

0172 chance [tʃæns] n 机会，机遇，可能性
Please give me a chance, let me show my talent.
请给我一个机会，让我展示我的才能。
　opportunity 机会，时机　　one more chance 再来一次

0173 chart [tʃɑːrt] n 图表
Please draw the chart out immediately.
请马上把这张图表绘制出来。
　graph 图表　　conversion chart 换算表

> 语法重点
> chart 和 table 都有"表"的意思，但 chart 是图表、图纸，table 是表格。

0174 chase [tʃeɪs] v / n 追逐，追赶，追求
The timid boy doesn't have the courage to chase the dog.
这个胆小的孩子没有勇气去追赶那只狗。
　sb. doesn't have the courage to do... 某人没有勇气做……

⊃ timid (P. 511)

0175 check [tʃek] v 核对 n 检查，支票
I go to the hospital for a check-up every year.
我每年都去医院进行体检。
　go to the hospital 只说去医院，不一定是去看病，也可能是去上班，go to hospital 主要指去医院看病或住院

0176 chick [tʃɪk] n 小鸡，少妇 a 胆小的
A group of chicks are looking for worms to eat in my yard.
在我的院子里，一群小鸡正在找虫子吃。

⊃ yard (P. 248)

0177 chicken ['tʃɪkɪn] n 鸡，鸡肉
She makes her living by selling chicken.
她靠卖鸡肉为生。
　sb. makes one's living by... 以……为生　　chicken 可指鸡、小鸡、鸡肉

0178 chief [tʃiːf] n 首领 a 主要的
Our chief purpose is to improve the life quality.
我们的主要目的是提高生活品质。
　major 主要的　　subordinate 次要的
　Chief Executive Officer 首席执行官

> 语法重点
> 不定式 to 在句中表目的。

0179 child [tʃaɪld] n 小孩，儿童
Don't be too hard on the child.
别对孩子太苛刻了。
- don't be too hard on... 别对……太苛刻

语法重点 child 的复数形式是 children，是不规则变化。

0180 Christmas ['krɪsməs] n 圣诞节
Many people think that Christmas is a festival to celebrate.
很多人认为圣诞节是一个值得庆祝的节日。
- Merry Christmas 圣诞快乐

0181 church [tʃɜːrtʃ] n 教堂，教会
There is a church near my home.
我家附近有一个教堂。
- chapel 小教堂
- go to church（去教堂）做礼拜

0182 city ['sɪti] n 城市，都市
I aspire to live in a small city.
我渴望去小城市生活。
- metropolis 都会
- country 农村

语法重点 "中等城市"是 medium-sized city；"大城市"可表达为 big city 或 large city。

0183 class [klæs] n 班级，阶级
We are from different classes.
我们来自不同的班级。
- grade 等级
- first class 头等，第一流，最高级

0184 clean [kliːn] a 干净的，清洁的
You must keep the room clean and tidy.
你们一定要保持房间干净、整洁。
- tidy 整洁的
- dirty 脏的

语法重点 keep 作"保持"讲，后面接双宾语，表示宾语保持什么样的状态。

0185 clear [klɪr] a 清楚的，明确的，明白的
You should make it clear to her that you don't agree with her plan.
你应该清楚地告诉她，你不同意她的计划。
- distinct 清楚的
- vague 模糊的
- make clear 显示，解释清楚

语法重点 it 在句中作形式宾语，表示强调。

0186 climb [klaɪm] v 攀爬，爬
I think mountain climbing is also a form of exercise.
我觉得爬山也是一种运动形式。
- ascend 攀登
- climb up 爬上去

→ mountain (P. 065)

0187 clock [klɑːk] n 时钟，仪表
This clock in my house has a long history.
我屋子里的这座钟有着悠久的历史。
- timer 时钟
- alarm clock 闹钟

→ history (P. 049)

0188 close(1) [kloʊz] v 关上，闭，结束

Please don't forget to close the window after work.
下班后不要忘记关窗。

同 shut 关　反 open 打开　搭 close the door 关门

语法重点
close 指"结束，了结"，end 指"终止，终结"。

0189 close(2) [kloʊz] a 接近的，紧密的

The two companies have established close relations of cooperation.
两家公司已经建立密切的合作关系。

同 intimate 亲密的　搭 close contact 近距离接触，紧密接触

语法重点
relation 指的是人、团体、国家等之间的关系；relationship 除了指人、团体之间的关系，还可指爱情关系。

0190 cloud [klaʊd] n 云，阴影

Dark clouds are a sign of rain, let's go home quickly.
乌云是要下雨的预兆，我们快点回家吧。

搭 in the clouds 心不在焉，在云层中　搭 be a sign of... 是……的预兆

0191 coast [koʊst] n 海岸，海滨（地区）

We set up a tent on the coast.
我们在海岸边搭帐篷。

同 seaside 海滨　搭 along the coast 沿着海岸

0192 coat [koʊt] n 外套，上衣

Whose coat is this?
这是谁的外套？

同 wrap 外套　同 trousers 裤子　搭 fur coat 皮毛大衣

语法重点
whose 是疑问代词，引导特殊疑问句，意思是"谁的"，指附属关系。

0193 cocoa ['koʊkoʊ] n 可可粉，可可饮料

Mother says chocolate is made from cocoa powder.
妈妈说巧克力是由可可粉制成的。

搭 cocoa bean 可可豆　搭 be made from... 由……制成的

语法重点
be made from 暗含的意思是看不出原材料。

0194 coffee ['kɔːfi] n 咖啡，咖啡色，咖啡粉

The woman is very dependent on coffee.
这个女人很依赖咖啡。

搭 a cup of coffee 一杯咖啡　搭 be dependent on... 对……依赖

⊃ dependent (P. 424)

0195 cola / coke ['koʊlə] / [koʊk] n 可乐，可乐树　n 可口可乐

Research shows that drinking Coca-Cola is bad for your teeth.
研究表明，喝可乐对牙齿不好。

语法重点
teeth 是 tooth 的复数形式，是不规则变化。

0196 cold [koʊld] a 冷的　n 冷，感冒

My cold has continued for a week.
我的感冒已经持续一周了。

搭 catch a cold 感冒

语法重点
从过去一直持续到现在的状态用现在完成时。

close(1) ~ correct

0197 color [ˈkʌlər] n 颜色，彩色
I have a variety of colors in my wardrobe.
我的衣柜里有各种颜色的衣服。
→ wardrobe (P. 804)

0198 come [kʌm] v 来，来到
The train is coming.
火车来了。
🔗 arrive 来到　　🔗 go 去　　🔗 come true 实现，成真

> 语法重点
> be coming 表达"即将到来"的意思，是一般将来时。

0199 common [ˈkɑːmən] a 普通的，共同的
The two of us don't have much in common.
我们两个没有太多共同点。
🔗 ordinary 普通的　　🔗 uncommon 不寻常的　　🔗 in common 共同的

0200 continue [kənˈtɪnjuː] v 继续，连续
Let's continue the class.
我们继续上课。
🔗 persist 持续　　🔗 discontinue 停止，中断　　🔗 continue with 继续做

> 语法重点
> class 指一般意义上的上课，侧重于课业的形式；course 指的是所学的课程，侧重的是课业的内容。

0201 cook [kʊk] v 烹调，烧菜　n 厨师
He is very interested in cooking.
他对烹饪很感兴趣。
🔗 chef 厨师　　🔗 be interested in... 对……感兴趣

> 语法重点
> cook 指的是擅长烹调的人或职业的厨师，而 chef 指（餐馆、酒店等）里面的厨师。

0202 cookie [ˈkʊki] n 饼干，（俚）家伙
I hate eating cookies.
我讨厌吃饼干。

0203 cool [kuːl] a 凉快的，冷静的
Today the weather is getting cool.
今天天气变凉爽了。
🔗 chilly 冷的　　🔗 warm 温暖的　　🔗 cool down 冷却，平静下来

> 语法重点
> get 在句中与形容词连用，表达"变得"的意思。

0204 corn [kɔːrn] n 谷物，玉米
Do you believe that cats like to eat boiled corn?
你相信猫咪喜欢吃煮熟的玉米吗？
🔗 cereal 谷物　　🔗 Do you believe that...? 你相信……吗？

> 语法重点
> boiled 可作形容词，表达"煮熟的"意思，同时也是 boil 的过去分词。

0205 correct [kəˈrekt] a 正确的　v 纠正
He insisted that his decision was correct.
他坚持认为自己的决定是正确的。
🔗 accurate 准确的　　🔗 incorrect 不正确的　　🔗 correct time 正确时间

> 语法重点
> correct 和 right 意思相近，correct 一般用于较正式的句子，指法律上、道德上等正确，主语一般是物，right 多用于口语，主语一般是人。
> → insist (P. 179)

025

0206 cost [kɔːst] **n** 价格，代价，成本 **v** 花费
I get from my mother that the chair cost $15.
我从妈妈那里知道这把椅子花了十五美元。
rate 价格，费用　production cost 生产成本
I get from... that... 我从……知道……

> 语法重点
> cost 的过去式是其原形，第三人称单数形式是 costs，句中的 cost 是其过去式。

0207 count [kaʊnt] **v** 计算，数，计数
Please count how many dogs there are in the yard.
请数一下院子里有多少只狗。
number 计算　count in 把……计算在内

> 语法重点
> how many 用于提问可数名词的数量。

0208 country [ˈkʌntri] **n** 国家，农村
I think different countries have different cultures, so we should respect the foreign guests.
我以为不同的国家有不同的文化，所以我们应该尊重外国客人。
state 国家　all over the country 遍及全国

> 语法重点
> country 和 culture 都是可数名词，句中指的是很多的国家和文化，所以两者都用复数形式。

0209 course [kɔːrs] **n** 课程，过程，一道菜
The course these adults take is an absolute doddle.
这些成年人学的课程简直太容易了。
process 过程　in the process of 在……的过程中

> 语法重点
> "选课" 是 take the course，"退课" 是 drop the course.
> ↪ adult (P. 004)

0210 cover [ˈkʌvər] **v** 覆盖，包括 **n** 盖子
Mother covers the quilt for me every night.
妈妈每天晚上都为我盖被子。
uncover 揭露，揭开　cover up 掩盖，盖住

> 语法重点
> 例句叙述的是每天都要做的事情，所以用一般现在时。

0211 cow [kaʊ] **n** 乳牛，奶牛
Who knows how many cows there are on the farm?
谁知道这个农场有多少头牛？

0212 cowboy [ˈkaʊbɔɪ] **n** 牛仔，牧童
She is fascinated with the cowboy.
她对那个牛仔很着迷。
sb. be fascinated with... 某人对……很着迷

↪ fascinate (P. 567)

0213 crow [kroʊ] **n** 乌鸦，鸦
Long time ago, a crow was the symbol of auspiciousness.
很久以前，乌鸦曾是吉祥的象征。
eat crow 被迫收回自己说的话　Long time ago, ... 很久以前，……

0214 cry [kraɪ] **v** 哭泣，叫喊 **n** 哭
Suddenly a loud cry broke the quiet night.
突然一声叫喊打破了平静的夜晚。
sob 哭泣，呜咽　laugh 笑　cry out 大声呼喊

> 语法重点
> quiet 作形容词时，主要表示环境或是人物性格的安静。

cost ~ dark

0215 cub [kʌb] n 幼童军，（狮、虎、熊、狐）幼兽，年轻人
The cub returned to his mother's arms.
这个年轻人回到了妈妈的怀抱。
- cub scout 幼童军　　... return to one's arms ……回到某人的怀抱

> **语法重点**
> 句中 return 作"返回"讲，指回到原来所在的地方。

0216 cup [kʌp] n 杯子，奖杯
Please wash the cups.
请把这些杯子洗一下。
- glass 杯子　　world cup 世界杯

0217 cut [kʌt] v 切割，剪，减少
She used scissors to cut cloth.
她用剪刀把布剪破了。

> **语法重点**
> cloth 是"布料"的意思，clothes 指"具体的衣服"，clothing 是"衣物的总称，概念上的衣服"。

0218 cute [kjuːt] a 可爱的，聪明的
It is such a cute dog that everyone wants to touch it.
它是如此可爱的一只狗，每个人都想抚摸它。
- lovely 可爱的　　boring 令人厌倦的　　cute girl 可爱的女孩

> **语法重点**
> it is such a / an + 形容词 + that 后一般接从句。
> ⇒ touch (P. 106)

0219 dad / daddy [dæd] / ['dædi] n 爸爸
The little girl likes to play with her daddy.
这个小女孩喜欢和爸爸一起玩。
- dad 爸爸　　mum 妈妈

0220 dance [dæns] v 跳舞 n 舞蹈
I don't mind dancing with him.
我不介意和他跳舞。
- dancing 跳舞，舞蹈　　dance floor 舞池

> **语法重点**
> mind 作动词"介意做某事"讲时，后接动词的 ing 形式。

0221 dancer ['dænsər] n 舞者，跳舞的人
My mother said that I have the gift of a dancer.
妈妈说我有成为舞蹈家的天赋。
- hoofer 舞者　　sb. has the gift of... 某人有……的天赋

> **语法重点**
> 妈妈说的话是过去说的，所以用 said，指自己一直都具备的才能，则用一般现在时。

0222 danger ['deɪndʒər] n 危险，危险事物
The real danger is that people don't realize the danger.
真正的危险是人们意识不到危险。
- risk 风险　　safety 安全　　hidden danger 隐患

0223 dark [dɑːrk] a 黑暗的，黑的
We should not be affected by the dark side of society.
我们不应该受社会阴暗面的影响。
- dismal 暗的　　bright 明亮的

> **语法重点**
> 句中要表达的是"被影响"，所以用被动语态 be affected。

0224 **date** [deɪt] n 日期，约会
Up to date, I haven't been to his house.
到目前为止，我还没去过他家。
📙 appointment 约会　　📗 date of birth 出生日期

0225 **daughter** ['dɔːtər] n 女儿
The couple has no daughter.
这对夫妇没有女儿。
📙 dau. 女儿　　📕 son 儿子

> 语法重点
> couple 是"一对"的意思，在这里作为一个整体用，所以动词用 has。

0226 **day** [deɪ] n 一天，白天
He works day and night for his son.
他为了儿子不分白天黑夜地工作。
📙 daytime 白天　　📕 night 晚上　　📗 every day 每天，每个白天

> 语法重点
> day 通常是泛指一天、一昼夜，而 date 是指具体的某年某月的某一天。

0227 **dead** [ded] a 死亡的，去世的，死去的
His father has been dead for five years.
他的父亲已经去世 5 年了。
📕 alive 活着的　　📗 sb. has been dead for... 某人已经去世……

0228 **deal** [diːl] n 交易 v 经营，处理
We should actively deal with the problems.
我们应该积极地处理问题。
📙 handle 处理　　📗 good deal 划算，好交易

> 语法重点
> deal 单独使用时是"成交"的意思；表达"处理"的意思时，与 with 连用。
> ↪ problem (P. 078)

0229 **dear** [dɪr] a 亲爱的，宝贵的 n 可爱的人，亲爱的人
You will always be my dearest friend.
你永远是我最亲爱的朋友。

0230 **death** [deθ] n 死亡
Don't be sad, for birth and death is the law of nature.
别伤心了，因为生死是大自然的规律。
📙 doom 死亡　　📕 birth 出生　　📗 death penalty 死刑

0231 **December** [dɪ'sembər] n 十二月
In December, I will attend a big wedding ceremony.
在十二月份，我要参加一个盛大的结婚典礼。
📙 I will attend... 我要参加……

> 语法重点
> attend 作"参加"讲时，是及物动词。
> ↪ attend (P. 126)

0232 **decide** [dɪ'saɪd] v 决定，决心，解决
Have you decided to give up the competition?
你已经决定要放弃比赛了吗？
📙 determine 决定，决心　　📕 hesitate 犹豫

date ~ direct

0233 deep [diːp] a 深的，深刻的
His smile left a deep impression on me.
他的笑容给我留下了深刻的印象。
同 profound 深刻的　反 shallow 浅的　搭 deep water 深层水，深水

0234 deer [dɪr] n 鹿
The deer ran away at the sight of the lion.
这群鹿一看到狮子就逃跑了。

> 语法重点
> deer 的单复数都是 deer。

0235 desk [desk] n 桌子
Where is Jack's desk?
杰克的桌子在哪里？
同 table 桌子　搭 front desk 服务台

> 语法重点
> 名字后面加 's 是名词的所有格形式，表示"某人的"意思。

0236 die [daɪ] v 死亡，灭亡
This old lady's only son died last week. It was a big blow for her.
这位老太太唯一的儿子上周死了，这对她来说是一个很大的打击。
搭 die of 因……死　搭 be a big blow for... 对……是一个很大的打击

> 语法重点
> blow 作名词时有"打击"的意思。

0237 different ['dɪfrənt] a 不同的，相异
The twins have different characters.
这对双胞胎有着不同的性格。
反 unlike 不同的　反 same 相同的　搭 different from 与……不同

> 语法重点
> character 指品性、品质方面的"性格"，它决定一个人对待生活中重大问题的态度。

0238 difficult ['dɪfɪkəlt] a 困难的
We must bravely face all kinds of difficult problems, and then find ways to overcome them.
我们要勇敢地面对各种难题，然后想办法克服它们。
同 hard 困难的　反 easy 容易的　搭 difficult choice 艰难的选择

0239 dig [dɪg] v 挖掘，采掘
Grandpa is digging holes to plant trees in the yard.
爷爷正在院子里挖洞种树。
反 bury 埋葬，掩埋　搭 dig out 掘出，发现

⇒ plant (P. 076)

0240 dinner ['dɪnər] n 晚餐，主餐
We are preparing a hearty dinner.
我们正在准备一顿丰盛的晚餐。
搭 dinner party 宴会　搭 sb. be preparing... 某人正在准备……

0241 direct [də'rekt] a 直接的　v 命令，指示
His direct expression made me at a loss.
他直接的表白令我不知所措。
搭 direct influence 直接影响　搭 make sb. at a loss 令某人不知所措

> 语法重点
> at a loss 还有"茫然，困惑"的意思。

0242 dirty [ˈdɜːrti] a 肮脏的，下流的 v 弄脏，玷污

His room is so dirty that nobody wants to enter it.
他房间里太脏以至于没人愿意进去。
⊜ be so + 形容词 + that... 如此……以至于……

> 语法重点
> so + 形容词或副词 + that 引导的结果状语从句，是"如此……以至于……"的意思。

0243 discover [dɪˈskʌvər] v 发现，偶然撞见

He is the person who first discovered the small lake.
他是第一个发现那个小湖的人。
⊜ find 发现 ⊝ miss 错过 ⊜ discover nature 探索自然

> 语法重点
> discover 是发现早就存在而不为人知的东西。

0244 dish [dɪʃ] n 盘子，碟

He can make very exquisite dishes.
他能制作很精美的盘子。
⊜ main dish 主菜 ⊜ sb. can make... 某人能制作……

> 语法重点
> dish 是可数名词。
> ⊃ exquisite (P. 719)

0245 do [də] v 做

I have formed the habit of doing exercise every day.
我已经养成了每天都做运动的习惯。
⊜ do well 做得好，进展得好

0246 doctor / doc [ˈdɑːktər] / [dɑːk] n 医生，大夫

It is reported that the doctor has a superb skill and noble medical ethics.
据报道，这名医生有着高超的医术和高尚的医德。
⊜ medic 医生 ⊝ patient 病人 ⊜ it is reported that... 据报道，……

⊃ noble (P. 329)

0247 dog [dɔːg] n 狗

In a sense, dogs and people are equal.
从某种意义上来说，狗和人是平等的。
⊜ pup 小狗 ⊜ hot dog 热狗

0248 doll [dɑːl] n 洋娃娃，玩偶

Barbie is the best-selling doll in the 20th century.
芭比娃娃是 20 世纪最畅销的玩偶。
⊜ dolly 洋娃娃 ⊜ barbie doll 芭比娃娃，没有头脑的人，徒有其表的人

> 语法重点
> best-selling 是由形容词 good 的最高级 best 和 sell 的 ing 形式组合而成的。

0249 dollar / buck [ˈdɑːlər] / [bʌk] n 元，美元

To tell you the truth, this gift cost me 100 dollars.
老实跟你说，这个礼物花了我 100 美元。
⊜ dollar depreciation 美元贬值 ⊜ To tell you the truth, ... 老实跟你说，……

0250 door [dɔːr] n 门，门口

My mother tells me the door to success opens only for the prepared people.
妈妈告诉我，成功之门只为有准备的人开启。
⊜ doorway 门口 ⊜ door to door 挨家挨户

0251 **dove** [dʌv] n 鸽子

Dove is one of the most common birds.
鸽子是最常见的鸟之一。
- be one of the most common... 是最常见的……之一

0252 **down** [daʊn] ad 向下　prep 沿着……向下

I want to note down what he says.
我想把他说的话记下来。
- downhill 向下　　up 向上　　go down 下降，降低

0253 **downstairs** [ˌdaʊnˈsterz] ad 向楼下　a 楼下的

Lily said that she would wait for me downstairs after school.
莉莉说放学后她会在楼下等我。
- belowstairs 在楼下　　upstairs 在楼上　　go downstairs 下楼

> **语法重点**
> downstairs 在句中表示地点。

0254 **dozen** [ˈdʌzn] n 一打，十二个

How much are a dozen socks?
一打袜子多少钱？
- twelve 十二个　　dozens of 几十，许多

> **语法重点**
> "一打"是十二个，所以后面要用复数形式 socks。

0255 **draw** [drɔː] v 图画，拖拉，画

I drew a conclusion that he dislikes women.
我得出结论，他不喜欢女人。
- draw lessons from 从……吸取教训
- sb. draws a conclusion that... 某人得出……结论

> **语法重点**
> drew 是动词 draw 的过去式。
> ⟳ conclusion (P. 276)

0256 **dream** [driːm] n 梦，梦想　v 做梦

I will do my best to realize my dream.
我要尽自己最大的努力去实现我的梦想。
- I will do my best... 我要尽自己最大的努力去做……

0257 **drink** [drɪŋk] v 喝水　n 饮料

He often goes to the pub for a drink.
他经常去那家酒馆喝酒。

> **语法重点**
> drink 作动词时本身就有"喝酒"的意思，所以说喝酒时后面可以不加 wine。

0258 **drive** [draɪv] v 驾驶，驱赶

It's hard to drive a car in the water.
在水里开车很困难。
- drive out 驱赶，开车外出　　it's hard to do... 做……很困难

> **语法重点**
> it 在句中是形式主语，真正的主语是 to drive a car in the water。

0259 **driver** [ˈdraɪvər] n 驾驶，司机

A drunken driver is a danger to the public.
喝醉的司机对公众是一个威胁。
- chauffeur 司机　　passenger 乘客　　the driver's seat 驾驶座

> **语法重点**
> 句中没指特定的某个司机，所以用不定冠词 a 修饰。

0260 dry [draɪ] a 干燥的 v 使干燥
Some people can't adapt themselves to the dry climate in the desert regions.
有些人无法适应沙漠地区的干燥气候。

> 语法重点
> desert 是"沙漠",dessert 是"甜点",注意区分。
> ⊃ adapt (P. 391)

0261 duck [dʌk] n 鸭子,鸭肉
Have you tried Peking duck?
你吃过北京烤鸭吗?
⊕ quacker 鸭子 ⊕ Have you eaten...? 你吃过……吗?

0262 duckling ['dʌklɪŋ] n 小鸭
Can you see a group of ducklings swimming in the pond?
你能看见一群小鸭子正在池塘里游泳吗?
⊕ Can you see...? 你能看见……吗?

> 语法重点
> pool 是天然形成的池塘,pond 通常指人工挖掘或是修造的池塘。

0263 during ['dʊrɪŋ] prep 在……期间
During my illness, my mother had been taking care of me.
在我生病期间,母亲一直在照顾我。
⊕ during the day 在白天

> 语法重点
> had been doing sth. 表达过去某种动作一直在持续。

0264 each [iːtʃ] pron 每个的 a 每,每个 ad 每个
We need to be patient to each person here.
我们对这里的每一个人都要有耐心。

> 语法重点
> each 更强调个人或个别,every 更强调全体或全部。

0265 eagle ['iːgl] n 老鹰
I have been dreaming of flying freely in the sky like the eagle.
我一直梦想着像鹰一样在空中自由飞翔。
⊕ I have been dreaming of doing... 我一直梦想着做……

0266 ear [ɪr] n 耳朵
His biggest characteristic is that he has a pair of big ears.
他最大的特征是有一双大耳朵。
⊕ be all ears 注意听,倾听

> 语法重点
> a pair of 表达"一双,一对"的意思,后面常接复数名词。

0267 early ['ɜːrli] ad / a 早的
Early to bed and early to rise is beneficial to the health of our body.
早睡早起有利于身体健康。
⊕ beforehand 事先 ⊗ late 晚的 ⊕ as early as 早在……的时候

⊃ bed (P. 013)

0268 earth [ɜːrθ] n 地球,泥土
Who on earth should take the responsibility?
究竟谁该承担责任呢?
⊕ dirt 泥土 ⊕ down to earth 实际的,不加渲染的

0269 **ease** [i:z] n 容易，自在 v 减轻，放松，缓和
I was struck with ease after finishing the task.
完成任务后，我突然感到一阵轻松。
⊚ allay 减轻，使缓和　⊚ ease down 放慢速度，使平静下来

语法重点
after 作介词表达"在……之后"，后接动词的 ing 形式。

0270 **east** [i:st] n 东方，东部 a 东方的 ad 向东方
The train he takes is moving toward east.
他乘坐的火车向东方行驶。
⊚ orient 东方　⊚ west 西方（的）

语法重点
toward 作介词用，表示朝向。

0271 **easy** ['i:zi] a 容易的，舒适的，随和的
It is not easy to struggle alone in the city.
独自一个人在城市奋斗很不容易。
⊚ uneasy 不自在的　⊚ go easy 安闲，从容不迫

语法重点
alone 在句中作副词，修饰动词 struggle。
⊚ alone (P. 006)

0272 **eat** [i:t] v 吃
After eating, I have to do the dishes.
饭后，我得洗餐具。
⊚ eat out 在外吃饭

0273 **edge** [edʒ] n 边缘，刀口
We live on the edge of the city.
我们住在城市的边缘。
⊚ border 边缘　⊚ on the edge of 濒于，在……边缘
⊚ on the edge 还有"坐立不安"的意思。

0274 **egg** [eg] n 蛋
Let's count the eggs.
让我们数一数鸡蛋的个数。
⊚ Easter egg 复活节彩色蛋　⊚ let's count... 让我们数一数……

语法重点
count 既可作及物动词，又可作不及物动词，表达"数……的数目"时是及物动词。
⊚ count (P. 026)

0275 **eight** [eɪt] n 八
To our surprise, she gave birth to eight children.
令我们吃惊的是，她竟然生了八个孩子。
⊚ to one's surprise, ... 令某人吃惊的是，……

0276 **eighteen** [ˌeɪ'ti:n] n 十八
The man is eighteen years older than his wife.
这个男人比他妻子大十八岁。
⊚ sb. be... years older than... 某人比……大……岁

语法重点
older 是 old 的比较级，old 的最高级是 oldest。

0277 **eighty** ['eɪti] n 八十
In my family, the proportion of females is eighty percent.
在我家，女性的比例是百分之八十。
⊚ the proportion of... is... ……的比例是……

语法重点
英语中"百分之多少"可用"数字 + percent"表达。

033

0278 **either(1)** ['aɪðər] a （两者之中）任一的 pron 任何一个
It turns out that they don't select either of us.
结果证明，他们不选我们当中的任何一个。
- neither 两者都不
- either of 两者之一

> **语法重点**
> select 是"精选"，即有所淘汰；choose 指一般意义上的选择。
> ⇒ select (P. 220)

0279 **either(2)** ['aɪðər] conj 或者
You can choose either the black one or the white one.
你可以选黑色的或者白色的。
- or 或者
- and 和

> **语法重点**
> either... or... 如果在句中用作主语，动词的单复数取决于 or 之后的那个词的单复数形式。

0280 **elephant** ['elɪfənt] n 大象
It's a pity that we did not see the elephant in the zoo.
遗憾的是，我们在动物园里没看到大象。
- African elephant 非洲象
- It's a pity that... 遗憾的是，……

0281 **eleven** [ɪ'levn] n 十一
Eleven plus five is sixteen.
十一加五等于十六。
- plus 还可替换成 and

> ⇒ plus (P. 205)

0282 **else** [els] ad 其他，此外 a 别的，其他的
There's nothing else but some old chairs in the room.
除了几把旧椅子，房间没有别的。
- other 别的，其他的
- someone else 其他人

> **语法重点**
> else 在句中是形容词。

0283 **end** [end] n 末端，结束
Let's put an end to this debate.
让我们结束这场辩论吧。
- ending 结束
- beginning 开始
- in the end 终于，最后

0284 **English** ['ɪŋglɪʃ] n 英语，英国人 a 英语的，英国人的
Most people agree that English is the most common language in the world.
大部分人认为，英语是世界上最通用的语言。
- in English 用英语

> **语法重点**
> "说英语的国家"可表达为 English-speaking countries。

0285 **enough** [ɪ'nʌf] a 足够的 ad 足够地，充分地
I don't have enough money.
我没有足够的钱。
- I don't have enough... 我没有足够的……

> **语法重点**
> enough 除了表示"足以满足需要的"外，还可以表示"数量很多使人感到心满意足的"意思。

0286 **enter** ['entər] v 进入
We are not allowed to enter the room.
我们不能进入房间。
- exit 退出
- enter in 进入，报关进口

> **语法重点**
> go into 也表示"进入"的意思。

either(1) ~ example

0287 equal ['iːkwəl] **a** 相当的，平等的
He always says that everybody is equal before the law.
他总说法律面前人人平等。
🔗 equivalent 相等的　🔗 unequal 不平等的　🔗 be equal to 等于

> 语法重点
> everybody 是第三人称单数，所以 be 动词用 is。

0288 even(1) ['iːvn] **ad** 甚至，更
They brushed straight by without even looking at the poor boy.
他们直接走过，甚至不看那个可怜的男孩一眼。
🔗 still 更　🔗 even if 即使，虽然

> 语法重点
> without 是介词，后面接名词或者动词 ing 形式。
> ⟳ straight (P. 228)

0289 even(2) ['iːvn] **a** 平坦的，相等的
The billiard-table in the room must be perfectly even.
房间里的那个撞球桌必须相当平整。
🔗 sb. / sth. must be... 某人 / 某物肯定是……

> 语法重点
> 句中 even 是形容词，必须用副词来修饰，所以用 perfect 的副词形式。

0290 evening ['iːvnɪŋ] **n** 傍晚，晚上
If the cat doesn't eat anything tomorrow evening, I'll take it to the vet.
如果小猫明天晚上还不吃东西，我就带它去看兽医。
🔗 eve 傍晚　🔗 morning 早上，上午　🔗 good evening 晚安

> 语法重点
> if 引导条件从句，从句中用一般现在时，主句用一般将来时。

0291 ever ['evər] **ad** 曾经，在任何时候，至今
Miss Liu is the kindest woman that she has ever seen.
刘女士是她曾经遇到过的最仁慈的女士。
🔗 ever since 从那时到现在　🔗 sb. has ever seen... 某人曾经见过……

0292 every ['evri] **a** 每个的，一切的
I will vacuum the interior every time I wash my car.
我每次洗车的时候都用吸尘器清理内部。

> 语法重点
> every time 引导时间状语从句，主句用一般将来时，从句要用一般现在时表示将来时。

0293 examination [ɪɡˌzæmɪˈneɪʃn] **n** 考试，检查，细查
I will finish this examination paper in ninety minutes.
我将在九十分钟内完成这份试卷。

> 语法重点
> in 后面接表示"一段时间"的名词，意思是"在……之内"，通常与将来时连用。

0294 examine [ɪɡˈzæmɪn] **v** 检查，调查
It is he that is sent to examine into the matter.
被派去调查那件事情的是他。
🔗 inspect 检查　🔗 examine and approve 审核

0295 example [ɪɡˈzæmpl] **n** 例子，榜样
Door-to-door delivery is right an example of our good services.
送货上门更是我们好的服务的表现。
🔗 sample 例子　🔗 for example 例如

> ⟳ delivery (P. 282)

0296 except / excepting [ɪkˈsept] / [ɪkˈseptɪŋ]
prep 排除，除……之外

I think LINE is the best way for communication except mobile telephone.
我认为 LINE 是除了手机之外最好的联系方式。
- include 包括
- except for 除了……以外

> **语法重点**
> be the best way for 中，for 是介词，后面接名词或动名词。
> ⊃ mobile (P. 326)

0297 eye [aɪ] **n** 眼睛

The couple don't usually see eye to eye on many matters.
这对夫妇经常在许多事情上意见不一致。
- in the eyes of 在……心目中，从……来看
- eye to eye 表示"看法完全一致"，可以替换为 agree perfectly。

0298 face [feɪs] **n** 脸

The doctor says there is no way to hide the freckles in his face.
医生说没办法掩盖他脸上的雀斑。
- in one's face 表示"在脸上"

0299 fact [fækt] **n** 事实

She seemed by implication to acknowledge that fact last night.
她昨晚似乎含蓄地承认了那件事实。
- truth 事实
- matter of fact 事实

> **语法重点**
> by implication 修饰 to acknowledge。

0300 factory [ˈfæktri] **n** 工厂，制造厂

They say the trouble is that our factory is running at full capacity.
他们说问题是我们公司正在全负荷运转。
- chemical factory 化工厂
- the trouble is that... 问题是……

> **语法重点**
> run at full capacity 表示"全负荷运转"，这里用现在进行时较好。

0301 fall [fɔːl] **v** 落下，跌倒，陷落

They know that the temperature has fallen to zero from the thermometer.
他们看温度计得知气温已经降到零度了。
- slump 下降，倒下
- ascend 上升
- fall ill 病倒

⊃ zero (P. 118)

0302 false [fɔːls] **a** 虚伪的，错误的，假的

I believe an open enemy is better than a false friend.
我相信虚伪的朋友比公开的敌人更坏。
- fake 假的
- false impression 错觉，虚假印象

> **语法重点**
> be better than 表示"比……好"，有比较的意思。

0303 family [ˈfæməli] **n** 家庭，家族，亲属

My best friend stopped smoking with the help of his family.
我最好的朋友在家人的帮助下戒了烟。
- household 家族
- family life 家庭生活

0304 **fan** [fæn] **n** 扇子，（运动等）狂热爱好者，风扇
I don't know this fan is broken.
我不知道这个电扇坏了。
🔄 electric fan 电风扇

0305 **far** [fɑːr] **ad** 远的，久远，非常
As far as I know, his car crashed into a big tree.
据我所知，他的车撞到了一棵大树。
🔄 far away 非常远　　🔄 as far as I know, ... 据我所知，……

语法重点
crash into 表示"撞上"，crash out 表示"撞毁，坠毁"。

0306 **farm** [fɑːrm] **n** 农场 **v** 务农
I heard a small percentage of the farm produce was ruined.
我听说农产品中的一小部分坏掉了。
🔄 plantation 农园，大农场　　🔄 fruit farm 果园

语法重点
a small percentage of 表示"一小部分"，因为 farm produce 是不可数名词，所以 be 动词用单数。

0307 **farmer** [ˈfɑːrmər] **n** 农夫
The farmer called his wife out of bed early at six.
这位农夫六点钟把妻子从床上叫了起来。

0308 **fast** [fæst] **a** 快速的，迅速的
I used to have a liking for fast cars.
我曾经很喜欢快车。
🔄 quick 快的，迅速的　　🔄 slow 慢的　　🔄 fast food 速食

0309 **fat** [fæt] **a** 胖的，多脂肪的，丰满的
You'll get fat if you continue to eat so many sweets.
你如果继续吃这么多的糖果，会发胖的。
🔄 chubby 圆胖的　　🔄 lean 瘦的

语法重点
get 后面加上形容词时，表示一种变化，意为"变成……"。
🔄 continue (P. 025)

0310 **father** [ˈfɑːðər] **n** 父亲
His father has the habit of smoking during meals.
他父亲有边吃饭边抽烟的习惯。
🔄 sb. has the habit of doing sth. 某人有……的习惯。

0311 **fear** [fɪr] **n** / **v** 害怕，担心，恐惧
I fear he is coming back soon.
恐怕他很快就要回来了。
🔄 for fear of 为了避免，唯恐　　🔄 I fear... 我恐怕……

语法重点
句中用现在进行时表示将来。

0312 **February** [ˈfebrueri] **n** 二月
I got to know him in February.
我在二月份认识了他。
🔄 in February 在二月　　🔄 sb. gets to know... 某人认识……

语法重点
get to know 侧重于认识的动作。

0313 feed [fi:d] v 喂，饲养
I think it doesn't pay to feed animals.
我认为饲养牲口不划算。
raise 饲养　　feed on 以……为食，以……为能源

＊animal (P. 007)

0314 feel [fi:l] v 感觉，觉得
He still felt sad after getting better.
康复后，他仍然觉得很伤心。

0315 feeling ['fi:lɪŋ] n 感觉，感情
I had a feeling of deep sorrow as I heard the news.
得知那个消息我深感遗憾。
affection 感情　　good feeling 好感

> 语法重点
> have a feeling of surprise 可以表示"感到吃惊"。

0316 few [fju:] a 少数的，很少的　pron 少数　n 少量
After a long flight they suffered from jet lag for a few days.
他们在长途飞行后，有几天时差不适。
quite a few 不少，相当多

⊃ suffer (P. 368)

0317 fifteen [ˌfɪf'ti:n] n 十五
It cost him fifteen dollars to repair the clock.
修这个钟他花了十五美元。

> 语法重点
> cost 主语是物；take 也表示"花费"，主语也是物，常用句型 it takes sb. ... to do sth.。

0318 fifty ['fɪfti] n 五十
The young man was given an advance of fifty dollars on his salary.
那个年轻人预支了五十美元薪水。
wage 也有"工资，报酬"的意思，二者的区别在于：salary 指的是有规律的、定期的基本工资，一般来说是按月的，而 wage 指的是报酬，尤其是指按小时、天和周来计算的报酬。

0319 fight [faɪt] v 打架，斗争，争吵　n 战斗，打架
I am always fighting with my sisters about the noise.
我常常因为噪声和妹妹们争吵。
fight for 为……而战　　fight with sb. about... 为……跟某人争吵

> 语法重点
> fight with 在本句中也可以替换为 quarrel with。

0320 fill [fɪl] v 装满，弥漫，填充，担任
I was filled with joy when I saw you again.
再次看到你，我无比高兴。
fill in 填写，填充

0321 final ['faɪnl] a 最后的，最终的，决定性的
It's indeed fortunate that his final attempt to fix it is successful.
他最后这次把它修好了确实很幸运。
final exam 期末考试　　it's indeed fortunate that... ……确实很幸运

> 语法重点
> 第一个 it 是形式主语，真正的主语是 that his final attempt to fix it is successful。

feed ~ floor

0322 find [faɪnd] **v** 发现，找到
She **found** somewhere to park the car at last.
最后她找到了地方停车。
⟹ discover 找到　⟸ lose 失去　⊕ find fault with 批评，抱怨

> **语法重点**
> at last 多指经主观努力，克服各种困难后才终于达到目的。

0323 fine [faɪn] **a** 很好的，晴朗的　**v** 罚款
The **fine** weather tempted them to go out for a walk.
好天气促使他们出去散步。
⟹ sunny 晴朗的　⟸ cloudy 阴沉的

> **语法重点**
> go out for a walk 表示"外出散步"，可以替换为"walk outside"。

0324 finger ['fɪŋər] **n** 手指，指针
My son had two **fingers** cut off by a knife while playing.
我儿子玩耍时被刀子切掉了两根手指。
⊕ in one's finger 在某人的掌控中，听某人支配

> **语法重点**
> have sth. done 意思是"让别人做某事"。
> ⟹ son (P. 095)

0325 finish ['fɪnɪʃ] **v** 结束，完成
Since we've **finished** our housework, let's play computer games and kill some time!
既然我们做完家务了，让我们打电脑游戏消磨时光吧！
⟹ commence 开始　⊕ finish line 终点线

> **语法重点**
> kill some time 表示"消磨时光"。"浪费时间"用waste time 来表示。"珍惜时间"是 value time。

0326 fire ['faɪər] **n** 火，开火　**v** 点燃，解雇
Keep a **fire** extinguisher available at all times.
任何时候都要放置即时可用的灭火器。

0327 first [fɜːrst] **a** 第一的，最初的　**ad** 首先，第一
The **first** thing he does after getting up is to make the bed.
他起床后的第一件事就是整理床铺。
⟹ primarily 首先　⟸ last 最后的　⊕ at first 首先，最初

> **语法重点**
> 句中含有一个从句，其中 thing 是先行词，引导词省略，he does after getting up 为定语从句。

0328 fish [fɪʃ] **n** 鱼
The idea of eating raw **fish** nauseates him.
他一想到吃生鱼就恶心。
⊕ nauseate 意思是"恶心"，可以替换为 disgust。

0329 five [faɪv] **n** 五
It has been **five** months since she left her hometown.
她离开家乡已经五个月了。
⊕ It has been... 已经有……的时间了

> **语法重点**
> since 后面接过去某个时间点，其主句用现在完成时。

0330 floor [flɔːr] **n** 地板，楼层
House prices have gone through the **floor** these days.
近期房价已经降得很低了。
⟹ ground 地面　⟸ ceiling 天花板

> **语法重点**
> go through the floor 中，floor 本意是"地面，楼层"，在此引申为"底部"。

0331 **flower** [ˈflaʊər] n 花
These roses have been in flower for three weeks.
这些玫瑰花已经开了三个星期。
🔄 blossom 花　　🔗 ... be in flower ……开花

0332 **fly** [flaɪ] v 飞行，坐飞机 n 苍蝇
If my son cleans his room, the pigs might fly.
如果我儿子整理自己的房间，猪都可以飞了。

> 语法重点
> 此句是使用虚拟语气，对将来事实进行假设。

0333 **fog** [fɔːɡ] n 雾
Let's get off after the dense fog melts away.
等浓雾消失后我们就出发。
🔄 mist 薄雾　　🔗 in the fog 困惑，迷茫

> 语法重点
> get off 是不及物动词短语，后面可以不接宾语。
> ⇨ dense (P. 424)

0334 **follow** [ˈfɑːloʊ] v 跟随，追赶，注意
What she said didn't make any sense. Don't follow it.
她说的话根本没有道理，不必照办。
🔗 ... not make any sense ……没有道理

0335 **food** [fuːd] n 食物
The famous singer contributed food and clothing for us.
那个知名的歌星给我们捐助食物和衣服。
🔗 ... contribute sth. for sb. ……向某人捐赠某物

> 语法重点
> donate sth. to sb. 也表示"向某人捐赠某物"。

0336 **foot** [fʊt] n 脚，英尺，底部
They are playing at the foot of the mountain.
他们在山脚下玩耍。
🔄 head 头　　🔗 on foot 步行

> 语法重点
> at the top of the mountain 表示"在山顶上"，halfway up the mountain 表示"在山腰上"。

0337 **for** [fər] prep 为了，因为
The girl gave up buying the skirt for the high price.
因为价格高，女孩没有买那条裙子。
🔄 against 反对

> ⇨ skirt (P. 223)

0338 **force** [fɔːrs] n 力量，武力，暴力 v 迫使，强制
You'd better make friends with those who will force you to lever yourself up.
你最好与那些让你不得不提升自己的人交朋友。
🔗 air force 空军　　🔗 force sb. to do sth. 迫使某人做某事

0339 **foreign** [ˈfɔːrən] a 外国的，外来的
You should contact the foreign guests right away.
你应该立刻与外国客人取得联系。
🔄 alien 外国的　　🔄 domestic 国内的

> 语法重点
> should 后面需接动词原形。

0340 **forest** ['fɔːrɪst] **n** 森林
The villagers put out the big forest fire at last.
村民们终于扑灭了那场森林大火。
- wood 森林　- rain forest 雨林　- sb. puts out... 某人扑灭……

> 语法重点
> put out 除了指"扑灭"，还可以表示"伸出，出版，打扰"。

0341 **forget** [fər'get] **v** 忘记
Don't forget to lock the door before going out.
出门前，别忘了锁门。
- neglect 疏忽，遗漏　- remember 记得

> 语法重点
> forget to do sth. 指"忘记要做某事"，forget doing sth. 指"忘记已经做过某事"。

0342 **fork** [fɔːrk] **n** 叉子，餐叉
Do you use a knife and fork or would you rather use chopsticks?
你是使用刀叉呢，还是宁愿用筷子？

> 语法重点
> Do you... or...? 表示"你是……还是……？"，给人两种选择，or 连接的两个部分要用对称结构。

0343 **forty** ['fɔːrti] **n** 四十
You must reduce speed to forty kilometres an hour.
你必须把速度减到每小时四十公里①。
- Life begins at forty. 人生四十才开始。

> 语法重点
> reduce speed to 中的 to 是介词，后面接名词。
> ⊃ reduce (P. 346)

0344 **four** [fɔːr] **n** 四
We have the option of a two-door or a four-door model.
我们可选择二门或四门的车型。
- on all fours 趴着

0345 **fourteen** [ˌfɔːr'tiːn] **n** 十四
I started earning a living for myself at fourteen.
我十四岁开始自己谋生。
- sb. starts doing sth. 某人开始做某事

0346 **free** [friː] **a** 自由的，免费的
Are you free for having a dinner with me tomorrow?
你明天有空和我一起吃饭吗？
- gratuitous 免费的　- chargeable 收费的　- for free 免费地

> 语法重点
> for 是介词，所以后面接动词的 ing 形式。

0347 **fresh** [freʃ] **a** 新鲜的，清新的
The teacher asked him to open the window to let in some fresh air.
老师请他打开窗户让一些清新的空气进来。
- new 新鲜的　- stale 不新鲜的

> 语法重点
> fresh 也可以作副词，意思是"刚刚，才"。

0348 **Friday** ['fraɪdeɪ] **n** 星期五
He knows he is going to leave here on Friday.
他知道他这周五要离开这里了。
- Black Friday 黑色星期五

> 语法重点
> 星期的前面用介词 on。
> ⊃ leave (P. 057)

① 1 公里 =1 000 米。

0349 **friend** [frend] **n** 朋友
I'd like you to meet my friend Kate.
我要给你介绍我的朋友凯特。
同 fellow 朋友　反 enemy 敌人　拓 net friend 网友

> 语法重点
> I'd 的完整形式是 I would。

0350 **frog** [frɔːg] **n** 青蛙
I saw the naughty child poke the frog with a stick.
我看见那个调皮的孩子用棍子拨动青蛙。
拓 with 表示"借用（工具）"的意思

> naughty (P. 194)

0351 **from** [frəm] **prep** 从，出自，来自
Before you repair the switch, heater must be disconnected from power supply.
你在修理开关前，务必切断暖气机的电源。
拓 go from 从……处出发

0352 **front** [frʌnt] **n** 前面的，正面的
There is a lawn in front of the house.
房子前有一片草坪。
反 rear 后面　拓 in the front 在前面

> 语法重点
> in front of 是指外部的前面，而 in the front of 指在内部的前面。

0353 **fruit** [fruːt] **n** 水果
My hometown abounds with fruits, especially apples.
我的家乡盛产水果，尤以苹果著称。

> 语法重点
> abound 为不及物动词，后面常接介词。

0354 **full** [fʊl] **a** 完整的，满的，充满的
He'll be full of energy in several months.
几个月后他就会感到精力充沛。
同 filled 满的　反 empty 空的　拓 full of 装满

0355 **fun** [fʌn] **n** 乐趣，玩笑　**a** 有趣的
I have made up my mind to get as much fun as possible in the future.
我已经下了决心以后要及时行乐。
同 joke 玩笑　反 seriousness 严肃　拓 for fun 开玩笑

> 语法重点
> 句子的主语是 I，所以 make up one's mind to do sth. 中的 one's 用 my。

0356 **funny** ['fʌni] **a** 有趣的，可笑的，滑稽的
What a funny coat he is wearing!
他穿的外套多么滑稽可笑啊！
反 serious 严肃的　拓 what + 形容词 + the... is / are ……多么

> 语法重点
> 此句是 what 引导的感叹句。

0357 **game** [geɪm] **n** 游戏，比赛
Why don't you go to a football game?
你们为什么不去看足球比赛呢？
拓 Why don't you...? 你们为什么不……呢？

> 语法重点
> why don't you 后面接动词原形，表示建议。

0358 garden ['gɑːrdn] n 花园

I intend to plant some flowers in my new garden.
我计划在新花园里种一些花。

> 语法重点
> intend to 后面接动词原形。

0359 gas [gæs] n 瓦斯，煤气，气体

He wanted to get some gasoline at the gas station nearby.
他要在附近的加油站加些油。

> 语法重点
> nearby 作形容词时，通常放在被修饰名词的后面。
> ⇒ gasoline (P. 300)

0360 general ['dʒenrəl] a 全体的，普遍的，全面的，一般的

In general, those who drink and drive will cause traffic accidents.
一般来说，酒后开车容易出车祸。
🔵 in general, ... 一般来说，……

0361 get [get] v 得到，达到，使得

Will you tell me how to get to the nearest post office?
你能告诉我最近的邮局在哪里吗？
🔵 get rid of 摆脱　　🔵 Will you tell me...? 你能告诉我……吗？

> 语法重点
> will 也可以替换为其他情态动词，如 could，would 或 can。

0362 ghost [goʊst] n 鬼，幽灵

The girl looked as if she had seen a ghost.
那女孩看起来就像她见到了鬼似的。

> 语法重点
> 此句用假设语气，从句表示与过去事实相反，动词用 had + 过去分词。

0363 gift [gɪft] n 礼物，赠品

This one is a gift and the other one is for his own use.
这个是送给别人的礼物，另一个是他自己用的。
🔵 present 礼物　　🔵 be for one's own use 某人自己用

> 语法重点
> 此句是个并列句，后面的句子中主语是 the other one，所以 be 动词用 is。

0364 girl [gɜːrl] n 女孩

I got off with a pretty girl in the park.
我在公园里结识了一位美丽的女孩。
🔴 boy 男孩　　🔵 I get off with... 我结识了……

> 语法重点
> get off with 后面通常接表示人的名词或代词。

0365 give [gɪv] v 给予，提供

She gave him her picture as a memento before going away.
她在离别前留给他一张照片当作纪念品。
🔵 supply 提供　　🔵 demand 需求　　🔵 give up 放弃

0366 glad [glæd] a 高兴的，乐意的

She is glad she could be of some help to him.
她很高兴能帮上他的忙。

> 语法重点
> "be of + 抽象名词" 相当于该名词对应的形容词意思。

0367 glass [glæs] n 玻璃，玻璃杯

He is thirsty, so please get him a glass of water.
他渴了，请给他一杯水解解渴。
🔵 a glass of... 一杯……　　🔵 get sb. sth. 给某人某物

> ⇒ thirsty (P. 235)

0368 glasses [glæsɪz] **n** 眼镜，双筒镜
I need to buy a pair of glasses.
我需要买一副眼镜。

0369 go [goʊ] **v** 去
All of them went to the airport to see him off.
他们都去机场为他送行了。
🔹 see sb. off 给某人送行

○ airport (P. 005)

0370 god / goddess [gɑːd] / [ˈgɑːdəs] **n** 男神 / 女神
He is forced to disbelieve in the existence of god.
他不得不怀疑上帝的存在。

【语法重点】
双重否定表示肯定，此句相当于 He doubts the existence of god. 他怀疑上帝的存在。

0371 gold [goʊld] **n** 黄金，金币 **a** 金制的，金色的
The color scheme of my room is green and gold.
我的房间的色彩配置是绿色和金黄色。
🔹 a voice of gold 金嗓子

【语法重点】
句中的主语 the color scheme 是单数，所以 be 动词用 is。

0372 good [gʊd] **a** 好的，上等的，优秀的
Be a good boy and clean the room now.
乖孩子，现在去打扫房间。
🔹 excellent 优秀的 🔹 bad 坏的 🔹 good quality 好品质

【语法重点】
此句是祈使句，动词 be 与 clean 并列，都用原形。

0373 goodbye [ˌgʊdˈbaɪ] **int** 再见
He just comes to say goodbye.
他就是来说声再见。
🔹 time to say good-bye 到说再见的时候了

0374 goose [guːs] **n** 鹅
It leads him on a wild-goose chase to open the window.
他白费了半天劲儿去开窗户。
🔹 a wild-goose 徒劳，白费力

【语法重点】
goose 是不规则名词，其复数形式是 geese。

0375 grand [grænd] **a** 雄伟的，壮丽的，豪华的，重大的
I suppose she believes I am a grand old rascal.
我看她一定认为我是个老滑头吧。

○ suppose (P. 369)

0376 grandchild [ˈgræntʃaɪld] **n** （外）孙子女
The old man lavishly kisses upon his grandchild.
老人一再地亲吻他的孙子。
🔹 grandparent （外）祖父母

0377 granddaughter [ˈgrændɔːtər] **n** （外）孙女
He left all his money to his granddaughter in the will.
在遗嘱中，他将所有的钱都留给了孙女。
🔹 sb. leaves... to... 某人把……留给……

【语法重点】
leave 是不规则动词，其过去式与过去分词都是 left。

0378 **grandfather** ['grænfɑːðər] n （外）祖父
His grandfather was in his anecdotage.
他的祖父已经年老。
- grandfather clock 落地式大摆钟　● be in one's anecdotage 年老

0379 **grandmother** ['grænmʌðər] n （外）祖母
Her grandmother always gargles with salt water after getting up.
她的奶奶起床后总是用盐水漱口。
- Don't try to teach your grandmother to suck eggs. 不要班门弄斧。

⟳ salt (P. 085)

0380 **grandson** ['grænsʌn] n 孙子，外孙
She entered the house supported by her grandson.
她由孙子扶着进了屋子。

0381 **grass** [græs] n 草，草地
He fell gently over upon the grass and fell asleep.
他轻轻地倒在草地上，睡着了。
- lawn 草地　● keep off the grass 勿踏草坪
- sb. fell gently over upon... 某人轻轻地倒在……上

语法重点
gently 是副词，修饰动词 fell。

⟳ asleep (P. 126)

0382 **gray / grey** [greɪ] / [greɪ] a 灰色的，暗淡的
The woman in gray hair is eating off a dish.
那个头发花白的女人正从盘子中取食。

0383 **great** [greɪt] a 大的，重要的，大量的
There is no doubt he is a great one for complaining.
毫无疑问，他是个抱怨大王。
- grand 极重要的　● puny 微不足道的　● great man 大人物

语法重点
great 的比较级是 greater，最高级是 greatest。

0384 **green** [griːn] a 绿色的，未成熟的
We all know that the regular taking of green food can promote one's health.
大家都知道常吃绿色食品能促进健康。
- ripe 成熟的　● green fruit 未熟的水果

语法重点
此句包含一个同位语从句，引导同位语从句的 that 叫作从属连词，它起连接作用，不能省略。

0385 **ground** [graʊnd] n 地面，立场
After the storm, a chasm appeared on the ground.
暴雨后，地上出现了一条裂缝。
- standpoint 立场　● to the ground 彻底地

⟳ storm (P. 228)

0386 **group** [gruːp] n 群体
What blood group is he?
他是什么血型？
- a group of 一组，一群　● "成群"可以用短语 in group 来表示。

0387 **grow** [groʊ] v 种植，生长，增加
I found the tulips grew larger and straighter.
我发现郁金香长得更大且更直了。
同 plant 种植　反 harvest 收获

语法重点
grow 后面接形容词比较级，表示变化。

0388 **guess** [ges] v 猜测，猜中 n 猜测，猜想
I can guess what he is doing now.
我能猜出来他现在在做什么。
同 imagine 猜测　同 prove 证实　同 guess what 猜猜看

语法重点
what 引导的宾语从句要用陈述语序。

0389 **guest** [gest] n 客人，宾客
I'm curious about why guests always give gifts at the reception.
我很好奇为什么客人们通常在宴会上赠送礼物。
同 caller 访客　同 host 主人　同 guest of honor 贵宾

0390 **guide** [gaɪd] n 向导，导游 v 指导，引导
The dog can act as a guide to a blind person since it has been trained.
这条狗能担任盲人的导盲犬，因为它受过训练。
反 misguide 误导　同 guideline 准则，指导路线

语法重点
act as 指"充当，起……的作用"，act for 指"代理，代为"。

0391 **gun** [ɡʌn] n 枪，炮
To hit the object, you have to move your gun.
要打中目标，你的枪也得动。

语法重点
to hit the object 是动词不定式，在句中表示目的。

0392 **hair** [her] n 毛发，头发
His hair is a bit too long and he wants to have it bobbed.
他的头发太长了，他想剪短一点儿。
同 hair dryer 吹风机

语法重点
a bit 修饰形容词，指"有点儿"；a bit of 修饰名词，指"一些"。

0393 **haircut** [ˈherkʌt] n 理发，发型
Do you think this is a nice haircut?
你觉得这是个漂亮的发型吗？
同 have a haircut 理发　同 Do you think...? 你认为……？

0394 **half** [hæf] n 一半 a 一半的
Mother told me it's a bad habit to leave things half done.
妈妈告诉我半途而废是一个坏习惯。
反 whole 整体，全部的　同 in half 分成两半

语法重点
things 与 do 是被动关系，所以用 done。

0395 **ham** [hæm] n 火腿
He sneaked past the woman and stole some hams.
他躲过那个女人，偷了一些火腿。
同 sb. sneaks past... 某人躲过……　同 ham 是可数名词

⇒ sneak (P. 635)

grow ~ head

0396 hand [hænd] n 手
He gave her his hand with mute thanks.
他向她伸手表示无言的谢意。
反 foot 脚　相 hand in hand 手牵手地，联合
句 do sth. with mute thanks 做某事以表示无言的谢意

> 语法重点
> thank 是抽象名词，同时也是可数名词。

0397 happen ['hæpən] v 发生
What would happen if I cannot afford to pay my monthly mortgage?
如果我付不出每月的房子贷款，会怎样呢？
同 occur 发生　句 happen to coincide 不约而同

> 语法重点
> happen 是不及物动词。

0398 happy ['hæpi] a 快乐的，高兴的
It is true that he is not happy.
他确实很不快乐。
同 cheerful 欢快的　反 unhappy 不高兴的

> 语法重点
> 句中 it 是形式主语，真正的主语是 that he is not happy。

0399 hard [hɑːrd] a 硬的，困难的 ad 努力地
You know flowers are pleasant to look at but hard to grow.
你知道的，看花容易栽花难。
反 soft 柔软的　相 hard disk 硬碟

> 语法重点
> 句中的两个短语 be pleasant to look at 与 hard to grow 都是以主动形式表示被动意思。

0400 hat [hæt] n 帽子
They're all wearing hats, so you can't see their faces.
他们都戴着帽子，所以你看不到他们的脸。
句 hat in hand 毕恭毕敬地，温顺地

> 语法重点
> put on 表"穿戴"的动作，而 wear 表示"穿戴"的状态。

0401 hate [heɪt] n/v 憎恨，厌恶
She hates me albeit I helped her.
尽管我帮助过她，可是她讨厌我。
同 loathe 憎恨，厌恶　反 love 爱，喜欢

> 语法重点
> albeit 在句中作连词，表示意思的转折。

0402 have [həv] v 拥有，得到
They have got the gall to ask him for help.
他们还有脸求他帮忙。
同 own 拥有

0403 he [hi] pron 他
He split up with his wife last year.
他去年与妻子离异了。

> 语法重点
> split 是不规则动词，其过去式和过去分词都是 split。

0404 head [hed] n 头
What was the final head count on his party?
最后有多少人来参加他的派对？
句 head office 总公司，总行

> 语法重点
> final head count 按单数处理，所以前面的 be 动词用 was。

047

0405 **health** [helθ] n 健康，医疗保健
My mother is solicitous about my health.
我妈妈很担心我的健康状况。

0406 **hear** [hɪr] v 听到，倾听
He is getting sick of hearing her voice.
他听够了她的声音。
同 listen 听　近 hear of 听说，听说过

0407 **heart** [hɑːrt] n 心，心脏，内心
I ate my heart out when I heard the news.
听到那个消息，我的心都碎了。
近 heart disease 心脏病　近 ... eat one's heart out ……心碎了

0408 **heat** [hiːt] n 热度 v （使）变热，（使）激动
The teacher tells us that chemical energy may be converted to heat.
老师告诉我们化学能可以转化为热能。
同 fever 发热　反 chill 寒冷　近 heat up 加热，加剧

> 语法重点
> hear 的意思是"听到"，侧重听的结果；listen to 的意思是"听"，侧重听的动作。

⊃ chemical (P. 138)

0409 **heavy** ['hevi] a 重的，沉重的
I'm sure of a heavy rain this evening.
我确信今天晚上有场大雨。
同 weighty 重的　反 light 轻的　近 heavy industry 重工业
注 大雨用 heavy rain 表示，而不是 big rain

0410 **hello** [hə'loʊ] int 哈喽，你好
It's time to say hello to the new year!
是时候迎接新年的到来了！
近 say hello to 也可以译作"向……问好"

0411 **help** [help] v / n 帮助，接济
I couldn't help laughing at his discomfiture.
我禁不住嘲笑他的窘态。
同 aid 帮助　近 with the help of 在……的帮助下　近 I couldn't help... 我忍不住……

> 语法重点
> couldn't help 后面接动词的 ing 形式。

0412 **her** [hər] a 她的 pron 她
He tried to persuade her to come to dinner.
他试着劝说她一起去吃晚餐。
近 persuade sb. to do sth. 说服某人做某事

> 语法重点
> 说服某人做某事也可以用 persuade sb. into doing sth.。

⊃ persuade (P. 336)

0413 **here** [hɪr] ad / n 这里
I think my success here depends upon effort.
我认为我的成功是通过努力得来的。

0414 **high** [haɪ] **a** 高的，高尚的 **ad** 高
Is she excited about entering high school?
她要上高中了，她会不会感到很兴奋呢？
🔄 high school 中学　🔄 Is sb. excited about...? 某人对……兴奋吗？

> **语法重点**
> excited 指"感到兴奋的"，exciting 则是"让人兴奋的"。

0415 **hill** [hɪl] **n** 小山，丘陵
At the top of the hill, the path curves to the right.
到了山顶以后，小路便向右转弯。
🔄 mound 高地　🔄 steep hill 陡坡，斜坡，陡峭的山坡

0416 **him** [hɪm] **pron** 他
Do not cling to him or he will be tired of you.
别总黏着他，不然他会厌倦你的。

> **语法重点**
> cling to 中的 to 为介词，所以后面的宾语用 him。
> ⇒ cling (P. 543)

0417 **his** [hɪz] **a** / **pron** 他的（东西）
My son is fond of his toy cars.
我儿子很喜欢他的玩具车。
🔄 be fond of... 喜欢，爱……

> ⇒ fond (P. 297)

0418 **history** ['hɪstri] **n** 历史
Every day of our life is a leaf in our history.
我们生命的每一天都是历史的一页。
🔄 ancient history 古代史

> **语法重点**
> 句中主语是 every day，是单数，所以 be 动词用 is。

0419 **hit** [hɪt] **v** 打，击，击中
The poor couple were hit by a bus and died on the spot.
那对可怜的夫妇被一辆公交车撞倒，当场死亡。
🔄 hit it off 情投意合　🔄 ... be hit by ……被撞倒

> **语法重点**
> hit 是不规则动词，其过去式、过去分词都是 hit。

0420 **hold** [hoʊld] **v** 握着，保持，抓住
I hold the opinion that you have a chance to defeat your opponent.
我认为你有机会打败对手。
🔄 hold on 不挂断电话，等一下，继续

> **语法重点**
> 句子中 that 引导同位语从句用以说明名词 opinion 表示的具体内容。

0421 **hole** [hoʊl] **n** 洞，孔，穴
I'm ignorant of why you dig a hole on the ground.
我不知道你为什么要在地上挖一个洞。
🔄 cave 洞　🔄 in the hole 负债，遇到经济困难

0422 **holiday** ['hɑːlədeɪ] **n** 假日
Make sure all the lights are switched off before you leave on holiday.
你出去度假前一定要把所有的灯都关了。
🔄 vacation 假期　🔄 go on holiday 去度假，正在休假

0423 **home** [hoʊm] **n** 家 **ad** 在家，回家
Please remind her to go home early.
请提醒她早点儿回家。

> **语法重点**
> home 在句中作副词，所以前面不用介词。

0424 **homework** ['hoʊmwɜːrk] **n** 功课
Thank you for not assigning homework this weekend.
感谢您这周末没有指派作业。
📖 schoolwork 家庭作业 📖 thank you for not... 谢谢你没有……

> ↻ assign (P. 398)

0425 **hope** [hoʊp] **v** 希望，期望，盼望
I hope the weather forecast is right this time.
我希望这次天气预报会准。
📖 expect 期望，盼望 📖 hope to do sth. 希望做某事

0426 **horse** [hɔːrs] **n** 马
His father eats like a horse.
他爸爸特别能吃。
📖 ride a horse 骑马 📖 sb. eats like a horse 某人饭量大
📖 drink like a fish 意思是"大喝"

0427 **hot** [hɑːt] **a** 热的，辣的
Don't overclothe your brother—he will be too hot.
别给你弟弟穿太多衣服，他会太热。
📖 cold 寒冷的 📖 hot pot 火锅

> **语法重点**
> 此句是祈使句的否定形式。

0428 **hour** ['aʊər] **n** 小时，钟点
They hired a taxi by the hour last night.
他们昨晚按小时租了一辆出租车。

> ↻ taxi (P. 101)

0429 **house** [haʊs] **n** 房子
No sooner had she left the house than it began to rain this morning.
今天早上她一离开家就开始下雨了。
📖 dwelling 住所 📖 no sooner... than... 一……就……

> **语法重点**
> no sooner... than... 引导时间状语从句，主句用过去完成时，than 后面的从句用一般过去时。

0430 **how** [haʊ] **ad** 怎么，怎样，多么，多少
How about having fish tonight?
今晚吃鱼怎么样？
📖 how about 用来询问别人的意见，相当于 what about

0431 **huge** [hjuːdʒ] **a** 巨大的，庞大的
The episode was a huge embarrassment for all the people concerned this morning.
今天早上这段小插曲，令所有相关人员都感到非常尴尬。
📖 tremendous 巨大的 📖 tiny 微小的 📖 huge amounts of 大量的

> **语法重点**
> all，any，some 等不定代词修饰的名词要放在其后。

0432 **human** [ˈhjuːmən] a 人的，人类的 n 人，人类
She cut herself off from all human contact last year.
去年她断绝了与所有人的联系。
- human being 人，人类
- ... cut oneself off from... ……与……断绝

0433 **hundred** [ˈhʌndrəd] n 一百
I think a hundred friends is too few.
我觉得一百个朋友太少。

> 语法重点
> a hundred friends 是一个整体，所以后面的 be 动词用 is。

0434 **hungry** [ˈhʌŋgri] a 饥饿的，渴望的
No wonder the boy is very hungry, he hasn't had food for three days.
难怪这个男孩这么饿，他已经三天没有吃任何东西了。

0435 **hurt** [hɜːrt] v 伤害，使疼痛 n 伤害，打击
She was hurt because she was not the one who did the dumping yesterday.
昨天她伤心是因为她被甩了，而不是她甩了别人。
- damage 伤害
- protect 保护
- get hurt 受伤

> 语法重点
> hurt 是不规则变化动词，其过去式、过去分词都是 hurt。

0436 **husband** [ˈhʌzbənd] n 丈夫
They, as a husband and a wife, never have any fights.
他们夫妻从不吵架。
- as a husband and a wife 也可以替换为 as a couple

0437 **ice** [aɪs] n 冰，冰块 v 结冰
Ice cream is popular among young people these days.
冰激凌目前深受年轻人的欢迎。
- be popular among / in... 在……中受欢迎

⊃ popular (P. 339)

0438 **idea** [aɪˈdiːə] n 想法，主意，意见
I have no idea where to have my bike repaired.
我不知道该去哪里修我的脚踏车。

0439 **if** [ɪf] conj 假如，如果
Try and see if you can ride the bike by yourself.
试试看，你能否自己骑脚踏车。
- provided 假如
- if any 若有的话，即便要

> 语法重点
> by yourself 的意思是"单独地，独自地"，在句中作状语。

0440 **important** [ɪmˈpɔːrtnt] a 重要的，重大的
To have breakfast is a very important thing that we should do.
吃早餐是我们应该做的一件非常重要的事情。
- significant 重要的
- unimportant 不重要的

> 语法重点
> 句子中不定式 to have breakfast 是主语，是一件事，所以 be 动词用 is。

0441 in [ɪn] prep 在……之内，在某方面 ad 向里，进入
In spite of vigilance, the children slipped into the yard.
尽管警戒很严，小孩们还是溜进了院子。
in between 在中间

语法重点
despite 用作介词时，与 in spite of 同义，都表示"尽管，虽然"，但 in spite of 语气较强，使用范围也较广。

0442 inch [ɪntʃ] n 英寸 v 慢慢移动
The snow is four inches deep at the moment.
目前雪积了四英寸①厚。
inch by inch 逐渐地

0443 inside [ˌɪnˈsaɪd]
n 内部 prep 在……里面 ad 在里面 a 里面的
He wore his sweater inside out yesterday.
他昨天把毛衣穿反了。
outside 外面的　　inside out 彻底地，里面翻到外面
类似的短语有 upside down，意思是"颠倒"。

⊃ sweater (P. 232)

0444 interest [ˈɪntrəst] n 兴趣，利息 v 使感兴趣
The old man was a confirmed bachelor and no women had any interest in him.
那个老人是个坚定的独身主义的单身汉，没有哪个女人对他感兴趣。
hobby 爱好　　places of interest 名胜

0445 into [ˈɪntə] prep 到……里面，进入
The young man beguiled his girlfriend into believing his story.
那个年轻人哄骗女朋友相信他的事情。
go into 走进，从事

语法重点
believe 一般是指相信某人说的话或所做的事，而 believe in 一般是强调相信某人。

0446 iron [ˈaɪərn] n 铁，熨斗 v 熨烫
The gates of the school are made of wrought iron.
学校的大门是用熟铁制成的。
an iron will 坚强的意志 / pig iron 生铁

0447 is [ɪz] v （用于第三人称单数）是，在
Is it necessary for you to buy an alarm clock in the store?
你有必要在商店里买一个闹钟吗？
Is it necessary for you to...? 你有必要……？

语法重点
句中 it 是形式主语，真正的主语是 to buy an alarm clock。

0448 it [ɪt] pron 它
Please remember to put anti-burglary chain on the door when you lock it.
锁门时请记得挂防盗链。
as it were 好像，可以说是

语法重点
it 代指 the door。

① 1 英寸 =2.54 厘米。

in ~ jump

0449 its [ɪts] **pron** 它的
Can you tell me when your garden is at its best?
你能告诉我你的花园什么时候最好看吗?
📖 Each day brings its own bread. 天无绝人之路。

> 语法重点
> its 对应前面的名词 your garden。

0450 jam [dʒæm] **n** 拥挤，果酱，堵塞，困境
They must be stuck in a traffic jam now.
他们现在肯定是遇上了交通阻塞。
📖 blocking 阻塞　📖 traffic jam 塞车

0451 January ['dʒænjueri] **n** 一月
They will get to his house on the 1st of January.
他们将在 1 月 1 日到他家。

> 语法重点
> 1 月 1 日也可以表达为 January lst。

0452 job [dʒɑːb] **n** 工作，职业
Her job is to take care of newborn babies.
她的工作是照顾新生婴儿。
📖 profession 职业　📖 job interview 求职面试

⊃ care (P. 020)

0453 join [dʒɔɪn] **v** 参加，加入
I'm sorry that I can't join you in the discussion tomorrow.
很遗憾，明天我不能参加你们的讨论了。
📖 participate 加入　📖 withdraw 退出　📖 join in 参加，加入

0454 joke [dʒoʊk] **n** 笑话，玩笑 **v** 说笑话，开玩笑
To his surprise, the beautiful girl treats his proposal as a joke.
令他惊讶的是，那个漂亮的女孩把他的求婚当作了一个玩笑。

> 语法重点
> joke 是可数名词。

0455 joy [dʒɔɪ] **n** / **v** 喜悦，欢乐
You will discover the joy of learning French.
你会发现学习法语的乐趣。
📖 pleasure 欢乐　📖 grief 悲伤　📖 with joy 高兴地

> 语法重点
> discover 表示偶然或经过努力发现客观存在的事物、真理或错误；find 指对某种事物的寻求，也指找到丢失的事物。

0456 juice [dʒuːs] **n** 果汁，汁液
Do you want any orange juice this time?
你这次还要橙汁吗?

> 语法重点
> any 常用在否定句与疑问句中。

0457 July [dʒuˈlaɪ] **n** 七月
She will be discharged from the hospital on July 31st, 2016.
她将于 2016 年 7 月 31 日出院。

0458 jump [dʒʌmp] **v** 跳跃，暴涨 **n** 跳跃，跳动
The naughty boy jumped into the water from the tree.
那个淘气的男孩从树上跳进了水里。
📖 jump over 跳过　📖 sb. jump into the... 某人跳进……

⊃ water (P. 111)

0459 June [dʒuːn] **n** 六月
All of my family members were at bay in June.
六月的时候我们全家人陷入了绝境。
⊕ ... be at bay ……陷入绝境

> **语法重点**
> attractive 是形容词，其比较级是在前面加 more。

0460 just [dʒʌst] **ad** 刚好，仅仅，刚才 **a** 公平的，公正的
I just want to make myself more attractive at the meeting.
我只是想让自己在聚会时看起来更好看些。
⊕ fair 公平的 ⊘ unjust 不公正的 ⊕ just now 刚才

0461 keep [kiːp] **v** 保持，保留
Keep in mind that protecting yourself is the most important thing when you are in danger.
记住危险的时候保护自己最重要。
⊕ maintain 维持 ⊘ break 打破 ⊕ keep up with 赶得上，和……保持联系

> **语法重点**
> important 是形容词，其最高级是在前面加 most。

0462 keeper [ˈkiːpər] **n** 保有者，看守人，饲养员，管理者
As a shop keeper, the man must keep accounts every day.
作为一个店主，那个男人必须每天记账。
⊕ administrator 管理人 ⊕ goal keeper 守门员

> **语法重点**
> 名词也可以修饰其他名词，一般用其单数形式，如句中 shop keeper 中的 shop。

0463 key [kiː] **n** 钥匙，关键 **a** 关键的，主要的
I looked for the lost key along the street for about two hours.
我沿着街寻找遗失的钥匙近两个小时。
⊕ crux 关键 ⊘ secondary 次要的 ⊕ key position 关键部位

0464 kick [kɪk] **v** 踢
Don't kick the little cat like that; it's cruel.
别那样踢小猫，太残忍了。
⊕ kick out 解雇，开除，把球踢出界 ⊕ don't... like that 不要那样……

0465 kid [kɪd] **n** 小孩，年轻人
He saw the kid step right in a pile of dog shit yesterday.
他昨天看见这个小孩正好踩在一堆狗屎上。
⊘ grown-up 成年人 ⊕ whiz kid 优等生，神童

> **语法重点**
> kid 多用于口语，表示"孩子很小"。child 表示"孩子"，多用于书面语中。

0466 kill [kɪl] **v** 杀戮，杀死
The angry man vowed to kill his wife's lover.
那个愤怒的男人发誓要杀死妻子的情人。
⊕ shoot to kill 往死里打 ⊕ sb. vows to... 某人发誓……

> **语法重点**
> kill 的主语可以是人也可以是物，但 murder 还含有"谋杀"的意思，其主语只能是人。

0467 kind [kaɪnd] **a** 亲切的，善良的 **n** 种类
His father isn't as kind as his mother is.
他父亲待人没有他母亲那么和善。
⊕ friendly 亲切的 ⊕ be kind to 对……好

> **语法重点**
> as... as 中间的形容词要用原形。

June ~ lack

0468 king [kɪŋ] n 国王

The king of the small country sought to look for the most beautiful woman in the world.
那个小国的国王努力寻找世界上最漂亮的女人。
🔄 queen 王后　🔗 monkey king 美猴王，孙悟空

> **语法重点**
> seek 指 "寻找，企图"，其过去式与过去分词都是 sought。

0469 kiss [kɪs] v / n 吻，轻触

It's time for us to kiss and make up.
我们该和好了。

> **语法重点**
> it's time to 后面接动词的原形。

0470 kitchen [ˈkɪtʃɪn] n 厨房

Their kitchen was small but well equipped.
他们的厨房空间虽小但设备齐全。
🔗 cookroom 厨房　🔗 kitchen knife 菜刀

> **语法重点**
> well equipped 前省略了 be 动词 was。

0471 kite [kaɪt] n 风筝

She had never learned to fly a kite.
她一直没有学会放风筝。

> **语法重点**
> 动词 learn 的过去式、过去分词都有两个：learn-learned-learned，learn-learnt-learnt。

0472 kitten / kitty [ˈkɪtn] / [ˈkɪti] n 小猫

The kitten was making noise, and I was fed up with it.
小猫一直闹，我受够它了。
🔗 kitten heels 中跟鞋　🔗 be fed up with... 受够了……

0473 knee [niː] n 膝盖

I am receiving physiotherapy on my damaged right knee.
因右膝受伤，我在接受物理治疗。
🔗 knee pad 护膝　🔗 sb. be receiving... 某人在接受……

> **语法重点**
> receive 的现在分词形式是去 e 加 ing，即 receiving。
> ↪ receive (P. 081)

0474 knife [naɪf] n 刀

The knife suddenly fell from my hand.
刀突然从我的手里落下。
🔗 blade 刀片　🔗 table knife 餐刀

> **语法重点**
> knife 的复数形式是 knives。

0475 know [noʊ] v 知道，认识

How do we know that the story is true?
我们怎样才能知道这个故事是真的？
🔗 know about 了解，知道……的情况，知道关于

> **语法重点**
> 前面有助动词 do，所以动词 know 要用原形。

0476 lack [læk] n 缺乏，无　v 缺乏，不足

In fact, she hates the lack of privacy in the dorm.
事实上，她讨厌宿舍里没有独处的机会。
🔗 lack of 缺乏　🔗 dorm 等于 dormitory。

055

0477 **lady** [ˈleɪdi] n 女士，夫人
It is common for a young lady to get married with a rich older man.
年轻女子嫁给有钱的老男人相当普遍。
◎ madam 女士，夫人　◎ lady first 女士优先

0478 **lake** [leɪk] n 湖泊
It is said that West Lake is known as the most beautiful lake in China.
据说西湖被誉为中国最美丽的湖泊。

> 语法重点
> be known as 一般不用于主动语态。

0479 **lamb** [læm] n 羔羊
It is obvious that the lambs were stolen.
很显然小羊们被偷了。
◎ ewe lamb 最宠爱的人　◎ It is obvious that... 很显然……

> ○ obvious (P. 330)

0480 **lamp** [læmp] n 灯，台灯
The gas lamp eventually lost ground to lights.
煤油灯最终被电灯取代。
◎ light 灯　◎ daylight lamp 日光灯

> 语法重点
> lost 的原形是 lose，lose 是不规则动词，其过去式、过去分词都是 lost。

0481 **land** [lænd] n 陆地，土地　v 靠岸，着陆
The news says these two countries disputed for many years over a small strip of land on their border.
新闻上说这两个国家为了边界上一块土地已经争执多年。
◎ continent 陆地　◎ on land 在陆地上

> ○ border (P. 264)

0482 **large** [lɑːrdʒ] a 大的，大量的
I regret that I have bought such a large house.
我后悔买了这么大的房子。
◎ big 大的　◎ large size 大尺寸的，大号，大码

0483 **last** [læst] a 最后的，上一个的　v 维持，持续
I was pressed to meet the last bus yesterday morning.
我昨天早上为了赶上末班车而焦头烂额。
◎ latest 最新的　◎ last of all 最后

> 语法重点
> "赶公交车"也可以用 catch the bus 来表达。

0484 **late** [leɪt] a 迟到的，晚的
I cautioned her not to be late again and again.
我一遍遍提醒她不要迟到。
◎ tardy 迟到的　◎ late for 迟到，来不及……

0485 **laugh** [læf] v 笑，发笑　n 笑声
The girl is no longer able to laugh after the breakup.
失恋后，女孩再也笑不出来了。
◎ weep 哭　◎ laugh at 嘲笑，因……而发笑

> 语法重点
> no longer 的意思是"不再"，修饰形容词 able。

lady ~ leave

0486 law [lɔː] **n** 法律，法规 **v** 起诉，打官司
It's their job to enforce the law.
他们的工作就是执法。
- legislation 法律　　- be at law 在诉讼中

> **语法重点**
> enforce the law 指"执法"；break the law 指"违法"。

0487 lay [leɪ] **v** 放置，躺，平放
Don't you dare lay a finger on that vase!
不许动那只花瓶！
- place 放置　　- don't you dare do... 不许做……

> **语法重点**
> lay 的过去式、过去分词、现在分词依次是 laid, laid, laying。

0488 lazy ['leɪzi] **a** 懒惰的，懒散的
He just likes to sleep like a lazy cat.
他只喜欢像懒猫一样睡觉。

> **语法重点**
> 句中第一个 like 是动词，意思是"喜欢"。第二个 like 是介词，意思是"像……一样"。

0489 lead [liːd] **v** 带领，引导，领先
I think these circumstances will lead up to war.
我觉得这些条件会导致战争。
- mislead 误导　　- lead in 导入

> **语法重点**
> lead up to 除了"导致"，还有"为……做准备"的意思。

0490 leader ['liːdər] **n** 领导者，领袖
Our support for the new leader is fraying at the edges.
我们对这位新任领导人的支持已经开始瓦解。
- chief 首领　　- follower 属下

0491 leaf [liːf] **n** 叶片，叶子
The giraffe eats tender leaves from the tall tree.
长颈鹿从高高的树上吃掉嫩叶子。
- leafage 树叶　　- in leaf 长满叶子的

↪ tender (P. 373)

0492 learn [lɜːrn] **v** 学习，学会，得知
It takes a long time to learn Japanese well.
把日语学好需要花很长的时间。
- study 学习　　- teach 教　　- learn of 听说，听到

0493 least [liːst] **a** 最少的，最小的 **ad** 最小地，最少地
I ride my bike for at least four times a week!
我每星期至少骑我的脚踏车四次！
- minimum 最小的　　- most 最多的　　- at least 至少

0494 leave [liːv] **v** 离开，出发
The room was in a disgusting state after my daughter left.
我女儿离开时，房间里一片狼藉。
- depart 离开　　- leave school 退学

> **语法重点**
> disgusting 本意是"令人尴尬的"，a disgusting state 意思是"一片狼藉"。

057

0495 left [left] a 左边的 n 左边
In Japan, people drive on the left-hand side of the road.
在日本，人们要靠左驾驶。
▶ right 右边　▶ turn left 向左转

↪ drive (P. 031)

0496 leg [leg] n 腿
My brother broke his leg while playing football.
我弟弟踢足球时腿骨折了。
▶ break a leg 祝好运，大获成功

语法重点
playing football 前省略了 he was。

0497 less [les] a 较少的，更少的 ad 更少地，较少地
The monthly rainfall in the town was less than 50 mm last month.
那个城镇上个月的降雨量不足 50 毫米。
▶ fewer 较少的　▶ more 较多的　▶ no less than 不少于，多……达

↪ rainfall (P. 492)

0498 lesson ['lesn] n 课，教训
I am disappointed that you could not learn the lesson of the experience.
你没能从这次经历中吸取教训，让我感到很失望。
▶ course 课程　▶ take lessons 上课

0499 let [let] v 让，允许
The owner had let the house fall into decay.
主人任由房子变得破烂不堪。
▶ let it be 顺其自然

语法重点
let 是不规则动词，其过去式、过去分词都是 let。

0500 letter ['letər] n 信件，字母 v 写下
Hey, here is a letter for you!
嗨，这里有你的一封信！
▶ character 字母　▶ to the letter 严格按照词句

0501 level ['levl] n 水平线，水准，标准
We live barely above the level of subsistence in this city.
我们的生活水平勉强在这个城市的最低水平线以上。
▶ standard 标准　▶ ground level 地平面

语法重点
barely 意思是"勉强"，用来加强语气。

0502 lie [laɪ] v 躺卧 n 谎言
Their words were next door to a lie.
他们的话和说谎差不多。
▶ fiction 谎言　▶ truth 实话　▶ tell a lie 说谎

语法重点
lie 当"说谎"讲时，其过去式、过去分词都是 lied。当"躺下"讲时，其过去式、过去分词是 lay, lain。

0503 life [laɪf] n 生命，生活
We should spare no effort to save this little girl's life.
我们应该不遗余力地去救这个小女孩的性命。

↪ spare (P. 505)

left ~ list

0504 lift [lɪft] **v** 举起，运送
I couldn't lift the stone and no more could she.
我搬不动那块石头，她也搬不动。
🔵 elevate 举起　🔴 lower 放下　🔷 lift up 举起，激励

> 语法重点
> 句中 no more could she 相当于 she couldn't lift the stone, either.

0505 light [laɪt] **n** 光线，灯光　**a** 轻的，浅色的，明亮的
Most of the cities in this country were affected by light noise pollution.
这个国家的多数城市受到轻度噪声污染。
🔷 light rail 轻轨，轻轨电车　🔷 be affected by... 受……影响

0506 like [laɪk] **v** 喜爱，想，愿意　**prep** 像，如同
What sort of person would like sleeping during daytime?
什么样的人喜欢白天睡觉呢？
🔵 enjoy 喜爱　🔴 dislike 不喜欢　🔷 if you like 如果你愿意的话

> 语法重点
> 句中 sort 的意思是"类型"，可以替换为 kind。

0507 likely ['laɪkli] **a** 有可能的　**ad** 很可能
It's likely that your father will come back next week.
你爸爸很有可能下周回来。
🔵 possible 可能的　🔴 unlikely 不可能的　🔷 most likely 最可能

> 语法重点
> likely 常指从表面迹象来判断有可能，possible 表示客观上的可能性。

0508 lily ['lɪli] **n** 百合花
We happened to see the water lily fold its petals.
我们碰巧看到莲花合拢花瓣。
🔷 water lily 睡莲　🔷 we happen to... 我们碰巧……

> 语法重点
> we happen to 后面接动词原形。

0509 line [laɪn] **n** 直线，界线，路线　**v** 排队
The man you want is on another line at the moment.
你要找的那个人正在接另外一个电话。
🔵 thread 线　🔷 in a line 排成一行

0510 lion ['laɪən] **n** 狮子
They kept the lion's skin as a trophy.
他们把狮子的皮作为纪念品保存起来。
🔷 lion tamer 驯狮者　🔷 ... keep sth. as... ……把某物当作……保存

> 语法重点
> kept 是动词 keep 的过去式，keep 是不及物动词，其过去式、过去分词都是 kept。

0511 lip [lɪp] **n** 嘴唇
Have you got something for chapped lips in your box?
你的箱子里有治嘴唇干裂的药吗？
🔵 labbro 嘴唇　🔷 upper lip 上嘴唇

> 语法重点
> something 一般用在肯定句中，用在疑问句时，表示询问者希望得到肯定的回答。

0512 list [lɪst] **n** 名单，目录，明细表
We are in torment after seeing the list.
我们看到那个目录后很痛苦。
🔷 price list 价目表

⮕ torment (P. 650)

0513 **listen** [ˈlɪsn] **v** 听
My mother put the radio on to listen to the music.
妈妈打开收音机听音乐。

0514 **little** [ˈlɪtl] **a** 少的，短的，微不足道的
I think there is very little likelihood of that happening.
我认为几乎没有发生那种事情的可能。
- big 大的   - little bit 一点点

> 语法重点
> little 表示"很少，几乎没有"，含有否定的意思。

0515 **live** [lɪv] **a** 活的 [paj] **v** 存活，生活，居住
We live on the outskirts of Beijing.
我们住在北京市郊。
- dwell 居住   - live with 和……生活在一起

> outskirts (P. 606)

0516 **long** [lɔːŋ] **a** 长的，长久的 **v** 渴望
How long will you be staying?
您打算住多久？
- tall 长的   - short 短的   - as long as 只要，和……一样长

0517 **look** [lʊk] **v** 看，朝着，注视
I'd like to look at the blue coat in the showcase.
我想看看橱窗内的那件蓝色的外套。
- look on 旁观   - I'd like to look at... 我想看看……

> 语法重点
> look at 与 see 都有"看"的意思，look at 强调看的动作，see 强调看到的结果。

0518 **lot** [lɑːt] **n** 很多，大量
I'm convinced that the best way to cure colds is to drink a lot of water.
我确信治疗感冒的最有效方法是喝大量的水。
- glut 大量   - dab 少量   - a lot 许多

> 语法重点
> a lot of 既可以修饰可数名词，也可以修饰不可数名词。
> cure (P. 148)

0519 **loud** [laʊd] **a** 大声的，喧吵的
The TV isn't loud enough and I turned it up.
电视声不够大，我把音量开大了一点儿。
- noisy 吵闹的   - quiet 安静的   - loud speaker 扩音器，增高话音

0520 **love** [lʌv] **n** / **v** 爱，喜欢
I loved you from the first sight I saw you.
从见你第一面时，我已经爱上了你。
- adore 喜爱   - abhor 憎恶，痛恨

> first (P. 039)

0521 **low** [loʊ] **a** 低的，少的
They have looked for the little boy high and low.
他们已经到处找过那个小男孩了。
- high 高的   - low price 低价

> 语法重点
> "到处"也可以用 here and there 或者 everywhere 来表达。

0522 lucky [ˈlʌki] a 幸运的，带来好运的
If my lucky number comes up, I will buy you a big house.
如果我走运的话，我就给你买一栋大房子。
- fortunate 幸运的 反 unlucky 不幸的 lucky dog 幸运儿

0523 lunch [lʌntʃ] n 午餐 v 吃午餐
We should make a habit of taking a nap after lunch.
我们应该养成午餐后小睡的习惯。
- have lunch 吃午餐

> **语法重点**
> make a habit of 后面接动词 ing。

0524 machine [məˈʃiːn] n 机器，机械
They want the machine manufactured to their own spec.
他们要求这台机器按他们的规格来制造。
- machinery 机器 machine parts 机器零件

0525 mad [mæd] a 发怒的，狂热的，着迷的
The cry of the baby nearly drove me mad.
孩子的哭声几乎使我发疯。
- crazy 疯狂的 sane 明智的 go mad 发疯，失去理智

> **语法重点**
> drive sb. mad 相当于 drive sb. to distraction，distraction 意思是"心烦意乱"。

0526 mail [meɪl] n 邮件，邮政
Many items of mail being sent to him were lost.
寄给他的许多邮件都遗失了。
- post 邮件，邮政 by mail 邮寄

> **语法重点**
> being sent to him 在句中用来修饰 mail。
> ⇒ item (P. 181)

0527 make [meɪk] v 制造，做
I made an appointment for you to see the girl.
我给你定了约见那个女孩的时间。

> **语法重点**
> make 是不规则动词，其过去式、过去分词都是 made。

0528 man [mæn] n 男人，人类
Jane averreds that she has seen the man before.
简斩钉截铁地说以前见过这个男人。
- woman 女人 sb. averreds that... 某人斩钉截铁地说……

> **语法重点**
> before 单独使用时，意思是"以前"，一般与完成时连用。

0529 many [ˈmeni] a 许多的
Many people think today is the time of reunion, but in fact it is not.
许多人认为今天是团圆的时候，但事实上不是。
- multiple 许多的 many a 许多的

> **语法重点**
> many 修饰可数名词。
> ⇒ reunion (P. 498)

0530 map [mæp] n 地图 v 绘制地图
Would you please make him a map showing the way to the zoo?
请你画张去动物园的地图给他好吗？
- Would you please...? 你能……吗？

0531 **March** [mɑːrtʃ] **n** 三月
We have to get back by March.
我们必须三月份之前回来。

> 语法重点
> 月份前面不加任何冠词。

0532 **market** [ˈmɑːrkɪt] **n** 市场，行情，销路
I think there is a good market for used cars.
我觉得二手车的需求量很大。
- market economy 市场经济
- there is a good market for... ……的需求量很大
- used cars 意思是"旧车"，也可以说 secondhand cars

0533 **marry** [ˈmæri] **v** 结婚，娶，嫁
The office gave her a present when she got married.
她结婚时，公司送了一件礼物给她。
- divorce 离婚
- marry up 结婚
- ... get married ……结婚了

0534 **master** [ˈmæstər] **n** 主人，硕士
He was considered a master of witty banter in the office.
他被认为是办公室里逗乐子的好手。
- great master 宗师，大师
- be considered a / an... 被认为是……

> witty (P. 805)

0535 **match** [mætʃ] **n** 火柴，比赛
Why did you get out of the football match this afternoon?
你为什么要逃避今天下午的足球比赛呢？
- league match 联赛
- get out of... 逃避……
- 足球比赛，一般英国人说 football match，而美国人说 football game

> afternoon (P. 004)

0536 **matter** [ˈmætər] **n** 物质，事情，问题
I will discuss this matter with her tomorrow.
我明天要和她讨论这件事情。
- no matter how 不管怎样

0537 **May** [meɪ] **n** 五月
The meeting is to be held on May 5th.
会议定于五月五日举行。

> 语法重点
> 具体的某一天前面用介词 on。

0538 **may** [meɪ] **aux** 可能，可以，能够
Buying household appliances may prove too costly.
购买家电可能会花很多钱。
- may be 也许，可能

> 语法重点
> buying household appliances 是句子的主语。

0539 **maybe** [ˈmeɪbi] **ad** 也许，大概
Maybe he has changed his mind.
或许他已经改变了主意。
- perhaps 也许，大概
- ... change one's mind ……改变主意

> 语法重点
> maybe 与 may be 意思相同，但用法不同。maybe 是副词，常位于句首。may be 中，may 是情态动词，be 是动词原形。

March ~ minute

0540 me [mi] *pron* 我
When do you think is convenient for me to visit you?
你认为我什么时候拜访你比较方便？

> 语法重点
> do you think 作插入语时，其语序为特殊疑问词 + do you think + 陈述句。
> ○ convenient (P. 145)

0541 mean [miːn] *v* 有……的意思，打算 *a* 吝啬的
In my opinion, passing the entrance exam means being admitted into college.
在我看来，通过入学考试意味着被大学录取。
• stingy 吝啬 • generous 慷慨的 • in the meantime 同时

0542 meat [miːt] *n* 肉
He smelt at the meat and told me it had gone bad.
他闻了闻这块肉，然后告诉我它已经坏了。
• sth. had gone bad 某物变坏了

> 语法重点
> go + 形容词（贬义），意思是"变得……"，表示一种变化。

0543 meet [miːt] *v* 遇见，见面
I rarely meet the guests face to face.
我很少和客户们见面。
• encounter 遇见 • meet with 符合，偶遇

> 语法重点
> face to face 是副词，而 face-to-face 是形容词，意思是"面对面的"。

0544 middle ['mɪdl] *a* 中间的，中等的
Please step to the middle, or you will block the door.
请往中间走，不然你就堵住门了。
• medium 中间的 • middle age 中年 • step to 相当于 walk to

0545 mile [maɪl] *n* 英里
It's about two miles over that way.
顺着那条路大约有两英里。

0546 milk [mɪlk] *n* 牛奶
Mix these fruits with the milk to make fruit salad.
把这些水果和牛奶调成水果沙拉。
• blend... with... to do sth. 把……和……混合在一起以做某事

> 语法重点
> milk 是不可数名词，没有复数形式。

0547 mind [maɪnd] *n* 注意，头脑，智力
Your words cut no ice with me—my mind was made up.
你说的话不起作用，我已下定决心了。
• state of mind 心境 • sth. cuts no ice with... 某物对……不起作用

> 语法重点
> sth. cuts no ice with 后面要接表示人的名词或代词。

0548 minute ['mɪnɪt] *n* 分钟，时刻 *v* 记录
Please wait a minute. I am engaged at the moment.
请稍等一会儿，我现在正在忙。
• wait a minute 等一下

> 语法重点
> be engaged 意思是"很忙"，可单独使用。短语 be engaged in... 的意思是"忙于……"。

063

0549 Miss [mɪs] n 小姐
Evidently, the man fell in love with Miss Black.
显然，那个人爱上了布莱克小姐。
🔗 Miss Universe 环球小姐　🔗 fall in love with sb. 爱上某人

语法重点
Miss 作"小姐"讲时，首字母一般要大写。

0550 miss [mɪs] v 错过，想念
I have to go now; otherwise I'll miss the last bus.
我必须现在就走，要不然就赶不上末班车了。

语法重点
otherwise 在句中作连词，意思是"否则的话"，等于 or。

0551 mistake [mɪˈsteɪk] n 错误，误会　v 误解，弄错
She acknowledged publicly that she had made a mistake.
她当众承认自己犯了个错误。
🔗 error 错误　🔗 by mistake 错误地

➔ acknowledge (P. 522)

0552 moment [ˈmoʊmənt] n 片刻，瞬间
Sorry, he just went out a moment ago.
抱歉，他刚才出去了。
🔗 in a moment 立刻　🔗 ... a moment ago 刚才……

语法重点
一段时间 + ago，意思是"……之前"，通常与一般过去时连用。

0553 mamma [ˈmæmə] n 妈妈
I didn't comply with my mamma's words when I was a little child.
我小的时候总是不听妈妈的话。
🔗 ... comply with... ……照……做，遵守……

0554 mommy [ˈmɑːmi] n 妈妈
Try your best, and mommy is always beside you.
尽力去做，妈妈永远在你身边。
🔗 try one's best 尽力

语法重点
try one's best to do sth. 表示尽力去做某事。

0555 Monday [ˈmʌndeɪ] n 星期一
She's covering for me on Monday.
她星期一会帮我代班。
🔗 on Monday 在周一　🔗 cover for... 帮……代班

➔ cover (P. 026)

0556 money [ˈmʌni] n 钱，财产
I am dreading borrowing money from him.
我正在为向他借钱的事发愁。
🔗 treasure 财富　🔗 make money 赚钱
🔗 money 泛指普通意义上的"钱"，cash 侧重指"现金"

0557 monkey [ˈmʌŋki] n 猴子
How many golden monkeys did you see?
你看到了多少只金丝猴？
🔗 monkey business 胡闹

0558 month [mʌnθ] n 月份

We often go shopping at the end of the month.
我们经常月底去购物。
⊕ month by month 逐月

> 语法重点
> at the beginning of the month 则是表示月初。

0559 moon [muːn] n 月亮，月球

It is said that the moon today is at its brightest and fullest.
据说，今天的月亮是最亮最圆的。
⊕ a blue moon 不可能的事

> 语法重点
> 月亮是独一无二的，所以前面加定冠词the。

0560 more [mɔːr] pron 更多的 ad 更多

More and more people choose to take a bus when they go out.
越来越多的人出门选择乘公交车。
⊕ many more 更多的 ⊕ more and more... 越来越多的……

> 语法重点
> much, many 的比较级都是 more，所以 more 后面可放可数名词或不可数名词。
> ⊃ choose (P. 139)

0561 morning ['mɔːrnɪŋ] n 早晨，上午

We all went to see them off on the morning of their departure.
他们离开的那个早上，我们都去送行了。
⊕ on the morning of... 在……的早上

> 语法重点
> "在早上"一般用 in the morning 来表示，但句子是"具体的某一天的早上"，所以前面用介词 on。

0562 most [moʊst] a 最多的，大多数的 ad 最（多）

Her eyes are her most striking feature.
她最引人注目的是那双眼睛。
⊕ maximum 最多的 ⊖ least 最少的 ⊕ most of 大部分

> 语法重点
> striking 的最高级是在前面加 most。
> ⊃ feature (P. 296)

0563 mother ['mʌðər] n 母亲，妈妈

Mother says to keep a pet is a waste of time.
妈妈说养宠物浪费时间。

0564 mountain ['maʊntn] n 山脉

After bidding them farewell, he left for the mountain to pray.
辞别了他们之后，他动身去山上祷告。
⊕ a mountain of flesh 大块头

> 语法重点
> leave for 表示"动身去……"，leave... for... 则是表示"离开……去……"。

0565 mouse [maʊs] n 老鼠，滑鼠

She is as quiet as a mouse.
她很文静。
⊕ rat 老鼠 ⊕ ... be as quiet as a mouse ……很文静

> 语法重点
> mouse 的复数形式是 mice。

0566 mouth [maʊθ] n 嘴，口

I can't stand it when people talk with their mouths full.
我无法忍受别人说话的时候满嘴食物。
⊕ hold one's mouth 住口，不作声 ⊕ I can't stand it when... 我无法忍受……

0567 move [muːv] v 移动，搬动

Let's move on to the prickly subject of where to set up the new factory.
我们继续讨论在哪里建新厂这个棘手问题吧。

反 stop 停止　同 move on 继续前进

语法重点
move on 中的介词 on 有"继续"的意思，go on 的意思是"继续"。
↪ subject (P. 230)

0568 movie / film ['muːvi] / [fɪlm] n 电影，影片

It is said that the movie is based on a real-life incident.
据说，这部电影是根据真实事件拍摄的。

同 film 电影　同 see a movie 看电影　同 be based on... 以……为基础

0569 Mr. ['mɪstər] n 先生

We have adopted Mr. Green as our manager.
我们接受格林先生做我们的经理。

语法重点
称呼男士，不管是已婚的还是未婚的，都可以用 Mr.。

0570 Mrs. ['mɪsɪz] n 太太，夫人

Mrs. Li remarked that she seemed a quiet girl.
李太太评论说，她看起来是个文静的女孩。

同 remarked that... 评论说……

语法重点
Mrs. 后面加上姓氏，用来称呼已婚的女士。

0571 Ms. [ˌem 'es] n 女士

Would Ms. Wang please come forward?
请王小姐到前面来好吗？

同 ... come forward ……上前

语法重点
Ms. 后面加上姓氏，用来称呼婚姻状况不明的女士。
↪ forward (P. 168)

0572 much [mʌtʃ] a 很多的　ad 很，几乎

I'm afraid I've taken up too much of your time.
恐怕我已经打扰您太久了。

同 almost 几乎　同 I'm afraid... 我恐怕……

语法重点
I'm afraid 后面省略了 that。

0573 mud [mʌd] n 泥巴，泥浆

He dirtied his trousers when he stepped on the mud.
他踩在烂泥里，把裤子弄脏了。

同 drag in the mud 玷污，诋毁　同 step on... 踩在……上

语法重点
mud 一般指"泥巴"，dirt 一般指"尘土，污渍"。

0574 mug [mʌɡ] n 大杯子，一杯的量

I had a mug of cocoa before going to bed.
临睡前，我喝了一杯可可。

同 a mug of 一杯

0575 music ['mjuːzɪk] n 音乐，乐曲

I like pop music a lot.
我很喜欢流行音乐。

同 melody 曲子　同 like... a lot 很喜欢……

move ~ never

0576 must [məst] aux 必须，很可能 n 必须做的事
No matter who he is, he must obey the rules.
不论他是什么人，都必须遵守规则。
- must be 一定　- no matter who... is... 不论……是什么人……

0577 my [maɪ] pron 我的
I lost my balance and fell down.
我没有站稳，就摔倒了。
- my own 我自己的　- ... lose one's balance ……失去平衡

↪ balance (P. 260)

0578 name [neɪm] n 名字
I'm sorry. There is no one here by that name.
对不起，这里没有叫那个名字的人。
- family name 姓　- ... by that name ……叫那个名字

> 语法重点
> by that name 在句中修饰 one。

0579 nation ['neɪʃn] n 国家，民族
The two nations warred upon each other for over a decade.
这两个国家互相打了十多年的仗。
- country 国家　- host nation 东道国　- ... for over a decade ……十多年

> 语法重点
> nation 与 country 都可以表示"国家"，但 nation 侧重指"国民或民族"，country 侧重指"国土或疆域"。

0580 nature ['neɪtʃər] n 自然界，本性
I have a forbearing nature and I accept troubles with a smile.
我较为宽容，遇到麻烦也能一笑了之。
- property 性能　- human nature 人性　- ... with a smile ……笑着……

> 语法重点
> nature 一般指人与生俱来的"性格、特点"。morality 指符合道德标准的行为，或用道德标准衡量某事，指社会的、个人的道德。

0581 near [nɪr] prep 在……附近，临近 ad 接近
Are there any parks near the theatre?
剧院附近有停车场吗？
- next 靠近　- away 在远处　- near by 在附近

> 语法重点
> near + 表示地点的名词，意思是"在……附近"，此时 near 作介词。

0582 neck [nek] n 脖子
The players are running neck and neck.
选手们并驾齐驱地跑着。
- cervix 颈部　- risk one's neck 赌命，拼命

0583 need [niːd] v 需要 aux 必须
I need someone to help me with the luggage.
我需要有人帮我搬行李。
- require 需要　- need for 对……的需要，需要……

> 语法重点
> someone 和 some 一样，一般用在肯定句中。

0584 never ['nevər] ad 从未，永不，从不
He is never concerned about being born a bastard.
他从不介意自己是私生子。
- ever 永远　- never before 以前从未有过

067

0585 **new** [nuː] **a** 新的，最近的
It seems that you feel ambivalent about your new job.
你似乎对新工作喜忧参半。
同 fresh 新的　　反 old 老的　　搭 new year 新年

0586 **news** [nuːz] **n** 新闻，消息
The news of her marrying a foreigner came as a bombshell.
她要嫁给一个外国人，这个消息令人震惊。
同 information 消息　　搭 good news 好消息

0587 **newspaper** ['nuːzpeɪpər] **n** 报纸
He felt dismal after reading a piece of bad news in the newspaper.
在报纸上读了一条不好的消息后，他心情忧郁。
同 courant 新闻　　搭 read the newspaper 看报

> **语法重点**
> in the newspaper 中的 the 可以去掉。

0588 **next** [nekst] **a** 最接近的，其次的　**ad** 其次，下次
We have decided to go camping next week.
我们已决定下个星期去露营。

> **语法重点**
> next + 表示时间的名词，意思是 "下一个……"。

0589 **nice** [naɪs] **a** 好的，可爱的，友好的，令人愉快的
It's been nice talking to you.
和你谈话很愉快。
同 pleasant 令人愉快的　　反 boresome 令人厌倦的
搭 nice to meet you 很高兴见到你

> **语法重点**
> it's 是 it has 的缩写。

0590 **night** [naɪt] **n** 夜晚
It must have rained last night for the road is wet.
路面是湿的，昨晚肯定下雨了。
同 evening 晚上　　反 day 白昼　　搭 good night 晚安，再见

> **语法重点**
> 句子表示对过去情况的推测，所以主句 must 后面接现在完成时。

0591 **nine** [naɪn] **n** 九，九个
That train gets there at nine o'clock on the button.
那班火车九点整到那里。
搭 nine to five 朝九晚五

> **语法重点**
> there 在句中作副词，所以前面省略了介词 to。
> ⊃ button (P. 135)

0592 **nineteen** [ˌnaɪn'tiːn] **n** 十九
They have nineteen days to stay here.
他们有十九天的时间可以待在这里。

> **语法重点**
> here 在句中作副词，前面不用任何介词。

0593 **ninety** ['naɪnti] **n** 九十
It is decided that we have to stay another ninety days.
已经决定了，我们不得不再停留九十天。
搭 ninety-nine times out of a hundred 几乎总是

> **语法重点**
> another 在句中的意思是 "又有，还有"，而不是 "另一个"。

new ~ note

0594 no / nope [noʊ] / [noʊp] **ad** 不，不是 **a** 没有的，不许的
There is no need to worry about it.
不必为那件事烦恼。
● no longer 不再

> 语法重点
> no 作形容词时，常位于名词前，用来表示否定。
> ↻ worry (P. 116)

0595 noise [nɔɪz] **n** 噪声，声音，响声
My mother always fires up at the noise.
我妈妈总是一听到噪声就生气。
● silence 寂静，无声　● make a noise 吵闹
● fire up at... 因……生气

0596 noisy ['nɔɪzi] **a** 吵闹的，嘈杂的
It is so noisy here that I can't do my homework.
这里太吵，我没法写作业。
● furious 狂怒的　● still 寂静的

> 语法重点
> so + 形容词或副词 + that 的意思是"如此……以至于……"，引导结果状语从句。

0597 noon [nuːn] **n** 正午，中午
We had a very tolerable lunch this noon.
今天中午我们吃了顿还算可以的午餐。
● midnight 午夜　● at noon 在中午

> 语法重点
> "今天中午"不能说成 today noon，要说 this noon。

0598 nor [nɔːr] **conj** / **ad** 也不，也没有
It neither increased nor decreased my income.
我既不会因此多赚些钱，也不会因此少赚些钱。
● neither 也不，也没有　● neither... nor... 既不……也不……

> 语法重点
> neither... nor... 的含义是否定的，连接任意两个并列成分。连接主语时，要遵循就近原则。

0599 north [nɔːrθ] **n** 北方，北部
It's very cold in the north in winter.
北方的冬天特别冷。
● to the north 向北方　● in the north 在北方

> 语法重点
> in the north of... 则是表示"在……的北方"。

0600 nose [noʊz] **n** 鼻子
When I gave her the present, she turned up her nose at it.
我送礼给她时，她对我的礼物不屑一顾。
● run at the nose 流鼻涕

> 语法重点
> 句中的 it 指代前面的 present。

0601 not [nɑːt] **ad** 不，没，不是
Please don't drive too fast. I'm not in a hurry.
请不要开太快，我不赶时间。
● if not for 要不是　● ... be in a hurry ……着急，……匆忙

> 语法重点
> fast 本身既可以作形容词，也可以作副词。句中 fast 作副词，修饰 drive。

0602 note [noʊt] **n** 笔记，便条
You should make a brief note on the telephone pad.
你需要在电话通信录上记下简短的话。
● minute 笔记　● take a note 记笔记

> 语法重点
> on the telephone pad 的意思是"在电话通信录上"，在句中表示地点。

069

0603 nothing ['nʌθɪŋ] pron 无事 n 没有，空
I have nothing to do with this matter.
我与这件事无关。
同 everything 一切   nothing but 只有，只不过

0604 notice ['noʊtɪs] v 注意，留心 n 通知
She is too proud to take notice of him.
她太骄傲以至于不理睬他。
public notice 公共启事，公告   ... too... to... ……太……而不能

> 语法重点
> too + 形容词或副词 + to + 动词原形，表示"太……而不能"，含有否定的意思。

0605 November [noʊ'vembər] n 十一月
They are expected to arrive there on November 5th.
他们有望在十一月五日抵达那里。
in November 在十一月

> 语法重点
> be expected to 后面接动词原形。

0606 now [naʊ] ad 现在，立刻 con 既然
I never dreamed of being your wife, but the fact is that I am your wife now.
我从未想过要当你的妻子，但是现在我成了你的妻子。
immediately 立刻   then 当时   up to now 到目前为止

> 语法重点
> the fact is 后面接句子，句子用陈述语序。
> ⇨ wife (P. 114)

0607 number ['nʌmbər] n 数字，号码
I'm afraid I have the wrong number.
恐怕我打错电话了。

0608 nurse [nɜːrs] n 护士，保姆 v 看护，护理
As a nurse, I am always full of thought for my patients.
作为护士，我对病人总是关心备至。

0609 OK [oʊ'keɪ] ad / a 可以的，好，不错
I'll pick you up tonight, OK?
今晚我去接你，好吗？
okay 好，不错   pick sb. up 接某人

> 语法重点
> OK 的用法很多，可以用作形容词、动词、名词、副词、感叹词等。

0610 ocean ['oʊʃn] n 海洋
Looking for the key there is like fishing for a needle in the ocean.
在那里找钥匙就像是大海捞针。
sea 海洋   Pacific Ocean 太平洋

> 语法重点
> ocean 与 sea 都有"海"的意思，区别在于 ocean 是指大洋或海洋的总称，sea 是指大海。

0611 o'clock [ə'klɑːk] ad 几点钟
I set the alarm clock for 7 o'clock.
我把闹钟定在七点钟。

> 语法重点
> o'clock 表示整点，有时会在后面加上单词 sharp，如 at 8 o'clock sharp，表示八点整，语气更强。

0612 **October** [ɑːkˈtoʊbər] **n** 十月
The number of travelers begins to tail off in October.
十月份游客开始减少。
🔗 October Revolution 俄国十月革命　🔗 ... tail off... ……变少

0613 **of** [əv] **prep** 属于……的
She often speaks ill of Jim behind his back.
她常在背后说吉姆的坏话。

> 语法重点
> 句子描述的是经常性、习惯性的动作，所以用一般现在时。

0614 **off** [ɔːf] **ad** 离开　**prep** 离开，在……之外
What time do you think is better for us to set off?
你认为我们什么时候出发比较好？
🔗 go off 离开，进行，睡去

> 语法重点
> set off 和 set out 都可以表示"出发"。

0615 **office** [ˈɔːfɪs] **n** 办公室
I'm sure flowers will add beauty to your office.
我确信花卉能美化您的办公室。
🔗 bureaux 办公处　🔗 office boy 杂务员

> 语法重点
> 句中的短语 add beauty to，可以用动词 beautify 替代，意思是"美化"。
> 🔗 beauty (P. 013)

0616 **officer** [ˈɔːfɪsər] **n** 官员，军官，高级职员
You mean the crime was committed with the connivance of a military officer?
你的意思是说，这项罪行是在一名军官的纵容下发生的？
🔗 wardroom 全体军官　🔗 staff officer 参谋

0617 **often** [ˈɔːfn] **ad** 常常，经常
Do you often contact your parents?
你经常和父母联络吗？
🔗 always 常常　🔗 seldom 很少　🔗 as often as 每当

> 语法重点
> 助动词 do 要与动词原形连用，因此后面的动词 contact 用的是原形。

0618 **oil** [ɔɪl] **n** 油
An expert says the oil spill will cause incalculable damage to the environment.
一位专家说，这次石油泄漏将对环境造成难以估计的损害。
🔗 petroleum 石油　🔗 vegetable oil 植物油

> 语法重点
> cause incalculable damage to 中的 to 是介词。
> 🔗 environment (P. 160)

0619 **old** [oʊld] **a** 老的，旧的，过时的
The old lady engaged herself in looking after her grandson.
这位老太太忙着照顾孙子。
🔗 engage oneself in doing... 忙于……

0620 **on** [ɑːn] **prep** 在……上面，关于
A young lady with graces appeared on the stage.
舞台上出现了一位优雅的年轻女士。
🔗 above 在……之上　🔗 beneath 在……之下　🔗 just on 将近，差不多

> 语法重点
> on 和 above 都可以表示"在……之上"的意思，above 指笼统的上方，on 含有表面接触的意思。

0621 **once** [wʌns] ad 一次，曾经
I had a date with the girl once before.
我以前和那个女孩约会过。
　once upon a time 曾经

○ before (P. 013)

0622 **one** [wʌn] n 一
All of us have to work together with one heart.
我们大家要齐心协力。
　no one 没有人

语法重点
with one heart 的意思是"齐心协力"，修饰动词 work。

0623 **only** [ˈoʊnli] ad 只有，仅仅，刚刚
We're going to have only one child.
我们只打算要一个孩子。
　just 仅仅　　only too 非常

语法重点
only 作副词，修饰 be going to（打算），在句中有加强语气的作用。

0624 **open** [ˈoʊpən] a 打开的，开放的
Suddenly, a butterfly flew in from the open window.
突然一只蝴蝶从开着的窗户飞了进来。
　in the open 在户外，在野外

语法重点
fly in 的意思是"飞进来"，句中用 fly 的过去式 flew。

0625 **or** [ɔːr] conj 或者
He spent days agonizing over whether to quit the job or not.
他用了几天时间苦苦思考是否要辞掉这个工作。
　or else 否则，要不然

0626 **orange** [ˈɔːrɪndʒ] n 柳橙，橘子
You can squeeze the juice from an orange.
你可以用橙子榨橙汁。

0627 **order** [ˈɔːrdər] n 顺序，规则，命令 v 命令，订购
In order to accomplish your target, you should work hard to improve yourself.
为了达到你的目标，你应该努力工作来提高自己。
　rule 规则　　in order 整齐，按顺序　　in order to... 为了……

语法重点
in order to 后面接动词原形。
○ target (P. 233)

0628 **other** [ˈʌðər] a 其他的，另外的
My father and mother are always bickering about something or other.
我父母总是在为这样那样的事情争吵。
　every other 所有其他的，每隔一个的

0629 **our** [aːr] pron 我们的
It's a pity our trip to Japan is cancelled.
真遗憾，我们去日本的旅行被取消了。

语法重点
前面的 trip 是单数形式，所以后面的 be 动词用 is。

once ~ papa / pa

0630 **out** [aʊt] prep 向外面地，在外面 ad 出，在外
Sorry, my parents won't allow me to stay out late.
对不起，我父母不会允许我在外面待得很晚。
- outside 在外面　- go out 出去　- ... stay out late ...... 在外待得很晚

语法重点
late 在句中作副词，修饰 stay out。

0631 **outside** [ˌaʊtˈsaɪd] n 外部 prep 在……外边 ad 在外面
Look, a compact sitting-room of the same genre is outside.
看，外面是间具有同样格调的小起居室。
- inside 在里面

0632 **over** [ˈoʊvər] prep 在……上方
A hawk is hovering over the hill.
一只鹰在小山丘上空翱翔。
- upon 在……之上　- under 在……下面
- over and above 除……之外，在……之上

语法重点
over 通常指"在……的（垂直）上方"。
↪ hover (P. 581)

0633 **own** [oʊn] a 自己的 v 承认，拥有
I advise you not to go out on your own at night.
我奉劝你在晚上别单独外出。
- at your own risk 由你自己负责

语法重点
on one's own 的意思是"某人自己，单独"，要注意与 of one's own（属于自己的）的区别。

0634 **page** [peɪdʒ] n 页面，张
His job is laying out the graphics on the page.
他的工作是设计页面上的图表。
- sheet 纸张　- home page 主页

0635 **paint** [peɪnt] v 油漆，绘画 n 油漆，颜料
I am engrossed in painting.
我全神贯注于绘画。
- varnish 亮光漆　- spray paint 喷漆

语法重点
be engrossed in 后面接名词或动名词。

0636 **pair** [per] n 一双，一对
I have two pairs of trousers to be washed and pressed.
我有两条裤子要洗和熨。
- couple 对　- a pair of... 一双……

语法重点
注意，two pairs of trousers 中，不仅是 trouser 要用复数形式，pair 也要用复数形式。

0637 **pants / trousers** [pænts] / [ˈtraʊzərz] n 裤子，长裤
Do you have pants to go with the jacket?
你们有和这件夹克搭配的裤子吗？
- short pants 短裤　- go with... 搭配……

语法重点
表示"与……很搭，搭配得好"时，要用 go well with。

0638 **papa / pa** [ˈpɑːpə] / [pɑː] n 爸爸
Ask your papa to help you ease off your belt a bit.
让你爸爸帮你把腰带松开些。
- papa 通常用在口语中，不如 father 正式

073

0639 **paper** [ˈpeɪpər] n 纸，报纸
I think Spring Festival couplets are written on red paper.
我认为春联是写在红纸上的。
· newspaper 报纸　· paper work 文书工作

> 语法重点
> 春联包括上联、下联及横批，所以 couplet 要用复数。

0640 **parent** [ˈperənt] n 父亲，母亲，家长
The judge said no parent can duck out of his / her duty to his / her children.
法官说没有一个父母可以逃避自己对孩子应尽的责任。
· child 孩子　· single parent 单亲父（母）

> 语法重点
> parent 指的是父母中的一方，所以后面的代词用 his / her。
> ⟳ duty (P. 158)

0641 **park** [pɑːrk] n 公园，停车场 v 停车，停放
We'll get to the amusement park soon.
我们很快会到游乐园。
· amusement park 游乐园

0642 **party** [ˈpɑːrti] n 派对，政党
I want to invite all of you to a party.
我想请你们所有人参加一个派对。
· get-together 聚会　· invite... to a party 请……参加派对

0643 **pass** [pæs] v 通过，经过，传递
It's impossible for you to pass the exam if you don't work hard to improve yourself.
如果你不好好学习提高自己，就不可能通过考试。
· pass the time 打发时间　· pass the exam 通过考试

> ⟳ improve (P. 178)

0644 **past** [pæst] a 过去的
I have built a solid friendship with my classmates in the past three years.
在过去三年里，我与同学们建立了深厚的友谊。

> 语法重点
> in the past + 一段时间，和现在完成时连用。

0645 **pay** [peɪ] v 付钱，偿还
You must pay a deposit for the library card.
你得为图书卡缴押金。
· compensate 偿还　· owe 欠钱　· pay for 为……付出代价

> 语法重点
> pay for 的主语是人。

0646 **pen** [pen] n 笔
We are required to write our exercises in pen.
要求我们用钢笔做练习。

> 语法重点
> in pen 相当于 with pen（用钢笔），表示一种方式。

0647 **pencil** [ˈpensl] n 铅笔
He bore hard upon the pencil and it broke.
他使劲压铅笔，然后铅笔就断了。

> 语法重点
> bear hard upon 的介词 upon 可以替换成 on。

paper ~ pig

0648 people ['piːpl] **n** 人们，人民
You know people have the right to wear what they like.
要知道，人们有权穿自己喜欢的衣服。
- common people 大众，平民

> 语法重点
> have the right to 后面要接动词原形。

0649 perhaps [pərˈhæps] **ad** 也许，可能
Perhaps he could assist in some way.
也许他能帮上什么忙。
- possibly 可能 反 certainly 确定地 or perhaps both 或者两者兼有

> 语法重点
> perhaps 通常放在句首。
> ⇒ assist (P. 257)

0650 person [ˈpɜːrsn] **n** 人
We can't find a suitable person to do that thing.
我们找不到一个合适的人选去做那件事。
- in person 亲自，外貌上

> 语法重点
> people 也可以表示"人"，其形式上虽是单数，却表示复数意义，若要表示几个人时要用 person。

0651 pet [pet] **n** 宠物
My son keeps a dog as a pet.
我儿子养了一条狗做宠物。
- pet food 宠物食品 keep... as... 养……作为……

> 语法重点
> a pet 对应前面的 a dog，如果养了几条狗做宠物，可以用 keeps several dogs as pets。

0652 piano [piˈænoʊ] **n** 钢琴
Lily is playing the piano in her room.
莉莉正在她的房间里弹钢琴。

> 语法重点
> 表示"弹奏乐器时"，乐器名称前一定要用定冠词 the。

0653 picture [ˈpɪktʃər] **n** 图画，照片
It is a picture of me in my school days.
那是我学生时代的照片。
- photo 照片 take pictures 照相

> 语法重点
> a picture of me 表示"照片上那个人是我"，a picture of mine 表示"那张照片属于我"。

0654 pie [paɪ] **n** 馅饼
What he said was only pie in the sky.
他所说的实在是很渺茫。
- pie in the sky 不能保证实现的诺言，空中楼阁

0655 piece [piːs] **n** 一件，块
I can do it. It's a piece of cake.
我能办得到的，这不费吹灰之力。
- in pieces 破碎，意见分歧
- a piece of cake 本意是"一块蛋糕"，也可以引申为"轻松的事"。

0656 pig [pɪɡ] **n** 猪
Look, a dead pig is lying on the ground.
看，地上躺着一头死猪。

> 语法重点
> lie（躺）的现在分词是 lying。

075

0657 **place** [pleɪs] n 地方，地点
It took us ages to find a place to park last night.
昨晚我们找了好半天才找到停车的地方。
同 district 行政区，地方 搭 working place 工作地点

> 语法重点
> to park 在句子中用来修饰 place。

0658 **plan** [plæn] n 计划
Our plan had some difficulties in being in operation.
我们在执行计划时遇到了一些困难。
同 scheme 计划 搭 make a plan 制订计划

⊃ operation (P. 479)

0659 **plant** [plænt] n 植物，设备，设施 v 种植
I am going to buy some potted plants.
我要去买些盆栽。
同 facility 设备，设施 搭 power plant 发电厂，动力装置

0660 **play** [pleɪ] v 玩耍，比赛
I often go to play football out of hours.
我在工作时间之外常去踢足球。
同 disport 玩耍 反 work 工作 搭 play the game 玩游戏

> 语法重点
> 球类运动前面不用任何冠词。

0661 **player** ['pleɪər] n 选手
He is second to none as a basketball player.
作为一名篮球队员，谁都赢不了他。

0662 **playground** ['pleɪgraʊnd] n 运动场，游乐场
There used to be a playground in the region.
这个地区曾经有个游乐场。
搭 there used to be... 曾经有……

> 语法重点
> there used to be 是 there be 句型和 used to do 句型的结合，表示过去曾经有，现在却没有了。

0663 **please** [pliːz] v 使高兴，使满意 ad 请
Wash your hands before you come in, please.
请先洗洗手再进来。
同 delight 使高兴 反 enrage 激怒 搭 please oneself 感到满意

0664 **pocket** ['pɑːkɪt] n 口袋，袋子
The key will be muddled up with something else in your pocket.
你的口袋里的钥匙会和其他东西混在一起。
同 sack 袋 搭 back pocket 后口袋

0665 **poetry** ['poʊətri] n 诗文，诗歌，诗集
His son has a gift for poetry.
他的儿子有作诗的天赋。
同 verse 诗篇 搭 ... have a gift for... ……有……的天赋

⊃ gift (P. 043)

0666 **point** [pɔɪnt] n 指出，观点，看法

My point is that we should go back now.
我的观点是我们现在应该立刻回去。
- perspective 观点
- point of view 观点，立场

语法重点
we should go back now 是对 point 的具体解释。

0667 **police** [pəˈliːs] n 警察

At that time, I sensed something was amiss and called the police.
那时候我觉得有点儿不对劲，我就叫了警察。
- copper 警察
- police station 派出所，警察局
- call the police = report to the police，表示"报警"

0668 **policeman** [pəˈliːsmən] n 男警察

I saw the policeman discharge his gun at the fleeing thief.
我看见警察向那个逃跑的小偷开了枪。
- traffic policeman 交通警察
- discharge... gun at... 向……开枪

语法重点
fleeing 表示正在进行的动作，说明贼正在逃跑。

0669 **pond** [pɑːnd] n 池塘

The little child dropped into the pond.
那个小孩子掉进了池塘里。
- mere 池塘
- drop into... 掉进……
- pond 一般指乡村由人工挖的可供喂养鹅、鸭等的水塘，pool 指自然形成的池塘

⊃ drop (P. 157)

0670 **pool** [puːl] n 游泳池，水塘

The pool was fenced off because it was dangerous.
这个水池很危险，所以用栅栏围起来了。

语法重点
pool 与 fence off 是被动关系，所以用被动语态。

0671 **poor** [pɔːr] a 贫穷的，可怜的

A poor boy called John was killed in the accident, too.
一个名叫约翰的可怜男孩也在这次意外中丧生。
- destitute 穷困的
- rich 富裕的
- poor people 穷人

语法重点
called John 修饰 boy。

0672 **popcorn** [ˈpɑːpkɔːrn] n 爆米花

He wants a pile of popcorn of the butyric flavor.
他想要一堆奶油味的爆米花。

0673 **position** [pəˈzɪʃn] n 地点，职位，立场，状态

You'd better shift your position from the horizontal.
你最好从水平姿势变换成其他姿势。
- in position 就位，在适当的位置，在原位

语法重点
句中 position 的意思是"姿势"，可以替换为 posture。

0674 **possible** [ˈpɑːsəbl] a 可能的，合理的

Do you think it is possible to arrive there on time?
你认为有没有可能准时到那里？
- impossible 不可能的
- if possible 如果可能的话

语法重点
be possible to do sth. 表示有可能做某事。

0675 power ['paʊər] n 力量，能力，权力
We've just had a power failure.
我们这里刚才停电了。
- electric power 电力，电功率
- ... have a power failure ……停电

0676 practice ['præktɪs] v 练习，实践
I plan to join a language club to practice English speaking.
我打算参加语言俱乐部来练习说英语。
- exercise 练习
- practice doing... 练习做……

语法重点
practice doing sth. 表示练习做某事。

0677 prepare [prɪ'per] v 准备，预备，筹划
If I had not prepared for my English exam, I would have attended your party.
如果我不用准备英语考试，我当初就去参加你的派对了。
- arrange 筹备
- prepare for... ……为……做准备

语法重点
句子用了虚拟语气，是对过去的一种假设，所以主句用 would + 现在完成时，条件句用过去完成时。

0678 pretty ['prɪti] a 漂亮的，美丽的 ad 相当地
My new car is pretty good and it stops on a dime.
我的新车很不错，它的刹车很灵。
- pretty face 漂亮的容貌
- ... be pretty good ……很好

语法重点
pretty 在句中作副词，修饰 good。
⇒ dime (P. 284)

0679 price [praɪs] n 价格，价值
What's the price of the blue coat?
那件蓝色外套多少钱？
- value 价值
- cost price 成本价格

语法重点
句中问的是 blue coat 的价钱，所以 price 用单数；同样地，be 动词用 is。

0680 print [prɪnt] v 列印，出版
They asked him to print the word in italics.
他们要求他用斜体印出这个词。
- publish 出版
- print out 印出
- in italics 表示"用斜体"，若是"用正体"则用 in block capitals

0681 problem ['prɑ:bləm] n 问题
With my help, she ought to have no problem.
有了我的帮助，她应该不会有什么问题。
- issue 问题
- solution 解答
- difficult problem 难题

语法重点
no problem 也可以单独使用，意思是"不麻烦，没什么事，很容易"。

0682 prove [pru:v] v 证明，证实，结果是
I will prove to the world that I am the best.
我要向全世界证明我是最棒的。
- certify 证明
- prove to be 结果是，证明为

语法重点
I will prove to the world 后面要接宾语从句。

0683 public ['pʌblɪk] a 公共的，公众的，公开的
He will be ashamed to show his face in public.
他不好意思抛头露面。
- overt 公然的
- secret 秘密的
- public opinion 民意，公众舆论

0684 pull [pʊl] v 拉，扯

Let's go over and help him pull the big box.
我们过去帮他拉那个大箱子。
　haul 拉，拖　　push 推　　pull up 拔起，停下来，阻止

0685 purple ['pɜːrpl] n 紫色

People decorate baskets with purple ribbons on that day.
在那一天，人们用紫色的丝带来装饰篮子。
　decorate... with... 用……来装饰……
　dark purple 的意思是"深紫色，暗紫色"，red purple 意思是"紫红色"

⊃ decorate (P. 150)

0686 purpose ['pɜːpəs] n 目的

Their main purpose is to raise money.
他们的主要目的就是募款。
　intention 目的　　on purpose 有目的地，故意地

语法重点
their main purpose is 后面可以接不定式或动名词。

0687 push [pʊʃ] v 推，按，挤

If you always push him too hard, he will go mad.
如果你总是逼他太紧，他会发疯的。
　push up 增加，提高，向上推　　push sb. too hard 逼某人太紧

语法重点
too 在句中的意思是"太"，是副词，修饰 hard。

0688 put [pʊt] v 放置，安置，使处于

It's time to put an end to their little caper.
是时候制止他们的胡闹了。
　put on 穿上，增加，假装　　... put an end to 制止，结束……

语法重点
句中 put an end to 就相当于 stop，表示制止。

0689 queen [kwiːn] n 王后，女王

To our surprise, the queen had a plain face.
让我们吃惊的是，那位女王相貌平平。
　emperor 皇帝，君主　　movie queen 影后

0690 question ['kwestʃən] n 问题，疑问

I'm afraid I won't be able to answer your question now.
恐怕我现在不能回答你的问题。
　query 疑问　　without question 毫无疑问

语法重点
句中的 answer 可以替换成 reply to（回答）。

0691 quick [kwɪk] a 快速的，灵敏的

I know he is quick on the uptake.
我知道他的理解力很强。
　rapid 快速的　　tardy 迟缓的　　quick temper 急性子，性情急躁

语法重点
he is quick on the uptake 是从句，充当 know 的宾语。

0692 quiet ['kwaɪət] a 安静的，宁静的，平静的

Keep quiet, your little sister is sleeping.
安静些，你的小妹妹在睡觉。
　serene 宁静的　　rowdy 吵闹的　　in quiet 安静地

0693 quite [kwaɪt] ad 相当地，完全，十分
It's quite straightforward to find my house.
找到我家相当容易。
- quite well 相当好，十分好

语法重点
quite 是副词，修饰形容词 straightforward。
→ straightforward (P. 641)

0694 race [reɪs] n 赛跑，竞争，人种 v 赛跑，竞赛
I am against race prejudice.
我反对种族歧视。
- competition 竞争　- I am against... 我反对……
- race prejudice 的意思是"种族歧视"；"种族平等"用 race equality 来表达

0695 radio ['reɪdioʊ] n 收音机，无线电
The astonishing news was given out over the radio.
这个令人震惊的消息是通过无线电发出的。
- wireless 收音机，无线电　- portable radio 便携式收音机

语法重点
"通过无线电"也可以用 by radio 来表达。

0696 railroad ['reɪlroʊd] n 铁路
To build a new railroad there will be a mammoth job.
在那里修建一条新铁路将会是一项巨大的工程。
- railway 铁路　- railroad track 铁轨

语法重点
To build a new railroad there 在句中作主语。

0697 rain [reɪn] n 雨 v 下雨
If it doesn't rain this weekend, will you go camping with us?
如果这个周末不下雨，你会和我们一起去露营吗？
- drizzle 毛毛雨　- a heavy rain 一场大雨

语法重点
rain 作动词用时，其否定形式是 it + 助动词 + not + rain。

0698 rainbow ['reɪnboʊ] n 彩虹
There is a beautiful rainbow hanging in the sky.
一条美丽的彩虹悬挂在天上。

语法重点
rainbow 与 hang 是主动关系，所以用 hang 的 ing 形式。

0699 raise [reɪz] v 举起，筹集，养育
I hope to raise my daughter to be a decent person.
我希望把女儿培养成优秀人才。
- arise 上升　- decline 下降　- raise up 举起，抬起

→ decent (P. 699)

0700 rat [ræt] n 老鼠，变节者，卑鄙的人
I occasionally see the rats in this house.
我有时会在这个房子里发现老鼠。

语法重点
occasionally 表示"偶尔，有时"，其表示的发生频率比较低。

0701 reach [riːtʃ] v 到达，伸出，达成
We didn't reach the village until it got dark.
我们直到天黑才到达那个村庄。
- extend 伸出　- reach for 伸手去拿
- not do... until... 直到……才……

语法重点
not... until... 中的 until 也可以替换成 till。

0702 read [riːd] v 阅读，理解
A man read the gas meter just now.
一名男子刚才来查看了燃气表。
- comprehend 理解
- read through 通读

> 语法重点
> read 是不规则动词，其过去式、过去分词都是 read。

0703 ready ['redi] a 准备好的，现成的
Run along and get ready for bed.
走，准备去睡觉。
- prepared 准备好的
- all ready 全部准备好，一切就绪

0704 real ['riːəl] a 真实的，正宗的，名副其实的
We'll never get to know the real England there.
我们在那里根本不会了解真正的英国。
- true 真正的
- unreal 不真实的
- real value 实际价值

> 语法重点
> real 表示的"真"，是相对想象、错觉、幻觉、伪造等而言的，是指现象与事实的一致性；而 true 表示的"真"，主要指符合特定的标准。

0705 reason ['riːzn] n 理由，原因，理性
What is the reason for the picture's appeal?
这幅画为什么具有吸引力呢？
- cause 原因
- result 结果
- by reason of 由于，因为
- What is the reason for...? ……是什么原因？

0706 receive [rɪ'siːv] v 收到，接到
Nothing is more important than to receive education for the girl.
对于这个女孩来说，没有比接受教育更重要的事情了。
- get 收到
- send 发送
- receiving mode 接收模式

> 语法重点
> 注意，"受教育"要用 receive education 来表达。

0707 red [red] a 红色的 n 红色
I have red eyes due to lack of sleep.
由于缺乏睡眠，我的双眼布满血丝。
- in red 穿红衣
- ... have red eyes ……双眼布满血丝

> lack (P. 055)

0708 remember [rɪ'membər] v 记得，记住
I remembered that he was the drunken man.
我记得他就是那个喝醉酒的人。
- recall 记起
- forget 忘记
- remember of 记得，想起

> 语法重点
> he was the drunken man 是从句，作 remember 的宾语。

0709 report [rɪ'pɔːrt] v / n 报道，报告
Can you tell me how to write this report?
你能告诉我如何写这份报告吗？
- news report 新闻报道
- Can you tell me how to...? 你能告诉我如何……吗？

0710 rest [rest] v / n 休息，静止
You deserve a rest after cleaning the house.
打扫完房子后，你应该休息一下。
- relax 休息
- proceed 继续进行
- have a rest 休息

> 语法重点
> after 在句中作介词，后面要接动词的 ing 形式。

0711 return [rɪˈtɜːrn] v / n 返回，归还
I'll certainly pass your message on to him as soon as he returns.
他一回来，我肯定把你的口信传给他。
revert 归还　depart 出发　return home 回家

0712 rice [raɪs] n 米，稻子
We mustn't waste a grain of rice.
我们不能浪费一粒米。

> 语法重点
> mustn't 的意思是"千万不能"，表示劝诫与警告。
> ➔ waste (P. 110)

0713 rich [rɪtʃ] a 富有的，丰富的，富裕的
I often dream about being a rich man.
我常常梦想成为一个富人。
wealthy 富裕的　poor 贫穷的　rich in 富有，富于

> 语法重点
> rich 与 wealthy 都有"富裕的"的意思，但 wealthy 还暗含有"富贵已久，有社会地位"的意思。

0714 ride [raɪd] v 骑乘 n 交通工具
The girl got on her bicycle and rode off.
女孩骑上脚踏车走了。
ride a bike 骑脚踏车　ride off 骑马（或脚踏车等）而去

> 语法重点
> ride 是不规则动词，其过去式、过去分词是 rode, ridden。

0715 right [raɪt] a 对的，右边的，向右的
You'd better put the dressing table on the right.
你最好把梳妆台放在右边。
correct 正确的　wrong 错误的　turn right 向右转

0716 ring [rɪŋ] n 环，戒指
He borrowed the wedding ring from his best friend.
结婚戒指是他从最好的朋友那里借来的。
diamond ring 钻石戒指　borrow... from... 从……借来……

> 语法重点
> ring 是"环形的圈，环状物"，而 circle 是"圆形的，圆状物"。

0717 rise [raɪz] v 上升，升起，起立
They all rose cheering to their feet.
他们都起立欢呼。
ascend 上升　drop 下降　rise up 上升，起立

> 语法重点
> rise 是不规则动词，其过去式、过去分词分别是 rose 和 risen。

0718 river [ˈrɪvər] n 河流，江
The children dived into the river to cool off.
孩子们跳进河里凉快一下。
dive into the river to do... 跳进河里干……

> 语法重点
> river 指"河，江"；stream 指"小河，小溪，水流"。

0719 road [roʊd] n 马路，途径，方法
Unluckily, the only road to the village was blocked by a fallen tree.
不幸的是，通往那个村庄的唯一道路被一棵倒下的树挡住了。
in the road 挡路　be blocked by... 被……挡住

> 语法重点
> "到……的路"要用介词 to。

0720 robot ['roʊbɑːt] n 机器人
I don't think a robot can think for itself.
我认为机器人不能独立思考。

> **语法重点**
> 在英语中，将 think, believe, suppose, expect, fancy, imagine 等单词后面的宾语从句的否定词转移到主句中，即主句的动词用否定式，而从句的动词用肯定式，这就叫"否定前移"，但在翻译时，主句用肯定，从句用否定。

0721 rock [rɑːk] n 石头，困境
Try to push the rock with all your might.
努力用全身力气推那块石头。
- rock music 摇滚乐
- do sth. with all one's might 用尽全力做某事

0722 roll [roʊl] v 滚动，转动
Two months rolled by, and the school finished at last.
两个月过去了，学校终于放假了。
- rotate 转动
- roll out 铺开

0723 roof [ruːf] n 屋顶，顶部
The roof collapsed under the weight of the snow last night.
昨晚屋顶被雪压坍了。
- housetop 屋顶
- floor 地板
- flat roof 屋顶平台

↪ collapse (P. 409)

0724 room [ruːm] n 房间，空间
I'd like to book a single room with a bath.
我想预订一间附卫浴的单人套房。
- drug room 药房
- I'd like to book... 我想预订……
- "双人房"要表示为 double room

0725 rooster ['ruːstər] n 公鸡
If you can pass the exam, the rooster will lay eggs.
如果你能通过考试，公鸡就会下蛋了。
- cock 公鸡
- hen 母鸡

> **语法重点**
> rooster 与 cock 都有"公鸡"的意思，cock 相对于 hen（母鸡）而言，更加侧重于表示性别，而 rooster 更加注重 roost（栖息，禽）。

0726 root [ruːt] n 根
Her stinginess is the root of trouble.
她的吝啬是苦恼的根源。
- at the root of 实质上，根本上
- be the root of... 是……的根源
- the root of all evils 表示"万恶之源"

0727 rope [roʊp] n 绳子，索
The thief let himself down by means of a rope.
那个小偷用一条绳子滑了下来。
- let oneself down by means of... 用……使某人下来

> **语法重点**
> means 的意思是"方法，方式"，表示单数。
> ↪ thief (P. 235)

0728 rose [roʊz] n 玫瑰，蔷薇
On Valentine's Day, she held a bouquet of roses.
情人节那天，她捧着一束玫瑰。
- red rose 红玫瑰
- hold a bouquet of... 捧着一束……

> **语法重点**
> on Valentine's Day 表示时间，也可以放在句末。

0729 round [raʊnd] **a** 圆的，球形的 **n** 一局，一轮
The girl came round soon.
女孩很快就醒了过来。
同 circular 圆形的 反 square 方形的 派 all round 到处

0730 row [roʊ] **n** 一列，排，划船 **v** 吵架
A row of boys are standing in front of the house.
一排男孩正站在房子前面。
同 range 排 派 in a row 连续，成一长行 派 a row of... 一排……

> 语法重点
> a row of 后面通常接名词的复数形式。

0731 rub [rʌb] **v** 摩擦
The girl rubbed her face with the back of her hand.
女孩用手背擦了擦脸。
同 scour 擦 派 rub out 擦掉

> 语法重点
> rub 的过去式与过去分词都是 rubbed。
> face (P. 036)

0732 rubber [ˈrʌbər] **n** 橡胶 **a** 橡胶的
The floor of the hall is covered with rubber to prevent slipping.
大厅的地板上覆盖着橡胶以防滑。
派 natural rubber 天然橡胶 派 be covered with... 用……覆盖

0733 rule [ruːl] **n** 规则，条例
I make it a rule to take a short walk after dinner.
我习惯在晚餐后散步。
同 regulation 规则 反 exception 例外 派 I make it a rule to... 我习惯……

> 语法重点
> make it a rule 后面要接动词不定式。

0734 run [rʌn] **v** 跑，运转，营运
He ran 100 meters in a surprising 12-second time.
他以惊人的十二秒时间跑完了一百米。
派 run away 逃跑，失控

> 语法重点
> run 是不规则动词，其过去式、过去分词分别是 ran 和 run。

0735 sad [sæd] **a** 悲哀的，难过的
I am so sad to hear that your grandmother has passed away.
听说你奶奶去世了，我十分难过。
同 downcast 悲哀的 派 so sad 如此悲伤，如此难过

> 语法重点
> pass away 是"死，去世"的一种委婉的表达方式。

0736 safe [seɪf] **a** 安全的，可靠的 **n** 保险箱
It is safe to cross the road with the help of the policeman.
在这位警察的帮助下过马路很安全。
同 secure 安全的 反 dangerous 危险的 派 safe from 没有……的危险

> 语法重点
> it is safe to 后面要接动词原形。

0737 sail [seɪl] **n** 帆 **v** 航行
Look, the boats are sailing on the water.
看，船正在水面上航行。

round ~ scare

0738 sale [seɪ] n 出售，促销
The mobile phone will be on sale next week.
这款手机将于下周上市。
反 purchase 购买　同 for sale 出售　同 be on sale 出售

> 语法重点
> "内销"用 domestic sale 来表示，"热销产品"则是 hot sale。

0739 salt [sɔːlt] n 盐 a 咸的
I taste the soup to see if he has put enough salt in it.
我尝了尝汤，看他是否放了足够的盐。
同 brackish 含盐的　同 in salt 撒了盐的，盐腌的

> 语法重点
> to 后面的不定式在句中表示目的。

0740 same [seɪm] a 同样的
Though we are the same age, you look younger than me.
虽然我们同岁，可是你看起来比我年轻。
同 uniform 相同的　反 distinct 截然不同的　同 in the same time 在同一时间

> 语法重点
> the same age 前面的主语必须是两个或两个以上的人。

0741 sand [sænd] n 沙
They were walking about on the sands with bare feet.
他们正赤脚在沙滩上四处漫步。
同 loose sand 一盘散沙　同 do sth. with bare feet 光脚做某事

> 语法重点
> 因为主语是"他们"，所以后面要用 feet（foot 的复数形式）。

0742 Saturday ['sætərdeɪ] n 星期六
He enjoyed a round of golf on Saturday mornings.
他喜欢在周六上午打一场高尔夫球。
同 Sat. 星期六　同 last Saturday 上周六

> 语法重点
> Saturday 的首字母 S 无论何时都要大写。
> ⤴ round (P. 084)

0743 save [seɪv] v 挽救，节省，保存
It will help you save much money if you travel by public transportation.
搭乘公共交通工具可以帮你省下很多钱。
同 economize 节省　反 waste 浪费　同 save energy 节约能源

> 语法重点
> it will help you 后面接省略 to 的不定式，也可接带 to 的不定式。

0744 saw [sɔː] n 锯子 v 用锯子锯
The man went away with a saw in hand.
那个人拿着锯子离开了。
同 rip 锯　同 saw blade 锯条

> 语法重点
> saw 正好与动词 see 的过去式同形，要注意区分。

0745 say [seɪ] v 说，讲
There's a lot to be said for eating reasonably.
合理饮食的好处不胜枚举。
同 say out 坦率说出

> 语法重点
> say 是不规则动词，其过去式、过去分词都是 said。

0746 scare [skeɪ] n 惊吓，惊恐 v 使惊吓，恐吓
If we make a noise, we'll scare off the thief.
我们如果发出声响，就会把小偷吓跑。
同 frighten 吓唬　同 scare away 把……吓跑

0747 scene [siːn] n 景象，场景
The workshop was a scene of feverish activity when the boss came in.
老板进来时，车间里是一片紧张繁忙的景象。
on the scene 在场，出现　　be a scene of... 是一片……景象

↪ workshop (P. 661)

0748 school [skuːl] n 学校，学院
Let me explain why I was late for school this morning.
让我解释一下今天早上上学迟到的原因。
go to school 去上学　　... be late for school ……上学迟到

0749 sea [siː] n 海，海洋
The doctor recommends sea baths for the benefit of my health.
医生劝我做海水浴以养生。

0750 season ['siːzn] n 季节，时期
How long does the rainy season last?
雨季会持续多久？
in season 应时的，当令　　How long... last? ……持续多久？

语法重点
rainy season 是单数，所以前面的助动词用 does。

0751 seat [siːt] n 座位，席位
Take a seat as soon as possible after you enter the hall.
进入大厅后，尽快找个座位坐下来。
window seat 靠窗的座位　　take a seat 相当于 be seated

0752 second ['sekənd] n 秒，第二
I flunked Chinese in second grade.
我二年级时中文不及格。

↪ flunk (P. 442)

0753 see [siː] v 看见
I saw two men fighting beside your door this morning.
今天早上我看到有两个人在你家门前打架。
watch 看　　see for oneself 自己去看

语法重点
this morning 表示"今天早上"，是一个固定搭配。

0754 seed [siːd] n 种子
Look, the farmers are scattering seeds.
看，农民们正在播种。

0755 seem [siːm] v 似乎，好像
Their children are always going to parties and seem to sleep out nearly every night.
他们的孩子总是去参加派对，好像几乎每晚都在外过夜。
appear 好像　　seem to be 看来，好像　　sleep out 在外过夜

语法重点
seem to 后面要接动词原形。

0756 **seesaw** ['siːsɔː] n 跷跷板
Price of the rice has gone up and down like a seesaw.
米的价格像跷跷板一样时涨时跌。
- go seesaw 动摇不定
- go up and down 时涨时跌

语法重点
句中的 gone 是动词 go 的过去分词形式。

0757 **self** [self] n 自己，自我，自身
It is easy for him to lose his self esteem.
他很容易失去自尊。
- ego 自我
- by one's self 独自，单独

0758 **selfish** ['selfɪʃ] a 自私的，利己的
I am disgusted with the behavior of the selfish woman.
我很讨厌那个自私女人的行为。
- asocial 自私的
- selfless 无私的
- selfish behavior 自私行为

语法重点
selfish 这个单词是由 self 加上词尾 -ish 构成的。
↪ behavior (P. 401)

0759 **sell** [sel] v 贩卖，出售
These kinds of pens are all sold out.
这些类型的钢笔全部卖完了。
- vend 出售
- buy 买
- sell well 畅销
- ... be sold out ……卖完了

语法重点
sell 是不规则动词，其过去式、过去分词都是 sold。

0760 **send** [send] v 寄送，派遣
We are obliged to send our children to school.
我们有义务送子女去上学。
- receive 收到
- send out 发送，派遣

语法重点
be obliged to 后面要接动词原形。
↪ oblige (P. 749)

0761 **sense** [sens] n 感觉，官能
We can't deny that he has a strong sense of time.
我们不能否认，他有很强的时间观念。
- sense of responsibility 责任感，责任心

0762 **sentence** ['sentəns] n 句子，判决 v 判决
I heard the judge handed down a very heavy sentence on her.
我听说法官给她判了很重的刑。
- condemn 判刑
- life sentence 无期徒刑
- hand down a sentence on... 给……判刑

语法重点
从句的时态要和主句一致，因此 hand down 要用过去时。

0763 **September** [sep'tembər] n 九月
It is September and time to pick the cotton; am I right?
九月了，摘棉花的时候到了，我说的对吗？

语法重点
time 之前省略了 it is。

0764 **serve** [sɜːrv] v 服务，侍候
I asked the waiter to come over to serve me.
我让服务生过来接待我。
- invite 招待
- come over to... 过来……

语法重点
serve 可以作及物动词，后面直接放服务的物件。

087

0765 **service** ['sɜːrvɪs] n 服务，公务部门
What do you think of this restaurant's service?
你认为这家餐厅的服务如何？
- waiting 服侍　　- room service 客房服务
- What do you think of...? 你认为……怎么样？

0766 **set** [set] v 设置，规定 n 集合，一套
I must set a limit to the expense of the trip.
我必须给这次的旅游定下预算。
- put 安置　　- a set of 一套，一副

> 语法重点
> I must set a limit to 中的 to 为介词，后面接名词或动名词。

0767 **seven** ['sevn] n 七，七个
It is required that they leave before seven o'clock.
他们得在七点之前离开。
- at sixes and sevens 乱七八糟　　- it is required that... 要求……

> 语法重点
> 一些表示建议、要求、命令等的动词（如 require, demand, suggest, advise 等）隐含说话者主观的意见，其后面的从句中，动词要用 should + 动词原形，should 可以省略。

0768 **seventeen** [ˌsevn'tiːn] n 十七
My sister was only seventeen when she joined the army.
我妹妹参军时才十七岁。
- sweet seventeen 豆蔻年华

0769 **seventy** ['sevnti] n 七十
My grandmother died at the age of seventy.
我奶奶享年七十岁。
- at the age of... 在……岁时

> 语法重点
> 七十几用 seventy- 加上具体的数字来表示。

0770 **several** ['sevrəl] a 几个的，若干的
Mary has lost her voice for several days.
玛丽的嗓子哑了好几天了。
- numerous 很多的　　- several times 好几次
- ... lose one's voice ……的嗓子哑了

> 语法重点
> lose one's voice 是延时性动作，可以与完成时连用。
> ⊃ voice (P. 110)

0771 **shake** [ʃeɪk] v 摇动
Shake the tablecloth before putting it away.
桌布收起来之前要抖一下。
- shake off 摆脱，抖落　　- put... away 把……收起来

> 语法重点
> 注意 put 的 ing 形式是 putting。

0772 **shall** [ʃəl] aux 将会，必须，应该
My idea is that we shall eat more fruits.
我的意见是我们要多吃水果。

> 语法重点
> shall 是情态动词，后面要接动词原形。

0773 **shape** [ʃeɪp] n 形状，身材，形式
The cake is in the shape of a heart.
蛋糕呈心形。
- form 形式　　- in shape 在外形上　　- be in the shape of... 呈……形状

0774 **shark** [ʃɑːrk] n 鲨鱼
The man was killed by a man-eating shark.
那个人被一条食人鲨杀死了。
　great white shark 大白鲨　　be killed by... 被……杀死

0775 **sharp** [ʃɑːrp] a 尖锐的，灵敏的，突然的
She has a sharp tongue, and no one likes her.
她言语刻薄，没有人喜欢她。
　反 dull 钝的　　sharp rise 激增，激涨

> 语法重点
> no one 是单数，所以 like 要用第三人称单数形式。

0776 **she** [ʃi] pron 她
She won't feel secure when she is alone in the house.
她一个人在家时感觉不安全。

> 语法重点
> feel 后面加上表示感情、感觉的形容词，意思是"感觉……"。

0777 **sheep** [ʃiːp] n 绵羊
Let's drive the sheep down the hill.
我们把羊赶下山吧。
　a black sheep 害群之马　　drive... down the hill 把……赶下山

> 语法重点
> sheep 的复数形式也是 sheep。

0778 **sheet** [ʃiːt] n 床单
The servant tore the sheet in half.
仆人把床单撕成了两半。
　coverlet 床单　　bed sheet 床单　　tear... in half 把……撕成两半

> 语法重点
> 句中 tore 是 tear 的过去式。

0779 **shine** [ʃaɪn] v 照耀，发光 n 光泽，光辉
We began to go home when the setting sun shone in.
夕阳西下时，我们开始回家。
　gleam 发光　　shine on 闪耀，照在……上

> 语法重点
> shine 是不规则动词，其过去式、过去分词都是 shone。

0780 **ship** [ʃɪp] n 船，舰 v 装运
Where is this ship bound for?
这船开往哪里？
　vessel 船　　merchant ship 商船

0781 **shirt** [ʃɜːrt] n 衬衫
Will you iron the shirt for me?
你能为我熨一下这件衬衫吗？
　blouse 衬衫　　stuffed shirt 自命不凡的人
　shirt 一般指男衬衫，而 blouse 一般指女衬衫。

　iron (P. 052)

0782 **shoe** [ʃuː] n 鞋子
The famous singer is as common as an old shoe.
那个著名的歌星很平易近人。
　boot 靴　　diving shoes 潜水鞋

0783 shop [ʃɑːp] n 商店，店铺
A new kind of chair is on display in the shop.
商店里展出了一种新椅子。
- store 店铺
- set up a shop 开店

> 语法重点
> 一般来说，store 指比较大型的仓库和仓库式商店，如超市、大型批发货场等，而 shop 一般指小型商店、小商铺等。

0784 shop [ʃɑːp] v 逛商店，买东西
I think it is a good idea to go shopping tomorrow.
我认为明天去逛街是个好主意。
- purchase 购买东西
- shop for 购买某物

> 语法重点
> I think it is a good idea 后面接动词不定式。
> ⊃ tomorrow (P. 105)

0785 shore [ʃɔːr] n 海岸
The ship is anchored off the shore.
船在海岸不远处抛了锚。
- coast 海岸
- off shore 离开岸边

> 语法重点
> shore 和 coast 都指邻接一大片水域的陆地，shore 指湖或海的边缘，或水边的狭长陆地，coast 可指邻接海或洋的较宽阔或狭长的地域。

0786 short [ʃɔːrt] a 短的，矮的，短缺的
Whenever you are short of money, just come to me.
你什么时候缺钱，都可以来找我。
- lacking 缺乏的
- long 长的
- short supply 供不应求

> 语法重点
> be short of 的意思是"缺少"，相当于 lack。

0787 shot [ʃɑːt] n 射击，发射，拍摄
You should have asked the doctor for a shot of penicillin.
你本应该让医生给你打一针青霉素。
- blast off 发射
- good shot 好球

> 语法重点
> you should + have done，意思是"你本应该……"，暗示实际上并没有做，有责备、惋惜、遗憾的意思。

0788 shoulder [ˈʃoʊldər] n 肩膀，肩部
Would you show me the place where I should put my shoulder bag?
你能告诉我应该把这个背包放在哪里吗？

> 语法重点
> where I should put my shoulder bag 在句中修饰 the place。

0789 shout [ʃaʊt] v 叫喊，喊叫
He always shouts at people when he gets angry.
他一生气就对人大喊大叫。
- exclaim 呼喊
- shout out 突然呼喊，大叫
- shout at... 对……叫嚷

> 语法重点
> always 通常用于一般现在时。

0790 show [ʃoʊ] v 显示，表现，流露 n 表演，展览
Would you like to show me the bus stop for the Palace Museum?
你可以告诉我去故宫博物院的公交车站在哪里吗？
- exhibit 展示
- hide 隐藏
- show up 露面

> 语法重点
> would you like to 后面接动词原形。

0791 shut [ʃʌt] v 关闭，停止
She shut the door after she came into the room.
她走进房间后就把门关上了。
- close 关闭
- open 打开
- shut away 隔离

> 语法重点
> shut 是不规则动词，其过去式、过去分词都是 shut。

0792 **shy** [ʃaɪ] **a** 害羞的，腼腆的，胆怯的
The child isn't shy at all with us.
这个小孩在我们面前一点儿也不害羞。
  同 blate 害羞的   反 bold 勇敢的   搭 not... at all 一点儿也不……

> **语法重点**
> not + 形容词 + at all 表示"一点儿也不……"，如 not happy at all 表示"一点儿也不高兴"。

0793 **sick** [sɪk] **a** 生病的，恶心的，晕的
I'm getting sick of hearing that.
我听够了。
  同 ill 有病的   反 healthy 健康的   搭 get sick 生病

> **语法重点**
> I'm getting sick of（我受够……了）后面接名词或动名词。

0794 **side** [saɪd] **n** 一边，方面
Well, you can park your car on either side of the street.
嗯，你可以把车停在街道的任何一边。
  同 aspect 方面   搭 side by side 并肩，一起
  搭 on either side of... 在……的任何一边

> **语法重点**
> either 表示"两者之一"，后面的 side 要用单数。
> ◎ either (P. 034)

0795 **sight** [saɪt] **n** 视觉，视力
All children are equal in the sight of the parents.
父母对所有孩子都一视同仁。
  同 vision 视力   搭 in sight 在即，在望

> **语法重点**
> 不管 in the sight of 后面接的人称是单数还是复数，sight 都用单数形式。

0796 **silly** ['sɪli] **a** 愚蠢的，傻的，糊涂的
Isn't it silly to see a movie that you know nothing about?
你不觉得看一部你一点儿都不了解的电影有点儿荒唐吗？
  同 foolish 傻的   反 sagacious 睿智的   搭 silly billy 傻瓜，笨蛋

> **语法重点**
> isn't it silly to 后面要接动词原形。

0797 **silver** ['sɪlvər] **n** 银色的，银器
I plunked down $350 for a silver necklace.
我花了 350 美元买一条银项链。
  同 silverware 银器   搭 plunk down... for... 为……花费

0798 **simple** ['sɪmpl] **a** 简单的，单纯的
He led a thrifty and simple life although he was an official.
他虽然当官，但生活俭朴。
  同 plain 简单的   反 complex 复杂的

> **语法重点**
> 句中的 led 是 lead 的过去式。

0799 **since** [sɪns] **prep** 自从 **conj** 因为，自从
Since we have a baby, we need a two-bedroom apartment.
我们有个小孩，所以要一个有两间卧室的公寓。

> **语法重点**
> since 在句中充当连词，意思是"因为"，相当于 because。

0800 **sing** [sɪŋ] **v** 唱歌
It's not easy to sing a song in front of people.
在众人面前唱歌不是件容易的事。
  搭 sing up 更用力地唱   搭 it's not easy to... 做……不容易

> **语法重点**
> sing 是不规则动词，其过去式、过去分词分别是 sang, sung。

0801 **singer** ['sɪŋər] n 唱歌者
Rumor has it that the famous singer lost her job.
传言说那位知名的歌手失业了。
- pop singer 流行歌手　● rumor has it that... 传言说……

0802 **sir** [sɜːr] n 先生
Your flight will be delayed for another two hours, sir.
先生，您的班机将再延迟两个小时起飞。
- mister 先生　● madam 女士

语法重点
sir 是对男性的尊称，一般不用在姓氏的前面，更不能在 sir 的前面加上姓氏。

0803 **sister** ['sɪstər] n 姐妹
You must tell me why you don't like my sister.
你必须告诉我你不喜欢我妹妹的原因。

语法重点
姐姐用 elder sister 来表达，妹妹用 younger sister 来表达。

0804 **sit** [sɪt] v 坐，坐落
The girl sat at her desk reading a novel.
女孩正坐在桌边看一本小说。
- stand 站立　● sit down 坐下

语法重点
sit 是不规则动词，其过去式、过去分词均是 sat。

0805 **six** [sɪks] n 六
The news that she has been pregnant for six months came through private channels.
她已怀孕六个月这个消息来源于小道消息。
- six to one 相差悬殊

0806 **sixteen** [,sɪks'tiːn] n 十六，十六个
In total, sixteen people were injured in a traffic accident last night.
在昨晚的交通事故中共有十六个人受伤。
- be injured in... 在……中受伤了

语法重点
in total 可以放在句首、句中或句末。
↪ total (P. 106)

0807 **sixty** ['sɪksti] n 六十
I will cease to write at the age of sixty.
我六十岁将停止写作。
- like sixty 飞快地　● I'll cease to... 我将停止……

语法重点
cease to 后面接动词原形，表示要停止这个动作。

0808 **size** [saɪz] n 尺寸，大小
What's the size of your normal group to Hong Kong?
你们去香港的旅游团一般有多大？
- measure 尺寸　● weight 重量　● life size 真人大小

语法重点
what's the size of 表面意思是询问尺寸、大小，句中用了其引申义，即询问规模。

0809 **skill** [skɪl] n 技巧，技能
Do you have the skill to ride a bike on a rope?
你能在绳子上骑脚踏车吗？
- accomplishment 技艺，技能　● job skill 工作技巧

语法重点
do you have the skill 后面要接动词不定式。

singer ~ smoke

0810 skin [skɪn] **n** 皮肤
Roughness of the skin can be caused by bad diet.
饮食不好可能引起皮肤粗糙。
🔄 sth. can be caused by... ……可能被……引起

⇨ diet (P. 283)

0811 sky [skaɪ] **n** 天空
It's pie in the sky. You'll never get the money.
那根本不可能，你永远也拿不到钱。
🔄 in the sky 在空中　🔄 ... be pie in the sky ……是不可能的事

0812 sleep [sliːp] **v** 睡觉 **n** 睡眠，睡觉
I slept like the dead last night and did not hear anything.
昨晚我睡得像死人，什么也没有听到。
🔄 Let sleeping dogs lie. 莫惹是非。

语法重点
sleep 也是不规则动词，其过去式、过去分词都是 slept。

0813 slow [sloʊ] **a** 慢的 **v** 放慢 **ad** 慢慢地
The new employees are slow to adapt to the rules.
新雇员对于那些规定适应得很慢。
🔄 quick 快的　🔄 do a slow burn 渐渐地生气

语法重点
be slow to 后面要接动词原形。
⇨ adapt (P. 391)

0814 small [smɔːl] **a** 小的
Americans play small tricks on friends and strangers on April Fool's Day.
不论是对朋友还是对陌生人，美国人都喜欢在愚人节时搞些恶作剧。

0815 smart [smɑːrt] **a** 伶俐的，聪明的，漂亮的，整齐的
I can see that you are a smart buyer.
我看得出你买东西很精明。
🔄 clever 聪明的　🔄 fool 傻的

语法重点
句中的 that 可以省略。

0816 smell [smel] **v** 闻，察觉 **n** 气味
You must have smelt the smell of dinner.
你一定闻到晚餐的味道了。
🔄 odor 气味　🔄 sense of smell 嗅觉

语法重点
"must + have done" 表示对过去情况的推测。

0817 smile [smaɪl] **v** / **n** 微笑
A smile of craftiness passed across her face.
她脸上掠过一丝狡黠的微笑。
🔄 laugh 笑　🔄 frown 皱眉　🔄 smile to yourself 暗笑

0818 smoke [smoʊk] **n** 烟 **v** 抽烟
Do they allow smoking in the cinemas?
他们允许在电影院里抽烟吗？
🔄 fume 烟　🔄 like smoke 飞快地

语法重点
do they allow 后面要接动词的 ing 形式。

0819 snake [sneɪk] n 蛇
I can't overcome my repugnance to eating snakes.
吃蛇真恶心，我可受不了。
🔗 a snake in the grass 潜伏的危险或敌人

> 语法重点
> I can't overcome my repugnance to 后面接名词或者动名词。

0820 snow [snoʊ] n 雪 v 下雪
My car is stuck in deep snow.
我的车陷进了深雪中。
🔗 Snow White 白雪公主　🔗 be stuck in... 陷于……

> 语法重点
> stuck 是动词 stick 的过去分词。

0821 so [soʊ] conj 所以，因此 ad 那么，这样，如此
Mom told me that it's not good for our teeth to eat so many sweet foods.
妈妈告诉我吃太多甜食对我们的牙齿不好。
🔗 thus 这样，如此　🔗 and so on 等等，诸如此类

> 语法重点
> so 在句中作副词，修饰 many。

0822 soap [soʊp] n 肥皂
I bought two cakes of soap last week.
我上周买了两块肥皂。
🔗 soap powder 肥皂粉　🔗 two cakes of... 两块……

> 语法重点
> soap 是不可数名词，表示复数时，其前面的量词 cake 要用复数形式。

0823 soda ['soʊdə] n 苏打
I would like a cup of tea and a bottle of soda as well.
我想要一杯茶，也要一瓶苏打水。
🔗 pop 汽水　🔗 soda water 苏打水

0824 sofa ['soʊfə] n 沙发
My son was asleep on the sofa.
我儿子在沙发上睡着了。
🔗 couch 沙发　🔗 sofa bed 沙发床　🔗 be asleep on... 在……上睡着了

⊃ asleep (P. 126)

0825 soft [sɔːft] a 柔软的，轻柔的
I've got to buy two soft berth tickets to Bei-jing for tomorrow.
我想买两张明天到北京的软卧票。
🔗 tender 柔软的　🔗 hard 硬的　🔗 soft in the head 头脑迟钝

⊃ ticket (P. 104)

0826 soil [sɔɪl] n 土壤，土地
The soil is adaptable to the growth of flowers.
土壤适宜花的生长。
🔗 earth 土地　🔗 barren soil 不毛之地

> 语法重点
> be adaptable to（适宜……）后面接名词或者动名词。

0827 some [səm] a 一些，若干 ad 大约，非常
I feel like having some dumplings.
我想吃一些饺子。
🔗 some of 一些　🔗 I feel like doing 我想要做……

snake ~ sound

0828 someone ['sʌmwʌn] **pron** 某人，有人
It is my pleasure to know someone like you.
能够认识到你这样的人是我的荣幸。
🔵 it is my pleasure to.... ……是我的荣幸

> 语法重点
> like you 在句中修饰 someone。
> ⊃ pleasure (P. 205)

0829 something ['sʌmθɪŋ] **pron** 某事
The letter has something to do with her husband.
这封信与她丈夫有关。

0830 sometimes ['sʌmtaɪmz] **ad** 有时候，间或
My mother often swore at me, sometimes for no reason at all.
妈妈经常骂我，有时毫无理由。

> 语法重点
> sometimes 是表示频度的副词，用法和 often, always 等一样。

0831 son [sʌn] **n** 儿子，孩子
She is badly cut up by the death of her son.
她因儿子的死极为悲伤。
🔵 like father like son 有其父必有其子 🔵 be cut up by... 因……而悲伤

0832 song [sɔːŋ] **n** 歌曲
The song has a good beat that we can dance to.
这首歌的节奏很强，我们可以跟着跳舞。

> 语法重点
> that we could dance to 用来修饰 beat。

0833 soon [suːn] **ad** 很快地，不久
But for your help, I couldn't have found my lost father so soon.
如果没有你的帮助，我不可能这么快找到我失踪的父亲。
🔵 quickly 很快 🔵 late 晚，迟 🔵 sooner or later 迟早

> 语法重点
> but for 可以与虚拟语气连用。

0834 sorry ['sɔːri] **a** 感到难过的，对不起的 **int** 对不起
I'm sorry, but I didn't notice you.
对不起，我没注意到你。
🔵 I'm sorry to say (that)... 很抱歉……

0835 soul [soʊl] **n** 灵魂，心灵，精神
I'm not going to sell my soul just to make money.
我不会为了赚钱而出卖自己的灵魂。
🔵 spirit 心灵，精神 🔵 body 身体 🔵 poor soul 可怜的人
🔵 sell one's soul to... 出卖某人的灵魂去做……

0836 sound [saʊnd] **n** 声音 **v** 听起来
It sounds like a reasonable solution to the problem.
这个解决问题的办法似乎比较合理。
🔵 sound asleep 熟睡的 🔵 It sounds like... 听起来似乎……

> 语法重点
> sound like 的意思是"听起来像"，其中的 like 为介词，所以其后通常接名词或代词作宾语。

095

0837 soup [suːp] n 汤
Eggs and tomatoes go well together in the soup.
汤中放入鸡蛋和番茄尝起来味道很好。
in the soup 在困境中　... go well together ……搭配得很好

0838 sour [ˈsaʊər] a 酸的，酸腐的，刻薄的
If we keep milk for a long time it will turn sour.
如果牛奶放得时间长了，它就会变酸。
be sour grapes 尖酸刻薄的人

> 语法重点
> it 代指前面的 milk。

0839 south [saʊθ] n 南方，南部 a 南方的
The harbor lies to the south of our city.
港口位于我们这个城市的南边。

> 语法重点
> lie to 表示"位于"，暗含的意思是两个地方不直接毗邻。

0840 space [speɪs] n 空间，太空
I know she took my parking space just to spite me.
我知道她为了使我恼怒而抢我的停车位。
space shuttle 太空梭　... to spite me ……使我恼怒

0841 speak [spiːk] v 说话，演讲，发言
The moment he spoke he regretted his words.
话一说出，他就后悔了。
speak out 大声讲　the moment... sb.... 一……某人就……

> 语法重点
> speak 是不规则动词，其过去式、过去分词分别是 spoke, spoken。

0842 special [ˈspeʃl] a 特殊的，特别的，专门的
Is there something special in your paintings?
你的画有什么特殊的地方吗？
particular 特别的　general 一般的，普通的

0843 speech [spiːtʃ] n 演说，演讲
It is important that we do not interrupt the speech of others.
不打断别人说话是很重要的。
address 演讲　silence 缄默　freedom of speech 言论自由

> 语法重点
> not 前面省略了 should。
> important (P. 051)

0844 spell [spel] v 拼写，拼成
How do you spell your name?
您的名字怎么拼写？

> 语法重点
> how do you 后面接动词原形。

0845 spend [spend] v 花费，浪费，度过
He had to spend some money again to have his watch repaired.
他又要花些钱去修表了。
cost 花费　earn 赚　spend a penny 去厕所

0846 spoon [spu:n] n 汤匙，调羹

My boyfriend was born with a silver spoon in his mouth.
我男朋友生于富贵人家。

- scoop 勺
- greasy spoon 下等餐饮

0847 sport [spɔ:rt] n 运动

What sport do you like among basketball, football or ping-pong?
在篮球、足球和乒乓球中你喜欢哪种运动？

> **语法重点**
> 三种或者三种以上的选择，要用 among... or...。

0848 spring [sprɪŋ] n 春天

Spring is just around the corner.
眼看春天就要到了。

> ↪ corner (P. 145)

0849 stair [ster] n 楼梯

I slipped and tumbled down the stairs.
我脚一滑滚下了楼梯。

- step 台阶，梯级
- the top of the stairs 楼梯的顶部

0850 stand [stænd] v 站立，忍受

He stood in various poses while he was photographed.
他照相时摆出了各种姿势。

- sustain 忍受
- stand on tiptoe 踮着脚

> **语法重点**
> stand 是不规则动词，其过去式、过去分词都是 stood。
> ↪ various (P. 380)

0851 star [sta:r] n 星星，明星

A little bird told me that new movie star would come to visit our city.
有人告诉我那个新电影明星要来我们城市。

- a little bird told me that... 有人告诉我……

0852 start [sta:rt] v 开始

I have to start packing and get ready for move next week.
我下周要开始打包行李准备搬家了。

- begin 开始
- end 结束
- start from 从……开始

> **语法重点**
> 例句中 move 作名词，意思是"搬家，移动"。

0853 state [steɪt] n 状况，国家 v 陈述，声明

Be sure to get in touch with him when you visit the States.
你去美国的时候一定要跟他联络。

- nation 国家
- be sure to... 一定要……

> **语法重点**
> the States 意思是"美国"，有时也用 the United States 来表示。

0854 statement ['steɪtmənt] n 陈述，声明

I think there's not a vestige of truth in the witness's statement.
我认为这个证人的证词没有丝毫的真实性。

- declaration 声明，宣布
- make a statement 发表声明

0855 **station** [ˈsteɪʃn] n 车站
I suggest that we leave early for the train station.
我建议我们早一点儿去火车站。
● police station 警察局　● I suggest that... 我建议……

0856 **stay** [steɪ] v 停留，逗留，保持
I must accustom myself to staying up late.
我必须使自己习惯晚睡觉。
● abide 停留　● go 去　● stay (at) home 待在家里

> **语法重点**
> accustom oneself to 中的 to 是介词，后面要接名词或者动名词。

0857 **step** [step] v 踏步，行走，路上 n 步骤，台阶
He's the first man to step out of the bus.
他是第一个下公交车的人。
● walk 行走　● out of step 步调不一致

0858 **still** [stɪl] ad 仍然，静止地 a 静止的
I think she still has chance to get into the university.
我认为她还有上大学的机会。
● yet 仍然　● still waters run deep 大智若愚

> **语法重点**
> have chance to（有机会做……）后面接动词原形。
> ● chance (P. 022)

0859 **stone** [stoʊn] n 石头
You are bound to move the big stone.
你肯定能搬动那块大石头。

0860 **stop** [stɑːp] v 停止，中断，阻止
Do you mean you won't stop your bad eating habits?
你的意思是说你不会停止不良的饮食习惯吗？
● cease 停止　● continue 继续　● stop work 停工

0861 **store** [stɔːr] n 商店
As far as I can remember, the store was closed down four years ago.
我记得那家商店在四年前倒闭了。
● shop 商店　● as far as I can remember, ... 我记得……

> **语法重点**
> 也可以用 close down 的主动形式来表示"倒闭"，如 the store closed down 表示"商店倒闭了"。
> ● close (P. 024)

0862 **story** [ˈstɔːri] n 故事
You should bring home to him the real meaning of the story.
你应该让他知道这个故事的真正含义。
● tale 故事　● short story 短篇小说　● bring home to sb. 让某人明白……

> **语法重点**
> to 是介词，所以后面接人称代词的宾格形式。

0863 **strange** [streɪndʒ] a 奇怪的，陌生的
Every time I hear the strange sound, I feel frightened.
我每次听到那个奇怪的声音，都会觉得害怕。
● ordinary 平常的，普通的　● strange to say 说来奇怪

> **语法重点**
> frightened 用来形容人，意思是"害怕的"；而 frightening 用来形容物，表示"令人恐怖的"。

098

station ~ sun

0864 street [striːt] n 街道，马路
Do you mind if I sit on the street to have a rest?
你介意我坐在马路上休息一会儿吗？
- road 马路
- on the street 在街上

> 语法重点
> have a rest 表示"休息一会儿"，rest 在句中作名词用。
> ⇨ rest (P. 081)

0865 strong [strɔŋ] a 强壮的，牢固的
Do you realize that the girl is fond of strong men?
你知道这个女孩喜欢强壮的男人吗？
- weak 弱小的
- Do you realize...? 你知道……吗？
- strong men 泛指所有强壮的男人

0866 student ['stuːdnt] n 学生，学者
I didn't mean to offend the foreign student.
我不是故意要冒犯那个留学生的。
- teacher 老师
- students' union 学生会

> 语法重点
> I didn't mean to 后面要接动词原形。

0867 study ['stʌdi] v 研究，学习
I am calling to ask something about studying.
我打电话来是想咨询一些有关学习的问题。
- study hard 努力学习
- I am calling to... 我打电话来……

> 语法重点
> study 也可以当作名词使用。

0868 stupid ['stuːpɪd] a 笨的，无聊的，乏味的
I have never seen such a stupid person.
我从没见过这么蠢的人。
- foolish 愚蠢的
- clever 聪明的
- I have never seen... 我从没过……

> 语法重点
> such + a / an + 形容词 + 名词单数表示"如此……的……"。

0869 such [sʌtʃ] a 这样的，如此的 ad 如此地
You are blessed in having such a good wife.
你娶到如此一位贤妻真是三生有幸啊。

> 语法重点
> have 的现在分词形式是去 e 加上 ing。

0870 sugar ['ʃʊgər] n 糖
I can't understand why you like eating sugar.
我搞不懂你怎么会喜欢吃糖。
- sand sugar 砂糖
- I can't understand... 我搞不懂……

> 语法重点
> sugar 表示"糖"时，通常作不可数名词。

0871 summer ['sʌmər] n 夏天，夏季
It is expected that this summer will be extremely hot.
预计今年夏天会非常热。
- summer resort 避暑胜地
- It is expected that... 预计……

> 语法重点
> 因为是"预计"的情况，所以 that 后面的从句要用一般将来时。
> ⇨ expect (P. 162)

0872 sun [sʌn] n 太阳
The truth is that the earth goes around the sun.
事实是，地球绕着太阳转。
- moon 月亮
- the setting sun 落日

> 语法重点
> sun 与 earth 都是独一无二的东西，所以前面必须加上定冠词 the。

0873 **Sunday** ['sʌndeɪ] n 星期日
I regret to tell you that I can't attend your party on Sunday.
我很遗憾地告诉你我不能参加你周日的派对了。

0874 **super** ['suːpər] a 超级的，极好的
I wish I have a super car.
我希望我能有一辆超级轿车。
- great 极好的
- poor 不好
- I wish... 我希望……

> **语法重点**
> wish 用于表达可以实现的愿望时，不用虚拟语气。

0875 **supper** ['sʌpər] n 晚餐
If you are not opposed, I'll eat supper with you.
如果你不反对，我想和你一起吃晚餐。
- dinner 晚餐
- have supper 吃晚餐
- if you are not opposed, ... 如果你不反对……

> **语法重点**
> if you are not opposed 在句中表示条件，用来引出后面的主句。

0876 **sure** [ʃʊr] a 确定的，肯定的 ad 当然，确实地
Make sure all mobile phones are turned off.
请务必关上所有手机。
- certain 确定的
- unsure 不确定的
- to be sure 当然

> **语法重点**
> mobile phones 与 turn off 是被动关系，所以句子用被动语态。

0877 **surprise** [sər'praɪz] v 使惊讶，使惊喜 n 惊奇，惊喜
His promotion to director took everyone by surprise.
竟然提拔他当主管，这让每个人都感到意外。
- to sb.'s surprise 让人惊讶的是
- ... take sb. by surprise ……让某人感到意外

○ promotion (P. 490)

0878 **sweet** [swiːt] a 甜的，可爱的 n 甜食
How sweet of you to come to see me!
你来看我多让人高兴啊！
- sour 酸的
- sweet words 甜言蜜语

0879 **swim** [swɪm] v / n 游泳
How often do you go swimming?
你多久游一次泳？
- sink or swim 不论成败

> **语法重点**
> how often 用来提问某动作或状态发生的频率。

0880 **table** ['teɪbl] n 桌子
Many a book is on the table.
桌子上有很多书。
- desk 书桌
- work table 工作台

> **语法重点**
> in the table 的意思是"在桌子里面"，注意与 on the table 的区别。

0881 **tail** [teɪl] n 尾巴，尾部
Soon the man came back with his tail between his legs.
很快，那个人垂头丧气地回来了。
- head 头
- go into tails 开始穿起燕尾服

○ between (P. 014)

0882 **take** [teɪk] v 拿，取用

It took a long time for her to forget it.
她花了很长时间才忘掉这件事。
- 同 carry 拿　反 give 给予　相 take for granted 认为……理所当然
- 句 it took a long time for sb. to... 某人花了很长时间……

语法重点
take 是不规则动词，其过去式、过去分词分别是 took, taken。

0883 **tale** [teɪl] n 故事，传说

Is there anyone who can tell a tale?
有人能讲故事吗？

语法重点
who can tell a tale 是定语从句，修饰 anyone。

0884 **talk** [tɔːk] v 说话，交谈，谈论

I tried to talk to her, but she refused.
我试图与她谈话，但她拒绝了。
- 同 converse 交谈，谈话　相 talk with 和某人交谈

语法重点
talk to sb. 意思是对某人讲话，介词 to 表示"方向"，表示一个人要对另一个人讲话，但是不表示对方也需要讲话，主要是强调告诉某人什么事。

0885 **tall** [tɔːl] a 高的，高大的

I am scarcely so tall as her.
我没有她这么高。
- 相 a tall order 难办的事情，难以完成的任务
- 句 be scarcely so tall as... 没有……高

语法重点
scarcely 的意思是"几乎不"，含有否定的意思。
⇒ scarcely (P. 506)

0886 **taste** [teɪst] n 味道，味觉　v 品尝

It tastes better if you put some sugar into the soup.
如果在汤里放些糖，喝起来味道会更好。
- 同 savor 滋味　相 have a good taste 有很好的品位

语法重点
taste 作感官动词，通常后面接形容词，译为"尝起来"。例句中的 taste 是接形容词 good 的比较级形式 better。

0887 **taxi** ['tæksi] n 计程车

Going to the park by taxi is the best choice.
搭计程车去公园是最好的选择。
- 同 cab 计程车　相 going to someplace by... 搭……去某地

语法重点
going to the park 是动名词短语。动名词兼有名词的性质，可以在句中作主语。

0888 **tea** [tiː] n 茶

Maybe you should have a cup of tea first.
我想你应该先喝杯茶。

0889 **teach** [tiːtʃ] v 教导，教授

My grandmother taught me how to sew.
我奶奶教我做针线活。

语法重点
teach 是不规则动词，其过去式、过去分词都是 taught。

0890 **teacher** ['tiːtʃər] n 老师

It was my teacher who was hit by the car.
被车撞的是我的老师。
- 同 instructor 教员，教师　反 student 学生

语法重点
it is / was + 被强调部分 + that + 句子其余部分…… 是强调句型，去掉 it is / was... that 剩下的还是一个完整的句子，其中 that 指代人时可以用 who 代替。

0891 tell [tel] v 告诉
The policeman told me to watch out for the man in black.
警察要我注意穿黑衣服的那个人。
to tell (you) the truth 说实话　　tell sb. to do sth. 告诉某人做某事

> 语法重点
> tell 是不规则动词，其过去式、过去分词都是 told。

0892 ten [ten] num 十
The books and pens cost ten dollars in total.
买书和钢笔总共花了十美元。
decade 十年　　ten to one 十有八九，很可能

> 语法重点
> 当 cost 的宾语表示数量、大小或程度时，cost 不用被动语态。

0893 than [ðən] conj / prep 比较
There's no seasoning other than the salt.
除了盐没别的调料了。

> 语法重点
> 该短语的意思是"除了"，than 之后的成分不包括在短语之前内容的范围内。

0894 thank [θæŋk] v 感谢 n 谢意
Thank you for handing the book to me.
谢谢你把书交给我。
appreciation 感谢　　thank you for... 谢谢你……

> 语法重点
> hand 除了有名词"手"的意思外，还可以作动词，其意思为"交，递"。

0895 that [ðæt] pron 那个
That shop was just opened last month.
那家店是上个月新开的。
this 这　　that is (to say) 也就是说

0896 the [ðə] art 这个，那个，这些，那些
The Greens hid in the basement for two whole weeks.
格林一家在地下室藏了整整两个星期。

> 语法重点
> "the + 姓氏"的复数形式，可以表示"一家人，一对夫妇"。
> ⊃ basement (P. 128)

0897 their [ðer] a 他们的，她们的，它们的
When did they announce their engagement?
他们什么时候宣布订婚的？

0898 them [ðəm] pron 他们，她们，它们
It's difficult for them to arrive here on time.
他们很难按时来到这里。

0899 then [ðen] ad 接着，那么，然后，当时
The girl stopped, and then picked up the purse.
女孩停下来，然后捡起了那个钱包。
by then 到那时　　and then 然后

> 语法重点
> and then 在句中起副词的作用，用于引导并列句。
> ⊃ pick (P. 203)

0900 there [ðer] ad 那里
Do you see the red apple over there?
你看见那里的红苹果了吗？
Do you see... over there? 你看到……在那里吗？

> 语法重点
> over there 表示离说话人比较远。

0901 **these** [ðiːz] pron 这些
These are the necklaces that she is looking for.
这些就是她要找的项链。

> 语法重点
> these 是 this 的复数形式，表示"这些"，其后所修饰的名词为可数名词的复数形式。

0902 **they** [ðeɪ] pron 他们
They are both from Beijing.
他们两个都来自北京。

0903 **thing** [θɪŋ] n 东西，事情
In given conditions, a bad thing can do good to you.
在一定条件下，一件坏事可能对你有利。
  the thing is 问题是，最重要的是　in given conditions, ... 在一定条件下……

> 语法重点
> thing 虽然是抽象名词，但是可数的。

0904 **think** [θɪŋk] v 想，认为
I have never thought that I can live in the villa.
我从没想过可以住在那栋别墅。
  consider 认为，考虑　think of 考虑

> 语法重点
> 频度副词一般放在动词之前，当句中有助动词时，频度副词要放在助动词之后。
> ⇒ villa (P. 802)

0905 **third** [θɜːrd] n 第三的，三分之一
More than two thirds of the children there are handicapped.
那里三分之二以上的孩子都有残疾。
  one third 三分之一　more than... 超过……

> 语法重点
> 英语中，分数的分子大于1时，分母须用复数形式。

0906 **thirteen** [ˌθɜːrˈtiːn] n 十三
I have written thirteen books till now.
迄今为止，我已经写了十三本书了。

> 语法重点
> till now（到现在为止）一般与现在完成时连用。

0907 **thirty** [ˈθɜːrti] n 三十
There are thirty households in our village in total.
我们全村共三十户人家。
  注意，thirty 不是直接由 3 的基数词 three + -ty 构成的，而是由 thir + -ty 构成的

0908 **this** [ðɪs] pron 这个
You must be able to use computer for this job.
要做这项工作你得会用电脑。

> 语法重点
> this 作指示代词，通常指距离说话人近的人或物。

0909 **those** [ðoʊz] pron 那些
Those people exclaimed with excitement when the magician stepped on the stage.
当魔术师走上台时，那些人兴奋地大叫。

> 语法重点
> those 是 that 的复数形式，后面接复数名词。

0910 **though** [ðoʊ] conj 虽然，尽管，然而
It didn't work even though I got the certificate.
尽管我取得了证书，但它没起作用。
  although 虽然，尽管　as though 好像，仿佛

> ⇒ certificate (P. 540)

0911 thought [θɔːt] n 想法，观念
There is a possibility that his thought is wrong.
他的想法很有可能是错的。
idea 想法　　lost in thought 陷入沉思

⊃ possibility (P. 207)

0912 thousand ['θaʊznd] n 一千
The population of our school is three thousand.
我们学校有三千人。
the population of... ……的人口

语法重点
thousand 与具体的数字连用，表示数目，通常用单数形式。

0913 three [θriː] n 三
He remains reading books for three hours in the library.
他在图书馆看了三个小时的书。
in twos and threes 三三两两

语法重点
remain 意思是"保持，持续"，通常后接形容词、动名词结构。

0914 throw [θroʊ] v 丢弃，扔
We saw the satellite was thrown into the space.
我们都观看了卫星被发射进入太空的场景。
throw away 扔掉，丢弃　　... be thrown into ……被发射进入

语法重点
throw 是不规则动词，其过去式、过去分词分别是 threw, thrown。

0915 Thursday ['θɜːrzdeɪ] n 星期四
Owing to your help, I finished my task before Thursday.
由于你的帮忙，我才在周四之前完成了工作。
owing to... 多亏……

语法重点
owing to 引导原因，其引导的从句既可以放在主句之前，也可放在主句之后，放在主句之前时需要用逗号和主句隔开。

0916 thus [ðʌs] ad 因此，从而，如此，这样
He identifies himself with his children, thus they love him.
他经常和孩子们打成一片，因此很受他们喜欢。
so 如此　　thus far 迄今，到现在为止

0917 ticket ['tɪkɪt] n 票券
I bought a lottery ticket to see if I can win a prize.
我买了张彩票，看看是否能中奖。
train ticket 火车票　　I do... to see if I can... 我做……看看是否……

0918 tie [taɪ] n 领带 v 系，捆绑
Tie up the puppy with a rope.
用绳子把小狗绑起来。
tie a knot 打结　　tie up... with... 用……把……绑起来

语法重点
tie up 后面可以接人或物。

0919 tiger ['taɪɡər] n 老虎
He killed the tiger with his bare hands.
他赤手空拳杀死了老虎。

0920 time [taɪm] n 时间，次数，倍

Your house is three times bigger than his.
你的房子比他的房子大三倍。
- kill time 消磨时间

> 语法重点
> time 当"时间"讲时不可数，当"次数"讲时可数。

0921 tiny ['taɪni] a 微小的，极小的

Not even a tiny mistake is allowed here.
在这里哪怕极小的错误都不能犯。
- little 小的　　large 大的

> 语法重点
> tiny 的意思是极其微小的，可能肉眼看不太清楚。

0922 tire ['taɪər] v 使……疲倦 n 轮胎

I proposed that we should take another tire for replacement.
我建议我们应该再多带一个轮胎来做备用。
- exhaust 使筋疲力尽　　tire chain 防滑链　　I proposed that... 我建议……

> 语法重点
> 主语 + propose + that 从句，从句中一般用 should + 动词原形的形式。
> ⇒ propose (P. 210)

0923 to [tə] prep 向着，对着 ad 去

All the flights to Japan were cancelled.
所有到日本的航班都已经被取消了。
- towards 向　　from 从　　go to 去

> 语法重点
> to 表示方向性。

0924 today [tə'deɪ] n 今天，现今

It's impossible to finish the work today.
今天根本不可能完成工作。
- Don't put off till tomorrow what should be done today. 今日事今日毕。

0925 together [tə'geðər] ad 一起，协调，一致

How about joining together to dance?
一起跳舞怎么样？
- alone 独自地　　hold together 团结一致
- join together to do sth. 一起做……

0926 tomorrow [tə'mɔːroʊ] ad 明天 n 明天，将来

I will have read the book by tomorrow morning.
明天早上之前我就能看完这本书。
- I will have done... 我将完成……

> 语法重点
> 将来完成时的结构为主语 + will / shall / be going to + have done。

0927 tone [toʊn] n 音调，语气

You'd better modify your tone if you want to get more friends.
如果你想得到更多的朋友，你最好说话婉转一点儿。
- you'd better... if... 你最好……如果……
- modify your tone 的意思是"说话婉转一点儿"，不要直译为"改变你的语气"。

> ⇒ modify (P. 597)

0928 tonight [tə'naɪt] **n** 今晚
I don't know whether we can enjoy the meteoric shower tonight.
我不知道今晚我们是否可以欣赏流星雨。
🔁 I don't know whether... 我不知道是否……

↪ shower (P. 221)

0929 too [tuː] **ad** 也是，太，而且，很
You added too much salt in the chicken soup.
你在鸡汤里放了太多的盐。

〈语法重点〉
much 作形容词修饰不可数名词。

0930 tool [tuːl] **n** 工具，手段
We don't have any tools to cure the festering sore.
我们没有工具来治疗已经溃烂的伤疤。
🔁 instrument 工具，手段　　🔁 tool box 工具箱

〈语法重点〉
any 的意思是"任何，任何一个"，放在名词前修饰名词。

0931 top [tɑːp] **n** 顶端 **a** 最高的，顶端的
The car drove along the road at the top speed.
那辆车以最高的速度在路上飞驰。
🔁 peak 最高的　　🔁 bottom 底部的　　🔁 top news 头条新闻

0932 total ['toʊtl] **a** 全部的，完全的 **n** 总数，总计
There are a total of eight people in the family.
家里共有八个人。
🔁 complete 完全的　　🔁 partial 部分的　　🔁 in total 总共

〈语法重点〉
a total of 后面要接名词的复数形式。

0933 touch [tʌtʃ] **n** 接触，联系 **v** 触摸，感动
I make a resolution not to get in touch with her.
我决定以后再也不和她联系了。
🔁 lose touch with... 和……失去联系

〈语法重点〉
get in touch with 的意思是"与……联系，和……接触"，介词 with 后面通常接人。

↪ resolution (P. 497)

0934 toward(s) [tɔːrd] / [tɔːrdz] **prep** 朝着，对着
Judged from her attitude towards him, she didn't forgive him.
根据她对他的态度判断，她还没有原谅他。
🔁 walk toward 朝……走去　　🔁 judged from... 从……判断

0935 town [taʊn] **n** 城镇，城市
The bus will not reach the small town if not fueled.
如果不加油的话，公交车是无法到达那个小镇的。

〈语法重点〉
本句的主语是 the bus，完整的条件句应该是 if the bus isn't fueled。

0936 toy [tɔɪ] **n** 玩具
You'll never guess who bought the toy car for me.
你永远猜不到谁买了那个玩具汽车给我。
🔁 plaything 玩具　　🔁 a toy car 玩具汽车

〈语法重点〉
you'll never guess 后面接宾语从句，从句中要用陈述语序。

0937 train [treɪn] **n** 列车 **v** 训练
The train had just left when we got to the station.
我们到达车站时，火车刚刚开走。
- in train 准备就绪

> 语法重点
> 句中的两个动作都发生在过去，而 left 在 got 之前就已经完成了，所以前者用过去完成时，后者用一般过去时。

0938 tree [triː] **n** 树
A tree fell down and gave us a fright.
一棵树倒了，吓了我们一大跳。
- family tree 家谱

0939 trip [trɪp] **n** 旅行，旅游
I am looking forward to going on a trip after graduation.
我希望毕业后去旅行。
- journey 旅行
- I am looking forward to... 我期望……

> 语法重点
> look forward to 中的 to 是介词，所以后面的动词要用 ing 形式。

0940 trouble ['trʌbl] **n** 麻烦，困难
You will get into trouble if you run into the policeman.
如果你们遇到警察就麻烦了。
- difficulty 困难
- in trouble 陷入困境

0941 true [truː] **a** 真实的，真的
We wish you make your dream come true.
我们祝福你能够梦想成真。
- real 真实的
- true love 真爱
- make... come true 使……成真

↻ dream (P. 031)

0942 try [traɪ] **v** 尝试，试图
I'm trying to figure out where to go in summer vacation.
我正考虑暑假去哪呢。
- attempt 试图，尝试
- try for 谋求
- I'm trying to figure out... 我正考虑……

> 语法重点
> "在暑假"通常用介词 in，有时候也用 during。

0943 T-shirt ['tiː.ʃɜːrt] **n** 短袖圆领衫
I'm supposed to wear a T-shirt and jeans.
我应该穿 T 恤和牛仔裤。
- tee-shirt T 恤
- I'm supposed to... 我应该……

↻ suppose (P. 369)

0944 Tuesday ['tuːzdeɪ] **n** 星期二
The departure time is 8:00 a.m. Tuesday.
起飞时间是周二上午八点。
- the departure time is... 起飞时间是……

> 语法重点
> 8:00 a.m. 表示上午八点，晚上八点用 8:00 p.m. 来表示。

0945 tummy ['tʌmi] **n** 肚子
After eating a big meal, my tummy hurts.
饱吃了一顿大餐后，我的肚子疼。
- stomach 胃，肚子

> 语法重点
> hurt 可以作及物动词，意思是"伤害，损害"，也可以作不及物动词，意思是"疼痛，有坏处"。

0946 **turn** [tɜːrn] v 转动，扭转
Most of my neighbors turn thumbs down on keeping dogs.
我的邻居大都反对养狗。
同 wheel 转动　反 fix 固定

⊃ thumb (P. 236)

0947 **twelve** [twelv] n 十二，十二个
Our team is composed of twelve members.
我们这队由十二个成员组成。
同 dozen 十二个　　同 section twelve 第十二部分
词 ... be composed of... ……由……组成

0948 **twenty** ['twenti] n 二十
The yard fell into disuse twenty days ago.
这个院子二十天前就废弃了。
词 twenty times 很多次　　词 ... fall into disuse ……废弃了

〈语法重点〉
fell 是动词 fall 的过去式。

0949 **twice** [twaɪs] ad 两次
The circle that I drew is twice larger than his.
我画的圈比他的大两倍。
同 think twice 再三考虑

〈语法重点〉
倍数 + 形容词 / 副词比较级 + than... 的结构用来作比较，than 后一般加名词或代词。

0950 **two** [tuː] n 二
I am sorry; I can only eat two eggs at a time.
对不起，我一次只能吃两个鸡蛋。

〈语法重点〉
注意 at a time 与 at one time 的区别，后者是指过去某一时间。

0951 **uncle** ['ʌŋkl] n 叔叔，舅舅
While my uncle was cooking, I was playing games.
叔叔做饭时，我在玩游戏。
词 Talk like a Dutch uncle. 谆谆教诲，小事大训。

〈语法重点〉
while 引导的时间状语从句的动词必须是延续性的，并且强调主句和从句的动作同时发生（或者相对应）。

0952 **under** ['ʌndər] prep 在……下面，低于
His marks are under their requirement.
他的分数没有达到他们的要求。
同 beneath 在……之下　　反 above 在……之上　　词 under consideration 在考虑中

〈语法重点〉
分数也可以用 score 来表示，score 也是可数名词。

0953 **understand** [ˌʌndərˈstænd] v 了解，懂得，明白，理解
From where I stand, it's easier to understand what he said.
在我看来，理解他的话比较容易。
同 comprehend 理解，领会　　反 misunderstand 误解

〈语法重点〉
easy 的比较级是变 y 为 i 再加上 er，即 easier。

0954 **unit** ['juːnɪt] n 单元，单位
My mother works at an auxiliary unit.
我的妈妈在一家附属单位工作。

0955 until [ən'tɪl] conj 直到……时候

Not until the girl is safely back can they rest easy.
要等女孩安全归来他们才放心。
- until present 直至现在
- not until... can... 直到……才……

语法重点
not until 引导时间状语从句，并置于句首时，主句要部分倒装。

0956 up [ʌp] ad 朝上地，往上 prep 向上

I lay on the bed staring up at the ceiling.
我躺在床上凝视着天花板。
- go up 上升，增长
- stare up at... 向上盯着……看

0957 upstairs [ˌʌp'sterz] ad 上楼地，往楼上

I will go upstairs to get the box down.
我上楼去把箱子搬下来。
- abovestairs 在楼上
- downstairs 在楼下
- walk upstairs 走上楼

语法重点
副词可和动词连用，其前面不需要加介词。

0958 us [əs] pron 我们

It is important for us to learn English well.
学好英语对于我们来说很重要。

语法重点
well 是 good 的副词形式，在句中修饰动词 learn。

0959 use [juːz] v 使用，利用 n 使用，用法

Many an old man doesn't know how to use a computer.
很多老人不知道怎么使用电脑。
- disuse 停止使用
- use sth. to do sth. 使用某物做某事

语法重点
many a / an 表示"许多"，后面接可数名词的单数形式，动词也按单数处理。

0960 useful ['juːsfl] a 有用的，有益的

It is useful for me to read books every day.
对我来说每天读书很有用。
- beneficial 有益的
- useless 无用的

语法重点
有时候也在 useful 前面加上 very，加强语气。

0961 vegetable ['vedʒtəbl] n 蔬菜，植物

It is well known to everyone that eating vegetables is good to our health.
众所周知，吃蔬菜对我们的健康有益。
- it is well known to everyone that... 众所周知……

0962 very ['veri] ad 非常地

Mentioning the matter that happened on National Day, he was very excited.
提到国庆节发生的那件事，他就很兴奋。
- quite 很
- very much 非常

语法重点
节日前通常不加任何冠词。
➲ national (P. 194)

0963 view [vjuː] n 视野，景色，观点

From my point of view, he is smarter than her.
在我看来，他比她聪明。
- opinion 观点
- have different views 有不同的观点

语法重点
from my point of view 是固定搭配，通常用于句首，也可以用 in my opinion 来表达。

0964 **visit** [ˈvɪzɪt] v / n 拜访，参观

Her ex-husband's visit caused her more distress than pleasure.
前夫的来访给她带来的痛苦大于快乐。
▶ pay a visit to 去拜访

语法重点
ex- 作词首附在名词前表示"以前的，前任的"。
↪ distress (P. 559)

0965 **voice** [vɔɪs] n 声音，嗓音

I miss his look and voice very much.
我非常想念他的外貌和声音。
▶ sound 声音   ▶ lose one's voice 嗓子哑了

0966 **wait** [weɪt] v 等待

The man with long hair seems to be waiting for you.
那个长头发的男子似乎是在等你。
▶ await 等待   ▶ wait a bit 等一下

语法重点
wait 为不及物动词，如果要接宾语，则后面须接介词 for。

0967 **walk** [wɔːk] v 走路，步行

The fuel has been used up, so they have to walk there.
油已经耗尽了，所以他们不得不步行去那里。
▶ walk away 走开   ▶ ... be used up ……用完了

0968 **wall** [wɔːl] n 墙壁

Climbing the Great Wall is my dream.
攀登长城是我的梦想。
▶ on the wall 在墙上   ▶ ... be my dream ……是我的梦想
▶ wall 的意思是"墙壁"，the Great Wall 是专有名词，意思是"长城"。

↪ climb (P. 023)

0969 **want** [wɑːnt] v 想要

When do you want me to give your car back?
你想要我在什么时候还车？

0970 **war** [wɔːr] n 战争，斗争

He was killed by a Japanese soldier in the Second World War.
他在"二战"中被一个日本兵杀死了。
▶ battle 战斗，斗争   ▶ peace 和平

0971 **warm** [wɔːrm] a 温暖的，暖和的，热情的

My mother is a warm-hearted woman.
我妈妈是一个热情的女人。
▶ enthusiastic 热情的   ▶ keep warm 保暖

0972 **waste** [weɪst] v 浪费，消耗 n 废物，浪费

We should make full use of our time rather than waste it.
我们应该充分利用时间，而不是去浪费它。
▶ save 节省   ▶ waste time 浪费时间

↪ full (P. 042)

0973 **watch** [wɑːtʃ] v 观看 n 手表

I will have repaired your watch before the sun goes down.
日落之前我会把你的表修理好的。
- regard 注视
- watch out 小心，提防

> 语法重点
> 将来完成时表示在将来某个时间之前已经完成了某个动作。

0974 **water** ['wɔːtər] n 水

To drink water here is a real sweat.
在这里喝水是一件难事。

> 语法重点
> a real sweat 意为"艰苦的工作"，在此结构中，sweat 用的是比喻意义，相当于 a difficult task。

0975 **way** [weɪ] n 道路，路线，方法

We will be on our way to London tomorrow.
明天我们就要启程去伦敦了。
- method 方法
- best way 最佳办法
- on one's way 在……的路上

> 语法重点
> 注意，in the way 的意思是"挡路"，与 on one's way 差别很大。

0976 **we** [wi] pron 我们

We pretend to have forgiven his misplay in the performance.
我们假装原谅了他在表演中的失误。
- pretend to do... 假装做某事

> 语法重点
> 不定式的完成形式要用 to have done。
> ↪ pretend (P. 341)

0977 **weak** [wiːk] a 弱的，无力的

We must cooperate with our comrades well, for a single person is very weak.
我们一定要和战友默契配合，因为一个人的力量是微弱的。
- be too weak to do sth. 太虚弱而不能去做某事

0978 **wear** [wer] v 穿戴，磨损

By the way, I think it is not suitable to wear shorts for her wedding.
顺便说一下，我认为穿短裤去参加她的婚礼不太合适。
- wear a seat belt 系安全带
- by the way, ... 顺便地，……

> 语法重点
> 说话者要转入一个新话题，通常要用 by the way 来引出这个话题。
> ↪ suitable (P. 368)

0979 **weather** ['weðər] n 天气，气象

We will go to the park in spite of the bad weather conditions.
不管天气多恶劣，我们都要去公园。
- weather forecast 天气预报

0980 **wedding** ['wedɪŋ] n 婚礼

Our wedding ceremony will be held at the Grand Hotel.
我们的婚礼将在圆山大饭店举行。
- marriage 婚礼，结婚
- golden wedding 金婚

> 语法重点
> wedding ceremony 中 wedding（婚礼）当形容词来用，修饰 ceremony（仪式）。

0981 **Wednesday** ['wenzdeɪ] n 星期三

The task will be done by Wednesday.
任务将会在星期三前完成。

> 语法重点
> will be done 是一般将来时的被动语态。

0982 week [wiːk] n 星期，周
All work will have been finished by the end of next week.
所有工作都将在下周末之前完成。
同 last week 上一周

语法重点
by the end of next week 通常与将来完成时连用。

0983 weekend [ˈwiːkend] n 周末
You know that I will be playing the piano at this time of the weekend.
你知道，周末的这个时候我会练钢琴。
反 weekday 工作日   搭 on weekend 在周末

语法重点
将来进行时的一般结构为 will / shall be + 动词的现在分词，表示将来某个时间正在进行的动作。
⊕ piano (P. 075)

0984 weigh [weɪ] v 有……的重量，衡量，称重，重达
This box weighs at least 100 pounds.
这个箱子至少有一百磅重。

0985 weight [weɪt] n 重量
She keeps walking to the office every day in order to lose weight.
为了减肥，她每天都走路去上班。
搭 a man of weight 重要人物

语法重点
keep 表示"保持"，其后一般接动词 ing 来表示"坚持做某事"。

0986 welcome [ˈwelkəm] v 欢迎 a 受欢迎的
Welcome you to pay a visit to our factory.
欢迎你来我们工厂参观。
同 greet 欢迎   反 unwelcome 不受欢迎的

语法重点
pay a visit to 为固定搭配，表达的意思是"拜访"，to 后面接表示人称或地点的名词或代词。

0987 well [wel] ad 很好地，相当地 a 健康的，适宜的
In a word, everything goes very well.
总而言之，一切都好。
句 All's well that ends well. 皆大欢喜。

语法重点
in a word（总之）用来表达一种总结性的概括，一般放在句首使用。

0988 west [west] n 西方，西部
It is common sense that the sun goes down in the west.
太阳从西边落下是基本常识。
句 it is common sense that... ……是常识

0989 what [wɑːt] pron 什么
What if I don't accept the invitation?
如果我不接受邀请会怎么样？
搭 no matter what 不管怎样

语法重点
what if 表示某种假设的情况，后接从句，从句的动词一般用一般现在时态或 should + 动词原形。

0990 when [wen] pron 什么时候
When shall we get down to this matter?
我们什么时候开始着手处理这个问题？
搭 since when 从那时以来，从什么时候开始

语法重点
get down 具有多种含义，如"下来，写下，使沮丧"等，而 get down to 则表示"开始或着手去做某事"。

0991 **where** [wer] `ad` 什么地方，在哪个地方 `conj` 在……地方

No matter where you are, I will find you.
不管你在哪里，我都要找到你。
- where it is 问题的关键所在，实际情况

> 语法重点
> no matter where 的意思和 wherever 相同，但前者只能引导状语从句，而后者除了引导状语从句，还可引导名词性从句。

0992 **whether** [ˈweðər] `conj` 是否，不管，无论

We can't decide whether to give way on this point.
我们不能决定在这一点上是否可以让步。
- if 是否
- whether to do sth. 是否做某事

0993 **which** [wɪtʃ] `pron` 哪个，哪些

One tire of my car which I bought yesterday has worn down.
我昨天买的一个汽车轮胎已经磨损了。
- can't tell which is which 分辨不出哪个是哪个

0994 **while** [waɪl] `conj` 在……时候，虽然，尽管 `n` 一段时间 `v` 消磨

You are well off while they are rather poor.
你非常富有，而他们却很贫穷。
- although 虽然，尽管
- after a while 过了一会儿

> 语法重点
> while 表示轻微的转折。

0995 **white** [waɪt] `a` 白色的，纯白的

How long will it take to go to the White House?
到白宫需要多长时间？

> 语法重点
> how long will it take to 后面要接动词原形。
> ↪ house (P. 050)

0996 **who** [hu:] `pron` 谁

Who is that speaking?
你是谁？
- 打电话时，如果询问对方身份，可用 Who is that speaking?，而不是 Who are you，其回答方式是 This is... speaking。

0997 **whole** [hoʊl] `a` 整个的，全部的，完整的

No wonder the whole team are against you.
怪不得整个队的人都反对你。
- entire 全部的
- as a whole 作为一个整体

> 语法重点
> the whole team 指的是全队的人，所以按复数处理，后面的 be 动词要用 are。

0998 **whom** [hu:m] `pron` 谁

To be honest with you, I know nothing about whom they are fighting for.
老实跟你说，我不知道这些人为谁打架。
- to be honest with you, ... 老实跟你说……
- fight 表示"奋斗，斗争"，而 fight for 的意思是"为……而战"。

> ↪ honest (P. 176)

0999 whose [huːz] pron 谁的
No one knows whose money was stolen.
没有人知道谁的钱丢了。
- no one knows... 没人知道……

> 语法重点
> no one 和 nobody 表达的意思相同，都表示"没有人"，但 nobody 还可以用来表示"小人物"。

1000 why [waɪ] ad 为什么 conj ……的理由，为什么
I don't know why she can't coexist with other girls.
我不知道为什么她不能与其他女孩和平共处。
- wherefore 为什么
- I don't know why... 我不知道为什么……

> 语法重点
> coexist with 的意思是"和……共同存在"，后面常接名词或代词。

1001 wide [waɪd] a 宽的，广泛的
If only he had wide interests.
他要是兴趣广泛就好了。
- broad 宽的，辽阔的
- narrow 狭窄的

> interest (P. 052)

1002 wife [waɪf] n 妻子
In view of his busy work, his wife didn't blame him.
鉴于他工作繁忙，他妻子没有责备他。

> 语法重点
> in view of 既可放在句首引导整个句子，也可以放在句中。

1003 will [wɪl] aux 将要，愿意，必须
I bet he will come back for you after a while.
我打赌他等一下会来找你。
- would 将
- will be 将是
- I bet... 我打赌……

> 语法重点
> while 在句中作名词。

1004 win [wɪn] v 赢得，获胜
Tell me which team won the game at last.
告诉我哪一队最终赢得了比赛。
- lose 失败
- win-win idea 双赢理念

> 语法重点
> win 后面不能接人，"战胜某人"不能用 win sb.，但可以说 sb. wins（某人赢了）。

1005 wind [wɪnd] n 风
During the winter, the wind is ferocious all the while.
整个冬天狂风肆虐。
- cold wind 冷风

> 语法重点
> all the while 表示自始至终的一段时间。

1006 window ['wɪndoʊ] n 窗户，视窗
I'll go to check out whether the window is open.
我过去看看窗子是否还开着。
- close window 关窗户
- I will do... 我将会做……

1007 wine [waɪn] n 酒，葡萄酒
People here always drink strong wine to keep the body warm.
为了保持身体温暖，这里的人们经常喝烈酒。
- liquor 酒
- mild wine 淡酒

> 语法重点
> 动词不定式通常可用来表示某种目的，相当于 in order to。

1008 **winter** [ˈwɪntər] n 冬天，冬季
In winter, they often go skating on the lake.
冬天，他们经常在湖面上溜冰。
⊃ skate (P. 360)

1009 **wish** [wɪʃ] v/n 希望，祝愿
To his parents' wish, he was enrolled by that college.
如父母所愿，他被那所大学录取了。
同 hope 希望　　as you wish 随心所欲

语法重点
to one's wish 的意思是"如某人所愿"，放在句首时，需要用逗号和主句隔开。

1010 **with** [ðɪð] prep 和……一起，用，随着，包括
I'll be with my family no matter what happens.
不管发生什么，我都会和家人在一起。
反 without 无，没有　　go with 伴随，与

1011 **woman** [ˈwʊmən] n 女人，女性
If I were you, I would fall in love with the woman.
如果我是你，我会爱上那个女人。
同 female 女性，女人

语法重点
fall in love with 侧重"爱上"的动作，短语 be in love with 强调的是"和某人陷入爱情"这个状态。

1012 **wood** [wʊd] n 木头，木材
I carved this piece of wood into a canoe.
我把这段木头雕成了一只独木舟。
wood door 木门　　carve sth. into... 将某物雕刻成……

语法重点
wood 当"木头"讲时不可数，woods 的意思是"森林"。

1013 **word** [wɜːrd] n 字词
All in all, I can learn about 50 words a day.
总的来说，我一天能学会 50 个单词。
big word 大话，吹牛　　All in all, ... 总的来说……

语法重点
word 还可以表示"话"，通常用复数形式。
⊃ learn (P. 057)

1014 **work** [wɜːrk] n 工作，职业 v 工作
It is a pity that I have to work and can't go to the party.
真遗憾，我要工作，所以不能去参加派对了。
同 job 工作，职业　　it is a pity that... 很遗憾……

语法重点
本句中的 work 作动词，work 作名词表示"工作、职业"时，通常表示不可数名词。

1015 **worker** [ˈwɜːrkər] n 工作者
I changed from a worker into a housekeeper after giving birth.
生了孩子后，我从一名工人变成了一名家庭主妇。
I change from... into... 我从……变成……

1016 **world** [wɜːrld] n 世界
Her novel made her known far and wide in the world.
她的小说使得她被世人所知。
同 globe 世界　　the World Cup 世界杯

1017 worm [wɜːrm] **n** 虫，蠕虫

It's difficult for birds to find worms in winter.
冬天，鸟儿很难觅到虫子。
- The early bird catches the worm. 早起的鸟儿有虫吃。（捷足先登）
- it's difficult for sb. to do... 做……对于某人来说很难

1018 worry [ˈwɜːri] **v** 担心，忧虑

I'm worrying whether she can complete the task before six.
我担心她是否能在六点之前完成任务。
- bother 烦恼，麻烦
- I'm worrying whether... 我担心是否……

> **语法重点**
> complete 当形容词讲时意思是"完整的，彻底的"，作动词则表示"完成"，是及物动词。
> ⊃ complete (P. 143)

1019 worse [wɜːrs] **a** 更坏的，更差的

What's worse, there's no water in the bottle.
更糟的是，瓶子里没有水。
- better 更好的
- what's worse, ... 更糟的是……

> **语法重点**
> 英语中要阐述一种更坏的情况时，通常用 what's worse，该短语要跟后面的句子用逗号隔开。

1020 worst [wɜːrst] **a** 最坏的，最差的，最不利的

Worst of all, the man even boxed the gate-keeper.
最严重的是，那人甚至出拳打了门卫。
- the worst 最坏的
- worst of all, ... 最严重的是……

> **语法重点**
> gate-keeper 是复合词，复合词的词性通常由最后那个单词的词性决定。

1021 write [raɪt] **v** 书写

It is vitally important for you to learn to write your own name.
你得学会写自己的名字，这非常重要。
- write down 写下

1022 writer [ˈraɪtər] **n** 作家，作者

I don't think the writer is good at handwriting.
我认为这个作家不擅长手写。
- freelance writer 自由撰稿人
- I don't think... 我认为……不

> **语法重点**
> handwriting 是由名词加动名词组合而成的复合词。

1023 wrong [rɔːŋ] **a** 错误的，有毛病的

I must say that you are wrong.
我必须说你错了。
- false 错误的
- right 对的

> **语法重点**
> say 和 speak 都表示"讲话"，say 主要强调说话的内容，而 speak 则主要强调说话的方式或动作。

1024 yam [jæm] / sweet potato **n** 甘薯，山药，番薯

The yam goods are there.
番薯在那里。

> **语法重点**
> 英语中一些名词在表达特定含义时，只有复数形式，如例句中的 goods，意思是"商品，货物"，其单数形式 good 通常作形容词，意思是"好的"。

worm ~ yucky

1025 year [jɪr] **n** 年，年份
Do you still remember the years when we were deskmates?
你还记得我们做同桌的那些日子吗？
🔗 for years 多年以来

> 语法重点
> 句中用的是 year 的复数形式，说明"我们做同桌"的时间要大于一年。

1026 yellow ['jeloʊ] **a** 黄色的 **n** 黄色
What will you choose, the red apple or the yellow one?
你会选哪一个，红苹果还是黄苹果？
🔗 maize 黄色的，玉米色   🔗 pale yellow 浅黄

> 语法重点
> 英语中为了避免重复，通常可以用 one 来代指之前所提到的人或物，如例句中的 one 就指代前面的苹果。

1027 yes [jes] **ad** 是的
I'd say yes to anything that he likes.
只要他喜欢的事物我都认同。
🔗 no 不   🔗 I'd say yes to... 对于……我都愿意

1028 yesterday ['jestərdeɪ] **n** 昨天
He didn't brush his teeth yesterday morning.
他昨天早上没有刷牙。
🔗 tomorrow 明天   🔗 the day before yesterday 前天

> 语法重点
> teeth 是 tooth 的复数形式。

1029 yet [jet] **ad** 还没，尚，仍然
The project hasn't been done yet.
计划还没有完成。
🔗 already 已经   🔗 and yet 然而，可是

> 语法重点
> yet 通常用在疑问句和否定句中。

1030 you [jə] **pron** 你，你们
I will go downstairs the moment you call.
你一打电话我就下楼。

> 语法重点
> the moment 的意思是"一……就……"，强调一种即时性，它引导的从句若用一般现在时，则主句用一般将来时。

1031 young [jʌŋ] **a** 年轻的
She used to be a teacher when she was young.
她年轻时是一位老师。
🔗 old 老的   🔗 sb. used to be... 某人曾经是……

> 语法重点
> used 还可用作 used to do sth. 表示过去常常做某事。其中 to 后接动词原形，而短语 be used to (doing) sth. 的意思是"习惯（做）……"，其中的 to 是介词。

1032 your [jʊr] **pron** 你的，你们的
Your appearance is changing year by year.
你的外貌年年都在改变。

1033 yucky ['jʌki] **a** 令人厌恶的
The yucky food almost made him throw up.
难吃的食物几乎要使他呕吐了。
🔗 disagreeable 厌恶的   🔗 fond 喜欢的

🔗 throw (P. 104)

1034 **yummy** [ˈjʌmi] a 好吃的，愉快的
Her mouth is watering when she smells the yummy flavor.
闻到诱人的香味，她的口水就流了下来。
🔄 delicious 美味的，可口的   🔄 unsavoury 难吃的

语法重点
water 当名词讲时，意思是"水"；当动词讲时，意思是"流泪，给……浇水"。

1035 **zero** [ˈzɪroʊ] n 零
The temperature fell to zero yesterday, and the water congealed into ice.
昨天温度下降至零度，水结冰了。
🔄 naught 零   🔄 scale zero 刻度零点

语法重点
ice 是物质名词，并且表示一般概念，前面不加任何冠词。
🔄 ice (P. 051)

1036 **zoo** [zuː] n 动物园
They took many photos in the zoo yesterday.
他们昨天在动物园里拍了很多照片。
🔄 zoo keeper 动物园管理员   🔄 sb. take photos in... 某人在……照相
🔄 photo 是名词 photograph 的简写。

MEMO

LEVEL 2
ability ~ zebra

LEVEL 2
ability ～ zebra

Review test
复习 Level 1 的学习成果，还记得以下单词是什么意思吗？

1 address ▸ _____
2 shut ▸ _____
3 hole ▸ _____
4 worse ▸ _____
5 lake ▸ _____
6 ease ▸ _____
7 born ▸ _____
8 light ▸ _____

Preview
单词重点预习，在开始之前先预习会让印象更深刻喔！

1 abroad ▸ _____
2 weekday ▸ _____
3 bet ▸ _____
4 indicate ▸ _____
5 sign ▸ _____
6 knowledge ▸ _____
7 president ▸ _____
8 discuss ▸ _____

语法重点预习，在开始之前先预习会让印象更深刻喔！

1 冠词，放在名词前面，可分成定冠词或不定冠词。
  - 定冠词：the，主要表示说话者与听话者都已经知道的事物。
  - 不定冠词：a / an，并没有特别指某事物；指首次提到的事物。

2 人称代词

项目	第一人称		第二人称		第三人称	
	单数	复数	单数	复数	单数	复数
主格人称代词	I	we	you	you	he / she / it	they
形容词性物主代词	my	our	your	your	his / her / its	their
名词性物主代词	mine	ours	yours	yours	his / hers / its	theirs
宾格人称代词	me	us	you	you	him / her / it	them

3 反身代词

第一人称		第二人称		第三人称	
单数	复数	单数	复数	单数	复数
myself	ourselves	yourself	yourselves	himself / herself / itself	themselves

4 集合名词：
  - 表示"整体"时，为单数；表示"个体"时，为复数。
  - 例如：army（军队）；audience（听众）；crowd（群众）；family（家人）

正确答案	Review test	1 名词 / 动词 / 住址；称呼　2 动词 / 关闭　3 名词 / 洞　4 形容词 / 更坏的
		5 名词 / 湖泊　6 名词 / 动词 / 容易；减轻　7 形容词 / 出生的　8 名词；形容词 / 光线；轻的
	Preview	1 形容词 / 在国外　2 名词 / 工作日　3 名词 / 动词 / 打赌　4 动词 / 指示
		5 名词 / 动词 / 标志；签名　6 名词 / 知识　7 名词 / 总统　8 动词 / 讨论

ability ～ zebra

0001 ability [əˈbɪləti] n 能力，能耐，才能
The dancer has ability, but she lacks the sense of collectivity.
那个舞者有能力，但是她缺乏团队意识。
同 aptitude 能力，才能　反 disability 无能

> 语法重点
> 动词有5种基本形态，主要包括原形、第三人称单数形式、过去式、过去分词和现在分词，例句中的 lacks 便为第三人称单数形式。

0002 abroad [əˈbrɔːd] a 在国外，到国外，在海外
If they can afford to, they will take a vacation abroad.
他们如果能够负担得起，就可以出国旅游了。
同 overseas 海外的　短 study abroad 出国留学

0003 absence [ˈæbsəns] n 缺席，没有，缺乏
Due to the absence of experience, the team failed in the game.
由于缺乏经验，这个队伍在比赛中失败了。
反 presence 出席　短 absence from 缺席，不在
辨 fail 当动词讲时，意思是"失败了"，常用在短语 fail in doing sth. 或 fail in sth. 中，表示"做某事失败了"。

> ⇒ fail (P. 163)

0004 absent [ˈæbsənt] a 缺席的，缺少的，心不在焉的
I see she was absent from the performance.
我知道她没有参加演出。
反 present 出席　短 absent from work 旷工

> 语法重点
> I see 后面可以接宾语从句，表示"知道（某件事）"。

0005 accept [əkˈsept] v 接受，同意，承认
Eventually, I accepted the invitation of the woman.
最终，我接受了那个女人的邀请。
同 adopt 接受　反 refuse 拒绝　短 accept sth. from sb. 从某人处接受某物

0006 active [ˈæktɪv] a 主动的，积极的，活跃的
Can you imagine the thin boy was active during the journey?
你想象得出来吗，那个瘦弱的男孩在旅途中十分活跃？
短 play an active role in... 在……发挥积极作用

> 语法重点
> thin boy 与 journey 是说话双方均知道的，所以前面用定冠词 the。
> ⇒ journey (P. 313)

0007 addition [əˈdɪʃn] n 增加，添加，加法
In addition, he will accompany you to the theatre.
此外，他还会陪着你去剧院。
反 subtraction 减少　短 in addition to 除……之外　短 In addition, ... 此外，……

> 语法重点
> 表示补充说明时，可以用 in addition，该短语跟后面的句子要用逗号分开。

怪物讲师教学团队的 7 000 "单词" + "语法"

0008 advance [əd'væns] **n** 使前进,发展,提高

They haven't been to that area before, so they should make preparation for the expedition in advance.
他们以前从没去过那个地方,所以得提前做好探险活动的准备工作。
- in advance 提前 - make preparation for... 为……做准备

> 语法重点
> so 在句中起连接作用,不单独作句子成分。

0009 affair [ə'fer] **n** 事物,事情,私事

I would never allow myself to get into so many love affairs.
我绝不允许自己陷入那么多的风流韵事。
- private affair 私事
- love 当名词讲时,意思是"爱",love affairs 的意思是"风流韵事",含有贬义。

> allow (P. 006)

0010 aid [eɪd] **v** 帮助,援助,有助于

If you had not aided me, I should have been scolded by the teacher.
要不是你帮助我,我今天就要被老师责备了。
- help 帮助 - financial aid 经济援助

0011 aim [eɪm] **n** 目标,目的,对准

The aim of the campaign is to remind people of the damage of wine.
这项活动的目的在于提醒人们注意饮酒的危害。
- goal 目的,目标 - aim to 目标在于 - the aim of... is... ……的目的就是……

0012 aircraft ['erkræft] **n** 飞行器,飞机,航空器

If the fog disappeared, the aircraft the travelers take would arrive on time.
如果雾散了,游客们乘坐的飞机就能准时到达。

> 语法重点
> on time 的意思是"按规定的时间做了某事"。

0013 airline ['erlaɪn] **n** 航线,航空公司

To save time, the visitors could transfer to an airplane with another airline.
为了节省时间,游客们可以换乘另一条航线的飞机。
- airway 空中航线 - airline company 航空公司

> 语法重点
> save 作动词,表示"节约,拯救",可以和名词或介词构成短语,如 save time(节省时间)等。

0014 alarm [ə'lɑːrm] **n** 警报,报警器,惊恐

If the guard had noticed the fire alarm at that time, the visitors would not be in hospital now.
如果当时警卫注意到火灾警报,游客们现在就不会躺在医院里了。
- fire alarm 火警

> 语法重点
> 例句用了虚拟语气,并且主句和条件句的动作发生时间不一致。

0015 album ['ælbəm] **n** 相簿,纪念册,专辑

Please put the photo taken on the scenic spot in the album and take good care of it.
把这张在景点照的照片放入相册中并好好保管。
- photo album 相册 - put sth. in... 把某物放到……里

> 语法重点
> 本句是动词原形开头,是祈使句。祈使句用来表示命令,或者提出请求和建议。

0016 **alike** [ə'laɪk] **a** 相像的，相同的
This picture you drew is alike to that one.
你画的这张画跟那张很像。
反 unlike 不同的　同 Great minds think alike. 英雄所见略同。

语法重点
alike 还可以作副词，在句中修饰动词。

0017 **alive** [ə'laɪv] **a** 活的，活泼的，有生气的
People said several visitors were alive in the air crash.
据说有几个游客在这次空难中生还。
同 lively 活泼的　反 dead 无生命的　同 come alive 活跃起来

→ several (P. 088)

0018 **almond** ['ɑːmənd] **n** 杏仁，杏树，杏仁状的东西
The doctor says it is bad to eat bitter almonds.
那名医生说吃苦杏仁不好。

语法重点
it is bad to 后面接动词原形。
→ bitter (P. 131)

0019 **aloud** [ə'laʊd] **ad** 大声地，出声地，高声地
It's impolite to talk aloud in public when you travel abroad.
你在国外旅游时，在公共场合大声交谈很不礼貌。
同 loudly 大声地　反 quietly 安静地　同 think aloud 自言自语

0020 **alphabet** ['ælfəbet] **n** 字母表，初步
What's the meaning of the alphabet on the wall of the theatre?
剧院墙上的字母是什么意思？
同 What's the meaning of...? ……是什么意思？

0021 **although** [ɔːl'ðəʊ] **conj** 虽然，尽管，可是
Although the woman is fat, she walks fast.
尽管那个女人很胖，但是她走得很快。
同 though 尽管

语法重点
在英语中，although 与 but 不可以同时使用。

0022 **altogether** [ˌɔːltə'geðər] **ad** 完全，总共，总而言之
There are about 2,000 visitors, as far as I know, in the scenic spot altogether.
据我所知，这个景点约有两千名游客。

语法重点
as far as I know 的意思是"据我所知"，通常放在句首，但也可放在句中作插入语，前后用逗号隔开。

0023 **amount** [ə'maʊnt] **n** 总额，数量，总数
I earned a large amount of money by selling goods in the park.
我在公园卖东西赚了一大笔钱。
同 quantity 数量　同 a considerable amount of... 相当多的……

语法重点
a large amount of 后面接不可数名词，其中 large 也可以替换为 great。

0024 **ancient** ['eɪnʃənt] **a** 古代的，古老的，远古的
In ancient Greece, many visitors swarm into the famous scenic spot every day.
在古希腊，每天都有很多的游客涌入这个著名的景点。
同 antique 古老的　反 modern 现代的　同 sb. swarms into... 某人涌入……

语法重点
国名前面通常不用任何冠词。

0025 **ankle** [ˈæŋkl] n 脚踝，踝关节
His ankle got hurt when he took a walk outside.
他外出散步时扭伤了脚踝。
gambrel 踝关节　　ankle joint 踝关节

> 语法重点
> 被动语态可以用"get + 过去分词"的结构，用来强调动作的结果，表示突发性的、偶然发生的事件。

0026 **anybody / anyone** [ˈenibɑːdi] / [ˈenɪwʌn]
pron 任何人，任何一个
Anyone of you could climb to the top of the mountain.
你们中的任何一个人都可以爬到山顶。

> 语法重点
> 不定代词 anyone 表示"任何人"，只能用来指人；而 any one 表示"任何的"，既可以用来指人，也可以用来指物。

0027 **anyhow** [ˈenihaʊ] ad 无论如何，不管怎样
Anyhow, they can only trust the guide to find their way home.
不管怎样，他们唯有相信导游才能找到回家的路。
anyway 无论如何，不管怎样　　... find one's way home ……找到回家的路

> 语法重点
> anyhow 可以放在句首，也可以放在句末。

0028 **anytime** [ˈenɪˌtaɪm] ad 在任何时候，无论何时
If you want to go traveling, you can call me anytime.
如果你想去旅游，随时打电话给我。
whenever 无论何时　　anytime 相当于 at any time。

0029 **anyway** [ˈenɪweɪ] ad 无论如何，不管怎样，总之
Anyway, she will be your loyal fan forever.
不管怎样，她永远都是你忠实的粉丝。
anyhow 无论如何

> 语法重点
> anyway 的用法同 anyhow，二者有时可以替换使用。

0030 **anywhere** [ˈenɪwer] ad 在任何地方，无论何处
I would like to go anywhere of the world if I have enough time.
如果有充足的时间，我要走遍世界。
get anywhere 有点儿成就

> 语法重点
> anywhere 可以用在肯定句中，意思是"任何地方"。

0031 **apartment** [əˈpɑːrtmənt] n 公寓，房间，套房
They are going to rent an apartment near the resort.
他们打算在那个度假胜地附近租一套公寓。
flat 公寓，房间　　service apartment 酒店式公寓
apartment 与 flat 都表示"公寓"，区别不大，美国人习惯用 apartment，英国人习惯用 flat。

0032 **appearance** [əˈpɪrəns] n 出现，外貌，露面
The actor is to have a plastic surgery for a good appearance.
为了拥有漂亮的外表，那个演员要去做整形手术。
looks 相貌，长相　　outward appearance 外观，外表
be to do sth. 要做……

> 语法重点
> "be to + 动词原形"也可以表示一般将来时，意思是按照计划将要做某事。
> ⇒ plastic (P. 338)

ankle ~ arrest

0033 appetite [ˈæpɪtaɪt] **n** 胃口，食欲，欲望
I went to a doctor for my bad appetite during my trip.
旅行中我胃口不好，去看了医生。
- desire 欲望
- enormous appetite 食欲旺盛

> **语法重点**
> 注意，go to a doctor 意思是"看医生"，go for a doctor 意思是"去请医生"。

0034 apply [əˈplaɪ] **v** 应用，申请，请求
How can he apply for a place for traveling abroad?
他如何才能申请去国外旅游的？
- demand 请求
- apply in person 亲自申请

> **语法重点**
> apply for 的意思指申请某事或请求某事。

0035 apron [ˈeɪprən] **n** 围裙，停机坪
The girl is playing with her friends wearing her mother's apron now.
女孩现在正穿着妈妈的围裙和朋友玩。

> **语法重点**
> 现在进行时的一般组成是：主语 + be 动词 + 动词的现在分词。

0036 argue [ˈɑːrgjuː] **v** 辩论，争论，讨论
They are arguing violently about where to spend their holiday.
他们正在就去哪里度假展开激烈的讨论。
- discuss 辩论，讨论
- argue with 争论，和……争吵

> **语法重点**
> 现在进行时表示在现在或近段时间内正在发生的事情，常用的时间有 now, at this time, these days。
> ↪ holiday (P. 049)

0037 argument [ˈɑːrgjumənt] **n** 议论，争论，争吵
The two singers were not having an argument when the man came in.
那个男人进来时，那两个歌手没有在吵架。
- debate 辩论
- argument about... 争论……

> **语法重点**
> 现在进行时的否定形式为：主语 + be 动词 + not + 动词的现在分词。

0038 armchair [ˈɑːrmtʃer] **n** 扶手椅，单人沙发，安乐椅
Is the traveler looking for an armchair?
那个游客是在找一把扶手椅吗？
- armchair traveler 神游旅行者（只阅读或听说关于旅行的事而不亲身旅行的人）

> **语法重点**
> 现在进行时变一般疑问句时，要将 be 动词放在句首，根据人称需要做相应的变化。

0039 arrangement [əˈreɪndʒmənt] **n** 安排，布置，整理
We should listen to the arrangement of the director carefully.
我们要仔细听取导演的安排。
- setting 布置
- arrangement for... 对……的安排

0040 arrest [əˈrest] **v** 逮捕，拘留，阻止
The policemen finally arrested the thief who always stole in the Palace Museum.
警察最终逮捕了那个总在故宫里行窃的小偷。
- apprehend 逮捕
- release 释放
- arrest sb. for... 因为……逮捕某人

> **语法重点**
> 个体名词是表示单个人或事物的名词，如例句中的 thief（小偷）。
> ↪ palace (P. 333)

0041 **arrive** [ə'raɪv] v 到达，抵达，达成
It was very late when the visitors arrived at the hotel.
当游客们抵达旅馆时已经非常晚了。
反 depart 离开，出发　近 arrive late 迟到

0042 **arrow** ['ærou] n 箭头，箭状物
Look, the athlete is discharging an arrow from a bow.
看，那个运动员正在射箭。
反 bow 弓　近 shoot an arrow 射箭

⊃ bow (P. 133)

0043 **article / essay** ['ɑːrtɪkl] / ['eseɪ] n 论文，物品，条款
You will be able to understand the article if you know the experiences of the author.
你如果知道作者的经历，就能读懂这篇文章。
近 article title 文章标题

语法重点
experience 当"经历"讲时是可数，当"经验"讲时是不可数。

0044 **artist** ['ɑːrtɪst] n 艺术家，美术家，艺人
As an artist, his father has an updated thought and travels abroad every year.
作为一名艺术家，他父亲的思想很前卫，每年都出国旅游。
近 maestro 艺术大师　近 make-up artist 化妆师

语法重点
as a / an 后面通常接表示职业的名词。

0045 **asleep** [ə'sliːp] a 睡着的，长眠的，麻木的
I couldn't be asleep for I had a cup of coffee before going to bed.
我上床前喝了杯咖啡，因此睡不着。
近 numb 麻木的　反 awake 醒着的　近 fall asleep 入睡，睡着

语法重点
coffee 是物质名词，物质名词是表示无法判断个体或数量的名词，如 water、milk、rice 等。

0046 **assistant** [ə'sɪstənt] n 助手，助理，助教
My assistant always goes to the gym at weekend.
我的助理周末经常去健身房。
近 helper 助手　近 gym 是 gymnasium 的简写。

0047 **attack** [ə'tæk] v 攻击，抨击，进攻
What surprised me was that he attacked the army in the afternoon.
让我吃惊的是他在下午向军队发动了攻击。
近 assault 攻击　反 defend 保卫　近 attack on 攻击

0048 **attend** [ə'tend] v 参加，出席，照顾
He attended the feast on his wife's behalf.
他代表妻子参加宴席。
近 join 参加　反 absent 缺席　近 attend a meeting 参加会议

⊃ feast (P. 441)

arrive ~ bakery

0049 attention [ə'tenʃn] n 注意，关心，关注
We should focus all our attention on climbing the hill.
我们应该把所有的注意力都放在爬山上。
≈ concern 关心　　● attract one's attention 吸引某人的注意

> 语法重点
> focus on 中的 on 可以替换为 upon。

0050 avoid [ə'vɔɪd] v 避免，避开，躲避
The travelers walked the path in order to avoid the heavy traffic.
游客们走小道以避开拥挤的交通。
≈ evade 逃避　　↔ face 面对　　● avoid doing... 逃避……

0051 baby-sit ['beɪbɪˌsɪt] v 当临时保姆，照看小孩
These nuns baby-sit the abandoned baby in turn.
这些修女们轮流照看这个弃婴。
● to baby-sit 给人当保姆　　● do sth. in turn 轮流做某事

↪ nun (P. 330)

0052 baby-sitter ['beɪbɪˌsɪtə] n 临时保姆
What you have to do is to find a scrupulous baby-sitter when you go travelling.
出去旅游时，你必须做的就是找个细心的保姆。
● what sb. has to do is to... 某人必须做的是……

> 语法重点
> 注意 baby-sitter 的拼写，里面有两个 t。

0053 backward ['bækwərd] a 向后的
I look backward from time to time when I am taking a walk.
我散步的时候时不时地向后看。
↔ forward 向前地　　● step backward 倒退，返回

> 语法重点
> 句中 look backward 这个动作发生在 taking a walk 这个动作正在进行的时候，所以前者用一般现在时，后者用现在进行时。

0054 backwards ['bækwərdz] ad 向后地
The water from the fountain kept the visitors moving backwards.
喷泉的水迫使游客们向后退。
≈ rearwards 在后面，向后面　　● looking backwards 回顾以往

> 语法重点
> 持续动词是用来表示主语保持或持续某种状态的动词，主要有 keep, remain, stay 等。

0055 bake [beɪk] v 烘烤，受热
He suggests baking more bread for the guests.
他建议为客人们多烤点面包。
● bake... for sb. 为某人烤……　　● sb. suggests doing sth. 某人建议做某事

> 语法重点
> suggest 的意思是"建议，提议"，还可用于 suggest itself to sb. 的结构，意思是"想到"。

0056 bakery ['beɪkəri] n 面包店，面包厂
It is suggested that we go to the bakery to buy some bread for the guests.
有人提议我们去面包店里为客人们买点面包。

> 语法重点
> it is suggested that（有人提议……）后面从句中的动词要用 should + 动词原形，例句中省略了 should。

127

0057 balcony [ˈbælkəni] n 阳台，包厢，楼座
We are playing cards in the balcony of my new house.
我们在我家新房子的阳台上玩扑克牌。
🔘 we are doing sth. in someplace 我们在某地正做某事

> **语法重点**
> 名词是有生命的，我们用"'s"结构来表示所有关系。如果名词是无生命的，我们就要用"名词 + of + 名词"的结构来表示所有关系。

0058 bamboo [ˌbæmˈbuː] n 竹子，竹竿
The reason why the pandas in the zoo died is that there was no bamboo.
动物园里熊猫的死因是没有竹子可以吃。
🔘 the reason why... is that... ……的原因是……

0059 banker [ˈbæŋkər] n 银行家，银行业者
The world-famous banker had a crush on Jane and invited her to watch a film.
那位享誉世界的银行家暗恋简，并请她看电影。
🔘 ... have a crush on sb. ……暗恋某人

> **语法重点**
> world-famous 是复合形容词，是由名词 world + 形容词 famous 构成的，且两个词之间要用连字符连接。
> ⟶ invite (P. 180)

0060 barbecue [ˈbɑːrbɪkjuː] n 烤肉，烧烤，烤架
They have a barbecue once a week.
他们一周吃一次烧烤。
🔘 barbecue sauce 烤肉酱

0061 bark [bɑːrk] n 狗吠叫，咆哮 v 吠叫
Suddenly, they heard a fierce burst of dog bark from the amusement park.
突然，他们听见游乐园里传来一阵凶猛的狗叫声。
🔘 ululation 吠声 🔘 one's bark is worse than his bite 刀子嘴，豆腐心

> **语法重点**
> a burst of 是一个固定短语，意思指"一阵"。

0062 basement [ˈbeɪsmənt] n 地下室，地窖，根基
I made it clear that you can't hide in the basement.
我已经明确说过，你们不能躲在地下室。
🔘 cellar 地下室，地窖 🔘 basement parking 地下停车场

> **语法重点**
> hide 表示"躲避，躲藏"时，既可以作动词，也可以作名词，例句中 hide 作不及物动词。

0063 basics [ˈbeɪsɪks] n 基础，基本要素，概要
You should get down to the basics of dance.
你应该从舞蹈的基础知识开始学起。
🔘 foundation 基础 🔘 sb. gets down to... 某人开始……

> **语法重点**
> get down to 中的 to 是介词，后面接名词或者动名词。
> ⟶ dance (P. 027)

0064 basis [ˈbeɪsɪs] n 基本原理，基础，底部
We should lay a solid basis for our performance.
我们应该为演出打下坚实的基础。
🔘 base 基础，底部 🔘 on the basis of... 根据，基于……

0065 battle ['bætl] n 战役，战斗，斗争

Both of his sons have sacrificed in the battle and he has no mood to travel.

他的两个儿子都在战争中牺牲了，他没有心情去旅游。

- combat 战斗
- in battle 在战争中，在战斗中

语法重点
现在完成时表示已经完成的动作对现在仍然造成影响，或是一直持续到现在的动作或状态，其一般结构为：主语 + have / has + 动词的过去分词。

0066 bead [biːd] n 有孔小珠，念珠，滴

It makes no sense to play with the crystal bead.

玩那个水晶珠根本毫无意义。

- draw a bead on 瞄准，把……作为靶子

语法重点
it makes no sense 后面通常接动词不定式。
↪ crystal (P. 554)

0067 bean [biːn] n 豆子，豆类植物

My hometown is famous for coffee beans and the waterfall.

我的家乡以咖啡豆和那个瀑布而出名。

- bean sprouts 豆芽
- someplace is famous for... 某地以……而出名

0068 beard [bɪrd] n 胡子，胡须，颌毛

She doesn't like her husband's littery beard and refuses to go out for a walk with him.

她不喜欢丈夫那杂乱的胡须，拒绝跟他外出散步。

- moustache 胡须
- full beard 络腮胡子，大胡子

语法重点
she doesn't like 后面可以接名词、动名词、不定式，也可以接宾语从句。
↪ refuse (P. 214)

0069 bedroom ['bedruːm] n 卧室，睡房，寝室

Her bedroom is situated on the second floor of the house and she is listening to music there.

她的卧室在房子的二楼，她正在里面听音乐。

- bedchamber 卧室，寝室
- master bedroom 主卧室

语法重点
be situated 后面可以接介词 in, at 或者 on，视情况而定。

0070 beef [biːf] n 牛肉，肌肉，力气

My husband wanted to eat beef for dinner.

我的丈夫晚餐想吃牛肉。

语法重点
beef 是物质名词，不可数。

0071 beep [biːp] n 哔哔声

The young traveler's phone continued beeping all the time.

那个年轻游客的手机一直发出哔哔声。

- bleep 发出哔哔声
- beep volume 提示音量

语法重点
continue 的意为为"保持，持续"，通常用来表示物体保持某一种状态；continue doing sth. 是固定搭配，表示"一直做某事"。

0072 beer [bɪr] n 啤酒

The visitor is allergic to dark beer.

那个游客对黑啤酒过敏。

- beer bottle 啤酒瓶
- be allergic to... 对……过敏

语法重点
dark beer 的意思是"黑啤酒"，dark（黑色的）是形容词，修饰 beer（啤酒）。

0073 beetle ['biːtl] n 甲虫，甲壳虫，木槌

How could the boy trample the beetle to death?

那个男孩怎么能把甲虫踩死呢？

语法重点
how could sb. 后面接动词原形。

0074 **beg** [beg] v 乞求，请求，恳求
These men near the zoo live by begging.
动物园附近的这些人以乞讨为生。
I beg your pardon. 对不起，请原谅，请再说一遍。

语法重点
live by 后面通常接谋生的工具或手段。

0075 **beginner** [bɪˈɡɪnər] n 初学者，新手，创始人
The young actor was still a beginner at this time last year.
去年的这个时候，那个年轻的演员还只是个新手。
learner 初学者　expert 专家　beginner's luck 新手的好运气

语法重点
一般过去时表示在过去的某个时间内发生的动作或存在的状态，常和 yesterday, last, once, before 等搭配使用。

0076 **belief** [bɪˈliːf] n 信念，信赖，信仰
You should keep your belief and never give up performing.
你要坚定信念，永不放弃表演。
faith 信仰，信任　... keep one's belief 某人坚定信念

语法重点
give up 可以单独使用，后面也可以加名词、动名词，加代词时将名词置于 give 与 up 中间。

0077 **believable** [bɪˈliːvəbl] a 可相信的
The waitress in red seems believable.
那个穿红衣服的女服务生看起来可以相信。
credible 可信的　unbelievable 不可信的
sb. seems + 形容词 某人看起来……

语法重点
seem 不能单独使用，后面必须接形容词，说明主语的状况、性质、特征等情况。
➔ waitress (P. 243)

0078 **belt** [belt] n 皮带，腰带，带状物
Every visitor fastened the seat belt, how come you didn't?
每个游客都系好了安全带，为什么你没有呢？
safety belt 安全带

语法重点
how come 通常用来表示责备、质问等。

0079 **bench** [bentʃ] n 长凳，工作台，替补队员
If you ask me, I think the man on the bench is a basketball enthusiast.
如果你问我，我认为坐在凳子上的那个人是篮球爱好者。

0080 **bend** [bend] v 弯曲，屈服，倾向于
If it is possible, bend over little by little to watch the goldfish.
如果可能的话，慢慢地弯下腰去观赏金鱼。
bow 弯腰　bend over 弯腰

0081 **besides** [bɪˈsaɪdz] prep 除……之外，此外，另外
Besides working, regular traveling is also important.
除了工作之外，定期旅游也很重要。
besides that 除此之外

语法重点
besides 短语通常放在句首，并用逗号与后面的内容隔开。

0082 **bet** [bet] v 打赌，下注，确信
You have to be over 18 to bet in this area.
在这个地方赌博者年龄不得低于十八岁。
gamble 赌博　bet on 就……打赌

语法重点
句子中第二个 to 表示目的性。

beg ~ bloody

0083 beyond [bɪ'jɑːnd] **prep** 超过，越过，除……之外
The amusement park has changed beyond recognition.
游乐园已经变得焕然一新。
反 within 在……之内　　近 beyond expression 无法表达，形容不出

> **语法重点**
> beyond recognition 是一个固定搭配，意思是指"面目全非，识别不出"，表示事物的面貌已经发生了很大的变化。

0084 bill [bɪl] **n** 账单，票据
I failed to pay my bill, so the network company cut off my Internet connection.
我没有支付账单，于是网络公司切断了我的网络连接。
近 account 账单　　搭 I fail to do sth. ..., so... 我没有做某事，于是……

> **语法重点**
> so 与 because 不能同时出现在一个句子中。
> ↪ network (P. 329)

0085 bind [baɪnd] **v** 捆，绑，约束，装订
The goat in the zoo was bound to a tree.
动物园里的那只山羊被绑在一棵树上。
反 untie 解开　　近 bind up 包扎，装订　　搭 be bound to... 被绑在……

> **语法重点**
> bind 是不规则动词，其过去式、过去分词都是 bound。

0086 bitter ['bɪtər] **a** 苦的，痛苦的，激烈的
That bitter medicine is good for your health is believable. If you get better, I will take you to the zoo.
良药苦口利于病还是可信的。等你好了，我带你去动物园。
反 sweet 甜的　　搭 to the bitter end 直到最后

> **语法重点**
> 主语从句是指由一个句子充当主语的句子，that, whether, what, who, which, where, when, how, why 等都可以引导主语从句。
> ↪ medicine (P. 190)

0087 blackboard ['blækbɔːrd] **n** 黑板
My opinion is that the information about when we go traveling on the blackboard is wrong.
我的意见是黑板上关于我们何时去旅游的信息是错误的。
近 chalkboard 黑板　　搭 blackboard eraser 黑板擦

0088 blank [blæŋk] **a** 空白的，空虚的，单调的
I gave the applicant the suggestion that he fill in all the blank forms.
我建议那个申请者把所有的空白表格都填写完整。
反 substantial 内容充实的　　搭 blank page 空白页

> **语法重点**
> 本句 that 引导的句子是一个同位语从句，是解释 suggestion 的具体内容的。

0089 blind [blaɪnd] **a** 眼盲的，盲目的，未察觉的
Since the actress was blind, she has been accustomed to the dark life.
自从眼睛瞎了之后，那个女演员已经适应了黑暗的生活。
近 sightless 看不见的　　反 conscious 意识到的
搭 be accustomed to... 习惯于……

> **语法重点**
> be accustomed to 中的 to 是介词，后面接名词或动名词。
> ↪ actress (P. 004)

0090 bloody ['blʌdi] **a** 血腥的，流血的，嗜杀的
She hates to watch the bloody war films.
她讨厌看血腥的战争片。
近 gory 血腥的　　搭 bloody Mary 血腥玛丽（酒名）

> **语法重点**
> "看电影"要用 watch film, 而不能使用 look film。

0091 board [bɔːrd]
n 木板，董事会 **v** 登（飞机、车、船等）

We had better ask the board for advice about where to spend the holiday.
关于去哪里度假，我们最好向董事会征求一下意见。
➤ ask sb. for advice about... 关于……向某人征求意见

> 语法重点
> ask for 的意思是"请求"，ask sb. to do sth. 的意思是"请求某人做某事"。

0092 boil [bɔɪl] **v** 沸腾，烧开，使蒸发

Look, the children are boiling some kind of liquid in the lab.
看，孩子们正在实验室里煮沸某种液体。
➤ freeze 冷冻   ➤ boil down to... 归结为……

> 语法重点
> lab 是 laboratory 的简写。

0093 bomb [bɑːm] **n** 炸弹 **v** 爆炸

The music fountain on the square is just like a time bomb.
广场上的音乐喷泉就像一颗定时炸弹。
➤ guided bomb 导弹   ➤ sb. / sth. be just like... 某人 / 某物就像……

> 语法重点
> time bomb 是一个名词短语，其中 time 是修饰词，bomb 是中心词。
> ⊃ fountain (P. 298)

0094 bony [ˈboʊni] **a** 骨头的

My uncle has turned from a strong man into a bony one after these years' riotous life.
经过多年的放荡生活，我叔叔从一个强壮的人变得骨瘦如柴了。
➤ boney 骨瘦如柴的   ➤ obese 肥胖的
➤ turn into 和 change into 都表示"改变，变成"，但是 turn into 主要侧重于状态上的改变，而 change into 则主要强调形式上的变化。

0095 bookcase [ˈbʊkkeɪs] **n** 书柜

Tom put those magazines into the bookcase.
汤姆把那些杂志放进书柜。
➤ bookshelf 书架   ➤ ladder bookcase 梯形书柜

> 语法重点
> 句中的主语 Tom 和动词 put 为主动关系，所以用的是主动语态。

0096 borrow [ˈbɑːroʊ] **v** 借用

Is it okay to borrow a camera from him?
可以向他借一台相机吗？
➤ lend 借出   ➤ borrow trouble 自找麻烦，杞人忧天

> 语法重点
> 注意 borrow 的意思是"借（入）"。

0097 boss [bɔːs] **n** 上司，老板

Let's invite the boss to that new disco.
我们邀请老板去那个新开的舞厅吧。
➤ employer 老板   ➤ employee 员工

> 语法重点
> invite sb. to 后面也可以接 party, wedding 等表示集体性活动的名词。

0098 bother [ˈbɑːðər] **v** 打扰，使不安

He won't bother the beautiful conductor anymore.
他不会再打扰那个美丽的售票员了。
➤ annoy 打扰   ➤ bother about 为……而烦恼

> 语法重点
> won't 是 will not 的缩写。

board ~ brick

0099 bottle [ˈbɑːtl] n 瓶子

The traveler gave the bottle a couple of shakes before drinking the juice.
那个游客喝果汁前把瓶子摇晃了几下。
- a bottle of 一瓶

> 语法重点
> shake 的意思是"摇晃"，可以作名词，也可以作动词。
> ↪ shake (P. 088)

0100 bow [boʊ] / [baʊ] n / v 弯腰 n 弓，船头

My father made a bow with the branch and rope to hunt for the bird.
为了猎取那只鸟，我父亲用树枝和绳子做了一张弓。
- stem 船首　- stern 船尾　- bow tie 领结
- 句中 hunt for 的意思是"捕猎，猎取"；除此之外，它还有"搜求，寻找"的含义。

> ↪ hunt (P. 177)

0101 bow [baʊ] v 鞠躬，致敬

The waiter in the bar refused to bow and scrape to every customer.
酒吧里那个服务生不愿奉承每个顾客。
- bow your head 低着头　- ... bow and scrape to sb. ……奉承某人

0102 bowling [ˈboʊlɪŋ] n 保龄球

He was invited by Lily to join her bowling club.
莉莉邀他加入她的保龄球俱乐部。

> 语法重点
> 例句用的是一般过去时的被动语态，其结构是"主语 + was / were + done"。

0103 brain [breɪn] n 头脑，大脑

Being in love with the girl addled the actor's brain.
爱上那个女孩使那个演员神魂颠倒。
- on the brain 念念不忘
- doing sth. addles one's brain 做某事使某人神魂颠倒

> 语法重点
> addle 的意思是"使腐坏，使混乱"，是及物动词。

0104 branch [bræntʃ] n 树枝，分支，分部

My mother made a slingshot from the branch of the tree and I liked to play with it.
妈妈用树枝做了一个弹弓，我很喜欢玩。
- headquarters 总部　- branch line 支线

> 语法重点
> branch 的复数形式是 branches，英语中以 ch 结尾的名词变复数时，一般是在其后加上 es。

0105 brand [brænd] n 品牌，商标

What is your favorite brand of wines?
你最喜欢哪种牌子的酒？
- logo 标志　- brand mark 商标

> 语法重点
> what is one's favorite 后面一般接名词单数，跟 is 相对应。

0106 brick [brɪk] n 砖头

The ballroom was built by those brick layers.
这个舞厅是由那些砌砖匠建造的。
- golden brick 金砖　- sth. be built by... 某物是由……建造

> 语法重点
> by 后面接表示人的名词或代词，表示 build 这个动作是由这个人发出的。

0107 brief [briːf] **a** 简短的，短暂的，短期的
It's my honor to make a brief introduction of the arrangement of the journey.
我荣幸地向你们简单介绍一下这次旅行的安排。
◎ prolonged 持续很久的   ◎ it's my honor to... 我很荣幸……

◎ arrangement (P. 125)

0108 broad [brɔːd] **a** 宽阔的，辽阔的
She won others' respect by her broad knowledge in music.
她因在音乐方面的渊博知识赢得了他人的尊重。
◎ expansive 广阔的   ◎ narrow 狭窄的
◎ sb. wins other's respect by... 因为……赢得他人的尊重

0109 broadcast ['brɔːdkæst] **n** 广播，广播节目
It's no use listening to the English broadcast every morning.
每天早上都听英文广播没什么用。
◎ live broadcast 现场广播   ◎ it's no use doing... 做……没有用

> **语法重点**
> 在名词短语中，修饰语为名词时，通常放在被修饰词的前面，如例句中 English 要放在 broadcast 的前面。

0110 brunch [brʌntʃ] **n** 早午餐
What do the visitors have for their brunch?
那些游客早午餐吃什么？
◎ brunch 是混合词，是 breakfast 和 lunch 混合而成。

0111 brush [brʌʃ] **v** 刷子，擦
No matter what you eat, brushing your teeth is the best way to fight cavities.
不管你吃什么，吃饭后刷牙都是抵抗蛀牙的最佳方式。
◎ rub 擦   ◎ brush off 刷掉

> **语法重点**
> no matter what 不能用来引导主语从句和宾语从句。

0112 bun [bʌn] **n** 小圆面包，小圆糕点
The buns would have been cooked well if I didn't go shopping.
如果我没有去逛街的话，小圆面包都已经做好了。
◎ have a bun in the oven 怀孕，身怀六甲

0113 bundle ['bʌndl] **n** 一束，包
I took a bundle of snacks to the park.
我带了一包零食去公园。

◎ snack (P. 224)

0114 burn [bɜːrn] **v** 燃烧，烧着
The trees were being burnt when they rushed out of the forest.
当他们从森林跑出时，那些树已经烧着了。
◎ blaze 燃烧   ◎ extinguish 熄灭   ◎ burn the midnight oil 熬夜

> **语法重点**
> burn 是不规则动词，其过去式、过去分词有两种，分别是 burn-burned-burned，burn-burnt-burnt。

brief ~ calm

0115 burst [bɜːrst] v 爆发
We all burst out laughing after hearing her joke.
听了她的笑话之后，我们都大笑起来。
🔁 blast 爆炸 🔁 burst into 闯入，突然发作

语法重点
burst out 后面一般放动名词。

0116 business [ˈbɪznəs] n 生意，商业，事务
He declined her invitation to the party because it conflicted with his business.
他谢绝了她的邀请，因为派对与他的生意冲突了。
🔁 trade 生意 🔁 do business 做生意

0117 button [ˈbʌtn] n 纽扣，按钮
No one is allowed to press that red button except the photographer.
除了摄影师以外，任何人都不能碰那个红色按钮。
🔁 no one is allowed to... except... 除了……任何人都不能……

语法重点
句中用被动语态可以加强语气。
➡ photographer (P. 203)

0118 cabbage [ˈkæbɪdʒ] n 甘蓝菜，卷心菜
The cabbage soup the woman made was tasty.
这个女人煮的白菜汤味道很好。

语法重点
made 是 make 的过去式。

0119 cable [ˈkeɪbl] n 缆线，电缆
The guide said the cable tunnel was destroyed by the earthquake.
导游说电缆隧道被这次地震破坏了。
🔁 telephone cable 电话电缆 🔁 be destroyed by... 被……破坏了

语法重点
例句用的是被动语态，因为动作的执行者不是人，而是一种没有生命的事物。
➡ destroy (P. 283)

0120 café [kæˈfeɪ] n 咖啡厅
Is that why the party was held in the café?
那就是派对在这家咖啡馆举行的原因吗？
🔁 coffeehouse 咖啡馆 🔁 an Internet café 可上网的咖啡厅

语法重点
当不知道或者是没有必要表达出动作的执行者时，通常用被动语态的结构。

0121 cafeteria [ˌkæfəˈtɪriə] n 自助餐厅
He is a frequent visitor to this cafeteria.
他是这家自助餐厅的熟客。
🔁 diner 餐馆 🔁 be a frequent visitor to... 是……的熟客

0122 calendar [ˈkælɪndər] n 日历，历法
I take it for granted the calendar on the wall of the park was taken down by my son.
我还以为公园墙上的日历是被我儿子取下来的。

语法重点
介词 by 表示"被，通过"，通常用于被动语态中，后跟动作的执行者或施加者。
➡ grant (P. 574)

0123 calm [kɑːm] a 平静的，冷静的 v (使)平静
Will you please calm down and have a cup of coffee?
请你冷静下来喝杯咖啡，好吗？
🔁 peaceful 平静的 🔁 excited 激动的 🔁 keep calm 保持安静

135

怪物讲师教学团队的 7 000 "单词" + "语法"

0124 **cancel** ['kænsl] v 取消，作废

Your decision to cancel the concert will disappoint your fans.
你取消这场音乐会的决定，会使你的歌迷失望。
- repeal 取消，废除   - cancel out 取消
- sth. will disappoint sb. 某事会让某人失望

0125 **cancer** ['kænsər] n 癌症，肿瘤

It is odd that the visitor died of cancer.
很奇怪，那个游客死于癌症。
- tumor 肿瘤   - cancer cell 癌细胞

> **语法重点**
> die of 后面接用来解释死亡原因的名词。
> ➔ odd (P. 330)

0126 **candle** ['kændl] n 蜡烛

It's clear that the candle on the stage will soon burn out.
很明显，舞台上那根蜡烛很快就会烧完。
- rush candle 微光   - it's clear that... 很明显……

> **语法重点**
> burn out 主要指燃料"耗尽"，也可以形容人"筋疲力尽"。

0127 **captain** ['kæptɪn] n 船长，舰长

Visitors may not be allowed to go backstage without the captain's permission.
没有船长的允许，游客们不许擅自进入后台。
- sailor 船员   - sb. may not be allowed... without... 没有……某人不许……

> **语法重点**
> 本句为了表达委婉或礼貌，不便提出动作的执行者，从而采用被动语态。

0128 **carpet** ['kɑːrpɪt] n 地毯

It looks that the floor of the auditorium was covered with carpet.
礼堂的地板上好像铺着地毯。
- rug 地毯   - red carpet 红地毯   - it looks that... 好像……

> **语法重点**
> 有些动词短语习惯用被动语态来表达，如 be born, be surrounded by.

0129 **carrot** ['kærət] n 红萝卜

There are enough carrots for the guests.
这边有足够的红萝卜给客人们吃。

> **语法重点**
> be 动词用 is 或 are 要根据 enough 后面的名词而定。

0130 **cart** [kɑːrt] n 手推车，马车

I made myself up as a cart driver.
我把自己化装成一个马车夫。
- put the cart before the horse 本末倒置，舍本逐末

> **语法重点**
> make up 除了有"化妆"的意思外，还可以表示"编造，弥补"。

0131 **cartoon** [kɑːrˈtuːn] n 卡通，漫画

The girl is like a cartoon character after getting dressed.
换上衣服后，那个女孩就像是一个卡通人物。
- title cartoon 动画字幕

0132 **cash** [kæʃ] n 现金
I was robbed of cash when I was walking along the river bank.
我在河边散步时现金被抢走了。
- currency 货币   - cash flow 资金流动

> 语法重点
> be robbed of 后面接 chance, purse, money 等名词。

0133 **cassette** [kə'set] n 卡式磁带
Before dancing, he inserted a cassette into the machine.
跳舞前，他把一盒录影带放入了机器。

↪ insert (P. 495)

0134 **castle** ['kæsl] n 城堡
The wall of the castle in the park requires repairing.
公园里那个城堡的墙需要修理。
- cloud castle 不切实际的计划   - sth. requires doing... 某物需要被……

0135 **cave** [keɪv] n 洞穴，山洞
The cave was surrounded by visitors all over the world.
山洞被来自全世界各地的游客包围了。
- rock cave 岩洞   - be surrounded by... 被……包围了

0136 **ceiling** ['siːlɪŋ] n 天花板
It's nothing to drink with boys, but her father hit the ceiling.
与男孩们喝酒没什么大不了，但这让她父亲勃然大怒。
- floor 地板   - hit the ceiling 勃然大怒

> 语法重点
> it's nothing to...（没有什么……）后面接动词原形。

0137 **cell** [sel] n 细胞
Actually, reasonable potation won't hurt nerve cell.
其实，适量饮酒不会对神经细胞造成伤害。

↪ reasonable (P. 346)

0138 **central** ['sentrəl] a 中央的，核心的
Let me tell you why the visitor was led into the central control room.
我来告诉你为什么那个游客会被带到中央控制室。
- chief 主要的   - central heating 中央暖气系统

0139 **century** ['sentʃəri] n 世纪，百年 a 百年的
Can you not understand, the game was invented in last century?
难道你不明白吗，这个游戏在上个世纪就发明出来了？
- century plant 龙舌兰

> 语法重点
> can you not understand 跟后面的句子要用逗号隔开。

0140 **cereal** ['sɪrɪəl] n 谷类作物
What about having a cup of cereal during the break?
休息的时候喝点麦片粥怎么样？
- grain 谷物   - cereal crop 粮食作物

> 语法重点
> what about 常在口语中出现，用于征求对方的意见。

0141 **chalk** [tʃɔːk] n 粉笔
The twins in the film are chalk and cheese.
这对双胞胎在电影中截然不同。
同 pastille 粉笔　　片 ... be chalk and cheese ……截然不同

↪ twin (P. 378)

0142 **change** [tʃeɪndʒ] v 改变
Every traveler has to change the flight, including you and me.
每个游客都得改航班，包括你和我。
同 alter 改变　　反 fix 固定　　片 change for the better 改善

0143 **character** ['kærəktər] n 个性，品质，人物
The actress is not strong enough in character and often depends on her boyfriend.
那个女演员在个性方面还不够坚强，总是依赖自己的男朋友。
同 personality 个性，品格　　片 main character 主要人物

语法重点
depend on 后面也可以接 sb. to do sth. 表示"指望某人去做某事"。

0144 **charge** [tʃɑːrdʒ] v 收费，控诉 n 责任
We will be charged if we keep our car parking outside the cinema when we watch the film.
如果我们去看电影，并把车停到电影院外面的话，我们要付费的。
同 accuse 控告　　片 free of charge 免费

语法重点
charge 是及物动词，可用于被动语态。

0145 **cheap** [tʃiːp] a 便宜的，廉价的
If you play golf, no wearing the cheap clothes.
去打高尔夫球时，别穿便宜的衣服。
同 inexpensive 便宜的　　反 expensive 昂贵的

语法重点
no doing 常用于简短的口语，如 no spitting（不要吐痰）。

0146 **cheat** [tʃiːt] v 欺骗
The travelers were cheated out of one hundred dollars by that cheater.
游客们被那个骗子骗了一百美元。
同 deceive 欺骗　　片 cheat on 对……不忠　　片 be cheated out of... 被骗了……

0147 **chemical** ['kemɪkl] a 化学的
Not only the actress but also the actor knows what a chemical change is.
那个女演员和那个男演员都知道化学变化。
片 not only... but also... do sth. 不但……而且……做某事

语法重点
not only... but also... 连接两个主语时，动词要跟其较近的那个保持一致。

0148 **chess** [tʃes] n 棋，国际象棋
There is little chance of my winning the chess game.
我赢棋的希望极小。
片 chess game 象棋比赛

语法重点
there is little chance of 后面通常接名词或者动名词。

↪ win (P. 114)

138

0149 childish [ˈtʃaɪldɪʃ] **a** 孩子气的，幼稚的
These adults danced around with childish delight.
这些大人像孩子一样欢乐地围在一起跳舞。
 ≈ babyish 幼稚的   ≠ adult 成年的，成熟的

0150 childlike [ˈtʃaɪldlaɪk] **a** 纯真的，孩子般的，单纯的
Although she is childlike, she is in charge of the whole ping pong team.
虽然她很单纯，但她现在已经负责管理整个乒乓球队了。
 ≈ childly 孩子似的   ≠ mature 成熟的   ⊕ be in charge of... 掌管……

0151 chin [tʃɪn] **n** 下巴，颌
She had her chin hurt in the PE class.
她在上体育课时，把下巴弄伤了。
 ≈ jaw 下巴   ⊕ double chin 双下巴

> 语法重点
> PE 是 physical education 的缩写。

0152 chocolate [ˈtʃɑːklət] **n** 巧克力
The little child began to cry when she took the chocolate and the toy away.
当她把巧克力和玩具拿走时，那个小孩子大哭起来。

> 语法重点
> the chocolate and the toy 也可以放在 away 后面。
> ↻ cry (P. 026)

0153 choice [tʃɔɪs] **n** 选择，挑选
I will take this song for choice.
我要选这首歌。
 ≈ option 选择   ⊕ by choice 出于自己的选择

0154 choose [tʃuːz] **v** 选择，决定
He was really stoked that they chose him for the team.
他们选他加入这个队伍，他兴奋极了。
 ≈ decide 决定   ⊕ pick and choose 挑挑拣拣

> 语法重点
> choose 是不规则动词，其过去式、过去分词分别是 chose, chosen。

0155 chopstick [ˈtʃɑːpstɪk] **n** 筷子
Their children are playing with the chopsticks which are a token of their love.
他们的孩子正在玩那些代表着他们爱情的筷子。
 ⊕ be a token of... 是……的象征

> 语法重点
> be a token of 是固定搭配，token 要用单数。

0156 circle [ˈsɜːrkl] **n** 圆圈
The foreign visitor admitted drawing a circle on the statue.
外国游客承认自己在雕像上画了一个圆圈。
 ≈ round 圆   ⊕ circle around 围绕
 ⊕ sb. admits doing sth. 某人承认做某事

> 语法重点
> 当宾语是动名词时，一般用主动语态。例句中的 drawing a circle 就是动名词，所以只能用主动语态。
> ↻ statue (P. 365)

0157 **citizen** ['sɪtɪzn] n 公民，市民

It is the duty of each and every citizen to protect the facilities of the park.
每个公民都有责任保护公园里的设施。
● senior citizen 老年人　● it is the duty of... to do sth. 做某事是……的责任

语法重点
each and every 的意思是"每个"，语气较强。
⊃ facility (P. 440)

0158 **claim** [kleɪm] v 要求，请求

I could claim to be an expert after coming back from the traveling.
旅游回来后，我可以说自己是专家了。
● demand 要求，请求　● claim for compensation 索赔
● I could claim to... 我可以声称……

0159 **clap** [klæp] v 鼓掌，拍手，轻拍

The audience clapped hands to welcome him coming back.
观众们鼓掌欢迎他回来。
● applaud 拍手喝彩，鼓掌　● clap eyes on 看见

语法重点
注意 clap 的过去式与过去分词都是重复词尾 p 再加 ed。

0160 **classic** ['klæsɪk] a 古典的，传统的，最优秀的

She likes music, except the classic one.
她喜欢音乐，但古典音乐除外。
● traditional 传统的　● modern 现代的

语法重点
except 的意思为"除……之外"，被除去的东西不包含在整体内。

0161 **claw** [klɔː] n 爪子

I am listening to music and wondering if the eagle caught the rabbit with its claws.
我边听音乐边想着老鹰是否用爪子抓住了兔子。
● in one's claws 在某人的魔掌下　● be wondering if... 想知道……

语法重点
claw 是可数名词，其复数形式是在后面直接加 s。

0162 **clay** [kleɪ] n 黏土，泥土

My son and daughter like making houses of sticks and clay.
我儿子和女儿喜欢用树枝和黏土盖房子玩。

语法重点
sb. likes making sth. of 后面接表示原材料的名词。

0163 **cleaner** ['kliːnər] n 清洁工，清洁工具

The path to the garden has been cleaned by the cleaner.
通往花园的小路已经被清洁工人打扫干净了。
● detergent 清洁剂　● be cleaned by... 被……打扫干净了

0164 **clerk** [klɜːrk] n 店员，办事员

I could not hide my amusement at the way the clerk was dancing.
看见那个职员跳舞的姿势，我忍不住笑出来。
● staff 职员　● sales clerk 售货员
● I could not hide my amusement at... ……让我忍不住笑出来

0165 clever ['klevər] a 聪明的，灵巧的

The compere always boasts about how clever her son is.
那个主持人总是吹嘘她的儿子是多么聪明。
- smart 聪明的　　- stupid 愚蠢的　　- be too clever by half 自作聪明
- clever 主要用来形容人或动物的脑子灵活，理解事物快。

0166 climate ['klaɪmət] n 气候

He had deliberately picked a city with a tropical climate to travel to.
他特意选了一个热带气候的城市去旅游。
- weather 天气，气象　　- climate change 气候变化
- climate 指一般比较长的时间，如一季的天气状况。weather 指某特定地区在一定时间内的气象情况。

0167 closet ['klɑːzət] n 衣橱

The accordion is stored in the hall closet.
手风琴一直搁在门厅的壁橱里。
- cupboard 橱柜　　- be stored in... 被储存在……

> 语法重点
> store 当名词讲是"商店"，当动词讲是"储存"。

0168 cloth [klɒːθ] n 布料，织物

I am tied up with the work to make cloth when I am free.
空闲的时候我总是忙于织布。
- cut one's coat according to one's cloth 量入为出

0169 clothe [kloʊð] v 帮……穿衣，穿上

All of the actors are always well clothed.
所有的演员都穿着考究。
- dress 给……穿衣　　- unclothe 脱去衣服　　- be clothed in... 穿着……

> 语法重点
> clothe 虽然在句中为被动形式，但和主语实际上表达的是一种主动的关系。

0170 clothes [kloʊðz] n 衣服，服装

I heard the clothes store was relocated to the center of the city.
我听说那家服装店搬迁到了那个城市的中心。
- garment 衣服，服装　　- be relocated to... 搬到……

center (P. 021)

0171 clothing ['kloʊðɪŋ] n 衣服，覆盖物

They took enough food and clothing for the traveling.
他们为这次旅游带了充足的食物和衣服。
- covering 覆盖物　　- a wolf in sheep's clothing 披着羊皮的狼，貌善心恶的人

> 语法重点
> 例句是个陈述句，其内容只是陈述事实，并无其他的感情色彩。

0172 cloudy ['klaʊdi] a 多云的，阴天的

The forecast says it will be cloudy next week, so we can travel as planned.
天气预报说下周是多云的天气，所以我们可以按计划旅游了。
- dark 昏暗的　　- clear 晴朗的

> 语法重点
> say 的主语除了人之外，也可以是物。

0173 **clown** [klaʊn] n 小丑，丑角
The star clown on the stage was considered as a master of witty banter.
舞台上那个小丑被认为是个逗乐子的专家。
- sb. / sth. be considered as a / an... 某人 / 某物被认为是……

0174 **club** [klʌb] n 俱乐部
Stop going to the new club in the town anymore.
不要再去镇上那家新开的俱乐部了。

语法重点
例句是祈使句，通常表示说话人向对方提出命令，语气较为强烈。
- town (P. 106)

0175 **coach** [koʊtʃ] n 教练
He has made great progress under the guidance of his coach.
在教练的指导下，他得到很大的进步。
- instructor 教练　- trainee 受训者
- sb. do sth. under the guidance of... 某人在……的指导下做某事

0176 **coal** [koʊl] n 煤炭，煤块
Do add some coal into the boiler.
一定要往锅炉里加一些煤。
- charcoal 炭　- coal mine 煤矿

语法重点
祈使句的动词之前加上助动词 do，表示强调，使语气更加强烈。

0177 **cock** [kɑːk] n 公鸡
Let us listen to her cock-and-bull story.
我们来听听她那荒诞的故事。

语法重点
使役动词 let 引导的句子结构通常为 let + 宾语 + 动词原形 + 其他成分，含有祈使意味。
- listen (P. 060)

0178 **cockroach / roach** [ˈkɑːkroʊtʃ] / [roʊtʃ] n 蟑螂
There's a big cockroach crawling on the floor of the museum!
有一只大蟑螂在博物馆的地板上爬！

0179 **coin** [kɔɪn] n 硬币，金钱
We flipped a coin to decide who would drink the wine.
我们用掷硬币的方法决定谁喝酒。
- piece 硬币　- flip a coin 抛钱币（决定）

语法重点
flip 的意思是"投，掷"，其过去式、过去分词都是重复词尾 p 再加 ed。

0180 **collect** [kəˈlekt] v 收集，取
The magnificent sights collect a large crowd of people.
壮丽的景色引来了一大群人。
- gather 收集　- scatter 分散，散开

语法重点
a large crowd of 后面可以接人，也可以接物。

0181 **colorful** [ˈkʌlərfl] a 彩色的，华美的，有趣的
I am engaged in collecting colorful candy papers.
我正在忙着收集五颜六色的糖果纸。
- colorless 无色的　- be engaged in... 忙于……

0182 comb [koʊm] n 梳子 v 梳理
Be still when I comb your hair before performance.
演出前我帮你梳头时，请不要动。
- 同 tease 梳理
- 反 clutter 使凌乱
- 搭 wooden comb 木梳

语法重点
comb 在句中作及物动词使用。

0183 comfortable ['kʌmftəbl] a 舒服的，充裕的
Collect yourself, since it's comfortable to sit on the grass.
放松一下，因为坐在草地上很舒服。
- 同 pleasant 舒适的
- 反 uncomfortable 不舒服的

语法重点
collect 表示"收集"的意思，但 collect oneself 意思为"镇定下来"，而不是"收集自己"。

0184 company ['kʌmpəni] n 公司
Why in God's name, the employees are dancing in the company.
天啊，员工们都在公司里跳舞。
- 同 firm 公司
- 搭 company name 公司名称

语法重点
why in God's name 中的 why 也可以替换为 what 或 how。

0185 compare [kəm'per] v 比较，对比
The young guide compares himself to Shakespeare, which annoys us.
那个年轻的导游把自己比作莎士比亚，这让我们感到很厌烦。
- 搭 beyond compare 非常好，无与伦比
- 搭 sb. compares... to... 某人把……比作……

0186 complain [kəm'pleɪn] v 抱怨，控诉，诉说
He is complaining about the latest movie.
他在抱怨最新的电影。
- 搭 complain of 抱怨，抗议
- 搭 sb. complain about... 某人抱怨……

语法重点
complain 也可和介词 of 连用，构成 complain of, 意思是"抱怨，抗议"。

0187 complete [kəm'pliːt] a 完整的 v 完成
Given that he goes traveling, we won't require him to complete the task today.
考虑到他去旅游了，我们不要求他今天完成工作了。
- 搭 complete the task 完成任务

语法重点
given 在句中可以引导从句来表明某种原因，而且从句一般放在主句之前。

0188 computer [kəm'pjuːtər] n 计算机
I bought a portable computer so that I can carry it during traveling.
我买了一台可携式计算机，以便在旅游时携带。
- 同 laptop 笔记本计算机
- 搭 computer software 计算机软件

语法重点
so that 的意思是"为了，以便"，引导目的状语从句。

0189 confirm [kən'fɜːrm] v 确认，批准，确定
What should I do if he calls to confirm the appointment?
如果他打电话来确认约会时间怎么办？
- 同 verify 证实
- 反 deny 否认，否定
- 搭 confirm sb. in... 使某人更坚定……

语法重点
confirm 是及物动词。
→ appointment (P. 396)

0190 **conflict** [ˈkɑːnflɪkt] / [ˈkɒnflɪkt] n / v 冲突，战斗

Never try to end the conflict between you and the athletes by fighting.
绝对不要试图靠打架来解决你和运动员们之间的冲突。

同 in conflict 有矛盾

> 语法重点
> 否定祈使句可用 never 来引导，强调不要再做某事。

0191 **Confucius** [kənˈfjuːʃəs] n 孔子

I arranged for them to visit the Confucius Temple tomorrow.
我已安排他们明天游孔子庙。

⊃ temple (P. 234)

0192 **congratulation** [kənˌɡrætʃuˈleɪʃn] n 恭喜，祝贺

The boy accepted his teammates' congratulations happily.
那个男孩高兴地接受了队友们的祝贺。

同 felicitation 祝贺，庆贺   同 congratulation on sth. 对……祝贺

> 语法重点
> 词尾 -mate 加在一些名词的后面，构成一个新的单词，其含义是"同伴"。

0193 **consider** [kənˈsɪdər] v 考虑，思考

She is very happy when being told that she was considered the most successful actress.
听说自己被评为最成功的女演员，她非常高兴。

同 all things considered 从全面考虑，总而言之

0194 **contact** [ˈkɑːntækt] n 联络，接触

Wish you have a good journey and keep in contact with me.
希望你旅途愉快，并且与我保持联系。

同 connect 联系   反 isolation 孤立

同 ... keep in contact with sb. ……与某人保持联系

⊃ keep (P. 054)

0195 **contain** [kənˈteɪn] v 包含，容纳

Hearing that news that they can go traveling, she couldn't contain herself for joy.
听到他们可以去旅游的消息，她高兴得不能自已。

同 comprise 包含   反 reject 排斥

0196 **control** [kənˈtroʊl] v / n 控制，操作

The man shows great self-control when others are teasing him.
那个人在别人开他玩笑时表现出极大的自制。

同 command 控制   同 control system 控制系统

> 语法重点
> control 是含义广泛的常用词，指对人或物施以约束或控制的力量。

0197 **controller** [kənˈtroʊlər] n 管理人，控制者，控制器

For my part, the controller needs to have a travel.
依我看来，总监需要去旅游。

同 inversor 控制器   同 for my part, ... 在我看来，……

conflict ~ cough

0198 convenient [kən'viːniənt] **a** 方便的，便利的
I want to know when it is convenient for us to have a date.
我想知道什么时候我们方便约会。
- handy 方便的 - inconvenient 不方便的 - convenient food 方便食品

> **语法重点**
> to have a date 是不定式短语，表示目的。

0199 conversation [ˌkɑːnvər'seɪʃn] **n** 会话，谈话，交谈
For your information, I had a successful conversation with the visitor.
你要知道，我和那个访客成功交谈了一次。
- talk 谈话 - conversation room 会谈室

> **语法重点**
> have a conversation 表示"交谈"，后面常接介词短语 with sb.，表示谈话的对象。
> ⊃ successful (P. 230)

0200 cooker ['kʊkər] **n** 烹调器具
The cooker I bought yesterday doesn't work, so let's go out for a picnic.
我昨天买的那个炉具不能用了，所以我们去野餐吧。
- gas cooker 煤气炉 - sth. doesn't work 某物坏了
- 注意 cooker 的意思是"炉具"，cook 的意思是"厨师"。

0201 copy / xerox ['kɑːpi] / ['zɪrɑːks] **v** 影印，复制，抄写
The painting she copied can pass for an authentic one.
她临摹的画足以乱真。
- duplicate 复制 - copy down 抄下来，记下来
- sb. / sth. can pass for... 某人 / 某物可以冒充……

> **语法重点**
> one 代指 painting。

0202 corner ['kɔːrnər] **n** 角落，转角
It's high time that they should fetch the ball in the corner.
他们是时候去捡回角落里的那个球了。
- street corner 街角 - it's high time... 是时候……

> **语法重点**
> it's high time 后面的句子常用虚拟语气，动词常用 should + 动词原形。

0203 costly ['kɔːstli] **a** 价格高的，昂贵的
I'm sick and tired of the singer's buying costly handbags.
我受不了那个歌手，她总是买价格昂贵的包包。
- expensive 昂贵的 - cheap 便宜的

> **语法重点**
> I'm sick and tired of 后面接名词或者动名词。

0204 cotton ['kɑːtn] **n** 棉花
It's your turn to put wads of cotton in your ears.
该你把小块棉花塞在耳朵里了。
- cotton cloth 棉布 - it's sb.'s turn... 该某人……

> **语法重点**
> turn 在句中作名词，意思是"（轮到的）机会"。

0205 cough [kɔːf] **n** 咳嗽
The director gave a little cough to announce her presence.
导演轻轻咳了一下，示意她已到场。
- tussis 咳嗽 - cough syrup 止咳糖浆

> **语法重点**
> cough 除了当名词使用，还可以当动词使用。
> ⊃ presence (P. 208)

145

0206 countryside [ˈkʌntrɪsaɪd] n. 乡下

Accompany your grandpa in the countryside when you are free lest he should feel lonely.
你有空时去乡下陪你爷爷吧，以免他觉得孤独。
🔄 rural area 农村   ⚡ city 城市

语法重点
lest 为连词，它引导的句子里的动词一般用"should + 动词原形"。

0207 county [ˈkaʊnti] n. 郡，县

Are you sure the super star's hometown is in a county?
你确定那位巨星的家乡在一个小县城里吗？
📝 hometown 的意思是"故乡"，homeland 的意思为"祖国"，和 motherland 同义。

⤷ hometown (P. 308)

0208 couple [ˈkʌpl] n. 夫妇

The couple at a neighboring table spoke in undertones.
邻桌的夫妇在低声交谈。
📖 ... speak in undertones ……低声交谈

0209 courage [ˈkɜːrɪdʒ] n. 勇气，胆量

I don't have the courage to talk about traveling with them.
我没有勇气和他们谈论一起旅游的事。
🔄 bravery 勇气，勇敢   ⚡ timidity 胆怯，胆小

语法重点
have the courage 后面通常接动词不定式。

0210 court [kɔːrt] n. 法院

As I see it, the best way to solve the dispute between you and the company is to take into court.
在我看来，解决你和那家公司之间问题的最好办法就是诉诸法律。
🔄 tribunal 法庭   📖 in court 在法庭上   📖 as I see it, ... 在我看来，……

0211 cousin [ˈkʌzn] n. 堂（表）兄弟姐妹

Would you mind if I introduce my cousin to you and invite you to my house tonight?
我把堂兄介绍给你，并邀请你今晚来我家，你介意吗？

语法重点
would you mind if 后面的条件句通常用一般现在时。

0212 crab [kræb] n. 螃蟹

The little boy takes the solider crab as his pet.
小男孩把这只寄居蟹当成是他的宠物。
📖 a case of crabs 失败

0213 crane [kreɪn] n. 鹤，起重机

The boy is climbing up the crane while other children are running after him.
其他孩子追那个小男孩的时候，他正在爬起重机。
🔄 derrick 起重机   📖 ... run after sb. ……追某人

语法重点
while 可连接两个同时进行的动作。
⤷ after (P. 004)

0214 crayon ['kreɪən] n 蜡笔，蜡笔画
The beautiful picture was drawn by my nephew with crayon.
这张美丽的画是我侄子用蜡笔画的。
- pastels 蜡笔　　- wax crayon 蜡笔　　- be drawn by... 由……画的

语法重点
介词 with 通常用来表示某种工具。

0215 crazy ['kreɪzi] a 疯狂的，荒唐的
It is crazy of him to go skating on the thin ice.
到这么薄的冰上溜冰，他真是疯了。
- mad 疯狂的　　- go crazy 发疯，疯狂

语法重点
在冰面上溜冰，所以用介词 on。

0216 cream [kri:m] n 奶油，乳酪，乳霜
The dresser spread some cold cream on the actor's face.
化妆师在那个演员的脸上涂了一些乳霜。

语法重点
cream 是不可数名词。
⊃ spread (P. 227)

0217 create [kri'eɪt] v 创造，造成
The actress's getting married again will create a scandal.
那个女演员再婚这件事情将引发丑闻。
- cause 引起　　- destroy 毁灭　　- create a role 创造角色

0218 crime [kraɪm] n 罪，罪行，犯罪
Could you please explain why the visitor committed a crime?
你能解释一下那个游客犯罪的原因吗？
- sin 罪　　- war crime 战争罪

语法重点
commit a crime 是固定搭配，意思是"犯罪"。

0219 crisis ['kraɪsɪs] n 危机，危急关头
Do you know if the man is having a mid-life crisis?
你知道那个男人是否正在经历中年危机吗？
- emergency 紧急情况　　- economic crisis 经济危机

语法重点
mid-life crisis 意思是"中年危机"，类似表达还有 financial crisis（金融危机）。

0220 crop [krɑ:p] n 农作物，收成
It's no good trying to harvest the crops, since they were trampled to death by the visitors.
没办法收获谷物了，因为游客把它们都踩死了。
- harvest 收成，收获；收割

语法重点
it's no good trying to 后面接动词原形。
⊃ trample (P. 651)

0221 cross [krɔ:s] n 十字形
When she appeared on the stage she was nervous by crossing her legs.
登台表演时，她双腿交叉，心情很紧张。
- cross off 删除　　- ... by crossing one's legs 双腿交叉……

0222 crow [kroʊ] **n** 乌鸦 **v** 啼叫，欢叫

The jewelry and ornaments the visitors want to buy are white crows.
游客们想买的珠宝饰品都是珍品。

● as the crow flies 笔直地
● 注意 white crow 不要翻译成"白色的乌鸦"。

↪ ornament (P. 605)

0223 crowd [kraʊd] **n** 人群，群众

The famous singer was engulfed by the waiting crowd.
那个著名的歌星被守候着的人群团团围住。

● throng 人群，群众 ● be engulfed by... 被……围住

0224 cruel [ˈkruːəl] **a** 残酷的，残忍的

I think it is cruel to confine the bird in a cage.
我认为把鸟关在笼子里太残忍了。

● brutal 残酷的 ● humane 仁慈的，人道的

语法重点
cruel 是形容词，其比较级和最高级分别是 crueller，cruellest。

0225 culture [ˈkʌltʃər] **n** 文化

The belief to respect the old is ingrained in our culture.
尊重老人这个理念在我们的文化中根深蒂固。

● civilization 文明 ● be ingrained in... 在……根深蒂固

语法重点
the old 的意思是"老人"。"the + 形容词"在英语中表示某一类人。
↪ belief (P. 130)

0226 cure [kjʊr] **v** 治疗

All of the experts in the hospital had no idea on how to cure the senator's disease.
医院里所有的专家对那个参议员的病都毫无办法。

● heal 治愈 ● kill or cure 孤注一掷

0227 curious [ˈkjʊriəs] **a** 好奇的，奇特的

The children are taking a curious glance at my new computer.
孩子们用好奇的眼光打量着我新买的计算机。

● odd 奇怪的，古怪的 ● incurious 无好奇心的

语法重点
例句中 glance 是名词，glance 也可以当动词，构成短语 glance at，意思是"浏览，扫视"，表示快速或者不经意地看。

0228 curtain / drape [ˈkɜːrtn] / [dreɪp] **n** 窗帘

He traveled to America behind the curtain.
他偷偷地去美国旅游了。

● drape 窗帘 ● take the curtain 谢幕 ● behind the curtain 秘密地

0229 custom [ˈkʌstəm] **n** 习俗，习惯，惯例

I think it would be better if you understand the custom there.
我认为如果你了解那里的风俗会更好。

● tradition 惯例 ● local custom 当地风俗
● custom 通常指经过一段时期在某国、某地区或一个社会中形成的传统行为方式。

crow ~ debate

0230 customer ['kʌstəmər] **n** 客户，主顾
They say the new law is enacted on behalf of the customers and visitors.
他们说这项新法律的制定代表了顾客们和游客们的利益。
Ⓢ client 顾客　Ⓢ customer service 客户服务

> 语法重点
> on behalf of 后面通常接人。

0231 daily ['deɪli] **a** 每天的，日常的
She has been much healthier since she began to do morning exercises.
自从开始每天做早操以来，她感觉身体好多了。
Ⓢ everyday 日常的　Ⓢ daily life 日常生活

0232 damage ['dæmɪdʒ] **v** 损坏，毁坏
I am sure drinking has damaged your health.
我确定饮酒已经损害了你的健康。
Ⓢ destroy 毁坏　Ⓢ sth. damages one's health 某事损害某人的健康

0233 dangerous ['deɪndʒərəs] **a** 危险的，不安全的
Generally speaking, my brother is fond of some dangerous sports.
一般来说，我哥哥喜欢一些危险的运动。
Ⓢ unsafe 不安全的　Ⓐ safe 安全的

> 语法重点
> generally speaking（一般来说）通常要与后面的句子用逗号分开。
> ⇨ fond (P. 297)

0234 data ['deɪtə] **n** 资料
Now the deleted data about the travelers is being recovered by the technicians.
现在那些被删除的游客资料正在由技术人员进行还原。
Ⓢ task data 任务资料　Ⓢ be recovered by... 由……还原

> 语法重点
> 例句用的是现在进行时的被动语态，其结构为 be 动词 + being + 动词过去分词，表示正在进行中的被动动作。

0235 dawn [dɔːn] **n** 黎明，开端
The delegation would take the flight which takes off at dawn of tomorrow.
代表团会搭乘明天黎明起飞的航班。
Ⓢ daybreak 黎明　Ⓐ dusk 黄昏　Ⓢ before dawn 黎明之前

0236 deaf [def] **a** 耳聋的
He likes the musician who is totally deaf.
他喜欢那个完全耳聋的音乐家。
Ⓢ dunny 聋的　Ⓢ deaf and dumb 聋哑的　Ⓢ ... be totally deaf ……完全失聪

⇨ musician (P. 193)

0237 debate [dɪ'beɪt] **n** / **v** 辩论，争论
No one expected that the public debate developed into a fistfight.
谁也没有料到公开辩论演变成了一场斗殴。
Ⓢ argue 辩论　Ⓢ under debate 在辩论中

⇨ public (P. 078)

0238 debt [det] n 债务

I could pay off my debt if I win a prize in the lottery.
如果我买彩票中奖的话，我就能还清债务了。
- liability 债务　　- in debt 欠债
- "得奖"也可以用 win an award 来表达。

0239 decision [dɪˈsɪʒn] n 决定，决心，决议

It's definite that her decision will upset a lot of fans.
她的决定肯定会使许多粉丝不开心。
- determination 决定，决心　　- come to a decision 做出决定
- It's definite that... 肯定……

⊃ definite (P. 423)

0240 decorate [ˈdekəreɪt] v 装饰，装修

Did you make any decision on how to decorate the room and where to spend the holiday?
你决定如何装修你的房间和去哪里度假了吗？
- adorn 装饰　　- decorate with 以……装饰

语法重点
make any decision 一般用在否定句和疑问句中。

0241 degree [dɪˈɡriː] n 程度，度数

I will award her a trip to America if she gets the master's degree.
如果她取得硕士学位，我将会奖励她去美国旅游一次。
- I will award sb. sth. 我会奖励某人某物

语法重点
例句中 if 引导真实的条件状语从句，表示一种可以实现的情况。
⊃ master (P. 062)

0242 delay [dɪˈleɪ] v 延迟，耽搁

The traveler wouldn't have to delay his plan if he had followed your instructions.
如果那个游客听你指示的话，你就不必延迟他的计划了。
- detain 耽搁　　- hurry 使匆忙　　- delay time 延迟时间

语法重点
follow one's instruction 意思是"遵循某人的指令"，one 在句中可以根据人称的不同而变换。

0243 delicious [dɪˈlɪʃəs] a 美味的，可口的

He hasn't eaten such delicious food since he began to travel around the world.
自从开始环球旅行，他好久没吃过如此美味的食物了。
- tasty 美味的　　- tasteless 没味道的

语法重点
since 后面接过去的某个时间点，其主句用现在完成时。

0244 deliver [dɪˈlɪvər] v 递送，发表

If I had delivered the gift there on time!
如果我能准时把礼物送到那里就好了！
- send 发送　　- if sb. had done... 要是……就好了

语法重点
这是一个省略了主句的虚拟语气结构，用来表示愿望。

0245 dentist [ˈdentɪst] n 牙医

I can't agree with the dentist more and I would give up drinking at night.
我完全同意牙医的意见，我将会戒掉晚上喝酒的习惯。
- I can't agree... more 我完全同意……

语法重点
can't 有时也用 couldn't 来代替。

0246 deny [dɪˈnaɪ] v 否认，不承认

The young father denies his daughter nothing and always plays with her.
年轻的父亲对女儿百依百顺，总是和她一起玩。
◉ reject 拒绝　◎ confirm 确认　◉ deny sb. nothing 对某人百依百顺

语法重点
denies his daughter nothing
双重否定表示肯定。
⇨ young (P. 117)

0247 department [dɪˈpɑːrtmənt] n 部门，科系，专长

It isn't my department to play the guitar.
弹吉他不是我的专长。
◉ section 部门　◉ Justice Department 司法部
◉ it isn't my department to... ……不是我的专长

0248 depend [dɪˈpend] v 依靠，依赖

The girls can depend on Tom since he is always ready to help others.
女孩们可以依靠汤姆，他总是很乐于助人。
◉ rely 依靠，依赖

0249 depth [depθ] n 深度

We lost our way in the depth of the forest yesterday.
昨天我们在森林深处迷路。
◉ in the depth of 在……的里面　◉ lose one's way in... 在……迷路了

0250 describe [dɪˈskraɪb] v 描写，形容

He is often described as the most handsome actor.
他经常被称为最英俊的演员。
◉ portray 描写　◉ describe with... 用……描述

语法重点
be described as (某人被称为……) 后面通常接名词或名词短语。

0251 desert [ˈdezərt] / [dɪˈzɜːt] n 沙漠 v 抛弃，丢弃

I've no idea if I can get some water in the hot and dry desert.
我不知道我能否在这又热又干的沙漠中得到一些水。
◉ abandon 遗弃　◉ retain 保留

语法重点
desert 还可以作形容词，意思是"荒凉的，不毛的"。

0252 design [dɪˈzaɪn] n / v 设计，计划

When we took photos in the park, the complicated design of the camera was beyond my depth.
我们在公园照相时，相机复杂的结构令我难以理解。
◉ devise 设计　◉ ... be beyond one's depth ……让某人难以理解

语法重点
beyond 是介词，意思是"超出，远于"。
⇨ depth (P. 151)

0253 desire [dɪˈzaɪər] n / v 渴望，向往

There is no reason for you to desire for traveling to the country.
你没有理由渴望去乡下旅游。
◉ aspire 渴望　◉ desire to do... 渴望做……

语法重点
there is no reason to 后面接动词原形。

0254 dessert [dɪˈzɜːrt] n. 餐后点心
Before the waiter moves on dessert we can play cards.
服务员上甜点前，我们可以玩扑克牌。
- dessert wine 甜酒
- sb. moves on sth. 某人端上某物

0255 detect [dɪˈtekt] v. 探测，发觉，察觉
The man was detected in the act of scrawling all over the antique wall.
那人在古墙上乱涂乱画被发现了。
- discover 发觉
- conceal 隐藏，掩盖

> 语法重点
> act 在句中作名词，意思是"行为，动作"。
> ⇨ antique (P. 534)

0256 develop [dɪˈveləp] v. 发展，开发
Any idea what develops healthy bodies? Does it include traveling often?
你知道什么对健康有益吗？包括经常旅游吗？
- exploit 开发
- develop into... 发展成为……

> 语法重点
> any idea 后面可直接接句子，而且这个句子要用陈述语序。

0257 development [dɪˈveləpmənt] n. 发展，生长
There are some inharmonious phenomena in the development of the tourism industry.
旅游业的发展中存在着一些不和谐现象。
- progress 发展
- decline 衰退
- career development 职业发展

0258 dew [duː] n. 露水
We can enjoy the morning dews here for the whole holiday.
整个假期我们都可以在这里欣赏晨露。

> 语法重点
> for the whole 后面接表示一段时间的名词，如 for the whole summer（整个夏天）。

0259 dial [ˈdaɪəl] v. 打电话
The traveler dialed the wrong number, but he threw it in the shopkeeper's dish.
那个游客拨错号码了，但他把这件事归咎于店铺老板。
- call 打电话
- dial the number 拨电话号码
- ... throw sth. in one's dish ……把某事归咎于某人

0260 diamond [ˈdaɪəmənd] n. 钻石
He didn't celebrate his parents' diamond wedding anniversary.
他没有庆祝父母六十周年钻石婚姻。
- sparkler 宝石
- diamond ring 钻石戒指

> 语法重点
> parents 是复数，其所有格是在后面直接加上"'"。

0261 diary [ˈdaɪəri] n. 日记，日记簿
The diary in the actress's schooldays is worthy of being kept.
那个女演员求学时记下的日记值得保存。
- journal 日记
- sb. / sth. be worthy of... 某人/某事值得……

> 语法重点
> be worthy of 加名词或者动名词。

dessert ~ disagreement

0262 dictionary [ˈdɪkʃəneri] n 字典
All the students are allowed to take part in the exam, on the condition that they can't use a dictionary.
所有学生都可以参加考试，条件是不能用词典。
⊜ lexicon 词典　⊕ look up in a dictionary 查词典

0263 difference [ˈdɪfrəns] n 差异，不同
Should there be another chance, try to eliminate the difference between you and your mother.
如果再有一次机会的话，要努力消除你和妈妈之间的分歧。
⊜ diversity 差异　⊗ likeness 相似

> 语法重点
> 虚拟语气中，表示对将来情况的假设时，可以用"should + 主语 + 动词原形"的倒装结构。
> ↪ eliminate (P. 433)

0264 difficulty [ˈdɪfɪkəlti] n 困难，争议，麻烦
Had it not been that difficulty, we would have arrived at the scenic spot in advance.
如果不是因为那个困难，我们已经提前到达景点了。
⊜ hardness 困难　⊗ ease 容易　⊕ do sth. in advance 提前做某事

> 语法重点
> 虚拟语气中，表示对过去情况的假设时，可以用"had + 主语 + 动词过去分词"的倒装结构。

0265 dinosaur [ˈdaɪnəsɔːr] n 恐龙
They all say that dinosaur museum is worth visiting.
他们都说那个恐龙博物馆值得参观。
⊕ ... be worth doing... ……值得做……

> 语法重点
> be worth doing 中的 doing，是用主动形式来表达被动含义。

0266 direction [dəˈrekʃn] n 方向，用法说明
She doesn't know the exact direction, so point out the way as she goes along.
她不太知道具体的方位，所以在沿途告诉她怎么走。
⊜ orientation 方向　⊕ wind direction 风向

> 语法重点
> 句中的 as 可以用 when 来代替。

0267 director [dəˈrektər] n 指挥者，导演，主管
I don't have a chance to travel with the director.
我没有机会和主管一起旅游。
⊜ conductor 指导者

> 语法重点
> I don't have a chance to 后面接动词原形。

0268 disagree [ˌdɪsəˈgriː] v 不同意
Don't tell me you disagree with the guide's words.
你不会是不同意导游的话吧。
⊜ dissent 不同意　⊗ agree 同意　⊕ agree to disagree 搁置争议，同意各自保留不同意见

> 语法重点
> don't tell me 后面一般接句子。

0269 disagreement [ˌdɪsəˈgriːmənt] n 意见不合，不一致，争论
His playing guitar loudly is a source of disagreement among the neighbours and him.
他大声弹吉他是他和邻居之间纷争的一个原因。
⊗ agreement 同意，一致　⊕ have disagreement 意见不合，有分歧

153

0270 **disappear** [ˌdɪsə'pɪr] v 消失，不见
To my delight, the taboo which forbids women to travel there is disappearing slowly.
让我高兴的是，禁止女人去那里旅游的禁忌正在逐渐消失。
≈ vanish 消失　↔ appear 出现　▶ disappear without trace 不翼而飞

⟹ forbid (P. 443)

0271 **discuss** [dɪ'skʌs] v 讨论，谈论
Let's fix a time for discussing where to spend the weekend.
我们约个时间来讨论去哪里度周末吧。
≈ debate 讨论　▶ discuss with sb. 与某人讨论

语法重点
let's fix a time for（我们约定时间做……）后面接名词或者动名词。

0272 **discussion** [dɪ'skʌʃn] n 讨论，谈论，叙述
Don't waste time having a discussion on that boring topic.
不要浪费时间谈论那个无聊的话题了。
≈ discourse 谈论　▶ beyond discussion 无讨论余地
▶ "讨论某事" 还可以用 talk over, talk about 等短语。

0273 **dishonest** [dɪs'ɑːnɪst] a 不诚实的
Don't you think that we should not make friends with dishonest people?
你不认为我们不该和不诚实的人交朋友吗？
≈ insincere 不诚实的　↔ honest 诚实的

语法重点
dishonest 后面加上 -ly，就构成了副词 dishonestly（不诚实地）。

0274 **display** [dɪ'spleɪ] v 展示，表现，夸示
Those precious items which were displayed yesterday were stolen.
昨天展出的那些珍贵展物被偷了。
≈ exhibit 显示，展示　↔ hide 隐藏　▶ display sth. to sb. 向某人展示某物

语法重点
display 也可以作名词，常用于短语 on display，意思是"展览，公开演出"。
⟹ precious (P. 341)

0275 **distance** ['dɪstəns] n 距离，路程
Keep your distance from the flowers in the garden!
和花园里的那些花保持距离！
▶ from a distance 从远方　▶ keep one's distance from... 跟……保持一定距离

0276 **distant** ['dɪstənt] a 遥远的，久远的
He will marry the girl from a distant place next month.
他下个月就要和这位来自远方的女孩结婚。
≈ remote 遥远的　↔ near 近的　▶ ... marry sb. ...和某人结婚

0277 **divide** [dɪ'vaɪd] v 分开
As a time-saving man, he always divides his weekend into several cuts.
作为一个节约时间的人，他总是将周末的时间分成几部分。
≈ distribute 分开　↔ unite 统一　▶ divide into 分成

语法重点
由两个词加连字符组成的形容词在句中可以修饰名词，而且一般放在被修饰名词的前面，如例句中的 time-saving。

0278 **division** [dɪˈvɪʒn] n 分割，分开
There is a clear division between his zone and mine, so be careful when you play basketball.
他的地盘和我的之间有明确的划分线，所以你打篮球时要注意一下。
 partition 划分，分开 consolidation 合并

0279 **dizzy** [ˈdɪzi] a 眩晕的
He felt dizzy and almost couldn't concentrate on TV.
他感到头晕目眩，几乎不能集中精力看电视。
 swimmy 眩晕的 feel dizzy 头晕

> 语法重点
> almost 与 nearly 都表示"几乎，差不多"，但 almost 表示的程度要更强一些。
> ⊃ concentrate (P. 412)
> ⊃ attract (P. 257)

0280 **dolphin** [ˈdɑːlfɪn] n 海豚
We were totally attracted by the dolphins just now.
刚才我们完全被海豚吸引住了。

0281 **donkey** [ˈdɔːŋki] n 驴子
It's donkey's years since he learned to play the guitar.
他学弹吉他已经好多年了。
 ass 驴 donkey's years 很久，很多年

0282 **dot** [dɑːt] n 点小圆点 v 点，点缀
There were some black dots on my face after I came back from the seaside.
我从海边回来后脸上有一些小黑点。
 point 点 dot frequency 点击率

0283 **double** [ˈdʌbl] a 两倍的，双重的，成双的
He hopes that they would become a double income after marriage.
他希望结婚后能组成一个双薪家庭。
 dual 双的 single 单一的 double room 双人房

0284 **doubt** [daʊt] n 怀疑，疑惑
There's no doubt that the performance will make some difference to them.
毫无疑问，这次演出会对他们造成一定的影响。
 mistrust 怀疑 trust 信任 have no doubts at all 毫无疑问

> 语法重点
> make some difference 表示"有影响，起作用"，有时 some 也可替换为 any 或 a。

0285 **doughnut** [ˈdoʊnʌt] n 甜甜圈
I have been thinking about why the doughnut is so delicious and the music is so melodious here.
我一直在想为什么这里的甜甜圈这么好吃，音乐这么好听。

> 语法重点
> I have been thinking about 后面可以接短语或是句子。
> ⊃ delicious (P. 150)

0286 **downtown** [ˌdaʊnˈtaʊn] n 闹区
The singers arrived at the hotel in the downtown on the dot of 9 o'clock.
歌手们九点钟准时到达了位于市中心的旅馆。
- downtown area 市中心

语法重点
on the dot of 常用在表达时间的名词之前，表示在几点钟准时发生某事。

0287 **doctor** [ˈdɑːktər] n 医生，博士
Health is not something that you can get back after visiting a doctor; you should exercise more.
健康并不是你在看过医生之后就可以重新得到的，你应该多运动。
- patient 病人

语法重点
something 是不定代词，它作先行词时，后面的引导词必须用 that。
➡ health (P. 048)

0288 **drag** [dræg] v 拖，拉，拽
I don't think it's necessary to drag politics into our conversation.
我觉得没必要把政治牵扯到我们的谈话中来。
- draggle 拖拽 - push 推

语法重点
drag into 的意思是"将……硬拉入"，介词 into 后面通常接名词或代词。

0289 **dragon** [ˈdræɡən] n 龙
I don't see that they will win the first prize in the dragon boat competition.
我认为他们不能在龙舟比赛中赢得第一名。
- like a dragon 凶猛地 - I don't see that... 我认为……不
- win the first prize 的意思是"取得第一名"，相当于 win the first place。

0290 **dragonfly** [ˈdræɡənflaɪ] n 蜻蜓
I don't think it's right to catch so many beautiful dragonflies in the park.
我觉得在公园里捉这么多美丽的蜻蜓是不对的。

0291 **drama** [ˈdrɑːmə] n 戏剧
They are anxiously awaiting the appearance of the famous drama actor from England.
他们在焦急地等待那个来自英国的著名戏剧演员。
- play 戏剧 - television drama 电视剧

语法重点
表示国别的名词要大写，如句中的 England。
➡ famous (P. 163)

0292 **drawer** [drɔːr] n 抽屉
All you have to do is to take pens out of the drawer.
你只要把笔从抽屉里拿出来就行。
- locker 储物柜 - drawer lock 抽屉锁

语法重点
all you have to do is 后面一般接动词不定式或者动词原形。

0293 **drawing** [ˈdrɔːɪŋ] n 绘图
The only motivation of my life is the desire for drawing art.
对绘画艺术的渴望是我生活唯一的动力。
- picture 图画 - go back to the drawing-board 重新开始

0294 **dress** [dres] n 连衣裙，女装
The actress insists that the dress for performance should be shorter.
那个女演员要求表演用的衣服要短一些。
🔘 formal dress 礼服　🔘 sb. insist that... 某人坚持……

语法重点
insist 的意思是"坚持"，后面接的宾语从句通常用虚拟语气，动词用"should + 动词原形"。

0295 **drop** [drɑːp] v 掉落，跌倒，下降
I dropped the ball into the water the minute I caught it.
我一抓到球就把它扔到了水里。
🔘 slump 下降　🔘 rise 上升　🔘 drop down 落下

语法重点
the minute 引导时间强调时间的短促性。
🔗 minute (P. 063)

0296 **drug** [drʌg] n 药品，麻醉药，毒品
It's nothing to be surprised about; the actor just bought some drug before acting.
没什么大惊小怪的，那个演员只是在表演前买了一些毒品。
🔘 medicine 药　🔘 a drug addict 吸毒上瘾的人

0297 **drugstore** [ˈdrʌgstɔːr] n 药房，杂货店
As a rule, visitors can buy the pills in the small drugstore at the entrance of the scenic spot.
一般来说，游客可以在景点入口处的小药房买到这些药丸。
🔘 pharmacy 药房　🔘 chain drugstore 连锁药房　🔘 as a rule, ... 一般来说……

0298 **drum** [drʌm] n 鼓
These children ran towards the man after hearing the beat of the drum.
这些孩子们听到鼓声就朝那个人跑去。
🔘 tambour 鼓　🔘 sb. runs towards... 某人朝……跑去

语法重点
句中 towards 也可以替换为 toward。

0299 **dryer** [ˈdraɪər] n 烘干机，吹风机，干燥剂
Oh my god, I forgot to pull out the plug of the dryer before I went out for a walk.
天哪，我出门散步前忘记把吹风机的插头拔掉了。

语法重点
pull out 的意思是"拔出"，后直接加名词，表示将某物拉出或拔出。

0300 **dull** [dʌl] n 乏味的，阴沉的
It is very dull to spend the weekend at home.
在家里度过周末很沉闷。
🔘 boring 乏味的　🔘 as dull as ditch-water 枯燥无味

语法重点
it is very dull 后面通常接动词不定式。

0301 **dumb** [dʌm] a 哑的，愚蠢的
Haven't you heard of the dumb boy who is a famous writer?
你没听说过那个哑巴男孩是一个著名的作家吗？
🔘 mute 哑的　🔘 acted dumb 装聋作哑

0302 **dumpling** ['dʌmplɪŋ] n 水饺
Have you ever eaten dumplings?
你吃过饺子吗？
🔊 boiled dumpling 水饺　🔊 Have you ever done...? 你做过……吗？

> 语法重点
> ever 的意思是"曾经"，常用于现在完成时。

0303 **duty** ['du:ti] n 责任，义务，尊敬
We should send our duty to gardeners and not destroy the plants when we are in the park.
我们在公园时应该尊敬园丁，不要破坏植物。
🔊 responsibility 义务，职责　🔊 one's bounden duty 应尽的义务

0304 **earn** [ɜ:rn] v 赚钱，赢得
In brief, we should distribute the money earned last year and go to travel.
简而言之，我们应该分配去年赚的钱并去旅游。
🔊 gain 赚到　🔊 consume 消耗　🔊 In brief, ... 简而言之，……

0305 **earthquake** ['ɜ:rθkweɪk] n 地震
We desire that our hometown should be rebuilt after the earthquake.
地震过后，我们希望能够重建家园。

> 语法重点
> desire 的意思是"希望"，后面的宾语从句用虚拟语气，动词用"should + 动词原形"。

0306 **eastern** ['i:stərn] a 东方的，东部的
The director said that the theme of the movie is about Eastern culture.
导演称这部电影的主题是关于东方文化的。
🔊 oriental 东方的　🔊 western 西方的，西部的

> 语法重点
> direct 的意思是"指出"，后面的宾语从句用虚拟语气，动词用"should + 动词原形"。
> ⇒ theme (P. 511)

0307 **education** [ˌedʒuˈkeɪʃn] n 教育
My parents sacrificed many things to pay for my education and took me abroad to travel.
我父母牺牲很多东西来支付我的学费，并带我去国外旅游。
🔊 sb. sacrifice... to do sth. 某人牺牲……做某事

> 语法重点
> pay for 除了"付钱，支付"，还有"付出代价"之意。

0308 **effect** [ɪ'fekt] n 影响
It seems that the film has little effect on these naughty children.
似乎这部电影对这些调皮的孩子没有影响。
🔊 influence 影响　🔊 cause 原因

0309 **effective** [ɪ'fektɪv] a 有效的，生效的，实际的
Television advertising should be the most effective way to popularize the toys.
电视广告是推广玩具最有效的方法。
🔊 practical 实际的　🔊 ineffective 无效的　🔊 effective time 有效时间

> 语法重点
> effective 是多音节词，其比较级与最高级分别是 more effective 和 most effective。

dumpling ~ encouragement

0310 effort ['efərt] n 努力，尝试
They climbed to the top of the mountain without effort.
他们不费力就登上了山顶。
≈ attempt 努力，尝试　≈ through one's efforts 通过某人的努力

0311 elder ['eldər] a 年长的，年龄较大的
The elder people have the priority to visit the museum.
老年人参观博物馆有优先权。
≈ older 年长的　≠ younger 较年轻的
≈ sb. has the priority to... 某人……有优先权

> 语法重点
> have the priority 后面接动词不定式
> ⊃ priority (P. 617)

0312 elect [ɪ'lekt] v 挑选，选择，选举
He was elected as the headman of their group without doubt.
他毫无疑问地被推选为他们的组长。
≈ select 选择　≈ president-elect 当选总统（尚未就职的）
≈ without doubt 的意思是"毫无疑问"，相当于 beyond doubt。

0313 element ['elɪmənt] n 元素，要素
All of the students should get familiar with the chemical elements.
所有学生都应该熟悉这些化学元素。
≈ factor 要素　≈ basic element 基本元素

0314 elevator ['elɪveɪtər] n 电梯
We can take an elevator to the top of tour tower.
我们可以搭电梯到观光塔顶。
≈ lift 电梯　≈ service elevator 服务梯，送货电梯

> 语法重点
> "乘电梯"也可以表达为 take the elevator。

0315 emotion [ɪ'moʊʃn] n 情绪，情感，感情
Whatever you do, you should take the boy's emotions into consideration.
不管你做什么，都应该考虑到男孩的情绪。
≈ sentiment 感情，情绪　≈ sb. takes... into consideration 某人顾及……

> 语法重点
> emotion 虽然是抽象名词，但它是可数的。
> ⊃ consideration (P. 277)

0316 encourage [ɪn'kɜːrɪdʒ] v 鼓励，激励
It is his desire that all the students should encourage each other.
他的愿望是所有学生都能够相互鼓励。
≈ inspire 激励　≠ discourage 使气馁

0317 encouragement [ɪn'kɜːrɪdʒmənt] n 鼓励，激励
His encouragement meant a great deal to the guests in the bar.
他的鼓励对酒吧里的客人来说意义重大。
≈ motivation 激励　≈ ... mean a great deal to sb. ……对某人意义重大

> 语法重点
> mean 当动词讲，意思是"意味着"，其过去式、过去分词是 meant。

0318 **ending** [ˈendɪŋ] n 结尾，结局
To sum up, the ending of the movie made us disappointed.
总之，这部电影的结尾让我们很失望。
同 conclusion 结局　反 beginning 开始　延 to sum up, ... 总之，……

> 语法重点
> 使役动词 make 的意思是"使，让"，通常用于"make sb. + 形容词"的结构中。

0319 **enemy** [ˈenəmi] n 敌人
I heard the boy's selfishness made many people his enemies.
我听说那个男孩因为自私树敌很多。
同 foe 敌人　反 friend 朋友　延 one's worst enemy 某人最大的敌人

> 语法重点
> 注意 enemy 的复数形式是变 y 为 i，再加上 es。

0320 **energy** [ˈenərdʒi] n 能量，精力
I was worn out and had little energy left after running.
我跑步后完全筋疲力尽，几乎没有什么剩余的精力了。
延 full of energy 精力充沛　延 sb. be worn out 某人筋疲力尽

> 语法重点
> little 修饰不可数名词，意思是"几乎没有"，含有否定的意思。

0321 **enjoy** [ɪnˈdʒɔɪ] v 享受，喜欢
It is hoped that I can sit beside the window to enjoy the pretty sights during the journey.
希望我能坐个靠窗的座位，以便好好欣赏沿途的美景。
同 like 喜欢　反 dislike 不喜欢　延 enjoy yourself 过得愉快

> 语法重点
> enjoy 的用法很广，后面可以接名词、代词、动名词，但不可以接动词不定式。
> ⊙ beside (P. 014)

0322 **enjoyment** [ɪnˈdʒɔɪmənt] n 享受，令人愉快的事
Music is my major source of enjoyment.
音乐是我快乐的主要源泉。

0323 **entire** [ɪnˈtaɪər] a 完整的，全部的
Ask him if we can book the entire restaurant for the party?
问他我们能不能包下整家餐厅来开派对？
同 overall 全部的　反 partial 部分的　延 entire life 一生一世

> 语法重点
> book 当名词讲是"书"，当动词讲是"预订"，相当于 reserve。

0324 **entrance** [ˈentrəns] n 入口，大门口
I appointed to meet her at the entrance of the cinema.
我约定在电影院门口和她碰面。
同 threshold 入口　反 exit 出口　延 front entrance 正门

0325 **envelope** [ˈenvəloup] n 信封
The man doesn't know why the flap doesn't stick to the envelope.
那个男人不知道为什么信封口粘不好。
延 sth. sticks to... 某物黏上……

> 语法重点
> stick to 后面也可以接动名词，意思是"坚持做……"。

0326 **environment** [ɪnˈvaɪrənmənt] n 环境
Maybe the visitors are unable to relate to the bad environment there.
或许游客们不能适应那里的恶劣环境。
延 sb. be unable to relate to... 某人不能适应……

> 语法重点
> relate to 还可以表示"与……有关，涉及"。

0327 eraser [ɪ'reɪsər] n 橡皮擦

Now open your eyes and guess where the eraser is.
现在睁开眼，猜猜橡皮擦在哪里。
- eraser tool 擦除工具
- ... open one's eyes ……睁开眼

> guess (P. 046)

0328 error ['erər] n 错误，过失，误差

The TV presenter checked it again to make sure there is no error.
节目主持人又核对了一遍，以便确保没有错误。
- mistake 错误
- correctness 正确
- in error 错误地

> 语法重点
> to make sure 在例句中表示目的。

0329 especially [ɪ'speʃəli] ad 尤其

I've got to be especially careful when I cycle on ice.
我在冰面上骑车时要格外小心。
- particularly 尤其
- especially important 尤其重要

> 语法重点
> I've 是 I have 的缩写。

0330 event [ɪ'vent] n 事件

I think the event is unavoidable to the actor.
我觉得这种事件对那个演员来说是不可避免的。
- occurrence 事件
- be wise after the event 事后诸葛

0331 exact [ɪg'zækt] a 正确的，确切的

He told me the exact date of departure.
他跟我说了出发的确切日期。
- accurate 精确的
- inexact 不精确的
- exact date 具体日期

> 语法重点
> 例句中的 he 与 me 都是人称代词。
> departure (P. 424)

0332 excellent ['eksələnt] a 极好的，优秀的，杰出的

He can do nothing but create excellent movies.
除了创作精彩绝伦的电影之外，他什么也不会。
- fantabulous 极出色的
- mediocre 中庸的

0333 excitement [ɪk'saɪtmənt] n 兴奋

She was happy that her performance aroused the excitement of the audience.
她很高兴自己的表演激起了观众们兴奋的情绪。
- wild with excitement 欣喜若狂
- sb. be happy that... 某人很高兴……

> 语法重点
> performance 的意思是"表演"，它还可以作"性能"讲。

0334 excuse [ɪk'skjuːs] v 原谅，请求宽恕 n 理由，辩解

The girl cannot come to the party, so she asks him to excuse her.
女孩不能来参加派对了，所以她请他原谅。
- reason 理由
- blame 责备，责怪

> 语法重点
> cannot 等于 can't。

0335 exercise [ˈeksərsaɪz] n 运动，练习

Do exercise in your free time and your health will be improved.
有空运动一下，你的健康状况会得到改善。

> 语法重点
> exercise 指"运动"时，既是可数也是不可数名词；当"练习"讲时，则是可数名词。

0336 exist [ɪɡˈzɪst] v 存在，生存

The boys can't exist without bread and water.
没有面包和水，这些男孩不能生存。
- survive 生存
- exist in 存在于

> 语法重点
> 句中 exist 可以替换为 live。

0337 expect [ɪkˈspekt] v 期待，盼望

The fans expected her to be the winner of the game.
粉丝们都期待她能成为比赛的赢家。
- anticipate 预期
- despair 失望，绝望
- as expected 不出所料
- expect sb. to do sth. 期待某人做某事

> 语法重点
> 动词不定式有表示将来的含义，例句中 to be the winner of the game 就发生在将来。

0338 expensive [ɪkˈspensɪv] a 昂贵的，高价的

I can't believe he bought the expensive car with all his savings and took his wife to Shanghai for a visit.
我真不敢相信他用所有的积蓄买了那辆昂贵的车，并带妻子去上海旅游了。

> 语法重点
> I 是第一人称，是"我"的主格形式，在句中主要作主语。

0339 experience [ɪkˈspɪriəns] n 经验

Riding a rollercoaster was a terrible experience for me.
坐过山车对我来说是一次可怕的经历。
- inexperienced 缺乏经验的
- work experience 工作经历

> 语法重点
> rollercoaster 有时也写作 roller coaster。
> ⊃ terrible (P. 234)

0340 expert [ˈeksp3ːrt] n 专家，能手

The actress is also an expert in writing.
那个女演员也是写作的专家。
- specialist 专家
- amateur 外行
- be an expert in... 是……的专家

> 语法重点
> be an expert in 后面接名词或者动名词。

0341 explain [ɪkˈspleɪn] v 解释

The girl asked the teacher to give her a chance to explain.
那个女孩请求老师给她一个解释的机会。
- explain oneself 为自己辩解
- give sb. a chance to... 给某人一个机会去……

0342 express [ɪkˈspres] v 表达，表示

I can't express how excited I was after watching the film.
我无法表达看完电影后我是多么激动。
- convey 表达
- suppress 抑制，压制
- I can't express... 我无法表达……

0343 extra [ˈekstrə] a 额外的

Do you have extra time to visit the old man?
你有额外时间去拜访那个老人吗？
- additional 额外的
- extra hours 额外时间，超时

> 语法重点
> you 是第二人称代词，表示"你，你们"，主格、宾格都是 you。

162

exercise ~ fearful

0344 eyebrow / brow ['aɪbraʊ] / [braʊ] **n** 眉毛
It is a trend for men to trim eyebrows this year.
今年，男士修眉是一种趋势。
 brow 眉毛   raise one's eyebrows 吃惊

➔ trend (P. 377)

0345 fail [feɪl] **v** 失败
You mean he failed at the pre-qualifying stage?
你意思是说他在预赛中被淘汰了？
 lose 失败   succeed 成功   fail to resolve 解决未果

语法重点
注意 you mean 引导的句子是疑问句，以问号结束。

0346 failure ['feɪljər] **n** 失败，失败者
We can't ascribe our failure to other teammates.
我们不能把失败归因于其他的队友。
 loser 失败者   success 成功   end in failure 以失败告终

语法重点
注意"队友"是 teammate，而不是 teamer。

0347 fair [fer] **a** 公平的 **n** 展览会
In this competition Tom was renowned as a fair judge.
在这次比赛中，汤姆赢得了公平裁判的荣誉。
 just 公平的   unfair 不公平的   by fair means or foul 不择手段地

0348 famous ['feɪməs] **a** 有名的
Have you ever been to that famous scenic spot?
你去过那个著名的旅游胜地吗？
 noted 著名的   nameless 无名的   Have you ever been to...? 你去过……吗？

语法重点
have been to 的意思是"去过"，暗含的意思是已经回来了。而 have gone to 的意思是"去了"，暗含的意思是去了，还没回来。

0349 fault [fɔːlt] **n** 错误，缺点，故障
Don't blame the stunt man; it's not his fault.
别责备那个替身演员了，那不是他的错。
 shortcoming 缺点   merit 优点   find fault 挑剔

0350 favor ['feɪvər] **n** 喜好，偏爱，特权
Could you do me a favor to take a photo of me?
请你帮我拍张照好吗？
 kindness 好意   malice 恶意   by favor 靠某人的偏爱

语法重点
could you do me a favor 后面要接动词不定式。

0351 favorite ['feɪvərɪt] **a** 最喜爱的
Can you tell me what your favorite movie is?
你能告诉我你最喜欢哪部电影吗？

语法重点
what your favorite movie is 是宾语从句，用陈述语序。

0352 fearful ['fɪrfl] **a** 害怕的，担心的，可怕的
The teacher is always fearful for the students.
老师总是为学生们担心。
 worried 担心的   fearless 大胆的   sb. be fearful for... 某人为……担心

163

0353 **fee** [fiː] n 费用，酬金
They will obtain an entrance fee after the entertainment.
娱乐表演之后，他们将获得一笔入场费。

⇨ obtain (P. 478)

0354 **female** ['fiːmeɪl] n 女性，雌性
We are liable for protecting the only female in our group.
我们有责任保护组里面这位唯一的女性。

0355 **fence** [fens] n 篱笆
It is regrettable that the horse unseated him at the first fence.
遗憾的是，马在过第一道篱笆时把他甩了下来。
hurdle 跨栏　　It is regrettable that... 遗憾的是……

0356 **festival** ['festɪvl] n 庆祝活动
As you know, the festival atmosphere didn't bring much happiness to them.
如你所知，节日的气氛并没有给他们带来多少欢乐。
holiday 节日　　as you know, ... 如你所知……

⇨ atmosphere (P. 399)

0357 **fever** ['fiːvər] n 发烧
She was pulled down by a sudden fever last night.
她昨晚突然发烧病倒了。
febricity 发烧　　have a fever 发烧

> 语法重点
> "昨晚"通常用 last night，而不是 yesterday night。

0358 **field** [fiːld] n 田野
Stop frolicking in the field as soon as possible.
快点停止在田地里玩耍。
farmland 田地　　hold the field 坚守阵地，坚持自己的主张

> 语法重点
> as... as possible 中间要加形容词的原级。

0359 **fighter** ['faɪtər] n 战士
It is stated that the strong fighter has never been knocked down by an opponent.
据说这位强壮的战士从未被对手打倒过。
fighter plane 战斗机　　it is stated that... 据说……

0360 **figure** ['fɪgjər] n 外形，图形，数字
Go and ask the accountant whether he got the total figure.
去问问会计他是否知道总额。

0361 **film** [fɪlm] n 电影
The majority of my friends have seen this film.
我的大多数朋友都已经看过这部电影了。
movie 电影

> 语法重点
> the majority of 后面接可数名词的复数形式，后面的动词按复数处理。

0362 fireman / firewoman ['faɪərmən] / ['faɪəwʊmɪn]
n 男 / 女消防员

A *fireman* found her pet cat and gave it back to her.
一个消防队员发现了她的宠物猫，并还给了她。
- pompier 消防队员　　● fireman uniform 消防员制服
- sb. gives... back to... 某人把……归还给……

0363 firm [fɜːrm] **a** 坚固的，坚定的 **n** 公司，商行

She told me the producer is very *firm* to her.
她告诉我，制片人对她要求非常严格。
- company 公司　　● hold firm to... 不放弃……　　● be firm to... 对……严格

▶ 语法重点
firm 的副词形式是 firmly。

0364 fisherman ['fɪʃərmən] **n** 渔夫

The guide said that being a *fisherman* isn't easy.
导游说做一个渔夫不容易。
- fisher 渔夫

▶ 语法重点
being a / an... is not easy 中 is 前面放的是代表职业的名词。

0365 fit [fɪt] **a** 合身，健康的 **v** 符合，适合

They all think this song *fits* you.
他们都认为这首歌适合你。
- healthy 健康的　　● unfit 不适合的　　● fit the bill 刚好符合要求

▶ 语法重点
fit 可以做形容词、名词或者动词，除了 be fit for sb.，其常用的固定搭配为 keep fit，意思是"保持健康"。

0366 fix [fɪks] **v** 修理，安装

Her radio was broken, who can *fix* it up?
她的收音机坏了，谁能把它修理好呢？
- mend 修理　　● fix up 修理，解决　　● ... fix up sth. ……修好某物

▶ 语法重点
it 指代 her radio。

0367 flag [flæg] **n** 旗帜

We reach the shore; have you seen the yellow *flag* over there?
我们到岸了，你看到那边的黄旗了吗？
- banner 旗帜　　● national flag 国旗　　● Have you seen...? 你看见……了吗？

↻ shore (P. 090)

0368 flash [flæʃ] **n** 闪光 **v** 闪光，闪现，掠过

This visitor is the only person who witnessed the sudden *flash*.
这名游客是唯一一个目睹那个突然闪光的人。
- blaze 闪耀　　● a flash of hope 一线希望

↻ witness (P. 518)

0369 flashlight ['flæʃlaɪt] **n** 手电筒，闪光灯

By using the little *flashlight*, he can finish reading the novel.
靠这支小手电筒，他可以读完这本小说。
- by doing..., sb. can... 透过……，某人能够……

▶ 语法重点
finish 后面一般接名词或者动名词。

0370 flat [flæt] a 平坦的，单调的 n 公寓
She walks into the flat with one of her fans.
她和其中一名粉丝一同走进公寓。
- apartment 公寓
- uneven 不平坦的
- feel flat 感觉无聊

语法重点
she 是第三人称单数，句子用一般现在时，所以动词要用第三人称单数。

0371 flight [flaɪt] n 飞行，航班
Nothing can stop the flight of time, so go traveling when you are young.
时间的飞逝是无法阻挡的，所以趁着年轻去旅游吧。
- fly 飞行
- flight number 航班班次

语法重点
flight 作动词表示"射击"。

0372 flood [flʌd] n 水灾，洪水 v 淹没，充满
Tens of thousands of visitors flood into the city in May every year.
每年五月，数以万计的游客涌入这座城市。
- inundate 淹没
- sb. floods into... 某人涌入……

语法重点
every day 和 everyday 都表示"每天"，但 every day 在句中修饰整个句子，而 everyday 在句中修饰名词。

0373 flour [ˈflaʊər] n 面粉
I spread the flour on my face to amuse my daughter.
为了逗女儿笑，我把面粉涂到了脸上。

语法重点
flour 是不可数名词。

0374 flow [floʊ] n 流动
The cyclists were nearly driven crazy by the flow of traffic.
脚踏车骑士们快被车流搞疯了。

语法重点
driven 是 drive（驾驶，驱使）的过去分词。

0375 flu [fluː] n 流行性感冒
How to avoid getting the flu when we are on holiday?
我们度假时，如何避免得流感呢？
- influenza 流感
- have the flu 患流感

语法重点
avoid 作动词，意思是"避免"，同动词 finish 一样，其后加动词时要用动词的 ing 形式。

0376 flute [fluːt] n 长笛
My sister always amuses herself by playing the flute.
我妹妹总是吹笛自娱。

0377 focus [ˈfoʊkəs] n 焦点 v 使聚焦
These reporters focus their attention on that movie star's private life.
这些记者关注的是那个电影明星的私生活。
- disperse 分散
- come into focus 明白易懂，清晰

语法重点
指示代词 that 既可以指在时间或空间上离说话者较远的人或物，也可指在心理上距离较远的物。
- attention (P. 127)

0378 foggy [ˈfɔːgi] a 多雾的
Don't you deem that foggy mountains are attractive?
你不觉得烟雾茫茫的群山很有魅力吗？
- fuzzy 模糊的
- foggy idea 模糊的思想

flat ~ formal

0379 following [ˈfɑːlouɪŋ] **a** 以下的，接着的，下列的
They held a big party the following evening.
他们第二天晚上举办了一个大派对。
≈ next 接着的 ≠ previous 之前的 ⊕ the following example 下面的例子

0380 fool [fuːl] **n** 傻子 **v** 愚弄，欺骗
Don't be a fool to think that he will take you to shoot arrows.
不要像傻瓜一样以为他会带你去射箭。
≈ fox 欺骗 ≠ sage 智者

> 语法重点
> don't be a fool to 后面接动词原形。

0381 foolish [ˈfuːlɪʃ] **a** 愚蠢的，荒谬的，可笑的
It surprises me that the tourist could be so foolish.
那个游客这么蠢，真是让我吃惊。
≈ silly 愚蠢的 ≠ wise 聪明的 ⊕ penny wise pound foolish 贪小便宜吃大亏
⊕ it surprises me that... ……真是让我吃惊

> ⊃ tourist (P. 375)

0382 football [ˈfutbɔːl] **n** 足球
After the game, he turned into a football fan.
那次比赛后，他成了一个足球迷。
≈ soccer 足球 ⊕ play football 踢足球

0383 foreigner [ˈfɔːrənər] **n** 外国人
These foreigners were requested to follow the customs of the city.
这些外国人被要求遵守这座城市的风俗。
≈ alien 外国人 ⊕ foreigner incident 涉外事件

> 语法重点
> 句中 request 当动词，作名词时常用的短语是 at sb.'s request（应某人之请求）。

0384 forgive [fərˈgɪv] **v** 原谅，宽恕
She will never forgive him for not accompanying her to travel.
她永远不会原谅他没有陪她去旅游。
≈ pardon 原谅 ≠ punish 惩罚 ⊕ forgive a debt 免偿债务

> ⊃ accompany (P. 390)

0385 form [fɔːrm] **n** 形式，形状 **v** 形成，建立
The only way to satisfy the boy is to find a form of entertainment which is fit for him.
唯一能让男孩满意的方法就是找到适合他的娱乐方式。
≈ shape 形状 ≠ content 内容 ⊕ form of value 价值形式

0386 formal [ˈfɔːrml] **a** 正式的，正规的
All of us have to wear formal dress for the party this evening.
今天晚上我们所有人应该盛装赴宴。
≈ official 正式的 ≠ informal 非正式的 ⊕ formal education 正规教育

> 语法重点
> all of 后面可以接可数名词，也可以接不可数名词。

167

0387 former [ˈfɔːrmər] a 之前的，前者的

It is unimaginable that he is the former member of the club.

他是俱乐部的前任成员，真是不可思议。

 earlier 以前   later 后来的，以后的

0388 forward [ˈfɔːrwərd] ad 向前，从今以后

Just keep moving forward and you will get to the foot of the mountain.

只要一直往前走，你就能走到山脚下。

 just keep doing sth. and you will... 一直……，你就会……

> 语法重点
> 祈使句之前加 just，可以有加强语气的作用。
> foot (P. 040)

0389 fox [fɑːks] n 狐狸，狡猾的人

As an actor, he is as crafty as a fox.

作为一名演员，他像狐狸一样狡猾。

 sb. be as... as a / an... 某人像……一样……

> 语法重点
> fox 的复数形式是在后面加上 es。

0390 frank [fræŋk] a 坦白的，直率的

They are frank and always friendly to the people who come here to spend holidays.

他们很直率，对来这里度假的人也很友善。

 outspoken 坦率的，直言的   pliable 圆滑的

> 语法重点
> be friendly to 后面一般接名词或代词。

0391 freedom [ˈfriːdəm] n 自由

Frankly speaking, he will lose his freedom if he becomes an actor.

坦白说，他如果成为演员就会失去自由。

 liberty 自由   freedom of speech 言论自由

> 语法重点
> frankly speaking（坦白地说）通常放在句首的位置，其后用逗号和句子隔开。

0392 freezer [ˈfriːzər] n 冷冻库

But for that pie in the freezer, we will suffer from hungry.

要不是冰箱里那块派，我们会挨饿的。

 refrigerator 冰箱   but for..., sb. will... 要不是……，某人会……

0393 friendly [ˈfrendli] a 友善的，友好的

There would be a friendly match between his school and mine tomorrow.

他的学校和我的学校明天有一场友谊赛。

 unfriendly 不友好的   friendly match 友谊赛

> 语法重点
> there would be 是 there be 句型的将来时。

0394 fright [fraɪt] n 惊骇，惊恐

When the earthquake took place, the visitors came out of the cave in a fright.

地震发生时，游客们都惊恐地从山洞里跑出来。

 horror 惊骇   stage fright 怯场

> 语法重点
> fright 是抽象名词，前面加上 a，可以使 fright 具体化。

0395 frighten ['fraɪtn] v 使害怕
Can you believe they can use crackers to frighten away wild animals?
你相信他们能以鞭炮吓走野兽吗？
- scare 惊吓，使害怕　- Can you believe...? 你相信……吗？

语法重点
句中 frighten 作不及物动词，它也可以当及物动词，后面直接接宾语。

0396 function ['fʌŋkʃn] n 功能
The main function of the machine is to amuse the people who are bored.
这款机器的主要功能就是娱乐无聊的人们。
- action 作用　- function key 功能键

语法重点
注意句中 bored 的意思是"感到无聊的、无趣的"，多形容人。
↪ amuse (P. 394)

0397 further ['fɜːrðər] a 较远的
Encouraged by the last victory, the player felt confident of further success.
在上次胜利的鼓舞下，该队员有信心再次获胜。
- farther 更远的　- closer 靠近的

语法重点
the player 和 encourage 是被动关系，所以 encourage 用过去分词。
↪ encourage (P. 159)

0398 future ['fjuːtʃər] n 将来，将来
I look forward to hearing from the man who is traveling in America in the near future.
我盼望着不久后收到那个在美国旅游的人的消息。
- past 过去　- predict the future 预测将来

语法重点
例句中 in the near future 表示"不久"，"遥远的将来"用 in the distant future 来表示。

0399 gain [geɪn] v 得到，获得
Some television stars would get into gossip to gain more publicity.
一些明星为了吸引更多公众的注意，不惜陷进八卦中。
- get 得到　- lose 失去　- gain a degree 获得学位

语法重点
get into 一般用来指卷入某种麻烦或不利的情况中。

0400 garage [gəˈrɑːʒ] n 车库
I found some children playing games there after I got into my garage.
进入车库后，我发现那里有几个孩子在游戏。

语法重点
got 是动词 get 的过去式。

0401 garbage ['gɑːrbɪdʒ] n 垃圾，废话
The smell of the garbage in the small park overpowered him.
那个小公园里垃圾的臭味使他无法忍受。
- rubbish 垃圾　- garbage can 垃圾箱

语法重点
名词 smell 不仅能表示普通的气味，也可以表示"臭味"。

0402 gardener ['gɑːrdnər] n 园丁，花匠
I spent the entire morning in helping the gardener trim these shrubs.
我花了整个上午的时间帮助园丁修剪这些灌木。
- I spend... in doing sth. 我花费……做某事

语法重点
I spend... in doing sth. 中的 in 可以省略。

0403 **gate** [geɪt] n 大门

I'm afraid the gate isn't wide enough to let the bus the travelers take in.
恐怕这大门不够宽，游客们乘坐的大巴士进不去。

语法重点
enough 前面是形容词原级。

0404 **gather** ['gæðər] v 聚集，集合

The notice says you should gather at the gate of the park.
通知说你们应该在公园门口集合。
反 distribute 分开

语法重点
notice 在句中作名词，意思是"通知，布告"。

0405 **generous** ['dʒenərəs] a 慷慨的，大方的

It was generous of the boss to drive us to the airport.
老板开车送我们去机场，他真是太慷慨了。
同 bountiful 慷慨的　反 mean 吝啬的

语法重点
generous 也常与介词 with 连用，表示"对……大方"。

0406 **gentle** ['dʒentl] a 温和的，轻柔的

Instead, the unexpected guest at the party was very gentle.
相反，派对上的这个不速之客很彬彬有礼。
同 mild 温和的　反 harsh 粗糙的，严厉的　搭 gentle smile 温柔的笑容

⇒ instead (P. 311)

0407 **gentleman** ['dʒentlmən] n 绅士

I think the man will be more attractive if he behaves like a gentleman.
我觉得如果那个男人的言行像绅士一样，他会更有魅力。
反 lady 淑女　搭 sb. behaves like a / an... 某人举止像……一样

语法重点
behave like 后面接名词或者代词，表示同其他人和物进行比较。

0408 **geography** [dʒɪ'ɑːgrəfɪ] n 地理，地理学

We are having our geography class at the moment, but they are watching a film.
我们现在正在上地理课，但是他们在看电影。
同 geographics 地理学　搭 ecological geography 生态地理学

0409 **giant** ['dʒaɪənt] a 巨大的

The workers in the zoo can't make the giant panda as a present to the visitor.
动物园里的工作人员不能把大熊猫作为礼物送给游客。
同 huge 巨大的　反 diminutive 小的，微小的

⇒ panda (P. 200)

0410 **giraffe** [dʒə'ræf] n 长颈鹿

Ask the children to get an eyeful of these giraffes.
让孩子们来看看这些长颈鹿吧。
同 camelopard 长颈鹿
搭 get an eyeful 单独使用，还有"一饱眼福，大开眼界"的意思。

0411 glove [glʌv] n 手套
The mate to this glove was left in the cinema just now.
这副手套的另一只刚才忘在电影院了。
- mitten 手套
- rubber glove 橡皮手套

语法重点
the mate to... 通常表示两个之中的"另一个"。
↳ glove (P. 171)

0412 glue [gluː] n 胶水
The child sticks to his mother like glue.
那个小孩寸步不离开母亲。
- gluewater 胶水
- super glue 万能胶

0413 goal [goʊl] n 目标
The goal the director set is impossible to achieve.
导演定下的目标是不可能完成的。
- target 目标
- set a goal 制定目标

语法重点
例句的主语是 the goal，所以 be 动词用 is。

0414 goat [goʊt] n 山羊
His refusal to my invitation really got my goat.
他拒绝了我的邀请，真是让我生气。
- old goat 好色之徒
- sth. gets one's goat 某事让某人发怒

0415 golden ['goʊldən] a 黄金的
They were planning to celebrate their golden wedding.
他们正在计划如何庆祝金婚。

↳ celebrate (P. 269)

0416 golf [gɑːlf] n 高尔夫球
I used to enjoy a round of golf on Saturday afternoons.
过去我喜欢在周六下午打一场高尔夫球。
- golf club 高尔夫球俱乐部

语法重点
enjoy 作动词时意思是"享受，喜欢"，其后加动词时要用动词 ing 形式，表示一种习惯性的爱好。

0417 govern ['gʌvərn] v 管理，统治，支配
You must govern your temper when you see the super star.
看到那位超级巨星时，你必须控制住情绪。
- rule 统治
- capacity to govern 治理能力

语法重点
"控制情绪"也可以用 keep one's temper 来表达。

0418 government ['gʌvərnmənt] n 政府
The solider was accused of being disloyal to the government last year.
去年，那名军人被指控对政府不忠。
- administration 政府
- the local government 当地政府

0419 grade [greɪd] n 等级，年级
You, she and I are in the same grade.
你、她和我在同一年级。
- degree 等级
- down grade 下坡，往下走

语法重点
英语中，单数人称代词顺序一般是你、他、我。

0420 grape [greɪp] n 葡萄
We, you and they like grapes and watching films very much.
我们、你们还有他们都非常喜欢葡萄和看电影。
sour grapes 酸葡萄，酸葡萄心理

语法重点
英语中，复数人称代词的顺序是我们、你们、他们。

0421 grassy ['græsi] a 多草的，像草的
Look, they are lying on the grassy hillside and playing cards.
看，他们正躺在长满草的山坡上玩牌。
herby 长满草的   sb. lies on... 某人躺在……上

0422 greedy ['griːdi] a 贪婪的
To our shock, the greedy singer is traveling in our city now.
让我们震惊的是，这个贪婪的歌手现在就在我们的城市旅游。
generous 慷慨的   to our shock, ... 让我们震惊的是……

语法重点
to our shock 是固定搭配，our 虽然意思是"我们的"，但 shock 依然用单数形式。

0423 greet [griːt] v 问候，迎接，致敬
He will greet you in the name of the host.
他将代表主人前来迎接你。
sb. does sth. in the name of... 某人以……的名义做某事

语法重点
in the name of 中的 in 也可以替换为 by。

0424 growth [groʊθ] n 成长，生长
He doesn't want to be an actor with the growth of age.
随着年龄的增长，他不再想当演员了。

语法重点
with the growth of 后面可以加名词，如 age, time, knowledge 等，表示"随着年龄、时间、知识等的增长"。

0425 guard [gɑːrd] v 守卫，看守
The stings of this flower are used to guard against the visitors who want to pick them up.
这种花的刺可以用来阻止那些想摘此花的游客。
defend 保卫，防守   violate 侵犯   be used to do sth. 被用来做……

0426 guava ['gwɑːvə] n 番石榴，芭乐
Welcome to have a taste of the guava juice.
欢迎来喝芭乐汁。

语法重点
welcome to 后面也可以接表示地点的名词，意思是"欢迎到……来"。

0427 guitar [gɪ'tɑːr] n 吉他
Indeed the guitar he plays does sound like a baby's cry.
事实上，他弹的吉他听起来的确像孩子的哭声。

语法重点
助动词 does + 动词原形，可以表示强调。

0428 guy [gaɪ] n 家伙，伙计
A guy with long hair lost his heart to the traveler from Beijing.
那个长头发的家伙爱上了这个来自北京的游客。
fellow 家伙，伙伴   ... lose one's heart to... ……爱上……

heart (P. 048)

0429 habit ['hæbɪt] n 习惯
I am not in the habit of watching TV.
我没有看电视的习惯。
custom 习惯   old habits die hard 本性难移

0430 hall [hɔːl] n 大厅，礼堂
How long was it from your house to the hall? I am afraid we will miss the play if we walk there.
从你家到礼堂有多远？我担心我们步行到那里会错过演出。
lobby 大厅   How long is it from... to...? 从……到……有多远？

语法重点
how long 不仅可以对距离提问，也可以对时间提问。

0431 hamburger / burger ['hæmbɜːrɡər] / ['bɜːrɡər] n 汉堡
He wanted to run onto the bus and made hamburger out of the disgusting driver.
他想冲上车把那个可恶的司机打一顿。
... make hamburger out of sb. 痛打某人

0432 hammer ['hæmər] n 榔头，槌子
It is regrettable that there's no hammer at hand for the passengers to smash the window.
遗憾的是手边没有槌子可以让乘客们用来砸烂窗户。
under the hammer 拿出拍卖

语法重点
at hand 不是"在手里"，而是"在手边"。
⊃ smash (P. 634)

0433 handkerchief ['hæŋkərtʃɪf] n 手帕
I saw the actress wave her handkerchief and throw the actor a kiss.
我看见女演员挥动手帕，给男演员一个飞吻。
... throw sb. a kiss 给某人一个飞吻

语法重点
wave 与 throw 并列，都是主语 I 看到的动作。

0434 handle ['hændl] v 处理，对待
The guide is the only person who knows how to handle the problem.
只有导游知道如何处理这个问题。
manage 处理   handle well 处理好

语法重点
only 有强调作用，本例句也属强调句型。

0435 handsome ['hænsəm] a 英俊的
The assistant isn't handsome, but it doesn't matter.
助理并不英俊，但这没有关系。

语法重点
it doesn't matter 中的 it 相当于形式主语，真正主语为语境里所述事情，本例句中 it 指代 but 前面所述事情。

0436 hang [hæŋ] v 悬挂，吊
The lanterns are hung at the gate of the park to illuminate the passers-by.
公园大门口挂着灯笼来为路人照明。
suspend 挂起   hang on one's lips 洗耳恭听

语法重点
passer-by（路人）的复数形式不是在词尾加 s，而是在 passer 后面加 s。
⊃ illuminate (P. 729)

0437 **hardly** ['hɑːrdli] ad 几乎不，简直不
I could hardly believe that I was paid to watch a film.
我不敢相信，看场电影还能得到报酬。
- barely 几乎不 - hardly ever 几乎从不
- I could hardly believe that... 我不敢相信……

语法重点
paid 是 pay 的过去分词。

0438 **hateful** ['heɪtfl] a 可恨的，可憎的
The old man used to be a hateful man, but now he is well bred.
那个老先生曾经是一个可憎的男人，但现在他非常有礼貌。
- detestable 可憎的 - adorable 可敬重的

0439 **healthy** ['helθi] a 健康的
What on earth should these women do to keep healthy?
这些女人到底该怎么做才能保持健康？
- robust 健康的 - unhealthy 不健康的 - healthy diet 健康的饮食

语法重点
on earth 这个介词短语可以用在疑问句中，加强语气，构成强调句。

0440 **heater** ['hiːtər] n 加热器
It's kind of you to help me move all these gas heaters in such a hot day.
在这么热的天帮我搬完所有的热水器，你真是太好了。
- warmer 加热器 - cooler 冷却器 - water heater 热水器

语法重点
to help me move all these gas heaters in such a hot day 是例句真正的主语。

0441 **height** [haɪt] n 高度，顶点
It is snowy all the year round in this height of the mountain and many visitors come here in summer.
这山在这个海拔高度终年都有积雪，很多游客都是在夏天来这里。
- altitude 高度 - absolute height 绝对高度

语法重点
英语中常用 it 来指代某种天气或者自然现象。
⊃ snowy (P. 224)

0442 **helpful** ['helpfl] a 有用的，有帮助的
It is my honor to get her helpful advice and I plan to travel next week.
得到她有用的建议实在是我的荣幸，我决定下周就去旅游。
- useful 有用的 - useless 无用的 - it is my honor to... ……是我的荣幸

语法重点
it is my honor to 常用于口语中，属于一种自谦或礼貌用语，后面一般要接动词原形。

0443 **hen** [hen] n 母鸡，雌禽
The hen my mother keeps brought off a brood of young last week, and the children are playing with them.
我妈妈养的那只母鸡上周孵出了一窝小鸡，孩子们正在和它们玩。

0444 **hero / heroine** ['hɪroʊ] / ['heroʊɪn] n 英雄 / 女英雄
The guide over there is the hero you are looking for.
那个导游就是你们要找的英雄。
- hero worship 英雄崇拜

0445 hide [haɪd] v 隐藏，躲藏

The dancer on the stage doesn't need to hide his light under a bushel.
舞台上那个舞者没必要隐藏他的才华。
- conceal 隐藏　- expose 暴露

语法重点
... doesn't need to hide one's light under a bushel 中 one 在句中根据人称的变化而变换。

0446 highway ['haɪweɪ] n 公路，交通要道

I'm thinking of crossing the highway and playing by the river.
我打算穿过公路去河边玩耍。

⊃ river (P. 082)

0447 hip [hɪp] n 臀部

I found a scar on his hip by accident and he told me he was hurt when he was playing basketball.
我偶然发现他的臀部有一个伤疤，他告诉我那是他打篮球时受的伤。
- pygal 臀部　- hip joint 髋关节

语法重点
by accident 一般用在句尾来修饰之前句子的内容。

0448 hippopotamus / hippo [ˌhɪpə'pɑːtəməs] / ['hɪpoʊ] n 河马

The hippopotamus plays with a red and yellow ball during the daytime.
河马在白天的时候玩一个红黄相间的球。

语法重点
play with 后也可以接人，意思是"和……一起玩"。

0449 hire ['haɪər] v 雇用，出租

The explorers hired a local villager to go across the river.
为了过河，探险家们雇了一个当地的村民。
- employ 雇用　- fire 解雇　- hire sb. to do... 雇某人做某事

语法重点
go across 主要强调穿越某个狭长的东西，如街道、河流、峡谷等。

0450 hobby ['hɑːbi] n 嗜好

His hobby is just the same as mine.
他的爱好和我的相同。
- cultivate one's hobby 培养某人的嗜好
- just the same as 语气比 as same as 要强烈。

⊃ mine (P. 192)

0451 holder ['hoʊldər] n 持有者，占有者

To tell the truth, he is the biggest holder of this project.
说实话，他是这个计划的最大持股人。
- possessor 持有人　- To tell the truth, ... 说实话，……
- 该句型为常用句型之一，常用来表示实情、真相等。

0452 homesick ['hoʊmsɪk] a 思乡的，想家的

When their conversation turned to Chinese food, he became homesick.
当他们的谈话转向中国菜时，他有些想家了。
- feel homesick 想家

语法重点
turn to 后面接物时，表示"转向……"；接人时，通常表示"求助于某人"。

0453 honest ['ɑːnɪst] a 诚实的，正直的

As an honest person, you should be faithful to your audience.
作为一个诚实的人，你该忠于自己的观众。
同 truthful 诚实的　反 dishonest 不忠实的　句 be faithful to... 忠实于……

⊃ faithful (P. 440)

0454 honey ['hʌni] n 蜂蜜

Don't bother them since they are on their honey moon.
别打扰他们，因为他们在度蜜月。
句 sb. be on honey moon 某人在度蜜月

0455 hop [hɑːp] v 跳过，单脚跳

The young dancer can hop and spin on his head.
这个年轻的舞者能单脚跳，并且以头支地旋转。

语法重点
hop 也可以作名词，与 hip（屁股）构成 hip-hop，是"街舞"的意思。

0456 hospital ['hɑːspɪtl] n 医院

The lonely visitor went to the hospital himself.
那个孤单的游客自己去医院了。

语法重点
句中的 himself 是反身代词，反身代词可以分为第一人称反身代词、第二人称反身代词、第三人称反身代词及不定代词反身代词四种形式，有单复数的变化。

0457 host [hoʊst] n 主人，主持人 v 主持，主办

The host frequently raised his glass during the feast last night.
昨晚的宴会上，主人频频举杯。
反 hostess 女主持人　句 raise one's glass during... ……的时候举杯

语法重点
注意 raise 不要写成 rise，前者意思是"举起"，是及物动词，后者意思是"上升"，是不及物动词。

0458 hotel [hoʊ'tel] n 旅馆，酒店

The hotel is perched on a steep hillside.
旅馆坐落在陡峭的山坡上。
同 inn 旅馆　句 be perched on... 坐落在……上

0459 however [haʊ'evər] ad 然而，可是

However, he made up his mind to travel by himself.
然而，他下定决心独自旅行。
同 but 然而，可是　句 however much 不论多少

语法重点
however 的意思同 but，表示转折，但后面接句子时要用逗号与该句分开。

0460 hum [hʌm] v 哼哼声

Everybody hums and haws when I refer to traveling.
我谈到旅游时，每个人都吞吞吐吐的。
同 buzz 发出嗡嗡声　句 hum and haw 吞吞吐吐

0461 humble ['hʌmbl] a 卑微的

Everybody says the famous actress is a humble woman indeed.
大家都说那个著名的女演员真的是个很谦逊的人。
同 modest 谦逊的　反 proud 骄傲的　句 eat humble pie 忍气吞声

语法重点
everybody 是单数，后面的动词用单三形式。

honest ~ ill

0462 humid ['hju:mɪd] **a** 潮湿的
It is very humid in the world-famous scenic spot.
这个世界闻名的景点非常潮湿。
同 dry 干的　　反 wet 潮湿的

> 语法重点
> world-famous 是形容词，修饰 scenic spot。

0463 humor ['hjʊmər] **n** 幽默的
You would know that the guide has a sense of humor.
你会发现那个导游很有幽默感。
词 sense of humor 幽默感

> ⊃ sense (P. 087)

0464 hunger ['hʌŋɡər] **n** 饥饿，渴望
He has the hunger for traveling but I also need that chance.
他渴望去旅游，但是我也需要那次机会。
同 appetite 欲望　　反 satiety 饱足

> 语法重点
> 句中 that 是指示代词，指示代词有单复数之分：this, that 是单数；these, those 是复数。

0465 hunt [hʌnt] **v** 打猎，搜寻
I'd like to know whether you can hunt for a fox in the forest.
我想知道你能否在森林里猎取到一只狐狸。
词 run with the hare and hunt with the hounds 两面讨好

> 语法重点
> I'd like to know 后面通常接句子，做 know 的宾语。

0466 hunter ['hʌntər] **n** 猎人
They saw the hunter creep up to the deer.
他们看到猎人蹑手蹑脚地走近那头鹿。
反 prey 猎物　　词 head hunter 猎头公司

> 语法重点
> sb. creeps up 中的 to 是介词，后面接名词或者代词。
>
> ⊃ creep (P. 279)

0467 hurry [hurry] **v** 催促，匆忙，赶紧
You should hurry up to arrive at the park on time.
你们得快点，以便准时赶到公园。
同 hasten 赶快，急忙　　反 delay 拖延　　词 hurry forward 加速向前
注 hurry up 也可以单独使用，意思是"快点，赶紧"，用在口语中，催促别人。

0468 ignore [ɪɡ'nɔːr] **v** 忽视，不顾，不理
The patient father ignores none of his daughter's requests even if she asks him to take her to the park at night.
那位耐心的父亲从不忽略女儿的任何要求，即使要求他晚上带她去公园玩儿也一样。
同 disregard 不理，忽视　　词 sb. does sth. even if... 某人……即使……

> 语法重点
> even if 后面接句子，相当于 although, though。

0469 ill [ɪl] **a** 生病的，坏的，有恶意的
I didn't play games because my son was seriously ill.
我儿子病得很严重，所以我没有玩游戏。
同 sick 有病的　　反 well 健康的　　词 ill at ease 不安的，感到拘束的

> 语法重点
> be ill 中间有时会加上 seriously 或 badly 这两个单词，表示"病得很严重"。

0470 imagine [ɪˈmædʒɪn] v 想象，设想，料想
I can't imagine what the lake in the park looks like.
我不能想象公园里那个湖是什么样子。
- assume 假定
- I can't imagine... 我不能想象……

> 语法重点
> I can't imagine 后面通常接句子或者动名词。

0471 importance [ɪmˈpɔːrtns] n 重要性
I know my performance is of no importance.
我知道我的表演无足轻重。
- significance 重要性
- unimportance 不重要

0472 improve [ɪmˈpruːv] v 改善
My father sent him a treadmill to help him improve his health.
我父亲送给他一台跑步机来帮助他改善健康状况。
- enhance 提高
- improve skill 提高技能
- ... send sb. sth. to... 为了……送某人某物

> 语法重点
> sent 是动词 send 的过去式。

0473 include [ɪnˈkluːd] v 包含
She has got many hobbies including listening to music.
她有很多爱好，包括听音乐。
- exclude 排除
- include in 包括在……中

> 语法重点
> including 常用于列举事物。

0474 income [ˈɪnkʌm] n 收入
I spend in excess of my income every month, so I don't have money to travel.
我每月都入不敷出，所以我没有钱去旅游。
- earnings 收入
- expenditure 支出

0475 increase [ɪnˈkriːs] / [ˈɪnkriːs] v / n 增加
Hang on; the number of the visitors is still increasing.
等一下，游客们的数量还在增加中。
- raise 增加
- decrease 减少
- increase speed 加速
- hang on 通常用在口语中，表示"等一下"，在电话用语中也较常用，表示"等等，别挂断"。

0476 independence [ˌɪndɪˈpendəns] n 独立，自主，自立
I think the independence of judgment is the symbol of an adult, so your son can't travel alone.
我认为独立判断是一个成年人的标志，所以你儿子还不能独自去旅游。

⇨ symbol (P. 232)

0477 independent [ˌɪndɪˈpendənt] a 独立的
I prefer independent travel to conducted tours.
比起观光团我还是喜欢独自旅行。
- dependent 依赖的
- I prefer... to... 比起……我更喜欢……

⇨ conduct (P. 549)

imagine ~ instant

0478 indicate ['ɪndɪkeɪt] v 指示，象征，显示
The alert indicates that there is no water left on the drinking fountain.
警报显示饮水机里没有水了。
↪ alert (P. 393)

0479 industry ['ɪndəstri] n 企业，产业
The industry here is less developed than that of the district, so the investors are disappointed.
这里的产业没有那个地区的发达，所以投资者们都很失望。
⊜ manufacturing 工业

> 语法重点
> "比……发达"用 be more developed than 来表示。
> ↪ district (P. 429)

0480 influence ['ɪnfluəns] n / v 影响，感染
Generally speaking, the media has a powerful influence on these famous singers.
一般来说，媒体对于这些著名的歌星有很大的影响。
⊜ affect 影响　⊜ positive influence 正面影响
▸ ... have a powerful influence on sb. ……对某人有很大的影响
▸ influence 作名词还可以构成短语 under the influence of，意思是"在……影响之下"。

0481 ink [ɪŋk] n 墨水
There's no ink in the pen for the visitor to go on his writing.
钢笔里没有墨水让那个游客继续写信了。

> 语法重点
> go on 后接名词或动名词。

0482 insect ['ɪnsekt] n 昆虫，虫子
I was bitten by an insect in the garden just now.
刚才我在花园里被虫子咬了一下。
⊜ worm 虫　⊜ insect damage 虫害　▸ be bitten by... 被……咬了

> 语法重点
> bitten 是动词 bite（咬）的过去分词。

0483 insist [ɪn'sɪst] v 坚持
The guide insisted setting off right away.
导游坚持要立刻出发。
⊜ persist 坚持　⊜ abandon 放弃　⊜ insist upon 坚持

> 语法重点
> insist 后面不仅可以接 that 从句，还可以接动名词。

0484 instance ['ɪnstəns] n 实例，场合，情况
I should apply to the manager in the first instance if I want to join the club.
如果我想加入俱乐部，首先应向经理提出申请。
⊜ example 例子　▸ in the first instance 起初，首先

0485 instant ['ɪnstənt] a 立即的，即时的
I think it is not enough having a cup of instant coffee before acting.
表演前只喝一杯即溶咖啡是不够的。
⊜ immediate 立即的　▸ instant mail 即时邮件

> 语法重点
> cup 的意思是"杯子"，除此之外，还可以用作量词，a cup of 就表示"一杯……"。

0486 instrument [ˈɪnstrəmənt] n 仪器，工具
He says the violin is one of the oldest instruments known to man.
他说小提琴是人们所知最古老的乐器之一。
同 appliance 工具　　词 instrument analysis 仪器分析

0487 international [ˌɪntərˈnæʃnəl] a 国际的
The guide in red is of international repute.
穿红色衣服那个导游享有国际声誉。
反 national 国家的　　词 international trade 国际贸易

0488 interview [ˈɪntərvjuː] n 面试
The famous dancer insisted on having the interview in public.
这位著名的舞蹈家坚持要当众接受采访。
同 cover 采访　　词 sb. insists on doing... 某人坚持做……

> 语法重点
> man 可以表示"男人"，还可以作为"人类"来讲，如例句中的 man 指的是"人"这个整体概念，而并非仅指男人。

> 语法重点
> insist on 表示对某事的强烈要求，其中的 on 为介词，后面接动名词。
> ⊕ public (P. 078)

0489 introduce [ˌɪntrəˈduːs] v 介绍
I went over to introduce myself to the foreign visitor emboldened by the wine.
我借酒壮胆，走上前去向那个外国游客做自我介绍。
同 present 介绍　　词 ... introduce oneself to sb. ……向某人做自我介绍

> 语法重点
> embolden 的意思是"给……壮胆，鼓励"，常用于以下结构 embolden sb. to do sth. 鼓励某人做某事。

0490 invent [ɪnˈvent] v 发明
The strangest thing is that the toy plane was invented by the boy.
谁也想不到，这个玩具飞机是这个小男孩发明的。

> 语法重点
> strange 是以字母 e 结尾的形容词，其比较级、最高级是直接在后面加上 r、st。

0491 invitation [ˌɪnvɪˈteɪʃn] n 邀请，邀请函
What in the world was the reason that made you refuse our invitation?
究竟是什么原因让你拒绝了我们的邀请呢？
词 at the invitation of 应……的邀请

> 语法重点
> in the world 的意思是"究竟，到底"，常用于疑问句中，用以加强语气。

0492 invite [ɪnˈvaɪt] v 邀请
Can you invite her to take part in the game?
你可以邀请她参加游戏吗？
反 refuse 拒绝　　词 invite sb. along 邀某人做伴
词 ... invite sb. to take part in... ……邀请某人参加……

> 语法重点
> take part in 指参加会议或群众性活动等，着重说明句子主语参加该项活动并在活动中发挥作用。

0493 island [ˈaɪlənd] n 岛
The small island is referred to as a fairyland on earth by the visitors.
这个小岛被游客们称为人间仙境。
同 isle 小岛　　词 sb. / sth. be referred to as... 某人 / 某物被称为……

instrument ~ joint

0494 item ['aɪtəm] **n** 项目，条款
He himself doesn't know which new item is his favorite, so he buys nothing at the shop.
他自己也不知道哪件商品是他最喜欢的，所以在商店里他什么也没有买。
🔄 article 物品，条款　　🔄 an export item 出口项目

> **语法重点**
> himself 为第三人称代词 he 的反身代词，置于代词 he 之后表示一种强调。

0495 jacket ['dʒækɪt] **n** 夹克，外套
The actor took off his down jacket before appearing on the stage.
登上舞台前，演员脱下了羽绒服。
🔄 coat 外套　　🔄 sb. takes off... 某人脱掉……

> **语法重点**
> 句子中 down 的意思是"绒毛，软毛"，是名词作形容词用，修饰 jacket（夹克）。
> ↪ stage (P. 227)

0496 jam [dʒæm] **v** 堵塞，塞满
Unfortunately, the policeman's gun jammed in the critical moment and the man was killed.
不幸的是，在那个千钧一发的时刻，警察的枪卡弹了，那个男人被杀了。
🔄 jam tomorrow 许诺但不兑现的东西，可望而不可及的事物

0497 jazz [dʒæz] **n** 爵士
The young man couldn't tell the difference between jazz music and pop music.
那个年轻人分辨不出爵士乐和流行音乐。
🔄 sb. couldn't tell the difference between... and... 某人不能区分……和……

> **语法重点**
> tell 除了可以表示"告诉"，也可以表示"区分"，常与介词 from 搭配使用。

0498 jeans [dʒiːnz] **n** 牛仔裤
The jeans are not the traveler's, that's because his are dark grey ones.
这条牛仔裤不是那个游客的，因为他的是深灰色的。
🔄 that's because... 那是因为……

> **语法重点**
> dark grey 的意思是"深灰色"，其中 dark 是形容词，修饰 grey（灰色）。

0499 jeep [dʒiːp] **n** 吉普车
I feel quite at ease when I sit in my new jeep and drive it to visit my friends.
坐在我新买的吉普车里去拜访朋友时，我感觉十分惬意自在。
🔄 Hummer jeep 悍马吉普车

> **语法重点**
> at ease 常用在 be 动词或感官动词 feel 之后，表示"自在安适"这种状态。

0500 jog [dʒɑːg] **v** 慢跑
It is my habit to take exercise by jogging every day.
我有每天慢跑的习惯。
🔄 jog one's memory 唤起某人的记忆　　🔄 it is my habit to... ……是我的习惯

> **语法重点**
> "做运动"也可以用 do exercise 来表达。

0501 joint [dʒɔɪnt] **n** 接缝　**a** 联合的，共同的
Amazingly, that picture is their joint work.
让人吃惊的是，那幅画是他们合作的作品。
🔄 a joint statement 联合声明

> ↪ picture (P. 075)

0502 **judge** [dʒʌdʒ] v 判断 n 法官，裁判
I am shocked to hear that the judge likes playing cards.
听说这个法官喜欢玩扑克牌，我很震惊。
- I am shocked to hear that... 听到……我很震惊

0503 **juicy** ['dʒuːsi] a 多汁的
Of course we can have some juicy fruits to quench our thirst.
我们当然可以吃一些多汁的水果来解渴。
- succulent 多汁的
- juicy peach 水蜜桃

语法重点
of course 除了可以用于回答别人的问题，也可以引导句子。

0504 **ketchup** ['ketʃəp] n 番茄酱
Come on, help yourself to the ketchup he made.
来，吃些他做的番茄酱。
- catsup 番茄酱
- a bottle of tomato ketchup 一瓶番茄酱

语法重点
help oneself 也可以单独使用，意思是"请自便"。

0505 **kindergarten** ['kɪndərgɑːrtn] n 幼儿园
The singer was abducted at the gate of the kindergarten yesterday.
昨天那个歌手在幼儿园大门口被绑架走了。
- nursery 托儿所
- sb. be abducted at someplace 某人在某地被绑架了

语法重点
注意 kindergarten 的拼写，不要写成 kindergarden。

0506 **kingdom** ['kɪŋdəm] n 王国
They lost themselves in the kingdom of Fairy Tales in the park.
在公园里，他们完全沉浸在童话王国里。
- realm 王国
- ... lose oneself in... 某人沉浸在……

语法重点
themselves 为第三人称代词 they 的反身代词，表示"他们自己"。

0507 **knock** [nɑːk] v 敲门，敲打
It was my fault to knock that vase in the museum.
把博物馆里的花瓶撞倒是我的错。
- knock at 敲（门、窗等）
- it is my fault to... ……是我的错

- fault (P. 163)

0508 **knowledge** ['nɑːlɪdʒ] n 知识
The boy is rich in knowledge although he has no money.
这个男孩学识渊博，尽管他很穷。
- information 知识
- be public knowledge 人所共知
- 与 be rich in 相反的短语是 be poor in（在……方面贫穷）。

0509 **koala** [koʊˈɑːlə] n 考拉
He had never seen a koala until he traveled to Australia last year.
去年去澳大利亚旅游之前他从来没有见过考拉。
- ... had never seen until sb. did 某人在……之前从没见过……

0510 ladybug / ladybird ['leɪdibʌg] / ['leɪdibɜːrd] n 瓢虫

I was fearful of the ladybug in the park.
我非常害怕公园里的瓢虫。

> 语法重点
> be fearful 后可以加 of + 名词，加动词，或加 that 从句。

0511 lane [leɪn] n 巷

It is general knowledge that this lane in the city is very narrow.
大家都知道，这座城市的这条小巷特别窄。
- alley 小路
- life in the fast lane 快节奏的生活（尤指带来财富和成功的激情生活）

> 语法重点
> knowledge 是不可数名词，所以前面没用任何冠词。
> ⊃ knowledge (P. 182)

0512 language ['læŋgwɪdʒ] n 语言

The girl is just ten years old, but she can speak three languages.
那个女孩只有十岁，但她可以说三种语言。
- tongue 语言
- foreign language 外语

> 语法重点
> 当某人称在句子中第二次出现时，一般用代词，如 she 指代 the girl。

0513 lantern ['læntərn] n 灯笼

Be careful, it is stated that a burning lantern in the park caused a fire yesterday.
小心，据说昨天公园里的一只燃烧的灯笼引起了一场火灾。
- glim 灯笼
- it is stated that... 据说……

0514 lap [læp] n 膝盖

I feel ashamed to sit on your lap to play games.
我不好意思坐在你腿上玩游戏。
- knee 膝盖
- in the lap of luxury 在奢侈的环境里

> 语法重点
> I feel ashamed to 后面接动词原形。

0515 latest ['leɪtɪst] a 最后的，最近的

He invited her to his house in their latest conversation.
在最近一次谈话中，他亲自邀请她去他家。
- earliest 最早的
- latest technology 最新科技

> 语法重点
> latest 是形容词 late 的最高级。

0516 lawyer ['lɔːjər] n 律师

I am becoming disenchanted with my job as a lawyer and plan to travel to Korea.
我对自己的律师工作渐渐地不抱幻想了，并打算去韩国旅游。
- attorney 律师

0517 leadership ['liːdərʃɪp] n 领导地位

Owing to his excellent leadership, the team won at last.
多亏他出色的领导才能，这一队最终赢了。
- owing to..., sb. / sth.... 多亏了……，某人 / 某事……

⊃ excellent (P. 161)

0518 **legal** ['liːgl] **a** 合法的，法定的，法律的
According to the legal process, the model will be released tomorrow.
根据法律流程，那个模特儿明天就会被释放。
同 legitimate 合法的　反 illegal 违法的　衍 legal action 法律诉讼

⊃ release (P. 347)

0519 **lemon** ['lemən] **n** 柠檬
The guest in the bar likes to put a squeeze of lemon in his drink.
酒吧里那个客人喜欢在饮料中放一点儿柠檬汁。

语法重点
a squeeze of 后面一般接不可数名词。
⊃ squeeze (P. 364)

0520 **lemonade** [ˌleməˈneɪd] **n** 柠檬水，汽水
Lemonade is the main contributor to the overweight of the traveler.
柠檬汽水是导致这个游客超重的罪魁祸首。
衍 词首 over- 表示"超出，超过"等含义，通常可以用在一些名词之前构成新词，如 overweight（超重）。

0521 **lend** [lend] **v** 借出
I criticized him for lending the camera to a stranger in the park.
我因为他把照相机借给公园里的一个陌生人而责怪他。
同 loan 借给　反 borrow 借入　衍 lend a helping hand 伸出援助之手

语法重点
criticize sb. for 后面接名词或者动名词。

0522 **length** [leŋθ] **n** 长度，距离
My teacher says it is a good practice to write to a certain length.
我的老师说，按照一定的长度进行写作是一种好的练习。
同 distance 距离　衍 at arm's length 疏远，在手臂伸得到的地方

语法重点
句中第一个 to 代表不定式，第二个 to 是介词，意思是"按照"。

0523 **leopard** ['lepərd] **n** 豹
Suppose he completed the painting of the snow leopard, what would he get?
假如他完成了那幅雪豹的画作，他能得到什么？

语法重点
suppose 后面可以接句子，表示假设，用虚拟语气。

0524 **lettuce** ['letɪs] **n** 莴苣；生菜
Tell the maid to take some more lettuce.
让女仆再拿一些生菜来。

0525 **library** ['laɪbreri] **n** 图书馆
She ran across him in the public library.
她在公共图书馆碰巧遇见他。
衍 public library 公共图书馆　衍 run across sb. 碰巧遇到了某人

legal ~ loaf

0526 lick [lɪk] **v** 舔食
I licked my upper lip and told the teacher I was not myself today.
我舔了舔上嘴唇，告诉老师我今天感到不舒服。
- lick somebody's boots 拍马屁
- ... be not oneself 某人感到身体不舒服

0527 lid [lɪd] **n** 盖子
I can cover the big pot with the lid and make soup for the guests.
我可以把那个大锅盖上锅盖，为客人们煮汤。
- cover 盖子
- pot lid 壶盖

> **语法重点**
> 情态动词 can 表示"能，会"，可以表示将来的情况，但不能用于将来时等结构。

0528 lightning ['laɪtnɪŋ] **n** 闪电
Sadly, the singer was struck by lightning and died instantly.
不幸的是，那个歌星被雷击了，很快就死了。
- sb. be struck by lightning 某人被雷击了

0529 limit ['lɪmɪt] **n** 限制，界限 **v** 限制
We limit our activities to running on the playground.
我们的活动范围仅限于在操场上跑步。
- restriction 限制
- within limits 适度地，在一定范围内

> **语法重点**
> we limit... to... 中的 to 是介词，所以后面只能接名词或者动名词。

0530 link [lɪŋk] **v** 连接，联系
I can't link these art works with the young man.
我不能把这些艺术作品和那个年轻人联想在一起。
- connect 连接，联系
- link with... 与……有关

> **语法重点**
> work 当名词讲，有"作品"的意思。

0531 liquid ['lɪkwɪd] **n** 液体
The nurse advised him to eat some liquid food.
护士建议他吃些流质食物。
- fluid 液体
- solid 固体

> **语法重点**
> 注意 advise 的名词形式是 advice，两个单词的拼写类似。
> ↳ advise (P. 253)

0532 listener ['lɪsənər] **n** 听者
There's no way I become the listener of that presenter.
我不可能成为那个主持人的听众。
- audience 听众
- there's no way... 不可能……

0533 loaf [loʊf] **n** 一块（面包）
It's hunger that goads the poor beggar to steal a piece of loaf.
饥饿驱使那个可怜的乞丐偷一块面包。
- bread 面包
- Half a loaf is better than none. 聊胜于无。
- loaf 作动词有"虚度光阴"的意思，常用固定搭配是 loaf around（闲混）。

0534 **local** ['loʊkl] a 当地的，地方性的
Don't be afraid of entertaining the boring local bigwigs.
不要害怕去招待当地那些无聊的大人物。
同 regional 地方的　　同 local calls 本地电话，市话

语法重点
don't be afraid of（别怕）后面接名词或者动名词。

0535 **locate** ['loʊkeɪt] v 使……坐落在……
You know the Great Pyramid is located in the middle of the desert.
你知道的，大金字塔位于沙漠中。

语法重点
表示客观事实时，要用一般现在时。

0536 **lock** [lɑːk] v 锁上，卡住
The visitor locked the door and stayed in the hotel room alone.
那个游客锁上门，独自待在旅馆房间里。
反 unlock 打开　　同 lock up 关起来　　同 sb. does sth. alone 某人独自做某事

0537 **log** [lɔːg] n 原木
There are two log cabins, one is for women visitors and the other is for men visitors.
有两间小木屋，一间给女游客，另一间给男游客。
同 as easy as falling off a log 十分简单，非常容易

语法重点
the other 指的是"两者中的另一个"。
⊃ cabin (P. 267)

0538 **lone** [loʊn] a 孤单的，寂寞的
The little girl was alarmed at being lone.
那个小女孩害怕孤独。
同 alone 孤独的　　反 busy 热闹的

0539 **lonely** ['loʊnli] a 独自的，寂寞的，荒凉的
The singer feels very lonely after his wife's death, so he always invites friends to his house.
那个歌星在妻子去世后感到很孤独，所以他总是邀请朋友到家里来。

0540 **lose** [luːz] v 失去，失败
The actor is, as it were, a man who is easy to lose his senses.
那个演员好像是一个很容易失去理智的人。
同 fail 失败　　同 lose your mind 失去理智

语法重点
as it were（可以说）常在句中作插入语，一般用在句中或句末。

0541 **loser** ['luːzər] n 失败者，输家
No one is a born loser; just be tough if you lose the game.
没有人生来就是失败者，如果你比赛失败了，要坚强些。
同 failure 失败者　　同 no one is a born... 没有人生来就是……

语法重点
动词 be 也属于动词原形，可以在句中用祈使语气来表示一种命令或请求。
⊃ tough (P. 512)

local ~ magician

0542 loss [lɔːs] **n** 损失，丧失，遗失
The old actor's death is a great loss to the entertainment business.
那位老演员的逝世是娱乐圈的重大损失。
🔄 losing 损失　　🔄 profit 获利　　🔄 cut one's losses 减少损失

↪ death (P. 028)

0543 lovely ['lʌvli] **a** 可爱的，令人愉快的，好看的
He found a lovely girl playing computer games there when he came into the hall.
他进入大厅时，发现一个可爱的女孩在里面玩电脑游戏。
🔄 cute 可爱的　　🔄 rebarbative 令人讨厌的

0544 lover ['lʌvər] **n** 爱人，爱好者
I enjoyed myself without the company of my lover.
没有爱人的陪伴，我仍然玩得很开心。
🔄 sweetheart 情人，爱人

0545 lower ['louər] **v** 降低，放下，抓住
I hope you wouldn't lower yourself to play games with your fan.
希望你不要降低身份，跟自己的粉丝玩游戏。
🔄 heighten 提高　　🔄 ... lower oneself to do sth. 降低某人的身份去做某事

🔖 语法重点
lower 同时也是形容词 low 的比较级。

0546 luck [lʌk] **n** 幸运，运气
The winner attributes his victory to luck.
那个赢家认为他的胜利是靠运气。
🔄 fortune 运气　　🔄 try one's luck 碰运气
💡 luck 常用于短语 good luck，意思是"祝你好运"，表示对人的祝福与鼓励。

0547 magazine ['mæɡəziːn] **n** 杂志
My favorite magazine is put out once a week.
我最喜欢的杂志一周出一期。
🔄 journal 杂志　　🔄 weekly magazine 周刊

↪ favorite (P. 163)

0548 magic ['mædʒɪk] **a** 神奇的 **n** 魔术
How did people feel about magic before 1,800 A.D.?
公元 1 800 年前，人们怎么看待魔术？
💡 How does sb. feel about...? 某人如何看待……？

0549 magician [mə'dʒɪʃn] **n** 魔术师，术士
Think about everything carefully before you choose to be a magician.
在决定成为一名魔术师之前，你要把所有事情都考虑清楚。
💡 think of 和 think about 都表示"考虑"，think of 除表示"考虑"外，还有"想要，打算，想出"等含义，而 think about 没有此种含义。

↪ choose (P. 139)

0550 **main** [meɪn] ⓐ 主要的
At that time, people always danced in front of the factory which was the main supplier of beer.
那时，人们总在这家工厂前跳舞，这家工厂是主要的啤酒供应商。
同 chief 主要的　反 secondary 次要的

语法重点
at that time 的意思为"在那时，在当时"，常用在过去时中，表示过去的某个时间所发生的情况。

0551 **maintain** [meɪn'teɪn] ⓥ 维持
The bar will take measures to maintain order.
酒吧将会采取措施来维持秩序。
同 preserve 保持　反 abandon 放弃

语法重点
take measures to 后面要接动词原形。
↳ measure (P. 190)

0552 **male** [meɪl] ⓝ 男性，雄性动物
The singer got mad at her husband's male chauvinism after marriage .
婚后，那名歌星对丈夫的大男人主义很生气。
同 man 男子　反 female 女性

语法重点
after 可以当连词，也可以当介词，后面接上名词，表示"在……之后"。

0553 **Mandarin** ['mændərɪn] ⓝ 普通话
It was not long before the foreign visitor learned to speak Mandarin.
没有多久，那个外国游客就学会讲普通话了。

语法重点
"讲某种语言"要用动词 speak。

0554 **mango** ['mæŋgoʊ] ⓝ 杧果
Sorry for my eating your mango.
原谅我吃了你的芒果。

语法重点
mango 的复数形式是 mangoes 或 mangos。

0555 **manner** ['mænər] ⓝ 方式，礼貌，习俗
It is not a good manner to talk at table, because the host will be angry.
吃饭时说话很不礼貌，因为主人会生气。

0556 **mark** [mɑːrk] ⓥ 标记，做记号
I was marked out for singing in chorus.
我被指定参加合唱团。

↳ chorus (P. 308)

0557 **marriage** ['mærɪdʒ] ⓝ 婚姻，结婚
They are trying to prepare for their marriage themselves and have a big party.
他们打算自己筹备婚礼并办一次盛大的派对。
同 wedding 结婚　反 divorce 离婚

语法重点
反身代词和被指代的名词属于一种对应的相互指代关系，二者在人称、词性和单复数上均要保持一致，如例句中的 they 和 themselves 的相互指代关系。

0558 **mask** [mæsk] ⓝ 面具，面罩
I admit that the man wearing the mask in the ball was a friend of mine.
我承认舞厅里那个戴面罩的人是我的一个朋友。

0559 **mass** [mæs] n 大量，堆

Have you heard that there was mass hysteria when the band came on stage?
你听说了吗？乐团登台时观众一片疯狂。

🔄 heap 堆，大量　　🔄 bit 少量　　🔄 in the mass 总体上

⊙ band (P. 010)

0560 **mat** [mæt] n 小垫子，席子

Wipe your shoes on the mat before you enter the bar.
你进酒吧前在垫子上擦一下鞋。

🔄 cushion 垫子　　🔄 bamboo mat 竹席
ℹ️ mat 也常用在短语 on the mat 中，意思是"受责备，受审问"。

0561 **match** [mætʃ] n 比赛 v 使相配

No kidding, the tie doesn't match your shirt and I advise you to change for another one if you want to take part in the party.
说真的，这条领带跟你的衬衫很不配，如果你打算参加派对的话我建议你换一条。

🔄 match with 使和……相匹配

语法重点
match 作不及物动词时，通常和介词 with 搭配使用。

0562 **mate** [meɪt] n 同伴，同事

The chief mate's wife was brought to bed, but he still went abroad to travel.
那位主任的老婆要生产了，但他还是去国外旅游了。

🔄 fellow 伙伴，同事　　🔄 soul mate 精神伙伴

0563 **material** [məˈtɪriəl] n 物质，材料

Recent studies show that these materials can be used to make footballs for people to play with.
最新研究表明这种材料可以用来生产足球，以供人们玩耍。

语法重点
material 既可以作可数名词，也可以作不可数名词。

0564 **meal** [miːl] n 餐，饭

I prepared a very elaborate meal for my guests.
我为客人们做了一顿精美的饭菜。

🔄 I prepare... for... 我为……准备……
ℹ️ meal 泛指任何一顿饭，通常用于短语 have a meal（吃饭）。

⊙ elaborate (P. 561)

0565 **meaning** [ˈmiːnɪŋ] n 意义，重要性

Speak point by point to get your meaning across, or the students will be at a loss.
一点儿一点儿地说，这样你的意思才能被人理解，不然学生们会不知所措。

🔄 significance 意义　　🔄 educational meaning 教育意义

语法重点
point by point的意思是"逐一，一点儿一点儿地"，在句中修饰动词speak。

0566 **means** [miːnz] n 工具，方法，财产

I will try every means to get a ticket of the concert.
我将会采用一切手段来得到演唱会门票。

语法重点
means 的单复数同形。

0567 measurable ['meʒərəbl]
a 可测量的，可预见的，重要的

My guess is that the girl surrounded by several bodyguards is a measurable singer.
我猜被几名保镖围着的那个女孩是一位重要的歌星。

- foreseeable 可预见的
- immeasurable 不可计量的

语法重点
surrounded by 在句中修饰 the girl。
↪ surround (P. 369)

0568 measure ['meʒər] **v** 测量，衡量 **n** 措施

It is objected that the new measure may hurt the fans' feelings.
有人提出反对，这个新的措施可能会伤害粉丝们的感情。

- scale 测量，衡量
- in good measure 充分地
- it is objected that... 有人反对……

0569 medicine ['medsn] **n** 医药，医学

The medicine is believed to date from the year of 1,700 A.D.
这种医学被认为是起源于公元 1700 年。

- drug 药
- sb. / sth. be believed to... 某人 / 某物被认为……

语法重点
date from 后面一般接表示时间的词。

0570 meeting ['miːtɪŋ] **n** 会议

I am delighted to see that the meeting hall was full of fans.
我很高兴看到会议厅坐满了粉丝。

- conference 会议
- a meeting of minds 达成一致，臭味相投

0571 melody ['melədi] **n** 旋律，曲调

My sixth sense tells me she is playing this beautiful melody.
第六感告诉我，她在弹奏这首优美的曲子。

- tune 曲调
- free melody 自由的旋律

0572 melon ['melən] **n** 香瓜，甜瓜

Let's share the melons equally before acting.
表演前让我们平分这些甜瓜吧。

- bitter melon 苦瓜
- let's share... equally 我们平分……吧

0573 member ['membər] **n** 成员，会员

They plan to enroll her as a member of the club next month.
他们打算下个月吸收她成为俱乐部会员。

- membership 成员，会员
- enroll sb. as a member of... 吸收某人为……的会员

语法重点
enroll 在句中作及物动词，当作不及物动词时，通常与介词 in 和 on 搭配使用。
↪ enroll (P. 562)

0574 memory ['meməri] n 记忆，记忆力

The singer advised us to observe a minute's silence in memory of the people who died in the accident.
那个歌手建议我们为事故中的死者默哀一分钟。
- sb. does sth. in memory of... 某人做某事以悼念……

> 语法重点
> 关系代词在从句中作主语时要用其主格形式，例句中的 who 就是关系代词的主格形式。
> ⇨ silence (P. 222)

0575 menu ['menjuː] n 菜单

The actor was in a hurry, so he told the waiter to bring the menu quickly.
那个演员很匆忙，所以他叫服务生快点儿拿菜单来。
- carte 菜单   - drop-down menu 下拉式功能表

> 语法重点
> in a hurry 通常用在 be 动词之后表示主语所处的匆忙的状态。

0576 message ['mesɪdʒ] n 讯息

Leave him a message to go fishing this afternoon.
给他留个口信，让他下午去钓鱼。
- urgent message 紧急通知   - leave sb. a message to... 留口信给某人……

0577 metal ['metl] n 金属

He took out a metal flask from his bag at the party.
在派对上，他从包包里掏出一个金属瓶子。
- reinforcement metal 钢筋

⇨ bag (P. 010)

0578 meter ['miːtər] n 米

The basketball star is about 2 meters tall.
那个篮球明星大约两米高。
- square meter 平方米   - sb. be... meter(s) tall 某人……米高

0579 method ['meθəd] n 方法，办法

It's easy to persuade the director if we get the right method.
只要我们的方法得宜，说服导演并不难。
- approach 方法   - teaching method 教学方法

> 语法重点
> to persuade the director if we get the right method 在句中作真正的主语。

0580 metro / subway / underground

['metroʊ] / ['sʌbweɪ] / [ˌʌndər'graʊnd] n 地铁

The posters of the concert are all over the metro carriage.
地铁的车厢里满满都是演唱会的海报。
- subway 地铁   - metro station 地铁站

> 语法重点
> all over 后面常接表示地点的名词，如 all over the world，表示"全世界"。

0581 military ['mɪləteri] a 军事的

None of the visitors understands these military terms.
没有一个游客懂这些军事用语。
- martial 军事的   - military use 军事用途

> 语法重点
> military 还可以作名词，the military 的意思是"军队，武装力量"。

0582 **million** [ˈmɪljən] **n** 百万
They consider the young actor as a man in a million.
他们认为这个年轻的演员是万中选一的人。

0583 **mine** [maɪn] **pron** 我的（东西）
I danced with his partner, and he danced with mine.
我和他的舞伴跳，他和我的舞伴跳。

> 语法重点
> mine 指代 my partner。
> ⇒ partner (P. 201)

0584 **minus** [ˈmaɪnəs] **prep** 减去
Every normal person would know that 8 minus 3 equals 5.
每个正常人都应该知道八减三等于五。
🔹 less 减去　🔹 plus 加　🔹 minus one 零下一度

> 语法重点
> every 的意思是"每个"，主要强调每个个体。

0585 **mirror** [ˈmɪrər] **n** 镜子
Whatever the kind woman says, she can't make the broken mirror whole again.
不管那个热心的女子说什么，都不能使破镜重圆。
🔹 ..., sb. can't make the broken mirror whole again ……，某人不能使破镜重圆

> 语法重点
> whatever 是复合疑问代词，复合疑问代词是由疑问代词和 ever 构成的，一般不用来引导问句。

0586 **mix** [mɪks] **v** 混合，掺入
I advise him to get out and mix more with people.
我建议他出去多跟人们往来。
🔹 blend 混合　🔹 ... mix with sb. ……与某人交往

> 语法重点
> 句中的 more 修饰 mix。

0587 **model** [ˈmɑːdl] **n** 模型
Your hobbies in your free time speak well for your model of life.
你空闲时的爱好说明你的生活方式很好。
🔹 matrix 模型　🔹 sth. speak well for... 某物说明……很好

> 语法重点
> hobbies 是名词 hobby 的复数形式。
> ⇒ hobby (P. 175)

0588 **modern** [ˈmɑːdərn] **a** 现代的，新式的
The modern amusement park is much better than it used to be.
这个现代化的游乐园比过去好得多。

> 语法重点
> better 是 good 的比较级。

0589 **monster** [ˈmɑːnstər] **n** 怪物
Somebody told me the monster in the movie is very frightening.
有人告诉我，电影里那个怪兽特别可怕。
🔹 green-eyed monster 嫉妒

0590 **mosquito** [məˈskiːtoʊ] **n** 蚊子
These runners are plagued by the ubiquitous mosquitos.
这些跑者正被无处不在的蚊子所困扰。
🔹 skeeter 蚊子　🔹 be plagued by... 被……困扰

> 语法重点
> mosquito 的复数形式有两种，mosquitoes 和 mosquitos。

0591 moth [mɔːθ] n 蛾

It is helpful to terminate this moth in the park.
这能帮助消灭掉公园里这只飞蛾。
- miller 蛾
- it is helpful to... 对……有帮助

语法重点
moth 是可数名词，其复数形式是 moths。
↪ terminate (P. 790)

0592 motion ['mouʃn] n 运动，动作

The warden in the park wanted to know who set this machine in motion.
公园里的管理员想知道是谁启动了机器。

0593 motorcycle ['moutərsaɪkl] n 摩托车

The racers can ride a motorcycle well, let alone a bicycle.
赛手们摩托车都骑得很好，脚踏车更不在话下了。
- ride a motorcycle 骑摩托车
- let alone... 更不用说……

0594 movable ['muːvəbl] a 可移动的，变动的

The point is the date of the activity is movable.
关键是活动的日期不固定。
- removable 可移动的
- immovable 不动的
- movable property 动产

语法重点
that 引导同位语从句，没有任何实际意义，在句中不作任何成分，只起到引导同位语从句的作用。

0595 MRT abbr 大众快捷运输

It was unfortunate that all the visitors missed the MRT at last.
不幸的是，所有的游客都没赶上大众快捷运输。
- mass rapid transit 捷运
- it is unfortunate that... 不幸的是……

0596 mule [mjuːl] n 骡子

The actress has fondly imagined that riding a mule is easy.
女演员天真地以为骑骡子很容易。
- sb. has fondly imagined that... 某人天真地认为……

语法重点
riding a mule 在从句中作主语。

0597 multiply ['mʌltɪplaɪ] v 增加

The mice in the park will multiply if there are no prevention measures.
如果没有预防措施，公园里老鼠的数量将会增加。
- increase 增加
- divide 除
- multiply by 乘以，乘上

语法重点
no 和 not 都表示否定，但在词义和使用场合上有一定的区别。no 可以作形容词、副词等词性，而 not 只能作副词，no 作形容词时等同于 not any。

0598 musician [mjuˈzɪʃn] n 音乐家

It is a pleasure to welcome the famous musician to give a performance.
热烈欢迎这位著名的音乐家来演出。

语法重点
it is a pleasure 后面通常接动词不定式。

0599 nail [neɪl] n 指甲，钉子

What you should do is to cut your nails.
你现在应该做的是剪指甲。

0600 naked ['neɪkɪd] a 裸体的，赤裸的
He is naked now after stripping off shorts in front of the swimming pool.
他在游泳池前脱掉短裤，现在是赤裸的。

> 语法重点
> strip off 就相当于 take off （脱掉）。

0601 napkin ['næpkɪn] n 餐巾
How does the golf player do with the paper napkin?
那个高尔夫运动员是怎么处理餐巾纸的？
⟲ serviette 餐巾　　table napkin 餐巾

0602 narrow ['næroʊ] a 狭窄的，有限的
By no means should the visitors adopt the guide's narrow viewpoint.
游客们决不能采纳导游那种狭隘的观点。

> 语法重点
> by no means 用在句首来表示强调，其后的句子用倒装语序。

0603 national ['næʃnəl] a 国家的，民族的
She is the most beautiful ranger of the national park I have seen.
她是我见过的最漂亮的国家公园看守员。

> 语法重点
> sb. is the... I have seen 中的省略号处应填上"形容词最高级 + 名词"。
> most (P. 065)

0604 natural ['nætʃrəl] a 自然的，天然的
It goes without saying that he is a natural athlete.
不用说，他是个天生的运动健将。
⟲ unartificial 自然的　　artificial 人工的　　natural landscape 自然景观

0605 naughty ['nɔːti] a 顽皮的，淘气的
It is naughty of you to pee in the swimming pool.
你在游泳池里小便真是顽皮。
⟲ mischievous 顽皮的，淘气的　　well-mannered 行为端正的

0606 nearby [ˌnɪr'baɪ] a 附近的　ad 在附近
I have to tell you there is no bar nearby.
我得告诉你附近没有酒吧。
⟲ vicinal 附近的　　faraway 遥远的

> 语法重点
> no 作形容词时，可以直接放在名词之前修饰该名词。

0607 nearly ['nɪrli] ad 几乎地，差不多地
She concerned for the racing-drivers and nearly got mad.
她一直为那些赛车手们担心，几近疯狂。
⟲ almost 几乎，差不多　　not nearly 根本就不

0608 neat [niːt] a 整洁的，简洁的
The garden is not neat enough; call someone to tidy it up.
花园不够整洁，找人把它整理好。
⟲ clean 清洁的，干净的　　dirty 脏的　　... tidy up sth. ……整理

> 语法重点
> not 作为副词可以用来修饰形容词，置于形容词之前起否定的作用。

naked ~ nest

0609 necessary ['nesəseri] a 必需的
It is both important and necessary to keep the scenery spot clean.
保持景点干净是重要且必要的。
- essential 必要的
- unnecessary 不必要的
- a necessary evil 必要之恶

⇒ scenery (P. 501)

0610 necklace ['nekləs] n 项链
The necklace is beautiful, hence I wear it to the party.
这条项链很漂亮，于是我戴着它去参加派对了。
- hence 相当于 so（所以，因此）。

0611 needle ['niːdl] n 针
The boy who fell from the horizontal bars sewed up the wound with a needle.
那个从单杠上摔下来的男孩用针来缝合伤口。
- look for a needle in a haystack 大海捞针

⇒ horizontal (P. 580)

0612 negative ['negətɪv] a 负面的，否定的，消极的
The negative answer of the actress made the public disappointed a lot.
女演员的消极回答让大众很失望。
- passive 消极的
- positive 肯定的
- negative effect 负面影响

0613 neighbor ['neɪbər] n 邻居
My neighbor listened to music throughout the night.
我的邻居彻夜听音乐。
- sb. does sth. throughout the night 某人彻夜做某事

语法重点
throughout 后面接表示时间的名词，可以表示"整个……"。

0614 neither ['naɪðər] pron 也不
He doesn't like skating, neither do I.
他不喜欢溜冰，我也不喜欢。
- both 二者都
- neither one 没有一个

语法重点
skate 是以不发音的 e 结尾的，所以其现在分词形式是去 e 加 ing。

0615 nephew ['nefjuː] n 侄子，外甥
No one can figure out why my nephew likes playing baseball so much.
没人知道我侄子为什么这么喜欢棒球。
- niece 侄女
- nephew relationship 叔侄关系

0616 nest [nest] n 鸟巢，窝
The quiet garden seemed like a little nest, peaceful and comfortable to us.
在我们看来，那个幽静的花园就像个小鸟窝，幽静又舒适。
- bird nest 鸟窝

⇒ peaceful (P. 202)

0617 **net** [net] n 网，网状物
It's funny that they use a broken fish net to catch fish.
他们用一张破网来捕鱼，真可笑。
web 网　　it's funny that... ……真可笑

0618 **niece** [niːs] n 侄女
As a matter of fact, his niece has practiced ballet for 5 years.
事实上，他的侄女已练了五年芭蕾舞。
nephew 侄子　　as a matter of fact, ... 事实上，……

0619 **nobody** ['noʊbədi] pron 没有人，无人
There's nobody on the square but these dancing women.
广场上除了这些跳舞的女人没有别人。
everybody 每个人　　nobody else 别无他人

> **语法重点**
> but 与 except 都表示"除……之外不再有……"的意思，但在表达上有细微的区别。but 主要侧重于其之前的名词，如例句中主要强调"没有人"，而 except 则强调其之后的名词。
> ○ square (P. 227)

0620 **nod** [nɑːd] v 点头
I nodded my head to agree with the plan that we go for a picnic on Sunday.
我点头表示同意周日去野餐的计划。
noddle 点头　　nod at... 朝……点头

0621 **none** [nʌn] pron 无一个
None of us would agree with such a stupid idea that we go to the park at night.
我们没有人同意晚上去公园这个愚蠢的想法。

> **语法重点**
> such 作形容词时含义为"这样的"，用在名词之前起修饰限定的作用，名词前若有冠词修饰，则冠词需要放到 such 之后。

0622 **noodle** ['nuːdl] n 面条
I like to taste all kinds of noodles in my free time.
空闲时我喜欢品尝各种面条。

0623 **northern** ['nɔːrðərn] a 北方的，北部的
I was stupefied by the magnificent northern scenery.
这北国风光使我吃惊。

0624 **notebook** ['noʊtbʊk] n 笔记本
I always keep a notebook at the elbow when I go traveling.
我旅游时，总是在手边放一个笔记本。
at the elbow 可以替换为 at hand.

0625 **novel** ['nɑːvl] n 小说 a 新颖的，奇特的
I spent a peaceful morning on the grassland, reading a novel.
我在草地上看小说，度过了一个宁静的上午。
fiction 小说　　backpack novel 平装小说

> **语法重点**
> 在句型 I spend a... on... 中，a / an 后面要接表示一段时间的名词，而 on 后面要放表示地点的名词。

0626 nut [nʌt] n 坚果，果仁

You will be off your nut if you consider the movie is good.

如果你认为这部电影很精彩，那你就错了。

- nuts and bolts 具体细节，基本要素
- nut 还常用于短语 be a tough nut to crack，意思是"很棘手"。

0627 obey [əˈbeɪ] v 服从，听从

I declare that those who don't obey the rules of the game will be punished.

我宣布不服从游戏规则的人将会受到惩罚。

- yield 屈服
- disobey 违反
- obey the law 遵守法律

语法重点
指示代词 those 为 that 的复数形式，表示"那些"，后面的动词要用复数形式。

0628 object [ˈɑːbdʒekt] n 物体 [əbˈdʒekt] v 反对

Some kind of unknown object has cut off the signal, so we cant' watch TV.

某种未知物体把信号切断了，所以我们不能看电视了。

语法重点
cut off 是动词短语，普通名词要放在 cut off 之后，而代词一般置于 cut 和 off 之间。

0629 occur [əˈkɜːr] v 发生，出现

Didn't it occur to you to have a chat with your friends?

难道你没有想到和朋友聊聊天吗？

- happen 发生
- occur as 以……形式出现

语法重点
occur 通常指按计划或规律在较为确定的时间"发生"的事；happen 常指那些偶然的或未能预见的"发生"。

0630 offer [ˈɔːfər] v 提供

Is it customary to offer gratuities to the guides here?

这里有给导游小费的习惯吗？

- provide 提供
- get 得到

0631 official [əˈfɪʃl] a 官方的

I think such kind of traveling is not official.

我认为这种旅行是不正式的。

- formal 正式的
- unofficial 非官方的
- official news 官方消息

语法重点
such kind of 后面接名词或者动名词。

0632 omit [əˈmɪt] v 省略，删节

The visitor omitted to take his camera.

那位游客忘记把他的相机拿走了。

- miss 漏掉
- omit to mention 略而不谈
- sb. omits to do... 某人忘了做……

0633 onion [ˈʌnjən] n 洋葱

I think onion is very delicious.

我觉得洋葱很好吃。

0634 operate [ˈɑːpəreɪt] v 操作，运转，动手术

You can't imagine my grandfather is learning to operate a computer recently.

你想不到我爷爷最近在学玩电脑吧。

- computer (P. 143)

0635 opinion [əˈpɪnjən] n 言论，观点
We don't arrive at an opinion on where to spend the holiday.
我们对去哪里度假还没有明确的意见。
- view 观点
- be a matter of opinion 见仁见智
- 注意"度假"用固定搭配 spend the holiday。

0636 ordinary [ˈɔːrdneri] a 一般的，平凡的，普通的
The host of the party is ordinary in his appearance.
举办这次派对的那个人相貌平平。
- common 普通的
- extraordinary 非凡的
- in the ordinary way 通常

⊃ ordinary (P. 198)

0637 organ [ˈɔːrɡən] n 器官
She was lucky that the ball didn't hit a vital organ.
她很幸运，球没有打中身体的重要器官。
- apparatus 器官
- internal organ 内脏

语法重点
动词与助动词搭配使用时，要用原形，所以 hit 用原形。

0638 organization [ˌɔːrɡənəˈzeɪʃn] n 组织，团体，机构
The organization she has just joined is cloaked in a shroud of secrecy.
她刚参加的这个社团笼罩着一种诡秘的气氛。
- community 团体
- be cloaked in... 笼罩着……

0639 organize [ˈɔːrɡənaɪz] v 组织，安排，筹办
I grow curious about who organized this event.
我很好奇谁组织了这次活动。
- arrange 安排
- I grow curious about... 我很好奇……

语法重点
I grow curious about 后面可以接名词、代词、动名词，也可以接句子。

⊃ curious (P. 148)

0640 oven [ˈʌvn] n 炉子，烤箱
He sat by the oven and had a chat with her.
他坐在烤炉旁边和她聊天。
- roaster 烤箱
- hot like an oven 热得像火炉

0641 overpass [ˈoʊvərpæs] n 高架道
What surprises me is that some street entertainers were giving performance on the overpass.
让我吃惊的是一些街头艺人正在天桥上表演。
- flyover 天桥
- underpass 地下通道
- pedestrian overpass 人行天桥

0642 overseas [ˌoʊvərˈsiːz] a 国外的 ad 在海外
It's extraordinary that he enjoys the overseas travel.
想不到他喜欢去国外旅行。
- abroad 到海外
- interiorly 在国内

语法重点
travel 在句中作名词。

⊃ extraordinary (P. 565)

opinion ~ painter

0643 owl [aʊl] n 猫头鹰
All that the girl can do is to take the wounded owl home.
女孩能做的就是带这只受伤的猫头鹰回家。
🔹 night owl 夜猫子

> 语法重点
> all that the visitor can do 是主语，后面的 be 动词与其保持一致，用 is。

0644 owner [ˈoʊnər] n 拥有者，所有人
To start with, the owner of the villa welcomed the guests personally.
首先，这栋别墅的主人亲自迎接客人。
🔹 possessor 所有人，持有人   🔹 legal owner 法定所有人

> 语法重点
> personally 是副词，修饰 welcomed，等于短语 in person（亲自）。

0645 ox [ɑːks] n 公牛
Because of lacking exercise, he is not as strong as an ox anymore.
由于缺乏锻炼，他不再像一头牛那样强壮了。
🔹 bull 公牛   🔹 sb. / sth. be not as... as... 某人 / 某物不像……一样……

> 语法重点
> not so... as... 中，so 和 as 中间要加形容词或副词的成分。

0646 pack [pæk] n 一包，包裹，一副
In short, all the gamers will receive a welcome pack.
总之，每位游戏玩家都会收到一个迎新包。
🔹 parcel 包裹   🔹 pack cards with 与……狼狈为奸

> 语法重点
> receive 表示客观上的"收到"，accept 表示主观上的"接受"。

0647 package [ˈpækɪdʒ] n 包裹，包装
The man distributed the packages of cigarettes to all the visitors.
那人把那些香烟分给了每个游客。
🔹 packet 包   🔹 sb. distributes sth. to... 某人把某物分给……

> 语法重点
> "一包香烟"可以用 a package of cigarettes 来表示，表示"多包香烟"时，package 也要变复数。
> ⇨ distribute (P. 429)

0648 pain [peɪn] n 痛苦，疼痛
He was injured when he was playing football and the drug has brought a brief respite from the pain.
他踢足球时受伤了，药物暂时缓解了疼痛。
🔹 ache 疼痛   🔹 pleasure 快乐   🔹 a pain in the neck 令人讨厌的人或事
🔹 respite 意思是"缓解"，常用于短语 put in respite（延期，暂缓）。

0649 painful [ˈpeɪnfl] a 痛苦的，令人不快的
It is painful that he can't play the guitar anymore.
他再也不能弹吉他了，这真叫人痛心。
🔹 enjoyable 令人愉快的   🔹 feel painful 感到疼痛

> 语法重点
> that he can't play the guitar anymore 是真正的主语，it 是虚语。

0650 painter [ˈpeɪntər] n 画家，油漆匠
You didn't expect that she is a painter and she can paint anything you want.
你没想到她是画家，能够画出你想要的任何东西。
🔹 portrait painter 肖像画家

> 语法重点
> 不定代词 anything 的意思是"任何事（物）"，其常用于否定句或疑问句中。

199

0651 **painting** ['peɪntɪŋ] n 绘画
Is there someone who can paint Chinese painting on the square?
广场上有人会画国画吗？
- picture 图画
- Is there someone who can...? 有人能……吗？

> **语法重点**
> 不定代词 someone 用来指人，意思是"有人，某人"，用作单数。

0652 **pajamas** [pə'dʒæməz] n 睡衣
It is paradoxical that she wears her pajamas to go for a walk.
她穿着睡衣外出散步，真是荒谬。

0653 **palm** [pɑːm] n 巴掌，棕榈
The boy held the ping-pong in the palm of his hand.
小男孩把乒乓球放在手心上。

> **语法重点**
> held 是动词 hold 的过去式。

0654 **pan** [pæn] n 平底锅
Warn the children not to play with the pan.
警告孩子们不要玩那个平底锅。
- frying pan 煎锅

0655 **panda** ['pændə] n 熊猫
People say that these pandas gave the most wonderful performance of the circus.
据说这些熊猫的表演是马戏团最精彩的节目。

> **语法重点**
> wonderful 是多音节的形容词，其比较级与最高级分别是在前面加上 more 和 most。
> ○ wonderful (P. 248)

0656 **papaya** [pə'paɪə] n 木瓜
There's nothing I can treat you except some papayas.
除了几个木瓜，我没有什么东西可以拿来招待你的。
- treat 当动词讲，除了有"对待，医治"的意思，还可以表示"款待"，相当于 entertain。

0657 **pardon** ['pɑːrdn] n / v 原谅，宽恕
I beg your pardon for the sudden visit last night.
对昨晚的突然拜访，我希望得到你的原谅。
- forgive 原谅，宽恕
- pardon my French 原谅我说脏话

> **语法重点**
> I beg your pardon for 后面通常接名词或者动名词。

0658 **parrot** ['pærət] n 鹦鹉
He is as sick as a parrot after coming back from the gym.
他从健身房回来后非常不高兴。
- as sick as a parrot 非常失望

> **语法重点**
> be as sick as a parrot 后面还可以接上介词 about，表示"对……很不高兴"。

0659 **particular** [pər'tɪkjələr] a 特别的，挑剔的，详细的
Well, any traveler who has particular request can speak it out.
嗯，任何游客有特殊要求都可以提出来。
- special 特别的
- common 一般的
- sb. speaks out... 某人提出……

> **语法重点**
> any 修饰 traveler（单数），后面的动词要用第三人称单数的形式。

painting ~ peace

0660 partner [ˈpɑːrtnər] n 伙伴，配偶，搭档
It is really a knotty problem to choose a partner for the game.
选个搭档去参加这个游戏真是件棘手的事。
- comrade 伙伴
- business partner 商业伙伴

0661 passenger [ˈpæsɪndʒər] n 乘客，旅客
All these passengers took advantage of the fine weather to travel.
这些乘客都是趁好天气出去旅游的。
- traveler 旅客
- passenger zone 乘客区
- 短语 take full advantage of 可以表示"充分利用"。

⊙ weather (P. 111)

0662 paste [peɪst] n 糨糊 v 粘贴
The naughty boy squeezed the paste into a ball.
那个淘气的男孩把糨糊揉成了球形。
- tomato paste 番茄酱

语法重点
paste 当动词讲时，常与介词 up 连用，构成短语 paste up，表示"（用糨糊）粘上"。

0663 pat [pæt] v 轻拍 n 轻拍，小块
I patted him on his head to encourage him to parachute.
我拍拍他的头，鼓励他跳伞。
- tap 轻拍
- a pat on the back 鼓励

0664 path [pæθ] n 路径，路线
Walk along the path and the garden is at the end of it.
沿着这条路走，花园就在路的尽头。
- route 路线
- walk along..., and someplace is... 沿着……走，某地就在……

0665 patient [ˈpeɪʃnt] a 耐心的 n 病人
Be patient to the pupils who pick off flowers.
你对摘花的小学生们要耐心点。
- sick 病人
- impatient 不耐心的
- patient history 病历

⊙ pupil (P. 211)

0666 pattern [ˈpætərn] n 图案，模式
The behavior of the guest in the bar deviates from the usual pattern.
酒吧里这个客人的举止与一般人不同。
- mode 模式
- pattern design 模型设计，图案设计

语法重点
pattern 当动词讲，意思是"模仿"，常用于短语 pattern oneself after（模仿……的样子）。

0667 peace [piːs] n 和平，平静
More importantly, all of you can have peace of mind by practicing Yoga.
更重要的是，练习瑜伽能让你们每个人心情平静。
- calmness 平静
- world peace 世界和平

语法重点
介词 by 的意思是"通过"，后面接动名词。

0668 **peaceful** [ˈpiːsfl] a 和平的，平静的，宁静的
As everybody knows, the peaceful countryside is fit for spending holidays.
大家都知道，宁静的乡村适合度假。
- pacific 平静的，和平的   反 unpeaceful 不和平的，不平静的
- as everybody knows, ... 大家都知道，……

↪ countryside (P. 146)

0669 **peach** [piːtʃ] n 桃子
He sent the peaches to everyone at the party.
他把桃子分给派对上的每个人。

语法重点
英语中，当名词以 s, x, sh, ch 结尾时，其复数形式通常是在词尾加上 es，所以 peach 的复数形式是 peaches。

0670 **peanut** [ˈpiːnʌt] n 花生
These peanuts thrown away by the visitors mean everything to that farmer.
这些被游客扔掉的花生对于那个农民来说就是一切。
- sb. / sth. means everything to... 某人 / 某物对……来说就是一切

0671 **pear** [per] n 梨子
The cheeks of the players are stuffed with pears.
玩家的脸颊里塞满了梨子。
- be stuffed with... 塞满……

0672 **penguin** [ˈpeŋgwɪn] n 企鹅
The movie *Mr. Popper's Penguins* will be shown tomorrow.
电影《波普先生的企鹅》明天就上映了。

语法重点
"上映"也可以用 be on 来表达。

0673 **pepper** [ˈpepər] n 胡椒粉
The pepper in the soup caused the guests to sneeze.
汤里面的胡椒呛得客人们直打喷嚏。
- red pepper 红辣椒   - cause sb. to do sth. 使某人做……

↪ sneeze (P. 504)

0674 **per** [pər] prep 每，每一
It is estimated that we can play golf once per week.
据估计，我们每周能打一次高尔夫球。
- it is estimated that... 据估计，……

语法重点
per 有时也可以替换为 a 或者 one。

0675 **perfect** [ˈpɜːrfɪkt] a 完美的
The path allows visitors to enter the yard in perfect safety.
游客们走这条小路就可以安全地进入那个院子。
- flawless 完美的   - Practice makes perfect. 熟能生巧。

0676 **period** [ˈpɪriəd] n 期间，时期
The scenic spot will be closed for an indefinite period.
这个景点将无限期关闭。
- time 时间   - transition period 过渡时期

0677 personal [ˈpɜːrsənl] a 个人的
The famous singer used to make a point of his personal honor.
那个著名的歌星过去很重视个人名誉。

0678 photograph / photo [ˈfoʊtəɡræf] / [ˈfoʊtoʊ] n 照片
In the park the family group together for the photograph.
在公园里，全家人聚在一起照相。
- picture 照片
- ... group together for... ……为了……聚在一起

语法重点 句中 family 虽然是单数，但由于强调的是家庭成员，所以是复数。

0679 photographer [fəˈtɑːɡrəfər] n 摄影师
Many photographers take pictures when the peonies are in bloom.
很多摄影师在牡丹花开的时候拍照。
- ... be in bloom ……开花
- be in full bloom 可以表示"盛开"。

0680 phrase [freɪz] n 短语
Lily had to learn these phrases, so she didn't follow us to the park.
莉莉要学习这些短语，所以她没有跟我们去公园。

语法重点 follow sb. to 后面也可以接动词原形，表示"跟随某人去做……"。
- follow (P. 040)

0681 pick [pɪk] v 挑选
The boy picked up the ball and handed it to another boy.
那男孩捡起球，把它交给另一个男孩。
- ... hand sth. to sb. ……把某物交给或递交给某人

语法重点 another 表示"另一个"，后面要接可数名词单数。

0682 picnic [ˈpɪk] n 野餐
Why not go out for a picnic on a sunny day?
天放晴了，为什么不去野餐呢？
- be no picnic 有困难或麻烦
- Why not do...? 为什么不……？

语法重点 表示天气的阴晴雨雪状况时，通常是将表示此类天气现象的名词变成形容词的形式，如例句中的 sunny（晴朗的），是名词 sun（太阳）重复 n 加 y 而构成的形容词。

0683 pigeon [ˈpɪdʒɪn] n 鸽子
Each of them took some food for the pigeon on the square.
他们每个人都为广场的这些鸽子带了一些食物。
- dove 鸽子
- put the cat among the pigeons 兴风作浪，挑起纠纷

0684 pile [paɪl] n 一层，一叠
Look, a pile of china dishes are resting on the acrobat's head.
看，杂技演员头上顶着一叠瓷碟。
- stack 堆，堆叠
- make a pile 发财

语法重点 china 这个单词，首字母小写时，意思是"瓷器"，大写时，意思是"中国"。

0685 pillow [ˈpɪloʊ] n 枕头
Lay down your head on your pillow to rest.
你把头枕在枕头上休息吧。
- pillow talk 枕边话，悄悄话
- lay down... 放下……

语法重点 lay down 除了"放下"，还有"制定，铺设，主张"的意思。

0686 pin [pɪn] n 大头针
The park is quiet and you can hear a pin drop.
公园里很安静，针掉在地上都可以听到。
clean as a new pin 非常整洁　… hear a pin drop 针掉在地上都可以听到

0687 pineapple ['paɪnæpl] n 菠萝
Have you thought about eating a pineapple?
你有没有想过要吃一个菠萝？
Have you thought about...? 你有没有想过……？

语法重点
have you thought about 后面一般要接动名词。

0688 ping-pong / table tennis ['pɪŋ pɔːŋ] / ['teɪbl tenɪs] n 乒乓球
She devotes herself to the foundation of the ping-pong association.
她致力于创立乒乓球协会。
devote oneself to... 致力于……

语法重点
反身代词有时在句中有强调作用，作宾语时则没有强调的效果。
↻ devote (P. 426)

0689 pink [pɪŋk] n 粉红色 a 粉红色的
As we know, people can enjoy the pink peach blossoms in the snowy weather here.
众所周知，这里的人们能够在雪天欣赏到粉红色的桃花。
in the pink 极健康　as we know, ... 众所周知……

语法重点
as we know 后面接句子，但不影响句子主要意思的表达，既可以放在句首，也可以放在句中。

0690 pipe [paɪp] n 管子，烟斗
He looked at his children and puffed contentedly on his pipe.
他看着他的孩子，心满意足地抽着烟斗。
put that in your pipe and smoke it 承认某事为客观事实，不能改变既成事实

语法重点
副词修饰动词短语时，一般放在中间，如句中的 puffed contentedly on。

0691 pitch [pɪtʃ] v 投掷
The explorers are scheduled to pitch their camps at 6.
探险者们计划六点开始搭帐篷。
encamp 扎营　at fever pitch 处于狂热状态

语法重点
be scheduled to（计划）后要接动词原形。
↻ schedule (P. 354)

0692 pizza ['piːtsə] n 比萨
The guest got full when he only ate half of the pizza.
客人吃了一半的比萨就饱了。
... get full ……饱了

语法重点
句中 ate 是动词 eat（吃）的过去式。

0693 plain [pleɪn] a 平坦的，简单的
She made it plain that she would go to see a film tonight.
她明确表示晚上要去看电影。
complicated 复杂的　in plain English 坦白地说
"看电影"也可以用 watch a film。

0694 **planet** ['plænɪt] n 行星
It was plain that he likes studying the planets in his free time.
很显然，他喜欢在空闲时间研究行星。
- major planet 大行星　- it was plain that... 很显然……

0695 **plate** [pleɪt] n 盘子，金属牌
When it comes to hobby, he likes making plastic plates most.
提到兴趣爱好，他最喜欢做塑胶盘子。
- dish 盘子　- a plate of... 一盘……

> 语法重点
> when it comes to 后面通常接名词或者动名词。
> ⊃ plastic (P. 338)

0696 **platform** ['plætfɔːrm] n 站台，讲台，平台
Many fans were still waiting at the station platform in the rain.
很多粉丝仍然冒雨在火车站站台上等待。
- platform ticket 站台票　- ... in the rain 冒雨……

> 语法重点
> "在某地"一般用介词 at 或 in，地方较大时用 in，小地方用 at，例如 at the station, in China。

0697 **playful** ['pleɪfl] a 爱玩的，幽默的
We were amused by the tricks of the playful girl.
我们都觉得那个调皮女孩的戏法很有趣。
- humorous 幽默的　- inhumorous 不幽默的　- be amused by... 以……为乐

0698 **pleasant** ['pleznt] a 愉快的，讨人欢喜的，舒适的
After passing through the training, we can enjoy a pleasant time.
训练过后，我们可以享受快乐时光。
- favorable 讨人欢喜的　- unpleasant 使人不愉快的，讨厌的

0699 **pleasure** ['pleʒər] n 愉悦，高兴，满足
It's been a pleasure to spend the weekend with you.
和你一起过周末真是太开心了。
- joy 高兴　- with pleasure 愉快地
- it's been a pleasure... ……真是太开心了

> 语法重点
> pleasure 是抽象名词，不可数，但在句中，表达的是具体的一件让人高兴的事，当可数名词处理。

0700 **plus** [plʌs] prep 加上　a 正的，超过的
A plus factor is that he has played the violin for ten years.
一个有利因素是他拉小提琴十年了。
- minus 减　- plus sign 加号　- a plus factor is... 一个有利因素是……

0701 **poem** ['poʊəm] n 诗作
It's the very mountain described in the poem.
这就是诗里面写的那座山。
- verse 诗　- narrative poem 叙事诗

> 语法重点
> very 修饰名词，可以加强语气，表示强调。
> ⊃ describe (P. 151)

0702 poet [ˈpoʊət] n 诗人
Unlike a poet, I write poems just for pleasure.
跟诗人不一样，我写诗只是出于兴趣。

> 语法重点
> unlike 后面通常接名词或者代词。

0703 poison [ˈpɔɪzn] n 毒，毒害
Selfishness is a poison in our society.
自私对社会有害。

0704 policy [ˈpɑːləsi] n 政策
The policy that the local government should control the number of the visitors has turned out to be a failure.
政府应该控制游客数量的政策最后以失败告终。
🔄 deal 政策   🔄 wise policy 英明决策

> 语法重点
> turn out to（以失败告终）后面要接动词原形。
> ☺ government (P. 171)

0705 polite [pəˈlaɪt] a 礼貌的，客气的
It's not polite to take French leave at the party.
派对上不辞而别是不礼貌的。
🔄 courteous 有礼貌的   ✗ impolite 不礼貌的   🔄 polite remarks 应酬的客气话

0706 population [ˌpɑːpjuˈleɪʃn] n 人口
The bulk of the population in the city plays cards at weekend.
这个城市的大多数人在周末玩牌。
🔄 resident population 常住人口   🔄 the bulk of... 大多数……

0707 pork [pɔːrk] n 猪肉
How could you prepare pork for the guests?
你怎么能为客人们准备猪肉呢？
🔄 roast pork 烤猪肉   🔄 How could you...? 你怎么能……？

> 语法重点
> how could you 表示责备的意思，后面要接动词原形。

0708 port [pɔːrt] n 港口
I'm convinced that the ships in the port are full of visitors.
我确信港口里那些船上满是游客。

0709 pose [poʊz] v 摆姿势，假装 n 姿势，姿态
The lake poses a great threat to the visitors.
这座湖对游客来说是一个威胁。
🔄 posture 摆姿势   🔄 strike a pose 装腔作势

> 语法重点
> pose a great threat to（造成一大威胁）中的 to 是介词，后面通常接名词或者代词。

0710 positive [ˈpɑːzətɪv] a 积极的，肯定的
In other words, enough water will make us positive when facing the arduous journey.
换句话说，充足的水能让我们积极面对艰辛的旅途。
🔄 active 积极的   ✗ negative 消极的   🔄 positive response 肯定回应

> 语法重点
> in other words 后面要接句子，用另一种表达方式来表达同样的内容，使句意更加清楚明了。

0711 possibility [ˌpɑːsəˈbɪləti] n 可能性，可能的事

There's no possibility for them to walk out of desert if they don't take any action.

如果不采取任何行动，他们不可能走出沙漠。

- probability 可能性
- impossibility 没有可能
- "采取一次行动"用 take an action 表示。

0712 post [poʊst] n 邮件，职位 v 邮递，通知 ad 快速地

It's conceivable that everyone has received the post about the weekend plan.

可想而知，每个人都收到了那封关于周末计划的邮件。

- mail 邮件
- by post 邮寄
- It's conceivable that... 可想而知……

语法重点
不定代词在句中作主语时，其后的动词单复数要和主语保持一致，所以例句中 everyone 后面的动词要用 has。

0713 postcard [ˈpoʊstkɑːrd] n 明信片

It is very considerate of him to send me a postcard before my birthday party.

他想得真周到，在我生日派对前寄明信片给我。

语法重点
动词 send 后面也可以接双宾语，句中 send me a postcard 等于 send a postcard to me。

0714 pot [pɑːt] n 壶，锅，罐

There is water and peanuts in the pot, help yourself.

罐里面有水和花生，请自便。

- kettle 壶
- keep the pot boiling 谋生

语法重点
there be 句型如果有并列的主语，be 动词要和就近的主语保持一致。
- peanut (P. 202)

0715 potato [pəˈteɪtoʊ] n 马铃薯

He would like to be a potato at weekends.

周末的时候，他喜欢懒散在家。

- mashed potato 马铃薯泥

0716 pound [paʊnd] n 磅，英镑 v 连续猛击

May I ask the shopkeeper to grind a pound of coffee for me?

我能请老板帮我磨一磅咖啡吗？

- pound on 重击，猛打
- May I...? 我可以……吗？

语法重点
may I 后面接动词原形，表示一种委婉的请求。

0717 powerful [ˈpaʊərfl] a 有力量的，强大的

The president's speech just now was a powerful spur to action.

校长刚才讲的话很有鼓动力。

- formidable 强大的
- powerless 无力的

语法重点
spur 的意思是"刺激"，抽象名词具体化。

0718 praise [preɪz] v/n 称赞，表扬

We are full of praise for the dolphin's performance.

我们对海豚的表演赞不绝口。

- compliment 赞扬
- blame 批评
- beyond praise 赞美不尽

语法重点
performance 是表示抽象概念的名词，也叫普通名词。

0719 **pray** [preɪ] v 祈祷，乞求

All the people in the park are praying for the drowning boy.
所有在公园的人都在为落水的男孩祈祷。
- beseech 乞求
- pray for pardon 祈求原谅
- pray for... 为……祈祷
- drowning 表示"落水的"，drowned 表示"淹死的"。

0720 **prefer** [prɪˈfɜːr] v 更喜爱

It is believed that most of people interviewed prefer TV to radio.
据说大多数接受采访的人都喜欢看电视多于听收音机。
- favor 偏爱
- it is believed that... 据说……

语法重点
prefer... to... 表示"比起……更喜欢……"，prefer 与 to 后面接的成分要一致，比如都是代词，都是名词，或者都是动名词。

0721 **presence** [ˈprezns] n 出席，到场

None of the visitors lost the presence of mind when the robbers approached.
当强盗们逼近时，游客们都很镇定。
- attendance 出席
- absence 缺席

语法重点
none 常和 of 连用，表示某个群体中没有任何一个，of 之后可以加名词或代词，通常用来作主语。

0722 **present** [ˈpreznt] / [prɪˈzent] n 现在 v 赠送

Jack and Tom's father was not present at the party.
杰克和汤姆的父亲没有出席那个派对。
- current 现在的
- at present 目前，现在
- be present at... 出席……

语法重点
英语中，在表示几个词共同的所有关系时，要在最后一个词后面加上 's。如例句中 Jack and Tom's father，是两人共同的父亲。

0723 **president** [ˈprezɪdənt] n 总统，主席

May I have the pleasure of dancing with president?
我能有幸和总统跳舞吗？
- May I have the pleasure of...? 我能有幸……？

语法重点
在称呼或表示官衔、职位的名词前不加冠词，所以例句中的 president 前没有冠词。
→ pleasure (P. 205)

0724 **press** [pres] v 按，压，逼迫 n 新闻界，出版社

One of my hobbies is to press wet snow hard to make snowballs.
我的一个爱好是把湿雪捏成雪球。
- squeeze 压榨，挤压
- press conference 记者招待会，新闻发布会

0725 **pride** [praɪd] n 骄傲

The woman takes pride in the winning of the game.
那个女人为赢得了这次比赛感到骄傲。
- conceit 自豪，自负
- modesty 谦虚
- swallow one's pride 忍气吞声

0726 **prince** [prɪns] n 王子

The prince was enamoured of a girl when he traveled in a small country.
王子在一个小国家旅游时迷恋上了一个女孩。
- princess 公主
- Prince Charming 白马王子

语法重点
enamoured 是动词 enamour 的过去分词，be enamoured of 就相当于 be crazy about。

pray ~ prize

0727 princess [ˌprɪn'ses] n 公主，王妃
Finally, the princess presented the performer with a bouquet of flowers.
最终，公主为表演者献上一束鲜花。

> 语法重点
> finally 可以放在动词之前，用来指经过漫长的等待后，某物终于出现或某事终于发生。

0728 principal ['prɪnsəpl] a 首要的 n 负责人
The principal of the activity said that we must go home before 11 at night.
活动的负责人说，我们必须在晚上十一点前回家。

0729 principle ['prɪnsəpl] n 原则，原理，道义
Mother doesn't allow me to go out with boys at night on principle.
出于原则，妈妈不允许我晚上和男孩子出去玩。
○ in principle 原则上　　○ ... on principle 出于原则……

0730 printer ['prɪntər] n 打印机，印刷工人
The printer takes it as a pleasure to watch you play computer games.
那个印刷工人很喜欢看你玩电脑游戏。
○ laser printer 激光打印机　　○ take it as a pleasure to... 很喜欢……

> 语法重点
> to watch you play computer games 是真正的宾语，it 是形式宾语。

0731 prison ['prɪzn] n 监狱
The man who destroyed the historical relics in the museum was put into prison by the police.
那个破坏博物馆文物的人被警方关进了监狱。
○ jail 监狱　　○ escape from prison 越狱
○ be put into prison 表示"被关进监狱"，come out of prison 表示"出狱"。

⊃ historical (P. 306)

0732 prisoner ['prɪznər] n 囚犯
I organized some artists to give a free performance for the prisoners.
我安排了一些艺人为犯人们免费演出。
○ convict 囚犯　　○ prisoner of war 战犯

0733 private ['praɪvət] a 私人的，秘密的
Worse still, her new celebrity is intruding on her private life.
更糟糕的是，最近的成名侵扰了她的私生活。
○ personal 私人的　　○ public 公共的　　○ private information 私人信息

> 语法重点
> worse 为 bad 的比较级形式，既可以作形容词，也可以作副词来用，意思是"更坏的"。它和 still 构成短语 worse still，表示"更糟糕的是，更坏的是"，一般放在句首，来表达一种更坏的情况。

0734 prize [praɪz] n 奖品，奖金
Needless to say, he will get the first prize in the singing competition.
不必说，他今年能拿到歌唱比赛的冠军。
○ award 奖品　　○ needless to say, ... 不必说，……

0735 **produce** [prəˈduːs] / [ˈprɔːduːs] v 产生 n 产品
The fans expect the actress to produce more and better works next year.
粉丝们期望这个女演员明年有更多更好的作品。
🔄 produce results 产生结果

0736 **producer** [prəˈduːsər] n 制造者
The producer of the roller coaster took responsibility for the accident.
过山车的制造商会对这次事故负责。
🔄 manufacturer 制造者　🔄 take responsibility for... 对……承担责任

> 语法重点
> 动词后加上 er 或者 r，变成名词，表示这个动作的发出者，如本句中的 producer，就是动词 produce 加 r 转变而来的。

0737 **progress** [ˈprɑːɡres] n / v 进展，进行
To be frank, the progress of the hiking is too slow.
坦白地讲，徒步旅行的进展速度太慢了。
🔄 advance 前进　🔄 be in progress 在进行中　🔄 to be frank, ... 坦白讲，……

> 语法重点
> to be frank 是动词不定式，在句中作插入语，一般放在句首。
> 🔄 frank (P. 168)

0738 **project** [prəˈdʒekt] / [ˈprɑːdʒekt] v / n 计划
She is enthusiastic over the project for building a new stadium.
她对于修建一个新的体育馆的计划很热衷。
🔄 scheme 计划　🔄 new project 新项目

0739 **promise** [ˈprɑːmɪs] v 承诺，答应，许诺，希望
I promised that I will go bowling with you tomorrow.
我承诺明天跟你一块去打保龄球。
🔄 permit 允许　🔄 a lick and a promise 潦草从事

0740 **pronounce** [prəˈnaʊns] v 发音，发表意见
Incidentally, the guests pronounced that the dinner was excellent.
顺便提一下，客人们说晚餐很不错。
🔄 declare 宣布　🔄 pronounce sentence of death 宣判死刑

> 语法重点
> incidentally 是插入语，插入语是指句子结构和成分之外的插入成分，只起到一种附加说明的作用，其在句子中的位置比较灵活，既可以放在句首，也可以放在句中或句尾。

0741 **propose** [prəˈpoʊz] v 提议，建议，求婚
She proposed that we should have a discussion about where to go.
她建议我们讨论一下要去哪里。
🔄 suggest 提议，建议　🔄 have a discussion... 讨论……

> 语法重点
> propose 后面接 that 从句时，从句一般用虚拟语气。

0742 **protect** [prəˈtekt] v 保护
Most important, all the young explorers should be well protected.
最重要的是要好好保护年龄小的探险者。
🔄 defend 保卫　🔄 protect the environment 保护环境

> 语法重点
> 一些形容词（短语）也可以作插入语，常放在句首。

produce ~ puppet

0743 proud [praʊd] **a** 骄傲的，自豪的
I feel proud of my brother, for he got the first prize in the piano competition.
我为哥哥感到骄傲，他赢得了钢琴比赛的第一名。
反 humble 谦虚的　搭 feel proud of... 为……骄傲

0744 provide [prəˈvaɪd] **v** 提供，供应
The book provides vital information regarding the scenic spots of the city to the visitors.
这本书为游客们提供这个城市景点的关键信息。
同 supply 供应　搭 provide... to... 向……提供……

> 语法重点
> 句中 regarding 的意思是"关于"，相当于介词 about。

0745 pudding [ˈpʊdɪŋ] **n** 布丁
The guest commented that the pudding was too sweet.
客人评论那个布丁太甜了。
搭 sb. comments that... 某人评论到……

> ⊃ comment (P. 410)

0746 pump [pʌmp] **n** 抽水机　**v** 抽取，灌输
Luckily, I borrowed a pump from a cyclist when travelling on the road.
幸运的是，在旅途中，我从一个骑脚踏车的人那里借到一个打气筒。

> 语法重点
> luckily 是副词，放在句首作插入语，也可以放在句中或者句末。

0747 pumpkin [ˈpʌmpkɪn] **n** 南瓜
My favorite food is pumpkin pie.
我最喜欢吃的食物是南瓜派。

0748 punish [ˈpʌnɪʃ] **v** 惩罚
The gardener didn't punish him for picking flowers.
园丁没有因为他摘花而惩罚他。
同 penalize 惩罚　反 forgive 原谅
搭 punish with... 用……惩罚　punish sb. for... 因为……惩罚某人

> ⊃ gardener (P. 169)

0749 pupil [ˈpjuːpl] **n** 小学生
The teacher checked off each pupil as they arrived at the zoo.
到动物园时，老师一一清点人数。
同 student 学生　反 master 教师　搭 check off... 核对……

0750 puppet [ˈpʌpɪt] **n** 傀儡，木偶
There's little chance for the little boy to play with his sister's puppet.
小男孩没有一点儿机会玩妹妹的木偶。
搭 puppet state 傀儡政权

> 语法重点
> chance 是不可数名词，所以前面用 little 来修饰。

0751 **puppy** ['pʌpi] n 小狗，幼犬
The most interesting thing is that a little puppy runs in the race.
最有趣的是还有一只小狗参加赛跑。
🔄 pup 小狗　🔄 puppy love 初恋

> **语法重点**
> little 除了表示数量上很少以外，作形容词时还有"小的，幼小的"之意，主要强调形体上的小，如例句中的 little puppy。

0752 **purse** [pɜːrs] n 钱包
I regretted that someone stole my purse when I was walking in the morning.
很遗憾，我早上散步时，有人偷走了我的钱包。
🔄 wallet 钱包　🔄 hold the purse strings 掌握开支，掌握财权
📌 purse 一般指女用钱包，wallet 一般指男用钱包。

⤴ regret (P. 347)

0753 **puzzle** ['pʌzl] v 困扰，使迷惑，使为难
What puzzled me so much is why she is so keen on the ballet.
让我感到很不解的是她为什么这么热衷于跳芭蕾。
🔄 confuse 使困惑　🔄 puzzle over 为……烦恼，苦苦思考

> **语法重点**
> be keen on 的意思是"热衷于……"，be 后面加上 so，语气更强烈。

0754 **quality** ['kwaːləti] n 品质
Moreover, there is a poetic quality to his playing.
而且，他的演奏富有诗意。
🔄 quality of life 生活品质

> **语法重点**
> moreover 的意同 and，但通常置于句首。

0755 **quantity** ['kwaːntəti] n 量
There are only a small quantity of tourists left in the zoo.
动物园里只剩下少数游客。
🔄 an unknown 未知数，难预测的事

0756 **quarter** ['kwɔːrtər] n 四分之一，一刻钟
I'm told that over a quarter of a million bicycle enthusiasts have been there.
我听说25万以上热爱骑脚踏车的人去过那里。
🔄 I'm told that... 我听说……

0757 **quit** [kwɪt] v 离开，停止，放弃
Time presses, so we have to quit some places.
时间紧迫，所以我们得放弃一些地方不去参观了。
🔄 abandon 放弃　🔄 quit smoking 戒烟　🔄 time presses, ... 时间紧迫，……

> **语法重点**
> quit 后面接动词时，通常要用动词的 ing 形式，表示"停止做某事，放弃做某事"。

0758 **quiz** [kwɪz] n 小考，恶作剧 v 盘问，对……进行测验
It is needless to say that he played basketball after taking part in the quiz.
不用说，参加完课堂测验他就去打篮球了。
🔄 test 测验　🔄 it is needless to say that... 不用说……

0759 rabbit ['ræbɪt] n 兔子

All of a sudden, the magician conjured a rabbit out of her clothes.
突然，魔术师从她的衣服里变出了一只兔子。
- hare 兔子
- all of a sudden（突然）等于 suddenly（突然）。

0760 rainy ['reɪni] a 下雨的

Strictly speaking, the rainy weather isn't fit for self-driving travel.
严格来说，雨天不适合自己开车出游。
- pluvial 多雨的
- rainless 少雨的
- prepare for a rainy day 未雨绸缪

语法重点
strictly 是副词，意思是"严格地，完全地"，和 speaking 搭配，构成短语 strictly speaking，意思是"严格来说"，通常用在句首，用来修饰其后的句子。

0761 range [reɪndʒ] n 范围，幅度

To tell you the truth, he is not within the age range that the tour group requests.
说实话，他不在旅行团所要求的年龄范围之内。
- scope 范围
- be within the age range... 在……的年龄范围

语法重点
句中 that 引导形容词从句，并在从句中充当宾语，因此可以省略。
↪ request（P. 349）

0762 rapid ['ræpɪd] a 迅速的

Do you find that only a few of the members can swim across such a rapid river?
你发现成员中只有很少的人能够游过这样湍急的河流吗？
- fast 迅速的
- slow 缓慢的
- make rapid strides 进展迅速，突飞猛进

语法重点
rapid 通常指突然或急速（且连续不断）的动作，而 fast 表示"快"，侧重指速度方面。

0763 rare [rer] a 稀有的，罕见的，珍贵的

It's extremely rare for it to be so cold in October in this touring city.
这个旅游城市十月份就这样冷是极其罕见的。

语法重点
October 的意思是"十月"，表示月份的名词，首字母都要大写。

0764 rather ['ræðər] ad 宁愿，相当

He would rather take the train to Beijing than by air.
他宁愿搭火车也不愿坐飞机去北京。
- would rather 宁可

语法重点
表示乘坐某种交通工具时，可以用"take + the + 交通工具"的结构，如 take the bus（搭公共汽车）等。

0765 reality [ri'æləti] n 真实，现实，实际

The film which was shown yesterday showed life in the country with great reality.
昨天上映的影片非常逼真地展现了农村的生活。
- actuality 现实
- in reality 实际上，事实上

0766 realize ['ri:əlaɪz] v 实现，认识，意识到，了解

Only then did she realize that it wasn't the way to the forest park.
直到这时她才知道，这不是到森林公园的路。

语法重点
only then 是否定副词短语，常置于句首，其后主要句子要用倒装结构。

0767 **recent** ['riːsnt] a 最近的
Recent events had no bearing on his decision to travel to Thailand.
近期的事件没有影响他去泰国旅游的决定。
latest 最近的　　ancient 古老的　　in recent years 近年来

0768 **record** ['rekərd] / [rɪ'kɔːrd] n 记录，唱片 v 记录，录下
We took many photographs to record our journey.
我们拍很多的照片来记录我们的旅程。
criminal record 犯罪记录　　take photographs... 照相……

photograph (P. 203)

0769 **rectangle** ['rektæŋgl] n 长方形，矩形
It was obvious that the little girl folded the paper into a neat rectangle.
很显然，小女孩折纸折成了一个整整齐齐的长方形。
oblong 长方形　　rectangle tool 矩形工具
it was obvious that... 很显然……

0770 **refrigerator / fridge / icebox**
[rɪ'frɪdʒəreɪtər] / [frɪdʒ] / ['aɪsbɑːks] n 冰箱
I'm embarrassed that there's little food in the refrigerator now to serve the guests.
很不好意思，冰箱里几乎没有食物来招待客人了。
portable refrigerator 携带式冰箱

语法重点
英语中，为了表达方便，可以将有些较长的单词的首尾字母去掉，只取中间的主体成分，所以有时 refrigerator 也写作 fridge。

0771 **refuse** [rɪ'fjuːz] v 拒绝
Trust me; none of them will refuse your invitation to the party.
相信我，他们都不会拒绝你的派对邀请。
decline 拒绝　　accept 接受　　refuse one's consent 不同意
trust me 为固定用法，一般不用 believe me 来表达。

0772 **regard** [rɪ'gɑːrd] n 注重 v 看作，注视，留意
In this regard, we will consider the feelings of the wounded players.
在这个方面，我们会考虑受伤球员们的感受。
disregard 忽视，漠视　　as regards 至于，关于
in this regard, ... 在这方面，……

语法重点
当表示有生命的名词本身带有短语或从句时，其所有格不用 's 的形式，而用 of 所有格，如例句中的 the feelings of the wounded players。

0773 **region** ['riːdʒən] n 区域，地区，地带
The bar is renowned as the best place of amusement in the region.
这个酒吧被誉为本地最好的娱乐场所。
area 地区，区域　　be renowned as... 被誉为……

语法重点
region 的使用范围较广，表示某种特定范围或具有某种特征的地区或区域；district 主要指某种专属的行政区域。

0774 regular ['rɛgjələr] a 有规律的，规则的

In reality, regular exercise is more helpful than all drugs.
事实上，有规律的锻炼比任何药物都有用。
同 inerratic 规则的　　反 irregular 不规则的　　扩 as regular as clockwork 极有规律

> **语法重点**
> in reality 用来表述一种"真相或真实情况"，常用在句首，用来引导整个句子。

0775 reject [rɪ'dʒɛkt] v 拒绝，驳斥

It was unwise of you to reject his invitation to go skiing.
你拒绝他去滑雪的邀请真是不明智。
同 refuse 拒绝　　反 accept 接受　　扩 rejection rate 拒绝率

0776 relation [rɪ'leɪʃn] n 关系，联系

The man in the tour group has some relations with the guide.
旅游团里的那个男人跟导游有关系。
扩 in relation to 关于……，涉及　　扩 have some relations with... 与……有关系

0777 relationship [rɪ'leɪʃnʃɪp] n 关系，亲戚关系

The actor and the actress only have a sexual relationship, and nothing else.
那个男演员和女演员之间只有性关系，仅此而已。
扩 causal relationship 因果关系　　扩 have a / an... relationship 有……的关系

> **语法重点**
> 副词 else 有"另外，其他"的意思，它和不定代词 nothing 连用构成 nothing else，表达的意思是"没有其他的，仅此而已"。

0778 repeat [rɪ'piːt] v 重复，重说，重做

Could you repeat the words in the song that you sang a moment ago?
你能重复一下刚才你唱的那首歌里的歌词吗？
同 reduplicate 重复　　扩 ... a moment ago 刚才……

> **语法重点**
> a moment ago 常用在一般过去时中，表示刚刚发生的某种情况。

0779 reply [rɪ'plaɪ] v 回复

Believe it or not, his idol replied to his email last night.
信不信由你，他的偶像昨晚回复了他的信件。
同 respond 回答　　反 question 询问　　扩 reply immediately 立即回答

> **语法重点**
> believe it or not（信不信由你）用在口语中，通常置于句首，和其后表达某种事实的主句用逗号隔开。

0780 reporter [rɪ'pɔːrtər] n 记者

The director said that the reporter did violence to the truth.
导演说这个记者扭曲了事实真相。
同 correspondent 记者　　扩 ... do violence to the truth ……扭曲事实真相

> **语法重点**
> 宾语从句的时态要与主句保持一致，所以从句中动词用的是 did。

0781 require [rɪ'kwaɪər] v 需要，规定

It's apparent that the flowers my father planted require watering.
很显然，爸爸种的那些花需要浇水了。
同 need 需要，需求　　扩 it's apparent that... 很显然，……

> **语法重点**
> 在动词 require 之后加动名词时，虽然是主动结构，但表达的是被动含义。
> ⊃ apparent (P. 255)

0782 **respect** [rɪ'spekt] v 尊敬，尊重 n 尊敬，方面
The boy suffering heart disease went bungee jumping without respect to the result.
那个有心脏病的男孩去高空弹跳，也不考虑后果。
同 esteem 尊敬　反 dishonor 使蒙羞　搭 respect oneself 自重
句 ... without respect to the result 不考虑后果……

⇨ disease (P. 285)

0783 **responsible** [rɪ'spɑːnsəbl] a 有责任的，负责的
The main problem is who should be responsible for these injured tourists.
主要问题是谁应该对这些受伤的游客负责。
同 conscientious 尽责的　搭 responsible for... 为……负责

0784 **restaurant** ['restrɑːnt] n 餐厅，饭店
The entertainment in the restaurant took hold of some foreigners.
这个餐厅的娱乐节目吸引了一些外国人。
同 hotel 饭店　搭 take hold of... 吸引……

⇨ entertainment (P. 435)

0785 **restroom** ['restruːm] n 洗手间
I happened to see her throwing up in the restroom of the zoo.
我碰巧看见她正在动物园的洗手间里呕吐不止。
同 bathroom 洗手间　搭 I happen to do... 我碰巧……

0786 **result** [rɪ'zʌlt] n 结果
I was disappointed at the result of the football game.
我对足球比赛结果很失望。
同 outcome 结果　同 cause 原因　搭 without result 徒劳地，毫无结果地

语法重点
"对……很失望" 也可以表达为 be disappointed with，be disappointed by。

0787 **review** [rɪ'vjuː] v / n 复习，回顾
The review written by the reporter was critical of the violence in the film.
记者写的这篇评论是批评影片里的暴力。
反 preview 预习　搭 review meeting 审核会　搭 be critical of... 批判……

语法重点
句中 the review 是主语，written by the reporter 修饰主语 the review。

0788 **riches** ['rɪtʃɪz] n 财产
After all, riches have wings.
毕竟钱财是身外之物。

语法重点
after all 用在句首时，用逗号和主句隔开。

0789 **rock** [rɑːk] n 岩石，摇滚乐
Last night, she listened to the whole disk about rock music without any stop.
昨晚，她一次就把整张摇滚音乐的光碟听完了。

0790 **rocky** ['rɑːki] a 多岩石的，困难重重的
It cost them ten hours to trek across the rocky terrain.
他们花了十个小时才艰难地穿过那片遍布岩石的地带。
- stony 石头的 - soft 柔软的 - rocky road 坎坷崎岖的路

0791 **role** [roʊl] n 角色，作用，职责
I didn't agree to play the role in the movie in the end.
我最终还是没有同意出演电影里这个角色。
- part 角色 - role model 榜样，模范

> 语法重点
> in the end 用在句尾，表示"最后、最终"，主要强调的是最终的结果。
> ⊃ agree (P. 005)

0792 **royal** ['rɔɪəl] a 王室的，皇家的
I received the invitation to the royal banquet.
我收到参加皇家宴席的请柬。

0793 **rude** [ruːd] a 粗鲁的，不礼貌的
Because of the rude behavior of the man, all of us were kicked out of the bar.
因为那个人行为粗鲁，我们所有人都被赶出了酒吧。
- polite 有礼貌的 - rude remarks 出言不逊，粗鲁的话

> 语法重点
> because of 表示"因为，由于"，其后接名词或动名词。

0794 **ruler** ['ruːlər] n 统治者，支配者
The key point which the ruler advocates is to do exercise every day.
那个统治者提倡的关键点是天天健身运动。
- governor 统治者 - the key point is that... 关键是……

> 语法重点
> 本句的主句是 the key point is...，which the ruler advocates 是定语从句，修饰主语 the key point。

0795 **runner** ['rʌnər] n 跑者，赛跑的人
She keeps running all the year round like a runner.
她全年都坚持锻炼跑步，如同跑者一般。

> 语法重点
> all the year round 指一年到头的情况都是如此，一般放在句尾。

0796 **rush** [rʌʃ] v 冲，奔跑，仓促行事，突袭
As I just mentioned, the tour bus rushed toward the crowds.
正如我刚才提到的那样，观光巴士朝人群冲了过去。
- rush up 催促
- rush 还可以当名词，意思是"匆忙，繁忙时候"，rush hour 指"上下班，高峰期"。

0797 **safety** ['seɪfti] n 安全
You should be watchful to ensure the safety of the travelers.
为了确保游客们的安全，你要格外小心。
- security 安全 - danger 危险 - safety device 安全装置

⊃ ensure (P. 562)

0798 **sailor** ['seɪlər] n 水手
As a result of the severe force of water, all the sailors lost their balance.
由于水的冲力太大，所有水手都失去了平衡。
● seaman 水手　● as a result of... 由于……

语法重点
as a result of 后接名词或动名词，用来表示原因，通常放在句首。
⊃ severe (P. 502)

0799 **salad** ['sæləd] n 沙拉，凉拌菜
All of her friends will back her up in this salad dish contest.
对于这次沙拉大赛，所有朋友都会支援她。
● will back up... 将会支持……

语法重点
her 是代词，要放在 back 与 up 之间。

0800 **salty** ['sɔːlti] a 咸的，盐的
He didn't taste the salty dish again all the way through the banquet.
在整个宴会中，他都没有再去碰那道太咸的菜。
● ... all the way through... 自始至终

语法重点
all the way 表示某种情况从头到尾的全过程，在句中一般作形容词使用，也可以表示"一路上"的意思。

0801 **sample** ['sæmpl] n 样品，样本
We should bring home to the supervisor that the sample was stolen.
我们应该让主管知道样本被偷了。
● specimen 样品，样本　● sample data 样本资料

0802 **sandwich** ['sænwɪtʃ] n 三明治
The poor hiker had to satisfy his hunger with a sandwich.
那个可怜的徒步旅行者不得不以三明治充饥。
● sandwich course 工读交替制课程　● satisfy one's hunger with... 以……充饥

语法重点
sandwich 的复数形式是 sandwiches，注意字母 d 不发音。

0803 **satisfy** ['sætɪsfaɪ] v 使满足
To satisfy her curiosity, they both told her where they would go.
为了满足她的好奇心，他们两个告诉了她他们要去哪里。
● please 使满意　● dissatisfy 使不满

语法重点
both 可以在句中作同位语，要放在作主语的名词之后。

0804 **sauce** [sɔːs] n 酱汁，调味剂，佐料
This kind of sauce goes with the fried fish well.
这种酱汁最适合做酥炸鱼了。
● ... go with... well 和……很相配

语法重点
well 修饰 go with，也可以放在 go 与 with 之间。

0805 **science** ['saɪəns] n 科学
The listeners all graduated from the science department of this university.
所有听众都是从这所大学的理工学院毕业。
● social science 社会科学　● graduate from... 从……毕业

语法重点
句中不定代词 all 作同位语，位于主语之后，动词之前。

0806 scientist ['saɪəntɪst] n 科学家

They are expecting the arrival of a famous scientist.
他们正期待一位著名科学家的来访。
- expect the arrival of... 期待……的到访

0807 scissors ['sɪzərzl] n 剪刀

That's not the right way to hold the scissors; and you will hurt other children.
你那样拿剪刀不对，会伤到其他的小朋友。
- a pair of scissors 一把剪刀

语法重点 that's not the right way 后面一般接动词不定式。

0808 score [skɔːr] n 成绩

She went mad with joy when she saw her boyfriend scored the winning goal.
看着男朋友射入获胜的一球，她感到欣喜若狂。
- marks 分数 - final score 最后得分

语法重点 句中 winning 不是动名词，而是形容词，修饰 goal。

0809 screen [skriːn] n 屏幕

She can't see the screen on account of the person in front of her.
由于前面的人挡住了她，所以她看不见屏幕。
- computer screen 电脑屏幕 - on account of... 由于……

0810 search [sɜːrtʃ] v 寻找

They searched the desert for the missing explorers.
他们在沙漠里寻找那些迷路的探险者。
- seek 搜索，寻找 - search out 查出，找到 - search... for... 在……寻找……

↔ desert (P. 151)

0811 secret ['siːkrət] n 秘密

You know whether the actor will appear or not is still kept as a secret.
你知道，那位演员是否出场现在仍是一个秘密。
- the secret of nature 自然的奥秘 - ... be kept as a secret... ……是一个秘密

语法重点 whether... or not 的意思是"是否……"，表示一种不确定的语气，作主语时其后的动词要用单数的形式。

0812 secretary ['sekrəteri] n 秘书，书记，部长，大臣

Someone will double for the secretary when he is on holiday.
秘书度假时，有人会来代替他。
- executive secretary 执行秘书 - double for... 代替……

0813 section ['sekʃn] n 部分，部门，章节

The section of the city is under threat from the large number of tourists.
该城市的这一地区由于游客太多而面临威胁。
- be under threat from... 受到……的威胁

语法重点 表示数量多时，要用 large 来修饰 number。
↔ threat (P. 374)

0814 **select** [sɪ'lekt] v 挑选，选择
At the same time, he selected a good place for camping.
同时，他还挑选了一个适合露营的好地方。
choose 选择　　at the same time, ... 同时，……

> 语法重点
> at the same time 表示在同一个时间发生某事，一般置于句首。

0815 **selection** [sɪ'lekʃn] n 选择，可选择的东西
There were a selection of movies for them to choose from.
有一系列的电影供他们选择。
option 选择　　natural selection 物竞天择　　choose from... 从……中挑选

0816 **semester** [sɪ'mestər] n 学期
Strive hard to have a good ending in the last semester and your parents will take you to the famous Ming Tombs.
在最后一个学期努力用功取得好成绩，你父母就会带你去参观明十三陵。
term 学期　　semester report 学期报告　　strive hard to... 努力用功去……

> 语法重点
> Ming Tombs（明十三陵）是一种特殊的建筑，属于专有名词，所以要大写。
> parent (P. 074)

0817 **separate** ['seprət] a 分开的 ['sepreɪt] v 分开
You can't separate the sheep from the goats in entertainment circle.
在娱乐圈，你无法分辨好人与坏人。
divide 分开　　unite 联合，统一　　separate... from... 分辨……与……

0818 **serious** ['sɪrɪəs] a 严肃的
The guide could make certain that the situation of the flood must be very serious.
导游可以确定水灾非常严重。
serious injury 重伤　　sb. can make certain that... 某人可以确定……

> 语法重点
> make 为使役动词，意思是"使"，certain 是形容词"肯定的"，二者组合形成短语 make certain，表示"弄清楚，确定"。

0819 **servant** ['sɜːrvənt] n 仆人
Tell the servant to lead the visitors in.
让仆人将客人领进来。
master 主人　　lead sb. in... 领某人进……

0820 **settle** ['setl] v 安放
I'm sure you will be tired of the merry-go-round of romance and settle down one day.
我知道你总有一天会厌倦那些风流韵事，会安定下来。
solve 解决　　be tired of... 厌倦……

> 语法重点
> merry-go-round 本意是"旋转木马"，但 the merry-go-round of romance 的意思是"风流韵事"。

0821 **share** [ʃer] v 分享，分担，分配
He asked me if I shared an affinity with him.
他问我是否跟他有相同的喜好。
allot 分配　　share and share alike 平均分配

> 语法重点
> share 还可以作名词，意思是"股份"，通常用复数。

select ~ sidewalk

0822 shelf [ʃelf] **n** 架子，隔板
She is forty years old and she's been left on the shelf.
她四十岁了，现在也嫁不出去了。
- on the shelf 束之高阁，闲置的
- ... be left on the shelf ……嫁不出去

○ old (P. 071)

0823 shell [ʃel] **n** 贝壳，外壳，炮弹
He picked up a beautiful shell by chance when walking by the seaside.
在海边散步时，他偶然捡到一个美丽的贝壳。
- come out of one's shell 不再冷漠，不再害羞
- ... by chance 偶然……

0824 shock [ʃɑːk] **n** 震惊
It was a shock for them to find there is no water left when travelling in the desert.
在沙漠旅游发现没水时，他们感到很震惊。
- cultural shock 文化冲击

0825 shoot [ʃuːt] **v** 射击
He began to shoot, and all of the tourists were shocked.
他开枪射击，所有游客都感到震惊。
- fire 射击
- shoot down 击落，否决
- be shocked by... 对……很震惊

> **语法重点**
> shoot 经常与 at 连用，表示"对……射击"。

0826 shorts [ʃɔːrts] **n** 宽松运动短裤
The man wanted to swim and he stripped down to his shorts and leaped into the river.
那人想要游泳，他把衣服脱得只剩下一条短裤，然后跳入河中。

> **语法重点**
> short 作形容词讲是"短的"，当名词讲时，意思是"短裤"，由于短裤是两条腿，所以一般都用复数。

0827 shower [ˈʃaʊər] **n** 阵雨，淋浴
I want to play cards; let's get started after taking the shower.
我想玩牌，我们洗完澡就开始吧。
- shower room 浴室
- Let's get started... 让我们开始……

> **语法重点**
> get started 表示开始行动，如果后面接名词要加"介词 in + 名词"，即 get started in sth.，如果接动词要加"介词 on + 动名词"，即 get started on doing sth.。

0828 shrimp [ʃrɪmp] **n** 小虾
I can't wait to catch shrimps in the stream.
我迫不及待要去小溪里捉虾了。
- I can't wait to... 我迫不及待……

0829 sidewalk [ˈsaɪdwɔːk] **n** 人行道
These young men are dancing to the music on the sidewalk.
这些年轻人在人行道上跟着音乐跳舞。
- pavement 人行道

> **语法重点**
> "伴随音乐跳舞"一般用介词 to，而不是 with。

0830 sign [saɪn] **n** 标志，符号 **v** 签名

She didn't show any sign of being moved after hearing the news that he would take her to America for their honey moon.
听到他要带她去美国度蜜月的消息，她没有任何感动的迹象。

> 语法重点
> 被动语态的动名词形式是"being + 动词过去分词"。

0831 silence ['saɪləns] **n** 寂静

Try to reduce the excited visitors to silence.
设法使这些兴奋的游客们安静下来。
反 noise 噪声　同 dead silence 寂静无声

0832 silent ['saɪlənt] **a** 沉默的，安静的，不吵闹的

The director asked her to keep silent and listen to him carefully.
导演让她保持安静，认真听他讲话。
同 quiet 安静的　反 noisy 喧闹的　词 ... keep silent 保持安静

> 语法重点
> listen to 一般不用于被动语态。

0833 silk [sɪlk] **n** 丝绸

This time we will travel along the old Silk Road which linked China with the West before.
这次我们要沿着丝绸之路旅行，过去它是连接着中国和西方国家的桥梁。
词 link... with... 把……和……连接起来

0834 similar ['sɪmələr] **a** 相似的，类似的

They hold similar views on the issue whether to let their daughter learn ballet.
他们在女儿是否该学芭蕾舞这个问题上观点相同。
同 alike 相似的　词 in a similar way 按同样的方式

> 语法重点
> hold similar views on 前面的主语必须是两个或者两个以上的人。
> ⇨ issue (P. 586)

0835 simply ['sɪmpli] **ad** 简单地，完全，简直

I simply cannot bear with the man who watches TV 24 hours a day.
我简直无法忍受那个一天 24 小时都在看电视的人。
同 fairly 简直　词 to put it simply 简单地说
词 I simply can't bear with... 我简直无法忍受……

> 语法重点
> 24 hours a day（一天 24 小时）是一种夸张的表达方法。

0836 single ['sɪŋgl] **a** 单一的，单个的

The man keeps single after divorcing his wife.
那个男人和妻子离婚后一直单身。

0837 sink [sɪŋk] **v** 沉没 **n** 水槽，沟渠

It's said that most of the passengers were moved into the rescue boats from the sinking ship, and only one is missing.
据说大部分乘客都从下沉的船上被移到救生艇上，只有一个乘客失踪了。
反 float 漂浮　词 move into... from... 从哪里移入……

> 语法重点
> 不定代词 one 在句中指代不确定的对象，而不是特指某个已知的人或物，如例句中的 one 并没有确定失踪的人是谁。

sign ~ slim

0838 skillful ['skɪlfl] a 熟练的，灵巧的
I dare not tell her parents her first dancing debut is neither skillful nor attractive.
我不敢告诉她父母，她的初次舞蹈表演既不灵巧，也没有吸引力。
- adept 熟练的　- unskillful 不熟练的　- be skillful in... 精于……

> 语法重点
> neither... nor 用来连接两个形容词或副词。
> - neither (P. 195)

0839 skilled [skɪld] a 熟练的，有技能的，需要技能的
Do you know that he is very skilled in video games?
你知道他玩电脑游戏很熟练吗？
- experienced 熟练的　- unskilled 不熟练的　- be skilled in... 擅长……
- video game 意思是"电脑游戏，电视游戏"，主要指电脑游戏或摇杆操作的电视游戏等。

0840 skinny ['skɪni] a 皮包骨的
The only problem on the stun man is that he is too skinny.
这个替身演员唯一的问题就是太瘦了。
- bony 瘦削的　- fat 胖的　- skinny jeans 紧身牛仔裤

> 语法重点
> only 在句中是形容词，修饰 problem。

0841 skirt [skɜːrt] n 裙子，下摆，边缘
The skirt is not the one that I plan to wear when traveling to Italy.
这条裙子不是我打算去意大利旅游时要穿的那条。
- be not the one that... 不是……的那一个

> 语法重点
> 不定代词 one 表示泛指的概念，但前面加上定冠词 the 时，则表示特指，the one 后一般加限制性定语从句。

0842 sleepy ['sliːpi] a 想睡的
The driver of the bus was sleepy and the bus ran into a lamppost.
公交车司机非常想睡觉，结果把车撞到路灯上了。
- slumberous 昏昏欲睡的　- wakeful 醒着的，不眠的　- feel sleepy 想睡觉

> 语法重点
> run into（撞上）后面接人时，意思是"偶然遇到"。

0843 slender ['slendər] a 苗条的，修长的
The girl with a slender figure likes playing bowling.
那个身材苗条的女孩喜欢打保龄球。
- slim 苗条的，修长的　- stout 肥胖的

0844 slide [slaɪd] v 滑动，下滑
Now you can slide down the grassy slope.
现在你可以顺着这草坡滑下去了。
- slide into... 不知不觉陷入……，不知不觉地沾染上……
- slide 表示在一个光滑的表面持续地滑动。

- grassy (P. 172)

0845 slim [slɪm] a 苗条的，细长的
The slim girl sank into the water when she was swimming.
那个苗条的女孩游泳时沉到了水里。
- slim down 使身材变苗条，裁员　- ... sink into... ……沉入……

> 语法重点
> sink into 既可以表示某种固体沉进液体里，也可以用来指液体渗入某种固体当中。

223

0846 **slip** [slɪp] v 滑动，溜走，滑落
I can slip you into the cinema without a ticket.
没有票我也可以带着你混进电影院。
slip through sb's fingers（尤指机会）被错过　　slip sb. into... 带某人溜进……

0847 **slipper** ['slɪpər] n 拖鞋
What do you say to wearing a pair of slippers to the party?
你觉得可以穿拖鞋去参加派对吗？
ballet slipper 芭蕾舞鞋　　What do you say to...? 你觉得……可以吗？

语法重点
what do you say to 后面要接名词或者动名词。

0848 **snack** [snæk] n 点心，速食，小吃
They had some snacks for breakfast in order to save time.
为了节省时间，他们早餐只吃了一些小吃。
refreshments 小吃，点心　　snack food 零食

语法重点
in order to 和 so as to 都用来表示目的，意思是"为了……"。in order to 既可以用在句首，也可以用在句中，so as to 只用在句中。

0849 **snail** [sneɪl] n 蜗牛
I feel that time moves at a snail's pace before the summer vacation.
我觉得暑假前的时间过得很慢。
at a snail's pace 极慢的　　... move at a snail's pace ……很慢

语法重点
time 是抽象名词，前面不用冠词。

0850 **snowy** ['snoʊi] a 多雪的，雪白的
They strode across the snowy road, singing happily.
他们高兴地唱着歌，大步地穿过积雪的道路。

0851 **soccer** ['sɑːkər] n 足球
Some boys were playing basketball and others were playing soccer.
一些男孩在打篮球，另外一些在踢足球。
football 足球　　soccer field 足球场

语法重点
others 是 other 的复数形式，指代"另一些"，表示一定范围内除去一部分后，剩余的另一些人或物。

0852 **social** ['soʊʃl] a 社会的，交际的，社交的
I don't like mixing with people of high social rank at the party.
聚会时，我不喜欢和社会地位很高的人交流。
sociable 社交的，好交际的　　unsocial 不善交际的，不合群的

语法重点
表示"社会地位低"通常用形容词 low。
rank (P. 345)

0853 **society** [sə'saɪəti] n 社会，社团
Encourage him to play basketball and take part in society parties.
鼓励他去打篮球，并参加社交聚会。
community 社会，社区　　encourage sb. to do... 鼓励某人做……

语法重点
party 是以 y 结尾的名词，其复数形式是变 y 为 i 加 es。
encourage (P. 159)

0854 sock [sɑːk] n 袜子

He stopped running and gave his socks a hitch.
他停止跑步，把袜子猛拉了一下。
- stocking 长袜
- pull one's socks up（努力）改进自己的表现或成绩

0855 soldier ['souldʒər] n 士兵

The thin soldier muttered about the boring movie.
那位瘦瘦的士兵咕哝地抱怨这场无聊的电影。
- mutter about... 咕哝着抱怨……

0856 solution [sə'luːʃn] n 解决方法

The swimming teacher didn't come up with any solutions to deal with the problem that he is afraid of water.
游泳教练想不出办法来解决他怕水这个问题。
- come up with... 想出……

语法重点
come up with 通常用来指想出某个主意或解决问题的方法，通常和 idea, solution 等词连用。

0857 solve [sɑːlv] v 解决

How to solve the problem that he is indulged in playing mahjong?
怎样解决他沉溺于打麻将这个问题呢？
- resolve 解决
- solve a puzzle 解决一个难题
- be indulged in... 沉溺于……

语法重点
be indulged in 后面要接名词或者动名词。
↪ indulge (P. 583)

0858 somebody ['sʌmbədi] pron 某人，有人

At the top of the mountain, the sudden screaming of somebody scared the tourists stiff.
山顶上，某人突然的尖叫声把游客们都吓呆了。
- someone 某人，有人
- scare stiff... 把……吓呆了

0859 somewhere ['sʌmwer] ad 某个地方，到某种程度，大约

To my judgment, the shy boy must be hiding somewhere in the room.
依我判断，那个害羞的男孩一定躲在房间的某个地方。

语法重点
to one's judgment 一般放在句首，相当于 according to one's judgment.

0860 sort [sɔːrt] n 种类，类别 v 整理，分类

I have no eye for this sort of quick-step dance.
我缺乏欣赏这种快步舞的眼光。
- classify 分类
- It takes all sorts to make a world. 世上的人无奇不有。

语法重点
have no eye for（缺乏眼光）后面接名词或动名词。

0861 source [sɔːrs] n 资源，发源地

The travelers looked up to determine the source of the waterfall.
游客们都向上看，以便确定瀑布的源头。
- origin 起源
- at source 在源头，在产地

↪ determine (P. 283)

0862 **southern** ['sʌðərn] **a** 南方的，南部的
In contrast, they are travelling in the southern part of the country.
相反，他们正在这个国家的南部旅游。
 southern hemisphere 南半球 in contrast, ... 相反，……

> **语法重点**
> in contrast 通常用在句首，表示一种语义上的转折。
> ⊃ contrast (P. 416)

0863 **soybean / soy** ['sɔɪbiːn] / ['sɔɪ] **n** 大豆
It's said the movie star only takes an interest in the soybean milk.
据说那位电影明星只对豆浆感兴趣。
 sb. takes an interest in... 某人对……感兴趣

0864 **speaker** ['spiːkər] **n** 演说者，发言者
The speaker is the life and soul of the party last night.
昨晚这名演讲者是派对的灵魂人物。
 lecturer 演讲者　 hearer 听者　 guest speaker 客座讲者

0865 **speed** [spiːd] **n** 速度，迅速
I think no horse has a speed comparable to his in the race.
我相信，赛马时没有一匹马的速度能比得上他的马。
 velocity 速度　 at speed 高速地，快地

> **语法重点**
> comparable to（比起来）可以放在句中，也可以放在句首，用于对两个或两个以上的人或物作比较。

0866 **spelling** ['spelɪŋ] **n** 拼写
I lost that pirated book with many spelling mistakes in it when I played in the park.
我在公园玩的时候弄丢了那本满是拼写错误的盗版书。

> **语法重点**
> 动词 pirate 的意思是"剽窃，非法翻印"，与 book 是被动关系，因此句中用它的过去分词形容 book。

0867 **spider** ['spaɪdər] **n** 蜘蛛
Amazingly, a spider is weaving a web in the cave when the visitors arrived there.
让人惊奇的是，当游客们到达那个洞穴时，一只蜘蛛正在那里结网。

> **语法重点**
> weave 的现在分词形式是去 e 加上 ing。

0868 **spinach** ['spɪnɪtʃ] **n** 菠菜
The spinach soup was served when we had a chat with the guest.
我们和客人聊天时，菠菜汤端了上来。
 spinage 菠菜　 ... be served 端上来……

> **语法重点**
> spinach 是不可数名词。

0869 **spirit** ['spɪrɪt] **n** 精神，灵魂
The rest of the audience seemed to be in low spirit because of the boring movie.
由于电影无聊，剩下的那些观众们似乎看起来无精打采。
 soul 精神，灵魂　 flesh 肉体　 ... be in low spirit ……无精打采

> **语法重点**
> the rest 表示"剩余的，其他的"，可修饰可数或不可数名词。

southern ~ steak

0870 spot [spɑːt] n 斑点，污点，地点

I don't know how to wipe off the spots on the souvenir which I just bought at the scenic spot.
我刚从景点买了个纪念品，不知道如何擦去上面的污点。
- scenic spot 风景区，景点

语法重点
句中用介词 on，说明那些污点是在纪念品的表面。

0871 spread [spred] v 散布，传播，展开

After that movie was shown, his good name had spread throughout the country.
电影上映后，他的好名声传遍了全国。
- spread like wildfire（尤指谣言、传闻、疾病）飞速地传开、蔓延等

语法重点
spread 是不规则动词，其过去式、过去分词都是 spread。

0872 square [skwer] n 正方形，广场 v 一致，使……成正方形

In this city, senior citizens often get together in the main square in the evenings.
在这个城市，老年人在傍晚时经常聚集在大广场上。
- plaza 广场
- get together in... 聚集在……

语法重点
老人通常用 senior citizen 来表达，而不是 old people。

0873 squirrel [ˈskwɜːrəl] n 松鼠

When we walked in the forest, we saw a grey squirrel scamper from limb to limb.
我们在森林里散步时，看到一只灰色的松鼠在树枝间跳来跳去。

0874 stage [steɪdʒ] n 阶段，舞台

I heard there was mass hysteria when the singer came on stage.
我听说歌手登台时观众一片疯狂。

0875 stamp [stæmp] n 邮票，图案

None of my friends occupied themselves in collecting stamps.
我没有一个朋友忙于集邮。
- postage stamp 邮票
- occupy oneself in... 忙于……

语法重点
none 和 no one 都可以用来形容人，表示"没有人"。作主语时，none 后的动词用单复数形式，而 no one 后的动词要用单数形式。
➔ occupy (P. 478)

0876 standard [ˈstændərd] n 标准，规格

They can enroll me as a member of the club, but I must live up to their standard.
他们可以接纳我成为俱乐部的一员，但我必须达到他们的标准。
- criterion 标准
- standard of living 生活水准
- I must live up to... 我必须达到……

0877 steak [steɪk] n 牛排

The girl tried to suck up to her partner with steak.
那个女孩试图用牛排来讨好她的搭档。
- steak knife 切肉排的刀
- suck up to... 讨好……

语法重点
suck up to 后面通常接人，表示"巴结某人，讨好某人"。

0878 **steal** [stiːl] v 偷窃

The thief stole the foreign visitor's money from under the police's nose.
小偷在警察的眼前偷走了外国游客的钱。
- scrump 偷窃
- steal the show 抢风头（尤指出其不意）

语法重点
from under 是双重介词，是英语语法中较为特殊的现象，其目的主要是使所表达的意思更确切、更全面。

0879 **steam** [stiːm] n 蒸汽，水汽；怒气

The visitor let off steam by yelling at the guide.
那个游客对导游大喊大叫，借以发泄怒气。
- at full steam 尽力地
- let off stream by doing... 通过……来发泄怒气

语法重点
let off 还可以表示"放屁"，一般用在口语中。
➔ yell (P. 386)

0880 **steel** [stiːl] n 钢铁，钢制品 a 钢的，坚强的

As a big shot in steel industry, he likes playing golf in his free time.
作为钢铁大王，他喜欢空闲时打高尔夫。
- strong 坚强的
- forceless 软弱的
- nerves of steel 钢铁般的意志
- ... in one's free time 在某人空闲的时候……

0881 **stick** [stɪk] n 棍棒 v 坚持，停留

He stuck to the promise that he should give her a big party.
他遵守了为她办一场盛大派对的诺言。
- stay 坚持
- stick to 坚持

语法重点
promise 不管是作名词还是作动词，后面接的 that 从句中的动词都要用 should + 动词原形。

0882 **stomach** ['stʌmək] n 胃，胃口，肚子

I have suffered from the pain in the stomach after I mealed in the scenic spot.
在景点吃完饭后，我一直胃痛。
- empty stomach 空腹
- I suffer from... 我遭受……

语法重点
表示身体某部位疼痛，一般用介词 in 或 on 来与 pain 搭配。

0883 **storm** [stɔːrm] n 暴风雨 v 起风暴

All of the tourists began to run toward the bus when the storm was coming.
暴风雨即将来临时，所有的游客都开始向巴士跑去。
- the calm before the storm 暴风雨前的宁静
- run toward... 跑向……

语法重点
toward 表示"跑"的方向。
➔ toward (P. 106)

0884 **stove** [stoʊv] n 炉子，火炉

They are playing cards to kill the time near the stove.
他们在火炉旁边玩牌以消磨时间。
- kill the time... 消磨时间……

语法重点
playing cards 中间不加定冠词 the。

0885 **straight** [streɪt] a 笔直的，坦率的 ad 笔直地，直接

Hold your back straight, or you will lose the game.
你要把背挺得笔直，不然你会输了比赛。
- direct 直接的
- bent 弯曲的
- go straight 改过自新，一直往前走

steal ~ strike

0886 stranger ['streɪndʒər] n 陌生人，外地人，新手
He is a stranger here and he knows nothing about where to play billiards.
他是一个外地人，对该去哪里打台球一无所知。
- newcomer 新手　- acquaintance 熟人
- perfect stranger 完全不认识的人

> 语法重点
> billiards 的意思是"台球"，与 play 连用时，中间不加任何冠词。

0887 straw [strɔː] n 稻草，麦秆，吸管
I don't care a straw for your opinion on where to spend the weekends.
关于去哪里度周末，我一点儿都不在乎你有什么看法。
- grasp at a straw 抓救命稻草　- I don't care a straw for... 我一点儿都不在乎……

> 语法重点
> care for 用在否定句时，中间加上 a straw 可以加强语气，是一种习惯用法。
> - opinion (P. 198)

0888 strawberry ['strɔːberi] n 草莓，草莓色
Keep away from the strawberry and come to play with your ball.
远离那些草莓，过来玩你的皮球吧。
- keep away from... 远离……

0889 stream [striːm] n 小河，水流　v 流动，流出
The visitors stepped across the stream and kept their feet dry.
游客们跨过了小溪，没有把脚沾湿。

0890 stress [stres] n 压力，强调　v 强调
I should stress that you'd better enjoy your weekends as much as possible.
我要强调一下，你最好尽可能享受周末时光。
- pressure 压力　- lay stress on... 重视，把重点放在……

> 语法重点
> possible 为形容词"可能的"，其和 as... as（像……一样）构成固定搭配 as... as possible, 表达的意思是"尽可能……的"，两个 as 之间要加形容词或副词的原级。

0891 stretch [stretʃ] v 伸展，延伸，拉长
I saw he stretch his leg and trip up the thief on TV.
我在电视上看到他伸出腿绊倒了小偷。
- extend 延伸　- shrink 收缩　- trip up... 绊倒……

> 语法重点
> 句中动词 stretch 和 trip 并列，都是 saw 看到的内容。

0892 strict [strɪkt] a 严格的，严谨的
The leader was strict with them for fear that they should have an accident.
领队对他们很严格，唯恐他们出意外。
- in the strict sense 严格来说　- for fear that... 唯恐……

> 语法重点
> for fear that 后的从句要用虚拟语气，动词用"should / may / might + 动词原形"。

0893 strike [straɪk] n 罢工，打击　v 打击
The strike hung up our traveling abroad.
这次罢工严重地延误了我们出国旅游。
- hit 打击　- strike a balance 找到折中办法，妥协

> 语法重点
> our traveling abroad 在句中作动词短语 hang up 的宾语。

0894 **string** [strɪŋ] n 细绳

The string broke with a snap when he was playing the guitar.
他弹吉他时，啪的一声，弦断了。
● chord 弦　● string sb. along 蓄意误导某人

0895 **struggle** ['strʌgl] v 奋斗，努力，斗争

In order to win the upcoming match fair and square, you'd better struggle hard.
为了光明正大地赢得这场比赛，你最好努力奋斗。
● struggle for... 为……奋斗　● ... fair and square 光明正大……

0896 **subject** ['sʌbdʒɪkt] n 主题

I suddenly changed the subject, which left him floundering helplessly.
我突然改变话题，使他茫然不知所措。
● topic 话题，主题　● ... leave sb. floundering helplessly ……让某人不知所措

语法重点
which left him floundering helplessly 在句中表示结果。

0897 **subtract** [səb'trækt] v 扣除

Subtract ten from twenty you have ten.
二十减十得十。
● deduct 减去　● add 加起来　● subtract from... 从……中扣除某物

0898 **succeed** [sək'siːd] v 成功

If you want to succeed, stop gambling as soon as you can.
如果你想成功，就尽快戒赌。
● fail 失败　● as... as you can 尽可能……

语法重点
as... as you can 中，两个 as 之间加形容词和副词，该短语通常置于句尾。

0899 **success** [sək'ses] n 成功

The actor showed off around after having gained the success.
获得成功后，那个演员到处炫耀。
● victory 成功　● failure 失败

语法重点
show off around（到处炫耀）通常用来表示一种贬义。
● around (P. 009)

0900 **successful** [sək'sesfl] a 成功的

The journey was successful and couldn't have been better.
这次旅行玩得真过瘾。
● unsuccessful 不成功的　● ... couldn't have been better ……不能再好了

0901 **sudden** ['sʌdn] a 突然的

The director's sudden death came as a bombshell.
那个导演突然死亡的消息让每个人都很震惊。
● abrupt 突然的　● gradual 逐渐的，平缓的　● sudden accident 突发事件

语法重点
bombshell 的意思是"炸弹，突发的惊人事件"，是可数名词。

0902 suit [suːt] n 一套衣服，诉讼 v 适合，方便

The super star wore a white suit to disguise herself for fear of being recognized.
那个巨星穿了一套白西装来掩饰自己，以免被别人认出来。

语法重点: for fear of（以免）后面通常接动名词。

0903 sunny ['sʌni] a 充满阳光的，晴朗的，明媚的

Let's bask ourselves on the sunny beach, OK?
我们在阳光灿烂的海滩上晒太阳，好吗？

- cloudless 晴朗的
- cloudy 多云的
- bask oneself on the sunny... 在……晒太阳

语法重点: 单词 OK 可以单独使用，用在问句中表示咨询对方的意见。
→ beach (P. 012)

0904 supermarket ['suːpəmɑːrkət] n 超市

In front of the supermarket, all the dancers throw themselves heart and soul into the performance.
超市前，所有舞者都尽心尽力地演出。

- supermarket chain 连锁超市
- throw heart and soul into... 倾尽全力做……

0905 supply [sə'plaɪ] v 供应，补给 n 供应

The explorer's water supply slowly diminished as the days wore on.
时间一天天过去，探险者的水在慢慢减少。

- provide 供应
- demand 需求
- in short supply 供应不足，供不应求

语法重点: supply 在句中作名词，"电源，电力供应"可以用 power supply 表示。
→ diminish (P. 704)

0906 support [sə'pɔːrt] v / n 支持，拥护

Her excellent performance made her win the audience's supports.
她那精彩的演出使她赢得很多观众的支持。

- sustain 支持
- ... win sb's supports ……赢得了某人的支持

0907 surface ['sɜːrfɪs] n 表面，外表

It's your turn to dive below the surface of the water.
该你潜水了。

- face 表面，外观
- on the surface 在表面上，在外表上

语法重点: it's sb.'s turn to（轮到某人）后面通常接动词原形。

0908 survive [sər'vaɪv] v 生存

If you continue playing with the fish, it won't survive.
如果你一直玩那条鱼的话，它会死的。

- survive from... 从……存活下来
- continue doing... 持续做……

0909 swallow ['swɑːloʊ] v 吞咽 n 燕子，吞咽

We said with one mouth that the answer to the riddle should be "swallow".
我们异口同声地说这个谜语的谜底应该是"燕子"。

- swallow one's words 收回自己的话
- ... with one mouth 一致地

语法重点: with one mouth 在句中作状语修饰动词。

0910 **swan** [swɑːn] n 天鹅 v 闲荡，游荡
I was amazed to see a beautiful swan swimming gracefully in the pond of the park.
我吃惊地看到一只漂亮的天鹅正在公园池塘中优雅地游水。
wander 游荡　All one's geese are swans. 自吹自擂。

> 语法重点
> be amazed to 后面要接动词原形。

0911 **sweater** ['swetər] n 毛衣
My greatest passion is knitting sweaters.
我最大的爱好是织毛衣。

> 语法重点
> 注意 knit 的 ing 形式是重复 t，再加 ing。
> ⊃ passion (P. 334)

0912 **sweep** [swiːp] v 打扫，拂
Jane was left to sweep up after the party.
派对结束后珍被留下来打扫。
clean 打扫　sweep the board 大获全胜　be left to do... 被留下来做……

0913 **swing** [swɪŋ] v 摇摆，旋转 n 摇摆，改变
I have been on the swing for about half an hour, now it's your go.
我荡秋千有半个小时了，现在该轮到你了。
swing into action 迅速采取行动

> 语法重点
> swing 是不规则动词，其过去式是 swang 或 swung，过去分词是 swung。

0914 **symbol** ['sɪmbl] n 象征，标志
The statue at the entrance of the scenic spot is the symbol of the leader.
景点入口处的那座雕塑是这个领导人的象征。
status symbol 社会地位的象征　be the symbol of... 是……的象征
symbol 主要表示某种象征意义的标志，而 signal 则主要指某种信号，也可以指灯光、声音或某种信号标志。

0915 **talent** ['tælənt] n 天才，天赋，才能
The young girl showed great talent for folk dance.
这个年轻的女孩在民族舞方面显示出很大的天赋。
a hidden talent 隐藏的才能　sb. shows talent for... 某人在……方面有天赋

> 语法重点
> great 用来加强语气，加深程度。

0916 **talkative** ['tɔːkətɪv] a 说话的，健谈的，多嘴的
He was annoyed by those talkative women.
他很讨厌那群叽叽喳喳的女人。
loquacious 多话的　taciturn 沉默寡言的

0917 **tangerine** ['tændʒəriːn] n 橘子，橘子树
I saw the farmers picking tangerines and collecting them in heaps.
我看到农夫们正在摘橘子并把它们摆放成堆。
orange 橘子　collect... in heaps 把……摆放成堆

collect (P. 142)

swan ~ teenager

0918 **tank** [tæŋk] n 坦克，箱，罐
I am longing for buying a fish tank to keep the goldfish.
我非常渴望买个鱼缸来养金鱼。
- oil tank 油罐
- I'm longing for... 我渴望……

> 语法重点
> long for 后面接名词、代词或者动名词。

0919 **tape** [teɪp] n 录音带
Judging from the tape, the singer's voice is very magnetic.
从磁带来判断，那个歌手的声音很有磁性。

> 语法重点
> judging from the tape 作插入语，后面接完整的句子。

0920 **target** ['tɑːrgɪt] n 目标，对象，靶子
What's the target audience of the performance?
这次表演以哪些人为对象？
- aim 目标
- target customers 目标客户
- What's the target of...? ……的目标是什么？

> 语法重点
> target 在句中作定语，修饰 audience。
> audience (P. 257)

0921 **task** [tæsk] n 任务
Hiking in such a hot day is no easy task.
在这样热的天徒步旅行真不是件容易的事。
- assignment 任务
- ... be no easy task ……不是件容易的事

0922 **tasty** ['teɪsti] a 好吃的
All of the guests can't hold back their appetite when facing the tasty food.
面对这么好吃的东西，所有的客人都控制不住自己的食欲了。
- delicious 可口的
- unsavory 难吃的

> 语法重点
> appetite 作"胃口"讲时是不可数名词。

0923 **team** [tiːm] n 团队
I think the success of the football team was largely due to his efforts.
这个足球队的成功在很大程度上是他努力的结果。
- group 组
- team spirit 团队精神
- be largely due to... 很大程度上由于……

> 语法重点
> due to 就相当于 because of，后面接名词、代词或者动名词。

0924 **tear** [ter] n 眼泪 v 撕破，扯下
In his fury the tourist tore the ticket to pieces.
盛怒之下，游客把门票撕得粉碎。
- tear one's hair 表示极大的悲伤、愤怒等
- in one's fury... 某人盛怒之下……

> 语法重点
> tear 是不规则动词，过去式、过去分词分别是 tore，torn。

0925 **teenage** ['tiːneɪdʒ] a 十几岁的，青少年的
It was clear that she was too old now for teenage parties.
很显然，她年龄太大了，不适于参加少年聚会。
- juvenile 青少年的
- it was clear that... 很显然……

> 语法重点
> old 在句中意思是"年龄大"，而不是"年老的"。

0926 **teenager** ['tiːneɪdʒər] n 青少年
These teenagers are expert in hip-hop.
这些青少年擅长跳街舞。
- teenager talents 后备人才
- be expert in... 擅长……

0927 telephone / phone ['telɪfoʊn] / [foʊn]
n 电话 **v** 打电话

The tourist telephoned the guide several times, but failed to get her in the end.
游客给导游打了好几次电话，但最终都无法联系上她。
phone 电话　on the telephone 在通电话

> **语法重点**
> telephone sb. 表示"打电话给某人"，也可以用 call sb. 替代。
> several (P. 088)

0928 television / TV ['telɪvɪʒn tiː 'viː] **n** 电视

There's live broadcast on the television about the football game tomorrow.
明天电视上有这次足球比赛的实况转播。
television program 电视节目

> **语法重点**
> television 有时会简写为 TV。

0929 temple ['templ] **n** 寺庙

The age of the temple is four times as long as the monk's.
寺院的年龄是那位僧人的四倍。
vihara 寺院　four times as... as... 是……的四倍……

> **语法重点**
> "一次"用 once 表示，"两次"用 twice，三次或以上用基数词加 times 来表示。

0930 tennis ['tenɪs] **n** 网球

The golden rule in tennis is to focus your attention on the ball.
打好网球的重要原则是眼要紧盯着球。

0931 tent [tent] **n** 帐篷

The guide said the wind would blow the tent away.
导游说风会把帐篷吹走。
tentage 帐篷　relief tent 救灾帐篷

> **语法重点**
> 情态动词 would 可以表示推测。

0932 term [tɜːrm] **n** 期限

I entered a swimming class before the term.
开学前我报了一个游泳班。
in the long term 长期

0933 terrible ['terəbl] **a** 可怕的，极度的，糟糕的

Her terrible joke frightened off all the foreign visitors.
她那个可怕的玩笑把所有的外国游客都吓跑了。
abominable 糟透的　superb 极好的　feel terrible 感觉不舒服

> foreign (P. 040)

0934 terrific [təˈrɪfɪk] **a** 可怕的，极好的，非常的

All the people at the party were having a terrific time.
参加派对的每个人都玩得开心极了。
marvelous 非凡的　inferior 差的

telephone / phone ~ thirsty

0935 test [test] n 测试，测验
I walked through the test, then went out to play basketball on the playground.
我草草地做完测验题，然后就去操场上打篮球了。
- experiment 试验　- simulation test 模拟试验

0936 textbook ['tekstbʊk] n 教科书
He left his textbook in the cinema.
他把课本忘在电影院了。
- textbook contents 教材内容　- left sth. in... 把某物忘在……

> **语法重点**
> "把某物忘在……"要用 left sth. in someplace，而不用 forget sth. in someplace。

0937 theater ['θɪətə] n 戏院
Last night, his performance won the praise of the audience in the theater.
昨晚，他的表演赢得了剧院里观众的赞美。
- home theater 家庭影院　- win the praise of... 赢得了……的赞美

> **语法重点**
> praise 是抽象名词，不可数。

0938 therefore ['ðeəfɔːr] ad 因此，所以
It was too hot; therefore the concert was put back from Monday to Wednesday.
天气太热了，因此音乐会从星期一延后到星期三。
- hence 因此　- and therefore 因此　- put back from... to... 从……延后到……

⊃ concert (P. 275)

0939 thick [θɪk] a 厚的，浓密的，粗的，（俚）太过分的
It is a bit thick to have a picnic on a rainy day.
雨天去野餐真让人受不了。
- dense 浓密的　- thin 薄的　- Blood is thicker than water. 血浓于水。

0940 thief [θiːf] n 小偷
My mother was set on by a thief in the park yesterday.
昨天，我妈妈在公园里遭到一个窃贼的袭击。
- burglar 窃贼　- be set on by... 被……袭击

0941 thin [θɪn] a 薄的，瘦的
Tell the boys it is dangerous to walk on the thin ice.
告诉那些男孩们，在薄冰上行走是危险的。
- lean 瘦的　- thick 厚的

> **语法重点**
> it is dangerous to 后面接动词原形。

0942 thirsty ['θɜːrsti] a 口渴的
Both of the children listened to the story with thirsty ears.
两个孩子都津津有味地听故事。
- be thirsty for... 渴望得到……　- listen to... with thirsty ears 津津有味地听……

> **语法重点**
> thirsty 作 ears（耳朵）的形容词，表示很认真地听。

⊃ listen (P. 060)

0943 **throat** [θroʊt] n 喉咙
The singer cleared his throat and began to sing.
那个歌手清了清嗓子，唱了起来。
- have a sore throat 喉咙痛
- clear one's throat... 清了清嗓子……
- throat 也常用于短语 have a bone in one's throat，意思是"难于启齿"。

0944 **through** [θruː] prep 通过，凭借
Contrary to our expectations, she slept through the party.
我们没想到她竟然从派对开始一直睡到结束。
- across 穿过
- look through 浏览，仔细查看

语法重点
slept 是动词 sleep 的过去分词。
⊃ expectation (P. 292)

0945 **throughout** [θruːˈaʊt]
prep 遍布，贯穿 n 自始至终，到处
The poor singer was booed and heckled throughout his singing.
那个可怜的歌手的演唱自始至终都遭到喝倒彩。

语法重点
throughout 作介词时强调贯穿、遍及的意思（时间、空间都可用），它还可以作副词，意思是"处处，始终"，通常放在句尾。

0946 **thumb** [θʌm] n 拇指
The slippers he wore made him stick out like a sore thumb at the party.
派对上，他穿拖鞋显得很尴尬。
- be all thumbs 笨手笨脚
- ... stick out like a sore thumb ……处境尴尬 / 引人注目

0947 **thunder** [ˈθʌndər] n 雷电，雷声
When we got to the top of the mountain, a sudden thunder made our hair curl.
当我们爬到山顶时，一阵响雷让我们感到毛骨悚然。

语法重点
hair 一般作不可数名词。
⊃ sudden (P. 230)

0948 **tip** [tɪp] n 尖端，小费
It is customary to give the guide a tip here.
在这个地方给导游小费是一种风俗。
- fee 小费
- it is customary to... ……是一种风俗

0949 **title** [ˈtaɪtl] n 头衔，题目，标题
He wanted to recall his words about the comments on the title of entertainment news.
他想收回他对这条娱乐新闻标题的评论。
- headline 标题
- recall one's words about... 收回有关……的话

语法重点
名词复数 words 通常表示"某人所说的话"。

0950 **toast** [toʊst] n 吐司，烤面包 v 烤，烘
There will be a great deal of toast at the party.
派对上会有大量的吐司面包。

语法重点
a great deal of sth. 表示"有很多……"，一般修饰不可数名词。

0951 toe [toʊ] n 脚趾

The shoe is pressing on the boy's toes and he couldn't walk anymore.
那个男孩的鞋子磨脚，他不能再走路了。
- finger 手指
- from head to toe 从头到脚
- press on... 强加于……

语法重点
情态动词 could 可以表示能力。

0952 tofu / bean curd ['toʊfuː] / [bin kɜːd] n 豆腐

My mother is adept at cooking dishes with tofu.
我妈妈最善于用豆腐煮菜了。
- beancurd 豆腐
- be adept at... 擅长……

0953 toilet ['tɔɪləʳt] n 洗手间

No wonder the tourist went to the toilet so frequently.
怪不得那个游客如此频繁地去洗手间。
- washroom 洗手间
- toilet articles 盥洗用品

语法重点
wonder 作名词，意思是"惊奇"，常用于 no wonder, no wonder that 的搭配中，表示"怪不得"，这类搭配常用于句首。

0954 tomato [tə'meɪtoʊ] n 番茄

Is it OK that the guests eat the tomatoes?
客人们可以吃番茄了吗？

0955 tongue [tʌŋ] n 舌头，语言

The singer was frightened on the stage and held his tongue.
那个歌手在台上很害怕，说不出话。
- wag one's tongue 唠叨不休
- ... hold one's tongue ……说不出话

语法重点
tongue 也常用于短语 bite one's tongue，意思是"忍住不说"。

0956 tooth [tuːθ] n 牙齿，齿状物

His teeth are sensitive to cold food.
他的牙齿对冰冷食物过敏。
- armed to the teeth 全副武装
- be sensitive to... 对……敏感

0957 topic ['tɑːpɪk] n 话题，主题

It's quite beyond him to speak on a topic on entertainment.
他实在讲不了关于娱乐的话题。
- theme 主题
- current topic 热门话题

语法重点
it's quite beyond sb. 后面常接动词不定式。

0958 tour [tʊr] n 旅行，观光，巡回

I map out a tour around the world after graduating from the university.
我计划大学毕业后进行一次环球旅行。
- travel 旅游
- tour group 旅行团
- I map out... 我计划……

语法重点
map 在句中作动词，map out 就相当于 plan（计划）。
➲ graduate (P. 301)

0959 towel ['taʊəl] n 毛巾

Do remember to bring your towel when go swimming.
去游泳时千万要记得带你的毛巾。
- bath towel 浴巾
- do remember to... 千万要记得……

语法重点
例句是一个强调句，助动词 do 无实际意义，只是用来加强语气。

0960 **tower** [ˈtaʊər] n 塔
Fancy her having been to the Eiffel Tower.
想不到她竟然参观过埃菲尔铁塔。
- ivory tower 象牙塔，空中楼阁　- fancy sb.'s doing... 想不到某人……

语法重点
fancy 后面也可以直接接动名词，也表示"想不到……"。
⊃ fancy (P. 295)

0961 **track** [træk] n 行踪
She has a deep love for track and field event.
她热爱田径运动。

0962 **trade** [treɪd] v / n 贸易，交易
They are travelling in Hong Kong which is said to be the biggest trade centre in Asia.
他们正在被认为是亚洲最大的贸易中心的香港旅游。
- business 交易　- be said to be... 被认为是……

语法重点
Asia 的意思是"亚洲"，表示大洋、洲的名词首字母要大写，如 Europe（欧洲）。

0963 **tradition** [trəˈdɪʃn] n 传统
It is a tradition to play majong here.
打麻将在这里是传统习惯。
- convention 惯例，习俗

语法重点
majong 与 play 连用时，中间不用任何冠词。

0964 **traditional** [trəˈdɪʃənl] a 传统的，习惯的
It is traditional to sing and dance on New Year's Day in the country.
在这个国家，新年这天唱歌跳舞是一种习俗。
- conventional 传统的　- it is traditional to do... 做……是习俗

语法重点
表示节日的名词一般要大写，如 New Year's Day。

0965 **traffic** [ˈtræfɪk] n 交通
The traffic in the city is very dangerous for the foreign visitors.
这个城市的交通对外国游客来说很危险。
- transportation 交通　- traffic jam 塞车
- be dangerous for... 对……来讲很危险

语法重点
traffic 还可以作动词，意思是"交易，买卖"。

0966 **trap** [træp] n 陷阱 v 设圈套
The boy put some cheese to lure the cat into his trap.
男孩放了一些乳酪来让小猫上钩。
- set a trap for... 为……设陷阱　- lure... into one's trap 引诱……上当

0967 **travel** [ˈtrævl] v / n 旅行
As you wish, your wife will get a free travel to Tokyo as the reward.
如你所愿，你妻子将得到赴东京免费旅行的奖赏。
- journey 旅行　- travel agency 旅行社　- as you wish, ... 如你所愿……

语法重点
去某地旅游，一般用介词 to，表示方向。

tower ~ trumpet

0968 treasure ['treʒər] n 宝物 v 珍藏，珍视
I hardly dreamt of finding a treasure map in the cave.
我没想到竟然在这个洞里发现一张藏宝图。
≈ wealth 财富　≈ priceless treasure 无价之宝

> 语法重点
> treasure 偏重于"金银财宝"之意；wealth 指物质财富，也可指精神财富。

0969 treat [triːt] v 对待，视为
It is a fairly shoddy way to treat an old tourist like this.
这样对待一位老年游客真是十分卑鄙。
≈ regard 看待，视为　≈ treat as... 对待，把……看作……

> 语法重点
> shoddy 的意思是"劣质的"，fairly 修饰 shoddy，加强语气。

0970 treatment ['triːtmənt] n 对待，处理
It appears that he will stop his traveling and go to hospital for treatment.
他好像要停止旅游，去医院接受治疗了。
≈ remedy 治疗　≈ it appears that... 好像……

> 语法重点
> go to hospital 的意思是"去医院看病"；go to the hospital 的意思是"去医院"，但不一定是去看病。
> ≈ appear (P. 008)

0971 trial ['traɪəl] n 试用
I won admiration for my comportment during the singing trial last year.
我去年在唱歌选拔赛中的表现得到了赞赏。
≈ experiment 实验　≈ trial and error 反复试验

0972 triangle ['traɪˌæŋɡəl] n 三角形
It happened that they are playing games on a triangle of grass beside the path.
碰巧，他们在路边的一块三角形草坪上玩游戏。
≈ love triangle 三角恋爱　≈ it happened that... 碰巧……

0973 trick [trɪk] n 诡计，花招
The tourist was on his toes, so he wasn't cheated by the old man's trick.
这个游客很机灵，所以没被那个老人的诡计骗到。
≈ play a trick on... 开……的玩笑，作弄……

> 语法重点
> trick 也可以作动词，意思是"欺骗，欺诈"，常用于 trick sb. into sth.（欺骗某人做某事）。

0974 truck [trʌk] n 卡车，手推车
At last, they drove a truck to drag the tour bus out of the river.
最终，他们开着一辆卡车将观光巴士从河中拖了出来。
≈ at last, ... 最终……

> 语法重点
> drove 是动词 drive 的过去式。

0975 trumpet ['trʌmpɪt] n 小喇叭，小号
Contrary to his brother, he likes blowing a trumpet.
和他的哥哥相反，他很喜欢吹喇叭。
≈ horn 喇叭　≈ blow one's own trumpet 自吹自擂，自卖自夸

> ≈ blow (P. 016)

239

0976 trust [trʌst] v / n 信任

We should trust the guide, for this is the only way that we can escape from the cave.
我们必须相信导游，因为这是我们从洞穴里逃出去的唯一办法。
- believe 信任　- distrust 不信任　- escape from... 从……逃脱

> 语法重点
> trust 后面常接人，即 trust sb.。

0977 truth [truːθ] n 真理，实情

The plain truth is that he has never played golf.
说白了，他从来没有打过高尔夫球。
- fact 事实，真相　- to tell the truth 说实话

> 语法重点
> golf 与 play 连用时，中间不加任何冠词。

0978 tube [tuːb] n 管子，软管

It is no use bringing a tube of toothpaste, for the hotel on the scenic spot provides every guest with a toothpaste and brush.
带牙膏没什么用，因为观光景点的旅馆为每位顾客提供牙膏和牙刷。
- test tube 试管　- it is no use... ……没用

> 语法重点
> it is no use 后面通常接名词。
> ⊃ scenic (P. 774)

0979 tunnel ['tʌnl] n 隧道，地道

He saw some naughty boys crawling into the tunnel when he was walking.
他散步的时候看到一些淘气的男孩爬进了隧道里。
- subway tunnel 地铁隧道　- crawl into... 爬进

> 语法重点
> 感官动词 see 之后可以加现在分词作补语，表示通过眼睛看到的某种正在发生的情况。

0980 turkey ['tɜːrki] n 火鸡，失败之作

It is said that the latest movie is a real turkey.
据说最近的那部电影是一大败笔。

> 语法重点
> latest 是"最近的"，不要翻译成"最晚的"。

0981 turtle ['tɜːrtl] n 乌龟

I saw a turtle crawling along the coastline.
我看到一只乌龟正在沿着海岸线爬行。
- turn turtle 翻船　- crawl along... 沿……爬行

> 语法重点
> "沿着……"通常用介词 along。

0982 type [taɪp] n 类型 v 打字

The bar offers a lot of diversions for every type of person.
这个酒吧为各种人提供许多消遣。
- kind 种类　- blood type 血型　- offer... for... 为……提供……

0983 typhoon [taɪ'fuːn] n 台风

Now the typhoon is deviating from the expected course; so tell the guests to stay at a safe place.
现在台风正在偏离预想的路线，所以通知游客待在安全的地方。
- hurricane 飓风　- be deviating from... 偏离……

> 语法重点
> 现在进行时可以表示现在正在进行的动作。

0984 ugly ['ʌgli] a 丑的
It is evident that the visitors don't like this ugly picture.
很显然，游客们不喜欢这幅丑陋的画。
🔗 it is evident that... 很显然……

0985 umbrella [ʌm'brelə] n 雨伞
To cut the chase, the umbrella in the bar was stolen by a man who drank there.
我就直说吧，酒吧里的那把伞是被一个喝酒的客人偷走的。
🔗 under the umbrella of... 在……的保护下

语法重点
动词不定式可以放在句首作独立成分，不和主句有意义上的联系，如例句中的 To cut the chase。
↻ chase (P. 022)

0986 underwear ['ʌndərwer] n 内衣
It never occurred to me for a moment that he came to the cocktail party with his underwear hanging out.
我一点儿也没想到他竟然衣冠不整来参加鸡尾酒会。
🔗 underclothes 内衣   🔗 outerwear 外衣

语法重点
it occurred to sb. 可以表示"某人想到……"，never 与 for a moment 都是用来加强语气的。

0987 uniform ['ju:nɪfɔ:rm] n 制服
The boxer gave the man in uniform a good beat.
拳击手把穿制服的人痛打了一顿。
🔗 school uniform 校服   🔗 give... a good beat 痛打某人一顿

语法重点
in 后面接表示衣服种类的名词，意思是"穿着……"。

0988 upon [ə'pɑ:n] prep 在……上面，紧接着，逼近
The director depended upon me to play this role in place of Jim.
导演让我代替吉姆扮演这个角色。
🔗 on 在……之上   🔗 under 在……之下   🔗 once upon a time 从前

语法重点
in place of 和 instead of 都表示"替代"，用法也基本相同，在句中可以互换使用，of 后接一般名词、代词、动名词。

0989 upper ['ʌpər] a 上面的，上部的，较高的
It's a wonder that he invited many poor men instead of the upper class for the party.
他邀请了一些穷人而不是上流人士来参加这次派对，真是难得。

语法重点
instead of 表示代词时，可以连接前后两个名词，强调用前者来代替后者。

0990 used [ju:st] a 习惯于，旧的
It's laughable that he is used to playing ping-pong before going to bed.
让人啼笑皆非的是，他已经习惯了睡前打乒乓球。
🔗 accustomed 习惯的   🔗 unused 不习惯的   🔗 get used to... 习惯于……

语法重点
used 后面的 to 是介词。

0991 used to ph 过去时常
It's hard to imagine there used to be a lot of sparrows in the park.
很难想象公园里以前有很多麻雀。
🔗 used to be 过去曾经是

语法重点
used 后面的 to 是不定式 to，后面要接动词原形。
↻ sparrow (P. 506)

0992 **user** [ˈjuːzər] n 使用者
The new game is sure to be popular among the young users.
这个新的游戏肯定会很受年轻用户的喜欢。

语法重点
be sure to 与 be sure of 都表示"必定"，但用法不同。be sure of 的主语为人，表示"某人对……有把握"，对某种情况有肯定的判断，而 be sure to 的主语既可以为人也可以为物，表示"一定，必然会"发生某种情况。

0993 **usual** [ˈjuːʒuəl] a 通常的，常见的，常有的
She dived into the game as usual without thinking.
她和往常一样不加思考便加入了这场游戏。
≡ common 通常的   ≠ unusual 不寻常的   ≡ as usual 像往常一样

0994 **vacation** [vəˈkeɪʃn] n 假期，休假
Why not swap houses with strangers in your vacation?
假期里为什么不与陌生人交换房屋呢？
≡ holiday 假期   ≡ on vacation 在度假

语法重点
房屋不只是一个，所以 house 用复数。

0995 **valley** [ˈvæli] n 山谷，溪谷
The valley the explorers are going to lies behind the small hill.
探险者们要去的山谷就在这座小山的背面。
≡ hollow 山谷   ≡ lie behind... 位于……的后面

↪ hill (P. 049)

0996 **value** [ˈvæljuː] n 价值，价格 v 估价，重视
There's a lot to be said for the value of walking after dinner.
晚餐后散步的好处不胜枚举。
≡ worth 价值   ≡ value judgment 价值判断

语法重点
after dinner 泛指"（任何一顿）饭后"。

0997 **victory** [ˈvɪktəri] n 胜利
The victory of the football game was at the cost of his injury.
这次足球比赛的胜利是他受伤换来的。
≡ be at the cost of... 以……为代价

0998 **video** [ˈvɪdioʊ] a 录影的 n 录影带
The problem with the video is that it is highly addictive.
录影带的问题在于它很容易让人上瘾。

0999 **village** [ˈvɪlɪdʒ] n 村庄
Is there anywhere that the mountaineer can have a rest in the village?
村里有供登山者休息的地方吗？
≡ country 乡村   ≠ city 城市

语法重点
anywhere 作先行词，后面的引导词必须用 that。

↪ rest (P. 081)

1000 **violin** [ˌvaɪəˈlɪn] n 小提琴
She was almost driven crazy each time I played the violin.
每次我拉小提琴，她就几乎要发疯。
- ... be driven mad ……要发疯

语法重点
time 作名词时除了可以表示"时间"，还可以表示"次数"。

1001 **visitor** [ˈvɪzɪtər] n 访客
The visitor is eager to get a good view of the famous waterfall.
那个游客急切地想更清楚地看看这条著名的瀑布。
- tourist 游客   visitor registration 访客登记处

⇒ waterfall (P. 244)

1002 **vocabulary** [vəˈkæbjəleri] n 词汇
He read the vocabulary again and again and forgot to play basketball.
他一遍又一遍地朗读词汇表，都忘了打篮球。
- glossary 词汇表   do... again and again 一遍又一遍做……

语法重点
副词 again 为"又一次，再一次"，副词由 and 连接构成 again and again 的结构，表示"再三地"，表示反复出现的现象。

1003 **volleyball** [ˈvɑːlibɔːl] n 排球
She said she likes volleyball least of all.
她说她最不喜欢打排球了。

语法重点
least 是 little 的最高级形式，least of all 的意思是"最不，尤其"，表达一种否定的语气。

1004 **vote** [voʊt] v 投票
I vote for having a picnic on Sunday.
我建议周日去野餐。
- ballot 选票   vote against 投票反对   I vote for... 我建议……

语法重点
vote for 后面要接名词或者动名词。

1005 **voter** [ˈvoʊtər] n 投票者，选举人
The man said he was not qualified to be a voter.
那个男人说他没有资格做选举人。
- elector 选举人   be qualified to... 有资格……

⇒ voter (P. 243)

1006 **waist** [weɪst] n 腰
Her waist is small and she is very suitable for dancing.
她的腰很细，很适合跳舞。
- loins 腰部   waist belt 腰带   be suitable for... 适合……
- 注意"腰细"用的是形容词 small。

1007 **waiter / waitress** [ˈweɪtər] / [ˈweɪtrəs] n 男服务生 / 女服务生
They had an argument with the waiter about the price of the wine in the bar.
在酒吧里，他们和服务生因为酒的价格发生了争吵。
- have an argument with... 和……发生了争吵

⇒ argument (P. 125)

1008 **wake** [weɪk] v 叫醒，唤醒，意识到
It's odd that the visitor woke up to find herself alone in the mountain.
很奇怪，那个游客醒来时发现只有她自己在山里。
sleep 睡觉　awake 唤醒　it's odd that... 很奇怪……

语法重点
woke 是 wake 的过去式。

1009 **wallet** [ˈwɑːlɪt] n 皮夹
That souvenir he bought from the scenic spot fell from his wallet and broke into pieces.
他从景点买的纪念品从皮夹里掉了出来，摔成了碎片。
digital wallet 电子钱包　... break into pieces ……摔成碎片

语法重点
介词 from 的意思是"从……"，表示方向。
↪ souvenir (P. 505)

1010 **waterfall** [ˈwɔːtərfɔːl] n 瀑布
The villager told the explorers that the waterfall never dries up all the year around.
村民告诉探险家，这条瀑布全年都不枯竭。
fall 瀑布　... all the year around 常年……

1011 **watermelon** [ˈwɔːtərmelən] n 西瓜
Mother cut the watermelon into several slices for the guests to eat.
妈妈把西瓜切成几块让客人们吃。
cut... into... 把……切成……

语法重点
slice 在句中作名词，意思是"薄片"。

1012 **wave** [weɪv] n 波浪，波纹　v 挥动，飘动
The flower vanished from sight with a wave of the magician.
魔术师手一挥花朵就不见了。
flutter 飘动　... vanish from sight ……消失不见

1013 **weapon** [ˈwepən] n 武器
I prize my guitar as a soldier prizes his weapon.
我珍爱我的吉他，犹如一个士兵珍爱他的武器。
arms 武器

语法重点
prize 在句中作动词，相当于 treasure（珍惜）。

1014 **wed** [wed] v 结婚，嫁，娶
They are opposed to wed after coming back from a tour of America.
他们反对从美国旅游回来后再结婚。
marry 结婚　divorce 离婚　be wedded to 固执，不肯放弃

语法重点
be opposed to 后面接动词原形。
↪ oppose (P. 479)

1015 **weekday** [ˈwiːkdeɪ] n 工作日
I am willing to overwork on weekdays if I can get the rewards.
如果有奖励的话，我愿意在工作日加班。
weekend 周末　on weekday 在工作日　I'm willing to... 我愿意……

语法重点
be willing to 是半助动词，功能介于动词和助动词之间，既带有助动词的性质，也可以直接作动词来用。

wake ~ wherever

1016 western ['westərn] `a` 西方的，西部的
It'd be foolish to watch the sun set beyond the western hills on such a cold day.
在这么冷的天看西方山上的夕阳真是够蠢的。

1017 wet [wet] `a` 湿的，潮湿的
When they dropped in on me, they were all wet through by the rain.
他们来拜访我时，全身都被雨淋透了。
- moist 潮湿的   - dry 干的   - drop in on... 顺道拜访某人

〔语法重点〕 drop in 后也可加介词 for，如 drop in for tea（来喝茶）。

1018 whale [weɪl] `n` 鲸
It was the first time for me to see a whale during the scuba diving this afternoon.
在今天下午的潜水活动中，我第一次看到了鲸。
- have a whale of a time 玩得很开心

〔语法重点〕 名词 scuba 有"呼吸器"之意，而 diving 为名词"潜水，跳水"，二者组合构成短语 scuba diving，表示"潜水"。

1019 whatever [wət'evər] `pron` / `ad` 不管什么，任何事物
Whatever happens, the football game will be held on schedule.
不管发生什么事，足球比赛都会如期进行。
- for whatever reasons 无论什么原因
- whatever happens, ... 不论发生什么……

〔语法重点〕 on schedule 就相当于 on time（准时）。

1020 wheel [wi:l] `n` 轮子，旋转 `v` 旋转，转动
To prepare so much food for the picnic would be to break a butterfly on the wheel.
野餐准备这么多食物有点儿小题大做了。
- behind the wheel 驾驶（车或船）
- ... break a butterfly on the wheel ……小题大做

- butterfly (P. 019)

1021 whenever [wen'evər] `conj` / `ad` 无论何时
Whenever you set out for the journey, I'll keep your company.
不管你什么时候出发去旅行，我都会陪着你。
- whenever possible 只要可能   - set out for... 出发去……

1022 wherever [wer'evər] `conj` / `ad` 无论何处
Wherever he travels, she will be by his side all the while.
无论他去哪里旅游，她都会在他身旁。
- go wherever 无论去哪里   - ... by one's side ……在某人的身边

- side (P. 091)

245

1023 **whisper** [ˈwɪspər] v 低声说出

Don't you know it's impolite to whisper in front of so many guests?
你难道不知道当着这么多客人的面窃窃私语很不礼貌吗？
- murmur 低声说
- shout 大声说
- whisper sth. to sb. 低声对某人说某事
- Don't you know...? 你难道不知道……吗？

语法重点
用 don't 来提问，语气更强烈，有责备的意思。

1024 **whoever** [huːˈevər] pron 不论任何人

Whoever can find the lost girl will get the reward of 1,000 dollars.
无论谁，只要能找到那个失踪的女孩，就能得到 1 000 美元的奖金。
- get the reward of... 得到……的奖赏

语法重点
reward 作名词，意思是"报酬，报答"，动词则表示"奖励，奖赏"。
⊃ reward (P. 499)

1025 **widen** [ˈwaɪdn] v 变宽，放宽

They will take steps to widen the garden in the park.
他们将会采取措施加宽公园里的那个花园。
- broaden 放宽
- narrow 变窄
- widen horizon 开阔视野
- take steps to do... 采取措施去做……

1026 **width** [wɪdθ] n 宽度，广度，宽阔

The young man paced out the length and width of the football ground.
年轻人用步伐量出足球场的长度和宽度。
- breadth 宽度
- pace out... 用步伐量……

1027 **wild** [waɪld] a 野生的，荒凉的，狂热的 n 荒野，荒地

After coming back from the long journey, he got down to his work about wild animals.
长途旅行回来之后，他开始研究野生动物的工作。
- feral 野生的
- domestic 驯养的
- get down to... 开始做……

1028 **willing** [ˈwɪlɪŋ] a 有意愿的，心甘情愿的

Are you willing that he should join us in the game?
你愿意让他加入我们的游戏吗？
- glad 乐意的
- unwilling 不情愿的
- Are you willing that...? 你愿意……吗？

语法重点
that 后面句子中的动词要用"should + 动词原形"。

1029 **windy** [ˈwɪndi] a 风大的，空谈的

He will be in company with her to go to that windy mountain region for relaxation.
他将陪她去那个风大的山区散心。
- wordy 冗长的
- brief 简短的
- windy night 多风的夜晚
- be in company with... 陪伴某人……

语法重点
句中的介词 for 表示目的。
⊃ region (P. 214)

1030 **wing** [wɪŋ] n 翅膀 v 飞过

The right wing of the bird was hit by a piece of stone.
鸟的右翅膀被一块石块打中了。
- on the wing 在飞行中
- be hit by... 被……击中

> **语法重点**
> 在被动语态中，be done by 后面通常接人，也可以接工具。

1031 **winner** ['wɪnər] n 赢家

The winner sang songs to amuse himself after the game.
比赛过后，获胜者唱歌自娱。
- victor 胜利者
- loser 失败者
- prize winner 得奖者

> **语法重点**
> sang 是 sing 的过去式，与 song 拼写类似。

1032 **wire** ['waɪər] n 电线，电报

The boy tied up the bird with the wire.
小男孩用电线将小鸟捆绑起来。
- telegram 电报
- wire fence 铁丝网
- tie up... with... 用……把……捆起来

1033 **wise** [waɪz] a 智慧的

It's wise to leave the park before the storm.
在暴风雨来临之前离开公园是明智的。
- intelligent 聪明的，智慧的
- stupid 愚蠢的
- as wise as an owl 非常聪明
- wise 常用来说明一个人有智慧、有谋略，也可指由于知识、经验丰富及良好的判断能力而正确处理人和事，常用于正式、客气的场合。

1034 **within** [wɪˈðɪn] prep 在……之内

It is fortunate that they succeeded in playing out the comedy within one hour.
幸运的是，他们成功地在一小时之内演完了那部喜剧。
- inside 在……之内
- outside 在……范围之外
- within sight 在视线内

> **语法重点**
> within 后面可以接表示距离、时间、范围的名词。
> ⟳ fortunate (P. 443)

1035 **without** [wɪˈðaʊt] prep 没有，在外面 ad 在外面

She is without question the best of all the players.
她无疑是所有选手中最好的。
- outside 在外面
- within 在内部
- without reason 无缘无故

> **语法重点**
> without question（毫无疑问）是插入语，不影响句子的结构。

1036 **wolf** [wʊlf] n 狼

The old man is a lone wolf and always walks on his own.
那个老先生是一个喜欢独处的人，经常一个人独行。
- eat like a wolf 狼吞虎咽
- ... be on one's own 独自做……

> **语法重点**
> on one's own 在句中一般置于动词之后，相当于 by oneself。

1037 **wonder** ['wʌndər] v 想知道

All of the tourists wonder that how they created such marvelous feats of engineering as the Great Wall.
所有游客都好奇他们是如何创造了像长城这样伟大的工程奇观的。

> **语法重点**
> such as 意思是"例如"，such... as... 意思是"像……一样……"，注意两者的区别。
> ⟳ marvelous (P. 322)

1038 wonderful [ˈwʌndəfl] a 令人惊奇的
They went into the country yesterday and had a wonderful time.
他们昨天到乡下玩得很愉快。
⊕ splendid 极好的 ⊖ bad 差的

1039 wooden [ˈwʊdn] a 木制的
The wooden bridge over the stream was made by the workers.
小溪上面的木桥是工人制造的。
⊕ wooden furniture 木制家具 ⊕ be made by... 由……制造

@ bridge (P. 017)

1040 wool [wʊl] n 羊毛，羊绒
I've decided to knit a sweater of wool for my husband in the free time.
我打算在空闲时间为丈夫织一件羊毛衫。
⊕ fleece 羊毛 ⊕ wool carpet 羊毛地毯 ⊕ I've decided to... 我决定……

〔语法重点〕
wool 是不可数名词。

1041 worth [wɜːrθ] a 有……价值，值……钱 n 价值，财富
It is worth while to discuss where to go for a picnic.
该去哪里野餐，值得讨论一下。
⊕ worthy 值得的 ⊖ unworthy 不值得的

〔语法重点〕
it is worth while（值得）后面常接动词不定式。

1042 wound [wuːnd] n 伤口
The visitor was wounded and his blood poured out of the wound.
那个游客受伤了，伤口血流如注。
⊕ trauma 创伤 ⊕ lick one's wounds 重整旗鼓，恢复元气

〔语法重点〕
例句中第一个 wound 是动词，第二个 wound 是名词。

1043 yard [jɑːrd] n 院子，场地
They were playing games in the yard at the front of the house.
他们在房前的院子里游戏。
⊕ courtyard 院子 ⊕ back yard 后院 ⊕ ... at the front of... 在……的前面

〔语法重点〕
at the front of 等于 in the front of。

1044 youth [juːθ] n 青年
I heard the man was a talented musician in his youth.
我听说那个男人年轻时很有音乐天分。
⊕ adolescence 青少年期 ⊕ ... in one's youth 在某人年轻的时候

1045 zebra [ˈzɪbrə] n 斑马
You are likely to see many wild animals on the grasslands, such as zebras and sheep.
你可能会在草原上看到很多野生动物，例如斑马和羊。
⊕ zebra crossing 斑马线，人行道   be likely to do... 很可能做某事

〔语法重点〕
"在草原上"要用介词 on。

LEVEL 3
aboard ~ zone

LEVEL 3

aboard ~ zone

Review test

复习 Level 2 的学习成果，还记得以下单词是什么意思吗？

1. leopard ▸ _____
2. encouragement ▸ _____
3. item ▸ _____
4. overseas ▸ _____
5. dumb ▸ _____
6. slender ▸ _____
7. accept ▸ _____
8. tradition ▸ _____

Preview

单词重点预习，在开始之前先预习会让印象更深刻喔！

1. motor ▸ _____
2. forever ▸ _____
3. necessity ▸ _____
4. rate ▸ _____
5. vivid ▸ _____
6. account ▸ _____
7. satisfactory ▸ _____
8. creative ▸ _____

语法重点预习，在开始之前先预习会让印象更深刻喔！

1. 有些英文单词加上"前缀"或"后缀"会引申出不同的意思，如果能够记得几个基本常见的词首或词尾的话，那么在考试中若碰到不懂的单词，就可以通过拆解单词来推断出单词的意思。

• 前缀

anti	对抗；反抗	auto	自动
co / con / com	共同；一起	cross	横越；穿过
dis	相反的	extra	超过；在……之外
hemi	一半	hyper	在……之上；过度
hypo	在……之下；低于	inter	在……之间
macro	大的	micro	小的
mis	错误；不	mon / mono	单一
under	在……之下；较低	un	不；打开

• 后缀

able / ble	能够	ship	身份关系；动作
ian / an /ar / er / or	人	aholic / holic / oholic	沉迷于……的人
ee	人	ant / ent	人；特质
free	没有……的	ion	状态；行动
ic	学科；特质	ist	人
ism	主义；行动	ly	有……特质
ive / ative / itive	具……特质	ness	状态；性质
ment	行为；结果	proof	具有防……的
ous / eous / ious	具……特质	y	做之后的结果；状态

|正确答案| Review test　1 名词／豹　2 名词／鼓励　3 名词／项目　4 形容词／副词／国外的；在海外
　　　　　　　　5 形容词／哑的　6 形容词／苗条的　7 动词／接受　8 名词／传统
　　　　　 Preview　1 名词／马达　2 副词／永远　3 名词／必需品　4 名词／比率
　　　　　　　　5 形容词／鲜明的　6 名词；动词／账户，理由；解释，报账　7 形容词／令人满意的　8 形容词／创造（性）的

LEVEL 3 aboard ~ zone

以中小学必考 2 000 单词范围为基础 / 符合美国三年级学生所学范围

0001 aboard [əˈbɔːrd]
ad 搭乘交通工具，在船（火车、飞机）上
Well, all the passengers who came aboard the ship could have a free meal.
嗯，船上的所有乘客都可以免费享用一餐。
🔄 on board 在船上，在飞机上   🔄 go aboard 上船，上飞机

语法重点
句中的 well 是感叹词，可以引起听话人的注意。

0002 acceptable [əkˈsɛptəbl] a 可接受的，受欢迎的
It is acceptable to have bacon and eggs today.
今天吃培根和蛋是可以接受的。
🔄 accepted 可接受的   🔄 unacceptable 不能接受的，不受欢迎的

语法重点
it is acceptable 后面通常接动词不定式。

0003 accident [ˈæksɪdənt] n 意外，事故
A traffic accident happened on the corner when we drank coffee.
我们喝咖啡的时候，那个转角发生了一起交通事故。
🔄 casualty 意外事故   🔄 accidents will happen 意外事故在所难免

语法重点
on / at / in the corner 都可以表示地点，意义略有不同。on the corner 表示在转角的邻近范围内，in the corner 表示在角落里的空间，而 at the corner 表示在转角的某一点。

0004 account [əˈkaʊnt] n 账户，理由 v 解释，报账
The man withdrew twenty thousand dollars from his bank account to invite his friends to dinner.
那个人从银行账户里取了两万美元请朋友吃饭。
🔄 reason 理由   🔄 send in account 报账

0005 accurate [ˈækjərət] a 精确的，准确的
The spelling must be accurate, or else, you are not allowed to have dinner.
拼写必须正确无误，否则，你不准吃晚餐。
🔄 correct 正确的   🔄 inaccurate 不准确的   🔄 or else... 否则……

语法重点
accurate 指通过努力达到符合要求的准确性，与事实无出入。
🔄 allow (P. 006)

0006 ache [eɪk] n 疼痛，隐痛
After having a big dinner, she had an ache in the stomach.
饱餐一顿后，她感到胃痛。
🔄 pain 疼痛   🔄 have an ache in... ……疼
🔄 ache 指人体某一部位较持久的疼痛，并且通常指隐痛，pain 可以与 ache 互换，但意义有所不同。pain 可以指一般疼痛，也可以指剧痛，也可以用来表示精神上的痛苦。

0007 achieve [ə'tʃiːv] v 达成，实现，完成
He could enjoy all kinds of delicacies if he achieved his goals.
如果目标实现的话，他就能享受各种美食。
- realize 实现　- fail 失败　- achieve one's goal 实现某人的目标

> **语法重点**
> goal 一般与 achieve 搭配，dream 一般与 realize 搭配。
> enjoy (P. 160)

0008 achievement [ə'tʃiːvmənt] n 成就，成绩
The cook is widely known for his achievement in dessert.
这位厨师因其甜食上的成就而出名。
- personal achievement 个人成就　- be widely known for... 因……而广为人知

0009 activity [æk'tɪvəti] n 活动，活跃
As a foodie, she is an active participant in the activity.
作为一名美食家，她积极参与这项活动。
- movement 活动　- mental activity 心理活动

0010 actual ['æktʃuəl] a 实际的，事实上的
We need take actual action immediately after making a decision to have hot pot.
决定去吃火锅后，我们要立刻采取实际行动。
- factual 实际的　- ideal 理想的　- make a decision to do... 决定做……

> **语法重点**
> need 在句中作情态动词，后面接动词原形。

0011 additional [ə'dɪʃənl] a 附加的，额外的
You need to pay additional expense if you order other dishes.
你如果点其他的菜，需要另外付费。
- extra 额外的　- additional tax 附加税

0012 admire [əd'maɪər] v 钦佩，赞美，羡慕
Ever since, thousands of guests have come to taste the delicious food and the cook has also been admired for it.
从那之后，成千上万的客人前来品尝美食，厨师也为此受到了赞美。
- praise 赞美　- despise 鄙视　- extremely admire 五体投地

> **语法重点**
> ever since 表示从某个动作或事件发生后，一直延续到现在，在句中可以独立使用，也可引导时间状语从句。

0013 admit [əd'mɪt] v 承认，允许进入
We celebrated in the big restaurant after I was admitted to Yale University.
我被耶鲁大学录取后，我们去那家大饭店庆祝。
- confess 承认　- expel 驱逐　- be admitted to... 加入……

> **语法重点**
> be admitted to 后接表示学校、机构等的名词，表示"被录取到某学校、机构等"。

0014 adopt [ə'dɑːpt] v 采取，收养，接受
The couple adopted an orphan who was picky about food.
这对夫妇收养了一个对食物很挑剔的孤儿。
- assume 采取　- desert 抛弃　- be picky about... 对……很挑剔

> orphan (P. 331)

achieve ~ adviser

0015 advanced [əd'vænst] **a** 先进的，高级的
The dishes taste better in the restaurant after introducing advanced technology.
引入先进技术后，这家餐厅的饭菜好吃多了。
同 senior 高级的　　派 advanced age 高龄，老年

0016 advantage [əd'væntɪdʒ] **n** 优势，有利条件
The cook takes advantage of his position to steal food.
这个厨师利用职务之便偷拿食物。
同 benefit 好处　　反 disadvantage 劣势　　派 take advantage of... 利用……

▷ position (P. 077)

0017 adventure [əd'ventʃər] **n** 冒险，奇遇 **v** 冒险，尝试
I was none the worse for my adventure, but was nearly starved to death.
这次冒险没有使我受到伤害，只是差点儿饿死。
同 venture 冒险　　派 spirit of adventure 冒险精神　　派 ... starve to death ……饿死

> **语法重点**
> none the worse 意思是"一点儿不差，还是，仍然"。

0018 advertise ['ædvərtaɪz] **v** 为……宣传，登广告，宣传
This kind of biscuit is delicious and it pays to advertise at the golden time.
这种饼干很好吃，在黄金时间段做广告很值得。
同 announce 通知　　派 advertise for 登广告征求

> **语法重点**
> golden 和 gold 作形容词都可以表示"金色的，金制的"，golden 还可以表示"珍贵的，幸运的"，而 gold 没有这样的含义。

0019 advertisement [,ædvər'taɪzmənt]
n 广告，公告，启事
I glanced at the food and beverage advertisement on the newspaper and then set it aside.
我看了一眼报纸上的餐饮广告，然后把它放在了一边。
同 advert 广告　　派 job advertisement 招聘广告

▷ beverage (P. 677)

0020 advice [əd'vaɪs] **n** 建议，劝告，忠告
I took my friend's advice and didn't have the fish.
我听从朋友的建议，没有吃那条鱼。
同 suggestion 建议　　派 take one's advice 采取某人的意见

> **语法重点**
> "吃东西"一般可以用动词 have 来表示。

0021 advise [əd'vaɪz] **v** 劝告，忠告，建议
Her parents advised her not to travel with the gang of scoundrels again.
父母劝她不要再和那群无赖一起旅行。
同 suggest 建议　　派 advise on... 就……提出建议

> **语法重点**
> a gang of 表示"一群，一伙"，常修饰表示坏人的名词。

0022 adviser [əd'vaɪzər] **n** 顾问，指导教授，劝告者
The adviser has a good appetite no matter what happens.
不管发生什么事，这个顾问都有好胃口。
同 consultant 顾问　　派 ... have a good appetite 有好胃口

0023 affect [əˈfekt] v 影响，感动，作用

The truth was that the rubbish near the table affected our appetite.
事实上，桌子旁边的垃圾影响了我们的食欲。

> affect 和 influence 都可以表示"影响"，但意义有所不同，affect 通常指某个物体或情势、环境所产生的消极影响，而 influence 则是指对人的思想、性格、行为等的潜移默化的影响。

0024 afford [əˈfɔːrd] v 承担得起，花费得起，提供，给予

We can't afford the bill and were kicked out of the hotel.
我们付不起账单，被赶出了旅馆。

- allow 给予
- can afford 买得起，有能力负担

语法重点
afford 后面常接名词、代词或动词不定式。

0025 afterwards [ˈæftərwərdz] ad 以后，后来

I tried my best to learn cooking, and soon afterwards I cooked well.
我尽全力学习煮饭，很快就有了一手好厨艺。

- try one's best to do sth. 尽力做某事

语法重点
soon afterwards 表示"不久以后，后来"，可放在句中的任何位置。

0026 agriculture [ˈæɡrɪkʌltʃər] n 农业，农学，农艺

Planting vegetables in vinyl house is very popular in modern agriculture.
在现代农业中，在温室里种植蔬菜十分普遍。

- farming 农业
- be popular in... 在……流行

语法重点
be popular in 后接表示某一个行业、领域或是地域等的名词。

0027 air-conditioner [er kənˈdɪʃənər] n 空调

We are having hot pot, so please turn on the air-conditioner.
我们在吃火锅，所以请把空调打开。

语法重点
turn on（打开）后接表示电器的名词或名词短语。

0028 alley [ˈæli] n 弄，巷，胡同

I have a cup of tea in the teahouse in this alley every afternoon.
每天下午我都在这条巷子里的那家茶馆喝茶。

- alleyway 胡同，小巷
- blind alley 死胡同，没有前途的职业

语法重点
"a + 器物名词 + of" 通常用来表示不可数名词的数量。

↪ alley (P. 254)

0029 amaze [əˈmeɪz] v 使惊讶，使吃惊

I was so amazed at the news that he was sent to hospital because he had eaten a roast frog.
听说他因为吃了一只烤青蛙而被送到医院，我十分吃惊。

- amaze sb. 让某人感到惊讶
- be amazed at... 对……感到惊异

语法重点
be amazed at 后面通常接名词、代词、动名词，相当于 be surprised at。

0030 amazement [əˈmeɪzmənt] n 惊奇，惊异

She was filled with amazement when I took her to a cafe.
我带她上咖啡馆时，她十分惊讶。

- astonishment 惊愕，惊讶
- ... be filled with amazement ……大为吃惊

语法重点
be filled with amazement 指很出乎某人的意料，主语通常是人。

affect ~ apparent

0031 **ambassador** [æmˈbæsədər] n 大使，代表
Newspapers are of vital importance to the ambassador from America.
对于这个从美国来的大使来说，报纸特别重要。

语法重点
from 意思是"来自"，表示方向。

0032 **ambition** [æmˈbɪʃn] n 抱负，雄心，野心
He has been filled with ambition to eat all kinds of snacks all around the world.
他立志要吃遍全世界的小吃。
= determination 决心 = be filled with ambition 志向远大

语法重点
be filled with ambition 通常后接不定式。
snack (P. 224)

0033 **angel** [ˈeɪndʒl] n 天使，天使般的人
I caught a glimpse of the girl in a restaurant; her way of eating is like an angel.
我在餐馆里瞥见过那个女孩，她吃饭的样子就像一个天使。
≠ demon 恶魔 = catch a glimpse of... 瞥见……

语法重点
catch a glimpse of 可以用于各种时态，通常不用于被动。

0034 **angle** [ˈæŋɡl] n 角度，角
The statue looks very ugly from this angle.
从这个角度来看，那个雕像很难看。
= do sth. from this angle 从这个角度做某事

语法重点
from this angle 通常与动词 look at, see 等感官动词连用。

0035 **announce** [əˈnaʊns] v 宣告，宣布，播报
It was announced that we would have a big dinner tonight.
我们收到通知，今晚将会有一顿丰盛的晚餐。
= declare 宣布 = announce sth. to sb. 向某人宣布某事

0036 **announcement** [əˈnaʊnsmənt] n 宣告，通告，声明
His sudden announcement of treating all the colleagues to dinner took us by great surprise.
他突然请所有同事吃饭，这让我们都很吃惊。
= declaration 宣布 = take sb. by surprise 让某人很吃惊
※ announcement 通常指公开宣布令人感兴趣或是好奇的消息，而 declaration 则是指正式而明确地公布某消息。

0037 **apart** [əˈpɑːrt] ad 分开，相距，分别地
Her outstanding ability for tasting red wine set her apart from other girls.
她独特的品酒能力使她在女孩中独具一格。
≠ away 离开 ≠ together 一起 = set... apart from... 使……与……不同

语法重点
set 是不规则动词，其过去式、过去分词都是 set。
outstanding (P. 480)

0038 **apparent** [əˈpærənt] a 明显的，表面上的
It is apparent that he had no intention of having a cup of coffee.
很明显，他不想喝咖啡。
= evident 明显的 ≠ unapparent 不明显的 = it is apparent that... 很明显……

语法重点
have no intention of 后面常接动名词。

255

0039 appeal [ə'piːl] v 呼吁，有吸引力
They appealed to the manager for a dinner party on Sunday.
他们向经理申请周日聚餐。
plead 恳求　appeal for 恳求　appeal to... 向……请求

0040 appreciate [ə'priːʃieɪt] v 欣赏，感激，赏识
We all appreciate your treating us to dinner.
谢谢你请我们吃饭。

0041 approach [ə'prəʊtʃ] v 接近，靠近 n 途径，方法
I decided not to approach her in fear of rejection.
我因怕她拒绝而决定不去找她。
way 方法　leave 离开　in fear of... 害怕……

> 语法重点
> approach 通常是指做某事的特殊方法，而 way 则是泛指，可以是一般的方法，也可以是具体的某种方式。

0042 approve [ə'pruːv] v 赞成，批准，同意
I will never approve of your eating such dirty food.
我永远不会赞成你吃这么脏的食物。
agree 同意　disapprove 反对　approve of... 赞成……

> 语法重点
> approve of 后面常接名词、代词、动名词。

0043 aquarium [ə'kweəriəm] n 水族箱，鱼缸；水族馆
We were all in high spirits when eating snacks stealthily in the aquarium.
在水族馆里偷偷吃零食时，我们都很兴奋。

spirit (P. 226)

0044 arithmetic [ə'rɪθmətɪk] a 算术的 n 算术，计算
I was surprised to find the little boy was good at arithmetic.
我惊讶地发现，那个小男孩的计算能力特别好。
arithmetic capability 计算能力　be surprised to... 对……感到惊奇

> 语法重点
> be surprised to 的主语通常是人，to 后面通常接动词原形，表示吃惊的原因。

0045 arrival [ə'raɪvl] n 抵达，到达
With the arrival of Jim, we began to sing.
随着吉姆的到来，我们开始唱歌了。
departure 离开　arrival at port 入港

> 语法重点
> with the arrival of 后面通常接名词和代词。

0046 ash [æʃ] n 灰烬
All of the books were burnt to ashes in the fire just now.
刚才，所有的书都在大火中化成了灰烬。
dust 灰尘　... be burnt to ashes ……化为灰烬

> 语法重点
> turn to ashes 也表示"化为灰烬"，多为比喻意义，并且不用于被动语态。

0047 aside [ə'saɪd] ad 在旁边，离开
I put the bread aside and began to drink milk.
我把面包放在一边，开始喝牛奶。
away 离开　aside from... 除……以外

> 语法重点
> put aside（放在一边）后面常接表示物的名词作宾语，宾语如果是 it，则必须放在 put 与 aside 之间。

0048 assist [ə'sɪst] v 帮助，协助

I asked my friends to assist in eating up the cake.
我请朋友们帮忙吃完这个蛋糕。
- aid 帮助　　- assist in 帮助　　- assist in doing sth. 帮忙做某事

0049 athlete ['æθliːt] n 运动员

After the failure, the athlete began to eat too much out of sheer boredom.
那次失败后，因为感到无聊，这个运动员开始无节制地大吃起来。
- player 运动员　　- Spanish athlete 吹牛者，胡说八道的人

语法重点
too much 表示"太多"，在句中用于修饰动词 eat。
⇒ sheer (P. 776)

0050 attempt [ə'tempt] v / n 企图，尝试

I attempted to eat the nasty dish, but failed.
我试图吃那道难吃的菜，但没有成功。
- make an attempt at 打算　　- attempt to do... 试图做……
- attempt 和 try 都可以表示"试图，努力"，但意义有所不同，attempt 通常用于较为正式的语境，表示已经在进展着的努力，但是未必有预期的结果，而 try 则是表示广义的努力或是尝试。

0051 attitude ['ætɪtuːd] n 态度，看法，姿势

He has a passive attitude towards the song.
他对这首歌采取负面的态度。
- standpoint 看法　　- have an attitude towards... 采取……的态度

语法重点
have an attitude 中，attitude 可以用相应的形容词修饰，也可以用介词 to 或 toward 表示对某人或某事的态度。
⇒ passive (P. 481)

0052 attract [ə'trækt] v 吸引，引来

The snack bar attracts guests from all parts of the country.
这家小吃店吸引了全国各地的客人。

0053 attractive [ə'træktɪv] a 吸引人的，有魅力的

Fine food is attractive to her.
美食对她很有吸引力。
- unattractive 没有吸引力的　　- be attractive to... 对……有吸引力

语法重点
be attractive to 中的 to 是介词，to 后面常接名词或代词。

0054 audience ['ɔːdiəns] n 观众，读者，拥护者

The audiences are forbidden to eat snacks in the cinema.
观众被禁止在电影院里吃零食。
- reader 读者　　- give audience to 听取
- be forbidden to do sth. 被禁止做某事

语法重点
forbidden 是动词 forbid 的过去分词。

0055 author ['ɔːθər] n 作者，作家

The famous author has a bad habit.
那个著名的作家有个坏习惯。
- writer 作家，作者　　- best author 畅销书作者

0056 **automatic** [ˌɔːtəˈmætɪk] a 自动的，无意识的
Ben stood up in an automatic movement after he finished dinner.
晚餐后，本不假思索地站了起来。
⊙ unconscious 无意识的　⊗ manual 手工的

语法重点
automatic 可以指机器自动装置，也可以指无意识的行动。

0057 **automobile / auto** [ˈɔːtəməbiːl] / [ˈɔːtoʊ] n 汽车
She ceased to eat for fear of staining the automobile.
担心把车弄脏，她停止了吃东西。
⊙ car 汽车　⊙ cease to do sth. 停止做某事
⊙ cease to do sth. 相当于 stop doing sth.

⊃ cease (P. 406)

0058 **available** [əˈveɪləbl] a 可用的，可得到的，有效的
He isn't available for living in China because he dislikes Chinese food.
他不适合住在中国，因为他不喜欢吃中国菜。
⊙ valid 有效的　⊙ available space 可用空间　⊙ be available for... 适合……

0059 **avenue** [ˈævənuː] n 大道
As we all know, he likes to have coffee in the café at the avenue.
我们都知道，他喜欢在林荫大道上那家咖啡馆喝咖啡。
⊙ boulevard 林荫大道　⊙ avenue to success 成功之道

语法重点
"喝咖啡"一般要用 have coffee 来表达。

0060 **average** [ˈævərɪdʒ] n 平均 a 平均的，一般的
I think there is nothing special about the dinner, and it is average.
我觉得晚餐的饭菜没什么特别，挺平常的。
⊙ general 一般的　⊙ average value 平均值

0061 **awake** [əˈweɪk] v 叫醒 a 醒着的，警觉的
Please awake him at 6 o'clock, or he will have no time to eat breakfast.
请在六点钟叫醒他，不然他就没时间吃早餐了。
⊙ wake 唤醒　⊙ asleep 睡着的　⊙ barely awake 半梦半醒
⊙ have no time to do sth. 没时间做某事

语法重点
"吃早餐"一般用 have breakfast 来表达，但在这里为了避免重复，句中用 eat。

0062 **awaken** [əˈweɪkən] v 醒来
He was awakened by his girlfriend and then went to have a cup of tea with her.
他被女朋友叫醒，然后跟她一起去喝茶。
⊙ awaken to 意识到　⊙ be awakened by... 被……叫醒

0063 award [ə'wɔːrd] n 奖励 v 授予，判给

He was awarded a gold metal in the competition, so he bought us a drink.
他在比赛中赢得了金牌，于是请我们喝酒。
- grant 授予
- award ceremony 颁奖仪式
- buy sb. a drink 请某人喝酒

语法重点
gold metal 表示"金牌，第一名"，silver metal 表示"银牌，第二名"，为固定表达，通常与动词 win 或 award 等动词连用。

0064 aware [ə'wer] a 知道的，意识到的

She wasn't aware of the problem that she had nothing to eat.
她还没有意识到她已经没有东西吃了。
- conscious 意识到的
- unaware 没意识到的
- be aware of... 意识到……

语法重点
be aware of 后面接名词、代词、动名词，也可以用 that 从句来代替 of 结构，动词 be 有时态和人称、数的变化。

0065 awful ['ɔːfl] a 可怕的，糟糕的

There, I cannot have a buffet because of the awful weather.
算了吧，天气很糟糕，我不能去吃自助餐了。
- terrible 可怕的，很糟的
- cannot do sth. 不能做某事

语法重点
感叹词 there 表示得意、鼓励、同情、悲哀、不耐烦、失望、安慰、挑衅、引起注意等，可译为"看，好啦"等，此句中的感叹词 there 表示失望。

0066 axe [æks] n 斧头，解雇，倒闭

If you can cleave a block of wood with the axe, I will give you some chocolates.
如果你能用这把斧头劈开一块木头，我就给你一些巧克力。
- hire 雇用
- get the axe 被解雇，被抛弃
- cleave... with... 用……劈开……

语法重点
a block of 表示"一块"，通常是指一块木头、石头、金属等，也可以指可以视为一个整体的大量事物，如股份、座位等。

0067 background ['bækɡraʊnd] n 背景，经历，幕后

He has a background in cooking and all of his friends like the dishes he cooks.
他学过烹饪，所有朋友都喜欢吃他做的菜。
- educational background 教育背景
- have a background in... 学过……，有……的背景

0068 bacon ['beɪkən] n 培根

Let me know if the bacon is cooked in a frying pan, because it tastes a little salty.
请告诉我培根是不是在平底锅里做的，因为它吃起来有点咸。
- bring home the bacon 赚钱养家，获得成功

语法重点
a little 表示"一点，稍微"，修饰形容词或是动词，表示程度。
- salty (P. 218)

0069 bacteria [bæk'tɪriə] n 病菌

He was suffering from a stomachache, it's because there were bacterium in the food he has just eaten.
他肚子疼，是因为他刚才吃的食物里有细菌。

语法重点
it's because 用于引述做某事或出现某种状况的原因，相当于 this is because。

0070 badly ['bædli] ad 坏地，严重地，极度地

I think the man is badly in need of water.
我认为这个人急需喝水。
- terribly 极度地
- be badly in need of... 急需……

语法重点
副词 badly 修饰 in need，强调程度。

0071 **badminton** [ˈbædmɪntən] n 羽毛球

He is fond of playing badminton and being out drinking on Sundays.
他喜欢在周日打羽毛球和出去喝酒。
- shuttlecock 羽毛球　● badminton field 羽毛球场

语法重点
on Sundays 表示"每逢周日"。
⊃ fond (P. 297)

0072 **baggage** [ˈbæɡɪdʒ] n 行李

Put your baggage on the rack and have a drink together with us.
你把行李放在行李架上，来和我们一起喝酒。
- luggage 行李　● excess baggage 超重行李
- baggage 通常是指大而重的行李，而 luggage 则是泛指旅行者的行李。

0073 **bait** [beɪt] n 诱饵 v 以饵引诱，逗弄

He hoped that the fish would nibble at the bait, if so, his children could have fish tonight.
他希望鱼来咬钩，这样的话，他的孩子今晚就有鱼吃了。
- rise to the bait 入圈套，上当受骗　● nibble at... 啃……，咬……

语法重点
nibble at 通常用于主动语态。

0074 **balance** [ˈbæləns] n 平衡，结余 v 权衡，使平衡

Can you keep balance between meals and snacks?
你能在主食和零食之间保持平衡吗？
- hang in the balance 悬而未决
- keep balance between... and... 在……和……之间保持平衡

语法重点
"失去平衡"用 lose balance 来表达。

0075 **bandage** [ˈbændɪdʒ] n 绷带 v 用绷带包扎

He was wounded when having hot pot, and now the nurse was twisting the bandage around his arm.
他在吃火锅时受伤了，现在护士正用绷带包扎他的手臂。
- fascia 绷带　● ... be wounded ……受伤了
- twist 通常是指转动或是扭动而使事物成弯曲状，而 crook 则是指参照某种样本或是模型来弯曲事物。

0076 **bang** [bæŋ] v 砰砰作响 n 巨响，重击

I went bang into a telephone pole and my milk spilt out.
我砰地撞到电线杆，我的牛奶洒了出来。
- bang into 撞上，偶尔遇见　● ... spill out ……洒了出来

语法重点
spill 是不规则动词，其过去式、过去分词都有两个，即 spill, spilled, spilled 或 spill, spilt, spilt。

0077 **bare** [ber] a 裸的，空的，仅有的

There is nothing to eat and they are on the margin of bare subsistence.
没有东西吃了，他们处在挨饿的边缘。
- naked 裸露的　● be on the margin of... 处于……的边缘

语法重点
bare 常用于短语，with one's bare hands 的意思是"赤手空拳地"。
⊃ margin (P. 470)

badminton ~ behave

0078 barely ['beɪli] *ad* 几乎不，仅仅，只不过

His income is barely enough to keep the wolf from the door.
他的收入只能让他勉强度日。
⊚ merely 仅仅，只不过　⊚ barely satisfactory 差强人意

0079 barn [bɑːrn] *n* 谷仓，牲口棚

I converted the barn into a garden, and always had coffee there.
我把那个谷仓改成了花园，我时常在那里喝咖啡。
⊚ barn door 谷仓门　⊚ convert... into... 把……转变成……

> **语法重点**
> convert into 可以用于主动语态，也可以用于被动语态。
> ⊃ convert (P. 551)

0080 barrel ['bærəl] *n* 大桶，枪管

His beer flowed out from the broken barrel, so he had to buy some from the shop.
啤酒从那个漏桶中流出来了，所以他得去商店里买一些。
⊚ bucket 桶　⊚ over a barrel 受人摆布，处于困境
⊚ flow out from... 从……流出来

0081 bay [beɪ] *n* 海湾，月桂树

Let me fill you in on why we have lunch near the bay.
让我来告诉你我们为什么要在海湾附近吃午餐。
⊚ at bay 在海湾，陷入绝境　⊚ let me fill you in on... 让我来告诉你……

> **语法重点**
> bay 也常用在短语 keep / hold sb. at bay，意思是"不让某人逼近"。

0082 beam [biːm] *n* 光线，光束　*v* 微笑，发光

The man drinking tea in the black was caught in the full beam of a searchlight.
那个在黑暗中喝茶的人被探照灯照中而暴露无遗。
⊚ on one's beam-ends 几乎倾覆，十分拮据　⊚ be caught in... 遇到……

> **语法重点**
> beam 常用在短语 a beam of 中，该短语表示"一束、一道、一线"，后面通常接表示太阳、月亮、灯的光线的名词。

0083 beast [biːst] *n* 野兽，畜生，凶残的人

It used to be said that when a man is drunk, he's a beast.
过去人们常说，一个人喝醉时很野蛮。
⊚ it used to be said that... 过去人们常说……

> **语法重点**
> drunk 在句中作表语，意思是"喝醉的"。

0084 beggar ['begər] *n* 乞丐，穷人　*v* 使贫穷，使不足

I opened my heart to the beggar and gave him something to eat.
我非常同情那个乞丐，给了他一点儿吃的。
⊚ Beggars can't be choosers. 饥不择食。

> **语法重点**
> 口语中 you lucky beggar 的意思是"你这幸运的家伙"。

0085 behave [bɪ'heɪv] *v* 表现，行为，举止

It is very impolite to behave so rudely at dinner.
吃饭时如此粗鲁真是没礼貌。
⊚ act 表现，举止　⊚ behave under oneself 低声下气

> **语法重点**
> behave 也可以跟 oneself 连用，意思是"自我检讨"。

0086 **being** [ˈbiːɪŋ] n 生命 a 现在的，目前的
An advantage of her being is that she can cook anything you want to eat.
她存在的好处之一就是她能做出你想吃的任何东西。
- existence 存在　- beingless 不存在的

语法重点
an advantage of... is that... 指"……的好处之一是……"，其中 advantage 是可数名词。
- advantage (P. 253)

0087 **belly** [ˈbeli] n 腹部
It seems that he has a wolf in his belly.
他吃起饭来像饿狼。
- abdomen 腹部　- go belly up 破产，倒闭

0088 **beneath** [bɪˈniːθ]
prep 在……之下，低于……　ad 在下方，在底下
Let me see if there is some bread beneath a pile of dead leaves.
让我看看那堆枯树叶下面是否有面包。
- below 在……下面　- on 在……之上　- beneath notice 不值得注意的

0089 **benefit** [ˈbenɪfɪt] n 利益，津贴 v 有益于，得益
We benefit a lot from having a glass of water after getting up in the morning.
早起后喝一杯水让我们受益颇多。
- gain 获利　- lose 受损失　- benefit from... 得益于……

语法重点
benefit from 通常用于主动语态，后接名词或是名词短语。

0090 **berry** [ˈberi] n 莓果，干果仁
I couldn't help eating the berry.
我忍不住吃莓果。
- coffee berry 咖啡豆　- couldn't help doing sth. 情不自禁做某事

0091 **bible** [ˈbaɪbl] n 圣经，有权威的书
He is reading the Bible.
他在读《圣经》。

0092 **billion** [ˈbɪljən] n 十亿
He has assets of billion dollars, but he always works with an empty belly.
他有十亿美元的资产，但总是饿着肚子工作。
- milliard 十亿　- few billion 几十亿

- empty (P. 290)

0093 **bingo** [ˈbɪŋɡoʊ] n 宾果游戏 int 看吧，瞧
Bingo! I have finished eating the big cake!
瞧，我把这个大蛋糕吃完了！
- bingo card 宾果卡　- finish doing sth. 完成做某事

语法重点
感叹词 bingo 表示欢喜、惊讶、赞叹等，多位于句首，句尾用感叹号表示，通常用于口语中。

0094 biscuit ['bɪskɪt] n 小饼干，淡褐色
The biscuits I ate last time left a deep impression on me.
上次吃的饼干给我留下了深刻的印象。
- cookie 饼干
- leave a deep impression on... 给……留下了深刻的印象

0095 blame [bleɪm] v 责怪，把……归咎于 n 责备，过失
My mother blamed me for my throwing the leftovers away.
我把剩饭倒掉，所以妈妈责备了我。
- criticize 批评
- take the blame 承担过错
- blame sb. for sth. 因某事而责怪某人

语法重点
blame 也常用在 be to blame 的结构中。

0096 blanket ['blæŋkɪt] n 毛毯，覆盖物
She wrapped herself in a blanket and shoveled the food into her mouth.
她身上裹着毯子，大口吃着东西。
- wrap... in... 把……裹在……里

语法重点
shovel 的意思是"铲起，大量投入"，在句中有比喻的意思。
↪ wrap (P. 385)

0097 bleed [bli:d] v 流血
A fish bone sticks in my throat and it bleeds.
一根鱼刺卡在我的喉咙里，喉咙流血了。
- bleed someone white 榨干某人的血汗，耗尽钱财
- stick in... 刺入……，插进……

0098 bless [bles] v 祝福，保佑
He is blessed with bread and water.
他很幸运，面包和水都有了。
- curse 诅咒
- be blessed with... 在……方面有福

语法重点
bread 与 water 都是抽象名词，且为不可数名词。

0099 blouse [blaʊs] n 短上衣
The woman in a yellow blouse told us they had a special on suitcase today.
那个穿黄衬衫的女人告诉我们，他们的行李箱今天特价。

语法重点
special 在句中作名词，意思是"特价"。
↪ suitcase (P. 644)

0100 bold [boʊld] a 大胆的，粗鲁的，无礼的
He should make so bold as to eat a puffer fish.
他竟然敢吃河豚。
- as bold as brass 厚颜无耻的，极其胆大妄为的
- make so bold as to do sth. 敢做某事

语法重点
情态动词 should 有"竟然"的意思。

0101 boot [bu:t] n 靴子，猛踢 v 踢，逐出
The boss gave him the boot because he stole stationery in the company.
他因为偷公司的文具而被老板开除了。
- kick 踢
- give sb. the boot 开除某人

语法重点
表示"遭到解雇"用 get the boot，该短语不用于被动语态。

0102 **border** [ˈbɔːrdər] n 边界，边境，边缘
Some foreigners crossed the border just to enjoy a quick snack.
有些外国人越过边境只是为了吃点儿小吃。
- edge 边缘　- cross the border 越界

0103 **bore** [bɔːr] v 使无聊，开凿 n 讨厌的人，麻烦事
Her everlasting eating candies bores her husband to death.
她不停地吃糖果，这让她的丈夫极度厌烦。
- bore sb. to death 让某人极度厌烦

0104 **brake** [breɪk] v 刹车 n 制动器，刹车
She braked hard in order not to hit the man who was standing in the middle of the road.
她急忙踩刹车，为的是不撞到那个站在马路中间的人。
- spoke 刹车　- brake system 刹车系统

> **语法重点**
> in order not to（为了不……）后面要接动词原形。

0105 **brass** [bræs] n 黄铜，铜管乐器，厚脸皮
He is as bold as brass to ask me for a piece of bread.
他厚颜无耻地向我要一块面包。
- brass wire 铜丝　- be as bold as brass to... 厚颜无耻地……

0106 **bravery** [ˈbreɪvəri] n 勇敢，大胆，华丽
They spoke highly of the bravery of the young man.
他们高度称赞那个年轻人的勇敢行为。
- courage 勇敢，胆量　- speak highly of... 高度赞扬……

> **语法重点**
> speak highly of 后面通常接表示精神、行为、信誉等的抽象名词，不用于被动语态。

0107 **breast** [brest] n 乳房，胸脯
He beat his breast at the news that his chocolates were eaten up by his sister.
得知妹妹吃完了他的巧克力，他捶胸顿足。
- bosom 胸怀　- beat one's breast 某人捶胸顿足

> **语法重点**
> beat one's breast 表示因自己的过错或是某种原因而伤心、痛苦、后悔等。

0108 **breath** [breθ] n 呼吸，气息
She has eaten for half an hour, barely pausing to draw breath.
她足足吃了半个小时，几乎没有停下来喘一口气。
- out of breath 喘不过气　- pause to do sth. 停下来去做某事

> barely (P. 261)

0109 **breathe** [briːð] v 呼吸，流露
She was able to breathe easily again after disposing of the rubbish.
处理掉所有的垃圾后，她又可以松口气了。
- breathe forth 吐气　- dispose of... 处理……

> **语法重点**
> breathe 后面可以接介词 in 和 out，分别表示"吸入"和"呼出"。

0110 **breeze** [briːz] n 微风，轻而易举的事

It is pleasant to enjoy the cool sea breeze and have a cup of coffee here.
在这里一边享受凉爽的海风一边喝着咖啡很惬意。

▶ pleasant (P. 205)

0111 **bride** [braɪd] n 新娘

The bride has never been a great one for rice.
新娘向来不喜欢吃米饭。
▶ bridegroom 新郎

0112 **brilliant** ['brɪliənt] a 明亮的，杰出的，才华横溢的

He had the good fortune to drink with some brilliant directors.
他有幸与几位杰出的主管人员一同喝酒。
▶ prominent 卓越的，杰出的　▶ commonplace 平凡的
▶ brilliant 和 intelligent 都表示"聪明的"，但意义有所不同，brilliant 通常是指才华出众、思维敏锐，而 intelligent 则是指智力优于常人，在理解、接受能力上超过常人。

0113 **brook** [brʊk] n 小溪 v 容忍，忍受

A brook flows through the small village.
一条小河流经这个小村庄。
▶ creek 小溪　▶ clear brook 清澈的溪流　▶ flow through... 流过……

语法重点
flow through 用来指江河溪流等流经某地，也可以接介词 into 表示所流向的地点。

0114 **broom** [bruːm] n 扫帚，金雀花

The cook picked up a broom to drive off the flies around the dish.
厨师拿起一把扫帚驱赶盘子周围的苍蝇。
▶ a new broom 新就职者，刚上任的新官　▶ pick up... 拿起……

语法重点
pick up 也可以表示"开车接，无意中学会，偶然结识"。

0115 **brow** [braʊ] n 眉毛，前额

He knitted his brow when he tasted the soup.
他品尝汤的时候皱起眉头。
▶ eyebrow 眉毛　▶ knit one's brow 某人皱眉

语法重点
knit one's brow 通常不用于被动，注意 knit 的过去式要重复词尾 t。
▶ knit (P. 315)

0116 **bubble** ['bʌbl] n 泡沫，气泡 v 起泡，冒泡

Oh my god, the soup in the pot is at the bubble.
天啊，锅里的汤在沸腾。
▶ foam 泡沫　▶ blow bubbles 吹肥皂泡　▶ ... be at the bubble ……在沸腾

0117 **bucket / pail** ['bʌkɪt] / [peɪl] n 水桶，一满桶

As for the current situation, the food she offered was just a drop in the bucket.
从目前的形势来看，她提供的食物不过是沧海一粟。
▶ pail 桶　▶ kick the bucket 死了，一命呜呼

语法重点
a drop in the bucket 比喻某人或某物在整个总量上所占的比重很小，其中 bucket 可以用 ocean 来代替。

0118 **bud** [bʌd] n 花蕾 v 发芽，萌芽

His bad habit of eating before going to bed should be nipped in the bud.
应该尽早把他睡前吃东西的坏习惯改掉。

🔵 sprout 发芽　🔵 be in bud 在萌芽状态，含苞待放

> **语法重点**
> bud 也可以与介词 in 构成短语 in bud，表示"萌芽，含苞欲放"，多用来描述花、树或是其他的植物。

0119 **budget** [ˈbʌdʒɪt] n 预算

In the final analysis, you must buy your food and water within a limited budget.
毕竟，你必须靠有限的预算来买食物和水。

🔵 financial budget 财政预算

↪ analysis (P. 394)

0120 **buffalo** [ˈbʌfəloʊ] n 水牛，野牛 v 威吓，欺骗

Regardless of the result, they killed all the buffaloes for their meat.
他们不计后果，为了吃肉而杀掉所有的野牛。

> **语法重点**
> regardless of（不顾）可置于句首，也可置于句中。
> ↪ regardless (P. 768)

0121 **buffet** [bəˈfeɪ] n 殴打，自助餐

Maybe it's better for you to come for buffet this Sunday.
你们这周日来吃自助餐可能会更好一些。

🔵 shock 打击　🔵 buffet car 餐车

0122 **bulb** [bʌlb] n 球茎，电灯泡，球状物

The bulb suddenly went out when we had supper in the house.
我们在屋里吃晚餐时，灯泡突然灭了。

🔵 incandescent bulb 白炽灯　🔵 ... go out ……熄灭

> **语法重点**
> go out 通常是指灯光、光线的熄灭，不用于被动语态，也可以表示"过时，出局"。

0123 **bull** [bʊl] n 公牛，警察

The man burnt his tongue when having the soup; he was a bull in a china shop.
那个人在喝汤时烫到了舌头，真是鲁莽。

🔵 a bull in a china shop 莽撞而笨拙的人

0124 **bullet** [ˈbʊlɪt] n 子弹，弹丸

They found a bullet in the beef.
他们在牛肉里面发现了一颗子弹。

🔵 pill 子弹，弹丸　🔵 bite the bullet 忍痛，咬紧牙关

0125 **bump** [bʌmp] v 碰，撞，撞击 n 肿块，撞击

The car bumped along the cranky mountain road.
汽车沿着蜿蜒曲折的山路颠簸而行。

🔵 clash 撞击　🔵 bump along... 沿着……颠簸而行

> **语法重点**
> bump along 的主语通常是交通工具，也可以用 bump down 来表达。

0126 bunch [bʌntʃ] n 一串，束，捆

How delicious the bunch of bananas taste!
那串香蕉吃起来真美味！
- cluster 串
- How delicious... taste! ……吃起来真美味！

语法重点
a bunch of 表示"一束，一串"，后接可数名词复数形式。

0127 burden ['bɜːrdn] n 负担，责任

He shoulders a heavy burden to support his families and buys food and water for them.
他肩负着养活家人的重担，并为他们买食物和水。
- debt burden 债务负担

语法重点
shoulder a heavy burden（肩负重担）通常用于主动语态，shoulder 也可以用 carry, bear 来代替。

0128 burglar ['bɜːrɡlər] n 小偷

A cat burglar slipped into her house and stole all the jewelry away.
一个飞贼溜进了她的家里，偷走了所有的珠宝。
- thief 贼
- burglar alarm 防窃报警器
- 英语中通常用动物来表示某种特殊的感情，并构成具有特定意义的结构，如 a cat burglar 表示"飞贼，身手敏捷的贼"，属于固定用法。

0129 bury ['beri] v 埋葬，隐匿

She always buries herself in searching for antique.
她总是专注于寻找古董。
- hide 隐藏
- dig 挖掘
- bury the hatchet 言归于好

语法重点
bury oneself in 后面接名词、代词、动名词，可用于主动语态，也可用于被动语态。

0130 bush [bʊʃ] n 灌木丛，矮树

There is no sense in beating around the bush.
说话拐弯抹角没有意义。
- shrub 灌木丛
- beat around the bush 旁敲侧击，拐弯抹角

语法重点
beat around the bush 是固定搭配，意思是"旁敲侧击，说话拐弯抹角"。

0131 buzz [bʌz] v 嗡嗡叫，匆忙 n 嗡嗡声，电话

There's a buzz going round that there will be a dinner party tonight.
传闻今晚将会举办一场派对。
- buzz word 术语，专门用语
- there's a buzz going round that... 传闻……

语法重点
buzz 在句中作名词，意思引申为"传闻"。
- dinner (P. 029)

0132 cabin ['kæbɪn] n 小屋

They drank themselves into oblivion in the cabin.
他们在小木屋里喝得不省人事。
- passenger cabin 客舱
- drink oneself into oblivion 某人喝得不省人事

0133 campus ['kæmpəs] n 校园，场地

Most of the college students are not pleased with the food on campus.
大多数大学生对学校的饭菜表示不满。
- campus life 校园生活
- be not pleased with... 对……不满意

语法重点
on campus 表示"在校内"，为固定用法，也可以用 on one's / the campus 来表示。表示相反意义可以用 off (the) campus（在校外）。

0134 **cane** [keɪn] n 手杖，藤条
He got the cane from his mother because he ate up all the honey.
他吃光了所有的蜂蜜，因而被母亲鞭打了。
≈ stick 手杖　◎ get the cane from... 被……鞭打

语法重点
get the cane 通常用于主动语态，也可以用被动结构 be given the cane 来代替。

0135 **canoe** [kəˈnuː] n 独木舟 v 乘独木舟
The little girl paddles her own canoe and always has nothing to eat.
那个小女孩自谋生计，经常没有东西吃。
◎ paddle one's own canoe 某人独立谋生

0136 **canyon** [ˈkænjən] n 峡谷
After breakfast, he paid a visit to the Grand Canyon.
早餐后，他参观了大峡谷。

语法重点
pay a visit to 后面接表示地点的名词。

0137 **capable** [ˈkeɪpəbl] a 能够的
I am sure he is capable of drinking so much wine.
我相信他能喝这么多酒。
≈ able 有能力的　≠ incapable 无能力的　◎ be capable of... 有能力……

语法重点
capable 通常是指有能力或是有条件做某事，常与介词 of 连用；而 able 则是指普遍意义上的能力，也可以指非凡的技能。

0138 **capital** [ˈkæpɪtl] n 首府，资本 a 资本的，首要的
The cook makes capital out of his authority and brings many dishes home.
那个厨师以权谋私，带了很多菜回家。
◎ fund 资金　◎ capital market 资本市场　◎ make capital out of... 利用……

语法重点
make capital out of 后面通常接表示某种状况、条件等的名词。

0139 **capture** [ˈkæptʃər] v / n 俘虏
The policemen fail to capture the thief who always steals bread in a bakery.
警察没能抓住那个总在面包店偷面包的贼。
≈ catch 捕捉　≠ release 释放　◎ fail to do sth. 没能做某事

0140 **carpenter** [ˈkɑːrpəntər] n 木匠，木工
The carpenter is skilled at tramping grapes for wine.
那个木工擅长酿葡萄酒。
≈ woodworker 木工　◎ be skilled at... 擅长……

语法重点
be skilled at 后面通常接名词、动名词，介词 at 可以用 in 来代替。

0141 **carriage** [ˈkærɪdʒ] n 婴儿车，火车车厢
It can't be denied that it is uncomfortable to have dinner in the carriage.
不可否认，在车厢里用餐很不舒服。
◎ it can't be denied that... 不可否认……

≋ deny (P. 151)

0142 **cast** [kæst] v 投掷，抛，铸造
The fly on the dish cast a damp over the guests.
饭菜上面的苍蝇让客人们很不高兴。
▷ damp (P. 422)

0143 **casual** ['kæʒuəl] a 偶然的，非正式的 n 临时工，便装
I think casual attire should not be proper for the banquet.
我认为穿便装参加宴会不合适。
informal 非正式的　　be proper for... ……合适

0144 **caterpillar** ['kætərpɪlər] n 毛毛虫
I would never dream of seeing a caterpillar in the soup.
我从来没想到会在汤里看到一只毛毛虫。
palmerworm 毛虫　　caterpillar track 履带

语法重点
would 是情态动词，用于所有人称。

0145 **cattle** ['kætl] n 牛，家畜，牲畜
In some sense, the cattle made the grade as prime beef.
在某种意义上，这头牛达到了上等牛肉的标准。
▷ prime (P. 488)

0146 **celebrate** ['selɪbreɪt] v 庆祝，庆贺
It is an occasion for us to celebrate in the pub.
这是值得我们去酒吧庆祝的时刻。
celebrate... with sb. 和某人一起庆祝……

0147 **centimeter** ['sentɪmiːtər] n 厘米
The bottle is 20 centimeters high.
那个瓶子有 20 厘米高。
tall 和 high 都可以表示"高"，但侧重点不同，tall 通常是指人高、树高，而 high 则是指物体的相对高度或是海拔。若是形容山高，二者都可以用。

0148 **ceramic** [sə'ræmɪk] a 陶器的
I couldn't stand to see him drink water with the ceramic.
我不能忍受看他用那个陶器喝水。
ceramic art 陶艺　　couldn't stand to do sth. 不能忍受做某事

0149 **chain** [tʃeɪn] n 锁链，链子，束缚
According to the expert, the food poisoning may set up a chain reaction in other restaurants.
根据专家的推断，此次食物中毒可能会引起其他餐厅的连锁反应。
▷ reaction (P. 346)

0150 **challenge** ['tʃælɪndʒ] n 挑战 v 向……挑战，质疑
It is a great challenge for me to eat such a big watermelon.
对我来说，吃这么大的一个西瓜是个相当大的挑战。
doubt 怀疑　　beyond challenge 无与伦比

语法重点
形容词是指用来描写和表述人或事物的性质、状态或特征的词，其在句中一般用来修饰名词，如例句中的 great。

0151 champion [ˈtʃæmpiən] n 冠军，优胜者，拥护者
The champion gets her fingers on everything that her brother does.
不管弟弟做什么事，那个冠军都要插手。
反 loser 失败者　同 get one's fingers on... 插手……

语法重点
get one's fingers on 是固定搭配，finger 要用复数形式。

0152 changeable [ˈtʃeɪndʒəbl] a 易变的，可改变的
The weather is changeable today, so he quits going out for a picnic.
今天的天气变化异常，所以他放弃了外出野餐。
同 variable 易变的　反 unchangeable 不能改变的
同 quit doing sth. 放弃做某事

参 picnic (P. 203)

0153 channel [ˈtʃænl] n 频道，海峡，通道
It is unbelievable that she can swim across the channel.
她居然能横渡海峡，这真难以置信。
同 route 通道　同 it is unbelievable that... ……难以置信

0154 chapter [ˈtʃæptər] n 章节，回，篇
In this chapter, you will learn how to cook western food.
在这一章，你将学习如何做西餐。
同 section 章节　同 a chapter of accidents 接踵而至的灾祸

语法重点
表示"在某一章节"，一般用介词 in。

0155 charm [tʃɑːrm]
n 魅力，吸引力，迷人　v 使着迷，施魔法
He is a man of charm and good at cooking.
他是一个有魅力的男人，而且很会做饭。
同 work like a charm 药到病除　同 ... be of charm ……有魅力

0156 chat [tʃæt] v / n 聊天
It's about time we had dinner and chatted with each other.
现在该是我们吃饭、聊天的时候了。
同 talk 交谈　同 chat about 闲聊，闲谈

语法重点
it's about time 后面从句中的动词要用过去时。

0157 cheek [tʃiːk] n 面颊，脸蛋
After finishing the meal, he kissed her on her snow-white check.
吃完饭后，他在她那雪白的脸颊上亲了一下。
同 cheek by jowl 紧密地　同 kiss sb. on... 亲某人的……

语法重点
有些名词和形容词也可以组合构成复合形容词，如例句中的 snow-white。

0158 cheer [tʃɪr] v 欢呼，喝彩　n 欢呼，激励
I think a good meal may bring cheer to their hearts.
我觉得一顿美食能使他们变得愉快。
同 glad 高兴　反 gloom 忧郁，阴暗　同 words of cheer 鼓励的话语

语法重点
情态动词 may 可以表示推测。
参 meal (P. 189)

0159 **cheerful** [ˈtʃɪrfl] a 兴高采烈的，快乐的
You're not your usual cheerful self after eating in the restaurant.
在那家餐厅吃过饭后，你就不像之前那么快乐了。

> 语法重点
> one's 要与 be 前面的主语保持一致。

0160 **cheese** [tʃiːz] n 乳酪
Cheese is a good lure for these children.
对于这些孩子来说，乳酪是个很大的诱惑。

> 语法重点
> cheese 是不可数名词。
> ↪ lure (P. 740)

0161 **cherry** [ˈtʃeri] n 樱桃，樱桃树
I could not forbear eating the red cherries.
我忍不住想吃那些红色的樱桃。
🔗 could not forbear doing sth. 忍不住做某事

> 语法重点
> 形容词修饰名词时，一般放在被修饰名词之前，如例句中的形容词 red。

0162 **chest** [tʃest] n 胸膛，胸腔
The girl nestled against his chest.
女孩依偎在他的怀里。
🔗 breast 胸部   🔗 on one's chest 心事重重   🔗 nestle against... 依偎在……

> 语法重点
> 句中的介词 against 也可以替换为 up 或 to。

0163 **chew** [tʃuː] v 咀嚼，嚼碎，深思
I chewed the gum and chatted with my mother.
我嚼着口香糖和妈妈聊天。
🔗 chew over 仔细考虑，详细讨论   🔗 chat with... 与……聊天

> 语法重点
> chew 还可以与介词 on 连用，构成短语 chew on，意思是"考虑"。

0164 **childhood** [ˈtʃaɪldhʊd] n 童年，幼年
I was fond of eating candies in my childhood.
我童年时喜欢吃糖果。

0165 **chill** [tʃɪl] n 寒冷，扫兴，寒心 v （使）寒冷
I was surprised at seeing that the meat was chilled.
看到肉结冻了，我很吃惊。

0166 **chilly** [ˈtʃɪli] a 寒冷的，冷淡的
The chilly wind made them discouraged to have dinner out.
寒风使他们放弃了外出吃饭的念头。
🔗 cold 寒冷的   🔗 hot 炎热的   🔗 chilly wind 寒风

> 语法重点
> 动态形容词是指带有某种动作含义的形容词，该类形容词通常是由动词转换变化而来，如例句中的 discouraged（气馁的）便属于动态形容词，是动词 discourage 的过去分词形式。

0167 **chimney** [ˈtʃɪmni] n 烟囱，烟道
I am confident that Santa Clause could come into the house through the chimney.
我坚信圣诞老人能够穿过烟囱进到屋里。
🔗 funnel 烟囱   🔗 I am confident that... 我坚信……

> 语法重点
> Santa Clause 的意思是"圣诞老人"，是常用的固定表达，首字母都要大写，也可以用 Father Christmas 来表达。

0168 **chip** [tʃɪp] n 碎片，碎屑 v 切下，将……切成条
It is irritating that the knife is too dull to cut the cucumber into chips.
这把刀太钝了，根本不能把黄瓜切成片，真恼人。
 patch 碎片   potato chips 马铃薯片

语法重点
通常情况下，由动词的现在分词或过去分词转化而来的形容词，仍具有动词的含义，因此属于动词形容词，如例句中的 irritating。

0169 **choke** [tʃoʊk] v 使窒息，阻塞，说不出话
The little boy was choked with a jelly.
小男孩被一个果冻噎住了。
 choke back 抑制，强忍   be choked with... 被……阻塞了

→ jelly (P. 313)

0170 **chop** [tʃɑːp] v 砍，劈，剁 n 砍，排骨
As expected, the hungry man began to eat chop suey.
不出所料，那个饥饿的男人开始吃炒杂碎。
 chop logic 咬文嚼字，强词夺理   as expected, ... 不出所料，……

0171 **cigarette** [ˈsɪɡəret] n 烟
He seems to like having cigarette with his drink.
他似乎喜欢在喝酒时抽烟。
 tobacco 烟草   cigarette holder 烟斗
 sb. seems to like... 某人看起来喜欢……

语法重点
cigarette 是可数名词。

0172 **circus** [ˈsɜːrkəs] n 马戏团，竞技场
He was spellbound by the circus performance and forgot to drink water.
他被马戏表演迷住了，忘了要喝水。

0173 **civil** [ˈsɪvl] a 市民的，国内的，文明的
She is very content with the civil life and likes the snacks here.
她很满意这里的平民生活，也喜欢这里的小吃。
 courteous 有礼貌的   uncivil 不文明的   civil war 内战

语法重点
be content with 强调自己认可某种情况，be satisfied with 也可以表示"对……满意"，但主要表示某种情况完全达到自己的预期。

0174 **classical** [ˈklæsɪkl] a 古典的，权威的，传统的
The classical musician was in an alcoholic stupor last night.
昨晚，那位古典音乐家醉得不省人事。
 traditional 传统的   classical literature 古典文学

语法重点
classical 的意思是"古典的，传统的"，而 classic 的意思是"经典的"，二者在含义上有一些差别。
→ alcoholic (P. 670)

0175 **click** [klɪk] v 点击滑鼠，一拍即合
Hamburgers have really clicked with young people in Beijing.
在北京，汉堡很受年轻人的喜爱。
 click here 点击这里   click with sb. 被某人喜欢

0176 **client** [ˈklaɪənt] n 客户，顾客，委托人
The client went out drinking and came back in an alcoholic haze.
那个客户出去喝酒，回来时醉醺醺的。
🔄 customer 客户　🔄 client service 客户服务

0177 **clinic** [ˈklɪnɪk] n 诊所，门诊部，科室
She took some bread to her husband's clinic as his breakfast.
她把一些面包送到丈夫的诊所，作为他丈夫的早餐。
🔄 ambulatorium 诊所　🔄 take... to... 把……拿到……

> 语法重点
> "牙科诊所"用 dental clinic 来表示。

0178 **clip** [klɪp] n 回纹针，别针 v 剪短，修剪
She was clipping her nails when I offered her a cup of tea.
我递茶给她时，她在剪指甲。
🔄 shear 修剪　🔄 clip one's nails 某人剪指甲

> 语法重点
> clip 的现在分词形式要重复词尾 p 再加 ing。
> 🔄 nail (P. 193)

0179 **clue** [kluː] n 线索，提示
I haven't got a clue about what he had this morning.
我一点儿都不知道他今天早上吃了什么。
🔄 hint 线索，暗示　🔄 not have a clue 毫无头绪　🔄 get a clue about... 知道……

0180 **cocktail** [ˈkɑːkteɪl] n 鸡尾酒，混合物，开胃品
It is conspicuous that the man enjoys cocktails.
很明显，那个人喜欢喝鸡尾酒。
🔄 it is conspicuous that... 很明显……

0181 **coconut** [ˈkoʊkənʌt] n 椰子，椰子仁
If you don't mind, I want to eat your coconut.
如果你不介意的话，我想吃你的椰子。

> 语法重点
> coconut 当"椰子"讲时是可数名词，当"椰子仁"讲时是不可数名词。

0182 **collar** [ˈkɑːlər] n 衣领，项圈
I accidentally splashed milk over the collar of my woolen coat.
我不小心把牛奶洒在羊毛外套的衣领上。
🔄 neck 衣领　🔄 blue collar 蓝领　🔄 splash... over... 把……洒在……上

> 语法重点
> 一些形容词可以表示事物的类别、来源或某种特殊性质等，但没有可以比较的性质，如例句中的 woolen（羊毛的），用来表示 coat 的性质，不能用来进行比较，是非等级形容词。

0183 **collection** [kəˈlekʃn] n 收集，聚集，收藏品
She is fond of drinking coffee while enjoying the collections in her room.
她喜欢边喝咖啡边欣赏房里的收藏品。
🔄 a collection of 一批，一些

> 语法重点
> 相对形容词指不可以在句中作独立成分的形容词，一般的形容词可以在句中独立使用，但相对形容词则必须和介词搭配使用，如句中的 fond。

0184 college ['kɑːlɪdʒ] n 学院

She hasn't got accustomed to the food in her college after a year.
一年过去了，她仍然没有适应大学里的食物。
⊙ university 大学   ⊙ at college 在大学读书

语法重点

accustomed 的意思是"习惯的，通常的"，是相对形容词，不能独立使用，一般用于 be accustomed to 或 get accustomed to 的结构中，表示"习惯于……"，be 侧重于表状态；get 则强调动作。

0185 colony ['kɑːləni] n 殖民地，侨居地

After living in the colony, you should accommodate yourself to the eating habits there.
住在侨居地后，你得适应那里的饮食习惯。
⊙ accommodate oneself to... 使某人适应……

➔ accommodate (P. 667)

0186 column ['kɑːləm] n 专栏，圆柱

He disagrees with the viewpoint about drinking in the column of yesterday's newspaper.
昨天的报纸专栏发表的有关喝酒的观点，他不能苟同。
⊙ water column 水柱   ⊙ disagree with... 不同意……

语法重点

disagree with 后一般加人物的名字或人称代词，表示"不同意某人的观点或意见"。

0187 combine [kəm'baɪn] v 合并，结合

You should combine theory with practice.
你应该把理论和实践结合起来。
⊙ connect 联合   ⊙ disconnect 拆开   ⊙ combine... with... 把……和……联合起来

语法重点

theory 与 practice 都是抽象名词，且为不可数名词。

0188 comfort ['kʌmfərt] v / n 舒适，安逸

She tried to comfort me by making soup when I was ill.
我生病时，她试着煮汤来安慰我。
⊙ ease 舒适   ⊙ discomfort 不适   ⊙ comfort sb. by... 通过……来安慰某人

0189 comma ['kɑːmə] n 逗号，间歇，小数点

Separate the two clauses by a comma and then come to have a cup of tea.
把这两个从句用逗号隔开，然后过来喝杯茶。
⊙ inverted comma 引号   ⊙ separate... by... 用……把……分开

语法重点

separate 后面一般接复数名词。

0190 command [kə'mænd] v 命令，指挥

The director commanded his men to drink some water before working.
主管命令手下工作前先喝点水。
⊙ command sb. to do sth. 命令某人做某事

0191 commercial [kə'mɜːrʃl] a 商业的，贸易的，营利的

I am blind to commercial operations.
我对商业运作一窍不通。
⊙ merchant 商业的   ⊙ commercial company 贸易公司
⊙ be blind to... 对……一窍不通

➔ blind (P. 131)

0192 committee [kəˈmɪti] n 委员会，受托人，保护人

He got into a wrangle with the committee about what to have for lunch.
他为午餐吃什么的事情跟委员会的人发生了争执。

≈ commission 委员会　≈ get into a wrangle with... 与……发生争执

0193 communicate [kəˈmjuːnɪkeɪt] v 沟通，交流，传达

She is very glad to communicate with you about how to improve the cooking skill.
她很高兴和你交流一下如何改进厨艺。

≈ convey 传达　≈ be glad to do sth. 乐意去做某事

语法重点
一些形容词之后可以加动词不定式形式，如例句中的 be glad to do sth.。

0194 comparison [kəmˈpærɪsn] n 对比，对照

I'm sure that the bread you make is without comparison.
我相信你做的面包是无与伦比的。

≈ by comparison 比较起来，相比之下

语法重点
一些形容词之后常可以接 that 从句来对某种情况进行具体的说明，如例句中的 I'm sure that.。

0195 compete [kəmˈpiːt] v 竞争，比赛，对抗

He is not certain whether he can get the upper hand when competing with her at the cooking competition.
和她比赛厨艺，他不确定自己能占上风。

≈ contest 竞争　≈ compete with 和……竞争

语法重点
whether 和 if 为"是否"的含义，表示一种选择关系，其引导的从句可以加在形容词之后。

⊃ certain (P. 022)

0196 complaint [kəmˈpleɪnt] n 抱怨，诉苦，投诉

If she is always busy working, she'll have no time for complaint about the unsavoury food.
如果她一直忙于工作，就没有时间抱怨饭菜难吃了。

≈ grumble 怨言　≈ be busy doing sth. 忙着做某事

0197 complex [kəmˈpleks] a 复杂的，合成的

She isn't in the mood to eat anything under such complex situation.
在如此复杂的情况下，她没有心情吃东西。

≈ complicated 复杂的　≠ simple 简单的

⊃ mood (P. 327)

❖ complex 与 complicated 都有"复杂的"意思，但 complex 指不是人为的而是自然而然形成的复杂，而 complicated 指人为造成的复杂。

0198 concern [kənˈsɜːrn] v 涉及，关心 n 关心，关心的事

He never concerns where to live.
他从不关心住哪里。

≠ unconcern 不关心　≈ concern about... 关心……

0199 concert [ˈkɑːnsərt] n 音乐会，一致，和谐

After finishing our work, we will set off for the concert.
做完工作后，我们就出发去听音乐会。

≈ accordance 一致　≠ disharmony 不和谐　≈ concert hall 音乐厅

0200 **conclude** [kənˈkluːd] v 做出结论

They concluded that eating raw tomato does no harm to health.
他们总结说，吃生番茄对健康无害。
conclude with 以……结束 sb. conclude that... 某人总结说……

语法重点
不定冠词 a / an 加上可数名词单数可以表示类别，如例句中的 a tomato。

0201 **conclusion** [kənˈkluːʒn] n 结论

In conclusion, all of us should not make any compromise on food safety.
总之，在食品安全问题上，我们所有人都不能妥协。
beginning 开始 ending 结尾 in conclusion, ... 总之，……

⇨ compromise (P. 548)

0202 **condition** [kənˈdɪʃn] n 情况

In this condition, we can only have steamed buns for supper.
在这种情况下，我们晚餐只能吃馒头。
situation 情况 in this condition, ... 在这种情况下，……

语法重点
condition 也可以表示"情况"，但要用其复数形式。

0203 **cone** [koʊn] n 圆锥形，锥形物，球果

The ice cream cone slid from his left hand and fell on the floor.
冰激凌筒从他的左手滑落掉到了地板上。
circular cone 圆锥 slide from... 从……滑落……

语法重点
slid 是 slide 的过去式。

0204 **confident** [ˈkɑːnfɪdənt] a 自信的，有信心的，有把握的

He is firmly confident that all of his friends will like the soup he makes.
他坚信所有的朋友都会喜欢他煮的汤。

0205 **confuse** [kənˈfjuːz] v 使困惑，使混乱

Don't confuse the books with these notebooks.
别把书和这些笔记本搞混了。
bemuse 使困惑 confuse the issue 混淆该问题
confuse... with... 把……与……搞混

语法重点
句中的 with 也可以替换为 and。

0206 **connect** [kəˈnekt] v 连接，接通，联系

It can be extremely difficult to connect coffee with salt.
很难把咖啡和盐关联起来。
combine 联合 connect up 连接，接上

0207 **connection** [kəˈnekʃn] n 连接，联系，关系

The delicious snacks are in connection with the clean kitchen.
这些好吃的零食跟这个干净整洁的厨房有关系。
link 联系 disconnection 切断 be in connection with... 与……有关系

0208 conscious [ˈkɑːnʃəs] **a** 有知觉的

He is conscious that who ate up those bananas.
他知道是谁吃了那些香蕉。
- aware 意识到的　- unconscious 无意识的
- sb. be conscious that... 某人知道……

0209 considerable [kənˈsɪdərəbl] **a** 值得考虑的

I find it very hard to imagine the small cake waste a considerable amount of time to make.
很难想象，制作这个小蛋糕竟然要花费相当多的时间。
- important 重要的　- a considerable amount of 相当多的
- I find it very hard to imagine... 很难想象……

> 语法重点
> time 是不可数名词。
> ↪ amount (P. 123)

0210 consideration [kənˌsɪdəˈreɪʃn] **n** 考虑，体贴

In consideration of his health, we were prepared to cook chicken soup.
考虑到他的健康，我们准备煮鸡汤。
- under consideration 考虑中　- in consideration of... 考虑到……

0211 constant [ˈkɑːnstənt] **a** 不变的，经常的

It was constant indulgence in wine that brought about her ruin.
长期酗酒导致了她的堕落。
- permanent 不变的　- inconstant 易变的　- constant temperature 恒温

0212 continent [ˈkɑːntɪnənt] **n** 大陆，洲

It is beyond doubt that they had little water to drink when staying in the continent of Africa.
毫无疑问，他们在非洲大陆时，几乎没有水喝。
- the continent of Asia 亚洲大陆
- it is beyond doubt that... 毫无疑问……

> ↪ doubt (P. 155)

0213 contract [ˈkɑːntrækt] **n** 契约 [kənˈtrækt] **v** 订约，收缩

I was hesitant about signing the contract during the dinner.
晚餐席间，我对是否签订这个合约犹豫不决。
- agreement 协议　- be hesitant about... 对……犹豫不决

0214 couch [kaʊtʃ] **n** 沙发

Worn out, he lied on the couch after finishing the dinner.
疲劳至极，他吃完饭后就躺在沙发上了。

> 语法重点
> 形容词也可单独在句中表示某种原因。

0215 countable [ˈkaʊntəbl] **a** 可数的

Don't duck out of counting the grapes; they are countable.
别逃避不去数葡萄，它们可以数得出来。
- computable 可计算的　- uncountable 不可数的

> 语法重点
> duck out of（逃避）后面要接名词、代词、动名词。

0216 **coward** ['kaʊərd] n 懦夫，胆小鬼 a 胆小的
The coward is in fear of eating the fish.
那个胆小鬼不敢吃鱼。
- weakling 懦弱的，怯懦者　- coward timid 胆小软弱
- be in fear of... 害怕……

0217 **cradle** ['kreɪdl] n 摇篮，发祥地
It is amusing that the baby is asleep in the cradle after feeding.
真有趣，婴儿吃奶后就在摇篮里睡着了。
- bassinet 摇篮　- in the cradle 在婴儿时期

> 语法重点
> be asleep 表达"正在熟睡中"这个状态。

0218 **crash** [kræʃ] v 碰撞，坠落
Every guest in the store was devastated by the news of the crash.
失事的消息使店里的每一位客人都感到震惊。
- strike 撞击　- crash program 应急计划
- "空难"用 air crash 来表达。

0219 **crawl** [krɔːl] v 爬行，卑躬屈膝
The boy crawled on his hands and knees to beg for food.
小男孩手脚并用爬着去乞讨食物。
- make one's flesh crawl 起鸡皮疙瘩，毛骨悚然

> 语法重点
> 手和膝盖都是两个，所以句中要用 hand 和 knee 的复数形式。

0220 **creative** [kri'eɪtɪv] a 创造（性）的，创作的
It derives from creative effort to make such a beautiful cake.
做出如此漂亮的蛋糕需要创造性的努力。
- creative thinking 创造性思维　- derive from... 来自……

> beautiful (P. 013)

0221 **creator** [kri'eɪtər] n 创造者，创作者
She was without doubt the creator of the new way of eating.
毫无疑问，她创造了这种新吃法。
- maker 制造者　- sb. be the creator of... 某人是……的创造者
- the Creator 可以表示"上帝"。

0222 **creature** ['kriːtʃər] n 生物，动物，人
After eating the poisonous bread, the creature went into its death throes.
吃了有毒的面包后，这个生命到了临终阶段。

> 语法重点
> throes 表示"疼痛"，一般用复数形式。

0223 **credit** ['kredɪt] n 信用，贷款 v 归功于，记入贷方
This dish does credit to the cook.
这道菜为厨师带来了声誉。
- honor 信用，荣誉　- discredit 无信用　- be to one's credit 使某人值得赞扬

> 语法重点
> dish 可以表示"一盘菜，一道菜"。

0224 creep [kriːp] v 蹑手蹑脚地走

Anorexia may creep up on you if you keep losing weight.
你如果继续减肥的话，就可能患上厌食症。
- crawl 爬行
- creep up 慢慢地爬上
- creep up on... 悄悄降临到……

语法重点
creep 是不规则动词，其过去式、过去分词都是crept。

0225 crew [kruː] n 一组工作人员

The crew said that there was something wrong with the breakfast.
工作人员说早餐有问题。
- staff 职员
- rescue crew 救护队

语法重点
形容词修饰 something, anything 等不定代词时，要放在不定代词之后。

0226 cricket ['krɪkɪt] n 蟋蟀，板球

The cricket player was the only person who had a barbecue yesterday.
这个板球运动员是昨天唯一一去吃烧烤的人。
- cricket game 板球游戏

语法重点
who 在宾语从句中作主语，不能省略。
➡ barbecue (P. 128)

0227 criminal ['krɪmɪnl] n 罪犯，犯人 a 犯罪的，违法的

Someone reported that the criminal was having lunch in a small restaurant.
有人举报说，那个罪犯正在一个小餐馆里吃午餐。
- offender 罪犯
- criminal law 刑法

语法重点
三餐前不加冠词。

0228 crisp / crispy [krɪsp] / ['krɪspi] a 脆的，卷曲的

This is the only way to keep the biscuits crisp.
这是唯一可以让饼干保持松脆的方法。
- fragile 脆的
- crisp air 空气清新

0229 crown [kraʊn] n 皇冠，王权，花冠

The man said that the crown was an attribute of kingship while drinking.
那个人喝酒的时候说，皇冠是王位的象征。
- take the crown 夺冠
- be an attribute of... 是……的象征

语法重点
crown 首字母大写可以表示"王国"。

0230 crunchy ['krʌntʃi] a 易碎的，发吱嘎声的

See to it that you buy some crunchy fresh vegetables suitable for the chafing dish.
务必买一些适合吃火锅的松脆新鲜蔬菜。
- delicate 易碎的
- see to it that... 务必……

语法重点
形容词在句中修饰名词时，需要放在名词后。
➡ suitable (P. 368)

0231 crutch [krʌtʃ] n 丁形拐杖，支柱 v 支撑

With the help of the crutch, the man walks slowly.
这个人拄着拐杖缓慢地行走。
- brace 支撑
- on crutches 拄着拐杖
- with the help of... 在……的帮助下

0232 cultural [ˈkʌltʃərəl] a (有) 文化的，(有) 教养的
The frequent guest in the tavern is a man of high cultural background.
酒馆里的那个常客是受过高等教育的人。
- underbred 没教养的 - cultural legacy 文化遗产
- "常客" 还可以用 regular guest 来表示。

↻ frequent (P. 298)

0233 cupboard [ˈkʌbərd] n 碗柜，橱柜
The candies are hidden in the cupboard.
糖果被藏在橱柜里。
- closet 壁橱 - a skeleton in the cupboard 不为人知的家丑
- be hidden in... 藏在……

〈 语法重点
hidden 是动词 hide（藏）的过去分词。

0234 current [ˈkɜːrənt] a 目前的，通用的
I think it's a good hobby to concern about the current fine food.
我认为关注时下流行的美食是一个好习惯。
- present 现在的 - future 将来的 - current money 通用的货币

〈 语法重点
描述性形容词是指对事物的性质或特征进行描述说明的形容词。

↻ concern (P. 275)

0235 cycle [ˈsaɪkl] n 循环
We must break out of the vicious cycle of starvation.
我们必须打破饥饿的恶性循环。
- circle 圆圈，周期 - break out of... 摆脱……

0236 dairy [ˈderi] n 牛奶店 a 牛奶的，乳制品的
It's necessary to keep down the price of dairy products.
有必要控制乳制品的价格。
- milky 牛奶的 - dairy farm 乳牛场 - it's necessary to... 有必要……

0237 dam [dæm] n 水坝，堤，障碍物 v 筑坝
They went at building the dam with a will.
他们努力着手修筑水坝。
- dam sth. up 抑制（情感等） - do sth. with a will 努力做某事

〈 语法重点
will 在句中作名词，意思是"意志，决心"。

0238 dare [der] v 竟敢，挑战，冒……的风险
Being hungry, none of them dare to climb up the mountain.
他们谁也不敢饿着肚子去爬山。
- risk 冒……的危险 - dare say 敢说 - dare to do sth. 敢做某事

〈 语法重点
dare 的否定式是 dare not，缩写为 daren't。

0239 darling [ˈdɑːrlɪŋ] n 心爱的人
My darling lost his memory after eating the poisonous mushrooms.
吃了那些有毒的蘑菇后，我的爱人就失忆了。
- beloved 爱人，心爱的 - lose one's memory 某人失忆

↻ poisonous (P. 485)

0240 **dash** [dæʃ] n 猛撞，突进，猛击
The robbers dashed into my house and robbed me of all the money.
抢匪们冲进我家，抢走了所有的钱。
🔄 dart 猛冲   🔄 cut a dash 神气，有气派

> 语法重点
> rob sb. of sth.（抢某人的某物）可用于被动语态。

0241 **deafen** ['defn] v 使耳聋，把……震聋
Rumor has it that the explosive sound of the bomb in the station deafened the man's ears.
谣言说，车站里炸弹的爆炸声把一个男人的耳朵震聋了。
🔄 be deafened by 被……震聋   🔄 rumor has it that... 谣言说……

> 语法重点
> that 后的句子是具体介绍 rumor 的内容。
> ⮕ explosive (P. 439)

0242 **dealer** ['diːlər] n 交易商
The dealer dressed up as a beggar to beg.
那个商人装扮成乞丐去乞讨。
🔄 trader 商人   🔄 dress up as... 装扮成……

> 语法重点
> dress up 单独使用还可以表示"打扮，装饰"。

0243 **decade** ['dekeɪd] n 十年，十年间
He has eaten about 4,000 apples in the last decade.
过去十年，他吃了将近四千个苹果。
🔄 golden decade 黄金十年

> 语法重点
> in the last decade 一般与现在完成时连用。

0244 **deck** [dek] n 甲板，层面
Standing on the deck, he is anxious about where to live tomorrow.
站在甲板上，他担心着明天住哪里。
🔄 board 甲板   🔄 clear the decks 准备战斗，准备行动
🔄 be anxious about... 担心……

> ⮕ anxious (P. 395)

0245 **deed** [diːd] n 行为，事迹
His foolish deed of stealing food in the shop will remain a blot on his escutcheon.
他从商店偷东西吃的愚蠢行为将永远成为他名誉上的污点。
🔄 action 行为   🔄 chivalrous deed 义举   🔄 remain a blot on... 是……的污点

0246 **deepen** ['diːpən] v 使……变深，使……强烈
It's evident to me that they should deepen the well if they want more water.
在我看来，如果他们想要更多的水，就得把井挖深。
🔄 intensify 使强化   🔄 it's evident to me that... 在我看来……

> 语法重点
> well 在句中作名词，意思是"水井"。

0247 **define** [dɪ'faɪn] v 下定义
I was asked to define the word "drunk".
我被要求给"醉酒"这个单词下定义。
🔄 regulate 规定   🔄 be asked to do sth. 被要求做某事

> 语法重点
> define sth. (as sth.) 表示"给……下定义"。

0248 definition [ˌdefɪˈnɪʃn] n 定义，阐释
No one can give a more precise definition of the word "full".
没有人能给"吃饱"这个单词下更确切的定义。
- sharpness 清晰度
- fine definition 高清晰度
- give a definition of... 给……下定义

> 语法重点
> precise 的比较级是在其前面加上 more。

0249 delivery [dɪˈlɪvəri] n 递送
Take delivery of the food at the station tomorrow.
明天到车站领取食物。
- on delivery 交货付款
- take delivery of... 领取……
- delivery 还可以表示"分娩"，an easy / difficult delivery 意思是"顺 / 难产"。

0250 democracy [dɪˈmɑːkrəsi] n 民主，民主制，民主国家
He was cynical that people suffered from hunger in a democracy.
他不相信在一个民主国家里，人们会挨饿。
- autocracy 专制统治，独裁
- sb. be cynical that... 某人不相信……

> 语法重点
> cynical 的意思是"愤世嫉俗的，怀疑的"，常与介词 about 连用。

0251 democratic [ˌdeməˈkrætɪk] a 民主的，民主党的
America is a democratic country.
美国是一个民主的国家。

0252 deposit [dɪˈpɑːzɪt] n 存款，定金 v 放置，存储
I can afford to buy many delicious snacks with my deposit.
我能用存款买很多美味的小吃。
- on deposit 在定期存款账户中
- afford to... 负担得起……

> 语法重点
> afford 后面可以接名词、代词，也可以接不定式。

0253 description [dɪˈskrɪpʃn] n 描述，刻画，说明书
I must say that the taste of the dish is beyond description.
我必须说，那道菜的味道无法形容。
- characterization 描写
- I must say that... 我必须说……

> 语法重点
> beyond 作介词，意思是"远于，超出"，beyond description 的意思是"无法形容"。

0254 designer [dɪˈzaɪnər] n 设计者，构思者
The famous designer has a propensity for drinking too much alcohol.
那个著名的设计师有酗酒的倾向。
- fashion designer 时装设计师
- have a propensity for... 有……的倾向

> 语法重点
> alcohol 是物质名词，且为不可数名词。
> propensity (P. 172)

0255 desirable [dɪˈzaɪərəbl] a 值得拥有的，令人向往的
It is desirable that we can eat so many delicious grapes.
我们能吃到这么多美味的葡萄真是太好了。
- satisfying 令人满意的
- it is desirable that... ……真是太好了

definition ~ dim

0256 **destroy** [dɪˈstrɔɪ] **v** 摧毁，破坏，消灭
It is said that the bacteria always takes our food as its food and destroys the surface of the teeth.
据说，细菌会从我们的食物中摄取它们自己的食物，并且破坏牙齿表面。
● damage 毁坏　● construct 建造　● totally destroy 完全摧毁

> **语法重点**
> take A as B 表达的含义为"把 A 视为 B"，和 consider... as 所表达的意思大致相同，但 take... as 含有"拿，带走"之意。

0257 **detail** [ˈdiːteɪl] **n** 细节，琐事，枝节
He depicted how to make pasta to me in great detail.
他向我详细讲解如何做意大利面。
● specific 细节　● do sth. in great detail 详细做某事

> **语法重点**
> in detail 常表示"详细地"，中间加上 great 加强语气。
> ● depict (P. 701)

0258 **determine** [dɪˈtɜːrmɪn] **v** 决定，确定，决心
To begin with, I determine to have a big meal.
首先，我决定大吃一顿。
● decide 决定　● determine on / upon sth. 决定做某事
● to begin with, ... 首先，……

> **语法重点**
> determine 也常与介词 on 或 upon 连用，意思是"对……下定决心"。

0259 **devil** [ˈdevl] **n** 魔鬼，淘气鬼，坏人
I found it flattering to have a dinner with the lovely devil.
和这个可爱的淘气鬼一起吃饭，我觉得很荣幸。
● demon 魔鬼　● angel 天使
● the demon drink 含酒精的饮料

> ● lovely (P. 187)

0260 **dialogue** [ˈdaɪəlɒɡ] **n** 对话，对白，磋商
The audience were eating when the actors carried on a dialogue in the middle of the stage.
演员们在舞台中央说对白时，观众们在吃东西。
● conversation 会话　● carry on... 进行……

> **语法重点**
> carry on 后面也可以接动名词，表示"持续做某事"。

0261 **diet** [ˈdaɪət] **n** 饮食
His sister is on a diet now.
他的姐姐现在正在节食。
● dieting 节食　● balanced diet 均衡饮食　● ... be on a diet ……在节食

0262 **diligent** [ˈdɪlɪdʒənt] **a** 勤奋的，用功的
For the future, I will be more diligent in cooking.
今后，我煮饭会更加勤奋。
● industrious 勤勉的　● lazy 懒惰的　● for the future, ... 今后，……

> **语法重点**
> diligent 也是多音节形容词，其比较级是在前面加上 more。

0263 **dim** [dɪm] **a** 微暗的，模糊的
Thanks to the dim light, I saw a man taller than me eating.
多亏了那昏暗的光线，我看见一个比我高的人在吃东西。
● vague 模糊　● bright 明亮的　● thanks to... 多亏了……

> **语法重点**
> 单音节形容词的比较级是直接在词尾加 er。

0264 dime [daɪm] n 一角硬币，数目极小的钱
Don't squander your dime in buying these toys.
不要把你的钱浪费在这些玩具上。
🔗 a dime a dozen 几乎一文不值的　🔗 squander... in... 把……浪费在……上

语法重点
squander... in 后面要接名词、代词和动名词。

0265 dine [daɪn] v 用餐，请……吃饭
He told me he would dine with her tonight.
他告诉我今晚要和她一起吃饭。
🔗 eat 吃，进食　🔗 dine out 在外吃饭　🔗 dine with sb. 与某人一起吃饭

语法重点
宾语从句中的动作在讲话人讲话时尚未发生，所以用一般将来时。

0266 dip [dɪp] v 浸泡，下沉，倾斜
He will talk about the food safety with me after he dips into this report.
浏览完这份报告后，他会和我谈谈食品安全的问题。
🔗 soak 浸　🔗 dip into... 从……中取出钱　🔗 dip into... 稍加研究……

语法重点
after 接时间从句时，动词可以用一般现在时表将来。

0267 dirt [dɜːrt] n 尘土，灰尘
Dirt and junk food are adverse to the growth of your son.
肮脏与垃圾食品对你儿子的成长很不利。
🔗 throw dirt at sb. 说某人坏话　🔗 be adverse to... 对……不利

语法重点
dirt 与 junk food 都是不可数名词，但它们并列作主语，所以 be 动词用 are。

0268 disappoint [ˌdɪsəˈpɔɪnt] v 使失望，使破灭
Don't disappoint your mother by going to school without breakfast.
不要不吃早餐就去上学，那会让你妈妈失望的。
🔗 despair 绝望　🔗 encourage 鼓励

语法重点
disappoint sb. by 后面一般接动名词。
🔗 without (P. 247)

0269 disappointment [ˌdɪsəˈpɔɪntmənt] n 失望，令人失望的人或事
To our disappointment, there is nothing to eat in the fridge.
令我们失望的是，冰箱里没有吃的。
🔗 depression 沮丧　🔗 to one's disappointment... 令某人失望的是……

语法重点
to one's disappointment 是固定搭配用法，不管 one's 是单数还是复数，disappointment 都要用单数。

0270 disco / discotheque [ˈdɪskoʊ] / [ˈdɪskətek]
n 迪斯科舞厅，迪斯科舞曲
You should dedicate yourself to singing instead of going to the disco.
你应该好好研究如何唱歌，而不是去舞厅跳舞。

语法重点
dedicate oneself to（致力于）中的 to 是介词，后面接名词、代词或者动名词。

0271 discount [ˈdɪskaʊnt] / [ˈdɪskaʊnt] v / n 打折，折扣
I will be only too glad to dine in your restaurant if you can offer a discount of twenty percents.
如果你打八折，我会非常乐意在你的餐厅里用餐。
🔗 deduct 减去，扣除　🔗 premium 额外费用

语法重点
短语 only too 表示"极，非常"，通常在句中作副词来修饰形容词，相当于 very，但比 very 语气更加强烈。

dime ~ dodge

0272 discovery [dɪˈskʌvəri] **n** 发现，发觉，被发现的物

His discovery is bound to be useful for making mooncakes.
他的新发现对于制作月饼肯定有帮助。
- find 发现
- make a discovery 发现

> 语法重点
> be bound to（必定）后面要接动词原形。

0273 disease [dɪˈziːz] **n** 疾病，病患，弊端

You will run the risk of disease if you eat the dirty food.
如果你吃了不干净的食物，就可能会患病。
- illness 疾病
- health 健康
- run the risk of... 有……的风险

> dirty (P. 030)

0274 disk [dɪsk] **n** 圆盘，唱片，磁片

Hand the disk to me and I will make you some tea.
把磁片递给我，我泡些茶给你喝。
- 注意，make tea 是泡茶，而 make water 是小便。

0275 dislike [dɪsˈlaɪk] **v** / **n** 不喜欢，厌恶，反感

I dislike to dine with him.
我不喜欢跟他一起吃饭。
- hate 厌恶
- likes and dislikes 好恶
- dislike to do sth. 不喜欢做某事

> 语法重点
> talk 为动词"说话"之意，其后加介词 to 构成 talk to 的结构，表示一方对另一方谈话。

0276 ditch [dɪtʃ] **n** 水道 **v** 丢弃，坠入沟中

He calls on the soldiers to have dinner in the ditch in case of the enemy's attack.
他号召战士们在战壕里吃饭，以防敌人进攻。
- trench 沟渠，战壕
- the last ditch 最后一道防线
- call on sb. to do sth. 号召某人做某事
- call on 单独使用，有"拜访"的意思。

0277 dive [daɪv] **v** / **n** 潜水，跳水，俯冲

Dive into the water to catch fishes, if so, he wouldn't suffer from hunger.
跳入河中捕一些鱼，这样的话，他就不用挨饿了。
- go diving 去潜水
- if so, ... 如果这样的话，……

> suffer (P. 368)

0278 dock [dɑːk] **n** 码头，船坞

The foods on the dock are in accordance with the ones that he demands.
码头上的那些食物和他想要的一致。
- wharf 码头
- put sb. in the dock 指控某人
- be in accordance with... 和……一致

> accordance (P. 667)

0279 dodge [dɑːdʒ] **n** 躲避，诡计 **v** 避开，躲避

He made a sudden dodge aside before the waiter splashed the soup over him.
在服务生把汤洒在他身上之前，他迅速闪到了一旁。
- avoid 躲避
- face 面对
- dodge an issue 躲避问题

> 语法重点
> 句中的介词 over 也可以替换为 on。

285

0280 **domestic** [dəˈmestɪk] a 内部的，家庭的，驯养的
The statics show that the demand for this drink in domestic supermarkets is as great as that of the overseas.
资料显示，国内的超市对这种饮料的需求和海外的需求同样旺盛。
- internal 国内的
- overseas 海外的
- domestic market 国内市场

> 语法重点
> 形容词的同级比较表达的含义为"和……一样，和……相同"，表示二者的程度相同。
> ⇨ demand (P. 423)

0281 **dose** [doʊs] n 一剂药，一服
It is rumored only one dose of this drink can alleviate your thirst.
传言说，服用小剂量的这种饮料就能缓解你的口渴。

0282 **doubtful** [ˈdaʊtfl] a 怀疑的，不确定的
It is doubtful whether he can drink the wine off at a time.
他能否一次喝完酒还值得怀疑。
- doubtful about... 对……怀疑
- it is doubtful that... ……还值得怀疑

> 语法重点
> at a time 意思同 once（一次），但用法不同，once 表示"一次"时一般不用在句末。

0283 **drain** [dreɪn] v 使流出，喝光，耗尽
Please stand by until we drain the glass dry.
站在一边等我们把这杯喝完。
- exhaust 耗尽
- drain away 逐渐消失或消退
- stand by... 站在……旁边

> 语法重点
> stand by 后面接人时，表示"支持某人"。

0284 **dramatic** [drəˈmætɪk] a 戏剧性的，引人注目的
She drank the milk in a dramatic gesture.
她动作夸张地喝着牛奶。
- dramatic irony 戏剧性讽刺

> 语法重点
> drank 是动词 drink 的过去式。
> ⇨ gesture (P. 300)

0285 **drip** [drɪp] v 滴下，漏出
The rain dripped into the bowl, but he didn't care about it at all.
雨水滴到了碗里，但他一点儿也不在意。
- drip down 滴下
- care about... 在意……

> 语法重点
> at all 放在否定句中，加强语气。

0286 **drown** [draʊn] v 溺水，淹死，淹没
He put down the wine glass and drowned himself in the past.
他放下酒杯，沉浸于回忆中。
- drown one's sorrows in drink 借酒浇愁
- drown oneself in... 沉浸在……

0287 **drowsy** [ˈdraʊzi] a 昏昏欲睡的，使人发困的
It's queer that he feels drowsy after lunch every day.
很奇怪，他每天午餐后都想睡觉。
- sleepy 昏睡的
- awake 醒着的
- drowsy eyes 睡眼朦胧

0288 drunk [drʌŋk] a 喝醉酒的，陶醉的 n 醉鬼

Evidently she got drunk and walked much slower than usual.
很显然她喝醉了，走路比平时要慢得多。
- tipsy 喝醉的
- drunk as a lord 酩酊大醉

> **语法重点**
> much 是副词，修饰比较级，意思是"更，更加"，起强调作用。

0289 due [duː] a 由于，应有的，应付的，预定的

At the banquet the guests took their seats in due order.
在宴会上，客人们依次就座。
- in due course 在适当时机
- take one's seat in due order 依次就座

0290 dump [dʌmp] v 抛弃，倾销 n 垃圾场

They throw the leftovers to the dump and it sends out an offensive odor.
他们把剩饭倒在垃圾场里，那里散发出难闻的气味。

> ⊃ offensive (P. 478)

0291 dust [dʌst] n 灰尘，尘土，粉尘 v 去掉……上的灰尘

It will be better if you can dust this bag of ham for me.
如果你能帮我掸去这火腿包上的灰尘就更好了。
- powder 尘土
- raise a dust 引起骚乱
- it will be better if... 如果……会更好

> **语法重点**
> ham 表示"火腿"时可数，当"火腿肉"讲时则不可数。

0292 eager ['iːgər] a 渴望的

I'm eager to know whether you have been there.
我很想知道你是否去过那里。
- anxious 渴望的
- be eager to... 急切……

0293 earnings ['ɜːrnɪŋz] n 收入，利润，报酬

I hear wine gobbles up half of his earnings.
我听说他一半的收入都用在喝酒上了。
- profit 利润
- loss 亏损
- business earnings 营业收益

> **语法重点**
> earning 是 earn 的现在分词形式，注意与 earnings 的区别。

0294 echo ['ekoʊ] n 回音，重复，共鸣

I drank a bottle of milk, shouted and listened for the echo.
我喝杯牛奶，大声喊着，然后聆听着回声。

> **语法重点**
> listen for 后面要接抽象事物，如 news, sound 等，强调内容。

0295 edit ['edɪt] v 编辑，校订

He keeps editing a book of his own poetry while drinking tea in his spare time.
空闲时间，他一直在喝茶、编诗集。
- revise 校订
- edit sth. out 在编辑过程中删除

> **语法重点**
> edit 常与介词 out 连用，意思是"删除"。

0296 edition [ɪ'dɪʃn] n 版本，版次

The edition of the cookery book is confined to 4,000 copies.
这一版烹饪书限量出售四千册。
- version 版本
- first edition 初版

> **语法重点**
> be confined to（限制）中的 to 是介词。
>
> ⊃ confine (P. 413)

0297 **editor** [ˈedɪtər] **n** 编辑，编者
The chief editor was unwilling to eat the steak.
主编不愿意吃牛排。
🔘 redaction 编辑 🔘 be unwilling to do sth. 不情愿做某事

> **语法重点**
> 与 be unwilling to do sth. 相反的短语是 be willing to do sth.（愿意做某事）。

0298 **educate** [ˈedʒukeɪt] **v** 教育，培养，训练
It takes patience to educate a child in using fork and knife.
教孩子使用刀叉需要耐心。
🔘 instruct 指导，教授 🔘 it takes patience to... ……需要耐心

> **语法重点**
> "在……上教某人"要用介词 in。

0299 **educational** [ˌedʒuˈkeɪʃənl] **a** 教育的，有教育意义的
Starvation and thirst may both be barriers to educational progress.
饥饿和口渴都会妨碍学业的进展。
🔘 instructional 教育的 🔘 be barrier to... 妨碍……

> **语法重点**
> be barrier to 中的 to 是介词，后面一般要接名词或者代词。

0300 **efficient** [ɪˈfɪʃnt] **a** 有效率的，能胜任的
He may as well give more food and water to those efficient workers.
他最好多发点食物和水给那些能干的工人。
🔘 competent 能胜任的 🔘 inefficient 无效率的
🔘 efficient operation 有效操作

0301 **elbow** [ˈelboʊ] **n** 手肘，扶手，急弯
I will eat more food if you are at my elbow.
如果你在我身边，我会吃得更多。
🔘 rub elbows with 与……交往 🔘 ... be at one's elbow ……非常近

> **语法重点**
> at one's elbow 是固定搭配，elbow 要用单数。

0302 **elderly** [ˈeldərli] **a** 年长的，年老的
It is curious that her food is even simpler than that of the elderly woman living next to her.
奇怪的是，她的食物甚至比隔壁老年妇女的食物还要简单。
🔘 aged 年老的 🔘 young 年轻的 🔘 the elderly 老年人

> curious (P. 148)

0303 **election** [ɪˈlekʃn] **n** 选举，推选，当选
He was too nervous to eat before the election.
选举前，他紧张得吃不下饭。
🔘 vote 选举 🔘 general election 大选
🔘 "赢得选举"可以用 win the election。

0304 **electric / electrical** [ɪˈlektrɪk] / [ɪˈlektrɪkl]
a 电的，带电的
The electric shortage had a great effect on our diet.
电力短缺对我们的饮食有很大的影响。
🔘 electrical 有关电的 🔘 have a great effect on... 对……有很大影响

> **语法重点**
> effect 之前加形容词 great 加强了语气。

0305 electricity [ɪˌlek'trɪsəti] n 电力，电学

The electricity supply in the dining room was cut off and we had dinner in the dark.
餐厅停电了，我们摸黑吃饭。
- magnetic electricity 磁电
- cut off... 切断……

0306 electronic [ɪˌlek'trɑːnɪk] a 电子的，电子学的

The new kind of machine is operated by an electronic pulse.
这款新型的机器是靠电子脉冲来操作的。
- electronic music 电子音乐
- be operated by... 由……操作
- electronic 是指跟电子（学）有关的，electric 是指任何电动的或发电的装置，被修饰的物体本身可带电。

> operate (P. 197)

0307 emergency [i'mɜːrdʒənsi] n 紧急事件

Emergency food supplies were brought in case of the storm.
为了预防暴雨，运来了应急食物。
- emergency ward 急诊室
- in case of... 假设……，万一……

> 语法重点
> in case of 表示预防某种不良情况的发生；而 in the case of 则表示"至于，就……来说"之意，一般用来引出某个议题。

0308 emperor ['empərər] n 皇帝，君主

The emperor attempted to eat noodles with a fork, but failed.
那个皇帝试图用叉子吃面条，结果失败了。
- sovereignty 君主
- empress 女皇
- attempt to do sth. 试图做某事

> 语法重点
> attempt to do sth. 侧重于指某一次具体地试图做某件事，而 attempt doing 的意思则表示一种长期的行为。

0309 emphasize ['emfəsaɪz] v 强调，着重

The governor emphasized that starving people were even more than before.
州长强调，挨饿的人甚至比以前还多。
- stress 强调
- emphasize on 强调

> 语法重点
> 副词 even 表示"更加"，可以修饰形容词的比较级。

0310 employ [ɪm'plɔɪ] v 雇用

After being employed as an editor, he is determined to commit himself to cooking.
被聘为编辑之后，他决心投身于烹饪这一行。
- hire 雇用
- dismiss 解雇
- be determined to do... 决定做……

0311 employment [ɪm'plɔɪmənt] n 雇用

Neither of us is currently in paid employment, so we have no money to get married.
我们俩目前都没有工作，所以没有钱结婚。

> 语法重点
> neither 表示"两者都不"，后面的 be 动词用单数。
> marry (P. 062)

0312 **employee** [ɪmˈplɔɪːˈ] **n** 员工
The employee gestured to the waiter to bring some more coffee.
那个员工打手势示意服务生再拿些咖啡。
🔹 gesture to sb. to do sth. 打手势示意某人做某事

语法重点
词尾 -ee，表名词，意思是"被动或主动的人"。

0313 **employer** [ɪmˈplɔɪər] **n** 雇主，老板
The man cherished a deep resentment towards his employer because of starvation.
那个人因为挨饿而对他的雇主怀恨在心。
🔹 boss 老板　🔹 cherish a deep resentment towards... 对……怀恨在心

⊃ cherish (P. 407)

0314 **empty** [ˈempti] **a** 空的，空洞的，空虚的
At first sight the fridge appeared to be empty, but there were many foods in fact.
乍看之下，冰箱是空的，其实里面有很多吃的。
🔹 vacant 空的　🔹 full 满的　🔹 on an empty stomach 空腹

语法重点
at first sight（乍看之下）可以放在句首，也可以放在句末。

0315 **enable** [ɪˈneɪbl] **v** 使能够，使可能
Clearly, his sharp teeth enabled him to eat meat.
很明显，他那锋利的牙齿确保他能够吃肉。
🔹 disable 丧失能力　🔹 enable sb. to do... 使某人能做……
🔹 注意，形容牙齿锋利用的是形容词 sharp。

0316 **energetic** [ˌenərˈdʒetɪk] **a** 精力旺盛的，充满活力的
It's possible that she doesn't feel energetic enough to go shopping.
很可能她觉得她没有足够的力气逛街。
🔹 active 活跃的　🔹 it's possible that... 很可能……

0317 **engage** [ɪnˈgeɪdʒ] **v** 使从事，雇用，订婚
It is not unusual for the fat woman to engage herself in eating all day.
那个胖女人天天忙着吃东西，这不足为奇。

0318 **engagement** [ɪnˈgeɪdʒmənt] **n** 婚约，雇用
She can't have dinner with him because she has a previous engagement.
她不能和他一起吃饭，因为她有约在先。
🔹 date 约会　🔹 engagement ring 订婚戒指

⊃ previous (P. 342)

0319 **engine** [ˈendʒɪn] **n** 发动机，机车
It might be a good idea to sit on the engine and have lunch.
坐在机车上吃午餐是个好主意。

0320 engineer [ˌendʒɪˈnɪr] n 工程师，机械师

The engineer was arrested for being drunk and disorderly last night.
昨晚，那个工程师因酗酒滋事而被捕。
- machinist 机械师
- software engineer 软件工程师
- be arrested for... 因……而被捕

语法重点
disorderly 表面上看像是副词，其实是形容词，意思是"无法无天的，凌乱的"。

0321 enjoyable [ɪnˈdʒɔɪəbl] a 快乐的

I feel very happy to have an enjoyable supper with my friends.
我很高兴和朋友们吃一顿愉快的晚餐。

0322 entry [ˈentri] n 进入，入口，登记

The entry of the fat man boosts our confidence to finish the big lunch.
那个胖子的加入增强了我们吃完这顿丰盛的午餐的信心。
- entrance 入口
- exit 出口
- entry to / into 准许进入

语法重点
boost ones' confidence 可以单独使用，也可以接动词不定式。
⊃ confidence (P. 412)

0323 environmental [ɪnˌvaɪrənˈmentl]
a 环境的，有关环境的

All the students should be conscious of the importance of the environmental protection.
所有学生都应该认识到环保的重要性。
- be conscious of... 认识到……

0324 envy [ˈenvi] v 羡慕，嫉妒

All of his friends envied him for having a good appetite.
他所有的朋友都羡慕他有个好胃口。
- satisfy 满意
- envy sb. 羡慕某人
- envy sb. for... 为了……而羡慕某人

0325 erase [ɪˈreɪs] v 擦掉，擦除

How can I erase the tomato juice from my coat?
我怎么才能把外套上的番茄汁擦掉呢？
- wipe 擦，消除
- How can I...? 我怎么才能……？

语法重点
erase 常与介词 from 连用，表示"把……从……抹掉"。

0326 escape [ɪˈskeɪp] v / n 逃离，泄露

My brother always sought escape in the bottle from hard realities last year.
去年我哥哥常常借酒消愁来逃避残酷的现实。
- ... seek escape in the bottle 借酒消愁

语法重点
sought 是动词 seek（寻找）的过去式。

0327 evil [ˈiːvl] a 邪恶的，有害的 n 邪恶，罪恶

It goes evil with her and she can't eat anything.
她的情况不妙，不能进食。
- wicked 邪恶的
- virtuous 善良的
- the evil eye 恶毒的目光

语法重点
anything 在句中的意思是"任何东西"。

0328 **excellence** [ˈeksələns] n 杰出，优点，优秀
Her ability of tasting red wine has reached a high degree of excellence.
她品尝红酒的能力已经达到炉火纯青的地步。
- merit 优点   - shortcoming 缺点
- ... reach a high degree of excellence ……达到炉火纯青的地步

0329 **exchange** [ɪksˈtʃeɪndʒ] v 交换，兑换
I should like to exchange my coffee with yours.
我想跟你交换咖啡。
- swap 交换   - exchange words 争吵，争论

语法重点
"与……交换"，常用介词 with。

0330 **exhibition** [ˌeksɪˈbɪʃn] n 展览，展示
After breakfast, he suddenly showed keen interest in exhibition.
早餐后，他突然对展览会表现出浓厚的兴趣。
- exposition 展览会   - show keen interest in... 对……表现出浓厚的兴趣

语法重点
keen 用来修饰 interest，加强语气。
- show (P. 090)

0331 **existence** [ɪɡˈzɪstəns] n 存在，生存
He was unaware of the existence of the milk in the kitchen until today.
直到今天，他才知道冰箱里有牛奶。
- presence 存在   - in existence 现存的   - be unaware of... 不知道……

语法重点
unware 的意思是"不知道"，含有否定的意思，和 until 用在一个句子里，可以翻译为"直到……才知道"。

0332 **exit** [ˈeksɪt] n 出口，退场
All of the guests in the hotel made a rush for the exit when the fire happened.
火灾发生时，旅馆里的所有人都慌忙冲向出口。
- emergency exit 紧急出口   - make a rush for... 慌忙冲向……

0333 **expectation** [ˌekspekˈteɪʃn] n 期待
It is beyond our expectation that the cake is salty.
真没想到，那个蛋糕竟然是咸的。
- against / contrary to (all) expectation(s) 出乎意料，意想不到

语法重点
it is beyond one's expectation 是固定搭配，不管 one's 是什么，expectation 都用单数。

0334 **expense** [ɪkˈspens] n 花费，代价
The expense of the food has gone beyond their budget.
这些食物的花费已经超出了他们的预算。
- cost 费用   - income 收入   - at one's expense 由某人付费

语法重点
go beyond（超出）后一般加名词。
- beyond (P. 131)

0335 **experiment** [ɪkˈsperɪmənt] n 实验，尝试
He handed the breakfast to his assistants before the experiment.
实验前，他把早餐递给助理。
- test 试验   - hand sth. to sb. 把某物递给某人

语法重点
短语 hand in 也可表示"递交"，也能表示下级向上级递交某物，但不可拆分。

0336 explode [ɪk'sploʊd] v 爆炸，爆发，激增

Given that the boiler might explode, we didn't cook dinner.
考虑到锅炉也许会爆炸，我们没有煮饭。

- burst 爆炸，爆发
- explode into 爆发出
- given that... 考虑到……

语法重点 given that 常用在句首，引导一种条件或假设的情况。

0337 export [ɪk'spɔːrt] v / n 出口

The export of this kind of milk powder has tripled over the past four years.
在过去四年里，这种奶粉的出口量增加了三倍。

- output 输出
- import 进口
- export product 出口产品

语法重点 over the past... years 常用于完成时。

0338 expression [ɪk'spreʃn] n 表达，表示

She had an anxious expression on her face when seeing the report.
她看到报告就愁容满面。

语法重点 have a / an... expression on one's face 的省略号处可以填上不同的形容词。

0339 expressive [ɪk'spresɪv] a 表现的，意味深长的

The boy was encouraged by his mother's expressive nod.
妈妈意味深长地点头鼓励了男孩。

- expressed 表达的
- be encouraged by... 被……所鼓励

语法重点 be encouraged by sb. 其后还可加动词不定式的形式时，表示"受到某人的鼓励去做某事"。

0340 extreme [ɪk'striːm] a 极度的，极端的 n 极端

Her points are always vey extreme and she always disputes with others during dinner.
她的观点总是很极端，而且她经常在吃饭时和别人吵架。

- excessive 极度的
- moderate 适度的
- dispute with sb. 和某人吵架
- dispute 语气较为强烈，表示"争论"之意，常用于各方坚持己见而引起的激烈争论，而 discuss 主要强调为解决某个问题进行"讨论"。

0341 fable ['feɪbl] n 寓言，神话，无稽之谈

I could not decide whether the story he told during the dinner was fact or fable.
我无法确定他晚餐时讲的故事究竟是事实还是无稽之谈。

- myth 神话
- fact 事实
- I could not decide... 我无法确定……

whether (P. 113)

0342 factor ['fæktər] n 因素，要素，因数

The factor of water and food is out of their expectation.
食物和水的因素超出了他们的预料。

- element 要素
- crucial factor 关键因素
- out of one's expectation 超出某人的意料

0343 fade [feɪd] v 消逝，褪色，凋谢

When their singing faded away in the distance, we began to drink coffee.
当他们的歌声逐渐消失在远方时，我们开始喝咖啡。

- discolor 褪色
- fade into 渐渐融入
- ... fade away ……逐渐消失

0344 faint [feɪnt] v / n 昏倒 a 微弱的，模糊的
He went off in a faint after eating the bread.
吃过面包后，他就昏过去了。
- dim 模糊的　- faint hope 微弱的希望　- ... go off in a faint ……昏过去了

语法重点
go off 单独使用可以表示"离开，睡去，变质"。

0345 fairly ['feɪrli] ad 公正地，相当地
She has got a fairly good idea of what to eat this evening.
她已经完全知道今天晚上要吃什么了。
- fairly and squarely 光明正大地　- get a fairly good idea of... 完全清楚……

0346 fairy ['feri] n 仙女，小精灵
Before sleep, some imaginative children made up fairy stories.
睡觉前，一些想象力丰富的孩子自己编造童话故事。
- elf 小精灵　- fairy story 童话故事　- make up... 编造……

⊃ imaginative (P. 456)

0347 faith [feɪθ] n 信念，信任
We should never lose faith, even if we are suffering from starvation.
即使挨饿，我们也绝不能丧失信念。
- belief 信仰，信赖　- doubt 怀疑　- in good faith 真诚地，诚意地

0348 fake [feɪk] n 冒牌货，欺骗 a 伪造的，假的
She is a real fake, and you can't count on her on buying car.
她是个真正的骗子，买车这件事你不能指望她。
- artificial 伪造的　- genuine 真的　- count on sb. 依靠某人
- count on 与 depend on 都表示"依靠"，但有细微的区别。count on 主要表示"指望"某人去做某事，而 depend on 则表示"依靠/依赖某人或某物"。

0349 familiar [fə'mɪliər] a 熟悉的，通晓的
Are you familiar with the well-dressed woman?
你熟悉那个衣着考究的女人吗？
- look familiar 面熟，眼熟　- be familiar with... 熟悉……

语法重点
副词和一些过去分词搭配可以构成一个形容词。

0350 fan [fæn] n 狂热者，风扇，扇子
The singer's eating habit gave rise to wild rumor among her fans.
这位歌手的饮食习惯引起了歌迷们的各种流言蜚语。
- enthusiast 狂热者　- fan club 崇拜者俱乐部

语法重点
give rise to（引起）主要指引起某种现象的出现，多指某种不良情况。

0351 fanatic [fə'nætɪk] n 狂热者，极端分子，盲信者
He is a puffer fanatic, but all of his friends tell him to get away from it.
他酷爱吃河豚，但他的朋友们都让他远离。
- get away from... 躲开……

0352 fancy ['fænsi] n 爱好 v 喜欢 a 悦目的，可口的

He fancied that girl and made an appointment with her yesterday.
他很喜欢那个女孩，昨天他们约会了。

- catch / take one's fancy 吸引某人
- make an appointment with sb. 和某人约会

0353 fare [fer] n 票价，车费，路费

The taxi fare rose on grounds of the petrol shortage, so we walked to the bookstore.
由于汽油短缺，出租车的费用上涨了，所以我们步行去书店。

- fee 费用
- taxi fare 出租车费
- on grounds of... 由于……

语法重点
ground 的复数形式可以表示"原因，理由"。
↪ shortage (P. 632)

0354 farther ['fɑːrðər] a 更远的，较远的

He beguiled the child to go farther with chocolates.
他用巧克力哄着孩子走远一些。

- further 更远的
- nearer 较近
- beguile... with... 用……哄……

语法重点
farther 与 further 都是形容词 far 的比较级。

0355 fashion ['fæʃn] n 风尚，样子

This kind of dress goes in and out of fashion quickly.
这种连衣裙很快流行起来，又很快不流行了。

- style 时尚，风格
- out of fashion 过时的

0356 fashionable ['fæʃnəbl] a 时髦的

He confirmed that they ate at a fashionable new restaurant.
他证实了他们在一家新开张的时尚餐厅吃饭。

- popular 流行的
- unfashionable 过时的
- sb. confirm that... 某人证实……

语法重点
confirm 为动词"证实，确定"，其后可加 that 从句来作宾语从句，表示"确定某种情况"，that 一般不省略，如例句中的用法。

0357 fasten ['fæsn] v 系紧，使固定，强加于

Fasten the horse to the tree, and then come to have a cup of tea.
把马拴在树上，然后过来喝杯茶。

- bind 绑
- loosen 松开
- fasten your eyes on... 注视着……

语法重点
fasten... to... 中的 to 也可以替换为介词 on。

0358 fate [feɪt] n 命运，宿命

By a strange quirk of fate we had lunch in the same restaurant.
真巧，我们居然在同一家餐厅吃午餐。

语法重点
by a strange quirk of fate 后面接句子，可以用逗号隔开，也可以直接放句子。

0359 faucet / tap ['fɔːsɪt] / [tæp] n 龙头，旋塞

Don't forget to switch off the faucet after you use it.
用完后别忘了关水龙头。

- switch off 和 turn off 都表示"关掉"，switch off 用法较正式，且主要表示上下按钮或插销的开关，而 turn off 较为口语化，表示关掉旋钮之类的开关或是电器等。

↪ switch (P. 370)

0360 fax [fæks] v 传真 n 传真机，传真件

There is great merit in fixing up the fax, for the boss will treat you to dinner and give you some money.
修好这台传真机大有好处，因为老板会请你吃饭，还会给你一笔钱。
- telefax 传真 - send a fax 发传真

0361 feather ['feðər] n 羽毛，轻的东西

He ruffled my feathers when we drank together in the bar, and my boyfriend gave him a lesson.
在酒吧喝酒时他惹怒了我，我男朋友给了他一个教训。
- birds of a feather 一丘之貉 - ruffle one's feathers 激怒某人

0362 feature ['fi:tʃər] n 特征，特色，容貌

He said that feature film has no charm for him, and then left the cinema.
他说对剧情片不感兴趣，就离开电影院了。
- characteristic 特征，特色 - common feature 共同特征

⊃ charm (P. 270)

0363 file [faɪl] n 档案，卷宗，文件

The principal keeps the announcement that he skips classes to drink on file.
校长把他逃课去喝酒的公告都存档了。
- document 文件 - on file 存档，归档 - keep... on file 把……存档

语法重点
that he skips classes to drink 在句中作 announcement 的同位语。

0364 firework ['faɪərwɜ:rk] n 爆竹

The feast ended up with a wonderful firework.
宴席以一场精彩的烟火表演结束。
- fireworks display 烟火表演 - end up with... 以……结束

语法重点
end up with 后面常接名词或者代词。

0365 fist [fɪst] n 拳头

I noticed that he stopped talking and clenched his fist.
我看到他停止说话并握紧了拳头。

0366 flame [fleɪm] n 火焰，热情，燃烧

It's impossible for them to broil turkey over a charcoal flame.
他们不可能在木炭上烤火鸡。
- blaze 火焰 - add fuel to the flames 火上浇油
- it's impossible for sb. to do sth. 某人不可能做某事

语法重点
for 后面要用人称代词的宾格形式。
⊃ charcoal (P. 684)

0367 flavor ['fleɪvər] n 味道

He said the kind of snack smelled stink, but in fact had delicious flavor.
他说这种小吃虽然很难闻，但是吃起来很有风味。
- savor 风味 - in fact... 事实上……

fax ~ fond

0368 **flea** [fliː] n 跳蚤
I'll put a flea in her ear if she still refuses to have breakfast.
如果她再不吃早餐的话，我就对她不客气了。
🔄 flea market 跳蚤市场　🔄 put a flea in one's ear 对某人不客气

> 语法重点
> put a flea in one's ear 是固定搭配，ear 要用单数。

0369 **flesh** [fleʃ] n 肉，果肉，肉体
Just thinking about eating snakes makes his flesh creep.
一想起吃蛇，他浑身都起鸡皮疙瘩。
🔄 spirit 精神，心灵　🔄 flesh and blood 血肉之躯，人性

> 语法重点
> flesh 是不可数名词。

0370 **float** [fləʊt] v 漂流
Strange thoughts floated through his mind when he ate the roast chicken.
他吃烤鸡时脑海里浮现了一些奇怪的念头。
🔄 float about / around（指传闻）广为流传　🔄 float through... 浮现……

0371 **flock** [flɑːk] n 一群，兽群，人群
A flock of guests in the hotel were scared off by the fire.
饭店里的一群客人被火灾吓跑了。
🔄 crowd 群众　🔄 a flock of... 一群……　🔄 be scared off by... 被……吓跑了

> 语法重点
> a flock of 后面常接可数名词的复数形式。

0372 **fold** [fəʊld] v 折叠，交叉，拥抱
He folded his arms when he felt uncomfortable after eating.
饭后感觉不舒服时，他抱紧了双臂。
🔄 enfold 折叠　🔄 fold one's arms 双臂在胸前合抱
🔄 fold one's arms 某人交叉双臂

0373 **folk** [fəʊk] n 民间，家属，亲戚
Don't grumble at the unsavory dishes of your school; difficulties help to forge you into an able folk.
别再抱怨学校的饭菜难吃了，困难有助于你成才。
🔄 grumble at... 抱怨……

> 语法重点
> 例句中 grumble 是不及物动词，当及物动词讲时，意思是"喃喃地说出"。
> ⓘ difficulty (P. 153)

0374 **follower** [ˈfɑːləʊər] n 跟随者，信徒，执行者
He made an attempt to throw the follower off, so he went to a bar and had a drink.
他试图甩掉跟踪他的人，于是进了一家酒吧喝酒。
🔄 the first follower 第一个追随者　🔄 make an attempt to do sth. 试图做某事

> 语法重点
> attempt 在句中作名词，attempt 还可以当动词，后面接 to do 表示"试图做"。

0375 **fond** [fɑːnd] a 喜欢的，深情的
My mother is fond of having a hand in everything, even what I eat and drink.
我妈妈喜欢什么事都插手，甚至连我的吃喝都要管。

> 语法重点
> have a hand in（插手管）后面通常接名词或者代词。

0376 forehead / brow ['fɔ:rhed] / [braʊ] n 前额，前部
My mother gave me a kiss on the forehead and asked me to have breakfast.
妈妈吻了我的前额，并要我去吃早餐。
同 forehead lines 抬头纹　同 give sb. a kiss 亲吻某人

语法重点
亲吻某个部位要用介词on。

0377 forever [fər'evər] ad 永远，老是
I'll bear the delicious food in mind forever.
我将永远记住那些好吃的食物。
同 eternally 永恒地　反 momentarily 暂时地　同 bear... in mind 记住……

⇒ bear (P. 012)

0378 forth [fɔ:rθ] ad 向前方，向外，露出
They set forth immediately after breakfast yesterday morning.
昨天早上吃过早餐后，他们就立即出发了。
同 forward 向前地　同 and so forth 等等　同 ... set forth ……出发

0379 fortune ['fɔ:rtʃən] n 幸运，财富，运气
I have had the good fortune to have dinner with him.
我有幸与他一起吃饭。
同 luck 运气　反 misfortune 不幸　同 seek one's fortune 寻找出路

语法重点
have the good fortune 后面一般要接动词不定式。

0380 found [faʊnd] v 建立，创立，创办
A bar was founded by the people here to memorize the old man.
人们在这里建了一家酒吧来纪念那位老人。
同 establish 建立，创办　同 founding father 创始人　同 be founded by... 被……所建造

语法重点
句子中，当动作的发出者不太重要时，一般用被动语态来表达。
⇒ memorize (P. 323)

0381 fountain ['faʊntn] n 喷泉，源泉，泉水
The villagers there live on the fountain from the mountain.
那里的村民都以山上的泉水为生。
同 spring 泉水　同 fountain pen 钢笔　同 live on... 以……为生

0382 freeze [fri:z] v 冷冻，冻结，僵硬，凝固
Big hotels always want to freeze out the smaller ones in this city.
在这个城市里，大饭店总是想排挤小饭店。
同 freeze one's blood 使充满害怕、恐怖的感觉　同 freeze out... 排挤

语法重点
in this city 也可以置于句首。

0383 frequent ['fri:kwənt] a 频繁的，经常的
The man is a frequent guest to the bar.
那个人是这家酒吧的常客。

语法重点
例句还可以这样表达：The man frequents the bar. 此时 frequent 作动词，意思是"常去"。

forehead / brow ~ gamble

0384 **friendship** ['frendʃɪp] n 友谊，友好
We held out the hand of friendship to him when he had nothing to eat.
当他没有东西吃时，我们向他伸出了友谊之手。
- fellowship 友谊   - hold out... 伸出……

0385 **frustrate** ['frʌstreɪt] v 挫败，使沮丧，使灰心
Doesn't it frustrate you that none of the guests likes the dishes you cook?
没有一个客人喜欢你做的菜，你不觉得沮丧吗？
- Doesn't it frustrate you that...? ……你不觉得沮丧吗？

0386 **fry** [fraɪ] v 煎炒，油煎，油炸
I'm considering some more pepper when frying the chicken.
我正考虑在炸鸡时多放一些胡椒粉。
- have bigger fish to fry 有更重要的事情要做   - I'm considering... 我正考虑……

> 语法重点
> more 是形容词 many / much 的比较级，用来修饰名词时，其前还可以加 some 或 much 等来加强语气，some more 表示"更多一些"，而 much more 的语气最为强烈，表示"多得多"。

0387 **fund** [fʌnd] n 资金，储备
The store is in want of more liquid fund to attract guests.
这家店需要更多的流动资金来吸引顾客。
- in funds 有钱花   - in want of... 需要……

> 语法重点
> want 作名词时意思是"缺乏，需要"，表示"需要某事物"时，要用 in want of，一般用于 be 动词之后。

0388 **fur** [fɜːr] n 毛皮，软毛，皮衣
She was rushed into going home, so she forgot her fur coat in the bar.
她被催着赶快回家，所以把皮大衣忘在了酒吧。

0389 **furniture** ['fɜːrnɪtʃər] n 家具
It took a lot of energy to move the furniture, so I had a big dinner after that.
搬家具费了我很大劲，所以搬完之后我大吃了一顿。
- furnishings 家具

> 语法重点
> furniture 是集合名词，一件家具通常用 a piece of furniture 来表示。

0390 **gallon** ['gælən] n 加仑
Two gallon of water is far from enough for these thirsty villagers.
对于这些口渴的村民来说，两加仑水远远不够。
- gal 加仑   - be far from enough for... 对于……来说远远不够

> 语法重点
> gallon 作为量词，当前面的数字大于一时，gallon 仍用单数。

0391 **gamble** ['gæmbl] v / n 赌博，冒险
Don't gamble with your life.
别拿你的生命冒险。
- risk 冒险   - take a gamble (on sth.) 赌博，冒险而为
- gamble with... 用……冒险

> 语法重点
> gamble 后面也可以接介词 in，表示"投资"。
> - life (P. 058)

299

0392 **gang** [gæŋ] n 一帮歹徒
It is unthinkable that a gang of criminals are drinking coffee in the café.
难以置信，一群罪犯正在这家咖啡馆里喝咖啡。
同 group 群　　a gang of thugs 一伙暴徒

语法重点
a gang of 后面接可数名词复数。
⊕ criminal (P. 279)

0393 **gap** [gæp] n 间隙
I think the most critical issue is to narrow the gap between the two dishes.
我认为最关键的问题是缩小这两道菜之间的差距。
同 generation gap 代沟　　the most critical issue is... 最关键的问题是……

语法重点
形容词的最高级前需要加上定冠词 the。

0394 **garlic** ['gɑːrlɪk] n 大蒜
My husband liked to eat pork which was seasoned with garlic.
我丈夫喜欢吃用大蒜调味的猪肉。

语法重点
season 在句中作动词，意思是"调味……"。

0395 **gas / gasoline** [gæs] / ['gæsəliːn] n 汽油，煤气，气体
The bandits set fire to the bar with gas and most of the guests were wounded.
歹徒们用汽油焚烧这家酒吧，大多数客人都受伤了。
同 step on the gas 踩油门，加速　　set fire to sth. 放火烧某物

0396 **gesture** ['dʒestʃər] n 姿势
She thrust the book away from her with an angry gesture.
她生气地把书猛地推开。
同 sign 手势　　thrust away... 推开……

语法重点
thrust 的意思是"猛推"，是不规则动词，其过去式、过去分词都是 thrust。

0397 **glance** [glæns] v 看一下
My brother cast a sneering glance at the card I made.
我弟弟轻蔑地瞥了一眼我做的卡片。
同 glimpse 一瞥　　反 stare 凝视　　at first glance 乍看之下，初看

0398 **global** ['gloʊbl] a 全球的，总的
I am a skeptic about the global water shortage.
我是全球水资源短缺的怀疑论者。
同 worldwide 世界性的　　global travel 环球旅行

0399 **glory** ['glɔːri] n 光荣，荣誉，壮丽
To a baker, the glory lies not in money but in the customers' compliment.
对于一个糕点师来说，荣耀不在于金钱，而在于顾客们的赞美。
同 honor 荣誉　　反 disgrace 耻辱　　eternal glory 永恒的荣耀

语法重点
not... but... 表示一种前否定后肯定的概念，not 和 but 之后既可以加名词、代词，也可以加介词短语等。

0400 glow [gloʊ] v / n 发光，发热

I lingered on the hill, drank a bottle of milk and enjoyed the beautiful glow of sunset.
我流连于山上，喝着牛奶并欣赏着美丽的落日余晖。
- shine 照耀 - linger on... 逗留在……

> **语法重点**
> linger 也可以与介词 away 连用，意思是"消磨"。

0401 gossip ['gɑːsɪp] n 八卦，闲话 v 散播流言蜚语

I looked down on those people who always talked about gossip at table.
我看不起那些喜欢在餐桌上传播流言蜚语的人。
- scandal 流言蜚语 - the latest gossip 最新八卦
- look down on... 看不起……

0402 governor ['gʌvərnər] n 州长，总督，管理者

The governor always yearns for the snacks in his hometown.
那个州长总是怀念家乡的小吃。
- yearn for... 对……充满渴望

> hometown (P. 317)

0403 gown [gaʊn] n 女礼服，长袍

I had no way to know the girl who was wearing a black gown.
我无法认识那个穿着黑色礼服的女孩。
- robe 礼服，长袍

> **语法重点**
> have no way to（没办法）后面要接动词原形。

0404 grab [græb] v 抓取

He wanted to grab at her bread, but she pushed him away.
他想抢她的面包，但被她推开了。
- clutch 抓住 - loosen 松开 - grab at... 抢……

> **语法重点**
> grab 还可以作及物动词，后面直接放宾语。

0405 gradual ['grædʒuəl] a 逐渐的，逐步的，平缓的

I have taken notice of the gradual change of the color of the meat.
我注意到了肉的颜色在逐渐变化。
- piecemeal 逐渐的 - rapid 迅速的 - take notice of... 注意到……
- take notice of 主要指"注意到某种情况的发生"，而 pay attention to 则表示"专心"，将注意力集中在某物或某件事情上。

0406 graduate ['grædʒuət] n 毕业生 v 毕业

The graduate is ruining his life by drinking every day.
那个毕业生每天都喝酒，这是在毁掉他自己的生活。
- graduate from... 从……毕业
- ruin 指通过一个过程而将某物一步步地彻底毁掉，而 destroy 主要强调通过具有杀伤性的力量将某物毁掉。

0407 **grain** [greɪn] n 谷粒，粮食，颗粒
Our family is almost self-sufficient in grain crops.
我们家的粮食现在已经差不多能自给了。
- cereal 谷物　- against the grain 与自己的性格、意愿格格不入

0408 **gram** [græm] n 克
I hear this kind of snacks is sold by gram.
我听说这种零食是以克为单位出售的。
- be sold by gram... ……按克出售

语法重点
by gram 是固定用法，gram 用单数形式。

0409 **grasp** [græsp] v 抓牢
He grasped the painting and kept staring at it.
他抓起图画，一直盯着它看。
- grasp one's meaning 领会某人的意思　- stare at... 盯着……看

语法重点
stare at 指凝视前方的人或物，含有一种惊奇或茫然之意。

0410 **grasshopper** ['græsha:pər] n 螳螂，蝗虫
The little grasshopper on the corn gave me quite a scare.
玉米上的小蝗虫真的让我吓了一跳。
- locust 蚱蜢，蝗虫　- give sb. a scare 吓了某人一跳

语法重点
scare 与 terrify 都可以表示"使害怕，使恐惧"，之后接名词或者人称代词。terrify 所表示的语气程度更强，表示非常恐惧，而 scare 的语气较弱。

0411 **greenhouse** ['gri:nhaʊs] n 温室，暖房
All of these vegetables are said to be bred in a greenhouse.
据说，这些蔬菜都是在温室里培育出来的。
- greenhouse effect 温室效应　- be said to... 据说……

语法重点
bred 是动词 breed（培育）的过去式。

0412 **grin** [grɪn] v 露齿而笑，咧着嘴笑
Seeing that the boy could have dinner himself, the young mother grinned with pleasure.
看到小男孩会自己吃饭，年轻的妈妈满意地笑了。
- grin and bear it 毫无怨言地忍受痛苦、挫折等

语法重点
注意 grin 的过去式要双写 n 再加上 ed。

0413 **grocery** ['groʊsəri] n 杂货店，食品店
It is just a short walk to the grocery.
到杂货店的路并不远。

语法重点
it is just a short walk to 中的 to 是介词，后面要接上表示地点的名词或者代词。

0414 **guardian** ['gɑ:rdiən] n 守护者，监护人
I think the legal guardian has the duty to ensure the kids won't starve.
我认为法定监护人有责任保证孩子不挨饿。
- keeper 保护人　- ward 受监护人　- have the duty to do sth. 有责任做某事
- duty 和 responsibility 都表示"责任"，但在实际表达中有所区别。duty 主要是指道德、伦理或者法律所规定的某种义务或责任，而 responsibility 则指某人主观上的责任或责任心。

↳ starve (P. 365)

grain ~ harbor

0415 guidance ['gaɪdns] **n** 引导，导航
Under the guidance of the boss, all the poisonous milk powder has been taken back.
在老板的指导下，所有的毒奶粉都回收了。
- direction 指导　　- ... be taken back ……被回收

→ powder (P. 341)

0416 gum [gʌm] **n** 口香糖，牙龈，树胶
I was pissed off by him and spitted the gum on his face.
我被他惹烦了，就把口香糖吐在了他的脸上。

语法重点
piss off 还可以表示"立即走开"，表示"惹……烦"时，一般要用被动语态。

0417 gymnasium / gym [dʒɪm'neɪziəm] / [dʒɪm] **n** 体育馆，健身房
The little boy gazed at those athletes who were drinking beers in the gym.
小男孩盯着那些正在体育馆里喝啤酒的运动员们看。
- stadium 体育馆　　- in a gym 在健身房　　- gaze at... 盯着……看

语法重点
gaze at 一般指"凝视远方"，且常含有一种"惊叹、羡慕"之意。

0418 hairdresser ['herdresər] **n** 美发师，美容师
He used to be a hairdresser, but he is very great at baking now.
他曾是一名理发师，但他现在对烘焙很精通。
- barber 理发师　　- be great at... 精于……

0419 hallway ['hɔːlweɪ] **n** 门厅，走廊，过道
The young man walked through the hallway to and fro in order to send lunch to those people in the house.
那个年轻人来来回回从走廊经过，是为了给屋子里的那些人送午餐。

语法重点
to and fro（来来回回）表示一种往返或重复的情况，在句中用作副词，修饰动词。

0420 handful ['hændfʊl] **n** 一把，一小撮，少量
He had good reasons to throw a handful of rice to the ground.
他有很好的理由扔一把米在地上。
- a handful of... 一把……，一小部分……，少量的……

语法重点
have good reason for 中的 for 为介词，后接名词、代词或者动名词。
→ reason (P. 081)

0421 handy ['hændi] **a** 便利的，手边的，现成的
The girl is handy with sewing.
那个女孩是缝纫的高手。
- come in handy 迟早有用　　- be handy with... 擅长……

0422 harbor ['hɑːrbər] **n** 港口，避难所　**v** 庇护
A worker in the harbor who ate a poisonous fish was in danger now.
港湾里的一个工人吃了有毒的鱼，现在很危险。
- harbor dues 入港税　　- ... be in danger ……处于危险中
- harbor 有时也写作 harbour。

303

0423 **harm** [hɑːrm] v / n 伤害，损害
This kind of food does more harm than good to our health.
这种食物对于我们的健康来说，弊大于利。
- hurt 损害　- do more harm than good to... 对……弊大于利

语法重点
比较级和最高级用来形容或修饰一种程度，只有形容词或副词才具有比较级或最高级形式，其他词性没有。

0424 **harmful** [ˈhɑːrmfl] a 有害的
Nobody knows whether this kind of drink is harmful to our health.
没有人知道这种饮料是否对我们的健康有害。
- destructive 有害的　- harmless 无害的

0425 **harvest** [ˈhɑːrvɪst] n / v 收获，收割
The harvest of apples last year was nothing less than that of the year before last year.
去年的苹果收成和前年的一样。
- crop 收获　- nothing less than... 和……一样

语法重点
主语是 harvest，所以 be 动词要是第三人称单数，而因为在讲过去的事情，所以用 was。

0426 **hasty** [ˈheɪsti] a 匆忙的，轻率的，急忙的
You should have thought twice before making your hasty decision to wear the dress.
匆忙决定要穿这件连衣裙之前，你本应该三思的。
- rushed 匆忙的，贸然的　- cautious 谨慎的　- ... think twice ……三思
- think twice 和 think over 都有"仔细考虑"之意，但 think over 主要指"认真考虑，仔细思考"，而 think twice 则表示"重新考虑"之意。

twice (P. 108)

0427 **hatch** [hætʃ] n 孵化，舱口 v 孵出，策划
The eggs can't be eaten if the chicks hatch out.
小鸡孵出来之后，鸡蛋就不能吃了。
- incubate 孵化　- down the hatch 干杯　- ... hatch out ……孵出来

语法重点
hatch out 用主动形式表示被动含义。

0428 **hawk** [hɔːk] n 老鹰，好战分子，贪婪的人
I don't know whether eating a hawk does harm to our health.
我不知道吃鹰肉是否会对我们的健康有害。

0429 **hay** [heɪ] n 干草
He stored some hay in case there would be snow.
他储存了一些干草，以防下雪。
- stover 干草　- hit the hay 上床睡觉　- in case... 以防……

0430 **headline** [ˈhedlaɪn] n 标题，新闻提要，头条新闻
It was not until he saw the headline of the newspaper that he got to know what he had eaten.
直到他看到报纸的头条新闻，他才知道自己吃了什么。
- title 标题　- hit the headlines 成为头条新闻

语法重点
it was not until... that... 是 not until 与强调句型 it was... that 的结合。

harm ~ hesitate

0431 headquarters [ˈhedkwɔːrtərz]
n 总部，司令部，指挥部

The headquarters made airdrops of food to refugees.
指挥部向难民们空投食物。
- command 司令部 - branch 分部

语法重点
headquarters 形式为复数，实际是单数，动词要按单数处理。
➲ refugee (P. 494)

0432 heal [hiːl] **v** 治疗，（使）愈合，使和解

He fell into a drunken stupor and got hurt, but now the wound healed.
他喝得不省人事并且受伤了，但是伤口现在已经好了。
- cure 治愈 - hurt 受伤 - heal up 痊愈，治愈
- ... fall into a drunken stupor ……醉得不省人事

0433 heap [hiːp] **n** 堆积，许多，大量

Put these apples in a heap now.
现在把这些苹果放成一堆。
- pile 堆，大量 - bit 少量

0434 heaven [ˈhevn] **n** 天堂

I feel like more in heaven than just being happy when I drink the red wine.
喝红酒时，与其说我感觉很快乐，倒不如说我如同身在天堂。
- hell 地狱 - seventh heaven 极乐 - more... than... 与其说……倒不如说……

语法重点
more... than... 表达一种语意上的增强，强调的是 more 之后的内容，和 than 之后的内容用来比较，如例句中的用法。

0435 heel [hiːl] **n** 脚后跟，（鞋、袜等的）后跟

Cool your heels and the coffee is nearly ready.
等一下，咖啡就好了。
- Achilles' heel 致命要害，薄弱环节 - cool one's heels 某人等一下

语法重点
cool one's heels 是固定搭配，heel 一定要用复数形式。

0436 hell [hel] **n** 地狱，阴间，苦境

Although dwelling in a shabby place which was just like the hell, I was sure of bread and water tomorrow.
虽然生活在一个破旧如地狱的地方，我依然坚信明天会有面包和水。
- heaven 天堂 - hell for leather 尽快地

语法重点
be sure of（肯定）后可以接名词、代词或动名词。
➲ shabby (P. 631)

0437 helmet [ˈhelmɪt] **n** 头盔，安全帽

The helmet protected him from being hurt in the accident happening.
在意外发生时，他的头盔保护他免受伤害。
- headguard 头盔 - steel helmet 钢盔 - protect sb. from... 保护某人不……

语法重点
accident 与 happen 是主动关系，所以 happen 用的是 ing 形式。

0438 hesitate [ˈhezɪteɪt] **v** 犹豫，不情愿

He never hesitates to eat pears whenever he sees them.
他一看见梨，就毫不犹豫地吃起来。
- hesitate at... 对……犹豫不决 - hesitate to do... 犹豫地做……

0439　hike [haɪk] **n** / **v** 健行，提高，增加
Nobody will accompany me to have a cup of coffee and hike other than him.
除了他之外，没有人会陪我喝咖啡和徒步旅行。
　take a hike 走路，滚开　　nobody... other than... 除了……没有人……

> 语法重点
> other than 表示"除了"，和介词 except, but 的意义和用法基本相同。

0440　hint [hɪnt] **v** 暗示，示意　**n** 暗示，线索
She dropped a hint to him by reaching out her fingers when she was having breakfast.
吃早餐时，她伸出手指来给他暗示。
　implication 暗示　　drop a hint to sb. 暗示某人

> 语法重点
> reach out 表示"伸出，伸展"，如伸出四肢等，其后一般加名词。

0441　historian [hɪˈstɔːrɪən] **n** 历史学家，史学工作者
The historian who committed himself to the study of history liked china best.
那位把全部精力都奉献给历史研究的历史学家最喜欢瓷器。
　commit oneself to... 致力于……

0442　historic [hɪˈstɔːrɪk] **a** 历史上著名的
The beginning of his eating fruits has historic meaning to his health.
他开始吃水果这件事对于他的健康具有历史意义。
　historic moment 历史性时刻　　have historic meaning to... 对……有历史意义

> 语法重点
> 例句的主语是 beginning，所以动词用 has。

0443　historical [hɪˈstɔːrɪkl] **a** 历史的，史学的
The shape of the vase is quite distinct from the historical records.
这种花瓶的外形和历史记载的不相符。

　⊃ vase (P. 381)

0444　hive [haɪv] **n** 蜂巢，蜂箱，蜂群
The dinning room was a hive of activity, and many guests were walking back and forth.
餐厅里一片繁忙的景象，许多客人们来来回回地走着。
　hive off 脱离编制，分出　　be a hive of activity 一片繁忙的景象

0445　hollow [ˈhɑːloʊ] **a** 中空的，空洞的，虚伪的
She seriously stared at the form in front of her with her hollow eyes.
她用那双凹陷的眼睛严肃地盯着面前的表格。
　empty 空的　　hollow cheeks 深陷的双颊

> 语法重点
> 副词用来修饰动词、形容词和其他副词或者是修饰整个句子，在句中常用来表示地点、时间、程度、方式或语气等，如例句中的 seriously。

0446　holy [ˈhoʊli] **a** 神圣的，圣洁的，令人景仰的
She lives a holy life and never eats meat.
她过着圣洁的生活，从不吃肉。
　godly 神圣的　　unholy 不神圣的　　live a... life 过……的生活

0447 **hometown** ['hoʊmtaʊn] n 故乡
I have been away from my hometown for about 20 years, but I can still visualize the taste of the food clearly.
我离开家乡已经将近 20 年，但我还能清晰地想象出那种食物的味道。
- homeland 故乡
- be away from... 离开……

语法重点
副词修饰动词时，如果动词是及物动词，之后有宾语，副词通常放在宾语之后，如例句中的副词 clearly.
↪ visualize (P. 803)

0448 **honesty** ['ɑːnəsti] n 诚实，正直
His teacher spoke in praise of him for his honesty.
他的老师表扬了他的诚实。
- integrity 诚实，正直
- dishonesty 不诚实，不正直
- in all honesty 诚实地，实在地
- speak in praise of... 表扬……

0449 **honor** ['ɑnɚ] n 荣誉，尊敬 v 尊敬，使荣幸
Undoubtedly, if he graduated with honors, his parents would take him to a big restaurant to celebrate it.
毫无疑问，如果他以优异的成绩毕业，他父母肯定会带他去大餐厅庆祝。
- glory 荣誉
- dishonor 耻辱，丢脸
- put on your honor 使立誓
- honor 作荣誉讲时，主要表示一种荣誉称号、奖励或者头衔，而 glory 的意思是"光荣，桂冠，荣誉"，主要表示某人因做出某种成就而获得声誉。

0450 **horn** [hɔːrn] n 角
The children rushed toward the dinning room eagerly after hearing the sound of horn.
听到喇叭声后，孩子们急切地冲向餐厅。
- rush toward... 朝……冲去

语法重点
当副词修饰的不及物动词之后接有介词短语时，该副词通常放在介词短语之后，如例句中的副词 eagerly 修饰动词 rushed，就被放在了 toward the dinning room 之后。

0451 **horrible** ['hɔːrɪbl] a 恐怖的，可怕的，令人恐惧的
To say truly, the food you cooked yesterday tasted really horrible.
说实话，你昨天煮的饭真难吃。
- terrible 可怕的
- To say truly, ... 说实话，……

语法重点
副词修饰不及物动词时，通常直接放在该动词的后面。

0452 **horror** ['hɔːrər] n 恐怖，战栗，厌恶
To his horror, they asked him to eat mice.
令他惊恐的是，他们竟然让他吃老鼠。
- To one's horror... 让某人惊恐的是……

0453 **hourly** ['aʊərli] a 每小时的，以小时计算的，随时的
The man who delivers mails comes here at hourly intervals, so you needn't worry.
那个送邮件的人每个小时来一次，所以你不用担心。
- hourly wage 按时计酬

语法重点
句中 needn't 是情态动词，后面直接放动词原形。
↪ interval (P. 734)

0454 **housekeeper** [ˈhaʊskiːpər] n 管家，主妇
The story goes that the housekeeper vowed not to cook anymore after that.
据说，从那之后那个主妇发誓再也不煮饭了。

语法重点
vow to do sth.（发誓做某事）的否定式是在 to 前加上 not。

0455 **hug** [hʌɡ] v / n 拥抱，紧抱
He hugged his daughter tightly before he leaved.
离开前，他紧紧地拥抱了女儿。
- embrace 拥抱
- hug yourself with joy 为自己感到高兴

语法重点
副词修饰动词时，可以起到表达某种方式的作用，如例句中的副词 tightly（紧紧地）用以修饰之前的动词 hugged（拥抱），表示以"紧紧地"方式"拥抱"。

0456 **humorous** [ˈhjuːmərəs] a 幽默的，诙谐的
She gave a humorous account of the snacks she had in America.
她风趣地讲述了她在美国吃到的小吃。
- witty 诙谐的
- inhumorous 不幽默的
- give an account of... 描述……

0457 **hush** [hʌʃ] v 使安静
After supper, she hushed her baby to sleep.
晚餐后，她哄宝宝睡觉。
- calm 使平静
- hush sth. up 防止某事张扬出去
- hush sb. to sleep 哄某人睡觉

0458 **hut** [hʌt] n 小屋，棚屋
I ate up the food in the hut.
我把小棚子里的食物吃光了。
- cabin 小屋
- eat up... 吃光……

0459 **icy** [ˈaɪsi] a 冰的，冷淡的
I will not chance eating icy food in such a cold day.
我不愿意在这样冷的天冒险吃冰冻的食物。
- cold 寒冷的
- fiery 炙热的
- chance doing sth. 冒险做某事

语法重点
chance 在句中作及物动词，意思是"冒……的险"。

0460 **ideal** [aɪˈdiːəl] a 理想的，空想的 n 理想
It is totally useless to talk about ideal food with the poor men who often starves.
和经常挨饿的那些穷人谈论理想的食物是完全没有用的。
- faultless 完美的
- real 现实的
- it is totally useless... ……完全没有用

语法重点
一些程度副词主要用来强调动作或者性质上的完整性，如例句中程度副词 totally。

0461 **identity** [aɪˈdentəti] n 身份，特征
The guard in the building quickly made certain of the guest's identity.
大楼里的警卫很快就确定了那名客人的身份。
- identity card 身份证
- make certain of... 确定……

语法重点
大部分的方式副词都是由形容词加上词尾 -ly 构成的。
- certain (P. 022)

0462 ignorance [ˈɪgnərəns] n 无知，愚昧
It is not surprised that the little boy is in sheer ignorance of this kind of drink.
那个小男孩完全不知道这种饮料，这不足为奇。
🔄 literacy 有文化   🔄 eliminate ignorance 消除愚昧

0463 image [ˈɪmɪdʒ] n 想象，形象，图像
She has the image of the tomatoes as being sweet and sour.
番茄给她的印象是甜甜的、酸酸的。
🔄 picture 图像   🔄 have the image of... as... 对……有……的印象

> **语法重点**
> as 后面通常接动名词。
> 🔗 sour (P. 96)

0464 imagination [ɪˌmædʒɪˈneɪʃn] n 想象，幻想
It is beyond imagination that she finished her supper in such a quick way.
她很快就吃完了晚餐，这真难以想象。

> **语法重点**
> 介词 in 可引导定语从句，相当于副词在句中的作用。

0465 immediate [ɪˈmiːdiət] a 立即的，目前的
The immediate sequel to his eating sashimi was the pain in his stomach.
他吃生鱼片的后果是立即肚子疼。
🔄 instant 立即的   🔄 mediate 间接的   🔄 immediate cause 直接原因

> **语法重点**
> 表示某个部位疼痛通常用介词 in。
> 🔗 stomach (P. 228)

0466 import [ˈɪmpɔːrt] v / n 进口，输入，引进
You should take it moderately on importing this kind of milk powder.
在进口这种奶粉时你们应该适可而止。
🔄 input 输入   🔄 export 出口   🔄 take it moderately on... ……适可而止

> **语法重点**
> 程度副词修饰动词，主要用来强调动作的程度。

0467 impress [ɪmˈpres] v 给……极深的印象，影响 n 印象
Surprisingly, such delicious foods didn't impress him at all.
奇怪的是，这么好吃的食物竟然没有给他留下任何印象。
🔄 impress on... 给……留下印象

> **语法重点**
> 副词常用在句首来修饰整个句子，如例句中的副词 surprisingly 在句中表达一种惊奇的语气。

0468 impressive [ɪmˈpresɪv] a 令人印象深刻的，感人的
The taste of the drink cut an impressive figure.
这种饮料的味道给人深刻的印象。
🔄 affecting 感人的   🔄 ... cut an impressive figure 给人深刻的印象

0469 indeed [ɪnˈdiːd] ad 确实，事实上
It is indeed unfortunate that he ate poisonous mushrooms and died.
他吃到毒蘑菇然后死了，这真是不幸。
🔄 really 真正地   🔄 indeed useful 确实有用

> **语法重点**
> indeed 作为副词，还可以单独使用，放在句首修饰整个句子。

309

0470 **individual** [ˌɪndɪˈvɪdʒuəl]
a 个人的，单独的 n 个人，个体
It's up to us to distribute food and water to each individual.
分发食物和水给每个人是由我们自己决定的。
同 separate 单独的 反 collective 集体的
词 it's up to sb. to do sth. 某人有责任做某事

0471 **indoor** [ˈɪndɔːr] a 室内的
As is known to us all, he likes to go indoor climbing.
众所周知，他喜欢室内攀岩。
反 outdoor 户外的 词 as is known to us all, ... 众所周知，……

> 语法重点
> 句中 go indoor climbing 和 drink coffee 是并列的两个动词短语。

0472 **indoors** [ˌɪnˈdɔːrz] ad 在室内，在屋里
It's best for you to stay indoors and do not go anywhere.
你最好待在屋里，哪里都不要去。
反 outdoors 在户外 词 keep indoors 待在家里，足不出户

> 语法重点
> 地点副词用来表示位置关系，如例句中 indoors，类似的副词还有 there, here, anywhere 等。

0473 **industrial** [ɪnˈdʌstriəl] a 产业的
Compared with the industrial area, there are many restaurants and bars here.
与工业区相比，这里有很多餐厅和酒吧。

> 语法重点
> compared with（与……相比）后面要接上做比较的物件。

0474 **inferior** [ɪnˈfɪriər] a 下级的，较低的，次等的
I admitted that the dish I cooked was inferior to his in taste.
我承认我煮的饭菜没有他煮的好吃。
同 lower 下级的 反 superior 高级的 词 be inferior to... 比……低级

> 语法重点
> 表示在某方面不如别人或者别的东西，一般用介词 in。
> 参 admit (P. 252)

0475 **inform** [ɪnˈfɔːrm] v 通知，告诉
They were informed to finish their work promptly.
他们都被通知赶快完成工作。
同 notify 通知 词 be informed of 听说 词 be informed to do sth. 被通知做某事

0476 **injure** [ˈɪndʒər] v 受伤，损害，损伤
Tell the waiter to be careful when he serves the dishes lest the boy should be injured.
告诉服务生端菜时要小心，以免小男孩受伤。
同 hurt 伤害 反 cure 治愈 词 ... lest... 以免……

> 语法重点
> lest 后面接句子，句子中的动词要用"should + 动词原形"。

0477 **injury** [ˈɪndʒəri] n 伤害，损害
It's no joke eating such spicy food when he is recovering from an injury.
他正在养伤，吃这么辛辣的食物可不是闹着玩的。
同 wound 受伤，创伤 词 add insult to injury 雪上加霜

0478 **inn** [ɪn] n 小旅馆
I have never realized that the price of the breakfast offered in the inn is so high.
我从未想到这家小旅馆的早餐价格竟如此之高。
≈ hotel 客栈，旅馆　◎ I have never realized that... 我从未想到……

语法重点
频度副词在句中一般放在实意动词之前，当句中有助动词时，则放在助动词之后。

0479 **inner** [ˈɪnər] a 内部的，里面的
I ate up the cake in response to an inner calling.
我受内心欲望的驱使吃完了那个蛋糕。
≈ internal 内部的　≠ outer 外部的　◎ in response to... 受……的驱使

0480 **innocent** [ˈɪnəsnt] a 无辜的，无知的
To prove that you were innocent and didn't eat the strawberries, you must show me your tongue.
如果你想证明自己是清白的，没有吃草莓，就伸出舌头让我看看。
≠ guilty 有罪的　◎ innocent victims 无辜的受害者

语法重点
to prove that（为了证明……）后面要接句子。
↪ tongue (P. 237)

0481 **inspect** [ɪnˈspekt] v 检查，视察
The traffic policeman held up a car so as to inspect if the driver has drunk.
交通警察拦住了一辆轿车，以便检查司机是否喝过酒。
≈ examine 检查　◎ inspect... for... 为了……而检查……　◎ hold up... 拦住……

0482 **inspector** [ɪnˈspektər] n 检察员，巡视员
The inspector had no qualms about eating without paying the bill.
对于吃霸王餐这件事，那个检查员并不觉得有什么不安。

0483 **instead** [ɪnˈsted] ad 作为替代，反而
First, they just had soup instead of a full meal at the dinner party.
首先，聚餐时他们没有吃全餐，只喝了汤。
◎ instead of... 代替，而不是……

语法重点
表示序列的副词，在句中要置于句首，并用逗号和之后的句子隔开，如例句中的 first。

0484 **instruction** [ɪnˈstrʌkʃn] n 指示，说明
You must strictly follow the expert's instructions and drink less, or you'll be in danger.
你必须严格按照专家的话去做，少喝酒，否则你会有危险。
≈ direction 指令，说明　◎ instruction book 说明书　◎ follow one's instructions 按照某人的话

语法重点
在句中修饰动词、形容词、副词或句子，并用来表示时间、地点、方式、程度、语气的副词称为一般副词。

0485 **internal** [ɪnˈtɜːrnl] a 内部的，内心的，国内的
Nonetheless, he is only interested in internal food.
然而，他只对国内的食物感兴趣。

语法重点
一些表示因果关系的副词在句中通常起到连接的作用，此类副词称为连接副词。
↪ nonetheless (P. 476)

311

0486 interrupt [ˌɪntəˈrʌpt] v 打扰 n 中断
I beg your pardon, but I don't mean to interrupt your lunch.
对不起,我不是故意要打扰你吃午餐的。
interfere 打扰,干涉　　I beg your pardon, ... 对不起,……

> **语法重点**
> mean to 主要用来表示目的,其否定形式 don't mean to 所表达的意思是"并不是有意去做某事",表示其目的不在于此。

0487 introduction [ˌɪntrəˈdʌkʃn] n 介绍,引进,序言
May I make an introduction of the dish to you now?
我现在可以向你介绍这道菜了吗?
presentation 介绍　　make an introduction of... 介绍……

> **语法重点**
> 时间副词是指在句中表示时间、顺序或频率的词。

0488 inventor [ɪnˈventər] n 发明者,创造者
This dish is named after the inventor.
这道菜是以那个发明者命名的。
be named after... 以……命名的

0489 investigate [ɪnˈvestɪɡeɪt] v 调查,研究
I felt obliged to deeply investigate the cause of the food poisoning.
我感觉有必要深入调查这次食物中毒的原因。
research 调查　　investigate into... 对……进行调查

↪ oblige (P. 749)

0490 ivory [ˈaɪvəri] n 象牙,乳白色 a 象牙制的,乳白色的
The chopsticks he is using are carved from ivory.
他正在用的筷子是用象牙雕成的。
opalescent 乳白色的　　be carved from... 由……雕成的

> **语法重点**
> 筷子是两只,所以 chopstick 要用复数形式。
> ↪ chopstick (P. 139)

0491 jail [dʒeɪl] n 监狱,拘留所 v 监禁,拘留
If you continue to steal food in the restaurant, you'll end up in jail.
你如果继续在餐厅里偷东西吃,最终会被抓进监狱的。
prison 监狱　　in jail 在狱中服刑　　continue to... 继续……
in jail 的意思是"坐牢", in the jail 的意思是"在监狱里",两者意思不一样。

0492 jar [dʒɑːr] n 罐子,震动 v 不协调,震荡
However, she can see nothing special on the dish except it is contained in a jar.
可是,除了装在一个广口瓶里外,她看不出这道菜有什么特别之处。

> **语法重点**
> 复合副词是指由两个独立的单词组合而成的副词,此类副词主要有 whatever, nowhere, somehow, somewhat, wherever, however 等。

0493 jaw [dʒɔː] n 下巴,颌
He saw his chance and threw his milk onto the girl's jaw powerfully.
他看准机会,将牛奶朝女孩的下巴狠狠地扔了过去。
chin 下巴　　the lower jaw 下颌

0494 jealous ['dʒeləs] **a** 嫉妒的，妒忌的，羡慕的

I am quite jealous of her because she can cook such delicious dishes.
我很嫉妒她，因为她能做出如此美味的菜。
- envious 羡慕的，嫉妒的
- be jealous of... 嫉妒……

0495 jelly ['dʒeli] **n** 果冻，胶状物

When he sees the lion, his legs feel like jelly.
他一看到那只狮子就两腿发软。
- ... one's legs feel like jelly ……两腿发软

> **语法重点**
> jelly 既可以作可数名词，也可以作不可数名词。

0496 jet [dʒet] **n** 喷射机，喷口，喷射

A jet plane is circling round and round clockwise above to airdrop food and water.
一架喷射机在上空顺时针盘旋着，空投食物和水。
- emission 喷射
- ... circle round and round ……盘旋着

> **语法重点**
> 有些副词是名词加词尾 -wise 组合而成，词尾 -wise 主要用来表示一种位置、方向或状态。
> ⇨ clockwise (P. 544)

0497 jewel ['dʒu:əl] **n** 宝石，受珍视的人或物

Orange juice is the jewel of all the drinks for me.
所有饮料当中，我最喜欢喝橙汁。
- gem 宝石，受人重视者
- be the jewel of... 最受……珍爱

> **语法重点**
> jewel 是可数名词。

0498 jewelry ['dʒu:əlri] **n** 珠宝，首饰

Under the escort of the safeguards, they conveyed the jewelry boxes without eating anything.
在保镖的护送下，他们没吃任何东西就去运送珠宝了。
- jewellery 珠宝，首饰

> **语法重点**
> under the escort of (在……的护送下) 是固定用法, of 后面通常接表示人的名词或代词。

0499 journal ['dʒɜ:rnl] **n** 期刊，日志，日记

I kept a journal about what I have eaten and drunk every day.
我每天吃了什么、喝了什么都记在日记里了。
- daily journal 日报
- keep a journal 写日记

0500 journey ['dʒɜ:rni] **n** 旅程，旅行，行程

They didn't prepare enough foods; consequently, they decided to cancel their plan for the journey.
因为没有准备足够的食物，因此他们决定取消旅行计划。
- make a journey 旅行
- consequently, ... 因此，……

> **语法重点**
> 因果连接副词是指用来连接具有因果关系的两个句子的连接副词，此类副词主要有 consequently（因此），hence（所以），therefore（所以），thus（因而）等。
> ⇨ cancel (P. 136)

0501 joyful ['dʒɔɪfl] **a** 高兴的

Did you have any recall of the joyful day when we had dinner together?
你还记得我们一起愉快吃饭的那天吗？
- happy 高兴的
- Did you have any recall of...? 你还记得……吗？

0502 jungle [ˈdʒʌŋgl] n 丛林，密林
God forbid that you should find anything to eat in the jungle.
你绝不会在丛林里找到任何吃的。
● chaparral 丛林，密林　● jungle law 丛林法则

⊃ forbid (P. 443)

0503 junk [dʒʌŋk] n 垃圾，破烂，废旧杂物
The cause why we never eat junk foods is that they are harmful to our health.
我们从来不吃垃圾食品的原因是它们对我们的健康有害。
● trash 垃圾　● junk price 赔本价钱
● the cause why... is that... ……的原因是……

语法重点
关系副词 why 引导的从句主要用来表示某种原因。

0504 justice [ˈdʒʌstɪs] n 公正，法官
The man who has a sense of justice is drinking milk now.
那个很有正义感的人现在正在喝牛奶。
● bring sb. to justice 使犯人归案受审　● have a sense of... 有……感

语法重点
have a sense of 后面可以接不同的名词表达不同的意思。

0505 kangaroo [ˌkæŋgəˈruː] n 袋鼠
Stop feeding food to the kangaroo, for it will be too full.
别喂袋鼠东西吃了，它会吃太饱的。
● feed... to... 给……喂食

语法重点
kangaroo 的复数形式是 kangaroo 或者 kangaroos。

0506 kettle [ˈketl] n 水壶，坑穴
Two hours have passed; however, the water in the kettle still doesn't boil up.
已经过去两个小时了，可是水壶里的水还没有烧开。
● pot 壶　● ... boil up ……沸腾

语法重点
boil up 也可以作及物动词短语，后面接宾语。
⊃ boil (P. 132)

0507 keyboard [ˈkiːbɔːrd] n 键盘
A story is going about that he spilt his water on the keyboard accidently.
据说，是他不小心把水洒在键盘上的。
● keyset 键盘　● keyboard shortcuts 快速键

语法重点
accidently 修饰动词 spilt。

0508 kidney [ˈkɪdni] n 肾脏，腰子
I am inept in making steak and kidney pie.
我擅长做牛肉腰子馅饼。
● kidney stone 肾结石　● be inept in... 擅长……

0509 kilogram [ˈkɪləgræm] n 千克
He set his goal to eat a kilogram of mooncakes.
他定下目标要吃掉一千克的月饼。
● kilo 千克　● set one's goal to... 定下目标……

0510 **kilometer** [ˈkɪləmiːtər] n 千米
They stopped to drink water per kilometer.
他们每走一千米就要停下来喝水。
- square kilometer 平方千米
- stop to do sth. 停下来去做某事

> **语法重点**
> 注意，stop doing sth. 的意思是"停止做某事"，意思与 stop to do sth.（停下来去做某事）不同。

0511 **kit** [kɪt] n 工具组，成套装备
I seized on my kit bag and ran out to have lunch.
我抓起工具袋就跑出去吃午餐了。
- toolbox 工具箱
- a first-aid kit 急救箱
- seize on... 抓住……

⊃ seize (P. 356)

0512 **kneel** [niːl] v 跪下
The beggar knelt down in front of the rich man to ask for food.
那个乞丐跪在那个富人的面前乞讨食物。
- ... kneel down ……跪下来

> **语法重点**
> kneel 是不规则动词，其过去式、过去分词都是 knelt。

0513 **knight** [naɪt] n 骑士，爵士，武士
I am furious that these knights get aggressive when they are drunk.
我很气愤，这些骑士一喝酒就寻衅滋事。
- I am furious that... 我很气愤，……

> **语法重点**
> knight 还可以当动词，意思是"封为爵士"。

0514 **knit** [nɪt] v 编织，密接，结合
My sister knits up sweaters faster than me.
我姐姐织毛衣比我快。
- unknit 拆开
- knit together 紧密结合，连接在一起
- knit up... 织……

> **语法重点**
> 形容词或副词的比较级主要用于两个人或物进行比较，表示"一个比另一个更加……"，如句中的 faster。

0515 **knob** [nɑːb] n 瘤，节，把手
He gave a wrench at the knob to open the fridge and look for food.
他猛地转了一下冰箱的把手，以打开冰箱找吃的。
- handle 把手
- adjusting knob 调节旋钮
- give a wrench at... 猛转……

0516 **knot** [nɑːt] n 结 v 打结
You should cut the knot by eating up all the food.
你应该快刀斩乱麻，把这些食物统统吃掉。

0517 **label** [ˈleɪbl] n 标签，标记 v 贴标签于，把……归类
I think the label should be firmly affixed to the package of the food.
我觉得这张标签应该牢牢地贴在食物的包装盒上。
- tag 标签
- trade label 商标
- be affixed to... 被贴在……

> **语法重点**
> 当动词后面接介词时，修饰该动词的副词要放在其前面。

⊃ package (P. 199)

0518 lace [leɪs] n 蕾丝
Didn't you like the dress with the lace collar?
你难道不喜欢那件有蕾丝衣领的连衣裙吗？
同 gymp 花边　　片 shoe lace 鞋带

0519 ladder ['lædər] n 梯子，门路，途径
I need another ladder which is longer than this one to pick off the apples.
我需要另外一架比这个长的梯子才能摘下那些苹果。
片 fire ladder 救火梯　　片 pick off... 摘……

语法重点
否定疑问句在句中主要表示说话者的某种惊讶、责难或赞叹等的情绪，语气比一般疑问句更为强烈。

语法重点
在定语从句中也可以用比较级的成分，表示定语从句主语和宾语之间的对比，如例句中的名词 ladder 之后的定语从句中的 one 和 ladder 进行对比。

0520 latter ['lætər] a 后面的
I will give up drinking in the latter part of the year.
后半年我将戒酒。
反 former 前者的

0521 laughter ['læftər] n 笑声
She tasted the bread I made and roared with laughter.
她吃了我做的面包，放声大笑。
同 cry 哭　　片 loud laughter 大声笑　　句 ... roar with laughter ……放声大笑

⊃ roar (P. 351)

0522 laundry ['lɔːndri] n 洗衣店，洗衣房
I am tired with washing clothes; let's send them to the laundry and have a cup of tea.
我洗衣服太累了，把它们送到洗衣房，然后喝杯茶。
片 laundry room 洗衣房　　片 be tired with... ……而劳累

语法重点
注意 be tired with 与 be tired of 的区别，后者表示"因……而厌倦"。

0523 lawn [lɔːn] n 草坪，草地
Keep off the lawn.
不要践踏草皮。
片 lawn mower 割草机　　片 keep off... 远离……

0524 leak [liːk] v 渗漏，泄露 n 泄露，漏洞
The bottle of milk is apt to leak if there is a hole.
如果有洞的话，那瓶牛奶会很容易漏。
同 seep 渗漏　　片 spring a leak 出现漏缝，用坏　　片 be apt to... 容易……

0525 leap [liːp] v / n 跳跃，跃过
His giving up eating meat was a leap in the dark.
他不吃肉是贸然的行动。
片 look before you leap 三思而后行　　句 ... be a leap in the dark ……是贸然行动

0526 leather ['leðər] n 皮革，皮制品
The bag he used to hold the food is made of leather.
他用来装食物的袋子是用皮革做的。
同 leder 皮革　　片 be made of... 由……做的

语法重点
be made of 暗含的意思是能看出原材料。

lace ~ lifeguard

0527 **leisure** [ˈliːʒər] n 闲暇，休闲
I am seldom at leisure to have a cup of coffee in the cafe.
我很少有空去咖啡馆喝杯咖啡。
- ease 悠闲　- leisure for 有空做某事　- ... be at leisure ……有空

> 语法重点
> seldom 表示"很少"，是频度副词，通常放在 be 动词后面。

0528 **lengthen** [ˈleŋθən] v 延长，延伸
Will you care to lengthen the dinner hour?
你介意延长晚餐的时间吗？
- elongate 延长　- shorten 变短　- Will you care to...? 你介意……吗?

> 语法重点
> Will you care to 后面要接动词原形。

0529 **lens** [lenz] n 镜头，透镜，镜片
We should first keep the camera lens clean.
我们应该先保持照相机镜头的清洁。
- contact lens 隐形眼镜　- keep... clean 保持……干净

0530 **liar** [ˈlaɪər] n 骗子
He had the temerity to drink my milk and called me a liar.
他竟敢喝我的牛奶，还说我撒谎。

0531 **liberal** [ˈlɪbərəl] a 自由主义的，慷慨的，开明的
I have a liberal attitude to eating snakes and mice.
我对吃蛇肉和老鼠肉看得很开。

> 语法重点
> have a liberal attitude to 中的 to 是介词，后面接名词、代词、动名词。

0532 **liberty** [ˈlɪbərti] n 自由，自主，自由权
He took the liberty of eating my food when I was away.
我不在的时候，他擅自吃我的食物。
- freedom 自由　- constraint 约束
- take the liberty of doing sth. 擅自做某事

0533 **librarian** [laɪˈbreriən] n 图书管理员
The librarian was in his cups and couldn't stand up.
那个图书管理员喝醉酒，站不起来了。
- bibliotheca 图书馆　- ... be in one's cups ……喝醉了酒

> 语法重点
> be in one's cups 是固定搭配，cup 要用复数。

0534 **lifeboat** [ˈlaɪfboʊt] n 救生艇
The secret of their survival is that there is some food in the lifeboat.
他们能够活下来的秘密就是救生船上有食物。
- emergency lifeboat 紧急救生艇　- the secret of... is to... ……的秘密是……

0535 **lifeguard** [ˈlaɪfɡɑːrd] n 救生员
The lifeguard was reluctant to hobnob with me.
那个救生员不愿意和我一起喝两杯。
- lifesaver 救生员　- lifeguard raft 救生筏　- hobnob with sb. 和某人喝两杯

↻ reluctant (P. 495)

0536 lifetime ['laɪftaɪm] n 一生，终身
He has never eaten a hamburger in his lifetime.
他一生从未吃过汉堡。
● once in a lifetime 一生一次

> 语法重点
> 句中的介词 in 可以替换为 during。

0537 lighthouse ['laɪthaʊs] n 灯塔
You don't have to eat the ice-cream which looks like a lighthouse.
你不需要吃那个看起来像灯塔的冰激凌。
● beacon 灯塔 ● lighthouse keeper 灯塔看守人

0538 limb [lɪm] n 肢，臂，脚，翼
If he drank up the water, all of us will be out on a limb.
如果他把水喝光了，我们都会有危险。
● life and limb 性命，生命 ● ... out on a limb ……有危险

0539 linen ['lɪnɪn] n 亚麻布，日用织品，亚麻织品
Before going out for a picnic, I sent my linen handkerchief to him as a souvenir.
去野餐之前，我把亚麻布手帕送给他留作纪念。
● wash one's dirty linen in public 公开谈论个人的事情或争吵的事
● linen 也常用在短语 shoot one's linen 中，意思是"故意抖出内衣的袖子"，表示自己是大人物，或表示不安。

● handkerchief (P. 173)

0540 lipstick ['lɪpstɪk] n 口红，唇膏
She put thick lipstick on her lips and it came off on the wine glass.
她嘴上涂了厚厚的口红，而口红印在了酒杯上。
● lippie 口红，唇膏 ● red lipstick 红色唇膏 ● come off... 脱离……

0541 litter ['lɪtər] n 废弃物，垃圾，杂乱
It is antisocial to throw away litter in public places.
在公共场所丢垃圾是没公德心的。
● rubbish 垃圾 ● leaf litter 落叶层

0542 lively ['laɪvli] a 精力充沛的，活泼的，栩栩如生的
Based on her lively description, we can get a general image of the beautiful city.
通过她那生动的描述，我们对美丽的城市有了大概的印象。

● description (P. 282)

0543 liver ['lɪvər] n 肝脏，生活者，居住者
You know excessive wine can result in injury to the liver.
你知道，饮酒过量会损害肝脏。
● hepar 肝 ● hot liver 热情的人，多情的人

> 语法重点
> 表示极限概念的形容词无比较级，如例句中的 excessive，意思是"过多的，过分的"，没有比较级。

0544 load [loʊd] v 装载 n 负荷，装载量

The good news that he began to take food has taken a load off her mind.
听到他开始进食的好消息，她放心了。
- burden 负担，载货量 - unload 卸货

语法重点
介词 off 有 "脱离" 的意思。
- mind (P. 063)

0545 lobby ['lɑːbi] n 大厅，游说团体 v 游说

The lobby was crowded with people who were having lunch.
大厅里挤满了吃午餐的人。
- ticket lobby 售票厅 - be crowded with... 挤满了……

语法重点
lobby 还常用于短语 lobby for，意思是 "为……游说"。

0546 lobster ['lɑːbstər] n 龙虾

The lobster I just ate lay heavy on my stomach.
我刚才吃的龙虾让我的肚子很难受。

0547 lollipop ['lɑːlipɑːp] n 棒棒糖

If I study still harder this term, he will buy me lollipops every day.
如果我这学期更加努力学习的话，他就会每天给我买棒棒糖吃。
- lolly 棒棒糖 - study harder... ……更加努力学习

语法重点
副词 still 可用于比较级之前对比较级进行修饰，有加强语气的作用。

0548 loose [luːs] a 宽松的，不牢固的

After eating the fish, I had loose bowels.
吃完那条鱼，我腹泻了。
- weak 不牢固的 - tight 紧的 - at a loose end 无事做，不知做什么好
- ... have loose bowels ……腹泻

0549 loosen ['luːsn] v 松开，放松，放宽

First of all, we should loosen the belt.
首先，我们得把腰带松一下。
- relax 放松 - tighten（使）变紧
- loosen one's tongue 使某人无拘无束地谈话

语法重点
first 是序数词，意思是 "第一"，用来构成短语 first of all（首先），通常置于句首，之后用逗号和后面的句子隔开。

0550 lord [lɔːrd] n 统治者

The lord has got some time for a cup of tea.
那个君王还有喝茶的时间。
- ruler 统治者 - live like a lord 养尊处优

语法重点
have 在句中充当助动词。

0551 loudspeaker [ˌlaʊd'spiːkər] n 喇叭

I made my opinion clear through the loudspeaker.
我通过扩音器清楚地表达了我的观点。
- amplifier 扩音器 - make clear... 表明……

语法重点
make clear 的宾语是代词时，该代词要放在 make 与 clear 之间。
- opinion (P. 198)

0552 luggage ['lʌgɪdʒ] n 行李
She has been informed that her luggage full of food and drink had already arrived.
她刚接到通知说，她那装满食物和水的行李已经运到了。
- baggage 行李   - luggage charges 寄存行李费

> **语法重点**
> luggage 后面省略了 which is。

0553 lullaby ['lʌləbaɪ] n 摇篮曲，催眠曲
Later on, the lullaby that he created became popular.
后来，他创作的摇篮曲流行起来。
- cradlesong 摇篮曲，催眠曲   - later on, ... 后来，……

> **语法重点**
> later 既可以作形容词，也可以作副词。作副词时和介词 on 连用构成 later on，意思是"以后，后来"，既可以放在句首，也可放在句尾。

0554 lung [lʌŋ] n 肺脏，呼吸器官
There is a connection between this kind of junk food and lung cancer.
这种垃圾食品跟肺癌有关。
- lung volume 肺活量
- there is a connection between... and... ……和……之间有关

> **语法重点**
> lung 也常用在短语 at the top of one's lungs，意思是"声嘶力竭地"。

0555 magical ['mædʒɪkl] a 神奇的，魔术的，有魔力的
That magical beauty who is sitting there alone seems to be in distress.
那个独自坐在那里的迷人美女看起来很伤心。
- magical impact 魔法效果   - ... be in distress ……伤心

⇨ distress (P. 559)

0556 magnet ['mægnət] n 磁铁，磁石
The dish in the restaurant is a magnet for its guests.
饭店里的这道菜吸引了客人们。
- aimant 磁铁   - bar magnet 条形磁铁   - be a magnet for... 吸引……

> **语法重点**
> be a magnet for 后面通常接表示人的名词。

0557 maid [meɪd] n 少女，女仆
The maid is eating with relish now.
那个女仆现在正津津有味地吃着。
- gilly 男仆   - maid of honor 伴娘   - ... with relish 津津有味地……

0558 major ['meɪdʒər] a 主要的，较多的 n 主修 v 主修
What is the major cause of her abstaining from food?
她绝食的主要原因是什么？
- chief 主要的   - minor 次要的   - major role 主角

0559 majority [mə'dʒɔːrəti] n 大多数，多数派
A majority of the people there starved themselves to death.
那里的大多数人是绝食而死的。
- minority 少数   - the silent majority 沉默的大多数

> **语法重点**
> a majority of 后面一般接可数名词的复数形式。

0560 mall [mɔːl] n 大型购物中心

Some of the guests are held up in the shopping mall and have no water to drink.
一些顾客被困在购物中心，没有水喝。
- plaza 购物中心
- shopping mall 大商场
- be held up in... 被困在……

语法重点
hold up 所表达的意思主要为"拦截，举起，支持"；表示"被滞留"在某种情况之中时，通常用 be held up in 的结构。

0561 manage ['mænɪdʒ] v 管理，做成

I'm sure that he can manage to finish the task.
我相信他能设法完成这项工作。
- manage with... 以……设法应付
- manage to do sth. 设法做到某事
- try to do sth. 意思是"尝试做某事"，不一定能做到，但 manage to do sth. 意思是"设法做到某事"，暗含的意思是做到了。

0562 management ['mænɪdʒmənt] n 管理，管理部门

The management is considering having a dinner to celebrate our anniversary.
管理部门正考虑为周年庆举办一次聚餐。
- governance 管理
- consider doing sth. 考虑做某事

语法重点
the management 是一个整体，如果强调的是部门里的人，那么后面的 be 动词要用 are。
↪ anniversary (P. 394)

0563 manageable ['mænɪdʒəbl] a 可管理的，易控制的

If we want to eat safe food, steps must be taken to reduce the problem to manageable proportions.
如果我们想吃到安全的食物，那么就必须采取措施将问题缩小到可控制的范围。
- accomplishable 可完成的
- unmanageable 难以处理的

↪ proportion (P. 617)

0564 manager ['mænɪdʒər] n 经理，管理者，管家

The manager exists on rice and water.
经理靠吃米饭和水过活。
- executive 经理
- deputy manager 副经理
- exist on... 靠……过活

0565 mankind / humankind

[mæn'kaɪnd] / [ˌhjuːmən'kaɪnd] n 人类

I heard that this kind of food made a greater contribution to mankind.
我听说这种食物对人类有更大的贡献。

语法重点
make a greater contribution to 中的 to 是介词，后面接名词、代词或者动名词。

0566 manner ['mænər] n 礼貌，规范，风俗

You should breed manners at table to children.
你应该教孩子们吃饭的礼节。
- politeness 礼貌
- bad manners 不礼貌，坏习惯
- breed sth. to sb. 教某人某事

0567 **marble** ['mɑːrbl] n 大理石，弹珠

He lost his marble after hearing that his lunch was eaten by others.
听说自己的午餐被别人吃掉了，他失去了理智。
- glass marble 玻璃球
- ... lose one's marble ……失去理智

0568 **march** [mɑːrtʃ] v 前进 n 游行示威

Some people dropped out, and some starved to death in the long march.
长途行进过程中，有些人脱队了，而有些人饿死了。
- parade 游行，列队行进
- halt 止步
- on the march 行进，行军

⊃ people (P. 075)

0569 **marvelous** ['mɑːrvələs] a 令人惊讶的，非凡的

He has a marvelous gift for singing.
他唱歌有非凡的天赋。
- extraordinary 非凡的
- commonplace 平凡的

0570 **mathematic / mathematical** [ˌmæθə'mætɪk] / [ˌmæθə'mætɪkl] a 数学的，精确的

There is nothing wrong with mathematical problems, so you can have lunch now.
数学题没有什么错误，所以你可以吃午餐了。

语法重点
wrong 修饰 nothing，要放在 nothing 的后面。

0571 **mathematics / math** [ˌmæθə'mætɪks] / [mæθ] n 数学

She is too nervous to eat anything when it comes to math.
一碰到数学课，她就紧张地吃不下东西。
- math 是 mathematics 的简写。

0572 **mature** [mə'tʃʊr] a 成熟的，考虑周到的

As a mature man, you should drink a cup of strong tea to sober yourself.
作为一个成年人，你应该喝杯浓茶让自己清醒一下。
- adult 成熟的
- immature 不成熟的
- sober up... 让……清醒

语法重点
"浓茶"用 strong 来形容表示。

0573 **mayor** ['meɪər] n 市长

The mayor tossed off the glass of water in one gulp.
市长一口气喝完了那杯水。
- burgomaster 市长
- deputy mayor 副市长
- toss off... 一饮而尽……

语法重点
gulp 意思是"一大口"，尤指液体。

0574 **meadow** ['medoʊ] n 草地，牧场

They are disputing about what to eat in the meadow.
他们在草地上争论着吃什么。
- grass 草地
- dispute about... 争论……

⊃ dispute (P. 428)

marble ~ mend

0575 meaningful ['miːnɪŋfl] a 有意义的，意味深长的
He threw a meaningful look at her before dinner.
晚餐前，他给她一个意味深长的目光。
- significant 有意义的，意味深长的
- meaningless 无意义的

> 语法重点
> throw a meaningful look at 后面通常接人。

0576 meanwhile ['miːnwaɪl] ad 同时
Meanwhile, he had a cup of tea.
同时，他喝了一杯茶。
- meantime 同时
- in the meanwhile 与此同时

0577 medal ['medl] n 奖章，勋章，纪念章
He received a medal in reward for eating the big watermelon in half a minute.
他因为在半分钟内吃掉了那个大西瓜而获得了一枚奖章。
- gold medal 金质奖章
- in reward for... 为了……而得奖

> 语法重点
> medal 常用于短语 one side of the medal，意思是"问题的一面"。
> ⊃ watermelon (P. 244)

0578 medical ['medɪkl] a 医学的，医药的，内科的
The man fainted after eating the food, but he had come to himself after the timely medical treatment.
那个人吃了食物之后就晕倒了，但经过及时治疗，他已经恢复了意识。
- medical insurance 医疗保险
- ... come to oneself ……恢复了意识

0579 medium / media ['miːdiəm] / ['miːdiə]
n 媒体，手段 a 中等的，适中的
The man who is drinking is medium in stature.
那个在喝酒的人身材中等。

0580 membership ['membəʃɪp] n 会员资格，会籍
He is eligible to apply for membership of the fine food association.
他有资格申请加入这个美食协会。
- qualification 资格
- be eligible to... 有资格……

⊃ association (P. 398)

0581 memorize ['meməraɪz] v 记住，背熟，记忆
The only thing she regretted was that she failed to memorize the name of the flower.
她唯一遗憾的就是没能记住那朵花的名字。
- remember 记住
- forget 忘记

> 语法重点
> 在例句中，was 后面省略了 that。

0582 mend [mend] v 修改
They will get started after they mend the car.
他们修好车后就会出发了。
- repair 修理
- break 弄坏
- It's never too late to mend. 改过不嫌迟。
- ... get started 开始……

> 语法重点
> get 后加动词过去分词，意思是"开始做某事"，主要表示一种人为的动作。

0583 **mental** ['mentl] a 心理的，精神的，思想的
He says people who have irregular eating habits may be predisposed to mental problems.
他说饮食不规律的人容易出现精神方面的问题。
⊛ spiritual 精神的　⊛ physical 身体的　⊛ be predisposed to... 有……倾向的

语法重点
be predisposed to 中的 to 是介词，后面一般接名词、动名词。

0584 **mention** ['menʃn] v/n 提到，说起
He likes drinking wine, not to mention good wine.
他喜欢喝酒，更别提好酒了。
⊛ reference 提及　⊛ don't mention it 不用介意
⊛ not to mention... 更不用说……

语法重点
not to mention 后面一般接名词或代词，用来跟之前提到的人或物做比较。

0585 **merchant** ['mɜːrtʃənt] n 商人，专家
As mentioned above, the merchant must be fond of eating noodles.
如上所述，那个商人肯定喜欢吃面条。
⊛ businessman 商人　⊛ retail merchant 零售商

语法重点
as mentioned above（如上所述）通常用在句首，在句中主要用于引出某种结论，表示通过以上的叙述得出某种结论。

0586 **merry** ['meri] a 快乐的
He never dreamed that he was merry after having only one glass of wine.
他没想到他只喝了一杯酒就醉了。
⊛ jolly 愉快的，欢乐的　⊛ gloomy 沮丧的　⊛ make merry 欢宴作乐，庆祝

0587 **mess** [mes] n 杂乱，脏乱
The table was in a mess after they had supper.
他们吃过晚餐后，桌上一团乱。
⊛ chaos 混乱　⊛ orderliness 有序，整齐　⊛ in a mess 一团乱

0588 **microphone / mike** ['maɪkrəfoʊn] / [maɪk]
n 麦克风，扩音器
She gave a tap at the microphone after lunch.
午餐后，她敲了一下扩音器。
⊛ radio microphone 无线话筒　⊛ give a tap at... 敲了一下……

语法重点
tap 在句中作名词，意思是"轻叩（敲）"。

0589 **microwave** ['maɪkrəweɪv] n 微波炉
Let's heat up the food in the microwave.
我们把食物放在微波炉里加热吧。
⊛ wavelet 微波　⊛ microwave oven 微波炉　⊛ heat up... 加热……

语法重点
heat 在句中作动词。
⊛ heat (P. 048)

0590 **might** [maɪt] n 能力，力量　v 可能，也许
We might eat fewer candies from now on.
从今以后我们少吃糖果为妙。
⊛ pigs might fly 无稽之谈，奇迹可能会发生　⊛ ... from now on 从今以后……

语法重点
from now on 既可用于句首，也可用于句尾。

mental ~ misery

0591 mighty [ˈmaɪti] **a** 强大的，巨大的
The mighty wind tore his food into pieces.
强劲的风把他的食物撕成了碎片。
- powerful 强大的 - weak 软弱的
- high and mighty 趾高气扬的 - tear sth. into pieces 将……撕成碎片

⟶ piece (P. 075)

0592 mill [mɪl] **n** 磨坊，工厂，磨粉机
After going through the mill, he can make all kinds of furniture.
受过艰苦的磨炼后，他能做出各种家具。
- paper mill 造纸厂 - ... go through the mill ……经受磨炼

0593 millionaire [ˌmɪljəˈner] **n** 百万富翁
The millionaire gave up drinking last year, but he was back on the booze now.
那个百万富翁去年戒酒了，但现在又开始喝了。
- ... be back on the booze ……又喝酒了

0594 miner [ˈmaɪnər] **n** 矿工
The miner drank himself into a stupor last night.
昨晚，那个矿工喝得烂醉。
- gold miner 淘金者 - drink oneself into a stupor 某人喝得烂醉

0595 minor [ˈmaɪnər] **a** 较小的，次要的
It isn't worthwhile worrying about minor problems and not having your dinner.
为这种小事担心，且都没吃饭，真是不值得。
- lesser 次要的 - major 主要的 - it isn't worthwhile... 不值得……

语法重点
it isn't worthwhile 后面通常要接动名词。

0596 minority [maɪˈnɔːrəti] **n** 少数人，未成年
The boy who is eating bread is in his minority.
那个吃面包的男孩尚未成年。
- nonage 未成年 - majority 多数

语法重点
his 跟主语 the boy 保持一致。

0597 miracle [ˈmɪrəkl] **n** 奇迹，令人惊奇的人或事
It was a miracle that she was able to survive without eating for ten days.
十天没有吃东西，她竟然活了下来，真是个奇迹。
- wonder 奇迹 - by a miracle 奇迹般地

语法重点
that 后面的句子是详细地介绍 miracle 的内容。
⟶ survive (P. 231)

0598 misery [ˈmɪzəri] **n** 悲惨
I think hunger is a prologue to misery for him.
我认为，饥饿对于他来说是痛苦的开始。
- grief 悲痛 - happiness 快乐，幸福 - be a prologue to... 是……的开始

语法重点
"对于某人来说"，一般用介词 for。
⟶ hunger (P. 177)

0599 missile ['mɪsl] n 飞弹，投射物
They got a fix on the missile launching site after meeting.
会议后，他们确定了导弹发射场的位置。
- dejectile 投射物　- long-range missile 远端导弹　- get a fix on... 确定……

语法重点
get a fix on 后面一般接表示地点的名词。

0600 missing ['mɪsɪŋ] a 失踪的，找不到的
The bread is most delicious, except for some missing pieces.
这个面包十分美味，除了缺失了的那几块。
- absent 缺少的　- except for... 除了……

语法重点
如果形容词或副词的最高级形式在句中是为了产生加强语气的作用，表示"十分，非常"的意思，那么最高级之前不加 the。

0601 mission ['mɪʃn] n 任务，使命，代表团
We guarantee to complete our mission.
我们保证完成任务。
- assignment 任务　- rescue mission 营救任务　- guarantee to... 保证……

语法重点
guarantee to 后面一般接动词原形。

0602 mist [mɪst] n 薄雾，迷蒙，朦胧不清
To enjoy the beautiful scenery in mist, we adhered to climbing the mountain without rest.
为了欣赏薄雾中的美景，我们坚持不休息就去爬山了。
- haze 薄雾　- adhere to... 坚持……

语法重点
adhere to 中的 to 为介词。

0603 mixture ['mɪkstʃər] n 混合物
I am hypersensitive to cough mixture.
我对止咳糖浆过敏。
- compound 混合物　- be hypersensitive to... 对……过敏

- cough (P. 145)

0604 mob [mɑːb] n 暴民，乌合之众　v 大举包围，蜂拥而入
The police kept the mob under control, so the hostages in the restaurant were free.
警察将暴徒制服了，所以餐厅里的人质自由了。
- a mob of... 一群……　- keep sb. under control 制服某人
- the mob 多含有贬义。

- hostage (P. 581)

0605 mobile ['moʊbl] a 可动的，易变的，活动的
The boss converted his car into a mobile snack bar.
老板把他的车改成了一个流动小吃店。
- locomotive 移动的　- immobile 固定的，不变的
- convert... into... 把……改成……

0606 moist [mɔɪst] a 潮湿的，湿润的
She can't love the moist weather and snacks here more.
她非常喜欢这里湿润的天气和小吃。
- damp 潮湿的　- dry 干燥的　- moist soil 湿地
- can't love... more 最喜欢……

语法重点
在一些情况下，比较级的否定结构可以表示最高级，表示"非常，最……"等含义，如例句中的 can't love... more。

0607 moisture ['mɔɪstʃər] n 湿气，水分，潮气

You can put the drier into the cabinet to soak up the moisture.
你可以在柜子里放些干燥剂来吸收湿气。
- humidity 潮气   - soak up... 吸收……

语法重点
soak up 是及物动词短语，后面可以接宾语。
⊃ cabinet (P. 404)

0608 monk [mʌŋk] n 僧侣，修道士

Some of the monks finished the noodles in no time.
一些和尚很快就吃完了面条。
- monastery 僧侣   - nun 修女，尼姑   - ... in no time 很快……

0609 mood [muːd] n 心情，情绪

I was tired and in no mood for eating.
我累极了，无心吃饭。
- feeling 情绪   - in a good mood 心情好   - be in no mood for... 无心……

0610 mop [mɑːp] n 拖把 v 用拖把拖，擦拭

After you finish your dinner, mop up the mess on the table.
吃完饭后，把桌子上的这些脏东西擦掉。
- swabber 拖把   - mop the floor 拖地板   - mop up... 擦掉……

0611 moral ['mɔːrəl] a 道德上的，精神上的

Stay away from people without moral principles when you drink.
喝酒时，要离没有道德原则的人远一点儿。
- ethical 道德的   - immoral 不道德的   - stay away from... 远离……

0612 motel [moʊ'tel] n 汽车旅馆

He has heaved up his dinner in the motel.
在汽车旅馆里，他把吃的饭都吐了出来。
- heave up... 吐出……   - motel 其实就是 motorist's hotel。

0613 motor ['moʊtər] n 马达，发动机，机动车

My motor car is at its best; come on, I will take you to the station.
我的汽车现在处于最佳状态，上来吧，我带你去车站。
- ... be at one's best 在……的最佳状态

语法重点
当最高级和物主代词连用时，通常用来表示一种最佳或最糟糕的状态或情况，如例句中的 at its best。

0614 murder ['mɜːrdər] n 谋杀，谋杀案 v 谋杀，损坏

He was arraigned for murder when he was having lunch in the afternoon.
下午吃饭时，他因谋杀罪而被传讯。
- assassinate 暗杀   - be arraigned for... 因为……被传讯

语法重点
在某个具体的时间点前，用介词 at。

0615 **muscle** ['mʌsl] n 肌肉，体力，力气
The man with strong muscles has never come to the café before.
那个肌肉发达的男人以前从没来过这家咖啡馆。
⦿ strength 力气　⦿ abdominal muscle 腹肌

语法重点
before 既可以作介词，也可以作副词。作副词时，通常在句中与现在完成时连用。

0616 **mushroom** ['mʌʃrum] n 蘑菇，暴发户
We think it a miracle that he survives after eating the poisonous mushrooms.
他吃完毒蘑菇竟然活了下来，我们认为这是个奇迹。
⦿ agaric 蘑菇　⦿ mushroom soup 蘑菇汤

⊃ miracle (P. 325)

0617 **musical** ['mjuːzɪkl] a 音乐的，悦耳的
We can taste of the snacks while watching the musical performance.
我们可以一边吃美食，一边观看音乐会。
⦿ harmonious 悦耳的　⦿ harsh 刺耳的　⦿ musical instrument 乐器

0618 **mystery** ['mɪstri] n 秘密，神秘，奥秘
In this way, I solved the mystery of the statue at last.
就这样，我终于解开了这个雕像的秘密。
⦿ secret 秘密　⦿ remain a mystery 仍然是个谜　⦿ in this way, ... 就这样，……

0619 **nanny** ['næni] n 保姆，奶妈
As of this evening, nanny has eaten three watermelons.
到今天晚上为止，保姆已经吃了三个西瓜了。

语法重点
as of 表示"到……为止"，表示某个时间点之前的一段时间，一般置于句首。

0620 **nap** [næp] n 午睡，打盹
You can take a nap after lunch till two o'clock.
午餐后你可以小睡一会儿，直到两点钟。
⦿ siesta 午后小睡　⦿ take a nap 睡午觉，小睡片刻

语法重点
介词 till 的意思是"直到……为止"，通常表示的是从现在到将来的某个时间点为止这一段时间。

0621 **native** ['neɪtɪv] a 天生的，当地的，本国的
Can you explain why this snack in your native land is so delicious?
你能解释一下，为什么你们家乡的这种小吃这么好吃吗？
⦿ foreign 外国的　⦿ native land 祖国，家乡
⦿ Can you explain why...? 你能解释一下为什么……？

0622 **navy** ['neɪvi] n 海军，船队
After retiring from the navy, my father settled down in this city and went to the café every day.
从海军退役之后，我父亲在这个小城市定居下来，并且每天都去喝咖啡。
⦿ royal navy 皇家海军　⦿ ... settle down ……定居下来

⊃ retire (P. 498)

0623 necessity [nəˈsesəti] n 必需品，需要

Is it a logical necessity that drinking too much wine leads to stomachache?
喝酒过多导致胃痛，这是个合乎逻辑的必然定律吗？
- need 需要
- out of necessity 出于必要

0624 necktie [ˈnektaɪ] n 领带

That necktie is the least one I will choose if I go to the banquet.
我要是去参加宴会的话，肯定不会选择戴那条领带。
- cravat 领带
- be the least... that... 不会……

语法重点
the least 后面加上名词，可以表示否定的意思。

0625 neighborhood [ˈneɪbərhʊd] n 邻近地区

I am quite a stranger in this neighborhood; can you tell me where the nearest restaurant is?
我完全迷路了，你能告诉我最近的餐厅在哪里吗？
- in the neighborhood of... 在……附近
- be a stranger in... 对……不熟悉

语法重点
be a stranger in 后面接表示地点的名词。
stranger (P. 229)

0626 nerve [nɜːrv] n 神经，勇气，敏感处

The wine always gets on my nerves.
酒总是让我觉得不安。
- courage 勇气
- ... get on one's nerves ……令人不安

语法重点
get on one's nerves 是固定搭配，nerve 要用复数形式。

0627 nervous [ˈnɜːrvəs] a 紧张不安的，焦虑的，神经的

After eating the chocolates, I am full of nervous energy.
吃过巧克力后，我精力充沛。
- agitated 焦虑的
- relaxed 放松的
- nervous system 神经系统

0628 network [ˈnetwɜːrk] n 网点，网络

It is generally appreciated that we can buy books and clothing through the network.
众所周知，我们可以通过网络买书和衣服。
- railway network 铁路网
- it is generally appreciated that... 众所周知，……

语法重点
介词 through 可以表示"通过"，后面要接表示途径的名词。

0629 nickname [ˈnɪkneɪm] n 绰号

Because I like eating apples, I am called by others as the nickname "apple" throughout my life.
因为爱吃苹果，我一生都被别人昵称为"苹果"。
- byname 绰号
- be called by sb. as the nickname... 被人昵称为……

语法重点
介词 throughout 的意思为"贯穿，遍及"，表示持续的一段时间。

0630 noble [ˈnoʊbl] a 贵族的，高贵的，高尚的

The man who is drinking coffee is of noble origins.
那个正在喝咖啡的男人出身高贵。
- aristocratic 贵族的
- ignoble 卑贱的
- ... be of noble origins ……出身高贵

语法重点
origin 表示"出身，血统"时，一般用复数形式。

0631　normal ['nɔːrml] **a** 正常的，正规的，精神健全的
He skipped normal meals to lose weight.
为了减肥，他不吃正餐。
　standard 正规的　　abnormal 反常的　　... lose weight ……减肥

◎ weight (P. 112)

0632　novelist ['nɑːvəlɪst] **n** 小说家
The novelist cut down on sugar to lose weight.
那个小说家为了减轻体重而开始少吃糖。

0633　nun [nʌn] **n** 修女，尼姑
It was a nun who ate these pears.
是一名修女吃了这些梨。

语法重点
it was a / an... who 是强调句型，who 之前要用表示职业、身份等的名词。

0634　oak [oʊk] **n** 橡树，栎树
We found these fruits in the oak tree.
我们在这棵橡树上找到这些水果。
　Big oaks from little acorns grow. 万丈高楼平地起。

0635　observe [əb'zɜːrv] **v** 观察，遵守，注意到
No words can express my feelings when I observe the little girl eating mice.
当我看到小女孩吃老鼠时，任何语言都难以表达我的心情。

语法重点
名词变复数通常在词尾加 s 或 es，而此句中的 mice 是不规则名词复数形式，由 mouse 变形而来。

0636　obvious ['ɑːbviəs] **a** 显然的
It is obvious that he lost his nerve after trying to eat the snakes many times.
显然在多次尝试吃蛇肉之后，他丧失了勇气。

◎ nerve (P. 329)

0637　occasion [ə'keɪʒn] **n** 场合，时机，机会
By occasion of her illness, we can't go out for a picnic.
她生病了，所以我们不能去野餐了。
　opportunity 时机，机会　　on occasion 有时，间或

0638　odd [ɑːd] **a** 古怪的，奇数的
It was odd of her to eat ice-cream in winter.
她在冬天吃冰激凌，这太奇怪了。
　peculiar 奇怪的　　an odd fish 古怪的人，难以理解的人

语法重点
odd 常用于名词短语，an odd fish，意思是"奇怪的人"。

0639　onto ['ɑːntə] **prep** 到……之上，向……上
She emptied the bread onto the plate.
她把面包全部倒在了盘子上。

语法重点
介词 onto 所表达的意思为"到……上，向……上"，强调的是一个移动的过程，从一个位置移动到另一个位置，而 on 的意思则为"在……之上"，主要用于强调地点。

normal ~ ought

0640 operator [ˈɑːpəreɪtər] n 操作者，技工
The children don't notice the farm operator is standing behind them.
那些孩子没有注意到农场主人已经站在了他们的后面。

> 语法重点
> 介词 behind 最常用的用法就是用来表示方位，意为"在……之后"，其后一般加名词或代词。

0641 opportunity [ˌɑːpərˈtuːnəti] n 机会
He took the opportunity to eat up all the candies.
他借机吃光了所有的糖果。
▸ chance 机会　▸ take the opportunity to do sth. 借机做某事

0642 opposite [ˈɑːpəzət] a 相对的，对面的，对立的
The girl sitting opposite to me was eating a big banana.
坐在我对面的那个女孩在吃一根大香蕉。
▸ contrary 相反的　▸ one's opposite number 与自己相当的人
▸ opposite to... 在……对面

> 语法重点
> opposite to 用来表示一种方位，如例句中的 opposite to me 就表示"正对着我"。

0643 optimistic [ˌɑːptɪˈmɪstɪk] a 乐观的，乐观主义的
She is not optimistic about the soup she is cooking.
她对自己正在煮的汤并不感到乐观。
▸ pessimistic 悲观的　▸ stay optimistic 保持乐观

> 语法重点
> be optimistic about（对……乐观）后面一般要接名词或代词。

0644 origin [ˈɔːrɪdʒɪn] n 起源，来源，出身
There is no denying that he knows the origin of the custom that people eat raw fish.
不可否认，他知道人们吃生鱼这个风俗的起源。
▸ source 来源　▸ country of origin 原产地，原产国

0645 original [əˈrɪdʒənl] a 起初的，有独创性的
There is no doubt that the original version of this picture is destroyed during the banquet.
毫无疑问，在宴会期间，这幅画的原作被毁坏了。
▸ imitative 仿制的　▸ original edition 原版
▸ there is no doubt that... 毫无疑问……

> 语法重点
> 当不知道动作的发出者是谁时，可以用被动语态来表示。
> ⊃ version (P. 801)

0646 orphan [ˈɔːrfn] n 孤儿
Please feel free to see these orphans when they are having dinner.
在这些孤儿们用餐期间，请随时来看他们。
▸ an orphan asylum 孤儿院

0647 ought [ɔːt] aux 应该
You ought to be ashamed of yourself for eating up your sister's candies.
你吃光了妹妹的糖果，应该感到羞耻。
▸ should 应该　▸ ought to do... 应该做……　▸ be ashamed of... 为……而羞耻

⊃ ashamed (P. 397)

0648 outdoor ['aʊtdɔːr] **a** 户外的，野外的，露天的
They took a chance to have an outdoor banquet.
他们将冒险举行一场露天宴会。
⊘ indoor 室内的　⊘ take a chance to do sth. 冒险做某事

0649 outdoors [ˌaʊt'dɔːrz] **ad** 在户外，在野外，露天
Let's have coffee in the yard for it's as cool as a cucumber outdoors.
我们去院子里喝咖啡吧，因为室外非常凉爽。
⊘ alfresco 在户外　⊘ indoors 在室内
⊘ 在美式口语中，outdoors 还常用于 all outdoors，表示"全世界，所有的人"的意思。

⊃ cucumber (P. 421)

0650 outer ['aʊtər] **a** 外部的，外面的
He is particular about outer man.
他对外表很挑剔。
⊘ outer space 太空，外太空　⊘ be particular about... 对……很挑剔

⊂ particular (P. 200)

0651 outline ['aʊtlaɪn] **n** 外形，大纲　**v** 概述
I asked him to make an outline of the article when he got ready to have dinner.
当他准备吃饭时，我让他写文章的大纲。
⊘ profile 轮廓　⊘ program outline 计划纲要　⊘ get ready to... 准备……

⊂ article (P. 126)

0652 overcoat ['oʊvərkoʊt] **n** 大衣
Leave off your overcoat when you enter the room.
进房间时把你的大衣脱下来。
⊘ light overcoat 风衣　⊘ leave off... 脱下……

0653 owe [oʊ] **v** 欠……债，感激，把……归功于
I owe it to you that I have a chance to eat such delicious food.
多亏你，我才有机会吃到这么美味的食物。
⊘ pay 偿还　⊘ owe sb. a debt 欠某人债务
⊘ I owe it to you that... 多亏你，我才……

0654 ownership ['oʊnərʃɪp] **n** 所有权，所有制
The café is under new ownership, so I don't want to go there anymore.
那家咖啡馆已换了新主人，所以我不想再去了。
⊘ property 所有权　⊘ ... be under new ownership ……已换了新主人

0655 pad [pæd] **n** 垫子，垫料
The pad is impregnated with water and you can't put your computer on it.
垫子上都是水，你不能把电脑放在上面。
⊘ liner 衬垫　⊘ mouse pad 鼠标垫

0656 pail [peɪl] n 桶，一桶之量

What do you mean by throwing the pail away and refusing to have breakfast?
你把桶扔掉并且不吃早餐是什么意思？
- bucket 桶子
- What do you mean by...? 你……是什么意思？

语法重点
what do you mean by 后面要接动名词。

0657 pal [pæl] n 伙伴

What do you think of having dinner with my pal?
你觉得和我的朋友一起吃饭如何？
- friend 朋友
- What do you think of...? 你认为……怎么样？
- pal 是非正式用语，一般用在口语中。

0658 palace ['pæləs] n 宫殿，豪华住宅，大厦

The robbers broke into the palace after having supper in the restaurant.
劫匪们在餐厅吃过晚餐就闯入了宫殿。
- mansion 大厦
- break into... 闯入……

○ robber (P. 351)

0659 pale [peɪl] a 苍白的，无力的，暗淡的

What made you think that she turned pale because she saw the cockroach on the table?
是什么让你觉得，她脸色发白是因为看到了桌上的蟑螂？
- faint 虚弱的
- turn pale 变得苍白（脸色）

0660 pancake ['pænkeɪk] n 薄煎饼，烙饼

I was all set to eat the pancake when he called me.
他打电话给我时，我正准备吃煎饼。
- flat as a pancake 十分平坦
- be all set to... 准备就绪……

语法重点
be all set to 后面要接动词原形。

0661 panic ['pænɪk] n 惊恐 a 惊慌的，恐慌的

We were in panic when told that there was no water to drink.
当被告知没有水喝时，我们都很恐慌。
- feel panic 感到恐慌
- ... be in panic ……恐慌起来

0662 parade [pə'reɪd] n 游行，检阅，阅兵

She is making a parade of her big cake.
她在炫耀自己的大蛋糕。
- pageant 盛会
- on parade 在游行

语法重点
make a parade of （炫耀）一般表示贬义。

0663 paradise ['pærədaɪs] n 天堂，乐园

It's sheer paradise to have a big dinner after being hungry for a long time.
饿了很长时间后饱餐一顿，真是莫大的享受。
- heaven 天堂
- hell 地狱
- it's sheer paradise to... ……是莫大的享受

0664 parcel [ˈpɑːrsl] **n** 包裹，一块地 **v** 分配，打包
The waiter bound up the parcel of leftovers for me in the restaurant.
在餐厅里，服务生帮我把装有剩菜的包装袋打包好。

> 语法重点
> bind 是不规则动词，其过去式、过去分词都是 bound。

0665 participate [pɑːrˈtɪsɪpeɪt] **v** 参与
You can participate with us in these tables.
你们可以跟我们共用这些桌子。
- participate in... 参加……
- participate with... in... 和……共用……

> 语法重点
> participate with 后面要接表示人的名词或代词。

0666 passage [ˈpæsɪdʒ] **n** 通道，走廊
I was accosted by a beggar when I was eating a piece of bread near the passage.
我在走廊附近吃面包时，一个乞丐向我乞讨。
- corridor 走廊
- respiratory passage 呼吸道
- be accosted by... 被……乞讨

0667 passion [ˈpæʃn] **n** 热情，酷爱
He flied into a passion because his breakfast was eaten up by others.
他大发雷霆，因为他的早餐被别人吃掉了。
- have a passion for 对……有强烈的爱好
- ... fly into a passion ……大发雷霆
- the Passion 可以表示"耶稣在十字架上的受难"。

0668 passport [ˈpæspɔːrt] **n** 护照，手段，保障
Your passport is out of date.
你的护照过期了。
- passport control 入境检查
- ... be out of date ……过期

0669 password [ˈpæswɜːrd] **n** 密码
I changed the password of the safe to keep out any stealing documents in it.
我更换保险箱的密码，以防有人偷里面的文件。
- password card 口令卡
- keep out... 挡住……

> 语法重点
> keep out 也可以作为祈使句来独立使用，如"Keep out!"的意思就为"严禁入内！"。
> steal (P. 228)

0670 patience [ˈpeɪʃns] **n** 耐心
It is beyond my patience that she refused to have breakfast again.
她再次拒绝吃早餐，这让我无法忍受。
- impatience 不耐烦，急躁
- lose patience 失去耐心
- it is beyond my patience that... ……让我无法忍受

0671 pause [pɔːz] **v** / **n** 暂停，中止
The dish in front of him gave pause to him.
面前的这道菜让他犹豫不决。
- stop 中止
- proceed 继续进行
- at pause 停止，踌躇，沉默
- ... give pause to sb. ……让某人犹豫不决

0672 pave [peɪv] **v** 铺，铺设，安排
The floor of the hall is paved with marble.
大厅的地板是用大理石铺成的。
🔗 pave the way for... 为……创造条件、做准备　🔗 be paved with... 铺满……

0673 pavement ['peɪvmənt] **n** 人行道，路面
I came to grief on the pavement.
我在人行道上滑倒了。
🔗 sidewalk 人行道　🔗 rigid pavement 混凝土路面

> **语法重点**
> come to grief 的本意是"遭受不幸，受挫"，但在例句中可以翻译成滑倒了。
> ↪ grief (P. 449)

0674 paw [pɔː] **n** 脚爪，爪子
He wanted to make a cat's paw of you when you had dinner together just now.
刚才你们一起吃饭时，他想利用你。
🔗 claw 爪子　🔗 fish and bears paw 鱼和熊掌
🔗 make a cat's paw of... 利用……

0675 pay [peɪ] **n** 薪水，工资 **v** 支付，缴纳
He was under no compulsion to pay for the jewelry.
没人强迫他买这些珠宝。
🔗 salary 工资

> **语法重点**
> be under no compulsion 可以单独使用，后面也可以接动词不定式。

0676 pea [piː] **n** 豌豆
You tip the peas into the pan and we can eat them after about ten minutes.
你把豌豆荚倒进锅里，大约十分钟后我们就可以吃了。
🔗 pease 豌豆　🔗 green peas 青豆　🔗 tip... into... 把……倒入……

> **语法重点**
> pea 是可数名词。

0677 peak [piːk] **n** 山顶
Living up to your expectations, we climbed onto the mountain peak and had lunch there.
我们不负众望登上了山顶，并且在那里吃了午餐。
🔗 foot 山脚　🔗 peak and pine（因悲哀）憔悴，消瘦　🔗 live up to... 不辜负……

🔗 expectation (P. 292)

0678 pearl [pɜːrl] **n** 珍珠，珍品
It's not the time to buy pearls.
现在不是买珍珠的时间。
🔗 pearl necklace 珍珠项链

> **语法重点**
> it's not the time to（不是……的时候）后面接动词原形。

0679 peel [piːl] **v** 削皮 **n** 果皮
Peel the apple with care.
削苹果时要小心。
🔗 skin 剥皮　🔗 peel... off 脱掉……　🔗 do sth. with care 小心做某事

0680 **peep** [pi:p] v 偷看，窥视 n 瞥见，偷看
He took a peep of the girl and put the love letter in her bag.
他偷偷看了女孩一眼，然后把情书放在了她的书包里。
- peek 偷看，窥视   peep of day 晨曦，破晓
- take a peep of... 偷偷看……一眼

➤ letter (P. 058)

0681 **penny** ['peni] n 便士，美分
I don't want to make penny of these apples.
我不想用这些苹果换钱。
- make penny of sth. 用某物换钱

0682 **perform** [pər'fɔ:rm] v 表演，执行，履行
He delegated me to perform the task and have dinner with the guests.
他委派我去执行那项任务，并和客人们一起吃饭。
- execute 执行   delegate sb. to do sth. 委派某人做某事

➤ task (P. 233)

0683 **performance** [pər'fɔ:rməns] n 表演，履行，表现
The singers gave an excellent performance when we had a cup of tea.
我们喝茶的时候，歌星们进行了精彩的演出。

0684 **permission** [pər'mɪʃn] n 许可，允许，同意
They have permission to eat these peaches.
他们获准吃这些桃子。
- prohibition 禁止   ask for permission 请求许可
- have permission to... 得到许可……

0685 **permit** [pər'mɪt] v 容许，许可 n 许可证，执照
I would not permit that you eat the cake.
我不允许你吃蛋糕。
- prohibit 禁止，阻止   work permit 工作许可证

语法重点
I would not permit that（我不允许）后面接的句子要用虚拟语气。

0686 **personality** [,pɜ:rsə'næləti] n 个性，特色，名人
It takes a very patient personality to have dinner with such a naughty boy.
跟这么顽皮的男孩一起吃饭需要极大的耐性。
- individuality 个性

0687 **persuade** [pər'sweɪd] v 说服，劝说
I failed in my attempt to persuade him to have a cup of coffee with us.
我没能说服他和我们一起喝杯咖啡。
- advise 劝告   dissuade 劝阻，劝止
- I failed in my attempt to... 我没能……

peep ~ pity

0688 pest [pest] **n** 害虫，讨厌的人
I can't eat anything when I see the pests on the vegetables.
我一看到蔬菜上的害虫就吃不下饭。
▸ vermin 害虫　　▸ pest control 消灭有害动物

0689 pickle ['pɪkl] **n** 腌渍物，泡菜，困境
He had a rod in pickle for you because you ate his cookie.
你吃了他的饼干，所以他伺机惩罚你。
▸ in the pickle 处境困难　　▸ has a rod in pickle for... 伺机惩罚……

> 语法重点
> has a rod in pickle for 后面要接表示人的名词或者代词。

0690 pill [pɪl] **n** 药丸
I was out of patience with the pills, so please give me a bowl of water.
我对这些药忍无可忍，所以请给我一碗水。
▸ tablet 药片　　▸ a bitter pill 苦药丸，不能不做的苦事，不得不忍受的屈辱
▸ be out of patience with... 对……忍无可忍

> 语法重点
> pill 是可数名词。
> ▸ patience (P. 334)

0691 pilot ['paɪlət] **n** 飞行员，驾驶员，领航员
The pilot inquired about the weather condition and asked the waiter to bring him a cup of coffee.
飞行员询问了天气情况，然后让服务生给他一杯咖啡。
▸ aviator 飞行员　　▸ airline pilot 航空公司飞行员　　▸ inquire about... 询问……
▸ 短语 test pilot 可表示"试飞员"。

> ▸ waiter (P. 243)

0692 pine [paɪn] **n** 松树，松木 **v** 消瘦，渴望
We have planted up to fifty pine trees; now we need to drink some water.
我们已经种了五十棵松树，现在需要喝点儿水。
▸ pine tree 松树　　▸ pine away (因悲哀）憔悴、消瘦（而死亡）

> 语法重点
> up to（多达）可以直接放在数词之前进行修饰。

0693 pint [paɪnt] **n** 品脱
Let's go out for a pint tonight, shall we?
我们今晚出去喝一品脱啤酒，好吗？

0694 pit [pɪt] **n** 坑洞，矿井，陷阱
He worked all his life down the pit.
他一辈子在矿井下工作。
▸ mine 矿井　　▸ ... all one's life 一辈子

0695 pity ['pɪti] **n** 同情，遗憾 **v** 鄙视
I pity you if you ate their food without permission.
如果你未经允许就吃他们的食物，我就鄙视你。
▸ out of pity 出于同情，出于怜悯

> ▸ permission (P. 336)

337

0696 plastic ['plæstɪk] n 塑胶，塑胶制品 a 塑胶的，可塑的
I peel away the plastic wrapping of the food and begin to eat.
我撕掉食品的塑胶包装，开始吃起来。
mouldable 可塑的　plastic bag 塑胶袋　peel away... 剥掉……

0697 plenty ['plenti] n 充分，大量 a 充足的，相当多的
Well, I have apples in plenty to eat.
嗯，我有大量的苹果可以吃。
enough 充足的　plenty time 充分的时间　... in plenty 大量的……

0698 plug [plʌg] n 插头，插座 v 塞，堵
The statue seems like a plug and I don't want to buy it.
那个雕像看起来像插头，我不想买它。
safety plug 安全塞　seem like... 看起来像……

0699 plum [plʌm] n 李子，梅子
He took away the biggest apple and he always took all the plums.
他把最好的东西拿走了，他总是挑出最好的东西占为己有。
plum job 好工作，肥差　... take all the plums ……挑出最好的东西据为己有

> **语法重点**
> plum 是可数名词。

0700 plumber ['plʌmər] n 水管工
I was sympathetic with this plumber and invited him to have dinner with me.
我很同情那个水管工人，我请他和我一起吃饭。

> **语法重点**
> be sympathetic with（同情）后面要接表示人的名词或者代词。
> ⊃ sympathetic (P. 509)

0701 pole [poʊl] n 杆，柱，极点
You must have been up the pole to eat so many candies at a time.
你一次吃这么多糖果，一定是发疯了。
up the pole 处于困境

> **语法重点**
> you must have been up the pole 后面通常接动词不定式。

0702 political [pə'lɪtɪkl] a 政治的，政党的
The political leader will be memorized for his charity for good.
这个政治领袖的仁慈将会被永远铭记。
political power 政治权力　be memorized for... 因为……被铭记

> **语法重点**
> for good 该短语所表达的意思为"永久地"，用来修饰整个句子。
> ⊃ charity (P. 406)

0703 politician [ˌpɑ:lə'tɪʃn] n 政治家，政客
These politicians are hostile to the idea of having western food.
这些政治家们反对吃西餐。
statesman 政治家　be hostile to... 反对……

> **语法重点**
> be hostile to 中的 to 是介词，后面要接名词、代词或者动名词。

plastic ~ portion

0704 politics [ˈpɑːlətɪks] n 政治学，政见
He talked about the politics in excitement over dinner.
饭间，他兴奋地谈起了政治。
- ... in excitement 兴奋地……

> 语法重点
> in excitement 在句中常当作形容词来表示某种状态，相当于副词。
> ↻ excitement (P. 161)

0705 poll [poʊl] n 投票，票数
I took a straw poll among these people to find out how many people like to eat a durian.
我在这些人之间做了一个调查，看看有多少人喜欢吃榴莲。
- vote 投票
- opinion poll 民意测验
- take a straw poll among... 在……中做调查

0706 pollute [pəˈluːt] v 污染，弄脏
You are past hope to have a picnic near the polluted lake.
你们不可以在这被污染的湖泊附近野餐。
- contaminate 污染，弄脏
- be past hope to do sth. 没有希望做某事

> 语法重点
> past hope 就相当于形容词 hopeless。

0707 pony [ˈpoʊni] n 小马
I have a pity on the pony and feed it with my water.
我很同情那匹小马，并拿我的水喂它。
- have a pity on... 同情……

0708 pop [pɑːp] n 流行的，爆裂声
That musician who is having dinner specializes in pop music.
那个正在吃饭的音乐家专攻流行音乐。
- pop culture 流行文化，通俗文化
- specialize in... 专攻……

↻ specialize (P. 781)

0709 popular [ˈpɑːpjələr] a 流行的，通俗的，大众的
If this kind of food is not popular in the market, you'll have to start over again.
如果这种食品在市场上不受欢迎，你们就必须从头再来。
- fashionable 流行的
- unpopular 不流行的
- ... start over ……重新开始

0710 porcelain / china [ˈpɔːrsəlɪn] / [ˈtʃaɪnə] n 瓷，瓷器
I had never eaten an orange and gave it a whirl sitting beside the porcelain.
我从没吃过橘子，就坐在瓷器旁试着吃了一个。
- china 瓷器
- give... a whirl 尝试……

0711 portion [ˈpɔːrʃn] n 部分，一份
Give a portion of each day to read books.
每天抽一部分的时间来看书。
- part 部分
- a portion of... 一份……

339

0712 **portrait** [ˈpɔːrtrət] n 肖像画，描写
His portrait is painted on the other side of the food's packing bag.
食品包装袋的另一面印着他的肖像。
同 portraiture 肖像画　同 head portrait 头像

> 语法重点
> 名词 side 有"面"的意思，表示"在……的另一面"时，常用 on one side of 表示。

0713 **postage** [ˈpoʊstɪdʒ] n 邮资
What's the postage for sending the book to Taipei?
把这本书寄到台北需要多少钱？
同 postage certificate 邮资凭证　同 What's the postage for...? ……要多少钱？

0714 **poster** [ˈpoʊstər] n 海报，广告，装饰画
The poster was nipped to pieces by the boys.
海报被男孩子们撕成碎片。
同 placard 海报　同 poster board 广告板，海报板

> 语法重点
> poster 是可数名词。

0715 **postpone** [poʊˈspoʊn] v 延迟
The news that the banquet was postponed made us in a bad mood.
宴会延期的消息让我们感到心情低落。
同 delay 延迟　反 advance 提前

0716 **postponement** [poʊˈspoʊnmənt] n 延迟，延期
There were various indications that the weather led to the postponement of ceremony.
种种迹象表明，是天气原因导致了典礼的延迟。
同 delay 延期　同 recruitment postponement 延缓征聘

⊃ indication (P. 457)

0717 **pottery** [ˈpɑːtəri] n 陶器
They were thrilled to find that the pottery could be used for cooking.
他们因发现这个陶器可以用来煮饭而欣喜若狂。
同 ceramic 陶瓷　同 be thrilled to... 因……而欣喜若狂

> 语法重点
> be thrilled to 后面要接动词原形。

0718 **pour** [pɔːr] v 倒，倾泻
We have to pour a great amount of milk into the sink.
我们不得不把大量的牛奶倒进水槽里。
同 spew 喷涌　同 It never rains but it pours 不鸣则已，一鸣惊人。
同 as the consequence... 由于……

⊃ amount (P. 123)

0719 **poverty** [ˈpɑːvərti] n 贫穷，贫乏
She poured out the series of misfortunes that led her to poverty when we had dinner together.
我们一起吃饭时，她倾诉导致她贫困的一连串的不幸。

> 语法重点
> pour out 当"倾诉"讲时，后面接表示出某种情感的名词。

portrait ~ prevent

0720 powder ['paʊdər] **n** 粉，火药 **v** 涂粉
She indulges herself in powdering her face during dinner.
晚餐期间，她沉溺于往脸上扑粉。
🔵 indulge oneself in（沉溺于）一般指对某种情况成瘾而无法自拔。

↻ indulge (P. 583)

0721 practical ['præktɪkl] **a** 实用的，实际的，明智的
The scheme to have a picnic in the park seems on the surface to be quite practical.
去公园野餐的方案表面上看起来似乎很实际。
🔵 actual 实际的　🔵 impractical 不实际的
🔵 for (all) practical purposes 事实上　🔵 ... on the surface 表面上……

↻ scheme (P. 629)

0722 prayer [prer] **n** 祷告，乞求
If you want to drink water, kneel in prayer now.
如果你想喝水，就跪下祈祷吧。
🔵 blessing 祷告　🔵 prayer book 祈祷书　🔵 ... kneel in prayer ……跪下祈祷

0723 precious ['preʃəs] **a** 珍贵的
Don't waste your precious time in drinking and you should persist in your dream.
不要把你的宝贵时间浪费在喝酒上，你应该坚持你的梦想。
🔵 valued 宝贵的　🔵 valueless 无价值的　🔵 precious belongings 贵重物品

语法重点
persist in（坚持）后面常接名词或动名词。

0724 preparation [ˌprepə'reɪʃn] **n** 准备，预备
They are working around the clock in preparation for the celebration.
他们正在为庆典的准备工作而昼夜不停地忙碌着。
🔵 in preparation 在准备中　🔵 in preparation for... 为……做好准备

0725 pressure ['preʃər] **n** 压力，压迫
It took great strength to resist the pressure of the authorities and get more food.
顶住当局的压力以得到更多的食物费了很多力气。
🔵 burden 负担　🔵 under the pressure 在压力之下

语法重点
it took great strength to 后面要接动词原形。

0726 pretend [prɪ'tend] **v** 假装，装作
It is all the better if you just pretend not to have had breakfast.
如果你假装没有吃早餐会更好。
🔵 feign 假装，装作　🔵 it is all the better if... 如果……会更好

语法重点
pretend 表示"假装时"，指在言行上装出是真的。

0727 prevent [prɪ'vent] **v** 预防，防止，阻止
Be careful when you eat a fish to prevent injuries to your throat.
吃鱼时要小心，以避免对你的喉咙造成伤害。
🔵 block 阻止　🔵 permit 许可

↻ throat (P. 236)

0728 previous ['pri:viəs] a 先前的，先于，在……之前
Previous to that, I have already had a lot of food.
在那之前，我已经吃了很多食物。
- former 从前的 - following 接着的，下列的
- previous to that, ... 在那之前，……

0729 priest [pri:st] n 牧师，神父，教父
The priest began to pursue his art world since his childhood.
那个牧师从儿时起就开始追求他的艺术世界。
- godfather 教父 - high priest 主教

> 语法重点
> pursue for 常用来指事业上的追求。
> childhood (P. 271)

0730 primary ['praɪmeri] a 主要的，初级的
What do you find the hardest thing in a primary school?
你觉得在小学里最困难的事是什么？
- secondary 次要的 - primary school 小学

0731 probable ['prɑ:bəbl] a 很可能发生的，大概的
It is hardly probable that he has already met her.
他不可能已经见过她了。
- likely 很可能的 - improbable 不大可能的
- it is hardly probable that... ……不可能

> 语法重点
> probable 的副词形式是probably。

0732 process ['prɑ:ses] n 过程 v 加工，处理
Your coffee is in the process of being boiled.
你的咖啡还在煮。
- course 过程 - be in the process of... 在……的过程中

0733 product ['prɑ:dʌkt] n 产品，产物，结果
Our new product stands out in the market, so I want to treat you to dinner tonight.
我们的新产品从市场中脱颖而出，所以今晚我想请你们吃饭。
- manufacture 产品 - product quality 产品品质
- stand out 的本意为"站出来"，在此表示"脱颖而出"。

> treat (P. 239)

0734 profit ['prɑ:fɪt] n 利润，收益 v 得益，获利
Many customers profit from the food festival.
很多顾客都从这次的美食节中得益。
- benefit 利益 - at a profit 获利，赚钱 - profit from... 从……中获利

0735 program ['proʊɡræm] n 节目，程序，计划
This dish lends itself to the cater program very well.
这道菜非常适合那个美食节目。
- procedure 程序 - lend oneself to... 适合……

> 语法重点
> itself 与前面的 this dish 保持一致。

previous ~ pub

0736 promote [prəˈmoʊt] **v** 促进，促销，升迁

I was promoted to manager, so I wanted to invite you to dinner for celebration.
我被提拔为经理，想邀请你们一起吃饭庆祝。

同 boost 促进　反 degrade 降低　延 promote sales 促销，推销商品

> **语法重点**
> be promoted to（被提拔为）中的 to 是介词，后面接表示职位的名词。

0737 proof [pruːf] **n** 证据，证物，证明

He was busy talking with her and didn't take notice of the proof.
他正忙着和她说话，没有注意到证物。

同 evidence 证据，证明　延 take notice of... 注意……

> **语法重点**
> notice 既可以作名词，也可以作动词讲，作名词时常用于 take notice of 的短语结构中，介词 of 后加名词。

0738 proper [ˈprɑːpər] **a** 适当的，正当的，真正的

It is proper that you should ask your mother if she has had supper.
你当然应该问问你的母亲，她是否已经吃晚餐了。

同 suitable 适当的　反 improper 不合适的　延 proper time 适当的时候

> **语法重点**
> it is proper that（应该）后面的句子一般要用虚拟语气。

0739 property [ˈprɑːpərti] **n** 财产，所有物，地产

My prime concern is to protect my property.
我最关心的是保护自己的财产。

同 public property 公共财产　延 my prime concern is to... 我最关心的是……

0740 proposal [prəˈpoʊzl] **n** 提议，建议，求婚

We are in two minds whether to accept his proposal to have a cup of coffee now.
他提议现在去喝一杯咖啡，我们对此犹豫不决。

同 suggestion 建议　延 ... be in two minds ……犹豫不决

0741 protection [prəˈtekʃn] **n** 保护，防卫

You can pick these persimmons and eat them under the protection of me.
你可以在我的保护下摘些柿子吃。

同 conservation 保护　反 invasion 侵犯
延 under the protection of... 在……的保护下

> **语法重点**
> persimmon 意思是"柿子"，是可数名词。

0742 protective [prəˈtektɪv] **a** 保护的，防卫的

It is obligatory for you to wear protective clothing when you work there.
你们在那里工作时，必须穿防护服装。

反 aggressive 侵略性的　延 protective clothing 防护衣

> **语法重点**
> protective 的副词形式是 protectively。
> 参 clothing (P. 141)

0743 pub [pʌb] **n** 酒吧，酒馆

Some people set on him when he drank in a pub.
他在一家小酒馆喝酒时，一些人把他揍了一顿。

延 set on... 袭击……

343

0744 punch [pʌntʃ] v 以拳头重击 n 打孔器，钻孔机
If you can fix the punch up, I will treat you a cup of coffee.
如果你能修理好那个打孔器，我会请你喝一杯咖啡。
- batter 猛击
- punch out 下班打卡

语法重点
I will treat you（我会请你）后面通常接名词。

0745 pure [pjʊr] a 纯粹的，纯的，纯洁的
He has never eaten western food, but it was pure guesswork on our part.
他从没吃过西餐，不过这纯属我们的猜测。
- stainless 纯洁的
- impure 不纯洁的
- ... on one's part ……就某人而言

⊙ western (P. 245)

0746 pursue [pərˈsuː] v 追补，追逐，从事
We should stand off those people who just drink to pursue pleasure.
我们要远离那些只会喝酒取乐的人。
- chase 追逐
- pursue after 追赶
- stand off... 远离……

0747 quarrel [ˈkwɔːrəl] v / n 争吵
I know your quarrel comes down to your eating habits.
我知道归根究底你们是为了不同的饮食习惯而吵架。
- quarrel about... 为……争吵
- come down to... 归根究底……

语法重点
come down to 后面要接表示原因的名词。

0748 queer [kwɪr] a 奇怪的，可疑的
I am queer for hamburgers these days.
我这几天迷上了吃汉堡。
- strange 奇怪的
- normal 正常的
- queer fish 怪人
- be queer for... 迷上……，一般用在美国俚语中。

0749 quote [kwoʊt] v 引用，引述，报价
I was impressed by the example he quoted at table.
我对他吃饭时举的那个例子印象深刻。
- cite 引用
- quote from... 引用自……
- be impressed by... 对……印象深刻

语法重点
quote 也可以当名词，意思是"引用，报价"，也可以表示"引号"，一般要用其复数形式。

0750 racial [ˈreɪʃl] a 种族的，人种的
Let me fill you in on what a victim of racial prejudice eats and drinks now.
让我来告诉你，种族偏见的受害者现在吃什么以及喝什么。
- ethnic 种族的
- racial discrimination 种族歧视

⊙ prejudice (P. 759)

0751 radar [ˈreɪdɑːr] n 雷达
Can I remind you to be careful with the radar when you go out?
我能提醒你，出去时要小心雷达吗？
- Can I remind you to...? 我能提醒你……?

0752 rag [ræg] **n** 破布，碎布，破衣服
Don't lose your rag if he refuses to eat the buns you make.
如果他不吃你做的馒头，你不要发脾气。
- in rags 衣衫褴褛　　- lose one's rag 发脾气

> 语法重点
> rag 表示"破衣服"的时候，要用复数形式。

0753 raisin ['reɪzn] **n** 葡萄干
There is no doubt about his eating up the raisins.
毫无疑问，是他吃完了葡萄干。
- there is no doubt about... 毫无疑问……

> 语法重点
> raisin 是可数名词。

0754 rank [ræŋk] **n** 等级，阶层 **v** 排列，分等级
He was demoted to the rank of ordinary soldier because of drinking.
因为喝酒，他被降为普通士兵。
- degree 等级，阶层　　- social rank 社会等级　　- be demoted to... 被降为……

> ordinary (P. 198)

0755 rate [reɪt] **n** 比率，速度，价格
The apple price is going down at the rate of one dollar per kilogram.
苹果价格以每千克一美元的速度往下降。
- price 价格　　- rate of exchange 汇率　　- at the rate of... 以……的速度

0756 raw [rɔː] **a** 生的，未加工的，不熟练的
I have told you that raw meat must be kept separate from cooked one.
我告诉过你生肉和熟肉必须分开存放。
- crude 未加工的　　- ripe 熟的　　- raw material 原料

> separate (P. 220)

0757 ray [reɪ] **n** 光线，射线，辐射
By this time, there's still a ray of hope for them to eat the barbecue.
到这时，他们仍有一线希望吃到烤肉。
- beam 光线　　- a ray of hope 一线希望　　- by this time, ... 到这时，……

0758 razor ['reɪzər] **n** 剃刀，刮胡刀
Don't fool with that razor when you have dinner.
吃饭时别玩弄那把剃刀。
- shiv 剃刀　　- shaving razor 剃须刀　　- fool with... 玩弄……
- razor 也常用在短语 on a razor's edge 中，表示"处于紧要关头"。

0759 react [riˈækt] **v** 反应，反攻
What will the boy react to your suggestion that we travel together?
那个男孩对你提出的我们一起旅行的建议有什么反应？
- respond 反应　　- react against 反抗　　- react to... 对……做出反应

> 语法重点
> react to 中的 to 是介词。

0760 **reaction** [ri'ækʃn] **n** 反应，回应，反动
My first reaction is to have a mouthful of water right away.
我的第一反应就是赶紧喝一口水。
- response 反应   - chemical reaction 化学反应

0761 **reasonable** ['riːznəbl] **a** 合理的，通情达理的
She is reasonable in her demands to eat in a famous restaurant.
她提出去有名餐厅用餐的要求是合情合理的。
- unreasonable 不合理的

0762 **receipt** [rɪ'siːt] **n** 收据，收条
I am in receipt of your parcel which is full of nuts.
我收到了你那个装满坚果的包裹。
- goods receipt 货物收据   - be in receipt of... 收到了……

➡ parcel (P. 334)

0763 **receiver** [rɪ'siːvər] **n** 收件人，听筒，接收器
He put down the bread and took up the receiver.
他放下面包，拿起电话听筒。
- acceptor 接受者   - take up... 拿起……

0764 **recognize** ['rekəgnaɪz] **v** 认出，意识到
There's no point in recognizing the stolen apple among these fruits.
从这堆水果中认出那个被偷的苹果毫无意义。
- deny 否认   - speech recognition 语音辨识
- there's no point in... ……毫无意义

语法重点
there's no point in 后面一般要接动名词。

0765 **recorder** [rɪ'kɔːrdər] **n** 录音机，记录仪
Would it be correct to use the recorder?
我们用这个记录仪是正确的吗？
- video recorder 录影机   - Would it be correct to...? ……正确吗？

0766 **recover** [rɪ'kʌvər] **v** 重新获得
The patient has an intense will to recover, if so he can drink with his friends.
那个病人热切地希望恢复健康，这样他就能和朋友一起喝酒了。
- retrieve 恢复   - relapse 复发   - recover oneself 恢复常态
- have an intense will to... 热切地希望……
- recover 多指丢掉的东西又重新得到。

➡ intense (P. 461)

0767 **reduce** [rɪ'duːs] **v** 减轻，缩小
You should reduce your intake of salt bit by bit.
你应该逐渐减少摄取食盐的量。
- decrease 减少   - increase 增加，加大   - do sth. bit by bit 逐渐做某事

0768 regional [ˈriːdʒənl] **a** 地区的，局部的，当地的
He was implicated in the regional conflict.
他被卷入地区冲突中。
- local 当地的　- regional government 地方政府

语法重点
be implicated in（卷入……中）后面所加的成分通常表示一种不好的情况。
⊃ conflict (P. 144)

0769 regret [rɪˈgret] **v** / **n** 后悔，惋惜，遗憾
I came to regret not having breakfast.
我开始后悔没有吃早餐。
- content 使满足　- regret doing 对做过的事情表示遗憾、后悔

0770 relate [rɪˈleɪt] **v** 和……有关
I find it hard to relate this little animal with a delicious dish.
我很难把这种小动物与美味的菜肴联系起来。
- narrate 叙述　- strange to relate 说也奇怪
- relate... with... 把……与……联系起来

0771 relax [rɪˈlæks] **v** 放松
Have a cup of coffee to relax yourself in due time.
在恰当的时机，喝杯咖啡来放松自己。
- loosen 放松　- tighten 绷紧　- relax oneself 放松自己

语法重点
in due time（在恰当的时机）一般用在句尾，有时也可以用在句首或句中。

0772 release [rɪˈliːs] **v** 释放，发行 **n** 释放，免除
I will release you from these unsavory foods.
我不会让你再吃这些难吃的食物了。

0773 reliable [rɪˈlaɪəbl] **a** 可靠的，可信赖的
I heard from a reliable source that you had nothing to eat.
我从一位可靠人士那儿获悉，你没有东西可以吃。
- dependable 可靠的　- unreliable 不可靠的　- reliable news 可靠消息

⊃ source (P. 225)

0774 relief [rɪˈliːf] **n** 解除，缓解
It is a great relief to have something to eat after the famine.
饥荒后能有东西吃真是让人松一口气。

0775 religion [rɪˈlɪdʒən] **n** 宗教，宗教信仰
My religion was a crutch to me when I suffered from hunger.
饥饿的时候，宗教信仰可以在精神上支撑我。
- freedom of religion 宗教自由　- be a crutch to... 是……的支柱

语法重点
religion 当"宗教"讲时是可数名词，当"宗教信仰"讲时，是不可数名词。

0776 religious [rɪˈlɪdʒəs] **a** 宗教的，虔诚的
He is in a trancelike state of religious ecstasy.
他的宗教狂热已使他处于恍惚之中。
- devout 虔诚的　- secular 世俗的　- religious culture 宗教文化

⊃ ecstasy (P. 712)

0777 **rely** [rɪ'laɪ] V 依赖，信任
He can cook and doesn't rely upon others.
他自己会煮饭，不依赖他人。
⊙depend 依靠，信赖　⊙rely on... 依赖……　⊙rely upon... 依靠……

0778 **remain** [rɪ'meɪn] V 余留，保持
You should eat less to cut back on expenditure and remain solvent.
你们应该少吃点儿以减少开支，以备急用。
⊙continue 仍旧，继续　⊙remain silent 保持沉默　⊙cut back on... 削减……

> 语法重点
> remain 后面一般要接形容词。

0779 **remind** [rɪ'maɪnd] V 提醒
I always remind myself that I should eat less.
我总是提醒自己要少吃。
⊙recollect 想起　⊙remind yourself 提醒自己
⊙remind 也常用在 that reminds me 中，意思是"我想起来了"，用来转换话题。

0780 **remote** [rɪ'moʊt] a 遥远的，偏僻的，远程的
The people who abide in the remote village still eat raw meat.
住在偏远村子的那些人仍然吃生肉。
⊙distant 遥远的　⊙remote education 远程教育　⊙abide in... 住在……

⊃ abide (P. 521)

0781 **remove** [rɪ'muːv] V 去掉，免除，搬迁
After lunch you can remove the cloth from the table.
午餐后，你可以把布从桌子上拿走。
⊙eliminate 消除　⊙replace 替换　⊙remove... from... 把……从……拿走

0782 **renew** [rɪ'nuː] V 更新，恢复
The most important thing is to renew your health and stop drinking in future.
最重要的是要恢复健康，并且以后要戒酒。
⊙refresh 恢复　⊙renew a friendship 重修旧好

> 语法重点
> the most important thing is 后面一般要接动词不定式。

0783 **rent** [rent] n 租金 V 出租，租用
The first thing to do is to rent an apartment.
第一件要做的事就是租一套公寓。
⊙lease 出租　⊙for rent 招租的，供租用的

⊃ apartment (P. 124)

0784 **repair** [rɪ'per] V / n 修理，补救
We can have a cup of tea when your bike is under repair.
你的脚踏车还在修理中，我们可以喝杯茶。
⊙mend 修理　⊙in good repair 维修良好　⊙be under repair ……在修理中

0785 replace [rɪˈpleɪs] v 取代，替换，偿还

We undertake to replace the ring if she don't like it.
如果她不喜欢这个戒指，我们保证退换。

- replace by... 取代，以……代替
- undertake to... 保证……

replace 是最普通用词，指任何形式的替代，尤指以新的替代旧的、老的和坏的等，指人指物均可。

➪ undertake (P. 797)

0786 replacement [rɪˈpleɪsmənt] n 取代，更换

It's hard to find a replacement for this assistant.
很难找到另一个人来代替这名助理。

- substitute 代替
- joint replacement 关节置换术

语法重点
find a replacement for（找一个替代品）后面可以接人，也可以接物。

0787 represent [ˌreprɪˈzent] v 代表，表现，象征

She was picked out from the staff to represent them to go to the banquet.
从全体员工中选出她来作为代表去参加宴会。

- delegate 委派为代表
- represent for... 代表……，象征……

0788 representative [ˌreprɪˈzentətɪv] a 代表的 n 典型

We need no more representatives other than you to go out for a picnic.
除了你之外，我们不需要别的代表外出野餐。

- delegate 代表
- legal representative 法人代表

0789 republic [rɪˈpʌblɪk] n 共和国，共和政体

We offer foods and water to the poor foreigners on behalf of the republic.
我们代表共和国，给这些可怜的外国人提供食物和水。

- commonwealth 共和国
- monarchy 君主政体
- parliamentary republic 议会共和国
- on behalf of... 代表……

➪ behalf (P. 530)

0790 request [rɪˈkwest] v / n 要求，请求

It is absurd that they should deny my request to offer them food.
他们拒绝我向他们提供食物的要求，真是荒唐。

- demand 要求
- grant 同意
- at one's request 应某人之请求

语法重点
it is absurd that（是荒唐的）后面的句子要用虚拟语气。

0791 reserve [rɪˈzɜːrv] v 保留，预订 n 候补，储存

The boy who is standing there has a reserve of talent.
站在那里的那个男孩有着极大的天赋。

- material reserve 物资准备
- have a reserve of... 有着极大的……

语法重点
reserve 前面可以用形容词来修饰，如 have a huge reserve of（有着极大的……）。

0792 resist [rɪˈzɪst] v 抵抗，抵制，反抗

He resisted eating bananas on that day.
那天他非常抗拒吃香蕉。

- rebel 反抗
- obey 服从
- resist doing sth. 抗拒做某事

0793 resource [ˈriːsɔːrs] n 资源，机敏，才干
If you don't save money, you will be lost without resource.
如果你不节省，你就会彻底完蛋。
🔄 natural resource 自然资源　　🔄 ... be lost without resource ……彻底完蛋

0794 respond [rɪˈspɑːnd] v 回答，反应
When I asked whether he had had breakfast, he was noticeably slow to respond.
当我问他是否已经吃过早餐时，他明显反应迟缓。
🔄 answer 回答　　🔄 ask 询问　　🔄 respond with 回复

> 语法重点
> noticeably 是副词，意思是"明显地"，修饰 slow。

0795 response [rɪˈspɑːns] n 回答，回应，答复
Her silence was a response to your invitation for dinner.
她的沉默就是对你邀请她吃饭的答复。
🔄 reply 回答　　🔄 enquiry 询问　　🔄 positive response 肯定回答

> 语法重点
> be a response to（是对……的回答）中的 to 是介词。

0796 responsibility [rɪˌspɑːnsəˈbɪləti] n 责任，职责，责任心
I have no responsibility to fulfill your needs of buying expensive clothing.
我没有责任来满足你买昂贵衣服的需要。
🔄 duty 责任　　🔄 have no responsibility to... 没有责任……

0797 restrict [rɪˈstrɪkt] v 限制，约束
I was restricted to drink one bottle of soda drinks every day in case of gaining weight last month.
为了防止增胖，我上个月被限制每天只能喝一瓶苏打饮料。
🔄 confine 限制　　🔄 unfetter 释放，使自由　　🔄 be restricted to... 被限制……

0798 reveal [rɪˈviːl] v 显示，透露，揭示
For pity's sake, don't reveal your identity before he has finished his lunch.
求求你，在他吃完午餐前，不要透露你的身份。
🔄 disclose 透露　　🔄 conceal 隐藏，隐瞒　　🔄 reveal secret 揭露秘密

🔗 identity (P. 208)

0799 ribbon [ˈrɪbən] n 丝带，缎带
The ribbon beside his bag is in similarity with mine.
他的袋子旁的那条丝带跟我的相似。
🔄 banderole 丝带　　🔄 in similarity with... 和……相似

🔗 similarity (P. 359)

0800 rid [rɪd] v 摆脱，除去
He drank some water to rid himself of thirst.
他喝了点水来解渴。
🔄 free 使自由　　🔄 be rid of... 摆脱……　　🔄 rid oneself of... 摆脱……

0801 **riddle** ['rɪdl] n 谜语 v 解谜，出谜题
Where he lived during those days was a complete riddle.
他那几天住在哪里完全是一个谜。

0802 **ripe** [raɪp] a 成熟的，熟的
The apples are ripe for eating.
这些苹果成熟了，可以吃了。
- mature 成熟的
- raw 生的
- be ripe for... 是……的时候

0803 **risk** [rɪsk] n 风险 v 冒险
He finished these tasks at the risk of his life.
他冒着生命危险完成了这些任务。
- danger 危险
- safety 安全
- at risk 有危险
- at the risk of... 冒着……的危险

0804 **roar** [rɔːr] v / n 吼叫，咆哮
He is roaring at his daughter because she refuses to drink milk.
女儿不喝牛奶，所以他正在对她咆哮。
- clamor 叫嚣
- roar at... 对……咆哮

语法重点
roar at 后面一般接表示人的名词或者代词。
refuse (P. 214)

0805 **roast** [roʊst] n 烘烤
Well, I think the roast hen is done to a turn.
嗯，我认为这鸡烤得正到火候。
- roast chicken 烤鸡
- ... be done to a turn ……烤得正到火候

0806 **rob** [rɑːb] v 抢劫，掠夺
They formed a plot to rob the bakery.
他们制订抢劫那家面包店的计划。
- plunder 抢劫
- form a plot to... 制订……的秘密计划

语法重点
rob 是及物动词。

0807 **robber** ['rɑːbər] n 强盗，盗贼
The robber was captured alive when I was having breakfast.
我在吃早餐时，强盗被活捉了。
- bandit 强盗
- suspected robber 抢劫嫌疑犯

0808 **robbery** ['rɑːbəri] n 抢劫案，盗取
Doesn't the man who is drinking look like that robber who's wanted for the jewel robbery?
那个喝酒的人像不像那个因抢劫珠宝而受到通缉的罪犯？
- theft 盗窃
- be wanted for... 因为……被通缉
- robbery 也常用在短语 daylight robbery 中，意思是"明目张胆的掠夺"。

0809 robe [roʊb] n 长袍，睡袍

He was clad in a rich robe encrusted with jewels when we had dinner together.
我们一起吃饭时，他身穿一件镶满宝石的华贵礼袍。
同 cope 长袍　　work robe 工作袍　　句 be clad in... 穿着……

> 语法重点
> rich 一般指"富裕的"，在例句中，rich 的意思是"华丽的"，修饰 robe。

0810 rocket ['rɑːkɪt] n 火箭　v 快速上升，猛增

The rocket will be lifted off after they come back.
他们回来后，火箭就会发射。
反 decline 下降　　词 get a rocket 受到严厉斥责

> 语法重点
> lift off 表达的意思为"起飞，发射"，通常用来表示火箭或导弹等的发射升空。

0811 romantic [roʊ'mæntɪk] a 浪漫的，传奇的，不切实际的

The girl has a romantic nature.
那个女孩天生多情。
同 amorous 多情的　　反 realistic 现实的　　词 romantic love 浪漫爱情

0812 rot [rɑːt] v / n 腐败，枯朽

It is perfect rot to believe him.
相信他才简直是荒唐。
同 decay 腐烂　　词 the rot sets in 情况开始变坏

> 语法重点
> it is perfect rot（真是荒唐）后面通常接动词不定式。

0813 rotten ['rɑːtn] a 腐化的，变质的

The morals of the man are rotten to the core.
那个男人道德败坏至极。
同 decayed 腐烂的　　反 fresh 新鲜的
词 a rotten apple 讨厌的家伙　　句 ... be rotten to the core ……坏到了极致

0814 rough [rʌf] a 粗糙的，艰难的

According to the rough estimate, he has eaten about one hundred grapes.
根据粗略的估计，他已经吃了近一百个葡萄。

↪ estimate (P. 437)

0815 routine [ruː'tiːn] n 例行公事，常规　a 例行的

I got myself bogged down in routine work and even had no time to have dinner.
日常事务把我绊住了，我甚至没有时间吃饭。
词 routine work 例行公事，常规作业

0816 rug [rʌg] n 小地毯，毯子

He reclined on a rug eating some potato chips.
他躺在地毯上吃薯片。
同 carpet 地毯　　句 recline on... 躺在……　　词 rug 一般指比较小的地毯。

↪ potato (P. 207)

0817 **rumor** ['ruːmər] n 谣言，传闻
Rumor has it that he doesn't eat meat.
有谣言说他不吃肉。
  gossip 传闻   rumor has it that... 有谣言说……

> **语法重点**
> rumor has it that 后面的句子可用各种时态。

0818 **rust** [rʌst] n 铁锈 v （使）生锈
These spoons will corrode with rust if you never use them to have soup.
如果你不用这些汤匙喝汤的话，它们就会因生锈而损坏。
  patination 生锈   rust remover 除锈剂
  ... corrode with rust ……因生锈而损坏

0819 **rusty** ['rʌsti] a 生锈的，荒废的
The girl in blue skirt is rusty in chess.
那个穿蓝色裙子的女孩对象棋生疏。
  go rusty 生疏   be rusty in... 在……方面生疏

> **语法重点**
> rusty 的比较级、最高级分别是 rustier, rustiest。
> chess (P. 138)

0820 **sack** [sæk] n 粗布袋，床铺 v 解雇，洗劫
Have your supper and hit the sack as early as possible.
吃完晚餐，早点上床睡觉。

0821 **sake** [seɪk] n 缘故，目的，利益
For God's sake, he didn't eat anything all day.
天啊，他一整天都没吃东西。
  reason 理由   for the sake of... 为了……的利益，为了

> **语法重点**
> for God's sake（天啊）可以放在句首或句尾。

0822 **satisfactory** [ˌsætɪsˈfæktəri] a 令人满意的
All in all, the dish you have cooked is very satisfactory.
整体来说，你煮的这道菜令人非常满意。
  content 满意的   unsatisfactory 不满意的

> **语法重点**
> all in all（整体来说）通常放在句首作插入语，主要用来表示一种总结性的概括。

0823 **saucer** ['sɔːsər] n 托盘，碟子
She put the saucer of milk on the table by the fire.
她把那碟牛奶放在炉边的桌子上。
  dish 碟子   ... by the fire ……在火炉旁

> **语法重点**
> 介词 by 含有"在……旁边，贴近，靠近"之意，用来表示某种位置关系。

0824 **sausage** ['sɔːsɪdʒ] n 腊肠
Considering that he has a big stomach, the sausage is for him.
考虑到他的胃口比较大，那根香肠归他了。
  wurst 香肠   ... be for sb. ……给某人

> **语法重点**
> considering 通常用来引导条件状语从句，用来表示某种条件。

0825 **saving** ['seɪvɪŋ] n 救助，储蓄，节省
It will be a saving to take a bus.
乘公交车能省钱。
  economy 节约   expense 开支

0826 scale [skeɪl] n 刻度，等级，规模
I think the value of the card my son made cannot be weighed in the scale of dollars and cents.
我儿子做的卡片的价值无法用金钱来衡量。
- dimensions 规模　- full scale 全尺寸　- in the scale of... 用……来衡量

0827 scarce [skers] a 稀少的，罕见的
Food and water are scarce with us.
我们缺少食物和水。
- scanty 缺乏的　- plentiful 丰富的　- be scarce with... ……缺少

> **语法重点**
> be scarce with 后面要接表示人的名词或者代词。
> - food (P. 041)

0828 scarecrow ['skerkroʊ] n 稻草人，可怕但无害的人
The little boys are frightened of the scarecrow.
那些小男孩很怕这个稻草人。
- jackstraw 稻草人　- be frightened of... 害怕……

> **语法重点**
> be frightened at 也可以表示"害怕"，但侧重于"突然吓了一跳"的含义。

0829 scarf [skɑːrf] n 围巾，披巾
The red scarf of the girl who is sitting there made her stick out.
那个坐在那里的女孩戴的那条红围巾使她显得很突出。

> **语法重点**
> scarf 的复数形式有两个，即 scarfs, scarves。

0830 scary ['skeri] a 骇人的，容易受惊的
How did she watch the scary movie and drink a cup of coffee calmly?
她是如何做到边看恐怖电影边镇定地喝咖啡的？
- chilling 使人恐惧的　- a scary movie 恐怖电影
- How did... do...? ……如何做到……？

0831 scatter ['skætər] v 散布，散开，驱散
Tell the children not to scatter about the banana peels.
告诉孩子们不要随地乱丢香蕉皮。
- disperse 驱散　- gather 收集，聚集　- scatter about... 乱丢……

0832 schedule ['skedʒuːl] n 时刻表，计划　v 计划，安排
If you hurry up, you will keep up with the new time schedule.
如果你快一点，就能赶上新的时间表。
- time-table 时间表　- a train schedule 火车时刻表
- keep up with... 赶上……

0833 scholar ['skɑːlər] n 学者，奖学金获得者
Some scholars turned against his opinion that people should eat less salt.
一些学者转而反对他提出的那个观点，即人们应该少吃盐。
- academic 学者　- turn against... 转而反对……

> **语法重点**
> scholar 是可数名词。
> - opinion (P. 198)

0834 scholarship [ˈskɑːlərʃɪp] n 奖学金，学问，学识

I set the goal to win the first scholarship and treat my parents a big dinner.

我设定目标，要赢得一等奖学金并请父母大吃一顿。

- fellowship 奖学金
- set the goal to... 定下目标……

语法重点
名词 goal 为"目标"之意，通常指一个人设定的要努力去达到的生活目标。

0835 scientific [ˌsaɪənˈtɪfɪk] a 科学的

She aspires to a scientific research.

她有志于一项科学研究。

- unscientific 不科学的
- aspire to... 有志于……

语法重点
aspire to 中的 to 也可以替换为 after。

0836 scoop [skuːp] n 勺子，独家新闻 v 挖空，舀取

Don't take using a scoop to have soup for granted.

不要认为喝汤用勺子是理所当然的。

- dip 舀
- scoop out 挖出
- take... for granted 认为……理所当然

语法重点
take... for granted 中间的省略号处要接名词、代词或者动名词。

0837 scout [skaʊt] n 童子军，侦查员 v 侦查，物色

He was mistaken for an enemy scout and nobody gave him foods to eat.

他被误认为是敌人的侦察兵，没有人给他食物吃。

语法重点
be mistaken for（被误认为）后面要接名词或者名词短语。

- enemy (P. 160)

0838 scream [skriːm] v 尖叫，发出刺耳声 n 尖叫声

I roared out her name to make her stop screaming and have something to eat.

我大吼她的名字，以让她停止尖叫并吃点东西。

- shriek 尖叫
- scream out 尖声喊叫，大叫
- roar out... 吼出……

0839 screw [skruː] n 螺丝，螺钉 v 拧紧

You should screw up your courage and finish the project.

你们应该打起精神完成这个项目。

- fasten 扣紧
- unscrew 旋松
- screw in 把……拧入
- screw up... 鼓舞……

0840 scrub [skrʌb] v 擦掉 n 灌木丛，擦洗

I got cream on my dress when I ate the cake and it wouldn't scrub off.

我吃蛋糕时连衣裙沾上了奶油，擦不掉了。

- scrub out 擦掉
- scrub off... ……擦掉

语法重点
scrub off 用主动形式表示被动的意思。

0841 seal [siːl] n 海豹，封条，印章 v 密封，盖印

No one can tear off the seal and eat in the restaurant without permission.

未经允许，没有人可以撕掉封条，并且在那家餐厅里吃饭。

- print 印章
- seal off 封闭，把……封锁起来

语法重点
without permission（未经允许）通常用于句尾。

0842 **secondary** ['sekənderi] a 第二的，从属的
Whether he has had his breakfast is a question of secondary importance.
他是否吃早餐是个次要的问题。
⊕ minor 次要的　⊗ primary 主要的

0843 **security** [sə'kjʊərəti] n 安全，保证，证券
He quickly ate up those snacks at the time when the security men entered.
保安人员进来的那一刻，他迅速吃掉了那些点心。
⊕ safety 安全　⊗ danger 危险　⊕ security force 保安部队

> **语法重点**
> at the time when（在……的时候）主要用来强调时间点，在某一刻发生了某事。

0844 **seek** [siːk] v 寻找，追求，试图
I have never sought to hide my idea when I want to eat something.
想吃东西时，我从不企图隐瞒自己的想法。
⊕ pursue 追求　⊕ seek refuge 寻求避难，寻求庇护

> **语法重点**
> seek 是不规则动词，其过去式、过去分词都是 sought。

0845 **seize** [siːz] v 抓，夺取，利用
Seize this opportunity to do whatever you like and I will be on your side.
抓住这个机会尽情做你喜欢的任何事情吧，我会支持你的。
⊕ grasp 抓住　⊗ loosen 松开　⊕ seize a chance 抓住机会

> **语法重点**
> on one's side（支持某人）主要表示一种情感上的态度。
> ⊕ opportunity (P. 331)

0846 **seldom** ['seldəm] ad 很少，难得
It is seldom that he eats so many candies.
他很少吃这么多糖果。
⊕ rarely 很少，难得　⊕ seldom or never 简直不，极难得

0847 **sensible** ['sensəbl] a 可感觉的，明智的，合情理的
No one was sensible of his suffering from hunger.
没人察觉到他正在挨饿。
⊕ be sensible of... 察觉到……

> **语法重点**
> sensible 的副词形式是 sensibly。

0848 **sensitive** ['sensətɪv] a 敏感的，灵敏的
If you don't eat the bread she bakes, it's difficult to avoid stepping on her sensitive feelings.
如果你不吃她烤的面包，就难免会伤害她脆弱的情感。

> **语法重点**
> it's difficult to avoid（很难避免）后面一般接动名词。

0849 **separation** [ˌsepə'reɪʃn] n 分离，分开，分居
After a long separation, they had a dinner happily together.
阔别多年后，他们一起愉快地吃了顿饭。
⊕ detachment 分离　⊕ after a long separation, ... 阔别多年后，……

> **语法重点**
> separation 当"分居"讲是不可数名词。

0850 **sew** [soʊ] v 缝上，缝纫
When he ate the boiled egg, his mother sewed some money into his coat.
他吃水煮鸡蛋时，妈妈把一些钱缝进了他的大衣里。
● sew together 缝合在一起　● sew... into... 把……缝进……

语法重点
sew 的过去式是 sewed, 过去分词有两个，sewed 和 sewn。

0851 **sex** [seks] n 性，性欲
I take it he likes to talk about sex during meeting.
我认为他喜欢在开会时谈论性。
● "与某人发生性关系" 可以用 have sex with sb. 来表示。

0852 **sexual** ['sekʃuəl] a 性欲的，性别的
I heard that the man is a person of gross sexual appetites.
我听说那个男人是个性欲旺盛的人。
● sexual relations 两性关系

↻ appetite (P. 125)

0853 **sexy** ['seksi] a 性感的，引起性欲的
He ended up having supper with a sexy girl.
他最后和一个性感的女孩共进晚餐。
● taking 迷人的　● sexless 性冷淡的　● end up doing sth. 最终做某事

0854 **shade** [ʃeɪd] n 阴凉处，遮蔽 v 遮蔽
They are having their lunch under the shade of the tree.
他们正在树荫下吃午餐。
● illuminate 照亮　● window shade 遮光窗帘

0855 **shadow** ['ʃædoʊ] n 影子，阴影，阴暗
You are casting your shadow over my dinner table and I can't see the dishes clearly.
你挡着我的餐桌了，我看不清楚。
● shade 阴影　● in the shadow 在阴暗处
● cast one's shadow over... 某人挡着……了

0856 **shady** ['ʃeɪdi] a 阴暗的，可疑的，荫凉的
He was strolling along the shady path and singing a love song.
他一边在林荫道上漫步，一边唱着情歌。
● sunny 阳光充足的　● keep shady 隐蔽，隐匿　● stroll along... 沿着……散步
● shady 还可以表示 "不正直的，名声不好的"，多用在口语中。

↻ stroll (P. 643)

0857 **shallow** ['ʃæloʊ] a 浅的，浅薄的
We came to the shallow river to have a picnic ahead of schedule.
我们都提前来到了这条浅河边野餐。
● low 浅的　● deep 深的　● ... ahead of schedule 提前……

0858 shame [ʃeɪm] **n** 羞耻，惭愧，可惜
The dish you made put me to shame.
你做的菜使我感到羞愧。
abashment 羞愧　　honor 荣誉，荣耀　　flush with shame 面红耳赤

> 语法重点
> put... to shame（让……感到羞愧）中，put 后面也可以接表示人的名词或者代词。

0859 shampoo [ʃæm'pu:] **n** 洗发水，洗头
It involves a lot of shampoo to wash your hair if they put the cream of the cake on it.
如果他们把蛋糕的奶油抹到你的头发上，你需要很多洗发水来洗头发。

> involve (P. 463)

0860 shave [ʃeɪv] **v** 修剪
I have to shave tonight.
我今天晚上要刮胡子。
trim 修剪　　shave off 剃掉，刮掉

0861 shepherd ['ʃepərd] **n** 牧人，牧师　**v** 带领，引导
The man who is eating a hamburger was born into a shepherd family.
那个正在吃汉堡的男人出生在一个牧师家庭。
guide 带领，引导　　shepherd dog 牧羊犬　　be born into... 出生在……

> 语法重点
> be born into 后面接表示家族、种族等的名词。

0862 shiny ['ʃaɪni] **a** 晴朗的，闪亮的，发光的
My son's drinking milk dates back to a shiny day in 2012.
我儿子喝奶这件事要追溯到 2012 年一个晴朗的日子。
lightless 不发光的　　date back to... 追溯到……

> 语法重点
> date back to 一般不用于被动语态。

0863 shorten ['ʃɔ:rtn] **v** 缩短，变短
They are discussing how to shorten the arm of the manager.
他们讨论怎么限制经理的力量。
lengthen 变长　　shorten the arm of... 限制……的力量

0864 shortly ['ʃɔ:rtli] **ad** 不久，简短地
Please wait a minute, and I will finish my supper shortly.
请稍等，我很快就吃完晚餐了。
instantly 立刻　　verbosely 冗长地
shortly before 前不久，在……之前不久

> 语法重点
> 有时为了句子表达的方便，习惯上将一些介词进行省略，如例句中的 wait 之后省略的介词 for，而直接用 wait a minute 来表达，这种情况常出现于口语中。

0865 shovel ['ʃʌvl] **n** 铲子，挖掘机　**v** 铲，铲起
Look out for the shovel when you walk there.
在那里走路时要当心铲子。
digger 挖掘机　　look out for... 小心……
look out 与 watch out 都表示"当心"之意，但 look out 还有表示"向外看"的意思，而 watch out 则没有这种用法，二者在表示"当心……"时，其后都加介词 for。

shame ~ sip

0866 shrink [ʃrɪŋk] v 收缩，退缩，萎缩
Instead of shrinking back from the meat, the vegetarian ate a piece of beef.
那个素食者吃了一块牛肉，而不是在肉食面前退缩。

→ vegetarian (P. 515)

0867 sigh [saɪ] n / v 叹息，叹气，惋惜
By contrast, some people only sigh when they have nothing to eat.
相比之下，一些人没有食物吃时就会唉声叹气。

语法重点
by contrast 后面接的句子表示一种对比的概念，意思要与之前的句子相反。

0868 signal ['sɪgnəl] n 信号，标志
There must be something wrong with the traffic signal.
交通信号灯一定是出问题了。
≈ mark 标志　　■ a signal of danger 危险的信号

语法重点
there be 和情态动词连用时，情态动词应该放在 there 和 be 之间的位置，如例句中的 there must be 的结构。

0869 significant [sɪgˈnɪfɪkənt] a 有意义的
A cake is significant for him on his 20th birthday.
20 岁生日这天，蛋糕对他来说很重要。
≈ important 重要的　　≠ insignificant 无意义的
■ be significant for... 对……很重要

0870 similarity [ˌsɪməˈlærəti] n 类似
In my eyes, there's no similarity between this ring and that one.
在我看来，这个戒指和那个戒指没有什么相似之处。
≈ analogy 类似　　≠ difference 差异，不同

语法重点
in my eyes 在句首用来引出某种观点。
→ between (P. 014)

0871 sin [sɪn] n 罪，罪孽
He thinks it's a sin to eat meat.
他觉得吃肉是一种罪过。
≈ evil 罪恶　　■ original sin 原罪

语法重点
it's a sin to（一种罪过）后面接动词原形。

0872 sincere [sɪnˈsɪr] a 真诚的，诚挚的
The man who is drinking is sincere and easy to get along with.
那个正在喝酒的男人很诚恳，很好相处。
≈ genuine 真诚的　　≠ insincere 不真诚的
■ ... be easy to get along with ……很好相处

0873 sip [sɪp] v / n 啜饮，小口喝
He took a sip of the tea and stood up.
他喝了一小口茶，站了起来。
≈ tiff 啜，饮　　■ take a sip 尝一口

语法重点
take a sip of 后面要接表示液体的名词。

359

0874 **situation** [ˌsɪtʃuˈeɪʃn] n 情势，局面，位置，状况
They have nothing to eat in the present situation.
在当前形势下，他们没有东西吃。
🔊 circumstance 情况　　🔊 current situation 现状

语法重点
in the present situation（在当前形势下）通常与一般现在时连用。

0875 **skate** [skeɪt] n 溜冰鞋，滑冰 v 溜冰，滑冰
I was in despair when I can't find my ice skates anywhere.
我到处都找不到溜冰鞋，真郁闷。

语法重点
地点副词 anywhere 所表达的意思为"在任何地方"，常用于否定句或疑问句中，在句中一般置于动词之后或句尾。

0876 **ski** [skiː] v 滑雪 n 滑雪板，雪橇
It's rotten not to be able to ski and have a picnic today.
今天不能去滑雪，也不能去野餐，真是太糟了。
🔊 go skiing 去滑雪　　🔊 it's rotten not to... 不能……太糟了

0877 **skip** [skɪp] v / n 略过，遗漏
He deserves to be punished for skipping school to drink.
由于逃课去喝酒，他应该受到惩罚。
🔊 skip rope 跳绳　　🔊 deserve to... 应该……

语法重点
deserve 为动词，意思是"应得，值得"，表示"做某事是值得的"时，后面可加 to be done 的结构，也可以直接加动词 ing 形式。
🔗 punish (P. 211)

0878 **skyscraper** [ˈskaɪskreɪpər] n 摩天大楼
Currently, there are about one hundred people taking photos in front of the skyscraper.
目前，大约有一百人在摩天大楼前面照相。
🔊 currently 表达的意思为"目前，当前"，表示当前所处的这个时间段，presently 也有"目前，现在"之意，还可以表示"不久，一会儿"。

0879 **slave** [sleɪv] n 奴隶，苦工 v 做苦工
Finally, the slaves who always starved rose against the slaveholders.
最终，饥饿的奴隶们起来反抗奴隶主。
🔊 bondman 奴隶　　🔊 slave labor 苦役　　🔊 rise against... 反抗……

🔗 starve (P. 365)

0880 **sleeve** [sliːv] n 袖子
I got the attention of the girl who was eating bread by plucking at my sleeve.
我拉袖子引起了那个正在吃面包的女孩的注意。
🔊 get the attention of... 引起……的注意

🔗 pluck (P. 614)

0881 **slice** [slaɪs] n 薄片，部分 v 切成薄片，割
I think it's best to slice into the cake from the middle.
我认为最好从中间把蛋糕切开。
🔊 proportion 部分　　🔊 thin slice 薄片　　🔊 it's best to do sth. 最好做某事

0882 slippery ['slɪpəri] a 容易滑的，油滑的，不可靠的

She is as slippery as an eel and leaves the unsavory biscuits to others.
她很滑头，把难吃的饼干留给其他人吃。
- the slippery slope 易导致失败、灾难等的情况

0883 slope [sloʊp] n 坡度，倾斜，斜坡，斜面

He slid down the slope and had lunch at the foot of the hill.
他滑下山坡，在山脚下吃午餐。
- lean 倾斜   - slope angle 倾斜角   - slide down... 从……滑下来

语法重点
slid 是动词 slide 的过去式。

0884 smooth [smuːð] a 平滑的，平稳的 v 使光滑，消除

Now you can blend the flour with the water to make a smooth paste.
现在你可以把面粉和水调成均匀的面糊。
- rough 粗糙的   - blend... with... 把……和……混合起来
- smooth 也常用于习语 in smooth water 中，意思是"进展顺利，一帆风顺"。

→ blend (P. 402)

0885 snap [snæp] v 猛咬，拍快照

Put down your bread and take a deep breath before snapping.
吃东西前，放下你的面包，再深吸一口气。

语法重点
breath 是名词，意思是"呼吸"，take a breath 就表示"吸一口气"。

0886 solid ['sɑːlɪd] a 固体的，实心的，结实的

The solid ice-cream will melt into water if it is being heated.
如果加热的话，固体的冰激凌能够融化成水。
- liquid 液体的   - solid state 固态   - melt into... 溶解成……

语法重点
动词 melt 的意思是"融化"，介词 into 表达的意思为"转入，进入"，而介词 away 则有"消失"的意思，因此 melt into 所表达的意思为"融化成"，而 melt away 则表示"（使）融化，（使）消散"之意。

0887 someday [səmdeɪ] ad 将来有一天

He will hit a streak of good luck someday and have enough money to buy whatever he wants to eat.
有一天他会走运，有足够的钱买他想吃的一切东西。

0888 somehow ['sʌmhaʊ] ad 不知何故，以某种方式

I must plough on somehow even if I have no water to drink.
尽管没有水喝，我仍然要坚持下去。
- plough on... 坚持……

0889 sometime ['sʌmtaɪm] ad 有些时候

Just be on alert, for he will get you drunk sometime.
一定要注意，因为他改天会把你灌醉。
- ... be on alert …… 当心一点

语法重点
alert 可作形容词、名词和动词，表示"警觉"之意。和介词 on 连用，构成 on alert（留神的，警觉的），常用在 be 动词之后。

0890 **somewhat** ['sʌmwʌt]
ad 多少，稍微，有点 pron 某物，一些

He seemed somewhat to be confused about what to eat tonight.
他似乎有点儿不明白今天晚上要吃什么。
- be confused about... 不明白……

⇒ confuse (P. 276)

0891 **sore** [sɔːr] a 疼痛发炎的，痛心的 n 痛处，伤口

He is in sore grief now, so don't bother him by these apples.
他现在正在极度悲痛之中，所以不要去叫他吃苹果了。
- aching 疼痛的   - ... be in sore brief ……处于极度悲痛中

0892 **sorrow** ['sɑːroʊ] n 悲伤，悲痛，悔恨

I'm in great sorrow now and I don't want to have dinner.
我现在感到很伤心，不想吃饭。
- grief 悲伤，悲痛   - happiness 幸福
- ... be in great sorrow ……处于极度悲痛中

0893 **spade** [speɪd] n 铲子，铁锹

Let's call a spade a spade.
我们还是有话直说吧。
- in spades 坦率地   - call a spade a spade... ……有话直说

0894 **spaghetti** [spə'geti] n 意大利面条

I hear she is a dab hand at cooking spaghetti.
我听说她是煮意大利面条的高手。
- pasta 意大利面   - be a dab hand at... 是……的高手

语法重点
be a dab hand at 后面一般接名词。

0895 **specific** [spə'sɪfɪk] a 特定的，明确的

What's the specific time of our meeting?
我们确切的开会时间是几点钟？
- definite 明确的   - general 普通的   - specific gravity 比重

语法重点
time 是不可数名词，所以前面 be 动词用 is。
⇒ meeting (P. 190)

0896 **spice** [spaɪs] n 香料，调味品，情趣

By putting some spice into the soup, you can make it delicious.
在汤里放些香料，汤会很美味。
- condiment 调味品   - spice up 使更活跃，加香料

语法重点
by 后面接动名词表示方式。

0897 **spill** [spɪl] v 使溢出，洒落 n 溢出，流

The milk spilled when I bent over to tie my shoes.
当我俯身绑鞋带时，牛奶洒了。
- cry over spilt milk 作无益的后悔   - bend over to do sth. 俯身去做某事

语法重点
spill 是不规则动词，其过去式与过去分词分别有两个，spill, spilled, spilled 或 spill, spilt, spilt。

0898 **spin** [spɪn] v / n 旋转，眩晕，纺织

They took a spin around the town in order to drink.
为了喝酒，他们坐车出去绕城转了一圈。
- take a spin around... 坐车绕……绕了一圈

0899 **spit** [spɪt] v 吐，吐出 n 唾液，唾沫

He spit out the milk.
他把牛奶吐了出来。
- spit on 向……吐唾沫 - spit out... 把……吐出来

0900 **spite** [spaɪt] n 恶意，怨恨 v 刁难，惹怒，冒犯

They cut off the power out of spite.
他们为了泄愤，将电源切断了。
- hatred 怨恨，敌意 - out of spite 出于恶意
- 注意 cut off 和 cut out 的区别，cut off 所表达的意思为"切断，砍下，剪切，迅速离开"等，而 cut out 则主要表示"删除或切去"之意。

⊙ power (P. 078)

0901 **splash** [splæʃ] v 溅，泼 n 泼溅声，斑点

Try not to let the soup splash on your hand.
小心别让汤溅到手上。
- spatter 溅，洒 - splash down 溅落 - splash on... 溅到……

0902 **spoil** [spɔɪl] v 弄糟，宠坏，溺爱，破坏

Can't we give up eating sweets before dinner because it will spoil our appetite?
我们不能在饭前不吃糖吗？因为会损害胃口。

语法重点
Can't we..?（我们不能……吗？）要放动词原形。

0903 **sprain** [spreɪn] v / n 扭伤

Do you by any chance know he got a foot sprain in his ankle when he went to have a drink in the bar?
你知道他在去酒吧喝酒时，脚踝严重扭伤了吗？
- twist 扭伤 - Do you by any chance know...? 你知道……吗？

语法重点
by any chance 是插入语，加强语气。

0904 **spray** [spreɪ] v 喷雾，扫射 n 喷雾，喷雾器，水沫

He trimmed off the sideburns and then sprayed.
他把鬓角修完并往头发上喷发胶。
- sprinkle 喷撒 - trim off... 修剪……

语法重点
注意 trim 的过去式是重复词尾 m 再加上 ed。
⊙ trim (P. 652)

0905 **sprinkle** ['sprɪŋkl] v 撒，洒 n 少数，少量

I saw he was sprinkling the flowers while eating when I came by his house.
当我从他家经过时，看到他正在边吃东西边浇花。
- spatter 洒 - a sprinkling of rain 小雨 - come by... 从……走过

语法重点
come by 后面通常要接表示地点的名词。

0906 **spy** [spaɪ] **n** 间谍，侦查 **v** 侦探，监视
These agents are chasing after the spy in the airport.
这些探员正在机场里追赶那名间谍。
同 detect 侦查　同 chase after... 追捕……

→ agent (P. 392)

0907 **squeeze** [skwiːz] **v** / **n** 挤，压榨，剥削
Do you have any good ways to squeeze out more juice to drink?
你有什么好办法挤出更多的果汁来喝吗？
同 crush 压榨　同 squeeze out 榨出，挤出

语法重点
do you have any good ways 可以单独作为句子，也可以在后面加动词不定式。

0908 **stab** [stæb] **v** / **n** 刺，戳，刺伤
The boy stabbed the other with a knife, then got away.
那个男孩用刀刺伤另一个男孩，然后就逃跑了。
同 stab sb. in the back 背地里中伤某人，背叛某人

语法重点
get away 主要强调"脱身"这个概念。
→ knife (P. 055)

0909 **stable** [ˈsteɪbl] **a** 稳定的，安定的 **n** 马厩，马棚
Finally the price of the oranges was stable.
最终橘子的价格稳定了。
同 steady 稳定的　反 unstable 不稳定的
辨 eventually 和 finally 都表示"结果"之意，eventually 主要侧重于动作或行为的结果，而 finally 通常表示所预计的情况终于发生了。

0910 **stadium** [ˈsteɪdiəm] **n** 体育场，运动场
It's sure that he will come over to the stadium.
他一定会来体育馆。
同 sports stadium 体育场，体育馆　同 it's sure that... 一定……

语法重点
come over 所表达的含义为"从远处来"，其主要强调一种距离感。

0911 **staff** [stæf] **n** 工作人员
Be sure that all the staff have enough water to drink.
一定要确保所有的员工都有足够的水喝。
同 crew 全体人员　同 be sure that... 一定要确保……

语法重点
be 动词也是属于动词的一种，以其原形开头的句子也是祈使句。

0912 **stale** [steɪl] **a** 不新鲜的，陈腐的，过时的
Do you think it is necessary to throw the stale bread away?
你认为有必要把变质的面包扔掉吗？
反 fresh 新鲜的　同 go stale 过时的，新鲜的
辨 throw away 主要用来指将垃圾或无用的东西等"扔掉，丢弃"。

0913 **stare** [ster] **v** / **n** 注视
He just stared at me in astonishment when hearing that there wasn't food left for him.
得知没有为他留食物后，他一直就那样吃惊地盯着我。
同 make sb. stare 使某人惊愕　同 ... in astonishment 吃惊地……

语法重点
"介词 in + 名词"可以表示状态，如例句中的介词 in 后加名词 astonishment 构成介词短语 in astonishment，用以表示"吃惊"这种状态。

0914 **starve** [stɑːrv] v 饿死

People who starve to death these days are beyond number.
这些天因饥荒而死的人数不清。
- famish 挨饿
- satiate 充分满足
- ... beyond number 数不清的……

0915 **statue** ['stætʃuː] n 雕像，塑像

As long as they are still sitting beside the statue, we can find them.
只要他们还坐在雕像旁，我们就能找到他们。
- bronze statue 铜像
- as long as... 只要……

0916 **steady** ['stedi] a 稳固的，平稳的

He gets a steady job to raise his family, that's to say, he can buy food and water for them.
他得到一份稳定的工作来养活家人，也就是说，可以为他们买食物和水。
- unstable 不稳定的
- steady job 固定工作
- that's to say, ... 也就是说，……

语法重点
that's to say 用在句中，前后两个句子意思相同。

0917 **steep** [stiːp] a 陡峭的，价格过高的

The mountain is too steep, and the traveler who has no equipment is at stake now.
那座山太陡了，那个没有带装备的游客现在很危险。
- precipitous 险峻的
- a steep increase 大幅度的增加
- ... be at stake …… 处于危险中

⊃ equipment (P. 436)

0918 **stepchild** ['steptʃaɪld] n 前夫或前妻生的孩子

His stepchild grew tired of the sameness of the dishes.
饭菜单调，他的继子都吃腻了。
- grow tired of... 对……腻了

0919 **stepfather** ['stepfɑːðər] n 继父

His stepfather caught a cold and didn't have supper tonight.
他的继父感冒了，晚上没有吃饭。
- ... catch a cold …… 感冒

0920 **stepmother** ['stepmʌðər] n 后母

My stepmother hasn't come to herself after eating the poisonous bread.
吃了有毒的面包后，我继母一直没从昏迷中醒来。

语法重点
come to oneself 用来表示某人从昏迷的状态醒过来，come 的过去分词还是 come。

0921 **stereo** ['steriʊ] n 立体音响

Wouldn't it be nice to play the stereo when we have supper?
我们吃饭的时候放音响不是更好吗？
- stereo system 立体音响系统

0922 **sticky** ['stɪki] a 黏的，闷热的，棘手的
He doesn't like this sticky food. Take it away.
他不喜欢这种黏黏的食物，把它拿开。
- sticky fingers 偷盗习惯　- take away... 拿走……

语法重点
因为 it 是代词，所以放在了 take 和 away 之间。

0923 **stiff** [stɪf] a 僵硬的，不灵活的
He was bored stiff after having noodles for three days.
连续吃三天的面条，他厌烦透了。
- rigid 僵硬的　- flexible 灵活的　- stiff as a ramrod 笔直

语法重点
be bored 表示"厌倦"，
be bored stiff 加强语气。

0924 **sting** [stɪŋ] v/n 刺，叮，苦恼
I'm sorry that my words stung you; I offer you a drink tonight.
很抱歉，我的话伤害了你，我晚上请你喝酒。
- a sting in the tail 直到最后才显现出来的坏处
- sorry 和 apologize 都表示"抱歉"之意。sorry 为形容词，通常用于口语中，表示"抱歉的，遗憾的"，而 apologize 为动词，一般用于较为正式的场合，表示郑重其事的道歉。

0925 **stir** [stɜːr] n 搅拌，骚乱 v 搅和，激起
It doesn't take much to stir milk into a cake mixture.
不用费力就能把牛奶搅和到做蛋糕的混合料中。
- rouse 激起　- still 静止，平静　- in stir 坐牢

语法重点
it doesn't take much（不费力）后面一般接动词不定式。

0926 **stitch** [stɪtʃ] n 针线 v 缝，绣
There's no need to stitch a button on my jacket.
没有必要在我的夹克上钉一颗扣子。
- sew 缝　- in stitches 捧腹大笑　- there's no need to do sth. 没必要做某事

0927 **stocking** ['stɑːkɪŋ] n 长袜
My stockings are crammed with chocolates now.
我的长袜里面塞满了巧克力。
- a pair of stockings 一双长袜　- be crammed with... 塞满了……

语法重点
cram 为动词，意思是"塞满"，其过去式、过去分词都是重复词尾 m 再加上 ed。

0928 **stool** [stuːl] n 凳子，便桶，大便
He perches on a stool at the bar and has drunk four bottles of wine by far.
他坐在酒吧里的一张椅子上，到现在已经喝了四瓶酒。
- fall between two stools 两头落空　- ... by far 到现在……

语法重点
by far 通常与现在完成时连用。
⇒ perch (P. 611)

0929 **stormy** ['stɔːrmi] a 暴风雨的，激烈的，粗暴的
We have reason to believe that she feels frightened sleeping alone at home in the stormy night.
我们有理由相信她对一个人在暴风雨之夜在家睡觉感到很害怕。
- fierce 激烈的　- calm 平静的　- stormy weather 暴风雨天气
- we have reason to believe that... 我们有理由相信……

sticky ~ style

0930 strategy [ˈstrætədʒɪ] n 战略
The new strategy about driving will take into effect soon.
关于驾驶的新策略很快就要生效了。
- tactic 策略，战略　· military strategy 军事部署　· ... take into effect ……生效

0931 strength [streŋθ] n 力量，力气，强度
The little girl doesn't have enough strength to life up the big box.
小女孩没有足够的力气将大箱子搬起。
- force 力量　· life up... 举起……

0932 strip [strɪp] n 长条 v 剥去，剥夺
He tore the bread in strips to eat.
他把面包撕成条来吃。
- peel 剥，剥落　· strip... down 卸掉……的所有零件进行清理或检修

> **语法重点**
> strip 用的是复数，说明"他"把面包撕成了不止一条。

0933 structure [ˈstrʌktʃər] n 构造 v 构造，建造
Am I allowed to have dinner in the restaurant the structure of which has changed?
我能不能在那家已改建的餐厅里吃饭？
- change 和 modify 都表示"改变"，change 表示进行大的或结构性的改变，如例句中的建筑结构改变，而 modify 则表示"修改，更改"，主要指较小范围地进行修改以示某事更适合所需。

· allow (P. 006)

0934 stubborn [ˈstʌbərn] a 顽固的，倔强的，难对付的
She is as stubborn as a mule, and your trying her to write a book is in vain.
她是一个非常顽固的人，你劝说她写书是没有用的。
- obstinate 倔强的　· docile 温顺的
- stubborn as a mule 非常顽固，非常倔强

· mule (P. 193)

0935 studio [ˈstuːdiəʊ] n 录音室，制片厂
The studio executive gave way to the staff.
电影公司经理对员工做出了让步。
- give way to... 向……做出让步

0936 stuff [stʌf] n 东西，原料，材料 v 塞满，填满
He found some green stuff on his way to the office.
在去办公室的路上，他发现了一些蔬菜。
- pack 塞满

> **语法重点**
> on one's way to 后面要接表示地点的名词。

0937 style [staɪl] n 风格，式样，时尚，类型
It took me a while to latch onto his style of eating steak.
我过了一会儿才明白他吃牛排的方式。
- fashion 时尚，样式　· in style 流行的，时髦的

0938 substance [ˈsʌbstəns] **n** 物质，财产

I personally think the reason why this mooncake is valuable is that it has rare substance in it.
我个人认为，这种月饼之所以贵是因为里面有稀有材料。

- in substance 实质上，基本上，事实上
- valuable 和 precious 都表示"贵重的"含义，valuable 主要指某物的价值很贵重，而 precious 则主要强调"宝贵"的含义，表示某物非常稀有。

↻ rare (P. 213)

0939 suburb [ˈsʌbɜːrb] **n** 市郊

I don't figure on so many people at the picnic in the suburb.
我们没有料到会有这么多人参加这次郊区的野餐。

- downtown 市中心
- in the suburbs 在郊区，在郊外
- figure on... 料想……

0940 suck [sʌk] **v / n** 吸，吸收，吸吮

Being thirsty, I had a suck of orange juice.
我口渴了，喝了一口橙汁。

- drink 吸收
- suck up (to sb.) 拍某人马屁

语法重点
being thirsty 表示喝橙汁的原因。

0941 suffer [ˈsʌfər] **v** 受苦，忍受，容忍

I couldn't bear to see others suffer from hunger.
我不忍看见别人挨饿。

- suffer from... 遭受，忍受，受……之苦
- I couldn't bear to... 我不忍心……

0942 sufficient [səˈfɪʃnt] **a** 充足的

It is sufficient to show that he has eaten up the chocolates.
这足以证明他吃光了所有的巧克力。

- adequate 充足的
- insufficient 不足的
- be sufficient to do sth. 足以做某事

0943 suggest [səˈdʒest] **v** 建议，暗示，表明

I presume to suggest that you should take more fruits.
我冒昧地建议你多吃些水果。

- advice 建议
- studies suggest that... 研究表明……

语法重点
suggest 当"暗示"讲时，后面接的 that 从句可不用虚拟语气。

0944 suicide [ˈsuːɪsaɪd] **n** 自杀，自取灭亡

She committed suicide because she got fired.
她因为被解雇而自杀。

- murder 谋杀
- suicide attack 自杀式袭击

语法重点
commit suicide（自杀）是固定搭配用法，通常用主动语态。

↻ commit (P. 410)

0945 suitable [ˈsuːtəbl] **a** 适合的，适宜的

I hope it is a suitable location for having a cup of tea.
我希望那是一个适合喝茶的地方。

- fitting 适宜的
- unsuitable 不适合的
- hope 和 wish 都可以表示"希望"，但意义有所不同。hope 通常是指对愿望的实行有一定的把握，而 wish 则是指难以实现甚至是不可能实现的愿望。

substance ~ survival

0946 sum [sʌm] n 总计，金额 v 总结，归纳
Do your utmost to count the sum of the apples.
尽你全力去计算苹果的个数。
- total 总数
- in sum 简言之，总而言之

> 语法重点
> do one's utmost to（尽某人的全力去）后面要接动词原形。
> ⇒ utmost (P. 799)

0947 summary ['sʌməri] n 摘要，总结 a 简略的，概要的
In summary, he doesn't like sweet food.
简言之，他不喜欢吃甜食。
- abstract 摘要
- in summary 总的说来，归纳起来

> 语法重点
> in summary 通常用于句首或是句末，相当于 in a word、in short。

0948 summit ['sʌmɪt] n 山顶，首脑会议
You will never make the summit if you don't have climbing ropes.
如果你没有登山绳，你永远到不了山顶。
- peak 山峰
- bottom 底部
- summit conference 高峰会议
- summit 和 peak 都可以表示"顶峰，顶点"，但意义有所不同。summit 通常是指努力、成就、事业的巅峰或是山的顶峰，而 peak 则侧重于山的顶峰。

0949 superior [suː'pɪriər] a 上级的，较好的 n 上级，高手
The taste of this grapefruit is superior to that of the one on the table.
这个柚子的味道比桌子上那个好。
- better 较好的
- inferior 差的，下级的
- be superior to... 比……好

> 语法重点
> superior 没有比较级与最高级。
> ⇒ grapefruit (P. 449)

0950 suppose [sə'poʊz] v 假定，料想，以为
I suppose they would like to come with us.
我猜他们会想要和我们一起去。
- assume 假定
- be supposed to do... 被期望或被要求做……
- suppose 通常是指某人自己的观点或是假设，缺乏确切的事实依据，而 assume 则是指没有根据的推测或是不合逻辑的推理。

0951 surround [sə'raʊnd] v 围绕
Do you enjoy being surrounded by all kinds of clothing?
你喜欢被各种衣服包围吗？
- encircle 包围，环绕
- Do you enjoy...? 你喜欢……吗？

0952 survey ['sɜːrveɪ] v 调查，审视 n 问卷，调查
According to the survey, only half of them have breakfast every day.
根据调查，他们中只有一半的人每天都吃早餐。
- examine 调查
- according to the survey... 据调查……

0953 survival [sər'vaɪvl] n 幸存，幸存者，残存
The man owed his survival to the bottle of water he brought.
他是因为带了一瓶水才幸免于难的。
- survival instinct 生存本能
- owe... to... 把……归功于……

0954 **survivor** [sərˈvaɪvər] n 生还者
It is just conceivable that the survivor lived on the watermelon these days.
那个幸存者这几天就靠这个西瓜生活，这不是不可能。
- victim 遇难者 - sole survivor 唯一的幸存者

0955 **suspect** [səˈspekt] / [ˈsəspekt] v 怀疑 n 嫌疑犯
I don't know why you suspect him of stealing the camera.
我不知道你为什么怀疑是他偷了相机。
- doubt 怀疑 - trust 信任 - suspect sb. of doing... 怀疑某人做……
- suspect 通常是指猜忌、怀疑，而 doubt 则是泛指因为没有确切证据或是证据不足而怀疑，无法肯定。

0956 **suspicion** [səˈspɪʃn] n 怀疑，猜疑，嫌疑
I have a suspicion that he is allergic to seafood.
我怀疑他对海鲜过敏。
- distrust 不信任 - belief 相信 - above suspicion 不受怀疑的

语法重点
have a suspicion 表示 "怀疑"，可以用介词 about 引述怀疑的物件。

0957 **swear** [swer] v 发誓，咒骂，诅咒
I sweared by Almighty God that I didn't steal her money.
我对万能的上帝发誓，我没有偷她的钱。
- vow 发誓 - swear blind 一口咬定 - I swear... 我发誓……

语法重点
Almighty God 意为 "万能的上帝"，为专有名词，首字母均要大写，也可以用 God Almighty。

0958 **sweat** [swet] v 出汗 n 汗，汗水，苦差事
Eating hot pot in such a hot day is a real sweat.
在这么热的天吃火锅是一件艰难的事情。

语法重点
在 be a real sweat（是一件艰难的事情）中，sweat 用的是比喻意义。

0959 **swell** [swel] v 肿起来，使鼓起 n 增大，膨胀
Their discontent about the dormitory gradually swelled into dispute.
他们对宿舍的不满渐渐演变成了争端。
- bulge 使膨胀 - shrink 收缩 - swell into... 演变成……

↪ dormitory (P. 430)

0960 **swift** [swɪft] a 迅速的，快速的，敏捷的
The man is swift to have his lunch.
那个男人迅速地吃了午餐。
- quick 迅速的 - slow 慢的 - be swift to do... 立即做……

0961 **switch** [swɪtʃ] n 开关，电闸 v 转变，转换
He suggested we switch the conversation to music.
他建议我们改为讨论音乐这个话题。
- shift 转换 - switch on 接通，开启 - switch... to... 把……转向……

↪ conversation (P. 145)

0962 sword [sɔːrd] n 剑

With a sweep of my sword I cut through the rope tied on the bag.
我挥剑把袋子上的绳子砍断了。

- a sword of Damocles 达摩克勒斯剑（比喻某人将有祸事临头）

0963 system ['sɪstəm] n 系统，制度，体制

We made an objection to the system that all the students should wear uniform.
我们反对让所有学生都穿制服的制度。

- education system 教育体制　　make an objection to... 反对……

⊙ uniform (P. 241)

0964 tablet ['tæblət] n 药片，碑，牌匾

To take two tablets of the medicine after dinner does good to your recovery.
饭后吃两片药有利于你的康复。

- troche 药片　　do good to... 对……有益

语法重点
a tablet of 意为"一片，一剂"，后接表示胶囊或是片状的药物名称，tablets of 为复数形式。

0965 tack [tæk] n 大头钉，行动方针 v 用大头针钉住，附加

We can hammer a tack into the wall.
我们可以在墙上钉一个钉子。

0966 tag [tæg] n 标签，标牌 v 给……加上标签

We can find the price tag attached to the packing bag of the chocolates.
我们能在巧克力的包装袋上找到价格标签。

- label 标签　　tag along 尾随，紧随　　attach to... 附在……上
- tag 和 label 都可以表示"标签"，但意义有所不同。tag 通常是指临时用的标签，而 label 则是指标明货物或是产品名称、重量、规格以及所有人信息的标签。

0967 tailor ['teɪlər] n 裁缝师 v 裁剪

The tailor who is well-known for making good suits is having a cup of tea now.
那个以制作精美西服而闻名的裁缝现在正在喝一杯茶。

0968 tame [teɪm] a 温和的，柔顺的 v 驯服，驯养

It is hardly conceivable that the tame girl made loud noise when she had soup.
简直难以想象，那个温顺的女孩喝汤时会发出很大的声音。

0969 tap [tæp] v 轻打，利用 n 轻拍，水龙头

I didn't realize that a little tap would scare you so much.
我并没有意识到，轻拍你一下会使你如此受惊。

- pat 轻拍　　on tap 散装的
- scare 通常是指受到惊吓而跑开或是停止正在做的事情，而 terrify 则是指极度惊恐。

0970 tax [tæks] n 税，负担 v 征税
The sales tax has always been a heavy burden on the boss of the bookstore.
对于这个书店的老板来说，营业税一直是个沉重的负担。
- levy 征税　- tax return 纳税申请表　- be a burden on... 是……的负担

0971 tease [tiːz] v 欺负，戏弄，取笑，挑逗
It was mean of them to tease the little boy about his lunch.
他们嘲笑那个男孩吃的午餐，真是太坏了。
- banter 开玩笑，逗弄　- tease about... 嘲笑……

> **语法重点**
> it was mean of sb. to do sth.（某人做……真是太坏了）中，不管 sb. 是单数还是复数，前面的 be 动词都用单数，与 it 保持一致。

0972 technical ['teknɪkl] a 技术的，工艺的
I entered a technical school to learn to design just two months ago.
就在两个月前，我进入一所技术学校学习设计。
- technological 技术的　- learn to do sth. 学习做某事

0973 technique [tek'niːk] n 技术，技巧，技能
I think it's a good idea to apply modern techniques to make bread.
我认为将现代技术应用于做面包，是个好主意。
- skill 技术，技巧　- technique of... ……的技术

0974 technology [tek'nɑːlədʒi] n 科技，工艺
Do you happen to know there is still much resistance to new technology on making ice-cream?
你知道吗，关于制作冰激凌的新技术仍然有很多的阻力？
- medical technology 医疗技术　- Do you happen to know...? 你知道……吗？

↪ resistance (P. 497)

0975 temper ['tempər] n 脾气，性情
You should find a proper way to control your temper when you see your son eating junk food.
当你看到儿子吃垃圾食品时，你应该找个合适的方法控制自己的脾气。
- in a bad temper 发怒，发脾气　- control one's temper 控制某人的脾气

0976 temperature ['temprətʃər] n 温度
He whispered to me that his temperature was up again after swimming.
他低声对我说他游泳后，体温又上升了。
- run a temperature 体温过高，发烧　- whisper to sb. 低声对某人说

> **语法重点**
> 表示体温低用形容词 low。

0977 temporary ['tempəreri] a 暂时的，临时的
Your temporary obesity was closely related to your eating habit.
你暂时的肥胖与饮食习惯有密切关系。

tax ~ thread

0978 tend [tend] v 易于做……
I tend to have bread and milk in the morning.
我习惯早上吃面包喝牛奶。
🔄 tend towards 走向　　🔄 tend to... 习惯于……

> **语法重点**
> tend to 通常后接动词原形。若表示"趋向，朝向"，可以用 tend to / towards，通常后接表示光线、状态等的名词。

0979 tender ['tendər] a 柔软的，嫩的
At the tender age of four, I began to like playing the guitar.
早在四岁时，我就开始喜欢弹吉他。
🔄 gentle 温和的　　🔄 tough 坚强的　　🔄 at a tender age 年幼而未成熟的

> **语法重点**
> at the tender age of（早在……岁时）后面接的表示年龄的数词一般较小。

0980 territory ['terətri] n 领土，区域，范围
Most animals will defend their territory against others to make sure they have enough to eat.
为了确保有足够的食物吃，大多数动物会抵制其他动物进入自己的领域。
🔄 district 区域　　🔄 defend against... 保护……不受……

> **语法重点**
> defend against 中的介词 against 通常可以与 from 互换，后接表示人或是表示攻击、伤害、控诉等的名词。

0981 text [tekst] n 正文，文本
The story he told was edited from the original text.
他讲的故事是根据原文改编的。
🔄 original text 原文　　🔄 be edited from... 根据……编辑的

> **语法重点**
> be edited from 一般不用主动语态。
> 🔄 original (P. 331)

0982 thankful ['θæŋkfl] a 感谢的，欣慰的
He is thankful to know that they have offered many foods to him.
得知他们给他很多食物，他十分感激。
🔄 appreciative 感激的　　🔄 be thankful for... 对……感激

> **语法重点**
> be thankful to 后接动词原形，引述原因，如句中所示。

0983 theory ['θɪri] n 理论，学说，原理
His plan for a picnic seems fine in theory, but I don't know whether it will work out.
他打算去野餐的计划从理论上来说是很好的，但我不知道能否实施。
🔄 in theory 理论上　　🔄 ... work out ……实现

0984 thirst [θɜːrst] n 口渴，渴望 v 渴望，渴求
I have a thirst for a hamburger now.
我现在渴望吃汉堡。
🔄 crave 渴望　　🔄 feel thirsty 感到口渴的　　🔄 have a thirst for... 渴望……

0985 thread [θred] n 线，思路 v 穿过，通过
He lost the thread of what he ate this morning.
他记不清自己早上吃了什么。
🔄 string 线　　🔄 lose the thread of... 记不清……
💡 thread 和 wire 都可以表示"线"，但意义有所不同。thread 通常是指用于纺织、缝纫等的细线，而 wire 则是指金属丝。

0986 **threat** [θret] n 威胁，恐吓

These people are under the threat of having nothing to wear.
这些人面临着没有衣服穿的威胁。
- danger 威胁
- carry out a threat 进行威胁
- under the threat of... 面临着……威胁

0987 **threaten** ['θretn] v 威胁，恐吓

Mother always threatens them with not letting them have supper.
妈妈总是用不准吃晚餐来威胁他们。
- threaten sb. with... 用……威胁某人

0988 **tickle** ['tɪkl] v 搔痒，逗乐

I am tickled pink that my son has eaten up the bread I made.
儿子吃完了我做的面包，我很高兴。
- tickle one's ribs 逗某人发笑
- ... be tickled pink ……十分满足

> **语法重点**
> be tickled pink 是固定用法，be 有时态和人称、数的变化，相当于 be tickled to death。

0989 **tide** [taɪd] n 潮汐，海浪，形势

I wonder when the tide can turn in our favor.
我想知道，形势什么时候会对我们有利。
- tendency 趋势
- ... in one's favor ……对某人有利

> **语法重点**
> in one's favor 通常用于动词之后，也可以表示"得到某人的赞同、好感"，其反义表达为 be out of one's favor。

0990 **tidy** ['taɪdi] a 整洁的

I have a good habit to keep my room tidy.
我有保持房间整齐的好习惯。
- ordered 整齐的
- untidy 不整齐的
- look tidy 看起来整洁
- have a good habit to do sth. 有做某事的好习惯

0991 **tight** [taɪt] a 紧的，牢固的，紧身的

I do my best to open the bottle of drink, but the cork is too tight.
我尽全力去打开这瓶饮料，但是盖子太紧。
- firm 牢固的
- loose 宽松的
- ... do one's best ……尽全力

0992 **tighten** ['taɪtn] v 变紧，勒紧，固定

I hear a new rule will come into effect to tighten the control on sales of alcohol.
我听说一项新的规定即将实施，以便加强对酒的销售控制。
- straiten 变紧
- loosen 松开
- tighten your belt 勒紧腰带，节衣缩食
- ... come into effect ……生效

> sale (P. 085)

0993 timber [ˈtɪmbər] n 木材，木料

Did you know that your father sold the timber to buy you a car?

你知道你父亲为了买车子给你，把木材卖了吗？

0994 tissue [ˈtɪʃuː] n 卫生纸，（动植物的）组织

What he said about his work was a tissue of lies.

他所说的关于他工作的那些话是一派胡言。

- a tissue of lies 一派胡言

> 语法重点
> a tissue of lies 是固定搭配，lie 要用复数。
> lie (P. 058)

0995 tobacco [təˈbækoʊ] n 烟草，烟丝，烟叶

He is enslaved to wine and tobacco, but she loves him all the same.

尽管他又酗酒又抽烟，她还是一样爱他。

- tobacco jar 烟灰缸
- be enslaved to... 沉溺于……
- cigar、cigarette、tobacco 都可以表示"烟"，但意义有所不同，cigar 通常是指雪茄，cigarette 是指纸烟、烟卷、香烟，而 tobacco 则是指烟草、烟叶、烟丝。

0996 ton [tʌn] n 吨，大量，许多

Even though he has tons of money, he doesn't often buy new clothing.

尽管他有很多钱，但是他也不常买新衣服。

- like a ton of bricks 严厉地
- Even though... 尽管……

> 语法重点
> tons of 表示"大量，很多"，通常用于口语中，后接可数名词复数或是不可数名词。

0997 tortoise [ˈtɔːrtəs] n 乌龟，迟钝的人

Have you considered cooking the tortoise he brought back from the beach?

你有没有考虑过用他从沙滩捡回来的乌龟做菜？

- turtle 龟
- tortoise shell 龟壳

> consider (P. 144)

0998 toss [tɔːs] v / n 抛，掷，摇荡

He angrily tossed a piece of bread to his sister while eating.

吃饭时，他生气地将一块面包扔向了妹妹。

- pitch 投，掷
- win the toss 猜中
- toss sth. to sb. 把某物扔向某人

0999 tourism [ˈtʊrɪzəm] n 观光

I can almost say snacks and tourism are the lifeblood of our city.

我几乎可以说小吃和旅游业是我们这个城市的命脉。

- sightseeing 观光
- I can almost say... 我几乎可以说……

> 语法重点
> lifeblood 是不可数名词。

1000 tourist [ˈtʊrɪst] n 观光客

Please put him through to the tourist agency.

请帮他接旅行社。

1001 tow [toʊ] **v** 拖曳 **n** 拖，拽，拖绳
He helped me to tow the box full of books to my house.
他帮我把装满书的箱子拖到了我家。
🔄 drag 拖　🔄 in tow 伴随，跟随　🔄 tow sth. to... 把……拖到……

1002 trace [treɪs] **v** 追踪，描绘 **n** 踪迹，痕迹
His hunger should be traced back to his not having breakfast this morning.
他之所以饿是因为早上没吃早餐。
🔄 trace sth. back to... 追踪到……

> 语法重点
> trace sth. back to 可以用于主动语态，也可以用于被动语态。有时，back 可以省去。

1003 trader ['treɪdər] **n** 商人，商船
The trader took a mouthful of the cake and then spat it out.
那个商人吃了一口蛋糕，又吐了出来。
🔄 dealer 商人　🔄 take a mouthful of... 吃了一口……

1004 trail [treɪl] **n** 踪迹，小径 **v** 拖，尾随
The boy left a trail of slime along the floor after eating the honey.
小男孩吃完蜂蜜，在地板上留下了一道黏液。
🔄 path 小路　🔄 blaze a trail 开辟道路，另辟蹊径
🔄 trail 通常是泛指跟踪，而 trace 则是指依据线索或是足迹而追踪，也可以指抽象意义上的寻找根源。

1005 transport [træns'pɔːrt] / ['trænspɔːrt] **v** / **n** 运输，输送
He has a deep fascination with all forms of transport.
他对所有的运输工具都很着迷。
🔄 convey 运输　🔄 be transported with delight 欣喜若狂

➔ fascination (P. 720)

1006 trash [træʃ] **n** 垃圾 **v** 废弃，捣毁
She thinks this kind of food is trash.
她觉得这种食品是垃圾。
🔄 rubbish 废物　🔄 trash bin 垃圾箱

1007 traveler ['trævələr] **n** 旅客
The traveler complained to us at the dishes in the restaurant.
那个游客向我们抱怨餐厅的菜不好吃。
🔄 tourist 旅行者　🔄 complain to sb. at sth. 向某人抱怨某事

> 语法重点
> traveler 有时也写作 traveller。
> ➔ complain (P. 143)

1008 tray [treɪ] **n** 托盘
How does his advice that we eat a tray of cake sound?
他建议我们吃一盘蛋糕，你觉得怎么样？
🔄 salver 托盘　🔄 How does... sound? ……怎么样？

> 语法重点
> a tray of 表示"一盘"，后接可数名词复数或是不可数名词，相当于 a plate of 或 a dish of。

1009 tremble ['trembl] v / n 颤抖

I was trembling with excitement at the good news that I can have supper in that restaurant.
听到我可以去那家餐厅吃饭的好消息，我兴奋地颤抖起来。

- tremble with... 因……而发抖
- tremble with excitement... 兴奋地颤抖

excitement (P. 161)

1010 trend [trend] n 趋势，倾向 v 倾向，趋向

How long will it take you to make clear of the trend of gas prices?
你搞清楚瓦斯价格的趋势需要多久？

- tendency 趋势
- How long will it take you...? ……要多久？

1011 tribe [traɪb] n 种族

It is supposed that the tribe still eats raw meat now.
据推测，这个部落现在还吃生肉。

- clan 部落
- It is supposed that... 据推测，……

语法重点
tribe 作为一个整体，按单数处理。

1012 tricky ['trɪki] a 狡猾的，巧妙的

I have no idea what could be done when facing with the tricky situation that my son doesn't sleep.
我儿子不睡觉，面临着这样棘手的形势，我不知道该做些什么。

- troublesome 麻烦的
- tricky mischief 诡计

1013 troop [tru:p] n 军队 v 群集，结队

There are a troop of people who are not great meat eaters in the restaurant.
餐厅里有一群吃肉不多的人。

- flock 群
- troop withdrawal 撤军

语法重点
a troop of 表示"一群，一队，一组"，通常是指人群或是鸟群、兽群，并且是正在移动中的，而复数形式 troops of 可以表示"多数，大群"。

1014 tropical ['trɑ:pɪkl] a 热带的，炎热的

In the tropical forest, they drink coconut milk after they cut down the trees.
在热带雨林里，他们砍倒树后，就喝椰子汁。

- tropic 热带的
- tropical plants 热带植物
- cut down... 砍倒……

1015 trunk [trʌŋk] n 树干，行李箱

Be careful of my trunk; it's full of painting.
小心我的行李箱，里面全是画。

- branch 树枝
- trunk line 干线
- be careful of... 小心……

1016 truthful ['tru:θfl] a 信任的，真实的

To be quite truthful with you, she is not interested in fiction movie at all.
跟你说实话，她对科幻片一点儿都不感兴趣。

- sincere 真实的
- untruthful 不诚实的

fiction (P. 441)

1017 **tub** [tʌb] **n** 木盆，浴缸
I was forced to buy a tub of ice cream for her.
我不得不买一盒冰激凌给她。
🔄 barrel 桶　🔄 in the tub 破产　🔄 be forced to do sth. 被强迫做某事

1018 **tug** [tʌɡ] **v** 用力拉
He gave a tug at my hair when I was playing ball.
我玩球时他拉了一下我的头发。
🔄 haul 拉　🔄 tug of war 拔河比赛　🔄 give a tug at... 拉了一下……

1019 **tulip** ['tu:lɪp] **n** 郁金香
I'm determined to plant a tulip bulb in the garden.
我决定在花园里种一株郁金香球根。
🔄 I'm determined to... 我决定……

→ determine (P. 283)

1020 **tumble** ['tʌmbl] **v** / **n** 跌倒，倒塌
He took a tumble down the stairs.
他摔下了楼梯。
🔄 tumble down 倒塌，垮掉　🔄 take a tumble down... 摔下了……

◁ 语法重点
表示"楼梯"时，stair 要用复数。

1021 **tune** [tu:n] **n** 曲调，调子　**v** 调音，调节
My mother always calls the tune about what to eat.
关于吃什么，总是我妈妈说了算。
🔄 melody 旋律，歌曲　🔄 tune... up 调整（乐器）使合调

◁ 语法重点
call the tune（发号施令）通常不用于被动语态，相当于 call the shots。

1022 **tutor** ['tu:tər] **n** 家庭教师，导师
He was taken in the charge of his tutor, even his meals were made by the tutor.
这男孩受他的家庭教师管理，甚至他的饭都是家庭教师煮的。
🔄 instructor 教员　🔄 student 学生　🔄 private tutor 私人教师，家庭教师

◁ 语法重点
be taken in the charge of（受……的管理）后面一般接表示人的名词或代词。

1023 **twig** [twɪɡ] **n** 细枝，嫩枝　**v** 理解，领悟
She still didn't twig why they ate up her apples.
她仍然不明白，为什么他们吃光了她的苹果。

1024 **twin** [twɪn] **n** 双胞胎之一　**a** 孪生的，成双的
I took Lily for her twin sister when we had dinner together.
一起吃饭时，我把莉莉当成了她的孪生妹妹。
🔄 take sb. for... 把某人当成了……

1025 **twist** [twɪst] **v** 扭转　**n** 弯曲，转折
The plastic box which contains chocolates tends to twist under pressure.
那个装巧克力的塑胶盒受到压力容易变形。
🔄 bend 弯曲　🔄 twist sb. round one's little finger 任意摆布某人
🔄 ... under pressure 在……的压力下

1026 typewriter ['taɪpraɪtər] n 打字机

The typewriter is always at your service after you have lunch.
你吃完午餐后，打字机随时都为你所用。
- typer 打字机
- at one's service 随时为某人服务

1027 typical ['tɪpɪkl] a 典型的，有代表性的

I hear this snack is typical of the region.
我听说这种小吃是本地区的特产。
- characteristic 特有的
- typical of 是……的典型特征
- be typical of... 是……的特产

1028 union ['juːniən] n 合并，联合，工会，联盟

The trade union is concerned with what the workers eat and drink.
工会关注工人们每天吃什么、喝什么。
- alliance 联合，联盟
- in union 一致地，共同地
- be concerned with... 关注……

1029 unite [juˈnaɪt] v 使联合，统一，团结

We must unite the students in asking the principal to improve the quality of the class.
我们必须使学生们团结，要求校长改善课堂品质。
- league 团结
- unite with 联合，混合
- unite sb. in doing sth. 团结某人做某事

> **语法重点**
> unite 通常用来指联合、团结、结合在一起，从而构成一个整体。
> ⇒ quality (P. 212)

1030 unity ['juːnəti] n 单一，一致

You must strengthen your unity facing with the problem when you have nothing to eat.
在面对没有东西可以吃的问题时，你们必须加强团结。
- accordance 一致
- inconformity 不一致
- facing with... 面对……

> **语法重点**
> 注意"加强团结"用动词 strengthen。
> ⇒ strengthen (P. 507)

1031 universe ['juːnɪvɜːrs] n 宇宙，万物，世界

Once upon a time, people knew nothing about the universe.
很久以前，人们对宇宙一无所知。
- cosmos 宇宙
- once upon a time, ... 很久以前，……
- universe 常用来指包括地球以及其他天体的广大空间，而 cosmos 则侧重于指和谐而有序的宇宙。

1032 unless [ənˈles] conj 除非，如果不

I won't speak to her unless she says sorry to me.
她不向我道歉，我才不会跟她说话呢。
- unless and until 直到……才
- speak to 对……讲话

> **语法重点**
> speak to 侧重主语对宾语讲话。

1033 upset [ʌp'set] v 使心烦意乱 a 心烦意乱
It was apparent that he was upset.
很明显他心烦意乱。
同 disturb 使不安 句 it was apparent that... 很明显……

⊕ apparent (P. 255)

1034 vacant ['veɪkənt] a 空的，空虚的，茫然的
She stared at her lunch with a vacant expression.
她茫然地凝视着自己的午餐。
反 full 满的 句 ... with a vacant expression 茫然地……

⊕ expression (P. 293)

1035 valuable ['væljuəbl] a 贵重的，有价值的
I have to tell you that this necklace is more valuable than that one.
我不得不告诉你，这条项链比那条还贵。
辨 valuable 多用来指具有相当价值，可高价出售的，且有益、有用的东西。

1036 van [væn] n 有盖小货车，面包车，前驱
The foodie is in the van of catering.
美食家站在餐饮业的前列。
同 police van 警车 句 in the van of... 站在……的前列

语法重点
in the van of 后面通常接抽象名词。

1037 vanish ['vænɪʃ] v 消失，绝迹
All my troubles will vanish away if my mother buys me many computer games.
如果妈妈买很多电脑游戏给我，我就无忧无虑了。
同 disappear 消失 反 appear 出现 句 vanish away... 消失……

1038 variety [və'raɪəti] n 多样化
I'm certain there are a variety of dishes on the table.
我确定桌子上有很多种菜。
反 monotony 单调 句 I'm certain... 我确定……
辨 kind 多用来指性质相同、特征很相似，多归为一类的人或东西，而 variety 则侧重强调各自的特点、形式不同、品质不同的种类。

1039 various ['veriəs] a 各式各样的，不同的
The small town is noted for its various snacks.
这个小镇因为各式各样的小吃而出名。
同 different 不同的 反 uniform 一致的 句 be noted for... 以……而出名

语法重点
various 侧重于强调种类的数目。

1040 vary ['veri] v 使变化，使多样化
Don't vary from the law of nature and eat seasonal fruits.
不要违反自然规律，要吃时令水果。
同 alter 改变 句 vary from... 违反……
辨 vary 则更强调不规则或断断续续地改变，而 change 则指任何变化，完全改变，侧重于与原来的情况有明显的不同。

upset ~ violet

1041 vase [veɪs] **n** 花瓶
Dear! You broke my favorite vase.
天哪，你竟然打碎了我最喜爱的花瓶。

> 语法重点
> dear 作感叹词，多用于句首，表示后悔、难过、吃惊、同情等。

1042 vehicle ['viːəkl] **n** 交通工具
There—the two vehicles collided with each other because both of the drivers were eating while driving.
瞧，两辆车相撞了，因为两个司机都是边吃东西边开车。

> 语法重点
> there 作感叹词时，多用于句首，表示引起注意，或得意、鼓励、同情等。
> ⇨ collide (P. 687)

1043 verse [vɜːrs] **n** 诗，韵文
I will give a lecture on American verse tomorrow.
我明天要做一个关于美国诗歌的讲座。

1044 vest [vest] **n** 背心，内衣，马甲
Oh, no! I forgot my vest in the café where we just had coffee.
不会吧！我把背心忘在刚才我们喝咖啡的那个咖啡厅了。
● waistcoat 背心，马甲　● lifesaving vest 救生背心

> 语法重点
> Oh, no!（喔，不会吧！）作感叹词，用于句首。多用来表示失望、懊恼等。

1045 vice-president [vaɪs 'prezɪdənt] **n** 副总统
The vice-president had a quick swig of water before speaking.
讲话前，副总统匆忙喝了一大口水。
● executive vice-president 执行副总裁

> 语法重点
> have a quick swig of（匆忙喝一口）后面要接表示饮料的名词。

1046 victim ['vɪktɪm] **n** 受害者，受骗者
I soon fell victim to hamburgers.
我很快就被汉堡迷住了。
● sufferer 受害者　● become the victim of 成为……的牺牲品

> 语法重点
> fall victim to（被迷住了）后面通常接物，不接人。

1047 violence ['vaɪələns] **n** 暴力，暴行
He finished his supper and slammed the door with violence.
他吃完晚餐，砰的一声猛地把门关上了。
● domestic violence 家庭暴力　● ... with violence 猛地……

1048 violent ['vaɪələnt] **a** 猛烈的，暴力的
With a violent movement, she shook the bread off her hand.
她一用力，甩掉了手上的面包。

1049 violet ['vaɪələt] **n** 紫罗兰，紫色 **a** 紫色的
Good heavens! My boyfriend sent me a bunch of violet!
天啊！男朋友竟然送给我一束紫罗兰！
● purple 紫色的　● shrinking violet 羞怯的人，畏首畏尾的人

> 语法重点
> Good heavens!（天啊！）作感叹词用，多用于句首，表示惊奇。

1050 **visible** [ˈvɪzəbl] a 可看见的，显而易见的
With the aid of the microscope, all viruses on the food are clearly visible.
在显微镜的帮助下，食物上的所有细菌都清晰可见。
noticeable 显而易见的　invisible 看不见的　barely visible 几乎看不见

语法重点
with the aid of（在……的帮助下）位置比较灵活，可用于句首，亦可用于句尾。

1051 **vision** [ˈvɪʒn] n 视力，视觉，幻觉
The beautiful waterfall came within our range of vision when we were eating and walking.
我们边走边吃时，美丽的瀑布进入我们的视野之中。
sight 视力　come into one's range of vision... 进入某人的视野

1052 **vitamin** [ˈvaɪtəmɪn] n 维生素
Wow! Apples are rich in vitamin E.
哇！苹果富含维生素 E。

语法重点
wow 用作感叹词时，常置于句首，用来表示赞赏、惊叹之意。

1053 **vivid** [ˈvɪvɪd] a 鲜明的，栩栩如生的
I have a vivid recollection of the shape of the statue.
我清楚地记得那雕像的形状。
live 生动的　dull 呆滞的，阴暗的　a vivid imagination 生动的想象

statue (P. 365)

1054 **volume** [ˈvɑːljuːm] n 音量，体积
What's the volume of the fridge which is full of food?
这个装满食物的冰箱体积有多少？
speak volumes 很有意义，含义很深
volume 也常用在短语 speak volumes for... 中，意思是"充分证明……的优点、品质"。

1055 **wag** [wæg] n / v 摇摆，摇头
It should be noted that he wagged his head when he saw the super star.
要注意，他看到这名超级巨星时摇了摇头。
tail wagging the dog 主次颠倒　It should be noted that... 要注意……

1056 **wage** [weɪdʒ] n 工资，代价，报酬
I was discontented with my wages because I can't buy enough food with it.
我对自己的薪资很不满意，因为它还不够我吃饭呢。
salary 工资　wage freeze 工资冻结
be discontented with... 对……不满意

语法重点
wage 指工资时，通常用复数形式。

enough (P. 034)

1057 **wagon** [ˈwægən] n 四轮马车，货车
How are you going to have your lunch in the small wagon?
你打算如何在这么小的马车里吃午餐呢？
carriage 四轮马车　on the wagon 戒酒
How are you going to...? 你打算如何……？

1058 waken ['weɪkən] v 叫醒，醒来

It looked as if he was wakened up, but he didn't sleep at all.
好像他是被叫醒似的，但是他根本就没睡。
- arouse 唤醒，醒来
- it looks as if... 看起来好像……

语法重点
waken 多用于被动态和引申意义。

1059 wander ['wɑːndər] v / n 徘徊，漫步，闲逛

Do constrain your mind not to wander from the dinner.
吃饭时克制着不让自己分心。
- have a wander 散步
- constrain one's mind not to do sth. 克制自己不做某事

1060 warmth [wɔːrmθ] n 暖和，热烈，热情，热心

Of one accord, they came out to enjoy the warmth of the sun after lunch.
午餐后，他们不约而同地去外面晒太阳。

语法重点
of one accord（不约而同）是固定搭配，one 不可以被 a 替换。
↳ accord (P. 667)

1061 warn [wɔːrn] v 警告，告诫

My sister warned me against the hot soup.
姐姐告诫我要小心热汤。
- caution 警告
- warn sb. off 通知某人离开或不要接触
- warn sb. against sth. 告诫某人小心某物

1062 wax [wæks] n 蜡 v 给……上蜡

How about lighting up a wax candle when we have supper?
吃晚餐时点支蜡烛怎么样？
- wax and wane 兴衰，盛衰
- light up... 照亮……

1063 weaken ['wiːkən] v 使……虚弱，变弱

What would you say of weakening the tea by adding water?
加些水把茶弄得淡一些，你觉得怎么样？
- 反 strengthen 加强，变强
- What would you say of...? 你认为……怎么样？

语法重点
what would you say of 后面通常接动名词。

1064 wealth [welθ] n 财富，财产

There is an old saying goes well "health is better than wealth," so don't hesitate to spend your money on eating something good.
有句谚语说得好，"健康胜于财富"所以别犹豫了，花钱吃点好吃的吧。
- fortune 财富
- 反 poverty 贫穷

↳ hesitate (P. 305)

1065 wealthy ['welθi] a 富裕的

The wealthy man cheated her into eating the steak.
那个富人骗她吃牛排。
- rich 富有的
- 反 poor 贫穷的
- cheat sb. into doing sth. 骗某人做某事

1066 **weave** [wiːv] v / n 编织，编造

Would you be so kind as to weave a garland of flowers?
能请你编一个花环吗？
- get weaving (on sth.) 精力充沛地或匆忙地开始做（某物）
- Would you be so kind as to...? 能否请你……？

1067 **web** [web] n 蜘蛛网，网，网络

I was enmeshed in the web of the debt because of drinking and gambling.
因为喝酒和赌博，我负债累累。
- net 网，网络
- a web of lies 一片谎言

语法重点
be enmeshed in（陷入）后面常接名词或者代词。
- debt (P. 150)

1068 **weed** [wiːd] n 野草 v 除草，淘汰

You'll never guess the café we used to go to is choked with weeds now.
你永远想不到，我们以前经常去的咖啡厅现在杂草丛生。
- weed sth. / sb. out 淘汰、剔除、除去（不需要的人或物）

语法重点
you'll never guess（你永远猜不到）后面通常接句子。

1069 **weep** [wiːp] v 哭泣，悲叹

All the children are weeping for starvation.
因为肚子饿，所有的孩子都在哭。
- sob 啜泣
- weep over... 因……而哭泣
- ... weep for... ……为……而哭

1070 **wheat** [wiːt] n 小麦，小麦色

You will be able to know what the wheat is if you have had cereal.
如果你喝过麦片粥，就会知道什么是小麦了。
- separate the wheat from the chaff 分清良莠
- you will be able to... if... 如果……，你将能够……

1071 **whip** [wɪp] v 鞭打，鞭策 n 鞭子

It's cruel to whip the child just because he was unwilling to wash his hands.
仅仅因为孩子不愿洗手就鞭打他，这太残忍了。
- flog 鞭打
- a fair crack of the whip 均等的机会

语法重点
it's cruel to（太残忍了）后面要接动词原形。

1072 **whistle** [ˈwɪsl] v 吹口哨，鸣汽笛 n 口哨，汽笛

Some people didn't hear the whistle for lunch, so some of them missed it.
有些人没听到午餐的哨声，所以他们之中的一些人没吃到饭。
- whistle in the dark 在惊险情况下尽力给自己壮胆。

- miss (P. 064)

1073 **wicked** ['wɪkɪd] **a** 邪恶的，缺德的

They supposed that the man was wicked, so they refused to have dinner with him.
他们认为那个人很坏，所以拒绝和他一起吃饭。
🔗 evil 邪恶的　🔗 virtuous 善良的

🔗 suppose (P. 369)

1074 **willow** ['wɪloʊ] **n** 柳树

What seems to be the trouble is the table beside which they are having dinner is made of willow.
问题好像在于，他们吃饭用的桌子是用柳木做的。

1075 **wink** [wɪŋk] **v** / **n** 眨眼，使眼色，闪烁

The girl showed much interest on the doll and winked at his mother to buy it.
那个女孩对洋娃娃表现出强烈的兴趣，向妈妈使眼色要买。
🔗 blink 眨眼　🔗 as easy as winking 非常容易，易如反掌

1076 **wipe** [waɪp] **v** 擦拭，除去，消除

Wipe out the bowl before you put soup into it.
盛汤前先把碗擦洗干净。
🔗 rub 擦　🔗 wipe away 擦去　🔗 ... wipe out... 擦洗干净……

1077 **wisdom** ['wɪzdəm] **n** 智慧，才智

The received wisdom is that he doesn't like playing cards.
大家一致认为他不喜欢玩牌。
🔗 wit 智慧　🔗 folly 愚蠢

语法重点
the received wisdom is that（大家一致认为）是习惯用法，注意 receive 用的是其过去分词形式。

1078 **wrap** [ræp] **v** 包裹，覆盖 **n** 围巾，包装材料

He wrapped himself up in a coat when he went out for shopping.
他外出购物时穿了一件外套。
🔗 cover 覆盖　🔗 unwrap 打开　🔗 wrap sb. up in cotton wool 过分保护某人
🔗 wrap oneself up in... 把某人裹在……里

语法重点
wrap 的过去式与过去分词都是重复词尾 p 再加上 ed。

1079 **wrist** [rɪst] **n** 手腕，腕部

He took me by my left wrist when we had coffee together.
我们一起喝咖啡时，他抓住了我的左手腕。
🔗 wrist joint 腕关节　🔗 take sb. by... 抓住某人的……

语法重点
take sb. by 后面要接表示身体部位的名词。

1080 **X-ray** ['eks reɪ] **n** X 光，X 光照片

What's the point of examining his stomach with the X-ray?
给他的胃照 X 光有什么意义？
🔗 What's the point of doing...? 做……有什么意义？

1081 yawn [jɔːn] v 打哈欠，张开 n 哈欠

He gave a yawn after lunch.
午餐后他打了个哈欠。
- make sb. yawn 使人打哈欠，使人厌倦
- give a / an... yawn 打了一个……的呵欠

语法重点
give a yawn 可以单独使用，也可以在 yawn 前加上不同的形容词。如 give an ostentatious yawn 可以表示"打了一个夸张的哈欠"。

1082 yell [jel] v / n 喊叫

He yelled at his mother because she didn't buy the shoes he wanted.
他因为妈妈没买他要的鞋子而对她大吼大叫。
- yell out 呼喊，大声地叫出
- ... yell at... ……对……大吼大叫
- yell at sb. about sth. 可以表示"因为某事对某人大吼大叫"。

1083 yolk [joʊk] n 蛋黄

Come on! He doesn't like the yolks.
拜托，他不喜欢吃蛋黄的。

语法重点
come on 多用在句首表示不耐烦，意思为"拜托！"，如例句所示；也表示催促、鼓励，意思是"快点，加油！"

→ proper (P. 343)

1084 zipper [ˈzɪpər] n 拉链

The banquet starts, but I couldn't find the proper way to sew in the zipper.
宴会已经开始了，可我没办法正确地缝上拉链。
- zip 拉链
- invisible zipper 隐形拉链

1085 zone [zoʊn] n 地区，区域，地带

They were required to meet the boss in the economic development zone.
他们被要求去经济开发区和老板见面。
- area 区域
- industrial zone 工业区
- ... be required to... ……被要求做……

语法重点
be required to 后面通常接动词原形。

→ economic (P. 431)

MEMO

LEVEL 4
abandon ~ youthful

LEVEL 4 | abandon ～ youthful

Review test

复习 Level 3 的学习成果，还记得以下单词是什么意思吗？

1 capital ▶ _____
2 wage ▶ _____
3 hatch ▶ _____
4 proper ▶ _____
5 decade ▶ _____
6 replace ▶ _____
7 territory ▶ _____
8 employee ▶ _____

Preview

单词重点预习，在开始之前先预习会让印象更深刻喔！

1 catalogue ▶ _____
2 deadline ▶ _____
3 identification ▶ _____
4 pirate ▶ _____
5 scarcely ▶ _____
6 embarrass ▶ _____
7 landmark ▶ _____
8 abstract ▶ _____

1 • 定冠词 the 的使用情况

指独特的、唯一的对象	搭配序数时
表示某一群体时	表示抽象概念时
表示方位或方向时	表示宇宙中的唯一物体时
表示国家	搭配被限定的专有名词时

• 不定冠词 a / an 的使用情况

等同于 one 时	搭配下定义的名词
搭配作同位语的单数可数名词	搭配引导句中的单数主语

• 零冠词的使用情况

称呼语或称谓	三餐、月份、星期、季节
学科、运动	by 引导的工具

2 句子中，主语和动词在数量上必须保持一致。

搭配单数动词的主语	单数名词、物质名词、抽象名词、名词短语、名词性从句 more than one / many a + 单数名词 the number of + 复数可数名词 an amount of / a great deal of + 不可数名词
搭配复数动词的主语	复数名词、few + 可数名词复数
依据较接近的主语而定	either... or... / neither... or... / not only... but also...
依据连词前面的主语而定	but / no less than / as much as / as well as

3 从句可分成：名词性从句、形容词性从句、副词性从句等，功能跟相应词性的用法相同。

| 正确答案 | Review test 1 名词；形容词 / 首府；资本的 2 名词 / 工资 3 名词；动词 / 孵化；孵出 4 形容词 / 适当的
5 名词 / 十年 6 动词 / 取代 7 名词 / 领土 8 名词 / 员工
Preview 1 名词 / 目录 2 名词 / 截止日期 3 名词 / 识别 4 名词；动词 / 海盗；盗版
5 副词 / 几乎不 6 动词 / 使困窘 7 名词 / 地标 8 形容词；名词；动词 / 抽象的；摘要；抽取

abandon ~ youthful

0001 abandon [əˈbændən] v 放弃，抛弃，放纵
It's not good for him to abandon himself to the virtual reality of the network.
他沉溺于网络的虚拟实境而不能自拔，真不好。
同 desert 遗弃　反 conserve 保存　词 ... abandon oneself to... ……沉溺于……

▶ 语法重点
与 abandon oneself to 具有相似含义的还有 surrender oneself to, addict oneself to 等。
⇒ virtual (P. 803)

0002 abdomen [ˈæbdəmən] n 腹部
What I'm getting at is you'll suffer from pain in your abdomen again if you eat ice-cream.
我的意思是，你吃了冰激凌，又会肚子痛了。
同 belly 腹部　类 lower abdomen 下腹部

0003 absolute [ˈæbsəluːt] a 绝对的，无约束的
I mean what he said is absolute libel.
我的意思是，他所说的完全是诽谤。
同 complete 完全的　类 absolute majority 超过半数，绝对多数

▶ 语法重点
what sb. said 作主语，动词用单数形式。

0004 absorb [əbˈzɔːrb] v 吸收，吸引……的注意，吞并
I have been tired of wearing silk socks, because they don't absorb sweat.
我厌倦穿丝袜，因为它们不吸汗。
词 I have been tired of... 我厌倦了……

0005 abstract [ˈæbstrækt] a 抽象的　n 摘要　v 抽取
My point of view is that his abstract theories are useless.
我的观点是，他的抽象理论没有什么用。
反 concrete 具体的　类 in the abstract 抽象地，在理论上

▶ 语法重点
that 从句是具体介绍 point of view 的内容。

0006 academic [ˌækəˈdemɪk] a 学术的　n 大学教师，学者
I thought academic success was not always an open sesame to a good job.
我认为，在校成绩好并非总是获得好工作的敲门砖。
词 sesame 作不可数名词，本意是"芝麻"，open Sesame 出自《天方夜谭》，表示用以开门的咒语。

⇒ success (P. 230)

0007 accent [ˈæksent] n 重音，强调　v 重读，强调
I don't like the boy because he speaks in his broad accent.
我不喜欢那个男孩，是因为他说话口音很重。
同 emphasis 强调　词 ... speak in one's broad accent 说话口音很重

389

0008 acceptance [əkˈseptəns] n 接受，认可，同意
Your words and opinion will receive wide acceptance.
你的话和观点将会得到广泛的认可。
同 adoption 接受 反 refusal 拒绝

语法重点
and 是并列连词，用以连接彼此是并列关系的单词、短语、分句或从句，被连接的两个部分彼此是独立的，在句法上是平等的。
查 opinion (P. 198)

0009 access [ˈækses] n 接近，入口 v 进入，存取
Don't worry; I have access to people who can help me.
别担心，我有办法接近能帮助我的人。
反 exit 出口 搭 access time 存取时间 搭 have access to... 有接触……的机会

0010 accidental [ˌæksɪˈdentl] a 偶然的，意外的
No matter how suspicious you are, my breaking your cup was really accidental.
不管你怎么怀疑，我打破你的杯子真的是意外。
反 planned 有计划的 搭 no matter how... 无论怎么样……

语法重点
动名词 my breaking your cup 在句中作主语。

0011 accompany [əˈkʌmpəni] v 陪伴，伴随……发生
I believe he can conquer anything if she accompanies him.
我相信，有她的陪伴，他可以征服一切。
同 companion 陪伴 搭 accompany by... 在……的陪同下
句 I believe... 我相信……

0012 accomplish [əˈkɑːmplɪʃ] v 达成，实现
He is afraid that he can't accomplish his ideal in his life.
他怕他这一生都无法实现他的梦想了。

语法重点
例句中的 that 是从属连词，常用的从属连词还有 whether，when，although，because 等。

0013 accomplishment [əˈkɑːmplɪʃmənt]
n 完成，成就，才艺
His laziness stands in the way of accomplishment of his plan.
懒惰是他实现自己计划的障碍。
句 ... stand in the way of... ……是……的障碍

0014 accountant [əˈkaʊntənt] n 会计师
She must have been defrauded of her money by the dishonest accountant.
她的钱肯定是被那个奸诈的会计骗走了。
搭 be defrauded of... 被骗走了……

语法重点
在英语中，冠词可以分为三类：不定冠词、定冠词以及零冠词，例句中的 the 就是定冠词。
查 dishonest (P. 154)

0015 accuracy [ˈækjərəsi] n 正确，精确度
No one can deny that it's hard to state the number of casualties with accuracy.
没人能够否认，准确地说出伤亡人数是困难的。
反 inaccuracy 不精确，错误 句 no one can deny that... 没人能否认……
辨 state 较正式，通常指用明确的语言或文字着重叙述事实，既强调内容，又注重语气。tell 是普通用词，指把某事告诉或讲述给某人听，可以用于口语或书面语。

0016 accuse [əˈkjuːz] v 控告，指责
He was accused of stealing; it was really astonishing.
他被指控犯有盗窃罪，真让人惊讶。
- condemn 谴责　- defend 辩护

语法重点
be accused of（被指控）后面通常接名词、动名词结构。

0017 acid [ˈæsɪd] n 酸，酸性物质 a 酸的，尖酸的
Learning from the last failure, I will be careful with acid this time.
从上次的失败中吸取教训，我这次要小心酸。

语法重点
learning from 可以表示"从……中学习"，还可表示"从……得到教训"，from 后一般接 sb. 或者 sth.。
- literature (P. 467)

0018 acquaint [əˈkweɪnt] v 使认识，使熟悉
I am acquainted with the Chinese Literature.
我对中国文学很了解。
- familiarize 使熟悉　- be acquainted with... 了解……

0019 acquaintance [əˈkweɪntəns] n 相识，了解，熟人
I'm not good at French, just having some acquaintance with it.
我不擅长法语，只是懂一点儿罢了。
- make one's acquaintance 结识某人，与某人相见

0020 acquire [əˈkwaɪər] v 取得，获得，学到
I'm very lucky, for I acquired the famous singer's autography just now.
我刚得到那个知名歌手的亲笔签名，真是太幸运了。
- gain 获得　- lose 失去　- an acquired taste 逐渐培养的爱好

0021 acre [ˈeɪkər] n 英亩
Nothing is more important than to have several acres of farmland for me.
对于我来说，没有什么比拥有几亩田更重要的事了。

语法重点
nothing is... than...（没有什么比……更……）中，is 后面要接形容词的比较级。

0022 adapt [əˈdæpt] v 改编，使适应
I will try my best to adapt myself to the new surroundings.
我要尽力使自己适应新环境。
- adjust 使……适应　- ... adapt oneself to... ……使自己适应……

语法重点
surrounding 作形容词，表示"周围的，附近的"，surroundings 作复数名词，表示"周围的事物，环境"。

0023 adequate [ˈædɪkwət] a 适当的，能胜任的，足够的
I wonder if she is adequate to the job.
我不知道她是否能胜任这项工作。
- sufficient 足够的　- deficient 不足的

语法重点
be adequate to（胜任）中的 to 是介词。

0024 adjective [ˈædʒɪktɪv] n 形容词 a 形容词的，从属的
I hate you for applying that adjective to me.
我讨厌你用那个字眼来形容我。
- dependent 从属的　- ... apply... to... ……把……应用于……

0025 adjust [ə'dʒʌst] v 调节，使适应
Now that you ask for my opinion, I tell you that you should adjust the focus of your camera.
既然你征求我的意见，那我就告诉你，你应该调节照相机的焦距。
同 adapt 使适应　　反 derange 扰乱，打乱　　派 now that... 既然……

0026 adjustment [ə'dʒʌstmənt] n 调整，调节，适应
I have to make adjustments to my thinking in order that I can survive in office.
为了保住这份工作，我必须转变观念。
同 adaptation 适应　　派 ... make adjustments to... ……在……上做出改变

0027 admirable ['ædmərəbl] a 令人钦佩的，极好的
An admirable performance means a great deal to me.
一场优美的表演对于我来说意义重大。
派 ... mean a great deal to sb. ……对某人意义重大

0028 admiration [,ædmə'reɪʃn] n 钦佩，赞赏
I was struck with admiration when I saw his works.
看到他的作品，我惊叹不已。
反 contempt 轻视　　派 be struck with admiration 大为惊叹

语法重点
be struck with admiration 的主语通常是人。

0029 admission [əd'mɪʃn] n 进入，认可，入场费
I think there is an increase in school admission of children.
我认为，入学儿童的数量有所增加。
同 recognition 承认　　派 admission of guilt 承认有罪

语法重点
不定冠词 a 或 an 可用于抽象名词前，使抽象名词具体化。如例句中的 an 用于抽象名词 increase（增加）来表示具体数量的增加。

0030 agency ['eɪdʒənsi] n 代理商，代理处，政府机构
Considering that the service of this travel agency is good, we choose it.
考虑到这家旅行社的服务较好，我们就选择了它。

语法重点
分词连词是由动词的分词形式转变而来的连词，例句中的 considering 就属于分词连词。

0031 agent ['eɪdʒənt] n 代理人，代理商，密探
You can ask an agent to keep the local people under control.
你可以让一个探员去控制当地的民众。

0032 aggressive [ə'gresɪv] a 侵略的，好斗的，有进取心的
I am angry that he puts forward some aggressive policies.
我对他提出一些侵略性的政策感到很生气。
同 belligerent 好战的　　反 defensive 自卫的　　派 aggressive behavior 攻击行为

派 forward (P. 168)

0033 agreeable [ə'griːəbl] a 令人愉快的，宜人的
I am agreeable to watch a film with him tonight.
我欣然同意和他今晚一起去看电影。
同 pleasant 令人愉快的　　反 disagreeable 不愉快的

语法重点
be agreeable to（同意）后面要接动词原形。

adjust ～ ambitious

0034 AIDS [eɪdz] `abbr` 艾滋病
No matter what you say, I still think AIDS isn't a serious infectious disease.
不管你们说什么，我都认为艾滋病不是一种严重的传染病。
◎ AIDS virus 艾滋病病毒　◎ no matter what... 不管……

> **语法重点**
> 不定冠词 a 只用于单数可数名词前，不强调数目概念，只用于泛指事物，说明其名称或种类。

0035 alcohol [ˈælkəhɔːl] `n` 酒精
On no account can we drink too much alcohol.
我们绝对不能饮酒过量。
◎ liquor 酒　◎ alcohol abuse 酗酒

> **语法重点**
> on no account can we（我们绝对不能）后面接动词原形。

0036 alert [əˈlɜːrt] `a` 机警的，灵敏的 `n` 警戒，警报
We should be on the alert for the cunning colleagues.
我们应该提防着狡猾的同事们。
◎ watchful 警惕的　◎ on the alert 警惕，提防

0037 allowance [əˈlaʊəns] `n` 零用钱
I am in favor of giving the allowance to the old couple.
我赞成把津贴给这对老夫妇。
◎ make allowance for... 考虑到……　◎ ... in favor of... ……赞成……
◎ 定冠词 the 有三种读音，如果用于元音之前，the 的读音就应该是 [ðɪ]。

⊙ favor (P. 163)

0038 aluminum [ˌæljəˈmɪniəm] `n` 铝
I think he will acknowledge that he stole the aluminum can on the table.
我想，他会公开承认他偷了桌上的那个铝罐。
◎ ... on the table 公开地……

⊃ acknowledge (P. 522)

0039 a.m. `abbr` 上午，午前
He talks as if he doesn't plan to come back before 11 o'clock a.m.
他说话的口气好像是不打算在上午十一点之前回来。
◎ p.m 下午　◎ talk as if... 说起来好像……

0040 amateur [ˈæmətər] `n` 业余爱好者 `a` 业余的
You have no choice but to let an amateur actor play the role.
你没有别的选择，只能让一个业余演员来扮演这个角色。
◎ specialist 专家　◎ ... have no choice but... ……别无选择，只能……

> **语法重点**
> have no choice but 后面要接动词不定式。

0041 ambitious [æmˈbɪʃəs] `a` 有野心的，有抱负的
I tell you I am ambitious to win the first place.
告诉你，我下决心要赢得第一名。

> **语法重点**
> be ambitious to（决心）后面要接动词原形。

393

0042 **amid / amidst** [ə'bɪmd] / [ə'bɪmd]
prep 在……之中，在……中间

Sorry to bother you, but I hope you can find him amid these people.
抱歉，打扰你了，但我希望你能在这些人中找到他。
⊙ around 在……周围　　⊙ deep amid thought 沉思

※ bother (P. 132)

0043 **amuse** [ə'mjuːz] **V** 使……欢乐，娱乐，消遣

Tell me more about the girl; she always amuses me.
再谈谈那个女孩吧，她总是逗我开心。
⊙ amuse oneself 是"自娱自乐"；amuse oneself with 是"以……自娱"。

0044 **amusement** [ə'mjuːzmənt] **n** 乐趣，消遣

He will take me to the amusement park and that's what I mean to do.
他要带我去游乐园玩，那正是我想要做的。
⊙ recreation 娱乐　　⊙ amusement park 游乐园

0045 **analysis** [ə'næləsɪs] **n** 分析，解析

Surfing the internet is the best way to get the analysis of the novel.
想要得到这本小说的分析，最好的办法是上网。
⊙ in the last analysis 总之，归根究底

语法重点
it's the best way（最好的办法）后面通常接动词不定式。

0046 **analyze** ['ænəlaɪz] **V** 分析，解析，研究

We should analyze the situation and find the way to solve the problem now.
现在我们应该分析形势，找出解决这个问题的方法。
⊙ synthesize 合成，综合　　⊙ analyze data 分析资料

※ situation (P. 360)

0047 **ancestor** ['ænsestər] **n** 祖先，祖宗

I learned that my ancestors came from Sichuan.
我得知自己的祖先是来自四川。
⊙ forefather 祖先　　⊙ descendant 后裔，子孙

0048 **anniversary** [ˌænɪ'vɜːrsəri] **n** 周年纪念日

That reminds me, I want to celebrate our 20th wedding anniversary in London.
那提醒我，我想去伦敦庆祝结婚二十周年。
⊙ wedding anniversary 结婚纪念日　　⊙ that reminds me, ... 那提醒了我，……

※ remind (P. 348)

0049 **annoy** [ə'nɔɪ] **V** 令人恼怒，使烦恼

It annoyed me that he didn't come to my house yesterday.
昨天晚上他没有来我家，这让我很气恼。
⊙ annoy sb. 令某人生气　　⊙ it annoyed me that... 让我气恼的是……

0050 **annual** [ˈænjuəl] a 年度的

The problem is the annual governmental conference won't be held in the city hall.
问题是一年一度的政府会议不在市政大厅举行。
- yearly 每年的　　- annual report 年度报告

⊃ conference (P. 412)

0051 **anxiety** [æŋˈzaɪəti] n 忧虑，担心，渴望

Her standing John up caused me great anxiety.
她让约翰空等一场，我感到很焦虑。
- ... stand sb. up ……让某人空等，放某人鸽子，多用来指约会爽约。

0052 **anxious** [ˈæŋkʃəs] a 忧心的，渴望的

I always feel anxious when I give a speech in public.
公开演讲时，我总是很焦虑。
- uneasy 心神不安的　　- easy 舒适的

0053 **apologize** [əˈpɑːlədʒaɪz] v 道歉，赔不是，辩解

I hope he will apologize to me on receiving my letter of complaint.
我希望，一收到我的投诉信，他就来向我道歉。
- apologize to... 向……道歉
- letter 是最普通用词，泛指一切形式的书信，尤指邮寄的信，correspondence 是集合名词，指全部的来往信件。

⊃ complaint (P. 275)

0054 **apology** [əˈpɑːlədʒi] n 道歉，认错，愧悔

You should make an apology to all the guests now.
你现在应该向所有的客人道歉。
- ... make an apology to sb. ……向某人道歉

0055 **appliance** [əˈplaɪəns] n 器具，器械，装置

I plan to sell a variety of drugs as well as medicine appliances.
我打算销售各种各样的药品和医疗器械。
- device 装置　　- domestic appliance 家用电器　　- ... as well as... ……和……

语法重点
a variety of 可修饰可数名词或不可数名词。

0056 **applicant** [ˈæplɪkənt] n 申请人，应征者

There's no way John was the eighth applicant for the job.
约翰绝对不可能是第八个申请这项工作的人。

语法重点
有些单词或短语在使用时，前面不允许加冠词，也就是零冠词。如句中的 John。

0057 **application** [ˌæplɪˈkeɪʃn] n 应用

I consider that they are writing an application for admission.
我认为他们正在写入学申请。
- application form 申请表　　- I consider that... 我认为……

语法重点
代词通常有明确的指代物件，之前不加任何冠词，如例句中的代词 they 在句中作主语，之前不加任何冠词。

0058 appoint [ə'pɔɪnt] v 任命，委派，指定
The question is that they may be reluctant to appoint a teacher to the vacant post.
问题是，他们可能不愿委派一名老师来填补那个空缺。
📘 assign 指派　📘 appoint as... 任命为……

0059 appointment [ə'pɔɪntmənt] n 任命，职位，约会
I am glad to hear that he got a good appointment yesterday.
听说他昨天找到了一个好工作，我为他高兴。
📘 keep one's appointment 守约　📘 I am glad to hear that... 听到……我很高兴

> **语法重点**
> 宾语从句与主句的时态可以不一致。

0060 appreciation [ə,pri:ʃi'eɪʃn] n 欣赏，感激，评价
I think he shows no appreciation of classic music.
我认为，他不会欣赏古典音乐。

> **语法重点**
> appreciation 当"欣赏，感激"讲时是可数名词，当"评价"讲时是不可数名词。

0061 appropriate [ə'proʊpriət] a 适当的，合适的，相称的
The example you cited wasn't appropriate for him.
你举的例子不适合他。
📘 suitable 适当的　📘 inappropriate 不适当的　📘 be appropriate for... 适合……
📘 appropriate 指专门适合于某人或某事，语气较重，强调"恰如其分"，而 suitable 指具有适合于某种特定场合、地位或情况等品质。

0062 approval [ə'pru:vl] n 认可，同意，批准
The news that he gave his approval to that project excited me.
他批准那项工程，这消息让我很兴奋。
📘 authorization 认可　📘 disapproval 不赞成

> **语法重点**
> 例句中的从属连词 that 在句中引导的是同位语从句，属于名词性从句。

0063 arch [ɑ:rtʃ] n 拱门，拱，拱状物 a 调皮的，淘气的
The way I see it, she gave us an arch smile in order to relax us.
我的看法是，她朝我们淘气地微笑是为了让我们放松。
📘 arch bridge 拱形桥　📘 the way I see it, ... 我的看法是……

> **语法重点**
> the way I see it 一般用在句首，后面要接表达自己观点的句子。

0064 arise [ə'raɪz] v 上升，产生，起源于
I believe the quarrel arose from a book.
我相信，这场争吵是由一本书引起的。
📘 originate 发源　📘 arise from... 起因于，由……引起

> **语法重点**
> arise 是不规则动词，其过去式、过去分词分别是 arose, arisen。
> 📘 quarrel (P. 344)

0065 arm [ɑ:rm] n 武器，手臂
It's his holding me by the arm that irritated me.
他抓住我的手臂激怒了我。
📘 weapon 武器　📘 bear arms 携带武器　📘 ... hold sb. by... ……抓住某人的……

> **语法重点**
> 定冠词 the 用在表示身体部位的名词前，如例句中的 the arm。

0066 arouse [əˈraʊz] v 唤起，激起，叫醒

Computer is the only thing that can arouse my interest.
只有电脑能引起我的兴趣。

- awaken 唤醒
- ... arouse one's interest ……引起某人的兴趣

语法重点
定冠词 the 可以用在形容词 only, very, same 等的前面表示强调，如例句中的 the only thing 就是强调"唯一的东西"。

0067 article [ˈɑːrtɪkl] n 物品，条款，文章

I don't want to make an outline of the article at night.
我不想在晚上写文章的大纲。

- outline (P. 332)

0068 artificial [ˌɑːrtɪˈfɪʃl] a 人工的，假的

I find his eyebrows are artificial in a glance.
我一眼就看出，他的眉毛是假的。

- fake 伪造的
- natural 自然的，天生的
- artificial respiration 人工呼吸
- ... in a glance 一眼就……

0069 artistic [ɑːrˈtɪstɪk] a 艺术的，美术的，精美的

We hold the opinion that the Louvre is one of the world's famous artistic centers.
我们认为，卢浮宫是世界有名的艺术中心之一。

- art 艺术的
- artistic work 艺术作品

语法重点
Louvre 是世界上独一无二的建筑物，所以前面要用定冠词 the。

0070 ashamed [əˈʃeɪmd] a 羞愧的，感到害臊的

I was ashamed to say I didn't go to his party.
我不好意思说我没有参加他的派对。

- compunctious 惭愧的
- feel ashamed 感到惭愧

语法重点
be ashamed to 后面要接动词原形。

0071 aspect [ˈæspekt] n 方面，方位，外貌

He loves me; that is because my aspect is fair and arresting.
他爱我，那是因为我漂亮、惹人注目。

- appearance 外貌
- that is because... 那是因为……

0072 aspirin [ˈæsprɪn] n 阿司匹林

Supposing she has a headache, give her two aspirins.
如果她头疼的话，就让她吃两片阿司匹林。

语法重点
supposing（假如）是分词连词，后面接句子。
- suppose (P. 369)

0073 assemble [əˈsembl] v 聚集，收集，装配

I think you don't need to assemble on the playground in the morning.
我认为，你们早上不需要在操场上集合。

- gather 收集
- dismiss 解散

0074 assembly [əˈsembli] n 集会，议会，装配

I believe the assembly will come to a close this Saturday.
我相信，大会将于本周六闭幕。

- assembly line 装配线
- ... come to a close ……闭幕

语法重点
表示星期的单词前不需要用冠词。

0075 assign [əˈsaɪn] v 分配，指定，指派
Provided the teacher doesn't assign homework for us, I will watch TV.
如果老师不指派作业给我们，我就看电视。
- distribute 分配 - assign sb. a task 指派某人一个任务
- assign 指按照某种原则进行的硬性分配，未必就是公平的，而 distribute 通常指以整体或定量分为若干份来分配。

0076 assignment [əˈsaɪnmənt] n 任务，功课
We can't emphasize the importance of the new assignment too much.
我们再强调新任务的重要性也不为过。

◎ emphasize (P. 289)

0077 assistance [əˈsɪstəns] n 帮助
The reason why I hate her is that she refused to give me assistance.
我讨厌她的原因是她拒绝帮助我。
- financial assistance 财政资助 - ... give sb. assistance ……帮助某人

语法重点
hate 表示人的情感，一般没有时态的变化。

0078 associate [əˈsoʊʃieɪt]
v 联合，联想 a 联合的 n 伙伴，朋友
Sorry, I always associate a highway with an accident.
对不起，我总是把高速公路和车祸联系在一起。
- associate with sb. 与某人交往 - ... associate... with... ……把……和……联系起来

0079 association [əˌsoʊʃiˈeɪʃn] n 协会，联想，结合
We must do something to join the association.
我们必须采取行动以加入这个社团。
- union 协会 - association with ……交往，与……联合

语法重点
we must do something 后面通常接动词不定式。

0080 assume [əˈsuːm] v 以为，承担，采用
I assume he has arrived in London.
我想他已经到伦敦了。

0081 assurance [əˈʃʊrəns] n 保证，确信，保险
I give you an assurance that I will buy you a present when I come back.
我向你保证，回来时一定买礼物给你。
- assurance company 保险公司
- I give you an assurance that... 我向你保证……

0082 assure [əˈʃʊr] v 向……保证，使确信，使放心
I assure you that I would never betray you.
我向你保证，永远不背叛你。
- convince 使确信 - I assure you that... 我向你保证……

◎ betray (P. 677)

0083 **athletic** [æθˈletɪk] a 运动的，强壮的
To tell the truth, I dislike the athletic star.
说实话，我不喜欢那个运动明星。
- strong 强壮的　- weak 虚弱的　- to tell the truth, ... 说实话……

0084 **ATM**
abbr 自动存提款机（= automatic teller machine）
To put it bluntly, I will never use an ATM.
直截了当地说，我永远都不会去用自动存提款机。
- ATM equipment 柜员机　- to put it bluntly, ... 直截了当地说……

0085 **atmosphere** [ˈætməsfɪr] n 气氛，氛围
I think the small town is still bathed in a festive atmosphere.
我觉得，这个小镇还沉浸在节日的气氛中。
- air 大气，空气　- be bathed in... 沉浸在……

0086 **atom** [ˈætəm] n 原子，微粒
I don't think a molecule is made up of atoms.
我认为，分子不是由原子组成的。
- be made up of... 由……组成

○ molecule (P. 598)

0087 **atomic** [əˈtɑːmɪk] a 原子的，原子能的
It is for the same reason that I don't understand the meaning of the word atomic.
我不明白单词 atomic 的意思，也是出自同样的原因。
- nuclear 原子能的　- atomic energy 原子能

0088 **attach** [əˈtætʃ] v 装上，贴上，使附属
As far as I'm concerned you needn't attach the label to the book.
就我看来，你不需要把标签贴到书上。
- detach 分离　- attach file 附件　- as far as I'm concerned... 就我看来……

0089 **attachment** [əˈtætʃmənt] n 附件，附属物，依恋
I think the little girl has a great attachment to her mother.
我觉得，那个小女孩十分依恋妈妈。
- adherence 依附　- segregation 分离　- attachment point 接合点

语法重点
have a great attachment to 中的 to 是介词，后面接名词或者代词。

0090 **attraction** [əˈtrækʃn] n 吸引力
I felt an immediate attraction for him at that moment.
在那一刻，我对他顿生爱慕。
- appeal 吸引力　- tourist attraction 观光胜地

语法重点
feel an immediate attraction for 后面一般接人。

0091 audio [ˈɔːdiəʊ] a 声音的 n 音响，设备
Be careful not to step on my audio components.
小心，别踩到我的音响设备。
同 vocal 声音的　反 video 视频的　搭 audio frequency 音讯

↪ component (P. 690)

0092 authority [əˈθɔːrəti] n 权力，权威，专家
I think we have no authority for the act.
我觉得我们无权这样做。

0093 autobiography [ˌɔːtəbaɪˈɒɡrəfi] n 自传，自传文学
I will spare no effort to write my autobiography.
我将不遗余力地写自传。

> **语法重点**
> spare no effort to（不遗余力地）后面接动词原形。

0094 await [əˈweɪt] v 等待，期待
There's no point in awaiting his letter for me.
对于我来说，等他的来信毫无意义。
同 expect 期待　反 despair 绝望　搭 await respectively 恭候

> **语法重点**
> await 是及物动词，相当于 wait for。
> ↪ letter (P. 058)

0095 awkward [ˈɔːkwəd] a 笨拙的，尴尬的
I was awkward for I forgot about his birthday.
我忘记了他的生日，真是尴尬。
同 clumsy 笨拙的　反 clever 聪明的，机灵的

> **语法重点**
> forget 作不及物动词时，常与 about 连用。

0096 backpack [ˈbækpæk] n 背包 v 背包徒步旅行
Both the box and the backpack are what I want.
箱子和背包都是我想要的。

> **语法重点**
> 主语是 the box 和 the backpack，所以 be 动词用 are。

0097 bald [bɔːld] a 秃头的，单调的
I won't buy him a comb because he is as bald as a coot.
我不会买梳子给他，因为他头上一根头发也没有。
同 hairless 秃顶的　搭 (as) bald as a coot 头顶全秃的

0098 ballet [ˈbæleɪ] n 芭蕾舞，芭蕾舞剧
Not only he but also I want to enjoy the ballet.
他和我都想看芭蕾舞剧。
搭 not only... but also... 不仅……而且……

> **语法重点**
> not only... but also 也适用于就近原则，如例句中动词 want 要与 I 保持一致。

0099 bankrupt [ˈbæŋkrʌpt] a 破产的 v 使破产
We must take action lest our company should go bankrupt.
为了不使公司破产，我们必须采取措施。
同 insolvent 破产的　搭 we must take action... 我们必须采取措施……

> **语法重点**
> "破产" 也可以用 go broke, become insolvent 来表达。

0100 bargain [ˈbɑːrɡən] v 买卖 n 便宜货，协议
I scorn to bargain with the shopkeeper.
我不屑于与店主讨价还价。

0101 barrier ['bæriər] n 路障，屏障
I think the chicken will not run away once I set a barrier.
我觉得，把栅栏建好之后，小鸡就不会乱跑了。
- obstruction 障碍
- once... 一旦……

> **语法重点**
> once 是从属连词，可引导名词性从句、形容词性从句。

0102 basin ['beɪsn] n 盆地，流域，盆子
To be frank, I don't like the color of the basin.
老实说，我不喜欢那个盆子的颜色。
- to be frank, ... 老实说，……

> frank (P. 168)

0103 battery ['bætri] n 电池，排炮，一系列
I was bored to death because a battery of questions troubled me.
一连串的问题困扰着我，我被烦死了。
- series 系列
- be bored to death 被烦死了

0104 beak [biːk] n 鸟嘴，鹰钩鼻
In my view, both those legs and the beak are made of paper.
在我看来，那些脚和鸡喙都是用纸做出来的。
- proboscis 喙，鼻子
- in my view... 在我看来……

> **语法重点**
> 一些表示身体部位的名词，通常用作复数形式，如 legs, eyes, arms, ears 等。

0105 beam [biːm] n 横梁，微笑，光束 v 发光，微笑
I think he is handsome when he beams at us with satisfaction.
我觉得，他满意地对着我们微笑时可帅了。
- smile 微笑
- on the beam 正确的

> satisfaction (P. 501)

0106 behavior [bɪ'heɪvjər] n 行为，举止，表现
As far as I could see, her behavior was unjustifiable yesterday.
在我看来，她昨天的行为是不合情理的。
- conduct 行为
- as far as I could see, ... 在我看来，……

0107 biography [baɪ'ɑːgrəfi] n 传记
For my part, the biography isn't interesting at all.
在我看来，那本传记一点儿也不有趣。
- celebrity biography 名人传记
- for my part, ... 在我看来，……

> **语法重点**
> at all 是用来加强语气，去掉 at all 也不影响句子的完整性。

0108 biology [baɪ'ɑːlədʒi] n 生物学
I will choose either biology or physics as my major.
我将选择主修生物学或物理。
- ... choose... as... ……选择……作为……

> **语法重点**
> 因为是在二者之中选一个作为主修，所以 major 用单数形式。
>
> physics (P. 484)

0109 **blade** [bleɪd] n 刀片，刀刃
In my heart, she is a good blade.
在我心中，她剑术高明。
- knife 刀 - leaf blade 叶片 - in one's heart... 在某人心中……

0110 **blend** [blend] v 混合 n 混合物
For your information, your coat doesn't blend with your skin color.
告诉你，你的外套和肤色很不搭。
- mix 使混合，混合物 - sort 分类 - blend in 混合，调和

0111 **blessing** ['blesɪŋ] n 祝福，有益之事
What a blessing I caught the last bus!
我赶上了末班车，真是幸运！
- wish 祝福 - curse 诅咒

语法重点
what a blessing（真是幸运）后面要接句子。

0112 **blink** [blɪŋk] v / n 眨眼
I hope you can finish it in a blink of an eye.
我希望，你能在一眨眼的工夫完成它。
- wink 眨眼 - on the blink 不灵，出故障

语法重点
in a blink of an eye（一眨眼的工夫）是固定搭配，eye 要用单数。

0113 **bloom** [bluːm] v 开花，繁盛 n 花，开花
I absolutely agree with his words that the flowers are in full bloom in June.
他说这花在六月最盛开，我完全同意。
- blossom 开花 - fade 凋谢 - in (full) bloom 开花

语法重点
在表示月份的名词之前不加冠词，如例句中的 June（六月）。

0114 **blossom** ['blɑːsəm] n 花，开花 v 开花，成长
I'm afraid I won't be able to wait till the trees are in blossom.
我恐怕不能够等到这些树开花了。
- flower 开花，花 - blossom out 开花

语法重点
I'm afraid I won't be able to 后面接动词原形。

0115 **blush** [blʌʃ] v / n 脸红
I'm not certain whether I will blush if I am scolded.
我不确定受到责备时会不会脸红。
- flush 脸红 - I'm not certain... 我不确定……

⊃ scold (P. 501)

0116 **boast** [boʊst] v 自夸，吹牛
I don't like boasting about my son's success at school.
我不喜欢夸耀儿子在学校学习成绩良好。
- modesty 谦逊 - boast about 自夸，吹嘘

0117 **bond** [bɑːnd] n 联结，协定，债券

I think about one third of us share a bond with animals every day.
我觉得，我们之中三分之一的人每天都与动物有关联。
- convention 协定
- ... share a bond with... ……与……有关联

> 语法重点
> 英语中，表示分数时，分子用基数词，分母用序数词。如例句中 one third 表示"三分之一"。

0118 **bounce** [baʊns] v 弹回，重新恢复

From where I stand, I hope this cheque doesn't bounce.
从我的立场来说，我希望这张支票不要遭到退票。
- rebound 反弹，弹回
- bounce back 受挫折后恢复原状

> 语法重点
> bounce 也可以作名词，当"弹性"讲时是可数名词，当"弹力"讲时是不可数名词。

0119 **bracelet** ['breɪslət] n 手镯，表带

I am angry that I have been under a cloud since her bracelet was lost.
自从她的手镯不见以后，我一直受到怀疑，这让我很生气。
- bangle 手镯
- be under a cloud 受怀疑

0120 **brassiere / bra** [brəˈzɪr] / [brɑː] n 胸罩，乳罩

The color of my brassiere leaves much to be desired.
胸罩的颜色让我不满意。

- desire (P. 151)

0121 **breed** [briːd] v 饲养，繁殖，养育

My goal is to breed many rabbits.
我的目标是养很多兔子。

0122 **bridegroom** ['braɪdgruːm] n 新郎

I can go on condition that the bridegroom is drunk.
我可以走，条件是新郎必须喝醉。
- groom 新郎
- bride 新娘

> 语法重点
> on condition that（条件是）要接句子。

0123 **broil** [brɔɪl] v 烤，炙

To be frank, his words made me broil with envy.
坦率地说，他的话让我妒火中烧。
- roast 烤
- broiled chicken 烤鸡
- ... broil with envy 妒火中烧

- envy (P. 291)

0124 **broke** [broʊk] a 一无所有的，破产的

To be honest, I think the man is as broke as you are.
说实话，我觉得那个人和你一样分文不剩。
- bust 破产了的
- to be honest, ... 说实话，……

0125 **brutal** ['bruːtl] a 野蛮的，残忍的，冷酷无情的

I think you should make an effort to protect your family in front of the brutal facts.
我觉得，在严峻的现实面前，你应该努力保护你的家人。
- lenient 仁慈的
- ... make an effort to do sth. ……努力做某事

0126 **bulletin** [ˈbʊlətɪn] n 公告，布告，期刊
I hope he will put up a notice on a bulletin board tomorrow.
我希望，他明天在布告板上张贴通知。
- announcement 公告   - news bulletin 新闻简报   - ... put up... ……张贴……

0127 **cabinet** [ˈkæbɪnət] n 橱，柜，内阁
I think you should never keep these things in the cabinet.
我认为，你绝不该把这些东西放在橱柜内。
- shoe cabinet 鞋柜   - you should never... 你绝不应该……

语法重点
用 keep 这个单词，意思是"把某物保存在……"，侧重于状态。

0128 **calculate** [ˈkælkjuleɪt] v 计算，估计，推测
What I should do now is to calculate the cost of the travel.
我现在要做的是计算旅行的费用。
- count 计算   - what I should do now is... 我现在要做的是……
- calculate 通常指要求细致精确和复杂的计算，以解决疑难问题，而 count 指逐一计算而得出总数。

0129 **calculation** [ˌkælkjuˈleɪʃn] n 计算，估计
After much calculation, I decide to give up smoking.
经过慎重考虑后，我决定戒烟。
- appraisal 估计   - preliminary calculation 预算

0130 **calculator** [ˈkælkjuleɪtər] n 计算机，计算者，计算图表
I should make good use of my money, so I plan to buy a pocket calculator.
我应该好好利用我的钱，所以我计划买一台携带型计算器。
- pocket calculator 携带型计算器

语法重点
I should make good use of （我应该充分利用）后面要接名词或者代词。

0131 **calorie** [ˈkæləri] n 卡路里，卡
I was not supposed to eat lower calorie vegetables.
我本不该吃低卡路里的蔬菜。

0132 **campaign** [kæmˈpeɪn] n 竞选活动，运动，战役
You should avoid taking part in such a big campaign.
你应该避免参加这么大的活动。
- movement 活动，运动   - election campaign 竞选活动

语法重点
you should avoid（你应该避免）后面要接动名词。

0133 **candidate** [ˈkændɪdət] n 候选人，应试者
You are not permitted to meet the candidate in private.
你不得私下与那个候选人见面。
- nominee 候选人   - be not permitted to... 不被允许……

语法重点
注意 permit 的过去分词是重复词尾 t 再加上 ed。
- permit (P. 336)

0134 **capacity** [kəˈpæsəti] n 容量，资格
I think the book is within the capacity of children.
我认为，孩子们能看懂这本书。
- ability 能力   - in one's capacity as... 以某种身份或立场

0135 cape [keɪp] n 海角，斗篷，披肩

I believe the freighter will go through the Cape of Good Hope.
我相信，那艘货轮会经过好望角。
- Cape of Good Hope 好望角
- ... go through... ……经过……

> 语法重点
> 表示"海峡"的名称前一般需要用定冠词 the。

0136 capitalism [ˈkæpɪtəlɪzəm] n 资本主义

Why in God's name? It's ignorant of you to use the phrase monopolistic capitalism here.
天啊？你在这个地方用垄断资本主义这个短语，真是无知。

⊃ ignorant (P. 455)

0137 capitalist [ˈkæpɪtəlɪst] n 资本家，资本主义者 a 资本主义的

I guess quite a lot of people are out of job in capitalist countries.
我猜，在资本主义国家里有许多人失业。
- capitalistic 资本主义的
- communist 共产主义的

> 语法重点
> quite 与单数名词连用，冠词放在其后。

0138 career [kəˈrɪr] n 职业，事业

I don't think she began her career as a zoologist at the age of 20.
我认为，她不是在 20 岁时开始动物学家职业生涯的。
- work 职业
- ... begin one's career as... ……开始……的职业生涯
- career 指经过专门训练，终身愿意从事的职业，而 work 指任何种类的工作，也泛指职业。

0139 cargo [ˈkɑːrɡoʊ] n 货物，船货

We should make every effort to salvage the cargo ship.
我们应该竭尽全力去打捞那艘货船。
- freight 货物
- cargo vessel 货轮

0140 carrier [ˈkæriər] n 运送者，行李架

To my joy, the medicine has killed the carriers of disease such as mosquitoes.
让我高兴的是，那种药杀死了蚊子之类携带病毒的昆虫。
- to one's joy... 让某人高兴的是……

⊃ mosquito (P. 192)

0141 carve [kɑːrv] v 雕刻，切割

To some extent, I dislike the statue carved last year.
在某种程度上，我不喜欢去年雕刻的那个雕像。
- carve out 雕刻，创业
- to some extent, ... 在某种程度上……

> 语法重点
> statue 与 carve 是被动关系，所以 carve 用的是过去分词形式。

0142 catalogue [ˈkætəlɔːɡ] n 目录

I lose my hope for life now after a catalogue of disasters.
一连串的灾难后，我现在对生活失去了希望。

0143 **cease** [siːs] v / n 停止，终止
I don't believe that he ceased breathing.
我不相信他停止了呼吸。
- stop 停止　- begin 开始　- ... cease doing sth. ……停止做某事

0144 **celebration** [ˌselɪˈbreɪʃn] n 庆祝，典礼，宗教仪式
Personally, I feel he will take part in her eightieth birthday celebrations.
我个人认为，他会来参加她的八十大寿的庆祝活动。
- festival 庆祝　- in celebration of... 为庆祝……

> 语法重点
> 10 以上的表示整十的数词，其序数词的构成方法是：先将十位数的基数词的词尾 -ty 中的 y 变为 i，然后加 -eth。

0145 **cement** [sɪˈment] n 水泥，接合剂 v 巩固，接合
I think cement is widely used in building work.
我认为水泥在建筑工程中应用很广。
- consolidate 巩固　- in cement 坚定不移的

0146 **CD** abbr 光碟
I hope you can forgive me for breaking your CD.
我把你的光碟弄坏了，希望你能原谅。
- CD player CD 播放机　- ... forgive sb. for... ……原谅某人……

0147 **chamber** [ˈtʃeɪmbər] n 寝室，会议厅，房间
On one hand I want to sleep, and on the other hand I want to watch the chamber concert.
一方面我想睡觉，另一方面我又想听室内音乐会。
- on one hand..., on the other hand... 一方面……，另一方面……

- concert (P. 275)

0148 **championship** [ˈtʃæmpiənʃɪp] n 冠军的地位，拥护
My dream is that I can take part in the 20th world championship.
我的梦想是，能参加第 20 届世界锦标赛。

> 语法重点
> 英语中表示序数词时，一般在数词之后加上 th。

0149 **characteristic** [ˌkærəktəˈrɪstɪk] n 特征，特性，特色
Generally speaking, I think this kind of tea has distinct characteristics.
整体而言，我认为，这种茶叶有明显的特征。
- feature 特点　- generally speaking, ... 整体而言，……

- distinct (P. 428)

0150 **charity** [ˈtʃærəti] n 慈善，仁慈，慈善机构
I strongly believe that both the charities he and his wife worked in are non-profit organizations.
我坚信，他和妻子工作的两个慈善团体都是非营利组织。
- mercy 仁慈　- cruelty 残忍　- I strongly believe that... 我坚信……

> 语法重点
> 定冠词通常位于名词或名词修饰语前，但是，名词前有 both 时，定冠词 the 就应该放在 both 之后，名词之前。

0151 **chemistry** ['kemɪstri] n 化学
I don't want to inform them to go to the chemistry lab.
我不想通知他们去化学实验室。
- organic chemistry 有机化学
- ... inform sb. to do sth. ……通知某人做某事

0152 **cherish** ['tʃerɪʃ] v 珍惜，爱护，怀有（希望、感情等）
Further, it's wrong for him to cherish possessions more than his wife.
另外，他重视财富胜过妻子是不对的。
- treasure 珍爱
- further, ... 另外，……

语法重点
句中表示说话人之前已经对听话人说了些话，通过 further 讲到 it's wrong... 这句话。
⇨ possession (P. 486)

0153 **chirp** [tʃɜːrp] v 鸟叫 n 叽喳声
I stopped up my ears so that I can keep the chirp of sparrows out.
我堵住耳朵，以便隔绝麻雀的叽喳声。
- cheep 吱吱叫
- ... so that... 以便……

0154 **chore** [tʃɔːr] n 家庭杂务
I am prepared to accept some remunerative chore.
我打算接受一些有报酬的杂务。
- trifles 琐事
- be prepared to do sth. 准备做某事

0155 **chorus** ['kɔːrəs] n 合唱团，歌舞团
I think your speech will be welcomed with a chorus of praise.
我认为，你的演讲会受到一片称赞。
- choir 合唱团
- in chorus 一齐，一致

语法重点
a chorus of 后面通常接表示声音的名词。

0156 **cigar** [sɪˈgɑːr] n 雪茄
I can't stand the smell of cigar smoke, but I'm not averse to the occasional cigar.
我不能忍受雪茄的气味，但我不反对偶尔抽一支。
- be adverse to... 反对……

⇨ occasional (P. 478)

0157 **circular** ['sɜːrkjələr] a 圆形的
I hope we can have a circular tour around the world before we get married.
我希望，在结婚之前我们可以环球旅行。
- round 圆的
- ... have a circular tour around the world ……环球旅行

0158 **circulate** ['sɜːrkjəleɪt] v 循环，散布，流通
I'm a firm believer in punishing the people who circulate false news.
我坚信散布流言者该受惩罚。
- scatter 散布
- I'm a firm believer in... 我坚信……

⇨ punish (P. 211)

0159 circulation [ˌsɜːkjəˈleɪʃn] **n** 循环，发行量，传播

I always thought his books had a circulation of one hundred thousand last year.
我一直以为，去年他的书销量是十万册。
- rotation 轮流　- in circulation 在流通中

> **语法重点**
> 在英语中，"十万"的表示方法为"不定冠词 a + hundred + thousand"，也可以表示为"基数词 one + hundred + thousand"。

0160 circumstance [ˈsɜːkəmstæns] **n** 情况，环境，详情

Under the circumstance, all of us should keep calm.
在这种情况下，我们都要保持冷静。
- condition 情况，环境　- under the circumstance, ... 在这种情况下，……

0161 civilian [səˈvɪliən] **n** 平民，百姓

It grieves me to see the civilian casualties there.
看到那里的平民伤亡，我感到很悲痛。
- populace 平民　- it grieves sb. to do... 做某事让某人很悲痛
- civilian 指相对于军人或官员的平民百姓，而 citizen 指拥有某国国籍或某地区合法身份的人，即公民。

↪ grieve (P. 450)

0162 civilization [ˌsɪvəlaɪˈzeɪʃn] **n** 文明，教养

In my opinion, human civilization is always on the move.
在我看来，人类文明一直都在进步。
- culture 文明，修养　- truculence 野蛮　- ... on the move 在进步

0163 clarify [ˈklærəfaɪ] **v** 澄清，阐明，净化

I'm curious to know what you have to clarify.
我很想知道，你必须澄清什么。
- explain 说明，解释　- clarify issues 澄清问题
- clarify 指把已发生的事件、情况说清楚，而 explain 指把某事向原来不清楚的人解释清楚。

↪ curious (P. 148)

0164 clash [klæʃ] **v** 相碰撞 **n** 冲突，碰撞声

I think there will be a clash between you and him.
我觉得，你和他之间将要起冲突。
- conflict 冲突　- reconciliation 和解

0165 classification [ˌklæsɪfɪˈkeɪʃn] **n** 分类，类别

I am dying to know the system of classification used in Chemistry.
我很想知道化学里的分类系统。
- category 分类，类别　- synthesis 综合　- be dying to... 渴望……

0166 classify [ˈklæsɪfaɪ] **v** 将……分类，归类

At first, I should classify these clothes according to quality.
首先，我应该把这些衣服根据其品质分类。
- categorize 分类　- synthesize 综合　- at first, ... 首先，……

> **语法重点**
> 按照词义，例句中的 at first 属于表示时间顺序的连词，意思是"首先……"，表示对要做的事情的先后顺序的安排。

0167 cliff [klɪf] n 断崖，绝壁

Don't bother me. I am busy with preparing for scrambling up the cliff.
别打扰我，我正忙着为攀爬峭壁做准备。
同 escarpment 悬崖，绝壁　　例 Red Cliff 赤壁

语法重点
be busy with（忙着）后面一般接动名词。
↳ scramble (P. 629)

0168 climax [ˈklaɪmæks] n 高潮，顶点

Your quarrel with the teacher will bring matters to a climax.
你和老师的争吵会使得事态发展到顶点。
同 summit 顶点　　例 come to a climax 达到顶点

0169 clumsy [ˈklʌmzi] a 笨拙的，不得体的

I'm sick and tired of the clumsy boy.
我对那个笨拙的男孩感到厌烦。
同 awkward 笨拙的　　例 I'm sick and tired of... 我对……感到厌烦

语法重点
clumsy 的比较级与最高级分别是 clumsier, clumsiest。

0170 coarse [kɔːrs] a 粗糙的，粗俗的，不精致的

I'm getting a little concerned about sleeping on the coarse blankets.
我对睡在粗硬的毯子上面有点儿担心。
同 rough 粗糙的　　反 delicate 精巧的

↳ blanket (P. 263)

0171 code [koʊd] n 代码，密码，准则

I am happy to tell you the postal code.
我很高兴告诉你邮递区号。
同 password 密码　　例 postal code 邮递区号

0172 collapse [kəˈlæps] v 崩塌，瓦解 n 倒塌

It's lucky that you didn't get hurt because of the collapse of the building.
你没有因为建筑物的倒塌而受伤，真是太幸运了。
同 founder 倒塌　　反 build 建立　　例 it's lucky that... 幸运的是……
辨 collapse 多用来指房屋等突然倒塌，而 fall 一般指由于失去平衡等。

0173 combination [ˌkɑːmbɪˈneɪʃn] n 结合，联合

I think he will carry on the business in combination with his brother.
我觉得，他会与哥哥合伙做生意。
同 unity 联合　　反 separation 分离，分开

语法重点
combination 一般用作不可数名词，但是，表示"混合物"时，是可数名词。

0174 comedy [ˈkɑːmədi] n 喜剧，滑稽，幽默

I am not sure whether I will go to watch the comedy which the actor plays in.
我不确定是否要去看那个演员演的喜剧。
同 humor 幽默　　反 tragedy 悲剧　　例 I am not sure... 我不确定……

0175 comic(1) ['kɑ:mɪk] n 连环漫画，喜剧演员
I'm grateful for your lending the two comics to me.
我很感激你能把那两本连环画借给我。
- comic books 漫画书
- be grateful for... 很感激……

> 语法重点
> 基数词是表示数目多少的数词，如例句中的 two。

0176 comic(2) ['kɑ:mɪk] a 滑稽的，喜剧的，有趣的
I am pleased to watch films with many comic scenes.
我很喜欢看有很多喜剧场景的电影。
- comical 滑稽的
- tragic 悲剧的

> 语法重点
> be pleased to（很喜欢）后面接动词原形。

0177 commander [kə'mændər] n 指挥官
I regretted not listening to the commander's order.
我后悔没有听指挥官的命令。
- comandante 指挥官
- ... regret doing sth. ……后悔做了某事

0178 comment ['kɑ:ment] n 意见 v 评论，发表意见
I feel unqualified to comment on her new hairstyle.
我觉得没有资格对她的新发型发表意见。
- remark 评论
- no comment 无可奉告

> 语法重点
> I feel unqualified to（我觉得没资格）后面接动词原形。

0179 commerce ['kɑ:mɜ:rs] n 商业
I remembered that you majored in international commerce last year.
我记得，去年你的主修是国际商务。
- international commerce 国际商务
- ... major in... ……主修……

> 语法重点
> major in 后面通常接表示学术、专业的名词。

0180 commit [kə'mɪt] v 犯罪，做错事，承诺
For one reason or another, I want to commit suicide these days.
不知什么原因，我这些天想自杀。
- sin 犯罪
- commit crime 犯罪，干坏事

⊃ suicide (P. 368)

0181 communication [kə,mju:nɪ'keɪʃn] n 交流，沟通
I don't want to commit myself on the reason of the communication disruption.
我不想对这次通信中断的原因表态。
- exchange 交流
- ... commit oneself on... ……对……表态

0182 community [kə'mju:nəti] n 社区，社会，团体
I think the young man will be integrated into the local community soon.
我想，那个年轻人很快就会融入当地人的圈子。
- organization 团体
- be integrated into... 融入……

⊃ integrate (P. 734)

0183 **companion** [kəmˈpæniən] n 同伴，伙伴，伴侣
I offer no comment on your companion on the train.
我没有对火车上你的那个同伴做评论。
同 fellow 伙伴　反 antagonist 敌手
短 ... offer no comment on... ……对……不做评论

0184 **competition** [ˌkɑːmpəˈtɪʃn] n 竞争，比赛
I don't know whether I will qualify for the second round of the competition.
我不知道我是否有资格进入第二轮比赛。
同 game 比赛　短 qualify for... 有……的资格

语法重点
在序数词的表示中，数词一、二、三的序数词表示方法没有一定的规律，分别表示为 first, second, third, 需要注意这三个特殊形式。

0185 **competitive** [kəmˈpetətɪv] a 竞争的，比赛的
Apart from this factor, French language teaching is a very competitive market in Beijing.
除去这个因素，法语教学在北京是个充满竞争的市场。
同 competitory 竞争的　反 cooperative 合作的　短 apart from... 除了……

0186 **competitor** [kəmˈpetɪtər] n 竞争者，对手
You should commit yourself to beating your competitor at that time.
那时候你应该专心致志于打败对手。
短 ... commit oneself to... ……专心致志于……

语法重点
commit oneself to 中的 to 是介词。
参 beat (P. 013)

0187 **complicate** [ˈkɑːmplɪkeɪt]
v 弄复杂，使难懂　a 复杂的
I didn't feel that I have complicated the problem.
我认为我没有把问题复杂化。
同 complex 复杂的　反 simplify 简化

语法重点
complicate 是规则动词，其过去式、过去分词都是直接在后面加上 d。

0188 **compose** [kəmˈpoʊz] v 构成，作曲，创作
I want to express my gratitude to you for helping me compose the song.
我要谢谢你帮我创作了这首歌。
同 constitute 组成，构成　同 compose oneself 镇静

语法重点
I want to express my gratitude to 中的 to 是介词。

0189 **composer** [kəmˈpoʊzər] n 作曲家，创作者
I think it is impossible for him to surpass the famous composer.
我觉得，他很难超越那个知名的作曲家。

参 surpass (P. 788)

0190 **composition** [ˌkɑːmpəˈzɪʃn] n 作文，作品，构成
He should apologize for not finishing the composition.
他应该为没完成作文道歉。
同 writing 作品　短 ... apologize for... ……为……道歉

0191 **concentrate** [ˈkɑːnsntreɪt] v 浓缩，专心，集中
I demanded that you concentrate your whole attention on the book.
我要求你把全部注意力都集中在书上。
同 focus 集中　反 distract 转移，分心

0192 **concentration** [ˌkɑːnsnˈtreɪʃn] n 浓度，集中，专心
I think you should read the book with great concentration.
我觉得，你应该聚精会神地看这本书。
同 thickness 浓度　反 distraction 分心

0193 **concept** [ˈkɑːnsept] n 概念，观念，思想
In my opinion, the girl has no concept of right and wrong.
在我看来，那个女孩没有是非概念。
同 design concept 设计理念　词 ... have no concept of... ……没有……的概念

> **语法重点**
> concept 指从众多实例中通过概括、归纳而形成的对事物本质、全貌及其内部联系的概念或看法。

0194 **concerning** [kənˈsɜːrnɪŋ] prep 关于
I am completely in the dark concerning how to get to the hotel.
我完全不知道如何去那家旅馆。

0195 **concrete** [ˈkɑːŋkriːt] a 具体的，有形的　n 混凝土
I will give you a concrete case to explain the theory later.
我会为你们举个具体事例来解释这个理论。
同 specific 具体的　反 abstract 抽象的

0196 **conductor** [kənˈdʌktər] n 指挥，售票员，导体
I am concerning myself over the young conductor now.
我现在很关心那个年轻的售票员。
同 lightning conductor 避雷针　词 ... concern oneself over... ……关心……

> **语法重点**
> myself 与主语 I 保持一致。

0197 **conference** [ˈkɑːnfərəns] n 讨论会，商谈
I am very pleased to have this opportunity to attend the press conference.
我很高兴能有机会参加这次记者会。
同 meeting 会议　词 bilateral conference 双边会议

> **语法重点**
> "新闻发布会"用 news conference 或者 press briefing 来表示。

0198 **confess** [kənˈfes] v 坦白，承认
I can hardly believe that he confessed the crime.
我几乎不敢相信他承认自己犯罪。
同 admit 承认　反 conceal 隐瞒

> **语法重点**
> I can hardly（我几乎不能）后面接动词原形。
> 参 crime (P. 147)

0199 **confidence** [ˈkɑːnfɪdəns] n 信心，信任，把握
I have every confidence that he will succeed.
我充分相信，他会成功。
同 trust 信任　词 in confidence 私下地

0200 confine [kənˈfaɪn] v 限制，禁闭 n 范围，限制

I confine to bed because of poor health.
因为身体不好，我得卧床休息。

- limit 限制
- confine within... 局限于……
- ... confine to... ……只限于……

0201 confusion [kənˈfjuːʒn] n 迷惑，混乱，混淆

I think I should summon up all my courage to go to work after one day's confusion.
我觉得，经过一天的迷茫后，我应该鼓足勇气去上班。

- order 顺序，规则
- in confusion 乱七八糟

语法重点
confusion 是不可数名词，指思绪混乱，无法进行正常的思维活动。
⊃ summon (P. 644)

0202 congratulate [kənˈɡrætʃuleɪt] v 恭喜，庆贺

I am reluctant to congratulate her on having passed the examination.
我不愿意祝贺她通过考试。

- compliment 道贺
- ... congratulate sb. on... ……为/向某人庆祝

⊃ reluctant (P. 495)

0203 congress [ˈkɑːŋɡrəs] n 会议，国会，代表大会

On this occasion, I don't want to talk about the congress.
在这样的场合，我不想讨论国会。

- parliament 国会
- on this occasion, ... 在这样的场合，……

语法重点
短语 in Congress 可以表示"在（美国）国会开会期间"。

0204 conquer [ˈkɑːŋkər] v 征服，战胜

My purpose is to conquer my disinclination to meet people.
我的目的是克服不愿与人交往的习惯。

- overcome 克服
- surrender 投降
- my purpose is to... 我的目标是……

0205 conscience [ˈkɑːnʃəns] n 良心，是非之心

I had a guilty conscience about not attending her wedding.
我因为没参加她的婚礼而感到内疚。

- on one's conscience 使人觉得自己做错了事或该做某事而未做

0206 consequence [ˈkɑːnsəkwəns] n 结果，后果，影响

Don't worry; I think it's of no consequence.
别担心，我觉得这不碍事。

- outcome 结果
- cause 原因
- in consequence 因此
- be of no consequence 不要紧

0207 consequent [ˈkɑːnsəkwənt] a 因结果而引起的

I think my failure in the exam was consequent on my illness.
我觉得，考试失败是由生病引起的。

- resulting 作为后果的
- causal 有原因的
- consequent reaction 后续反应
- be consequent on... 由……引起的

语法重点
illness 不具体，而是泛指一切疾病，强调生病的时间或状态，sickness 较口语化，可与 illness 换用，但还可表示恶心。

0208 conservative [kən'sɜːrvətɪv] a 保守的，守旧的

It seems to me that the young are less conservative than the old.
在我看来，年轻人比老年人不保守。
同 radical 激进的　扩 it seems to me that... 在我看来……

> 语法重点
> less 可以修饰多音节形容词，构成比较级形式。

0209 consist [kən'sɪst] v 组成，构成

I'm sorry to tell you that I will fire you because your actions do not consist with your words.
我很遗憾地告诉你，我要解雇你，因为你总是言行不一。
同 comprise 由……组成　扩 consist in 在于，存在于

0210 consistent [kən'sɪstənt] a 前后一致的

I have a disinclination for him because he isn't consistent with others in actions.
我讨厌他，是因为他的行动与别人不一致。
反 inconsistent 不一致的　扩 be consistent with... 与……相一致

0211 consonant ['kɑːnsənənt] n 辅音 a 一致的，符合的

I think the quality of the coat isn't quite consonant with its price.
我觉得，这件外套的品质和价钱不相称。
同 corresponding 一致的　反 vowel 元音　扩 be consonant with... 与……一致

0212 constitute ['kɑːnstətuːt] v 构成，制定

I'll fight you on constituting a committee.
我不同意你组建委员会。
同 compose 构成　扩 I'll fight you on... 我不同意你……

> 参 committee (P. 275)

0213 constitution [ˌkɑːnstə'tuːʃn] n 宪法，组织，体质

I can't imagine he doesn't even know what the constitution is.
我无法想象，他竟然不知道什么是宪法。
同 charter 宪章　扩 I can't imagine... 我不能想象……

> 语法重点
> 宪法是特指，所以前面用定冠词 the。

0214 construct [kən'strʌkt] v 建造

I think the rich man has the right to construct a factory here.
我认为，那个富人有权利在这里建厂。
同 build 建筑　反 demolish 拆除

0215 construction [kən'strʌkʃn] n 建造

I believe that the man had put a false construction on your words.
我相信，那个人是故意曲解你的话。
同 explanation 解释　反 destruction 破坏，摧毁

0216 constructive [kən'strʌktɪv] a 建设性的，构造上的

I meant it as a bit of constructive advice; I hope you won't take it as a personal insult.
我的本意是提一点建设性的意见，我希望你不要把这当作对你个人的侮辱。

- 同 anatomical 构造上的
- 搭 ... take... as... ……把……当作……

⊃ insult (P. 460)

0217 consult [kən'sʌlt] v 请教，查阅，商讨

We have to find a travel agent to consult about the travel things.
我们得找一个旅行社咨询出游事宜。

- 派 consulting room 诊察室
- 搭 consult about... 咨询……

语法重点
consult about 后面要接表示事物的名词结构。

0218 consultant [kən'sʌltənt] n 咨询者

I'm up for being a consultant anytime.
不管什么时候，我都喜欢做一名顾问。

- 同 adviser 顾问
- 搭 I'm up for... anytime 不管什么时候我都喜欢……

语法重点
I'm up for... anytime 是习惯用法，anytime 前不加任何介词。

0219 consume [kən'suːm] v 消费，吃喝，毁灭

I think he has consumed most of his time in playing computer games.
我觉得，他把大部分时间都花在打电脑游戏上了。

- 同 waste 消耗
- 反 produce 生产
- 搭 ... consume... in doing sth. ……在做某事上消耗了……

0220 consumer [kən'suːmər] n 消费者，用户，消费品

I will be consumed with these noisy consumers.
这些吵闹的顾客会让我心力交瘁。

- 同 customer 消费者
- 反 production 产品

⊃ noisy (P. 069)

0221 container [kən'teɪnər] n 容器

I was relieved after packing the goods into the container.
把货物装箱后，我松了一口气。

- 同 vessel 容器
- 搭 ... pack into... ……塞进……

0222 content [kən'tent] a 满足的 ['kɔntənt] n 内容，目录

I don't get very excited about the content of the will.
我对遗嘱的内容不感兴趣。

- 同 satisfaction 满足
- 反 discontent 不满

0223 contentment [kən'tentmənt] n 满足

I didn't expect to find contentment in playing the violin.
我没想到能从拉小提琴中得到满足。

- 同 fill 满足
- 反 discontentment 不满

语法重点
I didn't expect to（我没想到）后面接动词原形。

0224 **contest** ['kɑːntest] n 比赛，竞争 v 驳斥，争取
I don't have enough time to take part in the contest.
我没有时间参加比赛。
match 竞赛，比赛　　hold a contest 举办一场比赛

0225 **context** ['kɑːntekst] n 上下文，环境，背景
I don't know how to guess the meaning of words from the context of the article in class.
在课堂上，我不知道要怎么从文章的语境中猜出词义。
setting 环境，背景　　in context 联系上下文

> **语法重点**
> 个体名词 class 不用冠词，直接置于介词 in 后，表示该名词的深层含义，如例句中的 in class 表示"课堂上（指正在上课）"，若加上 the 则表示"在教室里"。

0226 **continual** [kən'tɪnjuəl] a 不断的，频繁的，连续的
I've had enough of the baby's continual crying.
小孩持续的哭声让我感到厌烦。
frequent 频繁的　　intermittent 断断续续的

> **语法重点**
> continual 强调重复或持续发生，连续之间允许有间断。

0227 **continuous** [kən'tɪnjuəs]
a 不断的，继续的，连续的
The continuous noise will drive me crazy.
连续不断的噪声会把我逼疯的。

> **语法重点**
> continuous 语意最强，强调在时间和空间上没有间断。
> noise (P. 069)

0228 **contrary** ['kɑːntreri] a 相反的，截然不同的
To be honest, my view is contrary to his.
老实说，我的观点和他的完全相反。
adverse 相反的　　same 相同的　　on the contrary 与此相反

0229 **contrast** ['kɑːntræst] n 对比 v 形成对照
In contrast with the city, I find the air in the countryside is fresher.
与城市相比，我发现农村的空气较新鲜。
compare 比较　　sharp contrast 鲜明对比

> **语法重点**
> in contrast with（与……相比）中的介词 with 可以用 to 来替换。

0230 **contribute** [kən'trɪbjuːt] v 捐献
I don't think he will contribute ten thousand dollars to the poor.
我觉得他不会捐一万美元给穷人。
donate 捐献　　contribute... to sb. 向某人捐助……

> **语法重点**
> 英语里没有"万"这一单位，万也用 thousand 表示，如例句中的 ten thousand 就表示"一万"，而不是"十千"。

0231 **contribution** [ˌkɑːntrɪ'bjuːʃn] n 捐献
I hope the building will be named after the man who made a generous contribution to us.
我希望，这栋大楼能以那个给我们慷慨捐助的人而命名。

contest ~ cooperation

0232 **convenience** [kənˈviːniəns] n 便利，适宜
He is sure to pick me up at his convenience.
他方便的时候肯定会来接我。
同 expedience 方便　反 inconvenience 不便　搭 convenience store 便利商店

0233 **convention** [kənˈvenʃn] n 公约，习俗，惯例
I think young people always set at naught every convention of society.
我觉得年轻人总是轻视所有的社会习俗。
同 custom 习俗　搭 by convention 按照惯例

关 society (P. 224)

0234 **conventional** [kənˈvenʃənl] a 习惯的
Teach our son some conventional morality in case he'll be a person with bad manners.
教我们儿子一些传统美德，以免他以后变成一个没教养的人。

语法重点
manner 的意思是"方式，风俗"，变为复数 manners 后，其意思是"礼貌"。

0235 **converse** [kənˈvɜːrs]
v 谈话　a 相反的，反向的　n 相反的事物
I can undertake that the converse of this argument is still true.
我保证，这个论点反过来也依然成立。
同 adverse 相反的　搭 converse about... 谈论……

关 argument (P. 125)

0236 **convey** [kənˈveɪ] v 转运，运输
I can't convey my views when facing so many people.
面对这么多人，我无法表达出自己的观点。
同 express 表达　搭 convey a message 传达信息

0237 **convince** [kənˈvɪns] v 说服，使确信，使信服
I think it's well-nigh impossible to convince the old woman.
我觉得要说服那个老妇人几乎不可能。
同 assure 使确信　搭 convince sb. of... 使某人相信……

0238 **cooperate** [koʊˈɑːpəreɪt] v 合作，协力，配合
I would like to cooperate with him in moving the house.
我愿意和他合作一起搬家。
同 collaborate 合作　搭 cooperate with... 与……合作

语法重点
cooperate with (……与……合作) 后面要接人。

0239 **cooperation** [koʊˌɑːpəˈreɪʃn] n 合作，协作
I really calculate on our cooperation; nevertheless, I have no time.
我真的期待与你合作，但是我没有时间。
同 collaboration 合作　搭 ... nevertheless... ……然而……

语法重点
按照词义，例句中的 nevertheless 属于表示转折关系的连词，意思是"尽管如此……，然而……"。
关 nevertheless (P. 476)

417

0240 cooperative [koʊˈɑːpərətɪv] **a** 合作的，协作的，共同的
I am grateful for their cooperative efforts; meanwhile, I look forward to working together next time.
我感谢他们的努力合作，同时也期待着再次合作。
反 parted 分开的　同 ... look forward to... ……期待……

语法重点
look forward to 中的 to 是介词，后面一般要接动名词。

0241 cope [koʊp] **V** 对付，对抗，妥善处理
I have confidence to cope with such a pile of work in one week.
我有信心在一周之内处理这么多工作。
同 cope with... 处理，应付……　同 ... have confidence to do sth. ……有信心做某事

⇒ confidence (P. 412)

0242 copper [ˈkɑːpər] **n** 铜，铜币
I subscribe to using copper because it conducts electricity better than iron does.
我赞成用铜，是因为铜的导电性比铁强。
同 copper mine 铜矿　同 ... subscribe to... ……赞成……

0243 cord [kɔːrd] **n** 电线，绳索，纽带
I don't assent to your idea that we tie the baggage with some cord.
我不同意你把行李用绳子绑起来。
同 string 细绳　同 I don't assent to... 我不同意……

0244 cork [kɔːrk] **n** 软木塞
I can't pull the cork out of the bottle, so I need your help.
我拔不出瓶塞，所以我需要你帮忙。
同 like a cork 轻松地　同 ... pull out of... ……拔出……

语法重点
help 一般当动词使用，例句中 help 作名词。

0245 correspond [ˌkɔːrəˈspɑːnd] **n** 符合，对应，通信
I don't want to make friends with her because her actions don't correspond with her words.
我不想和她交朋友，是因为她是个言行不一的人。
同 accord 符合　同 ... correspond with... ……与……一致

0246 costume [ˈkɑːstuːm] **n** 服装，戏装
This is the first time I have been here, and I am interested in the simple costume.
这是我第一次来到这里，我对那些简朴的服装很感兴趣。

语法重点
this is the first time sb.（这是某人第一次）后面要接现在完成时。

0247 cottage [ˈkɑːtɪdʒ] **n** 农舍，小屋，村舍
I calculate that the farm laborers' cottage is very simple and crude.
我估计，农场雇工的小屋非常简陋。
同 hut 小屋　反 mansion 大厦　同 I calculate that... 我估计……

⇒ crude (P. 697)

cooperative ~ cram

0248 council ['kaʊnsl] **n** 地方议会，理事会

It's a real bummer that the two warm-hearted women refused the awards driven by the local council.

那两个热心的女人拒绝接受地方议会颁奖给她们，真是让人失望。

同 committee 委员会 　student council 学生会

➤ award (P. 259)

0249 counter ['kaʊntər] **n** 柜台，筹码 **v** 对抗

You let me down countering my proposal with one of your own.

你以自己的一个建议来反对我的，这让我很失望。

同 resist 抵抗 　反 yield 屈服 　词 ... let sb. down ……让某人失望

➤ proposal (P. 343)

0250 courageous [kəˈreɪdʒəs] **a** 勇敢的，无畏的

It's courageous of her to do it by herself.

她居然自己去做那件事，真是勇敢。

同 brave 勇敢的 　反 sheepish 懦弱的

0251 courteous ['kɜːrtiəs] **a** 有礼貌的，殷勤的

I think we should be courteous to the old people wherever we are.

我觉得，无论在哪里，我们都要对老人有礼貌。

同 polite 有礼貌的 　反 uncourteous 粗鲁的

【语法重点】
be courteous to（对……有礼貌）中的 to 是介词。

0252 courtesy ['kɜːrtəsi] **n** 礼貌，好意

By courtesy, we'd better go to visit the man tonight.

为了礼貌起见，今晚我们最好去拜访那个人。

同 politeness 礼貌 　反 discourtesy 无礼

【语法重点】
by courtesy 后面加上介词 of 就表示"蒙……的好意，由于……的作用"。

0253 crack [kræk] **v** 破裂 **n** 裂缝，裂纹

I figure it's hard to crack these nuts.

我估计，弄掉这些坚果的壳是困难的。

同 fracture 破裂 　词 crack up 崩溃 　词 I figure... 我估计……

0254 craft [kræft] **n** 工艺，手艺，技术

I hold out no hope of his craft of wood carver.

我对他的雕刻技艺不抱什么希望。

同 skill 技术 　词 ... hold out no hope of... ……对……不抱希望

【语法重点】
craft 常用来指制作某些物品的手艺；skill 指某人具有专门知识，而且经验丰富又很熟悉。

0255 cram [kræm] **v** 把……塞进，塞满

I don't think the fat woman can cram into that car.

我觉得，那个胖女人进不了汽车。

同 fill 装满 　词 cram for 死记硬背 　词 ... cram into... ……塞入……

419

0256 creation [kri'eɪʃn] n 创造，创作
I feel there is a smelling of vinegar all over creation in my house.
我觉得，我的房子里到处都是醋的酸味。
◉ innovation 创新　◉ in all creation 到底　◉ ... all over creation in... 到处……

⇒ vinegar (P. 515)

0257 creativity [ˌkriːeɪˈtɪvəti] n 创造性，创造
I reckon it's his gifted creativity that attracted her.
我估计，是他那天才般的创造力吸引了她。
◉ originality 创力　◉ I reckon... 我估计……

0258 cripple ['krɪpl] n 跛子，残废 v 剥削，使瘫痪
It is painful that the accident crippled the pretty girl for life.
这次事故使这个漂亮的女孩终身残疾，真让人痛心。
◉ disable 使残废　◉ it is painful that... ……让人痛心

> 语法重点
> for life 的意思是"终身，一生"，是常用的副词短语。
> ⇒ painful (P. 199)

0259 critic ['krɪtɪk] n 批评家
It pleases me that the critic praised me.
那个批评家表扬了我，我真是太高兴了。
◉ commentator 评论员　◉ it pleases me that... ……我真是太高兴了

0260 critical ['krɪtɪkl] a 评论的，挑剔的
I am afraid that he is in a critical condition now.
我担心，他正处于危急状况中。
◉ crucial 决定性的　⊗ approbatory 认可的
◉ be in a critical condition 情况危急

> 语法重点
> critical 多指极为危急或缺乏的状况，而这种状况标志着某种转折。

0261 criticism ['krɪtɪsɪzəm] n 评论
I have to acknowledge that her criticism is right.
我不得不承认，她的批评是正确的。
◉ comment 评论　◉ I have to acknowledge that... 我不得不承认……

0262 criticize ['krɪtɪsaɪz] v 批评，评论，挑剔
I was furious at his criticizing.
我对他的批评感到很愤怒。

> 语法重点
> be furious at（对……感到愤怒）中的介词 at 可以替换为 with。

0263 cruelty ['kruːəlti] n 残忍，虐待
It's sickening to see such cruelty when we have dinner.
吃饭的时候看到这种残忍的行为，真让人反感。

> 语法重点
> it's sickening to（真让人反感）后面接动词原形。

0264 crush [krʌʃ] v 压碎，镇压，制服，压垮
My evaluation is that the machine is used to crush the wheat grains to flour.
我推测这种机器是用来把小麦粒轧碎制成面粉的。
◉ crunch 压碎　◉ crush in 压成，把……塞进

420

0265 **cube** [kju:b] n 立方
I ascertain that the cube of 3 is 27.
我确定 3 的立方是 27。
🔁 solid 立方体　🔁 cube root 立方根

0266 **cucumber** ['kju:kʌmbər] n 黄瓜
It rejoices me to know that we will have cucumbers for supper.
得知晚上要吃黄瓜，我很高兴。
🔁 cool as a cucumber 十分冷静

⇒ rejoice (P. 623)

0267 **cue** [kju:] n 线索
I think she always takes her cue from her mother.
我觉得，她总是看妈妈的眼色行事。
🔁 clue 提示　🔁 on cue 就在这时候
🔁 ... take one's cue from sb. ……看某人的眼色行事

0268 **cunning** ['kʌnɪŋ] a 狡猾的，诡诈的
That is to say, he is as cunning as a fox in my heart.
也就是说，在我心中他像狐狸一样狡猾。
🔁 sly 狡猾的　🔁 honest 实在的，可靠的

0269 **curiosity** [ˌkjʊri'ɑ:səti] n 好奇心，好奇，珍品
I would say he will give in to curiosity and open my letter.
我认为他会抑制不住好奇心，拆开我的信。

0270 **curl** [kɜ:rl] v 使……卷曲 n 卷曲，卷发
That's to say, I suggest she keep the hair in curl.
也就是说，我建议她留卷发。
🔁 wave 卷曲　🔁 unbend 变直　🔁 curl up 卷起

语法重点
that's to say（也就是说）属于表示解释说明的连词，后面的句子成分是对之前所说话语的解释。

0271 **curse** [kɜ:rs] v / n 诅咒
It's wrong of you to mutter a curse at your brother.
你低声咒骂弟弟是不对的。
🔁 swear 咒骂　🔁 bless 祝福　🔁 be cursed with... 因……而遭殃
🔁 口语中，可以用 the curse 来表示"月经"。

0272 **curve** [kɜ:rv] n 曲线，弧线，弯曲 v 使弯曲
I hold that the population curve will slow down.
我相信，人口曲线会趋向平缓。
🔁 straighten 变直　🔁 supply curve 供给曲线　🔁 I hold that... 我相信……

⇒ population (P. 206)

0273 **cushion** ['kʊʃn] n 垫子，软垫，缓冲
I was disgusted to see that he peed on the cushion.
看到他在垫子上小便，我很气愤。

⇒ disgust (P. 428)

0274 **damn** [dæm] v 骂……该死 int 该死 a 该死的
Damn me, but I'll prevent this kind of thing from happening on my wedding.
在婚礼上，我死也要阻止这种事情的发生。
同 bless 保佑　反 damn all 完全没有

语法重点
damn 常用在句中表示厌恶或愤恨的语气。
prevent (P. 341)

0275 **damp** [dæmp] a 潮湿的，有湿气的
I oppose that you buy damp wood which doesn't burn well.
我反对你买潮湿的木头，它们不好燃烧。
同 moist 潮湿的　反 dry 干的　句 I oppose that... 我反对……

0276 **deadline** ['dedlaɪn] n 截止期限
I trust that all the work will be done before the deadline.
我相信，所有工作都能在截止日期前完成。
句 meet the deadline 按期完成　句 I trust that... 我相信……

语法重点
定冠词通常位于名词或名词修饰语前，若名词之前有形容词 all，定冠词就要放在 all 之后、名词之前。

0277 **declare** [dɪ'kler] v 宣告，申报，声明
It's quite an honor to declare the meeting open.
我很荣幸宣布会议开幕。
同 announce 宣布　句 It's quite an honor to... ……很荣幸
辨 declare 侧重就某事清楚明白地正式宣布，而 announce 多指首次宣布大家感兴趣或可满足大家好奇心的事情。

0278 **decoration** [ˌdekə'reɪʃn] n 装饰，装潢
I am willing to hang up decorations in my house during the Spring Festival.
我愿意在春节的时候在屋子里挂一些装饰。
同 ornamentation 装饰　句 ... hang up in... ……悬挂

语法重点
在节日前一般不加冠词，但在 festival（节日）前要用定冠词 the。

0279 **decrease** [dɪ'kriːs] v / n 减小
I am conscious that the population here will decrease next year.
我知道这里的人口明年会减少。
同 reduce 减少　反 increase 增多　句 I am conscious that... 我知道……

conscious (P. 277)

0280 **defeat** [dɪ'fiːt] v 击败
At the news that they were defeated, I nearly want to kill myself.
听到他们战败的消息，我几乎想要自杀。
反 triumph 胜利　句 at the news that... 听到……的消息

0281 **defend** [dɪ'fend] v 保卫，防守，辩护
I am sure to defend our motherland provided that the enemy army invades.
如果敌军敢来侵犯，我肯定会保卫我们的国家。
同 protect 防护　反 assail 攻击

语法重点
provided that（如果……）后面接的句子通常用一般现在时。

damn ~ demonstrate

0282 **defense** [dɪ'fɛns] n 防御，保卫
I infer that the man there is the French Defense Minister.
我推断，那边那个人是法国的国防部长。
- protection 保卫 - assault 攻击 - I infer that... 我推测……

语法重点
定冠词可以用在表示民族的形容词前，表示整个民族。

0283 **defensible** [dɪ'fɛnsəbl] a 可防御的，可辩护的
If her plan is defensible in theory, I will carry it out.
如果她的计划在理论上站得住脚，我就把它付诸实践。
- easily defensible 易守难攻 - ... carry... out ……实施……

0284 **defensive** [dɪ'fɛnsɪv] a 保卫的，防御的，辩护的
I object to remaining on the defensive.
我反对继续采取守势。
- aggressive 侵略性的 - on the defensive 进行防御

语法重点
object to（反对）后面接名词、代词、动名词。
- object (P. 197)

0285 **definite** ['dɛfɪnət] a 明确的，一定的，有把握的
I am quite definite about his coming back.
我很确定他会回来。
- explicit 明确的 - indefinite 模糊的 - be definite about... 肯定……
- definite 指对所提到的事的范围及其细节毫无疑问，含有明确和确定界限的意味，而 explicit 指清楚明白，毫不含糊其辞，没有理解困难。

0286 **delicate** ['dɛlɪkət] a 精细的，纤细的
To be brief, I am angry that you broke my delicate glass.
一句话，你打破了我的精品玻璃杯，让我很生气。
- crude 粗糙的 - to be brief, ... 一句话，……

- brief (P. 134)

0287 **delight** [dɪ'laɪt] n 欣喜，快乐 v 使高兴，使欣喜
To my delight, my son is progressing in the writing skills.
令我高兴的是，我儿子的写作技能不断进步。
- in great delight 兴高采烈 - ... progress in... ……在……方面取得进展

0288 **delightful** [dɪ'laɪtfl] a 令人欣喜的，可喜的
On the whole, I had a delightful time in his house.
整体而言，我在他家玩得很高兴。
- pleasing 令人愉快的 - sad 难过的 - delightful taste 很好的滋味

语法重点
on the whole（整体而言）属于表示总结关系的连词，在句中是暗含也有些不愉快的事，但是总体上还是"玩得很高兴"。

0289 **demand** [dɪ'mænd] v / n 请求
I think yoga schools will be in great demand here.
我认为，瑜伽学校在这里将会很受欢迎。
- in demand 非常需要的，受欢迎的 - be in great demand 很受欢迎

语法重点
great 修饰 demand，表示需求的程度或者受欢迎的程度。

0290 **demonstrate** ['dɛmənstreɪt] v 显示，示范
I feel some disinclination to demonstrate that nothing lives in the Dead Sea.
我无心去证明，死海里没有生物。

0291 **demonstration** [ˌdemənˈstreɪʃn]
n 显示，示范，表达，示威游行

It's quite an honor to show you a simple demonstration of gravity.
为你们示范一个地心引力的简单证明，我觉得很荣幸。
同 march 示威游行　同 hold a demonstration 示威游行
辨 simple 指不复杂、不难懂、容易被理解的事物，而 easy 指不需要花费太多精力的工作或事，在实际运用中常与 simple 替换使用。

➦ gravity (P. 574)

0292 **dense** [dens] **a** 密集的，稠密的

I think the hills will be enveloped in dense fog tomorrow morning.
我觉得明天早上浓雾会笼罩群山。
同 thick 浓　同 dense fog 浓雾　同 be enveloped in... 被……包住

0293 **depart** [dɪˈpɑːrt] **v** 离开，出发

I'm opposed to the idea of departing tomorrow.
我反对明天就出发这个主意。
同 leave 离开　反 arrive 到达　同 depart (from) this life 去世，亡故
辨 depart 和 leave 均含"离开某处"之意，但两者有区别。depart 较正式，指经过周密考虑或郑重地离开，强调离开的起点，而 leave 侧重出发地而不是目的地。

0294 **departure** [dɪˈpɑːrtʃər] **n** 离去，出发，分歧

I do not doubt that your departure from Beijing University will set the world on fire.
我相信，你离开北京大学会引起轰动。
同 leaving 离开　反 arrival 到达　同 I do not doubt that... 我相信……

语法重点
表示大学名称的专有名词前不加冠词，如例句中的 Beijing University（北京大学）。

0295 **dependable** [dɪˈpendəbl] **a** 可靠的，可信赖的

It's quite necessary to get into the habit of making friends with dependable people.
有必要养成与可靠的人交朋友的习惯。
同 reliable 可靠的　同 get into the habit of... 养成……的习惯

0296 **dependent** [dɪˈpendənt] **a** 依赖的，从属的

I think he was dependent on charity because he had no means of subsistence.
我认为，他只能依靠救济，是因为他没有什么谋生手段。
同 reliant 依赖的　反 independent 独立的

语法重点
have no means of（没有办法）后面通常接名词或动名词。
➦ charity (P. 406)

0297 **depress** [dɪˈpres] **v** 使沮丧，使萧条

I can't go with you in that the bad weather depresses her.
你认为是坏天气使得她心情抑郁，我不同意。
同 deject 使沮丧　反 encourage 鼓励　同 depressed area 经济萧条地区

语法重点
depress 的第三人称单数形式是在其后加上 es。

424

demonstration ~ devise

0298 depression [dɪˈpreʃn] **n** 沮丧
We were heartbroken by the news that half the employees will be sheared during the depression.
大萧条期间我们公司要削减一半员工，这消息让我们很痛心。
🔄 recession 衰退　　🔄 be heartbroken by... 对……很痛心

> **语法重点**
> 定冠词通常位于名词或名词修饰语前，但如果名词前有 half，定冠词则要放在 half 之后、名词之前。

0299 deserve [dɪˈzɜːrv] **v** 值得
I didn't really deserve that you should be so kind to me.
我确实不值得你对我那么好。
🔄 I didn't really deserve that... 我确实不值得……

> **语法重点**
> really 修饰 deserve，加强语气。

0300 desperate [ˈdespərət] **a** 绝望的，不顾一切的
I was desperate when I knew I failed the exam.
我一得知自己考试失败，就绝望了。

☞ fail (P. 163)

0301 despite [dɪˈspaɪt] **prep** 不管
Despite the difficulties, you should throw yourself into your work.
尽管困难重重，你还是应该全心投入工作。
🔄 in despite of 尽管，不管　　🔄 ... throw oneself into... ……全心投入……

0302 destruction [dɪˈstrʌkʃn] **n** 破坏，毁灭
It is my belief that drinking will lead to his destruction.
我相信，酗酒会导致他的毁灭。
🔄 establishment 建立　　🔄 It is my belief that... 我相信……

0303 detective [dɪˈtektɪv] **n** 侦探 **a** 侦探的
I have great faith in the detective and I know he'll do well.
我对那个侦探有信心，我知道他会把事情办好。
🔄 private detective 私家侦探　　🔄 ... have great faith in... ……对……有信心

☞ faith (P. 294)

0304 determination [dɪˌtɜːrmɪˈneɪʃn] **n** 决心，决定
I think he is a man of determination.
我觉得他是个有决心的人。

0305 device [dɪˈvaɪs] **n** 装置，设备，策略
You can't leave your students to their own devices.
你不能听任你的学生们自由发展。
🔄 installation 装置　　🔄 mobile device 行动设备

0306 devise [dɪˈvaɪz] **v** 设计，策划，发明
To sum up, you should devise a new plan tonight.
总之，今晚你要设计出一个新计划。
🔄 plan 计划　　🔄 devise strategies 制订计划

> **语法重点**
> to sum up（总之）属于表示总结的连词，表示对上述话语的总结。

425

0307 devote [dɪ'vout] v 将……奉献

I think he didn't set out to devote his life to biology at the age of 20.

我觉得，他不是在 20 岁的时候开始致力于生物学的。

● devote to... 把……奉献给，把……专用于

> **语法重点**
> set out to（开始）后面接动词原形。

0308 diaper ['daɪpər] n 尿布 v 包上尿布

I believe in diapering the baby when he is asleep.

我赞成在孩子睡着的时候包尿布。

● didy 尿布 ● diaper pad 尿布垫

> **语法重点**
> I believe in（我赞成）后面一般接名词或者动名词。

0309 differ ['dɪfər] v 不同，有区别

I beg to differ from you on the opinion that we should go now.

恕我对你的看法不敢苟同，我不赞成我们现在离开。

● agree to differ 各自保留不同意见

0310 digest [daɪ'dʒest] v 消化，理解

For my money, this rich food doesn't digest easily.

在我看来，这种油腻的食物不易消化。

● absorb 吸收 ● for my money, ... 在我看来，……

0311 digestion [daɪ'dʒestʃən] n 消化，吸收，领悟

To my mind, the reason why the man can't eat too much rich food is that he has poor digestion.

在我看来，那人之所以不能多吃油腻食物，是因为他的消化能力不好。

● realization 领悟 ● to my mind, ... 在我看来，……

○ poor (P. 077)

0312 digital ['dɪdʒɪtl] a 数字的，手指的

I was disillusioned with the digital camera he bought for me.

我对他买给我的那台数码相机很失望。

● digital camera 的意思是"数码照相机"，有时也可以缩写为 DC。

0313 dignity ['dɪɡnəti] n 尊严，端庄

To me, a man's dignity depends upon his character.

在我看来，人的真正价值在于他的品格。

● beneath one's dignity 有失身份/尊严 ● To me, ... 在我看来，……

○ character (P. 138)

0314 diligence ['dɪlɪdʒəns] n 勤奋的，努力

I think all of us should cultivate the good habit of diligence and frugality.

我认为，我们都要养成勤俭节约的好风气。

● assiduity 勤勉 ● idleness 懒散 ● due diligence 尽职调查

○ cultivate (P. 698)

devote ~ discouragement

0315 **diploma** [dɪ'ploʊmə] **n** 文凭，毕业证书
I am confident of winning my diploma in three years.
我有信用三年时间取得毕业文凭。
 certificate 文凭，证书   I am confident of... 我有信心……

0316 **diplomat** ['dɪpləmæt] **n** 外交官，通权达变之人
I think the Premier Wang possessed an excellent gift for repartee as a diplomat.
我觉得，王总理具有外交官的卓越应对才能。
 ... possess an excellent gift for... ……有……的卓越才能

语法重点
在称呼或表示职位的名词前不加冠词。
 premier (P. 759)

0317 **disadvantage** [,dɪsəd'væntɪdʒ] **n** 不利，损害，损失
We will be at a disadvantage in this competition.
我们将会在这次竞赛中处于不利的地位。
 drawback 不利条件   advantage 有利条件

0318 **disaster** [dɪ'zæstər] **n** 天灾，大祸
To my thinking, these difficulties are caused by natural disasters.
在我看来，这些困难都是由自然灾害造成的。
 calamity 灾难   disaster area 灾区   to my thinking, ... 在我看来，……

 natural (P. 194)

0319 **discipline** ['dɪsəplɪn] **n** 纪律，学科
I think the college has a reputation for high standards of discipline.
我认为，这所大学是因纪律严格而闻名。
 ... have a reputation for... ……因……而出名

0320 **disconnect** [,dɪskə'nekt] **v** 分开，拆开
I have an objection to disconnecting the boiler from the water mains.
我反对将锅炉与供水总管分开。
 separate 使分离   connect 连接

语法重点
have an objection to（反对）中的 to 是介词。
 objection (P. 477)

0321 **discourage** [dɪs'kɜːrɪdʒ] **v** 使泄气
I will discourage him from continuing this project.
我要阻止他继续做这个计划。
 encourage 鼓励   discourage saving 抑制储蓄

0322 **discouragement** [dɪs'kɜːrɪdʒmənt] **n** 气馁
The play was a discouragement to me.
这部话剧让我灰心丧气。
 disheartenment 气馁   encouragement 鼓励

427

0323 **disguise** [dɪsˈɡaɪz] v 乔装
The man must have made his escape in disguise.
那人肯定是化妆后逃走的。
🔄 in disguise 伪装的，假装的　🔄 ... make one's escape ……逃跑

0324 **disgust** [dɪsˈɡʌst] v 使厌恶 n 作呕，厌恶
For the first time, my reaction was disgust when I saw the food.
我第一次看见那种食物就反感。
🔄 detest 厌恶　🔄 delight 高兴　🔄 with disgust 厌恶地

语法重点
disgust 作不可数名词，表示"对……反感"，可以与介词 at, with, for 连用。

0325 **dismiss** [dɪsˈmɪs] v 解散
I think she has been dismissed from her post because of drinking.
我觉得，她是因为喝酒而被解雇的。
🔄 discharge 解雇　🔄 employ 雇用　🔄 be dismissed from... 被从……解雇

语法重点
be dismissed from 是常用的搭配，介词 from 后面通常接表示职位的名词或代词。

0326 **disorder** [dɪsˈɔːrdər] n 无秩序
To my way of thinking, she has suffered from severe mental disorder.
在我看来，她患有严重的精神病。
🔄 confusion 混乱　🔄 to my way of thinking, ... 在我看来，……

语法重点
表示病情严重，通常用形容词 severe。
⇨ severe (P. 502)

0327 **dispute** [dɪˈspjuːt] v / n 争论，辩驳，争议
I excepted against his suggestion because it was very troublesome to arbitrate a dispute.
我反对他的建议，是因为仲裁争端很麻烦。
🔄 argue 争论　🔄 in dispute 在争论中　🔄 ... except against... ……反对……

0328 **distinct** [dɪˈstɪŋkt] a 有区别的，明显的，清晰的
I have the distinct impression that my boss is dissatisfied with me.
我清楚地感觉到，我的老板对我很不满意。
🔄 different 不同　🔄 indistinct 模糊的

语法重点
distinct 常与介词 from 搭配，表示"与……不同"。

0329 **distinguish** [dɪˈstɪŋɡwɪʃ] v 分辨
I am afraid I can't distinguish blue from green.
我恐怕分不清蓝色和绿色。
🔄 ... distinguish... from... ……把……与……分开

0330 **distinguished** [dɪˈstɪŋɡwɪʃt] a 卓越的
It occurred to me that she was the most distinguished scholar in the field.
在我看来，她是这一领域成就最为卓著的学者。
🔄 celebrated 著名的　🔄 unknown 默默无闻的

语法重点
distinguished 的比较级和最高级形式为 more distinguished, most distinguished，通常用作 be distinguished for / as。

0331 distribute [dɪˈstrɪbjuːt] **v** 分配，散发，分布

I give countenance to the suggestion that we take measures to distribute these goods.
采取措施来分销这些商品，我赞成这个建议。
- assign 分配
- assemble 集合
- exclusively distribute 总经销
- distribute 通常指以整体或定量分为若干份来分配，而 assign 指按照某种原则进行的硬性分配，也不一定是很公平的。

0332 distribution [ˌdɪstrɪˈbjuːʃn] **n** 分配，散发，散步

Our principle of distribution may meet with resistance.
我们的分配原则可能会受到抵制。

> **语法重点**
> principle of 的意思是"……的原则"，of 后面通常接名词。
> ⊃ resistance (P. 497)

0333 district [ˈdɪstrɪkt] **n** 辖区，地区，行政区

As far as I can tell, there is miles and miles of marsh in this district.
在我看来，这个地区有绵延无数英里的沼泽。
- As far as I can tell, ... 在我看来，……

0334 disturb [dɪˈstɜːrb] **v** 打扰，妨碍

I advise you not to disturb him in his work.
我建议你别打扰他的工作。
- upset 扰乱
- adjust 调整
- ... disturb sb. in... 在……方面打扰某人

⊃ advise (P. 253)

0335 divine [dɪˈvaɪn] **a** 神奇的，神圣的 **v** 占卜，预言

No one has a divine right to hurt others.
没有人天生就有权去伤害他人。

0336 divorce [dɪˈvɔːrs] **v** 与谁离婚，分离

I won't assent to divorcing from you.
我不会同意和你离婚。
- divorce rate 离婚率
- ... assent to... ……同意

> **语法重点**
> divorce from 表示"与……离婚"，也可以用于被动语态，即 be divorced from。

0337 dominant [ˈdɑːmɪnənt] **a** 支配的，占优势的

I don't think the company has achieved a dominant position in the world.
我觉得，这家公司在世界上并没有占据举足轻重的地位。
- dominant position 支配地位
- ... achieve a dominant position... ……有举足轻重的地位

> **语法重点**
> dominant 通常指居于支配地位，势力或影响最大。

0338 dominate [ˈdɑːmɪneɪt] **v** 支配，控制，统治

I think he has a strong desire to dominate over others.
我觉得他很想支配别人。
- control 控制
- have a strong desire to... 很想……

0339 **dormitory** ['dɔ:rmətɔ:ri] n 学生宿舍，寝室

I vote for the plan that a new dormitory and a new teaching building should be built.
我赞成建一栋新的宿舍和教学大楼的计划。
同 dorm 宿舍   同 ... vote for... ……赞成……

语法重点
如果在这两个名词前各有 a / an 修饰，则表示两个人或事物。
⊃ vote (P. 243)

0340 **download** [,daʊn'loʊd] v / n 下载

I hold by downloading a perpetual calendar from the internet.
我赞成从网络上下载一个万年历。
反 upload 上传 同 download center 下载中心 同 hold by... 赞成……

0341 **doze** [doʊz] v / n 打瞌睡

There's nothing like a little doze on the bed after lunch.
午餐后在床上睡一下是最好不过了。
同 nap 打盹儿 同 doze off 打瞌睡 同 there's nothing like... ……最好不过了

0342 **draft** [dræft] n 草稿，汇票 v 起草，征募

At the beginning, I was unwilling to draft a contract.
起初，我不愿意草拟合约。
同 recruit 征募 同 at the beginning, ... 起初，……

语法重点
at the beginning 属于表示时间顺序的连词，含有"起初"意思，和现在的情况做对比。

0343 **dread** [dred] v / n 惧怕，畏惧，忧虑

I have a dread of going out to work.
我害怕出去工作。
同 fear 惧怕 同 feeling of dread 恐惧感 同 ... have a dread of... ……害怕……
辨 dread 着重害怕的心理，常指胆怯和丧失勇气，fear 侧重指面临危险或灾祸时内心的恐惧。

0344 **drift** [drɪft] v / n 漂流，堆积

I think there will be some clusters of white clouds drifting across the blue sky.
我觉得，蔚蓝的天空会飘过几朵白云。
同 float 漂浮 同 drift along 随波逐流，任其自然

语法重点
drift across（从……飘过）后面通常接名词、名词短语或代词。
⊃ cluster (P. 544)

0345 **drill** [drɪl] v 钻孔，训练 n 训练，钻孔机

You need to drill the students in reading comprehension everyday.
你要每天让学生们做阅读理解训练。
同 train 训练 同 emergency drill 紧急演习
同 ... drill sb. in doing... ……训练某人做……

0346 **durable** ['dʊrəbl] a 耐穿的，持久的

I lean to buying this kind of durable materials.
我倾向于买这种耐用的材料。
同 perpetual 永久的 反 short-life 不耐用的

语法重点
lean to（倾向）中的介词 to 也可以替换为 towards。

dormitory ~ economical

0347 dusty ['dʌsti] **a** 覆着灰尘的，灰蒙蒙的
It delights me to know that it's not dusty in your city.
得知你所在的城市不是灰蒙蒙的，我很高兴。

0348 DVD abbr 高密度数字视频光盘；数字通用光盘
I am sold on buying lots of DVD of cartons for him.
我赞成多买一些动画片的光碟给他。
⊕ DVD 是由构词法中的首字母缩略法构成，原形为 digital video disk。

0349 dye [daɪ] **n** 染料，染色 **v** 染，染色
This dye doesn't take in cold water.
那种染料在冷水中不起作用。
反 bleach 漂白剂　　搭 of the blackest dye 最坏的

语法重点
dye 的现在分词与过去式、过去分词分别是 dyeing, dyed, dyed。

0350 dynamic [daɪ'næmɪk] **a** 动态的，有活力的
I rejoice that my dynamic son attracts a lot of girls.
我那有活力的儿子吸引了很多女孩子，我很高兴。
同 energetic 精力充沛的　　反 static 静态的　　搭 I rejoice that... 我很高兴……

⇒ rejoice (P. 623)

0351 dynasty ['daɪnəsti] **n** 王朝
I cannot say yes to his view that the poet lived in the Ming Dynasty.
他说那个诗人是明朝人，我不同意。
搭 change a dynasty 改朝换代　　搭 I cannot say yes to... 我不同意……

语法重点
在表示朝代的名词前需要用定冠词 the。

0352 earnest ['ɜːrnɪst] **a** 认真的，诚挚的，热切的
Sorry, I am deaf to your earnest words.
对不起，我听不进你的忠言。
同 sincere 诚挚的　　搭 in earnest 认真地　　搭 be deaf to... 听不进……

语法重点
earnest 用于短语 earnest money 中，意思是"订金，保证金"。

0353 earphone ['ɪrˌfon] **n** 耳机，听筒
I don't hold with her views on producing the new kind of earphones.
我不同意她关于生产这种新款耳机的观点。
同 headset 耳机　　同 wireless earphone 无线耳机　　搭 hold with... 赞同……

语法重点
view 是可数名词，表示"意见，看法"，通常与介词 on 或是 about 连用。

0354 economic [ˌiːkə'nɑːmɪk] **a** 经济上的，有利可图的
The unemployment will shoot up because of the deepening of the economic crisis.
失业人数会因为经济危机加剧而激增。
搭 economical 经济的　　搭 economic climate 经济形势　　搭 ... shoot up ……激增

⇒ crisis (P. 147)

0355 economical [ˌiːkə'nɑːmɪkl] **a** 经济的，合算的
I suggest you be economical with cooking oil when cooking.
我建议你烹饪时少用点儿油。

431

0356 economics [ˌiːkəˈnɑːmɪks] **n** 经济学
I vote that she studies economics in Tsinghua University.
我建议她去清华大学读经济学。
🔗 political economics 政治经济学　🔗 I vote that... 我建议……

语法重点
economics 作学科名词，视为不可数名词，意思是"经济学"，也可以表示"经济状况"。

0357 economist [ɪˈkɑːnəmɪst] **n** 经济学家，节俭的人
He considers the economist a great man. I'd like to take exception to that.
他认为那位经济学家是个伟大的人，我不同意他的看法。
🔗 saver 节俭的人　🔗 take exception to... 不同意……

0358 economy [ɪˈkɑːnəmi] **n** 经济，节约，节省
I think Mr. Lin is an important contributor to the economy of Shanghai.
我认为，林先生为上海经济做出了重要贡献。
🔗 thrift 节约　🔗 luxury 奢侈
🔗 be an important contributor to... 对……做出重要贡献

0359 efficiency [ɪˈfɪʃnsi] **n** 效率，功率，功效
I was most impressed with his work efficiency.
他的工作效率给我留下了很深刻的印象。
🔗 virtue 功效　🔗 cost efficiency 成本效率
🔗 be impressed with... 对……有深刻印象

🔗 impress (P. 309)

0360 elastic [ɪˈlæstɪk] **a** 有弹性的 **n** 橡皮圈，松紧带
I don't see it good to buy some new elastic.
我认为，再买一些松紧带是不对的。
🔗 flexible 灵活的　🔗 rigid 僵硬的，死板的

0361 electrician [ɪˌlekˈtrɪʃn] **n** 电气技师
We had better send for an electrician now.
我们现在最好派人去请个电工来。
🔗 wireman 电工　🔗 ... send for... ……派人去请

语法重点
send for 后面要接表示人的名词或代词。

0362 electronics [ɪˌlekˈtrɑːnɪks] **n** 电子学，电子器件
You should brush up your knowledge of electronics this week.
这周，你应该温习电子学知识。
🔗 electronic engineering 电子工程
🔗 brush up 在此表示"温习"，相当于 go over 或 review。

0363 elegant [ˈelɪɡənt] **a** 优雅的，雅致的
It was distressing to see he broke the elegant vase.
看到他打碎了那个别致的花瓶，真是痛心。
🔗 inelegant 不雅的　🔗 elegant furnishings 雅致的装饰

语法重点
it is distressing to（真是痛心）后面要接动词原形。

economics ~ emerge

0364 **elementary** [ˌelɪˈmentri] a 基本的，初级的，小学的
I nearly lose my interest in the elementary mathematics.
我几乎对基础数学失去了兴趣。
- basic 基本的
- advanced 高级的
- elementary education 初等教育
- ... lose one's interest in... ……对……失去兴趣

0365 **eliminate** [ɪˈlɪmɪneɪt] v 消除，根除，淘汰
I am obliged to eliminate all the possibility.
我不得不排除所有的可能性。
- avoid 消除
- add 增加，添加
- be obliged to do sth. 不得不做某事

⊃ oblige (P. 749)

0366 **elsewhere** [ˌelsˈwer] ad 在别处，到别处
I think about twenty percent of the city's residents are born elsewhere.
我觉得，这个城市的居民几乎有百分之二十是出生在异地。
- otherwhere 在别处
- living elsewhere 生活在别处
- be born 出生

语法重点
在英语中，百分数一般由"基数词 + percent"构成。

0367 **e-mail** [ˈiːmeɪl] n 电子邮件
To me, there are many communication tools, for instance, phone, e-mail and so on.
对于我来说，沟通工具很多，比如电话、电子邮件等。
- e-mail address 电子邮件地址
- ... for instance... ……例如，……

语法重点
for instance 属于表示解释说明的连词，后面要接被列举的事物。
⊃ instance (P. 179)

0368 **embarrass** [ɪmˈbærəs] v 使困窘，使为难
To be frank, I am embarrassed by these questions.
说实话，这些问题让我很窘迫。
- shame 使丢脸
- comfort 使缓和
- be embarrassed by... 因……感到窘迫

0369 **embarrassment** [ɪmˈbærəsmənt] n 难堪
I hope I can ease his embarrassment.
我希望能缓解他的困窘。
- aporia 窘迫
- comfort 舒适

0370 **embassy** [ˈembəsi] n 大使馆，大使馆全体成员
I am sure they will be familiar with the Japan Embassy before long.
我确定不久之后，他们将是日本大使馆的常客。
- embassy officials 大使馆官员
- ... before long 不久之后……

语法重点
before long 常在句中与将来时连用。

0371 **emerge** [iˈmɜːrdʒ] v 浮现，显现，暴露
I hope she can emerge from the accident unharmed.
我希望，她能在这次事故中脱险，毫无损伤。
- appear 出现
- submerge 淹没
- emerge from... 从……挣脱出来

0372 **emotional** [ɪˈmoʊʃənl] a 情感的，情绪的
By my reckoning, the teacher's emotional pep talk will stir up the students.
据我估计，老师的热情鼓励会让同学们倍感振奋。
同 emotive 感情的，情绪的　句 by my reckoning, ... 据我估计，……

↪ reckon (P. 622)

0373 **emphasis** [ˈemfəsɪs] n 重点
We had better put emphasis on all details that she told us.
我们最好重视她说的所有细节。
同 stress 强调　句 ... put emphasis on... ……重视……

语法重点
当先行词由 all 修饰时，引导词只能用 that，有时可以省略，如例句中的 that。

0374 **empire** [ˈempaɪər] n 帝国，大企业
Speaking my conscience, the collapse of the Empire can't be prevented.
说心里话，这个帝国的崩溃是不可避免的。
同 empery 帝国　句 ... speak one's conscience ……说心里话

语法重点
the Empire 表示"帝国"，是固定用法，其中 the 表示特指，Empire 的首字母必须大写。

↪ collapse (P. 409)

0375 **enclose** [ɪnˈkloʊz] v 围住，包住，附上
The two bowls enclose a vacuum, so I am afraid I can't pull them apart.
两个碗之间是真空的，所以我担心没办法将它们分开。
反 disclose 揭露　句 enclose with... 将……与……封入同一信封

0376 **encounter** [ɪnˈkaʊntər] v 遭遇，遇到，偶然碰到
I didn't think to encounter you here.
我没想到，会在这里遇到你。
同 encounter problems 碰到问题　句 I didn't think to... 没想到……

0377 **endanger** [ɪnˈdeɪndʒər] v 使……陷入危险，危害
Your action would endanger your health; worse still, it may endanger your life.
你的行为会危及你的健康，更糟糕的是，它可能危及你的生命。
反 ensure 使安全　同 endanger safety 危害社会安全

语法重点
worse still（更糟糕的是）属于表示递进关系的连词，暗含后面的后果比前面的严重。

0378 **endure** [ɪnˈdʊr] v 忍受，忍耐，持久
I can't endure to see he is so painful.
我不忍看到他如此痛苦。
同 tolerate 容忍　句 I can't endure... 我不能忍受……

语法重点
I can't endure 后面可以接动词不定式，也可以接动名词。

↪ painful (P. 199)

0379 **enforce** [ɪnˈfɔːrs] v 实施，执行，强迫
He has no right to enforce his own views on her.
他无权把自己的观点强加给她。
同 execute 执行　同 enforce a law 实施法律
句 ... have no right to do sth. ……无权做某事

0380 **enforcement** [ɪnˈfɔːrsmənt] n 施行，强制，实施
I think we lack the necessary enforcement machinery, but I am bashful in expressing my view.
我认为我们缺乏必要的执行机制，但我羞于表达自己的观点。

0381 **engineering** [ˌendʒɪˈnɪrɪŋ] n 工程学，工程
I was proud that my son got A's in many engineering exams.
我很骄傲，我儿子在很多次工程学考试中都得了 A。
近 project 工程　句 I am proud that... 我很骄傲……

语法重点
"'" 可以用于字母后表示字母的复数形式，如例句中的 A's。

0382 **enlarge** [ɪnˈlɑːrdʒ] v 扩大，增大，详述
I would like you to enlarge upon your suggestion.
我希望，你能详细谈谈你的建议。
近 amplify 扩大　反 diminish 缩小，变少　搭 enlarge on 详谈

语法重点
enlarge upon（详谈）中的介词 upon 也可以替换为 on。

0383 **enlargement** [ɪnˈlɑːrdʒmənt] n 扩张，扩建
I don't regard the enlargement of the company's overseas business activities favourably.
我不看好公司海外业务的扩展。
近 expansion 扩大　反 shrink 缩小

⇒ overseas (P. 198)

0384 **enormous** [ɪˈnɔːrməs] a 巨大的，庞大的
I think this kind of food has enormous sales potential.
我认为这种食品有很大的销售潜力。

⇒ potential (P. 615)

0385 **entertain** [ˌentərˈteɪn] v 使欢乐，使有兴趣
I think it is my time to entertain you at dinner.
我觉得，该由我来招待你们吃饭了。
近 serve 招待　搭 entertain an idea 抱着一种想法　句 it is my time... 该我……

0386 **entertainment** [ˌentərˈteɪnmənt] n 娱乐，款待，招待
Of course the guest will nag at your entertainment.
当然，那个客人会挑剔你们的款待。
近 treatment 对待　搭 ... nag at... ……挑剔……

0387 **enthusiasm** [ɪnˈθuːziæzəm] n 热衷，热心，巨大兴趣
I think he will show enthusiasm for traveling.
我想，他会热衷于旅游。
近 ardor 热情　反 pococurantism 冷淡

语法重点
enthusiasm 一般作不可数名词；表示"热衷的事物"时，则是可数名词。

0388 **envious** [ˈenviəs] a 羡慕的，妒忌的
I am envious of her new necklace.
我很嫉妒她的新项链。
近 jealous 妒忌的　搭 envious feeling 妒意

语法重点
be envious of（忌妒）后面可以接人，也可以接物。

0389 **equality** [iˈkwɑːləti] n 平等，相同，相等
I think that women should be on an equality with men.
我觉得，女人应该与男人平等。
- evenness 平等 - inequality 不平等 - be on an equality with... 与……平等

0390 **equip** [ɪˈkwɪp] v 配备
I will try my best to equip my daughter with a good education.
我要尽最大的努力，让女儿受到优质教育。

0391 **equipment** [ɪˈkwɪpmənt] n 装备，器材
I am sure the new system can be compatible with existing equipment.
我确定，新的系统会与现有的设备相容。
- facility 设备 - be compatible with... 与……相容

> **语法重点**
> equipment 通常用作不可数名词，多指成套的或重型的设备或装备。
> ⊃ compatible (P. 688)

0392 **era** [ˈɪrə] n 时代，年代
I deem the fall of the Berlin Wall marked the end of an era.
我认为柏林墙的倒塌标志着一个时代的结束。
- the end of an era 一个时代的终结 - I deem... 我认为……

> **语法重点**
> 专有名词 Berlin Wall 的意思是"柏林墙"，其前需要用定冠词 the。

0393 **errand** [ˈerənd] n 任务，差事，跑腿
It was an errand of mercy to me.
对于我来说，这是雪中送炭。

0394 **escalator** [ˈeskəleɪtər] n 手扶梯
The new store has escalators to carry customers from one floor to another.
新的店家有手扶梯载顾客从一层楼到另一层楼。
- elevator 电梯

0395 **essay** [ˈeseɪ] n 散文，随笔
I think the essay constitutes a direct threat to me.
我觉得这篇论文对我形成直接威胁。

0396 **establish** [ɪˈstæblɪʃ] v 建立，确立，创办
Moreover, the new rule has been established and none of us can modify it at random.
而且，新规则一经制定，我们任何人都不得任意修改。
- build 建立 - ruin 毁坏 - ... at random 任意地……

> **语法重点**
> 例句中的 moreover 表示递进关系，暗含除了其他的条件还有这个条件，而且更强调后者。
> ⊃ modify (P. 597)

0397 **establishment** [ɪˈstæblɪʃmənt] n 建立，机构
I could deduce that they're celebrating the establishment of the new college.
我推断，他们在庆祝新学院的成立。
- institution 机构 - I could deduce that... 我推断……

equality ~ exaggerate

0398 essential [ɪˈsenʃl] a 必要的，重要的
Vitamin and mineral requirements are essential for you.
对于你来说，维生素和矿物质是必须的。
⊙ necessary 必要的　　⊙ be essential for... 对……是必需的

> **语法重点**
> essential 后接 that 从句时，从句中的动词要用 "should + 动词原形" 来表示，should 可以省略。
> ⊙ vitamin (P. 382)

0399 estimate [ˈestɪmət] v / n 评估，估价
I estimate that she is the apple of her parents' eyes.
我估计，她是父母的掌上明珠。

0400 evaluate [ɪˈvæljueɪt] v 对……的评价，评估
I tell you not to evaluate a person on the basis of appearance.
我告诉你，不要以貌取人。
⊙ ... evaluate a person on the basis of appearance 以貌取人

⊙ appearance (P. 124)

0401 evaluation [ɪˌvæljuˈeɪʃn] n 估算，评价
Their opinions and evaluations are out of my expectation.
他们的意见和评价出乎我的意料。
⊙ be out of one's expectation... 出乎某人的意料

0402 eve [iːv] n 前夕
I am afraid he will fall ill on the eve of the race.
我担心他会在比赛前夕病倒。
⊙ on the eve of... 在……前夕

0403 eventual [ɪˈventʃuəl] a 最后的，可能的
I will never regret for what I said no matter what the eventual outcome is.
不管最后的结果是什么，我永远不会为自己说过的话后悔。
⊙ final 最终的　　⊚ initial 最初的　　⊙ regret for... 为……后悔

⊙ regret (P. 347)

0404 evidence [ˈevɪdəns] n 证据，根据，证词
On the basis of the evidence, I think he is innocent.
基于这些证据，我认为他是无罪的。
⊙ proof 证据　　⊙ (be) in evidence 显而易见的　　⊙ on the basis of... 基于……

> **语法重点**
> evidence 也常用于短语 show evidence of，意思是"证明，表明"。

0405 evident [ˈevɪdənt] a 明显的
It has become evident to me who betrayed me.
我已经清楚是谁出卖了我。
⊙ distinct 明显的　　⊚ uncertain 含糊的　　⊙ self evident 不言而喻的

0406 exaggerate [ɪɡˈzædʒəreɪt] v 夸大，夸张
I think he has a tendency to exaggerate things.
我觉得他倾向于夸大事实。
⊙ enormously exaggerate 大肆渲染

> **语法重点**
> have a tendency to（有倾向）后面可以接动词原形，也可以接名词。

437

0407 examinee [ɪɡˌzæmɪˈniː] **n** 应试者，受审查的人
I feel honored to be an examinee of the big company.
作为这家大公司的一名应试者，我觉得很荣幸。
㊉ candidate 应试者　㊉ examinee category 考生类别

语法重点
I feel honored to 后面要接动词原形。

0408 examiner [ɪɡˈzæmɪnər] **n** 主考人
The examiner won't let me through because my oral English is poor.
我的英语口语很差，考官不会让我及格的。
㊉ censor 检查　㊉ ...let...through ……让……及格

0409 exception [ɪkˈsepʃn] **n** 例外，除外
All of the dishes are good with the exception of this one.
所有菜都好吃，除了这一道。
㊉ with the exception of... 除……以外

语法重点
with the exception of 常与 all, every 等词用在同一个句子中，表示对比。

0410 exhaust [ɪɡˈzɔːst] **v** 耗尽
As far as I am concerned, too much exercise will exhaust him.
依我看，过多的运动会让他精疲力竭。
㊉ fatigue 疲劳　㊉ exhaust system 排气系统
㊉ as far as I am concerned, ... 依我看，……

0411 exhibit [ɪɡˈzɪbɪt] **v** 展示，展览 **n** 展品，展览
I would appreciate it if you take me to the exhibit.
如果你带我去看展览，我会非常感激。
㊉ I would appreciate it... ……我会非常感激

语法重点
exhibit 有很多意思，后面可以接表示物品的名词，表示展览或陈列某物；也可以接与情绪有关的名词，表示人的状态。
㊉ appreciate (P. 256)

0412 expand [ɪkˈspænd] **v** 扩大，增加，膨胀
In my opinion, this substance has no tendency to expand.
在我看来，这种物质没有膨胀的倾向。
㊉ enlarge 扩大　㊉ contract 收缩

0413 expansion [ɪkˈspænʃn] **n** 扩张，膨胀，扩充
I plan to give an impulse to industrial expansion next year.
我打算在明年促进工业的扩展。
㊉ inflation 膨胀　㊉ contraction 收缩

语法重点
give an impulse to（促进）中的 to 是介词。

0414 experimental [ɪkˌsperɪˈmentl] **a** 实验性的
If my memory serves me right, near the experimental farm exists a waterpower station.
如果我没记错的话，实验农场附近有一座水力发电站。
㊉ experimental data 实验资料

examinee ~ extent

0415 explanation [ˌekspləˈneɪʃn] n 解释，说明
Well, you should say a few words by way of explanation.
嗯，你得说几句话作为说明。
◉ by way of... 作为……

0416 explore [ɪkˈsplɔːr] v 探查，探险
If I were you, I would explore the Arctic regions.
如果我是你，我会探测北极地带。
◉ detect 探测 ◉ explore for oil 探勘石油

> **语法重点**
> 表示极地地带的专有名词前需要加冠词，如例句中的 the Arctic regions，以及 the North Pole, the Arctic Pole 等。
> ↪ arctic (P. 674)

0417 explosion [ɪkˈsploʊʒn] n 爆炸，激发，激增
The explosion just now gave me quite a scare.
刚才的爆炸声把我吓了一跳。
◉ nuclear explosion 核爆炸 ◉ ... give sb. a scare ……吓某人一跳

0418 explosive [ɪkˈsploʊsɪv]
a 爆炸性的，引发争论的 n 炸药
It's a problem, and above all, it is an explosive problem.
这是个问题，尤其是这个问题还容易引起争论。
◉ explosive force 爆炸力 ◉ ... and above all, ... ……尤其是，……

> **语法重点**
> above all 属于表示递进关系的连词，表示强调后面所叙述的事件。

0419 expose [ɪkˈspoʊz] v 使暴露
I am sure I will expose the shameful activity to the newspapers.
我确定要向报社揭露这无耻行径。
◉ disclose 揭露 ◉ hide 隐瞒 ◉ expose... to... 向……曝光

↪ shameful (P. 502)

0420 exposure [ɪkˈspoʊʒər] n 暴露，揭露
I have a yearning for having a room with a southern exposure.
我渴望有一间向南的房间。

↪ yearn (P. 806)

0421 extend [ɪkˈstend] v 延长，伸展
I am occupied with extending my garden, so I don't want to go to the party.
我正忙于扩建花园，所以我不想去参加派对。
◉ stretch 伸展 ◉ shrink 收缩 ◉ be occupied with... 忙于……
◉ extend 指时间或空间的延长，也可指影响和使用范围等的扩大，而 stretch 指长度的延伸以及宽度的增加。

0422 extent [ɪkˈstent] n 程度，范围，限度
I think it can hold back market competition to a great extent.
我认为，这在很大程度上阻止了市场竞争的发展。
◉ degree 程度 ◉ to some extent 在某种程度上

439

0423 facial [ˈfeɪʃl] a 脸的，面部的
I think the girl bears a strong facial resemblance to you.
我觉得，那个女孩的容貌和你十分相像。
facial expression 面部表情

➔ resemblance (P. 770)

0424 facility [fəˈsɪləti] n 设备，设施，便利
I wouldn't feel happy if they sent my daughter to the kindergarten with poor facilities.
如果他们把我女儿送到设备很差的幼儿园，我会不高兴。
plant 设备　leisure facilities 休闲设施

语法重点
facility 当"设备，设施"时，一般用复数形式。

0425 faithful [ˈfeɪθfl] a 忠实的，尽职的，忠贞的
If you want to get promoted, you will have to be faithful to your boss.
如果你想得到提拔，就得对老板忠诚。
faithful 多指对人对事或对诺言、誓言始终不渝，侧重于指在任何情况下都绝不改变。

0426 fame [feɪm] n 名声，名望，声誉
I think the woman has hankered after fame all her life.
我认为这个女人一生都在追求名声。
renown 名望　shoot to fame 一举成名　hanker after... 渴望……

0427 fantastic [fænˈtæstɪk] a 想象中的，奇异的，幻想的
I promise I won't give up the fantastic job.
我保证，我不会放弃这份好工作。
wonderful 极好的　terrible 很糟的

语法重点
I promise（我保证）后面的句子通常要用一般将来时。

0428 fantasy [ˈfæntəsi] n 空想，想象
To me, the movie was more of a horror story than an ironic fantasy.
在我看来，这部影片与其说是带有讽刺意味的奇幻片，不如说是恐怖片。
fancy 幻想　reality 真实　... more of... than... ……与其说……不如说……

➔ ironic (P. 736)

0429 farewell [ˌferˈwel] n 告别 int 再会，再见
I am afraid I have to make my farewell to you.
恐怕，我要与你们说再见了。
farewell party 欢送会　make one's farewell to... 与……说再见

0430 fatal [ˈfeɪtl] a 致命的，毁灭性的，决定性的
It would be fatal to bring the bag home.
把这个袋子带回家，可能招致灾难。
fatal error 致命错误　it would be fatal to... ……可能会招致灾难

语法重点
可以用 a fatal wound 来表示"致命伤，不治之症"。

0431 **favorable** ['feɪvərəbl] **a** 有帮助的，赞成的

I am favorable to going out for a walk.
我赞成出去散步。

> 语法重点
> be favorable to（赞成）后面要接名词、代词或者动名词。

0432 **feast** [fi:st] **n** 盛宴，宴会，节日 **v** 宴请

You shouldn't have troubled yourself to feast us with so many dishes.
你本不该用这么多菜宴请我们，太麻烦了。

🔄 banquet 宴请   🔄 feast one's eyes 饱眼福

> 语法重点
> 句子暗含的意思是本不该做某事，但是，实际上已经做过了。

0433 **ferry** ['feri] **n** 渡船，渡口 **v** 摆渡，运输

I think the boat is used to ferry the villagers to the bank.
我觉得，这小船是用来摆渡村民到河岸的。

🔄 ferry terminal 渡轮码头   🔄 ... ferry sb. to... ……把某人摆渡到……

> 语法重点
> 句中的第一个 to 是表示不定式的 to，第二个 to 是介词。

0434 **fertile** ['fɜːrtl] **a** 肥沃的，富饶的，多产的

It never occurred to me that your hometown is fertile of oranges.
我从没想到，你们家乡盛产橘子。

🔄 productive 多产的   🔄 be fertile of... 盛产……

0435 **fetch** [fetʃ] **v** 拿来，请来 **n** 相同物

Her bag is the exact fetch of the one I lost and I suspect she stole mine.
她的包包和我不见的那个一模一样，我怀疑是她偷了我的包包。

🔄 exact (P. 161)

0436 **fiction** ['fɪkʃn] **n** 小说，虚构，杜撰

To finish reading the fiction in two days is no easy work.
两天之内读完这本小说，不是件容易的事。

0437 **fierce** [fɪrs] **a** 猛烈的，凶猛的

I am sure I will get a beat on him after a fierce struggle.
我确定经过殊死的较量，我会比他占上风。

🔄 violent 猛烈的   🔄 fierce attack 重击   🔄 ... get a beat on sb. ……占某人的上风

🔄 struggle (P. 230)

0438 **finance** ['faɪnæns] **n** 财政，金融，资金

Of course I can get the position of director on the strength of my skill in finance.
我当然相信，凭着自己的理财本领，我可以得到主管这个职位。

🔄 capital 资金   🔄 on the strength of... 凭借……

> 语法重点
> finance 表示"资金"时，通常用复数形式。

0439 **financial** [faɪˈnænʃl] **a** 财政的，金融的

I am afraid the report is inconsistent with the financial affairs.
恐怕这份报告和那些金融事务不一致。

🔄 financial difficulties 财政困难   🔄 be inconsistent with... 与……不一致

0440 **firecracker** [ˈfaɪərkrækər] n 鞭炮
I think he was quite reckless of his own safety when he set off those firecrackers.
我想他点燃那些鞭炮的时候，完全都不顾及自己的安危。
同 banger 鞭炮　　　 be reckless of... 不顾及……

> **语法重点**
> firecracker 作可数名词，通常表示"鞭炮"，在美式英语中，表示"鱼雷，炸弹"。
> ⇨ reckless (P. 621)

0441 **fireplace** [ˈfaɪərpleɪs] n 火炉
I find it hard for me to wall up the fireplace at night.
我发现晚上把那个壁炉封住，对于我来说是困难的事情。
同 I find it hard for me to... 我发现……对我来说很难
注 evening 和 night 都有"夜，晚上"之意，但 evening 指日落到就寝之间的时间，night 指从日落到日出这段时间。

0442 **flatter** [ˈflætər] v 谄媚，奉承，取悦
I think she always flatters herself.
我觉得她总是自以为是。
同 be flattered by 深感荣幸　　　 ... flatter oneself... ……自鸣得意

0443 **flee** [fliː] v 逃走，逃离，逃避
I wouldn't stand that you fled from your duty.
我不能容忍你逃避责任。
同 escape 逃跑　　　 flee risk 逃离危险　　　 ... flee from... ……逃避……

> **语法重点**
> flee 是不规则动词，其过去式、过去分词都是 fled。
> ⇨ duty (P. 158)

0444 **flexible** [ˈfleksəbl] a 有弹性的，灵活的，可变通的
I think that the girl has a flexible mind.
我认为，那个女孩思维灵活。
同 pliable 柔韧的　　　反 inflexible 顽固的　　　 flexible working 弹性工作制

0445 **fluent** [ˈfluːənt] a 流畅的
She is fluent in a few languages, so I'm sure she can do this job.
她能流利地说好几种语言，我相信，她一定能胜任这项工作。
同 fluid 流畅的　　　反 faltering 支吾的　　　 be fluent in... 讲……很流利

> **语法重点**
> be fluent in 后面要接表示语言的名词。

0446 **flunk** [flʌŋk] v / n 失败，考试不及格
I don't want to flunk in the exam as you.
我不想和你一样考试不及格。
同 fail 失败　　　反 succeed 成功　　　 flunk out 因成绩不及格而被学校除名

0447 **flush** [flʌʃ] v / n 冲洗，脸红
I think he was in the full flush of success last year.
我认为，去年他的成就如日中天。
同 blush 脸红　　　 be in full flush of success 成就如日中天

0448 foam [foʊm] n 泡沫 v 起泡沫，吐白沫

In my view, where there is water, there is foam.
在我看来，有水的地方就有泡沫。
- bubble 泡沫
- where is... there is... 哪里有……就会有……

0449 forbid [fər'bɪd] v 禁止

I will forbid her going out at nights.
我要阻止她晚上外出。
- prohibit 禁止
- permit 许可，允许
- forbid sb. doing... 禁止某人做……

> **语法重点**
> at nights 中，night 用复数，说明不只是一个晚上。

0450 forecast ['fɔːrkæst] v / n 预测，预报

In my opinion, it would be premature to forecast the result.
在我看来，预言结果还为时过早。

> ○ premature (P. 759)

0451 formation [fɔː'reɪʃn] n 形成，组成，结构

I hate to disagree with you, but the formation of a new government is not as easy as you might think.
我不想和你有不同意见，但新政府的组建可能没有你想象的那么容易。
- structure 结构
- capital formation 资本形成，集资

0452 formula ['fɔːrmjələ] n 公式，方案，原则

I think that formula is very difficult to remember.
我觉得那个公式很难记。
- computational formula 计算公式
- be difficult to do sth. 很难做……

> **语法重点**
> formula 的复数形式可以表示为 formulas 或者 formulae。

0453 fort [fɔːrt] n 堡垒

I've always wanted to visit the old fort.
我一直想参观那个古堡。
- castle 城堡
- hold the fort 代他人尽责

> **语法重点**
> 用 want to 的完成式表示一直以来的想法。

0454 fortunate ['fɔːrtʃənət] a 幸运的，侥幸的

I am the fortunate possessor of a bright future.
我很幸运，我有个光明的前途。
- lucky 幸运的
- unfortunate 不幸的
- fortunate 指因好运或机会带来的成功和喜悦，lucky 指偶然机遇中的有利与幸运情况。

0455 fossil ['fɑːsl] n 化石，食古不化的人

At this distance of time, I consider it hard to date the fossil.
时隔这么久，我觉得很难确定这个化石的年代。

> ○ distance (P. 154)

0456 foundation [faʊn'deɪʃn] n 建立，基础，根基

It's her excellent performance that laid a foundation for her career.
是她出色的表现为她的事业打下了基础。
- basis 基础
- ... lay a foundation for... ……为……打下基础

0457 **founder** ['faʊndər] n 创立者，缔造者 v 沉没，失败

In my mind, they three are the founders of the university.
在我心中，他们三个是这所大学的创建人。
- builder 建立者
- founder member 创办人
- in my mind, ... 在我心中，……

语法重点
基数词在句中可用作同位语，如例句中的 three 就是充当主语 they 的同位语。

0458 **fragrance** ['freɪgrəns] n 芬芳，香味，香水

I hope the fragrance the flowers give out can relax you.
我希望花朵散发出来的香味能让你放松。
- aroma 芳香
- fragrance oil 香精
- give out... 发出……

relax (P. 347)

0459 **fragrant** ['freɪgrənt] a 芳香的，馥郁的

How fragrant the girl just passing by is!
刚走过去的女孩身上真香！
- aromatic 芬芳的
- smelly 发臭的
- pass by... 经过……

0460 **frame** [freɪm] n 骨架，框架，结构 v 镶框，制定

I will talk to him when he is in a better frame of mind.
他心情好些时，我会和他谈话。

语法重点
a frame of mind 可以表示"心情，心绪"，frame 前可以加上形容词来表示不同的心情。

better (P. 014)

0461 **freeway** ['friːweɪ] n 高速公路，快车道

I am afraid the tire will blow out on the freeway.
我担心会在高速公路上爆胎。
- expressway 高速公路
- have a flat tire 爆胎

0462 **frequency** ['friːkwənsi] n 频率，频繁

I have confidence in the frequency converter.
我对这个变频器有信心。
- periodicity 频率
- I have confidence in... 我对……有信心

0463 **freshman** ['freʃmən] n 新生，新手

I've had it up to here with the freshman.
我真受不了那个大一新生。
- 大一学生是 freshman，大二学生是 sophomore，大三学生是 junior student，大四学生是 senior student。

0464 **frost** [frɔːst] n 霜，严寒 v 结霜

These farmers should be cautioned to protect the vegetables from frost.
这些农民应该收到警告，保护蔬菜避免结霜。

语法重点
frost 当动词时，后面常接介词 over 与 up，表示"结霜"。

0465 **frown** [fraʊn] n / v 皱眉，蹙额

I frowned on her being late for school.
我因为她上学迟到而不高兴。
- mow 皱眉
- with a frown 皱着眉头
- frown on... 不高兴……

founder ~ furious

0466 frustration [frʌ'streɪʃn] **n** 挫折，失败，沮丧
I think it's wrong to drink in frustration.
心情不好就喝酒，我觉得是不对的。

0467 fuel ['fjuːəl] **n** 燃料，刺激因素 **v** 加燃料，刺激
I think this kind of fuel has the advantage of burning easily.
我认为，这种燃料有易燃的优点。
🔄 have the advantage of... 有……的优点

> 语法重点
> have the advantage of 后面可以接名词或者动名词。

0468 fulfill [fʊl'fɪl] **v** 实现，完成，满足
I have no experience in the work, so I am afraid I can't fulfill the task on time.
我对这个工作没有经验，所以我担心不能准时完成任务。
🔄 complete 完成　　🔄 fulfill one's promise 履行诺言

> 语法重点
> fulfill 后面常直接表示计划、任务、工作量的名词。

0469 fulfillment [fʊl'fɪlmənt] **n** 实现，完成，满足
I am sure he will try his best in fulfillment of his duty.
我确定，他会尽最大的努力来履行自己的职责。
🔄 fulfillment of a duty 履行义务　　🔄 in fulfillment of... 实现……

0470 functional ['fʌŋkʃənl] **a** 实用的
I think this telephone is out of order, but that one is functional.
我认为这部电话是坏的，不过那部可以用。
🔄 functional testing 功能测试　　🔄 be out of order 坏的

🔗 telephone (P. 234)

0471 fundamental [ˌfʌndə'mentl]
a 基础的，根本的，重要的
This book is fundamental to your study.
这本书对于你的学习来说是必不可少的。
🔄 basic 基本的　　🔄 unimportant 不重要的
🔄 be fundamental to... 对……来说必不可少

0472 funeral ['fjuːnərəl] **n** 葬礼，出殡
I shouldn't have scolded her since that's not her funeral.
这不关她的事，我本不该责怪她。
🔄 funeral expenses 丧葬费　　🔄 that's not one's funeral 不关某人的事

🔗 scold (P. 501)

0473 furious ['fjʊəriəs] **a** 狂怒的，猛烈的
My beloved trousers were flamed a hole by him, so I was furious with him.
我心爱的裤子被他烧了个洞，所以我对他很生气。
🔄 angry 愤怒的　　🔄 be furious with... 对……生气

> 语法重点
> trousers 是复数，所以 be 动词用 were。

445

0474 furnish [ˈfɜːrnɪʃ] v 供给，布置，装备
Shall we furnish the poor people with some supplies?
我们给这些穷人供应一些生活用品，好吗？
🔄 provide 提供　🔄 furnish with 供给，用……装饰

> 语法重点
> furnish... with... 中，一般 furnish 后面接人，with 后面接物。

0475 furthermore [ˌfɜːrðərˈmɔːr] ad 再者，而且，此外
Furthermore, I will leave for a date tomorrow.
而且，我明天便要离开去赴约。
🔄 moreover 而且　🔄 but furthermore 但除此之外

> 语法重点
> furthermore 表示递进，后面要接句子，而且一般用逗号跟后面的句子隔开。

0476 gallery [ˈɡæləri] n 画廊，美术馆，走廊
I don't like these paintings that are on show in the art gallery.
我不喜欢艺术馆展出的这些画。
🔄 play to the gallery 以大动作吸引旁观者　🔄 be on show 展出

0477 gangster [ˈɡæŋstər] n 一帮歹徒，匪徒
I think you are on the track of the gangster.
我想你们正在追踪那名匪徒。
🔄 be on the track of... 追踪……

↻ track (P. 238)

0478 gaze [ɡeɪz] v / n 注视
I am unhappy when my husband turned his gaze to the beautiful girl.
我丈夫把目光移到那个漂亮的女孩身上时，我很不高兴。

0479 gear [ɡɪr] n 排挡，齿轮，装备 v 调整，使适用于
You should change into first gear when you go down the hill.
下山时你应该换一挡。

0480 gene [dʒiːn] n 基因
Evidence is accumulating that the expert knows nothing about the structure of gene in fact.
越来越多的证据表明，其实那个专家对基因的结构一无所知。
🔄 gene mutation 基因突变

↻ accumulate (P. 668)

0481 generation [ˌdʒenəˈreɪʃn] n 世代，产生
The man was one of the best singers of his generation.
那人是他那一代中最优秀的歌星之一。
🔄 for generations 世世代代　🔄 of one's generation 在某一代人中

> 语法重点
> of one's generation 在句中表示范围。

0482 generosity [ˌdʒenəˈrɑːsəti] n 慷慨，大方
I am sure he will be knocked out by my generosity.
我确定，我的宽宏大量会让他感到吃惊。
🔄 bounty 慷慨　🔄 parsimony 吝啬

furnish ~ glimpse

0483 **genius** ['dʒiːniəs] n 天才，天赋
I think of myself as a genius in math.
我自以为自己是个数学天才。
- talent 天才　- idiot 傻瓜

0484 **genuine** ['dʒenjuɪn] a 真正的，真诚的，真实的
As time goes on, a genuine friendship will grow between them.
随着时间的推移，他们之间会产生真挚的友情。
- real 真实的　- as time goes on, ... 随着时间的推移，……

○ friendship (P. 299)

0485 **germ** [dʒɜːrm] n 微生物，萌芽
I will tell you if I have the germ of an idea.
如果我有初步的想法，就会告诉你。
- in germ 在萌芽中　- have the germ of... ……的开端

0486 **gifted** ['gɪftɪd] a 有天赋的
I think the boy is gifted with rare eloquence.
我觉得，那个男孩天生具有罕见的口才。
- talented 有才能的　- gifted child 天才儿童　- be gifted with... 天生具有……

○ eloquence (P. 713)

0487 **gigantic** [dʒaɪ'ɡæntɪk] a 巨人般的，庞大的
I was daunted by the gigantic word in this letter.
这封信里的这个长单词难倒我了。
- tremendous 巨大的　- small 小的　- be daunted by... 被……难倒了

语法重点
gigantic 指面积或体积的巨大，但多用于引申意义。

0488 **giggle** ['gɪgl] v / n 咯咯地笑，傻笑
Wouldn't it be a giggle to put his glasses away?
把他的眼镜藏起来，不是很有趣吗？

0489 **ginger** ['dʒɪndʒər] n 姜，生姜，精力
I think there is no ginger in the man over there.
我觉得那边那个人毫无生气。
- vigor 精力　- ginger juice 姜汁

语法重点
there is no ginger in（毫无生气）后面一般接表示人的名词或者代词。

0490 **glide** [glaɪd] v / n 滑动，滑翔，滑行
You should glide out of the room when he is sleeping.
你应该在他睡着时溜出房间。
- slide 滑动　- glide plate 滑板　- glide out of... 溜出……

0491 **glimpse** [glɪmps] v / n 瞥见，一瞥
I felt sad when I caught a glimpse of that paper.
瞥见那份试卷时，我很难过。
- peep 瞥见　- gaze 凝视　- catch a glimpse of... 匆匆看一下……

语法重点
caught 是 catch 的过去式，catch a glimpse of 相当于 catch sight of。

0492 globe [gloʊb] n 地球，地球仪，世界
I plan to travel around the globe next year.
我打算在明年进行环球旅行。
- Earth 地球
- travel around the globe 环球旅行

0493 glorious [ˈglɔːriəs] a 光荣的，壮丽的，辉煌的
It is a glorious thing to open the door for you.
为你开门是件光荣的事。

0494 goods [gʊdz] n 商品，动产
I was afraid that I would be alleged to have brought goods into the country illegally.
我怕我会被指控非法携带货物入境。
- commodity 货物
- deliver the goods 交货，履行诺言
- be alleged to do sth. 被指控……

语法重点
goods 视为复数名词，表示"货物，商品，动产"，作主语，动词用复数形式。

0495 grace [greɪs] n 优美，风度 v 使优雅
I will accept the gift sent by my friend with good grace.
我会欣然接受朋友送的礼物。
- disgrace 丢脸
- airs and graces 做作
- ... with good grace 欣然地……

- accept (P. 121)

0496 graceful [ˈgreɪsfl] a 优雅的，得体的
I think her success is closely linked to her graceful manner.
我觉得她的成功和优雅的举止息息相关。
- elegant 优雅的
- graceless 粗野的
- be closely linked to... 与……息息相关

0497 gracious [ˈgreɪʃəs] a 亲切的，优美的，高尚的
I assure you that she is a lovely and gracious woman.
我向你担保，她是个可爱又亲切的女子。
- friendly 亲切的
- I assure you that... 我向你担保……

语法重点
不定冠词 + 形容词 + and + 形容词 + 名词结构中，如果后一个形容词无冠词，则指同一个人或物，如例句中的 a lovely and gracious 表示的是同一个人。

0498 graduation [ˌɡrædʒuˈeɪʃn] n 毕业，毕业典礼
To be specific, your graduation thesis doesn't satisfy me.
具体地说，你的毕业论文让我不满意。
- To be specific, ... 具体地说，……

- specific (P. 362)

0499 grammar [ˈɡræmər] n 语法
I'll answer for it that the grammar book will be finished next week.
我保证下星期完成那本语法书。
- I'll answer for it that... 我保证……

globe ~ grief

0500 grammatical [grəˈmætɪkl] **a** 语法的
Except for some grammatical mistakes, your composition is well written.
除了几处语法错误之外，你这篇作文写得不错。
- grammatical rules 语法规则
- except for... 除了……

▷ composition (P. 411)

0501 grapefruit [ˈgreɪpfruːt] **n** 葡萄柚
Eating grapefruit doesn't make sense for these people.
对于这些人来说，吃葡萄柚没有什么意义。
- ... doesn't make sense ……没意义

语法重点
grapefruit 的复数形式可以是 grapefruit，也可以是 grapefruits。

0502 grateful [ˈgreɪtfl] **a** 感激的，令人愉快的
I was very grateful to you for your company.
我特别感谢你的陪伴。
- thankful 感激的
- ungrateful 不领情的

语法重点
be grateful to（感谢）后面一般接表示人的名词或者代词。

0503 gratitude [ˈgrætɪtuːd] **n** 感激，感谢，感恩
I promise you that I will not devoid of all gratitude if I succeed.
我保证，如果我成功了，绝不会忘恩负义。
- appreciation 感谢
- I promise you that... 我向你保证……

0504 grave [greɪv] **n** 墓穴 **a** 严肃的，庄重的
I feel impelled to express grave doubts about the plan they proposed.
我觉得，不得不对他们提出的计划深表怀疑。
- dig one's own grave 自掘坟墓
- I feel impelled to... 我觉得不得不……

▷ propose (P. 211)

0505 greasy [ˈgriːsi] **a** 油腻的，滑的，油滑的
For one thing I hate eating greasy food, for another it isn't good for my health.
一方面我不喜欢吃油腻的食物，另一方面，它也不利于身体健康。
- oily 油滑的
- insipid 清淡的
- greasy food 油腻的食物

语法重点
for one thing... for another（一方面……，另一方面……）连接两个并列的句子。

0506 greeting [ˈgriːtɪŋ] **n** 问候，打招呼
You should give her a warm greeting when she approaches.
当她走近时，你应该热情问候她。
- regard 问候
- greeting card 贺卡
- ... give sb. a warm greeting ……热情问候某人

0507 grief [griːf] **n** 悲伤
I swear grief and disappointment hastened the old man's death.
我肯定，悲哀和失望加速了那位老人的死亡。
- sadness 悲伤
- delight 高兴

语法重点
抽象名词表示一般概念时，通常不加冠词，如例句中的 grief and disappointment。

0508 grieve [griːv] v 悲伤，使痛苦
I shall not grieve for not passing the exam.
对于没通过考试，我一点儿也不难过。
... grieve for... ……为……难过

0509 grind [graɪnd] v 磨碎 n 磨，苦差事
I grinded my teeth when I saw they were having dinner together.
我看见他们在一起吃饭，气得咬牙切齿。
milling 磨　an axe to grind 另有所图，有不同意见
... grind one's teeth ……（因生气而）咬牙切齿

0510 guarantee [ˌgærənˈtiː] n 保证书 v 保证，担保
You must give a guarantee of good behavior.
你要保证行为端正。
assure 保证　under guarantee 保修期内　give a guarantee of... 保证……

0511 guilt [gɪlt] n 有罪，内疚
No matter where I went, the guilt will be eating into my conscience.
不管我走到哪里，内疚始终一直折磨着我的心。
compunction 内疚　sense of guilt 罪恶感　eat into... 侵蚀……

◎ conscience (P. 413)

0512 guilty [ˈgɪlti] a 有罪的，内疚的
I felt guilty by breaking her favorite vase.
打碎了她最心爱的花瓶，我感到非常内疚。
... feel guilty by doing sth. ……因为做某事而内疚
guilty 主要指某种行为违反道德标准，也可指违犯法律。

◎ favorite (P. 163)

0513 gulf [gʌlf] n 海湾，分歧
I've been thinking about in which year the Gulf War happened.
我一直在想海湾战争是发生在哪一年。
bay 海湾　a great gulf 鸿沟，根本的分歧

语法重点
表示战争名称的名词前需要用定冠词 the，如例句中的 the Gulf War（海湾战争）。

0514 habitual [həˈbɪtʃuəl] a 习惯性的
You must be a habitual visitor to his house.
你一定是他家的常客。
be habitual visitor to... 是……的常客

0515 halt [hɔːlt] v/n 停止，中止，暂停
I call for a halt to the attack towards the foreign people.
我呼吁停止对外国人的攻击。
cease 停止　come to a halt 停止前进，停下来

语法重点
call for a halt to（呼吁停止）中的 to 是介词。

0516 handwriting [ˈhændraɪtɪŋ] n 笔迹
I have a desire to see his current handwriting.
我非常渴望看到他现在的笔迹。
🔗 handwriting function 手写功能　　🔗 I have a desire to... 我非常渴望……

▶ current (P. 280)

0517 harden [ˈhɑːrdn] v 使硬化，使坚强
Don't you allow the clay to harden.
你不要让那些黏土变硬。
🔗 soften 使变软　　🔗 harden up 使坚硬

▶ 语法重点
祈使句一般无主语，为了强调主语，有时也有主语出现。祈使句的主语要重读，代词也要重读（陈述句的主语一般不重读）。

0518 hardship [ˈhɑːrdʃɪp] n 艰难，困苦
I think I can go through one hardship after another.
我相信，我可以经历一个又一个的困难。
🔗 difficulty 困难　　🔗 hardship consciousness 忧患意识

0519 hardware [ˈhɑːrdwer] n 硬件设备
I don't want to go to the hardware store in consequence of his words.
因为他说的话，我不想去那家五金行。
🔗 in consequence of... 由于……

▶ consequence (P. 413)

0520 harmonica [hɑːrˈmɑːnɪkə] n 口琴
I will steal a red and a black harmonica without reflecting on the consequences.
我将会不计后果地偷一支红色的和一支黑色的口琴。

▶ 语法重点
"不定冠词 + 形容词 + and + 形容词 + 名词"结构中，如果两个形容词都有冠词，则表示两个不同的东西，如例句中的 a red and a black harmonica 就表示两支口琴，一支红色的，一支黑色的。

0521 harmony [ˈhɑːrməni] n 一致
You should be in harmony with your colleagues.
你该与同事协调一致。
🔗 in harmony 和谐无间　　🔗 be in harmony with... 与……协调

0522 harsh [hɑːrʃ] a 刺耳的，严厉的，粗糙的
Don't be so harsh to the students who are naughty!
不要对调皮的学生太严厉！
🔗 severe 严厉的　　🔗 harsh times 非常时期　　🔗 be harsh to sb. 对某人严厉

▶ 语法重点
祈使句末尾通常用句号，如果要表示一种强烈的感情，也可以用感叹号。

0523 haste [heɪst] v / n 急忙，赶快
He went to school in haste just now.
他刚才急急忙忙去学校了。
🔗 hurry 匆忙　　🔗 composure 镇静，沉着　　🔗 in haste 匆忙地

0524 hasten [ˈheɪsn] v 赶忙，催促，加速
I should have hastened him to go to the Finance Ministry.
我本应该催他去财政部的。
🔗 hurry 赶快　　🔗 delay 延期　　🔗 hasten sb. to do... 催促某人做某事

▶ 语法重点
在某些表示组织机构的名词前要加定冠词 the。

0525 **hatred** ['heɪtrɪd] n 怨恨，憎恨，敌意
In my opinion, race hatred is common in the time of war.
在我看来，战争年代的种族仇恨很普遍。
- despite 憎恨
- deep hatred 深仇大恨
- in the time of... 在……的年代

→ race (P. 080)

0526 **headphone** ['hed,foʊn] n 双耳式耳机
You should wear the same headphone as your brother's.
你应该和弟弟戴一样的耳机。

0527 **healthful** ['helθfl] a 有益健康的，卫生的
I felt incapable of eating these healthful foods.
我感觉无法吃这些有益健康的食物。
- sanitary 卫生的
- ... feel incapable of doing sth. ……感觉无力做某事

0528 **helicopter** ['helɪkɑ:ptər] n 直升机
I haven't seen a helicopter for a long time.
我很久没有看到直升机了。
- whirlybird 直升机
- I haven't (done)... for a long time. 我很久没有……了
- helicopter 指直升机，而 aircraft 常用作集体名词，也可指一架飞机，其含义包括直升机和飞艇等。

0529 **herd** [hɜːrd] n 放牧的兽群
I don't think there will be a herd of sheep on the hill from a long distance.
我想，远处的山上不会有一群羊。

→ sheep (P. 089)

0530 **hesitation** [,hezɪ'teɪʃn] n 犹豫，踌躇
I will eat up the bread without hesitation.
我会毫不犹豫地把面包吃完。
- have no hesitation in saying 毫不犹豫地说
- ... without hesitation 毫不犹豫……

0531 **highly** ['haɪli] ad 高高地，很，非常
It is highly debatable whether she should accept his proposal.
她是否该接受他的求婚，还有待讨论。
- extremely 非常
- it is highly debatable that... ……还有待讨论

→ proposal (P. 343)

0532 **homeland** ['hoʊmlænd] n 祖国
I would adore to settle back in the homeland and eat the delicious snacks.
我非常乐意回家乡定居，吃美味的小吃。
- motherland 祖国
- homeland security 国土安全，国家安全

语法重点
adore to（喜欢）后面接动词原形。

hatred ~ host

0533 honeymoon [ˈhʌnimuːn] n 蜜月，初始的和谐时期
Do not bother her when she is on her honeymoon.
她度蜜月的时候不要打扰她。
🔗 honeymoon suite 蜜月套房　🔗 be on one's honeymoon 在度蜜月

0534 honorable [ˈɑnərəbəl] a 可尊敬的
You should be jealous of the honorable title.
你该忌妒这个光荣称号。
🔗 glorious 光荣的　🔗 honorable guests 嘉宾　🔗 be jealous of... 珍惜……
📖 title 指书名、剧码或其他文艺创作作品的题目，也可指荣誉称号。

➡ jealous (P. 313)

0535 hook [hʊk] n 钩子，钩状物　v 钩住
I can never be off the hook no matter what I do.
不管我做什么，都无法脱身。
🔗 hitch 钩住　🔗 hook in 勾住　🔗 ... be off the hook ……脱身

0536 hopeful [ˈhoʊpfl] a 有希望的，有前途的
I feel hopeful that we can find her even though the city is big.
尽管这个城市很大，我对找到她很乐观。
🔗 hopeless 没有希望的　🔗 be hopeful about... 对……抱有希望

0537 horizon [həˈraɪzn] n 地平线，眼界，见识
You should try to prevent the dispute on the horizon from happening.
你们应该试图避免这场即将发生的争端。
🔗 on the horizon 即将发生的，已露端倪的，临近的

▶ 语法重点
on the horizon 一般在句中放在被修饰词的后面。

0538 horrify [ˈhɔːrɪfaɪ] v 使害怕，使惊骇
Funny a book as it is, I was still horrified by some plots of it.
尽管这是一本很搞笑的书，我还是被一些情节吓到了。
🔗 alarm 使惊恐　🔗 reassure 使安心

➡ plot (P. 485)

0539 hose [hoʊz] n 水龙带，长筒袜　v 用软管浇水
I want to hose down a whole garden in one day.
我想在一天时间内来浇灌整个花园。
🔗 pipe 管　🔗 hose down... 用水管里的水冲洗……

0540 host [hoʊst] n 主办，主持
No one felt happy to have dinner with such a mean host.
没人乐意和这样吝啬的主人一起吃饭。
🔗 master 主人　🔗 guest 宾客　🔗 host country 东道国

▶ 语法重点
no one felt happy to（没有人会觉得高兴）后面要接动词原形。

➡ mean (P. 063)

0541 **hostel** [ˈhɑːstl] n. 青年之家，青年旅馆

Why didn't you live in the hostel near my house as I told you to?
你为什么不住我跟你说的我家附近的青年旅馆呢？
- Why didn't you...? 你为什么不……？

语法重点
why didn't you 后面要接动词原形。

0542 **household** [ˈhaʊshoʊld]
n. 家庭，户　a. 家庭的，家喻户晓的

It looks as though he was born in a respectable household.
他看起来好像是出生在一户有名望的人家。
- a household name 家喻户晓的名字　- it looks as though... 看起来好像……

语法重点
be born 的意思是"出生"，一般不用于主动语态。
⊃ respectable (P. 497)

0543 **housewife** [ˈhaʊswaɪf] n. 家庭主妇

I look down upon the housewife who is busy at housework all day.
我瞧不起那个整天忙家务的家庭主妇。
- materfamilias 家庭主妇　- be busy at... 忙于……

语法重点
be busy at 中的 at 可以替换为介词 with。

0544 **housework** [ˈhaʊswɜːrk] n. 家事

I think he is expert at getting out of housework.
我觉得他很会逃避家务。
- do housework 做家务　- be expert at... 在……方面的老手

⊃ expert (P. 162)

0545 **humanity** [hjuːˈmænəti] n. 人性，人道

The great chairman spent her lifetime in the service of humanity.
那位伟大的主席耗尽毕生的精力为人类服务。
- man 人类　- humanity spirit 人文精神

0546 **hurricane** [ˈhɜːrəkən] n. 飓风，暴风

I am sure many buildings will be demolished by the hurricane.
我确定，许多建筑物会被飓风摧毁。
- cyclone 飓风　- be demolished by... 被……摧毁

0547 **hydrogen** [ˈhaɪdrədʒən] n. 氢

Well, I believe water can be reduced to oxygen and hydrogen by electrolysis.
嗯，我相信用电解法可以把水分解为氧和氢。

语法重点
be reduced to 中的 to 是介词，后面一般接名词。
⊃ oxygen (P. 480)

0548 **iceberg** [ˈaɪsbɜːrɡ] n. 冰山，冷若冰霜的人

Something must be done to prevent the ship from crashing into the iceberg.
必须采取措施，避免轮船撞上冰山。
- floeberg 冰山　- the tip of the iceberg 冰山一角

0549 identical [aɪ'dentɪkl] a 相同的
I think he is identical in character with his sister.
我觉得，他的品性和他妹妹相同。
- alike 相同的
- different 不同的
- identical twin 同卵双生

语法重点
be identical with（和……完全相同）后面一般接表示人的名词或者代词。

0550 identification [aɪˌdentɪfɪ'keɪʃn] n 识别，身份证
You should take your identification card with you when you are in a strange place.
你在一个陌生的地方时，要随身带着你的身份证。
- recognition 识别
- identification card 身份证
- take... with sb. ……某人携带

0551 identify [aɪ'dentɪfaɪ] v 识别，认出，鉴定
He always identifies himself with us, thus we like him very much.
他经常和我们打成一片，因此很受我们喜欢。
- identify oneself 证明自己的身份
- identify oneself with... 与……打成一片

语法重点
identify oneself with 后面接表示人的名词或者代词。

0552 idiom ['ɪdiəm] n 惯用语，方言
You really have to do something about your study since both dialects and idioms are difficult to learn.
你真该为你的学业做点什么了，方言和惯用语都很难学。

○ dialect (P. 557)

0553 idle ['aɪdl] a 空闲的，懒散的，无聊的
It's wrong of you to drink in your idle time.
在空闲时间喝酒是不对的。
- diligent 勤勉的
- ... in one's idle time 在某人空闲的时候……

0554 idol ['aɪdl] n 偶像，神像
Let's bow down to the idol.
我们向神像行礼吧。
- fetish 偶像
- pop idol 流行偶像
- bow down to... 向……行礼

语法重点
bow down to 中的 to 是介词。

0555 ignorant ['ɪgnərənt] a 无知的，愚昧的，不知道的
I think he is ignorant of literature.
我觉得他不了解文学。
- learned 博学的，有学问的
- be ignorant of... 不了解……

0556 illustrate ['ɪləstreɪt] v 举图或实例说明
My hope is to draw a chart to illustrate my points.
我希望画个图表来说明我的观点。
- interpret 说明
- illustrate simply 简单地解释

○ chart (P. 022)

0557 **illustration** [ˌɪləˈstreɪʃn] n 图解，例证
By way of illustration, I'll refer to how a pig lives in the forest.
我将举例说明一头猪是如何在森林中生活的。
同 instruction 说明　同 by way of illustration... 举例说明……

0558 **imaginable** [ɪˈmædʒɪnəbl] a 可想象的，可想到的
It is imaginable that he will be angry if he gets the bad news.
可以想象，他得知那个坏消息会生气。
同 conceivable 可想象的　反 unimaginable 难以想象的

> 语法重点
> imaginable 一般要放在被修饰词的后面。

0559 **imaginary** [ɪˈmædʒɪneri] a 想象的，虚构的
It won't do any harm to draw an imaginary beast.
画一只虚构的怪兽，也没有什么坏处。
同 fancy 想象的　反 actual 真实的　同 imaginary line 虚线

0560 **imaginative** [ɪˈmædʒɪnətɪv] a 有想象力的，幻想的
It would be wonderful if all of you are imaginative.
如果你们都很有想象力，那就太好了。
同 it would be wonderful if... 要是……那就太好了

0561 **imitate** [ˈɪmɪteɪt] v 模仿，仿效，仿制
It makes a difference to me who you are imitating.
你在模仿谁，对我来说很重要。
同 emulate 模仿　同 imitate others 模仿别人

> 语法重点
> it makes a difference to 后面一般接表示人的名词或者代词。

0562 **imitation** [ˌɪmɪˈteɪʃn] n 模仿，效法
It is a wonder that all of your merchandise is imitation jewelry.
真不敢相信，你所有的商品都是伪造的珠宝。
反 invention 发明　同 in imitation of... 模仿……

> 语法重点
> 无生命的集体名词 merchandise 作主语时，动词用单数形式。
> ⇨ merchandise (P. 742)

0563 **immigrant** [ˈɪmɪɡrənt] n 外来移民，侨民
I think the machinery is tenanted by an immigrant from Korea.
我认为，这些机械是归一个韩国侨民所有。

> 语法重点
> 无生命的集体名词 machinery（机械）作主语时，动词用单数形式。
> ⇨ tenant (P. 648)

0564 **immigrate** [ˈɪmɪɡreɪt] v 迁入，移居
My plan is to immigrate to the United States.
我的计划是移民到美国。
同 immigrate to... 移民到……
同 immigrate 指自他国移入，长期定居，而 migrate 通常指大批人短期或定期地移居，指动物时，则指定期迁徙。

0565 immigration [ˌɪmɪˈgreɪʃn] n 移居，移民入境

I think it is not in conflict with the laws the immigration authority makes.
我想，这与移民局制定的法律没有冲突。

> 语法重点
> 表示机构名称的专有名词，作主语时应看作单数，动词用单数。
> authority (P. 400)

0566 impact [ˈɪmpækt] n / v 影响，冲撞

The news on the newspaper will have an impact on these people.
报纸上的新闻对这些人产生影响。
- influence 影响
- impact on... 对……有影响

0567 imply [ɪmˈplaɪ] v 暗示，暗含，暗指

He implies that we can have dinner together. Don't you understand?
他在暗示我们可以一起吃饭，你不明白吗？
- hint 暗示
- imply for... 意味着……
- imply that... 暗示……
- hint 指通过间接而有提示性的话语或表情来暗示某事，而 imply 侧重指话语、行为或情景中的一种暗示，听者或读者必须加以逻辑推断才能领会。

0568 impression [ɪmˈpreʃn] n 印象，感觉

I got the impression that he didn't forget the accident.
我感觉，他没有忘记那次意外。
- under the impression 在印象中
- I get the impression that... 我感觉……

0569 incident [ˈɪnsɪdənt] n 事件，事变，插曲

The film which is based on a real-life incident makes an indelible impression on me.
以现实生活中的事件为基础的那部电影，让我难以忘怀。

impression (P. 457)

0570 including [ɪnˈkluːdɪŋ] prep 包含，包括

I set my mind to read books at night, including vacations.
我下定决心在晚上看书，包括假日。
- include in... 包括在……中
- ... set one's mind to do sth. ……下定决心做某事

0571 indication [ˌɪndɪˈkeɪʃn] n 指示，表示，迹象

I don't want to give any indication of my feelings to you.
我不想向你展示自己的感情。
- instruction 指示
- indication function 指示功能
- give indication of... 展示……

0572 industrialize [ɪnˈdʌstriəlaɪz] v 使工业化

I'd like to know more about industrializing.
我想多了解一些关于工业化的东西。
- I'd like to know more about... 我想多了解……

> 语法重点
> industrialize 的现在分词、过去式、过去分词分别是 industrializing, industrialized, industrialized。

0573 **infant** [ˈɪnfənt] n 婴儿，幼儿 a 婴儿的，幼稚的

I think this is a good chance for you to look after the infant.
我认为，照顾那个婴儿对你来说是个很好的机会。

0574 **infect** [ɪnˈfekt] v 使感染

Keep away from me because I don't want to infect you with my cold.
离我远点，我不想把感冒传染给你。

- communicate 感染
- infect with... 传染……，感染……

0575 **infection** [ɪnˈfekʃn] n 传染，传染病，影响

His disease may be referable to virus infection.
他的病也许是由病毒感染引起的。

- contagion 传染病
- severe infection 重度感染，严重感染

语法重点
be referable to（可归因于）中的 to 是介词。

0576 **inflation** [ɪnˈfleɪʃn] n 膨胀

I think the government should bring up a hedge against inflation.
我认为，政府应该提出一项政策来预防通货膨胀。

- expansion 膨胀
- deflation 通货紧缩
- bring up... 提出……

against (P. 005)

0577 **influential** [ˌɪnfluˈenʃl] a 有影响力的，有权势的

I don't like him because he always tries to get in with the influential men.
我不喜欢他，是因为他总是试图巴结那些有影响力的人。

- influential factors 影响因素，影响因数
- get in with... 巴结……

语法重点
get in with 后面接表示人的名词或者代词。

0578 **information** [ˌɪnfərˈmeɪʃn] n 资讯，情报，资料

I would like to recommend the information to you.
我想推荐这个资料给你。

- I would like to recommend... 我想推荐……

0579 **informative** [ɪnˈfɔːrmətɪv] a 见闻广博的，情报的

In that case, I will buy an informative book.
既然那样，我要买一本资料丰富的书。

- informative reference 参考文献
- in that case, ... 既然那样，……

0580 **ingredient** [ɪnˈɡriːdiənt] n 组成成分，原料，因素

I think these kinds of ingredients are of great importance to cook the dish.
我觉得，做这道菜时，这几样原料很重要。

- active ingredient 有效成分
- be of great importance... 很重要

importance (P. 178)

0581 **initial** [ɪˈnɪʃl] **a** 开始的，字首的，最初的
I think recouping our initial investment is just around the corner.
我觉得我们马上就可以收回成本了。
同 earliest 最初的　反 final 最终的　搭 initial stage 初期

➪ investment (P. 463)

0582 **innocence** [ˈɪnəsns] **n** 清白，天真无邪，无罪
I am convinced of his innocence.
我确信他是无辜的。
同 blamelessness 无罪　反 guilt 犯罪，过失　搭 be convinced of... 确信……

0583 **input** [ˈɪnpʊt] **n** 输入　**v** 投入，输入资料
To me, our output should be proportional to the input.
在我看来，我们的输出应当与输入成比例。
反 output 输出资讯　搭 data input 资料登录

语法重点
be proportional to（与……成比例）中的 to 是介词。

0584 **insert** [ɪnˈsɜːrt] **v** 插入　**n** 插入物
I'll surely insert a picture into the fifth page of the dictionary.
我一定会在这本词典的第5页插入一张图片。
同 enter 进入　反 exit 退出　搭 I'll surely... 我一定会……

语法重点
I'll surely 后面要接动词原形。
➪ dictionary (P. 153)

0585 **inspection** [ɪnˈspekʃn] **n** 检查
I think we should make an inspection of the school.
我认为我们该去视察学校了。
搭 tour of inspection 出外巡视　搭 make an inspection of... 视察……

0586 **inspiration** [ˌɪnspəˈreɪʃn] **n** 灵感，鼓舞人心的人或事物
Maybe I can draw my inspiration from sleepwalking.
或许，我可以从梦游中获取灵感。
搭 ... draw one's inspiration from... ……从……中获取灵感
注 "名词＋动词"可以构成动词，如例句中的 sleepwalk，是由名词 sleep（睡眠）＋动词 walk 构成。

0587 **inspire** [ɪnˈspaɪər] **v** 鼓舞，激发，产生
Well, you should inspire your students to think more in the study.
嗯，你要鼓励学生在学习中多思考。
同 encourage 鼓励　反 discourage 使泄气　搭 inspire sb. to do... 鼓励某人做……

0588 **install** [ɪnˈstɔːl] **v** 安装，使……就职
It is essential that we install an air-conditioner in our house.
我们有必要在家里装一台空调。
同 fix 安装　搭 install program 安装程序

语法重点
it is essential that 后面接的句子中，动词要用 should 加上动词原形，should 可以省略。

0589 **instinct** [ˈɪnstɪŋkt] a 本能，直觉，天性
I think my son has an instinct for playing guitar.
我认为，我的儿子对弹吉他很有天分。

> 语法重点
> have an instinct for（对……有天分）后可以接名词，也可以接动名词形式。

0590 **instruct** [ɪnˈstrʌkt] v 教导，命令，通知
It's amazing that he instructs his sister in English.
他教妹妹英语，真让人惊讶。
- teach 教，教导
- study 学习
- instruct code 指令码

> 语法重点
> 注意，例句中的介词 in 不可以省略。

0591 **instructor** [ɪnˈstrʌktər] n 教师，讲师，指导书
Let's visit our history instructor at the weekend, OK?
周末我们去拜访历史老师，好吗？
- teacher 教师
- student 学生
- ... at the weekend 在周末……

0592 **insult** [ɪnˈsʌlt] v / n 侮辱，辱骂
My son got 0's in the final exam, which is taken as an insult by me.
我儿子在期末考试中得了很多零分，我认为这是对我的侮辱。
- humiliate 羞辱
- be taken as... 被看作……

0593 **insurance** [ɪnˈʃʊərəns] n 保险，保险费，安全保障
In my opinion, the insurance is grounded on trust.
在我看来，保险业立足于信用。
- assurance 保险
- insurance broker 保险经纪人
- be grounded on... 立足于……

- ground (P. 045)

0594 **intellectual** [ˌɪntəˈlektʃuəl]
a 智力的，聪明的 n 知识分子
It is high time that you invited the young intellectual to give a speech.
你早就该邀请那个年轻的知识分子来做演讲。
- clever 聪明的
- ignorant 无知的
- intellectual development 智力发展

> 语法重点
> it is high time that（早就该）后面的句子要用过去时。

0595 **intelligence** [ɪnˈtelɪdʒəns]
n 智慧，理解力，情报（工作）
It is important that she enter the intelligence services.
她进入情报部门很重要。
- information 情报
- intelligence test 智力测验

0596 **intelligent** [ɪnˈtelɪdʒənt] a 有才智的，聪明的
I have arrived at the conclusion that your boyfriend is intelligent.
我已得出结论，你男朋友很聪明。
- stupid 愚蠢的
- intelligent system 智慧系统
- I have arrived at the conclusion that... 我已得出结论……

- conclusion (P. 276)

0597 intend [ɪn'tend] v 想要，打算，意指

For the future, I intend to look after my baby with my sister.
今后，我打算和姐姐一起照顾我的孩子。

- intended target 预定目标
- for the future... 从今往后……

0598 intense [ɪn'tens] a 极度的，紧张的，强烈的

It's long been my dream to watch the intense match.
观看这场激烈的比赛一直是我的梦想。

- drastic 激烈的
- eased 放松的
- intense discussion 激烈的讨论
- it's long been my dream to... ……一直是我的梦想

0599 intensify [ɪn'tensɪfaɪ] v 加强，强化，加剧

It is likely that the government will intensify structural adjustment in this item.
政府有可能会在这个项目中增强结构调整力度。

- strengthen 增强
- weaken 变弱
- it is likely that... 有可能……

▷ structural (P. 643)

0600 intensity [ɪn'tensəti] n 强度，强烈，剧烈

It's really a challenge for me to read with the poor intensity of light.
在光的强度不足时看书，对我来说真是个挑战。

- strength 强度
- rainfall intensity 降雨强度

▶ 语法重点
it's really a challenge for me 后面一般接动词不定式。

0601 intensive [ɪn'tensɪv] a 强烈的，精细的，密集的

It makes no difference to me whether you have received intensive training.
你是否受过密集训练，对我来说无所谓。

- elaborate 精心制作的
- intensive care 特别护理

0602 intention [ɪn'tenʃn] n 意向，目的，打算

I have no intention of going shopping today.
我今天无意去逛街。

- purpose 目的
- good intentions 好意

▶ 语法重点
have no intention of（无意……）后面一般要接动名词。

0603 interact [ˌɪntər'ækt] v 互动，相互作用

I think these elements will interact with each other in this experiment.
我认为在这个实验中，这些元素会相互作用。

- interact on... 与……相互作用
- ... interact with... ……相互影响

▷ element (P. 159)

0604 interaction [ˌɪntər'ækʃn] n 互动，相互作用

It helps if his paper can express the concept of interaction design.
如果他的论文能体现交互设计的理念，那会有所帮助。

- social interaction 社会互动，社会干预，社会交往

▷ express (P. 162)

0605 **interfere** [,ɪntərˈfɪr] v 介入，妨碍
Don't interfere with his work.
别妨碍他工作。
- interfere in 干涉，干预
- interfere with... 妨碍……

0606 **intermediate** [,ɪntəˈmiːdiət]
a 中间的 v 干预

It goes without saying that the factory is till at an intermediate stage of development.
不用说，这家工厂还处在发展的中间阶段。
- secondary 中级的
- it goes without saying that... 不用说……

⇨ stage (P. 227)

0607 **Internet** [ˈɪntərnet] n 网际网络
It's a bad habit to surf the Internet all night.
彻夜上网是个坏习惯。
- on the Internet 在网上
- it's a bad habit to... ……是个坏习惯

0608 **interpret** [ɪnˈtɜːrprɪt] v 口译，解释
It's a pleasure to interpret the chairman's speech.
很高兴来翻译主席的演讲。
- account 解释
- interpret course 口译课程
- interpret 只能指口头翻译，而 translate 可以用来表示口头和书面的翻译。

⇨ chairman (P. 540)

0609 **interruption** [,ɪntəˈrʌpʃn] n 中断，停止，打岔
It's not like him to keep up physical training without interruption.
坚持锻炼不间断，不像是他的作风。
- suspension 暂停
- succession 连续

0610 **intimate** [ˈɪntɪmət] a 亲密的，私人的 v 暗示，透露
It's my first time of having an intimate candlelit dinner for two persons and I like it very much.
这是我的第一次温馨的二人烛光晚餐，我很喜欢。
- close 亲密的
- public 公开的
- intimate link 亲密联系

语法重点
当序数词前有代词时，不需要再加冠词，如例句中的 my first time。

0611 **intonation** [,ɪntəˈneɪʃn] n 语调，声调
It's been so long since I heard of his funny intonation; I want to laugh.
很久没听到他滑稽的语调了，我很想大笑。

语法重点
it's been so long since（很久）后面的句子通常要用一般过去时。

0612 **invade** [ɪnˈveɪd] v 侵略，侵袭
It won't take long before the cancer cells invade other parts of your body.
用不了多久，癌细胞就会侵袭身体的其他部分。
- intrude 侵入
- defend 防守

语法重点
part 是最普通用词，常指整体中可大可小的一部分，也可指整体中可分开的独立部分。

interfere ~ isolate

0613 invasion [ɪn'veɪʒn] n 侵犯，侵入

I think the invasion of tourists can bring life to the summer resort.
我觉得，大批游客的涌入会使这个避暑胜地热闹起来。
⊙aggression 侵略　⊛defense 防卫　⊙bring life to... 使……热闹起来

0614 invention [ɪn'venʃn] n 发明，创造，捏造

I don't know how he lit upon the idea for the invention.
我不知道他是如何想到那个发明的。
⊙Necessity is the mother of invention. 需要是发明之母。

语法重点
例句中，lit 是动词 light 的过去式。

0615 invest [ɪn'vest] v 投资，投入

It would be imprudent to invest all his money in the real estate.
他把所有的钱都投资在房地产上，是不明智的。
⊙input 投　⊙invest with... 授予……

⊃estate (P. 563)

0616 investment [ɪn'vestmənt] n 投资，投资额，投入

I think it is sensible in terms of an investment.
我认为，这件事从投资的角度来考虑是合理的。
⊙risk investment 风险投资　⊙it is sensible... ……是合理的

0617 investigation [ɪnˌvestɪ'ɡeɪʃn] n 调查，研究

The police must have arrived at a solution via scientific investigation yesterday.
昨天，警察肯定是通过科学的调查研究得出解决问题的办法的。
⊙research 调查　⊙under investigation 在调查研究中

语法重点
via 是介词，意思是"通过"，相当于 by。
⊃solution (P. 225)

0618 involve [ɪn'vɑːlv] v 牵涉，卷入

I think the project must be involved with state secrets.
我觉得，这项计划肯定涉及国家机密。
⊙include 包含　⊙involve others 牵累别人　⊙be involved with... 涉及……

0619 involvement [ɪn'vɑːlvmənt] n 牵连，参与

I don't know why he has always felt a deep involvement with dogs.
我不知道，他为什么对狗总是有着深厚的感情。
⊙feel a deep involvement with... 对……有深厚的感情

0620 isolate ['aɪsəleɪt] v 隔离，使孤立

I wonder why these thirteen hundred patients are isolated from other people.
我想知道为什么这 1 300 个病人要与其他人隔离。
⊙insulate 隔离　⊙be isolated from 与……被隔开

语法重点
英语中 1 100~1 900 常用 hundred 表示，如例句中的 thirteen hundred（1 300）。

463

0621 **isolation** [ˌaɪsəˈleɪʃn] n 隔离，孤立

The indication is that he wants to be in complete isolation from the outside world and I long for the life, too.
有迹象表明，他想过与世隔绝的生活，我也向往那种生活。

in isolation 单独地，独自地

◎ indication (P. 457)

0622 **itch** [ɪtʃ] v 抓痒，渴望 n 渴望，痒

To tell the truth, I have an itch to play chess now.
说实话，我现在很想下棋。

desire 渴望　　the seven-year itch 七年之痒

语法重点
have an itch to 后面要接动词原形。

0623 **jealousy** [ˈdʒeləsi] n 忌妒，猜忌

I am burning with jealousy at the moment.
我现在妒火中烧。

envy 妒忌　　... burn with jealousy ……妒火中烧

0624 **junior** [ˈdʒuːniər]

a 年轻的，资历较浅的 n 大三学生，年少者

He is junior to me in the company.
在公司里，他的职位比我低。

senior 高年级的　　be junior to... 比……职位低

语法重点
be junior to 也可以表示"比……年龄小"，其中的 to 是介词。

0625 **keen** [kiːn] a 敏捷的，热情的，热心的

I am keen to help these poor people.
我很愿意帮助这些穷人。

dull 迟钝的　　be keen on... 喜爱……，渴望……

语法重点
be keen to 后面接动词原形。

0626 **knuckle** [ˈnʌkl] n 关节 v 开始努力工作，屈从

The general opinion is that you have to knuckle down, but I don't think so.
大家普遍认为你应该专心练习，但是我不这么想。

语法重点
knuckle down 是不及物动词短语。
◎ general (P. 043)

0627 **labor** [ˈleɪbər] n 劳工，工人

I think a thousand one hundred and forty-nine labors will lose their jobs.
我认为，将会有 1 149 个工人失去工作。

rest 休息　　... lose one's job ……失业

语法重点
千位数由表示 1~9 的基数词 + thousand 构成，如果千位数的位置是"一"，该千位数可以表示为"one + thousand + 基数词 + hundred + (and) + 基数词 + 基数词"。

0628 **laboratory / lab** [ˈlæbrətri] / [læb] n 实验室

I hope that our laboratory can be kept in good order.
我希望，我们的实验室里能够保持井然有序。

be kept in good order 保持井然有序

0629 lag [læg] v 延缓，落后，滞留

I am afraid that I will lag behind him.
我害怕会落后于他。
- draggle 落后
- advance 前进
- lag behind... 落后于……

0630 landmark ['lændmɑːrk] n 地标，里程碑

In my opinion, the year 1949 is a landmark for the Chinese nation.
在我看来，1949 年是中华民族具有划时代意义的一年。
- milestone 里程碑
- be a landmark for... 是……的里程碑

语法重点
年份用基数词表示，一般写为阿拉伯数字，如例句中的 1949。
nation (P. 067)

0631 landscape ['lændskeɪp] n 风景，景色

It is universally acknowledged that Guilin's landscape is number one in the world, but I don't like it.
全世界都知道桂林山水甲天下，但是，我不喜欢那里。
- scenery 风景，景色

语法重点
例句中的 number one，还可以表示为 Number 1，或者缩写为 No.1。

0632 landslide / mudslide ['lændslaɪd] / ['mʌdslaɪd] n 山崩，滑坡，压倒性胜利

There seems to be some houses destroyed by a landslide; it was a pity.
看起来好像一些房子被山崩毁坏了，真是遗憾。
- landslide victory 以绝对优势取得胜利

destroy (P. 283)

0633 largely ['lɑːrdʒli] ad 大部分地，主要地

I think her conclusions were largely founded on guesswork.
我觉得，她的结论大部分都是基于猜测。
- chiefly 主要地
- largely right 基本上正确
- be founded on... 基于……

0634 lately ['leɪtli] ad 最近，不久前

I am angry that I have not seen anything of her lately.
近来我连她的影子也没有见到过，我很生气。
- recently 最近
- only lately 直到最近

语法重点
lately 用来指最近的一段时间，常与现在完成时连用。

0635 launch [lɔːntʃ] n 发射，下水 v 发射，发动

I estimate that thousands upon thousands people keep a watchful eye on the launch of the satellite.
我估计，成千上万的人在关注着这颗卫星的发射。
- start 启动
- clear launch 正确发射
- keep a watchful eye on... 关注着……

语法重点
基数词 thousand 相当于名词，有复数形式，其构成方法及读音与名词相同，表示不确定数目。
estimate (P. 437)

0636 lawful ['lɔːfl] a 合法的，守法的

It is not lawful to accept these thousands of dollars.
接受这上万美元是不合法的。
- legal 合法的
- unlawful 非法的
- lawful age 法定年龄

语法重点
基数词 thousand 相当于名词，其复数形式常与 of 连用，表示成千上万的。

0637 lead [liːd] v 带领，领先，导致 [led] n 铅

I think it was my teacher that led me into the world of music.

我认为是我的老师带我进入了音乐的殿堂。

lead up to... 作为……的准备，导致　　lead sb. into... 把某人带入……

0638 lean [liːn] v 倚，靠

I want to lean against the tree to have a rest.

我想靠着树休息一下。

incline 倾斜　　lean against... 靠着……

0639 learned ['lɜːrnɪd] a 有学问的，博学的

Those who are learned are not necessarily wise.

博学者未必都是聪明的。

lettered 有学问的　　unlearned 无学问的

> **语法重点**
> learned 作形容词时，表示"有学问的"，也可以视为及物动词 learn 的过去式、过去分词形式。

0640 learning ['lɜːrnɪŋ] n 学问，学识，学习

I will never boast of my learning.

我永远都不会夸耀自己的学识。

knowledge 学问　　boast of... 夸耀……

> boast (P. 402)

0641 lecture ['lektʃər] n 演讲

I take it as a pleasure to attend the famous scientist's lecture tomorrow.

明天我愿意去听那个知名科学家的演讲。

address 演讲　　deliver a lecture 发表演讲

> **语法重点**
> I take it as a pleasure to（我愿意）后面接动词原形。

0642 lecturer ['lektʃərər] n 讲师，演讲者

The lecturer should try to settle these people down.

那个讲师应该设法让这些人安静下来。

instructor 讲师　　guest lecturer 客座教授

settle sb. down 让某人安静下来

> **语法重点**
> settle... down 也可以用作 calm... down。
>
> settle (P. 220)

0643 legend ['ledʒənd] n 传说，传奇

I like nothing better than the legend about Robin Hood.

我最喜欢关于罗宾汉的传说。

folklore 民间传说　　I like nothing better than... 我最喜欢……

0644 leisurely ['liːʒərli] a 悠闲的，从容的 ad 慢慢地

I like taking a leisurely walk and appreciating the things in the historical museum.

我喜欢慢慢地走着，欣赏历史博物馆的东西。

easygoing 悠闲的　　engaged 忙碌的

> **语法重点**
> 在某些建筑物前需要用 the。

0645 **license** ['laɪsns] n 执照，特许

We are thinking of taking out a marriage license.
我们正打算领结婚证书。
- licence 许可证
- under license 获得许可
- we are thinking of... 我们打算……

0646 **lighten** ['laɪtn] v 照亮，启发

If you don't lighten the lantern, you must be ready to take the consequences.
如果你不点灯笼，就必须自食其果。
- abate 减轻
- darken 变得模糊
- lighten up 放松，不要生气

语法重点：take the consequences 后面也可以加上介词 of，表示"承担……的后果"。

0647 **limitation** [ˌlɪmɪ'teɪʃn] n 限制，限度，局限

It is a truth that I can't transcend the limitations of the ego.
我无法超越自身的局限性，这是事实。
- restriction 限制
- freedom 自由
- impose limitations 强加限制

语法重点：表示"局限"这个意思时，limitation 要用复数形式。

0648 **liquor** ['lɪkər] n 酒，烈酒

His wife will divorce him if he keeps being in liquor.
如果他总是喝得醉醺醺的，他妻子会和他离婚。
- wine 酒
- be in liquor... 喝醉

0649 **literary** ['lɪtəreri] a 文学的，文人的，书卷气的

She is considered to be one of the 17th century's literary giants, but I don't like her.
她被视为 17 世纪的文学巨匠之一，但是我不喜欢她。
- literary works 文学作品
- be considered to be 被认为是……

语法重点：be considered to be 后面常接形容词或名词。

0650 **literature** ['lɪtrətʃər] n 文学，文献

I think he has very eclectic tastes in literature.
我认为，在文学方面，他的兴趣非常广泛。
- document 文献
- ... have very eclectic tastes in... ……在……兴趣非常广泛

0651 **loan** [loʊn] n 贷款，借出 v 借出，贷给

It's so great that the bank makes a loan of five hundred thousand to us.
太棒了，那家银行贷给我们 50 万元。
- lend 借出
- borrow 借入
- on loan 借用，借贷

语法重点："……十万"的表示方法是：基数词 + hundred + thousand。

0652 **location** [loʊ'keɪʃn] n 位置，场所，定位

I think we should buy the house which is in a convenient location.
我觉得，我们应该买那间位置很方便的房子。
- site 场所
- on location 出外景，现场拍摄

语法重点：location 指某物设置的方向或地点。
- convenient (P. 145)

0653 **locker** ['lɑːkər] n 置物柜，冷藏室
You can hide in the locker room.
你可以躲在衣帽间里。
◎ locker room 更衣室　◎ hide in... 躲在……

0654 **logic** ['lɑːdʒɪk] n 逻辑，逻辑学，条理性
I think her words are against all logic.
我觉得，她的话完全不符合逻辑。
◎ logic operation 逻辑运算　◎ be against all logic 完全不合逻辑

0655 **logical** ['lɑːdʒɪkl] a 逻辑上的，合理的
It is logical that he borrow money from you.
他向你借钱是很自然的事。
◎ reasonable 合理的　◎ illogical 不合逻辑的
◎ it is logical that... ……是很自然的事

> 语法重点
> logical 的副词形式是在其后面直接加上 ly。

0656 **lotion** ['loʊʃn] n 化妆水，护肤液，乳液
In my opinion, the lotion has no use on her skin anyway.
在我看来，这乳液对她的皮肤一点效果都没有。
◎ body lotion 润肤乳液　◎ have no use on... 对……没有效果

0657 **lousy** ['laʊzi] a 卑鄙的，糟糕的，污秽的
You are dismissed for you are a lousy accountant.
你被辞退，是因为你是个不称职的会计。
◎ dirty 脏的　◎ cleanly 干净的　◎ be dismissed for... 因……被解雇

> ◎ dismiss (P. 428)

0658 **loyal** ['lɔɪəl] a 忠实的，忠心的
He will be loyal to his country forever.
他会永远忠诚于祖国。

0659 **loyalty** ['lɔɪəlti] n 忠诚，忠心
I want you to swear your loyalty to the Party.
我要你们宣誓效忠于党。
◎ brand loyalty 品牌忠诚度　◎ swear one's loyalty to... 宣誓效忠……

> 语法重点
> 在含有普通名词构成的专有名词前用 the，如例句中的 the Party。
> ◎ swear (P. 370)

0660 **lunar** ['luːnər] a 阴历的，月亮的
There is a better way to celebrate the lunar New Year.
还有个更好的办法来庆祝农历新年。
◎ solar 太阳的　◎ lunar module 登月舱

0661 **luxurious** [lʌɡˈʒʊriəs] a 奢侈的，豪华的
It's true that leading a luxurious life is always vacuous.
奢侈的生活总是很空虚，这是真的。
◎ extravagant 奢侈的　◎ economical 节约的　◎ it's true that... ……是真的

0662 luxury ['lʌkʃəri] n 奢侈，奢侈品

I think the luxury villa is worth at least seventy million dollars.
我认为这幢豪华别墅至少价值 7 000 万美元。
- extravagance 奢侈
- thrift 节俭
- be worth sth. 值……

语法重点
如果千万位数中除了千万位其他的位数上都为零，则表示为：基数词 + -ty + million。

0663 machinery [mə'ʃiːnəri] n 机械

You should phase in new machinery for increased automation next year.
明年，你们应该开始逐步采用新机器，以提高自动化程度。
- machine 机器，机
- phase in... 逐步引进……

语法重点
machinery 是总称，泛指机器，属于不可数名词。

0664 madam ['mædəm]
n 小姐，夫人，女士，太太

She is a little madam and we all dislike playing with her.
她有公主病，我们都不喜欢和她一起玩。

0665 magnetic [mæg'netɪk] a 磁铁的，有吸引力的

I want all the men to be ravished with my magnetic personality.
我要让所有的男人为我迷人的风度所倾倒。
- attractive 有吸引力的
- be ravished with... 为……所倾倒

0666 magnificent [mæg'nɪfɪsnt] a 壮观的，宏伟的

It is indeed the most magnificent building I have seen.
这确实是我见到过最宏伟的建筑。

- indeed (P. 309)

0667 makeup ['mek,ʌp] n 化妆品，组成，补充

I hope those who failed the exam can take a makeup exam next week.
我希望考试不及格的人下周参加补考。
- cosmetic 化妆品
- makeup cotton 化妆棉
- take a makeup exam 补考

0668 manual ['mænjuəl] a 手动的，体力的 n 手工，指南

I think he is your inferior in manual dexterity.
我觉得论手巧，他不如你。
- automatic 自动的
- manual operation 手动操作
- be one's inferior 不如某人

- inferior (P. 310)

0669 manufacture [,mænju'fæktʃər]
v 制造，捏造 n 产品，制造业

I want to use the equipment of our own manufacture.
我想用我们自己制造的设备。
- manufacture catalogue 产品目录

0670 manufacturer [ˌmænjuˈfæktʃərər] n 制造者，制造厂
It is good manners to visit the manufacturer first.
先拜访制造商是有礼貌的表现。
- maker 制造者
- it is good manners to do sth. 做某事是有礼貌的表现

0671 marathon [ˈmærəθɑːn] n 马拉松，耐力比赛
It takes a lot of stamina to run in the marathon.
跑马拉松很耗费体力。
- it takes a lot of stamina to do sth. 做某事很耗费体力

语法重点
marathon 首字母 m 有时也可以大写。

0672 margin [ˈmɑːrdʒən] n 边缘，余地
I hope there is no margin of error in your plan.
我希望，你的计划中不会有误差幅度。
- margin of error 误差幅度，误差界限

语法重点
margin 还可以作动词，意思是"围绕，给……加旁注"。

0673 maturity [məˈtʃʊrəti] n 成熟，到期
I think the girl has maturity beyond her years.
我觉得那个女孩过于老成。
- ripeness 成熟
- immaturity 不成熟

0674 maximum [ˈmæksɪməm] a 最大值的，顶点的 n 最大量
It's impossible that the car exceed the maximum speed.
那辆车不可能超越极限速度。
- minimum 最小的
- maximum amount 最高额

语法重点
maximum 没有比较级和最高级。
→ exceed (P. 564)

0675 measure [ˈmeʒər] n 尺寸，量度 v 测量，衡量
I'm hoping to measure the cliff before climbing it.
我希望攀爬悬崖前能先丈量一下。
- scale 测量
- I'm hoping to... 我希望……

0676 mechanic [məˈkænɪk] n 机械工
I hope I am paid by the month as a mechanic.
作为一名技工，我希望能按月领取工资。
- technician 技师
- auto mechanic 汽车修理工
- ... by the month 按月……

语法重点
定冠词 the 用在度量单位前，表示"每一"。

0677 mechanical [məˈkænɪkl] a 机械的，力学的，呆板的
Her smile is mechanical; she must be involved in the affair.
她笑得很勉强，一定是卷入了这件事中。
- flexible 灵活的
- be involved in... 卷入……中

语法重点
be involved in 不含贬义。
→ affair (P. 122)

0678 **memorable** [ˈmemərəbl] a 值得纪念的，难忘的

Feb. 13th was for me a memorable day because the lecture I attended that day had great influence on me.
对我来说，2 月 13 日是个值得纪念的日子，因为我那天听的演讲对我影响很大。

- have great influence on... ……对……有很大影响

> **语法重点**
> 为了简便起见，月份与日期连用时，月份常用缩写形式表示。缩写形式大部分都由其前三个字母表示，如例句中的 Feb.（二月）。
> - influence (P. 179)

0679 **memorial** [məˈmɔːriəl] a 纪念的 n 纪念碑，纪念物

I hope the memorial meeting can be held in the open air.
我希望，那个追悼会能在户外举行。

0680 **mercy** [ˈmɜːrsi] n 慈悲，怜悯，宽恕

You shouldn't show mercy to the beggar.
你不该怜悯那个乞丐。

- kindness 仁慈
- at the mercy of... 受……支配
- show mercy to... 对……很怜悯

0681 **mere** [mɪr] a 仅仅的，纯粹的

It's a mere waste of time talking to him.
和他谈话纯粹是浪费时间。

> **语法重点**
> it's a mere waste of time（纯粹是浪费时间）后面一般要接动名词。
> - aspect (P. 397)

0682 **merit** [ˈmerɪt] n 价值

I hope the boy who has merits in many aspects can become my boyfriend.
我希望，那个有很多优点的男孩能成为我的男朋友。

- merit pay 绩效工资
- have merit in... 在……有优点

0683 **messenger** [ˈmesɪndʒər] n 送信人

My letter was lost and the messenger should answer for the consequences.
我的信遗失了，那个送信人要对后果负责。

- postman 信差
- ... answer for the consequences ……对后果负责

0684 **messy** [ˈmesi] a 脏乱的，污秽的，麻烦的

He must be in a messy spot now.
现在他一定是陷入了窘境。

- dirty 肮脏的
- orderly 整齐的
- be in a messy spot 陷入窘境

0685 **microscope** [ˈmaɪkrəskoʊp] n 显微镜

It's inconceivable that the microscope was found under her bed.
这个显微镜最后在她床下找到了，太不可思议了。

- it's inconceivable that... ……太不可思议了

0686 **mild** [maɪld] a 温和的，柔和的，宽大的
I will give her a mild hint, hoping she will get it.
我会给她委婉的暗示，希望她能领会。
- gentle 温和的　　- harsh 严厉的
- ... give sb. a mild hint …… 给某人委婉的暗示

0687 **mineral** ['mɪnərəl] n 矿物，矿石，矿物质
I couldn't hide my disappointment when I knew there was no mineral.
当我知道那里没有矿物时，我掩饰不住自己的失望。
- ... hide one's disappointment …… 掩饰某人的失望

▷ disappointment (P. 284)

0688 **minimum** ['mɪnɪməm]
n 最小值，最低限度　a 最低的，最低限度的
The weather forecast says that the minimum temperature today is 2℃, so put on your down jacket when you go out.
天气预报说，今天的最低气温是2℃，所以你外出时要穿上夹克。
- lowest 最低的　　- maximum 最高的　　- minimum wage 最低工资

▷ 语法重点
在英语中，温度的表示方法为：基数词 + 表示温度的符号 "℃"。

▷ temperature (P. 372)

0689 **minister** ['mɪnɪstər] n 部长，大臣，牧师
I would contend that the minister is lying.
我倒是认为部长在撒谎。
- Minister of State 国务大臣　　- I would contend that... 我倒是认为……

0690 **ministry** ['mɪnɪstri] n 政府部门，内阁
I hope she can be on attachment to the Ministry of Defense from June 10th.
我希望从6月10日那天起，她能隶属国防部。
- Ministry of Economic Affairs 经济部　　- be on attachment to... 隶属……

▷ 语法重点
月份与日期连用时，月份常用缩写形式，即由其前三个字母表示，但是 May, June, July 三个月份要用完整的单词表示。

0691 **mischief** ['mɪstʃɪf] n 胡闹，淘气
Someone must have set the child on to do this piece of mischief.
一定是有人唆使那个孩子做这种胡闹的事。
- ... set sb. on to do sth. …… 唆使某人做某事

▷ 语法重点
must 后面接现在完成时，表示对过去情况的推测。

0692 **miserable** ['mɪzrəbl] a 不幸的，悲惨的，痛苦的
Talking of the past, I will feel miserable.
提起过去，我就觉得痛苦。
- deplorable 凄惨的　　- a miserable failure 惨败　　- talking of... 提起……

0693 **misfortune** [ˌmɪs'fɔːrtʃuːn] n 不幸，厄运，灾祸
He may be the one hundred and eleventh person who is dogged by his misfortune.
他应该是第111个被不幸纠缠的人。
- adversity 不幸　　- fortune 运气

▷ 语法重点
多位数序数词的后位个数如包含1~9时，后位数用序数词，前位数用基数词。

mild ~ monument

0694 mislead [ˌmɪsˈliːd] v 误导，欺骗
I don't want to see you are being misled by the man's wiles.
我不希望你被那个男人的花言巧语蒙混。
同 misdirect 误导　　反 lead 引导　　搭 be misled by... 被……蒙混住

语法重点
mislead 是不规则动词，其过去式、过去分词都是 misled。

0695 misunderstand [ˌmɪsʌndərˈstænd] v 误解，误会
I no longer fear that he would misunderstand me.
我不再害怕他会误解我。
反 understand 理解　　搭 misunderstand sb. 误解某人

语法重点
misunderstand 是不规则动词，其过去式、过去分词都是 misunderstood。

0696 moderate [ˈmɑːdərət] a 适度的，温和的，中等的
It's bad to drink, so remember to be more moderate in your drinking from now on.
喝酒不好，今后要记着适度饮酒。
同 mild 温和的　　反 excessive 过度的　　搭 be moderate in... ……要适度

0697 modest [ˈmɑːdɪst] a 谦虚的，适度的
I will remain modest even if I make a name for myself.
即使我出了名，也仍然会谦虚。
同 unobtrusive 谦虚的　　反 arrogant 自大的，傲慢的

语法重点
make a name for oneself 后面也可以接介词 in，表示"在……方面出名"。
参 remain (P. 348)

0698 modesty [ˈmɑːdəsti] n 谦虚，端庄
It is thought that modesty is a kind of virtue, but I don't think so.
人们认为谦虚是种美德，但是我不这么认为。
同 humility 谦虚　　反 arrogance 自大　　搭 it is thought that... 人们认为……

0699 monitor [ˈmɑːnɪtər]
n 监视器，屏幕，班长　v 监听，监视
It was miserable of you to steal the monitor.
你偷了屏幕真是可耻。

语法重点
it was miserable of you to 后面要接动词原形。
参 miserable (P. 472)

0700 monthly [ˈmʌnθli] a 每月一次的　ad 每月　n 月刊
Is it convenient for you to come here monthly? I need your help.
你能每月来一次这里吗？我需要你的帮忙。
搭 monthly salary 月薪　　搭 Is it convenient for you to...? 你是否方便……？

0701 monument [ˈmɑːnjumənt] n 纪念碑，历史遗迹
We should set up a monument in remembrance of the heroes.
我们应该建一座纪念碑来纪念那些英雄。
搭 historic monument 历史古迹　　搭 in remembrance of... 纪念……

0702 moreover [mɔːrˈoʊvər] ad 并且
Moreover, to go beyond the shibboleth is good for yourself.
另外，摆脱那些陈规陋习，对你自己有好处。

0703 mostly [ˈmoʊstli] ad 大多数地，主要地，通常
It was mostly in this respect that I found she wasn't as perfect as I thought.
主要是在这个方面，我发现她不像我想的那么完美。
⊙ mainly 主要地　⊙ it was mostly in this respect that... 主要是在这个方面，……

0704 motivate [ˈmoʊtɪveɪt] v 给……动机，促使，激发
You should motivate your students to study hard.
你应该激励你的学生努力学习。
⊙ encourage 激励　⊙ motivate sb. to do sth. 激励某人做某事

0705 motivation [ˌmoʊtɪˈveɪʃn] n 动机，目的，积极性
Is there any chance you could possibly tell me your motivation? I want to know it very much.
你有没有可能告诉我，你的动机是什么？我很想知道。

> 语法重点
> is there any chance you could possibly 后面接动词原形。

0706 mountainous [ˈmaʊntənəs] a 多山的，巨大的
I am unwilling to tell others I lived in the backward mountainous areas in my early ages.
我不愿诉别人，我小时候生活在落后的山区。
⊙ mountainous region 山地，山区　⊙ in one's early ages 在某人小时候

> 语法重点
> backward 可用于人或物，指向后的，落后的或迟钝的。

0707 mow [moʊ] v 收割 n 草堆，谷物堆
I think that as you sow you shall mow.
我认为，付出就会有收获。
⊙ mow down 割倒，摧毁

> 语法重点
> as you... you shall... 中，省略号处都要用动词原形。

0708 MTV abbr 音乐电视
Is there anything else that you want to know about MTV?
关于音乐电视，你还有别的想知道吗？

> 语法重点
> MTV 是由"music television"合成的，将两个词各取一部分，缩合成一个新词，前半部分表示属性，后半部分表示主体。

0709 muddy [ˈmʌdi] a 泥泞的，浑浊的
This was the moment when I made up my mind to avoid the muddy road.
就是在这个时候，我决心避开那条泥泞的道路。
⊙ sloppy 泥泞的　⊙ clear 清澈的　⊙ muddy water 浑水

> 语法重点
> this was the moment when 后面接的句子一般要用过去时。
> ⊙ avoid (P. 127)

0710 multiple [ˈmʌltɪpl] a 复合的，许多的 n 倍数
I don't think she excels in multiple-choice questions.
我认为，她不擅长做多选题。
⊙ numerous 许多的　⊙ few 很少的　⊙ excel in... 擅长……

0711 murderer ['mɜːrdərər] n 凶手
I hope the murderer will be put to death as soon as possible.
我希望那个凶手尽快被处死。
- convicted murderer 已定罪的凶手
- be put to death 被处死

0712 murmur ['mɜːrmər] v / n 低声说话
I believe he will pay the extra taxes without a murmur.
我相信，他会毫无怨言地交附加税。
- grumble 抱怨
- without a murmur 不抱怨，无怨言

→ tax (P. 372)

0713 mustache ['mʌstæʃ] n 小胡子
I think there is no one but likes his mustache.
我想，没有人会不喜欢他的小胡子。

语法重点
there is no one but 后面接动词第三人称单数形式。

0714 mutual ['mjuːtʃuəl] a 互相的
The little kingdom should confederate with other countries for mutual safety next year.
明年，这个小国应该与其他国家建立联盟，以求共同的安全。
- joint 共同的
- mutual respect 互相尊重
- confederate with... 与……联盟
- mutual 着重彼此共有或共用，局限于双方的关系；joint 强调至少两人或两方共同占用，侧重指一个统一体。

0715 mysterious [mɪ'stɪriəs] a 神秘的，不可思议的
They describe the woman to be a mysterious person, so I want to see what she looks like very much.
他们把那个女人描绘得很神秘，所以我很想知道她长什么样。
- mystic 神秘的
- describe sb. to be... 把某人描述成……

→ describe (P. 151)

0716 namely ['neɪmli] ad 意即，也就是
I have no intention to give up climbing the Himalaya, namely the highest mountain in this area.
我不打算放弃爬喜马拉雅山，它是这个地区最高的山。

语法重点
表示山脉名称的名词前，需要加冠词。

0717 nationality [ˌnæʃə'næləti] n 国籍，民族
I hope these people of no nationality can live happily.
我希望，这些没有国籍的人能快乐地生活。

0718 nearsighted [ˌnɪr'saɪtɪd] a 近视的
No doubt the nearsighted man won't satisfy my boss.
毫无疑问，那个近视的人不会让我的老板满意。
- telescopic 远视的
- nearsighted eyeglasses 近视眼镜

语法重点
no doubt（毫无疑问）后面接陈述句。

→ satisfy (P. 218)

0719 needy ['niːdi] a 贫穷的，缺乏的
I deem that it is my duty to help the needy.
我认为，帮助穷人是我的责任。
- affluent 富裕的，丰富的
- I deem that... 我认为……

0720 neglect [nɪˈɡlekt] v / n 忽视，忽略
I advise you not to neglect to visit your grandmother.
我建议你，别忘了去探望你的祖母。
- ignore 忽视
- neglect of duty 玩忽职守
- neglect to do sth. 忘记做某事

0721 negotiate [nɪˈɡoʊʃieɪt] v 谈判，洽谈
You should negotiate with them and ask if they can lend us four hundred million dollars.
你该和他们协商一下，问问他们能否贷给我们 4 亿美元。
- consult 商量
- the negotiating table 谈判桌
- negotiate with... 与……协商

语法重点
在英语中，"几亿"可以表示为"基数词 + hundred million"。

0722 nevertheless / nonetheless
[ˌnevərðəˈles] / [ˌnʌnðəˈles] ad 仍然，尽管如此
I have an eye for music; nevertheless, I know nothing about this song.
我对音乐很有鉴赏力，但是对这首歌一无所知。
- have an eye for... 对……很有鉴赏力

语法重点
have an eye for 是固定搭配，eye 要用单数形式。

0723 nightmare [ˈnaɪtmer] n 噩梦，梦魇，可怕的事
Staying in the Cayman Islands was a total nightmare to me.
在开曼群岛待的日子，对我来说，完全是一场噩梦。

语法重点
表示群岛名称的名词前需要加冠词。
- island (P. 180)

0724 nonsense [ˈnɑːnsens] n 胡说，废话，荒唐
What he said was all nonsense.
他全是在胡说。
- complete nonsense 一派胡言
- be all nonsense 全是胡说

0725 noun [naʊn] n 名词
It is indisputable that it's not right to use this noun here.
毫无疑问，在这里用这个名词是不对的。
- it is indisputable that... 毫无疑问……

0726 nowadays [ˈnaʊədeɪz] ad 当今，现在
Nowadays I am unwilling to wear my heart on my sleeves.
如今我不愿意轻易流露自己的感情。
- now 现在
- formerly 以前
- nowadays ages 当今时代

0727 nuclear [ˈnuːkliər] a 核心的，原子核，原子能的
I won't tell others I am a strident advocate of applications of nuclear power.
我不会告诉别人，我是核能应用的坚定拥护者。
- atomic 原子能的
- nuclear family 核心家庭

- advocate (P. 669)

0728 **numerous** ['nuːmərəs] a 为数众多的，许多的
It's my duty to send numerous necessities to the disaster area.
把难以计数的生活用品送往灾区，是我的责任。
🔄 it's my duty to do sth. 做某事是我的责任

🔗 necessity (P. 329)

0729 **nursery** ['nɜːrsəri] n 育儿室，苗圃
I plan to start up a nursery near my house.
我打算在家附近开办托儿所。
🔄 nursery school 幼儿园　🔄 start up... 创办……

0730 **nylon** ['naɪlɑːn] n 尼龙
It's beyond doubt that nylon doesn't knit up as well as pure wool.
毫无疑问，尼龙不像纯羊毛那样好织。
🔄 nylon bag 尼龙袋　🔄 ... beyond doubt 毫无疑问……

语法重点
knit up 在句中是用主动形式表示被动意义。

0731 **obedience** [ə'biːdiəns] n 服从，顺从，遵守
I can't make such a mob of blackguards act in obedience to my orders.
我无法让这群恶棍遵照我的命令行动。
🔄 act in obedience to... 服从……

0732 **obedient** [ə'biːdiənt] a 服从的，顺从的
You should be absolutely obedient to your teachers.
你要绝对服从老师们。
🔄 compliant 顺从的　🔄 be obedient to... 服从……

语法重点
absolutely 在句中修饰 obedient。

0733 **objection** [əb'dʒekʃn] n 反对，异议
How can you wave aside all our objections? You disappoint us.
你怎么能全然不顾我们的反对？你让我们感到失望。
🔄 dissent 异议　🔄 approval 赞成　🔄 wave aside... 把……丢在一边

🔗 aside (P. 256)

0734 **objective** [əb'dʒektɪv]
a 客观的，无偏见的　n 目的，目标
I will give an objective evaluation towards his performance.
我会对他的表演给出客观评价。
🔄 impersonal 客观的　🔄 subjective 主观的

🔗 evaluation (P. 437)

0735 **observation** [ˌɑːbzər'veɪʃn] n 观察，注意，评论
Please rest assured that I have good powers of observation.
请放心，我有很好的观察力。

0736 **obstacle** [ˈɑːbstəkl] n 障碍物，绊脚石
I feel pretty confident that all those obstacles are superable.
我很有信心，那些障碍都可以超越。
🔵 barrier 障碍　🔴 help 帮助　🟢 I feel pretty confident that... 我很有信心……

0737 **obtain** [əbˈteɪn] v 获得，得到
It is strictly forbidden to obtain information from the opponent in my company, but I don't care.
我们公司严禁从对手那里获取资讯，但是我并不在意。
🔵 acquire 获得　🔴 lose 失去　🟢 obtain knowledge 获取知识

(语法重点)
it is strictly forbidden to（严禁）后面要接动词原形。
⮕ opponent (P. 604)

0738 **occasional** [əˈkeɪʒənl] a 偶尔的，临时的
I think it's the occasional accident that brought them together.
我认为，那次偶然的事故让他们团结了起来。
🔵 accidental 偶然的　🔴 customary 习惯的　🟢 bring... together 使……团结起来

0739 **occupation** [ˌɑːkjuˈpeɪʃn] n 占据，职业，居住
People who have no fixed occupation are not allowed to enter my office.
没有固定职业的人不许进我的办公室。
🔵 occupational disease 职业病
🟢 ... have no fixed occupation ……没有固定职业

⮕ allow (P. 006)

0740 **occupy** [ˈɑːkjupaɪ] v 占据，占领，从事
You shouldn't have called upon workers to occupy the factory.
你不该号召工人占领工厂。
🔵 employ 使从事于　🟢 occupy in... 从事……　🟢 call upon... 号召……

0741 **offend** [əˈfend] v 冒犯，犯罪
To a great extent, your words offend him.
在很大程度上，你的话冒犯了他。
🔵 affront 冒犯　🟢 to a great extent, ... 在很大程度上，……

⮕ extent (P. 439)

0742 **offense** [əˈfens] n 冒犯，犯罪，进攻
It was silly of you to take offense at him.
你为他发怒，真是愚蠢。
🔴 defense 防卫　🟢 it was silly of sb. to do... 某人做某事真是愚蠢

0743 **offensive** [əˈfensɪv] a 冒犯的，令人不快的
What he did last night was offensive to me.
他昨晚的所作所为让我很不高兴。
🟢 be on the offensive 采取攻势，主动出击　🟢 be offensive to sb. 令某人不快

0744 opera ['ɑːprə] n 歌剧，歌剧作品
I don't want to be trained to be an expert in Beijing opera.
我不想被培养成京剧的专家。

0745 operation [ˌɑːpəˈreɪʃn] n 操作，经营，手术
I hope the new law will come into operation in 2018.
我希望，新法律能在 2018 年生效。
- be in operation （使某事物）生效，作用
- come into operation... 生效

> **语法重点**
> 如果表示年份的数字中间出现 "0"，通常不会读作单词 zero，而是读作字母 o 音。

0746 oppose [əˈpoʊz] v 反对，对抗
Their parents oppose their marriage, which will make a strong impact on them, in my opinion.
在我看来，他们的父母反对他们的婚姻，会对他们有很大的影响。
- 反 agree 同意
- as opposed to... 与……对照

> **语法重点**
> 句中 which 指代的是前面整个句子。
> ⇨ impact (P. 457)

0747 oral [ˈɔːrəl] a 口述的，口服的
It is a chance to practice your oral English.
这是你练习英语口说的机会。
- verbal 口头的
- written 书面的
- oral exam 口试

> **语法重点**
> it is a chance to 后面要接动词原形。

0748 orbit [ˈɔːrbɪt] n 轨道，势力范围 v 绕轨道而行
I am afraid he will go into orbit if he knows the news.
我怕，他如果得知那个消息，会暴跳如雷。

> **语法重点**
> go into orbit 是固定用法，注意，orbit 前面没有冠词。

0749 orchestra [ˈɔːrkɪstrə] n 管弦乐队
I was tempted to conduct the orchestra.
我很想指挥这个管弦乐队。

0750 organic [ɔːrˈɡænɪk] a 器官的，有组织的
I should like to know how bacteria decompose organic matter.
我想知道，细菌是如何使有机物腐烂的。
- organic chemistry 有机化学
- I should like to know... 我想知道……

> **语法重点**
> bacterium 是 bacteria（细菌）的单数形式。

0751 otherwise [ˈʌðərwaɪz] ad 否则，不同的
Take care a bit; otherwise I will smack you.
小心一点儿，否则我会揍你。
- differently 不同地
- similarly 同样地
- or otherwise 或相反

> **语法重点**
> take care a bit 一般用在句首，后面接表示警告、告诫的句子。
> ⇨ smack (P. 778)

0752 outcome [ˈaʊtkʌm] n 结果，后果
I was sitting on the thorns when I waited for the outcome yesterday.
昨天等待结果时，我如坐针毡。
- result 结果
- cause 原因
- sit on the thorns 如坐针毡

0753 outstanding [aʊt'stændɪŋ] **a** 杰出的
Given the opportunity, I will become an outstanding singer.
如果给我机会，我会成为一位杰出的歌手。

语法重点
given 与主语I是被动关系。

0754 oval ['oʊvl] **a** 蛋形的 **n** 卵形，椭圆形
It is well known to every one that the earth is oval, but I don't think so.
众所周知，地球是椭圆的，但是我不这么想。
- elliptical 椭圆的 - it is well known to every one that... 众所周知……

0755 overcome [ˌoʊvər'kʌm] **v** 克服，战胜
I was overcome with emotion when I saw him.
看到他，我很激动。
- surmount 克服 - submit 服从

语法重点
overcome 是不规则动词，其过去式、过去分词分别是 overcame, overcome。

0756 overlook [ˌoʊvər'lʊk] **v** / **n** 俯瞰，忽视
I don't know why he is incident to overlook her fault.
我不知道，他为什么这么轻易地宽容她的过错。
- disregard 忽视 - notice 留心 - overlook from... 从……俯视

语法重点
be incident to（易于）后面接动词原形。
- incident (P. 457)

0757 overnight [ˌoʊvər'naɪt] **ad** 整夜地
I'm worried that he will come back suddenly, so I will stay awake overnight.
我担心他会突然回来，所以我打算晚上不睡觉了。

0758 overtake [ˌoʊvər'teɪk] **v** 赶上
I was terrified out of my mind when he overtook me.
当他赶上我时，我吓呆了。
- exceed 超过 - be terrified out of one's mind 吓呆了

语法重点
overtake 是不规则动词，其过去式、过去分词分别是 overtook, overtaken。

0759 overthrow [ˌoʊvər'θroʊ] **v** / **n** 推翻，打倒
They plot to overthrow the government and I want to report them to the police.
他们蓄谋推翻政府，我想向警察举报他们。
- overturn 推翻 - overthrow cabinet 倒阁 - ... plot to do sth. 蓄谋做某事

语法重点
overthrow 是不规则动词，其过去式、过去分词分别是 overthrew, overthrown。

0760 oxygen ['ɑːksɪdʒən] **n** 氧；氧气
We should load ourselves with water, food and oxygen equipment when we go into the cave.
我们进入那个洞穴时，要携带水、食物和氧气设备。

- cave (P. 137)

0761 pace [peɪs] **n** 一步，节奏
Let's be fast to keep pace with him.
我们走快点，跟上他的速度。
- at a snail's pace 极慢地 - keep pace with... 赶上……

0762 **panel** ['pænl] n 仪表盘，嵌板
I am disappointed by the news that the panel discussion is postponed to next week.
专题讨论会延期至下周举行，我很失望。
- group 组
- be disappointed by... 对……很失望

语法重点
postpone 多指有安排的延期，并指明延期到一定时间。

0763 **parachute** ['pærəʃuːt] n 降落伞 v 跳伞
I would never dare to jump with a parachute without you accompanying.
没有你的陪伴，我永远也不敢跳伞。
- I would never dare to... 我永远也不敢……

语法重点
例句中的 to 也可以省略。

0764 **paragraph** ['pærəgræf] n 段落，节，短评
I hope the substance of our talk can be condensed into a paragraph.
我希望，我们谈话的要旨可以被压缩成一段话。
- section 节
- paragraph mark 段落符号
- be condensed into... 被压缩成……

↪ condense (P. 691)

0765 **partial** ['pɑːrʃl] a 部分的，偏袒的，偏爱的
I think the manager is always partial to his employees.
我觉得，那位经理总是偏袒自己的员工。
- employee 和 staff 都可表示"员工"，但 employee 指单个员工，而 staff 指全体工作人员。

0766 **participation** [pɑːrˌtɪsɪ'peɪʃn] n 参加，参与
I can't believe there is widespread disillusionment with his participation in politics.
我不相信人们对他参政普遍感到失望。

↪ widespread (P. 660)

0767 **participle** ['pɑːrtɪsɪpl] n 分词
I think it is wrong to choose the past participle for that question.
我觉得，那道题目选择过去分词是错误的。

0768 **partnership** ['pɑːrtnərʃɪp] n 合伙关系，合股经营
You had better go into partnership with him.
你最好和他建立合作关系。
- work in partnership with... 与……合作
- go into partnership with... 和……建立合作关系

语法重点
go into partnership with 后面接表示人或企业的名词或代词。

0769 **passive** ['pæsɪv] a 被动的，消极的
I hope I can take a passive role in the film.
我希望，我能在这部电影中扮演反派角色。
- negative 消极的
- active 积极的，主动的
- passive resistance 消极抵抗
- take a passive role in... 在……中扮演反派角色

0770 **pasta** [ˈpɑːstə] n 面团
Have you thought of eating pasta for supper? I'd love to have it very much.
你有没有想过晚餐吃意大利面？我非常想吃。
spaghetti 意大利面　Have you thought of...? 你有没有想过……？

语法重点
Have you thought of...? 后面一般接动名词。

0771 **pebble** [ˈpebl] n 小卵石，石子，水晶
He must have mistaken the egg for pebble.
他肯定是把那个鸡蛋当作鹅卵石了。
mistake... for... 把……当作……

0772 **peculiar** [pɪˈkjuːlɪər] a 独特的，古怪的
I think this kind of dialect is peculiar to the area.
我觉得，这种方言是这个地方特有的。
common 普通的　feel peculiar 感到奇特的　be peculiar to... 是……特有的

语法重点
be peculiar to 后面可以接人，也可以接物。
dialect (P. 557)

0773 **pedal** [ˈpedl] n 踏板 v 踩踏板，脚蹬，踩动
If you dare throw away the pedal, you must face the consequences of your action.
如果你敢扔掉那个踏板，就必须自食其果。
footplate 踏板　... face the consequences of one's action ……自食其果

0774 **peer** [pɪr] n 同辈，同等的人
In my opinion, he gets on well with his peers.
在我看来，他与同辈相处得很好。
peer group 年龄或地位相近的人　get on well with... 与……相处得很好

语法重点
peer 还可以当动词，常与介词 at, into 连用，意思是"凝视，盯着看"。

0775 **penalty** [ˈpenəltɪ] n 惩罚，罚球
To add insult to injury, I suffered a penalty.
更糟糕的是，我受到了惩罚。
punishment 惩罚　penalty kick（足球）罚球

语法重点
to add insult to injury（更糟糕的是）作插入语，后面接句子，表述一种更坏的情况。

0776 **percent** [pərˈsent] n 百分比，百分率，百分数
I estimate that the fire will reduced 10 percent of the houses to ashes.
我估计，大火会使 10% 的房屋化为灰烬。
percentum 百分比　reduce... to ashes 使……化为灰烬

语法重点
percent 前面是具体的数字时，percent 要用单数。

0777 **percentage** [pərˈsentɪdʒ] n 百分率，比例
I don't care about whether there are a small percentage of goods in the storage now.
我对现在仓库里是否有一小部分货物并不感兴趣。
centage 百分率　percentage points 百分点
I don't care about... 我对……不感兴趣

storage (P. 641)

0778 **perfection** [pərˈfekʃn] **n** 完美，完善
I think the dress can show off your figure to perfection. ⇨ figure (P. 164)
我认为，这件连衣裙能恰到好处地显示出你的身材。

0779 **perfume** [pərˈfjuːm] **n** 香水 **v** 使充满香气
I have no relish for buying perfume. ⇨ relish (P. 769)
我对买香水不感兴趣。
- stink 臭味   - perfume sprayer 香水喷瓶
- have no relish for... 我对……不感兴趣

0780 **permanent** [ˈpɜːrmənənt] **a** 永久的，固定的
I suspect that the boss allows her to become the permanent employee of our company.
我怀疑，老板会允许她成为我们公司的固定职员。
- everlasting 永久的   - transient 短暂的

0781 **persuasion** [pərˈsweɪʒn] **n** 说服，劝说，信念
I think it won't take much persuasion to let the salesman go away.
我认为，不用费什么口舌就可以让那业务员走开。
- faith 信念   - verbal persuasion 口头劝说

0782 **persuasive** [pərˈsweɪsɪv] **a** 有说服力的，令人信服的
You shouldn't be sceptical about these persuasive reasons.
你不该怀疑这些有说服力的理由。
- convictive 有说服力的   - be sceptical about... 怀疑……
- reason 强调通过逻辑推理而得出的结论性原因，而不是直接说明事情起因。

0783 **pessimistic** [ˌpesɪˈmɪstɪk] **a** 悲观的，厌世的，悲观主义的
I won't hear of his pessimistic views of work.
我不同意他对工作所持的悲观看法。
- optimistic 乐观的   - pessimistic feelings 悲观情绪
- I won't hear of... 我不同意……

0784 **petal** [ˈpetl] **n** 花瓣
I advise you to mark every petal with different colors.
我建议你为每一片花瓣都标记不同的颜色。
- petalage 花瓣   - mark... with... 在……上面标记……

> **语法重点**
> mark with 后面接名词或代词，表示用什么来做标记。

0785 **phenomenon** [fəˈnɑːmɪnən] **n** 现象，征兆，奇迹
I have doubts about the unnormal phenomenon.
我对这种不正常的现象表示怀疑。
- wonder 奇迹   - natural phenomenon 自然现象

0786 **philosopher** [fəˈlɑːsəfər] n. 哲学家，思想家
I take a pessimistic view of the philosopher's words.
我对那个哲学家的话持悲观见解。
≈ thinker 思想家　◎ take a pessimistic view of... 对……抱悲观见解

⚑ pessimistic (P. 483)

0787 **philosophical** [ˌfɪləˈsɑːfɪkl] a. 哲学的，冷静的
I think those philosophical views could serve as the guide of our behavior.
我认为，这些哲学思想可以作为我们行为的指导。
≈ calm 冷静的　⊘ uncool 不冷静沉着的　◎ philosophical argument 逻辑论证

〔语法重点〕
serve as（起作用）后面接名词或代词。

0788 **philosophy** [fəˈlɑːsəfi] n. 哲学，哲理
I believe you will find philosophy hard to learn at last.
到最后，我相信你会发现哲学很难学。
◎ philosophy of life 人生哲学

〔语法重点〕
句中动词 find 为"不完全及物动词"，只接一个宾语不能把句意表达清楚，必须接补语才可以。

0789 **photography** [fəˈtɑːɡrəfi] n. 摄影术
I can't wait to share with him my photography experience.
我迫不及待地想和他分享我的摄影经历。
≈ shoot 摄影　◎ ... share with sb.... ……与某人分享……

〔语法重点〕
photography 是不可数名词。

0790 **physical** [ˈfɪzɪkl] a. 身体的，物质的
Most important of all, you should keep in good physical condition.
最重要的是，你得保持身体健康。
≈ material 物质的　⊘ spiritual 精神的　◎ physical change 物理变化

〔语法重点〕
most important of all 是常用的形容词短语，通常置于句首，也可作插入语。

0791 **physician** [fɪˈzɪʃn] n. 内科医师，医生
You had better seek help from the physician right away.
你应该立即向内科医生寻求帮助。
≈ doctor 医生　⊘ patient 病人　◎ seek help from... 向……寻求帮助

0792 **physicist** [ˈfɪzɪsɪst] n. 物理学家，物理学研究者
I am doubtful the physicist isn't able to solve the problem.
我怀疑，那个物理学家无法解决这个难题。

0793 **physics** [ˈfɪzɪks] n. 物理学
To tell the truth, I'm not turned on by physics.
说实话，我对物理一点也不感兴趣。
◎ I'm not turned on by... 我对……一点也不感兴趣

0794 **pianist** [ˈpɪənɪst] n. 钢琴家，钢琴师
I wish to become a pianist when I grow up.
我希望长大后成为一名钢琴家。

〔语法重点〕
grow up 是用一般现在时表示将来。

0795 **pickpocket** [ˈpɪkpɑːkɪt] n 扒手，小偷

I foresee that the pickpocket will run away if we go near him.

我有预感，如果我们靠近那个小偷，他会逃跑。

- shoplifter 扒手
- I foresee that... 我有预感……

0796 **pioneer** [ˌpaɪəˈnɪr] n 拓荒者，先驱 v 开辟

I am proud of becoming the pioneer in the activity.

成为这次活动的先锋，我感到很自豪。

- forerunner 先驱
- be proud of... 以……为骄傲

0797 **pirate** [ˈpaɪrət] n 海盗，盗版者 v 盗版，剽窃

It is worthwhile to be a pirate this time.

这次，做个海盗还是值得的。

> 语法重点
> it is worthwhile to 后面接动词原形。
> → worthwhile (P. 661)

0798 **plentiful** [ˈplentɪfl] a 丰富的，充足的，大量的

The plentiful oil in this area was not my scene.

我对这个地区丰富的石油不感兴趣。

- abundant 丰富的
- scarce 稀有的
- be not one's scene 某人不感兴趣

0799 **plot** [plɑːt] n 阴谋，情节 v 密谋，绘图

I smell out a plot to assassinate the President and I want to call the police.

我发现了一个刺杀总统的阴谋，我想报警。

- conspiracy 阴谋
- hatch a plot 心怀鬼胎

> → assassinate (P. 675)

0800 **plural** [ˈplʊrəl] a 复数的 n 复数

I'm uninterested in the article which contains a lot of plural nouns.

我对那篇包含有许多复数名词的文章不感兴趣。

- complexor 复数
- singular 单数的

0801 **p.m. / pm** n 下午，午后

When they assign you more projects, you don't have a chance to go home at 6 p.m.

当他们指派更多计划给你的时候，你就没有机会在下午六点回家了。

- afternoon 下午，午后

> 语法重点
> p.m. 前面要加上具体的数词表示时间。

0802 **poisonous** [ˈpɔɪzənəs] a 有毒的，恶意的

I felt angry after he gave me a poisonous look.

他恶意地看了我一眼后，我觉得很生气。

- toxic 有毒的
- give sb. a poisonous look 恶意地看某人一眼

0803 **polish** ['pɑːlɪʃ] v 擦亮，磨光
You must polish up your English if you want to stay in the company.
你如果想留在公司，就得提高英语水平。
同 buff 擦亮　反 tarnish 玷污　搭 polish up... 改进……，提高……水平

0804 **pollution** [pəˈluːʃn] n 污染，污染物
We're just talking about the environmental pollution of this city, and we don't want to quarrel with you.
我们只是在讨论这个城市的环境污染问题，不想和你吵架。
同 contamination 污染　搭 pollution prevention 防止污染

联 quarrel (P. 344)

0805 **popularity** [ˌpɑːpjuˈlærəti] n 流行，普及，名望
There are indications that my popularity is ebbing and I feel anxious.
有迹象表明，我的声望正在下降，我感到很焦虑。
搭 enjoy great popularity 享有盛誉
搭 there are indications that... 有迹象表明……

语法重点
popularity 常用在短语 enjoy general popularity 中，意思是"受欢迎，得众望"。
联 indication (P. 457)

0806 **portable** ['pɔːrtəbl] a 可携带的
I need your help. When will it be convenient for you to repair my portable computer?
我需要你的帮忙。你什么时候方便修理我的可携式电脑？

语法重点
when will it be convenient for you to 后面接动词原形。

0807 **porter** ['pɔːrtər] n 搬运工，服务工，杂务工
I feel ashamed to tell others I worked as a porter before.
我羞于告诉他人我以前做过搬运工。

语法重点
work as a / an 后面要接表示职业的名词。

0808 **portray** [pɔːrˈtreɪ] v 画（人物），描述，饰演
I am angry that the film portrays him as a bad man.
电影把他描述成一个坏人，我很生气。
同 describe 描述　搭 portray sb. as... 把某人描述成……

0809 **possess** [pəˈzes] v 拥有，支配
I am possessed with the idea that he looks down upon me.
我总是有种感觉，他瞧不起我。
同 own 拥有　搭 be possessed of... 具有……

0810 **possession** [pəˈzeʃn] n 拥有，财产，所有
I think his factory is in possession of advanced manufacturing technology.
我觉得他的工厂拥有先进的制造技术。
同 property 财产　搭 in possession of... 拥有……

0811 precise [prɪˈsaɪs] a 精确的，严格的
To be precise, I don't like his way of speaking.
确切地说，我不喜欢他说话的方式。
- accurate 精确的　- incorrect 不正确的　- to be precise, ... 确切地说，……

语法重点
to be precise 可置于句首、句中或句尾，表示强调或是引出所要说的话。

0812 predict [prɪˈdɪkt] v 预测，预言，报告
It is hard to predict whether he will win the game.
很难预测出他是否会赢得比赛。
- it is hard to predict... 很难预测……

0813 preferable [ˈprefrəbl] a 更好的，更合意的
I think his suggestion is preferable to yours.
我认为他的建议比你的更好。

0814 pregnancy [ˈpregnənsi] n 怀孕，妊娠，含蓄
I am lukewarm about the news of her pregnancy.
我对她怀孕的消息不感兴趣。

语法重点
the news of 的意思是"关于……的消息"，后面接消息的内容。

0815 pregnant [ˈpregnənt] a 怀孕的，充满的，意味深长的
I think her words are pregnant with meaning.
我认为她的言辞富有意义。
- pregnant period 孕期　- be pregnant with... 富有……

0816 preposition [ˌprepəˈzɪʃn] n 介词，前置词
You'd better look up the preposition in the dictionary before you use it.
你用这个介词之前，最好先在词典里查阅一下。

0817 presentation [ˌpriːzenˈteɪʃn] n 赠送，介绍，陈述
You should make sufficient preparation for the product presentation tonight.
你今晚应该为产品介绍做好充分的准备。
- give a presentation 演讲，报告　- make preparation for... 为……做准备

语法重点
make preparation for 后面接名词或代词，表示介绍的物件。
- preparation (P. 341)

0818 preservation [ˌprezərˈveɪʃn] n 保存，维护，防腐
I think that picture is in good preservation in the museum.
我觉得那幅画在博物馆里保存得很好。
- conservation 保存　- discard 抛弃　- preservation measures 保全措施

0819 preserve [prɪˈzɜːrv] v 保存，保护，维持
In my opinion, you should preserve the animals from harm.
在我看来，你们应该保护这些动物免受伤害。
- protect 保护　- preserve food 保存食物

语法重点
preserve from...（保护……免遭伤害）后接表示损害或伤害的名词或代词。

0820 **prevention** [prɪˈvenʃn] n 预防，防止，阻止
I think this kind of medicine played a role in the prevention of the illness.
我认为这种药起了预防疾病的作用。
🌐 Prevention is better than cure. 预防胜于治疗。

0821 **prime** [praɪm] a 最初的，典型的
Out of question, this is the prime work we should do at present.
毫无疑问，这是我们当前要做的首要工作。
🌐 prime time 黄金时间　🌐 out of question, ... 毫无疑问，……

0822 **primitive** [ˈprɪmətɪv] a 原始的，简陋的
I think the stone implement can date from primitive society.
我认为这件石器可以追溯到原始社会。
🌐 original 原始的　🌐 primitive culture 原始文化

> 语法重点
> date from（追溯）后面通常接表示过去的时间。
> ⮕ implement (P. 730)

0823 **privacy** [ˈpraɪvəsi] n 隐私，秘密
He should be accused of infringing on their privacy.
他侵犯了他们的隐私，应该受到指责。
🌐 intimacy 隐私　🌐 privacy rights 隐私权　🌐 infringe on... 侵犯……

0824 **privilege** [ˈprɪvəlɪdʒ] n 特权，优惠　v 给特权，免除
It is a great privilege to be allowed into the hall.
被允许进入这个大厅是难得的事。
🌐 prerogative 特权　🌐 breach of privilege 滥用职权

0825 **procedure** [prəˈsiːdʒər] n 程序，手续，步骤
In my opinion, the results show clearly that the procedure is wrong.
在我看来，结果充分说明这种程序是错误的。
🌐 program 程序　🌐 normal procedure 常规程序

0826 **proceed** [proʊˈsiːd] v 进行，开始，着手
I hope you can proceed with the introduction in a minute.
我希望等一下你继续介绍。
🌐 begin 开始　🌐 proceed against 起诉，控告　🌐 proceed with... 继续进行……

> 语法重点
> proceed with 后面可接名词或代词，也可以用 go on with 来表达。

0827 **production** [prəˈdʌkʃn] n 生产，产量，成果
I aim to increase the production levels next year.
明年，我的目标是提高生产水准。
🌐 feedback 成果　🌐 in production 在生产中　🌐 aim to do sth. 计划做某事

> 语法重点
> aim 侧重指比较具体而明确的目标，通常指短期目标。
> ⮕ increase (P. 178)

prevention ~ promising

0828 productive [prəˈdʌktɪv]
a 生产的，富饶的，富有成效的

In my opinion, economic growth should be combined with productive forces.
在我看来，经济发展应该与生产力相结合。

● procreative 生产的　● productive capacity 生产能力

> **语法重点**
> be combined with（结合）后面接表示结合或联合的物件的名词或代词。

0829 profession [prəˈfeʃn] **n** 专业，职业，声明

I hope you can treat teaching as your lifelong profession.
我希望你能把教学当作终身职业。

● occupation 职业　● by profession 作为职业　● treat... as... 把……当作……

> **语法重点**
> treat as 后面接名词或代词。

0830 professional [prəˈfeʃənl] **a** 专业的，职业的，专门的

I don't plan to visit the professional athlete; please give my best wishes to him.
我不打算去拜访那个职业运动员，请代我问候他。

● occupational 职业的　● amateur 业余的

> **语法重点**
> Please give my best wishes to 中的 to 是介词，后面接名词或代词。

0831 professor [prəˈfesər] **n** 教授，老师

I want to say that your behavior is unbefitting of a university professor.
我想说，你的行为与大学教授的身份不相符。

● honorary professor 名誉教授　● be unbefitting of... 与……不相符

⊃ university (P. 514)

0832 profitable [ˈprɑːfɪtəbl] **a** 有利润的

I make a decision to read some profitable books from now on.
我下定决心，从现在起要读一些有益的书籍。

● helpful 有益的　● profitless 无益的　● profitable model 营利模式

0833 prominent [ˈprɑːmɪnənt] **a** 显著的，杰出的，突出的

I think his suggestion can play a prominent role in our work.
我觉得，他的建议在我们的工作中能发挥显著的作用。

● outstanding 杰出的　● anonymous 无名的
● play a part in... 在……中起作用

> **语法重点**
> play a part in 中的名词 part 也可以替换为 role。

0834 promising [ˈprɑːmɪsɪŋ] **a** 有前途的，有希望的

Please don't hesitate to ask me about the physical condition of the promising young man.
请随时询问我关于那个有为青年的健康状况。

● hopeful 有希望的　● hopeless 没有希望的
● please don't hesitate to... 请随时……

⊃ hesitate (P. 305)

0835 **promotion** [prəˈmoʊʃn] n 促进，升职，晋升
The news of her promotion came as a shock to me this morning.
今早，她升职的消息让我吃惊。
⊕ advancement 升职 ⊕ demotion 降职 ⊕ promotion opportunity 升职机会

⊕ shock (P. 221)

0836 **prompt** [praːmpt] a 即时的，迅速的 v 促使，推动
I hope you are prompt to do your work.
我希望你立即开始做你的工作。
⊖ slow 缓慢的 ⊕ prompt reply 立即回复 ⊕ be prompt to do sth. 立即做某事

0837 **pronoun** [ˈproʊnaʊn] n 代词
I want you to make a sentence with the pronoun.
我要你用这个代词造个句子。
⊕ personal pronoun 人称代词 ⊕ make a sentence with... 用……造句

0838 **pronunciation** [prəˌnʌnsiˈeɪʃn] n 发音，读音
I have to say that the pronunciation of the girl on the stage is terrible.
我不得不说，舞台上那个女孩的发音很糟糕。
⊕ I have to say that... 我不得不说，……

⊕ terrible (P. 234)

0839 **prosper** [ˈpraːspər] v 繁荣，成功
All of us should be thankful for her to make the company prosper again.
我们所有人都该感激她使公司重新繁荣起来。
⊕ flourish 兴旺 ⊖ decay 衰退 ⊕ boom prosper 蓬勃发展

语法重点
be thankful for（感激）后面通常接表示人的名词或代词。
⊕ thankful (P. 373)

0840 **prosperity** [praːˈsperəti] n 繁盛，兴旺
I think people's buying luxury goods is an index for the area's prosperity.
我认为，人们购买奢侈商品是一个地区繁荣的标志。
⊕ booming 兴旺 ⊖ declination 衰退 ⊕ be an index for... 是……的标志

0841 **prosperous** [ˈpraːspərəs] a 繁荣的，兴旺的
There are signs that the economy here is prosperous at present, but I think it won't last long.
有迹象表明，目前这个地区经济繁荣，但是我认为这持续不了多久。
⊕ flourishing 繁荣的 ⊕ prosperous places 繁华的地方

语法重点
at present 意思是"目前，现在"，可置于句首、句中或句尾，同义表达为 at the moment。

0842 **protein** [ˈproʊtiːn] n 蛋白质
I ask her to eat less protein from now on.
我要求她从现在开始少吃些蛋白质。

0843 **protest** [prəˈtest] / [ˈproʊtest] v / n 抗议
I think your protest against him makes no sense.
我觉得你对他的反抗没有任何意义。
- oppose 反对
- approval 赞成
- ... make no sense ……毫无意义

0844 **proverb** [ˈprɑːvɜːrb] n 谚语，格言
She is a proverb for carelessness and I don't want to work with her.
大家都知道她的粗心，我不想和她一起工作。

语法重点
be a proverb for（人尽皆知）后面接上表示性格、特征等的名词。

0845 **psychological** [ˌsaɪkəˈlɑːdʒɪkl] a 心理学的，精神的
I am disdainful of his psychological research.
我瞧不起他的心理学研究。
- mental 精神的
- physical 身体的
- psychological warfare 心理战

语法重点
psychological research 是常用的搭配方式，其中 psychological 作形容词修饰 research。

0846 **psychologist** [saɪˈkɑːlədʒɪst] n 心理学家
I think he is more a psychologist than a pathologist.
我觉得，与其说他是病理学家，不如说他是心理学家。

语法重点
be more... than... 当"与其说……不如说……"来讲时，连接并列的对等成分。

0847 **psychology** [saɪˈkɑːlədʒi] n 心理学
She must have had a background in social psychology.
她肯定受过社会心理学教育。
- psychics 心理学
- ... have a background in... ……受过……的教育

语法重点
在 social psychology 中，social 作形容词修饰名词 psychology。

0848 **publication** [ˌpʌblɪˈkeɪʃn] n 出版，发行，公布
We should try our best to make a good job of publication.
我们应该尽最大的努力做好出版工作。
- announcement 发表，公告
- make a good job of... 做好……的工作

0849 **publicity** [pʌbˈlɪsəti] n 名声，宣传，宣扬
I have no objection to publicity of the right kind.
我不反对正当的宣传。
- propaganda 宣传
- the glare of publicity 众人的关注

语法重点
have no objection to 中的 to 是介词。
objection (P. 477)

0850 **publish** [ˈpʌblɪʃ] v 出版，发行，发表
He threatened to publish a weighty refutation and I don't know what to do.
他威胁说要对发表文章进行有分量的反驳，我不知道该怎么办。
- issue 发行
- threaten to... 威胁做某事

语法重点
threaten to 后面要接动词原形。

0851 **publisher** [ˈpʌblɪʃər] n 出版者，出版社，发行人
It would be churlish to refuse the publisher's invitation.
拒绝那个出版社的邀请，未免失礼。

语法重点
it would be churlish 后面一般要接动词不定式。

0852 pursuit [pər'suːt] n 追求，追逐
I don't like him because he is in pursuit of money and fame all the time.
我不喜欢他，是因为他一直在追求金钱和名誉。
◎ in pursuit... 追捕…… ◎ be in pursuit of... 追求……

⊃ fame (P. 440)

0853 quake [kweɪk] n / v 地震，颤抖
I don't want to comment on the news that a building collapsed in the quake yesterday.
那则新闻说有栋建筑物在地震中倒塌，对此我不想评论。
◎ quiver 颤抖 ◎ comment on... 评论……

⊃ collapse (P. 409)

0854 quilt [kwɪlt] n 被子，被褥 v 缝，缝制
I think being wrapped in a quilt will be better.
我觉得，裹在被子里会好点儿。
◎ silk quilt 蚕丝被 ◎ be wrapped in... 裹在……里

0855 quotation [kwoʊ'teɪʃn] n 引文，报价
With regard to the quotation, I will talk with you face to face.
关于报价，我会和你面谈。
◎ offer 报价 ◎ quotation sheet 报价单

语法重点
with regard to（关于）通常置于句首，起引导或强调作用，相当于 regard to。

0856 rage [reɪdʒ] n / v 狂怒，大怒
I think he will flow into a rage if you slap him.
如果你甩他巴掌，我想他会勃然大怒。
◎ road rage 公路暴怒行为 ◎ ... flow into a rage ……勃然大怒

0857 rainfall ['reɪnfɔːl] n 降雨，降雨量
I hope I can live in an area which is abundant in rainfall.
我希望住在降雨量非常充足的地方。
◎ rainfall amount 雨量 ◎ be abundant in... 在……方面很充足

语法重点
be abundant in 后面接名词或名词短语。
⊃ abundant (P. 521)

0858 realistic [ˌriːə'lɪstɪk] a 现实的，现实主义的
We must be realistic about the problem.
我们必须实事求是地看待这个问题。

0859 rebel ['rebl] v 反抗，造反 n 造反者
I think it's money that leads to his becoming a rebel.
我认为，是金钱导致他成了造反者。
◎ renegade 叛徒 ◎ lead to... 导致……

语法重点
lead to 后面通常接名词或名词短语，表示结果或造成的影响。

0860 recall [rɪ'kɔːl] v / n 回想，取消，召回
It is enough for me to recall these students' names.
回忆这些学生的名字就够我受了。
◎ recollect 回忆 ◎ forget 忘记

语法重点
it is enough for me to 后面接动词原形。

0861 reception [rɪˈsepʃn] n 接待，招待会
You'd better give a reception to the guests yourself.
你最好亲自招待客人。
- entertainment 款待
- warm reception 热情接待
- give a reception to... 招待……

语法重点
give a reception to 中的 to 是介词。

0862 recipe [ˈresəpi] n 食谱，药方，秘诀
I agree in cooking dishes according to that recipe.
我同意按照那个食谱来做菜。

语法重点
agree in（同意）后面接名词或者动名词。

0863 recite [rɪˈsaɪt] v 背诵，列举
I do not doubt but that you can recite the article in two minutes.
我相信你能在两分钟内把文章背下来。

语法重点
I do not doubt but that 中的 but 也可以省略。

0864 recognition [ˌrekəɡˈnɪʃn] n 认出，识别，赏识
I think you will change beyond recognition after putting on make-up.
我觉得，你化妆后肯定会大变，让人难以认出。
- identification 识别
- speech recognition 语音辨识

语法重点
beyond 既可以指空间或时间上的超越，也可以用来形容思想或程度上的遥不可及。

0865 recovery [rɪˈkʌvəri] n 恢复，痊愈，复原
I am confident in your early recovery.
我相信你会早日康复。
- recuperation 恢复
- recovery room 恢复室
- be confident in... 相信……

语法重点
表示"从……中恢复过来"时，recovery 一般要与介词 from 连用。

0866 recreation [ˌriːkriˈeɪʃn] n 娱乐
I think where there is recreation, there is happiness.
我认为，哪里有消遣，哪里就有快乐。
- pastime 消遣，娱乐
- recreation ground 游乐场

0867 recycle [ˌriːˈsaɪkl] v 回收，再利用
I plan to recycle those beer cans in future.
我打算以后回收那些啤酒罐。
- reuse 再利用
- recycle bin 回收站

语法重点
in future 表示从现在开始以后要做某事，而 in the future 表示在距离现在一段时间的将来可能会发生的事情。

0868 reduction [rɪˈdʌkʃn] n 减少，降低，减价
You can't expect me to approve of the reduction during the Spring Festival.
你别指望我赞成春节时降价。
- decrease 减少
- increase 增加

语法重点
you can't expect me to approve of 后面一般接名词或者代词。
- approve (P. 256)

0869 refer [rɪˈfɜːr] v 参考，涉及，咨询
I hope you won't refer yourself to others.
我希望你不要求助于他人。
- consult 咨询
- refer drawing 参考图

语法重点
refer oneself to（求助于）中的 to 是介词。

0870 reference ['refrəns] n 参考，提及，查阅
Well, my words are only for your reference.
嗯，我的话仅供你参考。
- mention 提及　　- be for one's reference 供某人参考

0871 reflect [rɪ'flekt] v 反射，反省
I hope you can reflect on my suggestion.
我希望你能仔细考虑一下我的建议。
- reflect model 反射机制　　- reflect on... 仔细考虑……

⇒ suggestion (P. 508)

0872 reflection [rɪ'flekʃn] n 反射，沉思，倒影
I hope you made your decision on reflection.
我希望你是经过了再三考虑才做出决定的。
- meditation 沉思　　- on reflection 再三考虑

0873 reform [rɪ'fɔːrm] n / v 改革，革新，改良
I believe we will succeed in our reform.
我相信我们的改革会成功。
- reformation 改革　　- succeed in... 在……方面成功

⇒ succeed (P. 230)

0874 refresh [rɪ'freʃ] v 使清新
I want to have a cup of coffee to refresh myself.
我想喝杯咖啡提神。
- update 更新　　- exhaust 使筋疲力尽　　- refresh oneself 恢复精神

0875 refugee [ˌrefju'dʒiː] n 难民，流亡者
We should offer help to these poor refugees.
我们应该向这些可怜的难民提供帮助。
- refugee camp 难民营　　- offer... to sb. 向某人提供……

0876 refusal [rɪ'fjuːzl] n 拒绝，回绝
I bet he cares nothing for my refusal.
我打赌，他不在意我的拒绝。
- rejection 拒绝　　- acceptance 接受　　- care nothing for... 不在意……

> **语法重点**
> care nothing for 后面接名词或介词，表示具体的事物。

0877 regarding [rɪ'ɡɑːrdɪŋ] prep 关于，至于
I think he can provide better resolution for us regarding this problem.
我想，关于这个问题，他能为我们提供更好的解决办法。
- provide... for sb. 向某人提供……

⇒ resolution (P. 497)

0878 register ['redʒɪstər] v 注册，记录 n 登记簿，记录
I hope you can queue up to register.
我希望你们能排队登记。
- enroll 登记，注册　　- register for 注册　　- queue up to do sth. 排队做某事

reference ~ remark

0879 registration [ˌredʒɪˈstreɪʃn] n 注册，挂号
I think your marriage without registration won't be recognized by them.
我觉得他们不会承认你们未登记的婚姻。
- enrollment 登记
- be recognized by... 被……承认

↻ recognize (P. 346)

0880 regulate [ˈregjuleɪt] v 调节，管理，控制
I favour the idea that they should regulate the traffic.
他们应该管制交通，我赞成这个观点。
- adjust 调节
- I favour the idea that... 我赞成……的观点

0881 regulation [ˌregjuˈleɪʃn] n 调整，规则，管理
I require that the regulation allow of no variation.
我要求这个规则不得改变。
- rule 规则
- traffic regulation 交通规则

语法重点
allow of（容许）后面一般接名词或者名词短语。
↻ variation (P. 800)

0882 rejection [rɪˈdʒekʃn] n 拒绝，抛弃，抵制
I am afraid of her rejection to my proposal all the time.
一直以来，我都害怕她拒绝我的求婚。
- refusal 拒绝
- agreement 同意
- all the time 一直以来

0883 relative [ˈrelətɪv] a 相对的，比较的 n 亲属
I think the knife is relative to the murder.
我觉得这把刀和这件谋杀案有关。
- opposing 相对的
- absolute 绝对的
- be relative to... 与……有关系

语法重点
be relative to 中的 to 是介词。

0884 relaxation [ˌriːlækˈseɪʃn] n 放松，消遣，松弛
I advise you to keep a balance between relaxation and work.
我建议你在消遣和工作之间要保持平衡。

语法重点
keep a balance between... and... 在……处一般要放名词。

0885 relieve [rɪˈliːv] v 解除，救济
I don't know how to relieve him from his pain.
我不知道怎样才能让他摆脱痛苦。
- relieve of 解除
- relieve... from... 把……从……解脱出来

0886 reluctant [rɪˈlʌktənt] a 不情愿的，勉强的
I am reluctant to give suck to the baby.
我不愿意为那个婴儿喂奶。
- unwilling 不情愿的
- willing 乐意的

0887 remark [rɪˈmɑːrk] n / v 注意，谈论，评论
I would certainly disdain to remark on his picture.
我当然不愿意评论他的画。
- comment 评论
- personal remark 个人评论

语法重点
I would certainly disdain to 后面接动词原形。

495

0888 **remarkable** [rɪˈmɑːrkəbl]
a 值得注意的，卓越的，显著的
It's remarkable that his tongue can touch his nose.
他的舌头能触碰到鼻子，真是不寻常。

0889 **remedy** [ˈremədi] **n** 治疗，药物 **v** 治疗，补救
Your only remedy is to go and ask him for help.
你唯一的补救办法是去向他求助。
🔊 treatment 治疗

> 语法重点
> your only remedy is to 后面要接动词原形。

0890 **repetition** [ˌrepəˈtɪʃn] **n** 重复，反复
Let there be no repetition of such foolish questions.
别再问这种愚蠢的问题了。

> 🔊 foolish (P. 167)

0891 **representation** [ˌreprɪzenˈteɪʃn]
n 代表，陈述，描写，呈现
You should make a representation to your boss why you are late.
你得向老板说明为什么迟到。
🔊 statement 陈述　🔊 make a representation to... 向……说明

> 语法重点
> make a representation to 后面要接表示人的名词或者代词。

0892 **reputation** [ˌrepjuˈteɪʃn] **n** 评价，名声，名誉
I don't want to have a reputation for eccentricity.
我不想以行为古怪而出名。
🔊 renown 声誉　🔊 have a reputation for... 以……而出名
🔊 "好名声"用good reputation 来表示，"坏名声"用bad reputation 来表示。

0893 **rescue** [ˈreskjuː] **n** / **v** 援救，营救
I will brave death to rescue these people.
我会冒着生命危险去救这些人。
🔊 rescue workers 救援人员　🔊 brave death to do sth. 冒着生命危险做某事

0894 **research** [rɪˈsɜːrtʃ] **n** / **v** 研究，调查
I hope to research into the problem with you.
我希望和你一起研究这个问题。
🔊 study 研究　🔊 research into... 研究……

> 语法重点
> research 一般作名词，作动词时，是不及物动词。

0895 **researcher** [rɪˈsɜːrtʃər] **n** 研究员
I think it is an unexpected turn for the researcher.
我觉得，这对那个研究者来说是个出乎意料的转折点。
🔊 investigator 研究者
🔊 it is an unexpected turn for... 对……来说是个出乎意料的转折点

0896 **resemble** [rɪ'zembl] v 类似，像
I hope my baby will resemble his father in look.
我希望我的孩子长得像他父亲。
- resemble sb. in... 在……方面和某人很像

0897 **reservation** [ˌrezər'veɪʃn] n 保留
I want her to make a reservation in the restaurant.
我想要她在那家餐厅订位。
- booking 预订
- ... make a reservation …… 预订座位

语法重点
resemble 不用于被动语态。

0898 **resign** [rɪ'zaɪn] v 辞职，放弃
She shouldn't resign to her fate.
她不该听天由命。
- quit 辞职
- resign from 辞职
- resign to... 托付给……

语法重点
resign to 后面通常接名词，如例句。
fate (P. 295)

0899 **resignation** [ˌrezɪɡ'neɪʃn] n 辞职，放弃，听从
I will hand in my resignation letter to the boss tomorrow.
明天，我会将辞职信交给老板。
- resignation reason 离职原因
- hand in... 上交……

语法重点
hand in 表示将某物交给某人，比如将作业交给老师。

0900 **resistance** [rɪ'zɪstəns] n 抵抗，抵制，阻力
I perceive that you are not very satisfied with the resistance of the crowd.
我明白你对群众的抵抗不甚满意。
- rebellion 反抗
- obedience 服从
- I perceive that... 我明白……

0901 **resolution** [ˌrezə'luːʃn] n 决心，坚决，解决办法
I make a resolution not to get in touch with her in future.
我决心以后再也不和她联系。

语法重点
get in touch with 是常用短语，介词 with 后面通常接人。

0902 **resolve** [rɪ'zaːlv] v 决定，分解
I think it's up to me to resolve this problem.
我觉得这个问题应由我来解决。
- settle 解决
- resolve a dispute 解决争论
- it's up to sb. ... 该某人……

语法重点
it's up to sb. 后面一般接动词不定式。

0903 **respectable** [rɪ'spektəbl] a 值得尊敬的，体面的
As a matter of fact, I think she is a respectable artist.
事实上，我认为她是一位值得尊敬的艺术家。
- as a matter of fact, ... 事实上，……

0904 **respectful** [rɪ'spektfl] a 恭敬的，有礼貌的
You shouldn't look at the hypocrite with respectful eyes.
你们不该用恭敬的眼光看那个伪君子。
- polite 有礼貌的
- respectful behavior 有礼貌的行为

语法重点
look at 的意思是"看，考虑"，介词 at 后面接名词或代词，表示看的人或物。

0905 **restore** [rɪˈstɔːr] v 恢复，归还，复原
I think this medicine will restore you to health soon.
我觉得这种药能让你尽快恢复健康。
- recover 恢复　- restore sb. to... 使某人恢复……

语法重点 restore sb. to 中的 to 是介词，后面接名词或者名词短语。

0906 **restriction** [rɪˈstrɪkʃn] n 限制，约束
You will find out some disadvantage about trade restriction in the future.
以后，你们会发现贸易限制的一些弊端。
- limitation 限制　- find out... 发现……

语法重点 find out 是动词短语，也可以用 discover, find 等来表示相同的意思。

0907 **retain** [rɪˈteɪn] v 保持，保留，记住
I will do my utmost to retain the active and optimistic mentality.
我将会尽力保持积极乐观的心态。
- maintain 维持　- abandon 放弃　- do one's utmost... 尽最大努力……

0908 **retire** [rɪˈtaɪər] v 退休，撤退，就寝
I have quite a disinclination to retire from the factory.
我很不情愿从工厂退休。
- withdraw 撤退　- retire from... 从……退休

语法重点 have quite a disinclination to（很不情愿）后面要接动词原形。

0909 **retirement** [rɪˈtaɪərmənt] n 退休，退役，隐匿处
I hope she will be elected as the responsible person of the retirement community next year.
我希望明年她会当选为退休社区的负责人。
- retirement age 退休年龄　- be elected as... 被选举为……

语法重点 be elected as 后面接表示职务的名词。
- community (P. 410)

0910 **retreat** [rɪˈtriːt] v 撤退，改变
I am afraid we will be forced to retreat.
恐怕我们不得不撤退。
- withdraw 撤退　- advance 前进　- be forced to... 被迫做……

语法重点 be forced to 后面接动词原形。

0911 **reunion** [ˌriːˈjuːniən] n 再联合，团聚，重聚
I am sure you will be welcomed back to the reunion by them.
我确信他们会欢迎你回来团聚。
- gathering 聚会　- dissociation 分散

语法重点 be welcomed back to 中的 to 是介词，后面一般接名词或者名词短语。

0912 **revenge** [rɪˈvendʒ] v 替……报仇
I am afraid the criminal will take revenge on the police.
我担心罪犯会对警察实施报复。
- be revenged on sb. 向某人报仇　- take revenge on... 报复……

语法重点 take revenge on 后面接名词或代词，表示报复、报仇的对象。

restore ~ romance

0913 revise [rɪ'vaɪz] **v** / **n** 修正，修订
In light of these factors, we have to revise the plan.
鉴于这些因素，我们不得不修改这项计划。
- amend 修改 - final revise 最后校正

语法重点
in the light of（鉴于）是介词短语，后面一般接名词。

0914 revision [rɪ'vɪʒn] **n** 修正，修订本
At any rate, the plan you made last night needs revision.
不管怎样，昨晚你制订的那个计划需要加以修订。

0915 revolution [ˌrevə'luːʃn] **n** 革命，变革
I believe the revolution will be quickly snuffed out.
我相信那场革命会被迅速镇压。
- reformation 改革 - industrial revolution 工业革命
- be snuffed out 被镇压

0916 revolutionary [ˌrevə'luːʃəneri]
a 革命的，革新的 **n** 革命者
I want to cry at the mention of the revolutionary struggle.
一提到革命斗争，我就想哭。
- revolutionist 革命家

语法重点
at the mention of（一提到）后面接名词或者代词。
- struggle (P. 230)

0917 reward [rɪ'wɔːrd] **n** 报酬，奖金 **v** 奖赏，给……报酬
I think it is within my power to reward her for that.
我想我有权为那件事奖励她。
- remuneration 报酬 - punishment 惩罚

0918 rhyme [raɪm] **n** 押韵，韵文
In my opinion, meter and rhyme are assistants to your memory.
在我看来，押韵和格律有助于你记忆。

语法重点
be assistants to（有助于）中的 to 是介词。

0919 rhythm ['rɪðəm] **n** 节奏，韵律
I'm concerned that the boy has no sense of rhythm.
我担心那个男孩没有任何节奏感。
- I'm concerned that... 我担心……

- sense (P. 087)

0920 romance ['rəʊmæns] **n** 爱情小说，恋爱
I hear about the romance between them and want to do something for them.
我听说过他们之间的浪漫史，很想为他们做点儿什么。
- legend 传奇 - hear about... 听说……

语法重点
hear about 表示听说过某件事的详情；hear of 表示听说过某件事，却不一定了解详细情况。

0921 roughly ['rʌfli] ad. 大体上，粗暴地，粗鲁地
He shoved aside the pregnant woman roughly.
他把那个孕妇粗暴地推到了一边。
- crudely 粗鲁地 - softly 温柔地 - roughly equal 约等于

→ pregnant (P. 487)

0922 route [ruːt] n. 路线，路程
I want to take an indirect route in an attempt to kill the time.
我想绕路走，以消磨时间。
- itinerary 路线 - in an attempt to... 为了……

0923 ruin ['ruːɪn] n./v. 毁灭，毁坏
I think it's playing computer games that results in his ruin.
我认为玩电脑游戏导致了他的毁灭。
- destroy 毁灭 - in ruins 严重受损 - result in... 导致……

语法重点
result in 后面接结果，而 result from 后面接造成某种结果的原因。

0924 rural ['rʊərəl] a. 田园的，乡村的
I like his book which has a strong flavour of rural life.
他那本书有浓郁的农村生活气息，我很喜欢。
- urban 都市的 - rural planning 乡村规划

0925 sacrifice ['sækrɪfaɪs] n./v. 牺牲，献祭，供奉
You shouldn't get a promotion at the sacrifice of your health.
你不该以牺牲健康为代价来获得升职。
- at the sacrifice of... 以牺牲……为代价

语法重点
at the sacrifice of 是固定表达，介词 of 后面接名词或代词，表示具体的事物。

0926 salary ['sæləri] n. 薪水
I hope the manager can make an adjustment in my salary.
我希望经理能对我的薪水做出调整。
- wage 工资 - base salary 基本薪资
- make an adjustment in... 在……做出调整

→ adjustment (P. 392)

0927 salesman / saleswoman
['seɪlzmən] / ['seɪlzwʊmən] n. 男店员，女店员
It's contemptible of the saleswoman to inveigle the girl into buying four coats.
女店员诱骗那个女孩买了四件外套，真卑鄙。

0928 salesperson ['seɪlzpɜːrsn] n. 店员
I don't believe that the salesperson used to make a living by begging.
我不相信这个售货员曾经以乞讨为生。
- seller 售货员 - make a living by... 以……谋生

语法重点
make a living by 后面接表示方法或手段的名词或者动名词。

0929 **satellite** [ˈsætəlaɪt] n 卫星，人造卫星
I hope you can give attention to the information of the satellite.
我希望你能关注关于卫星的信息。
🔗 give attention to... 关注……

0930 **satisfaction** [ˌsætɪsˈfækʃn] n 满足，赔偿，补偿
I want all of you to leave with satisfaction.
我要你们每个人都满意地离开。
🔗 content 满足　🔗 discontent 不满　🔗 leave with satisfaction 满意地离开

0931 **scarcely** [ˈskersli] ad 几乎不，简直不，刚刚
I scarcely knew how to deal with the problem at that time.
那时我几乎不知道要如何处理那个问题。

0932 **scenery** [ˈsiːnəri] n 风景，景色，布景
They must be fascinated by the beautiful rural scenery.
美丽的农村风光肯定会让他们着迷。
🔗 landscape 风景　🔗 scenery spot 景点，风景区

> 语法重点
> be fascinated by 后面接景色或其他事物，也可以用 be captivated by 来表达。

0933 **scold** [skoʊld] v 责骂，训斥
I am very angry with him and want to scold him.
我很生他的气，想责骂他。
🔗 be angry with... 对……生气

> 语法重点
> be angry with 是常用的表达，介词 with 后面通常接表示人的名词或代词。

0934 **scratch** [skrætʃ] v 抓，搔 n 抓痕
I hope you can scratch your head for a solution to the question.
我希望你能好好思考，找出问题的答案。

0935 **screwdriver** [ˈskruːdraɪvər] n 螺丝起子
I don't want to get hold of the screwdriver because it's too cold.
我不想抓住这把螺丝起子了，太过冰冷。
🔗 turnscrew 螺丝起子　🔗 get hold of... 抓住……

> 语法重点
> get hold of 是固定用法，介词 of 后面接名词或代词，也可以用 seize hold of 来表达。

0936 **sculpture** [ˈskʌlptʃər] n / v 雕塑，雕刻
I bet they will marvel at the sculpture of Venus.
我打赌，他们会对这座维纳斯雕像惊叹。
🔗 incision 雕刻　🔗 marvel at... 对……惊叹

> 语法重点
> marvel at 后面通常接令人惊奇的事物。
> ⊃ marvel (P. 594)

0937 **seagull / gull** [ˈsiːɡʌl] / [ɡʌl] n 海鸥
I hope the dog to stop barking at the seagull.
我希望那只狗不要再对着海鸥叫。
🔗 bark at... 对……叫

0938 senior ['siːnɪə] a 年长的，资深的 n 年长者，大四学生
In respect of the age, I think I am senior to him.
论年龄，我觉得我比他年长。
　　older 年长的　　junior 下级的　　in respect of... 论……

0939 settler ['setlə] n 移居者，殖民者
I think these settlers' families can be traced back to 1805.
我认为这些定居者的家族可以追溯到1805年。
　　colonist 殖民者　　be traced back to... 追溯到……

> 语法重点
> be traced back to 也可用于主动语态。

0940 severe [sɪ'vɪr] a 严重的，剧烈的，严厉的
I am afflicted with a severe headache and want to go to hospital.
我正承受着严重的头疼，想去医院。
　　serious 严重的　　be afflicted with... 受……的折磨

> 语法重点
> be afflicted with 后面一般接没有生命的物体。

0941 shameful ['ʃeɪmfl] a 可耻的，猥亵的
I think it is shameful to sponge on my girlfriend.
我觉得依靠女朋友接济很可耻。
　　disgraceful 可耻的　　sponge on... 靠……接济过活

> sponge (P. 638)

0942 shaver ['ʃeɪvə] n 理发师，电动剃刀
I am eager to chatter up with the handsome shaver.
我急于和那个帅气的理发师搭讪。
　　barber 理发师　　chatter up with... 与……搭讪

> 语法重点
> handsome 作形容词，意思是"英俊的，帅气的"，通常用于形容男子的长相。

0943 shelter ['ʃeltə] n 避难所，庇护 v 保护，隐匿
I am unwilling to give shelter to them.
我不愿意给他们提供住宿。
　　refuge 庇护　　... give shelter to... ……给……提供住宿

> 语法重点
> shelter 常与介词 from 连用，表示"躲避……"。

0944 shift [ʃɪft] v / n 改变
I am pleased to lend you a hand to shift the stone.
我很高兴帮你搬石头。
　　shift one's ground (辩论中) 改变立场或方法
　　lend sb. a hand to do... 帮某人做……

0945 shortsighted [ˌʃɔːrt'saɪtɪd] a 近视的
It's very shortsighted of you to give up this opportunity.
你放弃这个机会，真是目光短浅。

0946 shrug [ʃrʌɡ] v / n 耸肩
I believe she can shrug off the unfair criticism.
我相信她不会理睬这不公平的批评。
　　hunch 耸肩　　shrug off... 不屑理睬……

> 语法重点
> shrug off 是固定搭配，后面通常接名词或代词。

0947 shuttle ['ʃʌtl] n 太空梭，梭子 v 穿梭

I say ditto to his idea about the shuttle.
我赞成他关于太空梭的观点。
- shuttle service 接送服务

0948 sightseeing ['saɪtsiːɪŋ] n 观光，游览

I feel it very shameful to have no money to do any sightseeing.
没钱去旅游，我觉得很丢脸。

- shameful (P. 502)

0949 signature ['sɪgnətʃər] n 签名，签字，署名

I think the signature isn't contemporaneous with the document.
我觉得签名和文件不是同时完成的。
- autograph 亲笔签名 - be contemporaneous with... 与……是同时的

0950 significance [sɪg'nɪfɪkəns] n 重要性

The speech has little significance for me.
这个演讲对我没什么意义。
- meaning 意义 - existing significance 存在意义

- speech (P. 096)

0951 sincerity [sɪn'serəti] n 真挚

To tell you the truth, I was deeply touched by her sincerity.
和你说实话，我被她的真诚深深地感动了。
- earnestness 诚挚 - hypocrisy 虚伪 - in all sincerity 衷心地

0952 singular ['sɪŋgjələr] a 单数的，非凡的，奇特的

He must have impressed the girl with his singular appearance.
他那奇特的外貌一定给女孩留下了深刻的印象。
- remarkable 非凡的 - impress sb. with... 给某人留下了……印象

语法重点
singular 也常用在短语 singular to say 中，意思是"说也奇怪"，一般用作插入语。

0953 site [saɪt] n 地点，位置，场所

I believe the man will give you the chance to find the site.
我相信那个人会给你们机会找到那个位置。
- location 位置，地点 - construction site 建筑工地

语法重点
give sb. the chance（给某人机会）后面一般要接动词不定式。

0954 sketch [sketʃ] n 概略，素描 v 素描，概述

I want to take that sketch map as an example to show you how to do the work.
我想以那张概略图为例来向你们展示怎么工作。
- draft 草图 - take... as an example... 以……为榜样

语法重点
在 take... as an example 结构中，如果 take 后面接人，表示"以……为榜样"；如果 take 后面接物，则表示"以某物为例"。

0955 sledge / sled [sledʒ] / [sled] n 雪橇，大锤
I have had enough of the old sledge and I want a new one.
我受够了那个旧雪橇，想买个新的。
sleigh 雪橇　have enough of... 受够……

语法重点
have enough of 后面可以接人，也可以接物。

0956 sleigh [sleɪ] n 雪橇 v 乘雪橇
I think the sleigh brims over with their hope.
我想那个雪橇载满了她们的希望。

0957 slight [slaɪt] a 轻微，纤细的
Maybe he has slight knowledge on the new subject.
或许，他对这门新学科略通一二。
slight earthquake 轻微地震

0958 slogan ['slougən] n 标语
I believe the tutor will think highly of the slogan.
我相信教练会高度评价这个口号。
campaign slogan 宣传口号　think highly of... 高度评价……

语法重点
在 think highly of 中，highly 作副词修饰动词 think，介词 of 后面接名词或代词，表示具体的人或物。

0959 smog [smɑːg] n 烟雾
Under the cover of the smog, you can approach the enemy secretly.
在烟雾的掩护下，你可以悄悄地接近敌人。
toxic smog 有毒烟雾　under the cover of... 在……的掩护下

语法重点
under the cover of 通常置于句首，用于引出下文或表示强调。
approach (P. 256)

0960 sneeze [sniːz] v 打喷嚏
I was shy of making a sneeze suddenly at dinner.
吃饭时我突然打了个喷嚏，我觉得很难为情。
sternutation 喷嚏　sneeze at 藐视，轻视

语法重点
be shy of 后面一般接动名词，表示对做某事感到害羞或难为情。

0961 sob [sɑːb] v / n 啜泣，呜咽
I am fed up with the woman who is sobbing out the whole event.
我受够了那个正在哭诉整个事件的女人。
pule 呜咽　sob out 哭诉

语法重点
sob 的现在分词、过去式、过去分词依次是 sobbing, sobbed, sobbed。

0962 socket ['sɑːkɪt] n 插座，插口
I think this kind of battery charger can plug into any socket.
我觉得这种电池充电器可以插入任何类型的电源插座。
power socket 电源插座　plug into... 插入……

battery (P. 401)

sledge / sled ~ sparkle

0963 software ['sɔːftweər] **n** 软体
I hope you can take charge of the software engineering of our company.
我希望你可以负责我们公司的软件工程。
- package 套装软体
- take charge of... 负责……

> 语法重点
> take charge of 后面通常接表示职务、事务的名词或代词，也可以用 be in charge of 来表达。

0964 solar ['soulər] **a** 太阳的，日光的，太阳能的
It's good that we can make use of solar energy to generate electricity.
我们能利用太阳能来发电，真是太好了。
- lunar 月亮的
- make use of... 利用……

↪ generate (P. 724)

0965 sophomore ['saːfəmɔːr] **n** 二年级学生
Maybe the girl who is good at painting is in her sophomore year.
或许那个擅长画画的女孩在读大二。
- underclassman 二年级学生
- be in one's sophomore year 在读大二

0966 sorrowful ['saːroufl] **a** 悲伤的，使人伤心的
It was a sorrowful day for all of us.
对于我们所有人来说，这都是个悲伤的日子。
- woeful 悲伤的
- cheerful 快乐的

> 语法重点
> be a sorrowful day for（对某人来说是个悲伤的日子）后面要接表示人的名词或者代词。

0967 souvenir [ˌsuːvə'nɪr] **n** 纪念品，纪念物
I think the souvenir can go back to my grandmother's childhood.
我觉得，这个纪念品可以追溯到我奶奶的童年。
- memento 纪念品
- go back to... 追溯到……

> 语法重点
> go back to 一般不用于被动语态。

0968 spare [sper] **a** 多余的，闲置的
I will mend the door in my spare time.
我会在闲暇时间修理那扇门。
- vacant 空闲的
- in one's spare time 在某人空闲的时候

0969 spark [spaːrk] **n** 火花 **v** 闪烁，冒火花
I think the spark is symbolic of hope.
我觉得这火花象征着希望。
- a bright spark 活泼的人
- be symbolic of... 是……的象征

↪ symbolic (P. 788)

0970 sparkle ['spaːrkl] **n** 闪烁，火花 **v** 闪耀，冒火花
If you tell him the good news, I believe his eyes will sparkle with excitement.
如果你告诉他那个好消息，我相信他的眼睛会闪耀着激动的光芒。
- twinkle 闪耀
- red sparkle 红色火焰
- sparkle with... 闪烁着……

> 语法重点
> sparkle with 后面接名词或者名词短语。

505

0971 **sparrow** ['spærou] n 麻雀
I am worried about the injured sparrow.
我担心这只受伤的麻雀。
- spadger 麻雀
- be worried about... 为……而担心

语法重点
be worried about 后面可以接名词或代词，表示担心的对象。

0972 **spear** [spɪr] n 矛，标枪
I was unwilling to catch fish with my spear.
我不愿意用长矛来捕鱼。
- lance 长矛
- be unwilling to do sth. 不愿做某事

0973 **species** ['spi:ʃi:z] n 种类，物种
I think this species is almost indistinguishable from that one.
我觉得，这个物种和那个物种几乎无法区分。
- variety 种类
- extinct species 灭绝物种
- be indistinguishable from... 很难和……区分

语法重点
species 的复数形式还是 species。

0974 **spicy** ['spaɪsi] a 辛辣的，香的
I am indisposed to have spicy food.
我不愿意吃辛辣食物。
- spicy food 辛辣食物
- be indisposed to... 不愿意……

语法重点
be indisposed to 后面接动词原形。

0975 **spiritual** ['spɪrɪtʃuəl] a 精神的，心灵的
I fancy that she regards her father as her spiritual pillar.
我猜她把父亲当作自己的精神支柱了。
- psychic 心灵的
- material 物质的
- I fancy that... 我猜想……

⊃ pillar (P. 612)

0976 **splendid** ['splendɪd] a 闪亮的，辉煌的，极好的
You should keep on working and get splendid achievement.
你应该坚持工作，取得辉煌的成就。
- splendid scene 壮丽景观
- keep on doing sth. 继续做某事

语法重点
keep on 表示继续做某事，或坚持做某事，后面也可以直接接名词。

0977 **split** [splɪt] v 劈开，分裂 n 裂口，分裂
I plan to split up with my wife next month.
我打算下个月与妻子离婚。
- split the difference （讲价时）各让一步，折中

语法重点
split up with 除了表示"与……离婚"外，还可表示"与……断交、分离"，后面一般接人。

0978 **sportsman / sportswoman**
['spɔːrtsmən] / ['spɔːrtswʊmən] n 男 / 女运动员
I wonder why he lays no claim to being a sportsman.
我想知道，他为什么不以运动员自居。
- lay no claim to... 不以……自居

0979 sportsmanship [ˈspɔːrtsmənʃɪp] n 运动家精神
All of the athletes should carry forward the sportsmanship.
所有运动员都要发扬体育精神。
- spirit 精神　- carry forward... 发扬……

> forward (P. 168)

0980 status [ˈsteɪtəs] n 地位
I think women in your country have very little status.
我觉得你们国家的女人没有什么地位。
- situation 情况　- social status 社会地位
- have very little status 没什么地位

0981 stem [stem] n 茎　v 起源于
I wonder if I can chop off these branches from the stem.
我想知道，我是否可以把这些树枝从枝干上砍掉。
- trunk 树干　- brain stem 脑干　- chop off... from... 从……砍掉

> branch (P. 133)

0982 stingy [ˈstɪndʒi] a 有刺的，吝啬的，小气的
Don't be so stingy with the money when your mother is ill.
当你的妈妈病了时，用钱不要那样吝啬。
- chary 吝啬　✗ generous 大方的　- be stingy with... 在……小气

0983 strengthen [ˈstreŋθn] v 加强，巩固
I intend to strengthen the reserve force in the face of the powerful enemy.
大敌当前，我打算加强后备力量。
- enhance 加强　✗ weaken 削弱　- in the face of... 面临……

> **语法重点**
> intend 多用于较正式的书面语中，指对将来做出打算，并力争实现。
>
> reserve (P. 349)

0984 strive [straɪv] v 努力，斗争
In any case, you must strive for your future.
无论如何，你都必须为你的将来而奋斗。
- struggle 奋斗　- strive together 共同努力　- In any case,... 无论如何，……

> **语法重点**
> in any case 可用于句首或句尾，表示强调。

0985 stroke [stroʊk] n / v 打击，中风，抚摸
I hope you can give the little dog a gentle stroke.
我希望你能轻轻抚摸那只小狗。
- at a stroke 一下子　- give... a stroke 摸一下……

> **语法重点**
> 在双宾语结构的简单句中，一般情况下间接宾语要在前，直接宾语要在后。

0986 submarine [ˌsʌbməˈriːn] n 潜水艇　a 水下的，海底的
I am afraid I can't fix the position on the submarine which submerges in the water.
我恐怕无法为那艘潜入水中的潜水艇定位。
- nuclear submarine 核潜艇　- fix the position on... 为……定位

submerge 指长时间的完全浸入，强调浸入液体的深层。

0987 **suggestion** [sə'dʒestʃən] n 建议，意见

I bridled at the suggestion that he made.
我瞧不起他提出的建议。
≈ advice 建议   direct suggestion 直接暗示

语法重点
bridle at（瞧不起）后面一般接表示物的名词或者代词。

0988 **summarize** ['sʌməraɪz] v 总结

It will be useful to summarize the main idea of this text for us.
总结这篇课文的中心思想，对我们会有用。
≈ generalize 概括   it will be useful to... ……有用

0989 **surf** [sɜːrf] v 冲浪，浏览 n 海浪

Believe it or not, I don't want to go surfing with him.
信不信由你，我不想和他一起去冲浪。
surf the Internet 上网

语法重点
believe it or not 一般用在句首。

0990 **surgeon** ['sɜːrdʒən] n 外科医生

I have no doubt that the surgeon is expert in treating leg disease.
我毫不怀疑这位军医擅长治疗腿部疾病。
≈ physician 内科医生   I have no doubt that... 我毫不怀疑……

0991 **surgery** ['sɜːrdʒəri] n 外科医学

I require that the doctor give a surgery to my son right away.
我要求医生立即为我儿子做手术。
give a surgery to sb. 为某人做外科手术

语法重点
在双宾语结构的简单句中，如果把间接宾语放在直接宾语之后，间接宾语前需要加介词 to 或 for。

0992 **surrender** [sə'rendər] n / v 投降，屈服，放弃

To tell you the truth, I will never surrender to her.
和你说实话吧，我永远不会屈服于她。
≈ resist 抵抗   surrender to... 屈服于……

语法重点
surrender to 中的 to 是介词，后面通常接表示人的名词、名词短语或代词。

0993 **surroundings** [sə'raʊndɪŋz] n 环境

You should acclimatize yourself to the new surroundings as soon as possible.
你应该尽快适应新环境。

语法重点
acclimatize oneself to 后面一般接名词或代词。
possible (P. 077)

0994 **suspicious** [sə'spɪʃəs] a 可疑的，多疑的

I am suspicious about the motive of the man over there.
我怀疑那边那个人的动机。
≈ doubtful 可疑的   convinced 深信的
suspicious of... 对……起疑   be suspicious about... 怀疑……

0995 **sway** [sweɪ] v / n 摇动
I fear that he is under the sway of bad men.
我担心他受到坏人的支配。
- hold sway 支配，统治
- be under the sway of... 受……的支配

> 语法重点
> under the sway of 后面要接表示人的名词或代词。

0996 **syllable** ['sɪləbl] n 音节
You should give stress to the third syllable.
你应该重读第三个音节。
- stressed syllable 重读音节
- give stress to... 重读……

0997 **sympathetic** [ˌsɪmpə'θetɪk] a 同情的，共鸣的，赞同的
I am very sympathetic to the poor orphan.
我很同情这个可怜的孤儿。

> 语法重点
> be sympathetic to 中的 to 是介词。
> ↪ orphan (P. 331)

0998 **sympathy** ['sɪmpəθi] n 同情，赞同，支持
I have no sympathy for you.
我不同情你。
- pity 同情
- letter of sympathy 慰问函

0999 **symphony** ['sɪmfəni] a 交响乐，交响曲
I can't work up much enthusiasm for the symphony.
我对这首交响乐不感兴趣。
- symphony orchestra 交响乐团

↪ enthusiasm (P. 435)

1000 **syrup** ['sɪrəp] n 糖浆
I want him to pass me the cough syrup.
我想让他把止咳糖浆递给我。
- cough syrup 止咳糖浆
- pass sb.... 递给某人……

1001 **systematic** [ˌsɪstə'mætɪk] a 有系统的，体系的
I think she should add some systematic knowledge to her thesis.
我认为她应该在她的论文中加入一些系统知识。
- scientific 系统的
- add... to... 把……加入……

> 语法重点
> 短语 add to 可以表示"增加"。

1002 **tap** [tæp] n 水龙头，窃听 v 轻拍，利用
You can borrow money from him; he has money on tap.
你可以向他借钱，他手头有钱。
- tap water 自来水
- have... on tap 可随时使用……

1003 **technician** [tek'nɪʃn] n 技师
I was greatly astonished that technician can't solve this problem.
技术员不能解决这个难题，我觉得很吃惊。
- technologist 技师
- laboratory technician 化验员，实验员

↪ astonish (P. 527)

1004 technological [ˌteknəˈlɑːdʒɪkl] **a** 科技的
I am firmly persuaded that technological progress will accelerate the pace of the life.
我坚信科技进步将会加快生活节奏。
technical 科技的　　technological innovation 技术创新

🔗 persuade (P. 356)

1005 telegram [ˈtelɪɡræm] **n** 电报　**v** 向……发电报
He could not make sense of the telegram.
他无法理解这封电报的意思。
wire 电报　　overseas telegram 海外电报　　make sense of... 理解……

1006 telegraph [ˈtelɪɡræf] **n** 电报，电报机　**v** 打电报，显示
I guess she heard on the bush telegraph that he will resign.
我猜她得到了他要辞职的小道消息。

1007 telescope [ˈtelɪskoʊp] **n** 望远镜　**v** 缩短，压缩
I put no trust in his theory about the telescope.
我不相信他那关于望远镜的理论。
binocle 望远镜　　through a telescope 用望远镜

1008 tendency [ˈtendənsi] **n** 倾向，趋势
I have a suspicion that he has a tendency to autosadism.
我怀疑他有自虐倾向。
trend 趋势　　globalized tendency 全球化趋势
I have a suspicion that... 我怀疑……

🔗 suspicion (P. 370)

1009 tense [tens] **a** 紧张的，绷紧的　**v** 拉紧，使紧绷
I think she is tense with expectancy.
我想她是因期待而神经紧张。
get tensed up 变得神经紧张　　be tense with... 因为……而紧张

语法重点
tense 还可以作名词，表示"时态"，如 past tense（过去时）。

1010 tension [ˈtenʃn] **n** 紧张，拉力，张力
I am not clear about how to dispel my tension mood.
我不知道该怎样消除自己的紧张情绪。
strain 张力　　high tension 高电压　　be clear about... 清楚……

1011 terrify [ˈterɪfaɪ] **v** 使恐惧
I think the little girl will be terrified to burst into tears.
我觉得小女孩会被吓得大哭起来。
gallow 使害怕　　reassure 使安心　　be terrified to do sth. 被吓得……

1012 terror [ˈterər] **n** 恐怖，惊骇
A snake is a terror to me.
蛇对我来说很可怕。
be a terror to sb. 对于……来说是可怕的

1013 theme [θiːm] n 主题，题目

I plan to give a talk on the theme of teenage crime.
我打算就青少年犯罪这个主题做一次报告。
- topic 主题
- theme park 主题乐园
- give a talk on... 就……做报告

1014 thorough [ˈθʌrəʊ] a 彻底的，详尽的

I think she has made a very thorough analysis on the situation.
我觉得她对形势的分析很透彻。
- radical 彻底的
- thorough understanding 彻底理解

语法重点
thorough 的副词形式是 thoroughly。

1015 thoughtful [ˈθɔːtfl] a 思考的，体贴的

I want to make friends with the girl who is thoughtful for others.
我想和那个对人很体贴的女孩做朋友。
- considerate 体贴的
- thoughtless 考虑不周的
- be thoughtful for... 对……很体贴

语法重点
be thoughtful for 后面一般接表示人的名词或者代词。

1016 timid [ˈtɪmɪd] a 羞怯的，害羞的

Your girlfriend comes across as a timid girl.
你女朋友看上去像是个胆小的女孩。
- bold 大胆的
- come across as... 给人的印象是……

语法重点
come across as 是常用搭配，as 后面接名词、形容词等表示修饰限定作用的词。

1017 tiresome [ˈtaɪəsəm] a 使人疲劳的，讨厌的

It would be too tiresome to eat in a restaurant without a waiter.
在没有服务生的餐厅里吃饭真是讨厌。
- tiresome work 吃力的工作
- it would be too tiresome to... ……真是讨厌
- waiter 多指饭店、旅馆等地方的男服务生，而 attendant 多指跟随某人并为其服务的人，比如侍者、随从等。

1018 tolerable [ˈtɒlərəbl] a 可容忍的，还不错的

Her mother shows that her behavior is tolerable, but I am fed up with her.
她母亲表示她的行为是可以容忍的，但是我受够她了。
- sufferable 可容忍的
- intolerable 无法容忍的

1019 tolerance [ˈtɒlərəns] n 宽容

I have no tolerance for his bad temper.
我不能容忍他的坏脾气。
- patience 容忍
- intolerance 不宽容
- tolerance limit 耐性限度

- temper (P. 372)

1020 tolerant [ˈtɒlərənt] a 宽容的，容忍的

You should be tolerant of youngsters.
你该对年轻人宽容一些。
- be tolerant of... 对……容忍
- be tolerant towards... 对……宽容

1021 **tolerate** ['tɑːləreɪt] v 宽容
I could not tolerate eating in my class.
我无法容忍有人在我的课堂上吃东西。
- stand 忍受　- tolerate doing sth. 容忍做某事

语法重点
tolerate 是及物动词，后面可以直接接宾语。

1022 **tomb** [tuːm] n 坟墓 v 埋葬
I shiver at the idea that I have to sleep in front of the tomb.
一想到要在坟前睡觉，我就害怕。
- grave 坟墓　- ancient tomb 古墓

⊃ shiver (P. 632)

1023 **tough** [tʌf] a 牢固的，艰难的，棘手的
Under the circumstances, I have to make a tough decision.
在这种情况下，我不得不做出一个艰难的决定。
- stiff 坚硬的　- tender 柔软的

语法重点
under the circumstances（在这种情况下）可以放在句首，也可以放在句末。

1024 **tragedy** ['trædʒədi] n 悲剧，灾难，惨事
Maybe the tragedy will leave a scar on my mind forever.
或许，这场灾难会给我留下永远的精神创伤。
- disaster 灾难　- comedy 喜剧　- leave a scar on... 给……留下创伤

1025 **tragic** ['trædʒɪk] a 悲剧的，悲惨的
I think it's tragic that he died at the age of eighteen.
他十八岁时去世，我觉得十分可悲。
- unfortunate 不幸的　- comic 喜剧的

语法重点
tragic 的比较级与最高级分别是 more tragic, most tragic。

1026 **transfer** [træns'fɜːr] / ['trænsfəː] v 转换 n 转账
I won't agree that you transfer your property to your lover.
我不会同意你将财产转让给情人。
- shift 转移　- transfer fee 转让费　- transfer... to... 把……转给……

语法重点
transfer 后面接名词或代词，表示接收的物件。
⊃ property (P. 343)

1027 **transform** [træns'fɔːrm] v 改变，转换
I bet that he will transform into a poor wretch overnight.
我打赌，他会在一夜之间变成穷光蛋。
- transform into... 转变成……

语法重点
transform into 后面接名词或代词，也可以用 switch into 来表达。

1028 **translate** [træns'leɪt] v 翻译，解释
You must make efforts to translate the article into English.
你必须努力把这篇文章译成英文。
- interpret 口译　- translate into... 翻译成

语法重点
make efforts to 后面接动词原形。

1029 **translation** [træns'leɪʃn] n 译文，译本
I advise you to be deep in translation during these two hours.
我建议你在这两个小时期间专心于翻译。
- interpretation 口译　- be deep in... 专心于……

1030 **translator** [trænsˈleɪtər] n 翻译者，译员
I hate translating since I get a handle on the beautiful translator.
自从对那个漂亮的翻译员有所了解后，我就很讨厌翻译。
- interpreter 口译者 　get a handle on... 对……有所了解

1031 **transportation** [ˌtrænspɔːrˈteɪʃn] n 运送，运输工具
I am afraid the transportation will be at a standstill soon.
我担心交通很快会瘫痪。
- carriage 运输 　transportation business 运输业
- be at standstill 处于停顿状态

1032 **tremendous** [trəˈmendəs] a 巨大的，惊人的
I think this will relieve him of a tremendous burden.
我想这将为他解决一个巨大的负担。
- vast 巨大的 　tremendous respect 极大的尊敬
- relieve sb. of... 使某人卸下……

→ relieve (P. 495)

1033 **tribal** [ˈtraɪbl] a 部落的，种族的
He must be proficient in several tribal lingoes.
他肯定精通几种部族语言。
- tribal cultures 部落文化 　be proficient in... 精通……

1034 **triumph** [ˈtraɪʌmf] n 胜利，喜悦 v 获胜，成功
I believe you will triumph at length.
我相信你们最终会胜利。
- success 成功 　failure 失败 　in triumph 胜利地，洋洋得意地

语法重点
at length（最后）强调经历了很长时间之后终于完成某件事情。

1035 **troublesome** [ˈtrʌblsəm] a 令人烦恼的，讨厌的
I'm not really into accepting the troublesome job.
我真不想接受那个讨厌的工作。
- messy 麻烦的 　I'm not really into... 我真不想……

语法重点
I'm not really into 后面一般接动名词。

1036 **tug-of-war** [ˈtʌɡˌəvˌwɔː] n 拔河，激烈竞争
I volunteer to take part in the tug-of-war.
我自愿参加拔河比赛。

语法重点
volunteer to 后面要接动词原形。
→ volunteer (P. 517)

1037 **twinkle** [ˈtwɪŋkl] v / n 闪耀，闪烁，眨眼
I feel disappointed that the meteor disappeared in a twinkle of an eye.
眨眼间那颗流星就不见了，我很失望。
- blink 眨眼 　in a twinkle 一眨眼工夫

1038 typist ['taɪpɪst] n 打字员
I want to recommend Jim as a typist.
我想推荐吉姆做打字员。
• typer 打字员　• recommend... as... 推荐……作……

> 语法重点
> recommend... as... 中，recommend 后面一般要接表示人的名词或者代词。

1039 underpass ['ʌndərpæs] n 地下道，高架桥下通道
Please tell me where the exit of this underpass is and I will be grateful to you.
请告诉我，这个地下通道的出口在哪里，我会很感激你的。
• underpass entrance 地道入口

• grateful (P. 449)

1040 unique [juˈniːk] a 唯一的，稀罕的
I think his style of painting is unique to mine.
我认为他的绘画风格和我的不同。
• distinct 独特的　• unique charm 独特魅力

> 语法重点
> be unique to（与……不同）中的 to 是介词，后面接表示人或物的名词或代词。

1041 universal [ˌjuːnɪˈvɜːrsl] a 世界性的
I think she is quite at home with English, which is called the universal language.
我认为她对被称为世界语言的英语很熟悉。
• widespread 普遍的　• individual 个别的　• be quite at home 熟悉……

1042 university [ˌjuːnɪˈvɜːrsəti] n 大学
I want to know why this hospital is affiliated with the local university.
我想知道这家医院为什么附属于当地大学。
• college 大学　• be affiliated with... 附属于……

> 语法重点
> university 是可数名词，其复数形式是 universities。

1043 upload [ˌʌpˈloʊd] v / n 上传档案
I have no heart for uploading the photos.
我没有心思上传照片。
• download 下载　• upload video 上传影片

> 语法重点
> have no heart for（没有心思）后面接名词或者动名词。

1044 urban ['ɜːrbən] a 都市的
I think the big supermarkets are concentrated in the urban centers.
我认为大超市集中在市中心。
• metropolitan 大都市的　• rural 农村的　• be concentrated in... 集中在……

• concentrate (P. 412)

1045 urge [ɜːrdʒ] v / n 催促，鼓励，要求
I have an urge to go on board as soon as possible.
我希望尽快登机。
• crowd 挤满，挤　• have an urge to do sth. 希望（很想）干……

typist ~ vinegar

1046 urgent ['ɜːrdʒənt] **a** 紧急的，紧迫的

I'm not in the right frame of mind to play because he is in urgent need of help.

他急需帮助，我没心思玩耍。

- urgent action 紧急行动
- I'm not in the right frame of mind... 我没心情……

> 语法重点
> urgent 的副词形式是 urgently。

1047 usage ['juːsɪdʒ] **n** 用法，惯例

I think the word has come into usage.

我认为这个单词已为大家所惯用。

- practice 惯例
- come into usage... 被大家惯用

1048 vain [veɪn] **a** 无益的

It is vain to try to persuade him.

试图说服他是没有用的。

- fruitless 徒劳的
- effective 有效的
- in vain 无结果地，徒然

> 语法重点
> in vain 后面通常要接动词不定式。
> persuade (P. 356)

1049 vast [væst] **a** 广大的，浩瀚的，巨大的

I believe he will make vast improvement in English.

我相信他的英语会有很大进步。

- gigantic 巨大的
- tiny 微小的

1050 vegetarian [ˌvedʒə'terɪən] **n** 素食主义者 **a** 素食的

It sounds funny to me that he is a vegetarian.

他是个素食者，这让我觉得很可笑。

- veggie 素食者
- vegetarian food 素食

> funny (P. 042)

1051 verb [vɜːrb] **n** 动词

In my opinion, the verb should be followed by a noun.

我认为这个动词后面要接名词。

- be followed by... 后面要接……

1052 very ['veri] **ad** 完全的，正是

I am very annoyed with him about his carelessness.

我对他的粗心大意非常恼火。

- quite 很
- before one's very eyes 公开地

> 语法重点
> be annoyed with 后面一般要接表示人的名词或者代词。

1053 vessel ['vesl] **n** 容器，血管，船舰

I want you to pour some liquid into the vessel.

我想让你倒一些液体到容器里。

- container 容器
- merchant vessel 商船
- pour... into... 把……倒入……

> 语法重点
> pour into 是一个动词短语，into 后面接名词或代词，表示进入的方向或地方。

1054 vinegar ['vɪnɪɡər] **n** 醋

You have to mix vinegar with other condiments together.

你得将醋与其他佐料混合在一起。

- table vinegar 食醋
- mix... with... 把……和……混合在一起
- mix 指将各种成分混合在一起，却不一定能看出原来的成分。

1055 violate ['vaɪəleɪt] **v** 违反，扰乱，侵犯
You can't violate the company's rules at will, or you will get punishment.
你不能任意地违反公司规定，不然你会受到惩罚。
同 violate contract 违反合约　　同 at will 任意……

↪ rule (P. 084)

1056 violation [ˌvaɪə'leɪʃn] **n** 违反，违背，妨碍
I think his behavior has been in violation of the law.
我认为他的行为已经违反了法律的规定。
同 infraction 违反　　同 violation of laws 违法　　同 be in violation of... 违反……

1057 virgin ['vɜːrdʒɪn] **n** 处女，未婚女子 **a** 纯洁的，原始的
I will keep an eye on the virgin voyage of that ship.
我会关注那艘轮船的处女航。
同 maiden 处女　　反 impure 不纯洁的　　同 ... keep an eye on... ……关注……

1058 virtue ['vɜːrtʃuː] **n** 美德，优点，长处
This pair of trousers has the virtue of durability.
这条裤子有耐穿的优点。
同 merit 优点　　反 shortcoming 缺点　　同 have the virtue of... 有……的优点

语法重点
this pair of trousers 按单数处理。
↪ trousers (P. 073)

1059 virus ['vaɪrəs] **n** 病毒，病原体
I want to keep my computer from being attacked by new viruses.
我想让我的电脑不受新型病毒的攻击。
同 virus infection 病毒感染　　同 be attacked by... 被……攻击
同 keep from 表示阻止某人做某事，或者阻止某物发生什么情况。

1060 visual ['vɪʒuəl] **a** 视觉的，视力的，看得见的
I am overwhelmed with delight when I see the film has excellent visual effects.
看到这部影片有着极好的视觉效果时，我高兴极了。
同 optical 视觉的　　反 unseen 看不见的

↪ overwhelm (P. 607)

1061 vital ['vaɪtl] **a** 生命的，重要的
It is vital that you sign your name on the document.
你在文件上签字是至关重要的。
同 dynamic 有活力　　反 nonsignificant 不重要的
同 it is vital that... ……是至关重要的

语法重点
vital 的比较级、最高级分别是 more vital, most vital。

1062 volcano [vɑːl'keɪnoʊ] **n** 火山
I think it is most risky to approach an active volcano.
我认为靠近一座活火山是非常危险的。
同 active volcano 活火山

1063 **voluntary** [ˈvɑːlənteri] a 自愿的，志愿的

I feel so good to do voluntary work in the orphanage.
在孤儿院做义工，我觉得很好。
🔄 compulsory 被强制的

➡ orphanage (P. 605)

1064 **volunteer** [ˌvɑːlənˈtɪr] n 志愿者，志愿兵 v 自愿

I hope he volunteers for the military service.
我希望他自愿去当兵。
🔗 volunteer for... 自愿……

1065 **vowel** [ˈvaʊəl] n 元音

It burns me up when he pronounces the vowel wrongly.
他读错那个元音时，我很生气。

1066 **voyage** [ˈvɔɪɪdʒ] n / v 航行，远行

You had better make your will preparatory to your voyage.
你最好在出航前立下遗嘱。
🔗 sailing 航海   🔗 preparatory to 在……之前

语法重点
preparatory to 后面一般接名词或者动名词。

1067 **walnut** [ˈwɔːlnʌt] n 核桃树

I think walnuts are a local specialty in his hometown.
我觉得核桃是他家乡的特产。

1068 **website** [ˈwebsaɪt] n 网站

It really made me angry when I found the information on the website.
在网上发现这个消息的时候，我真的很生气。
🔗 web 网   🔗 website design 网站设计

➡ information (P. 458)

1069 **weekly** [ˈwiːkli]

a 每周的，一周一次的   ad 每周一次   n 周刊，周报

I hope you can write to your parents weekly.
我希望你每周给父母写一封信。
🔗 weekly report 周报   🔗 write to sb. 写信给某人

1070 **welfare** [ˈwelfer] n 福利，福利事业，幸福

I think the welfare of the workers is bound up with the benefits of the factory.
我认为工人们的福利与工厂的效益密切相关。
🔗 welfare work 福利工作   🔗 be bound up with... 与……有密切关系

➡ bound (P. 534)

1071 **wit** [wɪt] n 机智

I don't think he is a man of little wit.
我认为他不是个头脑简单的人。
🔗 intelligence 智力   🔄 stupidity 愚蠢   🔗 at one's wits end 仓皇失措

1072 **witch / wizard** [wɪtʃ] / [ˈwɪzərd] n 女巫师，男巫师
I was curious how the witch cast a spell on the girl.
我很好奇女巫是怎样对小女孩施妖术的。

> 语法重点
> cast 是不规则动词，其过去式、过去分词都是 cast。

1073 **withdraw** [wɪðˈdrɔː] v 提取
They will withdraw if they run out of ammunition.
他们用完弹药就会撤退。
- deposit 存放
- withdraw deposit 提款
- run out of... 用光……

> 语法重点
> withdraw 作动词时，通常与介词 from 连用，表示"从……离开或撤回"。

1074 **witness** [ˈwɪtnəs] n 目击者 v 目击，见证
I think there is not a vestige of truth in that witness's statement.
我认为那个证人的证词没有丝毫真实性。
- as witness 以……为证明

> statement (P. 097)

1075 **wreck** [rek] n 残骸，失事 v 毁坏，遇难
I was devastated by the news of his death in the wreck.
获悉他在此次事故中去世的消息，我十分震惊。
- demolish 毁坏
- plane wreck 飞机残骸
- be devastated by... 为……感到震惊

1076 **wrinkle** [ˈrɪŋkl] n 皱纹，褶 v 使起皱纹
I hate to see that you wrinkle your forehead.
我讨厌看你皱眉。
- wrinkle up 使起皱纹
- wrinkle one's forehead 皱起眉头

> 语法重点
> wrinkle one's forehead 是固定搭配用法，forehead 要用单数形式。

1077 **yearly** [ˈjɪrli] a 每年的，一年一次的
I think your yearly payroll goes hand in hand with your capacity for work.
我认为你的年薪与你的工作能力密切相关。
- yearly turnover 年营业额
- go hand in hand with... ……与……密切相关

> 语法重点
> yearly 本身也可以作副词，意思是"每年，一年一次"。

1078 **yogurt** [ˈjoʊɡərt] n 优酪，酸乳
In my opinion, yogurt is a perfectly acceptable substitute for cream in cooking.
在我看来，优酪乳是烹饪时特别受欢迎的奶油替代品。
- be a substitute for... 是……的替代品

> substitute (P. 644)

1079 **youthful** [ˈjuːθfl] a 年轻的，青年的，有青春活力的
No matter what happens, I will try my best to keep youthful.
无论如何，我都要尽最大努力保持年轻。
- young 年轻的
- aged 年老的
- no matter what happens, I will... 无论如何，我都要……

LEVEL 5
abide ~ zoom

LEVEL 5 | abide ～ zoom

Review test

复习 Level 4 的学习成果，还记得以下单词是什么意思吗？

1. identify ▸ _____
2. resolve ▸ _____
3. deadline ▸ _____
4. guarantee ▸ _____
5. luxurious ▸ _____
6. hurricane ▸ _____
7. extend ▸ _____
8. wrinkle ▸ _____

Preview

单词重点预习，在开始之前先预习会让印象更深刻喔！

1. porch ▸ _____
2. hearty ▸ _____
3. mainstream ▸ _____
4. tuition ▸ _____
5. initiate ▸ _____
6. distinctive ▸ _____
7. scandal ▸ _____
8. longitude ▸ _____

语法重点预习，在开始之前先预习会让印象更深刻喔！

1 句子的种类与功用
- 句子一般可以分成以下两种：简单句和复合句。
- 句子的功用可分成：叙述、提问、命令、请求、感叹、祈使。

2 句子的语气可分：陈述、疑问、祈使、假设。
- 陈述：在陈述意见或事实时使用。
- 疑问：又可分为 Yes / No 问句、WH 问句、附加疑问句。
- 祈使：表示命令、禁止、劝告、请求等语气。
- 假设：在陈述内容与事实不符，或是尚未成真时使用。

3 名词跟数量词、限定词的搭配，整理如下：
- 可数单数名词：each，every，either，neither
- 可数单数名词、复数名词：other
- 复数名词：both，many，several，a few，few，a couple of
- 不可数名词：much，a little，little，a large amount of，a large quantity of，a great deal of
- 可数或不可数名词：all，half，some，any，enough，most，a lot of，lots of，plenty of

|正确答案| Review test 1 动词／识别 2 动词／决定 3 名词／截止期限 4 名词／动词／保证书；保证 5 形容词／奢侈的 6 名词／飓风 7 动词／延长 8 名词／动词／皱纹；使起皱纹
Preview 1 名词／玄关 2 形容词／衷心的 3 名词／形容词／主流；主流的 4 名词／教学 5 动词；名词／开始；初学者 6 形容词／区别的 7 名词／丑闻 8 名词／经度

abide ~ zoom

0001 abide [ə'baɪd] **v** 容忍，忍受，坚持
The salesgirl should abide such terrible conditions; it is really beyond me.
那个女售货员竟然能够忍受这样糟糕的环境，我真的想不通。
⊜ endure 忍耐，容忍　⊜ abide by 履行，遵守

语法重点
abide 表示"忍受，容忍"，通常用于否定句或是疑问句中，与情态动词连用，表示"遵守"时，通常与介词 by 连用。

0002 abolish [ə'bɑːlɪʃ] **v** 废止，革除
It's supposed that the tax on the products should be abolished.
据推测，这种产品的税收应当废除。
⊜ exterminate 消灭　⊜ establish 建立　⊜ it's supposed that... 据推测……

语法重点
abolish 通常是指废除某项法律、制度、习惯、风俗等，多用于正式文体。

0003 abortion [ə'bɔːrʃn] **n** 流产，堕胎
It's said that she had an abortion last week.
据说，她上周做了流产手术。
⊜ miscarriage 流产　⊜ pregnancy 怀孕　⊜ induced abortion 人工流产

语法重点
abortion 表示"流产手术"时为可数名词，表示"流产，堕胎"时为不可数名词。

0004 abrupt [ə'brʌpt] **a** 突然的，陡峭的，意外的
The customer took an abrupt departure just now.
刚才，那个顾客突然走掉了。
⊜ sudden 突然的，唐突的　⊜ abrupt change 突变，陡变

0005 absurd [əb'sɜːrd] **a** 不合理的，荒唐的，可笑的
It's indeed absurd of you to buy such an expensive pen.
你买这么贵的钢笔，真是荒唐。
⊜ ridiculous 荒谬的　⊜ reasonable 合理的

语法重点
absurd 的名词形式为 absurdity，副词形式为 absurdly。

0006 abundant [ə'bʌndənt] **a** 丰富的，充裕的
There is an abundant supply of fruit in the new supermarket.
新开的那家超市供应大量的水果。
⊜ plentiful 丰富的，充裕的　⊜ short 不足的

语法重点
abundant 通常与介词 in 连用。
⊜ supply (P. 231)

0007 academy [ə'kædəmi] **n** 高等教育，学院，专科学校
The writer was said to be a graduate of an art academy.
据说，那位作家毕业于一所艺术学院。
⊜ college 学院　⊜ academy award 奥斯卡金像奖　⊜ ... be said to... 据说……

0008 accustom [ə'kʌstəm] v 使……习惯于

It takes a while for the old man to accustom himself to the new living conditions.
那名老先生用了一段时间来适应新的居住环境。
🔗 accustom oneself to... 养成……的习惯

> **语法重点**
> accustom oneself to，也可以用作 be / get accustomed to，后接名词、动名词形式。

0009 ace [eɪs] n 杰出人才 a 一流的，卓越的

The man in trouble must have an ace up his sleeve.
那个处于困境中的男子必定有什么秘密王牌。
🔗 inferior 差的，下等的   🔗 an ace in the hole 暗中保留的王牌

0010 acknowledge [ək'nɑːlɪdʒ] v 承认，表示感谢

She alone refuses to acknowledge the need for sales promotion.
只有她拒绝承认促销活动的必要性。
🔗 admit 承认   🔗 deny 否认   🔗 acknowledge receipt 证实收到，回执

> **语法重点**
> acknowledge 作及物动词，表示"承认属实"，通常是指公开承认某事的真实情况，或是承认自己的错误，可以后接名词、不定式、从句。

0011 acne ['ækni] n 粉刺，痤疮

The product contains the effective anti-acne essence of tea trees.
这种产品含有高效抗痘茶树精华。

> **语法重点**
> essence 通常作不可数名词，表示"精髓，本质，要素"。

0012 admiral ['ædmərəl] n 海军上将，舰队司令

Just imagine her surprise on seeing the vice-admiral in the mall.
想想看，在购物中心看到那位海军中将，她是多么惊讶。

> **语法重点**
> surprise 表示"惊奇，惊讶"，通常用作不可数名词，指因为超出预料的或是意外的事情而感到惊讶。

0013 adolescence [ˌædə'lesns] n 青春期

Boys during adolescence seldom like going shopping with their mother.
很少有青春期的男生喜欢和妈妈一起去买东西。
🔗 youthhood 青春期，青少年时期   🔗 senescence 老年期

> **语法重点**
> adolescence 作不可数名词，表示"青春期"，指的是介于童年和成年之间的时期，约是 13 到 17 岁。
> 🔗 during (P. 032)

0014 adolescent [ˌædə'lesnt]
a 青春期的，青少年的 n 青少年

The adolescent girl feels like buying that simple dress without adornment.
那个少女想要买那件朴素毫无装饰的连衣裙。
🔗 hebetic 青春期的   🔗 gerontic 老年的

> **语法重点**
> adolescent 在句中作形容词。

0015 adore [ə'dɔːr] v 崇拜，爱慕，很喜欢

The little girl simply adores buying toys.
那个小女孩十分喜欢买玩具。
🔗 love 爱慕，极喜欢   🔗 abhor 憎恶，痛恨

> **语法重点**
> adore 通常用于口语中，不用于进行时态，其名词形式为 adoration，形容词形式为 adoring。

accustom ~ airtight

0016 adulthood [ˈædʌlthʊd] **n** 成年期，成人期
Regretfully, the millionaire became addicted to tobaccos in adulthood.
遗憾的是，那位百万富翁在成年时期染上了烟瘾。

> tobacco (P. 375)

0017 advertiser [ˈædvərtaɪzər] **n** 广告客户，刊登广告的人
If you'd like to, you can refer to the telephone directory to find the advertiser's number.
如果你想，可以从电话簿上找到那个广告客户的号码。
　adman 广告商　　advertiser company 广告公司

0018 affection [əˈfekʃn] **n** 影响，喜爱，感情
The teacher was held in great affection by those children.
那个老师很受那些孩子们喜欢。
　favor 喜爱　　hate 反感　　affection for... 对……的爱

> **语法重点**
> affection 表示"喜爱"，通常与介词 for、towards 连用，可作可数名词，通常用作复数形式，也可以用作不可数名词。

0019 agenda [əˈdʒendə] **n** 议程，日常工作事项
As a reputed company, quality should be put always at the top of the agenda.
作为一家信誉良好的公司，品质始终都应当是最重要的议题。
　agendum 议程，待办事项　　be put at the top of... ……是最重要的

> **语法重点**
> agenda 为复数名词形式，其单数形式为 agendum。

0020 agony [ˈægəni] **n** 痛苦，临死的挣扎
Whether to buy the dress or not, the woman was in an agony of indecision.
是否要买那件连衣裙，那位女士陷入了犹豫不决的痛苦中。
　in agony 痛苦不堪

0021 agricultural [ˌægrɪˈkʌltʃərəl] **a** 农业的，农艺的
The little town's economy mainly depends on agricultural products.
这个小镇的经济主要依靠农产品。
　industrial 工业的　　agricultural products 农产品

> **语法重点**
> agricultural 作形容词，无比较级和最高级形式，其名词形式为 agriculture。
> economy (P. 432)

0022 AI / artificial intellgence
n 人工智能
It is generally acknowledged that artificial intelligence has been commonly used in the intelligent robots research.
众所周知，人工智能被广泛应用于智能型机器人研究。
　it is generally acknowledged that... 众所周知……

0023 airtight [ˈeɪrtaɪt] **a** 密闭的，密封的，无懈可击的
The salesman wanted the cake to keep crisp, so he put it in an airtight container.
售货员想让饼干保持脆度，所以把它放在密封的容器中。
　tight 密闭的，密封的　　airtight container 密封容器

> crisp (P. 279)

523

0024 airway ['erweɪ] n 航线，导气管，通风孔
The sales manager suffered from an inflammation of the airways.
那位销售经理气管发炎了。

语法重点
airway 是可数名词。
suffer (P. 368)

0025 aisle [aɪl] n 走道，通道，侧廊
The salesman made the customers rolling in the aisles.
售货员逗得顾客们捧腹大笑。
walkway 走道　　down the aisle 沿教堂走道而去（至圣坛举行婚礼）
... make sb. rolling in the aisles ……让某人乐不可支（捧腹大笑）

0026 algebra ['ældʒɪbrə] n 代数
As for a salesman, it's not necessary to be good at algebra.
对于一名推销员而言，精通代数并不是必要条件。

语法重点
algebra 作不可数名词，视为学科名词，其形容词形式为 algebraic，其副词形式为 algebraically。
necessary (P. 195)

0027 alien ['eɪliən] a 外国的，不相容的 n 外国人，外星人
These unspoken rules in the marketing are alien to her nature.
营销业的潜规则与她的本性不符。
incompatible 不相容的　　compatible 相容的
alien beings 外星人　　... be alien to... ……与……不相容

0028 allergic [əˈlɜːrdʒɪk] a 过敏的
She wants to buy a pet cat, but her mother is allergic to cats.
她想买一只宠物猫，但是，她妈妈对猫过敏。
hypersensitive 过敏的　　allergic to... 对……过敏
allergic 作形容词，本意是表示"对……过敏的"，其延伸意义是表示"对……极讨厌的，强烈反感的"。

0029 allergy ['ælərdʒi] n 过敏症，反感，厌恶
The three-month-old baby has an allergy to some milk products.
那个三个月大的婴儿对某些乳制品过敏。
skin allergy 皮肤过敏　　have an allergy to... 对……过敏

0030 alligator ['ælɪɡeɪtər] n 短吻鳄鱼，短吻鳄皮革
Her sister wants an alligator handbag, but her family couldn't afford it.
她妹妹想要个鳄鱼皮手提包，可是她家里负担不起费用。

语法重点
alligator 作"短吻鳄（鳄科爬行动物）"讲时为可数名词，作"短吻鳄皮革"讲时，则为不可数名词。

0031 ally ['ælaɪ] n 同盟者，伙伴 v 使联盟，使联合
The salesgirl found an ally against the inhumane shopkeeper.
那位女店员找到了对抗不近人情的店主的盟友。

语法重点
ally 是可数名词。

0032 **alter** [ˈɔːltər] v 更改
Property prices have slightly altered in these two months.
这两个月的房地产价格有些轻微的变化。
- change 改变
- alter ego 密友，个性的另一面
- ... have done... these two months 这两个月，……做了……

0033 **alternate** [ɔːlˈtɜːnət] / [ˈɔːltərnət] v 轮流 a 轮流的
There is a pattern of alternate circles and squares on the wrapping paper.
包装纸上有一种圆形和方形相间的图案。
- commutative 交替的

wrap (P. 385)

0034 **altitude** [ˈæltɪtuːd] n 海拔高度，顶垂线
The boy is crying for the tree growing at an altitude of one thousand meters.
那男孩哭喊着想要的是生长在海拔 1 000 米处的那种树木。
- height 高地，高度
- in one's altitude 高傲自大
- altitude 作可数名词，指的是距离地面的海拔高度，而 height 则是泛指任何可以测量的高度。

0035 **ample** [ˈæmpl] a 充分的，丰富的，宽敞的
Well, these biscuits should be ample for you two.
好吧，这些饼干应该够你们两个吃了。
- abundant 丰富的
- insufficient 不足的
- be ample for... 足够……

biscuit (P. 263)

0036 **anchor** [ˈæŋkər] n 锚，抛锚停泊 v 抛锚，使固定
It's believed that the exchange rate can serve as an anchor in inflation control.
人们相信，在通货膨胀管控中，汇率可以发挥作用。
- inflation 作不可数名词，表示"通货膨胀"，而 deflation 表示"通货紧缩"，reflation 则是表示"物价回稳"。

inflation (P. 458)

0037 **anthem** [ˈænθəm] n 赞美诗，圣歌 v 唱圣歌庆祝
It's suggested that the anthem should be played to mark the open of the supermarket.
有人提议，奏圣歌来庆祝超市开业。
- chorale 赞美诗
- national anthem 国歌
- it's suggested that... 有人提议……

0038 **antique** [ænˈtiːk] n 古董，古玩 a 古老的，过时的
The old couple hesitated over whether to buy the antique mahogany table or not.
那对老夫妇犹豫是否要买那张红木古桌。
- old 古老的
- modern 现代的

hesitate (P. 305)

0039 **applaud** [ə'plɔːd] v 向……鼓掌，赞同，喝彩
They all applaud her decision to launch promotion activities.
他们都赞同她开展促销活动的决定。
◎ acclaim 称赞　◎ oppose 反对　◎ applaud one's decision 赞同某人的决定

◎ launch (P. 465)

0040 **applause** [ə'plɔːz] n 鼓掌欢迎，喝彩，欢呼
The customers broke into thunderous applause.
顾客们爆发出雷鸣般的掌声。

0041 **apt** [æpt] a 贴切的，有……倾向的，灵敏的
The salesman seems to be apt at communicating with customers.
这个推销员似乎很善于和顾客打交道。
◎ apt to... 易于，有……的倾向　◎ be apt at doing 善于做……

0042 **architect** ['ɑːrkɪtekt] n 建筑师，缔造者
I wonder whether you have any objection to the architect's plan for the new shopping center.
我想知道，对于这位设计师的新建购物中心设计图，你们是否有反对意见。
◎ designer 设计者　◎ have an objection to... 反对……

◎ objection (P. 477)

0043 **architecture** ['ɑːrkɪtektʃər] n 建筑学，建筑风格
I'm deeply impressed by the classical architecture of the commercial street.
商业街的古典建筑风格令我印象深刻。
◎ I'm deeply impressed by... ……令我印象深刻

0044 **arena** [ə'riːnə] n 竞技场
This is the largest indoor sports arena in the town.
这是这个城镇上最大的室内体育场。
◎ arena stage 中心舞台，圆形舞台

0045 **armor** ['ɑːrmər] n 盔甲　v 为……戴上装甲
It's said that a suit of armor of the general will be sold by auction.
据说，那位将军的一套盔甲将被拍卖。
◎ mail 盔甲　◎ ... will be sold by auction ……将被拍卖

语法重点
armor 作不可数名词，英式英语中则是用作 armour。
◎ auction (P. 676)

0046 **ascend** [ə'send] v 上升，登高，追溯
There is a long flight of stairs ascending to the entrance of the mall.
要走过长长的台阶，才能到达这个购物中心的入口处。
◎ climb 攀登　◎ descend 下降

applaud ~ astronomy

0047 ass [æs] n 驴子

She made an ass of herself—realizing that she left her purse at home at the checkout.
她做了件傻事，在结账处才意识到自己把钱包忘在家里了。
 on one's ass 处境恶劣，穷困潦倒，毫无希望
 ... make an ass of oneself ……出洋相

0048 assault [əˈsɔːlt] n 攻击，袭击 v 攻击，袭击

The roar of the traffic outside the mall was an assault on her nerves.
购物中心外的车辆喧嚣声刺激了她的神经。
 attack 攻击 defense 防守

0049 asset [ˈæset] n 财产，优点，有利条件

Good communication skills are undoubtedly an enormous asset to salesmen.
对于推销员来说，良好的沟通技巧无疑是极大的有利条件。
 capital 资本 handicap 不利条件 fixed asset 固定资产

> **语法重点**
> asset 作可数名词，表示"有价值的人或物"，而复数形式 assets 则是表示"资产"，它隶属于个人或是公司，可以抵偿债务或是在变卖后支付债务。
> enormous (P. 435)

0050 astonish [əˈstɒnɪʃ] v 使……吃惊

It astonished me that he should spend one thousand dollars on the counterfeit painting.
他竟然为那幅假画花了 1 000 美元，这令我感到惊讶。
 astound 使吃惊 ease 缓和

0051 astray [əˈstreɪ] a 迷路的，离开正道的 ad 迷路地

The misleading sign in the shopping center led him astray.
这家购物中心里的误导性标志使得他迷路了。
 stray 迷路的 go astray 误入歧途，迷路
 ... lead sb. astray ……使得某人迷路

> **语法重点**
> astray 可以作形容词，也可以作副词，无比较级和最高级形式，也可以取其比喻意义。

0052 astronaut [ˈæstrənɔːt] n 太空人，太空旅行者

I am astonished to hear that the salesman dreamed of becoming an astronaut.
听说那位推销员梦想着成为一名太空人，我十分惊讶。

0053 astronomer [əˈstrɒnəmər] n 天文学家

The telescope to astronomers is what the goods to salesman.
望远镜之于天文学家就如同商品之于售货员。

> **语法重点**
> astronomer 是可数名词。
> telescope (P. 510)

0054 astronomy [əˈstrɒnəmi] n 天文学

It is indeed a silly thing to talk about astronomy in the crowded supermarket.
在拥挤的超市里谈论天文学真是蠢事。

> **语法重点**
> silly 的比较级形式和最高级形式为 sillier, silliest，其名词形式为 silliness。

527

0055 attendance [əˈtendəns] n 出席，出席人数
In the trade fair, the dowager always had a bodyguard in close attendance.
在交易会上，那位贵妇总有一名保镖随身护卫。
㊀ presence 出席　㊁ absence 缺席　㊂ in attendance 出席，值班，负责

0056 auditorium [ˌɔːdɪˈtɔːriəm] n 礼堂，会堂，观众席
There was rapturous applause from every corner of the auditorium when the salesman appeared.
那位售货员出现的时候，礼堂里四处爆发出热烈的掌声。

㊂ applause (P. 526)

0057 auxiliary [ɔːɡˈzɪliəri]
a 辅助的，副的　n 辅助物，助动词，附属机构
You had better buy some medical auxiliaries in case of an emergency.
你最好买一些医疗辅助设备，以防紧急事件发生。
㊀ helping 辅助的　㊂ auxiliary equipment 辅助设备，附属设备

0058 awe [ɔː] n 敬畏　v 使敬畏，使畏怯
The crowd were awed into silence by the sternness of guide's voice.
导游严厉的声音吓得人群鸦雀无声。
㊀ fear 敬畏　㊁ contempt 轻蔑　㊂ be struck with awe 感到敬畏

语法重点
crowd 作集体名词，表示"人群"，指的是聚集在一起的群众整体。

0059 awhile [əˈwaɪl] ad 暂时，一会儿，片刻
Take it easy; we will not be going shopping yet awhile.
别着急，我们暂时还不会去购物。

语法重点
go shopping 与 do the shopping 都可以表示"购物"，但意义有所不同，前者指去逛街，并不一定会买东西，后者则是指买东西。

0060 bachelor [ˈbætʃələr] n 单身汉，学士
No one knows why the man remains a bachelor throughout his life.
没有人知道，那个男人为什么终生未娶。
㊂ bachelor degree 学士学位

0061 backbone [ˈbækboʊn] n 脊椎骨，骨干，毅力
In my mind, the experienced salesmen should be the backbone of the industry.
在我看来，经验丰富的推销员应当是这个行业的主要力量。
㊂ to the backbone 完完全全　㊂ be the backbone of... 是……的骨干力量

㊂ industry (P. 179)

0062 badge [bædʒ] n 徽章，标记　v 授给……徽章
The red hat is the badge of the clerks in the mall.
这家购物中心的店员都戴一顶红帽子。
㊀ edge 徽章　㊂ souvenir badge 纪念章　㊂ ... be the badge of... 是……的标记

attendance ~ barefoot

0063 ballot [ˈbælət] n 选票，投票用纸 v 投票
The customers held a ballot of members on the proposal.
顾客举行无记名投票，对这项提议进行表决。
◎ vote 投票　◎ secret ballot 无记名投票
◇ ... hold a ballot of members on... ……针对……举行无记名投票

> **语法重点**
> ballot 作可数名词，表示"无记名投票，无记名投票所得票数"；作不可数名词，表示"无记名投票制度"，也可以用作 ballot-paper。

0064 ban [bæn] v 禁止，剥夺权利 n 禁令，禁止
The company has been banned from the sale of milk products.
这家公司已被禁止从事乳制品销售。
◎ forbid 禁止　◎ permit 允许　◎ ban from 禁止

> **语法重点**
> ban 的过去式和过去分词形式为 banned, banned。

0065 bandit [ˈbændɪt] n 强盗，土匪
The supermarket was robbed by a band of bandits last night.
昨晚，那家超市被一群强盗抢劫了。
◎ robber 强盗　◇ be robbed by... 被……抢劫了

> ◎ rob (P. 351)

0066 banner [ˈbænər] n 横幅广告
This year may be a banner year for sales, I think.
我想，今年也许是销售状况最好的一年。
◎ banner ads 横幅广告，旗帜广告　◇ be a banner year for... ……是最好的一年

0067 banquet [ˈbæŋkwɪt] n 宴会 v 参加宴会，设宴
Her friends held a banquet for her after she bought a house in the city.
她在那座城市买了栋房子后，朋友们为她举行了宴会。
◎ state banquet 国宴　◇ ... hold a banquet for... ……为……举行宴会

0068 barbarian [bɑːrˈberiən] n 野蛮人 a 野蛮的
When it comes to the end-of-season sales, most housewives may behave like those barbarians.
季末清仓的时候，大多数的家庭主妇也许会表现得像那些野蛮人一样。
◎ civilized 文明的　◇ ... behave like those barbarians ……举止如同野蛮人

> **语法重点**
> barbarian 的形容词形式是 barbarous。

0069 barbershop [ˈbɑːrbərʃɑːp] n 理发店，四重唱
He had an unexpected encounter with his ex-girlfriend in the barbershop.
他在理发店巧遇了前女友。
◇ have an unexpected encounter with... 与……巧遇

> ◎ encounter (P. 434)

0070 barefoot [ˈberfʊt] a 赤足的 ad 赤脚地
When they entered the clothing shop, a barefoot girl suddenly ran out.
他们走进服装店的时候，一个赤脚的女孩突然跑了出来。
◎ shoeless 赤脚的　◎ calced 穿鞋的　◇ ... run out 跑出……

529

0071 **barren** ['bærən] a 不生育的，无益的

They had a barren discussion about the patterns on the wrapping paper.
他们对包装纸上的图案进行毫无意义的讨论。
- helpful 有益的   - barren land 荒地，不毛之地

0072 **bass** [beɪs] n 低音，鲈鱼 a 低沉的，低音的

Shoals of people always come to buy basses at this time of the year.
每年的这个时候都会有很多人来买鲈鱼。

> **语法重点**
> bass 的复数形式为 basses 或是 bass。

0073 **batch** [bætʃ] n 一批，一组，一群

These biscuits in the store are baked in batches of thirty.
这家店里的饼干是以 30 个为一炉进行烘烤。
- batch 作可数名词，可以表示"面包、糕饼的一炉"，也可以表示"人或物的一批"，还可以表示"电脑汇集处理的批次工作"。

0074 **batter** ['bætər] v 重击 n 面糊

The shopkeeper's face was battered to a pulp by those bandits.
那个店主的脸被那些抢匪打得血肉模糊。
- beat 打   - batter down 打烂

- bandit (P. 529)

0075 **bazaar** [bə'zɑːr] n 商场，市集

She came home with a box full of odds and ends bought from the bazaar.
她抱着满满一盒从市集上买来的零碎东西回家。
- plaza 市场   - charity bazaar 义卖

- odd (P. 330)

0076 **beautify** ['bjuːtɪfaɪ] v 美化

As Christmas is drawing near, the shopkeeper wants to buy some colorful lights to beautify the store.
随着圣诞节临近，那位店主想买些彩灯装饰店铺。
- adorn 装饰   - uglify 丑化   - as... is drawing near... 随着……临近

0077 **beforehand** [bɪ'fɔːrhænd] ad 事前

Her mother bought enough rice two weeks beforehand.
两周之前，她的妈妈就买了足够的大米。
- previously 预先   - afterward 后来   - tell beforehand 预言

> **语法重点**
> beforehand 作副词，通常用于句末，可以与时间段连用，也可以单独用。

0078 **behalf** [bɪ'hæf] n 代表，利益，支持

They collected money and bought daily necessities on behalf of the homeless.
他们为无家可归的人筹款、购置生活必需品。
- benefit 利益   - opposition 反对   - on behalf of... ……代表……
- sb. does sth. ... in behalf of... 某人为……的利益做某事

> **语法重点**
> in behalf of 表示"为……的利益"，等于 in one's behalf，介词 in 也可用 on。

0079 belongings [bɪˈlɔːŋɪŋz] n 所有物

You can't be too careful about your belongings while in the crowded shopping center.
在拥挤的购物中心，再怎么小心自己的财物都不为过。

- possessions 财产
- personal belongings 私人物品
- can't be too careful about... 对……再怎么小心都不为过

语法重点
belonging 作不可数名词，表示"所属关系"；belongings 为复数名词，通常是表示"财产，所有物"，用于口语中，也可以表示"家属，亲戚"。

0080 beloved [bɪˈlʌvd] a 心爱的 n 爱人

The salesgirl seems to be beloved of all children who have seen her.
似乎所有见过那个女店员的孩子们都会喜欢她。

- darling 心爱的人
- beloved wife 爱妻
- be beloved of / by... 为……所喜爱

0081 beneficial [ˌbenɪˈfɪʃl] a 有益的

It's universally acknowledged that vitamins are beneficial to our health.
世人皆知，维生素对健康有益。

- useful 有益的
- mutually beneficial 互利的，双赢的
- beneficial 和 profitable 都可以表示"有利的"，但意义有所不同，前者通常是指对健康、身心、事业等有益，而后者则是指实用的、可以获取利润的。

◎ vitamin (P. 382)

0082 bid [bɪd] v 出价

The old man bid five thousand dollars for the painting.
那位老人为这幅画出价 5 000 美元。

- inquire 询价
- bid for 投标，出价
- bid... for... 为……出价……

语法重点
bid 的过去式和过去分词形式均为 bid。

0083 blacksmith [ˈblæksmɪθ] n 铁匠，装蹄工，蹄铁

He is the only blacksmith to sell kettles for miles around.
他是方圆几英里内唯一卖水壶的铁匠。

- ironsmith 铁匠
- blacksmith welding 锻接，锻工焊接

◎ kettle (P. 314)

0084 blast [blæst] n 爆炸，冲击波 v 爆炸

When they went out of the mall, they encountered a blast of hot air.
他们走出购物中心时，一股热浪扑面而来。

- burst 爆炸
- (at) full blast 大力地
- sb. encounters a blast of... 一阵……扑向某人

0085 blaze [bleɪz] v 燃烧，着火 n 火焰，光辉，爆发

No one knows why the professor blazed up without warning.
没有人知道，那名教授为什么突然大怒。

- burn 燃烧
- quench 熄灭
- blaze a trail 开辟道路

0086 **bleach** [bliːtʃ] v 漂白，（使）变白 n 漂白剂

You had better soak the new shirt you bought yesterday in bleach to remove the stains.
你最好把昨天新买的衬衫泡在漂白剂中，以清除污垢。
- whitener 漂白剂　- soak... in... 把……泡在……中

语法重点
bleach 作可数名词，表示"漂白剂"；作不可数名词，表示"漂白，消毒"。而 bleaching-powder 则表示"漂白粉"。
↪ remove (P. 358)

0087 **blizzard** [ˈblɪzəd] n 暴风雪，大打击

A blizzard of e-mails came from the customers to enquire about the new product.
顾客发来大量的邮件，询问这种新产品。
- snowstorm 暴风雪　- enquire about... 询问……

0088 **blond** [blɑːnd] a 白肤碧眼金发的

She observed that the blond at the checkout was a foreigner.
她注意到，在结账处的那个金发女子是个外国人。
- fair-haired 金发的　- blond hair 金发　- sb. observes that... 某人注意到……

语法重点
blond 作可数名词，表示"有（金）黄色、浅色头发的人，尤指女子"，也可用 blonde。
↪ observe (P. 603)

0089 **blot / stain** [blɑːt] / [steɪn]

n 污渍，墨水渍 v 吸墨水，弄上墨渍或污渍

His being caught stealing in the supermarket will be a blot on the escutcheon forever.
他在超市中偷窃被抓，这将成为其永远的污点。
- stain 污点　- blot out 完全清除（思想、记忆等）
- ... be a blot on the / one's escutcheon ……成为名誉上的污点

0090 **blues** [bluːz] n 蓝调，忧郁，布鲁士 a 布鲁士的

The shopkeeper was in the blues because of those unsalable goods.
那位店主因为那些滞销货物而闷闷不乐。
- gloomy 忧郁的　- country blues 乡村蓝调

语法重点
goods 为复数名词，表示"货物，商品"，用于英式英语中，也可以表示"火车运载的货物"，而美式英语中则是用作 freight。

0091 **blur** [blɜːr] v 变得模糊

The early morning mist blurred the outline of the shopping center.
清晨的薄雾模糊了那个购物中心的轮廓。
- dim 使变模糊　- clarify 变得清晰
- ... blur the outline of... ……模糊了……的轮廓

语法重点
blur 作及物动词，其过去式和过去分词形式为 blurred，blurred，也可以用作可数名词，表示"模糊，模糊的东西"。

0092 **bodily** [ˈbɑːdɪli] a 身体上的，肉体的 ad 全部地

The clothing store will be moved bodily to a new site next month.
下个月，那家服装店将整体迁往新地址。
- integrally 整体地　- part 部分地　- bodily form 体型

0093 bodyguard [ˈbɑːdigɑːrd] n 护卫者
For lack of industry standards, the quality of bodyguard service greatly varied.
由于缺乏行业规范，保镖服务的品质参差不齐。
- bouncer 保镖 - for lack of... 由于缺乏……

→ standard (P. 227)

0094 bog [bɑːg] n 湿地，沼泽 v 使动弹不得
The discussion finally got bogged down in irrelevant details of the shopping list.
最终，这项讨论因为购物清单上的一些无关细节而终止。
- quagmire 沼泽 - bog down 停顿，陷入困境

语法重点
bog 作及物动词，其过去式和过去分词形式为 bogged, bogged, 通常用于被动语态，其本意为"陷入泥沼"，取其比喻意义，可以表示"陷入困境"。

→ detail (P. 283)

0095 bolt [boʊlt] n 门闩，螺栓 v 闩门
She has been dealing with the nuts and bolts of the marketing plan these days.
这些天，她都在思量营销方案的基本要点。

0096 bonus [ˈboʊnəs] n 分红，奖金，意外所得之物
Whoever buys a pound of chocolate from this store will get a box of biscuits as a bonus.
凡是从这家商店购买一磅巧克力的人都将得到一盒赠送的饼干。
- bonus share 红利 - get... as a bonus 得到……作为赠品

语法重点
bonus 作可数名词，其复数形式为 bonuses, 本意是"额外津贴"，其延伸意义是"意外的好处，额外赠送之物"。

0097 boom [buːm] n 隆隆声 v 急速增长，促进
It's supposed that this year should be a boom year for exports.
据推测，今年将是出口贸易繁荣发展的一年。
- prosperity 繁荣 - slump 衰落 - economic boom 经济繁荣

语法重点
boom 作可数名词，表示"人口、贸易等的突然增加"，也可表示"低沉的声音"，通常用作单数形式。

0098 booth [buːθ] n 货摊，亭子
There stands a telephone booth in front of the supermarket.
超市前面有个公用电话亭。
- kiosk 公用电话亭 - telephone booth 电话亭

0099 boredom [ˈbɔːrdəm] n 无聊，厌烦，厌倦
The little girl bought much ice-cream out of sheer boredom.
出于无聊，那个小女孩买了很多冰激凌。

语法重点
boredom 的动词形式为 bore, 形容词形式为 bored, boring, 副词形式为 boringly。

0100 bosom [ˈbʊzəm] n 胸怀，胸部，内心
She held the doll tightly to her bosom and asked her mother to buy it for her.
她把那个玩偶紧紧地抱在怀里，要妈妈买下它。
- bosom friends 知心朋友 - hold... to one's bosom 把……抱在怀中

语法重点
bosom 作可数名词，本意是"胸部，胸怀"，其延伸意义为"对某事物的关怀保护"，通常用作单数形式 the bosom of。

0101 **botany** [ˈbɑːtəni] n 植物学

You should know something about botany if you want to buy these flowers.
如果你想买这些花，就应该知道些植物学的知识。
- phytology 植物学
- agricultural botany 农业植物学

语法重点
botany 作不可数名词，表示"植物学"。

0102 **boulevard** [ˈbuːləvɑːrd]
n 林荫大道 a 娱乐性的 v 给……提供林荫大街

There happens to be a shopping center on Sunset Boulevard.
日落大道上恰好有一处购物中心。
- avenue 林荫大道

语法重点
boulevard 作可数名词，通常是指两旁植有树木的林荫大道。在美式英语中，则是表示"干道，大道"，首字母通常要大写。

0103 **bound** [baʊnd] v 跳跃，束缚 a 有责任的，一定的

I'm bound to say I don't like your new dress very much.
我必须说，我不太喜欢你新买的连衣裙。
- jump 跳跃
- be bound to 必定

语法重点
bound 与动词 bind（束缚）的过去式、过去分词同形，注意区分。

0104 **boundary** [ˈbaʊndri] n 边界，分界线，范围

As a driver, you had better keep in mind the boundary between acceptable and unacceptable behaviors.
作为一名司机，你最好牢记什么是该做的，什么是不该做的。
- keep in mind... the boundary between... and... 牢记……和……之间的界线

0105 **bowel** [ˈbaʊəl] n 肠子，内部

She will not go shopping with us because she suffers from a bowel complaint.
她腹泻，所以不会和我们一起去购物了。
- suffer from a bowel complaint 腹泻

语法重点
bowel 作可数名词，除作医学名词或是修饰语外，通常用作复数形式，也可以表示"最深的、最靠里面的部分"。
- complaint (P. 275)

0106 **boxer** [ˈbɑːksər] n 拳击手，装箱者

I feel bound to tell you that you had better stop talking about that heavyweight boxer in the crowded mall.
我觉得有必要告诉你，在这拥挤的购物中心里，你最好停止谈论那个重量级拳击手。
- pugilist 拳击手
- boxer shorts 四角裤

0107 **boxing** [ˈbɑːksɪŋ] n 拳击，装箱 v 将……装入盒中

You will be fired if you simply think about boxing while working as a policeman, I'll be bound.
我确信作为一名警察，如果你只是想着拳击，你一定会被解雇的。
- boxing match 拳赛
- ... I'll be bound 我确信……

0108 boyhood ['bɔɪhʊd] n 少年期

He has been a salesman going from door to door to sell products since boyhood.
从少年时代起，他就是个挨家挨户推销产品的推销员。
- sb. has been... since boyhood 某人从少年时代起就是……

> 语法重点
> boyhood 作不可数名词，但也可以与不定冠词连用，如 a happy boyhood。

0109 brace [breɪs] n 支架，托架 v 防备，支撑

All the salesmen have braced themselves for a supreme effort.
所有推销员都准备好全力以赴。
- support 支撑
- brace up 振作精神
- brace oneself for... 做好准备……

0110 braid [breɪd] n 辫子，穗带 v 编织

She feels like buying the dress which is trimmed with silk braid.
她想买那件有丝带装饰的连衣裙。
- plait 编织
- be trimmed with... 有……装饰的

> 语法重点
> braid 作不可数名词，表示"丝线、棉线编织的穗带"，作可数名词，表示"发辫，辫子"。
> trim (P. 652)

0111 breadth [bredθ] n 宽度，幅度，幅面

There are many pieces of material of different breadths for you to choose from.
这里有很多宽度不一的布料供您选择。
- width 宽度
- length 长度
- breadth of mind 心胸

0112 bribe [braɪb] n 行贿 v 受贿

The young man bribed his way into the supermarket.
那个年轻人靠贿赂进入这家超市工作。
- payola 贿赂
- bribe one's way into... 靠贿赂进入……

0113 briefcase ['bri:fkeɪs] n 公事包

After being given a bribe of five hundred dollars, the manager agreed to sell the briefcases at the trade price.
收了 500 美元的贿赂后，那位经理同意以批发价出售这些公文包。
- portfolio 公文包
- be given / offered a bribe of... 受……贿赂

bribe (P. 535)

0114 broaden ['brɔːdn] v 使……加宽，扩大，开阔

Two years' work in the mall has broadened the salesgirl's horizons.
在这个购物中心的两年工作经历，使得这个女店员拓宽了视野。
- extend 变大
- shrink 变小
- ... broaden one's horizons ……拓宽某人的视野

horizon (P. 453)

0115 bronze [brɑːnz] n 青铜，青铜制品

Those goods are all cast out of bronze.
那些商品都是用青铜铸成的。
- bronze work 青铜器
- be cast out of... 用……铸成的

0116 **brooch** [broʊtʃ] **n** 别针，领针

It's impossible for there to be any brooch at that price in the store.

这家商店里不可能有那个价位的胸针。

🔄 breastpin 胸针　🔄 brooch pin 胸针，胸针扣

语法重点

brooch 作可数名词，表示"女用胸针，领针"，一般用于英式英语中；美式英语中则用 pin。

0117 **brood** [bruːd] **v** 孵蛋，沉思 **n** 一窝，一伙

Actually, it's useless to brood over your fault.

事实上，对你所犯下的过错耿耿于怀也是没有什么用的。

语法重点

brood over 中的 over 也可以替换为 on 或者 about。

⚙ fault (P. 163)

0118 **broth** [brɑːθ] **n** 清淡的汤，培养基

"It doesn't help to cry over the split broth anyway," said the shopkeeper.

那位店主说，"无论如何，为打翻的肉汤哭泣也是无济于事的"。

🔄 Every cook praises his own broth. 老王卖瓜，自卖自夸。

🔄 it doesn't help to... ……无济于事

0119 **brotherhood** ['brʌðərhʊd]

n 兄弟关系，兄弟会，（总称）同行

We have dinner and go shopping together in complete brotherhood.

我们像兄弟一样一起吃饭一起逛街。

语法重点

brotherhood 作不可数名词，表示"兄弟关系，手足情谊"；作可数名词，表示"同业，同人"。

0120 **browse** [braʊz] **v** 浏览，吃草 **n** 浏览

They spent the whole afternoon browsing over books in the bookshop.

他们用整个下午的时间在书店里浏览书籍。

🔄 scan 浏览　🔄 scrutiny 细看　🔄 browse over... 浏览……

语法重点

browse 作不及物动词，表示"随意翻阅，牛羊等吃草"；作可数名词，表示"浏览"，通常用作单数形式。

0121 **bruise** [bruːz] **n** 瘀伤

The little boy was covered in bruises after falling off from the stairs in the mall.

那个小男孩从购物中心的楼梯上摔下来，身上有瘀青。

0122 **bulge** [bʌldʒ] **n** 肿胀，凸出部分，膨胀 **v** 膨胀，急增

There is usually a bulge in the sales of fruits in June.

水果的销售量通常在六月会有所增长。

🔄 inflation 膨胀　🔄 shrink 收缩　🔄 there is a bulge in... ……会有所增长

0123 **bulk** [bʌlk] **n** 体积，大批

These goods are cheaper if you buy them in bulk.

这些货物，如果你整批买的话，是较便宜的。

🔄 volume 体积，大量　🔄 in bulk 大批，大量

语法重点

bulk 作不可数名词，表示"体积，数量，容量，纤维素"；作可数名词，表示"巨大的形体或是身躯"。

brooch ~ calligraphy

0124 **bully** ['bʊli] v 霸凌，威吓 n 恃强凌弱者
The sales manager bullied these salesgirls into working hard by threatening them with dismissal.
那位销售经理用解雇来威胁那些女店员努力工作。
🔄 daunt 威吓　　🔗 ... bully sb. into doing... ……威胁某人做某事

> 语法重点
> bully 的过去式和过去分词形式为 bullied, bullied。

0125 **bureau** ['bjʊroʊ] n 局，处，社，所
The Bureau of Standards, Metrology & Inspection has put a ban on the product.
经济部标准检验局已经禁止出售这种产品。
🔄 innings 局　　🔄 education bureau 教育局　　🔗 put a ban on... 禁止……

> ↪ inspection (P. 459)

0126 **butcher** ['bʊtʃər] n 屠夫，屠杀者
The peddler was bullied by that ferocious butcher in the market.
那个小贩被市场上那个凶恶的屠夫欺负。
🔄 slaughterer 屠夫　　🔗 ... be bullied by... ……被……欺负

> 语法重点
> butcher 作可数名词，butcher's (shop) 则是表示"肉铺"。

0127 **cactus** ['kæktəs] n 仙人掌
The cactuses in the flower shop still bulk large in her memory.
那家花店里的仙人掌仍然让她记忆犹新。
🔗 ... bulk large in one's memory ……让某人记忆犹新

> 语法重点
> cactus 作可数名词，其复数形式为 cactuses 或是 cacti。

0128 **calf(1)** [kæf] n 小牛，犊皮，小腿
They planned to kill the fatted calf for Tom, the extraordinary salesman.
他们打算欢宴庆祝杰出推销员——汤姆的到来。
🔄 calf love 初恋　　🔗 ... kill the fatted calf for sb. ……欢宴庆祝某人到来/归来

> 语法重点
> calf 作可数名词，表示"小牛"，其复数为 calves；作不可数名词，表示"小牛皮革"，相当于 calfskin。
> ↪ extraordinary (P. 566)

0129 **calf(2)** [kæf] n 愚蠢的年轻人
There is no possibility that the calf will turn into an excellent manager.
那个愚蠢的年轻人不可能成为杰出的经理。
🔄 calf round 彷徨
ℹ calf 表示"傻头傻脑的年轻人，呆子"时，一般用在口语中。

0130 **calligraphy** [kə'lɪgrəfi] n 笔迹，书法
She bought some ink, writing brushes and paper because she wanted to teach herself calligraphy.
她想自学书法，所以去买了墨水、毛笔和纸张。
🔗 teach oneself... 自学……

537

0131 canal [kəˈnæl] n 运河，沟渠，管
If I had the chance, I would take the canal boat after coming back from shopping.
购物回来如果有机会，我要去坐运河船。
▶ if I had the chance..., I would... 如果有机会……，我要……

语法重点
canal 的动词形式为 canalize 或是 canalise。

0132 cannon [ˈkænən] n 大炮，火炮 v 碰撞
The little boy cannoned against a blind man on the corner in the supermarket.
在超市的转弯处，那个小男孩撞上了一位盲人。
▶ cannon fodder 炮灰，勇士们 ▶ cannon against / into... 与……相撞

0133 carbon [ˈkɑːrbən] n 碳
He wanted to make a carbon copy of the shopping list.
他想用复写纸复写一份购物清单。
▶ carbon dioxide 二氧化碳 ▶ make a carbon copy of... 用复写纸复写……

0134 cardboard [ˈkɑːrdbɔːrd] n 卡纸，纸板箱，硬纸板
There is no need for anxiety about the sales of these cardboard boxes.
没有必要为这些纸箱的销售而担心。
▶ strawboard 硬纸板 ▶ cardboard box 纸箱，纸板盒

▶ anxiety (P. 395)

0135 carefree [ˈkerfriː] a 无忧无虑的，不负责任的
She seems to take a carefree attitude to the sales of those cookies.
她似乎并不为那些饼干的销售而担忧。
▶ ... take a carefree attitude to / towards... ……对……并不担忧

0136 caretaker [ˈkerteɪkər] n 看管人，守护者 a 临时代理的
The old man has served as the caretaker in the shopping center for ten years.
那位老人已经在这个购物中心做了十年管理员。

0137 carnation [kɑːrˈneɪʃn] n 康乃馨，粉红色
She was seen to come out of the flower shop, holding a carnation in her hand.
有人看到，她手里拿着一支康乃馨，从那家花店出来了。

语法重点
carnation 作可数名词，表示"康乃馨"；作不可数名词，表示"淡红色"。

0138 carnival [ˈkɑːrnɪvl] n 嘉年华会，饮宴狂欢
A carnival atmosphere filled the shopping center.
这个购物中心充满了狂欢节的气氛。
▶ music carnival 音乐嘉年华
▶ a carnival atmosphere filled... ……充满了狂欢节的气氛

▶ atmosphere (P. 399)

0139 carp [kɑːrp] n 鲤鱼 v 吹毛求疵
She can always find something to carp about when living in the hotel.
住这家饭店的时候，她总是对某些事情吹毛求疵。
同 carp at 挑剔　　同 carp about... 对……吹毛求疵

0140 carton ['kɑːrtn] n 纸盒 v 用盒包装，制作纸箱
The little boy went to the store and bought a carton of milk.
那个小男孩走进那家商店，买了一盒牛奶。
同 carboard 纸板箱　　同 carton size 纸箱尺寸，包装尺寸

0141 category ['kætəgɔːri] n 分类，范畴
The books they bought fell into five categories.
他们买的书可以分为五类。
同 kind 种类　　同 fall into... categories 分为……类

> **语法重点**
> category 的复数形式为 categories，其动词形式为 categorize 或是 categorise。

0142 cathedral [kəˈθiːdrəl] n 大教堂
The store is next to a cathedral church; you will not miss it.
这家商店在教区总教堂旁边，你不会认错的。

0143 caution ['kɔːʃn] n 谨慎，警告 v 警告，劝……小心
You should exercise with extreme caution when dealing with customers.
与顾客相处时，你要极为小心。
同 warning 警告　　同 caution sb. about sth. 警告某人某事

> **语法重点**
> caution 作不可数名词，表示"小心，谨慎"；作可数名词，表示"警告，告诫"。

0144 cautious ['kɔːʃəs] a 谨慎的
If I were you, I would be particularly cautious about spending money.
如果我是你，我用钱会格外谨慎。
同 prudent 谨慎的　　反 careless 粗心的
同 be cautious of... 注意……，小心……　　同 be cautious about doing... 谨慎……

0145 celebrity [səˈlebrəti] n 名声
Those celebrities of stage and screen always live a luxurious life.
那些舞台和影视界名人总是生活奢侈。
同 fame 名誉　　同 celebrity charm 名人效应

> **语法重点**
> celebrity 作可数名词，其复数形式是 celebrities。

0146 celery ['seləri] n 芹菜
The woman who sells celery has a carping tongue.
那个卖芹菜的妇人言语刻薄。

同 tongue (P. 237)

... have a carping tongue ……言语刻薄

0147 **cellar** ['selər] n 地窖，藏酒 v 把……藏入地窖
The shopkeeper kept a good cellar.
那位店主藏有大量的葡萄酒。
同 basement 地下室　　同 storage cellar 地下储藏室

0148 **cello** ['tʃeloʊ] n 大提琴
There is no need for you to buy that expensive cello.
你没有必要买那把昂贵的大提琴。
同 there is no need for sb. to... 某人没有必要……

> 语法重点
> cello 作可数名词，复数形式为 cellos。
> 参 expensive (P. 162)

0149 **cellphone** ['selfoʊn] n 行动电话，大哥大
The man came to the checkout with his ear glued to the cellphone.
那个人打着电话来到结账处。
同 cellphone panel 手机面板

0150 **Celsius** ['selsiəs] a 摄氏的 n 摄氏度
It's eight degrees below zero Celsius today, but there are so many people in the supermarket.
今天是摄氏零下八度，然而，这家超市里还是有这么多人。
同 Celsius thermometer 摄氏温度计
同 it's... degrees below zero Celsius 摄氏零下……度

> 语法重点
> celsius 的缩写形式为 C。

0151 **centigrade** ['sentɪgreɪd] a 摄氏的
It's so cool in the mall, though it's thirty-nine degrees centigrade today.
今天有 39 ℃，这家购物中心却是如此凉爽。
同 Celsius 摄氏的　　同 degree centigrade 摄氏温度

> 语法重点
> centigrade 的缩写形式为 C 或是 cent。

0152 **ceremony** ['serəmoʊni] n 仪式，礼节
You don't have to stand on ceremony with strangers in the crowded store.
在拥挤的商店里，和陌生人不必拘礼。
同 celebration 典礼　　同 closing ceremony 闭幕典礼

> 语法重点
> ceremony 作可数名词，表示"仪式，典礼"，复数为 ceremonies；作不可数名词，表示"礼节，礼仪"。

0153 **certificate** [sə'tɪfɪkət] / [sər'tɪfɪkeɪt] n 证明书 v 发证书
You should have a medical certificate when buying medicine in the drugstore.
在这家药房买药，要持有医疗证明。
同 license 证明　　同 birth certificate 出生证明

> 参 drugstore (P. 157)

0154 **chairman** ['tʃermən] n 男主席
He took it upon himself to accompany the chairman to go shopping.
他擅自决定，陪董事长去购物。
同 chairperson 主席　　同 take it upon oneself to do... 擅自决定做……

cellar ~ chef

0155 chairwoman [ˈtʃerwʊmən] n 女主席，女议长
It was a big change in lifestyle after she became the chairwoman and she didn't have time to go shopping.
她当选女议长之后，生活方式有了极大的变化，她都没有时间去购物了。

0156 chant [tʃænt] v 唱，咏唱 n 赞美诗，祷文
I just can't stand the salesman who always chants his own praises.
那个推销员总是自夸，我实在无法忍受。
⊕ sing 唱歌　⊕ ... chant one's own praises ……自夸

◇ praise (P. 207)

0157 chatter [ˈtʃætər] v 不停地唠叨 n 唠叨，啁啾声
Please stop chattering on about your new necklace.
请停止谈论你新买的项链吧。
⊘ silence 沉默　⊕ chatter on about... 喋喋不休……

语法重点
chatter on about 中的介词 on 也可以替换为 away。

0158 checkbook [ˈtʃekbʊk] n 支票簿
He suddenly realized his checkbook was missing.
他突然意识到，自己的支票簿不见了。
⊕ chequebook 支票簿　⊕ balance checkbook 核对

语法重点
checkbook 用于美式英语中，英式英语中则用 chequebook 或是 cheque book。

0159 check-in
n 记录，登记，签到
There being nothing to be done, we have to wait at the check-in desk.
没有办法，我们只好在报到处等候。
⊕ registration 报到　⊕ check-in counter 入口检查处

0160 check-out n 检查，付款处
I wonder what time check-out is.
我想知道退房的时间。
⊕ I wonder what time... is 我想知道……是在什么时候

语法重点
check-out 作不可数名词，表示"退房，结账"，作可数名词，表示"付款柜台"，等于 check-out counter。

0161 checkup [ˈtʃɛkˌʌp] n 核对，检查，健康检查
Her mother asked her to get a medical checkup before she went shopping.
她妈妈要她购物前先去做体检。
⊕ examination 检查　⊕ checkup reporting 体检报告

0162 chef [ʃef] n 厨师，大师傅
If need be, you can ask the chef to buy some vegetables.
如果有必要，你可以让厨师买一些蔬菜。
⊕ kitchener 厨师　⊕ sous chef 副厨
⊕ if need be, you can... 如果有必要，你可以……

语法重点
chef 作可数名词，其复数形式为 chefs。
◇ vegetable (P. 109)

0163 **chemist** ['kemɪst] n 化学家，药店
She went to buy some aspirin at the chemist's on her way home.
回家的路上，她去那家药店买了些阿司匹林。
🔁 dispenser 药剂师　　🔁 sb. goes to buy sth. at someplace 某人在某地买某物

○ aspirin (P. 397)

0164 **chestnut** ['tʃesnʌt] n 栗子，栗色 a 栗色的
I feel a need to buy some roasted chestnuts.
我觉得有必要买一些炒栗子。
🔁 water chestnut 荸荠

0165 **chili** ['tʃɪli] n 红番椒
There is a great need for some chili peppers.
急需买一些辣椒。
🔁 chili paste 辣椒酱　　🔁 there is a great need for... 急需……

0166 **chimpanzee** [ˌtʃɪmpæn'ziː] n 黑猩猩
The shopkeeper who looks like a chimpanzee is said to be of good descent.
据说，那个看起来像黑猩猩的店主出身很好。
🔁 pongo 黑猩猩　　🔁 ... be of good descent ……出身很好

○ descent (P. 702)

0167 **choir** ['kwaɪər] n 唱诗班，合唱队 v 合唱
The salesman joined in a church choir on impulse.
那位推销员一时冲动就加入了教堂唱诗班。
🔁 chorus 合唱队　　🔁 bell choir 教堂钟
🔁 sb. does sth. on impulse 某人一时冲动做某事

○ impulse (P. 582)

0168 **chord** [kɔːrd] n 琴弦，和音，心弦
The salesman seemed to have struck a chord with the old granny.
那位推销员似乎打动了那位老奶奶。
🔁 touch a chord 触动某人的心弦　　🔁 strike a chord with... 打动/引起共鸣……

【语法重点】
chord 作可数名词。

0169 **chubby** ['tʃʌbi] a 圆胖的，丰满的
A little girl who was in a chubby sort of way asked her mother to buy a balloon just now.
刚才有个胖胖的小女孩要妈妈买气球。
🔁 pudsy 圆胖的　　🔁 thin 瘦的　　🔁 be in a chubby sort of way... 胖乎乎的……

【语法重点】
chubby 的比较级形式和最高级形式为 chubbier，chubbiest。

0170 **circuit** ['sɜːrkɪt] n 电路，环行，巡行
I think there may be a break in the circuit of the shop.
我想也许是商店里的电路断路。
🔁 be the circuit of 绕……环行　　🔁 ... a break in the circuit ……电路断路
🔁 "短路，漏电"可以用 short circuit 来表示。

0171 cite [saɪt] v 引述，表扬，举例

The salesgirl cited the high total sales as evidence of the popularity of the computers.
那位女店员列举庞大的销售总额以证明这批电脑的流行。
- reference 引用　● cite data 引用资料
- cite... as evidence of... 列举……以证明

⊃ total (P. 106)

0172 civic ['sɪvɪk] a 城市的，都市的，公民的

A new supermarket will be built in civic centre next week.
下周，市中心将新建一家超市。
- civic rights 公民权　● will be built in... 将被建于……

0173 clam [klæm] n 蛤蜊　v 保持沉默，挖蚌

When I mentioned the new handbag she bought yesterday, she closed up like a clam.
我提起昨天她新买的手提包时，她闭口不言。
- as close as a clam 一毛不拔的　● ... close up like a clam 闭口不言……

语法重点
clam 作可数名词。

0174 clan [klæn] n 部族，家族，帮派

The sales manager always clammed up when asked about his clan.
被问及他的家族时，那位销售经理总是闭口不言。
- tribe 宗族　● clam up... ……闭口不言

0175 clasp [klæsp] v 紧抱，握紧　n 扣子，紧抱

On seeing her in the supermarket, he went to her and held her hand in a firm clasp.
在超市里一看到她，他就走过去，紧紧握着她的手。
- grasp 抓紧　● disentangle 松开　● paper clasp 回纹针

语法重点
"握手"可以用 clasp hands 来表示。

0176 clause [klɔːz] n 从句，条款

There is a clause in the contract which says tenants should not sublease the flat to others.
合约条款规定，房客不得将公寓转租给别人。
- article 条款　● saving clause 附加条款　● sublease... to... 把……转租给……
- clause 作可数名词，指的是合约、遗嘱等法律文件中阐述具体义务、条件等的章节条款。

⊃ tenant (P. 648)

0177 cling [klɪŋ] v 黏住，依恋，坚持　n 紧抓，紧贴

They clung to each other and said goodbye at the exit of the mall.
在购物中心的出口，他们相互拥抱告别。
- cling film 保鲜膜　● ... cling to each other ……相互拥抱

语法重点
cling 的过去式为 clung。

0178 clockwise [ˈklɑːkwaɪz] a 顺时针方向 ad 顺时针方向地

She bought a bottle of juice and twisted the top in a clockwise direction.
她买了一瓶果汁，并按顺时针方向转开盖子。

反 anti-clockwise 逆时钟方向的

→ twist (P. 378)

0179 clover [ˈkloʊvər] n 苜蓿，养尊处优

Surprisingly, he has been in clover since he bought that four-leaf clover.
奇怪的是，自从买了那株四叶草之后，他一直过着优裕的生活。

片 in clover 生活优裕

0180 cluster [ˈklʌstər] n 一串，簇 v 群集，丛生

The girl bought a pot of rose and planted it in the garden, hoping there will be a cluster of roses next year.
那个女孩买了一盆玫瑰花，种在花园里，希望明年可以有一簇玫瑰花。

片 sb. did sth., hoping... 某人做某事，希望……

语法重点
cluster 作可数名词。

0181 clutch [klʌtʃ] v 紧握，企图抓住 n 离合器，掌握，抓紧

That girl bought the lovely cat from the pet store and clutched it to her chest.
那个女孩从那家宠物店买了一只可爱的猫咪，把它紧紧抱在怀中。

同 hold 抓住   反 loosen 松开   片 clutch at... 企图抓住……

0182 coastline [ˈkoʊstlaɪn] n 海岸线，海岸地形（或轮廓）

On the painting she bought last week is the beautiful landscape along the rugged coastline.
她上周买的那幅画上画着崎岖的海岸线附近的美丽风景。

同 shoreline 海岸线   同 mainland coastline 大陆海岸线

语法重点
coastline 作可数名词。
→ landscape (P. 465)

0183 cocoon [kəˈkuːn] n 茧，蚕茧 v 成茧状，把……紧紧包住

The baby was wrapped in a cocoon of blankets bought by his aunt.
那个婴儿被包裹在姑姑买的毛毯中。

同 silkworm cocoon 蚕茧   片 be wrapped in a cocoon of... 被包裹在……中

语法重点
cocoon 作及物动词，通常用于被动语态。

0184 coil [kɔɪl] v 盘绕 n 卷，线圈

Please buy a coil of yarn for me when you come back from work.
下班回来的时候，请帮我买一卷毛线。

片 shuffle off this mortal coil 死亡

clockwise ~ commission

0185 colleague [ˈkɑːliːg] **n** 同事，同僚

A colleague of hers just stared at the roses clustering round the window in the flower shop.

她的一位同事只是盯着花店窗户里四周丛生的玫瑰花。

- comrade 同事
- cluster round... 聚集在……周围
- colleague 作可数名词，指的是职业关系上的同事，为正式用词，而 partner 则是指事业上作为合伙关系的人。

0186 colonel [ˈkɜːrnl] **n** 陆军上校，中校

You can imagine there being a pleasant surprise seeing the colonel in the clothing store.

可以想象，看到那位陆军上校出现在这家服装店中，人们是多么惊喜啊。

- pleasant (P. 205)

0187 colonial [kəˈloʊniəl]

a 殖民地的 **n** 殖民地居民，殖民时代建筑

France, once a colonial power, now appears to be at the leading edge of fashion.

法国曾经是殖民强国，而今似乎走在了时尚尖端。

- ... be at the leading edge of... ……走在……尖端

0188 combat [ˈkɑːmbæt] **v** 战斗，减少 **n** 斗争，搏斗

We must unite to combat with counterfeit and shoddy products.

我们必须团结起来，与假冒伪劣产品斗争。

- fight 打架
- single combat 单挑
- combat with... 与……斗争

0189 comedian [kəˈmiːdiən] **n** 喜剧演员，丑角，滑稽的人

She briefly clasped hands before saying goodbye to that comedian.

她与那位喜剧演员匆匆握手告别。

0190 comet [ˈkɑːmət] **n** 彗星

Seeing her brother clasp that salesgirl to his chest, she was greatly surprised, as if she had seen Halley's comet.

看到哥哥把那位女店员紧紧抱在怀中，她惊讶极了，像是看到了哈雷彗星。

- clasp (P. 543)

0191 commentator [ˈkɑːmənteɪtər] **n** 时事评论家

The television commentator was seen to clasp a jade bracelet round her wrist.

有人看到，那位电视评论员将一个玉镯戴在手腕上。

- narrator 叙述者，解说员
- media commentator 时事评论员

语法重点
jewelry 作不可数名词，表示"珠宝"，英式英语中则用 jewellery。

0192 commission [kəˈmɪʃn] **n** 委托，委员会，佣金

Her sister has received the commission to design dresses for the clothing store.

她姐姐已经接下委托，为那家服装店设计连衣裙。

0193 commodity [kəˈmɑːdəti] n 日用品，货物
As a salesman with poor salary, every penny is a precious commodity to him.
作为一个薪水少得可怜的推销员，每一分钱对他而言都是很珍贵的。
- merchandise 商品
- be a precious commodity to... 对……而言是很珍贵的

语法重点
commodity 作可数名词，复数形式为 commodities。

0194 commonplace [ˈkɑːmənpleɪs]
a 普通的，平庸的 n 寻常的事物
I feel obliged to say that air travel is actually not at all exciting nowadays, just commonplace.
我不得不说，如今乘飞机旅行不足为奇，是件很平常的事。
- ordinary 普通的
- special 特别的
- commonplace book 备忘录

语法重点
commonplace 作形容词，通常含有贬义。
- nowadays (P. 476)

0195 communism [ˈkɑːmjunɪzəm] n 共产主义
Marx's ideas gave birth to communism.
马克思的思想使共产主义诞生了。

语法重点
communism 作不可数名词。

0196 communist [ˈkɑːmjənɪst] n 共产党员 a 共产主义的
In the following year he joined the Communist Party.
第二年他加入了共产党。
- capitalist 资本家，资本主义者

0197 commute [kəˈmjuːt] v 通勤，补偿 n 往返的路程
They all agreed to commute the annuity into the lump sum.
他们都同意，将年金改为一次性总付款。
- commute from 减刑
- ... commute... into... ……改变（付款方式）……

语法重点
... commute... into... 中的介词 into 也可以替换为 for。
- lump (P. 592)

0198 commuter [kəˈmjuːtər] n 通勤者，经常乘公共车辆往返者
The six o'clock train is usually packed with commuters from Oxford to London.
六点的那列火车通常挤满了从牛津到伦敦的通勤者。
- passenger 乘客
- be packed with... 挤满了……

语法重点
commuter 作可数名词。

0199 compact [ˈkɑːmpækt]
a 紧密的 n 连镜小粉盒 v 把……紧压在一起（压实）
No one knows why he insisted buying a compact mass of sand from that farmer.
没有人知道他为什么坚持向那位农民买一堆坚实的沙子。
- weak 不牢固的
- no one knows why... 没人知道为什么……

语法重点
compact 作及物动词时，通常用于被动语态。

0200 compass [ˈkʌmpəs] n 指南针，圆规，范围，界限

Why he shut down the store was beyond the compass of our mind.
我们想不通他为什么关闭那个商店。
- calliper 圆规
- be beyond the compass of... 超出……范围

语法重点
compass 指"圆规"时，通常用复数形式。

0201 compassion [kəmˈpæʃn] n 怜悯

The owner of the hotel took compassion on her suffering and offered a room for her.
那位旅馆主人同情她的遭遇，为她提供房间。
- sympathy 同情
- take compassion on... 同情……

语法重点
compassion 作不可数名词，通常与介词 on 连用。

0202 compassionate [kəmˈpæʃənət] a 怜悯的

The old man was offered some food for free on compassionate grounds.
基于值得同情的理由，那位老人得到了些免费的食物。
- kind 和善的
- compassionate release 保外就医

0203 compel [kəmˈpel] v 迫使

We were compelled to change the price under the circumstances.
在这种情况下，我们不得不改变价格。
- force 强迫
- compelling admiration 令人折服
- be compelled to... 被迫……

语法重点
compel 的过去式和过去分词形式为 compelled，compelled。
⊃ circumstance (P. 408)

0204 compliment [ˈkɑːmplɪmənt]
n 恭维，问候，道贺 v 恭维

Your accompanying me to go shopping is a great compliment.
你能陪我去购物，我真是太荣幸了。
- praise 称赞
- insult 侮辱
- compliment on... 称赞某人
- ... be a great compliment ……很荣幸

语法重点
compliment 表示"问候"时，常用作复数形式。

0205 compound [ˈkɒmpaʊnd] / [kəmˈpaʊnd]
n 合成物 v 组合

She wants to buy some salt which is a compound of sodium and chlorine.
她想买钠和氯的化合物——食盐。
- organic compound 有机化合物
- be a compound of... 是……的混合物

⊃ sodium (P. 780)

0206 comprehend [ˌkɑːmprɪˈhend] v 理解，包含，由……组成

We cannot comprehend why he bought so much paper.
我们无法理解他为什么买这么多纸。
- understand 理解

语法重点
comprehend 作及物动词，通常用于否定句中。

0207 comprehension [ˌkɑːmprɪˈhenʃn] **n** 理解力，领悟

The salesgirl had no comprehension of what the old man wanted to buy.
那位女店员不明白那位老人想买什么。

- understanding 理解　　- reading comprehension 阅读理解，阅读测验；life comprehension 人生领悟
- have no comprehension of... 不明白……

语法重点
comprehension 作不可数名词，表示"理解（力）"；作可数名词，表示"理解力练习"。

0208 compromise [ˈkɑːmprəmaɪz]
n 妥协，和解　**v** 妥协处理，危害

The intermediary tried to get the seller and the buyer to reach a compromise.
那位调停者试图让买卖双方和解。

- make a compromise 妥协　　- get... to reach a compromise 让……和解

语法重点
例句中 get 后面的宾语是两个或者两个以上的人。

0209 compute [kəmˈpjuːt] **v** 计算，估计，估算

The shopkeeper computed his losses in the fire at three thousand dollars.
那位店主估算，火灾造成的损失可达 3 000 美元。

- figure 计算　　- beyond compute 不可计量　　- compute... at... 估计……可达……

0210 computerize [kəmˈpjuːtəraɪz]
v 使电脑化，引进电脑设备

There is a possibility of the factory's being fully computerized.
那家工厂实现全电脑化是有可能的。

- cybernate 使电脑化，使电脑化

- possibility (P. 207)

0211 comrade [ˈkɑːmræd] **n** 同事，亲密的同伴

He stood quietly seeing his army comrade work as a bodyguard, unable to comprehend.
他静静地站着，看着自己的战友当了保镖，实在无法理解。

- mates 伙伴　　- opponent 敌人　　- ..., unable to comprehend 无法理解……

- comprehend (P. 545)

0212 conceal [kənˈsiːl] **v** 隐藏

The salesman tried his best to conceal his unemployment from his family.
那位推销员尽力隐瞒，不让家人知道他已经失业了。

- hide 隐藏　　- reveal 透露　　- conceal... from... 对……隐瞒……

语法重点
conceal 的名词为 concealment，为不可数名词。

0213 conceive [kənˈsiːv] **v** 构想

We cannot conceive why he likes going to that store.
我们想不透他为什么喜欢去那家商店。

- design 构思　　- conceive of 设想

comprehension ~ console

0214 condemn [kən'dem] v 谴责，指责，判刑

The oil produced by the factory has been condemned as unfit for human consumption.
这家工厂生产的油已被宣布不适合人们食用。
- denounce 谴责
- excuse 原谅
- be condemned to 被宣告

0215 conduct [kən'dʌkt] / ['kɒndʌkt] v 指导 n 引导

The foreigner asked an attendant of the hotel to conduct him to the door.
那位外国人要饭店的一位侍者领他去门口。
- conduct disorders 品行障碍
- conduct sb. to... 领某人到……

语法重点
conduct 的名词为 conduction。

0216 confession [kən'feʃn] n 承认

The young man made a full confession of his pilferage in the jewelry store.
对于在珠宝店行窃一事，那个年轻人供认不讳。
- derecognition 不承认
- make a full confession of... 对……供认不讳

0217 confront [kən'frʌnt] v 遭遇，面临，使对质

When confronted with the evidence of his pilferage in the store, the guy had to confess.
面对在商店行窃的证据，那人只得承认。
- face 正视
- avoid 避开
- confront with 使面临

confess (P. 412)

0218 consent [kən'sent] n 同意，赞成 v 同意

They finally consented to sell these shirts at a 10% discount.
他们最终同意，以九折出售这些衬衫。
- agreement 同意
- disagreement 反对
- consent to do 同意做……

discount (P. 284)

0219 conserve [kən'sɜːv] v 保存 n 蜜饯

We expect there to be a good way to conserve these strawberries.
我们期望，有好的办法来保存这些草莓。
- preserve 保存
- we expect there to be... 我们期望有……

0220 considerate [kən'sɪdərət] a 体谅的

It is considerate of you to bring me a doggie bag.
你真是太体贴了，帮我拿了打包袋。
- thoughtful 深思的
- it is considerate of... to... ……真是体贴……
- doggy bag 表示"餐厅中所用的打包袋"，也可用 doggie bag。

0221 console [kən'səʊl] v 安慰 n 操纵台

Nothing could console the old man whose purse was lost in the grocery store.
那位老人的钱包在杂货店中遗失时，什么都无法使他感到安慰。
- comfort 安慰，慰藉
- afflict 折磨
- game console 游戏机

grocery (P. 302)

549

0222 **constitutional** [ˌkɑːnstəˈtuːʃənl] a 宪法的，体质上的
The shopkeeper consoles himself with the thought that the new law is not constitutional.
那位店主聊以自慰地想，这项新法规不符合宪法。
⊙ essential 本质的　⊗ autocratic 独裁的，专制的，专横的

> **语法重点**
> constitutional 的名词形式为 constitutionalism，作不可数名词。
> ⊙ console (P. 549)

0223 **contagious** [kənˈteɪdʒəs] a 传染的，有感染力的
Customers pay the salesgirl a very charming compliment on her contagious smile.
那位女店员的微笑富于感染力，顾客都极为赞赏。
⊙ epidemic 流行的，传染性的　⊙ contagious disease 传染病

0224 **contaminate** [kənˈtæmɪneɪt] v 污染，玷污
Those salesmen always try to contaminate our minds with those lengthy speeches.
那些推销员总是试图用冗长的讲话来污染我们的思想。
⊙ dirty 弄脏　⊗ cleanse 洗净

0225 **contemplate** [ˈkɑːntəmpleɪt] v 凝视，沉思默想
The man contemplated what his wife would say if he bought that theater.
那人在想，如果他买下那家剧院，妻子会怎么说。
⊙ too dreadful to contemplate 不堪设想

> **语法重点**
> contemplate 作及物动词，通常是指长时间的思考，含有不确定的实际目的。

0226 **contemporary** [kənˈtempəreri] a 当代的，同时代的
The man in the shop is contemporary with me.
在商店里的那个人跟我是同时代的。
⊙ cotemporary 同时代的　⊙ be contemporary with... 与……同时代

> **语法重点**
> contemporary 作形容词，通常与介词 with 连用，也可当可数名词，表示"同时期的人"。

0227 **contempt** [kənˈtempt] n 轻蔑
The businessman treats the small hotel with contempt it deserves.
那位商人对这家小旅馆理所当然地嗤之以鼻。
⊙ despite 轻视　⊗ esteem 尊敬　⊙ hold in contempt 轻视

> **语法重点**
> contempt 作不可数名词，通常与介词 for 连用。
> ⊙ deserve (P. 425)

0228 **contend** [kənˈtend] v 争夺，竞争，声称
I would contend that we should try to make both ends meet.
我认为，我们应该尽力使收支相抵。
⊙ contend with... 与……斗争　⊙ I would contend that... 我认为……

> **语法重点**
> contend 作不及物动词，通常用作 contend with / against 或 contend for，表示"主张"，通常不用于被动语态。

0229 **continental** [ˌkɑːntɪˈnentl] a 大陆的，欧洲大陆的
The Englishman gave his consent for a continental lifestyle.
那个英国人同意采用大陆式的生活方式。
⊙ mainland 大陆的，本土的　⊙ give one's consent for... 同意……

constitutional ~ correspondence

0230 continuity [ˌkɑːntəˈnuːəti] n 连续性，继续，衔接

The middle-aged salesman's words lack continuity, always jumping from one subject to another.

那位中年推销员说话缺乏连贯性，总是东拉西扯。

- interruption 中断

> 语法重点
> continuity 作不可数名词。
> subject (P. 230)

0231 convert [kənˈvɜːrt] v 变换，使改变

The house was converted from a storage room to a shop.

那个房子由储物间改为了商店。

- transform 使……变形
- sustain 保持
- convert into... 使转变
- convert 指的是进行局部或是全体改造，使之具有新功能、新用途。

0232 convict [kənˈvɪkt] / [ˈkɔnvɪkt] v 证明谁有罪 n 囚犯

There is not enough evidence to convict him of theft in the supermarket.

没有足够的证据证明他在这家超市行窃。

- culprit 罪犯
- convict of 宣判有罪

0233 copyright [ˈkɑːpiraɪt] n 版权，著作权

The multinational corporation was sued for breach of copyright.

那家跨国公司因为侵犯版权而受到控告。

- patent 专利权
- copyright reserved 版权所有
- be sued for... 因……而被控告

> 语法重点
> copyright 通常与介词 on 连用，也可以作形容词，表示"获得版权保护的"。

0234 coral [ˈkɔːrəl] n 珊瑚，珊瑚色 a 珊瑚（色）的

I can hardly understand her preference for necklaces made of coral.

我无法理解她对珊瑚项链的偏爱。

> 语法重点
> coral 作不可数名词，表示"珊瑚"；作可数名词，表示"珊瑚虫"。

0235 corporation [ˌkɔːrpəˈreɪʃn] n 公司，企业，社团

The trading corporation's bankruptcy was beyond comprehension.

那家贸易公司的破产令人无法理解。

- transnational corporation 跨国公司
- ... be beyond comprehension ……令人无法理解

> comprehension (P. 548)

0236 correspondence [ˌkɔːrəˈspɑːndəns]

n 符合，对应，通信

There is a close correspondence between the customer's and the salesgirl's words.

那位顾客与女店员的说法十分相似。

- discordance 不一致
- in correspondence with 与……一致，和……保持通信联系

0237 corridor [ˈkɔːrɪdɔːr] n 走廊，通路
She cannot conceive that her purse was lost when walking along the corridor.
她无法相信经过走廊的时候，她的钱包就不见了。
- hallway 走廊
- sb. cannot conceive that... 某人无法相信……

0238 corrupt [kəˈrʌpt] a 堕落的 v 腐蚀，使堕落
She felt nothing but contempt for her husband who bought many expensive gifts for those corrupt officials.
她的丈夫买了很多昂贵的礼物送给那些腐败的官员，她十分鄙视。
- putrescent 腐败的
- corrupt practice 舞弊行为，行贿
- ... feel nothing but contempt for... ……对……鄙视

→ contempt (P. 550)

0239 counsel [ˈkaʊnsl] n 商议，诉讼律师 v 提供建议，劝告
You had better listen to the counsel of your sister and limit your expenditure to what is essential.
你最好听从姐姐的建议，把花费限制在必要的范围内。
- legal counsel 法律顾问，法律指导

【语法重点】
counsel 作不可数名词时，表示"劝告，建议"；作可数名词时，表示"诉讼律师"，单复数形式相同。

0240 counselor [ˈkaʊnsələr] n 顾问，律师，指导老师
At the thought of the high price, the mean counselor doesn't want that suit.
一想到那昂贵的价格，那个吝啬的顾问就不想买那套西装了。
- adviser 顾问
- at the thought of... 一想到……

0241 counterclockwise [ˌkaʊntərˈklɑːkwaɪz] ad 逆时针方向地
The little boy twisted the top of the bottle in a counterclockwise direction.
那个小男孩按照逆时针方向转瓶塞。
- contraclockwise 反时针方向的（地）

→ direction (P. 153)

0242 coupon [ˈkuːpɑːn] n 优惠券，票证
It was just at that moment that the shopkeeper conceived the notion of money-off coupons.
正是在那时候，这位店主想到了优惠券的主意。

0243 courtyard [ˈkɔːrtjɑːrd] n 庭院，院子，天井
Her mother contemplated buying some flowers to decorate the cobbled courtyard.
她妈妈在考虑买些花装点这个铺着鹅卵石的庭院。
- courtyard garden 庭院花园
- contemplate doing... 考虑做……
- contemplate 指长时间思考某事，并不强调确定的实际目的，consider 则是指一时的或是长时间的深入思考。

→ contemplate (P. 550)

0244 cowardly ['kaʊərdli]
a 怯懦的，懦弱的 **ad** 怯懦地，胆怯地

The shopkeeper was condemned as cowardly.
那位店主因胆小怯懦被指责。

- timorous 胆小的 ⊗ bold 胆大的 ≈ be condemned as... 因……而被指责

> **语法重点**
> cowardly 含有一定的贬义。

0245 cozy ['koʊzi]
a 温暖而舒适的，安逸的 **n** 保温罩

At the idea of buying a nice cozy little house, she was quite exciting.
想到要买一套美妙舒适的小屋子，她就很激动。

- comfortable 舒适的 ≈ cozy nest 安乐窝，温馨小窝
- at the idea of... 一想到……

> **语法重点**
> cozy 的比较级形式和最高级形式为 cosier, cosiest。

0246 cracker ['krækər]
n 薄脆饼干，爆竹

Out of compassion for the poor beggar, she bought a box of crackers for him.
出于对那个可怜的乞丐的同情，她买了一盒薄脆饼干给他。

- cookie 饼干 ≈ nut cracker 核桃钳

> ⊙ compassion (P. 547)

0247 crater ['kreɪtər]
n 火山口，弹坑

There appears to be a bomb crater in the small village.
这个小村庄里似乎有个弹坑。

- weld crater 熔池 ≈ there appears to be... ……似乎有……

0248 creak [kriːk]
n 嘎吱声 **v** 发出碾轧声，嘎吱作响

With the creak of the door, a little child entered the small store.
随着门的嘎吱声，一个小孩子走进了这家小商店。

> **语法重点**
> creak 和 creaking 都可以表示"嘎吱声"，前者是可数名词，后者作可数名词或不可数名词。

0249 creek [kriːk]
n 小河，小溪，克里克人

If we could not find a good way to sell these fruits, we would be up the creek.
如果我们不能找到办法出售这些水果，我们将会陷入困境。

0250 crib [krɪb]
n 粮仓，婴儿床 **v** 偷窃，限制，欺骗

It's hardly conceivable to her that the couple even could not afford the crib.
她几乎无法相信，那对夫妇连婴儿床都买不起。

- plagiarize 剽窃 ≈ it's hardly conceivable to sb. that... 某人几乎无法相信……

0251 crocodile ['krɑːkədaɪl]
n 鳄鱼，鳄鱼皮革

The shopkeeper shed crocodile tears when he drove away that poor beggar.
驱赶那个可怜的乞丐离开时，那位店主假装哭泣。

- crocodile tears 假装哭泣，假慈悲

0252 **crossing** [ˈkrɔːsɪŋ] **n** 十字路口
The old man who was knocked down by a car at the crossing aroused the rich man's compassion.
在十字路口被车撞倒的那位老人，引起了有钱男子的同情。
㊀ crossway 十字路口　㊀ zebra crossing 斑马线
㊀ ... arouse one's compassion ……引起某人的同情

0253 **crouch** [kraʊtʃ] **n** 屈膝　**v** 屈膝，蹲伏，卑躬屈膝
I have no idea why the girl suddenly drops down into a crouch.
我不知道那个女孩为什么突然蹲了下去。
㊀ squat 蹲坐　㊀ stand 站立
㊀ crouch down 蹲下，趴下　㊀ ... drop down into a crouch... ……蹲下……

语法重点
crouch 作不及物动词，表示"蹲伏"，通常后接介词 in, behind, beside 等构成的表示地点的短语。
㊀ drop (P.157)

0254 **crunch** [krʌntʃ] **v** 嘎吱作响地咬嚼　**n** 咬嚼声；紧要关头，危机
If it comes to the crunch, you can take the emergency exit in the mall.
关键的时候，你可以走购物中心的紧急通道。
㊀ credit crunch 信贷紧缩，信贷危机

0255 **crystal** [ˈkrɪstl] **n** 水晶，结晶体，晶粒
She hopes to hear compliment on the crystal necklace she bought yesterday.
她希望听到别人赞美她昨天买的水晶项链。
㊀ quartz 水晶　㊀ crystal clear 清澈透明的
㊀ hear compliment on... 听到……赞美

语法重点
crystal 作不可数名词，表示"水晶，精致玻璃制品"；作可数名词，表示"水晶石，化学结晶体"。
㊀ compliment (P. 547)

0256 **cuisine** [kwɪˈziːn] **n** 烹调，菜肴
They were disappointed at there being no restaurant with excellent cuisine.
这里没有什么菜肴精致的餐厅，他们感到失望。
㊀ cuisine 源自法语，为外来词。

0257 **curb** [kɜːrb] **v** 约束，制止　**n** 限制，马衔索
You must put a curb on your spending.
你必须限制开支。
㊀ inhibit 抑制，禁止　㊀ allow 允许
㊀ curb inflation 抑制通货膨胀　㊀ put a curb on... 限制……

0258 **currency** [ˈkɜːrənsi] **n** 货币，通用，流通
If you contemplate a visit to a foreign country, you should prepare some cash in local currency.
如果你想去国外旅游，要准备些当地货币。
㊀ money 钱，货币　㊀ currency exchange 货币兑换，外汇兑换

语法重点
currency 作可数名词或不可数名词，表示"货币，通货"；作不可数名词，表示"流通，通用"。

0259 curriculum [kəˈrɪkjələm] n 课程，全部课程

She can understand the French guest because French was on the curriculum in college.
她上大学的时候有法语课，所以她可以听懂那个法国客人的话。
- curriculum schedule 课程表
- ... be on / in the curriculum ……有……课程

语法重点
curriculum 是可数名词，其复数形式为 curriculums 或是 curricula。

0260 curry [ˈkɜːri] n 咖喱 v 制作咖喱料理

You really don't have to curry favor with those wealthy guests.
你真的不必讨好那些富有的客人。
- ... curry favor with... ……拍……马屁

语法重点
curry 的过去式和过去分词形式为 curried, curried。
- wealthy (P. 383)

0261 customs [ˈkʌstəmz] n 关税，海关

As for those articles for exportation, you have to pay customs on them.
对于那些出口商品，你要缴纳关税。
- tariff 关税
- customs entry 进口报关
- pay customs on... 为……缴纳关税

语法重点
customs 作复数名词，表示"海关"，也可以用作 the Customs。

0262 dart [dɑːrt] n 镖枪，飞奔 v 猛冲，飞奔

The shopkeeper rang off and made a dart for the storage room.
那位店主挂断电话，冲向储物间。
- pitch 投，掷
- make a dart for... 冲向……

语法重点
dart 作可数名词，表示"飞镖，飞奔，猛冲（通常用作单数形式）"；darts 作复数形式，单数意义，表示"掷镖游戏"。

0263 dazzle [ˈdæzl]

v 使眼花，使倾倒 n 耀眼的光，令人赞叹的东西

The little girl was dazzled by the colorful lights in the mall.
购物中心里的彩灯照得那个小女孩目眩。
- flash 闪光
- glare dazzle 眩光
- be dazzled by... 因……而目眩

语法重点
dazzle 作及物动词，通常用于被动语态。

0264 decay [dɪˈkeɪ] v 腐坏，衰败 n 腐烂

She bought many sweets in complete contempt of danger of tooth decay.
她买了很多糖果，完全不顾蛀牙的危害。
- rot 腐烂
- fall into decay 损坏，腐烂，衰败

0265 deceive [dɪˈsiːv] v 欺骗，蒙蔽，行骗

The old man was deceived into believing that the drug can cure his disease.
那位老人受骗了，他以为这种药可以治愈他的疾病。
- trick 欺骗，哄骗
- undeceive 不受欺骗

- disease (P. 285)

deceive ourselves 自欺欺人　be deceived into doing... 信以为真……

0266 declaration [ˌdekləˈreɪʃn] n 宣告，声明，宣言

At the bare idea of the declaration of income, the manager was deeply upset.
一想到收益申报表，那位经理极为沮丧。
announcement 公告，宣言　final declaration 最后声明

income (P. 183)

0267 delegate [ˈdelɪɡət] / [ˈdelɪɡeɪt] n 代表 v 委派……为代表

She was delegated to be in charge of the sales department.
她被委派监管销售部。
deputy 代表　chief delegate 首席代表　be delegated to do... 被委派做……

0268 delegation [ˌdelɪˈɡeɪʃn] n 委任

The delegation worked out a compromise agreement and decided to stay at the hotel for three days.
代表团制定出妥协方案，他们决定在这家旅馆停留三日。
delegation of authority 授权
... work out a compromise agreement ……制订出妥协方案……

语法重点
delegation 表示"代表团"时，是集合名词。
compromise (P. 548)

0269 democrat [ˈdeməkræt] n 民主主义者，民主人士

The democrat contributed five thousand dollars to a charity collection.
那位民主人士向慈善事业捐赠 5 000 美元。
contribute... to a charity collection 向慈善事业捐赠……

语法重点
Democrat 可作专有名词，表示"美国民主党成员、拥护者"，其缩写形式为 D 或是 Dem.。

0270 denial [dɪˈnaɪəl] n 否定，拒绝

The shopkeeper's repeated denial of the promised discount drove her out of her mind.
那位店主一再否认曾经诺过的折扣，这使得她失去了理智。
rejection 拒绝　affirmation 证实
... drive... out of one's mind 使……失去了理智

语法重点
denial 通常与介词 of 连用。

0271 descriptive [dɪˈskrɪptɪv] a 描写的，描述的，分类的

The owner of the restaurant was filled with compassion by the beggar's descriptive account of his suffering.
那个乞丐对其遭遇的描述，使得那位餐厅老板充满同情。
depictive 描写的，描述的　be filled with compassion... 充满同情……

语法重点
descriptive 的比较级和最高级形式为 more descriptive, most descriptive。
compassion (P. 547)

0272 despair [dɪˈspeər] n 绝望

The sale of those shoes has been the despair of the sales manager.
在那位销售经理看来，出售那些鞋子是毫无希望的。
hopelessness 绝望　in despair 在绝望中
be the despair of... 使……放弃希望

declaration ~ disbelief

0273 despise [dɪˈspaɪz] v 鄙视，看不起
The salesman was often despised for his meanness.
那位推销员总是因为吝啬而受人鄙视。
- slight 轻视　● despise reputation 浮名虚利
- be despised for... 因……而受人鄙视

0274 destination [ˌdestɪˈneɪʃn] n 目的地，终点，目标
Those travelers failed to comprehend the seriousness of the choice of their destination.
那些旅行者没有理解目的地选择的重要性。
- goal 目标　● start 起点　● ultimate destination 最终目的地
- destination 作可数名词，通常用作 arrive at / reach one's destination，也可表示"邮件、货物的投递处，收件人地址"。

0275 destiny [ˈdestəni] n 命运，定数，天命
Maybe it's her destiny to work as a sales assistant.
也许当个销售助理是她的命运。
- fate 命运　● ... it's one's destiny to... ……是……的命运

▷ assistant (P. 126)

0276 destructive [dɪˈstrʌktɪv] a 破坏的，否定的
The destructive fire drove the owner of the grocery store to despair.
那场毁灭性的大火使这位杂货店主陷入了绝望。
- harmful 破坏的，毁灭性的　● affirmative 肯定的
- drive... to despair 使……绝望

0277 devotion [dɪˈvoʊʃn] n 奉献，信仰，热爱
Being a solider requires a good comprehension of devotion to duty.
作为军人，要充分理解忠于职守的意义。

▷ require (P. 215)

0278 devour [dɪˈvaʊər] v 吞食，毁灭，全神贯注地看
Flames devoured a huge area of the buildings in the commercial district.
火焰吞没了商业区的大片建筑物。

▷ 语法重点
devour 是及物动词。

0279 dialect [ˈdaɪəlekt] n 方言，土语，地方话
There ought not to be dialect for the shopping guide in the mall.
这家购物中心不允许导购说方言。
- local dialect 地区方言　● there ought not to be... ……不应该有……

0280 disbelief [ˌdɪsbɪˈliːf] n 不信，怀疑
The shopkeeper darted a look of disbelief at that guy.
这位店主不相信地瞥了那个男人一眼。
- suspicion 怀疑　● belief 相信　● in disbelief 怀疑地，不相信

557

0281 **discard** [dɪsˈkɑːd] / [dɪsˈkɑːrd] v / n 抛弃，遗弃

The clerk had to discard all thought of buying fashionable clothes.
那个职员不得不放弃买时装的想法。
- desert 遗弃　　- preservation 保存
- into the discard 成为无用之物　　- discard all thought of... 放弃……想法

语法重点
discard 是及物动词。
- fashionable (P. 295)

0282 **disciple** [dɪˈsaɪpl] n 信徒，追随者

The customer there is an ardent disciple of Gandhi.
那边那个顾客是甘地的忠实信徒。
- protégé 门徒　　- be an ardent disciple of... 是……的忠实追随者

0283 **discriminate** [dɪˈskrɪmɪneɪt] v 歧视，区别，辨出

High-quality discriminated the cars produced by the factory from others of the same kind.
品质优异使得这家工厂生产的汽车与同类的其他车辆明显不同。
- distinguish 区别　　- discriminate between 区别
- discriminate... from... 使……与……区分开

0284 **dispense** [dɪˈspens] v 分送，实施，免除

He could dispense with the medicine, so you needn't buy for him.
他不必再吃这款药，所以你不需要给他买了。
- allot 分配　　- withhold 扣留　　- ... dispense with... ……用不着 / 摆脱……

语法重点
dispense 作及物动词，表示"分配"，通常用作 dispense... to...；作不及物动词，表示"免除"，与介词 with 连用。

0285 **dispose** [dɪˈspoʊz] v 配置，丢掉，销毁

There is no choice but to dispose of the furniture at a low price.
别无选择，只得低价出售这些家具。
- discard 丢弃　　- reserve 保留　　- dispose of 处理

0286 **distinction** [dɪˈstɪŋkʃn] n 区别，不同

The salesman drew a distinction between the rich and the poor in the area.
那位推销员对这个地区的富人和穷人加以区别。
- differentiation 区别　　- likeness 类似
- ... draw a distinction between... and... ……在……之间加以区别

0287 **distinctive** [dɪˈstɪŋktɪv] a 区别的，有特色的

Excellent cuisine should be distinctive of the restaurant.
菜肴精致应该是这家餐厅的特色。
- individual 个别的，独特的　　- be distinctive of... 是……的特色

- cuisine (P. 554)

discard ～ downward(s)

0288 distress [dɪ'stres] **n** 忧虑，悲伤，不幸

The loss caused in the robbery was a great *distress* to the shopkeeper.

在此次抢劫中所遭受的损失使那位店主极为难过。

- grief 悲痛
- distress warrant 扣押令
- ... be a great distress to... ……使……极为难过

0289 document ['dɑːkjumənt] **n** 文件，证件，文档

She typed a shopping list on the computer, but she forgot to save the *document*.

她在电脑上列了一张购物清单，却忘记了存档。

- paper 公文，文件
- document management 文件管理，资料管理
- ... save the document ……保存文档

> 语法重点
> document 是可数名词。

0290 doorstep ['dɔːrstep] **n** 台阶 **v** 上门访问

Seeing a group of foreigners turning up on the *doorstep*, the man was extremely excited.

看到一群外国人出现在门口，那位男人极为兴奋。

- camp upon / on one's doorstep 经常在某人门口纠缠

> 语法重点
> doorstep 作可数名词，其同义词还有 doorsill, doorway, threshold 等。

0291 doorway ['dɔːrweɪ] **n** 门口，门道

The owner of the restaurant darted an angry look at the beggar standing in the *doorway*.

那位餐厅老板狠狠地看了站在门口的那个乞丐一眼。

- threshold 门槛，入口
- ... dart an angry look at... ……狠狠地瞥了一眼……

0292 dough [doʊ] **n** 生面团，钱

He saw the baker knead the *dough* on a floured board and then leave it to rise.

他看到那位面包师在沾满面粉的案板上揉面团，然后等它发酵。

- big dough 巨款
- knead the dough on... 在……上揉面团
- dough 作不可数名词，本意是表示"制作面包、糕点等用的生面团"，用于俚语中，也可以表示"钱，现金"。

◎ rise (P. 082)

0293 downward ['daʊnwərd] **a** 向下的 **ad** 向下地

There is said to be a *downward* trend in price.

据说，价格出现下滑的趋势。

- upward 向上
- downward trend 向下趋势，下跌趋势

> 语法重点
> downward 用作副词，相当于 downwards。
> ◎ trend (P. 377)

0294 downward(s) ['daʊnwərd(z)] **ad** 向下，往下，以后

She was forced to sell the jade bracelet which was handed *downwards* from generation to generation.

她被迫出售那个世代相传的玉镯。

- downwards arrow 步步紧逼

559

0295 **drape** [dreɪp] v 垂挂，装饰，遮盖
The little girl draped her arms round her mother's neck and asked her to buy that doll.
那个女孩伸着手臂抱着妈妈的脖子，要她买那个洋娃娃。
同 hang 悬挂 片 drape one's arms round... 伸着手臂抱着……

0296 **dreadful** ['dredfl] a 可怕的
There might be a dreadful mistake; it was not she who bought that bracelet.
也许是大错特错了，她并没有买那个手镯。
同 fearful 可怕的 反 informidable 不可怕的 片 there might be... 也许有……

参 bracelet (P. 403)

0297 **dresser** ['dresər] n 梳妆台，外科手术助手
There is likely to be a downward trend in the price of the dresser.
这个梳妆台可能会降价。
片 there is likely to be... 可能会……

0298 **dressing** ['dresɪŋ] n 穿衣，调味料 v 穿着，装饰
There is nothing for it but to replace curry powder with salad dressing.
别无他法，只得用沙拉调味料来代替咖喱粉。
同 clothing 给……穿衣 反 strip 脱去衣服 片 dressing station 救护站

参 powder (P. 341)

0299 **driveway** ['draɪvweɪ] n 汽车道
We want there to be no snow on the driveway tomorrow so that we can go shopping.
我们希望明天车道上不会有积雪，那么我们就可以购物了。

0300 **duration** [du'reɪʃn] n 持续，持续的时间
They signed a sales contract of two years' duration with that clothing store.
他们与那家服装店签订了为期两年的销售合约。
同 continuance 持续，停留 反 interrupt 中断 片 for the duration 在整段时间内

语法重点
duration 作不可数名词，通常与介词 of 或是 for 构成短语。

0301 **dusk** [dʌsk] n 黄昏 a 微暗的 v 变暗
As dusk falls, she finally comes out of the jewelry store.
黄昏来临时，她终于从那家珠宝店走了出来。
同 dark 黑暗，夜，黄昏 反 dawn 黎明 片 as dusk falls... 黄昏来临时……

0302 **dwarf** [dwɔːrf] n 矮子 v 使受阻碍，使相形见绌
At the bare thought of *Snow White and the Seven Dwarves*, the schoolgirl went into that bookstore.
一想起《白雪公主和七个小矮人》，那个女学生就走进了那家书店。
同 mannikin 侏儒 反 giant 巨人 片 at the bare thought of... 一想起……

语法重点
dwarf 作可数名词，其复数形式为 dwarfs 或是 dwarves。

drape ～ embrace

0303 dwell [dwel] **v** 居住，思索，踌躇
There is no guessing what the salesman dwells on.
猜不到那位推销员在想些什么。
- ponder 沉思，考虑
- dwell upon 详述，细想

【语法重点】
dwell 作不及物动词时，常与介词 on, upon 连用。

0304 dwelling ['dwelɪŋ] **n** 住处，处所，居住
The clerk who lives in a portable dwelling dreamed of there being enough money to buy an apartment.
那个职员住在活动房屋中，他梦想能有足够的钱买一处公寓。
- shelter 住所
- dwelling narrowness 蜗居
- dream of there being... 梦想着有……

【语法重点】
dwelling 作不可数名词，表示"居住"；作可数名词，表示"住宅，寓所"。
- portable (P. 486)

0305 eclipse [ɪ'klɪps] **v** 被遮蔽
The brand of laptops remained in eclipse during the past ten years.
在过去的十年中，这种品牌的笔记本电脑默默无名。
- brighten 使明亮
- suffer an eclipse 黯然失色

0306 eel [iːl] **n** 鳗鱼，精明油滑的人
Delicious jellied eels of the restaurant dwelt in his mind.
这家餐馆鲜美的鳗鱼冻停留在他的记忆里。
- slippery as an eel 非常狡猾
- ... dwell in one's mind ……留在某人的记忆中

【语法重点】
dwell 作不及物动词，其过去式为 dwelt 或 dwelled。

0307 ego ['iːɡoʊ] **n** 自我，自己，自尊
Being unable to buy an apartment made quite a dent in the young man's ego.
买不起公寓，这大大地打击了那个年轻人的自尊。

【语法重点】
ego 的复数形式为 egos。
- apartment (P. 124)

0308 elaborate [ɪ'læbərət] / [ɪ'læbəret]
a 精心制作的 **v** 精心制作
There is nothing more exciting than an elaborate meal.
没有什么比一顿精心制作的餐点更振奋人心的了。
- elaborate on 详细说明
- there is nothing more... than... 没有比……更……的了

0309 elevate ['elɪveɪt] **v** 举起，提高，改善
The teacher bought many books, hoping to elevate the minds of her students.
那位教师买了很多书，他希望提高学生的素养。
- promote 提升
- lower 降低
- elevate the minds of... 提高……的素养

【语法重点】
elevate 作及物动词，通常用作 elevate... to...。

0310 embrace [ɪm'breɪs] **v** 拥抱，包括 **n** 拥抱
Seeing his girlfriend in the mall, he went over and held her in a warm embrace.
在购物中心看到女朋友，他走过去并热情地拥抱了她。

561

0311 endeavor [ɪn'devə] v. / n. 努力，尽力

Please make every endeavor to sell these bananas.
请尽力出售这些香蕉。
- endeavor in 致力于
- make every endeavor to... 尽力……

0312 enroll [ɪn'roʊl] v. 登记，招收，入学

The couple wanted to enroll their child in an elite school at any cost.
这对夫妇希望让孩子进入精英学校，他们为此不惜一切代价。
- register 登记，注册
- enroll in 参加
- ... do sth. ... at any cost ……不惜一切代价做某事

⊃ elite (P. 713)

0313 ensure [ɪn'ʃʊr] v. 保证

She went to buy some sleeping pills to ensure herself a good night's sleep.
为了确保自己能睡个好觉，她去买了些安眠药。
- guarantee 保证
- ensure public security 保安

⊃ pill (P. 337)

0314 enterprise ['entərpraɪz] n. 企业，计划，事业心

The trading company has become one of the most successful enterprises of its kind.
这家贸易公司已经成为同类企业中的佼佼者。
- enterprise management 企业管理
- become... of its kind 成为……同类中……

0315 enthusiastic [ɪn,θuːzi'æstɪk] a. 热心的，热情的，狂热的

The lady seems to be quite enthusiastic about buying fashionable clothes.
那位女士似乎极为热衷于购买时髦衣物。
- keen 热情的
- be enthusiastic about doing... 热衷于……

语法重点
enthusiastic 的比较级和最高级形式为 more enthusiastic, most enthusiastic，其副词形式为 enthusiastically。

0316 entitle [ɪn'taɪtl] v. 为书取名，给……权力（或资格）

The bearer of the coupon shall be entitled to a thirty percent savings.
这张优惠券的持有人可以享受 30% 的优惠。
- entitle to 给某人……的权利或资格
- ... be entitled to a... percent savings ……可以享受……优惠

语法重点
entitle 作及物动词，通常用于被动语态。

0317 equate [i'kweɪt] v. 使相等，相当于，等同

There is a tendency in youths to equate the luxurious lifestyle to happiness.
年轻人似乎倾向把奢侈的生活等同于幸福。
- equate... to / with 相当
- there is a tendency in... to do sth. ……中有……趋势

0318 erect [ɪ'rekt] a 直立的 v 竖立，建立

Why they decided to spend two thousand dollars erecting a statue in the square was beyond our comprehension.
他们为什么决定花 2 000 美元在广场上修建雕像，这让我们无法理解。
- construct 建造
- erect up 建立，竖起
- ... be beyond one's comprehension ……无法理解

0319 erupt [ɪ'rʌpt] v 喷出，突然发生，出疹

When her husband noticed the size of the bill, he erupted with anger.
看到巨额账单时，她的丈夫勃然大怒。
- burst 爆发
- erupt into 突然变成
- ... erupt with anger ……勃然大怒

> **语法重点**
> erupt with anger 中的介词 with 也可以替换为 in。

0320 escort ['eskɔːrt] n 护卫者 v 护送，陪伴

The lady went to the trade fair under the escort of two bodyguards.
在两名保镖的陪同下，那位夫人去了商品展览会。
- escort vessel 保镖
- do sth. under the escort of... 在……的陪同下做某事
- "陪某人回家"可以用 escort sb. home 来表示。

0321 estate [ɪ'steɪt] n 地产

He was most distressed to realize that he cannot buy an estate for his daughter.
意识到自己无力为女儿购置房产，他十分难过。
- real estate market 房地产市场
- be most distressed to... 对……十分难过

> distress (P. 559)

0322 esteem [ɪ'stiːm] n 尊重 v 尊敬，考虑，估计

The old man who bought many foods to these poor children was held in great esteem.
那位老人为这些可怜的孩子买了很多食物，人们都非常尊敬他。
- respect 尊敬
- scorn 藐视
- self esteem 自我尊重，自尊
- ... be held in great / high esteem... ……极为尊敬……

> **语法重点**
> esteem 作及物动词，通常不用于进行时态。

0323 eternal [ɪ'tɜːrnl] a 永恒的，永久的，无休止的

Her husband condemned her for her eternal chatter about shopping.
她的丈夫指责她喋喋不休地谈论购物。
- perpetual 永久的
- temporary 暂时的
- eternal life 永生，来世
- condemn sb. for... 为……指责某人

> **语法重点**
> eternal 作形容词，没有比较级和最高级形式。
>
> condemn (P. 549)

0324 ethics ['eθɪk] n 伦理学，道德规范，行为准则

The business ethics seems to be on the downward path.
商业道德似乎是在走下坡路。
- principles 行为准则
- social ethics 社会伦理学

> **语法重点**
> ethics 作复数形式，单数意义，也可以视为不可数名词。作主语时，动词用单数形式。

0325 **evergreen** ['evəgri:n] n 万年青 a 常绿的，永葆青春的

Tom came home in the dusk of the evening with the evergreen shrubs he bought.
黄昏时，汤姆带着他买的常绿灌木回到了家。

- indeciduous 常绿的，不落叶的
- evergreen tree 常青树

↪ shrub (P. 633)

0326 **exaggeration** [ɪg,zædʒə'reɪʃn] n 夸张，夸张的言语

It would be an exaggeration to say that he has never been to the supermarket.
要说他从来都没有去过超市，那是夸张的说法。

- it would be an exaggeration to say that... ……是夸张的说法

语法重点
exaggeration 作可数名词，表示"夸张的言语"；作不可数名词，表示"夸张，夸大"。

0327 **exceed** [ɪk'si:d] v 超过，胜过，超出

It's no exaggeration to say that the price of the desk will not exceed fifty dollars.
毫不夸张地说，这张桌子的价格不会超过50美元。

- surpass 超过
- exceed in 在……方面超过

0328 **excel** [ɪk'sel] v 胜过，优于 n 试算表

Her mother excels at bargaining with street vendors.
她的妈妈擅长与街头小贩讨价还价。

- better 胜过
- excel at / in doing... 擅长……

↪ bargain (P. 400)

0329 **exceptional** [ɪk'sepʃənl] a 例外的

The furniture in the store is only sold at a low price in exceptional circumstances.
只有在特殊情况下，这家商店里的家具才会以低价出售。

- truly exceptional 无与伦比的
- in exceptional circumstances... 在特殊情况下……

0330 **excess** [ɪk'ses] n 超过，过量，过度

The granny complained that she was charged an excess of five dollars over the amount on the bill.
那位老奶奶抱怨说，与账单上的数目相比，她多付了5美元。

- surplus 过剩
- to excess 过度，过分
- be charged an excess of... 多付了……

语法重点
excess 作可数名词，表示"超出的量"；作不可数名词，表示"过火，无节制"。

0331 **exclaim** [ɪk'skleɪm] v 惊叫

He exclaimed that the computer's price was unreasonable.
他叫着说，这台电脑的价格不合理。

- shout 叫喊
- exclaim over 感叹
- exclaim that... 叫喊……

0332 exclude [ɪkˈskluːd] v 把……排除

We cannot exclude the possibility that watermelons may be in excess of demand.
我们不能排除西瓜可能会供过于求的可能性。
- preclude 排除　　- include 包括　　- exclude ambiguity 消除不确定性
- ... exclude the possibility that... ……排除……可能性

0333 execute [ˈeksɪkjuːt] v 实行，处死，处决

The local government will execute a plan to reduce fuel consumption.
当地政府将执行一项计划，来减少燃料消耗。
- execute order 执行命令　　- execute a plan to... 执行计划，以便……
- execute 用于律法中，表示"使生效，实施"。

0334 executive [ɪɡˈzekjətɪv] n 执行者 a 执行的，行政的

The sales executive in the mall possesses excellent executive ability.
这家购物中心的营销主任具有杰出的管理才能。
- governor 主管人员　　- chief executive 董事长
- possess... ability 具有……能力
- "首席执行官，总裁"可以用 chief executive officer 来表示。

> possess (P. 486)

0335 exile [ˈeksaɪl] n 流亡，流亡者 v 流放，放逐

After an exile of eight years, her brother returned home and bought many gifts for the family.
背井离乡八年之后，她哥哥返家并买了很多礼物给家人。
- exile from 使流亡

0336 extension [ɪkˈstenʃn] n 延长，伸展

The young man has got an extension to pay the bill.
那个年轻人获准延期支付账单。
- decrease 减少　　- by extension 相关的　　- get an extension to... 获准延期……

> **语法重点**
> extension 作不可数名词，表示"延长，扩展"；作可数名词，表示"电话分机，延长期"。

0337 extensive [ɪkˈstensɪv] a 广泛的

The owner of the restaurant plans to carry out extensive repair work next month.
那个餐厅老板打算在下个月进行大规模的扩建工程。
- widespread 广泛的　　- extensive use 广泛应用

> **语法重点**
> extensive 的比较级和最高级形式为 more extensive，most extensive，其副词形式为 extensively，名词形式为 extensiveness。
>
> repair (P. 348)

0338 exterior [ɪkˈstɪriər] a 外部的，对外的 n 外貌，外表

The gentle man with a rough exterior bought some food for the beggar.
那个外貌粗犷、性情温和的男人为那个乞丐买了些食物。
- outer 外部的　　- interior 内部的　　- exterior scene 外景

0339 external [ɪk'stɜːrnl] a 外在的，外面的 n 外部，外观

As a supervisor, it's unwise to judge people by externals only.

作为一名主管，以貌取人是不明智的。

- surface 表面的
- external pressure 外部压力
- ... judge people by externals only …… 以貌取人

语法重点
external 作形容词，没有比较级和最高级形式。
↳ supervisor (P. 645)

0340 extinct [ɪk'stɪŋkt] a 已灭绝的，已废弃的

You can rely on there being fine weather tomorrow so that you can pay a visit to the extinct volcano.

你可以指望明天天气好，那么你就可以去看那座死火山了。

- dead 死亡的
- living 活着的
- become extinct 灭绝，绝种
- rely on there being... 指望有……

语法重点
例句中的 volcano（火山），是可数名词。

0341 extraordinary [ɪk'strɔːrdəneri] a 特别的

There could have been a plentiful supply of watermelons but for the extraordinary weather.

要不是这反常的天气，本该有充足的西瓜供应。

- there could have been... 本该有……

0342 eyelash / lash ['aɪlæʃ] / [læʃ] n 睫毛

She fluttered her eyelashes at her husband, hoping he would buy the necklace for her.

她对丈夫眨眼示意，希望丈夫为她买下这串项链。

- eyelash curler 睫毛夹
- flutter one's eyelashes at... 向……眨眼示意

语法重点
eyelash 作可数名词，表示"睫毛"，相当于 lash，通常用作复数形式 eyelashes。

0343 eyelid ['aɪlɪd] n 眼皮

She bought that expensive handbag without batting an eyelid.

她面不改色地买下那个昂贵的手提包。

- not bat an eyelid 没合眼
- do sth. ... without batting an eyelid …… 面不改色做某事
- the upper eyelid 表示"上眼皮"，the lower eyelid 则表示"下眼皮"。

0344 fabric ['fæbrɪk] n 纺织品，织物，组织

The textile fabric's price exceeded all expectations.

那些纺织品的价格超出所有人的预期。

- synthetic fabric 混合纤维
- ... exceed all expectations …… 超出所有人的预期

↳ exceed (P. 564)

0345 fad [fæd] n 一时的流行

There has been a fad for wearing blue shawls these days.

这段时间蓝色的披肩很流行。

- style 时尚
- there has been a fad for... …… 流行

external ~ feminine

0346 Fahrenheit [ˈfærənhaɪt]
a 华氏的，华氏温度计的 **n** 华氏温度计，华氏温标
It has been 102 degrees Fahrenheit for a few days, so the air-conditioners sell well.
这些天气温都是 102 ℉，所以空调很畅销。
● degree Fahrenheit 华氏温度　● sth. sells well 某物很畅销

> **语法重点**
> Fahrenheit 的缩写形式为 F，也可以用作 Fah. 或是 Fahr.。

0347 falter [ˈfɔːltər] **v** 结巴地说 **n** 踌躇，颤抖
The guy showed no sign of faltering when caught stealing in the supermarket.
在超市行窃被抓，那人却毫不畏缩。
● stammer 结巴地讲出　⊘ fluency 流畅，流利
● falter out 口吃地说出　●... show no sign of faltering ……毫不畏缩

0348 fascinate [ˈfæsɪneɪt] **v** 迷住
His daughter seems to be fascinated with the doll in the shop window.
他的女儿似乎被商店橱窗里的玩偶吸引了。
● attract 吸引　● fascinate the eye 看得入迷
●... be fascinated with... ……被……吸引

0349 fatigue [fəˈtiːg] **n** 疲劳，劳累 **v** 使疲乏
The young man has been fatigued with overtime work because he wanted to buy an apartment.
那个年轻人想买一栋公寓，所以总是加班工作而感到疲乏。
● exhaustion 精疲力竭　⊘ spiritedness 有精神
● visual fatigue 视觉疲劳　●... be fatigued with... ……因……而感到疲乏

> **语法重点**
> fatigue 作及物动词，通常用作被动形式。

0350 federal [ˈfedərəl] **a** 联邦的，联盟的
The store had received an order for office appliances from the federal agency.
那家商店收到了那个联邦机构购买办公用品的订单。
● federal government 联邦政府　● receive an order for... 接到……订单
● agency 作可数名词，用于美式英语中，可以表示"政府的特定机构"。

> ● appliance (P. 395)

0351 feeble [ˈfiːbl] **a** 虚弱的，无力的，无效的
She made a feeble attempt to explain the size of the bill.
她徒劳地试图解释那巨额的账单。
● make a feeble attempt to explain... 徒劳地试图解释……

> **语法重点**
> feeble 作形容词，其比较级和最高级形式为 feebler，feeblest。

0352 feminine [ˈfemənɪn] **a** 妇女的，阴性的，娇柔的
Handbags should be quite necessary from a feminine point of view.
从女性立场来看，手提包是十分必要的。

567

0353 fertilizer ['fɜːrtəlaɪzər] n 肥料
There is expected to be no artificial fertilizer anymore.
希望不会再有假肥料。
- compound fertilizer 复合肥料
- there is expected to be... 希望有……

▷ artificial (P. 397)

0354 fiancé / fiancée [ˌfiːɑːnˈseɪ] n 未婚夫/未婚妻
The girl in red dress is my fiancée.
那个穿红色连衣裙的女生是我的未婚妻。

0355 fiber ['faɪbə] n 纤维，光纤
The man of fine fiber bought many books in the bookstore.
那个性情文雅的人在这家书店里买了很多书。
- dietary fiber 膳食纤维，食用纤维

0356 fiddle ['fɪdl] n 小提琴 v 篡改，拨弄
The little boy fiddles about with the alarm clock his father bought for him yesterday.
那个小男孩在胡乱拨弄爸爸昨天给他买的闹钟。
- as fit as a fiddle 精神饱满
- fiddle with... 胡乱拨弄……

▷ alarm (P. 122)

0357 filter ['fɪltər] n 过滤器 v 过滤
It does not take long to filter coffee with this coffee filter her son bought the other day.
用她儿子前几天买的这个咖啡滤纸过滤咖啡，不会费太多时间。
- air filter 空气过滤器
- it does not take long to... ……不会花费太多时间

语法重点
the other day 一般与过去时连用。

0358 fin [fɪn] n 鳍，鱼翅
I'm glad we have come to an agreement about the price; tip me your fin.
很高兴，我们就价格议题达成一致，我们握个手吧。
- rear fin 尾翼
- tip / give... one's fin ……握手

0359 fishery ['fɪʃəri] n 渔业，水产业
They changed their dwelling to engage in inshore fishery.
他们搬家以从事近海渔业。
- aquaculture 水产业
- fishery resources 渔业资源
- ... change one's dwelling ……搬家

语法重点
fishery 作不可数名词，表示"渔业，捕鱼权"；作可数名词，表示"渔场"，通常用作复数形式 fisheries。

▷ dwell (P. 561)

0360 flake [fleɪk] n 小薄片，火星 v 脱落，切成薄片
When he got home, he flaked out in the sofa, since he wandered in the mall the whole day.
他在购物中心逛了一整天，所以回到家就瘫倒在沙发上了。
- spark 火星
- snow flakes 雪花
- flake out... 因筋疲力尽瘫倒或是入睡……

fertilizer ~ foil

0361 flap [flæp] v 拍打 n 飘动，摆动

The little girl was in a flap when she went lost in the supermarket.
在超市中迷路时，那个小女孩忐忑不安。
同 flutter 摆动　反 still 静止　派 be in a flap... 忐忑不安……

> 语法重点
> flap 的过去式为 flapped。

0362 flaw [flɔː] n 瑕疵

His explanation for the contract was full of flaws.
他对于那个合约的解释是漏洞百出的。
同 fault 缺点　反 merit 优点　派 security flaw 安全性漏洞

> 语法重点
> flaw 也可作及物动词，表示"使有缺陷"，通常用于被动语态。

0363 flick [flɪk] v 轻弹，轻拂 n 轻弹，快速的轻打

The cat's tail flicked from side to side, as if it were asking me to buy that ball of wool.
那只猫来回摇着尾巴，似乎是要我买那个毛线团。
派 flick through（快速）翻阅，浏览　派 ... flick from side to side ……来回摇动

> 语法重点
> flick 作及物动词，表示"轻打"，通常用作 flick... with / at；作不及物动词，表示"轻快地摇动"，其过去式为 flicked。

0364 flip [flɪp] n 轻弹，轻抛 a 无礼的 v 快速翻动

When he was told the mobile phone had been sold out after waiting in the line for three hours, he flipped his lid.
排队等了三个小时后，却被告知手机已经售完，他气得发狂。
派 flick 轻弹　派 flip through 匆匆查看　派 flip one's lid 失去自制

> 语法重点
> flip 的过去式和过去分词为 flipped, flipped。

0365 flourish [ˈflɜːrɪʃ] v 繁盛，兴旺

To my knowledge, this species of flower you bought flourishes in a cool climate.
据我所知，你买的那种花在凉爽的气候中会茁壮生长。
同 prosper 繁荣　反 decline 衰落
派 in full flourish 在全盛时，盛极一时　派 to one's knowledge... 就……所知

0366 fluency [ˈfluːənsi] n 流畅

The salesgirl built up a fluency in spoken English after working here for three years.
在这里工作三年之后，那位女店员练就了流利的英语口语。
同 volubility 流利　反 disfluency 不流利　派 build up a fluency in... 练就流利的……

> 语法重点
> build up a fluency in 后面一般接表示语言的名词。

0367 foe [foʊ] n 敌人，危害物，反对者

She met her bitter foe who had no fiber in the mall.
她在购物中心遇到那个缺乏人格的死敌。
同 enemy 敌人　反 friend 朋友　派 sworn foe 不共戴天的敌人

> 派 fiber (P. 568)

0368 foil [fɔɪl] n 金属薄片，箔纸 v 挫败

The deceiver was foiled in his attempt to rip us off.
那个骗子企图骗我们的钱，却没有成功。
派 conductive foil 导电箔　派 be foiled in one's attempt to... 企图……却没有成功

> 语法重点
> foil 作及物动词，通常用于被动语态。

0369 **folklore** [ˈfoʊklɔːr] n 民间传说，民间传统
The storybook she bought was adapted from a French folklore.
她买的那本故事书是根据法国民间传说改写的。
- Chinese folklore 中国寓言   - be adapted from... 由……改写

› adapt (P. 391)

0370 **forgetful** [fərˈgetfl] a 健忘的，疏忽的
In order to work out the marketing plan, the manager was always forgetful of his sleep and meals.
为了制订营销计划，那位经理总是废寝忘食。
- ... be forgetful of one's sleep and meals ……废寝忘食

语法重点
forgetful 的词根是 forget。

0371 **format** [ˈfɔːrmæt] n 格式 v 使格式化，安排……的格局
The novel she bought was a reissued version in a new format.
她买的那本小说是以新格式重新发行的版本。
- initialize 格式化   - date format 日期格式

› version (P. 801)

0372 **foul** [faʊl] a 肮脏的 v 弄脏，污染 n 犯规
She was determined to buy that apartment, by fair means or foul.
她决定买下那栋公寓，哪怕是不择手段。
- foul up 把……搞乱   - sb. ... by fair means or foul 某人不择手段……

语法重点
foul 的过去式和过去分词为 fouled, fouled。

0373 **fowl** [faʊl] n 野禽，禽肉 v 猎捕野禽
There would be a plentiful supply of fowl if there are no more foul-ups.
如果不再出差错，就会有充足的禽肉供应。
- poultry 家禽   - ... if there are no more foul-ups ……如果不再出差错

语法重点
fowl 作可数名词，表示"鸡"，复数为 fowls 或 fowl；作不可数名词，表示"鸡肉"。

0374 **fraction** [ˈfrækʃn] n 片段，分数
She decided to buy that bracelet after hesitating for the merest fraction of a second.
犹豫了一秒钟之后，她决定买下那个手镯。
- part 部分   - a fraction of 一小部分
- fraction 通常是指包含在整体中的一部分，侧重于指微不足道的小部分。

0375 **framework** [ˈfreɪmwɜːrk] n 架构，结构
They plan to explore the new commodity approach within the existing framework of practice.
他们打算，在现有惯例模式的框架结构中，寻找新的商品模式。
- structure 结构   - basic framework 基本框架

› commodity (P. 546)

0376 frantic ['fræntɪk] a 发狂似的
The shopkeeper was frantic with worry about the sales of watermelons.
那位店主为那些西瓜的销售而发愁。

0377 freight [freɪt] n 货物，运费 v 装货于
The ship freighted with cars stopped within a fraction of a meter of the dock.
那艘装载着汽车的船在离码头一米不到的地方停住了。
🔹 shipment 装载的货物　🔹 freight forwarder 货运代理（人）

语法重点
freight 的过去式和过去分词为 freighted, freighted。
🔹 fraction (P. 570)

0378 frontier [frʌn'tɪr] n 边境，边疆，新领域
The man was frantic to head for the frontier town to buy tobacco.
那人十万火急地赶往那个边疆城镇去买烟草。
🔹 border 边疆，边界　🔹 frontier point 界限点　🔹 be frantic to... 十万火急……

0379 fume [fju:m] n 烟，气，愤怒 v 冒烟，愤怒
She was fuming with rage at the spots of mud on her new dress.
她的新连衣裙沾上了泥污，她气得发狂。
🔹 smoke 烟　🔹 be fuming with rage at... 因……气得发狂

语法重点
fume 作不及物动词，表示"愤怒，冒烟"；作及物动词，表示"用化学药品烟雾处理木材"，其过去式为fumed。

0380 fury ['fjʊri] n 愤怒，暴怒
She was speechless with fury when her brother wanted to rip her off.
她的哥哥想骗她的钱，她气得说不出话来。
🔹 in a fury 在狂怒中　🔹 be speechless with fury... 气得说不出话来……

0381 fuse [fju:z] v 熔合 n 保险丝，引线
The sales manager is said to be on a short fuse.
据说，那位销售经理脾气暴躁。
🔹 light the fuse 造成紧张局面　🔹 be on a short fuse ……脾气暴躁

语法重点
fuse 为可数名词，用于英式英语中，美式英语中是fuze。

0382 fuss [fʌs] n 大惊小怪 v 小题大做，烦恼
There was a real fuss when the boy was caught stealing in the grocery store.
那个男孩在杂货店行窃被抓，真够他受的。
🔹 alarmism 大惊小怪　🔹 fuss about 激动，烦恼

语法重点
fuss 作不可数名词。

0383 gallop ['gæləp] v / n 飞奔，飞速发展
Tom gallops ahead of others in the sale of computers.
汤姆的电脑销售量远远超过了其他人。
🔹 spin 疾驰　🔹 go at a gallop 快速跑去
🔹 gallop ahead of... in... 在……远远超过……

语法重点
gallop 的过去式为galloped。

0384 **garment** ['gɑːrmənt] n 衣服 v 给……披上衣服
The new garment served as the perfect foil for the lady's fine complexion.
那件新衣服衬得那位女士容颜姣好。
- clothes 衣服
- serve as the perfect foil for... 极好地衬托出……

➔ complexion (P. 689)

0385 **gasp** [ɡæsp] v 喘气，倒抽气，渴望 n 喘气，喘息
The young man gasped in astonishment at the price of the apartment.
那栋公寓的价格惊得那个年轻人倒抽一口气。
- last gasp 奄奄一息
- gasp in astonishment at... 因……惊得倒抽一口气

0386 **gathering** ['ɡæðərɪŋ] n 聚集，采集 v 集合，推断
The salesman made a fuss of methods of information gathering.
那位推销员过于在意信息收集的方法。
- assembly 集会
- data gathering 资料搜集
- make a fuss of / over... 对……过于在意

0387 **gay** [ɡeɪ] n 男同性恋 a 快乐的，同性恋的
It's unwise to spend money with gay abandon.
挥霍钱财是不明智的。
- homosexual 同性恋者
- heterosexual 异性恋者
- ... spend money with gay abandon ……挥霍钱财

语法重点
gay 的副词为 gaily，表示 "欢乐地，轻率地"。

0388 **gender** ['dʒendər] n 性别
The users of the mascara make no distinction between the male and female genders.
这款睫毛膏同样适用于男性和女性。
- sexuality 性，性别
- make no distinction between... and... 不加区分……和……

➔ distinction (P. 558)

0389 **geographic / geographical** [ˌdʒiːə'ɡræfɪk] / [ˌdʒiːə'ɡræfɪkl] a 地理的
There is a fractional difference in the price of the grapes subjected to the geographical distribution.
受地域分布的限制，葡萄的价格有些许的差别。
- there is a fractional difference in... ……有些许的差别

语法重点
geographical 作形容词，无比较级和最高级形式，其名词 geography 表示 "地理学"。

0390 **geometry** [dʒɪ'ɑːmətri] n 几何学
The schoolboy was gasping for the geometry set in the store.
那个学童想要那家商店里的几何学绘图器。
- be gasping for... 想要……

garment ~ gobble

0391 glacier ['gleɪʃər] n 冰河，冰川
By way of introduction, the salesgirl gave her the background to the book about glacier plains.
作为介绍，那个女店员向她说明了这本关于冰川平原的书的写作背景。

> 语法重点
> glacier 源自法语，为外来词，其形容词为 glacial。

0392 glare [gler] v 怒视瞪眼，炫耀
When accused of stealing in the store, he just glared silently at the shopkeeper.
当他被指责在店中行窃时，他只是沉默地盯着那位店主。
- stare 凝视
- when accused of..., sb. ... 当被指责……时，某人……

> 语法重点
> glare 作不及物动词，通常与介词 at 连用。
> accuse (P. 391)

0393 gleam [gli:m] n 微光 v （使）闪烁，（使）闪亮
I don't know how to make the ball I bought gleam.
我不知道如何让我买的那个球发光。
- not a gleam of hope 毫无希望
- I don't know how to... 我不知道如何……

> 语法重点
> gleam 作不及物动词，与介词 in 或是 on 等连用。

0394 glee [gli:] n 喜悦，合唱曲
She cannot disguise her glee at the new mobile phone her father bought for her.
爸爸买新手机给她，她不禁喜形于色。
- glee feast 庆功宴，招待会

> 语法重点
> glee 作不可数名词，表示"欣喜"，通常与介词 at 连用；作可数名词，表示"三部、四部的重唱歌曲"。

0395 glitter ['glɪtə] v 闪烁，炫耀 n 灿烂的光辉，闪烁
She was in high glee to buy that ring glittering with diamonds.
她满心欢喜地买下了那枚闪闪生辉的钻戒。
- glow 闪烁
- be in high glee to... 满心欢喜地……

0396 gloom [glu:m] n 幽暗，阴暗，忧郁
She remained sunken in gloom for a week because her boyfriend did not buy gifts for her at Christmas.
圣诞节时，男朋友没有给她买礼物，她沮丧了一周。
- doom and gloom 凄惨，无望
- remain sunken in gloom... 沮丧……

> week (P. 112)

0397 gnaw [nɔ:] v 咬，啃，使苦恼，折磨
Fear and anxiety gnawed at his heart after he stole the ring from the store.
从那家店中偷了那枚戒指之后，他心中恐惧不安。
- gnaw at 啃，侵蚀
- gnaw at one's heart 心中受折磨

0398 gobble ['gɑ:bl]
v 大口猛吃，咯咯地叫 n （火鸡的）咯咯叫声
The boy bought a hamburger in the store and gobbled it down in a hurry.
那个男孩在这家商店买了个汉堡，并匆匆忙忙地吞了下去。
- gobble... down in a hurry 匆匆忙忙地吞下……

> 语法重点
> gobble 通常与介词 up 或是 down 连用。

0399 gorge(1) [gɔːrdʒ] n 峡谷，障碍物
The sight of robbery in the store made his gorge rise.
看到这家店里发生了抢劫案，他十分气愤。
≈ valley 山谷　≈ make one's gorge rise ……使……气愤

语法重点
gorge 通常是指两侧形成绝壁、中间夹有溪流的峡谷。

0400 gorge(2) [gɔːrdʒ] v 使吃饱，狼吞虎咽
The kids gorged themselves with biscuits mother bought for them.
孩子们狼吞虎咽地吃妈妈买来的饼干。
≈ devour 狼吞虎咽地吃　≈ gorge on 狼吞虎咽
≈ ... gorge (oneself) with / on... ……狼吞虎咽地吃……

0401 gorgeous ['gɔːrdʒəs]
a 绚丽的，美丽动人的，令人愉快的
She feels like going shopping in such a gorgeous weather.　≈ weather (P. 111)
天气如此美好，她想去购物。
≈ splendid 极好的

0402 gorilla [gəˈrɪlə] n 大猩猩，暴徒，打手
The gorilla with a dangerous gleam in his eyes came to buy a knife.
那个眼露凶光的恶汉来买了一把刀。
≈ ... with a dangerous gleam in one's eyes ……眼露凶光
≈ gorilla 作可数名词，源自希腊语，为外来词。

0403 gospel [ˈgɑːspl] n 福音，原则　a 传播福音的
You can take it as absolute gospel that the furniture in the　≈ absolute (P. 389)
mall is sold at a fifty percent discount.
这家购物中心的家具五折优惠，这是千真万确的。
≈ gospel truth 天经地义的事
≈ take it as absolute gospel that... ……是千真万确的

0404 grant [grænt] v 给予　n 拨款，补助金
Her grandpa granted his permission to buy that cat.　≈ permission (P. 336)
她的爷爷同意买那只猫。
≈ permit 许可　≠ disagree 不同意　≈ take for granted 认为……理所当然
≈ grant... permission to... 同意……

0405 gravity [ˈgrævəti]
n 重力，万有引力，地心引力，严肃，重要
The governments fail to realize the gravity of the fact that so many people rush to buy salt in large amounts.
这么多人急着大量购买食盐，政府却没有意识到这个事实的重要性。
≈ center of gravity 重心　≈ realize the gravity of... 意识到……的重要性

0406 **graze** [greɪz] v 吃草，轻擦 n 放牧，擦伤

The little boy grazed his leg against the stair in the shopping center.
那个小男孩在这个购物中心的台阶上擦伤了腿。

- feed 喂养
- graze on 吃（牛、羊等吃草）
- ... graze one's... on / against... ……在……擦伤了……

语法重点
graze 表示"牛、羊等吃草"时，通常与介词 in 或 on 连用；表示"擦伤"时，则通常与介词 against, along, on 连用。

0407 **grease** [griːs] n 油脂，润滑油 v 用油脂润滑，贿赂

The actress made a fuss about the price of grease paint.
那位女演员抱怨说，化妆品的价格太高。

- grease the wheels 使顺利进行，贿赂
- make a fuss about... 对……强烈不满

○ fuss (P. 571)

0408 **greed** [griːd] n 贪心，贪婪

The thief stared at the jewelry in the shop window and consumed with greed and envy.
那个满心贪婪与嫉妒的小偷盯着商店橱窗里的珠宝。

- covetousness 贪婪
- contentment 知足
- pure greed 十足的贪婪
- ... consumed with greed and envy ……充满贪婪和嫉妒

0409 **grim** [grɪm] a 严格的，冷酷的，残忍的

The salesman tried to persuade her into buying the shampoo like grim death.
那个推销员坚持不懈地劝说她买那款洗发水。

- dreadful 可怕的
- gentle 温和的
- grim reaper 死神

语法重点
grim 的比较级和最高级为 grimmer, grimmest。

0410 **grip** [grɪp] n 紧握，手提包 v 吸引，紧抓

The old man who was in the grip of despair bought a bottle of sleeping pills.
那位陷入绝望的老人买了一瓶安眠药。

- squeeze 紧握
- get a grip on 控制，把握关键
- ... be in the grip of despair 陷入绝望的……

○ despair (P. 556)

0411 **groan** [groʊn] v 呻吟，抱怨，嘎吱声 n 呻吟

The housewife was always groaning on about how much money she had to spend on meals.
那位家庭主妇总是抱怨她要为一日三餐花费那么多钱。

- moan 呻吟
- groan out 呻吟着说出
- ... be always groaning on about / over... ……总是抱怨……

0412 **gross** [groʊs]
n 总额 a 显而易见的，总的，恶劣的 v 总收入

In the gross, the apples in the store are sold by kilogram.
一般而言，这家商店里的苹果是按千克出售的。

- gross domestic product (GDP) 国内生产总值

语法重点
in the gross（一般，大体上）中的 the 也可以省略。

0413 growl [graʊl] v 咆哮 n 低吼
When they entered the pet store, a little dog growled at them.
他们走进那家宠物店的时候，一只小狗对他们狂叫。
bark 咆哮　　growl out 怒气冲冲

语法重点
growl 作不及物动词，表示"低吼"；作及物动词，表示"以低声的威胁口吻说"。

0414 grumble ['grʌmbl] v 抱怨，隆隆响 n 抱怨，隆隆声
The customer kept grumbling at being charged an excess of two dollars.
那位顾客一直抱怨说他被多收了两美元。
grumble away 发出连续、低沉的声音　　... grumble at (doing)... ……抱怨……

0415 guideline ['gaɪdlaɪn] n 指导方针，准则
You can choose books freely in the bookstore within certain broad guidelines.
在这家书店，你可以在某些广泛的准则范围之内自由选择书籍。
criterion 准则　　design guideline 设计方针，设计准则

0416 gulp [gʌlp] v 狼吞虎咽，哽住 n 吞咽，一大口
The little boy sobbed with loud gulps because his mother did not buy him that toy.
妈妈没有买那个玩具给他，所以那个小男孩大声抽泣。
swallow 吞咽　　... sob with loud gulps ……大声抽泣

sob (P. 504)

0417 gust [gʌst] n 一阵狂风，（感情）迸发 v （风）猛刮
The man felt a gust of anger when he found he bought a counterfeit painting.
发现自己买了一幅假画，那人很气愤。
a gust of 一阵　　... feel a gust of anger when... 当……时，感到十分气愤

语法重点
gust 通常与介词 of 连用。

0418 gut [gʌt] n 肠子，勇气 a 本能的 v 毁坏……的内部
The timid girl does not have the guts to buy flowers in the store around the corner.
那个胆小的女孩不敢去附近的那家店里买花。
courage 勇气　　gut feeling 直觉　　have the guts to... 有胆量

corner (P. 145)

0419 Gypsy ['dʒɪpsɪ]
n 吉卜赛人，吉卜赛语 v 流浪 a 吉卜赛人的
The gypsy bought a cup of coffee and emptied it at one gallop.
那个吉卜赛人买了一杯咖啡并且一口气喝完了。
gypsy camp 杂耍，马戏　　empty... at one gallop 一口气喝 / 吃完……
gypsy 也可以写作 Gypsy 或是 gipsy。

0420 hail [heɪl] **v** 向……欢呼
She bought a novel which was hailed as a masterpiece.
她买了一本被誉为杰作的小说。
⊜ welcome 欢迎　　⊜ hail from 来自　　⊜ be hailed as... 被誉为……

语法重点
hail 作及物动词，表示"热情地承认……为……"；作不及物动词，表示"来自某地"。
↪ masterpiece (P. 595)

0421 hairstyle [ˈheəstaɪl] **n** 发型
She grumbled at the barber about her new hairstyle.
她对理发师抱怨她的新发型。
⊜ hairdo 发型　　⊜ ... grumble at / to sb. about / over / at... ……对……抱怨……

0422 handicap [ˈhændikæp] **n** 障碍，不利条件　**v** 使不利
Not having a car seems to be a serious handicap in the country.
在这个国家，没有车似乎是极为不利的。

语法重点
handicap 通常用于被动语态，即 be handicapped by。

0423 handicraft [ˈhændikrɑːft] **n** 手工艺
The young man looked at those traditional handicrafts in the shop window.
那个年轻人看着商店橱窗里的那些传统手工艺品。
⊜ artifact 手工艺，手工艺品　　⊜ handicraft industry 手工业
⊜ handicraft 用于英式英语中，美式英语中则是用作 handcraft。

↪ traditional (P. 238)

0424 hardy [ˈhɑːrdi] **a** 强健的，能吃苦耐劳的
We grant the truth of what you say; the hardy man never buys down jackets in winter.
我们承认你所言属实，那个强健的人冬天从来都不买羽绒服。
⊜ strong 坚强的　　⊜ flabby 软弱的　　⊜ we grant the truth of... 我们承认……属实

语法重点
hardy 的比较级和最高级形式为 hardier, hardiest。

0425 harness [ˈhɑːrnɪs] **n** 马具，挽具　**v** 治理，给……上挽具
His father came home with the harness he bought in the gathering gloom.
天越来越暗的时候，他爸爸带着买来的马具回到了家里。
⊜ saddlery 马具　　⊜ in harness 一起合作，在日常工作中

0426 haul [hɔːl] **v** / **n** 拖，拉，运送
The boy was hauled over the coals for breaking the vase his mother bought.
那个男孩打破了妈妈买的花瓶，因此受到了严厉的斥责。
⊜ over the long haul 从长远观点看
⊜ be hauled over the coals for... 因……而受到严厉斥责

语法重点
haul 强调用力，却不强调方向。

0427 haunt [hɔːnt] **v** 思绪萦绕在心头　**n** 常去的地方
The businessman plans to revisit the haunts of his youth.
那个商人打算重游年轻时常去的地方。
⊜ haunt about 经常出没于

0428 hearty ['hɑːrti] a 衷心的，健壮的 n 朋友们，运动员
She gave her hearty approval and support to her husband's proposal to buy an apartment.
丈夫提议买一栋公寓，她对此竭诚赞同支持。
- devout 衷心的 - hypocritical 虚伪的 - hale and hearty 精力充沛的

⊃ approval (P. 396)

0429 heavenly ['hevnli]
a 天空的，非常合意的，令人愉快的
The bakery with heavenly cakes should be a favorite haunt of kids.
这家面包店有美味的蛋糕，这是孩子们常去的地方。

⊃ haunt (P. 577)

0430 hedge [hedʒ] n 篱笆，预防措施，障碍物
In wartime many people bought gold as a hedge against inflation.
在战争时期，很多人都购买黄金，以防通货膨胀。
- hedge one's bets 避免做出明确承诺
- do sth. as a hedge against... 做某事以防……

语法重点
hedge 作可数名词，本意是"用灌木等围成的树篱"，表示"障碍"时，通常与介词 of 连用；表示"预防措施"时，通常与介词 against 连用。

0431 heed [hiːd] n 留心，注意 v 注意，留心
The millionaire paid no heed to the price of the latest laptop.
那位百万富翁并不在意这台最新款笔记本电脑的价格。
- care 留心 - take heed of 留意 - pay no heed to... 不在意……

0432 heighten ['haɪtn] v 增高，加强
Those unsalable peaches heightened the shopkeeper's anxiety.
那些滞销的桃子加重了这位店主的忧虑。
- enhance 加强 - heighten vigilance 提高警觉

0433 heir [er] n 继承人
The young man who bought a large estate in the country was said to be heir of a large fortune.
据说，那个在乡下买大量地产的年轻人是大笔财产的继承人。
- inheritor 继承人 - lawful heir 合法继承人 - be heir of... 是……的继承人

⊃ fortune (P. 298)

0434 hence [hens] ad 今后
The price of petrol has been on the increase, hence the need for more money.
汽油价格已经上涨，所以需要更多的钱。
- hence with 拿开，带走 - ... be on the increase ……增加 / 上涨

0435 herald ['herəld] n 通报者，传令官 v 传达，预告

Forthcoming summer should be the herald of the watermelon season.

即将到来的夏天预示着西瓜旺季的到来。

- harbinger 先驱
- be the herald of... 预告……的来临

语法重点
herald 作可数名词，通常与介词 of 连用。

0436 herb [ɜːrb] n 草本植物

They faced with the grim prospect of large profits in kitchen herbs.

想从调味用草本香料中获取高额利润的前景黯淡。

- ... face the grim prospect of... ……前景黯淡

profit (P. 342)

0437 hermit ['hɜːrmɪt] n 隐士，小甜饼

He saw little prospect of buying sweet herbs from the hermit.

他觉得，向那位隐士购买甜香草是没有什么希望的。

- recluse 隐居者，隐士
- see little prospect of... 没有希望……

语法重点
例句中的 little 也可以替换为 no。

0438 heroic [həˈroʊɪk] a 英雄的，英勇的

Seeing the book about heroic myths in the bookstore, the schoolgirl's eyes gleamed with excitement.

在书店看到那本关于英雄故事的书，那个女学生眼中散发出激动的神情。

- courageous 勇敢的
- cowardly 胆小的

语法重点
heroic 作形容词，heroics 则是作复数名词，表示"夸张的言语、行为"。

0439 heterosexual [ˌhetərəˈsekʃuəl]

a 异性恋的，异性的 n 异性恋的人

The girl has a good grip of heterosexual intimacy.

那个女孩十分理解异性之间的亲密。

- have a good grip of... 十分理解……
- heterosexual 兼作形容词与可数名词，其具体意义须根据具体语境加以判断。

intimacy (P. 735)

0440 hi-fi ['haɪ faɪ] n 高级音响 a 音响高度传真的

I don't want to hear another grumble from you about the hi-fi records.

我不想再听你抱怨那些高传真的唱片。

0441 hijack ['haɪdʒæk] v 劫持，操纵 n 劫持，敲诈

Their plane was hijacked when they were on a visit to Canada.

他们搭飞机去加拿大的时候，遭遇了劫机事件。

- spoliate 掠夺，抢劫
- hijack an airplane 劫机
- be on a visit to... 去……观光

0442 hiss [hɪs] v 发嘘声 n 嘘声，嘶嘶声

The audience greeted the drama with boos and hisses.
观众对这场戏剧发出嘘声。
- boo 嘘声
- hiss off 把……嘘下去

语法重点
hiss 的过去式为 hissed。

0443 hoarse [hɔːrs] a 嘶哑的

The teacher's voice was as hoarse as a raven after talking with the student for an hour.
与那名学生谈了一小时之后，这位老师的嗓音沙哑。
- throaty 嘶哑的
- hoarse voice 声音嘶哑
- ... be as hoarse as a raven ……沙哑

0444 hockey ['hɑːki] n 曲棍球，冰球

The man kicked up a fuss about the price of the hockey stick.
那人对这柄曲棍球杆的价格强烈不满。

fuss (P. 571)

0445 homosexual [ˌhoʊməˈsekʃuəl] a 同性恋的

The old priest gave a glacial stare at the two homosexuals.
那位老神父冷冷地盯着那两个同性恋者。
- give a glacial stare at... 冷冷地盯着……

0446 honk [hɑːŋk] n 汽车喇叭声，雁叫声 v 发出雁叫声

When they entered the supermarket, he still did not stop fussing about the terrible honk of their car.
走进超市的时候，他仍然没有停止抱怨车的喇叭声。
- honk horn 按喇叭
- stop fussing about... 停止抱怨……

terrible (P. 234)

0447 hood [hʊd] n 头巾，车篷 v 罩上，覆盖

Weather permitting; we can drive the car with the hood down tomorrow to go shopping.
如果天气好的话，明天我们可以敞着车篷开车去购物。

0448 hoof [huːf] n 蹄，马蹄 v 走，以蹄踢

The butcher full of grumbles went to buy a cattle on the hoof and slaughtered it.
那个满腹牢骚的屠夫去买了头活牛然后宰杀了。
- ungula 蹄
- on the hoof 活着的，即兴地

语法重点
hoof 的复数形式为 hoofs 或是 hooves。

0449 horizontal [ˌhɔːrəˈzɑːntl] a 地平线的，水准的

The salesgirl was told bottles of wine should be kept horizontal.
那位女店员被告知，葡萄酒瓶应当平放。
- vertical 垂直的
- horizontal direction 水平方向
- be kept horizontal 平放

语法重点
horizontal 没有比较级和最高级形式。

hiss ~ hymn

0450 hostage ['hɑːstɪdʒ] n 人质
The robber took a little child hostage in the supermarket.
那个抢劫犯在超市里挟持了一名小孩子作为人质。
- captive 俘虏
- take sb. hostage 挟持某人作人质

0451 hostile ['hɑːstl] a 敌方的，不友善的
Most customers were hostile towards the price increase of daily necessities.
很多顾客都反对日用品价格上涨。
- enemy 敌方的
- be hostile to / towards... 对……反对

> 语法重点
> hostile 的比较级和最高级形式为 more hostile, most hostile。

0452 hound [haʊnd] n 猎犬 v 追逼，烦扰
The middle-aged man was hounded out of the supermarket by the guard.
那个中年人被保安赶出了超市。
- be hounded out of... 被逼离开……

> 语法重点
> be hounded out of 也可以用主动形式。

0453 housing ['haʊzɪŋ] n 住房供给，外罩
The new couple who are on a tight budget cannot afford to change the poor housing conditions.
那对新婚夫妇生活拮据，无力改变恶劣的居住条件。
- tenement 房屋
- ... be on a tight budget ……生活拮据

> budget (P. 266)

0454 hover ['hʌvər] v 盘旋，徘徊，彷徨
Seeing her husband buy a bracelet for her, a smile hovered on her lips.
看到丈夫为她买了个手镯，她露出了笑容。
- hover over 在……盘旋

> 语法重点
> hover 表示"盘旋"时，通常与介词 over 或 above 连用，表示"徘徊"时，通常与介词 around, over, about 连用，也可作 hover between... and...。

0455 howl [haʊl] n 号叫，（风等）呼啸
The price increase in daily necessities caused howls of protest from the customers.
日用品价格上涨引起了顾客们的抗议。
- roar 号叫
- gallop howl 奔腾呼啸
- cause howls of protest from... ……引起抗议

> 语法重点
> howl 作可数名词。
> increase (P. 178)

0456 hurl [hɜːrl] v 猛力投掷，大声叫骂
He hurled insults at the boy who was caught stealing.
他厉声辱骂那个行窃被抓的男孩。

0457 hymn [hɪm] n 赞美诗，圣歌 v 唱赞歌，赞美
There is little prospect of his buying a hymn book.
他不可能去买一本赞美诗集。
- Easter hymn 复活节赞歌
- there is little / no prospect of... 不可能……

> 语法重点
> prospect 作可数名词，表示"景象，景观"；作不可数名词，表示"有根据的希望，期望"。

0458 idiot [ˈɪdɪət] **n** 傻瓜

What an idiot he was to be charged an excess of thirty dollars over the amount on the bill.
他真笨，与账单上的数额相比，居然多付了三十美元。

0459 immense [ɪˈmens] **a** 巨大的，极好的

There are immense possibilities of buying these materials at a low price.
以低价购买这些材料，是很有可能的。
同 huge 巨大的　　反 small 小的，小型的
句 there are immense possibilities of doing... ⋯⋯有极大的可能

● material (P. 189)

0460 imperial [ɪmˈpɪrɪəl] **a** 帝国的，帝王的，宏大的

The shopkeeper dealt with the unreasonably troublesome customer with imperial generosity.
对于那位无理取闹的顾客，这位店主宽宏大量地应对。
同 regal 帝王的，王室的　　搭 imperial city 皇城，帝都

语法重点
imperial 无比较级和最高级。

0461 impose [ɪmˈpoʊz] **v** 征税

The local government decided to impose a further tax on luxuries.
当地政府决定对奢侈品进一步征税。
同 tax 对⋯⋯征税　　搭 impose on 强加于，欺骗
句 ... impose a further tax on... ⋯⋯对⋯⋯进一步征税
注 impose 通常是指某个案件中的处罚或是罚款，特别是政府征收某种税收的决定。

0462 impulse [ˈɪmpʌls] **n** 冲动，推动，驱使

Women always felt an irresistible impulse to buy fashionable clothes.
女性总有种无法抑制的冲动去购买时装。
搭 on impulse 一时冲动，心血来潮
句 feel an irresistible impulse to... 对⋯⋯有无法抑制的冲动

语法重点
impulse 作可数名词，表示"冲动，突如其来的念头"；作不可数名词，表示"冲动行事"。

0463 incense [ˈɪnsens] **n** 香 **v** 激怒

The young man felt deeply incensed by the girl's indifference.
那个女孩的冷漠让这个年轻人感到十分愤怒。

语法重点
incense 作及物动词，通常用于被动语态。

0464 index [ˈɪndeks] **n** 索引，指标

The increasing sale of luxuries could be regarded as an index of the town's prosperity.
奢侈品销售量日渐增长可以视为这个城镇经济繁荣的标志。
搭 index number 物价或人口指数
句 be regarded as an index of... 视为⋯⋯的标志

语法重点
index 作可数名词，其复数为 indexes 或 indices。

● prosperity (P. 490)

idiot ~ infinite

0465 indifference [ɪnˈdɪfrəns] **n** 不关心，中立，中性

It's a matter of complete indifference to me whether you buy that handbag.
你买不买那个手提包，对我而言，都无所谓。
- concern 关心
- indifference to... 对……漠不关心

0466 indifferent [ɪnˈdɪfrənt] **a** 不关心的

The businessman seems to be indifferent to the price increase in luxury goods.
奢侈品价格上涨，那位商人对此似乎并不关心。
- remain indifferent 保持中立
- be indifferent to... 对……漠不关心

▷ luxury (P. 469)

0467 indignant [ɪnˈdɪɡnənt] **a** 愤怒的，愤慨的

Many housewives are indignant at the price increase in daily necessities.
日用品价格上涨，很多家庭主妇都感到愤慨。
- wrathful 愤怒的
- indignant with sb. for... 因为……而对某人表示愤慨
- ... be indignant at / about / over... ……对……感到愤慨

0468 indispensable [ˌɪndɪˈspensəbl] **a** 不可缺少的，必需的

Computers seem to have become an indispensable part of our life nowadays.
如今，电脑似乎成为我们生活中必不可少的一部分。
- needed 必需的
- be indispensable to... 对……是必须的
- ... become an indispensable part of... ……成为……必不可少的一部分

> **语法重点**
> indispensable 通常是用来表示绝对必要性、不可缺少，语气较强。

0469 induce [ɪnˈduːs] **v** 引诱，劝，导致

The salesgirl tried to induce the old man to buy the walking stick.
那位女店员试图劝说那位老人买那根手杖。
- persuade 劝说
- induce sb. to do... 劝说某人做……

0470 indulge [ɪnˈdʌldʒ] **v** 沉迷，纵容，迁就

The clerk plans to indulge himself with a bottle of champagne in the pub.
那位职员打算去酒吧里喝一瓶香槟放纵一下。
- indulge in... 沉溺于……
- indulge oneself with... 放纵……

▷ champagne (P. 683)

0471 infinite [ˈɪnfɪnət] **a** 无限的，极大的

As a salesman, you need infinite patience to persuade people into buying your products.
作为一名推销员，你要有极大的耐心来劝说人们购买你的产品。
- endless 无尽的
- finite 有限的
- need infinite patience to do... 需要极大的耐心……

> **语法重点**
> infinite 无比较级和最高级形式。

583

0472 inherit [ɪnˈherɪt] v 继承，遗传得来

After inheriting an large fortune from his uncle, he bought an estate in the country.
从叔叔那里继承了大笔财产之后，他在乡下购置了一处房产。
- receive 收到　　- inherit property 继承财产
- inherit... from sb. 从某人那里继承……

⊕ uncle (P. 108)

0473 initiate [ɪˈnɪʃieɪt] / [ɪˈnɪʃiət] v 开始 n 初学者

The book his brother bought for him initiated him into the mysteries of science.
哥哥给他买的那本书让他初步了解了科学的奥秘。
- commence 开始　　- terminate 结束

0474 inland [ˌɪnˈlænd] ad 在内陆 a 内地的，内陆的

He seems to have indefinite faith in the medicine his son bought from that inland town.
对于儿子从那个内陆城镇买来的药，他似乎有着极大的信心。
- hinterland 内陆地区　　- coastal 沿海的　　- inland sea 内海

0475 innumerable [ɪˈnuːmərəbl] a 无数的，数不清的

The owner of the bookstore flew into a fury when he was told innumerable books were burnt in the fire.
得知无数的书籍在大火中焚毁，那位书店老板怒不可遏。
- infinite 无数的　　- finite 有限的
- ... fly into a fury when... 当……时……怒不可遏

语法重点
innumerable 无比较级和最高级形式，其副词形式为 innumerably。

0476 inquire [ɪnˈkwaɪr] v 询问，调查

The young mother inquired of the salesgirl where to buy milk powder.
那位年轻的母亲询问女店员在哪里可以买到奶粉。
- ask 问，询问　　- answer 回答，答复
- inquire about 打听　　- inquire of sb. ... 询问某人……

0477 institute [ˈɪnstɪtuːt] n 学会

Please send these goods to the agricultural institute with frantic haste.
请把这些商品迅速送到农学院。
- research institute 研究机构

⊕ agricultural (P. 523)

0478 insure [ɪnˈʃʊr] v 为……投保

The businessman insured himself for three thousand dollars.
那位商人为自己投保三千美元的人寿保险。
- insure against 给……保险以防……　　- insure oneself for... 为自己投保……人寿保险

0479 intent [ɪn'tent] **n** 意图，目的 **a** 专心的，专注的
The young couple were intent on buying an apartment.
那对年轻夫妇一心一意地要买一栋公寓。
反 distracted 注意力不集中的　搭 with intent 蓄意

0480 interference [ˌɪntər'fɪrəns] **n** 干涉，阻碍
Maybe we can expect cheap fares of airlines without interference from the government.
如果没有政府干预，我们也许可以期望航空公司设定便宜的票价。
近 intervention 调停，介入　搭 interference with 干涉，干扰

参 fare (P. 295)

0481 interior [ɪn'tɪriər] **a** 内部的，内地的 **n** 内部
She looked at the flower with an intent gaze; it is said to grow in the interior of the jungles of Africa.
她以专注的目光看着那盆花，据说它生长在非洲的内地丛林中。
近 inside 内部的　反 exterior 外部的　搭 interior design 室内设计

0482 interpretation [ɪnˌtɜːrprɪ'teɪʃn] **n** 口译
Their words suggested a different interpretation of the sales contract.
他们的话表明了对这份销售合约的不同理解。
近 explanation 解释　搭 interpretation method 判读方法
句 ... suggest a different interpretation of... ……表明对……的不同理解

语法重点
interpretation 作可数名词，表示"解释，说明"，通常与介词 of 连用；作不可数名词，表示"口译"。

0483 interpreter [ɪn'tɜːrprɪtər] **n** 口译员，翻译器
The interpreter watched the antique in the shop window with an intent expression.
那位译员以专注的神情看着商店橱窗里的古玩。
近 translator 译员，翻译机　搭 electronic interpreter 电子翻译器
句 ... watch... with an intent expression ……以专注的神情看……

参 antique (P. 525)

0484 intuition [ˌɪntu'ɪʃn] **n** 直觉
The man suddenly had an intuition about the gift he wanted to buy.
那人突然对自己想要买的礼物有种直觉。
搭 intuition thinking 直觉思维
句 ... have an intuition about... ……对……有种直觉

语法重点
intuition 作不可数名词，表示"直觉"；作可数名词，表示"凭借直觉感知的资讯"。

0485 inward ['ɪnwərd] **a** 向内的，内部的，本质上的
Judging by her inward nature, she will not buy those gaudy decorations.
从她的个性判断，她不会买那些花哨的饰物。
搭 judging by... 根据……判断

0486 inwards ['ɪnwərdz] ad 向内 n 内部，内脏
As to the reasons why customers seldom come to your store, you should turn your thoughts inwards.
对于为什么很少有顾客到你的商店来，你应当自省。
- inward passenger 入境旅客
- ... turn one's thoughts inward ……自省

0487 isle [aɪl] n 岛
She bought a plant which was said to grow on an isle.
她买了一株据说是生长在一个小岛上的植物。
- island 岛

plant (P. 076)

0488 issue ['ɪʃuː] v 发行，造成……结果 n 议题，发行物
They took issue with the shopkeeper about the price of the sweater.
他们就这件毛衣的价格和那位店主争论。
- social issue 社会议题
- take issue with sb. about... 针对……与某人争论

0489 ivy ['aɪvi] n 常春藤 a 常春藤联盟的
Intuition told her what her grandma wanted to buy were seeds of the English ivy.
直觉告诉她，奶奶想要买的是常春藤的种子。

语法重点
ivy 作不可数名词，其形容词形式为 ivied，Ivy League 则是专有名词，表示"常春藤联盟"，即为美国东部著名大学的统称。

0490 jack [dʒæk] n 起重机 v 用千斤顶顶起
Please lift this car with that jack.
请用那台起重机抬起这辆汽车。

0491 jade [dʒeɪd] n 玉，翡翠（色） v （使）疲倦
She had an intuition that there was something wrong with the jade bracelet.
她有种直觉，这个玉镯似乎有些不对。
- jasper 翡翠，碧玉
- green jade 翡翠，碧玉
- have an intuition that... 有种直觉……

intuition (P. 585)

0492 janitor ['dʒænɪtər] n 看门者，看管房屋的人，锅炉工
The janitor hailed curses down the kids who ran about at the entrance.
那位看门人大骂那些在入口处到处跑的孩子们。
- gatekeeper 守卫
- hail curses down... 大骂……

0493 jasmine ['dʒæzmɪn] n 茉莉，茉莉香料，淡黄色
I knew it by intuition that what she felt like buying was jasmine tea.
我凭直觉知道，她想买的是茉莉花茶。
- jasmine tea 茉莉花茶
- know... by intuition 凭直觉知道……

语法重点
intuition 作不可数名词，表示"直觉"。

inwards ~ jug

0494 jaywalk [ˈdʒeɪwɔːk] v 不守法穿越街道

When coming out from the bookstore, she heard a driver howl his displeasure at a boy who jaywalked.
从那家书店出来的时候，她听到一位司机对乱穿越马路的男孩怒吼。
- no jaywalking 禁止乱穿越马路
- howl one's displeasure at... 对……怒吼

> **语法重点**
> jaywalker 作可数名词，表示"乱穿越马路的人"，jaywalking 作不可数名词，表示"乱穿越马路"。

0495 jeer [dʒɪr] v 嘲笑，戏弄 n 嘲讽，讥笑的言语

He tried to resist an impulse to jeer at the new dress his wife bought.
他试图遏制自己的冲动，不去嘲讽妻子买的那件新连衣裙。
- taunt 嘲弄
- jeer at 嘲笑，嘲弄
- resist an impulse to do... 遏制做……的冲动

> impulse (P. 582)

0496 jingle [ˈdʒɪŋgl] n 叮当声 v （使）叮当作响

While waiting for his wife at the checkout, the man with an impatient gleam in his eye jingled keys in his hand.
在结账处等候妻子的时候，那个眼中露出不耐烦的人，手中拨弄着钥匙，叮当作响。
- tinkle 叮当声
- ... with an impatient gleam in one's eye ……眼中露出不耐烦

> gleam (P. 573)

0497 jolly [ˈdʒɑːli] a 快活的 ad 非常

The lady who looked jolly wandered in the shopping center from dawn to dusk.
那个看起来很愉快的女士在这家购物中心从早逛到晚。
- glad 高兴的
- jolly up 鼓励……积极起来

> **语法重点**
> jolly 的比较级和最高级形式为 jollier, jolliest。

0498 journalism [ˈdʒɜːrnəlɪzəm] n 新闻学，新闻工作

There is sure to be the book about journalism you want to buy in the bookstore.
这家书店一定有你想买的那本关于新闻的书。
- newspapering 报业
- there is sure to be... ……一定有……

0499 journalist [ˈdʒɜːrnəlɪst] n 新闻记者

The journalist was in his uncontrollable furies when the robbery took place in the supermarket.
超市中发生抢劫案，那位记者怒不可遏。
- photo journalist 摄影记者

0500 jug [dʒʌg] n 水壶 v 用陶罐煮

The housewife tried to curb an impulse to buy that lovely coffee jug.
这位家庭主妇试图控制自己的冲动，不去买那个漂亮的咖啡壶。
- curb an impulse to... 控制……冲动

> **语法重点**
> jug 作可数名词，用于英式英语中，美式英语中则是用作 pitcher。

0501 **jury** [ˈdʒʊri] n 陪审团，评奖团

The member of the jury who behaved so badly in the mall went down in our esteem.
那位陪审团成员在这家购物中心里举止恶劣，我们对他的看法一落千丈。
- trial by jury 陪审审判
- ... go down in one's esteem ⋯⋯看法一落千丈

语法重点
jury 作集体名词，通常用作 be / serve / sit on a jury。
esteem (P. 563)

0502 **justify** [ˈdʒʌstɪfaɪ] v 证明⋯⋯有理

We found it hard to justify his buying such a large estate.
我们无法理解，他怎么会买这么大的地产。
- ... find it hard to justify one's doing... ⋯⋯无法理解某人⋯⋯

0503 **juvenile** [ˈdʒuːvənl] n 青少年

To her immense relief, she still had enough money to buy those juvenile books.
让她感到极大安慰的是，她还有足够的钱买那些少年读物。
- teener 青少年
- juvenile delinquency 少年违法犯罪

0504 **kin** [kɪn] n 亲戚，家族 a 有亲属关系的，同类的

There is still an immense amount of money to buy gifts for your kin.
你还有很多钱可以买礼物给你的亲戚们。
- relative 亲戚
- of kin 有亲戚关系的，类似的

0505 **kindle** [ˈkɪndl] v 点燃，鼓舞，着火，激动

When she saw the comic book in the bookstore, the schoolgirl's eyes kindled with excitement.
在书店里看到这本漫画书，那个女生的眼中闪现出激动的光芒。

0506 **knowledgeable** [ˈnɑːlɪdʒəbl] a 渊博的，有知识的，聪明的

The bookseller seems to be quite knowledgeable about literature.
那位书商似乎对文学极有见地。

0507 **lad** [læd] n 男孩，伙伴，老朋友

He has been buying a Christmas card for his mother every year since he was a lad.
从幼时至今，他每年都买一张圣诞贺卡给妈妈。

0508 **lame** [leɪm] a 跛的，瘸的，蹩脚的

The lame old man got into a flap because of the shopkeeper's unpleasant expressions.
那位跛脚的老人因为店主的不悦目光而忐忑不安。
- lame duck 投机者，无用的人
- ... get into a flap ⋯⋯忐忑不安

语法重点
lame 的比较级和最高级形式为 lamer, lamest 或是 more lame, most lame。

0509 landlord ['lændlɔːrd] n 男房东

The landlord bought daily necessities for the young man who suffered great losses and was frantic with grief.
那位房东为了那个遭受极大损失、悲痛欲绝的年轻人买了些日用品。
🔄 ... be frantic with grief ……悲痛欲绝

⊙ frantic (P. 571)

0510 landlady ['lændleɪdi] n 女房东

The landlady who comes to buy bedclothes seems to be slightly off her rocker.
那位来买寝具用品的女房东似乎有点儿精神失常。
🔄 hostess 女主人   🔄 ... be slightly off one's rocker ……有点儿精神失常

▸ 语法重点
landlady 作可数名词，其复数形式为 landladies，在英式英语中，也可表示"酒店、寄宿舍的女店主"。

0511 laser ['leɪzər] n 激光

We cannot believe what you say for there to be no bar codes of these products in the store read by lasers.
我们无法相信你所说的这家店里的产品条码并不是以激光识别的。
🔄 laser beam 激光光束

0512 latitude ['lætɪtuːd] n 纬度，纬度地区，范围

They seem to allow their daughter too much latitude in spending money.
他们似乎对女儿的零用钱太过放任。
🔄 longitude 经度，经线   🔄 north latitude 北纬

▸ 语法重点
latitude 作不可数名词，表示"纬度（缩写形式为 lat）、行动、意见自由"，latitudes 则是表示"纬度地区"。

0513 lawmaker ['lɔːmeɪkər] n 立法者

The lawmaker said the imposition of the tax on luxury goods might cause a sharp rise in price.
那位立法者说，对奢侈品征税也许会导致价格急剧上涨。
🔄 legislator 立法   🔄 cause a sharp rise in... 引起……急剧上涨

▸ 语法重点
imposition 作不可数名词，表示"负担"，通常用作 imposition of... on / upon；作可数名词，表示"征税，欺骗"。

0514 layer ['leɪ] n 层，层次，铺设者

She did not want to buy that desk because there was a layer of dust on it.
她不想买那张桌子，因为桌子上有一层灰。
🔄 thickness 厚度，层

▸ 语法重点
dust 作不可数名词，用于修辞中，可以表示"遗骸"。

0515 league [liːg] n 联盟，联合会，社团

The two kinds of products appear to be not in the same league.
这两种产品似乎并不是同一个等级的。
🔄 association 协会，联盟   🔄 in league with... 与……密谋（联合），伙同

0516 **legislation** [ˌledʒɪsˈleɪʃn] n 立法

New legislation on the sale of tobacco cast a gloom over the businessman.
有关烟草售卖的新法规使得这位商人愁眉不展。
- statute 法令，法规 - legislation committee 立法委员会
- ... cast a gloom over... ……使……愁眉不展

语法重点
legislation 作不可数名词，表示"法律，立法"；law 作可数名词，表示"法律，法规"，泛指立法机构通过的成文、不成文的法律法规。

0517 **lessen** [ˈlesn] v 减少，贬低，看不起

You had better try to lessen the risk of excessive expenditure.
你最好尽力减少超支的风险。
- diminish 减少 - increase 增加 - lessen the risk of... 减少……的风险

→ excessive (P. 717)

0518 **lest** [lest] conj 以免

She was anxious lest they may fail to balance expenditure with income.
她担心他们会超支。

0519 **lieutenant** [luːˈtenənt] n 中尉，少尉

The lieutenant is demented with worry about the expenditure on weapons.
那位陆军中尉担心武器方面的开支。

→ weapon (P. 244)

0520 **lifelong** [ˈlaɪflɒŋ] a 终身的，永生不渝的

The young man dreamed of having a lifelong job so that he can have enough money to spend.
那个年轻人希望有个铁饭碗，那么，他就有足够的钱可以用了。
- womb-to-tomb 一辈子的 - lifelong learning 终身学习
- have a lifelong job 有铁饭碗

0521 **likelihood** [ˈlaɪklihʊd] n 可能性

There is a strong likelihood that she will buy that sweater.
她极有可能买那件毛衣。
- probability 可能性 - in all likelihood 十分可能

0522 **lime** [laɪm] n 石灰 v 撒石灰于

There is very little likelihood of his buying much burnt lime.
他不可能买很多生石灰。
- kalk 石灰 - slaked lime 熟石灰

语法重点
lime 作不可数名词，表示"石灰（quicklime），淡黄绿色（相当于 lime green）"，作可数名词，表示"酸橙，酸橙树"。

0523 **limp** [lɪmp] n 跛行 v 蹒跚 a 柔软的，无力的

The man who walked with a slight limp came to buy some lime juice.
那个走路有点儿跛的人来买了一些酸橙汁。
- hilch 跛行 - hobble limp 跛行

语法重点
limp 作不及物动词，通常与介词 about, along, away, off 等连用。

legislation ~ logo

0524 linger [ˈlɪŋər] v 继续逗留，缓慢消失
She wanted to go shopping at once, but her husband still lingered long over his meal.
她想立即去购物，然而，她的丈夫还在慢吞吞地吃饭。
⊜ remain 逗留　　⊝ leave 离开　　⊜ loiter linger 徘徊

> **语法重点**
> linger 作不及物动词，通常与介词 about, around, on 等连用。

0525 livestock [ˈlaɪvstɑːk] n 家畜，牲畜
The likelihood is that they will spend much money on livestock farming.
他们可能会花很多钱发展畜牧业。
⊜ livestock husbandry 畜牧业　　⊜ the likelihood is that... ……有可能

> **语法重点**
> livestock 作不可数名词，也可以视为集体名词，表示"牛、马、羊等家畜的统称"。

0526 lizard [ˈlɪzərd] n 蜥蜴
His brother's words reduced the likelihood that he will buy a lizard as a pet.
哥哥的话减少了他买只蜥蜴作宠物的可能性。
⊜ worm lizard 蚯蚓　　⊜ reduce the likelihood that... 减少……的可能性

> **语法重点**
> lizard 作可数名词，表示"蜥蜴"；作不可数名词，表示"蜥蜴皮革"。
> ⊜ likelihood (P. 590)

0527 locomotive [ˌloʊkəˈmoʊtɪv] n 火车头
The man who repaired the locomotive had to check an impulse to buy gifts for his daughter.
那个修理火车头的男子克制了想买礼物给女儿的冲动。
⊜ check an impulse to... 克制……冲动

0528 locust [ˈloʊkəst] n 蝗虫
An air of gloom settled over the farmer who could not afford the agentia to kill the locusts.
那位买不起除蝗药剂的农民十分忧郁。
⊜ grasshopper 蝗虫　　⊜ locust plague 蝗灾

> **语法重点**
> locust 作可数名词。

0529 lodge [lɑːdʒ] n 旅社 v 暂住，嵌入
There is no time to linger; let's lodge at the hotel.
没有时间拖延了，我们就住这家旅馆吧。
⊜ board and lodging 膳宿　　⊜ there is no time to linger... 没有时间拖延……

> **语法重点**
> lodge 作不及物动词，表示"寄宿，租住房屋"，通常与介词 at 或是 with 连用；作及物动词，表示"提供暂时住处，寄存"。

0530 lofty [ˈlɔːfti] a 非常高的
The salesman has a lofty position in the company.
那个推销员在公司里地位很高。
⊜ lofty ideal 崇高的理想　　⊜ have a lofty position in... 在……地位高

> **语法重点**
> lofty 的比较级和最高级形式为 loftier, loftiest。
> ⊜ position (P. 077)

0531 logo [ˈloʊgoʊ] n 商标
She bought four paper cups bearing the company's logo.
她买了四个印有这家公司标志的纸杯。
⊜ brand 商标　　⊜ ... bear / with... logo ……印有……标识

0532 **lonesome** [ˈloʊnsəm] a 孤独的，人迹稀少的，寂寥的
She went shopping all by her lonesome.
她独自去购物。
反 crowded 拥挤的 同 do sth. by / on one's lonesome 某人独自地……

0533 **longitude** [ˈlɑːndʒətuːd] n 经度
The gloom deepened as he learnt he cannot go to visit the island whose position was longitude 125 degrees east.
得知不能去那个东经125°的岛上观光，他越发郁闷。
同 shute 经线 同 west longitude 西经

0534 **lotus** [ˈloʊtəs] n 睡莲，莲花图案，莲属植物
You can command a broad prospect of lotus flowers in the hotel.
在这家旅馆可以眺望莲花的广阔景色。
同 padma 莲花 同 lotus land 安乐乡

0535 **lottery** [ˈlɑːtəri] n 彩票（奖券）
The boy rubbed his hands with glee at the thought of buying a lottery ticket.
想到要去买彩票，那个男孩开心得直搓手。
同 lottery ticket 彩票，奖券

> **语法重点**
> lottery 作可数名词，表示"彩票"，其复数形式为 lotteries，取其比喻意义，表示"碰巧的事"时，通常用作单数形式。

0536 **lumber** [ˈlʌmbər] n 木材，隆隆声 v 砍伐，笨重地行进
The lumber seller was said to have a mind lumbered with idle gossip.
据说，那个木材商脑子里尽是些流言蜚语。
同 timber 木材 同 ... have a mind lumbered with... ……脑子里尽是……

○ gossip (P. 301)

0537 **lump** [lʌmp] n 一块，团
She had a lump in her throat when she found her boyfriend bought a diamond ring for her.
发现男朋友买了一枚钻戒给她，她喉中哽咽。
同 block 块 同 lump sum 总额，汇总
同 ... have a lump in the / one's throat ……喉中哽咽

○ diamond (P. 152)

0538 **magnify** [ˈmæɡnɪfaɪ] v 扩大，夸大，夸张
She magnified the problem of money shortage, hoping to stop her husband buying that car.
她夸大了钱财短缺的困难，希望能阻止丈夫买那辆车。
同 broaden 放大 反 minify 变小 同 magnify the problem of... 夸大……问题

0539 **maiden** [ˈmeɪdn] n 少女 a 处女的，初次的
The woman's maiden name is Liu.
那个女人的娘家姓刘。
同 maiden flight 首航

lonesome ~ mansion

0540 mainland ['meɪnlænd] n 大陆，本土
It may cost much money to travel to the island lying off the coast of mainland Britain.
去那个远离英国大陆的岛上旅游也许会花费很多钱。
🔄 landmass 大陆　🔄 lie off the coast of... 远离……海岸

> **语法重点**
> lie off 表示"暂停工作，与陆地保持一段距离"，通常后接名词或是代词。

0541 mainstream ['meɪnstriːm] n 主流，主要倾向　a 主流的
Entertainment seems to have been absorbed into the mainstream of expenditures.
娱乐似乎已经成为消费支出的主流。

> **语法重点**
> mainstream 作可数名词，本意是"河川主流"，取其延伸意义，表示"思想、潮流的主流"时，通常与介词 of 连用。

0542 maintenance ['meɪntənəns]
n 保养，维修，抚养费，保持
The price maintenance may linger on for two weeks.
这个价格也许可以保持两周不变。
🔄 preservation 保持　🔄 maintenance man 维修工　🔄 linger on for... 延期……

> **语法重点**
> maintenance 作不可数名词，通常"维修"，用于律法中则可表示"赡养费"，通常用作 pay maintenance to.
> 🔄 linger (P. 591)

0543 majestic [mə'dʒestɪk] a 巨大的，壮丽的，庄重的
He has to find a hotel with majestic views.
他必须找家景致优美的旅馆。
🔄 magnificent 壮丽的　🔄 majestic views 壮丽的景色

0544 majesty ['mædʒəsti] n 雄伟，壮丽，庄严
The majesty of the mountain scenery impressed itself in our memory.
壮丽的高山景象给我们留下了深刻的印象。

> **语法重点**
> majesty 作不可数名词，表示"庄严"。Majesty 则是作可数名词，与所有格形式连用，以称呼王室成员。

0545 mammal ['mæml] n 哺乳动物
The curator need to collect more money to provide better surroundings for these marine mammals.
那位馆长需要募集更多的钱来为这些海洋哺乳动物提供更好的环境。
🔄 mammalian 哺乳类　🔄 mammal science 哺乳动物学

> 🔄 marine (P. 594)

0546 manifest ['mænɪfest] v 显示，表明　a 明显的，显然的
It is manifest to everyone that she bought a jade bracelet last week.
大家都知道，上周她买了个玉镯。
🔄 apparent 显然的　🔄 unconspicuous 不明显的　🔄 cargo manifest 载货清单

0547 mansion ['mænʃn] n 大厦，宅第
The rich man manifested little interest in buying that mansion.
那个富人对买那栋大厦没有什么兴趣。
🔄 manifest little interest in... 对……没有兴趣

> **语法重点**
> mansion 作可数名词。

0548 **maple** ['meɪpl] n 枫树，淡棕色
Carelessness was a lame excuse for your forgetting to buy that maple desk.
疏忽并不是你忘记买那张枫木书桌的充分理由。
🔄 maple leaf 枫叶

0549 **marginal** ['mɑːrdʒɪnl] a 边缘的，临界的，最低限度的
There is only a marginal improvement in the sale of tobacco.
烟草销售只是轻微好转。

0550 **marine** [məˈriːn] a 海洋的，航海的 n 船只，海军
Marine stores appear to be of marginal interest to the man.
那个男人似乎对船用物品不感兴趣。
🔄 marine biology 海洋生物学　be of marginal interest to... 对……不感兴趣

> **语法重点**
> marine 作形容词，无比较级和最高级形式。

0551 **marshal** ['mɑːrʃl]
n 司仪，执法官，元帅 v 整顿，配置
The marshal marshaled his thoughts and decided to increase the expenditure of money on weapons.
那位元帅整理了自己的思绪，决定增加购买武器的费用。
🔄 field marshal 陆军元帅　increase the expenditure of... 增加……的费用

> **语法重点**
> marshal 作可数名词，表示"元帅，高级军官"，通常用于构成复合词，如：执法官、警察局长、消防局长。

0552 **martial** ['mɑːrʃl] a 战争的
When the government imposed martial law, the price of daily necessities sharply increased.
政府实行军事管制时，日用品价格急剧增长。
🔁 militant 好斗的　🔄 peaceful 和平的
🔄 ... impose martial law ……实行军事管制

0553 **marvel** ['mɑːrvl] n 令人惊奇的事或人 v 对……感到惊奇
It was a marvel that she should buy such a cheap dress.
她居然买了一件这么便宜的连衣裙，真是不可思议。
🔄 marvel at 对……感到惊奇　it is a marvel that... ……真是不可思议

0554 **masculine** ['mæskjəlɪn] n 男性 a 男性的，阳性的
We marvel that she looks masculine in that garment.
我们大为惊奇的是，她穿上那件衣服有些男性化。
🔁 manly 男性的　🔄 feminine 女性的

> **语法重点**
> masculine 也可以作可数名词，表示"阳性词，阳性形式"。
> 🔗 garment (P. 572)

0555 **mash** [mæʃ] n 麦芽浆，马铃薯泥 v 把……捣成糊状
You go to buy some bangers and mash, and I will perform marvels at the kitchen stove.
你去买些香肠和马铃薯泥，我来做些美味佳肴。
🔁 mix 混合物　🔄 mash goods 麦芽汁产品

0556 massage [mə'sɑːʒ] n / v 按摩，推拿

The masseur gave him a relaxing massage for free.
那位按摩师免费为他做放松按摩。
- knead 按摩
- ... give sb. a relaxing massage ……为某人做放松按摩

0557 massive ['mæsɪv] a 大量的，大规模的

The young man bought a massive amount of alcohol yesterday.
那个年轻人昨天买了大量的酒。
- tremendous 巨大的
- light 轻的
- sb. buys a massive amount of... 某人买了大量的……

→ alcohol (P. 393)

0558 masterpiece ['mæstəpiːs] n 杰作，名著

She wanted to buy a masterpiece of that writer, but her mother treated her request with indifference.
她想买那位作家的杰出著作，但她妈妈对她的请求置若罔闻。
- masterwork 杰作
- ... treat... with indifference ……对……置若罔闻

0559 mayonnaise ['meɪəneɪz] n 美乃滋

Her husband was actually a marvel of patience and he could wait for an hour in line just to buy some mayonnaise.
她的丈夫是个极有耐心的人，他可以为了买美乃滋而排一小时的队。

语法重点
mayonnaise 作不可数名词，表示"美乃滋"，源自法语，也可写作 mayo。

0560 meantime ['miːntaɪm] n 同时

She went shopping; in the meantime, her daughter stayed at home and watched TV.
她去购物，同时，她的女儿在家里看电视。
- for the meantime 在此期间
- in the meantime 同时

0561 mechanics [mə'kænɪk] n 机械学，构成法，技术

Buying jewels is out of my territory, I am only interested in mechanics.
我不懂怎样买宝石，我只对机械学感兴趣。
- statistical mechanics 统计力学
- ... be out of my territory 我不懂……

语法重点
mechanics 作不可数名词，表示"力学，机械学"，the mechanics 则是作复数名词，表示"机件，工作部件，手法"。

→ territory (P. 373)

0562 mediate ['miːdieɪt] v 调解，斡旋

It's difficult to mediate between the buyer and the seller.
在买方和卖方之间调停斡旋是困难的。
- intercede 调停
- mediate between... and... 在……和……之间斡旋调停

0563 menace ['menəs] v 威胁，恐吓 n 威胁

The novel you bought creates an atmosphere of menace.
你买的那本小说营造了一种恐吓威胁的氛围。
- threat 威胁
- create an atmosphere of... 营造了一种……氛围

语法重点
menace 作不可数名词，表示"威胁"；作单数可数名词，表示"进行威胁的人或事物"，通常用作 be a menace to。

0564 mermaid ['mɜːrmeɪd] n 美人鱼，女子游泳健将
She bought a story book about the story of the Little Mermaid.
她买了一本关于小美人鱼的故事书。

0565 midst [mɪdst] n 中间，当中
A person in our midst should go to buy some butter.
我们之中有个人得去买些奶油。
同 centre 中部　　搭 midst link 中间环节

0566 migrant ['maɪɡrənt] n 移民，候鸟，迁移动物
The migrant who bought cotton plantations was said to lose his grip on reality.
据说那个购买了棉花种植园的移民不了解现实。
同 immigrant 移民　　搭 migrant worker 外来工

⇨ plantation (P. 613)

0567 mileage ['maɪlɪdʒ] n 行驶里数，好处，运费
His father bought a used car with a low mileage last month.
上个月，他爸爸买了一辆行驶里程数少的二手车。
同 mile 英里　　搭 gas mileage 每英里汽油消耗量

语法重点
mileage 作可数名词或不可数名词时，表示"英里数"；作不可数名词，表示"汽车里数津贴"，等于 mileage allowance。

0568 milestone ['maɪlstoʊn] n 里程碑
The figure marked a milestone in the history of the sale of rice.
这个数字是稻米销售历史上的里程碑。
同 landmark 里程碑　　搭 mark a milestone in the history of... 是……历史上的里程碑

0569 mingle ['mɪŋɡl] v 使混合，相交往
The seller mingled wine with water and sold to customers.
那个卖家以水兑酒，卖给顾客。
同 mix 混合　　搭 mingle with 混杂　　mingle... with... 用……和……混合

0570 minimal ['mɪnɪml] a 最小的，最低限度的
There is only a minimal amount of risk involved in the sale of daily necessities.
出售日用品只有最低限度的风险。
同 smallest 较小的　　反 maximal 最大的　　搭 minimal path 最短路径

语法重点
minimal 通常是指数量、程度最少或是最低，其副词形式为 minimally。
⇨ involve (P. 463)

0571 mint [mɪnt] n 薄荷，铸币场 v 铸造（硬币）
We would like a sprig of mint if it's not too much of an imposition to you.
要是不会为你添太多麻烦的话，我们想要一小枝薄荷。

语法重点
mint 作不可数名词，表示"薄荷"；作可数名词或不可数名词，表示"薄荷糖"；作可数名词，表示"铸币厂"。

mermaid ~ mold

0572 **miser** [ˈmaɪzər] n 吝啬鬼
You should never expect the miser to buy you a drink for a change.
永远不要指望让那个守财奴请你喝一杯。
moneygrubber 守财奴　　buy sb. a drink 请某人喝一杯

0573 **mistress** [ˈmɪstrəs] n 女主人，老板娘，情妇
His daughter always wanted to be mistress of her own affairs, so he did not buy clothes for her.
他女儿总是希望自己的事情可以自己做主，所以他没有买衣服给她。

affair (P. 122)

0574 **moan** [moʊn] v 呻吟，抱怨 n 呻吟声
The boy seems to be always moaning on about how little pocket money he has.
那个男孩似乎总是在抱怨零用钱太少。
groan 呻吟　　moan loud 呻吟大叫　　moan on... 抱怨……

0575 **mock** [mɑːk] v 嘲弄 a 模拟的，假装的
His friend mocked his attempts to buy that ring.
他的朋友嘲笑他自不量力地想买那个戒指。
deride 嘲笑　　make (a) mock of 嘲笑
mock one's attempts to... 嘲笑……不自量力

attempt (P. 257)

0576 **mode** [moʊd] n 方式，样式，流行
They had a good moan about the latest mode of the dress.
他们对最新款的连衣裙抱怨了一番。
style 风格　　flash mode 闪光灯模式

语法重点
mode 作可数名词，通常与介词 of 连用，表示"流行，样式"，通常作单数形式。

0577 **modernize** [ˈmɑːdərnaɪz] v 现代化 n 现代化事物
There is great mileage in spending money modernizing farming methods.
花些钱使耕作方式现代化是十分有益的。
there is great mileage in... ……是十分有益的

0578 **modify** [ˈmɑːdɪfaɪ] v 修改，修饰
His wife modified her position and agreed to buy that apartment.
他妻子改变立场，同意购买那栋公寓。
alter 更改　　modify password 修改密码
modify one's position 改变立场

语法重点
modify 通常是指细微的变化，其过去式和过去分词形式为 modified, modified。

position (P. 077)

0579 **mold** [moʊld] n 模型，性格 v 塑造，对……产生影响
The lady who always buys books is of gentle mold.
那位经常买书的女士性情温和。
model 模型　　be of gentle mold... 性情温和……

0580 molecule ['mɑ:lɪkju:l] n 分子，微粒
The perfume with activated molecules was regarded as a sign of femininity.
这种含有活性分子的香水被视为女性专用。
- microne 微粒
- polar molecule 极性分子
- be regarded as a sign of ... 被视为……的标志

◎ perfume (P. 493)

0581 monarch ['mɑ:nərk] n 君主，最高统治者
There is a limit to how much the monarch could spend on weapons.
那位君主可以花多少钱来买武器，是有限制的。
- sovereign 君主
- civilian 平民
- there is a limit to... ……是有限制的

0582 monstrous ['mɑ:nstrəs] a 怪异的，巨大的
It's absolutely monstrous to spend so much money on such inferior goods.
花那么多钱买这么劣质的东西，真是太不像话了。
- monstrous crimes 滔天罪行
- it's absolutely monstrous to... ……真是太不像话了

◎ inferior (P. 310)

0583 mortal ['mɔ:rtl] a 会死的
The collapse of the department store should be a mortal blow to the man.
对于那人来说，百货公司倒闭是致命的打击。
- fatal 致命的
- mortal enemies 不共戴天的敌人
- be a mortal blow to... 对于……来说是致命的打击

◎ 语法重点
mortal 没有比较级和最高级形式。

0584 moss [mɔ:s] n 苔藓，地衣 v 以苔藓覆盖
My mother asked me to buy some long thread moss, but I forgot it.
妈妈要我去买些发菜，我却忘记了。
- a rolling stone gathers no moss 滚石不生苔

0585 motherhood ['mʌðərhʊd] n 母性
His wife appeared to have not been ready for motherhood.
他的妻子似乎还没有做好当母亲的准备。
- maternalism 母性
- ... be ready for... ……为……做准备

0586 motive ['moʊtɪv] n 动机，目的
You had better question his motive in offering to buy that necklace for you.
你最好问清楚他买那串项链给你的动机。
- motivation 动机
- behavioral motive 行为动机
- ... question / examine one's motive in doing... 询问……的动机

◎ 语法重点
motive 作可数名词，表示"动机，原因"，通常与介词 for 连用。

molecule ~ mutter

0587 mound [maʊnd] n 土石堆，堆
Her mother gave her some money and asked her to send a mound of washing and ironing to the laundry.
她妈妈给了她一些钱，让她把一堆要洗熨的衣服送到洗衣店。
🔄 heap 堆　🔄 send a mound of... to... 把一堆……送到……

0588 mount [maʊnt] v 登，爬上 n 山
Those travelers buy some mountaineering equipment and plan to mount to the top of that mount.
那些游客买了些登山装备，打算登上那座山的顶峰。
🔄 mountain 山　🔄 mount to the top of... 登上……顶

语法重点
mount 作可数名词，表示"山"，现今也可以用于地名中，通常用缩写 Mt.。

0589 mower ['moʊər] n 割草者，割草机
It's believed that he had an ulterior motive for buying that rotary mower.
我们相信，他买那个旋转式割草机是有隐秘的动机的。
🔄 lawnmower 割草机

⊃ motive (P. 598)

0590 mumble ['mʌmbl] v 含糊地说 n 含糊，咕哝
The little girl mumbled that she wanted to buy some sweets.
那个小女孩咕哝着说，她想买些糖果。
🔄 murmur 低语　🔄 sb. mumbles that... 某人咕哝着说……

语法重点
mumble 表示"咕哝"，作不及物动词，通常用作 mumble about；作及物动词，通常用作 mumble... to sb. 或是后接宾语从句。

0591 muscular ['mʌskjələr] a 肌肉的，强壮的
The man with a muscular body feels disposed for shopping.
那个体格健壮的人愿意去购物。
🔄 muscular dystrophy 肌肉萎缩症　🔄 sb. feels disposed for... 愿意……

0592 muse [mjuːz] v 深思，谨慎地考虑 n 默想
He mused that it might take more money to buy that apartment.
他沉思着，要是买那栋公寓的话，也许要花费更多钱。
🔄 muse on 考虑　🔄 sb. muses that... 某人沉思……

语法重点
muse 表示"沉思自语地说"时，可以后接宾语从句。

0593 mustard ['mʌstərd] n 芥菜，芥末色
Tell that to the marines. She bought a mustard sweater.
我不相信，她竟然会买一件芥末黄的毛衣。
🔄 Tell that to the marines. 我不相信。

0594 mutter ['mʌtər] v 低声含糊地说，抱怨
She muttered away to herself as wandering in the supermarket.
在超市里闲逛的时候，她独自叽叽咕咕地说个不停。

⊃ wander (P. 383)

0595 mutton ['mʌtn] n 羊肉
His wife bought a leg of mutton from the butcher's.
他妻子在肉铺买了羊腿肉。
lamb 羔羊肉　　mutton skewer 羊肉串

▷ butcher (P. 537)

0596 myth [mɪθ] n 神话，神怪故事
The book seller who was as keen as mustard recommended the book about ancient Greek myth to her.
那位极为热心的书商向她推荐那本关于古希腊神话的书。
legend 传奇　　Greek myth 希腊神话
... be as keen as mustard ……极为热心的

▷ mustard (P. 599)

0597 nag [næg] v 使烦恼 n 马
She had been nagging her father all day long to buy her that laptop.
她整日地央求爸爸给她买那台笔记本电脑。
nag at 唠叨　　nag... to do 不停地央求……

语法重点
nag 的过去式和过去分词为 nagged, nagged。

0598 naive [naɪ'iːv] a 天真的，单纯的
It would be naive of us to think that we could afford that apartment.
如果我们认为自己买得起那栋公寓，就太天真了。
mature 成熟的
it would be naive of... to think that... 如果认为……就太天真了

0599 nasty ['næsti] a 令人作呕的
Being unable to buy that skirt left a nasty taste in the mouth.
无力购买那件裙子，让人觉得耻辱。
nasty laugher 奸笑　　... leave a nasty in the mouth ……觉得耻辱 / 厌恶

0600 navigate ['nævɪgeɪt] v 操纵，使通过
She doesn't like to go to that commercial district because she hates to navigate with difficulty through the crowd.
她不喜欢去那个商业区，因为她讨厌在人群中艰难前行。
navigate around 浏览

语法重点
navigate 作不及物动词，表示"领航"；作及物动词，表示"驾驶，航行"。

0601 newscast ['nuːzkæst] n 新闻报道
The betting was that people would not buy such milk products after listening to the newscast.
听过这个新闻广播之后，人们很有可能不会再买这些乳制品了。
evening newscast 晚间新闻　　the betting is that... 很有可能的是……

0602 nibble ['nɪbl] v 一点点地吃 n 轻咬，显出有兴趣

She nagged her sister for a new dress, while her sister just nibbled at the sandwich.
她不停央求姐姐给她买一件新连衣裙，姐姐只是漫不经心地咬着三明治。
● chew 咀嚼 ● nibble at 一点点儿地咬 ● nag... for... 不停地为……央求

语法重点
nibble 的过去式为 nibbled。

0603 nickel ['nɪkl] n 镍，五分镍币

Learning that the miser would not spend a nickel on food gave us a nasty shock.
得知那个吝啬鬼连五分镍币都不舍得花在食物上，我们大为震惊。

语法重点
nickle 作不可数名词，表示"镍"；作可数名词，表示"美国、加拿大的五分镍币"。

0604 nightingale ['naɪtɪŋɡeɪl] n 夜莺

She nagged her boyfriend into buying a nightingale for her.
她不断央求男朋友给她买一只夜莺。

语法重点
nightingale 作可数名词，表示"夜莺"；Nightingale 则是指姓氏"南丁格尔"。

0605 nominate ['nɑːmɪneɪt] v 提名，任命

We nominated you to do the shopping.
我们提议你去购物。
● nominate sb. 任命某人 ● ... nominate sb. to do... ……建议某人……

0606 nonetheless [ˌnʌnðə'les] ad 但是

The problem of money shortage has been nagging him for weeks; nonetheless, he did not tell it to his wife.
钱财短缺的问题已经困扰了他几个星期，但他没有和妻子说。

语法重点
nonetheless 作副词，也可以说 none the less，等于 nevertheless。
↪ nag (P. 600)

0607 nonviolent [ˌnɑn'vaɪələnt] a 非暴力的

They assumed that they could tackle the problem with the seller through nonviolent communication.
他们以为通过非暴力的沟通，就能解决与那位卖家的问题。
● peaceable 和平的 ● violent 暴力的 ● nonviolent means 非暴力手段

0608 nostril ['nɑːstrəl] n 鼻孔，鼻孔内壁

Their luxurious habits stunk in our nostrils.
他们奢侈的习惯令我们极为厌恶。
● nose 鼻子 ● ... stink in one's nostrils ……令……极为厌恶

语法重点
stink 的过去式为 stunk 或是 stank。

0609 notable ['noʊtəbl] a 显著的，著名的 n 名人

The notable writer made an absolute mint of money in the sale of the novel.
那位著名作家出售这部小说赚了一大笔钱。

语法重点
notable 也可以用作 be notable for / as，其副词形式为 notably。

◉ famous 著名的　◉ most notable 最值得一提

0610 noticeable ['noutɪsəbl] **a** 显著的，重要的

They expected noticeable improvement in the sale of jewelry.
他们期待珠宝销售额有明显的改善。
◉ obvious 显而易见的　◉ noticeable items 注意事项

◉ jewelry (P. 313)

0611 notify ['noutɪfaɪ] **v** 通知，告知，报告

You had better notify the school report card to his family as soon as possible.
你最好尽快将这份成绩单告知他的家人。
◉ inform 通知　◉ notify... to sb. 将……告知某人

语法重点
notify 的过去式和过去分词为 notified, notified。

0612 notion ['nouʃn] **n** 观念，意见，打算

His girlfriend appeared to have not the slightest notion of the price of the bracelet.
他女朋友似乎一点儿都不知道这个手镯的价格。
◉ conception 概念　◉ ingrain notion 根深蒂固的看法

0613 novice ['nɑːvɪs] **n** 初学者，新手，新信徒

The novice salesman appeared to have a nasty temper.
那个新售货员似乎脾气不好。
◉ beginner 初学者　◉ veteran 老手　◉ ... have a nasty temper ……脾气不好

◉ nasty (P. 600)

0614 nowhere ['nouwer] **ad** 任何地方都不

The shopkeeper has got nowhere with the sale of milk products by now.
到目前为止，那位店主的乳制品销售并没有什么进展。

语法重点
nowhere 作副词，表示"任何地方都不"；作不可数名词，表示"无人知道的地方"。

0615 nucleus ['nuːkliəs] **n** 原子核，核心，细胞核

The one thousand books bought last week form the nucleus of the library.
上周买的1 000本书是这个图书馆的核心部分。
◉ core 核心　◉ cell nucleus 细胞核
◉ ... form the nucleus of... ……构成……的主要部分

语法重点
nucleus 的复数形式为 nuclei 或 nucleuses。

0616 nude [nuːd] **a** 裸的，无装饰的，无效的　**n** 裸体

The nude statue bought by him was nowhere to be found.
他买的那个裸体雕塑找不到了。
◉ bare 赤裸的　◉ nude art 裸体艺术　◉ ... be nowhere to be found ……找不到

语法重点
nude 无比较级和最高级形式。

0617 oar [ɔːr] **n** 桨，划手　**v** 划（行）

She surely knew what gifts to buy for us, so you needn't shove your oar in.
她当然知道要买什么礼物给我们，所以你不必干涉。
◉ put one's oar in 插嘴　◉ ... shove one's oar in ……干涉

0618 **oasis** [oʊˈeɪsɪs] n 绿洲，乐土，慰藉物
The bookstore should be an oasis of calm in the noisy commercial district.
在喧闹的商业区，这个书店应是一方宁静之地。

语法重点
oasis 作可数名词，其复数形式为 oases。

0619 **oath** [oʊθ] n 誓约，咒骂
I will not buy that jade bracelet, on my oath.
我发誓，我不会买那个玉镯。
- pledge 誓言　- under oath 在法庭上宣过誓

语法重点
oath 作可数名词，其复数形式为 oaths。

0620 **oatmeal** [ˈoʊtmiːl] n 燕麦片
When his wife wanted to buy some oatmeal, he did not stick his oar in.
他的妻子想买些燕麦片，他没有干预。
- cornmeal 燕麦片　- instant oatmeal 即溶燕麦片
- stick one's oar in 干预……

0621 **oblong** [ˈɑːblɔːŋ] a 长方形的，矩形的 n 长方形
Her mother wanted the oblong table, but she had no notion of its price.
她妈妈想买这张长方形的桌子，但她不知道价格。
- rectangular 长方形的　- have no notion of... 不了解……

语法重点
oblong 作形容词，表示"长方形的"，等于 rectangular；作可数名词，表示"长方形"，等于 rectangle。

0622 **observer** [əbˈzɜːrvər] n 观察者，观察员
Observers noted the noticeable change in the price of daily necessities these two months.
观察员记下这两个月日用品价格的显著变化。
- viewer 观察者　- observer status 观察员身份

语法重点
observer 作可数名词，表示"观察员，旁观者"；也可表示"规则、宗教仪式的遵守者"，通常与介词 of 连用。

0623 **obstinate** [ˈɑːbstɪnət] a 顽固的，难于控制的
There is a very obstinate streak in the man who wants to buy a desk.
那个想买书桌的人很固执。
- stubborn 顽固的　- tame 顺从的　- obstinate disease 痼疾

0624 **occurrence** [əˈkɜːrəns] n 发生，出现，事件
Robbery seems to be of frequent occurrence in the commercial district.
这个商业区似乎经常发生抢劫事件。
- happening 发生　- random occurrence 随机事件

语法重点
occurrence 作可数名词，表示"事情，发生的事"；作不可数名词，表示"事情发生的频繁、事实"，用于正式文体中。
- commercial (P. 274)

0625 **octopus** [ˈɑːktəpəs] n 章鱼
The octopus bought by his father was nowhere to be seen.
他爸爸买的那只章鱼不见了。
- ... be nowhere to be seen ……不见了

0626 odds [ɑːdz] n 机会

The odds are in his favor because he is more experienced in selling daily goods.
他对于日用品的销售更有经验，所以可能会成功。
possibility 可能性　impossibility 不可能性　odds and ends 零碎物品

0627 odor [ˈoʊdər] n 气味，香气，味道

There is an odor of antiquity in the bookstore.
这家书店有种古色古香的格调。
fragrance 香气　stink 臭味

> **语法重点**
> odor 作可数名词，表示"香味，香气"；作不可数名词，表示"名声，声望"。

0628 olive [ˈɑːlɪv] n 橄榄

It's a waste of money buying so many olives.
买这么多橄榄是浪费钱。
it's a waste of money doing... ……是浪费钱

> waste (P. 110)

0629 opponent [əˈpoʊnənt] n 对手，敌手，对抗者

Opponents of the price increase in eggs hurled a few oaths at the seller.
那些反对鸡蛋价格上涨的人对那个卖家咒骂了几句。
objector 反对者　supporter 拥护者　political opponent 政敌
hurl a few oaths at... 对……咒骂几句

> **语法重点**
> opponent 作可数名词，表示"反对者"，通常与介词 of 连用；表示"对手"，通常与介词 at 或 in 连用。
> hurl (P. 581)

0630 optimism [ˈɑːptɪmɪzəm] n 乐观主义

The young man was full of optimism about the future despite having no money to buy a house.
虽然那个年轻人没钱买房，他对将来却很乐观。
be full of optimism about... 对……很乐观

> **语法重点**
> optimism 为不可数名词。

0631 orchard [ˈɔːrtʃərd] n 果园

His father was such an optimist that he believed he can buy all kinds of fruits in the orchard.
他爸爸十分乐观，他相信能在这个果园里买到所有品种的水果。

> **语法重点**
> orchard 作可数名词，表示"果园"；作不可数名词，表示"果园中果树的总称"。

0632 organizer [ˈɔːrɡənaɪzər] n 组织者，发起人

They were always at odds with the organizer over the expenditure.
他们常常为开支问题而与组织者争吵。
constitutor 组织者　personal organizer 个人备忘记事本

0633 orient [ˈɔːrient] n 东方　v 定方位

Tea and spices from the Orient once were in good odor with the aristocracy.
东方国家的茶叶和香料一度很受贵族阶级的欢迎。
east 东方　be in good odor with... 很受……欢迎

> **语法重点**
> orient 作可数名词，表示"东方"；the Orient 则是表示"东方诸国"。

0634 **oriental** [ˌɔːriˈentl] a 东方的，东方国家的

It's odds that his uncle will buy a painting with a typical feature of oriental art.

他叔叔可能会买一幅具有东方艺术典型风格的画。

- orient 东方的
- orient pearl 东方明珠
- it's odds that... ……有可能……

typical (P. 379)

0635 **ornament** [ˈɔːrnəmənt] n 装饰品，装饰

You had better not buy that clock which is simply for ornament.

你最好不要买那个只作装饰用的钟。

- decorate 装饰
- metal ornament 金属饰物

语法重点
ornament 作不可数名词，表示"装饰，点缀"；作可数名词，表示"装饰物，摆设"。

0636 **orphanage** [ˈɔːrfənɪdʒ] n 孤儿院，孤儿身份

They had a notion that the child from the orphanage stole money from the store.

他们以为那个从孤儿院来的孩子在这家店偷钱。

- have a notion that... 以为……

语法重点
orphanage 作可数名词，表示"孤儿院"；作不可数名词，表示"孤儿身份"。

0637 **ostrich** [ˈɑːstrɪtʃ] n 鸵鸟，逃避现实的人

It made no odds to me whether you buy that dress trimmed with ostrich feathers.

你是否买那件饰有鸵鸟羽毛的连衣裙与我无关。

语法重点
ostrich 作可数名词，其复数形式为 ostriches。

0638 **ounce** [aʊns] n 盎司

If he possessed an ounce of business sense, his store would not go into bankruptcy.

如果他有一点儿做生意的常识，他的商店就不会倒闭。

- ounce 作可数名词，表示"盎司"，重量单位，约为 28.35 克，其缩写形式为 oz。

语法重点
ounce 表示"少量，一点儿"，与动词的否定形式连用。

0639 **outdo** [ˌaʊtˈduː] v 胜过，优于

Not to be outdone, she was determined to make more money to buy a better apartment.

不想被人超过，她决定赚更多的钱，买一栋更好的公寓。

- surpass 超过
- outdo yourself 超越自我
- not to be outdone... 不想被超过……

语法重点
outdo 的第三人称单数形式为 outdoes，过去式为 outdid，过去分词为 outdone。

determine (P. 283)

0640 **outgoing** [ˈaʊtɡoʊɪŋ] a 外向的，即将卸任的

The shopkeeper appeared to have never been an outgoing type.

那个店主似乎并不是好交际的人。

- sociable 善于交际的
- outgoing passenger 出境游客

0641 output ['aʊtpʊt] n 生产，输出量，输出

It's noticeable that they should increase the literary output to meet demand.
很明显，为了满足需求，他们要增加出版物数量。

⊜ yield 产量　⊜ input 输入　⊜ output power 输出功率

> **语法重点**
> output 通常用作单数形式。

0642 outsider [ˌaʊtˈsaɪdər] n 门外汉，不大可能获胜的人

Just as the saying goes, the outsider sees the most of the game; you can ask your boyfriend about his opinion of the necklace.
正如俗语所说，旁观者清，你可以问问你男朋友对那条项链的看法。

⊜ just as the saying goes, ... 正如俗语所说，……

0643 outskirts ['aʊtskɜːrts] n 郊外，市郊，郊区

They bought a house on the outskirts of London last month.
他们上个月在伦敦市郊买了一栋房子。

⊜ suburbs 郊外　⊜ downtown 市区　⊜ on the outskirts 在郊外

> **语法重点**
> outskirts 作复数名词，表示"周边地区，郊区"，尤指市郊，通常与介词 of 连用。

0644 outward ['aʊtwərd] a 向外的，外面的

To all outward appearances, the boy who bought a sandwich was happy.
从外表来看，那个买了三明治的男孩很高兴。

⊜ surface 表面的　⊜ inward 向内的　⊜ outward appearance 外观

⊜ appearance (P. 124)

0645 outwards ['aʊtwərdz] ad 向外地，外表上

The man who looked outwards bought many books in mint condition.
那个向外看的人买了很多崭新的书。

⊜ return outwards 收益支出　⊜ ... look outwards 向外看……

0646 overall [ˌoʊvərˈɔːl] / ['oʊvərɔːl] a 全部的　ad 大体上

The overall cost of the computer including tax was four hundred dollars.
这台电脑的总价格，含税在内，是四百美元。

⊜ total 全部的　⊜ sectional 部分的　⊜ overall planning 整体规划

> **语法重点**
> overall 作副词时，表示"大体上"，通常用于句首或是句末。

0647 overdo [ˌoʊvərˈduː] v 使用……过度

Her mother appeared to overdo the worries about the expenditure.
她的妈妈似乎太担心开支了。

⊜ overdo your privilege 过度使用特权
⊜ overdo the worries about... 过分担心……

> **语法重点**
> overdo 的过去式和过去分词为 overdid, overdone。

0648 **overeat** [,ouvər'i:t] v 吃得过多

The odds are that he will overeat tonight because he bought many delicious snacks just now.
今晚他可能会吃得过多，因为他刚刚买了很多好吃的零食。
🔄 gluttonize 暴食　🔗 overeat oneself 吃得过量

🔹 delicious (P. 150)

0649 **overflow** [,əuvə'fləu] / [,ouvər'flou] v 泛滥 n 溢出

The market was overflowing with milk products, so the price was comparatively low.
市场上充溢着乳制品，所以乳制品价格相对较低。
🔄 inundate 淹没　🔄 be full to overflowing 满满的
🔗 be overflowing with... 充溢着……

语法重点
overflow 通常用于主动语态，其过去式为 overflew。

0650 **overhear** [,ouvər'hɪr] v 无意中听到，偷听到

She overheard her mother saying that she wanted to buy a new cupboard.
她无意中听到妈妈说想买个新碗柜。
🔄 hear 听到　🔗 overhear sb. say that... 无意中听到某人说……

0651 **oversleep** [,ouvər'sli:p] v 睡过头

I overheard him saying that he overslept and forgot to do the shopping.
我无意中听到他说，他睡过头且忘记了要去买东西。
🔗 overhear sb. saying that... 无意中听到某人说……

语法重点
oversleep 的过去式和过去分词为 overslept, overslept。

0652 **overwhelm** [,ouvər'welm] v 压倒

The girl was overwhelmed with joy when her mother bought her a laptop.
妈妈给她买了一台笔记本电脑，那个女孩不胜欢喜。
🔗 be overwhelmed by 使难以承受

语法重点
overwhelm 通常用于被动语态，其过去式和过去分词为 overwhelmed, overwhelmed。

0653 **overwork** [,əuvə'wɜ:k] / [,ouvər'wɜ:rk]
v 使工作过度 n 过劳

There was not an ounce of possibility that he can get enough money to buy that house unless he continued to overwork.
他没有半分可能凑到足够的钱买那栋房子，除非他继续加班工作。
🔄 overworking 过度工作　🔗 overwork oneself 劳累过度

语法重点
overwork 表示"滥用"时，多用被动语态。

0654 **oyster** ['ɔɪstər] n 牡蛎，守秘密的人，沉默寡言的人

He was as dumb as an oyster, so I did not know whether he wanted to buy the jacket.
他沉默不语，所以我不知道他是否想买这件夹克。
🔗 as close as an oyster 嘴很紧　🔗 ... be as dumb as an oyster ……沉默不语

语法重点
oyster 作可数名词，源自希腊语。

0655 ozone [ˈoʊzoʊn] n 臭氧，新鲜空气

His wife wanted to go on a trip and breathe in that ozone of seaside; he did not put in his oar.

他妻子想去旅行，呼吸海边的清新空气，他没有干预。

⊕ ozone layer 臭氧层　⊕ put in one's oar 干预……

> **语法重点**
> ozone 作不可数名词，表示"臭氧"。

0656 pacific [pəˈsɪfɪk] a 平稳的，太平的

The lady who was of pacific disposition went shopping with her sister yesterday.

昨天，那位性情温和的女士和妹妹一起去购物了。

⊕ gentle 温和的　⊕ warlike 战争的　⊕ pacific disposition 温和的性情

> **语法重点**
> pacific 作形容词，表示"和平的"；Pacific 则表示"太平洋的"。

0657 packet [ˈpækɪt] n 小包，小捆

The beggar was overwhelmed with gratitude when she bought a packet of biscuits for him.

她买了一小包饼干给那位乞丐，那位乞丐感激不已。

⊕ package 包裹

> **语法重点**
> packet 多用于英式英语中，美式英语中则用 package。
> ⊕ gratitude (P. 449)

0658 paddle [ˈpædl] n 桨球球拍 v 用桨划动，搬运

If you had used your common sense, you would not have bought such a paddle.

如果你有常识，就不会买这样的球拍了。

0659 pane [peɪn] n 窗格

We lay odds of three to one that he will not buy that pane of glass.

我们以三比一的赔率打赌，他不会买那块窗玻璃。

⊕ window pane 窗玻璃

> **语法重点**
> pane 作可数名词，表示"窗户上的单块玻璃"，可以用作数量表达 a pane of glass 或是 two panes of glass。

0660 paradox [ˈpærədɑːks] n 似是而非的言论

It's a paradox that the miser would spend so much money helping the earthquake victims.

那个吝啬鬼居然会花那么多钱帮助地震灾民，真是矛盾。

⊕ antinomy 自相矛盾　⊕ it's a paradox that... ……是矛盾的

0661 parallel [ˈpærəlel] a 平行的，相同的

When you go shopping, you can drive along the road which is parallel to the railway.

去购物的时候，你可以开车沿那条与铁路平行的路行驶。

⊕ comparable 相似的　⊕ different 不同的　⊕ in parallel 并行的
⊕ ... be parallel to / with... ……与……平行

0662 parlor [ˈpɑːrlər] n 客厅，起居室，店

She paddled her own canoe and bought an ice-cream parlor.

她靠自己的努力买了一家冰激凌店。

⊕ canoe (P. 268)

0663 participant [pɑːˈtɪsɪpənt] n 参与者
His father was an active participant in commodity transactions.
他的爸爸积极参与商品交易。

0664 particle [ˈpɑːrtɪkl] n 微粒
Actually, he has not a particle of malice in persuading you to buy that vase.
事实上，他劝你买那个花瓶并没有什么恶意。

◉ persuade (P. 336)

0665 partly [ˈpɑːrtli] ad 部分地，不完全地
She did not want to buy that desk partly because of dust particles on it.
她不想买那个书桌，有一部分原因是因为它上面有灰尘。
◉ half 部分地 ◉ wholly 完全地 ◉ partly because of... 有一部分原因是因为……

语法重点
partly 通常是指在某种程度上有几分、有些，没有比较级和最高级形式。

0666 passionate [ˈpæʃənət]
a 热情的，激昂的，易被情欲所支配的
There was not a particle of love in his buying roses for the passionate lady.
他给那位易动感情的女士送花，并没有半点儿爱意在内。
◉ intense 强烈的 ◉ there is not a particle of... in... ……没有半点……

0667 pastime [ˈpæstaɪm] n 消遣，娱乐
Photography, her favourite pastime, costs her a packet.
摄影是她最喜欢的消遣方式，这花了她一大笔钱。
◉ hobby 嗜好，娱乐 ◉ for a pastime 作消遣
◉ ... cost... a packet ……花了……一大笔钱

◉ sincerity (P. 503)

0668 pastry [ˈpeɪstri] n 酥皮点心
The man has not an ounce of sincerity in buying the pastries for his grandma.
那人买酥皮糕点给祖母，并没有半分诚心。
◉ pastry box 点心盒 ◉ ... have not an ounce of... ……没有半点儿……

语法重点
pastry 作不可数名词，表示"油酥面团"；作可数名词，表示"酥皮糕点"。
◉ sincerity (P. 503)

0669 patch [pætʃ] n 补丁，碎片 v 补缀
She would sew a patch onto the knee of her son's trousers rather than buy new trousers for him.
她宁愿在儿子的裤子膝盖处补补丁，也不愿买新裤子给她儿子。
◉ chip 碎片 ◉ patch up 解决

0670 patent [ˈpætnt] n 专利权 a 专利的 v 得到……专利权
It was patent to us that she likes to buy patent drugs.
我们都知道，她喜欢买专利药物。
◉ national patent 国家专利 ◉ it is patent to sb. that... 某人知道……

语法重点
patent 作形容词使用时，通常与介词 to 连用。

0671 patriot [ˈpeɪtrɪət] **n** 爱国者，爱国主义者
There was a feeling of optimism in the sale of that patriot's albums.
对于那位爱国人士的专辑销售前景，人们的看法十分乐观。
🔄 traitor 叛国者　　🔗 patriot act 爱国者法案

⊃ optimism (P. 604)

0672 patrol [pəˈtroʊl] **v** 巡逻 **n** 巡逻，巡查
A thousand dollars should go nowhere when you buy petrol cars.
要买巡逻车的话，一千美元也不算什么。
🔄 guard 守卫，警戒　　🔗 on patrol 在巡逻

语法重点
patrol 作不可数名词，表示"巡逻"；作可数名词，表示"巡逻者"。

0673 patron [ˈpeɪtrən] **n** 资助者，赞助人，老主顾
It's of immense importance to deal with those patrons.
和那些老主顾打交道是极为重要的。
🔄 customer 顾客　　🔄 seller 卖者　　🔗 patron saint 守护神

0674 peacock [ˈpiːkɑːk] **n** 孔雀，爱虚荣的人 **v** 炫耀
The lady who was as proud as a peacock always bought many fashionable clothes.
那位高傲的女士总是买很多时装。
🔄 peafowl 孔雀　　🔗 play the peacock 炫耀自己
🔗 be as proud as a peacock 得意扬扬的

⊃ fashionable (P. 295)

0675 peasant [ˈpeznt] **n** 佃农，农夫
Against all the odds, the peasant woman finally bought a house.
经过重重困难，那位农村妇女最终买了一间房子。
🔄 farmer 农民　　🔗 peasant household 庄户，农户

0676 peck [pek] **v** 啄食，小口地吃 **n** 大量，啄痕
Her mother bought a white dog last week, but it caused a peck of trouble to her family.
她妈妈上周买了一只白色的狗，但这只狗给她的家人带来许多麻烦。
🔗 peck at 啄　　🔗 cause a peck of trouble to... 给……带来许多麻烦

0677 peddler [ˈpedlər] **n** 小贩，毒贩
She bought a black cat with a white patch on its neck from that peddler.
她从那个小贩手中买了一只脖子上戴着白色斑点的黑色猫咪。

0678 peek [piːk] **v** 偷看 **n** 偷看，一瞥
The thief peeked into the shop window at the antique.
那个小偷隔着商店橱窗向里偷看那件古玩。
🔄 glimpse 一瞥　　🔄 gaze 凝视，注视　　🔗 peek into... at... 向……里偷看……

语法重点
peek 通常与介词 at, out, over 连用。

0679 peg [peg] n 钉子，栓子
The salesgirl made a mistake in the bill, which offered the customer a peg to hang his complaint on.
那位女店员弄错账单，使得那位客人有了不满的理由。
- offer the peg 现成的
- make a mistake in... 在……犯错了

0680 penetrate ['penətreɪt] v 刺入
A shrill cry suddenly penetrated the silence in the bookstore.
突然，一声尖叫划破了这家书店中的寂静。

语法重点
penetrate 表示"穿过"时，通常与介词 into 或 through 连用。

0681 perceive [pər'siːv] v 察觉，发觉，理解
She perceived a change in the price of agricultural products.
她发现农产品的价格有所变化。
- observe 注意
- perceive sb. do / doing sth. 察觉某人做某事

语法重点
perceive 的过去式和过去分词为 perceived, perceived，多用于主动语态。

0682 perch [pɜːrtʃ] n 栖息处 v 栖息
The parrot bought by his sister perched on the windowsill after giving him a sharp peck on the hand.
姐姐买的那只鹦鹉狠狠地啄了他的手之后，停留在了窗台上。

0683 performer [pər'fɔːrmər] n 实行者，演出者
The performer bought daily necessities for the earthquake victims.
那位演员为那些地震灾民购置了日用品。
- player 演员
- featured performer 主要演员

earthquake (P. 158)

0684 peril ['perəl] n 危险，冒险 v 置……于危险中
If you choose the product, you should face the possible perils of color fading.
如果选择这种产品，你会面临产品褪色的风险。

语法重点
peril 作不可数名词，表示"严重危险"，尤指死亡；作可数名词，表示"危险的事物或环境"，通常用复数形式。

0685 perish ['perɪʃ] v 灭亡，夭折，枯萎
He decided to buy the car; he shall do it or perish in the attempt, anyway.
他决定买那辆汽车，不论如何，拼死一搏。
- die 死亡
- survive 幸存
- perish the thought 打消念头

0686 permissible [pər'mɪsəbl] a 可允许的，容许的
It's permissible for consumers to slightly increase the price of the daily goods.
日用品价格轻微上涨，对于消费者而言，是可以的。
- admissible 可容许的
- unallowed 不允许的
- it's permissible for... to... ……对于……而言是可以的

daily (P. 149)

0687 **persist** [pərˈsɪst] v. 坚持，固执，持续

They persisted with the price increase despite opposition from consumers.
他们不顾消费者的反对，坚持涨价。
- continue 持续 - desist 停止 - persist in doing sth. 坚持做某事
- persist 通常含有贬义，指不听劝告，顽固坚持。

⊃ opposition (P. 750)

0688 **personnel** [ˌpɜːrsəˈnel] n. 人事部门

The personnel officer perceived that she can purchase train tickets at reduced price.
那位人事部负责人知道她可以买到优惠价的火车票。
- crew 全体人员 - personnel manager 人事部经理
- perceive that... 知道……

语法重点
personnel 表示"全体人员"，是单数形式表示复数意义，作主语时，动词用复数形式；也可以表示"人事部门"，视为不可数名词。

0689 **pessimism** [ˈpesɪmɪzəm] n. 悲观，悲观主义

There is a mood of pessimism in the manager about the sale of these cotton goods.
对于这些棉纺织品的销售，那名经理很悲观。
- optimism 乐观主义

语法重点
pessimism 为不可数名词。

0690 **pier** [pɪr] n. 码头，防波堤，桥墩

The seller who sold snacks along the pier was perceived to have difficulty in walking.
据观察所见，那个在码头附近卖零食的人，走路有些困难。
- harbor 港口，码头 - floating pier 浮动码头
- have difficulty in... 在……上有困难

0691 **pilgrim** [ˈpɪlɡrɪm] n. 朝圣者

The pilgrim pegged the landlord down to a price for the room.
那位朝圣者已经和店主谈妥了房间的价格。
- palmer 朝圣者 - peg sb. down to a price for... 就……与某人谈妥价格

⊃ landlord (P. 589)

0692 **pillar** [ˈpɪlər] n. 梁柱

In order to get enough money to buy the house, he went from pillar to post.
为了借到足够的钱买房，他到处奔走碰壁。
- ridgepole 栋梁 - ... go from pillar to post ……到处奔走碰壁

语法重点
pillar 作可数名词。

0693 **pimple** [ˈpɪmpl] n. 面疱，粉刺

The teenager with a pimple on his face had the hardihood to deny he stole the foods in the shop.
那个脸上有粉刺的少年厚颜无耻地否认他偷了商店里的食物。
- pimple skin 青春痘 - have the hardihood to do sth. 厚颜无耻地做某事

persist ~ plea

0694 pinch [pɪntʃ] **v** 捏，拧，掐掉，拮据

If it comes to the pinch, you can sell your apartment to get money.
必要时，你可以把公寓卖掉来筹钱。
- nip 捏
- at a pinch 必要时

0695 piss [pɪs] **n** 小便，撒尿 **v** 撒尿弄脏

He was pissed around for three days before they finally agreed to the price.
他们浪费了三天时间，才同意这个价格。
- urinate 小便
- shit 大便
- piss off 立即走开，使……讨厌

> **语法重点**
> be pissed around for 也可以用于主动语态。

0696 pistol ['pɪstl] **n** 手枪

It's marvelous how he wanted to buy an automatic pistol for his son.
他怎么会买一支自动手枪送给儿子呢，真是不可思议。
- gun 枪
- water pistol 玩具水枪

> marvelous (P. 322)

0697 plague [pleɪg] **n** 瘟疫，麻烦 **v** 折磨，造成麻烦

He avoided his sister like the plague in case she tried to borrow some money from him.
他极力回避妹妹，以免她试图向他借钱。
- plague with 用……来烦扰（折磨）人
- ... avoid... like the plague ……极力回避……

0698 plantation [plæn'teɪʃn] **n** 农场

He notified his wife that he would buy some bananas in the plantation.
他告知妻子，他想在种植园里买一些香蕉。
- grove 果园，树林
- tea plantation 茶园
- notify sb. that... 告知某人……

> notify (P. 602)

0699 playwright ['pleɪraɪt] **n** 剧作家

To make sure to get the playwright's autograph book, he offered over the odds for it.
为了确保买到那位剧作家的签名册，他出了高价。
- dramatist 剧作家
- offer over the odds for... 为……出高价

> autograph (P. 676)

0700 plea [pliː] **n** 借口，请愿，恳求

She refused to buy that bracelet on the plea that she could not afford it.
她以无力负担为由，拒绝购买那个手镯。
- petition 请愿
- on the plea of 以……为借口
- sb. refuses to do sth. on the plea that... 某人以……为由，拒绝……

0701 **plead** [pliːd] v 恳求

The little girl pleaded her mother to buy the doll.
那个小女孩请求妈妈买那个洋娃娃。

> 语法重点
> plead 作及物动词，其过去式和过去分词为 pleaded, pleaded 或是 pled, pled。

0702 **pledge** [pledʒ] n 誓约 v 发誓，典当

You should give a pledge never to tell others that he would buy his wife a ring secretly.
你要保证，不告诉别人他要偷偷买戒指给妻子。

● pawn 典当　● pledge oneself 宣誓

0703 **plow** [plaʊ] n 犁 v 耕，费力穿过

The farmer took it with a pinch of salt that his wife bought that plow at such a low price.
妻子用这样低的价格买了犁，那位农夫对此半信半疑。

> 语法重点
> plow 为可数名词；the Plow 则是作专有名词，表示"北斗星"。

● plow into 干劲十足地投入　● take... with a pinch of salt 对……半信半疑

0704 **pluck** [plʌk] v 摘，拔 n 拉

He plucked a rose for me from his garden, and then asked me to pay one dollar.
他从花园里为我摘了一朵玫瑰，然后要我付一美元。

● pick 采，摘　● pluck up 鼓起勇气
● pluck sth. for sb. from... 从……为某人摘……

0705 **plunge** [plʌndʒ] v 将……插入，使陷入

The two brothers were plunged into debt because of their extravagant lifestyle.
那两兄弟因为奢侈的生活方式而负债。

● debt (P. 150)

● take the plunge 冒险尝试

0706 **pocketbook** [ˈpɑːkɪtbʊk] n 袖珍本，女用钱包

The inflation will be most likely to hit the pocketbook of consumers.
通货膨胀极有可能影响消费者的购买力。

● pocketbook issue 民生问题　● be most likely to hit... 极有可能影响……

0707 **poetic** [poʊˈetɪk] a 诗意的，富有诗情的

She was so naive as to believe she could buy the entire poetic output of the famous poet.
她以为自己可以买到那位著名诗人的全部诗作，真是天真。

● entire (P. 160)

0708 **poke** [poʊk] v 戳，刺 n 戳，拨，钱袋

The twin sisters bought some chips and poked at them unenthusiastically.
那对双胞胎姐妹买了些薯条，无精打采地拨弄着。

● jab 戳，刺　● poke one's nose into 干预，探问

plead ~ precaution

0709 polar ['poʊlər] **a** 极地的，极性的 **n** 极线，极性
They made a packet with this kind of fish produced in the polar region and bought a villa.
他们靠这种产自极区的鱼赚了大钱，买了一栋别墅。
🔹 polar bear 北极熊 🔹 make / earn a packet with... 靠……赚大钱

▶ region (P. 214)

0710 porch [pɔːtʃ] **n** 玄关，门廊，入口处
She gave her boyfriend a quick peck on the cheek when he bought a bunch of roses and waited at the porch of her house.
男朋友买了一束玫瑰等在她家门廊处，她在他脸颊上飞快地吻了一下。
🔹 portico 门廊 🔹 porch climber 盗贼
🔹 give... a quick peck on the... 在……的……上飞快地吻一下

▶ peck (P. 610)

0711 potential [pəˈtenʃl] **a** 潜在的 **n** 潜力
The two brothers bought a novel which was a potential best seller.
那两兄弟买了一本有望成为畅销书的小说。
🔹 latent 潜在的 🔹 market potential 市场潜力

0712 poultry ['poʊltri] **n** 家禽
Most consumers seem to be pissed off with the price increase in poultry and eggs.
多数消费者似乎都对禽蛋类的价格变化感到厌烦。
🔹 fowl 家禽 🔹 poultry and eggs 禽蛋类 🔹 be pissed off with... 对……感到厌烦

语法重点
poultry 作复数名词，表示"家禽"；作主语时，动词用复数形式；作不可数名词，表示"家禽肉"。

0713 prairie ['preri] **n** 大草原，牧场，草原
He plucked up courage to tell his parent that he bought a prairie last week.
他鼓起勇气告诉父母，上周他买了一处牧场。
🔹 prairie fire 星火燎原 🔹 pluck up courage to... 鼓起勇气……

0714 preach [priːtʃ] **v** 传教，布道，鼓吹
The vicar who preached well did not want to know about his family living expenses.
那位讲道讲得很好的牧师对家庭生活开支不闻不问。
🔹 sermonize 布道 🔹 preach to 对某人谆谆告诫，向……传道

▶ expense (P. 292)

0715 precaution [prɪˈkɔːʃn] **n** 警惕
By way of precaution, he bought some food and vegetables in advance.
小心起见，他提前买了些食物和蔬菜。
🔹 take precautions against 采取措施预防

615

by way of precaution... 小心起见……

0716 **preference** ['prefrəns] n 偏好，优先，优先权
Choosing clothes should be a matter of preference.
挑选衣服是取决于个人爱好的事情。
同 favour 偏爱　　同 in preference to 优先于……

> **语法重点**
> preference 作不可数名词，表示"喜爱"，通常与介词 for 连用，表示"优惠，优待"，通常与介词 to / towards 连用；也可以作可数名词，表示"偏爱的事物"。

0717 **prehistoric** [,pri:hɪ'stɔ:rɪk] a 史前的，陈旧的
Her ideas on food and clothes appear to be prehistoric.
她对于衣食的观念是老旧的。
注 prehistoric 有时含有贬义。

0718 **prevail** [prɪ'veɪl] v 获胜，优胜
She did not recognize the potential for boom conditions prevailing in the region.
她没有意识到在这个地区生意兴隆的可能性。
同 recognize the potential for... 意识到……的可能性

⊃ potential (P. 615)

0719 **preview** ['pri:vju:] n 预习　v 预映
The news that they can attend the preview of the fashion collection plunged them into excitement.
可以去参加这次的时装预演的消息使他们十分兴奋。
同 rehearse 排练　　同 print preview 打印预览

⊃ plunge (P. 614)

0720 **prey** [preɪ] n 牺牲者　v 捕获
The thought that she was an easy prey for the dishonest salesman preyed on her mind.
想起自己那么轻易地被那个奸商敲竹杠，她就十分懊恼。

0721 **priceless** ['praɪsləs] a 贵重的，非常有趣的
When he lost that priceless treasure, he felt like such an idiot.
弄丢了那件无价之宝，他觉得自己蠢极了。
同 valuable 贵重的　　反 valueless 不值钱的　　同 priceless treasure 无价之宝

> **语法重点**
> priceless 的副词为 pricelessly。

0722 **prick** [prɪk] v 刺，戳
The latest sale figures pricked the bubble of his complacency about the prospect of the clothes.
最新的销售数额打破了他对于这些衣物销售前景大好的美梦。
同 penetrate 刺入　　同 prick up oneself 打扮自己
同 ... prick the bubble of... ……打破……美梦 / 幻想

0723 **prior** ['praɪər] a 在前的，优先的
There should be no price changes without the prior approval of consumers' association.
在消费者协会同意之前，价格不得有所改变。
同 previous 早先的　　反 posterior 其次的，较后的　　同 prior to 在……之前
注 prior 与 previous 通常可以互换，只是 prior 有较强的对比意味。

preference ~ proportion

0724 priority [praɪˈɔːrəti] **n** 优先权，优先考虑的事
Purchasing a comfortable apartment should be a top priority.
当务之急是买一栋舒适的公寓。
- give priority to 优先考虑
- ... be a top priority 当务之急是……

语法重点
priority 作不可数名词，表示"优先权"，通常与介词 over 连用；作可数名词，表示"优先的事物"。

0725 procession [prəˈseʃn] **n** 行列
Seeing a procession of customers coming to his store, he cannot help pinching himself in case it was all a dream.
看到顾客络绎不绝地来到自己的商店中，他忍不住捏了自己一下，生怕这只是一场梦。
- parade 队伍
- civilian procession 群众游行

⊃ pinch (P. 613)

0726 profile [ˈproʊfaɪl] **n** 轮廓，简介 **v** 描绘……轮廓
His wife muttered to him about the stamp she wanted to buy on which the chairman's head appear in profile.
他妻子低声对他说，她想买的那枚邮票上有主席的头像。
- outline 轮廓
- high profile 明确的立场
- mutter to sb. about (doing)... 低声对某人说……

⊃ mutter (P. 599)

0727 prolong [prəˈlɔːŋ] **v** 延长，拖延，延期
She pinched and scraped so that she could buy the drugs to help her father to prolong life.
她省吃俭用，以便买药来帮父亲延长寿命。
- delay 延期
- shorten 缩短
- prolong life 延年益寿

0728 prop [prɑːp] **n** 支撑物 **v** 支撑，使倚靠在某物上
When she wanted to buy that car, her husband's support was a great prop to her determination.
她想买那辆车的时候，丈夫的支持大大地坚定了她的决心。
- brace 支柱
- prop up 支撑，支持

⊃ determination (P. 425)

0729 prophet [ˈprɑːfɪt] **n** 先知
Don't get into a fuss about nothing; if you believed a prophet of doom, you would never start the business.
不要自寻烦恼，如果你相信那些悲观论调，这生意就永远都不可能起步。
- farseer 先知
- a weather prophet 气象预报员

0730 proportion [prəˈpɔːrʃn] **n** 比例，比率，部分
His son wanted to be his own master and spent a large proportion of his salary on photography.
他的儿子想要自己做主，把大部分的薪水都用于摄影上。
- ratio 比率
- out of proportion 不成比例，不相称
- ... be one's own master ……自己做主

617

0731 **prospect** ['prɑːspekt] n 预期，眺望处 v 勘探，有希望

The prospects for this season's sales of cars appear to be poor.
这一季的汽车销售，前景似乎不佳。
- outlook 前景　　- in prospect 展望，在期望中

语法重点
prospect 作可数名词，表示"景象，展望，有希望的候选人"；prospects 则是作复数名词，表示"成功的希望，前景"。

0732 **province** ['prɒvɪns] n 省，领域，部门

How to persuade him to buy the product is outside my province.
怎么说服他买产品不在我的职责范围内。
- territory 领域，地盘　　- be outside one's province 不在……的职责范围内

0733 **prune(1)** [pruːn] v 修剪（树木等），剪去

I'm afraid next month's expenditure will have to be drastically pruned.
恐怕下个月的开支必须大幅度削减。
- delete 删除　　- add 添加

0734 **prune(2)** [pruːn] n 西梅脯，西梅干，深紫红色

When his sister wanted to buy some prunes, he did not step in.
妹妹想买些西梅干，他没有干预。
- plum 梅子　　- sb. doesn't step in... 某人没有干预……

0735 **publicize** ['pʌblɪsaɪz] v 宣传，发表，为……做广告

The sales manager wants to launch an advertising campaign to publicize the new product, hoping others will not stick in their oar.
销售经理想为新产品展开宣传活动，希望其他人不会干预。
- proclaim 宣告　　- stick in one's oar 干预……

- campaign (P. 404)

0736 **puff** [pʌf] n 泡芙 v 喘气，趾高气扬

The boy bought a hamburger and vanished in a puff of smoke.
那个男孩买了汉堡，就一溜烟地不见了。
- puff out 吹灭，气喘吁吁地说　　- ... vanish in a puff of smoke ……一溜烟地不见了

- vanish (P. 380)

0737 **pulse** [pʌls] n 脉搏，脉冲，脉动

If you want to start the business, you should have your finger on the pulse.
如果你想做这单生意，就要充分地掌握最新情况。
- impulse 脉冲　　- ... have one's finger on the pulse ……充分地掌握最新情况……

0738 **purchase** [ˈpɜːrtʃəs] n 购买 v 买

The man's motive for purchasing these household appliances laid hidden.
那人购买这些家用设施的动机并不明确。

buy 买　　sell 卖　　purchase price 买价, 进货价格

▸ household (P. 454)

0739 **pyramid** [ˈpɪrəmɪd] n 金字塔 v 使……成塔尖形, 渐增

They began to regret the purchase of tins when they saw the pyramid of fruits in the store.
在这家店里看到摆成金字塔形的水果, 他们后悔买了那些罐头。

regret the purchase of... 后悔买……

0740 **quack** [kwæk]

n 呱呱叫, 江湖郎中　v（鸭子）发出嘎嘎声

The quack who always sold substandard medicine was in bad odor.
那个总是卖假药的庸医声名狼藉。

charlatan 庸医　　... be in bad odor ……声名狼藉

▸ medicine (P. 190)

0741 **qualify** [ˈkwɑːlɪfaɪ] v 使合格, 有合法权利

The coupon will qualify you to get ten dollars off.
这张优惠券可以让你少付十美元。

disqualify 取消资格　　qualify for 使合格
qualify sb. to... 使某人有资格……

0742 **quart** [kwɔːrt] n 夸脱

The businessman who was in ill odor came to buy a quart of vodka.
那个声名狼藉的商人买了一夸脱的伏特加。

... be in ill odor ……声名狼藉

语法重点
quart 的缩写形式为 qt。

0743 **quest** [kwest] n / v 探索, 追求

The elderly man spends all his life in quest of buying antiques.
那个老年人毕生都在追求买古董。

search 寻求　　the quest for 寻求　　be in quest of... 寻求……

语法重点
quest 通常与介词 for 连用。

0744 **quiver** [ˈkwɪvər] v 颤抖 n 颤动, 抖动

She quivered at the price which was out of all proportion to income.
看到与收入完全不成比例的高价, 她微微颤抖。

shake 抖动　　quiver with 颤动
be out of all proportion to... 与……完全不成比例

▸ proportion (P. 617)

0745 rack(1) [ræk] n 架子，行李架
The hungry old man took a peek at the toast rack in the bakery.
那位饥饿的老人偷偷地看着面包店里的面包架。
同 shelf 架子　似 luggage rack 行李架　派 take a peek at... 偷偷看……

⇒ peek (P. 610)

0746 rack(2) [ræk] v 使苦痛，折磨
The little girl asked her mother to buy that teddy bear in a voice racked by weeping.
那个小女孩用哭哭啼啼的声音要妈妈买那个泰迪熊。
同 torment 折磨　派 rack one's brains 绞尽脑汁

语法重点
rack 通常用于被动语态，指的是疾病、苦恼、情感等带来的苦痛。

0747 radish ['rædɪʃ] n 小萝卜
She was quite puffed by the time she got home with a bunch of radishes bought from the market.
提着从市场上买的一捆萝卜回到家时，她气喘得厉害。

0748 radius ['reɪdɪəs] n 半径
There are two supermarkets within a radius of five miles.
周围五英里的半径范围内，有两家超市。
同 semidiameter 半径　反 diameter 直径

⇒ mile (P. 063)

0749 ragged ['rægɪd] a 破烂的，粗糙刺耳的
Ragged old men should be common occurrence in the supermarket.
在这个超市里经常看到衣衫褴褛的老人。
同 shabby 破旧的　反 decent 大方的　派 be common occurrence 经常看到……

⇒ occurrence (P. 603)

0750 rail [reɪl] n 铁路
Our budget of this month completely went off the rails after you bought that ring.
你买了那枚戒指之后，我们这个月的预算开支就完全被打乱了。
同 track 轨道　似 by rail 搭火车　派 go off the rails 陷入混乱，失去控制

0751 rally ['ræli] n 大集会 v 恢复，集合起来
Her spirits rallied on hearing that her daughter bought a bunch of carnations for her.
听说女儿买了一束康乃馨给她，她又振作起了精神。
同 revive 恢复精神　似 rally point 集结点

语法重点
rally 作及物动词，表示"恢复精神"；作不及物动词，表示"集合"，通常用 rally round / to。

0752 ranch [ræntʃ] n 大牧场，大农场
The man who fell into bad odor had to sell the cattle ranch to buy a house.
那个声名狼藉的人只得卖掉那个牧牛场来买房子了。
同 farm 农场　派 ... fall into bad odor ……声名狼藉

0753 **rascal** ['ræskl] n 流氓，无赖
That rascal won't come to our store again, I trust.
但愿那个流氓不会再到我们店里来。
- sb. won't..., I trust 我希望……，某人不会……

0754 **ratio** ['reɪʃoʊ] n 比率
Female customers outnumbered male customers here in the ratio of four to one.
这里的女性顾客以四比一的比率多于男性顾客。
- percentage 百分比   - utilization ratio 利用率

> 语法重点
> ratio 作可数名词，表示"比率"，等于 proportion，通常用 the ratio of... to...，复数形式为 ratios。

0755 **rattle** ['rætl] v 发出咯咯声
She kept rattling on about expenditures, but nothing.
她围绕着费用开支喋喋不休，却是言之无物。
- patter 喋喋不休地说   - rattle off 飞快地说出
- rattle on about... 对……喋喋不休

> 语法重点
> rattle 表示"使紧张、恐惧"时，通常用被动语态。

0756 **realm** [relm] n 王国，领域，范围
A good prospect of sales might not be beyond the realms of possibility.
好的销售前景并非是没有可能的。
- domain 领域   - in the realm of 在……领域里

0757 **reap** [riːp] v 收割，收获
Buying his son a car might be within the realms of possibility after reaping a field of wheat.
收割田地里的麦子之后，也许能凑够钱给儿子买车。
- harvest 收获   - sow 播种   - reap the benefits of 获得益处

↪ wheat (P. 384)

0758 **rear** [rɪr] n 后面 v 抚养，培养
On the way to the rear entrance of the supermarket, his theme was moving into the realms of literature.
向超市后面的入口处去的时候，他把话题转到了文学的领域。
- bring up the rear 处在最后的位置
- ... be moving into the realms of... ……转到……领域

0759 **reckless** ['rekləs] a 鲁莽的
The businessman purchased a large number of estates with reckless abandon.
那个商人恣意地购置大量地产。
- careless 粗心的   - reckless driving 鲁莽驾驶
- do sth. ... with reckless abandon ……恣意做某事

↪ abandon (P. 389)

0760 reckon ['rekən] v 测量，认为

He reckoned that the price of milk products was a little too high.
他认为，乳制品的价格有点过高了。
同 think 认为　同 reckon on 依靠　同 reckon that... 认为……

语法重点
reckon 表示"认为……是……"时，通常用被动语态；表示"认为，想"时，通常用主动语态。

0761 recommend [,rekə'mend] v 推荐，介绍，劝告

I'm not the person to recommend how to get enough money for that apartment.
对于如何为那栋公寓凑到足够的钱，我并不能为此出什么主意。
同 recommend for 推荐

0762 reef [ri:f] n 暗礁，矿脉　v 收帆，缩帆

You had better not reckon on him to buy that coral reef for you.
你最好不要指望他买那个珊瑚礁给你。
同 rock 暗礁　同 coral reef 珊瑚礁　同 reckon on... to... 指望……

0763 reel [ri:l] n 卷轴　v 旋转，蹒跚

When they got home from the supermarket, they suddenly realized they had reckoned without the cotton reel.
从超市回到家的时候，他们突然意识到忘记买棉线轴了。
同 roller 卷筒　同 reel off 流畅地讲　同 reckon without... 没有把……考虑在内

0764 referee / umpire [,refə'ri:] / ['ʌmpaɪər]
v 裁判　n 裁判员，调解人

The referee reckoned that hire charges should be reckoned from the date of delivery.
那位调解人认为，租金应当是自货到之日算起。
同 mediator 调解人　同 chief referee 总裁判

● delivery (P. 282)

0765 refuge / sanctuary ['refju:dʒ] / ['sæŋktʃueri]
n 避难，庇护（者）

When collecting money to build the refuge for the homeless, they had many difficulties to reckon with.
对于筹钱为那些无家可归的人建庇护所，他们有很多的困难要考虑。
同 sanctuary 避难所　同 take refuge in 避难，求助于

语法重点
refuge 作不可数名词，表示"庇护"；作可数名词，表示"避难处"。

0766 refute [rɪ'fju:t] v 反驳，驳倒

His marketing theory was refuted down to the last point.
他的营销理论被驳斥得体无完肤。
同 contradict 反驳　反 admit 承认

0767 reign [reɪn] v 统治，支配 n 君主统治，在位期

There was an overall improvement in expenditure styles during the reign of the king.
在那位国王统治期间，消费方式有所改进。
- rule 统治
- reign over 统治，盛行

语法重点
reign 作不可数名词，表示"统治"，通常用 under the reign of；作可数名词，表示"统治时代"，用 during / in the reign of。

0768 rejoice [rɪˈdʒɔɪs] v 欣喜，高兴

She rejoiced to hear that her boyfriend bought a purse.
听说男朋友买了一个皮夹，她十分高兴。

0769 relic [ˈrelɪk] n 遗物，遗迹，纪念物

We rejoiced that they gave up changing the last remaining relic of ancient civilization into a commercial district.
我们十分高兴，他们放弃了把最后一处古文明遗址改为商业区的想法。
- memento 纪念品
- cultural relic 文物
- rejoice that... 十分高兴……

语法重点
relic 作可数名词，表示"遗物，遗迹"；relics 作复数名词，表示"部分遗骸，残存部分"。
- civilization (P. 408)

0770 reminder [rɪˈmaɪndər] n 提醒者

The incident served as a constant reminder how dangerous substandard medicine was.
这次事件时时提醒着我们，假药有多危险。

0771 repay [rɪˈpeɪ] v 偿还，报答

If I lend one hundred dollars to you to buy a bike, you should repay it to me by next week.
如果我借你一百美元买脚踏车，你要在下周之前还我。
- return 报答
- repay an obligation 报恩
- repay... to... 把……还给……

语法重点
repay 作及物动词，表示"偿还，付还"，为双宾语动词，用作 repay... to sb. 或是 repay sb. sth.。

0772 reproduce [ˌriːprəˈduːs] v 繁殖，生殖

She is reckoning on buying a copier that can reproduce colorful photographs.
她在考虑买一台可以复制彩色照片的影印机。

0773 reptile [ˈreptaɪl] n 爬虫类 a 爬虫类的，卑鄙的

You had better not buy such a reptile like a lizard as a pet.
你最好不要买类似蜥蜴之类的爬行动物作为宠物。

0774 republican [rɪˈpʌblɪkən] a 共和政体的，共和党的 n 共和党人

The Republican reckoned to limit the expenditure of money on weapons.
共和党考虑限制购买武器的开支。
- Republican Party 共和党

0775 resent [rɪ'zent] v 愤恨，对……表示愤恨
His wife resented his spending much money on alcohol.
他的妻子讨厌他花很多钱买酒。
同 hate 憎恨　似 strongly resent 强烈怨恨

语法重点
resent 作及物动词，后接名词、动名词形式。

0776 reside [rɪ'zaɪd] v 长久居住，驻扎，属于
The businessman who resides at 158 Fifth Avenue is reckoned to be the most extravagant man here.
那个住在第五大道 158 号的商人被认为是这里最奢侈的人。
同 inhabit 居住　似 reside in 居住于……　似 be reckoned to be... 被认为是……

➲ avenue (P. 258)

0777 residence ['rezɪdəns] n 居住，驻扎，住处
The price of the residence on that street was reckoned a little too high.
那条街上的住房价格有点儿过高了。
似 residence permit 居住许可证

语法重点
residence 作不可数名词时，表示"居住，居留期间"；作可数名词时，表示"住宅"。

0778 resident ['rezɪdənt] n 居民 a 居住的
The local resident was fined fifty dollars for buying smuggling articles.
那位当地居民因为买走私品被罚款五十美元。
似 permanent resident 永久性居民　似 be fined... for ... 因……而被罚款……

➲ smuggle (P. 779)

0779 resort [rɪ'zɔːrt] v / n 诉诸，求助，凭借
When it comes to the crunch, you can resort to selling the house.
危急时，你可以卖掉这座房子。
同 recourse 求援，求助　似 resort to 求助于，诉诸

0780 restrain [rɪ'streɪn] v 抑制，遏制，限制
It's hard to restrain her anger when she learnt that her husband spent all his money on gambling.
听闻丈夫把所有的钱都拿去赌博，她难以控制自己的怒气。
同 refrain 阻止　反 impel 推进　似 restrain from 阻止……去……
似 restrain one's anger 控制……的怒气

0781 resume [rɪ'zjuːm] / [rɪ'zuːm] v 重新开始 n 履历表
She said she bought a novel last week and gave a resume of the plot.
她说她上周买了一本小说并阐述了情节概要。
同 summary 摘要　似 personal resume 个人简历
似 give a resume of... 做……概要

语法重点
resume 作可数名词，表示"摘要"，通常与介词 of 连用。

resent ~ rib

0782 **retort** [rɪ'tɔːrt] v 反击，反驳
His wife retorted that it's quite necessary to buy that necklace.
他妻子反驳说，买那条项链是十分必要的。
- respond 应答　- question 质疑　- retort that... 反驳……

0783 **reverse** [rɪ'vɜːrs] v 颠倒 a 相反的 n 背面
Sales of fruits this month show a reverse trend to that recorded last month.
这个月的水果销售额与上月的情况相反。
- contrary 相反的　- same 相同　- in reverse 向相反方向

0784 **revive** [rɪ'vaɪv] v 复活
The sales figures revived fear of a small salary scale.
销售额唤起了人们对低薪的担忧。
　scale (P. 354)
- restore 复原　- revive economy 经济复兴
- revive fear of... 唤起对……的担忧

0785 **revolt** [rɪ'voʊlt] v / n 叛乱
The capitalist asked the police to put down the revolt with two thousand pounds.
那个资本家出两千英镑请警察来镇压叛乱。
- rebellion 反抗　- revolt against 反感，厌恶
- put down / quell the revolt 镇压叛乱

> 语法重点
> revolt 表示"反抗，反叛"时，通常与介词 against 连用；作"憎恶"时，通常用被动语态。

0786 **revolve** [rɪ'vɑːlv] v 旋转
The discussion revolved around the issue of purchasing office appliances.
这次讨论是以购买办公设施为中心。
　appliance (P. 395)
- revolve round 反复考虑，围绕……而旋转

0787 **rhinoceros / rhino** [raɪ'nɑːsərəs] / ['raɪnoʊ]
n 犀牛，钱，现金
The rhino horn should be the most extravagant purchase the miser had ever made.
那个犀牛角应当是那个吝啬鬼所买过的最奢侈的东西。
- money 钱　- ready rhino 现金（英俚语）

0788 **rib** [rɪb] n 肋骨，凸条花纹 v 嘲笑，开玩笑
He was constantly ribbed about his preference for buying barbecued spare-ribs.
他常常因为偏爱买烤猪排而被取笑。
- rib cage 胸腔　- be constantly ribbed about... 常常因为……而被取笑

625

0789 ridge [rɪdʒ] **n** 屋脊，山脉
The student bought the boots with ridges on the soles after revolving the amount of spending money in his mind.
仔细考虑过零用钱金额之后，那个学生买下了那双鞋底有条纹的靴子。

○ revolve (P. 625)

0790 ridiculous [rɪ'dɪkjələs] **a** 荒谬的，可笑的
Don't be ridiculous; you cannot buy that pearl necklace with your limited salary.
别傻了，就凭你那点儿有限的薪水，买不起那条珍珠项链的。
● make sb. ridiculous 使某人成为笑柄　● don't be ridiculous, ... 别傻了，……

> 语法重点
> ridiculous 的比较级和最高级为 more ridiculous, most ridiculous。

0791 rifle ['raɪfl] **n** 来福枪 **v** 快速搜寻，偷窃
It's ridiculous that the teenager should want to buy a rifle.
那个少年竟然想买一支来福枪，真是荒谬。
● it's ridiculous that... ……真是荒谬

0792 rigid ['rɪdʒɪd] **a** 严格的，刚硬的，僵硬的
Seeing the astronomical figures on the bill, the man was rigid with terror.
看到账单上的天文数字，那人吓得全身僵硬。
● stiff 僵硬的　● pliable 柔软的

○ terror (P. 510)

0793 rim [rɪm] **n** 边缘，框
We were revolted by his endless talking about the spectacles with gold rims he bought recently.
我们讨厌听他喋喋不休地谈论新买的那副金框眼镜。
● border 边缘

0794 rip [rɪp] **v** 扯裂，撕坏 **n** 裂口，裂缝
The little boy ripped the cover off the book, so his mother had to buy it.
那个小男孩把那本书的封面撕掉了，因此他妈妈只得买下它。
● tear 撕坏　● ... rip... off (...) ……撕下……

0795 ripple ['rɪpl] **n** 涟漪，波浪形 **v** 使泛起涟漪
A ripple of incredulity passed through her when she received the electrical bill.
收到电费账单时，她觉得不可置信。
● ripple effect 连锁反应

0796 rival ['raɪvl] **n** 对手 **a** 竞争的
The chain of supermarkets had no rival in the field of the retail of daily necessities.
在日用品零售方面，这家连锁超市无人能及。
● opponent 对手　● partner 伙伴　● rival firms 竞争公司

> 语法重点
> rival 表示"竞争对手"时，与介词 in 或 for 连用，通常是指在某项竞争、比赛中战胜对手。

0797 **roam** [roʊm] v 漫步
His wife roamed freely over the expenditures last month.
他妻子漫谈上个月的开支。
🔸 roam around 散步，闲逛　🔸 roam freely over... 漫谈……

0798 **robin** [ˈrɑːbɪn] n 知更鸟
His daughter wanted to buy a robin.
他的女儿想买只知更鸟。

0799 **robust** [roʊˈbʌst] a 强健的，耐用的，浓的
The ridiculousness of the scene made them laugh when the robust man in a gaudy shirt appeared in the store.
那个健壮的人穿着花哨的衬衫出现在店里，这滑稽的一幕逗得他们大笑。
🔸 sturdy 强健的　🔸 delicate 纤弱的

0800 **rod** [rɑːd] n 竿子，棒子
You are making a rod for your own back if you lend money to him to buy a car.
如果你借钱给他买车，那是自找麻烦。
🔸 ... make a rod for one's own back ……自找麻烦 / 自讨苦吃

【语法重点】
rod 作可数名词，表示"杆，棍"，多用于构成复合词。

0801 **rubbish** [ˈrʌbɪʃ]
n 垃圾，废话　v 把……说得一文不值，轻视
You had better not buy that novel which is actually a load of rubbish.
那本书其实就是废话连篇，你最好不要买。
🔸 garbage 废物，垃圾　🔸 appreciate 重视
🔸 rubbish dump 垃圾堆　🔸 ... be a load of rubbish ……废话连篇

【语法重点】
rubbish 作不可数名词，表示"垃圾"，表示"无聊的想法，胡说"，含有贬义，通常用作感叹语。

0802 **rugged** [ˈrʌɡɪd] a 粗糙的，崎岖的
Other cupboards will be dwarfed by the one which is famous for its rugged qualities.
这款以坚固耐用而闻名的碗柜使其他同类产品相形见绌。
🔸 flat 平坦的　🔸 be dwarfed by... 使……相形见绌

🔸 dwarf (P. 560)

0803 **rumble** [ˈrʌmbl] n 隆隆作响，打群架　v 发出隆隆声
My stomach is rumbling; let's buy something to eat.
我的肚子饿得咕咕叫，我们去买些东西吃吧。
🔸 boom 发出隆隆声　🔸 rumble into 隆隆地进入

【语法重点】
rumble 也可表示"车辆辘辘地驶过"，与介词 through 或 along 连用。

0804 **rustle** [ˈrʌsl] v 沙沙作响　n 沙沙声，急忙
When the waiter came to take his order, he made an insolent retort, rustling the menu.
服务生过来为他点餐的时候，他把菜单翻得沙沙响，傲慢地回绝。

0805 **sacred** ['seɪkrɪd] a 神圣的，受尊重的
Don't talk rubbish; what he bought were sacred writings.
别胡说八道，他所买的是宗教经典著作。
● holy 神圣的　● sacred flame 圣火
● don't talk rubbish, ... 别胡说八道，……

> 语法重点
> sacred 的比较级与最高级分别是 more sacred, most sacred。
> ● rubbish (P. 627)

0806 **saddle** ['sædl] n 马鞍　v 给……装鞍
His brother did not buy a saddle.
他哥哥并没有买过马鞍。
● sella 鞍　● in the saddle 在职

0807 **saint** [seɪnt] n 圣人
You must be a saint to be able to stand his extravagant tastes and habits.
你竟然能忍受他那奢侈的嗜好和习惯，真是个圣人。
● sadu 圣人　● demon 魔鬼　● patron saint 守护神

0808 **salmon** ['sæmən] n 鲑鱼，橙红色　a 浅橙色的
The salmon salad in the restaurant was rubbished by my mother.
这家餐馆的鲑鱼沙拉被我妈妈批评得一无是处。
● trout 鲑鱼　● salmon pink 鲑红色

> 语法重点
> salmon 作可数名词，表示"鲑鱼"，复数形式为 salmons；作不可数名词时，则表示"鲑肉，鲑红色"。

0809 **salute** [sə'luːt] v / n 招呼
The soldier reported to the officer about the expenditure of money on weapons after giving a salute.
敬礼之后，那位士兵向军官汇报用于购置武器的开支。
● hail 招呼　● military salute 军礼　● ... give a salute ……敬礼

0810 **sandal** ['sændl] n 凉鞋
It's ridiculous for you to buy a pair of sandals like that.
你竟然买那么一双凉鞋，真是荒谬。
● it's ridiculous for... to... ……真是荒谬

0811 **savage** ['sævɪdʒ] a 野蛮的　n 野蛮人　v 激烈抨击
The lady's remark was a savage attack on the quality of the laptop.
那位女士的评价是对这台笔记本电脑的品质的恶意攻击。
● be a savage attack on... 对……进行恶意的攻击

● remark (P. 495)

0812 **scan** [skæn] v 扫描，仔细地检查
She bought a novel which was savaged by readers and scanned it at bedtime.
她买了一本被读者们猛烈抨击的小说，在睡前浏览一遍。
● glance 浏览　● scan with 用……来看　● be savaged by... 被……猛烈抨击

sacred ~ scrape

0813 scandal ['skændl] n 丑闻，流言蜚语
His pilferage from the jewelry store caused a scandal in his family.
他在珠宝店行窃让家人很气愤。
同 disgrace 耻辱　同 make up a scandal 捏造丑闻

> **语法重点**
> cause a scandal in（在……激起义愤）中的 a 也可以省略。

0814 scar [skɑːr] n 伤痕，断崖 v 结疤，痊愈
The man with a scar on his face was caught pinching money from the cashbox in the store.
那个脸上有伤疤的人在这家店的钱箱中偷钱，当场被抓。
同 wound 伤疤　同 scar over 愈合　同 pinch... from... 偷……

0815 scent [sent] n 气味，香味 v 充满，得到……的暗示
The lady with scents of lavender pecked at her food in the restaurant.
那位有薰衣草香味的女士在餐厅里无精打采地吃着食物。
同 fragrance 香味　反 stink 臭味　同 by scent 凭嗅觉

0816 scheme [skiːm] n 计划，规划，诡计
The scheme that we go shopping in Hong Kong seems to be practical on the surface.
我们去香港购物的计划表面看起来似乎很实际。
同 plan 计划　同 scheme against 勾心斗角

参 practical (P. 341)

0817 scorn [skɔːrn] v 轻蔑，嘲弄 n 轻蔑，奚落
We all heap scorn on him for he can't afford to buy new uniform and schoolbag.
我们都嘲笑他买不起新制服和书包。
同 disdain 蔑视　同 pour scorn on 对……不屑一顾，嘲笑

参 uniform (P. 241)

0818 scramble ['skræmbl] v / n 杂乱地收集
The customers scrambled these goods up.
顾客们把这些商品弄乱了。
同 scramble for 争夺　同 sb. scrambles sth. up 某人把某物弄乱了

0819 scrap [skræp] n 小块，废料 v 废弃
I had a bit of a scrap with the salesman over there.
我跟那边的那个售货员有过争执。
同 not a scrap 一点儿也没有　同 have a bit of a scrap with... 与……有争执

> **语法重点**
> have a bit of a scrap with 后面接表示人的名词或者代词。

0820 scrape [skreɪp] v / n 刮，擦
We want to scrape together some money to buy a gift for the poor girl.
我们想凑钱为那个可怜的女孩买一份礼物。
同 raw 擦伤　同 scrape through 勉强通过　同 scrape together... 拼凑……

0821 scroll [skroʊl] n 卷轴，卷形物 v 卷动
The man who is buying a picture always wants to be on the scroll of fame.
那个正在买画的人老想名垂青史。
- scroll bar 卷轴
- be on the scroll of fame 名垂史册

0822 sculptor ['skʌlptər] n 雕刻家
The sculptor tried hard to bargain with the man.
雕刻家尽力与那个人讨价还价。

> 语法重点
> try hard to（尽力）后面接动词原形。

0823 secure [sə'kjʊr] a 安全的
What he hopes for is buying a can of secure milk powder.
他希望买到一罐安全的奶粉。
- safe 安全的
- insecure 不安全的
- secure against from 免受……（侵害等）
- what sb. hopes for is... 某人希望的是……

0824 segment ['segmənt] n 部分，弓形 v 分割，划分
Give me a segment of a tangerine to taste; if it is sweet, I will buy some.
给我一瓣柑橘尝尝，如果甜的话，我就买一些。
- portion 部分
- whole 整体

> tangerine (P. 232)

0825 sensation [sen'seɪʃn] n 轰动的事或人，知觉
He lost all sensation in his legs when he was at the supermarket.
他在超市购物时，腿部失去了知觉。
- feeling 感觉
- visual sensation 视觉
- lose all sensation in... 失去知觉……

0826 sensitivity [ˌsensə'tɪvəti] n 敏感度，多愁善感
All of us should keep the sensitivity to the market.
我们都应该保持对市场的敏感性。
- susceptivity 敏感
- light sensitivity 感光性

> 语法重点
> keep the sensitivity to（对……保持敏感性）中的 to 是介词。

0827 sentiment ['sentɪmənt] n 多愁善感
There is no time for sentiment for we have to go shopping now.
没有时间多愁善感，因为现在我们得去购物了。
- emotion 情绪
- there is no time for... 没时间……

0828 sergeant ['sɑːrdʒənt] n 陆军或海军陆战队中士
Sergeant Black wanted to go to the supermarket which is in the shadow of the hospital.
布莱克中士想去医院附近的超市。
- sarge 警官，军士
- be in the shadow of... 在……附近

> 语法重点
> 在英语中，表示称呼语或职务的单词，首字母必须大写。
> shadow (P. 357)

0829 series ['sɪriːz] n 系列，丛书

I heard that she gave forth a series of works in succession.
我听说她连续发表了一系列的作品。
- succession 连续
- series of 一系列
- give forth... 发表……

语法重点
series 之前可以有 long 等形容词修饰，of 后接名词。
➔ succession (P. 786)

0830 sermon ['sɜːrmən] n 讲道，讲道文章

Don't preach me a sermon, I just want to buy a computer.
请不要对我讲大道理，我只是想买一台电脑而已。
- preach sb. a sermon 是固定搭配，sermon 用单数。

0831 server ['sɜːrvər] n 侍者，餐具

Which kind of server do you want to buy?
你想要买哪一种托盘？
- waiter 侍者，服务生
- Which kind of... do you want to buy? 你想买哪一种……？

语法重点
server 是可数名词。

0832 setting ['setɪŋ] n 设定

The gruesome setting for the murder is the supermarket you always go to.
那起谋杀案令人毛骨悚然的背景就是你经常去的那家超市。
- surroundings 环境
- social setting 社会环境
- it is kind of... 有点儿……

0833 shabby ['ʃæbi] a 衣衫褴褛的，卑鄙的

The salesman even played a shabby trick on the customers.
那个售货员甚至对顾客们玩弄卑鄙的手段。
- seedy 破旧的
- play a shabby trick on... 对……玩弄卑鄙的手段

0834 sharpen ['ʃɑːrpən] v 使锐利，加剧

The salesman says this knife is designed to sharpen the pencils.
售货员说，这把刀就是为削铅笔而设计的。
- point 弄尖
- flatten 变平
- sharpen up 使……更敏锐

➔ design (P. 151)

0835 shatter ['ʃætər] v 破裂，毁坏 n 碎片

When I bought some pears, my glasses broke into shatters suddenly.
我买梨子的时候，眼镜突然碎了。
- break 打破
- repair 修理
- shatter into 使……粉碎
- break into shatters ……粉碎

0836 sheriff ['ʃerɪf] n 警长，郡治安官

The sheriff whose name is Tom Black is under no obligation to buy anything.
那个叫汤姆·布莱克的郡长不必买东西。
- nomarch 省长
- sheriff android 报警器

语法重点
在英语中，姓名中的名和姓的首字母都要大写。
➔ obligation (P. 749)

0837 **shield** [ʃiːld] **n** 盾，防护物 **v** 保护
To shield your eyes from the sun, you need to buy a pair of sunglasses.
想保护眼睛不受太阳光照射，你有必要买一副太阳眼镜。
同 shelter 庇护　反 risk 冒……的危险　搭 shield... from sth. 保护……不受

0838 **shiver** [ˈʃɪvər] **v** 发抖，哆嗦 **n** 冷战
At the thought of buying a snake home gave me the shivers.
一想起买一条蛇回家，我就吓得直哆嗦。
同 quake 发抖　反 calm 使平静　搭 shiver with 因……而发抖

0839 **shortage** [ˈʃɔːrtɪdʒ] **n** 不足，缺少，不足额
We have to buy some materials to make up for shortage.
我们需要买一些材料以弥补空缺。
反 abundance 富裕　搭 fund shortage 资金不足　搭 make up for... 弥补……

0840 **shortcoming** [ˈʃɔːrtkʌmɪŋ] **n** 短处，缺点
"Going shopping too often is her greatest shortcoming." her mother says.
她妈妈说："频繁购物是她的最大缺点。"
搭 doing sth. is one's greatest shortcoming 做某事是某人最大的缺点

> **语法重点**
> 例句中，直接引述别人的话时，要用引号。

0841 **shove** [ʃʌv] **v** 推，撞 **n** 猛推
Please shove up; I want to buy some grapes.
请借过，我想买点儿葡萄。
搭 shove off（命令）滚开

> **语法重点**
> shove up 是不及物动词短语，后面一般不接宾语。

0842 **shred** [ʃred] **n** 碎片，少许 **v** 撕成碎片
I think there was not a shred of falsehood in what the salesman said.
我觉得那个售货员没说一句假话。
搭 shred of 少量　搭 there is not a shred of falsehood in... ……没有一句假话

> **语法重点**
> shred of 通常用作单数，用于疑问句与否定句中，意思是"少量"。

0843 **shriek** [ʃriːk] **v** 尖叫，引人注意 **n** 尖锐的声音
The customer let out a piercing shriek after he saw the moldy bread.
那个顾客看到发霉的面包后，发出一声尖叫。
同 cry 叫　反 whisper 低声说，窃窃私语　搭 shriek with 发出尖叫
搭 let out... 发出……

> 参 bread (P. 017)

0844 **shrine** [ʃraɪn] **n** 神殿，庙 **v** 把……奉为神圣
The shrine is an object of pilgrimage, not a shopping center.
这座神殿是人们朝圣的对象，不是购物中心。
搭 be an object of... 是……的目的地

> **语法重点**
> shrine 也常用在习语 worship at the shrine of Mammon 中，意思是"一心想发财"。

0845 shrub [ʃrʌb] n 灌木，灌木丛

The visitors were shattered by the evergreen shrub in front of the museum.
观光客们都被博物馆前面的常绿灌木给震撼了。
🔄 bush 灌木　🔗 shrub zone 灌木带　🔗 be shattered by... 被……震撼了

语法重点
be shattered by 后面可以接人，也可以接物。
🔗 evergreen (P. 564)

0846 shudder [ˈʃʌdər] v 发抖，震动 n 颤动

The news that we don't have to go shopping on such a cold day sent a shudder through me.
得知我们不用在这么冷的天去购物的消息，我激动得浑身发抖。
🔄 shake 发抖　🔀 calm 镇静　🔗 shudder at 不寒而栗
🔗 send a shudder through sb. 使某人浑身发抖

0847 shutter [ˈʃʌtər] n 百叶窗，快门

Many a shop has put up the shutters owing to the bad weather.
许多商店都因为恶劣的天气停止营业了。
🔄 blind 百叶窗　🔗 shutter speed 快门速度
🔗 ... put up the shutters ……停止营业

语法重点
根据语法一致原则，当不定代词 many a 作主语或修饰主语时应看作单数，动词用单数。

0848 silkworm [ˈsɪlkwɜːrm] n 蚕

It was only two minutes before he bought some silkworms.
他只用两分钟的时间就买到了一些蚕。
🔗 it is only... before... 只用了……的时间就……

0849 simmer [ˈsɪmər] v 煨，炖 n 即将发作

Let's go to the supermarket to buy some foods after you simmer down.
等你平静下来后，我们一起去超市买点儿食品。
🔄 stew 炖　🔗 ... simmer down ……安静下来

0850 skeleton [ˈskelɪtn] n 骨骼，框架

The salesman gave us just the skeleton of her theory about how to buy a genuine antique.
那个售货员给我们提供了关于如何买到古玩真品的理论框架。
🔄 framework 框架　🔗 give sb. the skeleton of... 给某人提供……的框架

🔗 genuine (P. 447)

0851 skull [skʌl] n 头盖骨，骷髅头 v 击打头部

I have saved up enough money to buy the sweater with a design of a skull.
我已经存够钱来买那件带有骷髅头图案的毛衣了。
🔄 bone 骨头　🔗 out of one's skull 不正常　🔗 save up... 储蓄……

0852 slam [slæm] v 砰地关上
His answer to my request that we go shopping together was to slam the door.
我要求跟他一起去购物，他只是猛地关上门作为回答。
- bang 重击　- slam the door in someone's face 给……吃闭门羹

0853 slap [slæp] v / n 扇耳光
The customer gave the salesman a slap on the cheek.
顾客一巴掌打在售货员的脸上。
- smack 掌掴　- slap on 用掌拍打（某人）的（某部位）
- give sb. a slap on... 用巴掌拍打某人的……

⊙ cheek (P. 270)

0854 slaughter ['slɔːtər] v / n 屠宰
He slammed the door in my face and bought the slaughtered pig at last.
他拒绝听取我的意见，最终买下了那头被屠宰的猪。
- murder 谋杀　- protect 保卫　- slaughter room 屠宰场
- slammed the door in one's face 拒绝听取某人的意见

0855 slay [sleɪ] v 杀害，被（笑或爱）淹没
He was slain when he was buying a car.
他正在买汽车时被杀死。
- kill 杀死　- save 挽救　- be slain when... ……的时候被杀死

语法重点
slay 是不规则动词，其过去式、过去分词分别是 slew, slain。

0856 sloppy ['slɑːpi] a 不整洁的，草率的，稀薄的
I like going shopping in my sloppy clothes.
我喜欢穿着宽松随意的衣服去逛街。
- deliberate 深思熟虑的　- sloppy hat 软毡帽

语法重点
sloppy 的副词形式是 sloppily。

0857 slump [slʌmp] v 倒下 n 下降，消沉
She is in a slump in her career and can't afford to buy a fridge.
她处在事业的低谷，没钱买冰箱。
- sag 下垂　- ascend 上升　- slump badly 猛跌
- be in a slump in... 正处于……的低谷

⊙ fridge (P. 214)

0858 sly [slaɪ] a 狡猾的，暗中的，灵活的
The customer picked up a watch on the sly.
那个顾客偷偷地把那块手表偷走了。
- tricky 狡猾的　- as sly as a fox 像狐狸般狡猾

0859 smash [smæʃ] v 粉碎，猛撞 n 破碎，猛击
When you buy a bottle of drink, you have to give a smash on the vending machine.
你想买一瓶饮料的话，需要猛击那台自动贩卖机。

0860 snarl [snɑːrl] **v** 吠叫，纠缠，混乱 **n** 咆哮，混乱
Snarling at the salesman is useless.
对售货员咆哮是没有用的。
🔄 growl 咆哮　🔄 snarl at... 对……吼叫

> 语法重点
> 陈述句可以用来说明事实，也可以陈述看法，如例句。

0861 snatch [snætʃ] **v** 夺走，抓住 **n** 抢夺，一阵
Did you snatch the mobile phone from him when you go shopping together?
你们一起逛街的时候，你有没有把手机从他那里抢过来？
🔄 grasp 夺取　🔄 snatch at 抓住　🔄 snatch... from... 从……夺取……

> 语法重点
> 疑问句的主要交际功能是提出问题、询问情况，按其语法结构和交际功能可分为以下四种：一般疑问句、特殊疑问句、选择疑问句、反义疑问句。例句是一般疑问句。

0862 sneak [sniːk] **v** 偷偷地走 **n** 偷偷摸摸的人或事
It's dishonourable of us to have a sneak attack on him when he buys his breakfast.
我们在他买早餐的时候偷袭不光彩。
🔄 sneak in 偷偷地溜进　🔄 have a sneak attack on... 偷袭……

0863 sneaker ['sniːkər] **n** 鬼鬼祟祟做事的人，运动鞋
The man who is reduced to a skeleton likes to buy buns wearing sneakers.
那个瘦得皮包骨头的人喜欢穿着运动鞋买馒头。

🔄 skeleton (P. 633)

0864 sniff [snɪf] **v** 嗅，闻
I want to take a sniff at the roses before I buy them.
我想在买这些玫瑰花之前先闻一闻花香。
🔄 smell 嗅，闻　🔄 sniff out 发觉

> 语法重点
> take a sniff at（闻一闻）是固定搭配，sniff 要用单数。

0865 snore [snɔːr] **v** 打鼾 **n** 鼾声
His loud snore kept me awake, so I got up to go to the supermarket.
他的鼾声大得使我睡不着，所以我起床去超市了。
🔄 snore like a grampus 鼾声如雷　🔄 keep sb. awake 使某人睡不着

0866 snort [snɔːrt] **n** 喷气声，发哼声 **v** 哼着鼻子
He gave a snort of derision when I told him I bought a cheap cup.
当我告诉他我买了一个便宜的水杯时，他哼了一下鼻子表示嘲笑。
🔄 grunt 咕哝　🔄 snort at 对……发出哼声以示不满

0867 soak [soʊk] **v** 浸泡
He was soaked in the music and didn't want to buy anything.
他沉浸在音乐中，不想买任何东西。
🔄 steep 浸泡　🔄 dry 从……去掉水分　🔄 soak into 浸入
🔄 be soaked in... 沉浸在……

0868 **sober** ['soʊbər] a 没喝醉的，清醒的 v 使清醒，使沉着

When he sobers down, you can accompany him to buy some clothes.
等他安静下来，你可以陪他去买一些衣服。
同 lucid 神智清醒的，头脑清楚的　反 drowsy 昏昏欲睡的，催眠的

语法重点
sober down（安静下来）是不及物动词短语。

0869 **soften** ['sɔ:fn] v 使柔软，（使）温和，减轻

She was softened up with the free gifts the salesmen gave to her.
推销员送的赠品打动了她的心。

0870 **sole(1)** [soʊl] a 唯一的，单独的

To buy a cell-phone, the salesman is my sole trust.
如果要买手机的话，那个售货员是我唯一信赖的人。
同 only 唯一的　反 multiple 各式多样的　　sole proprietorship 独资（经营）
辨 sole 语气强于 only，指仅有一个或一群，只考虑这一个或这一群，only 是普通用词，常与 sole 换用，但侧重仅限于指定的人或物，而不需要更多。

0871 **sole(2)** [soʊl] n 脚底，鞋底，袜底

The nail pierced through the sole of the shoes he has just bought.
那根钉子刺穿了他刚买的鞋子的鞋底。

语法重点
sole 的复数形式有两个，即 sole 和 soles。

0872 **solemn** ['sɑ:ləm] a 严肃的，庄严的

She wore an extraordinarily solemn expression because her mother didn't buy the coat for her.
她脸上带着异常严肃的表情，因为她的妈妈没有买那件外套给她。

语法重点
expression 常与动词 wear 连用，表示脸上带着某种表情。

0873 **solitary** ['sɑ:ləteri] a 单独的，孤独的

She had been held in solitary confinement for half a month because she stole things in the supermarket.
因为在超市里偷东西，她被单独关押了半个月。
同 isolated 单独的　　solitary life 独居生活

语法重点
solitary 的副词形式是 solitarily。

0874 **solo** ['soʊloʊ] n 独唱，独奏，独唱曲

It was subsequently emerged that his solo attracted many customers in the supermarket.
随后的情况显示，他的独奏吸引了超市里很多的顾客。

⇒ emerge (P. 433)

0875 **sovereign** ['sɑ:vrən] n 君主 a 具有主权的，至高无上的

I think as a salesman, your character is of sovereign importance.
我认为作为一个推销员，你的人品最为重要。
同 supreme 至高的　　sovereign power 主权

0876 sow [soʊ] v 播种

It is too soon to sow yet and we haven't buy seeds.
现在还不到播种的时候，而且我们还没有买种子。
- seed 播种
- reap 收割
- sow discord 挑拨离间
- it is too soon to... 还不到……的时候

语法重点
sow 的过去式是 sowed，过去分词有两个，分别是 sowed 和 sown。

0877 spacecraft ['speɪskræft] n 太空船

His dream is to buy a spacecraft, but it's just a flight of fancy.
他的梦想是买一艘太空船，但这只是异想天开。
- spaceship 太空船
- ... be just a flight of fancy ……只是异想天开

- fancy (P. 295)

0878 specialist ['speʃəlɪst] n 专家，专科医生

My cousin is a specialist in literature and he loves buying jade.
我堂兄是文学方面的专家，而且他喜欢买玉石。
- expert 专家
- jackaroo 无经验者
- be a specialist in... 是……方面的专家

0879 specimen ['spesɪmən] n 样本，范例，某种类型的人

It was a specimen of her generosity to buy things.
这是她慷慨大方购物的一个实例。
- sample 样品
- take a specimen 取样
- it is a specimen of... 是……的一个实例

语法重点
specimen 是可数名词，复数为 specimens。
- generosity (P. 446)

0880 spectacle ['spektəkl] n 壮观，景象，场面

The drunken man made a spectacle of himself in the store.
那个酒醉的人在商店里大出洋相。
- make a spectacle of oneself 使自己出丑、出洋相

0881 spectator ['spekteɪtər] n 观众

He was content to stand by as an spectator when his wife was buying all kinds of clothes.
当妻子在买各种的衣服时，他满足于站在旁边做一个旁观者。
- onlooker 旁观者
- spectator sport 吸引大量观众的体育运动

语法重点
在美式英语中，spectator 还可以表示"女式运动鞋"，并多用其复数形式。

0882 spine [spaɪn] n 背骨，脊椎，刺毛

Hearing that his girlfriend has spent all his savings buying a car, a cold shiver ran down his spine.
得知女朋友用他所有的积蓄买了车，他打了一个寒战。
- ridge 背脊
- lumbar spine 腰椎，腰脊柱
- a cold shiver runs down sb.'s spine 某人打了一个寒战

语法重点
英语中的句号是实心点"."，而中文的句号是小圆圈"。"，句点一般用于一句话完全结束时。
- shiver (P. 632)

0883 **splendor** [ˈsplendər] n 灿烂，光辉，显赫
St. John has never gazed on such splendor in a supermarket.
圣约翰从没有在一个超市里见过如此辉煌壮丽的场面。
⦿ brightness 光辉　⦿ natural splendor 自然奇观　⦿ gaze on... 看到……

语法重点
句点也可以用于英文单词的缩写，如 St., Mr., Dr., U.S. 等。但要注意的是，当缩写的字母形成一个单词的时候，就不需要使用句点，如 IBM，DNA 等。

0884 **sponge** [spʌndʒ] n 海绵　v 用海绵擦
Don't sponge on your parents if you always want to buy luxuries.
如果你总是想要买奢侈品的话，就不要依赖你父母。
⦿ sponge off 依赖他人生活　⦿ sponge on... 依赖……

0885 **spotlight** [ˈspɑːtlaɪt]
n 聚光灯，探照灯　v 聚光照明，使公众注意
Since she likes to be in the spotlight, let her buy these things on behalf of us.
既然她喜欢出风头，就让她代表我们买这些东西吧。

语法重点
在英语中，逗点可以用于关联的从句之间，如例句中 since 引导的从句和 let 引导的从句间就是用逗点。

0886 **sprint** [sprɪnt] v 冲刺，全速短跑　n 全速短跑
We need to buy all these things on the list with a sprint of very hard work.
我们需要努力一阵子才能买到清单上所有的东西。
⦿ spurt 冲刺　⦿ all-out sprint 全力冲刺

0887 **spur** [spɜːr] v 刺激　n 刺激物
I always go shopping on the spur of the moment.
我总是一时兴起就去购物了。
⦿ spur on 驱使　⦿ do sth. on the spur of the moment 一时冲动之下做某事

⦿ moment (P. 064)

0888 **squash** [skwɑːʃ]
v 压扁，挤进　n 浓缩果汁，拥挤嘈杂的人群
After the salesman squashed the grapes into a pulp, we bought some.
等那个推销员把葡萄压榨成酱后，我们买了一些。
⦿ squash into 挤进　⦿ squash... into... 把……压榨成……

0889 **squat** [skwɑːt]
v 蹲下　a 蹲着的，矮胖的　n 蹲，擅自占用的土地
We need to get into a squat to pick out some good potatoes.
我们需要蹲下来才能挑到一些好的马铃薯。
⦿ crouch 蹲伏　⦿ stand 站立　⦿ squat down 蹲下
⦿ ... get into a squat ……蹲下来

0890 stack [stæk] n 干草堆，垛 v 堆积

I have a stack of emails in my inbox to deal with, so I have no time to buy vegetables.
我的收件箱里有很多电子邮件要处理，所以我没有时间买菜了。

- heap 堆积
- stack up 堆积，累计
- pile, stack, heap 都有"堆"的意思，pile 是一般用语，指把同种类的东西比较整齐地堆起来，stack 是指将同种类且同样大小的东西整齐地堆在一起，heap 指不分种类、杂乱地堆放。

0891 stagger ['stægər] v 蹒跚，使吃惊，使交错

I want to stagger work shifts to buy some daily necessities.
我得错开工作去买点儿日用品。

0892 stain [steɪn] v 弄脏，给……着色 n 污迹

This ink stain won't rub out and I need to buy some detergent.
这墨水渍擦不掉，我需要买一些清洁剂。

- spot 玷污
- cleanse 净化

语法重点
rub out（擦掉）用主动的形式表达被动的意思。
- rub (P. 084)

0893 stake [steɪk] n 股份 v 资助

I will stake you to a big house.
我会资助你买一间大房子。

- at stake 在危急关头
- stake sb. to sth. 资助某人取得某物

语法重点
stake sb. to sth. 中的 to 是介词。

0894 stalk [stɔːk] n 茎，高烟囱 n 跟踪 v 悄悄靠近

The sucker you want to buy is no better than a hollow stalk.
你想买的这个吸管比空麦秆子好不了多少。

- stem 茎，柄
- be no better than... 比……好不了多少

0895 stall [stɔːl] n 摊位，书摊，厩

He sneaked out to buy some fruits at a market stall.
他偷偷溜出去市场的货摊上买水果。

- booth 货摊，岗亭
- stall off 拖延
- ... sneak out ……偷偷溜出去

语法重点
sneak out 是不及物动词短语，后面一般不接宾语。

0896 stanza ['stænzə] n 诗的一节，局，场

I've read the third stanza before we made our way through the crowds of shoppers.
我们从购物的人潮中挤过去之前，第三节诗我已经读过了。

- verse 诗节
- make one's way through... 挤过……

0897 startle ['stɑːrtl] v 使惊吓 n 吃惊

His buying the expensive ring gave me a startle.
他买下那个昂贵的戒指，吓了我一跳。

- surprise 使吃惊
- calm 镇静
- give sb. a startle 吓了某人一跳

0898 **statesman** ['steɪtsmən] n 政客

The man who is anything of a statesman is buying a cake.
那个像政治家的男人在买蛋糕。
- politician 政治家
- elder statesman 政界元老
- be anything of... 像……
- statesman 的意思是"政治家"，含褒义，而 politician 的意思是"政客"，含贬义，要根据实际情况选择适当的词。

0899 **statistic** [stə'tɪstɪk] n 统计值，统计学

We have statistics for the last year about which kind of drink the customers like to buy.
我们有去年关于顾客最喜欢买哪种饮料的统计资料。
- correlations 统计
- statistics analysis 统计分析
- "进行统计"可以用 collect statistics 或 take statistics 来表示。

0900 **statistic / statistical** [stə'tɪstɪk] / [stə'tɪstɪkl]
a 统计的，统计学的

The salesman showed the price fluctuations in a statistical table to the customers.
售货员用统计表向顾客们展示价格的波动。
- statistical data 统计资料

0901 **steamer** ['stiːmər] n 轮船，蒸汽机

He put her aboard a steamer bearing in with London and went shopping alone.
他把她送上一艘驶向伦敦的轮船，然后独自去购物了。
- ferry steamer 渡轮
- bear in with... 开往……

语法重点
bear in with 的主语一般是"轮船"。
- aboard (P. 251)

0902 **steer** [stɪr] v 驾驶

We must steer by these pits to buy fruits there.
要去那边买水果，我们必须绕过这些坑。
- drive 驾驶
- steer clear of 绕开
- steer by... 绕过……

0903 **stereotype** ['steriətaɪp] n 刻板印象 v 使形成固定看法

The old woman always holds a stereotype to look upon buying luxuries.
那个老妇人总是用自己固有的观念看待购买奢侈品这件事。
- social stereotype 社会定型
- hold a stereotype to... 用固有的观念去……

0904 **stern** [stɜːrn] a 严格的，坚决的 n 船尾，臀部

The chef is very stern in buying rice.
这主厨购买稻米时极为严格。
- harsh 严厉的
- gentle 温和的
- from stem to stern 完全，从头到尾
- be stern in... 在……严格

语法重点
stern 的副词是 sternly。
- chef (P. 541)

statesman ~ straightforward

0905 stew [stuː] v 炖，煮，担忧 n 炖煮的菜肴，烦恼
There's no need to get in a stew and I believe you can buy a satisfying handbag.
没有必要烦恼，我相信你能买到一个满意的手提包。
- cook 烹调
- stew in one's own juice 自作自受
- get in a stew 烦恼

0906 stink [stɪŋk] v 发出恶臭，招人厌恶 n 恶臭，难闻的气味
Let me stink out the mosquitoes before we go shopping.
我们去购物前，让我把蚊子熏出去。

> **语法重点**
> 现代英语祈使句有两种类型：一种是第二人称祈使句；另一种是第一、三人称祈使句，如例句属于第一人称祈使句。

0907 stock [stɑːk] n 存货，股本
Is this kind of cloth in stock now?
这种布料现在有库存吗？
- out of stock 无现货的
- Is / Are... in stock? ……有库存吗？

0908 stoop [stuːp] v 弯腰
All of the customers have to stoop their head to enter the supermarket.
所有顾客必须弯腰才能进入超市。
- bend 弯曲
- stoop to 降低身份以求……
- stoop one's head 低下头

> **语法重点**
> stoop to 后加动词不定式表示 "降低身份以求……"，而 stoop to 后加动名词的意思是 "堕落到……的地步"。

0909 storage ['stɔːrɪdʒ] n 储存，储藏量
The storage of food is not enough for the whole family in winter and we have to buy some.
粮食的储存量不够一家人过冬，我们还要买一些。
- repository 仓储
- storage system 储存系统
- be enough for sth. 足够……

0910 stout [staʊt] a 肥胖的，牢固的 n 烈啤酒
This is the time for stout people to buy some diet pills.
是胖子们买减肥药的时候了。
- chubby 圆胖的
- brown stout 黑啤酒
- this is the time for... 是……的时候

- diet (P. 283)

0911 straighten ['streɪtn] v 弄直
She said she would straighten up her room after buying the eye-cream.
她说买过眼霜后她就整理房间。
- bend 弯曲
- straighten out 使成直线
- straighten up... 使……整齐

> **语法重点**
> 英语中，逗点用于直接引用的句子之前，但是如果句中含有间接引语，就不需要逗点。

0912 straightforward [ˌstreɪt'fɔːrwərd] a 直接的 ad 坦率地
They took a straightforward route to the beach after buying enough foods and water.
他们买了足够的食物和水后沿着直道去海滩了。
- aboveboard 率直地
- straightforward approach 直截了当的方法

> **语法重点**
> take a straightforward route to 中的 to 是介词，后面一般接表示地点的名词。

0913 strain [streɪn] v/n 拉紧，尽力

Their relationship is under great strain when they go shopping together.
他们一起购物时关系非常紧张。
📖 pull 拉　📖 loosen 松开　📖 strain at 紧拖
📖 ... be under great strain ……非常紧张

语法重点
strain 的复数形式可以表示"旋律"。

0914 strait [streɪt] n 海峡，困境 a 困难的，狭窄的，严格的

She took strait vows that she won't buy anything this month.
她立下严格的誓愿，这个月不买任何东西了。
📖 channel 海峡　📖 loose 宽松的

语法重点
strait 指短而窄的海峡，常用复数形式但表示单数，channel 则指比 strait 长而宽的海峡。

0915 strand [strænd] v 使搁浅 n 缕，不同的一个部分

She was stranded in the storm when you took a shower, wasn't she?
你淋浴时她被暴风雨困住了，是吗？
📖 ground 搁浅　📖 strand line 海岸线　📖 be stranded in... 被困在……

语法重点
在英语中，反问句之前要使用逗号。
📖 storm (P. 228)

0916 strap [stræp] n 带子 v 捆扎

The trousers of the child who is buying a lollipop are held on by an elastic strap.
那个正在买棒棒糖的小孩的裤子是用一根松紧带系着的。
📖 belt 带　📖 leather strap 皮带　📖 be held on by... 由……系着

0917 stray [streɪ] v 迷路 a 迷路的

Don't stray from the right subject when we talk about what to buy.
当我们在讨论买什么时请不要偏离正题。
📖 wander 迷路　📖 stray from... 偏离……

语法重点
stray from 是固定用法，介词 from 后面通常接名词或代词，表示偏离某个地方。

0918 streak [striːk] n 条纹，个性特征 v 疾驰，加上条纹

A streak of lightning flashed through the sky when we bought a fish in the market.
我们在市场买鱼时，一道光闪过天空。
📖 winning streak 连胜　📖 flash through... 闪过……

0919 stride [straɪd] v 迈大步走 n 大步，步伐

In a big stride did the customer come out of the store when the earthquake took place.
地震发生时，这个顾客一个箭步走出商店。
📖 steps 步伐　📖 take everything in stride 泰然自若

语法重点
例句用的是倒装结构，表示强调。

0920 stripe [straɪp] n 条纹 v 剥，夺去
He sniffed at the red striped T shirt I bought.
他对我买的那件红色条纹的 T 恤嗤之以鼻。
- magnetic stripe 磁条，磁片
- sniff at... 对……嗤之以鼻
- the Stars and Stripes 可以表示"星条旗（美国国旗）"。

➤ sniff (P. 635)

0921 stroll [stroʊl] v / n 散步，闲逛
I am going to take a stroll in the village after buying some tomatoes.
我准备买些番茄，然后到村里散步。
- stroll through 漫步走过
- take a stroll 散步

0922 structural ['strʌktʃərəl] a 结构上的，建筑的
The storm caused no structural damage to the supermarket that we were at.
风暴没有破坏我们所在超市的建筑结构。
- tectonic 建筑的
- structural design 结构设计

语法重点
structural 的副词是 structurally。

0923 stumble ['stʌmbl] v 绊倒，蹒跚，犯错误 n 绊倒，错误
He stumbled on his childhood friend when he was shopping.
他逛街时偶然遇到儿时的伙伴。
- stagger 蹒跚
- stumble across 偶然发现
- stumble on 偶然遇到

➤ childhood (P. 271)

0924 stump [stʌmp] n 残余部分，烟蒂 v 受窘，演说
We all went shopping and left him sitting on the stump.
我们都去逛街了，留下他一个人坐在树桩上。
- stump up 付出，拿出，买单
- leave sb. doing sth. 留下某人……

0925 stun [stʌn] v 使吃惊，使目瞪口呆 n 震惊，晕眩
I was stunned by his idea that he wanted to buy a villa.
我对他想要买一栋别墅的想法感到震惊。
- shock 震惊
- be stunned by... 对……感到震惊

0926 sturdy ['stɜːrdi] a 健壮的，坚定的，牢固的
You must sniff a sturdy man out to accompany you to buy the famous painting.
你必须找一个健壮的人来陪你买那幅名画。
- strong 牢固的
- weak 不牢固的
- sniff out... 找出……

0927 stylish ['staɪlɪʃ] a 时髦的，流行的，漂亮的
The customers in the supermarket are all stylish dressers.
这个超市里的顾客穿着都很时髦。
- fashionable 时髦的
- unfashionable 过时的
- stylish garment 流行服饰
- be a stylish dresser 穿着时髦

语法重点
stylish 后面加上词尾 -ness，构成名词 stylishness，意思是"时髦，新式"。

0928 submit [səb'mɪt] v 呈递，认为

I submit that we can buy a big box.
我想我们可以买一个大箱子。
- submit applications 提交申请
- I submit that... 我想……

0929 substantial [səb'stænʃl] a 实在的，坚固的，物质的

We made substantial changes to shopping.
我们在购物上做了重大变动。
- stable 牢固的
- immaterial 非物质的
- substantial increase 大幅度增长

语法重点
make substantial changes to（在……做出巨大的变动）中的 to 是介词。

0930 substitute ['sʌbstɪtuːt] v 用……代替 n 代替人

I had to find another one to substitute for her to go shopping with me.
我得找另一个人来代替她陪我去购物。
- replace 代替
- substitute A for B 用 A 代 B
- substitute for sb. to do sth. 代替某人做某事

0931 suitcase ['suːtkeɪs] n 手提箱，衣箱

You can pack all the things you have just bought into the suitcase.
你可以把你刚买的所有东西都放进这个手提箱里。
- trunk 衣箱
- pack... into... 把……装进

0932 sulfur ['sʌlfɚ] n 硫黄 v 用硫处理液化

I sneaked up on the man who was buying some sulfur.
我偷偷地接近那个买硫黄的男人。
- brenstone 硫黄
- sulfur dioxide 二氧化硫
- sneak up on... 偷偷地接近……

sneak (P. 635)

0933 summon ['sʌmən] v 召唤，鼓起（勇气）

I could not summon up the courage to ask him to buy the beautiful watch.
我鼓不起勇气要他买那漂亮的手表给我。
- summon up 鼓起（勇气），振作
- summon up the courage to... 鼓起勇气……

语法重点
例句中的 up 也可以省略。

0934 superficial [ˌsuːpərˈfɪʃl] a 表面的，肤浅的，一知半解的

The customer has a superficial knowledge of this kind of jewel.
那个顾客对这种珠宝略知皮毛。
- shallow 肤浅的
- deep 深刻的
- have a superficial knowledge of... 对……略知皮毛

语法重点
jewel 意思是"珠宝"，是可数名词。

submit ~ suspend

0935 superstition [ˌsuːpərˈstɪʃn] **n** 迷信，迷信行为，邪教
You must break down superstitions if you want to buy the new kind of wedding dress.
你想买这款新式婚纱，必须破除迷信。
- fetish 迷信　- eradicate superstition 破除迷信　- break down... 破除……

0936 supervise [ˈsuːpərvaɪz] **v** 监督，指导
I have to submit to his arrangement that I supervise the children when he goes shopping.
我不得不服从他的安排：他去逛街，我照顾孩子。
- control 管理　- I have to submit to... 我不得不服从……

⊙ arrangement (P. 125)

0937 supervisor [ˈsuːpərvaɪzər] **n** 监督者，检查员，导师
Between you and me, I think that our supervisor is a shopaholic.
我们私下说，我认为主管是一个购物狂。
- administrator 管理人　- accounting supervisor 会计主管，财务主管
- between you and me, ... 我们私下说，……

0938 suppress [səˈpres] **v** 镇压，抑制，隐瞒
I could not suppress a smile when I saw him buy the funny statue.
看到他买那个有趣的雕像，我禁不住笑了。
- repress 镇压　- suppress inflation 遏止通货膨胀

0939 supreme [suːˈpriːm] **a** 最高的，最大的
It was the supreme moment in his life when he bought the wedding ring.
买结婚戒指是他一生中最重要的时刻。
- uppermost 最高的　- lowest 最低的　- supreme court 最高法院

语法重点
supreme 没有比较级和最高级。

0940 surge [sɜːrdʒ] **n** 大浪　**v** 蜂拥而出，汹涌
The customers surge out of the supermarket before 10 p.m.
晚上十点前，顾客们从超市里涌了出来。
- storm surge 风暴汹涌　- surge out of... 从……涌了出来

0941 suspend [səˈspend] **v** 使中止
I have no alternative but suspend my experiment to buy books.
除了终止实验去买书，我别无选择。
- hang 悬挂　- advance 提前　- suspend payment 宣告破产

⊃ alternative (P. 671)

0942 **sustain** [sə'steɪn] v 支撑，供养，忍受

I do not have enough money to sustain your buying that expensive coat.
我没有足够的财力让你买下那个昂贵的外套。
- bear 承受 - sustain losses 蒙受损失
- I do not have enough money to sustain... 我没有足够的财力来……

0943 **swamp** [swɑ:mp] n 沼泽，困境 v 淹没，使陷于困境

He became bogged in the swamp on the way to hike.
他在徒步旅行的路上陷在了沼泽中。
- marsh 沼泽 - sb. becomes bogged in... 某人陷在……中

○ bog (P. 533)

0944 **swarm** [swɔ:rm] n 一大群，蜂群 v 云集，充满

When I went shopping, I found the waters in front of the supermarket swarm with life.
我去购物的时候发现超市前面的水里充满着生物。
- herd 群 - a swarm of 一群 - swarm with... 充满……
- swarm 通常指蜜蜂、昆虫群，而 herd 一般指大动物群，尤指家畜群，也可指人群。

0945 **sympathize** ['sɪmpəθaɪz] v 同情，同感，共鸣

I can't afford to buy the computer; he laughs in his sleeve instead of sympathizing.
我买不起那台电脑，他不同情，反倒暗笑。
- sympathize with 同情……，与……产生共鸣

语法重点
laugh in one's sleeve（暗笑）是固定搭配，sleeve 用单数。
○ sleeve (P. 360)

0946 **tackle** ['tækl] v 着手处理，解决 n 阻截，用具

I'll tackle him about buying which kind of book.
我得和他谈谈买哪一种书。
- deal 处理 - tackle with 解决，处理
- I'll tackle sb. about... 我得和某人谈谈……

语法重点
tackle 的宾语常为 question, problem 等，表示处理某种难题或困难。

0947 **tan** [tæn] n 棕褐色 v 晒黑，痛打 a 棕褐色的

The girl with tan skin sneaked into the supermarket to buy candies.
那个棕褐色皮肤的女孩偷偷溜进了超市买糖果吃。
- tan one's hide 痛打某人 - sneak into... 溜进……

0948 **tangle** ['tæŋgl] v 使纠缠 n 混乱，困惑

He doesn't know which bunch of flowers to buy because his mind is in a tangle.
他不知道要买哪一束花，因为他的思想还处于困惑之中。
- snarl 缠结 - tangle with 与……争吵，与……有纠葛
- be in a tangle 处于困惑之中

0949 tar [tɑːr] **n** 焦油，水手 **v** 涂以焦油
Don't buy the pipe for it is caked with tar.
别买那个烟斗，它里面渍了很多油。
⊙ tarre 焦油　　⊙ tar and feather 严厉惩罚

语法重点
cake 一般当名词用，意思是"蛋糕"，例句中 cake 作动词，意思是"使结成块"。

0950 tart [tɑːrt] **a** 酸的，刻薄的 **n** 果馅饼，妓女
I put little stock in the salesman because he sold tart apples to me last time.
我不太信任那个售货员，因为他上次卖给我的苹果很酸。
⊙ bitter 尖刻的　　⊙ egg tart 蛋挞
⊙ ... put little stock in sb. ……不大信任某人

0951 taunt [tɔːnt] **v** 辱骂 **n** 嘲弄，嘲弄的对象 **a** 很高的
I became a taunt to my friends because I didn't buy a car.
没有买车，我成了朋友们嘲讽的对象。
⊙ scoff 嘲笑　　⊙ taunt sb. with... 嘲笑某人……

语法重点
taunt 是及物动词。

0952 tavern ['tævərn] **n** 酒馆，客栈
He sneaked out of the tavern and went shopping.
他偷偷溜出小旅馆，去购物了。

⊙ sneak (P. 635)

0953 teller ['telər] **n** 叙述者，出纳员，泰勒（姓氏）
The teller bought all the fruits the man sold; it really takes the biscuit.
这位出纳员买下了那人卖的所有水果，实在是太离谱了。
⊙ cashier 出纳员　　⊙ ... take the biscuit ……极其可笑（离谱）

0954 tempo ['tempoʊ] **n** 拍子，节奏，速率
I can't adapt to the exhausting tempo of city life and even have no time to go shopping.
我不能适应这令人精疲力竭的城市生活节奏，我甚至都没有时间购物了。
⊙ rhythm 节奏　　⊙ I can't adapt to... 我不能适应……

语法重点
tempo 的复数形式有两个，tempos 和 tempi。
⊙ adapt (P. 391)

0955 tempt [tempt] **v** 诱惑，冒……的风险，使感兴趣
Just be careful not to be tempted off the straight path when you go shopping in the foreign countries.
你去国外购物时要小心，不要误入歧途。
⊙ attract 吸引　　⊙ tempt away 诱走
⊙ be tempted off the straight path. 误入歧途。

0956 temptation [temp'teɪʃn] **n** 诱惑，引诱
The toy I can't afford to buy was a strong temptation to my son.
我买不起的那个玩具对儿子来说是一个强烈的诱惑。
⊙ enticement 诱惑　　⊙ be a temptation to... 对……来说是一个诱惑

语法重点
be a temptation to 中的 to 是介词，后面接名词或者代词。

0957 **tenant** ['tenənt] n 房客，承租人 v 租赁，租借
The tenant sneaked a look at his book when he bought vegetables with his wife.
那个房客跟妻子一起买菜时偷偷地看书。
同 lessee 承租人　反 landlord 房东　组 sneak a look at... 偷看……

0958 **tentative** ['tentətɪv] a 暂时的，不确定的，犹豫不决的
They made a tentative arrangement to buy a pair of shoes this weekend.
他们暂定这个周末去买一双鞋。
同 provisional 暂时的　反 definitive 确定的

语法重点
tentative 的副词形式是 tentatively。

0959 **terminal** ['tɜːrmɪnl] a 末端的　n 末端
The man who is buying a pen is in the terminal stage of cancer.
那个正在买钢笔的人处于癌症晚期。
同 finishing 终点的　反 beginning 起点　组 bus terminal 公交车终点站，巴士站

cancer (P. 136)

0960 **terrace** ['terəs] n 大阳台，阳台，露台
I saw the man sneak a book into his bag in the terrace after I came back from the market.
我从市场回来看见那个男人在阳台上把一本书偷偷放在包里。
同 balcony 阳台　同 garden terrace 花园露台　组 sneak... into... 把……偷偷放在……

语法重点
terrace 也可以表示"阶梯看台，梯田"，但要用其复数形式。

0961 **thigh** [θaɪ] n 大腿
I will accompany you to buy a pair of thigh boots tomorrow.
我明天能陪你去买一双长靴。
组 accompany sb. to do sth. 陪同某人去做某事

0962 **thorn** [θɔːrn] n 有刺的植物，荆棘
I am swamped with researching the thorns and have no time to go shopping.
我正忙于研究荆棘，没空去购物。
同 acicula 刺　组 thorn in sight 眼中钉　组 I am swamped with... 我忙于……

0963 **thrill** [θrɪl] v 使兴奋　n 兴奋
It gave me a big thrill to know that he will buy me a car.
听说他要买辆车给我，我感到兴奋不已。
同 excitation 兴奋　组 thrills and spills 惊险刺激

语法重点
it gives me a big thrill to（让我兴奋不已）后面要接动词原形。

0964 **thriller** ['θrɪlər] n 恐怖小说或电影
If I don' buy the new thriller I will be on thorns.
如果不买那本新的惊险小说，我会如坐针毡。
同 chiller 惊险小说　组 ... be on thorns ……如坐针毡，焦虑不安

tenant ~ tiptoe

0965 throne [θroʊn] **n** 王权，君主
The young man who is buying a pair of ice skates is the heir to the throne.
那个正在买溜冰鞋的年轻人是王位继承人。
🔵 emperor 君主　🔵 take the throne 即位　🔵 be the heir to... 是……的继承人

0966 throng [θrɔːŋ] **n** 群众，一大群　**v** 群集，挤满
We pushed our way through a throng of customers.
我们从一大群顾客中挤过去。
🔵 crowd 群众，一伙　🔵 throng into 拥进
🔵 push one's way through... 从……挤过去

0967 thrust [θrʌst] **v** 用力推，插　**n** 插，讽刺
He thrust back the little stabs of homesickness by buying a lot of foods to eat.
他买很多食物吃以努力排遣涌上心头的思乡之情。
🔵 prod 刺　🔵 applied thrust 施加的推力　🔵 thrust back... 排遣……

语法重点
thrust 是不规则动词，其过去式、过去分词还是 thrust。
🔵 stab (P. 364)

0968 tick [tɪk] **n** 滴答声，记号　**v** 发出滴答声
She put a tick by the names of things she wanted to buy.
她在自己想买的东西名称前画上记号。
🔵 tictoc 发出滴答声　🔵 tick away (时间一分一秒) 过去

0969 tile [taɪl] **n** 瓷砖，贴砖
Many houses in the countryside are roofed in blue tiles.
农村很多房子都是用蓝瓦盖的。
🔵 be out on the tiles 纵情玩乐　🔵 be roofed in... 用……盖的

语法重点
在词尾 "ed, es" 等中 "e" 不发音，就不算是一个音节，如例句中的 roofed, tiles。
🔵 countryside (P. 146)

0970 tilt [tɪlt] **v** 使倾斜，抨击　**n** 倾斜，车盖
It has been predicted that the Earth will tilt on its axis, so let's buy some foods and water to store in case of famine and disease.
有人曾预言地球会倾斜，所以我们买些食物和水储存起来以防饥荒和疾病。
🔵 incline 倾斜　🔵 at full tilt 全速地，全力以赴地

0971 tin [tɪn] **n** 锡，罐头　**a** 锡制的　**v** 镀锡于
Send round to the grocer's for a tin of beer.
叫人到食品店去买一罐啤酒。
🔵 stannum 锡　🔵 a (little) tin god 受到不应得的崇敬之人或物

语法重点
send round to (派人去) 中的 to 是介词，后面接表示地点的名词。

0972 tiptoe ['tɪptoʊ] **n** 脚尖　**v** 用脚尖走　**a** 用脚尖
There are too many people there, so I need to stand on tiptoe to see what the peddler is selling.
那里人太多了，我需要踮着脚才能看到小贩在卖什么。
🔵 tip 尖部　🔵 on tiptoe 急切地

语法重点
stand on tiptoe (踮着脚尖) 是固定用法，tiptoe 用单数。

649

0973 toad [toʊd] n 癞蛤蟆，讨厌的家伙
I submitted myself to him and bought a lot of toads home.
我听说他买了许多蟾蜍回家。
🔹 I submit myself to... 我听从了……

语法重点
toad 是可数名词。
🔹 submit (P. 644)

0974 toil [tɔɪl] n 辛劳 v 长时间或辛苦地工作，跋涉
He wanted to buy the book which was a toil to read.
他想买那本读起来很费劲的书。
🔹 labor 劳工　🔹 rest 休息　🔹 toil up 艰难地往上行走
🔹 be a toil to... ……很费劲

语法重点
例句中 read 用主动形式表示被动的意思。

0975 token [ˈtoʊkən] n 象征 a 象征性的，装样子的
I want to buy him a present in token of my gratitude.
我想买一件礼物给他，以表示对他的感谢之情。
🔹 memento 纪念品　🔹 by the same token 同样地
🔹 do sth. in token of... 做某事以表示……

🔹 gratitude (P. 449)

0976 torch [tɔːrtʃ] n 火炬，火把，手电筒
He told her he has been carrying a torch for her about one year when they went shopping together.
他们一起逛街时，他告诉她他已经暗恋她近一年了。
🔹 firebrand 火把　🔹 carry a torch for... 暗恋……

语法重点
carry a torch for 后面要接上表示人的名词或者代词。

0977 torment [ˈtɔːment] / [ˈtɔːrment] n 痛苦 v 使痛苦
The man who is buying bread is tormented by toothache.
那个正在买面包的人因牙痛而受折磨。
🔹 torture 折磨　🔹 torment oneself 自寻苦恼
🔹 be tormented by... 因……而受折磨

0978 torrent [ˈtɔːrənt] n 急流，山洪 a 奔流的，汹涌的
Could you not bother me by a torrent of questions when I am doing shopping?
我买东西的时候你能不要用滔滔不绝的问题来烦我吗？
🔹 torrents of rain deluge 滂沱大雨
🔹 Could you not bother me by...? 你能不要用……来烦我吗？

语法重点
例句虽是疑问形式，但表示的是请求、劝告。

0979 torture [ˈtɔːrtʃər] v 拷打 n 拷问，折磨
He was tortured with anxiety and didn't want to go shopping.
他正为焦虑所苦，不想去购物。
🔹 trouble 折磨　🔹 savage torture 酷刑　🔹 be tortured with... 被……折磨着

0980 tournament [ˈtʊrnəmənt]
n 比赛，锦标赛，中世纪的骑士比武
I am aching to buy a new handbag after the tournament.
我渴望在联赛后买一个新的手提包。

toad ~ treasury

0981 toxic [ˈtɑːksɪk] **a** 有毒的 **n** 有毒物质

Don't buy a house in this city, because the atmosphere is seriously polluted by the toxic gases here.

别在这个城市买房了，因为有毒气体严重地污染了这里的空气。

- noxious 有毒的　　反 nontoxic 无毒的
- toxic waste 有毒废物　　be polluted by... 被……污染了

同 pollute (P. 339)

0982 trademark [ˈtreɪdmɑːrk] **n** 商标，特征

Through a careful inspect, I think the trademark of these goods was changed.

经检查，我觉得这些商品的商标都改了。

- logotype 商标　　registered trademark 注册商标

0983 traitor [ˈtreɪtər] **n** 叛徒，背叛者，背信弃义的人

The man who is buying flowers is denounced as a traitor by his friends.

那个买花的人被朋友们谴责为叛徒。

- betrayer 叛徒　　evil traitor 邪恶叛徒　　be denounced as... 被谴责为……

同 denounce (P. 700)

0984 tramp [træmp] **v** 践踏，步行 **n** 重脚步声徒步，流浪汉

The tramp frightened the shop assistant by talking to him.

那个流浪汉跟店员讲话，吓了那个店员一跳。

- vagabonds 流浪者　　on the tramp 走江湖，漂泊着
- frighten sb. by doing sth. 做某事把某人吓了一跳

0985 trample [ˈtræmpl] **v** 践踏，轻视 **n** 踩踏

Be careful not to trample on grass when you and your friends go to the park.

你和你的朋友去公园时不要践踏草坪。

- tread 践踏　　tramp on... 践踏……

0986 transparent [trænsˈpærənt] **a** 透明的，易识破的

Her lie was transparent when she checks out.

付账时，她的谎言被识破了。

- limpid 透明的　　反 opaque 不透明的　　transparent tape 透明带
- sb.'s lie be transparent when... 当……的时候，某人的谎言被识破了

0987 treasury [ˈtreʒəri] **n** 宝藏

It's said the treasury secretary combats extravagance and waste.

据说财政部部长反对铺张浪费。

- exchequer 国库，财政部
- sb. combats extravagance and waste 某人反对铺张浪费

同 combat (P. 545)

651

0988 **treaty** ['tri:ti] n 协定
The trade treaty will stimulate the market here.
这个贸易条约将会刺激这里的消费。
agreement 协议   peace treaty 和平条约

⊃ stimulate (P. 784)

0989 **trench** [trentʃ] n 沟，渠
The reporter who is buying a mask likes to be in the trenches.
那个在买口罩的记者喜欢去第一线。
dugout 防空壕   ... be in the trenches ……在第一线，在现场

语法重点
in the trenches 是固定搭配用法，trench 要用复数形式。

0990 **tribute** ['trɪbju:t] n 进贡，献礼，贡献
She began by paying tribute to the people who bought her products.
她首先向买她产品的人表示敬意。
glorification 赞颂   sb. pays tribute to... 某人向……表示感谢

语法重点
sb. pays tribute to 后面一般要接表示人的名词或者代词。

0991 **trifle** ['traɪfl] n 琐事，少许
Don't trouble yourself with such a trifle before you buy a car.
买车前，不要因为这样的小事而烦恼了。
small 小事   event 大事   trifle with 玩弄，心不在焉地做
don't trouble yourself with... 不要为……而烦恼了

0992 **trim** [trɪm] v 修剪 a 整齐的
I trimmed off the trousers after I bought them home.
那条裤子买回家后我修剪了一下。
ordered 整齐的   scruffy 不整齐的   ... trim off sth. ……修剪某物

0993 **triple** ['trɪpl] a 三倍的 v （使）成三倍 n 三倍之数
The number of customers in this supermarket triples today.
这个超市的顾客人数今天翻了三倍。
threefold 三倍的   triple jump 三级跳远
the number of... triples ……的数量翻了三倍

语法重点
"三级跳远"可以用 triple jump 来表示。

0994 **trot** [trɑ:t] v 小跑，快步走 n 疾走；现成译本，腹泻
I often go for a trot before buying foods in the morning.
早上我经常在买食物前小跑一会儿。
on the trot 一个接一个
trot 强调小跑时上下弹跳的动作，是介于跑与走之间轻快的快速运动。

0995 **trout** [traʊt] n 鳟鱼，鳟鱼肉
There is no trout left today; please come tomorrow.
今天没有鳟鱼了，明天再来吧。

treaty ~ understandable

0996 **tuck** [tʌk] v 使折叠，卷起 n 褶，祠
It was nip and tuck as to which one to buy.
到底买哪一个，很难说。
- bend 弯曲
- tuck away 藏起来，畅饮大吃
- it is nip and tuck as to... ……很难说

0997 **tuition** [tu'ɪʃn] n 教学，学费，教学
The salesman received tuition in marketing last year.
那个售货员去年学了营销学。
- schooling 学费
- postal tuition 函授

【语法重点】
sb. receives tuition in 后面也可接表示地点的名词，表示"在……受教育"。

0998 **tuna** ['tu:nə] n 鲔鱼
They took a long tramp to the city to buy tunas.
他们长途跋涉来到这个城市买鲔鱼。
- sb. takes a long tramp to... 某人长途跋涉到……

【语法重点】
tuna 是可数名词，其复数形式有两个，即 tuna 和 tunas。
- tramp (P. 651)

0999 **tyrant** ['taɪrənt] n 暴君，专横的人
The tyrant paid no attention to the salesman's cry and left without paying.
那个专横的人不理会售货员的叫喊，没付账就离开了。

1000 **undergraduate** [ˌʌndər'grædʒuət] n 大学生
The guest at the café has an undergraduate degree in psychology.
咖啡馆那个客人有心理学的学士学位。
- undergrad 大学生
- sb. has a / an... degree in... 某人有……的……学位

1001 **underline** [ˌʌndə'laɪn] / [ˌʌndər'laɪn]
v 在字下方画线 n 画在字下面的线
She showed partiality for the second-hand book with some sentences underlined.
她倾向于买那本句子带有底线的二手书。
- emphasize 强调，着重
- sb. shows partiality for... 某人倾向……

【语法重点】
underline 是及物动词。

1002 **underneath** [ˌʌndər'ni:θ] prep 在……的下面，在底下
The customer found there was a crack underneath the floor of the shop.
顾客发现，商店的地板下面有一条裂痕。
- below 在下面，低于
- above 在上面，超过

 crack (P. 419)

1003 **understandable** [ˌʌndər'stændəbl]
a 可理解的，能够懂的
It's quite understandable that she always buys cheap clothes.
她总是买便宜衣服，这很能让人理解。

653

1004 undoubtedly [ʌn'daʊtɪdli] **ad** 毋庸置疑地，肯定地
It was undoubtedly he who bought a fake.
买到赝品的肯定是他。
- doubtless 无疑地 - dubiously 可疑地 - undoubtedly true 无可置疑的

1005 update [ˌʌp'deɪt] / [ˌʌp'deɪt] **v** 更新，升级 **n** 更新
I update my best friend on what I have just bought.
我告诉最好的朋友我刚买了什么东西。
- refresh 更新 - degrade 降级，退化
- update sb. on... 向某人提供……的最新消息

1006 upright ['ʌpraɪt] **a** 挺直的，正直的 **ad** 直立地
He jerked upright in surprise when he saw the new cell phone I bought.
他看到我买的新手机后惊讶地跳了起来。
- vertical 垂直的 - horizontal 地平线的

1007 upward ['ʌpwərd] **a** 向上的，上升的 **ad** 向上地
There is an upward tendency in fruit prices.
水果价格有上涨的趋势。
- up 向上的 - down 向下的 - upward mobility 上进心
- there is an upward tendency in... ……有上涨的趋势

> **语法重点**
> upward 的副词形式是 upwardly，这个单词用得不多，因为 upward 本身就可以作副词。
> ⓒ tendency (P. 510)

1008 upwards ['ʌpwərdz] **a** 向上地，以上
Come this way, and these steps lead upwards to the front door of the supermarket.
走这边，这些台阶往上通向超市的正门。
- bottom upwards 倒置

1009 utter ['ʌtər] **v** 发出声音 **a** 完全的，彻底的
I am at an utter loss which skirt to buy.
我完全不知道该买哪条裙子。
- absolute 完全的 - halfway 不彻底的 - utter nonsense 一派胡言
- I am at an utter loss + 疑问词... 我完全不知道该……

1010 vacancy ['veɪkənsi] **n** 空白，失神
The vacancy of his expression made me doubt if he heard the salesman.
他茫然的神情让我怀疑他是否听到了售货员的讲话。
- blank 空白 - sth. makes sb. doubt if... 某事让某人怀疑……是否……

> ⓒ doubt (P. 155)

1011 vacuum ['vækjuəm] **n** 真空，真空吸尘器
He bought two vacuums in his innocence.
他傻傻地买了两台吸尘器。
- in a vacuum 脱离现实

> **语法重点**
> vacuum 是可数名词，其复数形式有两个，即 vacuums 和 vacua。

654

undoubtedly ~ venture

1012 vague [veɪg] **a** 含糊的
I have a vague idea of buying a present for her.
我隐约觉得要买一个礼物给她。

1013 vanity ['vænəti] **n** 自负，空虚，无价值的东西
His buying the car is just a boast out of vanity.
他买那辆车只是出于虚荣心。
- pretentiousness 自负
- ... be just a boast out of vanity ……只是出于虚荣心

→ boast (P. 402)

1014 vapor ['veɪpər] **n** 水汽，水蒸气
The salesman says, "Water in the pot will change to vapor after heated."
推销员说：" 锅里的水经过加热就会变成水蒸气。"
- steam 水蒸气
- vapor pressure 蒸气压力
- sth. changes to... 某物变成……

> **语法重点**
> 美式英语中 vapor 常写作 vapour。

1015 vegetation [,vedʒə'teɪʃn] **n** 草木，（植物）生长
The air is perfumed with the scent of vegetation in the flower market.
花卉市场的空气中充满了植物的香味。
- plant 植物
- vegetation period 生长期
- be perfumed with... 充满了……

1016 veil [veɪl] **n** 面纱，面罩，遮蔽物
My father draws a veil over the promise that he will buy me a bike.
父亲对要买一辆脚踏车给我的事情避而不谈。
- under the veil of... 以……为借口
- sb. draws a veil over... 某人避而不谈……

1017 vein [veɪn] **n** 静脉，风格，情绪，气质
I am not in the vein for shopping at the moment.
我现在没有心情购物。
- varicose vein 静脉曲张
- I am not in the vein for... 我没有心情……

→ moment (P. 064)

1018 velvet ['velvɪt] **n** 天鹅绒，意外之财 **a** 柔软的
I am arrayed in a red velvet to go shopping.
我穿着一件红色天鹅绒衣服去购物。
- velour 天鹅绒
- on velvet 处于有利地位，条件优裕

1019 venture ['ventʃər] **n** 冒险 **v** 敢于
I won't venture buying the washing machine.
我不敢买那台洗衣机。
- cower 退缩
- venture one's life 冒着生命危险
- I won't venture... 我不敢……

1020 verbal ['vɜːrbl] a 言词上的，用文字的，逐字的
The salesman at the door has a good command of verbal English.
门口那个推销员具有良好的英语口语表达能力。
同 oral 口头的　反 written 书面的　衍 verbal message 口信

1021 versus ['vɜːrsəs] prep ……对……
Let's buy some popcorn before watching the match which is Chelsea versus Manchester United.
看切尔西队对曼彻斯特联队的比赛前，我们去买点儿爆米花。

> 语法重点
> versus 可以缩略为 v. 或 vs.
> 参 popcorn (P. 077)

1022 vertical ['vɜːrtɪkl] a 垂直的，竖式的
He deceived her into the belief that he will buy her a ring if she can climb the vertical cliff.
他骗她相信，如果她登上那个陡峭的悬崖，他就买戒指给她。

> 参 deceive (P. 555)

1023 veto ['viːtoʊ] n 否决权，禁止 v 否决
He puts a veto upon my buying the high heels.
他不许我买那些高跟鞋。
同 neto 否决权　反 permission 允许　衍 veto power 否决权

1024 via ['vaɪə] prep 经由，通过
He bought the latest MP3 via a friend.
他通过一个朋友买到了最新款的 MP3。
同 through 通过　衍 sb. does sth. via... 某人通过……做某事

> 语法重点
> via 后面可以接人，也可以接物。

1025 vibrate ['vaɪbreɪt] v 振动，颤动
My heart vibrated with excitement when he bought me a bunch of roses.
当他买玫瑰给我时，我的心因兴奋而悸动。
同 wobble 使摇摆　反 steady 使稳固　衍 vibrate mode 振动模式

1026 videotape ['vɪdioʊteɪp] n 录影带 v 把……录在录影磁带上
There is nothing to stop him from buying videotapes.
没有什么办法可以阻止他买录影带。
衍 videotape player 放映机

> 语法重点
> videotape 是可数名词。

1027 viewer ['vjuːər] n 观看者，观察家
The anchorman's words evoke a strong response in the viewers.
主持人的话在观众中产生了强烈的反响。

verbal ~ vow

1028 vigor ['vɪgər]
- n 精力，（语言等的）气势，（动、植物的）强健
- The salesman recommended the pen to me with great vigor.
- 售货员很热情地向我推销那支钢笔。
- vigor and vitality 生机与活力
- ... do sth. with great vigor 以极大的热情做某事

> 语法重点
> 美式英语中，vigor 常写作 vigour。

1029 vigorous ['vɪgərəs] a 强有力的
- The man who is buying a car is yet in green vigorous senility.
- 那个买汽车的人老当益壮。
- dynamic 有活力的
- lifeless 无生命的
- vigorous exercise 剧烈的运动

1030 villain ['vɪlən] n 恶棍，反派角色，罪犯
- The man was wakened from sleep by the villain.
- 男人被坏人惊醒。
- rogue 小淘气
- hero 英雄
- sb. be wakened from sleep by... 某人被……惊醒

> sleep (P. 093)

1031 vine [vaɪn] n 藤蔓，攀爬植物
- My plan of going shopping died on the vine.
- 我去购物的计划夭折了。
- ... die on the vine ……夭折了

1032 violinist [ˌvaɪə'lɪnɪst] n 小提琴手
- The woman who is playing a violin is a great violinist by any standard.
- 不论以什么标准看，那个在演奏小提琴的女人都是伟大的小提琴家。
- fiddler 小提琴手
- principal violinist 首席小提琴手

> standard (P. 227)

1033 visa ['viːzə] n 签证
- The customer in the shop doesn't obtain a visa for England.
- 商店里那个顾客没有获得英国的签证。
- entry visa 入境签证
- sb. doesn't obtain a visa for... 某人没有获得……的签证

1034 vow [vaʊ] n 誓约，许愿 v 发誓
- I take a vow never to buy a book again.
- 我发誓再也不买书了。
- swear 发誓
- I take a vow never to... 我发誓再也不……

> 语法重点
> I take a vow never to 后面接动词原形。

1035 wade [weɪd] **v** 跋涉,猛烈攻击

The woman waded into the products we sold.
那个女人猛烈地抨击我们卖的产品。
- wade into sb. / sth. 猛烈攻击某人/某物

1036 wail [weɪl] **v** 号啕 **n** 痛哭,哭声

When he stepped out of the supermarket, he heard the girl wailing.
他走出超市时听到了女孩的哭叫声。

1037 ward(1) [wɔːrd] **n** 病房,受监护人,监视

The children who enter the supermarket should be in ward to adults.
孩子进入超市须由成人监护。
- sickroom 病房 - guardian 监护人 - maternity ward 产科病房
- be in ward to... 在……的监护下

⊕ adult (P. 004)

1038 ward(2) [wɔːrd] **v** 监护,挡住,避开,收容

She made a vain attempt to ward off the salesman.
她试图避开那个推销员,但没有成功。
- avoid 避开 - confront 面对 - ward off 挡住,避开
- sb. makes a vain attempt to... 某人试图……,但没有成功

1039 ware [wer]
n 商品,作……用的器皿 **v** 小心,避免 **a** 谨慎的

I think most of these wares are of poor quality.
我觉得这些商品大部分品质不好。
- goods 货物,商品 - kitchen ware 厨具

1040 warehouse [ˈwerhaʊs] **n** 仓库,货栈 **v** 存入仓库

The salesman thinks it's hard to clear off the old stocks in the warehouse.
售货员认为仓库里的存货很难处理掉。
- storehouse 仓库,储藏所 - warehouse specialist 仓库管理员

语法重点
warehouse 是可数名词。
⊕ stock (P. 641)

1041 warrior [ˈwɔːriər] **n** 武士

The warrior cajoled his girlfriend into buying him a new armor.
那个战士哄女朋友买新盔甲给他。

1042 wary [ˈweri] **a** 注意的,小心翼翼的,警戒的

I need to keep a wary eye on the customer over there.
我要密切注意那边那个顾客的举动。
- cautious 谨慎的 ⊗ unwary 不谨慎的

语法重点
keep a wary eye on(密切注意)后面可以接人,也可以接物。

1043 weary ['wɪri] a 疲倦的 v 使疲乏

I am weary of doing shopping alone.
我厌倦独自购物。
- tired 疲累的，厌倦的
- weary out 筋疲力尽
- be weary of... 对……厌倦
- weary 侧重指由于连续不断进行某项活动而造成的疲劳，以致感到厌烦，而 tired 泛指由工作紧张、劳动过度、休息不足等引起的疲乏。

1044 weird [wɪrd] a 怪诞的

The weird chothes he bought really gas me.
他买的奇装异服真是笑死我了。
- queer 奇怪的
- ordinary 平常的，普通的
- weird things 奇怪的事情

1045 wharf [wɔːrf] n 码头，停泊处 v 把货卸在码头上

We have to fetch up at the wharf before they auction the boat.
我们得在他们拍卖那艘船之前赶到码头。
- dock 码头
- wharf due 码头税

语法重点
we have to fetch up at（我们到达）后面要接表示地点的名词。
⇒ auction (P. 676)

1046 whereabouts [ˌwerəˈbauts] ad 在哪里，靠近什么地方 n 下落，所在之处

The courier couldn't bring to mind the customer's whereabouts.
那个送货员不记得顾客的住址。
- sb. couldn't bring to mind... 某人不记得……

1047 whereas [ˌwerˈæz] conj 然而，鉴于

I fix my attention on the foods whereas my husband does on the cigarettes in the supermarket.
逛超市时，我关注食品而我丈夫只看香烟。
- while 虽然，然而
- whereas now 但现在

语法重点
whereas 表示对比，一般可与 while 互换。
⇒ cigarette (P. 272)

1048 whine [waɪn] v 哀号，发牢骚 n 闹声，抱怨

"The vegetable price is rising." She spoke with a whine.
她抱怨着说，"蔬菜的价格又在涨"。
- complain 抱怨
- whine about 发牢骚
- sb. speaks with a whine... 某人抱怨……

1049 whirl [wɜːrl]

v 旋转，头晕目眩 n 回旋，混乱，尝试

My thoughts are in a whirl, so I don't want to go shopping.
我的思想很乱，所以不想去购物。
- twirl 快速转动
- give sth. a whirl 试试某物

语法重点
be in a whirl（很混乱）的主语一般是 mind, brain 等与思想相关的名词。

1050 whisk [wɪsk] **v** 拂，掸

The salesman whisked away the dust on the shelf.
售货员拂去那个架子上的灰尘。
- whisk off 匆匆离去
- sb. whisks away... 某人拂去……

▷ shelf (P. 221)

1051 whisky ['wɪski] **n** 威士忌

The young man sought solace in the whisky bottle at the bar.
那个年轻人在酒吧里借酒浇愁。
- whiskey 威士忌酒
- Scotch whisky 苏格兰威士忌酒

语法重点
whisky 是可数名词。

1052 wholesale ['hoʊlseɪl]
n 批发 **a** 批发的，草率的 **ad** 大规模地

The wholesale price of the hat is 10 dollars.
这顶帽子的批发价是 10 美金。
- retail 零售
- wholesale market 批发市场
- the wholesale price of... is... ……的批发价是……

1053 wholesome ['hoʊlsəm] **a** 有益健康的，合乎卫生的

It wouldn't be wholesome for her to do shopping there.
她去那里购物恐怕不安全。

1054 widespread ['waɪdspred] **a** 流传很广的，普遍的

There is widespread condemnation of the cashier's rude attitude.
收银员粗暴的态度遭到人们普遍的谴责。
- comprehensive 广泛的
- limited 有限的

语法重点
widespread 是多音节形容词，其比较级、最高级分别是 more widespread, most widespread。

▷ attitude (P. 257)

1055 widow ['wɪdoʊ] **n** 寡妇

The widow's heart is surcharged with grief and she doesn't want to eat anything now.
那寡妇特别忧伤，她现在什么都不想吃。
- relict 寡妇
- widower 鳏夫

1056 wilderness ['wɪldərnəs] **n** 荒野，荒地

He always goes shopping since he is in the wilderness.
自从风光不再，他经常去购物。
- wasteland 荒地
- howling wilderness 荒僻的旷野
- be in the wilderness 处于不重要的地位（尤指政治上）

1057 wildlife ['waɪldlaɪf] **n** 野生生物

Buying and selling animals is barred from wildlife sanctuaries.
野生动物保护区内禁止买卖动物。
- wildlife park 野生动物园
- be barred from... 禁止……

语法重点
wildlife 是不可数名词。

▷ sanctuary (P. 622)

whisk ~ wreath

1058 wither ['wɪðər] **v** 枯萎，以鄙视等态度慑服某人
The flowers withered and the princess cast it in the gardener's dish.
这些花都枯死了，公主把这归咎于园丁。
- fade 褪色，凋谢 反 bloom 开花，使茂盛
- wither away 枯萎，凋谢 cast sth. in sb.'s dish 把某事归咎于某人
- wither 指因无活力而丧失生生命力，而 fade 侧重指渐渐失去色彩和光泽。

➤ princess (P. 209)

1059 woe [woʊ] **n** 悲哀，不幸 **int** 用来表达悲伤或惊慌
Woe betide you if you stole the book I just bought.
如果你偷了我刚买的那本书，你会得到报应的。

1060 woodpecker ['wʊdpekər] **n** 啄木鸟
What do you want to do by buying a woodpecker?
你买一只啄木鸟干什么？
- hickwall 啄木鸟 What do you want to do by...? 你……想干什么？

语法重点
英语构词法中，名词 + 及物动词 + er / or 可以构成名词，如 woodpecker。

1061 workshop ['wɜːrkʃɑːp] **n** 工场
Roll up your sleeves in the workshop and go shopping freely in your free time.
在工场时好好工作，空闲时可以自由地购物。
- plant 工厂 camera workshop 摄影工作室
- roll up one's sleeves 卷起袖子（准备打架或苦干）

1062 worship ['wɜːrʃɪp] **v** 崇拜 **n** 礼拜，崇拜
He led his daughter to the church to worship God before going shopping.
去购物前，他带她女儿来教堂敬拜上帝。
- adore 崇拜 反 contempt 轻视 lead sb. to someplace 带某人到某地

语法重点
worship 的现在分词是 worshiping 或 worshipping，过去式是 worshiped 或 worshipped，过去分词是 worshiped 或 worshipped。

1063 worthwhile [ˌwɜːrθ'waɪl] **a** 值得做的
It is worthwhile to take a risk to buy the house.
冒险买那个房子是值得的。
- worthy 值得 反 unworthy 不值得的 take a risk to do sth. 冒险做某事

1064 worthy ['wɜːrði] **a** 有价值的，值得的
She doesn't esteem the salesman to be worthy of trust.
她认为那个售货员不值得信赖。
- valuable 有价值的 反 unworthy 无价值的，不值得的
- worthy of 值得，配得上的 esteem sb. to be... 认为某人是……

➤ esteem (P. 563)

1065 wreath [riːθ] **n** 花圈，圈状物 **v** 环绕
I am rather dubious about his idea to buy a wreath.
我对他想买花环的想法持怀疑态度。
- I am rather dubious about... 我怀疑……

➤ dubious (P. 712)

1066 **wring** [rɪŋ] v 绞，扭
Wring out your wet clothes before entering the room.
进房间前把你的湿衣服拧干。
- twist 拧，扭动
- wring someone's hand 紧握某人的手
- wring out... 拧干……

> 语法重点
> wring 是不规则动词，其过去式、过去分词都是 wrung。

1067 **yacht** [jɑːt] n 游艇，快艇 v 驾快艇
The poor man isn't worthy to buy a yacht.
那个穷人不配买游艇。
- by yacht 乘游艇
- sb. be not worthy to do sth. 某人不配做某事

→ worthy (P. 661)

1068 **yarn** [jɑːrn] n 纱线，毛线，故事 v 讲故事
I have a yarn with my mother while shopping.
我跟妈妈一边聊天一边购物。

> 语法重点
> I have a yarn with (和……聊天) 后面接表示人的名词或者代词。

1069 **yeast** [jiːst] n 酵母，泡，激动 v 发酵，起泡沫
I know which store keeps a large stock of yeast cake.
我知道哪家商店有大量的酵母饼存货供应。
- yeast cake 酵母饼
- keep a large stock of... ……有大量的……存货供应

1070 **yield** [jiːld] v 生产，让出 n 产量，收益
I will never yield to any mean seller.
我绝不会向任何卑鄙的商家屈服。
- yield to... 屈服于……
- I will never yield to... 我绝不会向……屈服

1071 **yoga** [ˈjoʊɡə] n 瑜伽
Let's take up yoga to aid relaxation after shopping.
买完东西，我们练瑜伽来帮助放松一下。
- yoga mat 瑜伽垫
- let's do sth. to... 为了……，我们……吧

→ relaxation (P. 495)

1072 **zinc** [zɪŋk] n 锌 v 在……上镀锌
The man wants to buy some brass which is an alloy of copper and zinc.
那个人想买铜锌合金——黄铜。
- Zn 元素锌的符号
- be an alloy of... 是……的合金

1073 **zip** [zɪp] n 拉链 v 用拉链拉上或扣上
Zip your lips when you buy foods.
买食物的时候闭上你的嘴。
- zip file 压缩档
- zip one's lips 闭上嘴

1074 **zoom** [zuːm] v 将画面推近或拉远
This new kind of camera can zoom out on people.
这款新相机可以使人像缩小。
- zoom in 放大
- ... zoom out on sb. / sth. ……缩小某人 / 某物

LEVEL 6
abbreviate ~ zeal

LEVEL 6 abbreviate ~ zeal

Review test
复习 Level 5 的学习成果，还记得以下单词是什么意思吗？

1. abortion ▸ _____
2. grease ▸ _____
3. eclipse ▸ _____
4. magnify ▸ _____
5. potential ▸ _____
6. reverse ▸ _____
7. infinite ▸ _____
8. token ▸ _____

Preview
单词重点预习，在开始之前先预习会让印象更深刻喔！

1. zeal ▸ _____
2. intimidate ▸ _____
3. therapy ▸ _____
4. accelerate ▸ _____
5. sequence ▸ _____
6. pedestrian ▸ _____
7. controversy ▸ _____
8. excessive ▸ _____

语法重点预习，在开始之前先预习会让印象更深刻哦！

1 从句可分成：名词性从句、形容词性从句、副词性从句等，功能跟相应词性的用法相同。
2 分词短语具有形容词的性质，用来修饰名词。
- 主动语态的简单式，使用现在分词。
- 被动语态的简单式、被动语态的完成式，使用过去分词。
- 被动语态的进行式，使用 being + 过去分词。
3 英文句中有时在强调某项信息或是句子结构不平衡时，会使用倒装句。
- 将表示时间、地点、频率或修饰动作状态的副词短语直接放到最前面。
- 将要强调的宾语往前移，但注意若肯定语意的宾语前移，主语与动词不用倒装；若否定语意的宾语前移，主语与助动词要倒装。
- 主语的结构较大，主语补语的结构较小，可将两者位置互换成"主语补语 + be 动词 + 主语"。
4 动词基本上可分成以下几类：
- 及物动词：后面需接宾语语意才完整的动词。
- 不及物动词：后面不需接宾语语意就完整的动词。
- 感官动词：表示主语感受到的动作或状态的动词。
- 使役动词：驱使宾语从事或接受动作的动词。

|正确答案| Review test 1 名词 / 流产 2 名词；动词 / 油脂；用油脂润滑 3 动词 / 被遮蔽 4 动词 / 扩大
5 形容词 / 潜在的 6 动词；形容词；名词 / 颠倒；颠倒的；背面 7 形容词 / 无限的 8 名词；形容词 / 象征；象征性的
Preview 1 名词 / 热心 2 动词 / 恐吓 3 名词 / 治疗 4 动词 / 使增速
5 名词 / 连续 6 名词 / 行人 7 名词 / 丑闻 8 形容词 / 过度的

abbreviate ～ zeal

0001 abbreviate [əˈbriːvieɪt]
v 缩写 **n** 使用缩写词的人，缩短

Mister can be abbreviated to Mr. in commercial correspondence.
在商务信函中，Mister 可以缩写为 Mr.。
近 shorten 缩短　反 lengthen 变长
词 in abbreviate 简言之　词 be abbreviated to... 被缩写为……

语法重点
be abbreviated to 中的 to 用作介词，其后接缩略词。

0002 abbreviation [ə,briːviˈeɪʃn] **n** 缩写，简化，缩写词

The buyer said that kg was the abbreviation of kilogram.
那个采购员说，kg 是 kilogram 的缩写。
近 shortening 缩短　反 amplification 详述
词 be the abbreviation of... 是……的缩写

参 kilogram (P. 314)

0003 abnormal [æbˈnɔːrml] **a** 反常的，变态的

It's abnormal for you to missend the email.
你发错邮件，这很不正常。
近 unnatural 反常的　反 normal 正常的
词 abnormal behavior 异常行为，变态行为
词 it's abnormal for sb. to... 某人……是不正常的

0004 aboriginal [,æbəˈrɪdʒənl]
a 土著的 **n** 土著居民，土生生物

The manager had no idea of this aboriginal story.
那个经理不知道这个土著居民的故事。
词 aboriginal rights 原住民权利　词 ... have no idea of... ……不知道

0005 aborigine [,æbəˈrɪdʒəni] **n** 原住民

At that instant, a negotiator suddenly spoke aborigine language.
在那一刻，一名谈判员突然说了原住民语。

参 instant (P. 179)

0006 abound [əˈbaʊnd] **v** 充满

The warehouse abounded with computer equipments.
仓库里有很多电脑设备。
反 lack 缺乏　词 abound in 盛产，富于　词 abound with... 充满……

参 warehouse (P. 658)

665

0007 absentminded [ˌæbsənt'maɪndɪd] a 茫然的，恍惚的
The supervisor was absentminded about everything at the meeting.
在会议上，主管对任何事都心不在焉。
同 abstracted 心不在焉的　反 sedulous 聚精会神的
句 be absentminded about... 对……心不在焉

0008 abstraction [æb'strækʃn] n 抽象，抽象概念
The secretary looked at the memo with an air of abstraction.
秘书茫然地看着备忘录。

> 语法重点
> abstraction 的形容词是 abstractional。

0009 abundance [ə'bʌndəns] n 富足
It is said that the financier had an abundance of wealth.
据说，那位金融家非常富有。
同 plenty 充分，丰富，很多　反 shortage 不足，缺乏
句 in abundance 丰富，充足　句 ... have an abundance of... ……有大量……

> 语法重点
> have an abundance of 的主语通常是人，介词 of 后面接名词或代词，表示所拥有的事物。

0010 abuse [ə'bjuːs] v 虐待 n 滥用
He advised the superior not to abuse his privilege.
他建议上司不要滥用特权。
同 ill-use 虐待，凌辱　同 abuse of 滥用
句 ... advise sb. not to do... 建议某人不要做……

> 语法重点
> to do 不定式的否定形式通常是在 to 之前加否定词 not。

0011 accelerate [æk'seləreɪt] v 使增速
The trade regulations will be carried out to accelerate the development of economy.
贸易法规的实施是为了加快经济的发展。
同 quicken 加速　反 retard 延迟

0012 acceleration [ækˌselə'reɪʃn] n 加速，加速度
The factory needed a truck with a good acceleration.
工厂需要一辆加速性能很好的货车。

> 语法重点
> with a good 后面通常接名词，用以表示某人或某物具备某种优越的品质或性能。

0013 accessible [æk'sesəbl] a 可接近的，易懂的
Business information was accessible to the leader.
领导者很容易得到商业资讯。
反 inaccessible 难达到的　句 be accessible to sb. 某人容易接近……

0014 accessory [æk'sesəri] n 配件
The operator was charged with being the accessory to this commercial espionage.
那个接线生被指控为这个商业间谍的共犯。
同 accomplice 共犯　句 sb. be charged with doing... 某人被指控做……
析 espionage 作名词表示"间谍（活动）"，具有相似含义的还有 spy 等。

扩 operator (P. 331)

0015 accommodate [əˈkɑːmədeɪt] v 使……适应，容纳

This conference room can accommodate five hundred persons at most.
这个会议室最多可容纳五百人。
- contain 包含
- accommodate oneself to 使适应于
- someplace can accommodate... at most 某地最多可容纳……
- at most 表示"最多"，具有相似含义的还有 not more than, at best 等。

0016 accommodation [əˌkɑːməˈdeɪʃn] n 适应，住宿

Food and accommodation have become a great problem to the staff.
对于员工们来说，食宿已经变成一个大问题。
- lodging 住房
- accommodation bill 空头汇票

0017 accord [əˈkɔːrd] v 和……一致，给予 n 一致，符合

Don't buy the salesman's story because his conduct always doesn't accord with his words.
不要相信那个销售员的话，他总是言行不一。
- cotton 一致
- disaccord 不一致
- accord with 与……一致
- don't buy one's story, ... 不要相信某人的话，……

语法重点
accord with 常用于否定句。
- conduct (P. 549)

0018 accordance [əˈkɔːrdns] n 一致，和谐，授予

In accordance to your request, we will deliver goods as soon as possible.
根据你方的要求，我方会尽快发货。
- conformity 一致
- discordance 不一致
- in accordance with 与……一致
- in accordance to... 根据……

0019 accordingly [əˈkɔːrdɪŋli] ad 因此，于是，依据

Please inform them of our order for goods and they would act accordingly.
请通知他们我们的订货单，他们会照做的。
- inform sb. of... 通知某人……

- inform (P. 310)

0020 accountable [əˈkaʊntəbl] a 可说明的

The shipping company should be accountable for the accident.
船运公司应该对事故负责。
- accountable for 对……应负责任
- sb. be accountable for... 某人对……应负责任

0021 accounting [əˈkaʊntɪŋ] n 会计

It is said that there is no love left between the accounting and the production departments.
据说，会计部门和生产部门之间关系很不好。
- accountancy 会计工作
- accounting department 会计部门

怪物讲师教学团队的 7 000 "单词" + "语法"

0022 accumulate [əˈkjuːmjəleɪt] **v** 累积，堆积
The rainwater in the freight car had accumulated to a depth of half a meter.
货车里面的雨水已经有半米深了。
🔵 gather 聚集　🔴 dissipate 使消散　🟢 accumulate to... 积累到……

> **语法重点**
> half 表示"一半"，通常与名词搭配表示"一半"。
> 🔗 depth (P. 151)

0023 accumulation [əˌkjuːmjəˈleɪʃn] **n** 累积，累积量
You must clean away all the accumulations of dirt in the meeting room in one hour.
你们必须在一个小时内清理掉会议室里的所有灰尘。
🟢 clean away... 清除……

0024 accusation [ˌækjuˈzeɪʃn] **n** 指控
There is a hint of accusation in this letter of complaint.
这封投诉信里暗含着指责。
🔵 charge 控告　🟢 accusation of 控告　🟢 there is a hint of... 暗含……

> 🔗 complaint (P. 275)

0025 acquisition [ˌækwɪˈzɪʃn] **n** 获得，采集
All the employees must spend much time on the acquisition of English.
所有职员都必须花大量时间来学习英语。
🔵 getting 获得　🟢 merger and acquisition 收购兼并
🟢 spend time on the acquisition of... 花费时间学习……

> **语法重点**
> the acquisition of 后面可以接表示语言或技能的名词或代词。

0026 activist [ˈæktɪvɪst]
n 行动主义者，积极分子　**a** 激进主义的
He has been an activist investor for so long time.
他成为一名激进投资者很长时间了。
🔵 militant 好斗者　🟢 have done... for so long time 做……很长时间

0027 acute [əˈkjuːt] **a** 尖锐的，敏锐的，急性的
The assistant said that there was an acute shortage of folders.
助理说资料夹严重短缺。
🔴 dull 钝的　🟢 acute disease 急性病
🟢 there is an acute shortage of... ……严重短缺

> 🔗 shortage (P. 632)

0028 adaptation [ˌædæpˈteɪʃn] **n** 改编，适应性的改变
It is not in conformity with good social adaptation.
这不符合良好的社会适应能力。
🔵 adjustment 调节　🟢 social adaptation 社会适应，适应能力

0029 addict [ˈædɪkt] v 使沉溺 n 入迷的人

The girl was not much of a secretary addict.
那个女孩并不是很喜欢秘书工作。
- drug addict 吸毒者
- addict 通常与其他名词构成固定搭配用法。

0030 addiction [əˈdɪkʃn] n 上瘾，吸毒成瘾，癖好

The boss came here to help his assistant overcome addiction to drugs.
老板来这里是为了帮助他的助理克服毒瘾。
- indulgence 嗜好
- come here to do sth. 来这里做某事

语法重点
addiction to 表示"对……上瘾"，其中 to 用作介词，后面接名词或代词。
↻ overcome (P. 480)

0031 administer [ədˈmɪnɪstər] v 管理，实施，给予

Internal affairs of the company are administered by professionals.
公司内部事务由专业人员进行管理。
- administer justice 执法
- be administered by... 由……管理

0032 administration [əd,mɪnɪˈstreɪʃn] n 行政

Many new employees are ingratiating themselves with the administration department.
很多新员工都在讨行政部门的欢心。
- governance 管理
- ingratiate oneself with sb. 讨某人的欢心

0033 administrative [ədˈmɪnɪstreɪtɪv] a 行政上的

The administrative burden will be lifted from the company next year.
公司的行政负担将于明年解除。
- executive 行政的
- administrative law 行政法
- be lifted from... 解除……

语法重点
be lifted from 的主语为需要解除的事物，而介词 from 后面接被解除的物件。
↻ burden (P. 267)

0034 administrator [ədˈmɪnɪstreɪtər] n 统治者

The company was starved for a network administrator.
公司急需一位网络系统管理员。
- conductor 领导者
- be starved for... 急需……

0035 advocate [ˈædvəkət] / [ˈædvəkeɪt] n 提倡者 v 提倡

The corporate leaders didn't advocate reforming the management system.
公司领导人并不主张进行管理体制改革。
- support 拥护
- impugn 指责
- advocate doing sth. 主张做某事

0036 affectionate [əˈfekʃənət] a 充满深情的

This superior was so affectionate towards his subordinates.
这位主管非常疼爱他的下属。
- caring 表示关怀或关心的
- uncaring 漠不关心的
- be affectionate towards sb. 疼爱某人

↻ subordinate (P. 785)

0037 affirm [əˈfɜːrm] v 断言，坚持声称，承认
I dare affirm that this is a junk mail.
我敢肯定这是一封垃圾邮件。
- declare 宣布　- copyright affirm 版权声明
- I dare affirm that... 我敢肯定……

junk (P. 314)

0038 aggression [əˈɡreʃn] n 侵略，攻击，进攻
Their termination of contract was condemned as aggression.
他们解除合约的行为被谴责为一种挑衅行为。
- invasion 入侵　- be condemned as... 被谴责为……

0039 alcoholic [ˌælkəˈhɔːlɪk] a 含酒精的，酒精中毒的
It's a pity that the excellent leader had degenerated into an alcoholic.
遗憾的是，那位优秀的领导者已经堕落成为一名酗酒者。
- inebriate 酒醉的　- nonalcoholic 不含酒精的
- alcoholic beverage 酒精饮料　- degenerate into... 堕落为……

pity (P. 337)

0040 alienate [ˈeɪliəneɪt] v 使疏远，使不友好，转让
You can't alienate from your colleagues or superiors.
你不能疏远你的同事或上司。
- endear 使亲密　- alienate from 使疏远　- ... alienate from sb. ……疏远某人

0041 alliance [əˈlaɪəns] n 联盟
This private enterprise has decided to be in alliance with the labor union.
这家私营企业决定与工会联盟。
- union 联盟　- strategic alliance 战略联盟　- be in alliance with... 与……联盟

enterprise (P. 557)

0042 allocate [ˈæləkeɪt] v 分配，把……拨给
Key cards should be allocated to every employee.
出入证应该分配给每一名员工。
- assign 分配　- allocate for 为……而分配
- be allocated to sb. 将……分配给某人

0043 alongside [əˌlɔːŋˈsaɪd] ad 在旁边，并排地　prep 在旁边
The secretary stood alongside of the president in the press conference.
在记者招待会上，秘书站在总裁的身边。
- abreast 并列地　- come alongside 靠过来

语法重点
alongside 是由副词 along 与名词 side 构成的副词，也可用作介词。

affirm ~ amplify

- stand alongside of... 站在……旁边

0044 **alternative** [ɔːlˈtɜːrnətɪv]
a 二选一的，供选择的 **n** 选择

There was no alternative for the manager to agree with this plan.
经理别无选择，只好同意这个方案。
- substitute 替换物
- have no alternative 没有其他选择
- there is no alternative for sb. to do sth. 某人别无选择，只好做某事

0045 **ambiguity** [ˌæmbɪˈɡjuːəti] **n** 意义不明，歧义

The argument between them resulted from the ambiguities in the contract.
他们的争论是由合约中的歧义引起的。
- definitude 明确
- result from... 起因于……，……由……造成

→ argument (P. 125)

0046 **ambiguous** [æmˈbɪɡjuəs] **a** 含糊不清的

The manager was given an ambiguous reply when he asked about the minutes of the meeting.
经理询问会议记录时，得到了一个含糊不清的答复。
- equivocal 模棱两可的
- clear 清楚的
- ask about sth. 询问某事

0047 **ambulance** [ˈæmbjələns] **n** 救护车，野战医院

Two firemen helped this injured worker into the ambulance.
两名消防员扶这个受伤的工人上救护车。
- auxilium 帮助
- air ambulance 空难救护
- help sb. into... 帮助某人进入……

语法重点
injured 作形容词表示"受伤的"，可以与定冠词 the 连用，构成 the injured 表示"受伤的人"。

0048 **ambush** [ˈæmbʊʃ] **n** 埋伏，伏兵 **v** 伏击

The opponent would lay an ambush for the delegation.
对手将设下埋伏等待代表团的到来。
- trap 陷阱，圈套
- lay an ambush for... 设下埋伏等待……

→ opponent (P. 604)

0049 **amiable** [ˈeɪmiəbl] **a** 友善的

Could you tell me whether he was an amiable cooperator or not?
你能告诉我他是否是一个友善的合作者吗？
- pleasant 和蔼可亲的
- abominable 讨厌的
- amiable tumor 良性肿瘤
- Could you tell me whether...? 你能告诉我是否……？

语法重点
amiable 作形容词用于修饰名词 cooperator。

0050 **amplify** [ˈæmplɪfaɪ] **v** 扩大，详述

It's the assistant who told me how to amplify the sound of the microphone.
是助理告诉我如何扩大麦克风的声音的。
- enlarge 扩大
- weaken 使变弱

0051 analects [ˌænəˈlekts] n 文选，论集
As the editor-in-chief, have you read the newly-published *The Analects of Confucius*?
作为主编，你读过那本新出版的《论语》吗？
同 anthology 选集　关 The Analects of Confucius《论语》

语法重点
在英语中，表示书名或期刊的名称一般要用斜体来表示，如例句中的 *The Analects of Confucius*。

0052 analogy [əˈnælədʒi] n 类比，比拟
There was analogy between this contract and that one.
这两份合约有相似之处。
同 similarity 相似　搭 draw an analogy between 指出……之间的相似处
句 there is analogy between... and... ……和……有相似之处

语法重点
analogy 是可数名词，其复数形式是 analogies。

0053 analyst [ˈænəlɪst] n 分析者，化验员
I do believe he is a market analyst.
我确信他是一名市场分析员。
搭 news analyst 评论员　句 I do believe... 我确信……

语法重点
助动词 do 用于动词前，起强调作用。

0054 analytic / analytical [ˌænəˈlɪtɪk] / [ˌænəˈlɪtɪkl] a 分析的，解析的
Please improve your analytical skills as soon as possible.
请尽快提高你的分析能力。
搭 analytical method 分析法　句 please do... as soon as possible 请尽快做……

0055 anecdote [ˈænɪkdoʊt] n 趣闻轶事，逸事，秘史
It had never been more than an anecdote about the company development.
那只不过是一个有关公司发展的趣闻轶事罢了。
根 ana 轶事　句 it had never been more than... 那只不过是……

0056 animate [ˈænɪmeɪt] / [ˈænɪmət] v 赋予生命 a 有生命的
These scientists still made no clear distinction between animate and inanimate organisms.
这些科学家还无法清楚地辨别有生命和无生命的生物体。
同 lived 有生命的　反 inanimate 无生命的　搭 animate cartoon 动画片

关 distinction (P. 558)

0057 annoyance [əˈnɔɪəns] n 烦恼，使人烦恼的事
The leaders always took their annoyance out on the new employees.
领导者们总是拿新员工出气。
同 worry 担心　反 pleasure 令人高兴的事　搭 relieve annoyance 解除烦恼

语法重点
take one's annoyance out on sb.（对某人出气）中的 one's 可以根据需要变换不同的人称。

0058 anonymous [əˈnɑːnɪməs] a 匿名的，无特色的
If you agree to have anonymous vote at the meeting, just let you be.
如果你同意在会议上进行不记名投票，就随你便吧。
同 innominate 匿名的　反 onymous 署名的　搭 let sb. be 随某人的便

0059 antarctic [æn'tɑːrktɪk] a 南极的，南极地区的 n 南极洲

It's your duty to reconsider the Antarctic Treaty.
你们有责任重新考虑南极条约。

- south-polar 南极的
- antarctic circle 南极圈

语法重点
it's one's duty to do sth.
（某人有责任做某事）中的 one's 可以使用不同的人称代词。

0060 antenna [æn'tenə] n 触角，感觉，天线

The workers were permitted to erect antenna on the roof of the company.
允许工人在公司的屋顶安装天线。

- sb. be permitted to... 允许某人……

erect (P. 563)

0061 antibiotic [ˌæntibaɪ'ɑːtɪk] n 抗生素

I grant you liberty to sell these antibiotic ointments on the market.
我允许你们在市场上销售这种抗生素软膏。

- microbiotic 抗生素
- I grant sb. liberty to do... 我允许某人……

0062 antibody ['æntibɑːdi] n 抗体

Until recently, this antibody drug began to sell well.
直到最近，这种抗体药物的销量才有所提升。

- antitrope 抗体
- until recently, ... 直到最近，……

语法重点
sell well 表示"畅销"，一般用主动语态。

0063 anticipate [æn'tɪsɪpeɪt] v 预期，期望

The manager anticipated making a clean sweep in the product launch.
经理期望在产品发布会上大获全胜。

- foresee 预见
- anticipate problems 预见到问题
- anticipate doing sth. 预期做某事

sweep (P. 232)

0064 anticipation [ænˌtɪsɪ'peɪʃn] n 预期

The president was in anticipation of more people attending this business party.
总裁期待有更多的人来参加这次的商业派对。

- expectation 期待
- in anticipation 预先
- be in anticipation of... 期待……
- anticipation 指基于先见、预知的期待或希望，多指好的事情，而 expectation 指盼望某事发生或认为某事会发生。

0065 antonym ['æntənɪm] n 反义词

As a lawyer, he knew that defendant was the antonym of plaintiff.
作为一名律师，他知道被告是原告的反义词。

- opposite 反义词
- synonymy 同义词
- be the antonym of... 是……的反义词

0066 applicable [əˈplɪkəbl] **a** 适用的，适当的
This program is applicable to all office softwares.
这种程序适用于所有的办公软体。
- suitable 适当的
- unsuitable 不适合的
- applicable scope 适用范围
- be applicable to... 适用于……

0067 apprentice [əˈprentɪs] **n** 学徒，徒弟 **v** 使……做学徒
I am an apprentice to the worker there.
我是那边那个工人的徒弟。
- novice 初学者
- veteran 老手
- be an apprentice to... 是……的徒弟

> **语法重点**
> be an apprentice to 中的 to 是介词，后面接表示人的名词或者代词。

0068 approximate [əˈprɑːksɪmət] **a** 近似的 **v** 接近，近似
This product questionnaire is approximate to perfect.
这份产品调查问卷近乎完美。
- approximate value 近似值
- be approximate to... 近似于……

↪ questionnaire (P. 764)

0069 aptitude [ˈæptɪtuːd] **n** 才能，资质，倾向
This entrepreneur has a strong aptitude for management.
这位企业家有很强的管理才能。
- talent 才能
- academic aptitude 学术才能
- have an aptitude for... 有……的才能

0070 arctic [ˈɑːrktɪk] **a** 北极的，极寒的 **n** 北极圈
This instrument was designed for arctic exploration.
这个仪器是为北极探险而设计的。
- antarctic 南极的
- arctic circle 北极圈
- be designed for... 为……而设计

↪ exploration (P. 719)

0071 arrogant [ˈærəgənt] **a** 自大的
The manager was waking up that this salesman was extremely arrogant.
经理开始认识到，这名业务员极其傲慢。
- haughty 傲慢的
- humble 谦逊的
- be waking up that... 开始认识到……

0072 artery [ˈɑːrtəri] **n** 动脉，要道
That a main artery would be built in this city is true.
这座城市真的要修建一条主干道。
- mainstream 主流
- vein 静脉
- carotid artery 颈动脉

> **语法重点**
> 此句型是一个典型的主语从句。

0073 articulate [ɑːˈtɪkjələt] / [ɑːˈtɪkjuleɪt]
a 清晰的 **v** 清晰的发音
The agent struggled to articulate his view on retail.
那个代理商竭力表明自己对于零售的看法。
- enunciative 发音清晰的
- inarticulate 不善辞令的
- struggle to do sth. 竭力做某事

0074 artifact [ˈɑːrtɪfækt] n 人工制品，手工制品

Could you help me check whether the stone was an artifact?
能否请你帮我一个忙，查看一下这个石头是不是人造的？
- Could you help me do...? 你能帮我……？

0075 assassinate [əˈsæsəneɪt] v 行刺，暗杀

Their plan to assassinate the business magnate was uncovered by the secretary.
他们刺杀那个商业巨头的计划被秘书发现了。
- be uncovered by... 被……发现

0076 assert [əˈsɜːrt] v 主张

You must seek opportunities to assert yourself at the stockholders' meeting.
在股东大会上，你一定要寻找机会维护自己的权利。
- affirm 断言，确认   - assert oneself 坚持自己的权利
- seek opportunities to do sth. 寻求机会做某事

> **语法重点**
> assert oneself 中的 oneself 是反身代词，可以变换成不同的人称。
> opportunity (P. 331)

0077 assess [əˈses] v 估定财产的价值

It's too early to assess his capacity now.
现在对他的能力进行评估还为时过早。
- evaluate 估价   - it's too early to do sth. now 现在做……还为时过早

0078 assumption [əˈsʌmpʃn] n 前提

Send a telegram on the assumption that the fax machine is broken.
假设传真机坏了，就发电报。
- do sth. on the assumption that... 假设……，就……

0079 asthma [ˈæzmə] n 气喘，哮喘

This medical corporation is selling drugs which were contraindicated in patients with asthma.
这家医药公司正在销售对哮喘病人禁用的药物。
- wheezing 哮喘，气喘   - allergic asthma 过敏性哮喘

0080 asylum [əˈsaɪləm] n 收容所，政治避难

That is why most of the financiers seek for political asylum.
这就是大多数金融家寻求政治庇护的原因。
- shelter 避难所，收容所   - that is why... 这就是为什么……

> **语法重点**
> 例句是由 why 引导的从句，强调结果。

0081 attain [əˈteɪn] v 达成，获得，完成

For us, it's of great importance to attain the sales target.
对我们来说，完成销售目标非常重要。
- accomplish 完成，实现   - fail 失败   - attain success 获得成功

> target (P. 233)

0082 attendant [əˈtendənt] a 伴随的 n 服务人员，侍者

Those attendants set about arranging the exhibition hall.
那些服务人员开始布置展览厅。
- waiter 服务生
- room attendant 客房服务生
- set about doing sth. 开始做某事

exhibition (P. 292)

0083 attic [ˈætɪk] n 阁楼

You could not take down the attic which was used to store goods.
你们不能拆除那个用于存放货物的阁楼。
- garret 阁楼
- attic faith 坚定的信念
- take down sth. 拆卸某物

0084 auction [ˈɔːkʃn] v / n 拍卖

Due to economic crisis, they had to put these facilities up for auction.
由于经济危机，他们不得不把这些设备拿去拍卖。
- sale 拍卖
- sale by auction 拍卖
- put... up for auction 把……拿去拍卖

crisis (P. 147)

0085 authentic [ɔːˈθentɪk] a 真实的，有根据的

Do you know whether this trade secret is authentic?
这个商业机密是否可信你知道吗？
- actual 真实的
- spurious 假的
- authentic proof 确证
- Do you know whether...? ……是否……你知道吗？

0086 authorize [ˈɔːθəraɪz] v 授权，批准，向……授予权威

Under no circumstances will the bank authorize this loan.
在任何情况下，银行都不会批准这项贷款。
- under no circumstances will sb. do... 在任何情况下，某人都不会……
- authorize 特指权威性的允许与认可，allow 侧重指听任、默许，用在正式场合时表示客气的请求。

0087 autograph / signature [ˈɔːtəɡræf] / [ˈsɪɡnətʃər] n 签名

What made the editor-in-chief happy was that he got the famous writer's autograph.
主编很开心，是因为他得到了那位名作家的签名。
- signature 签名
- autograph album 纪念册

语法重点
由 what 引导的主语从句表示结果，后面的从句表示原因时，后面的从句要用 that 引导，而不用 because。

0088 autonomy [ɔːˈtɑːnəmi] n 自治，自主权

The principals of the branch offices had full autonomy in their own markets.
分公司负责人对其管辖的市场享有充分的自主权。
- self-rule 自治
- local autonomy 地方自治
- sb. has autonomy in... 某人在……享有自主权

语法重点
形容词 full 用于修饰名词 autonomy。

0089 aviation [ˌeɪviˈeɪʃn] n 航空，航空学

These researchers are masters of aviation industry.
这些研究人员是航空业方面的专家。
- aeronautics 航空学
- be a master of... 精通……，控制……

0090 awesome [ˈɔːsəm] a 令人敬畏的

We should do our utmost to live through this awesome economic crisis.
我们应该尽全力来度过这场可怕的经济危机。
- do one's utmost to do sth. 尽全力做某事

⊃ utmost (P. 799)

0091 barometer [bəˈrɑːmɪtər] n 气压计，晴雨表

Stock index is a barometer of the market economy.
股票指数是市场经济的晴雨表。

0092 beckon [ˈbekən] v 向……示意，召唤，吸引

The administrative director beckoned to the waiter when the banquet began.
宴会开始时，行政主管朝服务生招了招手。
- gesture 做手势
- beckon foe 诱敌深入
- beckon to sb. 向某人招手

⊃ administrative (P. 669)

0093 besiege [bɪˈsiːdʒ] v 包围，围攻，拥挤在周围

The principal was constantly besieged by the reporters in the press conference.
在记者会上，负责人不断受到记者的打扰。
- siege 包围
- be besieged with... 被 ... 弄得应接不暇
- be besieged by... 被……打扰

> 语法重点
> 副词 constantly 用于修饰动词 besiege。

0094 betray [bɪˈtreɪ] v 背叛，辜负，泄漏

It's out of character to betray your colleagues at work.
在工作中背叛你的同事很不像你。
- deceive 欺骗
- betray oneself 原形毕露

0095 beverage [ˈbevərɪdʒ] n 饮料

I really want to know why you drank so much alcoholic beverage in the party.
我真的很想知道你为什么在派对上喝那么多酒精饮料。
- alcoholic beverage 酒精饮料
- I really want to know... 我真的很想知道……

0096 bias [ˈbaɪəs] n 偏见，偏袒 v 使有偏见

The customers had a bias against import commodity.
顾客对进口商品心存偏见。
- prejudice 偏见
- impartiality 公正
- a bias for... 对……的偏爱
- have a bias against... 对……有偏见

⊃ commodity (P. 546)

0097 binoculars [bɪˈnɑːkjələrz] **n** 双筒望远镜，双筒镜
You are expected to put this binoculars on sale. ◁ 语法重点
你应该廉价出售这个双筒望远镜。
you are expected to（你应该）后面通常接动词原形。

0098 biochemistry [ˌbaɪoʊˈkemɪstri] **n** 生物化学
The scientists made a plan about researching the plant biochemistry.
科学家们制订计划来研究植物生物化学。
🔁 make a plan about doing sth. 制订计划做某事

0099 biological [ˌbaɪəˈlɑːdʒɪkl] **a** 生物学的，与生物学相关的
What do you mean by specializing in biological engineering?
你主修生物工程是什么意思？
🔁 biologic 生物的　🔁 What do you mean by...? 你……是什么意思？

⊃ specialize (P. 781)

0100 bizarre [bɪˈzɑːr] **a** 奇异的
What made you think that the new colleague had a bizarre behavior? ◁ 语法重点
你为什么认为那个新同事行为怪异？
what makes you think that 中的 makes 运用了一般现在时，也可以用一般过去时。
🔁 grotesque 奇怪的　🔁 usual 平常的　🔁 bizarre behavior 怪诞的行为
🔁 What makes you think that...? 是什么让你认为……？

0101 bleak [bliːk] **a** 荒凉的，无希望的
It's a surprise that the project leader looked bleak.
令人惊奇的是，那位专案负责人看起来很沮丧。
🔁 it's a surprise that... 令人惊奇的是……

0102 blunder [ˈblʌndər] **n** 大错 **v** 跌跌撞撞地走，犯错误
It's a blunder to let him know about our investment plan.
让他了解我们的投资计划是一个错误。
🔁 blunder away 挥霍掉，抛弃　🔁 it's a blunder to do sth. 做某事是一个错误

⊃ investment (P. 463)

0103 blunt [blʌnt] **a** 钝的，率直的 **v** 使迟钝，使减弱
The house agent is blunt about his career life.
那位房产经纪人对自己的职场生活直言不讳。
🔁 dull 钝的　🔁 blunt question 直白的问题　🔁 be blunt about... 对……直言不讳

0104 bombard [bɑːmˈbɑːrd] **v** 轰炸，攻击 **n** 射石炮
The manager bombarded the secretary with the sales report.
经理不停地向秘书追问有关销售报表的事情。
🔁 attack 攻击　🔁 bombard sb. with... 不停向某人追问……

0105 bondage ['bɑːndɪdʒ] n 奴隶身份

This professor is always in bondage to his self-conceit and arrogancy.
这名教授总是被自负和自大所束缚。
- break the bondage 打破束缚
- be in bondage to... 受……的束缚

0106 boost [buːst] n / v 促进

Merger of company gave the enterprise revenue a big boost.
公司合并使企业效益大大提高。
- promote 促进
- boost morale 鼓舞士气
- give... a big boost 使……大大提高

↪ revenue (P. 771)

0107 bout [baʊt] n 一阵，回合

What will you do if you fail your interview this bout?
如果这次你面试失败了，你会做什么？
- round 一回合
- toilet bout 抽水马桶
- What will you do if...? 如果……，你会做什么？

0108 boycott ['bɔɪkɑːt] n 杯葛 v 抵制，拒绝参加

Most of the customers have decided to put this fake commodity under a boycott.
大多数消费者决定联合抵制这项伪劣商品。
- revolt 反抗
- secondary boycott 间接抵制
- put... under a boycott 联合抵制……

0109 breakdown ['breɪkdaʊn] n 故障

Why on earth did the excellent student suffer from mental breakdown?
那个优秀的学生究竟为什么会精神崩溃？
- mental breakdown 精神崩溃
- Why on earth did sb. ...? 某人究竟为什么……？
- on earth 表示 "究竟"，而 on the earth 表示 "在地球上"。

↪ mental (P. 324)

0110 breakthrough ['breɪkθruː] n 突破

This sales team made a breakthrough in dominating the Asia market.
这个销售团队在占据亚洲市场方面有所突破。
- breakthrough point 突破点
- make a breakthrough in... 在……方面有所突破

↪ dominate (P. 429)

0111 breakup ['breɪk,ʌp] n 中断

Breakup of marriage didn't have an influence on his work.
婚姻破裂并未对他的工作造成影响。
- breakup of marriage 婚姻破裂
- have an influence on... 对……有影响

0112 **brew** [bruː] v 酿制，冲泡，即将发生 n 冲泡
The assistant brewed up a cup of tea for the visitor.
助理为访客倒了一杯茶。
- ferment 酝酿 - brew up 酿造 - brew up... for sb. 为某人沏茶
- a cup of tea 是固定用法，表示"一杯茶"。

0113 **brink** [brɪŋk] n 悬崖边缘
It is said that the transnational corporation is on the brink of bankrupt.
据说，那家跨国公司就要倒闭了。
- rim 边缘 - on the brink of 在……边缘 - be on the brink of... 濒于……

语法重点
运用 be on the brink of 这个句型时，介词 of 后面一般接表示灾难、死亡等不好的事件。
- bankrupt (P. 400)

0114 **brisk** [brɪsk] a 活泼的，敏锐的，清新的
It's great to work with a brisk colleague.
与一个做事干脆利落的同事共事是很愉快的。
- brisk trade 贸易繁荣 - it's great to... ……是好的

0115 **brochure** [broʊˈʃʊr] n 小册子，介绍指南
He can vouch for the authenticity of these recruitment brochures.
他能够保证这些招聘简章的真实性。
- booklet 小册子 - sales brochure 销售手册

语法重点
vouch for（担保）后面也可以接表示人的名词或代词。

0116 **brute** [bruːt] n 残暴的人 a 残酷的
Actually, the headman of this factory was usually a brute to the workers.
事实上，这家工厂的负责人经常虐待工人。
- brute force 强力 - be a brute to... 虐待……

语法重点
actually 作副词置于句首，用于修饰整个句子。

0117 **buckle** [ˈbʌkl] n 扣环 v 用搭扣扣紧，变形
You can benefit a lot if you buckle down to this new job.
如果你认真做这份新工作，你会受益颇多。
- buckle down 倾全力 - buckle down to... 认真做……

语法重点
buckle down to 后面通常接名词、代词或名词短语。

0118 **bulky** [ˈbʌlki] a 庞大的，笨重的，体积大的
The worker was incapable of moving this bulky cargo.
那名工人搬不动这件超大货物。

语法重点
be incapable of（不能）后面一般接动名词，表示"不能做某事"。

0119 **bureaucracy** [bjʊˈrɑːkrəsi] n 官僚，官僚机构
Bureaucracy did grave damage to the interest of corporation.
官僚作风严重损害了公司利益。
- bureaucratism 官僚主义 - do grave damage to... 严重损害……

语法重点
do damage to 句型中，to 是介词，后面接名词或代词。

0120 **burial** [ˈberiəl] n 埋葬，葬礼，坟墓

Won't you attend the chairman's burial?
你不想参加董事长的葬礼吗？
- burial ground 坟地
- Won't you do...? 你不想……吗？
- attend 侧重指参加或出席会议、学术活动，join 一般指加入党派、团体或游戏活动。

0121 **byte** [baɪt] n 字节

Double byte is a computer terminology, is that right?
双字节是电脑用语，对吗？
- ..., is that right? ……，对吗？

语法重点
computer terminology 是固定用法，表示"电脑术语"。

0122 **caffeine** [ˈkæfiːn] n 咖啡因，茶精

What would you think of that I buy a bottle of drink without caffeine for the manager?
你认为买一瓶不含咖啡因的饮料给经理怎么样？
- caffeine test 咖啡因试验
- What would you think of that...? 你认为……怎么样？

语法重点
drink 在例句中用作名词，表示"饮料"。
- bottle (P. 133)

0123 **calcium** [ˈkælsiəm] n 钙

Calcium is found abundantly in the dairy products produced by this company.
这家公司生产的乳制品中含有很多钙。
- be found in... 存在于……

语法重点
abundantly 作副词，修饰动词 found。

0124 **canvas** [ˈkænvəs] n 帆布，油画

The maintainer took out a plier from a canvas bag.
那名维修工从一个帆布包里拿出了一把钳子。
- painting 绘画
- canvas shoes 帆布鞋
- sb. takes out... from... 某人从……中拿出

0125 **capability** [ˌkeɪpəˈbɪləti] n 能力，容量，生产率

This leader had the capability to deal with budgetary deficit.
这位领导人有能力应付预算赤字。
- capacity 能力
- design capability 设计能力
- have the capability to do sth. 有能力做某事
- capability 多指人能够胜任某项工作的能力，也指本身所具有的潜在能力，而 capacity 侧重指人的潜在能力，通常指才智及悟性能力。

0126 **capsule** [ˈkæpsl] n 胶囊，航太舱，密封舱

The following is the production process of this capsule.
下面是这种胶囊的生产流程。
- in a capsule 概括地说
- the following is... 下面是……

语法重点
the following is 句型中，如果所指物体是复数，则 is 可以换成 are。
- process (P. 342)

0127 caption ['kæpʃn] n 标题 v 加上说明（字幕）
Could you think up a caption which summarizes the conference?
你能想出概括会议内容的标题吗？
- Could you think up...? 你能想出……吗？

○ summarize (P. 508)

0128 captive ['kæptɪv] n 俘虏，被监禁的人 a 被俘虏的
The principal said that the truck was taken captive by the gangsters.
负责人说，那辆货车被歹徒劫持了。
- prisoner 囚犯   - be taken captive 被俘   - be taken captive by... 被……劫持

0129 captivity [kæp'tɪvəti] n 监禁
The great majority of the corrupt officials were kept captivity for two years.
大多数的受贿官员都被监禁了两年。
- embarment 囚禁   - freedom 自由   - in captivity 受限制的
- be kept captivity for... 被关了……

0130 carbohydrate [,kɑːrbou'haɪdreɪt]
n 碳水化合物，糖类食物
The reason for her getting fat is that she usually has too many carbohydrates in the office.
她发胖是因为经常在办公室里吃过多的碳水化合物食品。
- the reason for... is that... ……的原因是……

语法重点
too many 表示"过多"，一般修饰可数名词复数。

0131 caress [kə'res] v 抚摸，亲吻 n 接吻，拥抱
The female colleague gave my hand a caress.
那位女同事抚摸了一下我的手。
- petting 爱抚   - loving caress 亲吻   - sb. gives... a caress 某人抚摸……

语法重点
female 通常用于名词前，表示性别。
○ female (P. 164)

0132 carol ['kærəl] v 颂歌，歌唱庆祝 n 圣诞之歌
Maybe it's better for all the staff to go caroling together.
全体员工一起唱圣诞颂歌，可能会更好一些。

0133 cashier [kæ'ʃɪr] n 出纳员，收银员 v 解职，丢弃
This senior accountant ever worked as a cashier in a district bank.
这名资深会计曾经在一家地方银行当出纳员。
- cashier district 收银区   - work as... 担任……

0134 casualty ['kæʒuəlti] n 伤亡人员，受害者
This laid-off worker was a casualty of the company's layoff.
这名被解雇的工人是公司裁员的受害者。
- sufferer 受害者   - be a casualty of... 是……的受害者

语法重点
laid-off 是一个合成形容词，表示"被解雇的"。

caption ~ champagne

0135 catastrophe [kə'tæstrəfi] **n** 大灾难，灾祸

No one knows that this catastrophe insurance has been abolished.
没有人知道这项重大事故保险已经取消了。
- calamity 灾难
- luck 运气
- no one knows that... 没有人知道……

0136 cater ['keɪtər] **v** 迎合，承办酒席

As a service industry, we must cater to all the clients.
作为服务业，我们必须满足所有顾客的需求。
- humor 迎合
- cater for 为……提供所需
- ... cater to sb. ……满足某人的需要

> **语法重点**
> cater to 后面接 sth. 时，表示"考虑"。

0137 cavalry ['kævlri] **n** 骑兵，骑兵部队，装甲部队

All the people saw the cavalry charge down on a little girl via video.
通过影片，所有人都看到骑兵向一个小女孩冲去。
- trooper 骑兵
- charge down on... 向……冲去
- charge down 也可以表示"把……记在某人账上"。

0138 cavity ['kævəti] **n** 洞，穴，凹处，蛀牙

It is absurd that there is a big cavity in the boss's tooth.
老板的牙上有个大洞，真是荒唐。
- hole 洞，孔
- oral cavity 口腔
- it is absurd that... ……真是荒唐

> absurd (P. 521)

0139 cemetery ['seməteri] **n** 公墓

The chairman was buried in a private cemetery after he passed away.
董事长去世后，被埋在了私人墓地里。
- graveyard 墓地
- be buried in... 被埋在了……

0140 certainty ['sɜːrtnti] **n** 确实

I know with certainty that where the book of tender is.
我确切知道投标书放在了哪里。
- doubt 怀疑
- with certainty 确定无疑地
- I know with certainty that... 我确切知道……

0141 certify ['sɜːrtɪfaɪ] **v** 证明，担保，发证书（或执照）给

The applicant has been certified as a senior accountant.
那位应聘者已经拿到高级会计师证书。
- guarantee 保证
- honorary certify 荣誉证书
- be certified as... 拿到……的证书

> **语法重点**
> be certified as 句型中，as 后面通常接某种职称。
> senior (P. 502)

0142 champagne [ʃæm'peɪn] **n** 香槟酒，平原

The waiters served up champagne after the business dinner began.
商务宴会开始后，服务生端上香槟酒。

> **语法重点**
> serve up（端上）后面通常接表示食物或饮料的名词。

683

0143 **chaos** ['keɪɑːs] n 大混乱，无秩序，混沌
The president's disappearance threw the whole company into chaos.
总裁的失踪使整个公司陷入一片混乱。
- disorder 混乱　- cosmos 秩序　- in chaos 混乱
- throw... into chaos 使……陷入混乱

0144 **characterize** ['kærəktəraɪz]
v 具有……的特征，赋予……特色
The administrative assistant's work is characterized by patience and carefulness.
那位行政助理的工作特点是耐心和细心。
- depict 描述　- characterize as 把……描述成
- be characterized by... 具有……的特征

> **语法重点**
> be characterized by 句型中，介词 by 后面通常接表示性质或特点的名词。
> ↪ administrative (P. 669)

0145 **charcoal** ['tʃɑːrkoʊl] n 木炭，炭画笔　v 用木炭画，炭烤
One third of the clients thought this activated charcoal was easy to use.
有三分之一的顾客认为这种活性炭使用起来很方便。
- xylanthrax 木炭　- activated charcoal 活性炭　- be easy to use 使用方便

0146 **chariot** ['tʃæriət] n 双轮战车　v 驾驭
I will never allow you to watch chariot race during work-time.
我绝不允许你在工作时间看战车比赛。
- prison chariot 囚车　- I will never allow... 我绝不允许……

0147 **charitable** ['tʃærətəbl] a 温和的，宽厚的，慷慨的
Embarking in charitable causes could earn the company a good reputation.
从事慈善事业可以为公司赢得好名声。
- charitable donation 慈善捐款　- embark in... 从事……，参与……

↪ embark (P. 714)

0148 **cholesterol** [kəˈlestərɔːl] n 胆固醇
Many employees got fat, which was not a predictor of high cholesterol level.
很多员工发胖，并不表示他们的胆固醇很高。

0149 **chronic** ['krɑːnɪk] a 慢性的，长久的，习惯性的
Chronic gastritis always coexists with work stress.
慢性胃炎总是与工作压力同时存在。
- acute 急性的　- chronic disease 慢性病　- coexist with... 与……共存

0150 chuckle ['tʃʌkl] v 咯咯地笑 n 轻笑声

After giving a little chuckle, the assistant leveled with the manager.
轻声一笑之后，助手对经理说了实话。
- chuckle unceasingly 窃笑不已
- level with sb. 对某人说实话
- level with 也可以表示"和……同一水准"。

0151 chunk [tʃʌŋk] n 厚块，相当大的部分

The student sought his bed after completing a fair chunk of her article.
那个学生写完大部分的文章后，就睡觉了。
- seek one's bed 就寝

→ article (P. 126)

0152 civilize ['sɪvəlaɪz] v 使文明，教育

Pre-job training was intended to civilize those inexperienced new employees.
职前培训的目的在于教育那些毫无经验的新员工。
- educate 教育
- be intended to... 意图是……

0153 clamp [klæmp] v 夹住 n 夹子，夹钳

The secretary clamped the folder to the pen container.
秘书把资料夹夹在笔筒上。
- clamp down on 对……进行压制
- clamp sth. to... 用夹具把某物固定在……上

0154 clarity ['klærəti] n 清楚，明确，清晰度

With this knowledge, the stenographer could classify with clarity.
了解这些，速记员就可以清楚地进行分类。
- lucidness 透明
- 反 ambiguity 不明确
- with clarity 清楚地
- with this knowledge, ... 了解了这些，……

语法重点
knowledge 通常用作不可数名词，在使用时要用单数。
→ classify (P. 408)

0155 cleanse [klenz] v 净化，使……清洁，清洗

After work, her business is to cleanse the office.
下班后，她的任务是清理办公室。

0156 clearance ['klɪrəns] n 清洁

There is not enough clearance for the locker being put in the office.
办公室里没有足够的空间来放置储物柜。
- removel 清除
- customs clearance 结关
- there is not enough clearance... 没有足够的空间……

语法重点
例句中的 locker 是被放在办公室里，所以要用被动语态。

0157 clench [klentʃ] v 握紧，抓紧 n 抓紧

This new employee felt a clench in his head when seeing the superior.
看到上司时，这位新员工感到头部一阵揪紧。

语法重点
feel a clench in（感到……揪紧）句型中，介词 in 后面通常接某个身体部位。

0158 clinical [ˈklɪnɪkl] a 门诊的，冷静的
The institute of medicine was doing clinical trial on the drugs of your company.
医学研究院正在对你们公司的药物进行临床试验。
◎ clinical trial 临床试验 ◎ ... do clinical trial on... ……对……进行临床试验

◎ trial (P. 239)

0159 clone [kloʊn] v 复制动植物
Many employees said that the manager was a younger clone of the chairman.
很多员工说，经理是董事长年轻时的翻版。
◎ copy 复制 ◎ genetic clone 基因复制 ◎ be a clone of... 是……的翻版

0160 closure [ˈkloʊʒər] n 关闭 v 使结束，使停止辩论
The principal was meant to declare the closure of the factory.
负责人打算宣告工厂关闭。
◎ termination 结束 ◎ opening 开始 ◎ be meant to... 打算……

◎ declare (P. 422)

0161 coffin [ˈkɔːfɪn] n 棺材，蹄槽 v 收殓
It's strange that there was a coffin at the gate of the company.
令人奇怪的是，公司的门口竟然放着一副棺材。
◎ coffin chamber 墓室 ◎ it's strange that... 令人奇怪的是……

0162 coherent [koʊˈhɪrənt] a 一致的
Maybe some coherent explanation should be added to the memorandum.
或许应该在备忘录中增加一些有条理的说明。
◎ consistent 一致的 ◎ incoherent 不连贯的 ◎ be added to... 增加到……

0163 coincide [ˌkoʊɪnˈsaɪd] v 同时发生，相符
My opinion coincided with that of the group leader.
我的意见与组长的意见一致。
◎ happen to coincide 不约而同 ◎ coincide with... 与……相一致

语法重点
在英语中为了避免重复，通常用 that 指代前文中出现过的同一事物，如例句中的 that 指代 opinion。

0164 coincidence [koʊˈɪnsɪdəns] n 巧合，符合，一致
It's no coincidence that the president was against this project.
董事长反对这项方案并非偶然。
◎ concurrence 一致 ◎ by coincidence 碰巧

0165 collective [kəˈlektɪv] a 共同的，集合性的
These two sales teams held together for collective reputation.
这两个销售团队为了集体的荣誉而团结在了一起。
◎ hold together for... 为了……团结在了一起

◎ reputation (P. 496)

clinical ~ commence

0166 collector [kə'lektər] n 收集者，收集器，收税员
Not a few personal collectors attended the auction.
很多私人收藏家出席了拍卖会。
- gatherer 收集者
- dust collector 吸尘器

⊙ auction (P. 676)

0167 collide [kə'laɪd] v 碰撞，冲突，抵触
They were struck with horror when seeing two trucks collided.
他们看到两辆货车相撞时，大吃一惊。
- clash 冲突
- compromise 妥协
- collide with 与……冲突
- sb. be struck with horror when... ……的时候，某人大吃一惊

⊙ horror (P. 307)

0168 collision [kə'lɪʒn] n 相撞，冲突
Her suggestion was in collision with the topic of the conference.
她的建议与会议的主题相冲突。
- conflict 冲突
- in collision 相撞，在冲突中
- be in collision with... 与……相冲突

0169 colloquial [kə'loʊkwiəl] a 口语的，会话的
"Yeah" is a colloquial word for "yes".
"yeah"是"yes"的口语。
- informal 通俗的
- written 书面的
- colloquial words 口语词汇

0170 columnist ['kɑːləmnɪst] n 专栏作家
The manager tried to talk the columnist out of gossiping.
经理试图说服那个专栏作家不要八卦。
- weekly columnist 每周专栏作家
- talk sb. out of doing... 说服某人不做……

0171 commemorate [kə'meməreɪt] v 纪念
This monument was built to commemorate the company's tenth anniversary.
这座纪念碑是为庆祝公司成立十周年而兴建的。
- celebrate 庆祝
- commemorate stamps 纪念邮票
- be built to... 为……而兴建

> **语法重点**
> be built to 后面通常接动词原形。
>
> ⊙ monument (P. 473)

0172 commence [kə'mens] v 开始，着手，获得学位
We immediately commenced preparing for the media session.
我们马上开始筹备记者会。
- begin 开始
- end 结束，终止
- commence business 开始营业
- commence doing sth. 开始做某事
- begin 含义广泛，多用于指行动、工作等的开始，而 commence 是书面正式用词，语气庄重，特指有正式程序或一定仪式。

687

0173 **commentary** [ˈkɑːmənteri] n 评论
They had no right to have a commentary on our investment plan.
他们没有权利对我们的投资方案做出评论。
🔵 comment 评论　🔵 commentary on 对……的评论

语法重点
have no right 后面可以接动词不定式，也可以接动名词，表示"没有权利做某事"。

0174 **commitment** [kəˈmɪtmənt] n 犯罪，承诺
The manager considered it useless that this salesman made such a commitment.
经理认为这名业务员做这样的一个承诺没有用。
🔵 compliance 承诺　🔵 make a commitment 承诺
🔵 consider it... that... 认为……怎么样

语法重点
当 consider 后面有宾语补足语时，要用 it 作形式宾语，并且将 that 引导的宾语从句后置，如例句所示。

0175 **communicative** [kəˈmjuːnɪkeɪtɪv]
a 畅谈的，好社交的
He wasn't feeling communicative at the meeting today.
他今天开会时不爱说话。
🔵 conversational 健谈的　🔵 communicative competence 交际能力

0176 **companionship** [kəmˈpæniənʃɪp] n 友谊，友好交往
I provided companionship to him when working overtime last night.
我昨晚陪他加班。
🔵 fellowship 友谊　🔵 provide companionship to sb. 陪伴某人

0177 **comparable** [ˈkɑːmpərəbl] a 可比较的，类似的
All the employees knew that this kind of comparable data was often lacking.
员工们都知道，这种可比较的资料通常缺乏。

0178 **comparative** [kəmˈpærətɪv] a 比较的，相对的
With the help of the secretary, the cooperative programme was accomplished with comparative ease.
在秘书的帮助下，合作方案被比较容易地完成了。
🔵 relative 相对的　🔵 absolute 绝对的，完全的
🔵 sth. be accomplished with ease 某事被轻松地完成了

语法重点
comparative 作形容词用于修饰后面的名词 ease。
🔵 accomplish (P. 390)

0179 **compatible** [kəmˈpætəbl] a 能共处的，相容的
To be honest, he was compatible with the lawyer.
老实说，他跟律师志趣相投。
🔵 harmonious 和谐的　🔵 incompatible 矛盾的
🔵 compatible with 与……和谐相处　🔵 be compatible with sb. 与某人志趣相投

0180 compensate ['kɑːmpenseɪt] v 补偿，抵消

The company has decided to compensate the customers for all their losses.
公司决定赔偿顾客们的所有损失。
- compensate for 赔偿
- compensate sb. for sth. 为了……而赔偿某人

语法重点
compensate sb. for sth. 句型中，for 后面接赔偿的原因，而不是赔偿的事物。

0181 compensation [ˌkɑːmpenˈseɪʃn] n 补偿，报酬

These injured employees gained subsidy as the compensation for their losses of office.
这些受伤的员工得到补助作为失去职位的补偿。
- do sth. as the compensation for... 做某事作为……的补偿
- loss of 表示"损失"，还可以表示"茫然的"。

0182 competence ['kɑːmpɪtəns] n 能力，胜任，称职

His supervisor could testify to his good communication competence.
他的主管能够证实他具有良好的沟通能力。
- incompetence 不称职
- core competence 核心竞争力
- testify to... 证明……

supervisor (P. 645)

0183 competent ['kɑːmpɪtənt] a 有能力的，应该做的

He was competent to manage the whole Marketing Department.
他有能力管理整个营销部门。
- capable 有能力的
- incapable 无能力的
- be competent for 胜任
- be competent to do sth. 有能力做某事

0184 compile [kəmˈpaɪl] v 收集，编辑

The researcher was trying to compile the report.
研究员在努力编制那份报告。
- be trying to do sth. 正在努力做某事
- compile 虽然可表示"编辑，编纂"，但是词典类的编辑一般用 compile 或 compiler，而报刊类的编辑用 edit 或 editor。

0185 complement ['kɒmplɪmənt] / ['kɑːmplɪment] n 补充物 v 补充

As a new employee, he needed a complement of this aspect.
作为一名新员工，他需要补充一下这方面的知识。

语法重点
need a complement of 后面通常接补充的对象。
aspect (P. 397)

0186 complexion [kəmˈplekʃn] n 气色，局面，性质

Actually, the color of her wedding dress went well with her complexion.
其实，她的结婚礼服的颜色很适合她的肤色。
- color 肤色
- go well with... 与……相配

语法重点
go well with 中的 go 需要根据内容进行相应的时态变化。

0187 complexity [kəm'pleksəti] n. 复杂，难懂
The principal was studying the complexity of this planning graph.
负责人正在研究这幅错综复杂的规划图。
- complicacy 复杂性
- brevity 简洁，简短

➔ graph (P. 725)

0188 complication [ˌkɑːmplɪ'keɪʃn] n. 复杂，混乱
The employees' suspicion was a complication to the new policy.
员工的猜疑是使新政策复杂化的一个因素。
- chaos 混乱
- simplification 简单化
- illness complication 并发症
- be a complication to... 是使……复杂的一个因素

➔ suspicion (P. 370)

0189 component [kəm'pounənt] n. 成分，组件
The maintainer said that this screw was not the component of the engine.
那名维修工说，这个螺丝不是这台发动机的零件。
- constituent 成分
- key component 主要组成部分
- be the component of... 是……的部件
- engine 泛指或大或小、简单或复杂的机械、机器，又可指产生动力的发动机，而 motor 通常指小型或轻型马达、发动机。

0190 comprehensive [ˌkɑːmprɪ'hensɪv] a. 广泛的，理解的
This employee handbook is a comprehensive guide to the company systems.
这本员工手册是介绍公司制度的一本全面指南。
- extensive 广泛的
- be a comprehensive guide to... 是……的全面指南

➔ employee (P. 290)

0191 comprise [kəm'praɪz] v. 由……构成
The interview team was comprised of the manager and the department head.
面试团队由经理和部门负责人构成。
- contain 包含
- exclude 排除
- be comprised of... 由……组成
- comprise 和 compose 都可表示"组成"：comprise 指整体是由几个独立的部分所组成，而 compose 多用被动语态，指将两个或两个以上的人或物放到一起形成一个整体。

0192 concede [kən'siːd] v. 承认，让步，认输
The president conceded the right to complaint to this employee.
总裁给予这名员工申诉的权利。
- confess 承认
- concede to 让步
- concede sth. to sb. 给予某人做某事的权利

0193 conceit [kən'siːt] n 自负，幻想，观点 v 幻想，理解

I had to say that the man was full of conceit.
我不得不说，那名男人十分自负。

- full of conceit 自高自大
- be full of conceit ……是自负的

0194 conception [kən'sepʃn] n 概念，构想，怀孕

The scientist has got a pretty strange conception of cooperation.
那名科学家对合作的见解很独特。

- notion 概念，想法
- artistic conception 意境
- ... have got a pretty strange conception of... 对……的见解很独特

语法重点
pretty 作副词，修饰 strange。

0195 concession [kən'seʃn] n 让步，妥协，优惠

We wouldn't make any concession to the other side before the negotiation came to an end.
谈判结束之前，我们不会向对方做出任何妥协。

- compromise 妥协
- intransigence 不妥协
- make a concession to sb. 向某人妥协

语法重点
make concession 中的 concession 之前可由 some, any 等词修饰。
- negotiation (P. 747)

0196 concise [kən'saɪs] a 简洁的，简要的

Tell the secretary to make this report concise and to the point.
告诉秘书把这份报告做得简明扼要一些。

- brief 简洁的
- redundant 多余的
- concise money 短期资金
- make sth. concise and to the point 使……简明扼要

0197 condense [kən'dens] v 压缩，精简，使更紧密

It's necessary to condense this long report into a brief summary.
需要将这份长篇报告简缩为一份摘要。

- compress 压缩
- condense into 把……压缩
- condense sth. into... 把某物缩短成……

- summary (P. 369)

0198 confer [kən'fɜːr] v 商议，授予

He was conferring the change of personnel with the general manager in the conference room.
他正在会议室里与总经理商议人事变动。

- consult 商议
- confer with 协商
- confer sth. with sb. 与某人商议某事

0199 confidential [ˌkɑːnfɪ'denʃl] a 秘密的，表示信任的

She said in a confidential tone, "it's time to clock off."
她悄悄说："该下班了。"

- secret 秘密的
- keep confidential 保密
- say in a confidential tone 悄悄说
- clock off 表示"打卡下班"，而"打卡上班"一般表示为 clock in。

691

0200 **conform** [kən'fɔːrm] v 遵守，顺从，相似
You'd better conform your marketing plan to the target.
你最好使自己的销售计划与目标相符。
- conform with 符合，与……一致
- conform... to sth. 使……与某物相符

0201 **confrontation** [ˌkɑːnfrən'teɪʃn] n 对抗，面对，遭遇
The assistant found that the manger was so infatuated with films about military confrontation.
助理发现经理居然对军事对峙电影非常着迷。
- military (P. 191)

0202 **congressman / congresswoman** ['kɑːŋɡrəsmən] / ['kɑːŋɡrəswʊmən] n 美国男 / 女众议员
He dared say that there's not much prospect of the man's being elected as a congressman.
他敢说，这名男子当选为国会议员的希望不大。

语法重点
congressman 的复数形式 congressmen；congresswoman 的复数形式 congresswomen。

0203 **conquest** ['kɑːŋkwest] n 征服，克服，战利品
The male colleague made a conquest of the secretary.
那名男同事赢得了秘书的芳心。
- capture 战利品
- alien conquest 外星人入侵
- make a conquest of sb. 赢得某人的芳心

语法重点
male 用于名词 colleague 之前表示性别。
- colleague (P. 545)

0204 **conscientious** [ˌkɑːnʃi'enʃəs] a 诚实的
She got praise from the manager because she was conscientious.
她由于办事认真而受到经理的表扬。
- earnest 认真的
- halfhearted 不认真的
- get praise from sb. 受到某人的赞扬

0205 **consensus** [kən'sensəs] n 共识
Each department reached a consensus on this issue.
各个部门就此问题达成共识。
- accordance 一致
- discordance 不一致
- reach a consensus 达成共识
- reach a consensus on... 就……达成共识

0206 **conservation** [ˌkɑːnsər'veɪʃn] n 保存，保护
You should be in conservation of the paper in the office.
在办公室里要注意节约用纸。
- preservation 保存
- be in conservation of... 节约……

0207 **consolation** [ˌkɑːnsə'leɪʃn] n 安慰，慰问
This employee was good at finding consolation in the work.
这名员工善于在工作中寻求安慰。
- comfort 安慰
- consolation money 抚恤金

语法重点
find consolation in（在……中寻求安慰）后面一般接名词。

0208 **conspiracy** [kənˈspɪrəsi] n 阴谋，反叛，共谋

These several employees admitted the conspiracy to reveal company secrets.
这几名员工承认他们共谋泄露公司机密。

- conspiracy theory 阴谋论
- admit the conspiracy to... 承认……的阴谋

语法重点
admit the conspiracy to 后面通常接动词原形，表示"共谋做某事"。

0209 **constituent** [kənˈstɪtʃuənt]
a 组成的，构成的 n 成分，选民

The researchers would extract the active constituent of coffee.
研究人员将会提取咖啡中的活性成分。

⊃ extract (P. 719)

0210 **consultation** [ˌkɑːnslˈteɪʃn] n 商议，商讨会，请教

This company would be in consultation with the WTO.
该公司将会与世界贸易组织进行磋商。

- counsel 商议
- be in consultation with... 与……磋商
- WTO 全称是 World Trade Organization，表示"世界贸易组织"。

0211 **consumption** [kənˈsʌmpʃn] n 消耗

This country planned to reduce consumption by putting the workers out of work.
这个国家打算通过使工人失业来降低消费。

- consumption tax 消费税
- reduce consumption by... 通过……来降低消费

0212 **contemplation** [ˌkɑːntəmˈpleɪʃn] n 沉思，意图

These new employees were lost in contemplation of the grand assembly room.
这些新员工被豪华的会议室深深吸引。

- under contemplation 规划中的
- be lost in contemplation of... 被……深深吸引

语法重点
be lost in contemplation of 的主语一般指人。

⊃ assembly (P. 397)

0213 **contestant** [kənˈtestənt] n 竞争者，参加竞赛者

My order is that all the contestants gather in the meeting room at once.
我命令所有参赛者马上到会议室集合。

- competitor 竞争者
- contestant name 参赛者姓名

0214 **contractor** [kənˈtræktər] n 立契约者，收缩物

The contractor would estimate for the reestablishment of the school.
那位承包商将会对学校的重建进行估价。

- general contractor 总承包人
- estimate for... 对……估价

⊃ estimate (P. 437)

0215 contradict [ˌkɑːntrəˈdɪkt] v 反驳
Honestly speaking, it's really saucy of you to contradict your parents.
老实说，你顶撞父母，真是无礼。
- deny 否认　- applaud 赞同　- contradict oneself 自相矛盾
- it's saucy of sb. to do sth. 某人做某事是无礼的
- contradict 指肯定地否认、反对或反驳某事，坚持相反的意见，deny 侧重否认意见或言论的真实性，尤指否定他人的指控或责难。

0216 contradiction [ˌkɑːntrəˈdɪkʃn] n 反驳
I heard that the assistant was in contradiction with the manager.
我听说助理与经理之间有矛盾。
- in contradiction to 与……矛盾　- be in contradiction with... 与……有矛盾

> 语法重点
> be in contradiction with 句型中，with 后面通常接表示人的名词或代词。

0217 controversial [ˌkɑːntrəˈvɜːrʃl] a 争论的，可疑的
Merger of enterprise is a highly controversial topic.
公司兼并是一个颇有争议的话题。
- disputed 有争议的　- unsuspicious 不怀疑的
- controversial issues 争议的问题

> 语法重点
> 在此句型中，highly 作副词修饰后面的形容词 controversial。

0218 controversy [ˈkɑːntrəvɜːrsi] n 争论
Her being elected as the secretary general was beyond controversy.
她当选为秘书长是无可争议的。
- debate 辩论　- sth. be beyond controversy ……无可争议

0219 conviction [kənˈvɪkʃn] n 定罪
The corporate juridical person has had his conviction set aside.
那位公司法人已经被撤销定罪。
- damningness 定罪　- acquittal 赦免

↪ corporate (P. 695)

0220 coordinate [kəʊˈɔːdɪneɪt] / [koʊˈɔːrdɪneɪt] v 协调 a 同等的
The president was willing to coordinate closely with the company.
总裁很乐意与那家公司密切合作。
- adjust 调整　- coordinate with 使协调，配合
- coordinate closely with... 与……密切合作

> 语法重点
> coordinate closely with 句型中，with 后面可以接人，也可以接团体或组织。

0221 cordial [ˈkɔːrdʒəl] a 热诚的
Luckily, they negotiated in a cordial atmosphere.
幸运的是，他们在亲切的气氛中进行协商。
- cordial service 服务周到
- do sth. in a cordial atmosphere 在亲切的气氛中做某事

0222 core [kɔːr] n 核心，中心部分

The manager was trying to get straight to the core of the problem.
经理正在试图了解问题的核心。

- center 中心
- at the core of 在……的中心
- get straight to... 了解……

> 语法重点
> get straight to 后面一般接名词。
> - straight (P. 228)

0223 corporate [ˈkɔːrpərət] a 法人的，全体的，公司的

At no time would they reveal the corporate secrets.
他们绝不会泄露公司机密。

- corporate culture 企业文化
- at no time would sb.... 某人绝不……

> 语法重点
> at no time 后面一般接倒装句。

0224 corps [kɔːr] n 军团，校友会

It's said that he was a member of the diplomatic corps.
据说，他是外交使团中的一员。

- corps of engineers 陆军工兵部队
- be a member of... 是……的一员

0225 corpse [kɔːrps] n 尸体

The Colonel wrapped the corpse of the soldier with a piece of cloth.
上校用一块布将这名军人的尸体包裹起来。

- ptoma 尸体
- wrap sb. / sth. with... 用……包裹某人 / 某物

> 语法重点
> a piece of 表示"一片，一块"，修饰不可数名词，表示复数概念时，需要将 piece 变为 pieces，如 two pieces of news。

0226 correspondent [ˌkɔːrəˈspɑːndənt]
n 通信者 a 相应的，一致的

The negotiation result was correspondent with their expectation.
这个谈判结果与他们预料的一致。

- special correspondent 特派员
- be correspondent with... 与……相一致
- expectation 和 hope 都可"期望，指望"：expectation 指期待某事发生或假设某事能发生，多含揣想的意味，而 hope 通常指建立在愿望基础上的期待，这种期待可能发生或实现，但也可能不会实现。

0227 corruption [kəˈrʌpʃn] n 堕落，贪污，讹误

It must be pointed out that enterprise corruption is inadvisable.
必须指出企业贪污是不可取的。

- crime of corruption 贪污罪

> 语法重点
> it must be pointed out that（必须指出）句型是"it + 动词（短语）的被动式 + that 从句"结构的具体应用。

0228 cosmetic [kɑːzˈmetɪk] a 化妆品的 n 装饰品，化妆品

It's only a cosmetic measure to hold press conference.
召开记者会只是一种装饰门面的措施。

- decoration 装饰品
- cosmetic defect 外观不良

> 语法重点
> it's only a cosmetic measure 后面可以接动词不定式。
> - measure (P. 470)

0229 cosmopolitan [ˌkaːzməˈpaːlɪtən]
a 世界性的，四海为家的 **n** 世界主义者

The World Exposition would be held in this cosmopolitan city.
世博会将会在这个国际都市举行。
- worldwide 全世界的
- regional 地区的
- be held in... 在……举行

0230 counterpart [ˈkaʊntərpaːrt] **n** 极相像的人或物

In this company, operation department is the counterpart of sales department.
在这家公司，营运部就相当于销售部。
- be the counterpart of... 相当于……

→ operation (P. 479)

0231 coverage [ˈkʌvərɪdʒ] **n** 覆盖，覆盖范围

There's little coverage of insurance coverage in this contract.
这份合约里几乎没有保险责任范围。
- decken 覆盖
- media coverage 媒体报道
- there's little coverage of... 几乎没有……
- insurance coverage 表示"保险责任范围"，是常用的保险用语。

0232 covet [ˈkʌvət] **v** 垂涎

Most employees thought that it's a sin to covet.
多数员工认为，贪得无厌是一种罪过。
- desired 渴望的
- it's a sin to... ……是一种犯罪

【语法重点】
it's a sin to 后面通常接动词原形。

0233 cramp [kræmp]
n 抽筋，绞痛 **v** 使痉挛，使扫兴 **a** 狭窄的

My girlfriend couldn't move because she got cramp in her left leg.
我的女朋友不能动是因为她的左腿抽筋了。

【语法重点】
get cramp in（抽筋）后面一般接身体部位。

0234 credibility [ˌkredəˈbɪləti] **n** 可信度，确实性

This employee has gained credibility with the president.
这名员工已经获得总裁的信任。
- gain credibility with... 获得……的信任

0235 credible [ˈkredəbl] **a** 可信的

The manager's demission seemed credible to most of the employees.
经理的离职在大多数员工看来是可信的。
- believable 可信的
- unreliable 不可靠的
- credible information 可靠消息
- seem credible to sb. 在某人看来是可信的

0236 **criterion** [kraɪˈtɪriən] n 标准，准则

Remember that it is the only authorized evaluation criterion.
记住，这是唯一被认可的评估准则。
- standard 标准
- evaluation criterion 评估标准

> 语法重点
> remember that 是一个祈使句型，表示命令或要求。
> evaluation (P. 437)

0237 **crook** [krʊk] n 弯曲，骗子 v 使弯曲 a 不正当的

The salesman was a crook and I demanded an apology from him.
那个推销员是一个骗子，我要求他向我认错。
- demand an apology from sb. 要求某人认错

0238 **crooked** [ˈkrʊkɪd] a 弯曲的，歪扭的

It's strange that he kept on giving me a crooked grin.
奇怪的是，他不停地对我歪斜着嘴笑。

0239 **crucial** [ˈkruːʃl] a 关系重大的

The customers' trust is crucial to the company.
顾客的信任对于公司来说至关重要。
- critical 关键的
- crucial error 关键纰漏

> 语法重点
> be crucial to（对……至关重要）后面一般接名词或代词。

0240 **crude** [kruːd] a 天然的，粗糙的

The malevolent leader actually gave a crude caricature of the fact.
那个心术不正的领导者居然歪曲事实。
- crude oil 原油

> 语法重点
> give a crude caricature of 后面一般接表示事物的名词或代词。

0241 **cruise** [kruːz] v 巡航，漫游 n 巡逻，游览

All the member will go on a cruise to Paris next month.
全体成员将于下个月搭船去巴黎。
- range 漫游
- go on a cruise to... 乘船去……

0242 **cruiser** [ˈkruːzər] n 游艇，巡洋舰，警察巡逻车

The cruiser that the reporters took was knifing through the sea.
记者们乘坐的观光游艇正穿过大海。
- knife through... 穿过……

0243 **crumb** [krʌm] n 小块 v 捏碎，裹上面包屑用油煎

My only crumb of comfort is that the boss offers me a high salary.
唯一值得我安慰的是，老板给我的工资很高。
- bread crumb 面包碎屑
- my only crumb of comfort is that... 唯一值得我安慰的是，……

> salary (P. 500)

0244 crumble ['krʌmbl] v 粉碎，崩溃，瓦解

Due to economic downturn, this small enterprise finally crumbled to dust.
由于经济不景气，这家小型企业最终倒闭了。
- disintegrate 瓦解
- crumble to dust ……化为乌有

0245 crust [krʌst] n 面包皮，硬外皮

The slothful employee had the crust to ask for salary increase.
那名懒散的员工居然有脸要求加薪。
- continental crust 大陆地壳
- have the crust to... 在做……上厚颜无耻

语法重点
have the crust to 后面通常接动词原形

0246 cultivate ['kʌltɪveɪt] v 培养

The students should cultivate the good habit of conscientiousness and diligence.
学生要养成认真勤奋的优良习惯。
- foster 培养
- cultivate talents 培养人才
- cultivate the habit of... 培养……的习惯

diligence (P. 426)

0247 cumulative ['kjuːmjəleɪtɪv] a 累积的，渐增的

The stepmother's rigor would have a cumulative effect on the child.
继母的苛刻会逐渐对小孩产生影响。
- accumulated 累积的
- decrescent 渐减的
- have a cumulative effect on... 对……逐渐产生影响

0248 customary ['kʌstəməri] a 习惯上的，合乎习俗的

It's customary with him to wear a suit when attending business dinner.
他习惯在出席商业宴会时穿西服。
- usual 通常的
- it's customary with sb. to do sth. 做某事是某人的习惯

0249 daffodil ['dæfədɪl] n 黄水仙，鲜黄色 a 淡黄色的

The potted flower on the table was something in the nature of daffodil.
桌上的那盆花有点儿像水仙。
- be something in the nature of... 有点儿像……

0250 dandruff ['dændrʌf] n 头皮屑，头垢

The dandruff on the job hunter's head left a bad impression on the interviewer.
那名求职者头上的头皮屑给面试官留下不好的影响。
- dandruff remover shampoo 去头皮屑洗发水
- leave an impression on sb. 给某人留下印象
- interviewer 表示"主持面试的人"，其反义词是 interviewee，表示"被面试的人"。

hunter (P. 177)

0251 daybreak ['deɪbreɪk] n 黎明

The man was routed out of bed by the phone call from his mother before daybreak.
天还没亮，这名男子就被他妈妈打来的电话叫起来了。
- dawn 拂晓
- at daybreak 天亮时

0252 deadly ['dedli] a 致命的，非常有效的 ad 极其

The shock resulted from negotiation failure was deadly to the company.
谈判失败给公司造成了致命打击。
- fatal 致命的
- deadly poison 致命毒药
- be deadly to... 对……是致命的

> failure (P. 163)

0253 decent ['diːsnt] a 端正的

It is not decent to have a casual wear in the meeting.
开会时穿便服是不得体的。
- proper 正派的
- indecent 下流的
- decent job 体面的工作
- it is not decent to... ……是不得体的

0254 decisive [dɪ'saɪsɪv] a 决定性的，坚定的，果断的

Benefit maximization was a decisive factor in negotiating.
利益最大化是谈判的决定性因素。
- definitive 决定性的
- indecisive 优柔寡断的
- decisive battle 决战
- ... be a decisive factor in doing sth. ……是做某事的决定性因素

> benefit (P. 262)

0255 decline [dɪ'klaɪn] v 下降，拒绝 n 衰微，晚年

The female sales agent declined to have dinner with the client.
那位女业务代表拒绝与客户共进晚餐。
- refuse 拒绝
- accept 接受
- decline stage 衰退期
- sb. declines to do... 某人拒绝……
- decline 和 reject 都可表示"拒绝"：decline 指婉言谢绝他人的帮助或邀请等，而 reject 多指由于某物（事、行为）不能让人满意而被当面直截了当地拒绝。

0256 dedicate ['dedɪkeɪt] v 以……奉献

This scientist dedicated his life to the mechanical research.
这位科学家毕生致力于机械研究。
- devote 奉献
- dedicate to 专心从事
- dedicate one's life to... 献身于……

> 语法重点
> dedicate one's life to 后面通常接名词或代词。

0257 dedication [ˌdedɪ'keɪʃn] n 奉献，献身精神

In no case should the employees abandon professional dedication.
员工们绝不能丢弃敬业精神。
- professional dedication 敬业精神
- in no case should sb. ... 某人绝不

> 语法重点
> in no case 位于句首时，引起的倒装通常为部分倒装。
> professional (P. 489)

能……

0258 deem [di:m] v 认为，视为，主张
Some employees deemed it wise to take shift leave.
部分员工认为轮班休假是明智的。
🔗 deem highly of 高度评价 🔗 deem it... to do sth. 认为做某事为……的

0259 defect [ˈdiːfekt] n 缺陷 v 叛逃，背叛
We couldn't ignore the defect in the company system.
我们无法忽视公司制度的缺陷。
🔗 congenital defect 先天性缺陷

语法重点
the defect in 后面一般接名词或代词。
👉 ignore (P. 177)

0260 deficiency [dɪˈfɪʃnsi] n 不足，缺点，缺陷
On no condition would the principal find the deficiency of this scheme.
负责人绝不会发现这个方案的缺陷。
🔗 shortage 缺乏 🔗 enough 充足

语法重点
on no condition 位于句首时，所引起的倒装句通常为部分倒装。

0261 degrade [dɪˈɡreɪd] v 降级，使丢脸
Don't degrade yourself by cooperating with the small company.
不要跟那家小公司合作来自贬身份。
🔗 downgrade 使降级 🔗 promote 晋升 🔗 degrade yourself 贬低自己
🔗 don't degrade yourself by... 不要……而自贬身份

0262 deliberate [dɪˈlɪbərət]
a 深思熟虑的，慎重的 v 权衡，熟虑
Several department managers were deliberating on the corporate affairs.
几位部门经理正在商议公司事务。
🔗 intentional 故意的 🔗 hasty 轻率的 🔗 deliberate on... 商议……

👉 corporate (P. 695)

0263 delinquent [dɪˈlɪŋkwənt]
n 违法者 a 拖欠债务的，不尽责的
The small company was usually delinquent in paying its payment for goods.
那家小公司经常拖欠货款。
🔗 derelict 玩忽职守者 🔗 be delinquent in... 拖欠……

0264 denounce [dɪˈnaʊns] v 指责，正式指控，告发
The accountant denounced this company to the tax bureau.
那名会计向税务局告发了这家公司。
🔗 denounce sb. for... 因……谴责某人 🔗 denounce... to... 向……告发

语法重点
denounce... to 后面通常接名词。

700

0265 **density** ['densəti] n 浓密，浓度，愚钝

As the biggest sales market, this area has a high population density.
作为最大的销售市场，这个地区的人口密度很高。
population density 人口密度

⊕ population (P. 206)

0266 **dental** ['dentl] a 牙齿的，牙科的 n 齿音

A medicine salesman had looked into this dental clinic.
一位药品推销员对这家牙科诊所进行调查。
dental braces 牙套　look into... 调查……

0267 **depict** [dɪ'pɪkt] v 描述

Rules for the operation were depicted to a nicety by him.
操作规则被他描述得非常详细。
describe 描绘　depict... as... 把……描绘成……

0268 **deprive** [dɪ'praɪv] v 剥夺，夺去

Many casual laborers are deprived of the right to take vacations.
很多临时工被剥夺休假的权利。
deprive of 剥夺，失去　be deprived of... 被剥夺了……

0269 **derive** [dɪ'raɪv] v 衍生出，源于，提取

Some employees reflected that they could derive pleasure from their work.
一些员工反映他们能够从工作中获得快乐。
acquire 获得　derive from 来自　derive sth. from... 从……中获得某物

⊕ pleasure (P. 205)

0270 **deputy** ['depjuti] n 代表 a 副的，代理的

I heard that the deputy manager was the virtual head of the restaurant.
我听说副经理是那家餐厅的实际负责人。
deputy chief 副局长　be the virtual head of... 是……的实际负责人

0271 **descend** [dɪ'send] v 下降，遗传，屈尊

This afternoon, some investment counselors descended on the manager.
今天下午，一些投资顾问突然来访问经理。
drop 下降　ascend 上升，攀登
descend from 由……传下来的　descend on sb. 突然访问某人

⊕ counselor (P. 552)

0272 **descendant** [dɪ'sendənt] n 子孙 a 下降的，祖传的

This gear design was the descendant of the mechanical device.
这个齿轮设计是那个机械装置的衍生物。
offspring 后代　forefather 祖先　be a descendant of... 是……的衍生物

0273 descent [dɪ'sent] n 下降，倾斜，血统
All the shareholders in this company are of Asian descent.
这家公司的所有股东都是亚洲血统。
- blood 血统　- ascent 上升　- be of good descent 出身好

语法重点
be of... descent（出身……）句型中，of 后面通常接形容词来修饰名词 descent。

0274 designate ['dezɪgneɪt] v 指定 a 指定的，选定的
The secretary was designated to make an appointment with the client.
秘书被指派和客户约见面。
- appoint 任命　- designate as 指派为
- be designated to do sth. 被指派做某事

0275 destined ['destɪnd] a 命运注定的，前往的
This impractical investment plan was destined to fail.
这个不切实际的投资方案注定会失败。
- predestined 注定的　- destined to 注定

语法重点
destined 表示"命中注定的"时，后面接 to (do) sth.；表示"前往的"时，后面接介词 for。

0276 detach [dɪ'tætʃ] v 派遣，分开
Taking vacations could make the employees detach themselves from the work pressure.
休假能够使员工从工作压力中解放出来。
- detach from 从……分离　- detach oneself from sth. 使某人从某事中解放出来

语法重点
detach oneself from sth. 中，oneself 可以变换为不同的人称。
- pressure (P. 341)

0277 detain [dɪ'teɪn] v 阻止，耽搁，拘留
The police was instructed to detain the principal of this law office.
警察奉命拘留这家律师事务所的负责人。
- hold 拘留　- free 释放　- be instructed to do sth. 被命令做某事

0278 deter [dɪ'tɜːr] v 使断念
She deterred her boyfriend from tearing up these letters.
她阻止男朋友撕毁这些信件。
- deter from 防止　- deter sb. from doing sth. 阻止某人做某事

0279 deteriorate [dɪ'tɪriəreɪt] v 恶化，变坏
It was pathetic to watch the company's condition increasingly deteriorate.
看到公司局势日益恶化，真是可怜。
- degenerate 恶化　- deteriorate further 进一步恶化

语法重点
it was pathetic to（很可怜）后面一般接动词原形。

0280 devalue [ˌdiː'væljuː] v 使贬值，降低（某事物）的价值
It's unfair to devalue other colleagues' work at discretion.
随意贬低其他同事的工作是不公平的。
- depreciate 贬值　- appreciate 增值，涨价
- devalue the currency 货币贬值

语法重点
it's unfair to（不公平）后面通常接动词原形。

0281 **diabetes** [ˌdaɪəˈbiːtiːz] n 糖尿病，多尿症

He retired after he was diagnosed as diabetes.
被诊断患有糖尿病之后，他就退休了。

> 语法重点
> be diagnosed as（被诊断为……）后面通常接表示疾病的名词。
> ↪ diagnose (P. 703)

0282 **diagnose** [ˌdaɪəgˈnoʊs] v 诊断，判断

This employee got fired because he was diagnosed with schizophrenia.
这名员工被辞退了，因为他被诊断患有精神分裂。

- diagnose as 诊断为
- be diagnosed with... 被诊断罹患……
- get fired 是一个固定搭配，表示"被解雇"。

0283 **diagnosis** [ˌdaɪəgˈnoʊsɪs] n 诊断，调查分析

The president planned to have a second test to confirm the diagnosis this afternoon.
总裁准备今天下午去复查以确诊。

> 语法重点
> have a second test to 后面一般接动词原形。

- accurate diagnosis 确诊
- have a second test to... 复查……

0284 **diagram** [ˈdaɪəgræm] n 图表，图解 v 用图表示

The assistant said that on the back of the fax was a process flow diagram.
助理说传真的背面是一张加工流程图。

> ↪ process (P. 342)

- chart 图表
- flow diagram 流程图
- on the back of... is... ……的背后是……

- diagram 和 illustration 都可表示"画，图"：diagram 多指科技书籍或文献中具有概括解说作用的图表或图样，而 illustration 指插入书页之间，帮助说明的任何插图或图解。

0285 **diameter** [daɪˈæmɪtər] n 直径

The engineer said that this wheel had a diameter of one meter.
那名工程师说，这个轮子的直径是一米。

- radius 半径
- inside diameter 内径
- have a diameter of... 的直径是……

0286 **dictate** [ˈdɪkteɪt] v 听写，控制，支配

I remembered that the manager dictated a notice to the assistant.
我记得经理向助理口授了一项通知。

> 语法重点
> dictate... to 句型中，to 后面通常接名词或代词。

- dictate to sb. 命令，向……口授

0287 **dictation** [dɪkˈteɪʃn] n 口述，听写，命令

The manager thought highly of her because she was adept in taking dictation.
经理很器重她，因为她善于记录命令。

> 语法重点
> be adept in（善于）后面可以接名词或动名词。

0288 **dictator** [ˈdɪkteɪtər] n 独裁者，发号施令者

The principal was a dictator, so we felt impotent to resist him.

那名负责人是一个独裁者，我们无力反抗他。

- autocrat 独裁者
- feel impotent to... 感到无力……

语法重点
feel impotent to 后面通常接动词原形。
→ principal (P. 209)

0289 **differentiate** [ˌdɪfəˈrenʃieɪt] v 辨别

Many employees couldn't differentiate between job responsibility and job description.

很多员工无法区分工作职责和工作说明。

- distinguish 区别
- differentiate... from... 将……区别开来
- sb. couldn't differentiate between... and... 某人无法区分……与……

→ description (P. 282)

0290 **dilemma** [dɪˈlemə] n 窘境，进退两难

The order from the president made the Minister in a dilemma.

总统的命令使部长左右为难。

- predicament 窘况
- ethical dilemma 道德困境
- make sb. in a dilemma 让某人处于进退两难的境地（左右为难）

0291 **dimension** [daɪˈmenʃn] n 尺寸，面积

The shareholders were talking about the dimension of the new corporation.

股东们在讨论新公司的规模。

- measurement 尺寸
- two dimension 二维
- talk about... 讨论……

0292 **diminish** [dɪˈmɪnɪʃ] v 缩小，降低

You must do all you can to diminish the cost of production.

你们必须尽力减少生产成本。

- reduce 降低
- increase 加大
- diminish inflammation 消炎

语法重点
you must do all you can to（你们必须尽力）后面接动词原形。

0293 **diplomacy** [dɪˈploʊməsi] n 外交，外交手腕

The president didn't support the viewpoint that international trade problems should be solved by diplomacy.

总裁不支持这个观点，即国际贸易问题应该通过外交途径来解决。

- support the viewpoint that... 支持……的观点

0294 **diplomatic** [ˌdɪpləˈmætɪk] a 外交的，有手腕的

This diplomat was renowned for his extensive diplomatic relations.

这位外交官因其广泛的外交关系而出名。

- diplomatic immunity 外交豁免权
- be renowned for... 因……而出名

→ extensive (P. 565)

0295 **directory** [dəˈrektəri] n 号码簿

All the customers' names and phone numbers have been listed in the telephone directory.
所有顾客的名字和电话号码已经被列在电话簿上了。
- directory inquiries 地址簿　- be listed in... 在……列出

0296 **disability** [ˌdɪsəˈbɪləti] n 无能，无资格

The company finally decided to come to terms with this applicant with physical disability.
公司最终决定接受这名残疾求职者。
- disablement 无能　- ability 能力　- physical disability 肢体残疾
- come to terms with... 接受……

> applicant (P. 395)

0297 **disable** [dɪsˈeɪbl] v 使……无能，使伤残

Violent collisions disabled this printer from working.
剧烈的碰撞使这台打印机无法工作了。
- cripple 使残废　- disable from 使……不能做

> **语法重点**
> disable sb. / sth. from（使某人 / 某物不能……）后面通常接动名词。
>
> collision (P. 687)

0298 **disapprove** [ˌdɪsəˈpruːv] v 反对

The department manager disapproved of this budget proposal.
部门主管不赞成这项预算草案。
- disfavor 不赞成　- approve 赞成　- disapprove of 不赞成
- sb. disapproves of... 某人不赞成……

0299 **disastrous** [dɪˈzæstrəs] a 灾害的，破坏性的

The failure of the investment plan was nothing to him in comparison with the disastrous consequence.
与那个灾难性的结果相比，投资计划失败对他来说并不算什么。
- disastrous result 灾难性的结果
- ... be nothing to sb. in comparison with... 与……相比，……对某人不算什么

0300 **discharge** [dɪsˈtʃɑːrdʒ] v 排出，放电 n 释放

Yesterday the employee was discharged from the company.
昨天那名员工被批准离开公司。

> **语法重点**
> be discharged from（批准离开……）中，from 后面通常接名词或代词。

0301 **disciplinary** [ˌdɪsəˈplɪnəri]

a 纪律的，执行纪律的，惩戒性的

Whoever breaks the rules of the school deserves disciplinary treatment.
不管谁违反学校规定，都要受到纪律处分。
- disciplinary punishment 纪律处分
- whoever... deserves... 不管谁……，都要受到……

> **语法重点**
> whoever 引导从句时，从句的动词不能用将来时或进行时，且从句的位置较为灵活。

705

0302 disclose [dɪsˈkloʊz] v 透露，透漏
The leader wouldn't disclose details of the negotiation.
那名领导人不会透露谈判的细节。
- reveal 揭露 - conceal 隐瞒 - disclose information 泄露信息
- disclose details of... 透露……的细节

⊕ detail (P. 283)

0303 disclosure [dɪsˈkloʊʒər] n 透露，被公开的秘密
This accountant received punishment for disclosure of financial information.
这名会计因透露财务资讯而受到处罚。
- exposure 揭露 - disclosure of... 披露/透露……

0304 discomfort [dɪsˈkʌmfərt] n 不安 v 使……不安，使苦恼
The manager's anger caused his discomfort.
经理的怒气令他感到不安。
- trouble 烦恼 - physical discomfort 身体不适

语法重点
cause one's discomfort（令某人感到不安）中的 one's 可以指代各种人称。

0305 discreet [dɪˈskriːt] a 谨慎的，小心的
Every shareholder was discreet about the investment decision.
每一位股东都对投资决策守口如瓶。
- cautious 谨慎的 - be discreet in 对……谨慎
- be discreet about... 对……守口如瓶

0306 discrimination [dɪˌskrɪmɪˈneɪʃn] n 歧视，区别，辨别
She was exempt from gender discrimination when applying.
在应聘时，她没有遭受性别歧视。
- prejudice 偏见 - racial discrimination 种族歧视
- be exempt from... 被免于……

⊕ gender (P. 572)

0307 disgrace [dɪsˈɡreɪs] n 不名誉 v 使丢脸，贬黜
On behalf of the company, you couldn't bring disgrace on it.
作为公司的代表，你不能给公司丢脸。
- shame 使丢脸 - in disgrace 失宠，丢脸
- bring disgrace on... ……给……带来耻辱
- disgrace 侧重在别人，尤其在众人面前丢脸，而 shame 指由不光彩或不道德的行为引起的惭愧感或羞耻感。

0308 disgraceful [dɪsˈɡreɪsfl] a 可耻的，丢脸的
It's disgraceful that you slandered your colleague for promotion.
你为了获得晋升而诋毁同事，真是可耻。
- shameful 可耻的 - disgraceful conduct 可耻行为
- it's disgraceful that... ……是可耻的

disclose ~ displease

0309 dismantle [dɪsˈmæntl] v 拆开，废除，取消
The worker asked for help to dismantle the engine.
这名工人为了拆除发动机而寻求帮助。
- disassemble 拆开 - assemble 装配
- ask for help to do sth. ……求助做某事

0310 dismay [dɪsˈmeɪ] v 使沮丧，使气馁 n 失望，气馁
The department manager was dismayed by these emergency situations.
部门经理被这些突发状况搞得焦虑不安。
- disappointment 失望 - in dismay 沮丧地

> **语法重点**
> be dismayed by（被……弄得焦虑不安）后面通常接不好的事情。

0311 dispatch [dɪˈspætʃ] n 派遣，急件 v 派遣，分派
Under the direction of the manager, the assistant solved these problems with dispatch.
在经理的指导下，助理迅速处理这些问题。

0312 dispensable [dɪˈspensəbl] a 非必要的，可有可无的
The president looked on publicity department as dispensable.
总裁认为宣传部可有可无。
- needless 不必要的 - necessary 必要的
- sb. looks on... as... 某人认为……怎么样

- publicity (P. 491)

0313 disperse [dɪˈspɜːrs] v 解散
The safeguards in the department store were making an attempt at dispersing the crowd.
百货公司的警卫正试图驱散人群。
- spread 散开 - gather 聚集

> **语法重点**
> make an attempt at（试图）后面可以接名词、代词或动名词。
> - safeguard (P. 773)

0314 displace [dɪsˈpleɪs] v 替代，使离开原位
This new employee would displace her as the researcher.
这名新员工将取代她当研究员。
- supplant 代替 - displace oneself 移置
- displace... as... 取代……来作为……
- displace 常用来指用某物挤掉某物，内含强迫之意，但并不意味着原先之物已完全丧失作用。

0315 displease [dɪsˈpliːz] v 得罪
The fact that he was demoted displeased him.
被降职的事实让他感到很生气。
- be displeased at... 对……感到不快
- the fact that... displeases sb. ……的事实让某人生气

707

0316 disposable [dɪˈspoʊzəbl]
a 用完即丢弃的，可供使用的
This investment plan was only aimed at people with disposable income.
这项投资计划仅针对那些有可支配收入的人。
反 reusable 可重复使用的　　同 disposable chopsticks 卫生筷
片 be aimed at... 旨在……

> **语法重点**
> be aimed at 后面可以接名词或动名词。
> 参 income (P. 178)

0317 disposal [dɪˈspoʊzl] **n** 处理，处置，布置
You can have the waste paper at your disposal.
你可以随意使用这些废纸。
同 arrangement 布置　　同 have sth. at one's disposal ……供某人支配

0318 disregard [ˌdɪsrɪˈɡɑːrd] **v** 不理会，漠视　**n** 忽视，漠视
In disregard of my advice, he was determined to resign.
他无视我的劝告，执意要辞职。
同 ignore 不理睬　　反 regard 注重　　同 disregard of 不顾
片 in disregard of..., sb.... 不顾……，某人……

0319 dissident [ˈdɪsɪdənt] **a** 有异议的　**n** 持异议者
The president gave the order that all the dissidents should be cast out from the company.
总裁命令说，所有持异议者都要被驱逐出公司。
片 be cast out from... 被驱逐出……

0320 dissolve [dɪˈzɑːlv] **v** 使溶解，解散
Almost all the shareholders dissolved in laughter when hearing the good news of participation in profit.
听到分红的好消息，几乎所有的股东都情不自禁地笑了起来。

参 participation (P. 481)

0321 dissuade [dɪˈsweɪd] **v** 劝阻，劝止，劝诫
The manager dissuaded him from being of two minds at work.
经理劝他不要在工作中三心二意。
反 encourage 鼓励　　同 dissuade from 劝阻
片 dissuade sb. from doing sth. 劝某人不要做某事

0322 distort [dɪˈstɔːrt] **v** 曲解，使变形
He deliberately distorted reality in order to catch the supervisor's attention.
为了引起上司的注意，他故意歪曲事实。
同 misrepresent 歪曲　　同 distort a statement 曲解事实
片 catch one's attention 引起某人的注意

参 reality (P. 213)

disposable ~ diversion

0323 distract [dɪˈstrækt] v 转移

Chatting to make friends distracted him from work.
聊天交友使他在工作时分心。
- disturb 打扰
- distract one's attention 分散某人注意力
- sth. distract sb. from... 某物使某人在……上分心

语法重点
make friends 表示"交朋友"，且 friends 要为复数形式。

0324 distraction [dɪˈstrækʃn] n 分心

He kept silent at work only because he had no desire for distraction.
他在工作时不说话只是因为不想分心。
- concentration 专心，集中
- with distraction 心不在焉地

语法重点
have no desire for（不想）后面通常接名词。

0325 distrust [dɪsˈtrʌst] v 不信任，怀疑 n 不信任

You are familiar with the department supervisor, so you have no reason to distrust him.
你了解那位部门主管，所以没有理由不相信他。
- doubt 怀疑
- trust 信任
- with distrust 疑惑地
- have no reason to do sth. 没有理由做某事

0326 disturbance [dɪˈstɜːrbəns] n 扰乱，混乱，烦恼

He wanted to finish this business plan without any disturbance.
他想不受任何干扰地完成这份商业计划书。
- uneasiness 担忧
- do sth. without disturbance 不受干扰做某事

0327 diverse [daɪˈvɜːrs] a 不同的，各式各样的

This business party was a composite of the leaders from diverse industries.
这个商业聚会汇集来自不同行业的领导人物。
- different 不同的
- a diverse range of 各式各样的

语法重点
be a composite of（汇集了）后面通常接名词。

0328 diversify [daɪˈvɜːrsɪfaɪ]
v 使……多样化，进入新的商业领域

The manufacturers were encouraged to diversify into new products.
制造商们被鼓励实现产品多样化。
- simplification 简单化
- diversify one's interests 培养多方面兴趣

语法重点
be encouraged to do sth.（被鼓励做某事）的主语一般指人。
☞ encourage (P. 159)

0329 diversion [daɪˈvɜːrʒn] n 转换，转向，消遣

The manager's talk created a diversion of the employees' attention.
经理的讲话分散了员工们的注意力。
- distraction 分心
- create a diversion of... 分散……

709

0330 diversity [daɪˈvɜːrsəti] n 不同点

There is no diversity between these two business proposals.
这两份商业计划书没有差异。
- unicity 单一性
- species diversity 物种多样性
- there is no diversity between... ……之间没有差异

0331 divert [daɪˈvɜːrt] v 使转向，转移

The supervisor wanted to divert the attention of the employees from the vacation.
主管想把员工的注意力从休假上转移开。
- distract 转移
- divert from 转移
- divert attention of sb. from... 把某人的注意力从……上转移开来

vacation (P. 242)

0332 doctrine [ˈdɑːktrɪn] n 教义，教条，主义

The students have no interest in the doctrine of surplus value.
学生们对剩余价值学说不感兴趣。
- belief 教义
- have no interest in... 对……不感兴趣

0333 documentary [ˌdɑːkjuˈmentri]
n 纪录片 a 记录的，文书的

The foreign trade corporation agreed to make payment against documentary draft.
那家外贸公司同意凭跟单汇票付款。
- documentary film 纪录片
- make payment against... 凭……付款

draft (P. 430)

0334 dome [doʊm] n 圆屋顶，圆顶房，穹顶

I have to tell you a truth that my work room is just under the dome of the building.
我不得不告诉你一个事实，就是我的工作室就在那座建筑物的圆顶之下。
- I have to tell you a truth that... 我不得不告诉你一个事实……

0335 donate [ˈdoʊneɪt] v 捐赠，赠送

This transnational corporation donates money to the charity every year.
这家跨国公司每年都为慈善事业捐款。
- donate money 捐款
- donate money to... 为……捐款

语法重点
donate money to 后面通常接表示人或团体组织的名词。

0336 donation [doʊˈneɪʃn] n 捐赠之物

Every employee in the company made donation to the charity.
公司的每一位职员都向慈善事业进行捐赠。
- endowment 捐赠
- blood donation 捐血
- make donations to... 向……捐赠

语法重点
make donation of 也表示"捐赠"，但 of 后面要接所捐赠的物品，如 make donation of money 表示"捐钱"。

0337 donor ['doʊnər] n 捐赠人

The company had no way of confirming which employee was the donor.
公司没办法确定哪一名员工是捐赠人。
- contributor 捐助者
- have no way of... 没办法……

语法重点
have no way of 后面通常接动词名词，表示"没办法做某事"。
⊃ confirm (P. 143)

0338 doom [duːm] n 厄运 v 注定，命定

This impractical investment plan was doomed to fail.
这项不切实际的投资计划注定要失败。
- doom to 使遭受……的厄运

语法重点
be doomed to 后面可以接动词原形，表示"注定发生某事"。

0339 dosage ['doʊsɪdʒ] n 药量，服法，配药

I hear excessive dosage of that drug resulted in injury to the boss's liver.
我听说老板过量服用那种药，肝脏受到了损害。
- dose 剂量
- result in injury to... 对……造成了伤害

语法重点
excessive dosage of 后面通常接名词。
⊃ excessive (P. 717)

0340 drastic ['dræstɪk] a 猛烈的

Drastic measures were needed by the president to run the company.
总裁需要采取严厉措施来治理公司。
- severe 严厉的
- mild 温和的
- drastic action 剧烈反应

语法重点
be needed by（被……所需要）的主语一般是指物的名词或代词。

0341 drawback ['drɔːbæk] n 撤回，缺点，不利条件

The only drawback to this proposal is the high cost.
这项提议的唯一缺点是成本过高。
- shortcoming 缺点
- strength 优点

0342 dreary ['drɪri] a 沉闷的，枯燥的，乏味的

It's said that she has had a dreary day of it.
据说她已经为此生了一天闷气。
- tedious 沉闷的
- dreary job 枯燥的工作

0343 drizzle ['drɪzl] n 毛毛雨 v 下毛毛雨

We didn't pay a visit to the workshop because it drizzled off and on all day.
我们没有去工作室参观，是因为一整天都下着毛毛雨。
- downpour 大雨
- breeze and drizzle 微风细雨
- do sth.... off and on ……断断续续地做某事

0344 drought [draʊt] n 干旱，旱灾

The foundation turned its attention to the drought area.
基金会把注意力转向干旱地区。
- flood 洪涝
- drought resistance 抗旱性

语法重点
turn one's attention to（把注意力转向）后面一般接名词。

0345 dual ['du:əl] a 成双的，两重的
This young man had dual role as manager and shareholder.
这个年轻人有经理和股东的双重身份。
- double 双重的   - single 单一的   - have dual role as... 有……的双重身份

> 语法重点
> have dual role as 中，as 后面一般接表示职位或头衔的名词。

0346 dubious ['du:biəs] a 半信半疑的，犹豫不决的
The committee members were dubious about this corporate reform.
委员们对这次公司改革心存疑虑。
- uncertain 迟疑不决的   - be dubious of 对……表示怀疑
- be dubious about... 对……表示怀疑

- committee (P. 275)

0347 dynamite ['daɪnəmaɪt]
n 炸药，具有爆炸性的事物 v 破坏 a 极好的
What was astounding was that the cargo ship was blown up with dynamite.
令人震惊的是，那艘货船被炸药炸毁了。
- explosive 炸药   - be blown up with... 被……炸毁

0348 ebb [eb] n 退潮，衰退 v 跌落，减少
At present, his career was still at a low ebb.
目前，他的事业还处于低潮期。
- lessen 减少   - flow 涨潮   - ebb tide 退潮
- be at a low ebb ……处于低潮，衰败

> 语法重点
> at present 修饰整个句子。

0349 eccentric [ɪk'sentrɪk] a 反常的 n 古怪的人
As far as I know, the administrative assistant had the name of an eccentric.
据我所知，行政助理有怪人之称。
- queer 古怪的   - normal 正常的   - have the name of... 有……之称

- administrative (P. 669)

0350 ecology [i'kɑ:lədʒi] n 生态，社会生态学，个体生态学
This landscaping enterprise has been determined to keep ecology in balance.
这家园林绿化企业决心要保持生态平衡。
- bionomics 生态学   - plant ecology 植物生态学

> 语法重点
> keep... in balance（保持……平衡）句型中，keep 后面一般接表示事物的名词或代词。

0351 ecstasy ['ekstəsi] n 入迷，忘形，迷幻药
All the negotiators were in an ecstasy of delight when hearing the good news.
听到这个好消息时，所有的谈判代表都欣喜若狂。
- delight 高兴   - go into ecstasies 兴高采烈

dual ~ eloquent

0352 edible [ˈedəbl] ⓐ 可食用的

He said that the meals cooked in the staff canteen were edible after a fashion.
他说员工餐厅的饭菜勉强可以食用。
- eatable 可以吃的
- edible oil 食用油
- do sth. after a fashion 勉强做某事

0353 editorial [ˌedɪˈtɔːriəl]
ⓝ 社论，重要评论 ⓐ 编辑的，社论的

It has been decided that Linda would be the editor-in-chief of the editorial department.
已经决定让琳达当编辑部的主编。
- compilatory 编辑的
- editorial office 编辑部

> **语法重点**
> it has been decided that（已决定）句型是"it + 动词（短语）+ that 从句"结构的具体应用，属于有形式主语 it 和 that 引导的主语从句的固定用法。

0354 electron [ɪˈlektrɒn] ⓝ 电子

On the contrary is an electron microscope with the most advanced technology.
与此相反的是一种运用最先进技术的电子显微镜。
- electron microscope 电子显微镜
- on the contrary is... 与此相反的是……

◎ contrary (P. 416)

0355 eligible [ˈelɪdʒəbl] ⓐ 能当选的，合格的，符合条件的

This principal was eligible to give orders to the employees.
这位负责人有资格对员工发号施令。
- qualified 有资格的
- unqualified 没有资格的
- eligible children 适龄儿童
- be eligible to do sth. 有资格做某事

0356 elite [eɪˈliːt] ⓝ 精英，掌权人物

He had no opportunity to learn from the elites in the company.
他没有机会向公司里的精英们学习。
- elite education 精英教育
- have no opportunity to do sth. 没有机会做某事

> **语法重点**
> 此句型也可以表达为 have no chance to do sth.。

0357 eloquence [ˈeləkwəns] ⓝ 雄辩，修辞法

The customers were charmed by this salesman's eloquence.
顾客们被这位推销员的口才迷住了。
- elocution 辩论术
- social eloquence 社交口才
- be charmed by... 被……迷住

0358 eloquent [ˈeləkwənt] ⓐ 辩才无碍的，有说服力的

This excellent shopping guide was eloquent about her sales techniques.
这名优秀的导购员善于谈论她的销售技巧。
- well-spoken 善于言辞的
- be eloquent about... 善于谈论……

◎ technique (P. 372)

0359 embark [ɪmˈbɑːrk] v 上船或飞机
This young man embarked on a business career last year.
这个年轻人去年开始经商。
- disembark 下船（车）
- embark cargo 装货
- embark on... 从事……

0360 emigrant [ˈemɪɡrənt] a 移居他国的，侨居的 n 移民
I heard that the multinational president was an emigrant from Europe.
我听说，这家跨国公司的总裁，是一位从欧洲移居过来的侨民。
- migration 移居
- immigrant 移民
- emigrant bird 候鸟
- be an emigrant from... 来自……的侨民
- emigrant 和 immigrant 都可表示"移民，侨民"，但 emigrant 作"侨民"讲，指移居在国外的人，而 immigrant 作"移民"讲，指从国外移居的人。

0361 emigrate [ˈemɪɡreɪt] v 移居外国
He emigrated to America for the reason of job transfer.
他因为工作调动而移民到了美国。
- emigrate from... 离开本国前往……
- emigrate to... 移民到……

语法重点
emigrate to 后面通常接地点名词。
transfer (P. 512)

0362 emigration [ˌemɪˈɡreɪʃn] n 移民出境
My father had emigration for the reason of working in Canada.
我爸爸因在加拿大工作而移民。
- emigration rate 迁出率
- for the reason of... 因为……

0363 emphatic [ɪmˈfætɪk] a 强调的，加强语气的
This new employee has achieved a series of emphatic victories.
这位新员工已经取得一系列的显著胜利。
- achieve a series of... 取得一系列的……

语法重点
a series of 与名词构成名词短语，作主语时应看作单数，动词用单数。
achieve (P. 252)

0364 enact [ɪˈnækt] v 制定，颁布，充当角色
There's no use enacting this plan.
制订这项计划已经没有用了。
- enact plan 制订计划
- there's no use doing... ……没有用

0365 enclosure [ɪnˈkloʊʒər] n 围墙，圈占，附件
All the workers were led to an enclosure.
所有工人都被带到了一个围场里。
- attachment 附件
- shower enclosure 淋浴间

语法重点
be led to（被带到）后面通常接地点名词。

0366 encyclopedia [ɪnˌsaɪkləˈpiːdiə] n 百科全书
Many teachers thought this encyclopedia was of great use.
很多老师认为，这本百科全书很有用。
- cyclopaedia 百科全书
- ... be of great use ……很有用

语法重点
be of great use 的主语一般是物。

embark ～ EQ

0367 endurance [ɪnˈdʊrəns] **n** 耐力，持久（力），忍耐力

The manager's harsh criticism was beyond her endurance.
经理的严厉批评让她忍无可忍。
🔗 be beyond one's endurance 令某人忍无可忍

⊕ criticism (P. 420)

0368 enhance [ɪnˈhæns] **v** 增加价值

There is an opportunity to enhance your writing skill now.
现在有一个机会，可以提高你的写作技能。
🔗 heighten 加强　　🔗 weaken 削弱
🔗 there is an opportunity to do sth. 有机会做某事

0369 enlighten [ɪnˈlaɪtn] **v** 启发，教导，照耀

The secretary didn't enlighten the vice president about this condition.
秘书没有向副总裁讲明这种情况。
🔗 enlighten wisdom 启迪智慧　🔗 enlighten sb. about... 向某人讲明……

语法重点
enlighten 后面直接接人时，表示"启迪某人"。

0370 enrich [ɪnˈrɪtʃ] **v** 使富有，给……添加肥料，使……美味

These new employees needed to develop an ability to enrich themselves.
这些新员工需要发展充实自我的能力。
🔗 fertilize 使肥沃　🔗 emaciate 使贫瘠　🔗 enrich oneself 充实自我

语法重点
develop an ability to（发展……的能力）后面通常接动词原形。

0371 epidemic [ˌepɪˈdemɪk]

n 传染病，风尚等的流行　**a** 极为盛行的

Recently, a flu epidemic has swept through the whole company.
最近，一场流感席卷了整个公司。
🔗 epidemic disease 流行病　🔗 sweep through... 席卷……

0372 episode [ˈepɪsoʊd] **n** 一个事件

This episode was an embarrassment for the corporate leaders.
这个小插曲使公司领导人感到十分尴尬。
🔗 incident 插曲　🔗 be an embarrassment for sb. 使某人尴尬

语法重点
be an embarrassment for sb. 的主语一般是不好的事情。
⊕ embarrassment (P. 433)

0373 EQ abbr 情商

The general manager thought that the employees' IQ couldn't take the place of EQ.
总经理认为，员工的智商不能代替情商。
🔗 IQ 智商　🔗 take the place of... 代替……
🔗 EQ 是个缩略词，全称是 Emotional Quotient，表示"情商"。

0374 equation [ɪˈkweɪʒn] **n** 方程式，等式，相等

There is a large portion of engineers who has no idea of this rate equation.
大部分工程师不知道这个速率方程式。
- equivalence 相等　- inequality 不等
- there is a large portion of... 有一大部分……

语法重点
a portion of 与名词构成名词短语作主语时，应看作单数，动词也用单数，portion 之前还可以用 small, large 等形容词修饰。
- portion (P. 339)

0375 equivalent [ɪˈkwɪvələnt] **a** 相当的　**n** 对等物，当量

The new employee's pay was the equivalent of one thousand dollars a month.
新员工的薪水相当于每个月一千美元。
- equal 相等的　- equivalent dose 等效剂量
- be the equivalent of... 相当于……

0376 erode [ɪˈroʊd] **v** 侵蚀，逐渐毁坏，损害

Profit margin has been eroded by the fierce competition in the futures market.
期货市场的激烈竞争降低了利润率。
- corrode 侵蚀　- heighten 增强　- erode morale 减弱士气
- be eroded by... 被……所降低

- margin (P. 470)

0377 eruption [ɪˈrʌpʃn] **n** 爆发

After the volcanic eruption, some geologists planned to make an on-the-spot investigation in this area.
火山喷发后，一些地质学家打算在这个地区进行实地考察。
- outburst 爆发　- volcanic eruption 火山喷发
- make an on-the-spot investigation in... 在……进行实地考察

语法重点
on-the-spot 是个合成词，表示"现场的"。

0378 escalate [ˈeskəleɪt] **v** 扩大

The quarrel between these two technicians had escalated into a dispute.
这两名技师之间的争吵已经逐步升级为一场纠纷。
- descend 下降　- slowly escalate 逐步晋级　- escalate into... 逐步升级为……

语法重点
escalate into 所涉及的一般是不好的事情。
- quarrel (P. 344)

0379 essence [ˈesns] **n** 本质，精髓，香精

This clause is of the essence in the labor contract.
这项条款在劳动合约中至关重要。
- substance 实质　- in essence 大体上　- be of the essence 至关重要

0380 eternity [ɪˈtɜːrnəti] **n** 永远，永生，不朽

The manager's speech at the meeting lasted for an eternity.
经理在会议上的讲话持续了很长时间。
- timelessness 永恒　- last for an eternity ……持续很长时间
- speech 指一般的发言或讲话，可能是事先准备的或是即席的，而 address 指在庄严隆重的场合做精心准备的演讲或正式演说。

0381 ethical ['eθɪkl] a 道德的，伦理的

Every employee should take his or her ethical principle into account.
每位员工都要考虑自身的道德原则。
- moral 道德的
- ethical issues 伦理问题
- take sth. into account 考虑……

0382 ethnic ['eθnɪk] a 种族的，部落的

In the meantime, all the employees should learn ethnic culture.
在此期间，所有员工都要学习民族文化。
- racial 种族的
- in the meantime, ... 在此期间，……

meantime (P. 595)

0383 evacuate [ɪ'vækjueɪt] v 撤离，腾出，撤退

It's impossible to evacuate so many employees in such a short time.
不可能在这么短的时间内疏散这么多员工。
- personnel evacuation 人员疏散
- it's impossible to do sth. 不可能做某事

0384 evolution [ˌiːvə'luːʃn] n 发展，进化论，形成

Product evolution was out of the principal's imagination.
产品的演变过程超出负责人的想象。
- social evolution 社会演化
- the evolution of... ……的发展

imagination (P. 309)

0385 evolve [i'vɑːlv] v 发展，使进化，发出

This small company finally evolved into a transnational enterprise.
这家小公司最终发展成为一个跨国企业。
- develop 发展
- evolve from... 由……进化
- evolve into... 发展成……

0386 excerpt ['eksɜːpt] / ['eksɜːrpt] v 摘录，引用 n 摘录，引用

This business information excerpted from the business letter.
这些商业信息摘录于那封商业信函。
- citing 引用
- written excerpt 文字节录
- excerpt from... 引用自……

0387 excessive [ɪk'sesɪv] a 过度的，过多的

This employee took an excessive interest in her personal appearance.
这名员工过分注重个人外貌。

appearance (P. 124)

0388 exclusive [ɪk'skluːsɪv]

a 排外的，专用的 n 独家新闻，专有物

All the other people are shareholders exclusive of him.
除了他之外，其他人都是股东。
- inclusive 包含的
- exclusive report 独家报道
- exclusive of... 不包括……

0389 **execution** [ˌeksɪˈkjuːʃn] n 实行，成功，效果

The president said that he couldn't put this project into execution.
总裁说，他无法实施这个方案。
- accomplishment 完成　- a stay of execution 延期执行
- put... into execution 使……得以实施

→ project (P. 210)

0390 **exert** [ɪɡˈzɜːrt] v 运用，使受（影响等），用（力）

He exerted himself more at work for promotion.
为了获得晋升，他更加努力工作。
- exert sell 强行推销　- exert oneself 尽力，努力

0391 **exotic** [ɪɡˈzɑːtɪk] a 异国情调的，奇异的，吸引人的

The customers have a partiality for these exotic products.
顾客们特别喜欢这些异国产品。
- foreign 外国的　- native 本国的　- have a partiality for... 特别喜爱……

0392 **expedition** [ˌekspəˈdɪʃn] n 探险，迅速

Minority employees agreed to go on an expedition to the South Pole.
少数员工同意去南极探险。
- go on an expedition to... 去……探险
- expedition 和 tour 都可表示"旅行"：expedition 指有特定目的的远征或探险，而 tour 指最后返回出发地，旅途中有停留游览点，距离可长可短，目的各异的周游或巡行。

0393 **expel** [ɪkˈspel] v 逐出，把……除名，排出（气体）

He was expelled from the company for absenteeism.
他因旷职而被公司开除。
- expel from 驱逐出，开除　- be expelled from... 被开除……

0394 **expertise** [ˌekspɜːrˈtiːz] n 专门知识，专家的意见

The boss tells us not to be vague on matters of technical expertise.
老板告诉我们在技术专长的问题上不能含糊。
- skill 技能　- technical expertise 专业技术

◁ 语法重点
be vague on（在……上面含糊）后面一般接名词或者名词短语。

0395 **expiration** [ˌekspəˈreɪʃn] n 期满，呼气

The manager would consider this proposal at the expiration of the contract.
合约到期后，经理会考虑这项提议。
- aspiration 呼气　- inspiration 吸气　- expiration of policy 保险单期满
- at the expiration of... 结束……

→ proposal (P. 343)

0396 **expire** [ɪk'spaɪər] v 终止，失效，断气

They had not finished the task, so they wanted to push back the expire date.
他们还没有完成任务，因此想延后截止日期。

- die 死亡
- birth 出生
- expire date 截止日期
- push back... 把……向后推

expire 是委婉用词，引申为吐出最后一口气，断气而死，而 die 是最普通用词，指某人或某物失去生命而永远不存在。

0397 **explicit** [ɪk'splɪsɪt] a 明确的，直言的，不隐瞒的

He was explicit about his intention to get promotion.
他对自己升职的意图直言不讳。

- clear 清楚的
- vague 含糊的
- be explicit about... 对……直言不讳

intention (P. 461)

0398 **exploit** [ɪk'splɔɪt] n 功绩 v 剥削，开发

These salesmen exploited markets to the best of their ability.
这些业务员尽全力开拓市场。

- feat 功绩
- exploit markets 开拓市场
- to the best of one's ability 尽力做……

ability (P. 121)

0399 **exploration** [ˌeksplə'reɪʃn] n 探索，研究

They made a plan for the exploration of international market.
他们为探索国际市场而制订一个计划。

- study 研究
- make a plan for the exploration of... 为探索……制订计划

0400 **exquisite** [ɪk'skwɪzɪt]
a 精巧的，优美的 n 过分讲究穿戴的人

After a short space, this exquisite artwork began to be sold by auction.
片刻之后，这件精美的艺术品开始拍卖。

- pretty 优美的
- after a short space,... 片刻之后，……

语法重点
after a short space 用于修饰整个句子。

0401 **extract** [eks'trækt] / ['ekstrækt] v 用力取出 n 提取物

The secretary extracted a contract from the folder.
秘书从资料夹里取出一份合约。

- seaweed extract 海藻精华
- extract sth. from... 从……取出

0402 **extracurricular** [ˌekstrəkə'rɪkjələr] a 课外的，业余的

I heard that the president took an active part in extracurricular activities when he was young.
我听说，总裁在年轻时积极参加课外活动。

- extracurricular activity 课外活动
- take an active part in... 积极参加……

0403 eyesight ['aɪsaɪt] n 视力，观察，眼力
You should allow for his poor eyesight when you make arrangement of work.
你在安排工作时要考虑到他的视力不佳。
同 vision 视力　同 allow for... 考虑到……

⊙ arrangement (P. 125)

0404 fabulous ['fæbjələs] a 惊人的
Most of the students had a fabulous time at the banquet.
在宴会上，大多数学生都玩得很开心。
同 unbelievable 难以置信的　同 have a fabulous time 玩得很开心

⊙ banquet (P. 529)

0405 facilitate [fə'sɪlɪteɪt] v 帮助
Please take down the customers' telephone numbers to facilitate contact with them.
请记下顾客的电话号码，以便与他们联系。
同 assist 帮助　同 facilitate contact with sb. 方便与某人联系

0406 faction ['fækʃn] n 派系
These factions would produce an effect on our business.
这些小集团会对我们的生意造成影响。
同 junta 派别
同 produce an effect on... 对……产生影响

0407 faculty ['fæklti] n 全体教员，能力
The manager was drunk, so he was not in control of his elaborative faculty.
经理喝醉了，无法控制自己的思考能力。
同 faculty member 教职工　同 be in control of... 控制……

0408 familiarity [fə,mɪli'ærəti] n 熟悉，认识
Most of the employees in this company have familiarity with English.
这家公司的大多数员工都精通英语。
同 familiarity with... 熟悉……，精通……

0409 famine ['fæmɪn] n 饥荒，饥饿，极度缺乏
Many canned goods have been out of stock in case of famine.
为了预防饥荒，很多罐头食品都已经没有库存。

0410 fascination [,fæsɪ'neɪʃn] n 魅力，迷恋
Many customers have a fascination with this sexy advertisement.
很多顾客都为这个性感广告所着迷。
同 charm 魅力　同 have a fascination with... 对……着迷

⊙ advertisement (P. 253)

0411 feasible ['fi:zəbl] ⓐ 可实行的，可能的
It's feasible for the manager to approve the budget.
经理可能会批准这项预算。
㊦workable 可行的 ㊦infeasible 不可行的
㊦it's feasible for sb. to do sth. 某人可能做某事

0412 federation [ˌfedəˈreɪʃn] ⓝ 联邦政府
The man in black was the chairman of the trade federation.
那个穿黑衣服的人是贸易联盟的主席。
㊦league 联盟 ㊦be the chairman of... 是……的主席
㊧chairman (P. 540)

0413 feedback [ˈfiːdbæk] ⓝ 回应，自动调节
Most of the employees got feedback on their work.
大多数员工都收到对各自工作的回馈。
㊦response 反应 ㊦get feedback on... 获得……回馈

0414 fertility [fərˈtɪləti] ⓝ 肥沃，丰产，繁殖力
Fertility rate would exert an effect on the development of economy.
人口出生率会对经济发展产生影响。
㊦productivity 生产力 ㊦fertility rate 生育率
㊦exert an effect on... 对……产生影响

0415 fidelity [fɪˈdeləti] ⓝ 忠诚，逼真，尽责
There is nothing like these knights' fidelity and confidence.
没有什么能比得上这些骑士的忠心和信心。
㊦faithfulness 忠诚 ㊦disloyalty 不忠实
㊧knight (P. 315)

0416 fireproof [ˈfaɪərpruːf] ⓐ 防火的 ⓥ 使防火，使耐火
It's irresponsible not to inspect this kind of fireproof paint.
没有对这种防火涂料进行检验是不负责任的。
㊦fireproof material 耐火材料 ㊦it's irresponsible to... ……是不负责任的
㊧inspect (P. 311)

0417 flare [fler] ⓥ 闪耀 ⓝ 闪光，反射
Dad flared up when he heard the bad news.
听到这个坏消息后，爸爸大发脾气。
㊦blaze 燃烧 ㊦extinguish 熄灭 ㊦flare up 突然发怒

0418 fleet [fliːt] ⓝ 船队 ⓐ 快速的 ⓥ 疾驰，消磨
A fleet of limousines stopped in front of the building.
一队豪华轿车停在大楼门前。
㊦fast 快速的 ㊦slow 慢的 ㊦a fleet of... stopped in front of... 一队……停在……前
㊟a fleet of 专指车队或舰队。

0419 flicker ['flɪkər] n 闪烁 v 闪烁，飘扬，昏倒
Till the end, there was still a flicker of hope in these negotiators' heart.
直到最后，这些谈判代表还是心存一丝希望。
  screen flicker 屏幕闪烁   there was a flicker of hope in... ……有一丝希望

0420 fling [flɪŋ] v 扔，抛 n 投掷，一时的放纵
Last year, this actress flung herself into show business.
去年，这位女演员投身于演艺事业中。
  cast 投掷   at one fling 一鼓作气地

> **语法重点**
> fling oneself into（投身于）后面通常接表示事业的名词。

0421 fluid ['fluːɪd] n 流体 a 流体的，易变的
This professor was immersed in the study of fluid mechanics.
这位教授全心投入流体力学的研究中。
  liquid 液体   solid 固体   be immersed in... 全身心投入……

0422 flutter ['flʌtər] v 拍翅 n 激动不安，飘扬
The news of terminating the contract put them into a flutter.
解除合约的消息使他们仓皇失措。
  float 飘动   flutter the dovecotes 掀起风波
  put... into a flutter 使……仓皇失措

↻ terminate (P. 790)

0423 foresee [fɔːr'siː] v 预知，有先见之明
Nobody could foresee a great change for the financial market.
没有人能够预知金融市场上的巨大变化。
  foretell 预言   foresee the future 预见将来
  foresee a great change for... 预知……的巨大变化

0424 formidable ['fɔːrmɪdəbl] a 可怕的，令人敬畏的
These researchers had a formidable task ahead of them.
这些研究员都面临着一项艰巨的任务。
  function formidable 功能强大   have... ahead of sb. 某人面临着……

0425 formulate ['fɔːrmjuleɪt] v 系统地说明
Little by little, this marketing promoter formulated his sales strategy to us.
这位营销专员逐步地向我们阐述他的销售策略。

↻ strategy (P. 367)

0426 forsake [fər'seɪk] v 抛弃，断念，摒弃（坏习惯）
You should forsake this idea for the sake of the customers.
为了客户的利益，你应该放弃这种想法。
  abandon 放弃   conserve 保存   for the sake of... 为了……

> **语法重点**
> forsake 后面接人时，表示"离弃某人"。

0427 forthcoming [fɔːrθˈkʌmɪŋ] a 即将到来的 n 来临

All the employees were gearing up for the forthcoming annual meeting.
所有员工都在为即将到来的年会做准备。
- coming 即将到来的 - gear up for... 为……做准备

≈ annual (P. 395)

0428 fortify [ˈfɔːrtɪfaɪ] v 增强，鼓励，使坚定，构筑防御工事

The wine fortified with brandy sold well in the market.
这种用白兰地强化的葡萄酒在市场上很畅销。
- strengthen 加强 - recede 减弱 - fortify with... 以……加强

0429 foster [ˈfɔːstər] v 养育 a 养育的，领养的

These financiers had a responsibility to foster economic growth.
这些金融家有责任促进经济增长。
- cultivate 培养 - foster home 寄养家庭
- have a responsibility to do sth. ……有责任做某事

语法重点
economic 作形容词，用于修饰后面的名词 growth。

0430 fracture [ˈfræktʃər] n 破裂，骨折 v （使）折断

This cleaner should be held responsible for the bone fracture of the assistant.
这位清洁工应该为助理的骨折负责。
- break 折断 - repair 修复 - be held responsible for... 为……负责

0431 fragile [ˈfrædʒl] a 易碎的，脆弱的

Tell the workers to move these fragile goods with great care.
告诉工人们，小心搬运这些易碎货物。
- breakable 易碎的 - solid 结实的 - with great care 小心……

≈ goods (P. 448)

0432 fragment [ˈfrægmənt] n 碎片，碎块

She was sweeping up the glass fragments on the floor.
她正在清扫地板上的玻璃碎片。
- sentence fragment 句子碎片 - sweep up... 清扫……

0433 frail [freɪl] a 脆弱的，意志薄弱的，易损的

The frail girl was taken to the rest room.
那名虚弱的女孩被带到休息室。
- fragile 易碎的 - tough 结实的 - be taken to... 被带到……

0434 fraud [frɔːd] n 欺骗，骗子

This senior accountant was jailed for three years for accounting fraud.
这位高级会计师因做假账而被监禁三年。
- be jailed for... 因……而入狱

0435 freak [friːk] n 畸形的人 v 使强烈反应 a 奇异的
The manager suddenly got angry, which freaked the secretary out.
经理突然发火，把秘书吓坏了。

0436 fret [fret] v 使苦恼，磨损 n 烦躁，磨损处
The assistant was fretting over the analysis report.
助理正在为这个分析报告而着急。
⊜ worry 烦恼　⊜ fret about... 因……焦急　⊜ fret over... 为……着急

↻ analysis (P. 394)

0437 friction [ˈfrɪkʃn] n 摩擦
There was friction between these several trainees.
这几名实习生之间出现了摩擦。

语法重点
there is friction between(……之间出现摩擦) 后面通常接表示人的名词或代词。

0438 galaxy [ˈɡæləksi] n 银河
This security company had a galaxy of sales personnel.
这家证券公司拥有一批销售人员。
⊜ have a galaxy of... 有一群……

0439 generalize [ˈdʒenrəlaɪz] v 一般化，概括，归纳
The manager generalized about this development planning when the meeting came to an end.
会议结束时，经理概述了这个发展计划。
⊜ summarise 概括　⊜ specialize 详细说明　⊜ generalize about... 概述……

0440 generate [ˈdʒenəreɪt] v 产生，引起
These mashines were utilized to generate profit for the company.
这些机器用于为公司创造利润。
⊜ create 造成　⊜ generate revenue 产生收入　⊜ be utilized to... 被用于……

↻ utilize (P. 799)

0441 generator [ˈdʒenəreɪtər] n 发电机，发生者
During the past three years, this holding company has been a good cash generator.
在过去三年中，这家控股公司的营利状况很好。
⊜ signal generator 信号发生器　⊜ be a cash generator ……是赚钱机器

0442 genetic [dʒəˈnetɪk]
a 基因的，遗传（学）的 n 遗传学
There remained a question about genetic products to be discussed.
还剩下一个关于基因产品的问题需要讨论。
⊜ inherited 遗传的　⊘ acquired 后天的

语法重点
there + remain 结构表示还剩下某人、某物或某事，意义比 there be 结构更为生动贴切，其中的 remain 需要根据时态做出相应的变化。

freak ~ graphic

0443 genetics [dʒəˈnetɪks] **n** 遗传学
According to the schedule, there would follow a seminar about genetics.
按照日程安排，随后将会有一个关于遗传学的研讨会。
🔄 hereditism 遗传学　　🔄 there follows... 随后……

> **语法重点**
> there + follow 这个句型表示随后将会有某人、某物或某事，其中的 follow 需要根据时态做出相应的变化。
> ⇨ seminar (P. 774)

0444 glamour [ˈɡlæmər] **n** 魅力，诱惑力
These fashionable clothes cast a glamour over all the customers.
这些时尚的服装吸引所有顾客。
🔄 fascination 魅力

> **语法重点**
> cast a glamour over（迷住）后面通常接表示人的名词或代词。

0445 glassware [ˈɡlæswer] **n** 玻璃器皿
This store specially hired out glassware for banquets.
这家商店专门为宴会出租玻璃器皿。
🔄 chemical glassware 化学玻璃器皿　　🔄 hire out... 出租……

0446 glisten [ˈɡlɪsn] **v** 闪耀，闪亮 **n** 闪光，闪耀
All the people's eyes glistened with tears when they knew the negotiation failed.
得知谈判失败，所有人眼中都闪烁着泪花。
🔄 twinkle 闪耀　　🔄 glisten with 闪耀着

> **语法重点**
> glisten with 也可以表示眼睛里闪烁出某种感情。

0447 gloomy [ˈɡluːmi] **a** 幽暗的，令人沮丧的
The manager was missing and all the employees felt gloomy.
经理失踪了，所有员工都感到愁闷。
🔄 obscure 昏暗的　　🔄 feel gloomy 感到愁闷

0448 GMO **abbr** 基因改造生物
Many manufacturers are suspicious of this GMO.
很多制造商都怀疑这种基因改造生物。

> **语法重点**
> GMO 是 Genetically Modified Organism 通过首字母缩略法缩略而成。

0449 graph [ɡræf] **n** 图表，曲线图 **v** 用曲线图表示
This sales graph was defined to be a warning figure.
这张销售图表被定义为一张警示图。
🔄 graph paper 方格纸　　🔄 be defined to... 被定义为……
🔄 graph 和 chart 都可表示"图"：graph 多指用纵横坐标之间关系的曲线表示两个量之间的图表，而 chart 指航海地图，也指图表。

0450 graphic [ˈɡræfɪk] **a** 图解的
They gave a graphic description of the product launch.
他们生动描述了那场产品发布会。
🔄 graphic arts 图像艺术

⇨ launch (P. 465)

725

0451 grill [grɪl] n 烤架 v 烧烤, 拷问
The manager planned to grill the secretary about this issue.
经理打算向秘书盘问此事。
- barbecue 烧烤
- grill sb. about... 向某人盘问……

语法重点
grill 后面接表示食物的名词时, 表示"烧烤某物"。

0452 grocer ['grousər] n 食品杂货商
This grocer went down to other distributors.
这名零售商被其他分销商打败了。
- grocery store 杂货店
- go down to... 被……击败

0453 grope [group] v 摸索, 探索
The boy was groping for the switch in the dark room.
男孩在黑漆漆的房间里摸索开关。
- fumble 摸索
- grope around 摸索
- grope for... 摸索……

switch (P. 370)

0454 guerrilla [gə'rɪlə] n 游击队
The company threatened to take guerrilla marketing strategy.
那家公司威胁说要采用游击营销战略。
- bushfighting 游击战

语法重点
threaten to (威胁) 后面通常接动词原形。

0455 habitat ['hæbɪtæt] n 栖息地, 产地
This factory made away with the habitat of the animals.
这家工厂摧毁了动物们的栖息地。
- natural habitat 自然栖息地
- make away with... 摧毁……

0456 hack [hæk] n 劈, 砍 v 砍, 出租
Yesterday someone hacked into the Department of Defense's computer system.
昨天, 有人侵入了国防部的电脑系统。
- chop 砍
- hacking cough 干咳
- hack into... 侵入……

0457 hacker ['hækər] n 黑客
He said that the company systems were vulnerable to the hacker attack.
他说, 公司系统容易受到黑客攻击。
- computer hacker 电脑黑客

语法重点
be vulnerable to (易受……的伤害) 后面通常接名词或代词。

vulnerable (P. 804)

0458 harassment ['hærəsmənt] n 骚扰, 扰乱, 烦乱
These female employees had no patience with sexual harassment.
这些女员工无法容忍性骚扰。
- persecution 烦扰
- have no patience with... 不能容忍……

0459 hazard ['hæzərd] n 危险，公害
This investment plan put the company in hazard.
这项投资计划使公司处于危险之中。
- risk 危险
- safety 安全
- put... in hazard 使……处于危险中

0460 hemisphere ['hemɪsfɪr] n 半球
This measure would imperil their interests in northern hemisphere.
这项措施将会危及他们在北半球的利益。
- semisphere 半球
- brain hemispheres 大脑半球

northern (P. 196)

0461 hereafter [,hɪr'æftər] ad 随后，从此以后
We should pay close heed to the economical situation hereafter.
今后，我们要密切关注经济形势。
- forwards 今后
- before 以前

语法重点
pay close heed to（密切注意）后面通常接名词或代词。

0462 heritage ['herɪtɪdʒ] n 遗产，继承物，传统
He inherited heritage from his father.
他从父亲那里继承了遗产。
- inheritance 遗产
- cultural heritage 文化遗产
- inherit... from sb. 从某人手里继承……

0463 heroin ['herouɪn] n 海洛因，吗啡
An idea came to the manager's mind that the box with heroin in was still in the office.
经理突然想起，那个装有海洛因的箱子还放在办公室里。

0464 highlight ['haɪlaɪt] n 强光，最重要的事情 v 强调
The president's speech was the highlight of the conference.
总裁的讲话是这次会议的高潮。
- stress 强调
- be the highlight of... 是……的精彩之处

0465 honorary ['ɑːnəreri] a 名誉上的，挂名的
The company conferred the honor of honorary employee on him.
公司授予他"荣誉员工"的称号。
- honorary president 名誉主席
- confer... on sb. 授予某人……

confer (P. 691)

0466 hormone ['hɔːrmoun] n 荷尔蒙，激素
This new machine was used for extraction of growth hormone.
这台新机器被用于提取生长激素。
- incretion 激素
- plant hormone 植物激素
- be used for... 用于……

0467 **hospitable** [hɑː'spɪtəbl] a 好客的，热情友好的
The employees are hospitable to these visitors.
员工们对这些参观者非常热情友善。

> 语法重点
> be hospitable to（对……热情友好）后面通常接表示人的名词或代词。

0468 **hospitality** [ˌhɑːspɪ'tæləti] n 好客
These foreign investors were overwhelmed by the hospitality of the receptionists.
这些外国投资商为接待员的热情好客感动不已。

0469 **hospitalize** ['hɑːspɪtəlaɪz] v 使住院治疗，就医
It's said that the designer was hospitalized for high blood pressure.
据说，设计师因患高血压而住院接受治疗。

> 语法重点
> be hospitalized for（因……而住院治疗）后面通常接表示疾病的名词。

0470 **hostility** [hɑː'strɪləti] n 敌意，愤怒反抗
The shareholders' hostility to this proposal was known to us all.
我们都知道，股东们反对这项提议。
 同 hatred 敌意　 近 show hostility 表现出怒气
 搭 hostility to... was known to... 都知道……反对……

> 语法重点
> hostility to 后面通常接名词或代词。
> ↪ proposal (P. 343)

0471 **humanitarian** [hjuːˌmænɪ'teriən]
n 人道主义者　a 人道主义的，博爱的
Many leaders in the company thought of themselves as humanitarians.
很多公司领导者把他们自己视为人道主义者。
 近 humanitarian aid 人道主义援助　 搭 think of... as... 把……看作

0472 **humiliate** [hjuː'mɪlieɪt] v 侮辱，羞辱
It's not the manager's intention to humiliate you.
那位经理不是有意要羞辱你的。
 同 disgrace 丢脸　 反 honor 尊敬
 搭 it's not one's intention to do sth. 某人不是有意要做某事

0473 **hunch** [hʌntʃ] n 直觉，预感　v 隆起，向前移动
He had a hunch about the success of this negotiation.
他有预感，这次谈判会成功。
 同 anticipation 预感　 近 have a hunch that 总怀疑

> 语法重点
> have a hunch about（预感到）后面通常接名词。

0474 **hurdle** ['hɜːrdl] n 跨栏，障碍　v 跨越某物
Insufficient raw material was the biggest hurdle for producing.
原材料不足是生产的最大障碍。
 同 obstacle 障碍　 近 brush hurdle 树篱　 搭 be a hurdle for... 是……的障碍

0475 **hygiene** [ˈhaɪdʒiːn] n 卫生学，保健法
As the receptionist of the company, you should be careful about your personal hygiene.
作为公司的接待员，你要注意个人卫生。
- health 卫生　- dental hygiene 口腔卫生　- be careful about... 当心……

◎ personal (P. 203)

0476 **hypocrisy** [hɪˈpɑːkrəsi] n 虚伪
The customers always railed against the hypocrisy of the salesmen.
顾客们总是抱怨这些推销员的伪善行为。
- untruthfulness 虚伪　- sheer hypocrisy 自欺欺人　- rail against... 抱怨……

0477 **hypocrite** [ˈhɪpəkrɪt] n 伪君子，伪善者
He was more than a hypocrite, and also a bigot.
他不仅仅是个伪君子，还是个很顽固的人。
- pseudo 伪君子　- be more than... 不仅仅是……

0478 **hysterical** [hɪˈsterɪkl] a 歇斯底里的
The teacher kept a watchful eye on the hysterical student.
老师注意到了那个歇斯底里的学生。
- keep a watchful eye on... 注意

0479 **illuminate** [ɪˈluːmɪneɪt] v 照明，照亮
The principal would illuminate his opinion with data report.
负责人将用资料报告来阐述他的观点。
- explain 说明　- illuminate... with... 用……来阐述……

◎ data (P. 149)

0480 **illusion** [ɪˈluːʒn] n 错觉，假象
These several representatives had an illusion about winning the negotiation.
这几名代表对赢得谈判抱有一丝幻想。
- delusion 幻想　- create an illusion 造成一种错觉

语法重点
have an illusion about （对……抱有幻想）后面通常接动名词。

0481 **immune** [ɪˈmjuːn] a 免疫的，豁免的
The company's reputation was immune to the payment in arrears.
公司的信誉没有受到拖欠货款的影响。
- exonerative 免除的　- immune response 免疫反应
- be immune to... 不受……的影响

◎ reputation (P. 456)

0482 **imperative** [ɪmˈperətɪv] a 命令式的 n 必要的事
It's imperative that we must amend the blueprint.
至关重要的是，我们必须修改蓝图。
- necessary 必要的　- needless 不必要的
- it's imperative that... 至关重要的是……

0483 implement ['ɪmplɪment] / [ˈɪmplɪment] **n** 工具 **v** 实施
The president made a promise to implement this plan.
总裁承诺，会履行这项计划。
- fulfill 履行 - implements of production 生产工具
- make a promise to do sth. 承诺做某事

0484 implication [ˌɪmplɪˈkeɪʃn] **n** 含义，暗示，暗指
The manager nodded, with the implication that he agreed to this arrangement.
经理点头，意味他同意这项安排。
- by implication 暗示地 - with the implication that... 言外之意是……

0485 implicit [ɪmˈplɪsɪt] **a** 含蓄的，绝对的
The soldiers had implicit faith in their colonel.
士兵们绝对相信他们的上校。
- colonel (P. 545)

0486 imposing [ɪmˈpoʊzɪŋ] **a** 壮观的，威风的 **v** 强迫
The interviewer had a favorable impression on this imposing applicant.
面试官对这个仪表堂堂的求职者很有好感。
- impressive 给人印象深刻的 - imposing appearance 气宇轩昂

0487 imprison [ɪmˈprɪzn] **v** 监禁
After getting fired, he imprisoned himself in this room.
被炒鱿鱼后，他就将自己囚禁在这间房间里。
- incarcerate 监禁 - liberate 释放 - imprison for 被监禁
- imprison oneself ……自我囚禁

0488 incentive [ɪnˈsentɪv] **n** 刺激，鼓励
There is no incentive to make the employees work overtime.
没有激励政策促使员工加班。
- stimulus 刺激 - incentive system 奖励制度

语法重点
there is no incentive to 后面通常接动词原形。

0489 incidental [ˌɪnsɪˈdentl]
a 附带的，偶然发生的 **n** 伴随事件
His speech was only incidental to the meeting.
他的讲话只是这次会议的一个陪衬。
- accidental 偶然的 - incidental music 配乐

语法重点
be incidental to（是……的陪衬，……是次要的）后面通常接名词或代词。

0490 incline [ɪnˈklaɪn] / [ˈɪnklaɪn] **v** （使）倾斜 **n** 倾斜
These negotiators inclined to blame the opportunity for their failure.
这些谈判代表倾向于将失败归咎于机遇。
- incline to... 倾向于……，有意于……

语法重点
incline to 后面通常接动词原形，表示"有意做某事"。

0491 **inclusive** [ɪnˈkluːsɪv] a 包含的
The folder is inclusive of all the meeting materials.
所有的会议资料都包含在这个资料夹里。
≈ containing 包含的 ≠ exclusive 排外的 ● be inclusive of... 把……包括在内

0492 **indignation** [ˌɪndɪgˈneɪʃn] n 愤怒，义愤
He was filled with indignation at the employees' frequent working overtime.
他为员工们经常加班而满心愤慨。
≈ anger 愤怒 ● be filled with indignation at... 为……而满心愤慨

☞ frequent (P. 298)

0493 **inevitable** [ɪnˈevɪtəbl] a 不可避免的，必然的
It is inevitable to terminate the cooperation with that company.
终止与那家公司的合作，是不可避免的。
≈ inescapable 不可避免的 ≠ avoidable 可避免的
● inevitable consequence 不可避免的后果

语法重点
it is inevitable to（是不可避免的）后面通常接动词原形。
☞ terminate (P. 790)

0494 **infectious** [ɪnˈfekʃəs] a 传染的，有传染力的
It is beyond all doubt that this receptionist's laughter is infectious.
毫无疑问，这位接待员的笑容具有感染力。
≈ contagious 传染性的 ● it is beyond all doubt that... 毫无疑问……

0495 **infer** [ɪnˈfɜːr] v 推断，暗示
The scientist inferred a fact from these data.
科学家从这些资料中推断出一个事实。
≈ deduce 推断 ● infer... from... 从……中推断……

0496 **inference** [ˈɪnfərəns] n 推理，推断
The secretary drew the inference that the manager would agree to this project.
秘书推断经理会同意这个方案。
≈ conclusion 结论 ● make inferences 做出结论

语法重点
draw the inference that（推断）后面接同位语从句。

0497 **ingenious** [ɪnˈdʒiːniəs] a 心灵手巧的
He expected there to be some ingenious designs.
他期待能有一些别出心裁的设计。
≈ clever 熟练的 ≠ clumsy 笨拙的 ● expect there to be... 期待……

语法重点
动词 + there to be 结构中的动词，往往是 expect, want, intend, mean, consider, like, hate 等接不定式作宾语的动词。

0498 **ingenuity** [ˌɪndʒəˈnuːəti] n 心灵手巧，设计新颖，巧妙
This employee showed ingenuity in designing.
这名员工在设计方面很有创造力。
≈ originality 独创性 ≠ copy 模仿

语法重点
show ingenuity in（在……方面有创造力）后面可以接名词或动名词。

0499 **inhabit** [ɪnˈhæbɪt] v 居住，（动物）栖息于
This apartment was inhabited by most of the employees.
大多数员工都住在这个公寓里。
- live 居住 be inhabited by... 居住于……
- inhabit 和 settle 都可表示"居住"：inhabit 强调人或动物居住在某个地区并已适应某种特殊环境，而 settle 侧重指某人定居于城市、国家或地区，而不指居住的住所。

0500 **inhabitant** [ɪnˈhæbɪtənt] n 居民，住户
There lived many inhabitants in this employee apartment.
这个员工公寓里有很多住户。
- resident 居民 inhabitant tax 居民所得税

语法重点
there + live 这个句型表示在某地生活/住着某些人，意义比 there be 结构更为生动贴切，其中的 live 需要根据时态做出相应变化。

0501 **inherent** [ɪnˈhɪrənt] a 天生的
The ability of designing was inherent in him.
他天生具有设计才能。
- instinctive 天生的 acquired 后天的

语法重点
be inherent in（天生）后面通常接表示人的名词或代词。

0502 **initiative** [ɪˈnɪʃətɪv] n 主动的行动，主动权，提案
The supervisor thought that they must take the initiative in negotiating.
主管认为，他们必须在谈判中采取主动。

语法重点
take the initiative in（在……中采取主动）后面通常接动名词。

0503 **inject** [ɪnˈdʒekt] v 注射，引入，投入
The bank decided to inject one billion dollars into this company.
银行决定向这家公司投入十亿美元。
- inflood 注入 elicit 引出 inject... into... 向……投入……

0504 **injection** [ɪnˈdʒekʃn] n 注射，注入，充满
The doctor gave every employee a preventive injection.
医生为每一名员工打了预防针。
- hypodermic injection 皮下注射 give sb. an injection ……给某人打针

➲ preventive (P. 760)

0505 **injustice** [ɪnˈdʒʌstɪs] n 不公正，冤枉
It's said that these employees were all the victims of injustice.
据说，这些员工都遭受过不公平待遇。
- inequity 不公平 justice 公平 injustice undone 沉冤得雪
- be the victim of... 遭受……

➲ victim (P. 381)

0506 **innovation** [ˌɪnəˈveɪʃn] n 革新，创新
This technological innovation would save the company much time.
这项技术创新将会为公司节省大量时间。
- reformation 革新 innovation theory 创新理论

inhabit ~ institution

0507 innovative [ˈɪnəveɪtɪv] **a** 创新的
The company organized the competition with the purpose of cultivate the employees' innovative awareness.
为了培养员工的创新意识，公司举办了这场比赛。
🔄 innovative approach 创新方法　🔄 with the purpose of... 为了……

▷ cultivate (P. 698)

0508 inquiry [ɪnˈkwaɪrɪ] **n** 询问，打听，调查
The principal made an inquiry into this strike.
负责人对此次罢工进行了调查。
🔄 questioning 质问　🔄 inquiry about... 打听……
🔄 make an inquiry into... 对……进行调查

0509 insight [ˈɪnsaɪt] **n** 洞察力，领悟，了解
The principal gained an insight into this cooperation.
负责人对这次合作有着深入的了解。
🔄 perception 洞察力　🔄 gain an insight into... 了解……

0510 insistence [ɪnˈsɪstəns] **n** 坚持，强调，极力主张
They were united in their insistence that the manager should reconsider this proposal.
他们一致坚持认为，经理应该重新考虑这项提议。
🔄 emphasis 强调　🔄 insistence on... 坚持……
🔄 be united in one's insistence that... 一致坚持认为……

▷ proposal (P. 343)

0511 installation [ˌɪnstəˈleɪʃn] **n** 就任，装置，设施
Upon most occasions, equipment installation was carried out after work.
在大多数情况下，设备安装都在下班时进行。
🔄 device 装置　🔄 accelerating installation 加速装置
🔄 upon most occasions,... 在大多数情况下，……

▷ occasion (P. 330)

0512 installment [ɪnˈstɔːlmənt]
n 分期付款，（分期连载的）部分
The company allowed the customer to pay for this refrigerator by installment.
公司允许顾客用分期付款的方式来为这台冰箱付款。
🔄 portion 部分　🔄 entirety 全部
🔄 pay for... by installment 用分期付款来为……付费

语法重点
pay by installment 表示"分期支付"，而"用现金支付"可以表达为 pay in cash。

0513 institution [ˌɪnstɪˈtuːʃn] **n** 机构，习俗，制度
The list was without reference to this financial institution.
名单中没有提及这家金融机构。
🔄 public institution 公家单位　🔄 without reference to... 没有提及……

733

0514 **intact** [ɪnˈtækt] a 完整无缺的，未受损伤的
All the goods in the warehouse remained intact.
仓库里的所有货物都完好无损。
🔊 complete 完整的　🔊 incomplete 不完整的　🔊 remain intact 完好无损

0515 **integrate** [ˈɪntɪɡreɪt] v 整合，使……成为一体
Many graduates couldn't integrate into the career life.
很多毕业生无法融入职场生活。
🔊 merge 合并　🔊 separate 使分离　🔊 integrate into... 与……成为一体

🔗 graduate (P. 301)

0516 **integration** [ˌɪntɪˈɡreɪʃn] n 整合，一体化，混合
These men's aim is to realize regional integration.
这些男人的目标是实现区域一体化。
🔊 coalition 结合　🔊 separation 分离　🔊 aim is to... 的目的是……

语法重点
此句型中，to 后面通常接动词原形。

0517 **integrity** [ɪnˈteɡrəti] n 正直，诚实，完整
This matter was a threat to the company's business integrity.
这件事情威胁到这家公司的商业信誉。
🔊 honesty 诚实　🔊 dishonesty 不诚实　🔊 be a threat to... 对……构成威胁

0518 **intellect** [ˈɪntəlekt] n 智力，理解力，才智非凡的人
These corporate leaders are famed for their intellect and perseverance.
这些公司领导人以智慧和毅力而出名。
🔊 ignorance 无知　🔊 be famed for... 以……而出名

0519 **intersection** [ˌɪntərˈsekʃn] n 十字路口，交点
They decided to modify the architectural drawing with a view to this intersection point.
考虑到这个交叉点，他们决定修改建筑图纸。
🔊 junction 交叉点　🔊 intersection line 交叉线　🔊 with a view to... 考虑到……

🔗 modify (P. 597)

0520 **interval** [ˈɪntərvl] n 间隔，区间
The secretary reminded the general manager at intervals at the meeting.
秘书在会议上不时地提醒总经理。
🔊 time interval 时间间隔　🔊 do sth. at intervals 不时做某事

0521 **intervene** [ˌɪntərˈviːn] v 介入，干涉，阻挠
The model couldn't intervene in this advertisement campaign.
模特儿不能干预这次的广告活动。
🔊 intervene in 干预，插手　🔊 intervene in sth. 干预某事

🔗 campaign (P. 404)

0522 **intervention** [ˌɪntərˈvenʃn] **n** 介入，干涉，调解

This measure was used as a pretext for the market intervention.
这项措施成为市场干预的借口。
- interference 干预
- be used as a pretext for... 成为……的借口

0523 **intimacy** [ˈɪntɪməsi] **n** 亲密，亲近

It's said that the secretary had intimacy with the negotiator.
据说，秘书与那位谈判者关系密切。
- closeness 亲密
- alienation 疏远
- inappropriate intimacy 过度亲密

语法重点
have intimacy with（与……关系密切）后面通常接表示人的名词或代词。

0524 **intimidate** [ɪnˈtɪmɪdeɪt] **v** 恐吓

This commercial espionage intimidated him into stealing company information.
这名商业间谍威胁他窃取公司资料。
- intimidate into 恫吓使之做某事
- intimidate sb. into doing sth. 威胁某人做某事
- intimidate 和 startle 都可表示"惊吓，惊恐"：intimidate 特指恐吓某人，迫使其做某事，而 startle 强调突然使人惊骇或震惊。

steal (P. 228)

0525 **intrude** [ɪnˈtruːd] **v** 侵入，把观点强加于他人

I would not intrude upon you if you were busy with your work.
如果你工作很忙，我就不打扰你了。
- interrupt 打扰
- intrude on 干涉，介入
- intrude upon... 侵入……

0526 **intruder** [ɪnˈtruːdər] **n** 侵入者，妨碍者，爱管闲事的人

The intruder suddenly jumped at the famous singer.
那个闯入者突然向那名知名歌手扑去。
- raider 侵入者
- jump at... 扑向……

0527 **invaluable** [ɪnˈvæljuəbl] **a** 无价的

He gained invaluable experience from his last job.
他从上一份工作中获得了宝贵的经验。
- precious 宝贵的
- valueless 无价值的
- gain experience from... 从……获得经验

语法重点
last job 通常不解释为"最后的工作"，而要解释为"上一份工作"。

0528 **inventory** [ˈɪnvəntɔːri] **n** 清单，目录，商店存货

The warehouse keeper lost the inventory on his way back to the office.
那名仓库管理员在回办公室的路上弄丢了库存单。
- list 目录
- merchandise inventory 库存商品

语法重点
on one's way back to（在某人回……的路上）后面通常接表示地点的名词。

怪物讲师教学团队的7 000"单词"＋"语法"

0529 investigator [ɪnˈvestɪɡeɪtər] **n** 调查者，审阅者
He had ever been an investigator of the insurance company.
他曾是保险公司的一名调查员。
- researchist 调查者　- be an investigator of... 是……的调查员

0530 IQ **abbr** 智商，与……相同，进口限额
Most of the employees' IQs were above average.
大多数员工的智商都在中等偏上。
- ... be above average ……高于平均水准

> **语法重点**
> IQ 是 Intelligence Quotient 的首字母缩写。
> - average (P. 258)

0531 ironic [aɪˈrɑːnɪk] **a** 挖苦的，冷嘲的
It is ironic that so many employees kept silent about this issue.
具有讽刺意味的是，这么多员工都对此事保持沉默。
- ironic strategy 反讽策略　- it is ironic that... 具有讽刺意味的是……

0532 irony [ˈaɪrəni] **n** 讽刺，反语，冷嘲
The secretary usually said to other employees with slight irony.
秘书经常略带讽刺地对其他员工说话。
- sarcasm 讽刺　- say to sb. with slight irony 略带讽刺地对某人说话

> **语法重点**
> with irony 表示"讽刺地"，通常在句中做副词使用。

0533 irritable [ˈɪrɪtəbl] **a** 暴躁的，过敏的
This reporter felt irritable after waiting in the office for an hour.
在办公室里等了一个小时后，这名记者感觉很烦躁。

> **语法重点**
> wait in 表示"在……等待"，后面通常接等待的地点。

0534 irritate [ˈɪrɪteɪt] **v** 使生气，使不适，使疼痛
This department manager had a bad temper, so you'd better not irritate him.
这位部门经理脾气不好，你最好别去惹他。
- provoke 激怒　- appease 安抚　- have a bad temper 脾气不好

0535 irritation [ˌɪrɪˈteɪʃn] **n** 烦躁，令人恼火的事
The manager felt an irritation against this new employee.
经理对这名新员工感到很气愤。
- incentive 刺激　- displeasure 不愉快

> **语法重点**
> feel an irritation against（对……感到气恼）后面通常接表示人的名词或代词。

0536 joyous [ˈdʒɔɪəs] **a** 高兴的，充满欢乐的
The man made these children's travel to Europe so joyous.
这名男子使这些小孩的欧洲之旅非常快乐。
- glad 高兴的　- sorrowful 伤心的　- make... joyous 使……快乐

> **语法重点**
> 此句型中，make 后面可以接人，也可以接表示物的名词或代词。

investigator ~ legendary

0537 kernel ['kɜːrnl] **n** 果核的仁，核心，谷粒

The kernel of this meeting is to discuss the annual vacation.
这次会议的核心是商议年假。
- main 要点
- the kernel of... is... 的核心是……

◎ discuss (P. 154)

0538 kidnap ['kɪdnæp] **v** 绑架

All the members hit the panic button when they heard that the leader was kidnapped.
听到领导者被绑架时，所有成员都非常惊慌失措。
- abduct 绑架
- kidnap case 绑架案
- hit the panic button 是美国俚语，表示"过于惊慌失措，非常恐惧"。

0539 lament [lə'ment] **v** 哀悼，悲叹 **n** 悲痛之情，悼词

The corporate leaders lamented over all the economic losses.
公司领导人为所有的经济损失懊悔不已。
- bewail 悲叹
- lament for 哀悼，为……而悲痛
- lament over... 为……而懊悔

0540 lava ['lɑːvə] **n** 熔岩，火山岩

A moment later, the father's anger spilled out like lava.
片刻之后，父亲的怒气就像火山爆发似的迸发出来。

语法重点
a moment later 表示"片刻之后"，相当于 after a moment 等。
◎ spill (P. 362)

0541 layman ['leɪmən] **n** 一般信徒，门外汉

He was just a layman, so he didn't know how to judge this design drawing.
他只是个门外汉，不懂得如何评价这幅设计图。
- adept 内行，能手
- judge of... 判断……

0542 layout ['leɪaʊt] **n** 规划，安排，设计

The layout of the factory was designed by the architect.
工厂的规划是由那名建筑师设计的。
- design 设计
- layout plan 平面图

语法重点
be designed by（由……设计）后面通常接表示人的名词或代词。

0543 LCD abbr 液晶显示器

The salesman said that this panel was cheaper than the LCD one.
那名推销员说，这种面板比液晶显示器面板更便宜。
- LCD driver 液晶驱动器
- be cheaper than... 比……更便宜

语法重点
LCD 是 Liquid Crystal Display 的首字母缩写。

0544 legendary ['ledʒənderi] **a** 传说的 **n** 传说集

This foreign trade corporation was legendary for its integrity.
这家外贸公司以诚信而闻名。
- rumorous 传说的
- be legendary for... 以……而闻名

737

0545 **legislative** ['ledʒɪsleɪtɪv] a 立法的 n 立法权
It's said that this legislature was shorn of legislative power.
据说，这个立法机关被剥夺了立法权。
- nomothetic 制定法律的　- legislative body 立法机构
- be shorn of... 被剥夺……

▷ legislature (P. 738)

0546 **legislator** ['ledʒɪsleɪtər] n 立法者
Half of the legislators agreed on this economic statute.
有一半立法者同意这项经济法规。
- lawmaker 立法者　- half of... agreed on... 半数……同意……

语法重点
half of 后接可数名词的复数作主语时，应看作复数，动词要用复数形式。

0547 **legislature** ['ledʒɪsleɪtʃər] n 立法机关，州议会
This company addressed a petition to the local legislature.
这家公司向当地的立法机关提交了请愿书。
- legislative body 立法机关

语法重点
address a petition to（向……提交请愿书）后面通常接名词或代词。

0548 **legitimate** [lɪ'dʒɪtɪmət] / [lɪ'dʒɪtɪmeɪt]
a 合法的 v 使合法
Economic downturn was a legitimate reason for layoff.
经济不景气是裁员的正当理由。
- lawful 合法的　- illegitimate 非法的　- legitimate power 合法权力

语法重点
be a legitimate reason for（是……的正当理由）后面可以接名词或动名词。

0549 **lengthy** ['leŋθi] a 漫长的
This lengthy meeting finally came to an end.
这个漫长的会议终于结束了。
- interminable 冗长的　- lengthy explanations 冗长的解释
- come to an end 结束

0550 **liable** ['laɪəbl] a 容易……的，有义务的，有……倾向的
What you have done was liable to give offence to the customers.
你们的做法可能会惹火顾客。
- probable 可能的　- be liable for... 对……有责任

语法重点
give offence to（触怒）后面通常接表示人的名词或代词。

0551 **liberate** ['lɪbəreɪt] v 使自由
The assistant would liberate you from the busy work.
助理会让你从繁忙的工作中解脱出来。
- discharge 放出　- restrain 约束
- liberate sb. from... 使某人从……中解脱出来

0552 **liberation** [ˌlɪbə'reɪʃn] n 解放，释放
All the prisoners in this jail panted after liberation.
这座监狱里的囚犯都渴望解放。
- deliverance 释放　- captivity 囚禁　- pant after... 渴望……

legislative ~ literate

0553 likewise [ˈlaɪkwaɪz] ad 同样地，也，又
The writer worked overtime on the weekend and expected the editor to do likewise.
作者在周末加班，并且期望编辑也这么做。
🔹 too 也　🔹 and likewise 和……一样
🔹 expect sb. to do likewise 期望某人也照样做

> **语法重点**
> likewise 和 too 都可表示 "也"：likewise 是书面语用词，而 too 多用于口语，且在肯定句中通常用于句末。

0554 limousine / limo [ˈlɪməziːn] / [ˈlɪmoʊ] n 大轿车
The president got inside the limo companied by the secretary.
总裁在秘书的陪同下进入了豪华轿车。

🔗 inside (P. 052)

0555 liner [ˈlaɪnər] n 班机，衬垫，画线者
The corporate leaders had decided against taking the passenger liner to Paris.
公司领导人决定不乘坐客机去巴黎。
🔹 decide against doing sth. 决定不做某事

0556 linguist [ˈlɪŋgwɪst] n 语言学家
One of the negotiators was a Spanish linguist.
其中一名谈判商精通西班牙语。
🔹 philologer 语言学家　🔹 be a... linguist 精通……语言

0557 liter [ˈliːtər] n 升
The assistant went to buy one liter of juice after getting the work done.
完成工作后，助理去买了一升果汁。

0558 literacy [ˈlɪtərəsi] n 识字，有文化
He was doing research on the workforce literacy.
他正在研究员工的读写能力。
🔹 illiteracy 文盲　🔹 do research on... 研究……

0559 literal [ˈlɪtərəl] a 逐字的
The secretary said that this contract was a literal translation from English.
秘书说，这份合约是从英文直译过来的。
🔹 verbatim 逐字的　🔹 literal meaning 字面意思
🔹 be a literal translation from... 从……直译过来

🔗 translation (P. 512)

0560 literate [ˈlɪtərət] a 能读写的 n 识字的人，有学问的人
The supervisor said that he only breakfasted with literate persons.
上司说，他只和有文化修养的人一起吃早餐。
🔹 learned 有学问的　🔹 illiterate 文盲的　🔹 breakfast with... 与……共进早餐

> **语法重点**
> breakfast 原本是名词表示 "早餐"，属于抽象名词，在例句中转化为动词，表示 "吃早餐"。

739

0561 longevity [lɔːnˈdʒevəti] n 长寿，寿命
This family business was distinguished by its longevity.
这个家族企业以其历史悠久而著称。
 ephemer 短命   be distinguished by... 以……为特征

distinguish (P. 428)

0562 lounge [laʊndʒ] n 休息室 v 懒洋洋地躺，闲逛
He got fired for he lounged away his working time.
他因消磨工作时间而被开除了。
 lounge bar 豪华酒吧   lounge away... 虚度……

0563 lunatic [ˈluːnətɪk] n 疯子 a 疯狂的，愚蠢的
This timid employee pleaded for a peaceful life in the lunatic workplace.
这名胆小的员工祈求在混乱的职场中平静地生活。
 crazy 疯狂的   plead for... 请求……，为……辩护

plea (P. 613)

0564 lure [lʊr] v 诱惑 n 吸引力，诱惑物
The manager of another company lured her into job hopping.
另一家公司的经理引诱她跳槽。
 tempt 诱惑   lure sb. away 吸引某人离开
 lure sb. into doing... 引诱某人做某事
 job hopping 是常用搭配，表示"跳槽"。

0565 lush [lʌʃ] a 多汁的，豪华的 n 醉汉 v 喝醉
Although the president was a lush, he was the life of the party.
虽然总裁是个酒鬼，但他是派对的中心人物。

0566 lyric [ˈlɪrɪk] a 抒情的，感情丰富的 n 歌词，抒情诗
He said that this song's lyric gave expression to the employees' mood.
他说，这首歌的歌词表达出员工们的心情。
 emotional 感情丰富的   epic 叙事诗   lyric poetry 抒情诗

语法重点
give expression to（表达出）后面一般接名词。

0567 magnitude [ˈmæɡnɪtuːd] n 巨大
Judging from this proposal, most of the employees had not realized the magnitude of it.
从这个提议判断，大多数员工都没有意识到它的重要性。
 consequence 重要性   judging from... 根据……判断

语法重点
现在分词短语 judging from 在例句中作插入语，也可以用 judging by 来代替。

0568 malaria [məˈleriə] n 疟疾
What they were producing was an effectual preventive for malaria.
他们正在生产的是一种有效的疟疾预防药。
 paludism 疟疾   malaria control 疟疾防治

语法重点
be a preventive for（是……的预防药）后面通常接表示疾病的名词。

longevity ~ medication

0569 **manipulate** [mə'nɪpjuleɪt] v 操作，控制
He always manipulated her to steal information from the company.
他总是让她从公司窃取资料。
🔄 handle 操作　🔄 manipulate sb. to do... 控制某人做某事

0570 **manuscript** ['mænjuskrɪpt] n 手稿，原稿
The editor made a mark with pencil in the manuscript.
那名编辑用铅笔在手稿上做记号。
🔄 scripture 手稿　🔄 make a mark with... 用……做记号

> 语法重点
> make a mark with 后面通常接表示工具或用具的名词。
> 👉 editor (P. 288)

0571 **mar** [mɑːr] v 毁损，糟蹋 n 污点，障碍
What they did marred the smooth running of the meeting.
他们的举动破坏了会议的顺利进行。
🔄 damage 毁坏　🔄 mar one's career 毁掉某人的前程
🔄 mar the smooth running of... 破坏……的顺利进行

0572 **massacre** ['mæsəkər] n 大屠杀，惨败 v 彻底击败
The manager wanted to collect evidence to massacre the company.
经理想收集证据来彻底打败那家公司。
🔄 slaughter 屠杀

> 语法重点
> collect evidence to（收集证据）后面通常接动词原形。

0573 **mastery** ['mæstəri] n 熟练，掌握，控制权
Most of the salesmen have had mastery of the sales skills.
大多数业务员已经掌握了销售技巧。
🔄 command 控制　🔄 have mastery of... 掌握……

0574 **mattress** ['mætrəs] n 床垫，空气垫
The mattresses produced in this factory are of good quality.
这家工厂生产的床垫品质很好。
🔄 bedpad 床垫　🔄 spring mattress 弹簧床垫　🔄 be of good quality 品质好

👉 factory (P. 036)

0575 **mechanism** ['mekənɪzəm] n 机械装置，结构，途径
The operational mechanism of this machine was beyond the researchers' comprehension.
研究人员不理解这种机器的运作机制。
ℹ️ mechanism 指运行系统，简单的机械装置，而 apparatus 指具有特殊用途的装置。

0576 **medication** [ˌmedɪ'keɪʃn] n 药物，药物治疗
She saw her boss being on medication when she walked into the office.
她走进办公室时，看到老板在服药。
🔄 drugs 药　🔄 oral medication 口服药　🔄 be on medication 在服药

> 语法重点
> walk into 是个常用的动词短语，表示"走进，不慎陷入"等。

0577 **medieval** [ˌmedɪˈiːvl] a 中世纪的，中古时代的
The manager was a man with a medieval attitude toward the employees.
那位经理是个以中世纪的古老态度来对待员工的人。
⊛modern 现代的　⊛medieval warfare 中世纪战争

> 语法重点
> with a medieval attitude toward（用中世纪的古老态度对待）后面通常接名词或代词。
> ⊛attitude (P. 257)

0578 **meditate** [ˈmedɪteɪt] v 沉思，策划
The president was meditating on this proposal.
总裁正在沉思这份提案。
⊛propose 打算　⊛meditate on 沉思

0579 **meditation** [ˌmedɪˈteɪʃn] n 沉思，冥想
Many leaders were lost in meditation at the meeting.
在会议上，很多领导人陷入了深思中。
⊛deliberation 熟思　⊛be lost in... 迷失在……

0580 **melancholy** [ˈmelənkɑːli]
n 忧郁，悲哀　a 忧郁的，阴沉的
She had a strain of melancholy after she got fired.
被炒鱿鱼后，她有点忧郁。

⊛strain (P. 642)

0581 **mellow** [ˈmeloʊ] a 成熟的，柔和的　v 成熟，变柔和
She grew more mellow after marrying for three years.
结婚三年后，她变得更加成熟了。
⊛full-grown 成熟的　⊛immature 未成熟的
⊛grow more mellow 变得更加成熟了

0582 **mentality** [menˈtæləti] n 智力，思想，精神力
The secretary had a different mentality from the manager.
秘书与经理的心理不同。

> 语法重点
> have a different mentality from（……与……有着不同的心理）后面通常接表示人的名词或代词。

0583 **merchandise** [ˈmɜːrtʃəndaɪs]
n 商品，货物　v 买卖，经商
This company provided merchandise for each supermarket.
这家公司为各个超市提供商品。
⊛merchandise export 商品出口　⊛provide merchandise for... 为……提供商品

0584 **merge** [mɜːrdʒ] v 合并
This company was merged with a holding company.
这家公司与一家控股公司合并了。
⊛combine 结合　⊛divide 分开　⊛merge together 混合
⊛be merged with... 与……合并

0585 **metaphor** ['metəfər] n 隐喻，暗喻，象征

This hard-working employee was usually a metaphor for workaholic.
这名努力工作的员工通常是工作狂的象征。
- parabole 隐喻　　simile 明喻　　be a metaphor for... 是……的象征

> **语法重点**
> 副词 + 现在分词可以合成形容词，如例句中的 hard-working 就是由副词 hard（努力地）+ 现在分词 working（工作）构成的。

0586 **metropolitan** [,metrə'pɑːlɪtən] a 大都市的

These graduates planned to get in the metropolitan career life.
这些毕业生准备投身进入大城市的职场生活中。
- urban 城市的　　rustic 乡村的
- metropolitan district 都市区　　get in... 进入……

> career (P. 405)

0587 **migrate** ['maɪgreɪt] v 迁徙，移居，迁移

These girls migrated to Canada for job hunting.
为了找工作，这些女孩移居到了加拿大。
- transplant 迁移　　migrate attribute 迁移特性
- migrate to... 移居到……

0588 **migration** [maɪ'greɪʃn] n 迁移，移居

The secretary said that there was nothing wrong with the data migration.
秘书说，资料移转没有任何错误。

0589 **militant** ['mɪlɪtənt] a 好战的 n 激进分子

The failure of the negotiation didn't foul up the employees' militant spirit.
谈判失败并没有挫伤员工们的斗志。
- aggressive 好斗的　　foul up... 搞糟……

> **语法重点**
> militant spirit 可以表示"斗志"。

0590 **miller** ['mɪlər] n 磨坊主人，碾磨工，蛾

Could I bother you to hand this contract to the miller?
能麻烦你把这份合约交给那个磨坊主人吗？
- Could I bother you to...? 能麻烦你……？

> **语法重点**
> could I bother you to 后面通常接动词原形。

0591 **mimic** ['mɪmɪk] v 模仿 n 复写品或仿制品 a 模仿的

This high-tech robot was an amazing mimic.
这台高科技机器人有着惊人的模仿能力。
- imitate 模仿　　mimic diagram 模拟图
- ... be an amazing mimic ……有惊人的模仿能力

> robot (P. 083)

0592 miniature ['mɪnətʃər]
a 小型的，微小的 **n** 微小的模型，缩影

This model was a miniature of the whole constructional engineering.
这个模型是整个建筑工程的一个缩影。
- minute 微小的 **反** large 大的 **词** in miniature 小型
- miniature 指由正常体积微缩的物体，而 minute 指小得难看见，有时需用显微镜才看得见。

engineering (P. 435)

0593 minimize ['mɪnɪmaɪz]
v 使减到最少

He has minimized the importance of this plan.
他已经将这个计划的重要性贬至最低。
- reduce 减少 **反** maximize 最大化 **词** profit minimize 利润最小化
- minimize the importance of... ……贬低……的重要性

0594 miraculous [mɪ'rækjələs]
a 奇迹的，不可思议的

These salesmen won a miraculous victory over the opponents.
这些业务员战胜了对手，赢得了奇迹般的胜利。
- incredible 不可思议的

opponent (P. 604)

0595 mischievous ['mɪstʃɪvəs]
a 淘气的，有害的

The mischievous employee was clever at programming.
那名淘气的职员擅长程序设计。
- naughty 淘气的 **词** mischievous smile 恶意的微笑

语法重点
be clever at（擅长）后面通常接动词原形。

0596 missionary ['mɪʃəneri]
a 传教的 **n** 传教士

A missionary accepted an offer of employment of this school as a teacher.
一名传教士受聘为这所学校的老师。
- shepherd 牧师 **词** accept an offer of employment of... 应聘……

0597 mobilize ['moʊbəlaɪz]
v 动员，组织，动员起来

The president mobilized all the employees to brainstorm.
总裁动员所有员工集思广益。
- organize 组织 **词** mobilize support 动员支持
- mobilize sb. to do... 动员某人做某事

语法重点
brainstorm 作动词表示"集体讨论，集思广益以寻找"。

0598 modernization [ˌmɑːdərnə'zeɪʃn]
n 现代化，现代化的事物

For this reason, we should achieve enterprise modernization.
为此，我们要实现企业现代化。
- update 现代化 **词** for this reason, ... 为此，……

miniature ~ motto

0599 mold [moʊld] n 模型 v 形成，塑造，对……产生影响
The manager wanted to mold all the employees into supermen.
经理想把所有员工都塑造成超人。
- casting mold 铸模
- mold sb. into... 把某人塑造成……

0600 momentum [moʊˈmentəm] n 动量，气势
It's said that this strike was gaining momentum.
据说，此次罢工势头正猛。
- gather momentum 不断兴起

> **语法重点**
> gain momentum 的主语一般是某个过程或运动。

0601 monopoly [məˈnɑːpəli] n 垄断，垄断商品
They were determined to smash up the monopoly in the field of production.
他们决心打破生产领域的垄断。
- monopoly on... 对……的垄断
- smash up... 击毁……

▶ smash (P. 634)

0602 monotonous [məˈnɑːtənəs] a 单调的，无抑扬顿挫的
It is monotonous to sort out these sales data every day.
天天整理这些销售资料很无聊。
- tedious 单调乏味的
- various 各种各样的
- it is monotonous to do sth. 做某事很无聊

▶ sort (P. 225)

0603 monotony [məˈnɑːtəni] n 单调，无聊
These employees were eager to relieve the monotony of their work.
这些员工很想缓解单调乏味的工作。
- boredom 无聊
- break the monotony 打破单调

> **语法重点**
> relieve the monotony of（缓解单调乏味的）后面通常接表示物的名词。

0604 morale [məˈræl] n 士气，信念，风纪
The department manager was bolstering up the morale of the employees.
部门经理正在鼓舞员工们的士气。
- restore morale 恢复士气
- bolster up the morale of... 鼓舞……的士气

0605 morality [məˈræləti] n 道德，道德准则
It is revolting to his morality of career.
这违反了他的职业道德。
- virtue 品德
- personal morality 个人品德
- it is revolting to... 这违反了……

0606 motto [ˈmɑːtoʊ] n 座右铭，箴言
Serving the customers is the employees' motto.
为顾客服务是员工们的座右铭。
- proverb 格言
- school motto 校训
- be one's motto 是……的座右铭

745

0607 mournful ['mɔːrnfl] a 令人悲痛的，使人伤心的
The retired old employee looked so mournful.
那位退休的老员工看起来很悲伤。
- melancholy 使人悲伤的　- mournful eyes 悲伤的眼神
- ... looks mournful ……看起来很悲伤

> 语法重点
> 句中的 so 作副词，修饰形容词 mournful。

0608 mouthpiece(1) ['maʊθpiːs] n 话筒
The secretary quickly put her hand over the mouthpiece.
秘书急忙用手捂住话筒。
- telephone mouthpiece 电话话筒　- put one's hand over... 用手捂住……

0609 mouthpiece(2) ['maʊθpiːs] n 喉舌，代言人
The model was the mouthpiece of this company.
那名模特儿是这家公司的代言人。
- spokesman 代言人　- be the mouthpiece of... 是……的代言人

0610 municipal [mjuːˈnɪsɪpl] a 市政的，地方政府的
The municipal government gave the go-ahead for this bidding document.
市政府批准了这份标书。
- municipal engineering 市政工程　- give the go-ahead for... 批准……

› document (P. 559)

0611 mute [mjuːt] a 沉默的 n 哑巴
Most of the employees were mute on this proposal.
大多数员工对此项提议保持沉默。
- voiceless 无声的　- mute sound 静音　- be mute on... 对……保持沉默

0612 mythology [mɪˈθɑːlədʒi] n 神话，虚构的事实
This writer was skillful in rewriting Chinese mythology.
这位作家善于改写中国神话。

> 语法重点
> be skillful in（善于）后面通常接动名词。

0613 narrate [nəˈreɪt] v 叙述，旁白说明，讲故事
The singer held tears to narrate one thing to the guests at the party.
在派对上，这名歌手含泪叙述一件事情给宾客们听。
- relate 叙述　- narrate character 叙事对象

> 语法重点
> hold tears to（含泪……）后面接动词原形。

0614 narrative ['nærətɪv] n 叙述 a 叙事体的，善于叙述的
It's a narrative about how this entrepreneur established a business.
这是一个关于这名企业家如何创业的故事。
- story 故事　- narrative structure 叙事结构

› establish (P. 436)

0615 narrator [nəˈreɪtər] n 叙述者，解说员

The woman was the narrator of this product launch.
那名女人是这次产品发布会的解说员。
- teller 讲述者
- be the narrator of... 是……的解说员

语法重点
be the narrator of 的主语一般是指人的名词或代词。

0616 nationalism [ˈnæʃnəlɪzəm] n 民族主义，民族自豪感

The president had a longstanding interest in economic nationalism.
总裁一直对经济民族主义很感兴趣。
- statism 国家主义

0617 naturalist [ˈnætʃrəlɪst] n 自然主义者 a 自然的，博物学的

This naturalist put forth a new theory.
这名自然主义者提出了一种新理论。
- spontaneous 自然的
- put forth... 提出……

- theory (P. 373)

0618 naval [ˈneɪvl] a 海军的，军舰的

This naval base planned to advertise for sailors.
这个海军基地准备登广告招聘水手。
- marine 海的
- naval base 海军基地
- advertise for... 登广告招聘……

0619 navel [ˈneɪvl] n 肚脐，中央，中心

The company put a ban on the employees' ring in their navel.
公司禁止员工在肚脐上挂环。

语法重点
put a ban on（禁止）后面通常接名词。

0620 navigation [ˌnævɪˈgeɪʃn] n 航海，航海术，导航

Electromagnetic interference has become a threat to the satellite navigation.
电磁干扰已经成为卫星导航的威胁。
- sailing 航行
- navigation canal 通航运河

语法重点
become a threat to（成为……的威胁）后面通常接名词或代词。

0621 negotiation [nɪˌgoʊʃiˈeɪʃn] n 协商

Cooperating with each other was an essential precondition for the negotiation.
互相合作是谈判的必要前提。
- treaty 谈判
- break off negotiations 中断谈判

语法重点
be an essential precondition for（是……的必要前提）后面通常接名词或代词。
- essential (P. 437)

0622 neon [ˈniːɑːn] n 霓虹灯，氖

The store's neon could flash in turn after repair.
修理之后，商店的霓虹灯能够交替闪烁。
- neon signs 霓虹灯广告
- ... flash in turn ……交替闪烁

0623 **neutral** ['nuːtrəl] a 中立的，不偏不倚的
The manager said in a neutral voice, "You are fired."
经理以不动声色的口吻说："你被解雇了"。
- litmusless 中性的　　secund 偏向一方的　　neutral nation 中立国

0624 **newlywed** ['nuːliˌwɛd] n 新婚者
All the employees raised their glasses to propose a toast to the newlyweds.
所有员工举起酒杯，向这对新婚夫妇敬酒。
- raise one's glass to propose a toast to... 举起酒杯向……敬酒

> **语法重点**
> raise one's glass to propose a toast to 后面通常接表示人的名词或代词。
> toast (P. 236)

0625 **newscaster** ['nuːzkæstər] n 新闻播报员
I heard that this new employee was in competition with the experienced newscaster.
我听说，这位新员工正在与那位经验丰富的新闻广播员竞争。
- be in competition with... 与……竞争

> **语法重点**
> newscaster 是由 news 和 broadcaster 两个词混合而成的一个新词，前半部分表属性，后半部分表主体。

0626 **nomination** [ˌnɑːmɪ'neɪʃn] n 提名，被提名
It's said that the assistant gained a nomination for the best employee.
据说，助理获得最佳员工的提名。
- appointment 任命　　nomination speech 提名演说

> **语法重点**
> get a nomination for（获得……的提名）后面通常接表示奖项的名词。

0627 **nominee** [ˌnɑːmɪ'niː] n 被提名者，候选人，被任命者
The manager said that this new employee was the last one who could be raised as a nominee.
经理说，这名新员工是最不可能获得提名的人。
- appointee 被任命者　　nominator 提名者　　nominee company 托管公司
- be the last one... 最不可能……

> **语法重点**
> 在英语中，可以用形容词 last 修饰名词或形容词来加强语气，表达说话者的情感，意思是"最不……的"。

0628 **norm** [nɔːrm] n 基准，规范（劳动）定额
These stenographers have been above the norm in shorthand.
这些速记员的速记能力已经超过标准。
- criterion 标准　　have become the norm 已经变成惯例
- be above the norm in... ……超过标准

0629 **notorious** [noʊ'tɔːriəs] a 恶名昭彰的，声名狼藉的
This accountant was notorious for embezzling public funds.
这名会计因贪污公款而声名狼藉。
- infamous 声名狼藉的　　notorious conduct 丑行
- be notorious for... 因……而声名狼藉

> **语法重点**
> be notorious for 和 be famous for 都表示"以……出名"，但 be notorious for 一般用于不好的名声，而 be famous for 则用于好的荣誉或名誉等。

neutral ~ oblige

0630 nourish ['nɜːrɪʃ] v 养育，施肥于，怀抱，使健壮
The manager said that he could find nothing to nourish his suspicion.
经理说，他找不到任何怀疑的根据。

> 语法重点
> find nothing to（找不到）后面通常接动词原形。

0631 nuisance ['nuːsns] n 麻烦事，损害
The irresponsible telephone operator made a nuisance of herself.
那个不负责任的接线员真让人讨厌。
- make a nuisance of oneself 某人惹人讨厌

> 语法重点
> make a nuisance of oneself 句型中，oneself 指代被讨厌的人。

0632 nurture ['nɜːrtʃər] v / n 养育，培育，滋养
The company was duty-bound to nurture these new employees.
公司有责任培养这些新员工。
- foster 养育　　nurture life 孕育生命
- be duty-bound to do sth. 有责任做某事

> 语法重点
> duty-bound 是个合成词，表示"义不容辞的"。

0633 nutrient ['nuːtriənt] n 营养物，养分 a 营养的，滋养的
The researchers were making a study of these nutrients.
研究人员正在仔细研究这些营养物质。
- make a study of... 仔细研究……

0634 nutrition [nuːˈtrɪʃn] n 营养
This new product could provide nutrition for the elders.
这种新产品能够为老年人提供营养。
- nourishment 营养　　provide nutrition for... 为……提供营养

> 语法重点
> provide nutrition for 后面常接表示人的名词或代词。

0635 nutritious [nuːˈtrɪʃəs] a 有营养的，滋养的
It's so important to choose nutritious work meals.
选择有营养的工作餐是非常重要的。
- alible 有营养的　　innutritious 缺少养分的　　it's important to... ……是重要的

> 语法重点
> it's important to 后面通常接动词原形。
> meal (P. 189)

0636 obligation [ˌɑːblɪˈɡeɪʃn] n 义务，责任
Every employee was under the obligation to maintain the company image.
每一名员工都有责任维护公司形象。
- duty 责任　　be under the obligation to... 有责任……

> maintain (P. 188)

0637 oblige [əˈblaɪdʒ] v 使不得不做……
The manager was obliged to cancel the meeting due to critical situation.
由于紧急情况，经理不得不取消会议。
- force 强迫　　free 使自由　　be obliged to... 被迫……

> 语法重点
> be obliged to 相当于 be forced to, to 后面接动词原形。

749

0638 obscure [əbˈskjʊr] **a** 阴暗的，费解的 **v** 使变模糊
This warehouse was too obscure for looking for anything.
这个仓库太昏暗了，什么都找不到。
- dim 变模糊
- obscure glass 毛玻璃
- be too obscure for... 太昏暗而无法……

0639 offering [ˈɔːfərɪŋ] **n** 供奉，提议，课程 **v** 提供
We had the pleasure in providing you with the offering price.
我们很高兴地为您提供发行价。
- offering service 提供服务
- have the pleasure in... 很高兴……

→ pleasure (P. 205)

0640 offspring [ˈɔːfsprɪŋ] **n** 子孙
The president's offspring could take over this company.
总裁的子女可以接管这家公司。
- descendant 子孙
- take over... 接管……

0641 operational [ˌɑːpəˈreɪʃənl] **a** 操作上的，可使用的
Operational management was hemmed in by company system.
操作管理受到了公司制度的限制。
- handling 操作的
- be hemmed in by... 受到……的限制

0642 opposition [ˌɑːpəˈzɪʃn] **n** 反对，相反，反对者
Most of the employees were in opposition to this vacation plan.
大多数员工都反对这项休假计划。
- favour 赞成
- be in opposition to... 反对

→ vacation (P. 242)

0643 oppress [əˈpres] **v** 压迫，压制，压抑
Only a few workers were oppressed by the private enterprises.
只有少数工人遭受私营企业的压迫。
- suppress 压制
- liberate 解放
- spirit oppress 精神压迫

语法重点
be oppressed by（遭受……的压迫）后面可以接表示人或团体组织的名词或代词。

0644 oppression [əˈpreʃn] **n** 压迫，被压迫的状态，压迫物
Oppression from the company provoked the employees to rebellion.
公司的压迫激起了员工们的反抗。
- pressure 压迫
- liberation 解放
- political oppression 政治迫害

语法重点
provoke sb. to（激起……）后面通常接名词或代词。

0645 option [ˈɑːpʃn] **n** 选择，选择权
The manager had no option but to resign.
经理除了辞职，别无选择。
- choice 选择
- put option 卖出期权
- have no option but to do sth. 别无选择只好做某事

0646 **optional** [ˈɑːpʃənl] a 非必需的，可选择的，随意的
The rest of the product summaries are optional.
剩下的产品目录是可以选择的。
- elective 选择的
- compulsory 必修的

> **语法重点**
> the rest of 后接可数名词的复数形式作主语时，应看作复数，动词用复数，如例句。

0647 **ordeal** [ɔːrˈdiːl] n 严酷的考验，折磨
Continuous work overtime was an ordeal for the employees.
连续加班对员工们来说是一种折磨。
- illusage 折磨
- be an ordeal for... 对……来说是一种折磨

> **语法重点**
> be an ordeal for 后面通常接表示人的名词。

0648 **orderly** [ˈɔːrdərli] a 整齐的，有秩序的
The employees walked out of the meeting room in an orderly fashion.
员工们井然有序地走出会议室。
- tidy 整洁的
- messy 杂乱的
- orderly sequence 有条不紊
- do sth. in an orderly fashion 井然有序地做某事

> fashion (P. 295)

0649 **originality** [əˌrɪdʒəˈnæləti] n 独创性，独特
As a whole, this designer was a man of great originality.
整体来说，这名设计师是个很有创造力的人。
- novelty 新颖
- emulate 效仿
- be a man of... 是个……样的人

> **语法重点**
> be a man 表示"做个男子汉，拿出勇气来"，是常用的短语，其主语通常是人。

0650 **originate** [əˈrɪdʒɪneɪt] v 产生，起源于，创造
The architect said that this architectural style originated in Europe.
那名设计师说，这种建筑风格起源于欧洲。
- emanate 发源
- originate from... 发源于……

0651 **outbreak** [ˈaʊtbreɪk] n 爆发，突然发生
The outbreak of flu started last week in the company.
公司于上周开始爆发流感。
- eruption 爆发
- mass outbreak 大规模流行

> **语法重点**
> the outbreak of 指疾病或暴动的爆发。

0652 **outfit** [ˈaʊtfɪt] n 全套装备，工具 v 装备
You should have a go to outfit yourself.
你应该试着打扮自己。
- tool 工具
- have a go to do sth. 试着做某事

0653 **outing** [ˈaʊtɪŋ] n 郊游，散步 v 伸出，揭露
Most of the employees agreed to go on an outing to the seaside.
大多数员工同意去海滨游玩。
- excursion 远足
- on an outing 户外活动
- go on an outing to... 去……郊游

0654 **outlaw** ['aʊtlɔː] n 歹徒 v 宣布……为不合法，将……放逐

The outlaw was caught in the assembly room.
那名歹徒在会议室里被抓住了。
- gangster 歹徒　- be caught in... 在……被抓住

🔗 assembly (P. 397)

0655 **outlet** ['aʊtlet] n 排气口，出路，排遣

The secretary found an outlet for her anger.
秘书找到了发泄怒火的途径。
- exit 出口　- inlet 入口　- outlet valve 排气阀
- outlet 通常指流体（如水、电以及怒火等）的"出口，入口"，而表示人的"入口，出口"要用 entrance, exit 等。

0656 **outlook** ['aʊtlʊk] n 观点，看法，展望

The president changed his outlook on this proposal.
总裁改变了对这项提议的看法。
- view 观点　- change one's outlook on... 改变对……的看法

🔗 proposal (P. 343)

0657 **outnumber** [ˌaʊt'nʌmbər] v 数量胜过……

Female employees outnumbered male ones by fifty.
女员工比男员工多五十人。
- overnumber 数目超过，比……多　- outnumber by... 多……

0658 **outrage** ['aʊtreɪdʒ]
n 暴行，愤慨 v 激起……的义愤，激怒

Most of the employees were outraged by this unreasonable arrangement.
大多数员工为这个不合理安排而震怒。
- anger 愤怒　- be outraged by... 为……所震怒

0659 **outrageous** [aʊt'reɪdʒəs]
a 粗暴的，无法容忍的，反常的

The outrageous client was driven out by the manager.
那个蛮横的顾客被经理赶了出来。
- bearish 粗暴的　- be driven out by... 被……赶出来

【语法重点】
drive out 表示"驱赶，开车外出"，而 be driven out 是其被动形式。

0660 **outright** ['aʊtraɪt]
a 公然的，直率的 ad 完全地，即刻

The president gave an outright denial to the bankrupt things.
总裁断然否认破产的事情。

【语法重点】
give an outright denial to（断然否认）后面通常接名词或代词。

- downright 直率的 - incomplete 不完全的

0661 **outset** [ˈaʊtset] n 开头

At the outset of the business, all the employees were full of ambition.
事业刚起步时，所有的员工都踌躇满志。
- start 开始 - ending 结尾 - outset date 起始日期
- at the outset of... 在……开始

语法重点
与 at the outset 具有相似含义的还有 at the start 等。
- ambition (P. 255)

0662 **overhead** [ˌoʊvərˈhed] a 在头顶上，架空的

The teacher put the folders in the overhead locker.
老师把资料夹放在上头的柜子里。
- aloft 在头顶，在高处 - put... in... 把……放在……里

语法重点
在英语构词法中，介词 + 名词可以构成形容词，如例句中的 overhead。

0663 **overlap** [ˌəʊvəˈlæp] / [ˌoʊvərˈlæp] v 部分重叠 n 重叠

Interview time overlapped with the beginning of the meeting.
接见时间与会议开始的时间是重叠的。
- repeat 重复 - overlap with... 与……重叠

0664 **overturn** [ˌəʊvəˈtɜːn] / [ˌoʊvərˈtɜːrn]
v 使翻转，使倾覆 n 翻转

The manager backed down after his proposal was overturned.
经理在自己的提议被推翻后做出了让步。

语法重点
在英语构词法中，副词 + 动词可以构成动词，如例句中的 overturn 就是由副词 over（从一边到另一边）+ 动词 turn（翻转）构成的动词。

0665 **pact** [pækt] n 契约，协定，条约

The corporate leaders decided to make a pact with those representatives.
公司领导人决定与那些代表达成协议。
- treaty 条约 - trade pact 贸易协定

语法重点
make a pact with（与……达成协议）后面通常接表示人的名词或代词。

0666 **pamphlet** [ˈpæmflət] n 小册子

The pamphlets have been given out to every employee.
小册子已经分发给每一位员工。
- booklet 小册子 - be given out 分发……

语法重点
be given out 是 give out 的被动形式。

0667 **paralyze** [ˈpærəlaɪz] v 瘫痪，使麻痹，使惊愕

This problem would sooner or later paralyze the company.
这个问题迟早会使公司陷于瘫痪。

0668 **parliament** [ˈpɑːrləmənt] n 议会，国会

It's said that the president of this company was elected to parliament.
据说，这家公司的总裁当选为议员。
- congress 国会 - parliament buildings 议会大厦

语法重点
be elected to（当选为）后面通常接表示机构或组织的名词。

0669 **pathetic** [pəˈθetɪk] `a` 悲惨的，可怜的
It's pathetic that all these senior employees got fired.
这些老员工都被辞退了，真是可悲。
- poor 可怜的
- it's pathetic that... ……很可悲

0670 **patriotic** [ˌpeɪtriˈɑːtɪk] `a` 爱国的
Many foreign businessmen were penetrated with patriotic feeling.
很多外商都满怀爱国情怀。
- traitorous 背叛的
- be penetrated with... 充满……

→ penetrate (P. 611)

0671 **PDA** `abbr` 掌上电脑
The manager got information from the PDA.
经理从掌上电脑中获取资讯。
- get information from... 从……中获取信息

语法重点
PDA 是 Personal Digital Assistant 的首字母缩写。

0672 **peddle** [ˈpedl] `v` 叫卖，忙于琐事
The female colleague usually peddled gossip round the office.
那位女同事经常在办公室里到处说闲话。
- peddle munitions 贩卖军火

语法重点
peddle gossip round（在……说闲话）后面通常接表示地点的名词。

0673 **pedestrian** [pəˈdestriən] `n` 行人，步行者
The workers were in the construction of the pedestrian subway.
工人们正在建造人行隧道。
- walker 步行者
- pedestrian crossing 斑马线
- be in the construction of... 建筑……

→ subway (P. 191)

0674 **peninsula** [pəˈnɪnsələ] `n` 半岛
It was difficult to imagine how this company built a factory in this peninsula.
很难想象，这家公司要如何在这个半岛上建立一家工厂。
- Arabian Peninsula 阿拉伯半岛
- it is difficult to imagine... 很难想象……

0675 **pension** [ˈpenʃn] `n` 退休金，年金
This company had a disinclination to pay pension fund.
这家公司不愿意缴纳退休基金。
- pension fund 退休基金

语法重点
have a disinclination to（不愿意）后面通常接动词原形。

0676 **perception** [pərˈsepʃn] `n` 感觉，观念，洞察力
She minded her boyfriend's perception of this thing.
她很在意男朋友对此事的看法。
- sense 观念
- aesthetic perception 美感
- mind one's perception of... 在意……对……的看法

0677 **perseverance** [ˌpɜːrsəˈvɪrəns] n 坚持不懈，不屈不挠

The employees showed great perseverance in the preparation for the exhibition.
员工们在筹备展览时表现出坚强毅力。
- doggedness 坚持不懈
- ... show great perseverance in... ……在……方面表现出坚强毅力

语法重点
show great perseverance in 后面通常接名词或代词。

0678 **persevere** [ˌpɜːrsəˈvɪr] v 坚持不懈，不屈不挠

These programmers persevered with the programming.
这些程序员坚持不懈地进行程序设计。
- persist 坚持　　abandon 放弃　　persevere in 坚持
- persevere with... 坚持……

0679 **persistence** [pərˈsɪstəns] n 固执，持续，保留时间

By sheer persistence, the salesman signed the contract.
那名业务员全凭坚持不懈签订了合约。
- continuance 持续　　by sheer persistence, ... 全凭坚持不懈，……

→ sheer (P. 776)

0680 **persistent** [pərˈsɪstənt] a 固执的

The manager felt embarrassed by the reporter's persistent questioning.
那名记者连续不断的提问使经理感到很尴尬。
- continual 连续的　　discontinuous 间断的
- feel embarrassed by... 为……感到尴尬

0681 **perspective** [pərˈspektɪv] n 透视图，远景，观点

The old man told the girl to keep things in perspective.
这名老人告诉女孩，要正确地看待事物。
- viewpoint 观点　　perspective figure 透视图

0682 **pesticide** [ˈpestɪsaɪd] n 杀虫剂，农药

The scientist hastened the development of a new pesticide.
科学家们加紧研制一种新的杀虫剂。
- insecticide 杀虫剂　　the development of... ……的发展

→ hasten (P. 451)

0683 **petroleum** [pəˈtroʊliəm] n 石油

This company didn't agree to advance the price of the petroleum.
这家公司不同意提高石油的价格。
- gasoline 石油　　petroleum product 石油产品
- advance the price of... 提高……的价格

0684 **petty** [ˈpeti] a 小的，器量小的
The assistant was bothered by the petty task all day long.
助理整天都为烦琐的工作而烦恼。
- trivial 琐碎的
- petty cash（通常指小额的）零用现金
- be bothered by... 为……而烦恼

0685 **pharmacist** [ˈfɑːrməsɪst] n 药剂师
This pharmacist must meet the interviewer by appointment.
这名药剂师必须预约会见面试官。
- druggist 药剂师
- licensed pharmacist 执业药师
- meet sb. by appointment 预约会见某人

appointment (P. 396)

0686 **pharmacy** [ˈfɑːrməsi] n 药房，制药业
This company had solved the problem of pharmacy equipment.
这家公司已经解决了药房设备的问题。
- dispensary 药房
- solve the problem of... 解决……的问题

0687 **phase** [feɪz] n 阶段，方面 v 分阶段实行
This factory was still in the first phase of construction.
这座工厂还处于建造的第一阶段。
- stage 阶段
- be in the first phase of... 处于……的第一阶段

0688 **photographic** [ˌfoʊtəˈɡræfɪk] a 摄影的，摄影用的
It's said that this architect had a photographic memory for the planning map.
据说，这名建筑师对规划图具有摄影般精确的记忆力。
- photographic equipment 摄影设备

0689 **picturesque** [ˌpɪktʃəˈresk] a 美丽的，生动的，奇特的
The reporter had a picturesque description of this exhibition.
记者生动地描述了本次展览。
- vivid 生动的
- have a picturesque description of... 生动描述……

语法重点
picturesque 作形容词，用于修饰后面的名词 description。

0690 **pierce** [pɪrs] v 刺穿，穿入
The workers wanted to pierce holes in the steel plate.
工人们想在钢板上打洞。
- transpierce 刺穿
- pierce through 刺破
- pierce holes in... 在……上打洞

plate (P. 205)

0691 **piety** [ˈpaɪəti] n 虔敬
The believers in this church are eminent for piety.
这间教堂的信徒以虔诚闻名。
- godliness 虔诚
- impiety 不虔诚
- filial piety 孝顺
- be eminent for... 以……著称

petty ~ poacher

0692 **pious** [ˈpaɪəs] **a** 虔诚的，可嘉的
You should always remember that you need to be a pious employee.
你必须牢记你要当一名尽责的员工。
🌐 you should always remember that... 你必须牢记……

🌐 employee (P. 290)

0693 **pipeline** [ˈpaɪplaɪn] **n** 管道，管线 **v** 用管道运输
The construction of this factory was in the pipeline.
这座工厂的建设正在筹划当中。
🌐 in the pipeline 在进行中

0694 **pitcher** [ˈpɪtʃər] **n** 投手，水壶
Mother asked me to fetch a pitcher of water.
妈妈要我拿一壶水过来。
🌐 hurler 投掷者 🌐 a pitcher of 一壶

🌐 fetch (P. 441)

0695 **plight** [plaɪt] **n** 誓约，困境 **v** 宣誓，订婚
The president was in sympathy with these employees' plight.
总裁非常同情这些员工的困境。
🌐 difficulty 困境 🌐 plight one's troth 订婚 🌐 be in sympathy with... 同情……

0696 **pneumonia** [nuːˈmoʊniə] **n** 肺炎，急性肺炎
It's said that the general manager came down with pneumonia.
据说，总经理染上肺炎病倒了。
🌐 pulmonitis 肺炎 🌐 bronchial pneumonia 支气管肺炎
🌐 come down with... 染上……病

0697 **poach** [poʊtʃ] **v** 烹调，偷猎，窃取
The manager wanted to poach employees from this company.
那位经理想挖走这家公司的员工。
🌐 filch 窃取 🌐 poach on someone's territory 侵犯他人的权利
🌐 poach employee from... 从……挖走员工

0698 **poacher** [ˈpoʊtʃər] **n** 偷猎者，侵入他人地界者
The poacher beat a hasty retreat before the workers came.
工作人员到来之前，那名盗猎者就仓皇逃跑了。
🌐 intruder 入侵者 🌐 poacher turned gamekeeper 监守自盗
🌐 beat a hasty retreat 仓皇逃跑

🌐 retreat (P. 498)

0699 pollutant [pə'luːtənt] **a** 受污染的 **n** 污染物质
This pollutant would have a bad effect on the workers' health.
这种污染物会对工人们的健康造成不好的影响。
- contamination 污染物 - have a bad effect on... 对……造成不好的影响

0700 ponder ['pɑːndər] **v** 仔细考量，沉思
The manager was pondering on this proposal in the office.
经理正在办公室里考虑这个提议。
- consider 考虑 - ponder over 沉思 - ponder on... 考虑……

0701 populate ['pɑːpjuleɪt] **v** 居住在……，繁殖，增加
The apartment was populated by most of the students.
大多数的学生都住在这个公寓里。
- inhabit 居住 - thickly populated 人口密集

语法重点
be populated by（聚居）后面可以接表示动物或人的名词或代词。

0702 posture ['pɑːstʃər] **n** 姿态 **v** 做出某种姿势
The president adopted an uncompromising posture on this decision.
总裁对这项决议采取毫不妥协的态度。
- pose 姿势 - good posture 良好姿势
- adopt an uncompromising posture on... 对……采取毫不妥协的态度

语法重点
uncompromising 表示"不妥协的"，作形容词用于修饰后面的名词 posture。

0703 precede [prɪ'siːd] **v** 处在……之前，领先
They touched upon this question in the several meetings that preceded.
在前面的几次会议中，他们都谈及这个问题。
- follow 跟随 - precede by 为……加上前言 - touch upon... 涉及……

0704 precedent ['presɪdənt] **n** 前例，惯例 **a** 先前的
This successful entrepreneur set a precedent for those people who wanted to establish a business.
这位成功的企业家为那些想要创业的人开创了先例。
- antecedent 先前的 - following 下面的 - without precedent 史无前例
- set a precedent for... 为……开先例

- successful (P. 230)

want 和 expect 都可表示"希望"：want 一般指想要的是渴望得到的东西，能弥补实际需要，而 expect 通常指有很大程度的把握，但仍含有预料之意，或预计某事或某行动的发生。

0705 precision [prɪ'sɪʒn] **n** 精准，精密，精密度
The secretary made the sales report with precision.
秘书准确无误地制作了销售报表。
- fidelity 精确 - do sth. with precision 准确无误做某事

pollutant ~ premier

0706 predecessor ['predəsesər] n 前辈，前任者
It's said that the new manager was more mature than the predecessor.
据说，新经理要比前任经理更成熟一些。
📘 successor 继承者　📗 be more mature than... 比……更成熟

📙 mature (P. 322)

0707 prediction [prɪ'dɪkʃn] n 预言，预告，预报
The analyst would make a prediction about the exhibition.
分析员将会对展览做出预测。
📘 forecast 预报　📘 earthquake prediction 地震预报
📗 make a prediction about... 对……做出预测

0708 preface ['prefəs] n 序言，前言　v 以……开始
The principal prefaced his speech with the company's brief introduction.
这位负责人以公司的简介作为讲话的开场白。
📘 introduction 引言　📗 preface... with... 以……作为……的开场白

0709 prejudice ['predʒudɪs] n 偏见，成见
The president had a prejudice against the new employee.
经理对这名新员工抱有偏见。
📘 bias 偏见　📗 have a prejudice against... 对……有偏见

> 语法重点
> have a prejudice against 后面通常接表示人的名词或代词。

0710 preliminary [prɪ'lɪmɪneri] a 初步的，预备的
The girl was taking preliminary steps in preparation for the annual conference.
女孩正在为年会做初步准备。
📘 rudimentary 初步的
📗 take preliminary steps in preparation for... 为……做初步准备

📙 preparation (P. 341)

0711 premature [ˌpriːmə'tʃʊr]
a 过早的，早产的　n 早产儿，早熟
The investment conference was brought to a premature end.
招商发布会过早地结束了。
📘 pronatis 早产儿　📘 premature incubator 早产婴儿保温箱

0712 premier [prɪ'mɪr] n 首相
The president gave an interview to the vice premier in the meeting room.
总裁在会议室里接见了副总理。
📗 premier cycle 第一阶段

> 语法重点
> give an interview to（接见）后面通常接表示人的名词或代词。
> 📙 interview (P. 180)

759

0713 prescribe [prɪˈskraɪb] v 开药方，指示
You have to keep in mind that the company prescribed how the employees should behave.
你必须牢记，公司规定了员工们该有的行为举止。
- order 命令
- you have to keep in mind that... 你必须牢记……

0714 prescription [prɪˈskrɪpʃn] n 处方
The nurse said that the medicine was available on prescription.
护士说，这种药只能凭处方购买。
- recipe 处方
- prescription medicine 处方药
- ... be available on prescription ……凭处方购买

→ available (P. 258)

0715 preside [prɪˈzaɪd] v 主持，充当会议主席
The sales manager would preside over this meeting.
销售部经理将会主持这次会议。
- direct 指挥
- preside over... 主持……

0716 presidency [ˈprezɪdənsi] n 公司总裁职位，管辖
Last year this shareholder was elevated to presidency.
去年，这位股东晋升到总裁的职位。

语法重点
be elevated to（晋升至）后面通常接表示职务的名词。

0717 presidential [ˌprezɪˈdenʃl] a 总统的，总统制的
The secretary booked a presidential suite for the general manager.
秘书为总经理预订了总统套房。
- book... for... 为……预订……

语法重点
此句型中，book 作动词表示"预订"。
→ suite (P. 787)

0718 prestige [preˈstiːʒ] n 声望
The manager had high prestige among all the employees.
经理在所有员工中具有很高的威信。
- reputation 声望
- high prestige 崇高威望

语法重点
have high prestige among（在……中有很高的威信）后面通常接复数名词。

0719 presume [prɪˈzuːm] v 假设，揣测
They presumed to change the marketing plan.
他们擅自改变了营销计划。
- guess 推测
- presume on 利用
- presume to do... 擅自做……

0720 preventive [prɪˈventɪv] a 预防的 n 预防，预防措施
The manager said that we should take preventive actions.
经理说我们应该采取预防措施。
- precautionary 预防的
- preventive action 预防措施

0721 **productivity** [ˌprɑːdʌkˈtɪvəti] n 生产力，生产率

These new machines have increased productivity in the products.
这些新机器提高了产品的生产效率。
- fertility 生产力
- labor productivity 劳动生产率

≈ machine (P. 061)

0722 **proficiency** [prəˈfɪʃnsi] n 熟练，精通

All these employees made proficiency in computer operation.
这些员工都能熟练操作电脑。
- conversancy 熟练
- make proficiency in... 熟练掌握……

≈ operation (P. 479)

0723 **profound** [prəˈfaʊnd] a 深刻的，渊博的

The reform had a profound effect on the development of the company.
这项改革给公司的发展造成了深远影响。
- deep 深奥的
- shallow 肤浅的
- profound effect 深刻的影响
- have a profound effect on... 对……造成深远影响
- profound 语气较强，较为庄重，多指抽象的事物，多用于比喻，而 deep 是普通用词，指由上到下，或由表及里的深度，可指具体或抽象事物。

0724 **progressive** [prəˈɡresɪv] a 进步的，向前进的

Corporate globalization is a progressive idea.
公司全球化是一种进步思想。
- ongoing 前进的
- conservative 保守的

0725 **prohibit** [prəˈhɪbɪt] v 制止，阻止

The company prohibited the employees from dressing in skirt.
公司禁止员工穿裙子。
- prevent 阻止
- allow 允许
- prohibit parking 禁止停车
- prohibit... from doing... 禁止……做……

0726 **prohibition** [ˌproʊəˈbɪʃn] n 禁止，禁律

The residents approved of the prohibition of smoking in the public place.
居民们赞成禁止在公共场所吸烟的规定。

语法重点
the prohibition of 后面通常接动名词。

0727 **projection** [prəˈdʒekʃn] n 设计，投射，突起物

The secretary took the new employees into the projection room.
秘书带新员工们进入了放映室。
- projection room 放映室

语法重点
take sb. into（带某人进入）后面通常接地点名词。

0728 **prone** [proʊn] a 容易……的，有……倾向的
I heard recently the man was prone to angry.
听说这名男子最近很容易发怒。
- apt 有……倾向的
- scandal prone 有丑闻的
- be prone to... 易于……

0729 **propaganda** [ˌprɑːpəˈgændə] n 宣传，宣传运动
The manager asked the secretary to find information on the propaganda department.
经理要秘书收集有关宣传部的信息。

0730 **propel** [prəˈpel] v 推动
The principal's ambition propelled him into embezzling public funds.
这位负责人的野心促使他贪污公款。
- shove 猛推
- propel... into doing... 促使……做……

※ fund (P. 299)

0731 **propeller** [prəˈpelər] n 推进器
The president has agreed to appropriate the fund for these propellers.
总裁已经同意拨款购买这些螺旋桨。

语法重点
appropriate the fund for（为……拨款）后面可以接动名词。
※ appropriate (P. 396)

0732 **prose** [proʊz] n 散文，单调 v 用散文写
This prose writer had a taste for writing poetry.
这位散文作家爱好诗歌写作。
- essay 散文
- have a taste for... 爱好……

0733 **prosecute** [ˈprɑːsɪkjuːt]
v 对……起诉，告发，从事检察官
The trainee accountant was trying his best to prosecute his duties.
那名实习会计正在努力履行他的职责。
- undertake 从事
- prosecute sb. 起诉某人

语法重点
be trying one's best to（某人正在尽力）后面通常接动词原形。

0734 **prosecution** [ˌprɑːsɪˈkjuːʃn] n 起诉
The company called for the prosecution of those business espionages.
公司要求起诉那些商业间谍。
- conduct 实施
- defense 防守
- call for the prosecution of... 要求对……进行起诉

语法重点
call for the prosecution of 后面通常接被起诉的对象。

0735 **prospective** [prəˈspektɪv] a 预期的，将来的，可能的
The salesman said that this old man was a prospective customer.
那名推销员说，这位老人是一个潜在顾客。
- anticipated 预期的
- past 过去的

0736 provincial [prəˈvɪnʃl] a 省的，地方的 n 乡下人
He thought the manager had provincial attitudes.
他认为经理思想迂腐。

0737 provoke [prəˈvoʊk] v 对……挑衅，激怒，驱使
The student didn't provoke the teacher to anger.
这名学生没有惹老师生气。
- irritate 激怒
- appease 安抚
- provoke sb. to... 惹某人……

0738 prowl [praʊl] v 徘徊，潜行 n 悄然潜行
He was on the prowl for the book sewer.
他在四处寻找订书机。
- on the prowl 积极地寻找某物
- be on the prowl for... 四处寻找……

0739 punctual [ˈpʌŋktʃuəl] a 准时的
This new employee is always punctual for work.
这位新员工总是准时上班。
- unpunctual 不准时的
- punctual person 守时的人
- be punctual for... 准时……

0740 purify [ˈpjʊrɪfaɪ] v 使纯净，使洁净
The scientists wanted to purify this substance from the food.
科学家们想从食物中提取出这种物质。
- clarify 得到净化
- purify water 纯水
- purify... from... 从……中提取……

※ substance (P. 368)

0741 purity [ˈpjʊrəti] n 纯净
The researchers wanted to prove the purity of drinking water.
研究人员想检验饮用水的纯度。
- high purity 高纯度
- prove the purity of... 检验……的纯度

0742 qualification [ˌkwɑːlɪfɪˈkeɪʃn] n 资格，限制，资历
This accountant has obtained an accounting qualification certificate.
这名会计已经取得会计资格证书。
- capacity 资格
- disqualification 取消资格
- qualification test 资格考试
- obtain a... qualification certificate 获得……资格证书
- obtain 和 get 都可表示"获得"：obtain 着重通过巨大努力、要求而得到所需或盼望已久的东西，而 get 使用广泛，可指任何方式得到某物，也不一定要经过努力。

※ certificate (P. 540)

0743 quarrelsome [ˈkwɔːrəlsəm] a 爱争吵的
It's said that the employee had a quarrelsome disposition.
据说，那名员工生性爱吵架。

0744 **quench** [kwentʃ] v 抑制

Drinking a bottle of water couldn't quench the athlete's thirst.
喝一瓶水不能使这名运动员解渴。
- suppress 压制　- burn 燃烧　- quench a fire 灭火
- quench one's thirst ……使某人解渴

athlete (P. 257)

0745 **query** [ˈkwɪri] n 询问，问号　v 质疑

The principal had query about this contract.
负责人对这份合约有疑问。
- question 问题　- have query about... 对……有疑问

0746 **questionnaire** [ˌkwestʃəˈner] n 问卷

All the members were asked to fill in questionnaires.
要求所有成员填写调查问卷。
- questionnaire survey 问卷调查　- be asked to fill in... 被要求填写……

0747 **racism** [ˈreɪsɪzəm] n 种族主义，人种偏见

The president said that racism and ageism would not seep into the interview.
总裁说，种族歧视和年龄歧视不会影响到面试。
- prejudice 偏见　- seep into... 影响到……

interview (P. 180)

0748 **radiant** [ˈreɪdiənt] a 光芒四射的，明亮的，辐射的

The manager was radiant with joy after getting promoted.
获得升职后，经理高兴得容光焕发。
- dim 暗淡的　- radiant power 辐射功率

语法重点
be radiant with joy（高兴得容光焕发）的主语一般是表示人的名词或代词。

0749 **radiate** [ˈreɪdieɪt] v 散发，辐射

Joy and satisfaction radiated from all the contestants.
所有参赛者都流露出喜悦与满足的表情。
- release 发射，释放　- radiate from... 从……发出

0750 **radiation** [ˌreɪdiˈeɪʃn] n 辐射，发射

Many female employees feared the long term effects of radiation.
不少女员工害怕辐射造成的长期影响。
- emission 发射　- absorbed radiation 吸收辐射
- fear the long term effects of... 害怕……造成的长期影响

0751 **radiator** [ˈreɪdieɪtər] n 辐射体，冰箱

The clerk said this electric radiator was in short supply.
店员表示这种电暖气缺货。

supply (P. 231)

quench ~ rational

0752 radical ['rædɪkl] **a** 根本的，彻底的 **n** 激进分子，基础
It's said that this department manager was quite radical in demand.
据说，这位部门经理要求十分偏激。
🔵 thorough 彻底的　🔵 superficial 表面的

> 语法重点
> be radical in（在……方面偏激）后面通常接名词。

0753 raft [ræft] **n** 木筏，橡皮艇，大量 **v** 筏运
These principals put forward a raft of new proposals.
这些负责人提出大量新的提议。
🔵 life raft 救生筏　🔵 put forward a raft of... ……提出大量……

0754 raid [reɪd] **n** 突击，突然搜查 **v** 袭击，劫夺
The police made a raid on this law office.
警察突然搜查这家律师事务所。
🔵 invade 侵袭　🔵 raid on 袭击　🔵 make a raid on... 突然搜查

0755 random ['rændəm] **a** 随意的 **n** 随机 **ad** 随机地
The principal carried out random spot checks on these products.
负责人对这些产品进行随机抽查。
🔵 at random 随意地　🔵 carry out random spot checks on... 对……进行随机抽检

🔗 carry (P. 021)

0756 ransom ['rænsəm] **n** 赎金，赎罪 **v** 赎回，赎救
The scoundrel held a shareholder for ransom.
歹徒劫持一名股东以勒索赎金。
🔵 redeem 赎回　🔵 hold... for ransom 劫持……以勒索赎金

0757 rash(1) [ræʃ] **n** 疹子，爆发，同时大量出现的事件
Most of the employees broke out in rash after they ate seafood last night.
昨晚吃了海鲜后，大多数员工都长出了疹子。
🔵 break out in... 突然出现……

0758 rash(2) [ræʃ] **a** 轻率的，鲁莽的
The manager was regretful for the rash decision he had made.
经理为他所做的那个轻率的决定而感到后悔。
🔵 impulsive 冲动的　🔵 rash decisions 鲁莽的决定
🔵 be regretful for... 为……感到后悔

🔗 decision (P. 150)

0759 rational ['ræʃnəl] **a** 理性的，出于理性的
The shareholders finally came to a rational decision.
最终，股东们做出一个理性的决定。
🔵 sensible 明智的　🔵 ... come to a rational decision ……做出一个理性的决定

765

0760 ravage ['rævɪdʒ] **v** 毁坏，劫掠 **n** 破坏
His workroom was ravaged by a group of people.
他的工作室被一群人毁坏了。
◎ damage 毁坏　◎ be ravaged by... 被……毁坏

⊙ group (P. 045)

0761 realism ['riːəlɪzəm] **n** 现实主义，唯实论
These employees showed realism in their work.
这些员工在工作中表现出了务实精神。
◎ actualism 现实主义　◎ idealism 理想主义
◎ show realism in... 在……中表现出务实精神

0762 realization [ˌriːələ'zeɪʃn] **n** 领悟，实现
The manager came to the realization that this project was impractical.
经理逐渐意识到，这个方案不可行。
◎ understanding 认识　◎ come to the realization that... 逐渐意识到……

⊙ project (P. 210)

0763 rebellion [rɪ'beljən] **n** 叛乱，反抗
This job gave him a sense of rebellion.
这份工作给他一种叛逆感。
◎ revolt 反抗　◎ support 支持　◎ rise in rebellion 叛乱
◎ give... a sense of... 给……一种……感觉

0764 recession [rɪ'seʃn] **n** 后退，衰退期
Many transnational enterprises were mired in economic recession.
很多跨国企业都陷入了经济衰退的境地。
◎ depression 不景气　◎ prosperity 繁荣

⊙ economic (P. 431)

0765 recipient [rɪ'sɪpiənt] **n** 接受者，收信者
The president acquired a taste for the recipient of the letter.
总裁对这封信的收信者很感兴趣。
◎ receiver 接受者　◎ acquire a taste for... 对……感兴趣

0766 recommendation [ˌrekəmen'deɪʃn]
n 推荐，介绍，劝告
No longer would the supervisor write recommendation letter for the employees.
主管再也不会为员工写推荐信了。
◎ no longer would... 再也不会……

语法重点
no longer 位于句首所引起的倒装句通常为部分倒装，如果动词为 be 的一般现在时或一般过去时，则为完全倒装。

0767 reconcile ['rekənsaɪl] **v** 调解，使甘心
Finally the girl was reconciled with her boyfriend.
最终，那个女孩和她男朋友和好了。
◎ reconcile to 顺从　◎ be reconciled with... 与……和解

ravage ~ refund

0768 recreational [ˌrekri'eɪʃənl] **a** 娱乐的
The meeting room was set aside for recreational equipments.
这个会议室被留出来放置娱乐器材。
- recreation ground 游乐场
- be set aside for... 为……留出

⊙ aside (P. 256)

0769 recruit [rɪ'kruːt] **v** 征募，吸收（新成员） **n** 新兵，新成员
The factory made bold to recruit child laborers.
这家工厂胆敢招收童工。
- enlist 应募
- recruit registration 新人报到

语法重点
make bold to（擅自……，胆敢……）后面通常接动词原形。

0770 recur [rɪ'kɜːr] **v** 重现，再发生，诉诸
The manager recurred to the problem at the meeting.
经理又在会议上提起了这个问题。
- recrudesce 再发作
- recurring decimal 循环小数
- recur to... 重新提起……

0771 redundant [rɪ'dʌndənt] **a** 多余的，累赘的，解雇的
Ten employees were made redundant from their job last month.
上个月有十名员工被解雇了。
- excessive 过多的
- ... be made redundant from one's job ……被解雇

0772 refine [rɪ'faɪn] **v** 使优美，精炼，改善
They decided to refine the sales program.
他们决定改进这个销售方案。
- improve 改善
- refine rate 净化率
- refine on... 改进……

⊙ sale (P. 085)

0773 reflective [rɪ'flektɪv] **a** 反射的，反映的
These opinions were reflective of the employees' attitude.
这些意见反映出了员工们的态度。
- reflective thought 反省思考
- be reflective of... 反映出……

⊙ attitude (P. 257)

0774 refreshment [rɪ'freʃmənt] **n** 恢复精神，爽快
The secretary didn't partake of those employees' refreshment.
秘书没有吃那些员工的点心。
- spiritual refreshment 精神恢复
- partake of... 吃光……

0775 refund ['riːfʌnd] / [riː'fʌnd] **n** / **v** 退还
Most of the customers asked for a refund.
大多数顾客都要求退款。
- repay 偿还
- tax refund 退税
- ask for a refund ……要求退款

767

0776 **regardless** [rɪˈgɑːrdləs] ad 不注意的
Regardless of the weather, they would visit the factory.
不论天气如何，他们都会来参观工厂。
同 notwithstanding 尽管，仍然　　同 regardless how 无论如何
衍 regardless of... 不管……

0777 **regime** [reɪˈʒiːm] n 政权，制度
They should take the liberty of changing the monetary regime.
他们想擅自更改货币体制。
同 government 政体　　同 legal regime 法律制度

语法重点
take the liberty of（擅自……，斗胆……）后面通常接动名词。
参 liberty (P. 317)

0778 **rehearsal** [rɪˈhɜːrsl] n 排练，彩排
The emcee said the opening ceremony was in rehearsal.
司仪说开幕典礼正在排演中。
同 training 训练　　同 in rehearsal 在彩排中

0779 **rehearse** [rɪˈhɜːrs] v 排练，预演
Several musicians were rehearsing for the opening ceremony in the auditorium.
几名音乐家正在礼堂里为开幕式进行排练。

语法重点
rehearse for（为……进行排练）后面通常接表示活动的名词。

0780 **rein** [reɪn] n 缰绳 v 驾驭，严格控制
The supervisor kept a tight rein on these new employees.
主管对这些新员工严加管制。
同 restrain 控制　　同 draw rein 节省开支，放弃努力

语法重点
keep a tight rein on（对……严加约束）后面通常接表示人的名词或代词。

0781 **reinforce** [ˌriːɪnˈfɔːrs] v 增强
Reinforcing the management is a matter of great account.
加强管理是一件很重要的事情。
同 strengthen 加强　　同 reinforced concrete 钢筋混凝土
衍 ... be a matter of great account ……是很重要的事

0782 **relay** [ˈriːleɪ] v 接替 n 接力赛，替班
The secretary said she would relay your message.
秘书说她会转达你的口信。
衍 ... relay one's message ……转达某人的口信

0783 **relevant** [ˈreləvənt] a 相关的，相对的
The chief editor told me that copyright was relevant to patent.
主编告诉我，版权和专利权有关。
同 concerned 有关的　　反 inappropriate 不恰当的　　同 relevant range 相关范围
衍 be relevant to... 和……有关

参 copyright (P. 551)

0784 **reliance** [rɪ'laɪəns] n 信赖，所信赖的人或物

It would reduce the manager's reliance on you.
这会减少经理对你的信任。
- dependence 依靠
- self reliance 自力更生

语法重点
reduce one's reliance on（减少某人对……的信任）后面通常接表示人的名词或代词。

0785 **relish** ['relɪʃ] n 美味，调味品 v 品尝，调味

The assistant had no relish for vacation.
助理对休假不感兴趣。

语法重点
have no relish for（对……不感兴趣）后面可以接名词或动名词。

0786 **remainder** [rɪ'meɪndər] n 剩余物，余数

The remainder of the materials was put in the folder.
剩余的资料都放在了资料夹里。
- trust remainder 信托财产的指定继承人
- be put in... 被放在……里

0787 **removal** [rɪ'muːvl] n 除去

The removal of the general secretary blew the employees' mind.
秘书长的免职令员工们十分震惊。
- move 移动
- blow one's mind 令某人十分震惊

0788 **renaissance** ['renəsɑːns] n 复活，复兴，文艺复兴

The president said the commodity economy was experiencing a renaissance.
总裁说，商品经济正在复兴。
- reconstruction 复兴
- early renaissance 文艺复兴初期

0789 **render** ['rendər] v 给予，使得

You should render an account of the negotiation result.
你们需要报告谈判结果。
- render certain 确保
- render an account of... 报告……

result (P. 216)

0790 **renowned** [rɪ'naʊnd] a 著名的，有声誉的

The merchant was renowned throughout the business circle.
那位商人在商业界闻名遐迩。
- famous 著名的
- be renowned throughout... 在……出名

merchant (P. 324)

0791 **rental** ['rentl] n 租金，租金额

The company rented the office building at an annual rental of 3,000 dollars.
公司以每年3 000美元的租金租这个办公大楼。
- letting 租金
- accrued rental 应计租金
- rent... at an annual rental of... 以每年……租金租……

0792 **repress** [rɪˈpres] **v** 抑制，镇压，压抑
You should repress your emotion at work.
在工作中你要克制住自己的感情。
suppress 镇压　　repress one's emotion 克制某人的感情
↪ emotion (P. 159)

0793 **resemblance** [rɪˈzembləns] **n** 类似，相似性
Many employees said that the manager bear a resemblance to the president.
很多员工说，经理与总裁相像。
similarity 相似性　　imparity 不同　　bear a resemblance to... 与……相像

0794 **reservoir** [ˈrezərvwɑːr] **n** 水库，蓄水池，蓄积
All the salesmen had a vast reservoir of initiative.
所有的业务员都蕴藏着很大的积极性。
storage 存储　　oil reservoir 油箱　　have a reservoir of... 蕴藏了……

0795 **residential** [ˌrezɪˈdenʃl] **a** 居住的
The residential building was under construction.
那座住宅建筑正在建造中。
resident 居住的　　residential area 住宅区
be under construction 正在建造中

0796 **resistant** [rɪˈzɪstənt] **a** 抵抗的，反抗的
I had no idea why the intern was resistant to speaking at the meeting.
我不知道实习生为什么抗拒在会议上发言。
recalcitrant 反抗的　　compliant 顺从的　　corrosion resistant 抗腐蚀

语法重点
be resistant to（抵抗……的）后面一般接表示不好的人、物或者事件等，具有相似含义的还有 stand up against 等。

0797 **resolute** [ˈrezəluːt] **a** 坚决的，刚毅的，不动摇的
They were resolute in opposing the proposal.
他们坚决反对这项提议。
firm 坚定的　　irresolute 优柔寡断的　　a resolute refusal 断然的拒绝

语法重点
be resolute in（坚决）通常接动名词。
↪ oppose (P. 479)

0798 **respective** [rɪˈspektɪv] **a** 个别的，各个的
The employees in this department had their respective duties.
这个部门的员工都有各自的职责。
each 各自的　　... have one's respective duties ……有各自的职责

0799 **restoration** [ˌrestəˈreɪʃn] **n** 恢复，归还，复位
The elevators in the company were closed for restoration.
公司里的电梯因整修而关闭。
recovery 恢复　　waste recovery 废物回收
... be closed for... ……因……而关闭

770

0800 **restraint** [rɪ'streɪnt] n 抑制，遏制，克制
The researcher told me the whole plan without restraint.
研究员毫无保留地告诉了我整个计划。
🔄 suppression 抑制　🔄 incitement 刺激
🔄 tell... without restraint 毫无保留地告诉……

0801 **retail** ['riːteɪl] n / v / ad 零售
This printer retailed at 200 dollars for each.
这种打印机零售价为每台 200 美元。
🔄 resale 零售　🔄 wholesale 批发　🔄 ... retail at... ……以……价格零售

0802 **retaliate** [rɪ'tælieɪt] v 报复，反击，回敬
The employee who got fired intended to retaliate upon the manager.
那名被炒鱿鱼的员工打算报复经理。
🔄 avenge 报复　🔄 retaliate upon... 报复……

🔗 intend (P. 461)

0803 **retrieve** [rɪ'triːv] v 收回，恢复 n 恢复
Failure of the negotiation has been beyond retrieve.
谈判失败已经无可挽回。
🔄 to retrieve a hopeless situation 扭转乾坤

🔗 failure (P. 163)

0804 **revelation** [ˌrevə'leɪʃn] n 揭发，发觉，启示
He got fired after the revelation of his embezzlement of public funds.
他贪污公款的事情被揭露之后就被解雇了。
🔄 disclosure 披露　🔄 revelation about 披露
🔄 get fired... after the revelation of... 揭露……之后被开除

0805 **revenue** ['revənuː] n 税收，收入，总收入
There would be a shortfall in sales revenue in this company.
这家公司的销售收入将会不足。
🔄 income 收入　🔄 expenditure 支出　🔄 sales revenue 销售收入
🔄 there would be a shortfall in... 将会有……不足
ℹ️ revenue 专指国家或企业的收入，主要指国家的税收，而 income 主要指个人收入，包括劳动所得和利润。

0806 **revival** [rɪ'vaɪvl] n 复兴，重新上演
The revival of trade cheered most of the entrepreneurs up.
贸易振兴使大多数企业家都非常高兴。

0807 **rhetoric** ['retərɪk] n 修辞，华丽的文辞
I was swayed by his rhetoric into signing a contract with this company.
我被他说服，才跟这家公司签订合约。

🔗 sway (P. 509)

0808 **rhythmic** [ˈrɪðmɪk] a 有节奏的，周期性的
Many receptionists were thudding about in a rhythmic movement in the hall.
很多接待员在大厅走来走去。

0809 **ridicule** [ˈrɪdɪkjuːl] n 嘲笑 v 嘲笑，使……受嘲笑
The assistant wanted to draw down ridicule on the new employee.
助理想使那名新员工受到嘲笑。
- sneer 嘲笑　　- arouse ridicule 引起讪笑
- draw down ridicule on... 使……受到嘲笑
- ridicule 多指有意地用言语戏弄某人，以使之显得渺小、不重要，此种嘲笑善意恶意均可，而 sneer 指除了用讽刺言语讥笑外，还带有轻蔑的表情。

0810 **rigorous** [ˈrɪɡərəs] a 严格的，荒谬的，可笑的
Scarcely had the rigorous pre-job training begun when some job-hunters couldn't bear it.
严格的职前培训刚开始，一些求职者就受不了了。
- severe 苛刻的

【语法重点】
Scarcely... when...（一……就不能……）位于句首所引起的倒装为部分倒装，如果动词为 be 的一般现在时或一般过去时，则为完全倒装。

0811 **riot** [ˈraɪət] n 暴乱，极度丰富 v 骚乱，浪费
Most of the employees rioted in busy work.
大多数员工都热衷于繁忙的工作。
- run riot 撒野，闹事　　- riot in... 热衷于……

0812 **rite** [raɪt] n 仪式，习惯，礼拜式
Barely had the business rite began when there was a power failure.
商务礼仪刚开始，就停电了。
- tradition 惯例　　- business rite 商务礼仪

【语法重点】
barely... when...（一……就……）位于句首所引起的倒装为部分倒装，如果动词为 be 的一般现在时或一般过去时，则为完全倒装。

0813 **ritual** [ˈrɪtʃuəl] n 仪式，例行公事 a 例行的
He had to make the ritual noises in business negotiation.
在商业谈判中，他不得不说一些客套话。
- ceremony 仪式　　- sleep ritual 睡眠仪式

【语法重点】
make the ritual noises（说客套话）的主语通常是表示人的名词或代词。

0814 **rivalry** [ˈraɪvlri] n 对抗
These new employees had rivalry with each other.
这些新员工之间相互竞争。
- business rivalry 商业竞争　　- have rivalry with... 与……竞争

0815 **rotate** [ˈroʊteɪt] v 旋转
The maintainer rotated the wheel with his hand.
那名维修工用手转动这个轮子。
- rotate direction 旋转方向　　- rotate... with... 用……转动……

- wheel (P. 245)

rhythmic ~ sanctuary

0816 rotation [roʊˈteɪʃn] n 旋转，轮流，自转
The assistant and the secretary wanted to clean the meeting room in rotation.
助理和秘书想轮流打扫会议室。
🔄 rotation speed 旋转速度　🔄 do... in rotation 轮流做……

0817 royalty [ˈrɔɪəlti] n 王室，版税
The writer could get royalty on these books.
那名作家可以从这些书中得到版税。
🔄 royal family 皇族　🔄 get royalty on... 从……得到版税

0818 ruby [ˈruːbi] n 红宝石 a 红宝石色的 v 使带红宝石色
The ruby necklace would come under the hammer.
那条红宝石项链将会被拍卖。
🔄 ... come under the hammer ……被拍卖

🔗 hammer (P. 173)

0819 safeguard [ˈseɪfɡɑːrd] v 保护 n 保护措施，护照
They examined all the systems to safeguard against programming errors.
他们检查了所有的系统以防止出现程序错误。
🔄 precaution 预防措施　🔄 infringe 侵犯　🔄 safeguard measure 保护措施
🔄 safeguard against... 防范……

0820 saloon [səˈluːn] n 厅，大轿车
The principal said this saloon was made over from a shopping mall.
负责人说这个展览场是由一个大商场改造而成的。
🔄 bar 酒吧　🔄 be made over from... 由……改造而成

0821 salvation [sælˈveɪʃn] n 救助，解救办法
Those bankrupt enterprises have been beyond salvation.
已经无法拯救那些破产的企业了。
🔄 deliverance 解救　🔄 ... be beyond salvation ……无法拯救

0822 sanction [ˈsæŋkʃn] v / n 认可，处罚
The law would take sanctions against these illegal enterprises.
法律会对这些违法企业进行制裁。
🔄 permit 准许　🔄 interdict 禁止　🔄 economic sanction 经济制裁
🔄 take sanctions against... 对……实行制裁

🔗 law (P. 057)

0823 sanctuary [ˈsæŋktʃueri] n 圣堂，庇护
The government was unlikely to give sanctuary to illegal enterprises.
政府不可能为违法企业提供庇护。
🔄 refuge 避难所　🔄 right of sanctuary 庇护权，居留权

语法重点
give sanctuary to（为……提供庇护）后面通常接名词或代词。

0824 **sane** [seɪn] a 神志正常的，稳健的
The principal of this firm was a sane person.
这家企业的负责人是一个很有头脑的人。

0825 **sanitation** [ˌsænɪˈteɪʃn] n 公共卫生，卫生设备
Viewed from the sanitation point, this water cooler was disqualified.
从卫生角度来看，这台饮水机不合格。

0826 **scenic** [ˈsiːnɪk] a 风景的，舞台的 n 风景胜地
The scenic resort was marked as reconstruction center.
这个风景区被标记为改造中心。
- picturesque 风景如画的　　- scenic spots 景点
- be marked as... 被标记为……

center (P. 021)

0827 **scope** [skoʊp] n 范围，余地
You can finish the task within the scope of your capacity.
你可以在能力范围之内来完成这项工作。
- extent 范围　　- give scope to 给予充分发挥……的机会
- do... within the scope of... 在……的范围内做……

0828 **script** [skrɪpt] n 笔迹，手稿
The script has been delivered to the director.
剧本已经转交给导演。
- film script 电影剧本

语法重点
be delivered to（转交给）后面通常接表示人的名词或代词。
director (P. 153)

0829 **sector** [ˈsektər] n 扇形，部分，防区
It was a branch of the financial sector.
它是财政部门的一个分支。
- be a branch of... 是……的一个分支

0830 **seduce** [sɪˈduːs] v 引诱，诱使……堕落
They decided to seduce the manager with wealth.
他们决定用钱财来收买经理。
- lure 引诱　　- seduce from 诱开　　- seduce... with... 用……来收买……

语法重点
此句型中，seduce 后面接表示人的名词或代词，而 with 后面接表示物的名词。

0831 **selective** [sɪˈlektɪv] a 有选择性地
The interviewer was selective about these applicants.
面试官很注意挑选这些应聘者。
- elective 选择的　　- selective service 义务兵役制

applicant (P. 395)

0832 **seminar** [ˈsemɪnɑːr] n 研讨班，研讨会
The teacher was preparing material for the seminar.
老师在准备研讨会所用的材料。
- prepare material for... 准备……用的材料

0833 senator ['senətər] n 参议员

The president of that company could go on to be a senator.
那家公司的总裁可以继续出任参议员。
- councilor 评议员
- senior senator 资深参议员
- go on to... 继续……

0834 sentimental [ˌsentɪ'mentl] a 感伤的，多愁善感的

Many employees were sentimental about their prospect.
很多员工为自己的前途而多愁善感。
- emotional 情绪化的
- rational 理性的
- be sentimental about... 为……而多愁善感

→ prospect (P. 618)

0835 sequence ['siːkwəns] n 连续，继续，次序

The secretary sorted files according to the sequence of time.
秘书按照时间顺序来整理文件。
- succession 连续
- time sequence 时间顺序
- do... according to the sequence of... 按照……顺序来做……

0836 serene [sə'riːn] a 宁静的，晴朗的，清澈的

The man looked as serene as he always did when he heard the bad news.
听到这个坏消息时，男子看起来像往常一样平静。
- pacific 平静的
- furious 狂怒的
- all serene 一切平静，平安无事
- look as... as sb. always did 某人像往常一样看起来……

0837 serenity [sə'renəti] n 平静

The doctor's face had an expression of serenity the whole day.
一整天，医生的脸上都带着平静的表情。
- calm 平静
- ... have an expression of... ……有……的表情

语法重点
the whole day 表示"整天"，在句中表示时间。

0838 serving ['sɜːrvɪŋ]

n 服务，上菜 a 用于上菜的 v 服务，提供

The secretary couldn't come to the telephone because she was serving the customers.
秘书在招待客户，所以不能接电话。

→ telephone (P. 234)

0839 session ['seʃn] n 开会，一段时间

The staff knew the importance of the session.
员工们知道这次会议的重要性。
- in session 在开庭，在开会，在上课
- know the importance of... 知道……的重要性

0840 setback ['setbæk] n 挫折，阻碍，退步
It's said that there had never been setback in the president's career.
据说，总裁在事业上从未遇到过挫折。
≈ frustration 挫折　≠ progress 进步
there had never been setback in... ……从未有挫折

0841 sewer ['suːər] n 缝制工　v 从……排污水
A worker kicked the tool cabinet into the sewer.
一名工人把工具箱踢进了下水道。
≈ sewage 下水道　book sewer 订书机　kick... into... 把……踢进……
⊙ cabinet (P. 404)

0842 shed [ʃed] v 流出，去除，散发　n 棚
The manager shed light on the feasibility of the system at the meeting.
经理在会议上阐明这项制度的可行性。
shed leaves 落叶　shed light on... 阐明……
⊙ system (P. 371)

0843 sheer [ʃɪr] a 全然的，陡峭的　ad 垂直地　v 偏离
Those employees' proposal was totally sheer nonsense.
那些员工的提议完全是无稽之谈。
sheer off 转向（离开）　... be sheer nonsense ……是一派胡言
⊙ nonsense (P. 476)

0844 shilling ['ʃɪlɪŋ] n 先令（币值单位）
Those applicants who took the King's shilling were given a prior consideration.
那些当过兵的求职者优先考虑。
take the King's shilling 入伍，当兵
... be given a prior consideration 优先考虑……

0845 shoplift ['ʃɑːplɪft] v 在商店内行窃
The employee who shoplifted got the bounce.
那名在商店偷盗的员工被解雇了。

0846 shrewd [ʃruːd] a 精明的，敏锐的，狡猾的
This girl was shrewd at shorthand.
这个女孩在速记方面很在行。
shrewd in money matters 精打细算　be shrewd at... 对……在行

0847 shun [ʃʌn] v 避开，避免
From that moment on, the student shunned his teacher.
从那时起，学生就有意避开他的老师。
≈ evade 回避　≠ face 面对　from that moment on, ... 从那时起，……

setback ~ skim

0848 siege [siːdʒ] n 包围，围困
Many reporters laid siege to the hospital.
很多记者包围了这家医院。
🔄 surrounding 周围

> **语法重点**
> lay siege to（包围）后面通常接名词或代词。

0849 signify ['sɪgnɪfaɪ] v 表示……的意思，意味着
It doesn't signify, so you can take back your resignation letter.
这无所谓，所以你可以收回你的辞职信。
🔸 signify much to 对……很重要　🔸 it doesn't signify, so... 这无所谓，所以……

0850 silicon ['sɪlɪkən] n 硅
This factory pioneered the use of silicon steel.
这家工厂率先使用硅钢。

🔗 pioneer (P. 485)

0851 simplicity [sɪm'plɪsəti] n 简单，朴素
For simplicity, the secretary copied the report.
为了简单起见，秘书复印了这份报告。
🔸 simplicity of style 简朴的风格　🔸 for simplicity, ... 为了简单起见，……

0852 simplify ['sɪmplɪfaɪ] v 简化，使单纯
His assistance could simplify my task.
他的协助可以简化我的工作。
🟰 clarify 简化　🟥 complicate 使复杂

> **语法重点**
> simplify one's task（简化某人的工作）中的 one's 可以变换成不同的人称。
> 🔗 assistance (P. 398)

0853 simultaneous [ˌsaɪml'teɪniəs]
a 同时发生的，同时存在的
This meeting was simultaneous with that one.
这个会议与那个会议同时召开。
🔸 simultaneous interpretation 同步口译
🔸 be simultaneous with... 与……同时进行

0854 skeptical ['skeptɪkl] a 怀疑的
The shareholders were skeptical about the proposal.
股东们对这项提议表示怀疑。
🟰 disbelieving 怀疑的　🟥 certain 确信地
🔸 be skeptical about... 对……表示怀疑

0855 skim [skɪm] v 去除，擦过，略读
You could skim through the product catalog.
你可以浏览产品目录。
🔸 skim off 撇去　🔸 skim through... 浏览……

0856 slang [slæŋ] n 俚语，黑话，漫骂 v 用俚语说
Come to the bargaining table and stop slanging.
回到谈判桌上来，不要再漫骂了。
- jargon 行话
- army slang 军队俚语

0857 slash [slæʃ] v 砍，严厉批评，大幅削减 n 猛砍，斜线
The manager said that there was nothing in prospect to slash costs in the company.
经理说公司没有希望大幅度削减开支。
- slash price 砍价
- there was nothing in prospect to... ……没有希望

0858 slavery ['sleɪvəri] n 奴隶身份，苦役
The young man was sold into slavery to work as a miner.
那个年轻人被卖为奴隶做矿工。
- bondage 奴役
- ... be sold into slavery ……被卖为奴隶

※ miner (P. 325)

0859 slot [slɑːt] n 狭缝，投币口，时间段 v 插入
The manager slotted her nephew into a job in the personnel department.
经理把她的侄子安排在人事部工作。
- time slot 时间空当
- slot... into a job 给……安排工作
- slot machine 表示"自动贩卖机"。

※ nephew (P. 195)

0860 slum [slʌm] n 贫民窟 v 访问贫民区
The entrepreneur was ever brought up in a slum.
那名企业家曾在贫民窟长大。
- rookery 贫民窟
- ... be brought up in a slum ……在贫民窟长大

0861 smack [smæk] n 滋味，掌掴，海洛因 v 拍 ad 直接地
It's said that the woman gave the salesman a smack.
据说，那名女人打了那名业务员一巴掌。
- indirectly 间接地
- give... a smack 打……一巴掌

0862 smallpox ['smɔːlpɑːks] n 天花
My colleague was inoculated against smallpox when he was a child.
我的同事小时候打过预防天花的预防针。
- smallpox virus 天花病毒

语法重点
be inoculated against（接种预防）后面通常接表示疾病的名词。
※ colleague (P. 545)

0863 smother ['smʌðər] v 窒息，遮掩 n 窒息物，浓烟
He tried to smother his anger after reading this file.
看到这份文件后，他试图抑制住自己的怒气。
- smother up 隐蔽
- smother one's anger 抑制住某人的怒气

slang ~ socialist

0864 smuggle ['smʌgl] v 走私

The corporate leader was arrested for smuggling out drugs.
那名公司领导人因私运毒品而被逮捕。
- contraband 走私
- smuggle through 走私运出
- smuggle out... 私运……

0865 snare [sner] n 陷阱，诱惑 v 捕捉，诱惑，陷害

The commercial espionage allured the secretary into a snare.
那名商业间谍引诱秘书落入圈套。
- trap 陷阱
- spell snare 圈套
- allure... into a snare 引诱……落入圈套

> commercial (P. 274)

0866 sneaky ['sniːki] a 鬼鬼祟祟的

It is a sneaky way of stealing company secrets.
这是一种卑鄙的窃取公司机密的方式。
- furtive 鬼祟的
- frank 直率的

> 语法重点
> it is a sneaky way of（这是一种卑鄙的……的方式）后面通常接动名词。

0867 sneer [snɪr] n 嘲笑，讥笑的表情 v 讥笑，冷笑

Most of the employees sneered at the contract.
大多数员工都嘲笑这份合约书。
- mock 嘲笑
- sneer down 以嘲笑拒绝
- sneer at... 嘲笑……

0868 soar [sɔːr] v 往上飞舞，暴涨

It is considered that insurance claim would soar.
有人认为保险索赔会急剧增加。
- slump 下降，衰落
- it is considered that... 有人认为……

0869 sociable ['souʃəbl]

a 社交的，随和的 n 恳亲会，对座四轮马车

The leader of public relations department was a sociable person.
公关部主管是一个很爱交际的人。

0870 socialism ['souʃəlɪzəm] n 社会主义

Most of the firms declared for market socialism.
大多数企业表示拥护市场社会主义。
- capitalism 资本主义
- declare for... 表示拥护……

> declare (P. 422)

0871 socialist ['souʃəlɪst] n 社会主义者

Domestic enterprises gave strong backing to socialist market economy.
国内企业给予社会主义市场经济强大支持。

> 语法重点
> give strong backing to（给予……强大支持）后面通常接名词或代词。

0872 **socialize** ['soʊʃəlaɪz] v 社会主义化，使适应社会需要
It's rude of you not to socialize with your colleagues in the office party.
你在公司聚会上不跟同事们交谈是很无礼的。
🔁 socialize with 交际，交往

> 语法重点
> it's rude of you（你……很无礼）后面通常接动词不定式。

0873 **sociology** [ˌsoʊsiˈɑːlədʒi] n 社会学
The investor said that economic sociology emphasized the importance of market.
那位投资商说，经济社会学强调市场的重要性。
🔁 emphasize the importance of... 强调……的重要性

0874 **sodium** ['soʊdiəm] n 钠
The researcher said that sodium chloride contained in the food was above standard.
研究人员说，这种食物中的氯化钠超标。
🔁 ... be above standard ……超过标准

▶ standard (P. 227)

0875 **solidarity** [ˌsɑːlɪˈdærəti] n 团结
Putting it mildly, these new employees had no lack of solidarity.
说得好听一点，这些新员工不缺乏团结。
🔁 unanimity 团结   🔁 abruption 分裂

> 语法重点
> putting it mildly 意思是"说得委婉些"，在句中为现在分词作插入语。

0876 **solitude** ['sɑːlətuːd] n 孤独，隐居处，幽静，荒野
They were busy with work, without the opportunity for solitude.
他们工作很忙，没有独处的机会。
🔁 loneliness 孤独   🔁 in solitude 单独地

> 语法重点
> without the opportunity for（没有……的机会）后面通常接名词。

0877 **soothe** [suːð] v 安慰，使平静，减轻痛苦
The old man took the girl in his arms and soothed her.
那名老先生将女孩搂在怀里来安慰她。
🔁 soothe 着重以安慰减轻悲痛、愤怒或激动，使人理智地平静下来，也可指药物等减轻病痛，而 relieve 指解除或缓解某人的病痛、担心或忧虑等，常用被动语态。

0878 **sophisticated** [səˈfɪstɪkeɪtɪd] a 世故的，高级的
It's said that the lawyer was sophisticated for his ways of social communication.
据说，律师在社交方面老于世故。
🔁 be sophisticated for one's ways of... 某人在……方面老于世故

▶ social (P. 224)

0879 sovereignty ['sɑːvrənti] n 统治权，独立国

The decision was vital to consumer sovereignty.
这项决议对消费者主权来说非常重要。
- reign 统治，支配

语法重点
be vital to（对……极其重要）后面通常接名词或代词。

0880 spacious ['speɪʃəs] a 宽敞的，广阔的

Who reserved the spacious meeting room was unknown to them.
他们不知道是谁预订了这个宽敞的会议室。
- expansive 广阔的
- narrow 狭窄的

语法重点
be unknown to（不知道）后面要接表示人的名词或代词。

0881 span [spæn] n 一段时间 v 持续，包括

The new product had a life span of three years.
这种新产品的使用寿命是三年。
- extent 长度，范围
- life span 寿命，使用期限
- have a life span of... 的使用寿命是……

0882 specialize ['speʃəlaɪz] v 专攻

The company specialized in fixing the graduates up with jobs.
这家公司专门负责为毕业生安排工作。
- specialize in 专门研究，负责
- fix... up with... 给……安排……

0883 specialty ['speʃəlti] n 专业，特点 a 特色的，专门的

His specialty design gained the manager's recognition.
他的专业设计获得了经理的认可。
- profession 专业
- specialty shop 专卖店
- gain one's recognition 获得某人的认可

- recognition (P. 493)

0884 specify ['spesɪfaɪ] v 具体指定，详细说明

The principal specified the size of each exhibition hall.
负责人指定了每个展厅的大小。
- specify by 用……说明
- specify the size of... 指定……的大小

- exhibition (P. 292)

0885 spectacular [spek'tækjələr] a 可观的 n 壮观的演出

The manager would work with us on the spectacular trade fair.
经理将与我们一起工作，来举办盛大的贸易展销会。
- spectacular view 壮观景色
- work with... on... 与……共同做……

0886 spectrum ['spektrəm] n 光谱，系列，幅度

It's said that the company accumulated wealth across a broad spectrum of assets.
据说，这家公司以各种各样的资产形式积累财富。

0887 speculate ['spekjuleɪt] v 沉思，猜测，推断
What the employees speculated was none of the manager's business.
员工们猜测什么都和经理无关。
⊙ guess 猜测　⊙ speculate about 思索

0888 sphere [sfɪr] n 球体，范围
The market has always been within the sphere of influence of the European company.
这个市场一直属于欧洲公司的势力范围。
⊙ field 领域　⊙ sphere of influence 势力范围，影响范围
⊙ be within the sphere of influence of... 在……的影响范围之内

⊙ influence (P. 179)

0889 spike [spaɪk]
n 大钉，细高跟　v 加烈酒于，以大钉钉牢
The secretary drew the lag spike out from the tool box in the office.
秘书从办公室的工具箱里取出了螺丝钉。
⊙ crampon 钉鞋　⊙ lag spike 螺丝钉　⊙ draw out... 取出……

0890 spiral ['spaɪrəl] a 螺旋的，盘旋的　n 螺旋　v 盘旋上升
The company's profits began to spiral down this month.
这个月公司的利润开始急剧下降。
⊙ screw 螺旋　⊙ spiral down 急剧下降

0891 spire ['spaɪər] n 螺旋，塔尖　v 给……装尖塔，螺旋形上升
The company's spire swam into the president's ken.
公司的尖顶滑入总裁的视线。

0892 spokesman / spokeswoman
['spoʊksmən] / ['spoʊkswʊmən] n 男／女发言人
The manager wouldn't reveal the identity of the spokeswoman.
经理不会透露这位女发言人的身份。
⊙ reveal the identity of... 透露……的身份

⊙ identity (P. 308)

0893 spokesperson ['spoʊkspɜːrsn] n 发言人，代言人
The model was the spokesperson for this product.
那名模特儿是这个产品的代言人。
⊙ brand spokesperson 品牌代言人
⊙ be the spokesperson for... 是……的代言人

⊙ product (P. 342)

0894 sponsor ['spɑːnsər] n 赞助者 v 发起

It's said that all the cost was borne by the sponsor.
据说，所有费用都由赞助商承担。

- sponsor by 由……主办
- be borne by... 由……承担
- cost 和 expense 都可表示"价格，费用"：cost 指生产某东西的成本，也泛指商品的价格，可与 price 换用，而 expense 常指实际支付的费用的总数额，有时也指钱的花费。

0895 spontaneous [spɑːnˈteɪniəs] a 自然发生的，本能的

These employees were spontaneous in their behavior.
这些员工在行为上是自发的。

- instinctive 本能的
- be spontaneous in... ……是自发的

behavior (P. 401)

0896 spouse [spaʊs] n 配偶

The president's spouse was conscientious in her work.
总裁的配偶在工作方面非常认真。

- mate 配偶
- be conscientious in one's work 某人工作认真

0897 sprawl [sprɔːl] v 蔓延 n 随意扩展，蔓延

A client laid in a sprawl in the office.
一名顾客四肢伸开，躺在办公室里。

0898 squad [skwɑːd] n 小队

The squad car was hard on the corporate leader's track.
警车正在追踪那名公司负责人。

corporate (P. 695)

0899 stability [stəˈbɪləti] n 稳定，稳定性，巩固

The company's stability needed the involvement of all the staff.
公司的稳定需要全体员工的参与。

- firmness 稳固
- instability 不稳定
- economic stability 经济稳定

0900 stabilize [ˈsteɪbəlaɪz] v 使稳定，使坚固

These salesmen's top priority was to stabilize the market.
这些业务员的首要任务是稳定市场。

- fix 固定
- loosen 松散
- stabilize prices 稳定物价

priority (P. 617)

0901 stalk [stɔːk] v 蔓延，追踪 n 主茎，高烟囱

As you see, I was stalking the singer.
如你所见，我在悄悄跟踪歌手。

- stem 茎
- as you see, ... 如你所见，……

0902 stammer [ˈstæmər] v 结结巴巴地说，口吃 n 结巴

One of the applicants got a bad stammer.
其中的一名应征者口吃严重。

- stumble 结巴
- stammer trip 结巴
- get a bad stammer ……口吃严重

0903 staple ['steɪpl]
n 订书钉，原料 **v** 用订书机装订 **a** 主要的
The secretary said that the report was stapled to some letters.
秘书说那份报告和一些信件钉在了一起。
- staple of money 货币交易市场
- be stapled to... 被钉在……上
- letter 和 note 都可表示"信"：letter 泛指一切形式的书信，尤指邮寄的信，而 note 指内容直截了当的短信或便条，正式或非正式均可。

0904 stapler ['steɪplər] **n** 订书机，装订工
The assistant found the stapler was not working.
助理发现订书机坏了。
- be not working ……坏了

0905 starch [stɑːrtʃ] **n** 淀粉，形式主义 **v** 上浆，浆硬
The failure of the negotiation took the starch out of the employees.
谈判失败使员工们丧失了勇气。

> **语法重点**
> take the starch out of (使……失去勇气) 常用于口语中，of 后面一般接表示人的名词或代词。

- nearly (P. 194)

0906 starvation [stɑːrˈveɪʃn] **n** 饥饿，饿死，绝食
The foundation decided to give financial help to those people who nearly died of starvation.
基金会决定救济那些快要饿死的人。
- hunger 饥饿
- give financial help to... 救济……

0907 stationary ['steɪʃəneri] **a** 不动的，常备军的 **n** 驻军
The stationary fixture in the office was in need of repair.
办公室里的固定夹具需要修理。
- stationary value 平稳值
- ... be in need of repair ……需要修理

0908 stationery ['steɪʃəneri] **n** 文具，信笺
Several salesmen traveled in some office stationery.
几名业务员到处推销一些办公文具。
- office stationery 办公文具

- salesman (P. 500)

0909 stature ['stætʃər] **n** 身高，声望
The applicant who was short in stature was eliminated.
那名身材矮小的应聘者被淘汰了。
- shape 身材
- middling stature 中等身材
- be short in stature 身材矮小

0910 stimulate ['stɪmjuleɪt] **v** 刺激，激励，激发
All the new employees were stimulated by the challenge.
所有新员工都受这项挑战所激励。

> **语法重点**
> be stimulated by (受到……的激励) 后面通常接表示物的名词。

staple ~ subscribe

0911 stimulation [ˌstɪmjuˈleɪʃn] **n** 刺激，激发，促进
The activity provided plenty of stimulation for the employees.
这项活动给予员工们很多启发。
🔄 provocation 激发　🔄 provide plenty of stimulation for... 给予……很多启发

0912 stimulus [ˈstɪmjələs] **n** 刺激，激励
Under the stimulus of economic recession, this company decided to lay off employees.
在经济衰退的刺激下，这家公司决定裁员。
🔄 stimulation 刺激　🔄 under the stimulus of... 在……的刺激下

↪ recession (P. 766)

0913 strangle [ˈstræŋgl] **v** 勒死，使……窒息　**v** 窒息而死
The scoundrel strangled an employee to death.
那名歹徒将一名员工掐死了。

〔语法重点〕
此句型中，strangle 后面通常接表示人的名词或代词。

0914 strategic / strategical [strəˈtiːdʒɪk] / [strəˈtiːdʒɪkl]
a 战略的，战略性的
This proposal was the strategic fulcrum of the financial budget.
这项提议是财务预算的战略支点。

↪ budget (P. 266)

0915 stunt [stʌnt]
v 妨碍，表演特技　**n** 特技，发育不良的动植物
Don't pull a stunt, and you should work hard.
不要耍花招，你应该努力工作。
🔄 publicity stunt 作秀　🔄 pull a stunt ……耍花招

0916 subjective [səbˈdʒektɪv] **a** 主观的　**n** 对象，主题
He thought that resignation was a subjective matter.
他认为辞职是一个主观问题。
🔄 objective 客观的　🔄 ... be a subjective matter ……是一个主观问题

0917 subordinate [səˈbɔːdɪnət] / [səˈbɔːrdɪneɪt]
a 下级的　**v** 使服从
These several employees were subordinate to him.
这几名员工是他的下属。
🔄 inferior 下等的　🔄 superior 上好的

〔语法重点〕
be subordinate to（次于……，从属于……）后面通常接表示人的名词或代词。

0918 subscribe [səbˈskraɪb] **v** 订阅
The company subscribed to newspaper for each department.
公司为每一个部门都订购报纸。
🔄 subscribe to 订购（报刊等）

〔语法重点〕
subscribe to 后面接表示刊物的名词。

0919 subscription [səb'skrɪpʃn] n. 订阅，捐款，募捐
This company decided to raise money by subscription. ⊕ raise (P. 080)
这家公司决定靠募捐的方法来筹钱。
⊙ raise money 募款

0920 subsequent ['sʌbsɪkwənt] a. 伴随发生的，后来的
They discussed the proposal subsequent to the meeting.
他们在会议之后讨论这些提议。
⊙ following 随后的　⊘ early 早的　⊙ subsequent to 在……之后

0921 substitution [ˌsʌbstɪ'tuːʃn] n. 代替，替换，取代
They decided to use the office in substitution for the meeting room.
他们决定用办公室来代替会议室。
⊙ stead 代替　⊙ use... in substitution for... 用……代替……

0922 subtle ['sʌtl] a. 微妙的，狡诈的，头脑灵活的
The researchers would make a subtle observation to these materials. ⊕ observation (P. 477)
研究人员会对这些材料进行细致入微的观察。
⊙ delicate 微妙的　⊙ subtle distinction 微妙的差别
⊙ subtle 侧重有洞察、领悟事物细微差别以及微妙关系的能力，而 delicate 侧重指需要谨慎处理和对待。

0923 suburban [sə'bɜːrbən] a. 郊外的，在郊区的 n. 郊区居民
Suburban commercial buildings sprang up.
郊区的商业大楼如雨后春笋般涌现出来。
⊘ downtown 市中心的　⊙ suburban district 郊区　⊙ ... spring up ……涌现

0924 succession [sək'seʃn] n. 连续，继任，继承
The applicant had ever taken a succession of jobs.
那名应聘者曾经做过一连串的工作。
⊙ series 连续　⊙ a succession of 一连串
⊙ take a succession of... 做了一连串的……

0925 successive [sək'sesɪv] a. 连续的，接连的
Debt crisis occurred in successive years in this company. ⊕ occur (P. 197)
这家公司连年发生债务危机。

0926 successor [sək'sesər] n. 继任者
The successor of the president was able to manage the company all by himself.
总裁的继承人能够独立经营这家公司了。
⊙ inheritor 继承人　⊙ legal successor 法定继承人
⊙ do... all by oneself 某人独立做……

0927 suffocate ['sʌfəkeɪt] v 使窒息

Those employees who were trapped suffocated from a lack of oxygen.
那些被困住的员工因缺少氧气而窒息。
- stifle 使窒息
- suffocate from a lack of... 因缺少……而窒息

⊙oxygen (P. 480)

0928 suite [swiːt] n 套房，一套物件，随员

The manager invited me to her suite for business.
经理邀请我去她的套房谈生意。
- invite me to... 邀请我到……

0929 superb [suːˈpɜːrb] a 极好的，高品质的

The sound in the concert hall was in superb condition.
音乐厅里的音响效果极好。
- excellent 极好的
- be in superb condition 状况极好

0930 superiority [suːˌpɪriˈɔːrətiː; nuː] n 优越，优势

Most of the employees believed in the superiority of this measure.
大多数员工都相信这项措施的优越性。
- advantage 优势
- inferiority 劣势
- overwhelming superiority 绝对优势

0931 supersonic [ˌsuːpərˈsɑːnɪk] a 超声波的，超声速的

The engineers decided to improve on this supersonic plane.
工程师们决定改良这架超声速飞机。
- supersonic aircraft 超声速飞机
- improve on... 改进……

⊙improve (P. 178)

0932 superstitious [ˌsuːpərˈstɪʃəs] a 迷信的，有迷信观念的

The old man was quite superstitious, so you weren't satisfied of him.
那名老男人很迷信，你别相信他。
- fetishistic 迷信的
- be satisfied of... 相信……

0933 supervision [ˌsuːpərˈvɪʒn] n 监督，管理

I mean there to be close supervision to the staff.
我的意思是，要好好监督员工们。
- governance 监督
- I mean there to be... 我的意思是要……

语法重点
there be 句型作动词 mean 的宾语时，一般用 there to be 的形式。

0934 supplement [ˈsʌplɪmənt] / [ˈsʌplɪment] n / v 补充

What the supervisor likes best is Sunday supplement.
周日增刊是主管的最爱。
- increase 增加
- decrease 减少

语法重点
supplement 主要指使书、报等内容更完善而额外增加的部分。

0935 surpass [sər'pæs] v 超过，超越，胜过
The newcome employee will soon surpass us in technology.
这个新来的员工很快会在技术上超过我们。
- exceed 超过
- surpass sb's imagination 出乎意料
- surpass sb. / sth. in... 在……方面超过某人 / 某物

0936 surplus ['sɜːrpləs] n 过剩，盈余 a 多余的
The manager said the surplus equipment should be handed in to the factory.
经理说多余器材应该交回工厂。
- excess 过剩
- deficit 赤字，不足
- surplus value 剩余价值
- be handed in to... 被交给……
- surplus 通常指数量过剩，而 excess 指超过限度、标准或界线。

＞ factory (P. 036)

0937 suspense [sə'spens] n 暂时停止，悬念
I waited in great suspense for the boss's decision.
我焦急万分地等待老板的决定。

0938 suspension [sə'spenʃn] n 暂停，悬挂
The mistake led to his suspension from office.
他因为这个错误暂时停职。
- hang 悬挂
- suspension bridge 吊桥
- lead to one's suspension from office 让某人暂时停职

0939 swap [swɑːp] v 交换，用……作交易 n 交换
My colleague wants to swap her working scheme for mine.
我的同事想跟我换一下工作方案。
- exchange 交换
- swap... for... 跟……交换……

＞ scheme (P. 629)

0940 symbolic [sɪm'bɑːlɪk] a 象征的，符号的
It's symbolic of his formal retirement.
这意味着他正式退休了。

语法重点
it is symbolic of（象征着……）后面一般接名词或者名词短语。

0941 symbolize ['sɪmbəlaɪz] v 象征，用符号表现
The document symbolizes the manager's failure, so he is in utter despair.
这份文件说明经理失败，所以他彻底绝望了。
- token 象征
- be in utter despair 彻底绝望

0942 symmetry ['sɪmətri] n 对称，匀称
I will seek my boss's advice about the symmetry of the house I designed.
关于我设计的这座房子的对称性问题，我将征求老板的意见。
- balance 匀称
- I will seek one's advice... 我将征求某人的意见……

0943 symptom ['sɪmptəm] n 症状，征兆

The manager told us to keep a tab on the newcome colleague's symptoms.
经理让我们注意那个新同事的病症。
- premonitory 征兆
- early symptom 早期症状
- keep a tab on... 注意......

语法重点 symptom 通常指作为医学诊断的疾病征兆。

0944 synonym ['sɪnənɪm] n 同义词

My boss is a synonym for wisdom in the company.
在我们公司，老板就是智慧的代词。
- antonym 反义词
- ... be a synonym for... ......是......的代词

- wisdom (P. 385)

0945 synthetic [sɪn'θetɪk] a 综合性的，合成的

Making synthetic leather is an ordeal for these workers.
制作人造皮革对于这些工人来说是件痛苦的事情。
- synthetic fiber 人造纤维
- ... be an ordeal for sb. ......对某人来说是个折磨

0946 tact [tækt] n 老练

I have no tact in dealing with my classmates.
我太傻了，不会和同学们相处。

语法重点 tact 是不可数名词。

0947 tactic ['tæktɪk] n 战术 a 按顺序的

The little boy must use surprising tactics to win the competition.
为了赢得比赛，那个小男孩必须采用出人意料的手段。
- strategy 战略
- defense tactic 防守战术
- use... tactic to... 用......的手段......

0948 tariff ['tærɪf] n 税率，价目表 v 交关税

There is a very high tariff on the product, so the manager gave up buying.
这种产品的关税很高，所以经理放弃采购。
- duty 关税
- import tariff 进口关税
- there is a very high tariff on... ......的关税很高

0949 tedious ['tiːdiəs] a 沉闷的

He said the tedious job simply ate him up.
他说单调乏味的工作简直把他烦死了。
- dreary 沉闷的
- exciting 兴奋的
- ... eat sb. up ......快把某人烦死了

- simply (P. 222)

0950 temperament ['temprəmənt] n 气质，性情

Our landlord is a young man with an artistic temperament.
我们的房东是一个很有艺术家气质的年轻人。

怪物讲师教学团队的7 000"单词"+"语法"

- disposition 性情
- sb. be a / an... with... temperament 某人是个具有……气质的……

0951 tempest ['tempɪst]
n 大风暴，骚动 **v** 使遭受暴风雨（或雪），使骚动

No tempest is capable of shattering my decision to resign.
任何惊涛骇浪都不能动摇我辞职的决心。
- a tempest in a teapot 小题大做

语法重点
no tempest is capable of（任何惊涛骇浪都不能）后面接动名词。
- resign (P. 497)

0952 terminate ['tɜːrmɪneɪt] **v** 使停止，结束

I heard your contract will terminate next week.
我听说你的合约下周就到期了。
- end 结束
- terminate a contract 终止合约
- terminate 强调有一个空间和时间的限度，届时必须终止，end 着重事情的完成，也指某种活动因达到目的而自然结束或由于某种原因而突然中止。

0953 textile ['tekstaɪl] **n** 纺织品 **a** 纺织的

The manager told us textile prices had been marked down.
经理告诉我们纺织品降价了。
- spinning 纺织的
- textile industry 纺织工业

语法重点
be marked down（降价）的主语一般是表示商品或者价格的名词。

0954 texture ['tekstʃər] **n** 结构，手感，纹理

Cotton fabric the workers produce has a pleasant texture.
工人们生产的棉布手感很好。

0955 theatrical [θi'ætrɪkl]
a 戏剧的，剧场的 **n** 戏剧表演，戏剧演员

I have no time to have dinner because of working overtime, to say nothing of the theatrical district.
因为加班，我连吃饭的时间都没有，更谈不上去剧院了。
- dramatic 戏剧的
- theatrical performance 戏剧表演
- I have no time to..., to say nothing of... 我没时间……，更别说……了

0956 theft [θeft] **n** 盗窃，失窃案例

My colleague was prosecuted for theft yesterday.
昨天我同事因偷窃被告发了。
- stealing 偷窃
- identity theft 身份盗用

语法重点
sb. be prosecuted for（某人因为……被告发）后面接名词或者动名词。

0957 theoretical [ˌθiːə'retɪkl] **a** 理论上的，假设的，空论的

His resigning tomorrow is only a theoretical possibility.
他明天就辞职只是一种假设。
- ... be only a theoretical possibility ……只是一种假设

语法重点
theoretical 的副词形式是 theoretically。

0958 therapist ['θerəpɪst] **n** 治疗学家，特定疗法技师

I just want to be a family therapist after resigning.
我只想在辞职后做一个家庭治疗师。

语法重点
want 一般指想要的东西是渴望得到的东西，能弥补实际需要。

0959 therapy [ˈθerəpi] n 治疗，理疗

My brother underwent aversion therapy for his addiction to drinking last year.
去年，我哥哥因为酗酒成瘾而接受厌恶疗法的治疗。
- treatment 治疗，疗法　　- radiation therapy 放射治疗

> 语法重点
> 例句中，underwent 是动词 undergo（经历）的过去式。

0960 thereafter [ˌðerˈæftər] ad 此后，以后

I was sold out by one of my friends, thereafter we didn't speak to each other.
我被一个朋友出卖，此后我们互相不理睬。
- afterward 以后　　- previously 以前　　- soon thereafter 不久以后

> 语法重点
> be sold out by（被……出卖）后面常接表示人的名词或者代词。

0961 thereby [ˌðerˈbaɪ] ad 因此，由此

The manager has this matter up his / her sleeve, thereby you needn't worry.
经理对这件事有应急计划，所以你不用担心。
- hence 因此　　- have sth. up one's sleeve 某人对某事有应急计划

> 语法重点
> have sth. in one's sleeve 是固定搭配，sleeve 用单数。

0962 thermometer [θərˈmɑːmɪtər] n 温度计，寒暑表

Watch out for thermometer in the laboratory.
密切注意实验室里的那个温度计。

> 语法重点
> watch out for（密切注意）后面可以接人，也可以接物。
> - laboratory (P. 464)

0963 threshold [ˈθreʃhoʊld] n 门槛，入门

I can't use a computer at the threshold of my job.
刚开始工作时，我不会用电脑。
- gateway 门　　- on the threshold of 在……的开始

0964 thrift [θrɪft] n 节约，茁壮成长

Our boss said that to practice thrift is a virtue.
我们老板说，节俭是美德。
- thrift store 旧货店，二手店　　- ... be a virtue ……是美德

> 语法重点
> thrift 的名词形式是 thriftiness，该名词是不可数名词。

0965 thrifty [ˈθrɪfti] a 节俭的，茁壮的，茂盛的

The thrifty housewife said she got something on our manager.
这个勤俭持家的主妇说，她抓住了我们经理的把柄。
- economical 经济的　　- wasteful 浪费的　　- thrifty people 节俭的人
- ... get something on sb. ……抓住某人的把柄
- thrifty 侧重节缩开支，积蓄收入，而 economical 指正当使用财物，强调节省，避免浪费。

0966 thrive [θraɪv] v 兴旺，繁荣，旺盛

The company thrives on our boss's good management.
我们公司的兴旺发展得益于老板的良好管理。
- boom 使兴旺　　- decline 下降　　- thrive on... 以……成长

0967 throb [θrɑːb] n 悸动，脉搏 v 抽痛，跳动

My heart was throbbing with excitement when he interviewed me.
当他面试我的时候，我兴奋得心直跳。
- epigastric throb 心悸
- throb with... ……跳动

语法重点
throb 的现在分词 throbbing，过去式与过去分词都是 throbbed。
- excitement (P. 161)

0968 toll(1) [toʊl] n 通行费，损失，长途电话费

Hard working takes a heavy toll of her body.
辛苦工作使她的身体受到了伤害。
- toll station 收费站
- take a heavy toll of... 对……造成损失

0969 toll(2) [toʊl] n 钟声 v 敲钟

We went out of the company along with the sound of the toll every day.
每天我们伴随着钟声走出公司。
- ring 铃声
- sound of a tolling bell 缓慢而有规律的钟声
- do... along with... 伴随着……做……

语法重点
- along (P. 006)

0970 topple ['tɑːpl] v 使倒塌，摇摇欲坠，将……推翻

The assistant toppled over onto the floor when the super star came in.
这名超级巨星进来时，助理摔倒在了地板上。
- topple down 推翻，跌落
- topple over onto... 摔倒在……上

0971 tornado [tɔːr'neɪdoʊ] n 龙卷风，大雷雨

A tornado whirled into the city when we were having a meeting.
我们在开会时，一场龙卷风袭击了这座城市。
- whirlwind 龙卷风
- cyclone tornado 龙卷风，飓风
- whirls into... 席卷了……

语法重点
tornado 是可数名词，其复数形式有两个，tornados 和 tornadoes。

0972 trait [treɪt] n 特色，显著的特点

One of the manager's less attractive traits is criticizing us in public.
经理有个不大讨人喜欢的特点，就是喜欢当众责备我们。
- characteristic 特点
- personality trait 人格特质
- one of sb's less attractive traits is... 某人有个不大讨人喜欢的特点是……

0973 tranquil ['træŋkwɪl] a 安静的，平静的，宁静的

There is a tranquil expression on my boss's face at the meeting.
开会时，老板的脸上有种安详自若的表情。
- quiet 安静的
- noisy 嘈杂的

语法重点
there is a / an... expression on one's face（某人脸上有种……的表情）中，expression 前面可以加上不同的形容词。

0974 tranquilizer ['træŋkwəlaɪzər] n. 镇静剂，止痛药

The tranquilizer can be up your sleeve during work.
工作时，你可以私下准备一些镇静剂。
- narcotic 镇静剂，麻醉药
- tranquilizer gun 麻醉枪
- ... be up one's sleeve 秘密备用……

语法重点
up one's sleeve 是固定搭配，sleeve 用单数。

0975 transaction [træn'zækʃn] n. 交易，业务

The manager left the transaction of the matter to me.
经理把这个业务交给我办理。
- transaction volume 交易量
- leave... to... 把……交给……办理

0976 transcript ['trænskrɪpt] n. 副本

The secretary sneaked a peek at the transcript of the interview.
秘书偷偷看了一眼采访内容的文字稿。
- copy 副本
- sneak a peek at... 偷偷看了一眼……

sneak (P. 635)

0977 transformation [ˌtrænsfər'meɪʃn] n. 转变，转换

I want to make the transformation from an ordinary employee to a manager.
我想由一个普通的员工变身成为一名经理。
- make a transformation from... to... 从……变成……

0978 transistor [træn'zɪstər]
n. 电晶体，晶体管收音机，半导体收音机

Grandfather takes a transistor everywhere.
爷爷去哪里都带着一个晶体管收音机。
- take... everywhere 去哪里都带着……

0979 transit ['trænzɪt] n. 运输，转变 v. 横越，运送

You should make an effort to protect the products in transit.
在运送过程中，你应该努力保护好这些产品。
- pass 通过
- in transit 在运输中
- you should make an effort to... 你应该努力……

effort (P. 159)

0980 transition [træn'zɪʃn] n. 过渡

His transition from an employee to a boss is hard.
他从一个员工变为老板，过程非常艰辛。
- conversion 转变
- transition from... to... 由……转化成……

0981 transmission [træns'mɪʃn] n. 传达，传动，发射

I think the document will be delayed in transmission.
我觉得这份文件会在传递中被耽误。
- transmittal 传输
- data transmission 资料传输

0982 transmit [træns'mɪt] **V** 传达，发射
Please transmit the document to the manager right away.
请立即把这份文件传给经理。
- release 发射
- transmit... to... 把……传给……

0983 transplant [træns'plɑːnt] / [træns'plænt] **V** / **N** 移植
I hated being transplanted from this office to that one.
我不喜欢从这个办公室移到那个办公室。
- implantation 移植
- organ transplant 器官移植
- be transplanted from... to... 从……移到……

语法重点：例句中用的是 be transplanted from... to... 的比喻意义。

0984 trauma ['trɔːmə] **N** 外伤，痛苦经历，挫折
The girl's fear at the elevator may have its root in a childhood trauma.
那个女孩对电梯的恐惧可能源于童年时期的创伤。
- psychological trauma 心理创伤，精神创伤
- have its root in... 源于……

语法重点：trauma 的复数形式是 traumata。
elevator (P. 159)

0985 tread [tred] **V** 踩，步行于 **N** 踩，踏板
She didn't really mean to tread on the manager's toes.
她不是真的有意要冒犯经理。
- tread out 踩出，平息
- tread on one's toes 冒犯某人

0986 treason ['triːzn] **N** 叛逆，不忠，背信
One of my friends was suspected of treason.
我的一个朋友被怀疑犯有叛国罪。
- betrayal 背叛
- loyalty 忠诚
- treason felony 背叛罪
- be suspected of... 被怀疑……

0987 trek [trek] **V** 艰苦跋涉 **N** 牛车旅行，艰苦的跋涉
It's a long trek from my house to the night market.
从我家到夜市很远。
- trek up 跋涉
- it's a long trek from... to... 从……到……很远

语法重点：trek 的过去式、过去分词都是 trekked。

0988 tremor ['tremər] **N** 颤抖，震颤声
There was a slight tremor in the manager's voice when he told us the good news.
经理通知我们这个好消息时，他的声音略微有点儿颤抖。
- trembling 发抖

voice (P. 110)

0989 trespass ['trespəs] **V** 擅自进入，侵犯 **N** 罪过，打扰
Don't trespass upon the staff during working hours.
工作时间不要打扰员工。
- intrude 闯入
- trespass on 侵犯，非法侵入，妨碍
- don't trespass upon... 不要打扰……

transmit ~ truce

0990 trigger ['trɪgər] n 扳机 v 触发，引起
I heard the boss is quick on the trigger.
我听说老板很机灵。
- attract 引起
- quick on the trigger 机灵的
- be quick on... 在……方面动作迅速

0991 triumphant [traɪ'ʌmfənt] a 胜利的，欢欣鼓舞的
All of my colleagues made a triumphant return.
我们的同事全部胜利而归。
- successful 胜利的
- unsuccessful 失败的
- triumphant return 凯旋
- make a triumphant return 胜利而归

> 语法重点
> triumphant 的副词形式是 triumphantly。

0992 trivial ['trɪviəl] a 琐碎的，平常的
The girl works herself up about the most trivial things during working hours.
工作时间内，最琐碎的事情也能让那女孩变得很激动。
- trivial matters 无关重要的事情

0993 trophy ['troʊfi]
n 战利品，奖杯 a 显示身份或地位的，有威望的
The image of the girl holding up the trophy is still etched on my memories now.
我现在还记着女孩举着奖杯的样子。
- memento 纪念品
- ... be etched on one's memories 某人铭记……

> 语法重点
> trophy 的复数形式是 trophies。
> ⇒ memory (P. 191)

0994 tropic ['trɑːpɪk] n 热带，热带地方 a 热带的
We sit in the classroom and imagine the tropic sun glared down on us.
我们坐在教室，想象着热带的太阳整日灼晒着我们。

0995 truant ['truːənt]
n 逃学（者），逃避责任（者）；玩忽职守 a 玩忽职守的
v 翘课，偷懒
The secretary wasn't reprimanded for playing truant before.
秘书以前没有因玩忽职守而受到过斥责。
- play truant 翘课，旷课
- be reprimanded for... 因为……而受到斥责

0996 truce [truːs] n 停战，停止争辩 v 停止争执
Let's call a truce to avoid the boss's suspicion.
我们休战吧，以免引起老板的怀疑。
- armistice 停战
- renounce truce 终止停战
- let's call a truce to avoid... 为了避免……，我们休战吧

> 语法重点
> truce 常用在 "A truce to nonsense!" 口语中，意思是 "别讲废话！"。
> ⇒ suspicion (P. 370)

0997 **tuberculosis** [tuːˌbɜːrkjəˈloʊsɪs] **n** 肺结核
She was infected with tuberculosis last year.
她去年被传染了肺结核。
- pulmonary tuberculosis 肺结核
- be infected with... 染上……

> **语法重点**
> be infected with 后面接上表示疾病的名词。

0998 **tumor** [ˈtuːmər] **n** 肿瘤，肿块，赘生物
What's the relation between malignant tumor and cancer?
恶性肿瘤和癌症有什么关系？
- knob 肿块，肿瘤
- malignant tumor 恶性肿瘤
- What's the relation between... and...? ……和……之间有什么关系？
- "良性肿瘤"用 benign tumor 来表示。

0999 **turmoil** [ˈtɜːrmɔɪl] **n** 骚动，混乱，焦虑
The critic's criticism put him in turmoil.
评论家的批评让他很焦虑。
- turbulence 骚乱
- financial turmoil 金融危机
- puts sb. in turmoil 让某人很焦虑

◁ criticism (P. 420)

1000 **twilight** [ˈtwaɪlaɪt] **n** 黎明，黄昏，暮年，衰退期
Don't leave me in the twilight of my career, please.
请不要在我事业的衰退时期离开我。

1001 **tyranny** [ˈtɪrəni] **n** 暴政，专横，暴行
I resign in an effort to counter the boss's tyranny.
我辞职是为了对老板的专横表示抗议。
- misrule 暴政
- democracy 民主
- do... in an effort to... 为了……做……

1002 **ulcer** [ˈʌlsər] **n** 溃疡，腐坏物，弊病
My mother was stricken by stomach ulcer last year.
我妈妈去年罹患了胃溃疡。
- sore 溃疡
- duodenal ulcer 十二指肠溃疡
- be stricken by... 罹患……

1003 **ultimate** [ˈʌltɪmət] **a** 最后的，最终的
The ultimate responsibility for the labor trouble undoubtedly lies in the management.
毫无疑问，资方应当为此次劳资纠纷负完全责任。
- final 最终的
- original 最初的
- ultimate goal 最终目标
- the ultimate responsibility for... lies in... ……为……负完全责任

> **语法重点**
> ultimate 的副词形式为 ultimately。

1004 **unanimous** [juˈnænɪməs] **a** 全体一致的
The employees were unanimous in their oppositions to the salary reduction.
雇员们都一致反对削减薪水。
- inconsistent 不一致的
- be unanimous in (doing)... 一致……

◁ opposition (P. 750)

1005 uncover [ʌnˈkʌvər] v 揭开……的盖子，揭露

It was she who uncovered a plot against the sales manager.
是她揭露了那位销售经理的阴谋。

- disclose 揭露
- hide 隐藏
- uncover the secret 揭开秘密
- uncover a plot against... 揭发反对……的阴谋

1006 underestimate [ˌʌndərˈestɪmeɪt] / [ˌʌndərˈestɪmət] v / n 低估，看轻

The director appeared to have underestimated the cost of the business trip.
那位主管似乎低估了这次出差的费用。

- undervalue 看轻
- overestimate 评价过高
- underestimate oneself 妄自菲薄

语法重点
underestimate 作及物动词，表示"低估经费、时间、困难等，看轻某人"，作不及物动词，表示"估价过低"。

1007 undergo [ˌʌndərˈɡoʊ] v 经历，经受

They underwent great hardship at the beginning of the program.
这个计划开始时，他们遭遇了极大的困难。

- suffer 遭遇
- undergo treatment 正在治疗

语法重点
undergo 的过去式和过去分词形式为 underwent, undergone。
- hardship (P. 451)

1008 undermine [ˌʌndərˈmaɪn] v 侵蚀……的基础

His confidence was seriously undermined by repeated failures of his efforts to get a promotion.
努力谋求晋升，却屡次失败，他的信心受到严重的打击。

1009 undertake [ˌʌndərˈteɪk] v 试图，保证，从事

I cannot undertake that she will undertake the task.
我不能保证她会接手这项任务。

- undertake commitment 承担责任
- undertake that... 保证……

语法重点
undertake 表示"承担，负责任"时，通常接名词、名词短语作宾语，表示"同意，保证"时，则是接不定式、that 从句作宾语。

1010 undo [ʌnˈduː] v 打开

Always remember that even a small mistake might undo all our efforts.
要时刻记得，即便是一个小小的失误，也可能使我们前功尽弃。

语法重点
undo 的过去式和过去分词形式为 undid, undone。

1011 unemployment [ˌʌnɪmˈplɔɪmənt] n 失业，失业状况，失业人数

Due to the economic crisis, more and more workers faced unemployment.
由于经济危机，越来越多的工人面临失业。

- joblessness 失业
- employment 就业
- unemployment rate 失业率
- face unemployment 面临失业

语法重点
unemployment 作不可数名词，表示"失业，失业状况，失业人数"，不用冠词修饰。

1012 unfold [ʌn'foʊld] v 打开，呈现

It's a scandal that the director unfolded the business secret to their opponent.
那位主管把商业机密告诉了对手，真是可耻。
- unfold a map 展开地图
- it's a scandal that... ……真是可耻

1013 unify ['juːnɪfaɪ] v 统一，使成为一体

Never should you underestimate the difficulty of unifying each department.
你永远都不要轻视统一各个部门的困难。
- unite 联合
- disrupt 使分裂

> **语法重点**
> unify 的过去式和过去分词为 unified, unified，其名词为 unification，作不可数名词。
> underestimate (P. 799)

1014 unlock [ˌʌn'lɑːk] v 开……的锁，开启，揭开

The manager was in a savage mood and left before the assistant unlocked the door.
那位经理非常生气，等不及助理开门就走了。
- unfasten 解开
- lock 锁上
- unlock code 解锁密码

> **语法重点**
> mood 作可数名词，通常是表示"情绪，气氛（通常用作单数形式）"。

1015 unpack [ˌʌn'pæk] v 打开包裹取出东西

She saw the sales manager unpack the contract from the drawer.
她看到那位销售经理从那个抽屉里取出了合约。
- pack 包装
- unpack... from... 从……中取……

1016 upbringing ['ʌpbrɪŋɪŋ] n 养育，培养，家教

His son who had a strict upbringing became a director in the multinational company.
他那个受到严格教育的儿子成了那家跨国公司的一名主管。
- nursing 养育
- have a... upbringing 受到……的教育

> **语法重点**
> upbringing 作不可数名词，表示"抚育，养育"，通常是指儿童、幼年时期受到的教育，可以用形容词 strict, religious, sheltered 等修饰。

1017 upgrade ['ʌpgreɪd] v 升级，改善 n 升级，上坡

He was upgraded to the director of the sales department last week.
上周，他晋升为销售部主管。
- promote 提升
- downgrade 退步
- on the upgrade 上升的
- be upgraded to... 晋升为……

> week (P. 112)

1018 uphold [ʌp'hoʊld] v 支持，维护，举起

The manager who had a savage temper found it hard to get employees to uphold his verdict.
那位性情粗暴的经理发现，难以让雇员们支持他的裁决。
- support 支持
- uphold verdict 维持原判
- have a savage temper 性情粗暴

> **语法重点**
> uphold 的过去式和过去分词形式为 upheld, upheld。

unfold ~ utmost

1019 uranium [juˈreɪniəm] **n** 铀
It was decided by a unanimous vote that he should undertake the task to research into enriched uranium.
大会一致决定，由他来接手研究浓缩铀的任务。

> 语法重点
> uranium 作不可数名词。
> ⓔ enrich (P. 715)

1020 urgency [ˈɜːrdʒənsi] **n** 急迫，急事，紧要
It's a matter of urgency that the marketing plan be prepared by next week.
营销计划须于下周之前准备妥当，这是当务之急。
ⓢ haste 急忙　ⓟ in case of urgency 一旦发生紧急情况
ⓒ it's a matter of urgency that... ……是当务之急

1021 urine [ˈjʊrən] **n** 尿，小便
The assistant always passes his urine before he punches out.
那位助理总是在下班打卡之前去小便。
ⓢ pee 尿　ⓟ urine test 尿检　ⓟ pass / discharge one's urine ……小便

> 语法重点
> urine 作不可数名词，表示"小便"。
> ⓔ punch (P. 344)

1022 usher [ˈʌʃər] **n** 接待员，引座员 **v** 引领，陪同
You can ask the secretary to usher you into the manager's office.
你可以让那位秘书引领你去经理办公室。

1023 utensil [juːˈtensl] **n** 用具，器皿
The clerk underestimated the cost of the writing utensils by twenty percent.
那位职员对书写用具的花费低估了百分之二十。
ⓢ tool 用具　ⓟ kitchen utensil 厨房用具

> 语法重点
> utensil 作可数名词，通常用作复数形式，表示"用具，器皿"，尤指日常家庭生活中所用的器具。

1024 utility [juːˈtɪləti] **n** 效用 **a** 有多种用途的
It's a problem of great urgency that we should design the utility furniture.
当务之急是设计多功能家具。
ⓢ multipurpose 多种用途的　ⓟ of no utility 没用的

> 语法重点
> utility 作不可数名词，表示"效用，功用"；作可数名词，表示"公用事业"，如铁路、公路、电力、自来水、瓦斯事业等。

1025 utilize [ˈjuːtəlaɪz] **v** 利用，使用
The research group tried to utilize solar power as a source of energy.
那个研究组试图将太阳能作为能源。
ⓢ use 使用　ⓟ utilize... as... 利用……作为……

1026 utmost [ˈʌtmoʊst] **a** 最大的 **n** 极限
We have done our utmost to help you with that task.
我们已经尽最大的努力来帮助你做那项工作。
ⓢ limitation 极限　ⓟ do one's utmost to... 竭尽全力……

1027 **vaccine** [væk'siːn] n 疫苗 a 疫苗的
We should have a contract with them for the supply of vaccine.
就疫苗供应一事，我们应当与他们签订合约。
- vaccinum 疫苗
- have a contract with... for... 就……与……签订合约

1028 **valiant** ['væliənt] a 勇敢的，坚定的 n 勇敢的人
It was a valiant attempt to apply for a job in the well-known company.
向那家知名的公司申请职位，是很勇敢的尝试。
- timid 胆小的
- it was a valiant attempt to... ……是很有价值的尝试

↪ attempt (P. 257)

1029 **valid** ['vælɪd] a 有效的，正当的
They insisted that the contract was held to be valid.
他们坚持认为，这份合约是有效的。
- available 有效的
- invalid 无效的
- valid contract 有效合约
- ... be held to be valid ……是有效的

1030 **validity** [və'lɪdəti] n 正当，有效性
I'm afraid the period of validity of the sales contract has expired.
恐怕，这份销售合约的有效期已满。
- availability 有效性
- invalidity 无效
- the period of validity of... has expired ……的有效期已满

1031 **vanilla** [və'nɪlə] n 香草 a 香草的
We had a contract with their company to supply concentrated vanilla.
我们和他们公司有供应香草香精的合约。
- vanilla ice cream 香草冰激凌
- have a contract with... to... 和……有……合约

> **语法重点**
> vanilla 作可数名词，指花味香醇的热带兰科植物；作不可数名词，指由香子兰荚中提取或是人工合成的香精。

1032 **variable** ['veriəbl] a 可变的，变数的 n 可变因素
I wonder why the quality of your work is distinctively variable.
我想知道，为什么你的工作品质时好时差。
- mobile 易变的
- invariable 不变的

1033 **variation** [ˌveri'eɪʃn] n 变化，变动，变异
The currency exchange rate does not seem to show much variation this season.
这一季的货币兑换率似乎并没有太大的变动。
- variety 变化
- invariability 不变

> **语法重点**
> variation 作可数名词或不可数名词，表示"变化，变动"，通常与介词 of 或是 in 连用；用于音乐中，则是作可数名词，表示"变奏（曲）"。

show much variation 显示出很大的变动

1034 vend [vend] v 叫卖，发表，声明

The manager questioned the validity of the assumption that someone vended customers' personal information.
那位经理对某人出售顾客个人信息的推测感到有些怀疑。
- sell 出售　反 purchase 购买　近 vend an opinion 公开发表意见
- question the validity of... 对……提出疑问

≈ assumption (P. 675)

1035 vendor ['vendər] n 摊贩，自动售货机，供应商

You said she once worked as a street vendor.
你说，她曾经是个街头小贩。
- street vendor 小贩

1036 verge [vɜːrdʒ] n 边缘，界限　v 接近，趋于

The news that she was fired brought her to the verge of tears.
听到自己被解雇的消息，她都快哭了。
- edge 边缘　近 on the verge of 接近于，濒临于
- ... bring... to the verge of tears ……使……快哭了

≈ tear (P. 233)

1037 versatile ['vɜːrsətl] a 多才多艺的，通用的

The company whose main products were versatile tools was said to be on the verge of bankruptcy.
据说那家主要生产万用工具的公司濒临破产了。
- ... be on the verge of bankruptcy ……濒临破产

1038 version ['vɜːrʒn] n 版本，说法，译文

There seems to be different versions of the manager's resignation.
对于经理辞职一事，似乎有不同的说法。
- latest version 最新版本
- there seems to be different versions of... ……似乎有不同的说法

1039 veteran ['vetərən] n 老兵，老手　a 经验丰富的

The veteran was elected as the chairman of the chamber of commerce by a unanimous vote.
那位老兵以全数通过当选为商会主席。
- experienced 经验丰富的　反 inexperienced 缺乏经验的

≈ commerce (P. 410)

1040 veterinarian / vet [ˌvetərɪ'neriən] / [vet] n 兽医

The vet's complaints appeared to be all variations on a theme.
那位兽医的抱怨，说来说去似乎也都是那么回事。

🔹 ... be all variations on a theme ……都是一回事

1041 vibration [vaɪˈbreɪʃn] n 震动，感受
The interviewer got good vibrations from the interviewee.
那位面试者给面试官留下了好印象。
🔹 get good vibrations from... 给……留下好印象

1042 vice [vaɪs] n 邪恶，缺点
Carelessness should be one of the assistant's little vices.
粗心大意是那位助理的缺点之一。
🔹 weakness 缺点 🔹 be one of one's little vices ……是……的缺点之一

> **语法重点**
> vice 作不可数名词，表示"罪恶，恶劣行径"；作可数名词，表示"缺点，坏习惯"。

1043 vicious [ˈvɪʃəs] a 邪恶的，剧烈的，堕落的
The manager's vicious look gave her bad vibrations.
那位经理恶狠狠的样子给她留下了不好的印象。
🔹 wicked 邪恶的 🔹 virtuous 善良的 🔹 vicious circle 恶性循环
🔹 give... bad vibrations 给……留下了不好的印象

1044 victimize [ˈvɪktɪmaɪz] v 欺骗，使受害，使牺牲
The accountant was victimized for discovering undisposed deficit.
那位会计因为发现未处理的账目亏空而遭惩处。
🔹 ... be victimized for (doing)... ……因……而遭（不公正）惩处

🔹 discover (P. 030)

1045 victor [ˈvɪktər] n 胜利者，获奖者
With so many variations, it's hard to estimate who will be the victor in the competition for the contract.
有那么多变数存在，难以判断谁会争取到这份合约。
🔹 winner 胜利者 🔹 loser 失败者 🔹 a victor of... ……的获胜者

🔹 variation (P. 800)

1046 victorious [vɪkˈtɔːriəs] a 得胜的
Our company was victorious over theirs in the competition for the contract.
我们公司胜过他们公司，争取到了这份合约。
🔹 triumphant 成功的 🔹 unsuccessful 失败的
🔹 be victorious over... in... 在……胜过……

> **语法重点**
> victorious 作形容词，通常没有比较级形式，其副词形式为 victoriously。

1047 villa [ˈvɪlə] n 别墅，公馆，住宅
The manager raised valid objections to the plan for building a villa there.
对于在那里修建别墅的计划，那位经理提出了有力的反对。
🔹 raise valid objections to... 提出有力的反对……

1048 vineyard [ˈvɪnjərd] n 葡萄园，工作场所
The workers needed in the vineyard were always subject to variation.
这个葡萄园里所需要的工人是经常变动的。

1049 virtual ['vɜːrtʃuəl] a 事实上的

It's said that a virtual state of competition existed between the two companies.
据说，这两家公司实际上是处于竞争状态。
- actual 实际的　- virtual reality 虚拟世界
- a virtual state of... exist between... ……实际上处于……状态

> **语法重点**
> virtual 的副词形式为 virtually。

1050 visualize ['vɪʒuəlaɪz] v 使可见

She cannot visualize what her life would be like if she lost the job.
她无法想象，如果失去这份工作，她的生活将会是什么样子。
- visualize what... would be like if... 想象如果……将会是什么样子

1051 vitality [vaɪ'tæləti] n 生命力

The new editor appeared to be bursting with vitality and imagination.
那位新编辑似乎充满活力和想象力。
- energy 活力　- debility 衰弱　- be bursting with... 充满……

1052 vocal ['voʊkl] a 声音的，直言不讳的 n 声乐作品

Most interviewees were vocal about their expectation of the salary.
大多数面试者都对薪资期望值直言不讳。
- outspoken 直言不讳的　- concealed 隐瞒的
- be vocal about... 对……直言不讳

> **语法重点**
> vocal 的副词形式为 vocally；作可数名词时，通常用复数形式 vocals，表示"爵士乐的歌唱部分"。

1053 vocation [voʊ'keɪʃn] n 职业，使命，天命

I'm afraid you have missed your vocation; you should have been a good teacher.
恐怕你是入错行了，你本该是一位好老师。
- profession 职业　- a sense of vocation 使命感
- miss one's vocation 入错行

1054 vocational [voʊ'keɪʃənl] a 职业的，行业的

She was the virtual head of the vocational training.
她是这次职业培训的实际负责人。
- professional 职业的　- amateurish 业余的
- vocational education 职业教育

↻ virtual (P. 803)

1055 vogue [voʊg] n 流行，时髦的事物 a 流行的

Electronic products of the company had a great vogue three years ago.
三年前，这家公司的电子产品风靡一时。
- fashion 时尚　- outmoded 过时的　- in vogue 正在流行
- have a great vogue 风靡一时

↻ electronic (P. 289)

1056 **vomit** [ˈvɑːmɪt] v 呕吐，喷出 n 呕吐（物），催吐剂

The young man vomited up all he had eaten after coming home from the banquet.
从宴会上回到家之后，那名年轻男子把所吃的东西都吐了出来。
- spew 呕吐　　- emetic vomit 催吐剂
- ... vomit (up) all... have eaten ……把所吃的东西都吐了出来

※ banquet (P. 529)

1057 **vulgar** [ˈvʌlɡər] a 通俗的，粗俗的，乡土的

The man dressed in cheap and vulgar clothes had little vocation for interpretation.
那个穿着廉价而低俗衣服的人不适合做口译。
- coarse 粗俗的　　- elegant 高雅的　　- have little vocation for... 不适合……

1058 **vulnerable** [ˈvʌlnərəbl] a 易受伤害的，有弱点的

Her unemployment left her feeling vulnerable and helpless.
失业使得她六神无主，十分无助。
- be vulnerable to 易受……攻击（伤害）　　- leave... feeling... 使……觉得

语法重点
vulnerable 作形容词，通常与介词 to 连用。

1059 **wardrobe** [ˈwɔːrdroʊb] n 衣柜，衣橱，藏衣室

It's a matter of the utmost importance to provide wardrobes with different sizes for consumers.
为顾客提供不同尺寸的衣柜是极为重要的。
- it's a matter of the utmost importance to... ……是极为重要的

语法重点
wardrobe 作可数名词，表示"衣柜"；作集体名词，表示"个人、剧团的全部衣物"。

1060 **warfare** [ˈwɔːrfer] n 战争，冲突

In those countries engaged in warfare, it's hard to visualize supporting your family with the poor salary from work.
在那些交战国中，难以想象要用微薄的工资来养家。
- war 战争　　- psychological warfare 心理战　　- visualize doing... 想象……

1061 **warranty** [ˈwɔːrənti] n 保证书，担保，批准

You had better make sure that your laptop is still under warranty.
你最好确保你的笔记本电脑还在保修期内。
- guarantee 保证　　- warranty period 保修期
- be still under warranty 还在保修期内

1062 **waterproof** [ˈwɔːtərpruːf] a 防水的

They made a valiant attempt to design the waterproof clothing.
他们做了大胆的尝试来设计防水衣服。
- rainproof 防水的　　- make a valiant attempt to... 做大胆的尝试……

语法重点
waterproof 作形容词，表示"防水的"，无比较级和最高级形式；作可数名词，表示"防水衣服"，通常用复数形式 waterproofs。

804

vomit ~ wrestle

1063 whatsoever [wɒtˈevər] ad 不管什么样的
There is no evidence whatsoever to show that the scientist wants to resign.
并没有什么证据表明，那位科学家想要辞职。
- whatever 无论什么
- none whatsoever 完全没有

语法重点
whatsoever 作副词，表示"任何，无论什么"，通常用于否定句中，以加强语气，多与 no 或是 none 连用。

1064 windshield [ˈwɪndʃiːld] n 挡风玻璃
He saw through the windshield that the guard held the worker's arm in a vice-like grip.
通过挡风玻璃，他看到，那名警卫紧紧地抓住了工人的手臂。
- windshield wiper 雨刷
- ... hold one's arm in a vice-like grip ......紧紧地抓住......的手臂

1065 withstand [wɪðˈstænd] v 耐得住，抵挡，反抗
The assistant's ability to withstand pressure had been tested to the utmost.
那位助理对压力的承受已经达到极限。
- revolt 反抗
- surrender 屈服
- ... be tested to the utmost ......达到极限

语法重点
withstand 的过去式和过去分词形式为 withstood, withstood。

1066 witty [ˈwɪti] a 反应灵敏的，诙谐的，机智的
But for the witty remarks, the question of the reporter will put the senator in a vulnerable position.
要不是有幽默的妙语，那个记者的问题将会使参议员处于危险的境地。
- humorous 幽默的
- put... in a vulnerable position 使......处于危险的境地

语法重点
witty 作形容词，比较级和最高级形式为 wittier, wittiest，其副词形式为 wittily。

1067 woo [wuː] v 追求，求爱，争取……的支持
We have been pushed to the utmost limits of endurance by the manager who woos success.
我们已经被那位想要获得成功的经理逼得忍无可忍了。
- woo the voters 争取选民的支持
- ... be pushed to the utmost limits of endurance ......被逼得忍无可忍

语法重点
woo 的过去式和过去分词形式为 wooed, wooed。
- endurance (P. 715)

1068 wrench [rentʃ] v 扭伤，曲解 n 痛苦
He angrily wrenched his arm away when she tried to explain the matter to him.
她想对他解释这件事的时候，他生气地把手臂挣脱开了。
- twist 拧
- monkey wrench 活动扳手，螺旋钳

1069 wrestle [ˈresl] v 与……摔跤 n 摔跤，斗争
They wrestled with great difficulty in the competition for the contract.
为了争取到这份合约，他们在竞争中努力克服了极大的困难。
- wrestle out 拼命做
- wrestle with great difficulty in... ……努力克服困难

语法重点
wrestle 表示"努力对付，制服"时，通常与介词 with 连用。
- difficulty (P. 153)

1070 yearn [jɜːrn] **v** 怜悯，渴望，想念
The assistant yearned to get a promotion.
那位助理渴望获得晋升。
🔄 yearn for 渴望   🔄 yearn to do... 渴望……

语法重点
yearn 表示"渴望，向往"时，后接介词 for 或是不定式。

1071 zeal [ziːl] **n** 热心，热情，奋发
The new manager always works with great zeal.
那位新来的经理总是热情洋溢地工作。
🔄 enthusiasm 热情   🔄 indifference 冷淡   🔄 zeal for 热心
🔄 ... work with great zeal ……热情洋溢地工作

语法重点
zeal 作不可数名词，表示"热情，热心"，侧重于指为实现某个目标、追求向往的事业等所表现出来的高度热忱。
🔗 always (P. 006)

MEMO

LEVEL 1-6   7 000 单词总复习

#	单词	词性	中文
1	m_____e	动词	给……动机
2	whisky	▸	▸
3	s_____n	名词	车站
4	g_____y	形容词	多草的
5	harassment	▸	▸
6	layout	▸	规划
7	manifest	动词；形容词	▸ ；
8	f_____y	名词	工厂
9	betray	动词	▸
10	r_____y	名词	真实
11	scroll	名词；动词	▸ ；卷动
12	leadership	名词	▸
13	e_____n	名词	爆发
14	a_____t	名词；动词	账户；
15	s_____e	动词	努力
16	gravity	名词	▸
17	n_____y	动词	通知
18	edition	名词	▸
19	j_____y	名词	忌妒
20	restriction	▸	▸

正确答案：1 motivate 2 名词/威士忌 3 station 4 grassy 5 名词/骚扰
6 名词 7 显示；明显的 8 factory 9 背叛 10 reality
11 卷轴 12 领导地位 13 eruption 14 account/解释 15 strive
16 重力 17 notify 18 版本 19 jealousy 20 名词/限制

LEVEL 1-6
7 000 单词总复习

21	revenge	▶ 动词	▶
22	endure	▶	▶ 忍受
23	f___ h___	▶	▶ 繁盛
24	lament	▶ 动词；名词	▶ ；
25	g___ e___	▶ 名词；动词	▶ 保证书；
26	p___ e___	▶ 动词	▶ 坚持不懈
27	uphold	▶ 动词	▶
28	s___ r___	▶ 名词	▶ 晚餐
29	v___ e___	▶ 形容词	▶ 易受伤害的
30	fence	▶ 名词	▶
31	c___ e___	▶ 动词	▶ 污染
32	trial	▶ 名词	▶
33	p___ g___	▶ 动词	▶ 延长
34	s___ s___	▶ 形容词	▶ 可疑的
35	abolish	▶ 动词	▶
36	mean	▶ ；形容词	▶ 有……的意思；
37	h___ e___	▶ 动词	▶ 侮辱
38	i___ e___	▶ 形容词	▶ 不可避免的
39	prevail	▶ 动词	▶
40	c___ r___	▶ 名词	▶ 竞争者

【正确答案】 21 替……报仇　22 动词　23 flourish / 动词　24 哀悼；悲痛之情　25 guarantee / 保证
26 persevere　27 支持　28 supper　29 vulnerable　30 篱笆
31 contaminate　32 试用　33 prolong　34 suspicious　35 废止
36 动词 / 吝啬　37 humiliate　38 inevitable　39 获胜　40 competitor

版权专有 侵权必究

图书在版编目（CIP）数据

怪物讲师教学团队的7000"单词"+"语法" / 怪物讲师教学团队著.—北京：北京理工大学出版社，2019.7
ISBN 978-7-5682-7242-1

Ⅰ.①怪… Ⅱ.①怪… Ⅲ.①英语—词汇—自学参考资料 ②英语—语法—自学参考资料 Ⅳ.①H313 ②H314

中国版本图书馆CIP数据核字（2019）第134990号

北京市版权局著作权合同登记号图字：01-2017-3510
简体中文版由我识出版社有限公司授权出版发行
怪物讲师教学团队的7000"单字"+"文法"，怪物讲师教学团队著，2015年，初版
ISBN：9789869203708

出版发行 /	北京理工大学出版社有限责任公司
社　　址 /	北京市海淀区中关村南大街5号
邮　　编 /	100081
电　　话 /	（010）68914775（总编室）
	（010）82562903（教材售后服务热线）
	（010）68948351（其他图书服务热线）
网　　址 /	http://www.bitpress.com.cn
经　　销 /	全国各地新华书店
印　　刷 /	天津久佳雅创印刷有限公司
开　　本 /	710毫米×1000毫米　1/16
印　　张 /	51
字　　数 /	1336千字
版　　次 /	2019年7月第1版　2019年7月第1次印刷
定　　价 /	166.00元

责任编辑 / 梁铜华
文案编辑 / 梁铜华
责任校对 / 刘亚男
责任印制 / 李志强

图书出现印装质量问题，请拨打售后服务热线，本社负责调换